William H. Emerson III
Bradford House
52 Bradford St.
Albany, NY 12206

THE KING'S PEACE
1637-1641

THE
GREAT REBELLION

THE
KING'S
PEACE

1637-1641

C. V. WEDGWOOD

COLLINS
ST JAMES'S PLACE, LONDON

FIRST IMPRESSION 1955
SECOND IMPRESSION 1955
THIRD IMPRESSION 1960
FOURTH IMPRESSION 1964
FIFTH IMPRESSION (REVISED) 1969
SIXTH IMPRESSION 1974
SEVENTH IMPRESSION 1978

ISBN 0 00 211403 8

Made and printed in Great Britain by
William Collins Sons & Co. Ltd., Glasgow

To
GEORGE MACAULAY TREVELYAN, O.M.

ACKNOWLEDGMENT

Although this book has been in my mind for many years it would not have been finished by 1954—if finished at all—without the perfect conditions for work generously given to me by the Institute for Advanced Study, Princeton. I would like to take this occasion of expressing my admiration for the Institute and its work under the humane guidance of Dr. Robert Oppenheimer and my gratitude to my friends there, more especially to the late Professor Edward Meade Earle without whose kindly persistence in urging me to cross the Atlantic I should not have enjoyed those months of exhilarating and peaceful endeavour.

CONTENTS

CONTENTS

LIST OF ILLUSTRATIONS

INTRODUCTION

The King's Peace is a narrative history of the British Isles for the four years in the reign of King Charles I which immediately preceded the Civil Wars. I hope in later volumes to describe the course of these wars and the Republican experiment that followed them. The story is not simple; it involves three separate countries, England, Scotland and Ireland, and two civilisations of a wholly different type, the Normanised Anglo-Saxon and the Celtic.

The Scots first revolted against the King because he would have compelled them to religious conformity with England. The Irish next rose, not against the King, but against English and Scottish settlers and the aggressive Protestantism of the English Parliament. They established an independent government at Kilkenny for upwards of eight years. The English, who appealed last to arms, fought—with assistance and diversions from the Scots, Irish and Welsh—a war for religious and political principles which ended in the death of the King on a public scaffold. This, being much resented in Scotland, precipitated a war within Scotland and another between Scotland and England.

European governments, aware of the strategic importance of the British Isles in their own wars, intervened with open or secret help. The French, the Dutch and the Danes offered to mediate between King Charles and his subjects. The Pope sent his nuncio, and the Kings of France and Spain sent their ambassadors to the Irish at Kilkenny. A German prince fixed hopeful eyes on the not quite vacant English throne. English settlements in the Netherlands, Scottish settlements in the Baltic, groups of English traders in Leghorn, Constantinople and Madras felt the far vibrations of the war. So did the young colonies on the eastern fringe of America's vast continent, and the island outposts in the West Indies.

The civil wars of the British Isles had an effect on European politics, on the dominion of the Mediterranean and the rise and decline of colonial empires, but essentially they were the intimate concern of our islands and sprang from the explosive energy, diverse ideals and colliding interests of their inhabitants. The principles for which they fought and the problems that they tried to solve are alive to-day; the conflict between the authority of the State and the liberty of the subject, between public responsibility and private conscience is not, and probably never will be, fully resolved. The doctrines they created, the laws they made or unmade, the sufferings and triumphs of individuals, their nobility and their baseness—all are part of the tradition we inherit and within which we live and think. We are still so much involved with this conflict that passion and propaganda colour all that has been written about it. It is not yet an academic study which we can approach with scientific indifference and cannot become so while a vital current of continuous belief runs through it to us. The final, dispassionate, authoritative history of the Civil Wars cannot be written until the problems have ceased to matter; by that time it will not be worth writing.

A writer approaching a controversial and lively subject on which much has been written owes it to the reader to make his own position at least as clear as it is to himself. The causes of the Civil Wars have been analysed, the rights of the combatants have been judged and weighed by Churchman and Dissenter, Whig and Tory, Liberal and Marxist, utilitarian and romantic. The religion, the political morality and the philosophies of his own time colour the outlook of every writer, however conscientious, although, wise in his own generation, each may add something to our understanding of the past. No historian has ever been, or will ever be, omniscient in his knowledge or infallible in his deductions. None can see the whole and undivided truth.

The contemporary could not do so either. Puzzled by the variety of events which came so confusingly upon him from day to day, and ignorant of much that time alone would bring to light, he steered his way through his own world—as we do now—by the imperfect judgment of an ill-informed mind. But the contemporary knew one thing that the historian can only imagine: he knew what it felt like to be alive at that time, to experience those religious doubts, political fears, and economic pressures as a part of his life. He may not have known or suspected influences which have been later revealed; but he knew what he experienced in his mind or suffered in his flesh, and he knew what beliefs and what interests he admitted to be the motives of his action. " Here we are subject to error and misjudging one another," said Strafford on the scaffold. The day-to-day events of history arise at least in part from error and misjudgment. On this level falsehood itself is a part of truth.

Before history can be put into a coherent perspective it is often necessary to clear away the misinterpretations and the half-knowledge by which contemporaries lived. But the application of modern methods of research, together with modern knowledge and prejudice, can make the past merely the subject of our own analytical ingenuity or our own illusions. With scholarly precision we can build up theories as to why and how things happened which are convincing to us, which may even be true, but which those who lived through the epoch would neither recognise nor accept. It is legitimate for the historian to pierce the surface and bring to light motives and influences not known at the time; but it is equally legitimate to accept the motives and explanations which satisfied contemporaries. The two methods produce different results, but each result may be a fair answer to the particular question that has been asked. They become misleading only if either is accepted as the whole truth.

I have not attempted in this book to examine underlying causes, but rather to give full importance and value to the admitted motives and the illusions of the men of the seventeenth century. I have sought to restore their immediacy of experience.

History experienced is not simple for those who experience it, as every intelligent inhabitant of the twentieth century is aware, and it is impossible to express the full significance of contemporary confusion without sacrificing some, though I hope not all, appearance of clarity. I have tried to describe the variety, vitality and imperfections as well as the religion and government of the British Isles in the seventeenth century in an opening section, deliberately avoiding analysis and seeking rather to give an impression of its vigorous and vivid confusion. Otherwise this book is intended as a straightforward and chronological narrative. I have preferred to describe events as far as possible in the order in which they happened, although this necessarily means a shifting of interest from theme to theme and from place to place. A narrative which sorts out the muddled strands of day-to-day events makes smoother reading, but only a resolute insistence on chronology can make the immediate pressures and confusions which acted on contemporaries clear to the modern reader.

The highest ideals put forward in this generation of conflict were noble; the men who fought or worked for them were less noble than the ideals, for the best of men do not consistently live on the highest plane of virtue, and most men live far below it. The idealisation of certain figures in the Civil War has led, later, to exaggerated condemnations, but a cynical view of human frailty is no help to the historian, and human values can be fairly assessed only if an honest effort is made to understand the difficulties and prejudices of each of the people concerned. These mental acrobatics cannot always be successful, but the attempt to perform them is always illuminating.

This book covers only a few years, and many of the people in it cannot be fully understood until their lives are seen as a whole. It is my aim to show the unfolding of certain characters and the emergence of others and to comment on them, as far as possible, from evidence relating only to the years described. Clarendon's account of Charles I, for instance, together with most of the best known descriptions of the King, belong to a later epoch, are coloured by the knowledge of his end, and are therefore misleading if their evidence is allowed to influence a study of him as he was between the years 1637 and 1641.

The behaviour of men as individuals is more interesting to me than their behaviour as groups or classes. History can be written with this bias as well as another; it is neither more, nor less, misleading. The essential is to recognise that it answers only one set of questions in only one way. Few methods of historical study do more, and no harm will be done by any of them so long as the limitation is understood. This book is not a defence of one side or the other, not an economic analysis, not a social study; it is an attempt to understand how these men felt and why, in their own estimation, they acted as they did.

BOOK ONE

THE HAPPIEST KING IN CHRISTENDOM

June 1637

We have no other intention but by our government to honour Him by Whom Kings
reign and to procure the good of our people,
and for this end to preserve the right and
authority wherewith God hath vested us.

CHARLES I

O thou, that dear and happy isle,
The garden of the world erewhile,
Thou Paradise of the Four Seas
Which Heaven planted us to please,
But—to exclude the world—did guard
With wat'ry, if not flaming, sword:
What luckless apple did we taste
To make us mortal and thee waste?

ANDREW MARVELL

CHAPTER ONE

COURT AND COUNTRY

CHARLES, King of Great Britain and Ireland, in the thirty-seventh year of his age and the thirteenth of his reign, believed himself to be the happiest King in Christendom. He said as much in the warm June of the year 1637 to his eldest nephew and godson, the Elector Palatine, Charles Louis, who with his next brother Rupert had been on a long visit to his Court. They were the sons of the King's only sister Elizabeth, whose husband, once Elector Palatine and King of Bohemia, had lost in the German wars all that he possessed.

King Charles's claim was not extravagant. He was, to all immediate observation, singularly blessed in the inward tranquillity and the outward peace of his dominions. He had not wished to be involved in the bloody turmoil of Europe even for his sister's and her children's sake. As one of his many courtier poets had prettily expressed it:

> Tourneys, masques, theatres better become
> Our halcyon days; what though the German drum
> Bellow for freedom and revenge, the noise
> Concerns not us, nor should divert our joys;
> Nor ought the thunder of their carabins
> Drown the sweet airs of our tun'd violins.[1]

The benevolent authority which King Charles sought to exercise over his people was reflected in many a noble and civilised achievement of the arts. With the help of courtier-

21

landowners, inspired by the Crown, the embellishment of the capital proceeded apace. The piazza at Covent Garden, surrounded by splendid town houses for the nobility and dominated by the handsome new church of St. Paul, was all but finished. London's greater St. Paul's, the huge, decrepit medieval cathedral, had been purged of the hucksters who used the nave as a market place; the citizens who had for years tipped their rubbish into the crypt had been compelled to find another place for it. A magnificent portico in the Italian manner was being erected to beautify the outmoded Gothic façade.

The King's Surveyor General, the virtuoso Inigo Jones, had some admirable ideas for a new London, spacious, sweet and clean. London Bridge through the narrow arches of which, at high tide, the Thames flowed in dangerous rapids, was doomed to demolition; the crazy structure of houses surmounting it was grotesque and old fashioned, and for the last few years had become dangerous and unsightly owing to a fire which had left, on the north side, only burnt-out shells patched with boards. All this would soon be replaced by a stone structure, modelled on the bridge of Sant' Angelo in Rome, and worthy of a great capital and a great river. In the architectural schemes of Inigo Jones the new London already appeared to be, in outward form as it was in size, the greatest city in Europe.

In practice the King met with irritating opposition. When he decided to demolish the inferior little church of St. Gregory to free St. Paul's from surrounding clutter, the parishioners of St. Gregory sulked; they did not think their church inferior and they too had spent good money on improvements. Other more exasperating incidents interfered with the building of the capital. A fine vista had been planned in the suburban fields of Long Acre, but before work could be started on it, wooden hovels appeared overnight and by morning were full of clamouring squatters.

Apart from opposition there were the usual checks to which building operations are subject—bad weather, delays in delivery of material, mistaken plans which had to be rectified. The superb series of paintings commissioned by the King from Sir Peter Paul Rubens for the ceiling of his new banqueting house at Whitehall was ready more than a year before there was any ceiling to which to attach them. They had to be rolled up and stacked in the workshop of the master at Antwerp. When the ceiling was ready for them they were found to have cracked, and Rubens, who had put his highest efforts into their composition, had to devote some weeks' personal work to them before they were again ready for transportation to England. By the summer of 1637 they were at last safely in their appointed places, and revealed, to those who curiously or admiringly examined them, an allegorical tribute to the late King James of blessed memory.

At each corner symbolic groups illustrated the triumph of peace, wisdom and authority over strife, falsehood and faction: a serpent-headed Medusa writhed under the feet of her conqueror, and Hercules grappled successfully with the Hydra of rebellion. Along each side buxom children, who staggered beneath cornucopias or tumbled among garlands of flowers, conveyed the general idea of prosperity. The three great pictures in the centre showed the late King bestowing order, justice, peace and the benefits of true religion on his people, before mounting to heaven where a throng of Christian angels and pagan gods united to exchange his earthly crown for a celestial one.

In one of these pictures two ample nymphs representing the sister kingdoms of England and Scotland dandled between them a baby boy whose prancing legs and outstretched arms seemed to foretell at once the greatest energy and the noblest aspiration. This child portrayed King Charles himself as an infant. In prosaic fact, he had been a sickly little thing with no resemblance to the bouncing Flemish baby used by Rubens as a model, but the higher truth of allegory is not bound to pedantic details. The pictures illustrated the vision which both King Charles and his father had for their people—peace, order, justice.

A literal-minded critic might have found fault with the whole splendid composition of cloud-capped domes and sky-borne deities. These had little to do with the archipelago scattered out north-westward from the mainland of Europe, the British Isles, with their seven thousand miles of coast, towering crag and jagged reef battered by Atlantic storms, chalk ramparts above the green Channel, dune and quicksand, shelving shingle and crumbling cliff: the beacon on the headland, the bell on the rock, the fishing boats on the beach, the nets drying on the sea wall, the bales unloaded on the busy quays; and inland, the cornfields and the pastures, the sheep on the downs, the cattle in the hills, forest and park, moor and mine, impenetrable mountain and impassable bog; and the King's seven million subjects (more or less) crammed in towns, snug in villages, lonely in moorland farmstead or island croft; or far off on the rocky shore of Newfoundland, the wooded hills of Massachusetts, the warm islands of the Caribbean; or east or west on the world's wide oceans in some *Mary Rose* of Bristol, *Andrew* of Leith, *Patrick* of Galway.

All this was but vaguely comprehended in the vast allegorical design. The painter had not been asked, and had not been expected, to represent the geographical character of the King's dominions or the activities of his subjects. He had been asked to represent certain large and noble ideas, and he had, largely and nobly, acquitted himself of his task. It was not for him to reconcile the vision with the facts. That task fell to the King.

The races, customs, languages, religions and interests of the King's subjects were as various as the landscape of his dominions. The greater number of them lived in England which, with the adjoining principality of Wales, accounted for about five millions; Scotland and Ireland with the islands off their coasts had not above a million each.

A contemporary scholar reckoned that twelve languages were spoken in the British Isles. Only one of these, English, was officially recognised, and the aggressive, conquering language, now in its vigorous golden age, was bounded on the North and West by the older Celtic tongues, once the general speech of the land—moribund Cornish in the extremity of the western peninsula, lively lilting Welsh throughout the principality, and various forms of the melancholy, guttural Irish dialects in the Scottish Highlands, the Western Isles, the Isle of Man, and throughout Ireland. Norse dialects were spoken in the Orkney and Shetland Islands, French persisted in the Channel Islands and French or Dutch among the self-contained communities of refugees who had settled in the south and east coast towns during the last century.

The King's dominions were encircled and invaded by the sea. On the western littoral, jagged headlands and rocky cliffs fronted the stormy onslaught of the Atlantic ocean; on the eastern shores the sandy coastline slowly retreated before the pressure of the North Sea. The sea penetrated far into the interior, up the broad estuaries of Thames and Severn, Humber and Tyne, the Firths of Forth and Clyde and the narrow fjords of Loch Fyne, Loch Long, Loch Linnhe; it grasped whole handfuls from the Irish coast in wide bays and low-shored, labyrinthine loughs. In places the King's dominions were bogged and saturated by the sea, with acres of salt marsh, mud-flat and quicksand.

At least half the King's subjects derived their living directly or indirectly from the sea. Hundreds of fishing hamlets lay along his coasts. The delicacies and riches of the rocks and waters were eagerly sought. On the Cumbrian and Scottish shores the mussel beds yielded pale irregular pearls. The oysters of Colchester and Whitstable were famous; so were Selsey cockles and the shrimps of the sandy Lancashire shores. The Thames estuary had its teeming population of sprats and eels; eels, larger and richer, were the boast of northern Ireland, and lampreys were the speciality of the Severn estuary. Pilchards from Plymouth and Penzance were famous in far countries; mussels were the pride of Minehead. Plump sea-gulls were in demand, and the tiny, naked new-hatched gannet were carried away by the basket load from the Bass Rock to be swallowed, at one succulent, greasy mouthful, by revellers in Edinburgh. Berwick had long been famous for salmon and shellfish but had recently fallen upon evil times; the fisher folk, tempted by the possibility of a record haul, had broken the Sabbath and gone out in their boats. Since that time the salmon had deserted Berwick whose present distress was held up as a warning to all who despised the commandments.

From the North Sea the Yarmouth herring boats brought home by the barrel-load the silvery, living harvest of the deep, and fisher folk came in their cobles from as far north as the coast of Durham and as far west as Lyme to sell their herring on the Yarmouth quays to be split and smoked and marketed. From the ports of East Anglia—Lynn, Southwold, Dunwich, Aldeburgh—the Iceland ships went out for codling. On fish quays up and down the kingdom, housewives bargained for plaice and sole, cod and mackerel, turbot, skate, whiting and " poor John," as they familiarly called the vulgar hake, the Friday fare of the people. Sturgeon and whale, cast up on the coast, were for the King's use.

Far to the north the adventurous Scots were discovering the treasures of the Greenland whale fisheries, but the English Muscovy Company disputed the profitable fishing rights of the icy waters, and English money and resources weighted the scale against Scottish enterprise. Fishing rights in Scotland's own waters were savagely contested, for lowland intruders were opposed by the fierce people of the Highland coasts and the Hebrides, and the aggressive Hollanders fell upon both alike.[2] Round the Orkney Islands the Dutch not only trespassed on the fishing but had, on occasion, fired on the poor coracles of the Orcadians, wilfully damaged the breeding grounds of their sea-birds, and plundered their villages.

Where the coasts were low-lying, hundreds of salt pans yielded the mineral wealth of the deep; refineries at Newcastle, Colchester and Chester perfected it. Where the coast was rocky, seaweed was carted inland to enrich the soil. On cliffs and sandhills men gathered samphire and sought for ambergris among the sea-drift on the shore, to sell to the kitchens of the rich. The river delicacies were also prized—fresh-water eels from Abingdon, Severn greyling, and Arundel mullet.

Thousands of small craft plied with goods and passengers from one little port to another. Stubby trows from Swansea carried the coal of South Wales across the Bristol Channel; Minehead and Barnstaple exchanged wares and travellers with Tenby and the ports of southern Ireland, Waterford, Wexford, Youghal, Kinsale and Cork. Fifty sail from these Irish ports would put into the Severn estuary for the Bristol fair in July. The small ships of Perth, Arbroath and Montrose connected the villages of Scotland's eastern seaboard better than the indifferent roads of the interior; those of Glasgow and Greenock linked the western Highlands with the Isles and Ireland. Hull, Yarmouth, King's Lynn, Ipswich and Harwich commanded England's east coast carrying trade. A fleet of three hundred ships carried Newcastle coal to London. Dumbarton and Whitehaven sent colliers to Dublin, and the Irish Mail (wind and weather permitting) went from Chester. Ayr and Irvine traded to France; Leith, Dundee, Aberdeen and Stonehaven to Norway, Denmark and the Low Countries. A cross-Channel traffic from Dartmouth and Exeter brought in the flax and hemp of Normandy and Brittany and exported it again as sail cloth and buckram. Gloucester, queenly among the meads of Severn, assembled the woolsacks of the Cotswold country for shipment to Bristol and beyond. Travellers for France took ship at Dover; for the Low Countries and Germany, at Harwich or from London.

From Bristol, Plymouth, Southampton ships set sail for the Atlantic crossing with a hundred or two hundred men, women and children bound for the American colonies, and supplies of malt and meal, shirts and shoes, cloth and hardware for the settlers already there. Having discharged their cargo they turned northward, bought in Newfoundland fish, sold it two thousand miles away at Cadiz in Spain, and so came home again rich with Spanish wines.[3]

The King's subjects made a living from the sea in other ways besides fishing and merchandise. Lundy Island, the Orkneys, the Scilly Islands sheltered pirates; on the Hebrides, on the Blasket islands, on the Cornish coast and on the black, appalling cliffs of county Clare, delusive fires might burn by night to lure the lost vessel to the mercy of reefs and robbers. The great men of these parts, in return for a share in the profits of piracy and wrecking, would sometimes help their wilder neighbours and tenantry in deceiving and defying the government. A recent attempt to convert Stornoway into a more reputable port by settling merchant folk within it had been stubbornly defeated by the inhabitants. The depredations by sea and land of the Clan Macdonald had been fairly checked on the mainland of Scotland, but it was not two years since the *Susanna* of Limerick, driven against the coast of Lewis by a stormy sea, had been systematically plundered by the Macdonalds under one of their principal chieftains. Between northern Ireland and the Western Isles native coracles plied a traffic in crude liquor and fugitive criminals. They defied alike His Majesty's customs and His Majesty's justice, and preyed from time to time on the English-speaking settlers from London or the Scottish lowlands who were trying to turn the wild Ulster of the O'Neills and Macdonnells into a farming and flax-raising country.

Outside the great ports of the kingdom, foreign ships might be ill received. A Dutch ship damaged by Dunkirk pirates in the Channel had limped into Seaford for help and shelter, but the men of Seaford robbed the crew, ransacked the ship and stood at sulky defiance when the King's government commanded them to make good the damage. The inhabitants of Dunbar turned out with horses and wagons to carry off the cargo of a foreign ship that ran ashore a few miles from their town. A Dutch East Indiaman, storm-driven into an Irish port, forestalled any possible hostility by covering the place with its great ordnance and landing a party to kidnap the son of its richest citizen. The crew of another, which had taken refuge from pirates in a remote Irish haven, terrorised the inhabitants, and refused to pay customs on the goods sold to lighten the burden. As the cargo was of spices, worth two hundred thousand pounds, the King's Deputy in Dublin considered the possibility of forcibly detaining and seizing it all, a design which was foiled

because this armed giant of the ocean was more than a match
for the English vessels sent to deal with it.[4]

Dunkirk pirates made English waters unsafe. The Barbary
corsairs raided the Devon and Cornish coasts and, repeatedly,
those of southern Ireland, so that the slave-markets of Africa
knew the fair-skinned boys and girls of Plymouth, Barnstaple
and Baltimore.

The King was enlarging his navy to protect his people. He
envisaged the addition of two major warships to his naval
strength every year, while experiments were being made with
a new type of ship, the small swift-sailing whelps. At Deptford
where Drake's *Golden Hind* still lay at anchor slowly rotting,
crowds gathered to watch the amazing progress of the greatest
ship ever to be built in England. Still nameless, she rose majestic
in the stocks, while the best craftsmen in the country completed
the carving, the gilding and the paint which gave elegance and
richness to her formidable bulk.

The King's principal shipyards lay along the southern shore
of the Thames estuary. A few miles farther up the river, the
gigantic London and its satellite villages, the centre of maritime
and mercantile England, covered five miles of its northern and
three miles of its southern bank with houses, quays and towers.
Westward, the buildings ran out along the river bank as far as
Westminster; painted barges, cushioned and capacious, were
moored at the watergates of the great lords' houses that fringed
the Strand. Traffic came and went by water, bearing lawyers
to Westminster Hall and officials, servants, courtiers to the
King's sprawling palace-village of Whitehall. Eastward from
the Tower, the Ratcliff Highway joined Wapping, Shadwell
and Limehouse, mariners' villages looking out upon the great
ships at anchor in the estuary, with green country and windmills
at their backs; they bought in the produce of Essex, coarse hard
cheeses and salted meat, to provision the outgoing ships. On
the south bank, houses and quays were continuous through
Rotherhithe and Southwark; thence they trailed away into the
region of disreputable gaiety, the pleasure gardens and bear pits,

theatres and brothels of Blackfriars and Bankside. A strip of marshland divided this district from the Archbishop's low-lying red-brick palace at Lambeth and the fields whence, on warm summer evenings, young Londoners went bathing. This great urban conglomerate numbered already close on a quarter of a million souls. In two wide half-circles, north and south, the outlying villages reached inwards to London, as London reached outwards towards them. They grew hay for London horses and vegetables for London tables; their windmills ground the corn for London bread and their innkeepers and dairy maids provided ale and cheesecakes, plums and cream for Londoners on holiday afternoons.

In the recently opened Hyde Park, on London's western perimeter, rich citizens strolled with courtiers and visiting gentry. The occupants of smart coaches showed themselves off in the Ring; there was horse racing and foot racing, two bowling greens, a gaming house and an eating house, and dairymaids walked round with milk for the thirsty. For the humbler citizens of London, Finsbury fields were a favourite walking place although of late years much spoiled by the brick-works which supplied London's builders. Within the city itself Moorfields was set aside for citizens' wives and maids; here they could hang out their laundry or spread it on the grass; shady trees, specially planted, bore the names of those who had placed them there, and wooden shelters had been put up against sudden rain. It was pleasant by daylight but with nightfall it grew disreputable, even dangerous.

London was first and foremost a seaport. The tidal river lapped at the streets' end; high masts and furled sails closed the narrow vistas of its ancient alleys. Greater than all the other seaports of the realm together, London was the mart of the known world. The Venetian envoy, who had experience in ships and shipping, reckoned that twenty thousand craft, small and great, were to be seen from London in a day. Rowing-boats and ferry-boats carried the citizens upstream and down, or from bank to bank; heavy barges distributed goods from London up river, and brought back to London the produce of the Thames valley. Merchantmen from Antwerp and Amsterdam, Calais and Bordeaux, Lisbon, Leghorn and Cadiz, Bergen, Hamburg and Archangel, Constantinople, the East and the West Indies, rode at anchor in the Pool or unloaded at the wharves. Some were privately owned, others belonged to trading companies— the Muscovy Company, the Levant Company, the West India Company and the Merchant Adventurers. Greatest of all towered the huge ships of the East India Company, " mobile, maritime fortresses " embattled against piracy and storm.[5]

London was a huge port and a huge town and, at its worst, as dark and wicked as such towns are. In the porch of St. Paul's, in the arcaded shopping centre of the New Exchange, the "coney catcher" loitered to ensnare some wide-eyed country rabbit with a little money in his foolish paws. The "jeering, cunning courtesan, the rooking, roaring boy" conspired to wheedle and bully unsuspecting fools. All day the shouts of oyster and tripe women, the swearing of draymen, the creak and clatter of hackney coaches dazed and deafened the newcomer, and after sunset

" riotous sinful plush and tell-tale spurs
Walk Fleet Street and the Strand, when the soft stirs
Of bawdy ruffled silks turn night to day." [6]

London was not a safe place for the innocent, although those accustomed to it, born in " the scent of Newcastle coal and the hearing of Bow bells," knew how to avoid the dangers, and the more experienced revellers who came in for a spree, like Sir Humphrey Mildmay who got home " mad, merry and late " after " playing the fool with two punks in a barge on the Thames," were very well able to take care of themselves.[7] But country boys and girls, driven to the capital by bad times or tempted by tales of easy money, drifted through disappointment and disaster into the criminal depths of the city, to die in the common gaol or of the " Tyburn ague " on the gallows.

As the town grew, and it was growing fast, its gaieties

increased. Bear gardens and pleasure gardens spread along Bankside, puppet-theatres showed *Bel and the Dragon* and other apocryphal matter; peep-shows advertised *The Creation of the World* represented to the life in pasteboard. The two principal theatres, now both covered in and lit by wax candles, attracted the rich and fashionable. Blackfriars on Bankside carried on the Shakespeare-Burbage tradition, with Taylor, thought to be the greatest Hamlet yet seen, and Swanston's much praised Othello; the portly comedian Lowin played Falstaff and the whole Jonsonian gallery of grotesques, and the fair youth Stephen Hammerton drew tears with his Juliet and Desdemona. Christopher Beeston's company at the Cockpit in Drury Lane concentrated on more modern topical works. These two had the highest reputation though half a dozen lesser theatres, more old-fashioned, open-roofed and playing by daylight, still drew large audiences. A French company brought over the neo-classical drama from Paris but the Londoners, taking it into their heads to be scandalised at seeing women on the stage, pelted them with rotten apples. The Queen, who patronised the company, was indignant, and after a little the Londoners forgot their moral views and accepted the novelty.

The tidal Thames, creeping into the heart of the city up many an open inlet, ditch and hithe, did something to purify the town. Fresh water had been brought within reach by the New River Company which had diverted the river Lea to Islington. But rosemary and jasmine were in constant demand to disguise the putrid smells of streets and houses. London children already suffered badly from rickets, and the various epidemic diseases vaguely defined as plague caused ten thousand deaths in the bad year 1636. In the following year, still bad, there was something over three thousand victims.

The respectable citizens of London drew together against the underworld of the criminal, the drunken, the defeated. Their city might be one of the wickedest in Europe; it was also, as a natural consequence, one of the most austerely pious. The virtues of plain living and hard work were extolled and practised;

the Bible and the hundred churches stood firm against the ballads and the playhouses. Religion was a fighting force in the city because it could never cease from fighting, " the miles between Hell and any place on earth being shorter than those between London and St. Albans."

Out of London and into London came and went carriers' carts by road and barges by water. The King's posts started for Edinburgh thrice weekly, but for the most part citizens relied on independent carriers and, except when they found it useful, looked with some resentment on government enterprise. Provincial carriers called at least once in the week, and sometimes more than once, at various London taverns; for Oxford and Northampton the carts left daily. The industrious John Taylor, doggerel poet, scribbler, traveller and busybody, had compiled a *Carriers' Cosmography* listing the available services, but his work had not been easy: the carriers had taken him at first for a government spy collecting information " to bring carriers under some new taxation."

For all heavier goods water-transport was generally esteemed better than the roads, which were rough at best, impassable in bad weather, and not free from thieves. The coastal boats loaded their cargo into barges in the reaches below London and the barges carried goods up the Thames to Reading and up the Lea to Ware. West coast shipping came into Gloucester whence the Severn barges carried the freight to Shrewsbury. The Yorkshire Ouse served northern Yorkshire, the Trent the midlands. The rivers, well-disposed by nature and assisted by the ingenuity of man, had made the English a relatively united and economically interdependent people. Water-transport could not link the wilder country of Wales and had not been exploited in Ireland. The rivers of Scotland, the rapid Forth, the headstrong Tay, the sandy silted Clyde, were beyond the control of seventeenth-century engineering. With few bridges, with troublesome fords often swollen by rain, they emphasised the divisions of Scotland. The elements of unity and prosperity were concentrated in England.

Next after the sea, the King's subjects drew their living from wool and all the industries surrounding it. They herded sheep on the Sussex and Wiltshire downs, in the rich pastures of Cotswold, in the Thames valley, on the Lancashire fells and the Lincolnshire and Yorkshire wolds, in the Scottish lowlands and the Welsh mountains. Wool towns had grown up wherever streams gave water-power enough to drive the mills which washed and whitened it. In manufacture the regions had their specialities. Scotland's plaids protected both highlanders and lowlanders against the rigours of the climate and were exported to all the colder regions of Europe; they were Scotland's principal export and worth more than all the rest together. Wales made coarse friezes, so did North Devon; Carmarthen specialised in flannel. Blankets from Witney in Oxfordshire were famous all over England. Bolton and Manchester wove the soft-textured woollens confusingly called cottons—confusingly because Manchester was already importing Smyrna cotton for her fustians and dimities. (Derby, Macclesfield, Leek and Nottingham, were abandoning wool for the manufacture of silk.) Bradford specialised in rugs and cushions; Kendal in Westmorland, Bewdley in Worcestershire, and Monmouth in the Welsh marshes specialised in stockings and caps. Woodstock and Ilminster made gloves. The best cloth came mostly from the south, although Leeds and Halifax led the way for Yorkshire with fine broadcloth; in general, broadcloth was made round Reading and Newbury and in the Wiltshire towns. Wiltshire cloth was sold over all Europe, and some, shipped by enterprising city merchants to Ragusa, was marketed far within the dominions of the Turk. Coggeshall and Colchester were the centres of the coarse cloth manufacture—the baize and serges—of southern East Anglia; their wares went in bulk to religious houses abroad, and friars of Spain, Portugal and Italy were clothed by the Puritan weavers of Suffolk and Essex. Norwich, once the leading wool town of England, had lost its supremacy and was visibly declining. Gloucester was now, after the all-conquering London, queen of the wool trade strategically placed on the navigable Severn, linked by it to Shrewsbury where the fleeces of Wales were sold, and to Bristol the greatest outgoing port, after London, in the realm. Gloucester also drew to herself the famous fleeces of the white, square-bodied, long-necked Cotswold sheep, the greatest wool-bearers in the country.

York was for the north what Gloucester was for the west; and York claimed also to be what London was for the south. It was the northern centre for the exchange and distribution of raw wool and the finished cloth. But York was also the second capital of England, the seat of an Archbishop, the centre of the King's government in the north parts and, in its own opinion, in no way inferior and in many ways superior to London. Its magnificent walls, its lofty Minster, its forty churches, proclaimed a greatness which defied decline. While the King beautified London, his representative at York, the Lord President of the North, had majestically extended his official residence in the noblest European manner. It was rivalled by the mansion of a private gentleman, Sir Arthur Ingram, whose palatial Italianate house and garden were the wonder of the city. As for good fare York boasted that it could do better than London; northern appetites were hearty and "the ordinary in York would be a feast in London."

The making of cloth was, for the most part, a cottage industry. Women and children sat at their doors carding, spinning or knitting. In East Anglia the big windows of the cottages gave light to the looms which were the livelihood of the family. There were enterprises also on a larger scale, especially in Wiltshire and East Anglia. At Colchester a Dutch settler employed five hundred men and women, and was so hated by the independent weavers that, in a lean year, they burnt his mill.

The factory was not the only enemy of the English weaver. Merchants found it increasingly profitable to sell raw wool abroad, instead of finished cloth. Home fashions too were changing; boots were making long woollen hose superfluous, and linen caps were neater and more comfortable than woollen. Weavers, knitters, spinners everywhere, but especially in Essex, suffered the enforced idleness which brought want and hunger.

High in importance in his subjects' lives, after the sea and the sheep, was the mineral wealth of the King's dominions. In recent years the " Black Indies " of the Durham minefields had begun to yield their riches; coal was mined too in Lancashire, Derbyshire, South Wales and in southern Scotland, and surface workings were frequent over all the English midlands. Some of the northern mines were deep; one shaft went down three hundred feet, reputedly the deepest in Europe, and at Culross on the coast of Fife the workings ran far out under the sea. Coal was a principal export from Scotland, but in England coal was rapidly replacing wood as the favourite fuel, and little went abroad. It came by sea from Newcastle to London and thence by barge inland. At first it had been carried partly in vessels from the east coast ports and partly in London ships, but of late years Newcastle citizens had developed their own coal fleet of over three hundred vessels. With the rising demand for coal the Newcastle hostmen, as the middlemen who transported and shipped the fuel were called, had become rich and powerful. The London faggot-mongers, as their trade in wood declined, had tried to wrest the transport of the new fuel from the " Lords of Coal " in the north, but the King favoured Newcastle and contemplated granting the hostmen a monopoly of the transport. London, now warmed almost wholly by coal fires, envied the rising wealth of the black seaport in the north.[8]

While the quarrel between the transporters raged, the coal miners everywhere remained an outcast minority, a black, savage people living in hovels round the primitive workings. In Scotland men worked so unwillingly in the mines that the old principle of serfdom had been revived by statute in Fife, and the miners were held by law, from generation to generation, in a bondage whence there was no escape. Women and children helped the men, and in some places it was said that whole families camped underground from week's end to week's end, coming up only on the Sabbath for compulsory kirk. In both England and Scotland the absconding felon or homeless vagabond was liable to be forced into this despised and dangerous toil. The miners kept themselves apart from the rest of the population and retained, not unnaturally, terrible and diabolic beliefs. They worked with unprotected tallow candles, and none knew better than they the fearful things that the demons from Hell could do when they unloosed the fire hidden in the depths of the earth.

The miners who worked for metal were more respected, although they too formed a class apart from their neighbours. Often, like the tin-miners of Cornwall, they lived under laws of their own. The lead mines of Mendip were worked by yeomen-miners; by the "custom of the hill" a man might stake his claim to his own small working wherever he struck lucky and set up his windlass. Lead workings pock-marked these hills for miles, causing roads to cave in and creating pitfalls for grazing cattle.

Copper was mined in Westmorland; copper, zinc and silver in the west country where German workers had been brought in by Queen Elizabeth. There were brass foundries near Bristol. King and Court entertained the highest hopes of the veins of silver opened up in South Wales by the indefatigable prospector Thomas Bushell.

Iron, after coal, was the chief mineral wealth of the country. It was a principal industry of Sussex and was worked also in Staffordshire, Derbyshire and Westmorland. Some doubt was felt about the workings in the Forest of Dean; as wood was still used for smelting the ore, the King feared that expansion of the iron works would destroy too much of the forest. The forests of Sussex had already been consumed, and in Worcestershire they were fast disappearing because wood was needed for the salt refineries which had sprung up near the saline springs. Unlimited destruction of timber could not be allowed, English oak being of the first necessity for shipbuilding. Recent experiments in smelting with coal might, it was hoped, solve this critical problem.

English ironmongery lacked distinction. The coarse knives of Sheffield and the cheap swords of Birmingham were widely despised but widely used. The swordsmiths of Hounslow had a higher reputation, and Ripon was distinguished for the excellence of its spurs. A smear of black country ran right across south Staffordshire whose " iron men " returned the hostility and contempt with which the sheep-herding " moorlanders " of north Staffordshire looked upon them. Iron-working was a domestic industry given over to nails and pins, and families worked industriously each at its own small forge. In Staffordshire too there was a local pottery industry, conducted in the same humble domestic manner. But earthenware pitchers and trenchers were not much used outside the clay regions; in general, wooden trenchers and leather bottles were used by the poorer sort, pewter by the better off. The finest harness and leather work was made on the edge of the Cotswolds, at Chipping Norton, or Burford, as famous for saddles as was Woodstock for gloves.

The islands were well supplied with building stone. The quarries of Scotland yielded granite. Marble was worked in Derbyshire and northern Ireland, alabaster in Lincolnshire, Staffordshire and on both sides of the Bristol Channel, at Penarth and at Minehead. There were slate quarries in Wales, Cornwall and Northampton. The Cotswolds had their own beautiful limestone; Devon and Dorset mansions were built from the fine yellow stone of Hamden Hill above Montacute.

The beautiful limestone from Portland in Dorset was coming into fashion and black marble from Ireland was sometimes used for decoration: materials were brought from great distances to produce a sophisticated and European style of architecture. But in much English building local styles and materials still prevailed. Brick was common for large buildings over most of the South although in the North and West timber was much used. A conservative people, the English retained Gothic details of decoration in spite of cosmopolitan Renaissance influence, and English carpenters showed remarkable skill in reproducing the ingenuity of Gothic stonecarving in their decorative woodwork. Inigo Jones, responding to the European fashion, denied to his workmen their individual fantasies; he—like the King in another sphere—decreed that the single mind of the master-architect should plan the entire building with all its ornaments. But outside the capital city medieval freedom of invention lingered yet; the carved lintels of Worcestershire doorways and the plaster ornamentation of Essex and Suffolk houses displayed the simple, gay imagination of the craftsmen who made them. While Inigo Jones conceived of London as a sophisticated European city, John Abell, master architect of Herefordshire, built the last and largest masterpieces of the local style, the elaborate and ambitious timber town-halls of Hereford and Leominster. The masons and builders of Scotland, by tradition and culture more closely connected with Europe and especially with France, had brought to maturity a style in which Renaissance detail was combined with the asperities of the native manner. Turrets, lintels, and doorways, which recalled the softer landscape of the Loire, lightened the harsh architecture evolved in a cold climate and an unstable society, and carved staircases and painted walls and ceilings showed the taste of the richer and more modern lords and citizens.

England was rich in mineral springs, some of only local fame, others famous throughout the land. Bath was the oldest and, though much fallen from its Roman splendour, still a place of considerable resort for health and pleasure. Visitors could enjoy organised entertainments such as dancing and fencing matches, but the chief amusement was to watch the sick people, of all ages and sexes, stark naked but for linen caps, sitting immersed in the great bath. The younger spa, Tunbridge, which offered good public rooms and gaming tables, was temporarily the more fashionable; the fortunate visitor might see " six earls and lords in a morning at the Wells."

The saline springs of Droitwich and the medicinal waters of Buxton and Matlock were locally famous. Physicians spoke marvels of the waters at Knaresborough but they attracted the attention of the curious rather than the sick, because of their petrifying action.

Mining and manufacture notwithstanding, the King's dominions were still essentially rural. His people lived in small communities, were proud of local achievements, prejudiced in the local interest, and very close to the soil.

The countryside offered many simple delights. Izaak Walton and his companions could pass a summer's day in happy argument on the relative merits of their favourite sports, catch trout and chub in the clear streams, listen to the milkmaids singing and watch with tranquil interest the striped caterpillars on the leafy trees and the painted butterflies in the meadows. John Milton in one of his rare idle hours may have seen such dancing in the chequered shade as he attributed to " the upland hamlets." Girls as pretty if not as eloquent as Perdita gave out posies at the sheep-shearing. On winter evenings the young jigged and danced by firelight at Leap Candle or the Cushion Dance; all the year long they had their singing rounds and games, Sellenger's Round, John Come Kiss Me, and Barley Break. Rush-bearing ceremonies, blessing of cornfields and of springs, crowning the May Queen, roasting geese at Michaelmas and sucking pig at Lammas, varied the laborious year. Free beer flowed merrily at Whitsun-ales and harvest festivals, and boys in wigs and petticoats bounced about on hobby-horses to the uproarious delight of all. In strongly Protestant districts traditional Hallowe'en jollities were being ingeniously transferred to Gunpowder Treason Day on November 5th. But religious disapproval so far had had little effect on the celebrations which marked the end of August when London's Bartholomew Fair lasted close on a fortnight, and all over Lancashire and Somerset the wakes were held, usually in the churches, with dancing, drinking, pipe, tabor and fiddle. During the time of general holiday between Christmas and Twelfth Night a Lord of Misrule was still sometimes elected to preside over the festivities, and the old mockery of church ceremonies, permitted in medieval times, was occasionally indulged, but at greater peril. The King, when he came to hear of it, viewed with grave disapproval a swineherd's impersonation of an Anglican priest at a mock marriage. At all times of year, bridals and christenings were an excuse for merry-making and the distribution of gifts, garters, posies, ribbons and—if they could be afforded—gloves. In the lowlands of Scotland the poor people had thriftily invented the " penny bridal," an occasion when each guest paid his penny towards the day's revelling. As anyone could become a guest at such feasts, they were the occasion of noisy mirth, on which the respectable frowned and the Kirk made determined but unsuccessful war.

In the summer months picnic parties from the towns rode out into the country with baskets full of pasties, and London apprentices carried their girls to Islington, Tottenham and Hogsden for cheese cakes and cream. The rich and fashionable favoured the Three Pigeons at Brentford for week-end parties. The sports and pleasures of the gentlefolk were hawking and hunting, and bowls as they grew older; they matched their hawks and greyhounds against each other, and their horses at the local race meetings which were becoming regular events. Sometimes, as at Kiplingcotes in Yorkshire, a piece of plate was the reward of the winner. Newmarket and Epsom Downs were already famous, and horses, like Bay Tarrell, a Newmarket winner, and Toby, whose owner, a London merchant, had gilded his hoofs, were popular favourites. With racing went the bagpipes, and the winner was escorted through the crowds to their shrill music.

Travelling pedlars and mountebanks entertained the villages with their wares and their news; they performed simple operations, drew teeth, cut corns, lanced boils and successfully straightened wry-necked children by cutting the tendons. The crowder, or fiddler, ready to play for any festivity, the rope-dancer, the juggler, and the showman with a bear, or perhaps a monster, were popular figures in the villages and country towns. In Scotland a solitary camel, the King's property, was leased out to a warden who was permitted to show him off, by tuck of drum, at all times of day except during divine service.[9]

In their leisure time students and apprentices competed with the bow; village boys played ninepins, cudgels, or a rough kind of football. In some places local sports were annually held. The famous Cotswold Games, sponsored by jolly Captain Dover, took place every year on a broad-topped down that still bears his name. From miles around came men and boys to compete in running, wrestling, quarter staff and shooting, for a great distribution of prizes and favours. The enterprise enjoyed royal favour and aimed at creating a new Olympia. The King's Court had graced it once with their presence and several poets had celebrated it in rhyme.

The people had the free and spontaneous gaiety of those who live in the moment because the next may bring disaster. The happy lovers who in the summer embraced "between the acres of the rye," would in a famine-stricken winter cling together for warmth before a cold hearthstone. They enjoyed the good times, they endured the bad. Drought, frost, fire, flood were the enemies of all who lived by the land.

With the easy laughter and song went also a primitive delight in violence. Cock-fighting and bull- and bear-baiting were the sports of all classes when they could get to them, and a light-hearted squire like Sir Humphrey Mildmay in Essex would from time to time let out his bull to be baited by the village dogs. Cock-throwing, which meant pelting the poor birds with sticks or stones, was a traditional annual sport among village boys. The ducking of scolds, or leading them through the village bitted and bridled, and compelling their husbands to ride the pole were occasional village amusements. Domestic quarrels were violent in all classes of society; a London regulation forbade wife-beating after nine in the evening because of the noise. Gentlemen who were known to "fling cushions at one another's heads only in sport and for exercise" descended with ease from horse-play to fisticuffs; blows were exchanged on very small provocation and in the most unseemly places. The

Murgatroyds, for instance, annoyed because another family walked into church ahead of them, knocked down and trampled on their rivals, causing a disturbance the echoes of which were several years dying away in the ecclesiastical courts.

The physical conditions of life were not easy for anyone. Few anodynes were known and none were effective; rich and poor alike suffered with little help all the varied torments of the flesh. Familiarity with pain bred, in all classes, a certain stoicism, a deep acceptance of suffering as part of the necessary order of the world and a willingness to inflict it and to see it inflicted.

The King's dominions differed greatly in the quality and character of their soil. In many regions, village communities still endeavoured to be self-supporting in necessities. Small crops of rye, barley and oats, beans and peas were sown in strips in the common field. Hogs pastured on the common or the beech mast in the woods, and were mostly slaughtered at Michaelmas when their lean flesh, smoked, provided the winter meat, and their bladders, blown up, made footballs for the winter's sport. Even in the Scottish Highlands the cattle-herding clans had their sparse crops of oats, sown and reaped by their women. Only in parts of Ireland nomadic communities still existed who scorned the plough and lived, year in and year out, on the milk and flesh of their cattle, such edible grasses and seaweeds as grew without their help, and, from time to time, the plunder of an English settler's barn.

The cattle-farming of the Celtic peoples in Scotland and Ireland survived from early times; their herds of lean and shaggy beasts had the freedom of the mountains and wilds. The Highland clans, ennobling the struggle for provender with the bloody romance of clan feuds, disputed their difficult country among themselves. No one else wanted it. But in Ireland, whose low-lying, spongy meadows provided good pasture, settlers from England and southern Scotland were thrusting the native people and their herds back into the bogs while they introduced better breeds of cattle and more economic methods.

Sheep-breeding in England had, for the time being, reached

its utmost expansion. The towns which had fattened upon it had to be fed with other things than fleeces; experiments were made and methods discussed for increasing the yield of the earth, improving crops, developing wheat and barley in place of the cruder rye and oats. More and more land—for there was still much waste and forest land in England—was used for growing corn and raising cattle. Cattle for milk and meat and hides were being extensively bred in Devon and Somerset, in Herefordshire and the Midlands. The old complaint of the poor in the previous century that the sheep had eaten up the arable land was changed to a new one—that the cultivated land was eating up the common and the forest. The poor man needed the common and the forest so that he could collect firewood and pasture his hogs. Great landowners from time to time enclosed the waste land, but they were not the only encroachers. The yeoman and the labourer also made their surreptitious advances, and small hamlets grew up on the edge of forest and heath, the penurious outposts of landless squatters.

The regions had their specialities. The Sussex wheatear, a tiny bird, was praised as "a little lump of flying sugar equal to the best ortolans of France." In Kent acres of cherry trees provided a favourite fruit for London. In Herefordshire and Worcestershire, and in Somerset, especially about Taunton, and in Gloucestershire, "that rich and fruitful garden-shire",[10] the far-spread apple orchards filled the autumn vats for cider. Hampshire claimed the sweetest honey in the kingdom; so did Bishop Auckland. Cheddar was famous for cheese, Banbury for cheese and cakes, Tewkesbury for mustard, Pomfret and Nottingham for licorice, and wide fields of crocus round Saffron Walden explained its name. About London for twenty or thirty miles the towns and villages were set in a chessboard of vegetable gardens, cultivated in the Dutch manner, growing asparagus, young green peas, cauliflower and carrots for the luxury market of the capital.

The dairy produce of Devon was gaining reputation, and the fat cattle of Herefordshire ambled along the drove roads, at a comfortable rate of eight miles a day, to their doom in Smithfield market. Northumberland boasted plump chickens and all manner of poultry. There was not much to be said for Cumberland or Westmorland where travellers from the south were shocked at the poverty and smallness of the hamlets, the bare feet and uncouth accent of the people. Carlisle cathedral, to the southerner, was nothing but " a great wild country church," and the city's aldermen wore blue bonnets, like roving Scots, instead of felt or beaver hats. But game birds and venison were plentiful in the north parts and " a huge standing water called Windermere " produced a most delicious fish called a char.[11]

The poverty of Cumberland, which shocked southern travellers, was equalled by the poverty which met the English traveller's eyes when he crossed the Border. Even in a gentleman's house flitches of bacon hung from the rafters in the smoke of the best room, and the lady of the place did not always wear stockings. The women of the one-roomed, turf-thatched, mud-floored hovels wore their petticoats kilted above the knee, but their feet and ankles were clean because they trod their washing instead of handling it.

The best of Scotland was not on the Border. In Lothian, cattle and sheep at pasture, and strips of oats and barley surrounded Edinburgh with an air of modest prosperity. The stone-built capital of Scotland, wedged between rock and loch, its tall forbidding tenements crowned by the airily graceful lantern tower of St. Giles, was like no other town in the islands. It was not, by any but Scottish standards, a rich town; the winds that whistled through its ravine streets blew upon marketing women shrouded in heavy plaids—the material of which, as an English traveller snobbishly remarked, his countrymen made saddle cloths. They were a hard-working, hard-headed people indifferent to outward appearances, very sure of themselves, independent and proud.

West from Edinburgh in the Lennox and in Clydesdale good mixed farming was to be found, orchard, corn and grazing land, fissured here and there with new workings of coal. The city of

Glasgow which commanded at once its outlet to the sea and the system of roads, such as it was, that linked the south-west of Scotland had flourished considerably. It had as yet little reputation as a port, for the sandy Clyde was too shallow to take any but the smallest ships.

The region of Galloway was relatively prosperous because of the steady traffic that passed through its little ports for northern Ireland; it was also famous for sheep and mettlesome Galloway nags. Other regions of good farming, especially for barley and oats, were the carse of Gowrie, the gracious region between Perth and Montrose, and that strangely blest strip of land north of Cairn Gorm, fringing the northern sea, the " golden planure " of Moray. The cattle, deer and small wild animals of the Highlands, otters, badgers and ferocious martens, provided furs and hides which were a valuable export; even the skins of wolves which still roamed the wilder mountains had their price. Beyond the Highlands, the people of the more open northern lands of Ross and Caithness lived upon fish and cattle, a spare, hard existence which did not prevent the men of Caithness from being, in the opinion of the loquacious traveller William Lithgow, " the best and most bountiful Christmas keepers (the Greeks excepted) that ever I saw in the Christian world." [12]

In England and in the more fertile parts of Scotland intelligent farmers and landowners were considering ways of improving their methods and their land. In England the prevalence of common-field farming made large-scale experiments difficult, and in Scotland the system of land tenure, by which leases were terminable from year to year, discouraged long-term planning. But experiment was in the air. New crops and new methods were discussed by the educated. Potatoes and turnips were being tried but had not gained any popularity. Lucerne, clover and sainfoin had been suggested as possible crops to provide winter fodder for cattle, and thus make the wholesale slaughter of beasts every autumn unnecessary. But the ideas put forward by progressive theorists who wished to enclose all the common land and so curtail the spread of cattle diseases were highly

unpopular. Occasionally a landowner like Sir Richard Weston
at Sutton Place in Surrey conducted experiments in irrigation
and the improvement of soil on a large scale. The King had
given authority for the draining of some of the fen country, and
a successful beginning had been made with Hatfield Chase, a
water-logged region between Yorkshire and Lincolnshire which
the Dutch engineer Vermuyden had reclaimed. But farmers
complained that the local price of corn had gone down owing
to the plentiful harvests from the new land.

Vermuyden was now reclaiming the fenlands round Ely, a
scheme in which the Court was interested and into which the
Earl of Bedford and a number of other distinguished shareholders had put large sums of money. This improvement, and
others like it, was bitterly opposed by the fenmen who had long
lived by fishing and fowling and had no inclination to see their
hunting-grounds turned over to grazing:

> For they do mean all fens to drain and water overmaster,
> All will be dry and we must die, 'cause Essex calves want
>   pasture. . . .
> The feather'd fowls have wings to fly to other nations,
> But we have no such things to help our transportations.
> We must give place (oh grievous case) to horned beasts and
>   cattle,
> Except that we can all agree to drive them out by battle.[13]

The fenmen decided on battle. They assailed Vermuyden's
workmen with showers of stones and repeatedly destroyed the
works.

New manures, new methods of sowing and ploughing, the
introduction of new domestic animals were also discussed.
Richard Childe, with some knowledge of the East, seriously
considered the introduction of the elephant: a beast " very
serviceable for carriage, fifteen men usually riding on his back
together, and he is not chargeable to keep." [14]

New fruits and plants were assiduously cultivated by the

rich. The King's gardener John Tradescant had introduced a small French willow tree, excellent for making baskets, as well as the merely ornamental acacia and lilac. His interesting botanical garden, recently opened at Lambeth, was rivalled by that created for the university of Oxford by Lord Danby. But experimental gardens, beautiful or medicinal, were being made everywhere; Sir Arthur Ingram's at York, ornamented with statues in the Italian manner, was famous and so was the fine garden of Moray House in Edinburgh. Many a country gentle-man spent time and trouble introducing new fruits to his orchard and new flowers to his garden—the better kinds of apples and pears and such novelties as apricots, vines and raspberry canes, the Portugal quince, figs, melons, currants and damsons, walnuts, almonds and the edible chestnut. The flowering peach and laburnum were already popular, and Sir John Oglander in the Isle of Wight, recorded proudly in his diary that he had planted " in one knot all sorts of French flowers and tulips . . . Some roots cost me 10d. a root." [15]

Neither the cultivation of their gardens nor wider schemes for reclaiming land could assuage the land hunger of the English or the lowland Scots. The Scots indeed had for generations now emigrated by families to the Baltic shores of North Germany and Poland, there to build up the Scottish–Baltic trade. The number of these foreign-dwelling Scots was estimated at nearly thirty thousand. But for new land both Scots and English looked towards Ireland. Scots and English intruders flourished in Ulster, English intruders in Munster; dairy farming had begun round Waterford and in Wicklow where English cattle had been introduced; good crops of rye and barley grew round Dublin; the government was encouraging the cultivation of flax for linen in Ulster; there was a growing export trade in Irish timber.

Another promised land awaited the adventurous on the farther side of the Atlantic Ocean, where pioneers were planting their English cultivation and their English names—Plymouth, Taunton, Boston, Ipswich—on the shores of a gigantic unknown continent. Not very many of the King's subjects lived in this perilous land, in his opinion too far from his control: from Newfoundland to the Caribbean, not more than fifty thousand. For King Charles it sometimes seemed fifty thousand too many. If his people wanted more land, let them go to Ireland where he could watch over their religion, education and morals. The stream of adventurers went for other causes than the need for land alone; far from his paternal vigilance they practised uncouth religions and strange politics. He was considering whether it would not be wise to prohibit their going altogether.

The structure of society was still hierarchic, although with differences in the nature and the rigidity of the hierarchy in different regions. In England at the topmost level were noblemen of the old school who kept two hundred servants of all degrees, from their Master of the Horse and Gentleman Ushers, their Yeomen of the Buttery and Pantry, to laundresses and grooms, and who went on journeys with a trumpeter to give notice of their coming.[16] At the lowest level was the day labourer with one coarse shirt to his back, earning a night's lodging and a share of pease-pudding, and enjoying from time to time the free spectacle of the great lord and his train passing by. Great as was the distance between high and low, no insurmountable barriers separated, one from the other, the many classes in between. There was unceasing movement up and down. A man might rise or sink by his own good fortune or his own endeavours. Gentility was to be acquired by intellect or valour or wealth; by English custom, all clergy, all university students, all lawyers and any man who had held command in an army might write himself down " gentleman ", no matter who his father had been. In every generation tradesmen and yeomen made their way into the gentry not to mention the clerks and secretaries who rose by service to the great lords or the Court. The last step into the nobility was open to those who could pay the price for it either by direct purchase or by services to the Crown. The older nobility might look with contempt on these sons and grandsons of aldermen financiers and clerks, these earls and barons who had paid cash down for their titles—Middlesex, Portland, Clare, Cork—but they received them in their houses and eagerly sought their daughters in marriage.

The downward movement was as persistent as the upward, and the feckless gentleman who wasted his estates could drop in a few years to the criminal depths of society. The attempt to save the situation by abducting an heiress was made more often than it succeeded. In the summer of 1637 Sarah Cox, a rich orphan of fourteen, was snatched from a party of schoolgirls walking on Newington common and carried away screaming by a young gentleman in a coach. Although she was forcibly married that day, her friends rescued her next morning, and her enterprising husband was thrown into prison.[17]

Love occasionally found a way and if the poor suitor won the lady's heart his chances were usually good. A city heiress, on the eve of her wedding to the dull husband of her guardian's choice, whispered to the handsome younger son of a poor Scots lord that " her affection was more to him, if his were so to her she would instantly go away with him." Receiving the necessary encouragement, she drove to Greenwich with him that night and married him.[18]

The nearness of the Court unsettled London wives and daughters. Courtiers had more persuasive manners than citizens, and the citizen's wife, showing off her new coach in the Ring at Hyde Park, might easily make a flattering conquest of some fine gentleman. An invitation to a Court masque or play might follow, and not all the excited young women who hurried to Whitehall in their best finery brought back an unsullied virtue to the paternal or conjugal hearth. " There is not a lobby nor chamber, if it could speak, but would verify this," declared a censorious writer. It was an insolent common boast of young courtiers that they had cuckolded half a dozen aldermen. In the City of London the moral reputation of the Court stood very low: the Queen was rumoured to be Harry Jermyn's mistress, or else Lord Holland's, nor was the King held blameless. These scandals were baseless, but jealous citizens repeated, magnified and believed them.

English women enjoyed unusual freedom; the tradition went far back and had much to do with the movement between class and class. When the Reformation closed the nunneries to the younger daughters of the rich or nobly born, they did not remain mewed up, unmarried, because there were no suitors good enough. They married where and how they could: the nobleman's younger daughter married the squire, the squire's younger daughter married the tradesman, the schoolmaster's or vicar's daughter might marry the yeoman, even the labourer, and so on to the lowest rungs of the social ladder. These women were a powerful, secret force, diffusing the pretensions and confidence of gentility in the humblest ranks of English society.

There was no legal and only a limited traditional objection to marriages which outraged the conventions. If the gentleman's daughter ran off with the footman her family might refuse to see her again but it was not an essential point of honour, as it would have been in some contemporary European countries, to wipe out the stain by killing the low-born seducer.

No English tradition prohibited gentlemen from following the professions or concerning themselves with trade. For the small squire it was nothing unusual to practise as a doctor or solicitor or to "get a ship and judiciously manage her." [19] Richer men adopted more ambitious courses. The powerful companies which financed colonial ventures and trade with Russia, Turkey and the East counted noblemen among their directors and shareholders. Many great families were already drawing their fortunes from coal and iron, not merely because these had been found on their lands but because they had themselves opened the mines and organised transport and marketing. The Willoughbies at Wollaton had started glass-furnaces to absorb the produce of the coal mines on their estates. The Byrons, on the strength of a rising fortune in coal, had become *entrepreneurs* and money-lenders on a large scale in the Midlands;

the Robartes family, whose fortune was built on wool and tin, had done the same in Cornwall; the Ashburnhams were the largest iron masters in Sussex; the Lumleys financed the alum works at Hartlepool, and the Lambtons the salt refineries at Sunderland. Sir John Winter, of an ancient Roman Catholic family, leased the iron mines of the Forest of Dean from the King, and with the help of a cousin, Lord Herbert of Raglan a pioneer in experimental engineering, had greatly developed them. He had also acquired interests in the South Wales coal mines, and in the course of the next generation was to fore-shadow that marriage between coal and iron from which, in good time, the Industrial Revolution would be born. The Lowthers in Cumberland were developing the mines of Whitehaven, linked with a fleet of ships to transport their produce to Ireland.

England had long since accepted the fusion of the feudal landowner with the industrialist and the merchant. The squire's younger sons were, in the order of things, apprenticed to trades unless their abilities fitted them for the law or the Church. Only the ardently adventurous or irremediably stupid were sent abroad with horse and arms to become soldiers in foreign service.

In all the larger towns, and above all in London, the short-haired apprentices who thronged about the place counted among their number gentlemen's sons, yeomen's sons, the sons of professional men and of citizens. There were distinctions between them of course; gentlemen's sons were naturally apprenticed to the wealthiest and most respectable men. The irascible master worked off his temper on the poor widow's son rather than the baronet's younger brother. But within the framework of the great corporations and before the laws of the city all were alike apprentices, and common interests, hopes and pleasures broke down the barriers of inheritance.

Instructive handbooks enabled the self-made to learn the manners and outlook of the class into which they had penetrated. Richard Brathwaite's *The English Gentleman* and *The English Gentlewoman Drawn out to the Full Body* enjoyed considerable popularity. So did Henry Peacham's more ambitious *The Compleat Gentleman* which aimed at improving the accomplishments of the gentry and instructed them in science, literature and art as well as fishing and heraldry. His *The Worth of a Peny* and *The Art of Living in London* were directed at the many young men who fell a prey to the cheats and temptations of the great city. The anonymous *A Precedent for Young Pen-men* instructed the uneducated, with numerous examples, in the art of polite letter-writing.

The movements and alliances between the classes did not prevent the careful observance of the differences between them; there would have been less point in climbing the social ladder had it been otherwise. None were more anxious to preserve the privileges of their order than those who had but recently risen to occupy it. The merchant who had married his daughter to a lord stood bare-headed in her presence until she gave him leave to cover. The citizen's coach made way for the knight's coach when they met in a narrow place. Relations who had come down in the world often entered the house of their more fortunate kinsfolk as servants and had no more than the rights of servants; the good-natured Ralph Josselin, a country vicar, recorded a generous resolution in his diary: " My sister Mary is come under my roof as a servant, but my respect is and shall be towards her as a sister." [20] Bowing, curtsying, taking off the hat, entering a room, sitting at table were all strictly regulated, although some conventions were declining, and old people grumbled at the free and easy manner of the young.

Some sports were for gentlemen only, special clothes belonged to certain professions. A labourer might play at ninepins but not at bowls, and his wife and daughter must wear petticoats and bodices as separate garments, not gowns like gentlewomen. Lord Stamford was indignant when a sporting vicar trespassed on his land with greyhound in leash and hawk on wrist and a hunting dress of a most uncanonical colour. A blacksmith's wife who ventured forth in a gown suitable to a merchant's wife was hooted back into the smithy by the people of Ludlow.

But some conventions at least were growing slack. A petition had only recently been presented to the King praying him to prohibit the wearing of boots to the lower orders while there was yet time, for "divers inferior persons, both tradesmen and others . . . wear boots as familiarly as any nobleman or gentleman, the which abuse doth not only consume much leather vainly but doth much hurt unto divers poor people which would have much employment by . . . knitting of hose." [21]

The family atmosphere of town and country life was declining but apprentices and sons still shared the house and table of the master and father, servants and family ate together in farmhouses, and in some parts of the country the honest labourer could still count on his Sunday dinner either at the squire's table or at that of a neighbouring farmer. Order of precedence was carefully preserved, and in a few houses the old phrase "below the salt" retained its actual and not merely its metaphorical meaning; the massive salt cellar divided masters from servants. But in the houses of the rich, by this time, separate tables or even separate rooms had become the custom.

Some great houses, particularly in the more rural North, retained the custom of piling the broken meats into tubs and setting them out for the poor, but fashions in food as well as fashions in living were bringing this medieval custom to its end. Foreign dainties, Italian sauces, "French kickshaws," as they were called, and the new elaborate ways of serving food with more emphasis on candied fruit and flowers, on elegance than on substance, were not suited to the old custom. Conservative writers already lamented the roast beef of old England as a thing of the past. Yet solidity had not wholly disappeared from a diet in which, for festive occasions, roast fawn stuffed with suet dumplings, boar's head with lemon, turkey stuffed with pheasant which was in turn stuffed with capon, made their appearance, and the autumn delicacy of all classes was the luscious sucking pig.

Local practice varied greatly, but such in the main was the structure of English society: a clearly defined hierarchy from landless labourer to nobleman, from unskilled journeyman to Mayor—but a hierarchy without barriers, a steep ladder on which men and women passed continually up and down.

This situation was not reproduced in the adjoining lands. The gentry of Wales were as a rule poorer and simpler than the gentry of England. " You can sooner find fifty gentlemen of £100 a year than five of £500," recorded an observer from England, or, as a traditional jingle put it of one Welsh county:

> Alas, alas, poor Radnorshire,
> Never a park, nor ever a deer,
> Nor ever a squire of five hundred a year
> Save Sir Richard Fowler of Abbey Cwm Hir.[22]

But the Welsh gentleman in his stone-built farmhouse, with salmon hanging in the smoke of his chimney, a dresser with wooden trenchers upon it, fixed benches round the fire and about the walls, and a woven cloth for the parlour table on a Sunday, lived a traditional and patriarchal life among servants and tenantry who looked upon him as something more than employer and landlord and felt for him and his a tribal loyalty and pride. Often he still did not trouble himself to have an English surname; knowing well by oral tradition that he was descended from royal stock, he scorned the English insistence on family names; himself he was David Evans ; his son, called Evan from his grandfather, would be Evan Davis. His life, impoverished reflection of the Celtic tradition, had a simplicity and poetry of its own, but even in its decadence Celtic society was more rigid than the competitive, make-your-own-way society of England.

Ambitious Welsh boys sought their fortunes not at home but in England, where their alert faces, quick tempers and musical accent were teasingly accepted. Eloquence and imagination often carried them far in the church or in the law; John Williams, Bishop of Lincoln, was only the most remarkable of the many Welsh bishops in the British Isles, and two of the

King's twelve Judges, John Trevor and William Jones, were Welshmen. Some of these distinguished Welshmen would come home in mature years, settle benevolently among their poor countrymen, patronise and encourage local talent and offer the wealth and fame won in England to swell the diminished glories of their native Wales. More often the emigrant Welsh, successful or unsuccessful, stayed in their adopted country, and the names of Jones and Trevor, Vaughan, Evans and Morgan would be found, sparsely, in parish registers over all the English midlands, the south and west.

In Wales itself the poverty of the people and the patriarchal structure of society made it possible for a few great landowners to wield immense influence and power—families like that of Herbert, carrying half a dozen titles, or Somerset, whose head, the Earl of Worcester, lived at Raglan. Here in Wales the old feudal system superimposed four centuries earlier on the Celtic world had persisted, strengthened by the profound loyalties, rivalries and hatreds of the Celtic tradition.

In Scotland, where the Celtic world, hostile and unsubdued, had been penned into the Highlands, the situation was unlike that in Wales and England. Lowland Scotland, predominantly Anglo-Saxon in race and English in speech, kept perpetual watch on the untamed Highlands, but the feudal organisation imposed on this southern region in the twelfth century had acquired a patriarchal quality from contact with the Celt. The King himself in Scotland was not—as in England—regarded as the feudal overlord and fountain of justice and authority; he was regarded patriarchally as the head of the family. He was King of *Scots* not of Scotland, a ruler with a personal relationship to his people.

The Scottish laird, simply clad in homespun, with his blue bonnet on his head, ruled among his tenantry and servants with the intimacy, affection and arbitrariness of a father. He kept open house for travellers; he relieved the poor at his gate; his people called him by the name of his estate and he called them by the names of their farms. This gave a deceptively friendly air to a relationship which was dictatorial and could be tyrannous. The tenant Scots held their land upon annual lease, and the landlord who found minerals upon his estate, as many now did, might reduce his dependent farmers to landless men overnight at the year's end. The lowland Scots were discovering the mineral wealth of their country and developing shipping and trade of all kinds; compared to England theirs was a harsh and difficult world, where economy and stubborn toil alone yielded rewards. The belief that the Lord had His Chosen People and rewarded them, gave a terrible intensity to Scotland's struggle to establish herself in the pattern of European economics, with her wool, coal, timber and fur exports and her fisheries. The Lord placed coal mines upon the lands of His Chosen; since theirs was the earth and the fulness thereof, it was clear that those who were dispossessed, or forced down the mines in the process, were none of the Lord's people. The belief was not cynical; it was often associated with a strenuousness of austerity and prayer that showed—if in a strange fashion—a deep sense of gratitude and responsibility for the Lord's well-placed gifts.

In the highlands the Celtic clan system generally prevailed, although the ancient clan loyalties were here and there crossed by feudal conceptions of land tenure. The Mackintosh, for instance, was accepted as chief in districts which, by feudal tenure belonged to Huntly, chief of the Gordons. Conversely he was feudal overlord of other regions inhabited by the Cameron clan. This confusion of rights was fruitful of trouble in a land where clan chiefs still in practice had rights of life and death over their people; whatever laws the Crown might pass to curtail this jurisdiction, such men as Argyll, Huntly, Seaforth had a moral and actual power over Campbells, Gordons, Mackenzies which extended to every part of their lives. Among themselves the highlanders were tenacious of their enmities: Campbell slew Macdonald, and Macdonald Campbell whenever they could. The Mackenzies were at feud with the MacLeods, the Gordons with the Crichtons, and every man's hand was against the Mac-Gregors and MacNabs. The land was terrible and bloody, but with a wild beauty dear to those who knew it. In the late summer the clans gathered for the hunting; lesser quarrels were temporarily at rest while for long days over the great hills, they encircled and drove the deer. Sometimes, in the summer days the young men camped together in the meadow land by Tay or Spey, enjoyed the season's sport, swam, wrestled, leaped, danced, through the warm nights when dawn came after sunset with scarce a resting time between. In highland games or highland wars, the sons of the greater chiefs, who had been at the French Court or the English and had learnt the delicacies and graces of cosmopolitan civilisation, slept on the ground among their clansmen, wore—with a cultured elegance—the plaid and trews of their native land, spoke Gaelic, listened to the interminable songs of bards and the sharp music of the pipes, and watched the sword dances and the revels by the long sunset light and the glow of the turf fires.

Some of the southern nobility came north for the hunting; those whose lands lay along the highland frontier—Montrose, Ogilvy, Mar, Eglinton—were usually present. These had adopted some of the highland ways, probably "had the Gaelic," sometimes called themselves chiefs although they were in effect merely heads of families. Their function in the strategy of Scotland was to prevent highland incursions into the richer lands of the South, but over centuries of strife they had learnt to admire and imitate the very things they fought. Sometimes too a foreign visitor was welcomed to the highland hunting; an intruding cockney John Taylor, clad in a kilt lent him by the Earl of Mar, squatted on the unfamiliar, uncomfortable ground throughout the weird dances and wondered why these extraordinary people did not cut down their pine forests and trade them as masts to the shipyards of the world.

Between lowlands and highlands an armed neutrality reigned, broken from time to time by cattle-raiding. The highlanders, who knew that the land had been all theirs until the Saxon came, esteemed it no robbery to steal back something of their own. Lawlessness of the same kind prevailed on the English border.

The late King James, when he succeeded to the English throne, had tried to pacify the borders with a strong hand, and for a time his armed patrols, his hangings and deportations of the border reivers, Scots and English, had brought an illusory calm. But the tradition of valiant robbery and lawlessness was too strong to die in a few years. Under the relaxed vigilance which marked King Charles's reign, the borders had gone back to their old way of life and by 1635 great parts of the country were terrorised by armed gangs who lived by robbery, kidnapping and ransom and revenged themselves so horribly on any who informed against them that few dared do so. The treacherous slaughter of the Laird of Troughend, the subject of one of the finest of the border ballads, was a part of this tale of blackmail and vengeance.

In Scotland the Celtic North and the Anglo-Saxon South were separated by the geographical division of highlands and lowlands. No division so convenient existed in Ireland where alien invaders from England had forcibly thrust themselves upon an angry Celtic land. The first settlers, the Normans, had become in the course of centuries acceptable to the Irish chiefs. The great family of Butler—Earls of Ormonde—were cross-bred with Irish families; so were the Fitzgeralds, the St. Legers, and the de Burghs commonly called Burke.

In the last seventy years new settlers had descended upon Ireland, first from England, then from the lowlands of Scotland. These were calculating, adventurous, competitive, bent on developing the latent possibilities of an undeveloped land, and Protestant, with a Protestant government behind them. The wild Irish were as alien to them as the American Indians to the settlers across the Atlantic. Against these pushful newcomers, the Irish and the Norman-Irish drew together—aristocrats, with their retainers and their clans, a patriarchal society against upstarts.

Apparent peace prevailed, and the royal government, as represented by Lord Deputy Wentworth, hopefully cherished the ambition of seeing Ireland " enclosed and husbanded, beautified with towns and buildings and stored with an industrious well-conditioned people." Dublin at least had been improved with handsome modern additions to the Castle, a pleasant meeting place for coaches and equestrians at Phœnix Park, and a theatre for which the fashionable James Shirley had written the opening play. The Deputy ostentatiously placed his own son at Trinity College (which Queen Elizabeth had founded) as an encouragement to other distinguished residents to do the same. Under government patronage Christopher Syms had composed a new Latin grammar specially designed for use in Irish schools and published recently in Dublin.

Appearances were deceptive. The Irish retained their religion and their unconquered independence of spirit. Their clans remained loyal to their chieftains, whether these were exiles far away, like the Red O'Neill, or friendly to the English government, like Randall MacDonnell, Earl of Antrim, or Murrough O'Brien, Earl of Inchiquin, chiefs respectively of the largest clans in the north and south. Scattered nomadic hordes still lived in the shelter of the hills and bogs, levying blackmail on their neighbours and raiding the settlers when they dared. The worst danger was not from them but from the covert hostility of an entire population. Here in Ireland, sooner than any thought or feared, the struggle of eleven hundred years between the Saxon and the Celt was to burst into a new and terrible blaze.

The same clash of ideas and interests was reproduced in miniature midway between the Irish and the English shores on the Isle of Man. Twelve miles across and thirty-three miles in length, it belonged to Lord Strange, the Earl of Derby's eldest son. He found its lively, loquacious inhabitants faithful to their old customs in spite of benevolent attempts to bring their peculiar system of land tenure into line with that of his other possessions on the English mainland, and to reform their laws. The greatest native family was that of Christian. Its present head was especially powerful because of his many sons; illegitimacy mattered little among the Manxmen and the head of the Christian family bore patriarchal sway over his people. His opposition compelled Lord Strange to modify his policy; for the time being he had accepted Captain Christian as Dempster, which meant that he virtually ruled the island in Lord Strange's name.

The Celtic populations were a significant and possibly a dangerous minority in the King's dominions. They represented an antique challenge to the modern world in a way that the French-speaking Channel Islanders and occasional groups of foreign refugees did not. At the moment, the Channel Islanders were resentfully and jealously guarding their ancient privileges against government encroachment, but they shared with the English and the Lowland Scots much the same outlook on society and the world, although they might have lesser differences of interest and opinion.

Another kind of society, secret and submerged, persisted in the King's dominions: the gypsies. They were known to the people as wanderers and vagabonds, distinguished from the ordinary vagabonds and thieves who roamed the country by a peculiar language and a closer organisation. Ballads occasionally romanticised them but the law persecuted them, and in the lowlands of Scotland to be a gypsy might in itself prove a capital offence.

Such were the peoples over whom King Charles reigned, and to whom he wished to give the blessings of peace, justice, order and true religion, under the unquestioned authority of the Crown. The ideal was constantly before his eyes but the intellectual and æsthetic fashion of the day, strongly bent towards allegory, obscured the practical difficulties of the task. The King lived in a world of poetic illusions and could not but be affected by them. For him and his courtiers, the most ordinary events were swiftly wreathed in pastoral or classical disguise. The Countess of Anglesey gave an evening party for the Queen and at once the poets summoned the goddess Diana and bade the stars shoot from their spheres;[23] Lord Bridgewater's three children made a long journey, and Comus with all his rout sprang eloquently forth to provide a masque and a moral to celebrate their reunion with their parents.

A young poet, hailing a new arrival at Court, cried out:

" What's she, so late from Penshurst come.
More gorgeous than the mid-day sun
That all the world amazes?
Sure 'tis some angel from above,
Or 'tis the Cyprian Queen of Love
Attended by the Graces."[24]

But it was only the Lady Dorothy Sidney with the usual duenna and waiting women.

Arcadian scenes were rhymed and sung, with splendid or with humble staging, in many a school or college hall or private house. Almost every year the King himself acted in a Christmas masque, and, recently, the most expensive masque ever mounted —it cost over £20,000—had been put on in his honour by the lawyers of the Inns of Court. It had represented the Triumph of Peace, and the masquers, about two hundred of them, had ridden through the streets of London by torchlight in the quaint and gorgeous finery designed for them by Inigo Jones.

The King had approved of this masque, written by the skilful and much favoured James Shirley. It too had enacted that same allegory which he had commissioned Rubens to portray. Peace, Law and Justice had, with song and dance, triumphed over folly, faction and idle criticism.

The allegorical trick in poetry and compliment insensibly spreads to other things and becomes almost a habit of mind. The King seemed sometimes to treat administration and politics as though the peace and contentment of the realm were indeed assured because, at his Christmas revels, a golden chariot upon a white cloud had descended against the heavenly backcloth bearing Peace, " in a flowery vesture like the Spring," with buskins of green taffeta, a garland of olives on her head and a branch of palm in her hand.[25]

King Charles had been nourished from childhood in a deep understanding of the sanctity and responsibility of the sovereign's part. His father, long since, had written a book, *Basilicon Doron*, a short impressive manual on the duties of a King, intended for the instruction of his eldest son; that eldest son, Prince Henry, had died, and the younger boy, then his father's cherished Baby Charles, had inherited, along with all else that would have been his brother's, the wisdom and policy enshrined in this book. He must, as a boy, have carefully turned over on his stammering tongue and conscientiously pondered in his mind such sentences as these:

[A good King] acknowledgeth himself ordained for his people, having received from God a burden of government, whereof he must be countable.

His father, in this book, repeatedly emphasised that the relationship between King and people is that of a father to his children, and that his authority, like that of a father, is founded in the immutable decree of the Almighty. Just as no misconduct on the part of a father can free his children from obedience to the fifth commandment, so no misgovernment on the part of a King can release his subjects from their allegiance. But the King, like the father, has duties and must answer to God if he scants them. This, in essence, was the doctrine of Divine Right as digested and set out by the late King James and as it had been imprinted on the mind of his son. Other writings by the old King were extant, and these too had been studied by the young Charles. " A good King will frame his actions to be according to the law," he had written in his tract on *The True Law of Free Monarchies*, " yet he is not bound thereto but of his good will." In fact it lay with the King to keep or break, make or unmake the laws. In his *Defence of the Right of Kings*, provoked by the rise of certain impertinent theories of popular and clerical rights against the Crown, he had declared:

" My brother princes and myself, whom God hath advanced upon the throne of Sovereign Majesty and supreme dignity, do hold the royal dignity of His Majesty alone, to whose service, as a most humble homager and vassal, I consecrate all the glory, honour, splendour and lustre of my earthly Kingdom."

With a profound sense of his holy office, therefore, and a deep conscientiousness, the earnest and self-disciplined Charles had taken up the burden of kingship, in the early hours of March 27th, 1625, when it pleased Almighty God to call King James to Himself. He was twenty-four. At his coronation he had defied tradition. He had refused to make the solemn rite an occasion for vulgar display and had omitted the customary procession, so popular with Londoners. He had also carefully revised the coronation oath in accordance with his views, swearing to maintain the liberties and laws of the country only in so far as they did not clash with his prerogative. He had eschewed as far as possible the pompous trappings of royalty and had worn white for his consecration. The text chosen for the sermon—it aroused some comment at the time—was *Be thou faithful unto death and I will give thee a Crown of Life*.

The King's ideals were clear from the first. He wanted his subjects throughout his dominions to accept his absolute authority with unquestioning obedience and to belong with uniform and regular devotion to the Church established by law. This was the only just basis of government as he saw it; this once achieved he would—*of his good will*, and not by any legal obligation—protect their traditional rights and freedoms within the framework of the laws, and ensure equal justice, order, and as far as in him lay, prosperity and security to his good people.

No ruler can pursue an effective policy at home or abroad without money, and the revenues of the Crown were inadequate. It lay with Parliament to vote money to the sovereign, and the King had found, within a few months of his accession, that Parliament was very far from accepting his view that it existed and functioned only by his good will. In the first five years of his reign he had quarrelled with three Parliaments in succession. In 1629 he had got rid of the third, in spite of a violent attempt on the part of his principal opponents to prevent the dissolution.

CHARLES I
by Anthony Van Dyck

He had committed the leaders of the tumult to prison without trial, made peace abroad, and settled down to conduct his own affairs in his own way.

The King had shelved his problems, not solved them, and the beauty and order with which he had surrounded himself deceived him into the belief that his authority in his kingdoms was as absolute as his authority at Court. He turned away from less pleasing realities, contemplated with pardonable satisfaction his beautiful palaces, his well-behaved Court, his bishops and chaplains, and took this seemly shining surface to indicate an untroubled deep.

His Court reflected his own personality and ideals. He never criticised his father, but he had early perceived the incongruity of King James's theory of monarchy with the jovial squalor in which he chose to live. In his most impressionable years, the young Charles had been for many months at the Court of Spain, wooing the Infanta. The wooing had come to nothing but he had brought back from Spain the memory and the knowledge of a Court ceremonial after his own heart. On his accession the broad Scots jokes and the drunken romps which had amused his father abruptly ceased. Babbling quarrels in ante-room and corridor were stilled. From the Gentlemen of the Bedchamber to the waiters at the sideboard, each man precisely knew where to be and when, at which table to take meat, when to attend prayers, when the King would rise, when sleep, when ride, when give audience, and who, with staff of office in hand or napkin on arm, should walk before him or stand behind his chair. The formality of the Court on all official occasions was rigorous and extreme. The King, alone of European princes, was served on bended knee, and when the French ambassador complained because neither chair nor stool was set for his wife —as was done for the English ambassador's wife in France—he was told that on official occasions no lady of the English Court except the Queen herself, not even the Princess Royal, was allowed to sit in the royal presence.[26] King Charles lived, with no vulgar ostentation, but with elegance and ceremony.

The reform was partial only and did not extend beyond the King's immediate circle. The rabbit-warren palace of Whitehall was a village in itself; in its streets, alleys and outbuildings, a crowded world of dependents, professional courtiers, servants' families and servants' servants lived parasitically on the Court. The Venetian envoy, considering the King's surroundings with a critical mind, condemned his housekeeping as extravagant.[27]

The disorders of such hangers-on were not before the King's eye. He ruled his immediate surroundings with an absolute authority. Had it not been for the licensed gaiety of his French Queen, the Court would have been intolerably strict. She, who loved dancing, masquing, plays and music, enlivened Whitehall and Hampton Court with elegant and innocent frolic. Not only did she and the King take part in the Christmas masques and often bring professional players to Court to perform for royal birthdays or Twelfth Night revels, but she herself, breaking all precedent, had been known to attend public performances at the theatre in person.

The wilder young courtiers looked for additional pleasure, far from the restraint of their monarch's presence; they frequented the gaming tables of Piccadilly, the race course of Hyde Park, the taverns of Westminster and the Strand with their legal or literary gossip, or the expensive, disreputable pleasure gardens south of the river, where, it was said, a single supper with Bess Broughton, or her like, might stand a man in twenty pounds, not to mention what the lady's favours would cost him. But the Court remained, none the less, the focal point of society and the ultimate standard of taste and manners.

It was also an intellectual centre, the meeting place of talent and wit, not less than fashion and beauty. The poets and writers gathered in the gardens of St. James's and Whitehall or the Queen's drawing-room at Somerset House; here they neatly turned their *vers de société* or circulated prose *Characters* and satirical epigrams to amuse the ladies. Suckling risked the mischievous innuendo, Lovelace was frivolous and musical, Davenant musical and courtly. Less talented courtiers with pretensions to poetic gifts circulated their work anonymously and were often mortified at its reception.

The courtiers' talent spilled over into the life of the capital when they turned to drama and mounted their own plays at the London theatres, often with great splendour. The King, as patron, critic and censor, sometimes intervened: he persuaded Suckling to change a tragic to a happy ending, and, with a surprising realism, he discouraged his master of the revels, Sir Henry Herbert, from removing the realistic expletives from the dialogue of Davenant's social comedy, *The Wits*.

The King cultivated music more than poetry; his small private orchestra entertained him as he sat at meat with choice pieces of secular music or, in the Chapel Royal, performed delicate and complex sacred airs, to the scandal of some of his subjects who thought that God's house was no place for Italian fiddlers.

The King's greatest achievement was the superb collection of works of art which he had been accumulating since he was Prince of Wales. Rubens himself had described him as "*le prince le plus amateur de la peinture qui soit au monde.*" His own excellent taste and the advice and gifts of intelligent agents had enabled him to fill his palaces with the rarest and the greatest collection in Europe. He possessed antique marbles and Florentine bronzes, delicate ivories, cut crystal, and the most rich and curious work of the goldsmith and medallist. Many of the noblest works of the Italian masters hung upon his walls—Titian's great "Entombment," Mantegna's incomparable "Triumph of Julius Caesar," Tintoretto's "Nine Muses," white-limbed on sun-dappled Parnassus, Correggio's "Marriage of Saint Catherine," portraits by Raphael, allegories by Giorgione; the works of the Bassano and Carracci families, of Giulio Romano and the younger Palma filled the gaps. Of contemporary artists, he commissioned paintings from Rubens and possessed those of Rembrandt; he employed in work for his Court and collections Anthony Van Dyck, Daniel Mytens, Gerard Honthorst, Wenceslas Hollar, Francis Klein, the ageing Italian master Orazio Gentileschi with his talented daughter Artemisia; Balthasar

Gerbier, miniaturist, architect and indefatigable busybody of the studio and sale room, assisted and advised him, and he had secured for the chief artist at the mint, the skilled French engraver Briot.

He had bought the magnificent cartoons drawn by Raphael for the Vatican tapestries and sent them to the English tapestry works at Mortlake to be copied, while he commissioned Van Dyck to design appropriate borders for the woven pictures. He had also given encouragement to the Mortlake works by commissioning great numbers of hangings for his palaces. In spite of all, the works had got into difficulties, and Charles, with some idea of making the industry a royal monopoly, bought them for the Crown.[28]

The fashion in tapestries, pictures, and classical decoration set by the King in his palaces at Whitehall, Greenwich, Oatlands and Hampton Court was followed by his nobility and courtiers. Lord Arundel's house was rich in Italian marbles; Lord Pembroke had the famous double-cube room at Wilton decorated by Van Dyck; the splendours of the Marquis of Winchester's Basing House were legendary; at Ham House the King's friend Will Murray had ceiling and wall decorations in paint and plaster work of great elaboration, some of them copied from the architecture depicted in the Raphael cartoons his master had bought.

Although the arts were his chief delight the King respected and encouraged the sciences. The physicians who enjoyed the honour of his patronage included pioneers of the new learning like Sir Theodore de Mayerne, the great exponent of clinical medicine who had probably saved the Queen's life at the premature birth of her first child, and William Harvey, the discoverer of the circulation of the blood.

The numerous lords and gentlemen who meddled with scientific and mechanical matters also felt the attraction and solicited the patronage of the Court, partly, but not exclusively, in the hope of acquiring profitable patents for their inventions. Lord Herbert of Cherbury had rooms in the royal palace to give him easier access to the papers he needed for his projected work on the life of Henry VIII; in the intervals of history he solicited the King's attention for various practical inventions of his own —gun-carriages, naval equipment, and a floating bathing establishment to be installed on the Thames. The talented son of the old Earl of Worcester, Edward Somerset, devoted his ingenuity to water pumps and hydraulic lifts for his father's castle at Raglan on the Welsh border, but when business brought him to Whitehall he gained the intelligent approbation of the King. Sir Francis Kynaston, courtier and poet, secured the King's patronage for a school that he founded for young noblemen, but was less fortunate in getting him to adopt a new kind of furnace for use in warships. Charles Cavendish, the Earl of Newcastle's brother, an amateur mathematician who was in touch with many foreign scholars, doubtless had the King's approbation in his several attempts to persuade the French mathematician Claude Mydorge and the French philosopher René Descartes to make peaceful England their permanent home.[29]

The English Court was the abode of ceremony, elegance and learning. It was also the abode of beauty. The noble ladies in silks of pale saffron and coral pink, sky-blue, willow-green and oyster, their ringleted hair framing plump, oval faces, went by water to Blackfriars and had their likenesses recorded by Anthony Van Dyck: Lucy, Countess of Carlisle, bold and handsome; Lady Ann Carr, pensive, dangling her gloves; Lady Mary Villiers, with palm and lamb as Saint Agnes.

The courtiers were depicted in masque attire, nonchalant in buskins with a shepherd's crook like Lord d'Aubigny, or with appropriate accessories—curly-headed George Digby, Lord Bristol's scholar son, with papers and a globe, the connoisseur Lord Arundel with a choice marble statue, Algernon, Earl of Northumberland, Lord High Admiral of the Kingdom, with an anchor and a naval battle behind him, Viscount Wentworth, the Lord Deputy of Ireland, with one of the huge Irish wolf-hounds which he bred at his hunting lodge near Dublin.

The smaller luxuries which surrounded these men and women have been etched in loving detail by Wenceslas Hollar, the Bohemian drawing master of the King's children: the lace collars and cuffs, the knots of satin ribbon, the fur muffs, the painted fans, the embroidered gloves, the jewelled hat-bands and silver shoe-roses, the fringed velvet and tiffany masks to shield their waxen skins from wind and sun.

The small, fastidious King presided fittingly over his well-ordered Court. By nature reserved, he was isolated still more by that slight impediment of the speech which made him shun all but formal contacts, except with his familiars. Even his friends he kept at their distance, but with a regular and courteous demeanour that all understood and some, who were formal themselves, grew to like. He was constant in his conduct, predictable, disliking steadily those whom he disliked, holding with great firmness to his opinions and his friends, even when the opinions proved mistaken and the friends faithless, and resolute in the fulfilment of his duty.

He was as fine a judge of horseflesh as he was of painting, and in Sir John Fenwick of Wallington he had a trainer and breeder of high repute, one that " bred the best horses ever was in England for coursing, famous over all the world." [30] In the hunting field the King's formality thawed a little, but never wholly. Deft and lightly made, he rode well; it was necessary that he should. The chase was his passion as it had been his father's, but he was not, like his father, as often in a ditch as in the saddle. " Have I three Kingdoms and must you fly into my eye?" old King James had apostrophised an intruding insect; but the flies, if any, which made this mistake with King Charles were removed without comment. The unseemly, the ludicrous, the merely human were excluded from his public life, and almost all his life was public. Even when he had a hunting accident it was of a high, dramatic kind. Mistaking green weed for a grassy hollow he plunged once in full career into a morass in which his horse floundered irrecoverably. He himself escaped through the prompt assistance of his attendants, and with the utmost coolness, changed clothes with a courtier, mounted a fresh horse and continued the chase.[31]

But though he moved from palace to palace with a restlessness on which foreign ambassadors remarked, he did not know his people well and was a stranger to the greater part of his own dominions. On his journeys he followed always much the same route. He had hunted in the New Forest and visited the Isle of Wight; he went frequently to Newmarket for the races, or to stay with the Earl of Pembroke at Wilton; he had been received at the university of Oxford and he knew the Thames valley and his deer parks at Windsor, Richmond, Oatlands and Theobalds. Once since his manhood, he had travelled to Scotland and back, had seen the wolds of Lincolnshire, had climbed the two hundred and seventy steps of the tower of York Minster to admire the prospect, had crossed the coalfields of Durham, the Northumbrian moors and the hills of Lothian. He had played golf on the links at Leith, and made a progress as far as Perth and Brechin, but, unlike all his ancestors, he had not hunted the deer with the highland clans. He had never been to Wales. He had never visited Ireland. He had inspected his ships of war at Chatham and Gravesend, and had watched, from the sedate summer residence he had built for his Queen at Greenwich, the sails that passed up and down the broad estuary of the Thames to London, but he did not know the seaports of his kingdom or the mariners and merchants on whom the prosperity of his State was so largely built. At his council table, or more informally by conversations in the halls and embrasures of his palaces, he settled a huge number of technical questions relating to taxation, to industry, manufacture and shipping, to the regulation of trade, and the quarrels of his subjects. Through these he had learnt a good many things about the manufacture of salt, soap, pins, and beaver hats, the cloth trade, the importation of wine, the herring fisheries, the oyster beds, the forests, the mines, the foundries and the glass works.

The reports which his Council received regularly from the Justices of the Peace, informed him, if he wished to know, of the general state of the country, the rise or decline of the number of vagabonds, the arrangements for apprenticing orphan children and relieving the industrious poor.

71

The King had a high sense of duty towards the people whom he regarded as a sacred trust from God, but this was compatible with an open dislike of their proximity and their opinions. It was only, perhaps, when he touched for the King's Evil at Easter and Michaelmas that he allowed the vulgar to approach closely to his royal person, and even then each invalid who presented himself to be cured had to produce a certificate signed by a clergyman, a churchwarden and a justice of the peace before he might enter the palace gates.[32]

He had never had the painful experience from which his father, as a young man, had learnt so much; he had never confronted insolent opponents face to face and had the worst of the argument. No national danger had compelled him to go out among his people and share their perils. He was, at this time, not only the most formal but the most remote and sheltered of all European kings.

Less virtuous monarchs escaped from formality in the arms of low-born mistresses, but for the chaste Charles, no Nell Gwynne, prattling cockney anecdotes, opened a window into the lives of his humbler subjects. What he knew of men, he knew chiefly by report and study. Like many shy, meticulous men, he was fond of aphorisms, and would write in the margins of books, in a delicate, beautiful, deliberate script, such maxims as " Few great talkers are good doers " or " None but cowards are cruel."[33] He trusted more to such distilled and bottled essence of other men's wisdom than to his own experience, which was, in truth, limited; his daily contact with the world was confined within the artificial circle of his Court and the hunting field. He was to say, much later, in tragic circumstances, that he knew as much law as any gentleman in England. It was true; but he had little conception of what the laws meant to those who lived under them.

Admired by some and feared by many, he was not greatly loved. He neither solicited nor gained the affection of his people from whom he expected neither more nor less than duty. In the smaller circle of his Court he was of those who exclude love when they exclude familiarity. His servants knew him to be punctilious and just, a stranger alike to impulses of anger or good humour. In later years the respect which he had from all his household grew into love, but it was his misfortune, not his graciousness, which melted their hearts. In his time of unquestioned power very few felt for him, personally as a man, that unreasonable, human attachment which sweetens service and softens authority.

Yet the King was capable of deep and tender attachment when his secretive affections were touched. His love for his wife, though it had been slow to come, was now the strongest personal emotion in his life.

Queen Henrietta Maria was the opposite of her husband in outward manner and in temperament, and their marriage had opened in storm and rebellion on her side, in a coldness amounting almost to cruelty on his. She was nine years his junior and had come to him as an effervescent girl of fifteen, very fond of dancing. He had objected to her gaieties and to the conduct of the French companions who encouraged her. They had been sent away, leaving the tear-stained child to the mercy of her solemn husband and his overbearing favourite the Duke of Buckingham. For three unhappy years she lived forlorn and neglected; only after the murder of Buckingham, in 1628, did she become pregnant for the first time.

She was not strong and her spine was a little crooked. Her first child, a boy, survived only a few hours and she rose from her bed with the bloom of her youth withered. She had always had bad features, with a long nose and prominent teeth; now the freshness of her complexion and her dimpled charm had gone, though the ivory quality of her skin and her large, brilliant eyes still commanded admiration.

The loss of her looks mattered nothing, for Charles, on Buckingham's death, had transferred his devotion instantly and wholly to his wife. He was in love, with the single-mindedness of those who give their affection to few, but to those few entirely. Beloved, the little Queen flowered again; her vivacity, her charm, and a good dressmaker hid all defects. She knew that she was not a beauty but she made the world think that she was. The dancing, on which the King had frowned, was now permitted, and her wit and gaiety made her husband's Court such as she had always wanted. Year by year her mental ascendancy over her husband increased; he sought her advice on every subject, except religion, and had been heard to regret that he could not make her a member of his council. Only in religion was there no understanding between them, for she was as devoted to the Church of Rome as he to the Church of England.

Sufficient to themselves, the King and Queen were not greatly interested in their growing family. Princes and Princesses were born at regular intervals, at cost of great suffering to the Queen. Suitable attendants were appointed to wait on them and they enjoyed every care proper to their station, but although they accompanied their parents occasionally on a Maying party or courtly revel and Van Dyck painted the Royal Pair awkwardly dandling a couple of babies, neither the King nor the Queen was truly at home in the nursery. Not until years later, when they were themselves separated, did either of them indulge in demonstrations of emotional love for their children.

The Queen had not her husband's studious temperament and slow, ruminative mind. She understood things quickly and superficially; he understood them deeply, or not at all. But like many slow thinkers, he greatly admired a quick wit, and like many doubtful and hesitative men, he was easily impressed by the capacity to make a decision, however ill-conceived or impulsive.

The fusion of their two influences—his for stateliness and form, hers for liveliness and style—had made their Court within a few years the "most sumptuous and happy in the world." [34] The achievement was considerable but it was shallow. It bore no relation to the unsolved problem of government.

BOOK I CHAPTER I REFERENCES

1. Thomas Carew, *Poems*, Oxford, 1949, p. 77.
2. Lipson, *Economic History*, Oxford, 1948, III, p. 152.
3. *Acts of the Privy Council, Colonial Series*, I, pp. 264–83.
4. *Strafford MSS. XI*, October-November 1637 *passim*.
5. *Relazioni dagli Ambasciatori Veneti*, ed. Barozzi and Berchet, Venice, 1863, ix, pp. 307–8.
6. Vaughan, *Works*, Oxford, 1914, i, p. 11.
7. Ralph, *Sir Humphrey Mildmay: Royalist Gentleman*, New Brunswick, 1947, p. 25.
8. See Nef. *The Rise of the British Coal Industry*, London, 1932, I. *passim*.
9. *Register of the Privy Council of Scotland*, 1633–5, p. 126.
10. *A Short Survey of 26 Counties*, ed. Wickham Legg, London, 1904, p. 83.
11. *Ibid.*, pp. 37, 43.
12. Lithgow, *Rare Adventures and Painful Peregrinations*, Glasgow, 1906, p. 433.
13. Dugdale, *History of Embanking*, London, 1662, p. 391.
14. Hartlib, *Legacie*, London, 1651.
15. *A Royalist's Notebook. The Commonplace Book of Sir John Oglander*, ed. Bamford, London, 1936, p. 84.
16. Brathwait, *Household of an Earl*, London, 1821.
17. *Calendar of State Papers, Domestic Series*, 1637, pp. 422, 547, 565.
18. Knowler, *The Earl of Strafford's Letters and Despatches*, London, 1739, ii, p. 142.
19. Oglander, p. 75.
20. Ralph Josselin, *Diary*, ed. Hockliffe. *Camden Society*, 1908, p. 15.
21. *Bankes MSS.*, 60/19.
22. Rhys and Brynmor Jones, *The Welsh People*, London, 1906, p. 449; Rowlands *Cambrian Bibliography*, Llanidloes, 1869, p. 195.
23. Davenant, *Works*, London, 1673, p. 218.
24. Waller, *Poems*, London, 1893, p. 62.
25. Shirley, *Works*, London, 1833, vi, p. 274.
26. *Calendar of State Papers, Venetian Series*, 1636–9, p. 421; Burnet, *History of my own Time*, ed. Airy, Oxford, 1897, i, p. 28.
27. Barozzi and Berchet, ix, p. 310.
28. W. G. Thompson, *History of Tapestry*, London, 1906, pp. 299, 309, 351 ff.
29. Rigaud, *Correspondence of Scientific Men*, Oxford, 1841, i, pp. 22–3.
30. *Historical Manuscripts Commission, Report X, Appendix IV*, p. 108.
31. *Calendar of State Papers, Venetian Series*, 1636–9, p. 64.
32. Crawford, *The King's Evil*, Oxford, 1911, pp. 165–215.
33. The aphorisms quoted are from his copy of Bacon's *Advancement of Learning*, Oxford, 1640, preserved in the British Museum.
34. Barozzi and Berchet, ix, p. 393: " la piu sontuosa e la piu allegra del mondo."

CHAPTER TWO

FAITH AND FOREIGN POLITICS

THE King, in agreement with most serious thinkers of his time, believed that good government must be founded on true religion. The first essential was that his people should believe rightly and worship God in the manner most acceptable to Him. What that manner was, the Church alone could teach. Unhappily schism in the Catholic Church and vulgar sectarianism with its hundred disputing tongues made it exceptionally difficult in the seventeenth century to know which belief and which form of worship was right.

The overwhelming majority of the King's subjects, whatever their doctrines, their education or their interests, were simply and sincerely religious. They did not doubt that their souls were immortal or that Christ had died to redeem them. Some of them remembered this daily, most of them remembered it on Sunday, and a few perhaps not more than once or twice a year. But it was to them a cardinal fact in life, and in death. From the felon jauntily going to the gallows, with a bold face and a pious word, to the nobleman (of whom there would soon be many) mounting the steps of the scaffold, almost all faced death with an unquestioning belief in a life to come. The nobleman shared with the felon the uplifting and unshaken conviction that the Son of God Himself had, for his redemption, gone the selfsame way. To die without that hope, to die—as men said—" desperately " was an unusual and terrible thing.

The desire to believe and the capacity to believe were still almost equally strong. This was true, with a minority of individual exceptions, of all the King's subjects, in spite of the differences of wealth, breeding and education which divided them.

King Charles counted among his people some of the finest and most cultivated minds in Europe and some of the most primitive. The leading scholars at the universities of Oxford, Cambridge, St. Andrew's, Aberdeen, and the more recently founded Trinity College, Dublin, ranked with the best in the world. Theology dominated the universities but the classics, philosophy, ancient history, mathematics and medicine were also taught. Francis Glisson, lecturing on anatomy at Cambridge, supported William Harvey's new theory of the circulation of the blood, a theory angrily attacked by the Scottish scholar Alexander Ross, who, not content with challenging Harvey and Glisson, was soon to hurl himself with ironical eloquence upon the Italian astronomer Galileo, pulverising him—as he hoped— in a book entitled *The Earth No Wandering Star except in the Wandering Heads of the Galileans*.

London was a centre of scientific activity. At Gresham College, Henry Gellibrand, professor of astronomy, was investigating the magnetic north. The Barber Surgeons company had built an anatomy theatre from designs by Inigo Jones, where public lectures drew distinguished audiences; sometimes banquets were provided, after which the Barber Surgeons, to their chagrin, missed a number of their silver spoons.

Anatomy and all the natural sciences had a great following both amateur and professional. Sir Kenelm Digby was working on an exhaustive inquiry into the *Nature of Bodies* in which he discussed, with other questions, what part of the animal was the first to be formed, whether animals can think and " how the vital spirits are sent from the brain into the intended parts of the body without mistaking their way." Thomas Browne, a physician of considerable reputation who had just settled at Norwich, was compiling an immense and varied store of learning for the book in which he would examine and deal justly with a multitude of common superstitions and vulgar errors in the interests of scientific truth. In Yorkshire, a precocious boy, William Gascoigne, scanned the stars and made improvements in the telescope. It was not three years since the posthumous publication of Dr. Muffet's *Insectorum Theatrum* had opened the way towards the science of entomology.

Mathematicians pursued their solitary calculations. John Napier from his castle tower near Edinburgh had opened the century with the publication of the first tables of logarithms; at another Scottish castle Sir Thomas Urquhart of Cromarty pondered, in his eccentric overcrowded brain, the practice of trigonometry, squaring the circle and the invention of a universal language. William Oughtred had recently published his *Clavis Mathematica*. John Wilkins at Cambridge took time off his mathematical studies to speculate on the habitability of the moon and on an invention, left incomplete, which might have been a telephone. At Cambridge, too, young Seth Ward, poor and studious, wrestled with the problems of geometry. But arithmetic, even in its elementary complexities, was for scholars: in merchants' counting-houses the clerks used the abacus for their sums, although a few now employed an elementary slide rule attributed to John Napier and familiarly known as Napier's Bones. The highly educated and efficient Lord Deputy of Ireland, wishing to reckon fifteen times four, wrote down fifteen four times and added it up. The multiplication table was not at that time taught with the A B C.

The ancient languages of the East and the antiquities of the British Isles exerted a simultaneous attraction upon many scholars. William Bedell, Bishop of Kilmore, the leading Hebrew scholar of the day, had devoted himself since he had gone to Ireland to the study of the Irish language and antiquities and was carefully rendering the Old Testament into Irish. Abraham Wheelocke, Professor of Arabic at Cambridge, who was no less learned in the Persian tongue, after preparing a refutation of the Koran, was translating the works of the Venerable Bede into modern English. Edward Pococke, Professor of Arabic at Oxford, had been granted a sabbatical year to travel dangerously in the Turkish dominions in search of the manuscript treasures of Greek and Syrian monasteries.

The traffic was not all in one direction; Christian refugees from the Turkish dominions sometimes reached England. A Cretan scholar, Nathaniel Canopis, had been brought to Oxford by Archbishop Laud where, from Balliol College, he disseminated his grave learning and amused his colleagues by brewing a black drink from roasted coffee berries.

Scholars in universities and in their homes collected libraries and worked assiduously, together or alone, on problems of history, archæology and etymology never before considered. It was the dawn of the great dictionaries, the surveys, the monumental volumes which laid the foundations of future learning in many different fields. Florio's Italian dictionary, Cotgrave's French dictionary, Minsheu's Spanish dictionary were on the shelves of the learned, as well as Minsheu's remarkable etymological dictionary of nine languages. William Camden's *Britannia* was already a standard work; Dugdale had begun the researches into English ecclesiastical history which culminated in the publication of his *Monasticon*. Henry Spelman had issued the first volume of his glossary of legal terms and was still deeply engrossed midway between M and Z. Dodsworth, Archer, D'Ewes and others were following in the footsteps of Robert Cotton and William Lisle in the study of Anglo-Saxon, revealing the history hidden in place names and the origins of the English language, customs and laws.

The casual tourist had picked up the prevailing intellectual curiosity and would go out of his way to see druidical circles as remote as " Long Meg and her Daughters " in Cumberland. All who crossed the border paused to contemplate the great grass-grown bastion which they vaguely called the Picts Wall. Stonehenge drew travellers to and from the west; Inigo Jones asserted that it had been built by the Romans but other scholars contested this. Visitors to the strange caves of Wookey Hole would play the recorder in order to appreciate the echo.

Lesser, more simply practical or light-hearted speculations

and inventions were discussed. Richard Norwood had paced
the distance from London to York, a primitive method of
measurement which was surprisingly accurate. "Way-wisers"
or small machines attached to the leg, or a coach wheel, for
measuring the distance travelled, were a discussed novelty.
Rival methods of abbreviated writing, the various new steno-
graphies, claimed public attention. John Babington, one of His
Majesty's gunners, had borrowed time from his more serious
occupations to write a volume on fireworks in which he described "the manner of making the best sort of stars," and "how
to make Fisgigs which some call serpents," with such other
skilful wonders as coats of arms correctly blazoned or a fortress of
fireworks whence mechanical musketeers emerged to fire off
rockets—"which being well and orderly performed will give much
content."

The London booksellers and printers, congregated about
St. Paul's, had an eager market for their wares, paper volumes
displayed on trays before their shops, opened at an interesting page.
There were books and to spare, good, bad, indifferent, grave,
gay, useful, pious. Each was registered at the King's Stationery
Office; the harvest for the year 1637 included a commentary on
Aristotle by Thomas Hobbes, translations of St. Ambrose,
Symmachus, Virgil, Martial and Petrarch; numerous histories
ancient and modern; practical handbooks—*The Complete
Cannonier or the Gunner's Art*, *The Attorney's Academy*, *The Hus-
bandman's Practice*, *A Discourse of Bees*; some works on navigation,
on medicine, on midwifery; Taylor's guide to the posts called
The Carriers' Cosmography; the latest plays of Fletcher, Heywood,
and Shirley; *The Merry Jests of the Cobbler of Canterbury* and
other familiar joke books; a large number of "dainty new
ditties," poems, elegies and anagrams; a new issue of *The Wise
Men of Gotham* and other old favourites like the lives of Dick
Whittington and Old King Cole; St. Francis de Sales' *Devout
Life* in English, a new translation of the *Golden Ass* of Apuleius,
and *A Posy of Godly Prayers* from an unknown hand.

In the literary haunts of London—Ben Jonson's old Devil

ARCHBISHOP LAUD
by an Unknown Artist

Tavern, or the newer fashioned Rose in Covent Garden, or the Globe, where the walls were painted to represent Arcady—young gentlemen of London and visitors from the provinces talked of the latest books and plays. In country houses, small and great, societies of intelligent men and women met to debate on faith or philosophy, to read their works aloud, to sing or dance together to the pretty music of the virginals or the deeper tones of the small organs which had become popular in many homes. Some have left a name and fame behind, like Great Tew where Falkland's circle met; the pleasures of other great houses are echoed in contemporary letters, Lord Leicester's Penshurst, Lord Northumberland's Syon, Lord Northampton's Compton Wynyates, Lord Newcastle's Bolsover.

Smaller houses, the homes of scholars, clergymen, citizens and gentlemen, offered the delights of good conversation and sometimes also curiosities and things of beauty to look at. The Provost of Eton, Sir Henry Wotton, collected many friends about him in his peaceful old age to talk of painting and literature, to look at the Venetian pictures that adorned his walls, and to examine such curiosities as " a piece of Crystal Sexangular, grasping divers several things within it, which I bought among the Rhaetian Alps." [1] At the house of his friend Izaak Walton, citizen and ironmonger of London, the talk was of literature and the quiet delights of fishing. Samuel Hartlib, another London citizen, collected about him those interested in education, philosophy or the improvement of husbandry. William Oughtred, in his vicarage at Albury, gathered round him his disciples in the study of mathematics, but would from time to time retire to his room for two or three days together, refusing all food and interruptions, until he had solved the insistent problem tracking through his brain. The poet Drummond, at his secluded Hawthornden in the Lothian hills, discussed poetical and political problems with his kinsmen and friends. Dr. Henry King, in his deanery at Rochester, composed verses and sermons and put together a choice library which he intended to bequeath to the Cathedral.

Such were the pleasures to be found among the most civilised nobility, clergy, gentry and citizens. The average level was not so high. The majority of country houses offered coarse entertainment to the mind: the talk was of dogs, hawks, horses, harvest prospects and local quarrels; the books were manuals on hawking or land tenure, a handbook on the law, the Bible, Foxe's "Book of Martyrs", possibly a play-book bought when last the owner visited London, with *Guy of Warwick*, *Palmerin of England* or some other romance.

Education of a kind was widespread at least in England. The grammar schools and ancient foundations like Eton, Westminster, Winchester, Charterhouse and St. Paul's, took the sons of citizens and gentry, of the clergy and the professional classes, sometimes those of the nobility. It was more usual for the nobility to have a tutor resident in the house, and for the richer gentry to send the boys to live with a private schoolmaster where five or six pupils, looked after as part of his family, occupied all his scholastic attention. From such establishments, quite as often as from the ancient and famous schools of the realm, the most eminent men emerged.

Hours were long, and six in the morning the usual time for school to begin. Long before daylight on a winter morning schoolboys would be on their way, breakfasting, as they went, on a piece of bread and honeycomb or a lump of cheese. At school Latin was the basis of all learning; the boys of the middle and upper classes, when they had mastered the language, proceeded to learn all other subjects, including their own religion, in the Latin tongue. The careful, comprehensive and fundamentally simple catechism which had been prepared in the last century by Dean Nowell for the use of older children was composed in Latin so as to fit into the grammar school curriculum. History, philosophy, geography and all appreciation of poetry or great literature came through the study of ancient and modern Latin classics. History written in English, like Holinshed's Chronicle, or the many recent books on European history were for recreation: so was Raleigh's great *History of the World*

—a favourite book among Puritans—which Oliver Cromwell recommended for leisure reading to his idle son Dick.

As Latin was still the universal language of the educated, and modern works both of information and of literature were composed in it, this technique of education did not exclude the boys from contemporary knowledge. On the contrary it brought them into contact with European culture and the greatest of Renaissance and Reformation thinkers. The works of Erasmus, of Melanchthon, of Linacre and of George Buchanan were studied in the grammar schools. Some schools preferred the works of Christian to pagan writers and commended the study of Mantuan, Palingenius or Cornelius Schön, poets and dramatists of the sixteenth century, before those of Lucan, Virgil, Seneca or Terence. The vast corpus of George Buchanan's works, for instance, provided in themselves for English, and still more for Scottish, boys a liberal education; his writings included plays, epigrams and pastorals, a prose history of Scotland as educational as Livy, and, for political philosophy, his *De Jure Regni* which expounded the theory of a strictly limited monarchy.

The immense influence of Buchanan in the schools had been viewed with disquiet by the late King James, and the Archbishop of Canterbury at this present time was trying to popularise in Scottish schools the fluent verse of Arthur Johnston, recently appointed rector of the university of Aberdeen. Johnston, whose religious views were more favourable to the monarchy than those of Buchanan, had achieved a fair measure of contemporary fame by his recent versification of the psalms in Latin.

The basic Latin of seventeenth-century education did not create uniformity of knowledge or outlook. The majority of Latin-educated boys had no more of the pagan classics than a handful of quotations. Their knowledge, philosophy and outlook on life were drawn from the Latin writers of the last century. But a worldly minority among the nobility and richer gentry had studied the pagan classics, had travelled abroad and had tasted the graces and the civilisation of the antique world in its Renaissance revival. They liked the colour, the imagination, the wit, wisdom and nobility of the Latin poets; they quoted the *Metamorphoses* of Ovid, the Satires of Persius and —more rarely—Juvenal, and above all the stoical and republican sentiments of Lucan's *Pharsalia*. Seneca, beloved of the Elizabethans, was going out of fashion, and Virgil was second to Lucan in favour.

Newer methods were discussed rather than practised. Samuel Hartlib was arranging for the publication in English of the important work on education written by the Bohemian exile John Comenius, and some men of learning hoped that the famous educationist might be persuaded to make his home in the island.

The grammar schools did not undertake to teach the elements of reading and writing. The children of professional men and the gentry were taught their alphabets at home by their mothers, but the ability to read and write was not uncommon among the poor in England, especially in the South. Working women left their children to be minded by some stay-at-home labourer, a cobbler, tailor, weaver, or carpenter. To keep them quiet, he made them learn their letters from a hornbook or battledore with the alphabet pasted upon it, which was handed from pupil to pupil. Dame's schools existed in some villages, but the cobblers' "petty schools" were more usual and some of these amateur schoolmasters, the "abecedarians" as they were called, were patient and clever; one carpenter cut out the letters on blocks of wood, others made up little rhymes, invented small rewards, alternated mental and manual work with play. Girls commonly had less of this schooling than boys; they were not so liable to mischief as their brothers, needed less "minding," and were early able to help their mothers at work. The wilder regions, where farmsteads and hamlets were far apart and no such cobblers' schools existed, were served by travelling pedagogues. These vagabonds of the teaching profession would spend a month or two in one small settlement and then pass on, often following a regular circuit that brought them back once in every three or four years to teach a new gaggle of little children to read and write. The craftsmen who kept school had a halfpenny or a penny a week for each child. The travelling pedagogue was given his keep in one yeoman's kitchen or another, and received presents from grateful parents. It was very simple, primitive and unorganised, but it worked reasonably well. Among the country folk the women were usually illiterate but most intelligent men could read.

They could read: but they had little to read. They read the Bible, for that most decent families possessed. They read Foxe's " Book of Martyrs," the most widespread and popular work of history in England, a copy of which was sometimes kept, along with the Bible, in the parish church. They read elementary books of devotion like *The Practice of Piety* and *The Whole Duty of Man*. Reading little, they took the printed word gravely, pondered it much and remembered it well. The more intelligent thought seriously, because the habit of prayer was usual, and concentrated prayer encourages coherent thinking. In respectable families the parents would possess a cheap catechism and would keep their children thoroughly exercised in it. Furthermore, in all the great schools, in some of the petty schools and in almost every home of whatever kind, everyone sang. The women sang at their carding and knitting and spinning, in the dairy and the kitchen; the men sang at the carpenter's bench, at the loom and the forge, or as they followed the plough. A favourite manual of musical instruction, especially devoted to the singing of the psalms, was reprinted two hundred and thirty-five times in the course of the century.

Where the villages lay thickest, where the market towns were busiest, there the psalms and the Bible-reading, Foxe's book and the works of Knox made their strong impression. For simple people, over the greater part of England and southern Scotland, certain ideas and phrases were written deep on the waxen minds of childhood. An astonished Italian reported that " they give their sons Hebrew names and call their daughters after the virtues and have quite abandoned those in use among Christians." [2] The Old Testament was commonly better known to these people than the New, and unconsciously they acquired the outlook, because they acquired the words, of the Chosen People. To the confident, self-reliant and assertive characteristics of the Anglo-Saxon were added tenacious Jewish fatalism and an unyielding confidence in a God who was theirs against the world.

The danger which might arise from the opinions of people who were serious, literal-minded and only in the most elementary sense *educated* was evident to authority. For this reason the Crown insisted on the importance of catechising children in the hope of keeping the speculations of the humble within the disciplined limits laid down by the Church. From time to time efforts were made to establish some kind of uniformity in the books used for instruction by village pedagogues. In theory, if not always in practice, all A B C's were issued by royal authority, so that nothing but the most orthodox and innocuous prayers or sentences could be found in them. King James had attempted unsuccessfully to coerce all the village dominies in Scotland into using a text book called *God and the King*, an obsequious treatise by an English divine.

Where the Celtic languages prevailed the scene was different. The adaptable Welsh had partly brought their native culture into line with English fashions. Welsh, alone of the Celtic languages, could claim a reasonable if not a very large number of printed books. A Welsh-Latin dictionary had been compiled and two Welsh aldermen of London had arranged for the printing of a cheap edition of the Bible in Welsh—at five shillings, to suit the slender purses of Welsh farmers. The Common Prayer had been officially translated and a Welsh poet, Edmund Prys, had versified the psalms. Rhys Prichard, an enterprising clergyman, taught his flock in rhyming Welsh, simplifying and even singing the Bible story. But Welsh was no longer the speech of the educated. The Welsh gentry spoke English and sent their sons to English-speaking schools. They did not trouble much with their daughters, and Vicar Prichard, in an angry outburst at the attitude of his compatriots, exaggerated and underlined the different education of Welsh and English girls: an English tinker's daughter could read, he said, when a Welsh squire's daughter could not. Literacy offered little advantage to those who only spoke Welsh, and the poor rarely troubled to learn their letters. Their crafts, their traditions and much of their literature, they handed on by word of mouth.

What was partly true in Wales was wholly true of the Scottish highlands and of Ireland. No useful comparison can be made between the literate Englishman or lowlander and the unlettered Celt. The two did not represent different levels of the same culture; they represented different ways of life and thought. The highlander and the wild Irishman had skills of hand and eye, and a hardiness lost to the southerners; they had knowledge of legend and history and poetry by memory and oral tradition. They had their own code of honour and respected the laws of their ancient, half-shattered society, older than the Norman Conquest, and older than the English invasion. The Anglo-Saxon thought them barbarous, but they thought him vulgar.

The gentry, in the Celtic regions, sometimes sent their sons to English-speaking seats of learning; the highland Scots to Aberdeen and St. Andrews, the Irish to Trinity College, Dublin. But if they were true to the old religion, as many of them were, they sent their sons abroad. Many a young Irish or Scottish chief had his education in France or Flanders, Italy or Spain. They avoided thereby the crude contamination of the Anglo-Saxons but they hardly preserved the purity of their own traditions: Ireland's most distinguished poet of this epoch, Piers Ferriter, a chief dwelling on the Blasket Islands, wrote Petrarchan lyrics in his native tongue.

Romantics and antiquaries regretted that the Reformation and the printed word had had a deadening effect on the natural imagination of the people. John Aubrey lamented that " the many good books and variety of turns of affairs have put all the old Fables out of doors, and the divine art of printing and gunpowder have frighted away Robin Goodfellow and the fairies." His nurse, he said, " had the history from the Conquest down to Carolus I in Ballad." But the English about the year 1637 had not put fables quite out of doors. While some, aspiring to education and picking up undigested knowledge from the new Anglo-Saxon studies, angrily declared that the common people of England were the oppressed descendants of the conquered Saxons while all the nobility were tyrannous Normans, others still accepted the ancient legend that Brutus, a great grandson of Aeneas, had conquered Britain from the giants Gog and Magog. As the power and energy of their country grew, they were well pleased to think that Britain was now what Rome had once been—the legitimate heir of Trojan greatness.

The people were still in many things, and even in their cities, very close to nature and the springs of life. The voices of wind and water, the signs of sun and moon, stars and clouds, the movements of birds, the baying of dogs, had not lost their messages and meanings. Goblins and fairies flittered in the autumn dusk; Robin Goodfellow had " his creambowl duly set " and sometimes, with human connivance, left threepence in the slippers of industrious maids. Pigwiggin afflicted the lazy with cramps; Billyblind chuckled on the hearthstone of the north country cottage; the water nixies clutched at the ankles of the late traveller wading the swollen burn. The wise, wizened faces of the little folk stared at the lone hunter crossing the moors at dusk. At many a cool spring in a shady hollow, sanctified by the name of a maiden saint, loveless girls and barren wives performed rites which had been old when Saint Frideswide was young. Pagan festivals survived, sometimes crudely Christianised; boys and girls decked the houses of town and country with green branches on May Day and danced riotously round the maypole, though the religious, with some justification, abhorred the practice. Crops and wells were blessed with old pagan rites and at harvest festivals straw dolls were plaited and carried in triumph.

In the wilds of Lochaber from time to time a green man would be seen, one that had been killed between daylight and starlight and belonged neither to earth nor heaven. Some thought these apparitions were only the unhappy dead but others thought them one of the many forms taken by the devil. The strong forces of nature, with the advent of Christianity, had become confused with the devil, and after the lapse of centuries witchcraft had become indivisibly compact of pagan and Christian beliefs. The devil, in many forms, bestrode the islands from end to end. Sometimes he was " a proper gentleman with a laced band," as when he came to Elizabeth Clarke at Chelmsford; at other times you might know him, as Rebecca Jones of St. Osyth did, by his great glaring eyes. He was cold and sensual and rather mean: he offered Priscilla Collit of Dunwich only ten shillings for her immortal soul; she gave it to him and off he went without paying. Respectably dressed in " brown clothes and a little black hat," he spoke in friendly terms to Margaret Duchill of Alloa in Scotland; " Maggie, will you be my servant?" he asked, and when she agreed he told her to call him John and gave her five shillings and powers of life and death over her neighbours.[3]

In England the devil kept low company for the most part. He comforted poor, half-crazed, hungry old women, cackling ill-naturedly at their neighbours and growing foolish over a mangy cat, a tame sparrow or a friendly toad on which they bestowed a comical or high-sounding name, Pyewacket, Jeremary, or Grizel Greediguts. In Scotland he was said to have more distinguished clients. From the spikes on the Tolbooth in Edinburgh grinned the white skull of the Earl of Gowrie, reputed a warlock in his time, as other noblemen had been. The devil drove with Lord Carnegie in a coach-and-six over tracks where no coach could go. The devil had had a hand in it when Sir John Colquhoun of Luss seduced his sister-in-law Lady Katherine Graham, and while the fugitive couple hid in London, their shocked and distinguished families solemnly pleaded witchcraft as the cause of their sin. What witchcrafts flourished among the Celtic peoples it is hard to say, but the English and the lowland Scots viewed their dark powers with apprehension. The Irish, it was certain, could call up vapours from their bogs to the destruction of whole armies.

The frontier between legitimate country lore and black magic was but feebly marked; in general the wise woman or " cunning man " who collected simples and knew how to brew drugs or pronounce spells to cure the ills of men and horses, to take away the toothache, banish warts and ease the pains of childbed, was not likely to be persecuted as a witch, in England at any rate. In Scotland, a more austere religious faith made all rites and jargons suspect, and women who muttered old Latin rhymes or were guilty of touching a sick cow with a blue pebble or other such conduct were within reach of the law though it rarely fell upon them for such things alone.

The " healing touch " was an old English belief. The government sometimes took action against those who claimed to have it, for to heal by touch was the King's sacred prerogative. A seventh son of a seventh son—these were popularly thought to have the power—had practised near London, but his cures were examined by the College of Physicians and dismissed as fraudulent; he turned out not even to be a seventh son. A little boy of five in Somerset, who was incontrovertibly a seventh son of a seventh son, was carried from village to village by his father and made many cures; no money was paid, only fruit and sugar-plums, garters, points and ribbons. The Bishop of Bath and Wells, instructed to look into the matter, was lenient; he let off the father with a caution and sent them both home.[4]

The suppression of superstition and dubious healing rites was but a small part of the King's task. In the matter of witchcraft he had shown himself enlightened, and had intervened to save a group of Lancashire women from malicious persecution. His principal task was the more lofty one of imposing right beliefs and right religious practices on all his subjects, however complex or however simple their minds, however civilised or primitive their way of thought.

To King Charles the Church was the soul of the State, without which the body politic would be inert and lifeless matter. At this tranquil and apparently successful time in his career his feelings for the Church were chiefly apparent in his vigorous determination to destroy its opponents and to enforce upon all his people obedience to its canons. But implicit always in this attitude of his was an inner spiritual passion. His church policy was the outcome not of calculation but of conviction; he was ready to die for it.

In 1637 it seemed impossible that any such sacrifice would be asked of him, yet had the wild hypothetical question been put to him he would not have hesitated in his answer. When he was still a prince, he had been overheard to say to friends that he could not be a lawyer for " I cannot defend a bad nor yield in a good cause." [5]

The sentiment expressed very exactly the King's temperament; when he thought a cause was good he would not yield, and by "not yielding" he did not mean that he would yield on sufficient persuasion, or the day after to-morrow, or the year after next; he meant that he would not yield. This capacity for total resistance showed in these sunnier times as an occasional inconvenient obstinacy: occasional, because the number of things about which the King had completely made up his mind were few. On most subjects his hesitations and indecisions were notorious and embarrassing. But on the question of the Church he was immovable; it was the central pillar of his life, and his attitude to his own royal authority was but a part of his profound conviction of the unique rightness of the Church of England.

He was of the intractable stuff of which martyrs are made—not the swift, ecstatic martyrs who run upon death in a high impulsive fervour, but the sad, thoughtful martyrs who follow over long, patient years some logical sequence of thought and action which always may, and sometimes must, bring them to disaster. It is hard to understand and impossible to do justice to the situation which developed in England unless this peculiar quality of King Charles is seen from the outset as an integral part of it. In 1637 his actions might well be interpreted as those of a King who sought to strengthen the authority of the Crown by extending the authority of the Church. But this was the least part of them; for when it became apparent that their effect was precisely the opposite, that the logic of his policy was leading him not towards a serene magnificence of Kingship but to the mortal hazards of war, to capture, even to death, he would not turn aside.

Charles was the first King who had been brought up from childhood as a member of the Church of England. His predecessors had accepted the Church in maturity, as a convenient framework of belief. Charles had drawn in its doctrine with the innocent acceptance of childhood; the Church of England was to him, as it had been to none of his predecessors, the established order of things.

For the first time, the Anglican Church had as its head a Defender of the Faith who had never considered the possibility of defending any other faith. As if in response to this first monarch, so truly its own, it had flowered into a new beauty, of words, of form, and here and there a shining saintliness. The careful argumentation of Lancelot Andrewes and the menacing thunder of John Donne had been familiar to the King in the early part of his reign, but now a gentler, more pastoral inspiration breathed from the younger generation of preachers, Jeremy Taylor, Henry Hammond, William Cartwright. Many of them wrote poetry; a delicate sensibility to beauty lit up the meditations and prayers which they composed as they contemplated the Infinite from a college study or a vicarage window or the garden of a wealthy patron. They were a minority, as men of sensibility and talent necessarily are, but they set up a vibration in the Anglican community which has not died away. They loved the temperate beauty of their Church, not wantonly glorious like the Church of Rome, nor aggressively plain like that of Geneva. As George Herbert gratefully wrote:

> Blessed be God, Whose Love it was
> To double-moat thee with His grace,
> And none but thee.

The King had at his right hand an Archbishop after his own heart. He had always liked and approved of William Laud, although his father had feared the meddling temperament of the little man and had been unwilling to give him preferment. Under King Charles, Laud had been raised first to the see of London, then to that of Canterbury.

A man of great learning, a profound believer in ritual and hierarchy, Laud was more of a tidier-up and setter-in-order than a true reformer, but he had boundless energy and clear, if limited, vision. His ideal was a Church, rigidly and efficiently organised, its services reverently conducted according to a uniform ritual, its hierarchy sagely established, and the whole population gathered together into one docile flock. This vision exactly matched the King's. It became the corner-stone of a deep personal respect and friendship which made it possible for Charles to overlook the Archbishop's social failings. These were less kindly viewed by many of his colleagues on the King's council who found him troublesome, tactless and ill-bred. The son of a Reading tradesman, he had never acquired the poise suitable to his exalted position, and his appearance—" a little, low, red-faced man "— was much against him. He was irritable, opinionated, apt to shout in argument and to slap about impatiently with his hands. He did not have the sense to avoid the absurd; his enemies can be forgiven for their angry amusement when, at the dedication of St. Catherine Cree Church, the splendid opening phrase, " Be ye lift up, ye everlasting doors: and the King of Glory shall come in," was immediately followed by the entry of stout little Laud. In spite of his shortcomings he had an element of greatness, a selfless and singleminded devotion to his religion and his duty. Like the King, he worked not for what he thought to be expedient, but for what he thought to be right, and, like the King, he would not abandon it.

Under the King's and the Archbishop's influence, outward beauty was much regarded. Inigo Jones designed simple, handsome churches in the Renaissance manner, and re-modelled, on chastely luxurious lines, the chapels of the great. Italianate façades and porticoes were wedded incongruously to older buildings. A hybrid style, later to be called Laudian Gothic, was evolved. There was a revived interest in Church plate, vestments, hangings, screens, lecterns, pulpits, fonts, furniture of all kinds, even in painted glass.

Small organs, many of which came from Germany, beautifully carved and gilded, were introduced into private chapels, churches and cathedrals. Singing of the most elaborate kind was encouraged and cherished; new music was composed for the King's chapel and cathedral choirs. The Church flowered in a new beauty of holiness.

George Herbert, a younger son of a noble house, bred to the Court, had abandoned a wordly career and created during his brief devoted ministry the pattern of the Anglican parish priest. Nicholas Ferrar, of a wealthy family, to whom preferment stood open, had withdrawn from the world to Little Gidding in Huntingdonshire, where with his mother and brother and his brother's children he had created a community devoted to prayer, contemplation, good works and religious studies. Poor widows lived on the charity of this community and village children learned their psalms from the pious ladies with a penny prize for the word-perfect and Sunday dinner afterwards for all.[6]

The good preachers, the sensitive writers, the fine, holy and devout men in the Anglican Church were a minority. The King, who drew towards him divines after his own heart, too easily believed that those he saw were, if not typical, at least dominant in the Church. Factious dissent and criticism seemed to him only the last mutterings of an ancient storm soon to be quiet for ever.

He was wrong in every way. His Church was young and insecure, doctrinally divided, imperfectly organised, open to criticism and but feebly rooted in the affections of the people. At the time of its establishment by law under Queen Elizabeth many points of doctrine had been left vague in order that as many as possible of her subjects might be brought in without offence to conscience. The Church was Protestant because it repudiated the Pope but it was officially spoken of as Catholic and it had retained the episcopal hierarchy. This reformation seemed inadequate to the large number of English Protestants who had come under the Calvinist or Baptist influences which flowed into the country with the Netherlands trade. The first demanded the reorganisation of the Church without bishops, on the model of Geneva; the second demanded liberty for congregations of the faithful to choose their own way of worship. Of the two the Calvinist group was the more intellectual, the more highly conscious and the stronger, for the Baptists and their like declined by their very nature towards an anarchy of subdivision.

Apart from those who fully understood the doctrine and organisation of Calvinism, a great number of Protestants in England tended, by temperament, through the verbal interpretation of the Bible or through animosity to the Church of Rome, to lean away from the Catholic and towards the Protestant elements in the Church of England. The term Puritan, used indiscriminately for all these, had no definite and no official meaning: it was a term of abuse merely. It might be applied equally to a devout cobbler expounding the scriptures according to a theory of his own, or to a dutiful member of the Anglican communion who had done no more than hazard the opinion that the surplice was a remnant of Rome.

For the last half-century the English Church had been striving towards a greater clarity and uniformity of worship and doctrine, but the movement had not been continuously in the same direction. Archbishop Whitgift had compelled the more in-transigent Calvinist clergy to leave the Church, and his successor Richard Bancroft had worked with pastoral severity to suppress extreme Protestant doctrines. George Abbot, Bancroft's successor, had reversed this policy. He had favoured the more Protestant clergy and discouraged those whose practices showed too close an approximation to Rome.

The doctrines of Arminius, the Dutch theologian who had challenged Calvinism at Leyden, were at this time gaining currency in England and bringing with them a return to ritual. Abbot detested their tenets, but the intellectual fashion was too strong for him; more and more of the promising young men at the universities adopted Arminian views. When King Charles ascended the throne, the division between the Arminians and the school of churchmen whom Abbot approved was already deeply marked. When Abbot retired, Charles himself put forward William Laud, the most distinguished of the Arminians, to take his place. Laud reverted, inevitably, to the anti-Puritan policy of Bancroft and Whitgift. But he could not undo the work of Abbot. The English Church, from bishops downwards, was full of those who disapproved of the Arminians, and Laud's favour towards them was popular neither with laity nor with clergy. " What do the Arminians hold?" went the ill-natured joke—" All the best livings in England." Both pastors and flock were deeply, bitterly divided.

The crucial question was the relationship of the Anglican Church to Rome. The creed spoke of " one holy Catholic Church " but this meant different things to different men. A man who, like the Archbishop or the King, believed that truth was one and indivisible must necessarily wish to see Catholic Christendom re-united. Certain of the Anglican clergy shared the wish, although the intensity of their desire and the ways in which they would have liked to implement it varied greatly. The sincere and unhappily bewildered Godfrey Goodman, Bishop of Gloucester, was one of the few leading churchmen who doubted the rightness of the Anglican position and would have welcomed a return to the communion of Rome at the price of concessions.[7]   Archbishop Laud and his chief supporters saw in the Anglican doctrine and ritual the true Catholic faith, deplored the errors of Rome and were steadfast against them. But Rome, for them, represented an error in Catholicism which might one day be set right.   It was very different from vile heresies like Calvinism and Baptism.   They would protect their flocks with all their strength against conversion to Rome, but they felt the Roman error to be less fundamental and less dangerous to the souls in their care than the sectarian heresies.

The bishops who survived from Archbishop Abbot's time were essentially Protestant and had no thought at all of undoing the work of the Reformation.   Several of them were distinguished for discretion and integrity but they were not fortunate in their leadership.   Bishops Davenant of Salisbury and Hall of Exeter, learned and worthy men, were neither of them ambitious for domination.   The able and diplomatic Bishop Morton of Durham was equally unwilling to thrust himself forward in Church politics.   Leadership of the group who wished to conciliate the Puritans fell therefore to John Williams, Bishop of Lincoln, a super-subtle Welshman against whom the Archbishop waged a continual war.   Williams believed, honestly and charitably, that the Church could prosper only through alliance and friendship with the best of the Puritans.   But his honesty of motive did not go with honesty of method.   Mistakenly meddling in the early quarrels of Charles and his Parliaments, Williams had forfeited the King's favour and laid himself open to the grave charge of revealing state secrets.   In attempting to defend himself against this charge, the excitable and over-ingenious prelate had involved himself in an offence even more grave—that of suborning witnesses.   The King, dropping the original accusation, had substituted the new one, and Williams, after trying every trick of evasion and postponement, was to face the King's council in the summer of 1637 on this disgraceful charge.   So shocking a crime made him at the moment more of a liability than an asset to the conciliatory party in the Church.

The Archbishop, well knowing this, pressed the charge home with the intention of wrecking, at one blow, both Williams and the policy for which he stood.

The division between the best men in the Church was one grave difficulty that the King had to face. Another problem was the inadequate resources and organisation of the Anglican Establishment. At the untidy Reformation made by Henry VIII the economic foundations of the Church had been irreparably damaged. The hierarchy and the administrative framework had survived and been reaffirmed under Elizabeth, but it was another matter to restore enough Church property to maintain the Anglican Church with the dignity of its Roman predecessor. The bishoprics had been so plundered that Elizabethan, Jacobean and Caroline bishops were reduced to the oddest expedients. The Bishop of St. David's tore off and sold all the lead on the episcopal palace. The Bishop of Lichfield recklessly deforested his land to get the profit of the timber. Other bishops converted the short leases of their tenants into life-rents for sums of ready money. This was a help to the bishop who made the arrangement but left his successor poorer than before, and King Charles had vigorously—and vainly—prohibited the practice.[8]

Since the Reformation, tithes had in some places been commuted for money, and in others been alienated to the lay patrons of the living. The value of money had declined in the past eighty years and often changes in agriculture had altered the value and quantity of the payments in kind. Friction over tithes between the clergy and their parishioners or their patrons was frequent, and was intensified by the contention of Puritan dissidents that they did not wish to pay any minister who was not of their own way of thinking, or even that to pay tithes at all was a form of simony, the gifts of the Holy Ghost not being for sale. All these quarrels brought to popular notice the least spiritual aspect of the Church and its ministers.

Patronage of church livings had at the Reformation been greedily swallowed up by laymen of all sorts, landowners or corporations, who had frequently taken a large part of the endowments as well. The smallness of the incomes from preferments led to unashamed pluralism. A churchman who by astute courting of the right patrons had procured several livings for himself could delegate his religious duties to one or two poor curates hired at miserable wages. The pluralist himself, it was said, " weareth cassocks of damask and plush, good beavers and silk stockings, can play well at tables or gleek, can hunt well and bowl very skilfully . . . and can relish a glass of right claret."[9] The absentee was rarely an advertisement for the spiritual qualities of the Church, nor was the starveling curate who filled his place.

The parson's status in the social hierarchy was doubtful; manual labour was frowned on but he had to work his glebe. Parishioners in one village complained because the parson played ninepins with the butcher, and in another, because he undertook odd jobs of thatching in his spare time. No doubt much depended on the reputation and general behaviour of individuals: many of these disappointed educated men, exiled in remote places, found solace in drink and low company, and thatching or playing ninepins with the butcher were only one part of the conduct which was felt to misbecome their office— for when the neatly dressed parson's wife of Fladbury tripped down the village street with her milk pail on her head like a dairymaid she got nothing but indulgent smiles and commendation for her Christian simplicity.[10]

Ordination was inadequately controlled. Orders were sold or forged, or given by bishops on insufficient inquiry into the character and education of the candidate. The Puritan Baxter's account of the Anglican clergy round Kidderminster at about this time—decrepit and doddering or else drunk and immoral— represents the Church as seen by a vehement critic, but these dark colours were true to a part of the reality. The Church had neither the men nor the organisation to meet all the needs of the people. Wales was wretchedly neglected for lack of priests and of those appointed to Welsh parishes few could speak or preach in Welsh. In Herefordshire it was said that in over two hundred churches and chapels there were not twenty incumbents fit or willing regularly to preach a sermon.[11]

Serious-minded men and women, some but not all of whom were extreme Protestants, tried to remedy the shortcomings or the absence of the local clergy by meeting independently for prayer and Bible reading. It was an easy step from this to expounding and preaching. A gentleman living in Exeter, for instance, with a comfortable household employing seven or eight servants, held "a conference upon a question propounded once a week in his own family"—a debate upon the scriptures in which his children and servants joined.[12] However innocently such discussions began, they created a dangerous liberty of argument, and the established Church discouraged them, mildly or vigorously according to the temper of the bishop in charge. Attacks provoked defiance and bred fanaticism; in districts where Puritanism was deeply rooted, family gatherings insensibly grew into conventicles, meeting secretly when they were forbidden. The steady increase in the number of these conventicles was, for all those who had the interests of the Establishment at heart, one of the most disquieting phenomena of the sixteen-thirties.

A group of Puritans, earlier in King Charles's reign, had embarked on a scheme for providing respectable clergy by private enterprise. They bought in advowsons which had become secularised at the Reformation, and presented to them ministers of their own choosing. In this way they planned, little by little, to place men of good morals and sound doctrine—according to their way of thinking—in a great number of parishes. They had not gone far before they were stopped. In Laud's opinion their action was a plot—" in a cunning way, under a glorious pretence, to overthrow the Church government, by getting into their power more dependency of the clergy, than the King and all the Peers and all the Bishops in all the Kingdom had." [13]

From his own point of view Laud was right, but so, from their point of view, were the Puritan gentry who had given time, thought and money to the project. Both wanted to propagate what they took to be right doctrine and both wanted control of the best instrument of instruction and propaganda in the country—the pulpit.

Whitgift and Bancroft in their efforts to reorganise the Church had made great use of one effective weapon, the ecclesiastical Court of High Commission for inquiring into abuses. Under Bancroft clashes with the common lawyers began to arise; the High Commission, as the guardian of public morals, claimed jurisdiction in numerous domestic disputes and also in cases arising on, or in connection with, church land. Disputes over tithes also brought the interests of the Church into contact and collision with the common law [14] and the possibilities of ecclesiastical encroachment on territory belonging to the secular courts yearly increased; the old medieval conflict between spiritual and secular justice was thus revived. The danger to the Church arising from this clash with the common law was immediate and practical, for the pretensions of the High Commission Court created an alliance between the common lawyers and the Puritans.

Archbishop Laud used the High Commission vigorously, both to enforce his doctrinal and ritualistic ideas and to maintain the purity of English morals. Those summoned before the Court were compelled to take the so-called *ex officio* oath before answering the searching questions which might be put to them. Refusal to take the oath or to answer any question was treated as a plea of guilty. This practice above all roused the anger of the lawyers and caused popular critics to compare the High Commission, with sincere exaggeration, to the Spanish Inquisition.

Meanwhile, causes for quarrel with the extreme Protestants both clergy and laity, increased from year to year. Candles multiplied in the churches of the young, fervent Arminian clergy whom Laud favoured; images of saints and of the Virgin were restored or introduced; the Communion table was set up altarwise at the east end of the chancel. The Arminian clergy wore not only the surplice but vestments; a silly woman in Norwich, seeing something red, asked why the Mayor was officiating in church. Music came back to the cathedrals; choir boys were taught to come in two by two and not to turn their backs to the altar; priests bowed towards it; some even used the sign of the Cross.

The more extreme opponents clamoured derisively about these " apish anticks," these cringings and duckings and caperings, and a great number of simple people were truly perturbed and bewildered at what they believed to be a return to Rome. Knowing their Bible and Foxe's " Book of Martyrs," and remembering, in grisly detail, how some of their immediate forefathers had endured martyrdom rather than yield to the idolatries of Rome, they were profoundly unwilling to betray the faith which had thus been sealed and sanctified to them. It was useless to explain to such people that an image is not in itself idolatrous but only becomes so when it is worshipped as an idol; this seemed to them mere sophistry against the forthright words of the second commandment: *Thou shalt not make unto thee any graven image.*

So also with the commandment to keep holy the sabbath day, a commandment notoriously flouted by the Papists. In some regions of the country, where the old religion was still strong, the sabbath-keepers and the sabbath-breakers came into open conflict. In Lancashire and in Somerset wakes and holy days were enthusiastically celebrated by some, in defiance of the pious disapproval of others. King James had attempted to make an end of the people's quarrels by issuing a judgment of Solomon in the matter. In 1618 he had published the *Book of Sports* declaring what games might lawfully be played on Sundays after church: he included dancing for both sexes, vaulting, archery, and maypoles and morris dances in season. The King had prefaced his Book with the argument that if sports were made unlawful, the people would be driven to tipple in alehouses where they would learn to indulge themselves in " idle and discontented speeches."

The Book was, in intention, both politic and humane but it

met with great opposition. King Charles reissued it in 1633 with instructions that the vicar of each parish see that its provisions be thoroughly made known. He was widely reported to have commanded the clergy to read it from the pulpit, and some do indeed seem to have understood his orders in this way, for one, who read the book, followed it with the fourth commandment, adding, " Dearly beloved, you have heard the commandment of God and Man: obey which you will."

The Archbishop's more indiscreet supporters often aroused the animosity of their flock. A vicar of Grantham provoked derision because he genuflected with such extravagance as to lose his balance. A little later, when he tried to move the communion table to the east end of the chancel, his parishioners burst into the church to stop him. The vicar tugged at one end, they at the other, till he gave up the unequal contest, shouting to them to keep their old trestle, he would build a stone altar instead. They would have no " dressers of stone " in their church, they retorted and, led by a couple of aldermen of their city, went off in a party to complain to the Bishop. The vicar followed after, " pale and staring in his looks," pitifully telling the Bishop that his parishioners had threatened to burn his house.

The diocese was Lincoln and the Bishop John Williams, the conciliator. He asked them all to supper and tried to patch up the quarrel. Later he wrote to the vicar: " Whether side soever, you or your parish, shall yield unto the other, in these needless controversies, shall remain in my poor judgment, the more discreet, grave and learned of the two: and by that time you have gained some more experience in the cure of souls, you shall find no such ceremony equal to Christian charity." [15] Not long after he published, anonymously, in a pamphlet entitled *Holy Table: Name and Thing* his own moderate opinion on the place of the communion table in churches. The Archbishop regarded this attempt to propound a calmer view of the controversy with nothing but resentment.

Other church dignitaries were intransigent with their flocks for more secular reasons. At Chester no mayor had entered the cathedral for twelve years, owing to a dispute about the place allotted to him. At last a mayor, who had begun life as a cathedral chorister, tried to heal the breach but no sooner did he attempt to take his seat in the cathedral than the Dean reopened the old dispute and the mayor did not come again.[16]

Sometimes the internal dispute in the Church flared up between members of a cathedral chapter. A prebend of Durham, John Cosin, persuaded the chapter to beautify this most splendid of cathedrals in a worthy manner: great candlesticks gleamed on a high altar of " branched marble " and old defaced carvings of saints and angels were restored. A rival Puritan member of the cathedral chapter, Dr. Smart, in a thundering sermon on idolatry condemned him as " our young Apollo, who repaireth the Choir and sets it out gaily with strange Babylonish ornaments." The Court of High Commission silenced Smart, who lost his place in the cathedral and was fined five hundred pounds. The sentence purchased a temporary victory for Cosin at far too high a price; in the angry Puritan world Smart became the proto-martyr in a new era of persecution.[17]

Whatever the occasional extravagances of the Laudians, the conduct of the English in Church at this epoch stood in need of reformation. Lack of money and the disappearance of endowments had caused many churches to fall into decay and some altogether into disuse. Many were filthy, with unglazed windows, and mud floors like cow byres. Squatters took possession of neglected chapels; in Wiltshire several families were found camping in one, using suitable tombstones as cheese presses.[18] The abhorrence of idolatry taught by the Puritans had degenerated into open disrespect for church buildings. The parish church was often the parish meeting place, not only for sober business but for dancing and drinking parties. Sporting parishioners brought their dogs and hawks to divine service and the poorer sort pastured their hogs in the graveyard. An indignant sexton in Suffolk found the local squire sheltering from a storm with his horse inside the sacred building.

Much Communion plate had vanished at the Reformation and its place was often meanly supplied by wicker and earthenware bottles and vulgar tavern pots. The Calvinist practice of giving the sacrament at a table placed in the middle of the nave was usual; this, in Laud's angry phrase, made the church into an alehouse. He exaggerated, but the central position of the Communion table encouraged the congregation to use it as the common repository for hats and gloves, and to loll upon it with their elbows during the sermon.[19]

Social distinctions were more carefully preserved than reverence towards God. The gentry, and the London apprentices, thought it beneath their dignity to sit bareheaded during the sermon. In Bristol it was customary to wait for the mayor before beginning the sermon, or, if he came early, to begin the sermon immediately, omitting all the rest of the service. The clergy in many towns seem to have thought it right or at least advisable to " give good-morrow to Mr. Mayor, though in the middle of the Lesson." Conversely a respectful ploughman, joining in the responses, was alleged to have answered the vicar's *The Lord be with you* by *And with your worship's spirit.*

Such was the situation which the King and the Archbishop undertook to reform. Not long after the unseemly tumult between the vicar of Grantham and his parishioners, Laud began to insist that the communion table in every church in the kingdom be moved to the east end of the chancel and protected by rails " one yard in height and so thick with pillars that dogs may not get in." [20] The wearing of the surplice, bowing at the name of Jesus, and the churching of women after child-birth (another ceremony repugnant to the extreme Protestants) were likewise to be enforced.

Year after year, by means of visitations and prosecutions in the ecclesiastical Court, the Archbishop pressed on with his counter-reformation, provoking at each new clash and at each new prosecution a deeper resentment against himself and against his King.

The intensity with which his orders were enforced varied

from diocese to diocese. In the south and south-west, the old and cautious Bishop Davenant of Salisbury and the gentle and humane Bishop Hall of Exeter were anxious not to drive good men into opposition for trifles or to provoke animosity among the people. Neither of these bishops was popular at Whitehall, and Charles had had each of them in turn—and Hall more than once—on his knees before the Privy Council for offending his religious susceptibilities. The Dean of Winchester, also, pleaded to be excused from bowing at the name of Jesus because of the offence which this gave to the ignorant and to weaker vessels who might be alienated and lost to the Church.[21]

Very different was the spirit of the vehement Arminian, Matthew Wren, who had been appointed to the see of Norwich in the heart of East Anglia, the stronghold of Puritanism. The vigour of his visitations and the searching character of the questions which were put to the people had, within the space of two years, created a sullen, vindictive resentment throughout his diocese. He inquired not merely into the state of churches and churchyards, the order of services, the dress of the clergy, the existence of conventicles, the employment of chaplains or tutors by private families, but asked whether any man had heard any other speak anything against the King's authority, or if any in the parish did " presume to make matters of divinity their ordinary table-talk." If there were any who took " the liberty of their trencher-meetings . . . rashly and profanely to discourse of Holy Scripture " it was the duty of their neighbours to " name the persons, times and places, as far as you know, or have heard or can remember." [22] This gave dangerous encouragement to informers, provoked suspicion and ill-feeling from many honest, earnest Christians, and instituted a prying, exacting inquiry which was deeply resented. The number of prosecutions in the diocese and the number of the clergy suspended for Puritan conduct or doctrine was, in truth, nothing out of the ordinary. But the anger aroused by the bishop's policy was not assuaged because he was less terrible in deed than in word.

A recently published pamphlet called *News from Ipswich* had given the Puritans of London an exaggerated account of the troubles in East Anglia. Written in a confused but passionate manner, full of rhetoric, but also full of lively details, the pamphlet was widely bought and read before the government could stop it. The source of the publication was never revealed. It bore the statement " printed in Ipswich," but no Ipswich printer had set it up. A popular London preacher, Dr. Henry Burton, the Puritan rector of St. Matthew's, Friday Street, made *News from Ipswich* the subject of two sermons, in which he loudly condemned not only Bishop Wren but all bishops as " upstart mushrumps." This was not the first time that Burton had offended and he cannot have been greatly surprised at finding himself once again the object of government prosecution. In June of the year 1637 he faced his trial before the King's council, with two other opponents of the bishops.

The authorship of *News from Ipswich* had been traced to William Prynne, once a barrister, now a prisoner in the Tower of London. Some years before he had been condemned for the publication of a violent attack on the stage, a work as erudite as it was intemperate, entitled *Histriomastix*. The book was alleged to contain references to the dancing and masquing at Court and thus to offend the King's—and more especially the Queen's—Majesty. Prynne had been fined £5,000, had stood in the pillory, had had his ears cut off, and been sent to the Tower for life. Oxford had taken away his degree, Lincoln's Inn had expelled him, and the Inns of Court, to show their abhorrence of his opinions, had presented Shirley's famous and fabulously expensive masque, *The Triumph of Peace*, as a special compliment to the Court.

Prynne's powerful intellect and massive learning were constricted within the rigid bonds of his fanatical prejudices. He had no interests outside the study, no wife, few friends, and he advocated his Calvinist convictions with the glum ferocity of the professional pedant. He was an exasperating, unloved, unlovable man but his single-minded and ill-placed courage were to make him, over the years, into a popular public character.

Side by side with Henry Burton and William Prynne stood John Bastwicke, one of Burton's parishioners. By profession a doctor, Bastwicke had also been in trouble before and had been imprisoned in the Gatehouse for publishing in the Latin tongue attacks on the bishops. Early in 1637 he had changed his manner, though not his matter, and published an attack in plain English. All three men were thus before the Council for the same offence: a deliberate attempt to undermine the hierarchy of the Church. Prynne, Burton and Bastwicke might each individually be dismissed as a cantankerous eccentric. But they voiced an opposition which was steadily growing.

The opposition was serious, although often expressed in an ignorant, factious and ridiculous manner. Henry and Susan Taylor, from a Norfolk village, had, for instance, loudly babbled that bishops were lazy fellows, that tithes were unlawful, that the Anglican service was no different from the Mass and—with an unexpected veering from Protestantism to Popery—that the clergy should not marry.[23] The vicar of Llanidloes, who let his parishioners shoot birds in the nave and cut up his surplice for towels, was of much the same mettle as the Essex woman who pegged up her laundry in the chancel, crying that if parson brought his old linen into the church, so would she; or the good wife in Wolverhampton who, on being told to wear a veil for her churching, impudently clapped a dinner napkin over her head. Now and again the extremist fringe showed signs of mental derangement; the crazy Lady Eleanor Davies, who had the reputation of a prophetess, marched into Lichfield cathedral with a bucketful of pitch and splashed it over the altar hangings; she was assisted by the town clerk and his wife, both of whom seem to have been sane.[24] All this was ridiculous; but the popular emotions and the deeper convictions which underlay these incidents were not ridiculous.

The King's attitude to sermons stirred the Puritans more deeply than his attitude to ceremonies. The sermon, the expounding of the scriptures, was their great strength; when a parson was himself weak in this kind of eloquence it was not unusual for him to engage, often at the expense of the parish, a lecturer to do the preaching for him. The great majority of these were Puritan clergy who, in present circumstances, were unlikely to get any higher preferment. Where Puritanism was strong, parishioners sometimes joined together for the godly purpose of paying for extra sermons, usually mid-week lectures. In this way, without any direct contravention of the authority of the Church, extreme Protestantism was poured forth from a great number of pulpits.

The King and the Archbishop, determined to stop the abuse, decreed that one sermon on Sunday, on a strictly uncontroversial topic, was alone to be permitted. Suitable sermons for general use were available, to help the less eloquent, in the *Book of Homilies*. At afternoon service a general catechism was to take the place of the sermon. As for the mid-week sermons, they were only to be allowed under strict diocesan supervision. Two more Puritan devices were forbidden: the church bell was not to be rung in a special manner to distinguish a service with a sermon from one without, and popular preachers were no longer to hold their services either later or earlier than those of neighbouring clergy, to enable people from outlying parishes to combine them, on a Sunday, with compulsory worship in their own church. In future there was to be no question of sermon-hungry parishioners straying into other folds to taste forbidden fruit.[25]

Apart from this general prohibition, the Archbishop and the bishops who supported his policy, from time to time suspended individual clergy or prohibited them from preaching. In Wales, the ignorance of the people and the isolation of farms and hamlets caused a few conscientious clergy to preach out of doors, in farm houses, or at irregular hours. William Wroth of Llanfaches, accused of such practices before the High Commission, pleaded with Celtic passion. He had seen " thousands of immortal souls around me, thronging to perdition, and should I not use all means to save them? " He was deprived of his cure none the less; so was William Erbury, of St. Mary's Cardiff and his curate, Walter Craddock. These three devout evangelists were strongly marked with Puritanism and, on losing their cures, continued to preach privately in despite of the law; Craddock ("a bold ignorant young fellow," said the High Commission) took his staff and scrip and roamed the hills of South Wales expounding the word of the Lord to the people in their own tongue. But even the gentle Rhys Prichard, who was no Puritan, was in trouble with authority for his unconventional practice of teaching the scriptures by making and singing Welsh songs with his flock. The Archbishop, whose first bishopric had been the South Welsh diocese of St. David's, was willing enough that the light of the gospel should shine in Wales, but it must shine only as he directed.

Clergy who had clashed with the Archbishop did not easily escape his vigilance. Thomas Shepard, a young man who shortly after his ordination had been chosen as their lecturer by the people of Earl's Colne in Essex, was one of those forbidden either to preach or to exercise any other religious function. He vainly argued his case in an interview with Laud, but the Archbishop trembled with rage and looked, Shepard recorded, "as though blood would have gushed out of his face." Shepard and his friends, who were no more courteous to Laud than he to them, spoke of him among themselves as the swine sent "to root up God's plants in Essex." Uprooted, Shepard fled to Yorkshire where he took refuge in a private household, but his retreat was discovered and he sailed for the wider freedom of New England.

New England and the other settlements far across the Atlantic were a source of nagging annoyance to the Archbishop and the King. It was difficult to know for sure, and almost impossible to stop, what was going on in those places. The Archbishop did his best by persistently interfering with the efforts of Puritans to raise money for "godly ministers" to go out to the congregations across the Atlantic. The stream of emigration of Puritan congregations and their clergy went on none the less and the

King was now seriously considering a total prohibition of all further sailings.

An annoyance of another kind came from the Protestant shores of Europe. English clergymen ordained by Calvinists in Holland somehow made their way into the English Church, and several protests to the Prince of Orange not to permit this irregular ordination of Englishmen had hitherto been in vain. Enclaves of foreign Calvinism also remained within the King's dominions. The Channel Islanders had received the Reformation from France and were indifferent to the English-speaking version of it later dispensed to them. Allowances had to be made for the Channel Islanders; they enjoyed a good many separate rights, owing to their status as part of the lost Duchy of Normandy. Administrative quarrels, bitter and frequent at this time, were not Laud's province: religion was. He went to work with more restraint and wisdom than usual. The difficulty was that all instruction in the islands had to be in French, and teachers were usually trained at the Huguenot academy at Saumur. Laud endowed three fellowships for Channel Islanders at Oxford in the hope that good education and pure doctrine would flow forth together from his own university.

The refugee churches, founded by fugitives from the Spanish Netherlands or France, and scattered over the south and south-east—at Norwich, Colchester, Maidstone, Sandwich, Canterbury, Southampton and London—came in for rougher treatment. Wren attacked them in the Eastern counties, Laud in the diocese of Canterbury. Their reason for existence as communities was questioned and they were commanded to attend the English parish churches and dissolve their separate organisation. Their English fellow citizens took their side; quite apart from the religious aspect of the matter, the towns which sheltered them did not want their own parishes to become responsible for the poor and infirm of communities which had hitherto always looked after their own.[26]

The English Church covered England and Wales and enclosed at least two-thirds of the King's subjects, willingly or unwillingly,

the fold. The Churches of Ireland and Scotland, which
engaged the King's attention, offered different problems.
Church of Ireland was, in organisation, doctrine and liturgy,
same as that of England, and the King usually sought the
advice of Laud in making appointments to Irish bishoprics, in
spite of the primacy, over the Irish Church, of James Ussher,
Archbishop of Armagh.

Ussher's Anglican flock consisted chiefly of settlers and their
families. Ineradicable and all-pervasive, the Old Religion commanded the allegiance of the Irish; the Roman priests and
bishops had their loyalty although cathedrals, churches, chapels,
and episcopal residences and revenues were in the hands of
strangers, and their own clergy lived on the charity of the
faithful by the sufferance of the government.

Abroad, in Rome, in Spain, in the Spanish Netherlands,
Irish friars kept in constant touch with their brethren at home.
Plots for the return of Ireland to the Church, with the help of
Spain, were continuously in the air. A mysterious figure, the
titular Archbishop of Cashel, moved secretly between Ireland and
Spain; it was said that the Spaniards paid him a thousand ducats
a year for his services, and the Lord Deputy Wentworth had
hitherto been unsuccessful in identifying and seizing upon
him.[27]

The Church of Ireland was adrift like a raft on an alien sea,
and had not even the universal approval of the settlers who were
inclined, especially in Ulster, towards the anti-episcopal doctrines
of Calvin. It was at least fortunate in the Primate, James Ussher,
Archbishop of Armagh. He was " a tall, proper, comely man,"
of a fine but austere presence, studious and frugal habits and
simple, courteous bearing. Ussher's Protestantism was enriched by great learning, guided by a high intelligence and
informed by a genuine, though concealed, warmth of heart. He
was a man of strong, unbending character but he was not provo-
cative. Laud, who did not agree with him, respected both his
knowledge of Ireland and his integrity; he never willingly
went against him either in his appointments or his policy, and

the Irish Church had been allowed to retain an essentially Protestant character. The English Church in Ireland had, however, suffered no less than the Church at home from the unscrupulous plundering of its revenues since the Reformation. The ceaseless law suits about property and endowments between the clergy and the laity made it unpopular with the wealthy settlers and sometimes contemptible to the pious.[28]

In Ulster the Lowland Scots who had come over in the last twenty-five years were emphatically Calvinist, often gave trouble to their bishops and were sometimes abetted in it by their own clergy. Since defiance of authority could not in any circumstances be tolerated, Archbishop Ussher, though not altogether happy about the matter, was at one with the Lord Deputy Wentworth in disciplining the recalcitrant. A number of the more stubborn had been deprived of their livings and made to leave the country. The Bishops of Down and Derry were the firmest in carrying out this policy, a circumstance which (because of the refrain of the old song—*hey derry down derry*) provoked a grim smile even among the Puritans.

Some of these expelled Scottish clergy had set sail for New England, but contrary winds had driven them back to the Ayrshire coast, where they were joined by others who had had to leave Ireland. Their forlorn condition touched the good people of these parts, especially the women, and the strongminded housewives of Ayr came to Edinburgh to plead their cause. When the King's councillors tried to pass them by, their spokeswoman laid a muscular hand on the arm of the foremost with " Stand, my lord, in Christ's name, till I speak to you." [29]

Most of the King's councillors in Scotland were anxious to yield to Calvinist opinion whenever possible, for the religious situation, complicated by economic anxieties and national pride, was more immediately dangerous there than in either of his other kingdoms. Seventy years before, Scotland had been the scene of a violent Calvinist Reformation. The bitterness of feeling between Calvinist and Catholic had been further intensified by the racial antagonism of Saxon and Celt; the old religion survived in the restless highlands but the industrious people of the lowlands turned to the new.

King James VI had sidled his way through the savage factions of his nobility until he achieved effective authority over the warring elements in the Scottish state. Catholicism survived illegally in the wilds, but he made the nation's official religion Protestant, while steadily discouraging its more extreme manifestations. By the exercise of patience and ingenuity and the offer or distribution of bribes, King James had persuaded succeeding Assemblies of the Kirk to accept the return of episcopacy and to pass orders for church worship and organisation—the famous Five Articles of Perth—by which kneeling to receive the sacrament, confirmation by bishops and the principal fasts and feasts of the Church were restored. Further he had not tried to go, and he had been constant always to one important principle of policy: to do nothing likely to unite the interests of the nobility with those of the extreme Calvinists. He had been careful, when restoring the bishops, to make no attempt to restore also the episcopal revenues seized by Scots lords at the Reformation. The Jacobean bishops were humble and cautious men careful to placate the secular lords. King James had, moreover, left the parish organisation of the Kirk intact, so that the system of moral and religious control in each village and community was on the Geneva model, with elders and frequent meetings to maintain discipline and to control alike the minister and the people.

King Charles was unwilling to acquiesce in this middle part. When he visited Scotland—which was not until the ninth year of his reign—he introduced the full Laudian ceremony at the chapel of Holyrood. The coronation was marked by a clash of wills with the Lord Chancellor, who threatened to resign rather than give precedence, at the King's request, to the Archbishop of St. Andrews. "I will not meddle further with that old cankered goutish man," said the King angrily as he yielded the point. In outward form the coronation was, otherwise, according to the King's desire, but the hearts of his nobility did not go with their hands. Lord Rothes, who carried the Sword at the ceremony, attempted some days later to present a petition against the bishops.[30]

Parliament, meeting during the King's visit, passed some further reforms in ceremonial with only a narrow majority—some said with no majority at all, but by the juggling of the clerk who was a King's man. Charles noted the names of all who had voted against the measure and when, not long after, one of them, Lord Balmerino, was found to be in possession of a draft of another petition against prelacy, the King had him arrested on a charge of high treason. Tried by the King's council and condemned by a casting vote, Balmerino was then graciously reprieved by the King. He felt no gratitude, only a smouldering resentment at a monstrous proceeding.

The passions raised by the Balmerino trial and the unwillingness of so many of his lords and people to accept further changes in ceremony and ritual should have opened the King's eyes to the difficulties which lay before him in trying to make the Scottish Church as like the English as possible. But the King was in no position to make dispassionate judgment. The courtier-Scots whom he kept about him in England were willing and obedient Anglicans; those who had been most forward and most favoured in Scotland during his visit had also been, either from conviction or from policy, episcopalian in sympathy. Drummond, the poet-scholar, who had composed the official welcome to the King, was a convinced episcopalian; so were several distinguished scholars and clerics, expecially those from the university of Aberdeen. The distinction and eminence of these Scottish episcopalians concealed from the King the relative smallness of their numbers. A Court religion will always be in some degree a fashionable religion, and in Edinburgh in the thirties persons of rank frequently attended the Anglican service at the Chapel Royal. The Anglican service was also used by one or two of the younger bishops in their chapels and at New College, St. Andrews—all this with no noticeable protest, or none that reached the King's ears. He came to believe, on evidence all too slight, that the old stubbornness of the Calvinist Scots had weakened, and continued firmness would break it down altogether.

More truly religious and less wary than his father, Charles had from the outset abandoned political caution when faith and the honour due to the Church were in question. His attempt to make the Chancellor give way to the Archbishop, and his regular appointment of bishops to the vacant places on his council in Scotland, was deeply disturbing to the Scots. When in 1635 the Chancellor died, the Archbishop of St. Andrews was appointed in his place. The nobility, who were willing enough to tolerate bishops as inferiors, were indignant at this new elevation. They saw in it an attempt by the King to govern Scotland by means of his own prelatical nominees. The situation was not improved by the character of some of these. The Archbishop was old and careful to placate when he could. But the younger generation of bishops were bolder men, more zealous for the King's policy; they were prepared to outface the nobility and to respond to rudeness, not with Christian resignation but with episcopal dignity. Personal quarrels occurred even at the council table. So far from strengthening his council in Scotland by appointing bishops to it, the King weakened it by multiplying causes for hostility and division among its members.

The Scots nobility, on and off the Council, had another reason for resenting the King's religious policy. He had already proclaimed his intention of restoring to the Church some, if not all, of the property which they had seized. His two principal Scots courtiers, Lennox and Hamilton, had agreed to sell back to the Crown, for the Church, lands that their fathers had taken. The good example was not followed by other lords, who felt a growing apprehension for the safety of their property.

The King had not revisited Scotland, but in the four years since his coronation he had continued, undeflected, in his church policy. The clergy who supported him, mainly in the region of Aberdeen, moved further in the direction of English practice and ritual. A Jesuit missionary reported the appearance in Scottish churches of organs and altars, the wearing of the surplice and the singing of matins and evensong. The form of worship seemed to him "an imitation of the Mass."[31] The powers of a High Commission Court were now conferred on the Scots bishops, who thus, like the English, acquired the right to discipline the unruly. A new Book of Canons, something on the English model, had been sent to Scotland to replace the *Book of Discipline* of John Knox. These things aroused a muttering resentment, but the opposition had as yet no organisation; the alliance between the nobility, who felt their power and property in danger, and the discontented clergy and laity had not fully come into being.

The Book of Canons, which brought the organisation of the Scots Church into line with that of England, was to be followed by a new Prayer Book which should do the same for the order of worship. It was ready by the year 1636 but on the advice of the King's council in Scotland its introduction was postponed for several months.

The council was divided in opinion. The bishops naturally approved of the Book; several of their fellow councillors did not, and most of them foresaw serious opposition. The Book was presented in a manner bound to offend the sensibilities of the Scots. No Assembly of the Kirk and no Parliament had been called to discuss it, and although it had been drawn up by Scotsmen, they had gone to London to draft it in consultation with the English Archbishop. Furthermore, the King had prefaced it with a royal command to all ministers to use it and a sentence of outlawry on all who refused. A beautiful and dignified liturgy thus reached the Scots in a manner and in a form which could not but be offensive. It looked like an assault on their political as well as their religious independence.

The danger, as the King's council knew, lay as much in the ambitions of the discontented peers as in the religious fervour of people and ministers. What would Rothes and Balmerino do, given the opportunity? Their religious feelings might not go very deep, but suspicion of anything that smacked of Popery touched at once their prejudices, their dearest interests and seventy years of continuous tradition. As a ruffianly old nobleman said, when religion was discussed: "If I have lain with never so many whores, I'll never lie with the whore of Babylon." If the bigotry, greed and ancient feudal authority of the nobles should come together with the fervour of the people, great trouble would certainly follow.

For this reason the council asked for postponement, and only at the repeated instance of the King, at last, and with trepidation, fixed a Sunday at the end of July 1637 for the official introduction of the new order of worship throughout the country.

In Scotland and in England dislike and suspicion of Catholicism went with certain simple and far-reaching political prejudices. Both countries had experienced, to a greater or lesser degree, the reverberations of Europe's religious wars. Both had recollections of attempted foreign interference in the Roman Catholic interest, but in England the prejudice against Catholicism was closely linked with the hatred of Spain. It was the heritage of the Armada and the Elizabethan seamen. When the King had visited the Isle of Wight as a young man he had been surprised to see an inn sign representing a friar clawed by a lion. When he asked its meaning, his host, the genial John Oglander, boasted "we serve all papists and priests in that manner." [32] John Oglander was far from being an extreme Protestant, still less a Puritan; he spoke from the fulness of an Elizabethan heart.

King Charles made little allowance for such prejudices, and did not understand the confusion of thought in many of his subjects' minds. At York he had carefully arranged for the restoration of the shrine of Saint William; both he and Laud spoke respectfully of the saints, and it was alleged that a cleric who had referred disparagingly to Saint George had been made to apologise for his irreverence. The Archbishop had certainly prosecuted a man for publishing an almanack in which the names of Protestant martyrs from Foxe's Book were substituted for those of saints.

Side by side with the harassing of Calvinists, Baptists and other Protestant critics of the Church, went a policy of comparative toleration for Roman Catholics. In his marriage treaty the King had undertaken to repeal the more oppressive of the laws against them. Parliament had compelled him to break this promise, but in the long intermission of Parliaments after 1630 the King had found a way out. He did not repeal the laws but he exempted his Catholic subjects by individual letters patent, in return for a sum of money; this policy was advantageous as well as tolerant.

In other ways, the laws rusted. It was by law a capital offence for an English priest to be found in the country, but priests went openly about London. The Franciscans had returned, theoretically in secret, although their presence was generally known; the English province had been re-founded, and the Jesuits, who were jealous, spoke of them as Archbishop Laud's trencher-flies, a term which seems to have arisen from Laud's purely intellectual interest in the suggestions put forward by one of them, Franciscus a Sancta Clara, for the reconciliation of the Anglican and the Roman Churches. Another eminent exile, Mary Ward, the founder of a new religious order in Germany, the *Englische Fräulein*, came home with a small band of nuns and found a temporary resting place for them in Yorkshire.

The Catholic, or potentially Catholic, minority in the country was still in some districts a large one, able to give help and protection to the priests. In London, the bulk of the respectable population was strongly Protestant; the priests worked among the poor, the outcasts and the plague-stricken. Sometimes these London priests were under arrest and lived in prison awaiting trial, but by day they were allowed out on bail to perform their priestly functions. The further course of the law against them was held up indefinitely by the mercy of the King. This curious situation aroused some critical comparisons with the plight of one or two Protestant preachers and writers whom the King's justice had confined to prison without such unofficial privileges.

In Ireland the penal laws had been temporarily suspended in return for a large sum of money. Roman Catholics were allowed to practise at the bar and to hold positions of public trust. No obstacles were put in the way of the private practice of their religion although public services and large gatherings of the faithful were expressly forbidden, as were also pilgrimages, processions and all open demonstrations of faith.

In Scotland, where the majority was strongly Calvinist, the King's attempts to alleviate the persecution of his Catholic subjects were less successful. The Catholic cause was, for one thing, closely connected with the Gordon clan and its chief the Marquis of Huntly, a circumstance which confused the religious problem with the enmities of the clans and the traditional hostility between highlands and lowlands. All that the King had contrived to do was to grant special privileges to Huntly and his family.

Jesuit missionaries were active in Scotland, and, in the region round Aberdeen where Huntly's power was greatest, they conducted a regular ministry among the faithful. The air of secrecy and conspiracy which surrounded a religion carried on in so limited and dangerous a manner was especially strong in Scotland. In 1630 a principal member of Huntly's family had perished with several companions in a fire at Frendraught, a house belonging to the Crichtons. The Crichtons, though apparently reconciled, were hereditary enemies of the Gordons, and foul play was suspected. If the horrible business had indeed been a murder and not an accident, it was probably the result of personal enmity and nothing more, but a religious motive was half suspected. The Catholics told a tragic tale of the heroism of the young victim who had expounded the true faith to his companions as the flames crept up the tower in which he was trapped. This, with the evident unwillingness of those responsible for justice in Scotland to bring the crime home to the Crichtons, suggested that religious feuds were involved and that

Protestant sympathisers were determined to shield the murderers of a prominent Catholic, in spite of all that the King could do to have the culprits punished.[33]

The King's concessions to Catholics might not have provoked so much unfavourable comment from his Protestant subjects had not the open practice of Catholicism at Court attracted general attention. The Queen was the focus of fashionable Catholicism: a new and elegant allure lit up the old religion, and many lords and ladies flocked to the services in the Queen's chapel at Somerset House. Some went to be in the fashion but some were potential converts. The Queen's confessor, a charming and cultivated Scottish Benedictine, Robert Philip, often debated religious points with interested courtiers, and the existence of what was almost a Roman Catholic mission at Court made a bad impression on Puritan Londoners. The King, although he was indignant when any of his courtiers became converts, encouraged the intelligent and cultivated priests who surrounded his wife. He dearly loved a theological argument, and these men, unlike the Calvinists, talked a language which he approved and understood. He felt himself in many ways very close to them.

When the Queen had shown him a beautiful diamond cross, a gift sent to her by her godfather Pope Urban VIII, he had smiled and said that he must change his opinion of Roman priests: he had until this time believed that they would take but never give. The innocent jest gave rise to malicious speculation as to what the King had meant by the promise to change his opinion.

With his ideal of unity and uniformity, Charles truly wished to see Catholic Christendom made whole again. But, like the Archbishop and the Laudian clergy, he was convinced that this could only be through concessions made by the Pope to the Anglican communion. He stood out with resolute firmness against the appointment of a Roman Catholic bishop to look after the faithful in England. The establishment of a dual system of bishoprics, Roman and Anglican, would have implied acceptance of schism. Compliments between his Court and the Vatican were, however, frequent, and the Pope presented him with a splendid bust done by the famous Bernini from Van Dyck's painting.

The Vatican had exchanged agents with King Charles's Court in 1636. The King had sent to Rome the Scot Sir William Hamilton an optimistic Roman Catholic who talked hopefully of the coming return of Great Britain to the Church. Father George Con, the Vatican agent in England, was also a Scotsman but of a more realist temperament: he recognised the ultimate intransigence of both sides and he was alive to the strength of Puritan opinion in England. An intelligent and highly educated man, Con had a threefold attraction for the King, as a fellow Scotsman, a connoisseur of the arts and a cultivated conversationalist. Although he had no intention of changing his religion, Charles received and welcomed him with friendly familiarity and on one occasion had kept the chapter of the Knights of the Garter waiting for more than half an hour while he showed Con some new acquisitions to his collection. The slight to the greatest knightly order in the kingdom naturally provoked comment.

In other ways the King's affection for his wife and her friends made him indiscreet. He once accompanied her on a visit to the small community of Capuchins under her protection at Somerset House, inspected their chapel and their cells and stayed to share their humble and friendly supper.[34]

Charles himself, strong in the consciousness of his innocence, had no patience with the foolish misunderstandings to which his conduct gave rise, and punished with severity those who propagated slanders. A man who asserted that the King attended Mass with the Queen was fined £5,000, but while the King continued his favours to Roman Catholics, such harshness was in vain; his critics merely assumed that he chose an occasional victim to gloss over the awkward truth. Archbishop Laud, who fully recognised the danger, regretted the King's encouragement of Con and implored him to restrain the influence of some of the Queen's other protégés. Two of her courtiers troubled him especially, Toby Mathew and Wat Montagu; the former was the son of an Anglican bishop, the latter of the pious and sternly Protestant Earl of Manchester. Both were recent and eloquent converts to Rome, and both were clever men. Montagu was the more serious, Mathew the more amusing. He delighted in and played up to a reputation for entertaining silliness—as, for instance, when he offered to make some of the new drink, *chocolate*, for the Queen and did indeed do so, but absentmindedly drank it all up himself. Under this mask of levity, he was a man of a keen, inquiring mind, widely read and alert to all the latest explorations in the sciences. Not the least charm of fashionable Roman Catholicism at this time was that it represented also the *avant-garde* of intellectual life. Lord Herbert of Raglan and Sir Kenelm Digby, both Catholics, stood with Toby Mathew among the foremost amateur scientists of the age, and it was a group consisting principally of Catholics who a few years before, had tried to found a society devoted to the new learning.

The Archbishop was aware of the impression made by the King's encouragement of Roman Catholics. The popular argument was ignorant, incorrect, but deadly: if the King, the head of the Anglican Church, persecuted honest Protestants and smiled upon the Papists, it followed that the Church itself was being led back to Rome. The King's indiscreet and harmless relations with his wife's friends made his, and Laud's, religious policy suspect, not only to extremists and fanatics, but to the substantial majority of his Protestant subjects.

The misapprehension was deepened and embittered by the part which England under King Charles had come to play, or rather *not* to play, in the politics of Europe. Educated men had certain broad conceptions of foreign policy and of England's position and part in European affairs. For the last seventy years western Europe had been divided into two warring camps: the intense struggle between the Habsburg dynasty, ruling in Spain and Austria, and the Bourbon dynasty, ruling in France, had extended and confused the religious wars arising out of the Reformation. The Habsburg dynasty had taken upon themselves a crusade against the heretic; as a result, the French King, although officially Catholic, usually found it wise to sustain the Protestant forces with advice, money and arms, while the Vatican, which also had political interests to consider, tended to support France against Spain. In England this criss-cross of dynastic and religious interests was not widely understood, and the war appeared simply as a religious struggle or as a fight against the dominance of Spain. When, in Elizabeth's time, the English had entered the conflict they had fought against Spanish sea-power which barred their own adventurous expansion in the Americas, and with equal if confused zeal against the Church of Rome and the Spanish Inquisition. The fact that the Roman Catholic powers were not all on the same side in the war, and that the Vatican had moved steadily into alliance with France against Spain, meant very little to the average uninformed Englishman.

The last twenty years had been marked, in Europe, by a resurgence not of the Spanish but of the Austrian Habsburgs who, in the first decade of the Thirty Years War, had regained a large part of central Europe and of the German states for the Catholic Church. The plight of their co-religionists was brought home to the Protestant English by the presence in their midst of refugee German and Bohemian divines, often in such want that they sent their children in quest of alms from door to door. The words " the Protestant Cause " had become a catch-phrase in political discussion. Without very much conception of what the King could do to help the Cause, alehouse politicians—and a fair number of intelligent critics as well—blamed him for doing nothing. In Europe the Protestant Cause was sustained against Spain and Austria in the fields of Germany and Flanders by the Dutch and the Swedes, on the Rhine principally by the French, and at sea, against the Spaniards, by the Dutch alone. The King of England's great ships did nothing more distinguished than squabble with neighbouring Protestant powers about fishing rights.

Clashes with the Dutch in the Narrow Seas and in the Indies, where the merchants of both nations competed for trade, were becoming yearly more violent. But the average Englishman's feeling for the Protestant Cause was stronger than his feelings of rivalry so long as the Dutch were at war with Spain. The Hollanders could still therefore count on English volunteers for their armies and on sympathy from most, if not all, the English people. King Charles's subjects were not so deeply gratified as they should have been when the King, instead of assisting the Protestant Cause, turned his naval guns against the Dutch and with a show of force compelled their government to accept England's prior rights over the herring fisheries. The King, who was anxious to silence critics and to impress on his subjects the importance of what he had done, had a silver medal struck for the occasion. It was a most beautiful piece of work by Briot and bore the lovely text: *Justice and Peace have kissed one another*, but the symbolism represented the intention rather than the achievement of the treaty. The Dutch took little notice of the agreement, and incidents between their fishing boats and the Navy continued much as before.

A Court which favoured the Catholics, a Church which persecuted the Calvinists, a navy which fired only on the Dutch—the simplified picture was open to a dangerous interpretation. Neither at home nor abroad did the policy of King Charles appear Protestant. In the opinion of many it was not even neutral: in 1630 the King had made a treaty with Spain by which Spanish silver was to be minted in England and transported in English ships to Antwerp, where it was needed to pay the Spanish armies which were fighting the Dutch. To Spain the advantage of this arrangement was that the money, shipped by a power which was technically neutral, was safe from interception by the Dutch navy. The advantage to King Charles was that he received a share of each load of bullion for the English mint. This, as the Dutch complained, was a very odd kind of neutrality. In effect the King had become the pensioner and helper of Spain.[35]

The Protestant critics of the King's policy were bound together by the sentimental cult of the King's only sister Elizabeth. She had been married in 1613 to the young Elector Palatine, a Protestant and Calvinist alliance which had been extremely popular. Her husband had some years later accepted the crown of Bohemia from the insurgent Protestants of that country, an action which had precipitated the Habsburg crusade against Protestantism in the imperial dominions. In the course of the struggle the unhappy man had lost not only Bohemia but his title of Elector and all his hereditary German lands. Elizabeth had left behind in her own country a pleasing impression of her youth, liveliness and beauty. This had since been overlaid with visions both noble and tragic: Elizabeth, crowned Protestant Queen of Bohemia; Elizabeth, "our blessed undaunted lady," sharing the rigours of her husband's wintry flight from Prague; Elizabeth, Queen of Hearts, rallying to the drooping Protestant Cause the chivalry of northern Europe; Elizabeth, a fertile mother of many beautiful children (cheap woodcuts of her with an increasing troop of little ones were very popular in London); finally, Elizabeth the tragic widow defending the forlorn rights of her eldest son. At the core of these visions was a living woman of charm, character and considerable beauty. Those who troubled to make the short journey to The Hague, where she lived as a pensioner of the Dutch government, found their fervour for her cause stimulated by her conversation. A few of the more austere Calvinists were shocked by the frivolity of her family, who were greatly given to acting plays, but most visitors were impressed by her courage and high spirits.

The Queen of Bohemia herself was attached to her brother, King Charles, and was grateful for the help which he sent her. But it was known—how could it be otherwise?—that she regretted his inability or unwillingness to take on her behalf any effective action in war or diplomacy. The visit to the English

Court of her son, the Elector Palatine, Charles Louis, had strikingly emphasised the King's failure in this respect. The young man had come seeking help from his uncle, hoping that the King would find the time ripe for intervention in the European war against the Spanish-Austrian power. It was plain for all to see, in the summer of 1637, that he had been turned away, if not quite empty-handed, at least gravely disappointed. He had hoped that a defensive and offensive alliance might be signed with the King of France, now fighting the Spanish-Austrian power on the Rhine, in Flanders and on the Pyrenees, that the English navy would join with the Dutch in the attack on Spanish sea-power, and King Charles take up the part once played by Queen Elizabeth. As nephew of the King he would then have had the help and prestige he needed to regain his father's forfeited lands in Germany.

The King had, however, made difficulties even about recognising the precedence to which, as an Elector, his nephew thought himself entitled, and on one occasion he had had to listen to a Court sermon denouncing the Calvinist doctrines in which he had been educated and for which his father had fought. The King, after a brief wavering in the direction of an alliance with France against Spain and Austria, had sunk again into his uncertain neutrality. "Mutability and confusion reign here," lamented the Venetian envoy, while the Spaniard, in a burst of rage at the King's vacillations, declared to a fellow ambassador that no Court in the world conducted diplomacy so strangely as did the English; they did not listen, they did not understand, and they changed their opinions at every moment. A wild scheme by which the Elector's younger brother Rupert was to command a fleet for the conquest of Madagascar was all the talk of the Court for some weeks, and Davenant celebrated the imaginary venture in a poem. At another time the King spoke of placing fifteen warships at the disposal of the Elector. But in the end Charles continued to devote his naval energies to the herring quarrel with the Dutch, while all that he gave the young Elector was advice to go to the wars himself and make a reputation. He was, at least, generous about personal allowances to both the princes, and added a sizeable lump sum with which the Elector could hire some soldiers, but, as his courtiers said, he was willing to pay to get rid of his poor relations.[36]

The Elector had a cool head and a cool heart. Early in the proceedings King Charles had had to reprimand the young man's secretaries for putting too many military and diplomatic schemes into his head. The reprimand may have been intended for the Elector himself, who was thereafter no less active but more discreet. He privately canvassed the opinions of the Venetian and Dutch ambassadors in London on his own affairs and his uncle's policy.[37] He also cultivated the friendship of the more eminent Protestant critics of the King, especially those with naval and colonial interests.

The alliance of colonial adventure with militant Protestantism, which had sprung from the first clashes of English seamen with Spain, had grown stronger when the policy of the Crown became favourable to Catholics at home and to Spain abroad. English naval enterprise of late, had developed in a manner likely to prove dangerous should it come to an open conflict between the Court and its critics. By the peace with Spain in 1604 King James I had relinquished the claim of Englishmen to trade in the West Indies. Undeterred, English captains continued to trade under foreign flags. They used as their bases ports in the Netherlands, in southern Ireland and in North Devon. The illicit nature of their traffic made them bold, self-reliant and unscrupulous. Fiercely conscious of their English race, reputation and religion, they were at the same time indifferent to and contemptuous of the authority of the royal government, which neither recognised nor protected them. One of England's major commercial interests and one of the chief sources of national and local pride thus eluded the royal authority altogether. A new tradition, which had ripened through a long generation, had created something like an opposition, rather than a loyalty, between the most adventurous English seamen and the Crown. While the King struck pretentious medals about herring treaties, his subjects defied Spain, the traditional enemy, at their own expense and under any flag but their own.

Foremost of the men who financed and sometimes took part in this underhand expansion of sea-power was Robert Rich, Earl of Warwick. He was the son of Penelope Devereux, immortal as the *Stella* of Sir Philip Sidney's poems. By her unloved husband (" that Rich fool, who by blind fortune's lot, the richest gem of love and life enjoys ") Penelope had been the mother of two sons—this Robert, and a younger, Henry, now Earl of Holland and a favourite of Queen Henrietta Maria. By her lover, the Earl of Devonshire, Penelope had had a third son. Mountjoy Blount, now Earl of Newport and a prominent man at Court. These three men were on friendly family terms with their cousin, the living Earl of Essex, Penelope's brother's son. Another friend, the Earl of Hertford, had married the Earl of Essex's sister. Of this family group Holland and Newport alone were figures at Court. Warwick, an active seaman who had himself once led an expedition to the West Indies, preferred his country houses and the ships and dockyards to Hampton Court and Whitehall. Essex and Hertford had both as young men suffered humiliation and unhappiness at the hands of the Court. Essex, at twenty-four, had been compelled by King James I to allow his wife, whom the King's favourite wished to marry, to divorce him on the score of impotence. He had served in the Low Countries since then and had the reputation of a good soldier, a good Protestant and an honest unpretentious fellow. Hertford had in youth loved and secretly married the Lady Arabella Stuart, cousin of King James. The alliance had been thought to endanger the throne to which Arabella and Hertford had each a tenuous claim. The lovers were parted, Hertford fled the country and Arabella died, mad, in the Tower. At fifty his tragic romance was a thing of memory; he was comfortably re-married to the sister of Essex, and the father of a family—a stodgy, uninspired gentleman of Protestant views, neither in nor out of favour with the Court, but not particularly attached to it.

These kinsmen had other associates and friends, Lord Saye and Seal, Lord Brooke, John Hampden a rich Buckinghamshire landowner, and John Pym a West country squire of great business ability. Both these latter had been prominent opponents of the King in the last Parliament and all were active in advocating and financing colonial ventures.

The Elizabethan wars with Spain had created the alliance between strong Protestantism and colonial expansion of which these men were the most outstanding representatives. At home, they protected and encouraged the Protestant clergy. In the settlements across the Atlantic they placed ministers of the same kind. New England was becoming a refugee centre for laymen and clergy unwilling to accept the Laudian rule; astonishing in its religious and intellectual vigour, the little settlement of Boston had already in 1636 founded a college for Puritan theology and Puritan learning in the New World. John Harvard, graduate of Emmanuel College, Cambridge, the chief centre of Puritan thought at home, had left four hundred books and seven hundred pounds to create a second Cambridge by the Charles river in Massachusetts.

But the ideals and interests of the leading Puritan-adventurers and their antagonism to the Crown were concentrated in particular in the Caribbean settlements controlled by the Providence Company of which Warwick, Saye, Brooke and Hampden were all shareholders. Warwick's courtier brother Lord Holland, another shareholder, protected the company's interests at Whitehall. Oliver St. John, a leading Puritan barrister, was the company's solicitor and its secretary was John Pym.

The Company had founded the settlement of Providence, on the small Caribbean island now known as Santa Catalina, with a two-fold intention. The outpost, with its two neighbouring islands Association and Henrietta, was well placed as a naval base for the harrying of Spain; but the new settlements were also to be models of primitive virtue. In Providence, Henrietta and Association sin would be unknown and simple purity reign supreme. The Company drew up regulations, forbidding cards and dice and permitting only chess as an evening recreation for the people, with other stern and simple rules. Whoring, drunkenness, profanity would not be tolerated. A carefully chosen minister—a German Calvinist refugee from the Palatinate—was brought home in disgrace for singing catches on a Sunday.

The business of these three godly settlements was chiefly to keep watch on Spanish ships and prey on them when possible. The Earl of Warwick and his friends were sincerely trying to create three nests of pirates with the behaviour and morals of a Calvinist theological seminary. Other difficulties beside moral ones afflicted the Providence settlements. Only negroes could work effectively in the climate, but this involved the company in the African slave trade; moreover the negroes grew mutinous and further importation had to be stopped. There was little water. A plague of rats swept the settlements. The cultivation of tobacco and cotton both failed to pay—tobacco because of the King's interference with the trade, and cotton because the means to dress the raw material for export were lacking. Fruit and sugar canes alone seemed to do well, and hogs throve. But Spanish, French and Dutch hostility menaced the islands on every side, and in 1635 the Spaniards raided and totally destroyed the settlement at Association.

The shareholders of the Company met in London, either at Lord Brooke's house or at Warwick's; John Pym was at one or other of the houses more often than the rest, for the main burden of organisation rested on him. He was an efficient manager and administrator, with a quick, resourceful wit, a good memory, and an astonishing capacity for acquiring, digesting and using information.

The shareholders of the Providence Company undoubtedly talked politics together. They could hardly have avoided it, since their religious and colonial interests were so much affected by the King's church policy and by his friendship with Spain. Some or all of them certainly paid their respects to the Elector Palatine during his long and disappointing visit to his uncle's Court. At one moment during that visit, the King, in a tentative movement towards a change of foreign policy, went so far as to give verbal consent to a war of reprisals on the Spaniards in the Caribbean—a war to be waged at the Company's expense and with its own ships. Faced with a continual tale of loss and disaster, the Company had considered moving the colony to the mainland but the possibility of recouping their losses through licensed piracy brightened the outlook, and in the summer of 1637 the shareholders sank another £100,000 in the enterprise and decided to go on with it.[38] Their original ideals had dismally faded and an enterprise which had began with the genuine intention of planting a godly commonwealth, had deteriorated into a scheme for licensing pirate captains in return for a share of the profits. The records of the Providence Company are depressing, but it was, for all that, the heir of the Elizabethan tradition.

The King's private permission to the governors of the company to pursue their own war on Spain did not in their eyes counterbalance the rest of his foreign policy. Saye, Brooke, Warwick, Hampden, Pym and their friends felt as strongly as any in England that in failing to support the Elector Palatine the King was betraying the Protestant Cause and losing the opportunity of a war both profitable, honourable and just.

The King's religious policy and his foreign policy worked together to increase the misgivings of his opponents about the future of their country under his unquestioned rule. A small fact, a mere accident, to which Prynne had drawn attention in his *News from Ipswich*, seemed to clinch the matter. In the reissue of the Prayer Book for the year 1636 the prayer for Elizabeth, Queen of Bohemia, and her family had been omitted. Prayers for the King's sister had been said as long as Charles was childless and she was heiress-presumptive to the throne. By 1636 he had five living children: the number of his relations who could reasonably be included by name in a prayer was naturally limited, but the exclusion of Elizabeth was loaded with dark significance by her brother's critics.

The King treated such follies with contempt, but he was

mistaken in doing so. The various parts of his policy were open not simply to misinterpretation, but to the *same* misinterpretation. There lay the danger: his religious policy and his foreign policy united too many of his subjects in the same resentments and the same fears.

BOOK I CHAPTER II REFERENCES

1. Logan Pearsall Smith, *Life and Letters of Sir Henry Wotton*, Oxford, 1907, i, p. 218.
2. *C.S.P. Ven*, 1636–9, p. 305.
3. Matthew Hopkins, *Discovery of Witches*, London, 1647; *Scottish Historical Review*, IV, p. 42.
4. *H.M.C. Report VII, App. II*, p. 229.
5. Laud, *Works*, Oxford, 1847, iii, p. 147.
6. *Ferrar Papers*, ed. Blackstone, Cambridge, 1938.
7. See Geoffrey Soden's *Godfrey Goodman* (London, 1953) for a refutation of the belief that this unhappy man was in fact reconciled with Rome while holding an English bishopric.
8. Cardwell, *Documentary Annals of the Church*, Oxford, 1839, ii, pp. 195–6.
9. *The Curates Conference, Harleian Miscellany*, London, 1808, i, p. 497.
10. *C.S.P.D.*, 1637–8, p. 539; *Ibid.*, 1639, p. 108; Symonds, *Diary of the marches of the royal army*, ed. C. E. Long, Camden Society, 1859, p. 27.
11. *H.M.C. Portland MSS.*, III, p. 79.
12. *Chronicles of the First Planters*, ed. A. Young, Boston, 1846, p. 346.
13. Laud, *Works, IV.*, pp. 303–6; see also Isobel M. Calder, in *American Historical Review*, LIII.
14. See *History*, XXVI (1941) for M. James's full and lucid exposition of the tithes question.
15. Williams, *Holy Table: Name and Thing*, Lincoln, 1637, pp. 7–9, 20.
16. *C.S.P.D.*, 1638–9, pp. 141–2.
17. Fuller, *Church History*, London, 1655, Book IX, viii.
18. *C.S.P.D.*, 1637, pp. 298, 484–6, 491, 499, 518.
19. Hessels, *Ecclesiae Londine-Bataviae Archivum*, Cambridge, 1897, III, ii, p. 1681; I. S. Williamson, *History of the Temple*, London, 1924, p. 393 n.
20. Cardwell, p. 202.
21. *Winchester Cathedral Statutes*, Oxford, 1925, p. 92.
22. *Articles of Visitation of the Diocese of Norwich*, 1636.
23. *C.S.P.D.*, 1637, p. 582.
24. *Ibid.*, p. 531; 1637–8, pp. 219, 382.
25. *Ibid.*, 1637, p. 519.
26. Hessels, III, ii, pp. 1645–1749 *passim*.
27. *Strafford MSS.*, XI, folio 322–3.
28. The MS. *Memoirs* of Richard Augustine Hay in the Advocates Library at Edinburgh

contain an illuminating account of a lawsuit by the bishop of Clogher; the *Lismore Papers*, ed. Grosart, London, 1886, throw light on some of the conflicts of the Irish Church with the Earl of Cork.

29. Blair, *Life*, Wodrow Society, Edinburgh, 1848, p. 154.
30. Balfour, *Historical Works*, Edinburgh, 1825, II, pp. 141–2; Guthry, *Memoirs*, London, 1702, pp. 10–11; James Wilson, *History of Scots Affairs*, Edinburgh, 1654, p. 8–9.
31. Forbes Leith, *Memoirs of Scottish Catholics*, London, 1909, i, pp. 164–72.
32. Oglander, p. 15.
33. Forbes Leith, i, pp. 57, 92, 97 ff.
34. See Gordon Albion, *Charles I and the Court of Rome*, London, 1935; A. O. Meyer, *Charles I and Rome*, American Historical Review, 1913, p. 23; C.S.P. Ven, 1636–9, pp. 70, 120, 149–51, 217–18.
35. Feavearyear, *The Pound Sterling*, Oxford, 1931, pp. 82 ff.; see also *Clarendon State Papers*, Oxford, 1767, ii, pp. 712–80.
36. *C.S.P. Ven*, 1636–9, pp. 108, 130 f, 140 f, 184 f, 220, 234–6.
37. *Ibid.*, pp. 94, 107.
38. *C.S.P. Colonial*, 1574–1660, pp. 249, 255, 264–5; see also A. P. Newton, *Colonising Activities of the English Puritans*, Yale, 1914.

THE KING'S PEACE AND THE KING'S REVENUE

THE distrust created by the King's church policy would have been less damaging to his prospects had he been successful in practical administration. A government which is not trusted can be effective only if it is feared, and Charles might have achieved something of what he wished to achieve had his administration been conducted in such a manner as to command respect and compel obedience.

England was the richest, most influential and most valuable of his dominions, and on English administration his true power was based. No reputable English lawyer would at this time have contested the proposition that " the law of Royal Government is a law fundamental." [1] But the way in which this government was to be exercised gave rise to argument. The King believed that it rested with his good will alone to respect and uphold his people's liberties, but a contemporary legal work aptly expressed another view, " English laws are rather popular than peremptory, rather accepted than exacted." [2] In practice the administration of the laws rested on the consent and co-operation of the King's subjects, countrymen and citizens, justices of the peace, constables, sheriffs and lords lieutenant throughout the country, to whom power was delegated. " The authority of a King is the keystone which closeth up the arch of government," one of the King's principal supporters had said. But the arch was made up of many other stones beside the keystone. To change the metaphor: the King was the fountain of justice. But the river of justice which flowed from the monarch divided into multitudinous smaller streams and canals irrigating the whole country, with, as it were, their own locks, weirs and fishing rights: they retained only a theoretical and remote consciousness of the fountain whence their waters came.

The King personally appointed the judges, whose first duty, as he saw it, was to maintain his authority. Francis Bacon, his father's Chancellor, had described the judges as "lions under the throne." If the lions roared in such a manner as to shake rather than support the throne, it was plain sense, and plain duty, to silence them. Neither James I nor Charles I had hesitated to do so. James had removed Lord Chief Justice Coke, the loud-mouthed champion of the common law, and Charles dismissed Lord Chief Justice Crewe when he refused to uphold the legality of one of the royal demands for money. To make his authority over the judicial bench clear beyond doubt the King had altered the formula by which judges were appointed. In the past judges had held office *quamdiu se bene gesserint*, or as long as they behaved rightly. In King Charles's time the judges were appointed *durante bene placito*, or during the King's good pleasure.

The King was careful to discourage all studies which seemed likely to produce a wrong attitude in lawyers. The antiquary Sir Robert Cotton found warrant in Anglo-Saxon institutions and in the baronial wars of Henry III for doctrines of government unfavourable to the King; his library was impounded and he himself excluded from Court favour. The King also prohibited further publication of Sir Edward Coke's commentaries on the laws, seized his papers and relegated the ex-Chief Justice to apoplectic silence in a country exile.

Such actions would have been politic had the King found nominees of worth and character to fill the Bench, but his choice fell too often upon the merely ambitious, the complaisant, or those with money to offer. John Finch and John Bramston, who had been the Chief Justices since 1635, were learned and ingenious lawyers, but Finch was too unscrupulous, vain and ambitious to command respect, and Bramston was weak and malleable. Edward Littleton and John Bankes, respectively Solicitor-General and Attorney-General, were men of greater integrity; these were respectable appointments. But as a rule the prices of remunerative places were whispered round Whitehall and the prospects of the bidders openly discussed for months at a time.[3]

While, as lions under the throne, the judges grew to look like sheep or even jackals, respect for them declined. This did not affect the popular esteem in which the law was held, for the law had an existence independent of the King's theories or the corruption of the Bench, and therein lay its strength.

Justice was administered throughout the kingdom in a multitude of small local courts, and the governors of England, in all that affected the daily life of the subject, were the local justices of the peace—small gentry in the countryside, aldermen in the cities. At Quarter Sessions the justices, gathered together in the county town, fixed the rate of wages and discussed the state and needs of the county. They were competent to try all crimes except treason or offences by the King's servants. These cases, together with a few which presented exceptional problems of law, would be reserved for trial by the King's judges at the Assizes.

Between sessions the justices saw to the daily affairs of the village, apprenticed boys to trades, disciplined unruly servants, ordered idlers into the fields at harvest time, licensed or suppressed alehouses, punished rogues and vagabonds, put bastard children out to nurse, sent lewd women and incorrigible beggars to the house of correction, relieved the sick, poor and disabled, encouraged lawful and discouraged unlawful sports, and saw to the maintenance—such as it was—of roads and bridges.

The innumerable petty disputes over boundaries and trespass, which occurred in a countryside very little enclosed and cultivated on the strip system, were mostly settled by the old manorial courts—the Court Leet or the Court Baron—both of which still survived. Here the lord of the manor or his steward sat in the chair of justice, to deal with trespass, poaching, and injury to park land, but also to rebuke eavesdroppers, scolds, drunkards and trouble-makers.

Neither lords of manors, stewards nor justices of the peace in town or country were by custom or necessity deeply versed in the law, though many of them had been for a while at the Inns of Court in London. The little learning they had then acquired, and one of the many convenient handbooks specially written for them, gave them all the technical help they needed in a task in which experience and common sense were fully as important as knowledge of the law.

This widely delegated judicial system had its focal point at Westminster, in whose ancient hall and in the buildings which abutted against it, the four courts of King's Bench, Common Pleas, Exchequer and Exchequer Chamber held their sessions. The boundaries between the first two courts were indistinct; the King's Bench was supposed to deal in general with actions of the Crown against subjects, the Common Pleas with actions between subject and subject. Each had a Lord Chief Justice and three judges attached to it, and had power to rectify the errors committed by the inferior courts of the kingdom. The Exchequer Court, whose four judges were confusingly called Barons of the Exchequer, dealt with cases arising out of taxation. The Court of Exchequer Chamber, so called merely from the place in which it met, was used when the judges of all three courts assembled to decide on some particularly difficult case.

The hearings of all these courts were open. Justice in England was conducted in a bustling, public manner. Westminster Hall was divided into smaller courts by partitions shoulder-high; several cases might be going on at once, within sight and earshot of each other and of the crowds who sauntered past. What was true of Westminster Hall was equally true of lesser courts in cities and villages. The administration of English law was a familiar, instructive and entertaining spectacle in the midst of ordinary life, and the audience followed it with the half-professional interest of those who were sometimes actors themselves in the daily drama. As plaintiff or defendant, as witness or surety, or as a minor official of the court, the great majority of the population would be at one time or another directly involved with the law. Not only the wealthy and powerful knew and used it; the journeyman and the wagoner, the labourer and the boatman larded their alehouse conversation with the mis-remembered jargon of the courts and had a crude conception of the law's logic and of their rights under it. " Every plough-man with us," wrote a contemporary lawyer, " may be a senes-chal in a Court Baron: he can talk of essoins, vouchers, wither-nams and recaptions." [4]

Familiarity bred not contempt but affection. There is little evidence at this epoch in England of any real fear of the law. Its purpose was to uphold the rights of Englishmen, and on the whole Englishmen saw to it that the law did so. Certainly there was corruption of many kinds, bribery and intimidation being the most common; certainly the law, administered entirely by men of substance and property, bore harshly on the outcasts of society. But society was composed of interlocking, inter-dependent groups, and it was in the interests of all parties, squires, tenants, yeomen and hired servants, to maintain equable if not always equitable relations. Vagabonds and " masterless men "—a term still much in use—were the only constant victims of the law, and they were not always helpless. Tradition told of a rogue who had brought and won an action for damages because the pillory had collapsed under him and nearly caused him a fatal injury.[5]

For the rest, the English passion for litigation, common to all classes, reveals the general attitude to the law. It was an attitude at once proprietary and resolute: the law existed to defend and confirm each man in his proper station; it was a servant or a guard, but not a master. In England, furthermore, lawyers and laymen were not sharply divided into hostile groups. This was true even of the humbler sort, since the labourer knew, understood and sometimes played a part in his local court; but it was far more true of the educated classes. West of London, straggling down both sides of Holborn towards the river, lay the Inns of Court—Lincoln's Inn, Gray's Inn, and the Inner and Middle Temple. Hither, more often than to Oxford or Cambridge, the country gentleman or the rich citizen sent his sons to see a little of life and to learn a little law. Rich young men and poor young men lived together in this district; rowdies like Augustine Garland and Nicholas Love of Lincoln's Inn who had just been disciplined for holding the porter under the pump,[6] solemn students like Matthew Hale who read for sixteen hours a day, intellectuals discussing music, philosophy, literature and the fine arts, like John Hutchinson and Edward Hyde. They shared the same lectures, ate in the same halls, attended the same chapels, and participated in some of the same hilarities at the Christmas revels. The Inns of Court were the third university of England, and in point of influence the first. Here above all, through innumerable youthful friendships, was forged that alliance between the men who made, the men who interpreted and the men who administered the law, which opposed a solid bulwark against royal or clerical encroachment on the law's authority.

The King controlled the appointment of Judges, but he could not control the operation of the law: the machine had a life of its own. At the Assizes the King's Judges instructed the local justices of the peace on the royal policy, issued general recommendations for the future and reprimanded them when the King's policy had not been properly carried out. But in the last resort the King's commands were obeyed only if the justices wanted them to be obeyed; and no effective means existed whereby the justices could be coerced into carrying out any measure which was generally unpopular. The King's council could prosecute, reprimand or remove a few recalcitrant justices but if the majority were to oppose him he could not reprimand or remove the entire bench; who, then, would be left to carry on the necessary affairs of the countryside?

Queen Elizabeth had kept her justices in salutary fear of the royal authority by calling the incompetent to order before the council; but her fingers were on the pulse of the country and she had avoided collision with public opinion. In this way she had created and maintained a delicate equilibrium between the authority of the Crown and the demands of the subject. She had been respected and feared, but she had also been popular, and she had never allowed any crisis to arise in which her power was pitted against the will of her justices or her people.

King Charles had too high an opinion of the Crown's authority to consider the necessity of maintaining this equilibrium. At the outset of his non-Parliamentary rule he had determined, wisely enough, to bring the justices into regular contact with the Crown by requiring them to make semi-annual reports to the royal council. This plan for more regular and stricter control had coincided with a number of interesting royal proclamations designed to improve the administration of the Poor Law, to prevent the spread of epidemics, to avert famine or a shortage of corn, to control unhealthy and ill-considered building and to relieve the distress of debtors or the chronically disabled. This double move foreshadowed what might have been a benevolent social policy directed and controlled by the Crown, and intended to increase the central power of the King's council at the expense of local and parish authorities.

But the success of the experiment depended on the vigour with which it was prosecuted. After a year or two the social legislation ceased, the proclamations were neglected and surveillance flagged. When, for instance, the King attempted to relieve distress among cloth workers by a government scheme for buying in raw wool and redistributing it to the spinners and weavers of each district, it was found that the central government lacked the administrative skill, the authority and the expert knowledge either to compel or to persuade the full co-operation of the justices. The misconceived scheme was allowed to drop but it damaged the prestige of the central government and strengthened, in the justices of the peace, feelings of resentment and contempt.

Although administration thus eluded the King's control, he

was still the fountain of justice. He exercised, through the Privy Council and through his Court of Chancery, the power to rectify the errors of any court in the realm, and the errors were many.

High costs and corruption were the prevalent diseases of the courts. Lawyers had their fees and documents cost money; every Court swarmed with hangers-on, clerks, copyists, doorkeepers, each expecting something for his pains, each ready to give extra assistance to the litigant who paid him most, and to do an ill turn to the litigant who forgot to pay him at all. Round Lincoln's Inn and the Temple false witnesses hung about for hire.[7] Suits could be endlessly delayed by the ingenuity or malice of clerks bribed for this purpose, and the delay might be as bad as loss. No one doubted that a rich and powerful man could win a case against a poor man, if by no other means than by spinning it out until his opponent fell into debt and cried for mercy. The deliberate ruining of some unhappy victim by this means was a frequent subject of contemporary plays, and surviving records give examples of it. Vindictive and false prosecutions occurred; a great landowner might have half the justices of a county in his pocket. Most of those in authority took bribes and, according to the Venetian ambassador who was shocked at the practice, regarded it as harmless and natural.[8]

The law remained serviceable in spite of all. The majority of cases before the courts were not between ill-matched litigants, nor did every powerful man in England abuse his power. For the most part, cases were between equals, where the difference between a fourpenny or sixpenny bribe did not grossly affect the scales of justice. Corruption, intimidation and general dishonesty were held in check by the practical conviction that, within certain limits, the law must be made to work.

When so much was known to be amiss with the ordinary courts of the realm, the King might have strengthened his position and undermined the influence of the common law by demonstrating the superiority of justice directly dispensed by the Crown. He did not take this opportunity. Widespread as was criticism of the ordinary courts of justice, few if any were heard to praise the superior honesty, speed and cheapness of those directly controlled by the King.

The Court of Chancery, which existed specifically to give a remedy to the subject when there was no remedy at Common Law, was at this time admittedly the most expensive, slow and corrupt court in the Kingdom, and was used quite as frequently as any other court in the realm to forward the interests of the great, more especially those with influence in the royal circle, against those whom they wished to weaken or ruin. The Court of Wards, for several generations the most unpopular court in the Kingdom, was feared and hated by the gentry because it had insensibly become nothing but a means of raising revenue for the Crown at the expense of any estate inherited by a minor, any disputed will or inheritance. Both these Courts were famous for interminable and expensive delays, for the number of their predatory clerks and their extortionate charges.[9]

The reputation of the King's Court of Star Chamber, the most important of the prerogative courts, was better, although it was not free of taint. The Star Chamber was simply the King's inner council, with the two Chief Justices in addition, acting as a court of law. The Council's functions had been developed in this way since the time of Henry VII for the express purpose of defending the King's humbler subjects against the unscrupulous powerful. The Star Chamber could and did punish bribery and intimidation; it intervened to stop the deliberate persecution of a small man by a wealthy enemy in the law courts; it called incompetent country justices to order. For more than a century it had held in check the bribing nobleman or the corrupt magistrate who flouted justice too outrageously. But a court created to check abuses had developed abuses of its own, and malicious prosecutions in the Star Chamber were not unknown. King Charles, moreover, had used it to silence critics of the Court, Church or government and, on occasion, critics or libellers of his friends and ministers. Intending to make his subjects fear his authority, he had in a few cases

authorised very heavy fines and humiliating punishments. His
subjects were not intimidated; they lost faith in the Star Chamber
as a source of protection and became suspicious of it.

Three other courts depended on the King's council: the
Court of the North at York, the Court of Wales and the Marches
at Ludlow, and the Court of Castle Chamber in Dublin. These
too were designed to extend the punitive and protective powers
of the King to the furthest parts of his dominions, and to open
for the subject a direct path to the justice of his Sovereign or his
Sovereign's immediate Deputy. Placed in York, Ludlow and
Dublin, they were intended to give the Lord President of the
North, the Lord President of Wales and the Marches, and the
Lord Deputy of Ireland the necessary powers to control the
pretensions and possible violence of the over-mighty lords who
in these remoter regions might overawe and oppress His Majesty's
lesser subjects. Of the three the Court of Wales had the least to
do and was the least criticised. It performed its functions effectively under the mild and pompous guidance of the Earl of
Bridgewater whose chief concern was to keep clear of political
quarrels.[10] The Lord President of the North and the Lord
Deputy of Ireland was one and the same man, the Viscount
Wentworth, a governor of a sterner vision than Bridgewater,
and facing both in the North and in Ireland a harder task. He
had striven manfully to combine the defence of the humble
against the mighty with the disciplining of the King's critics.
In York, and more especially in Dublin, Wentworth had on
occasion defended the interest of this or that inarticulate
farmer or weeping widow against the tyranny and dishonesty of
the great landowners. In Ireland at least, the King's justice had
gained with the smaller men a popular reputation for speed and
efficiency. But in England the benefits Wentworth had bestowed were disregarded, and the severity with which he had
punished his opponents was common talk. Sometimes, and not
always on the happiest occasions, these Courts worked together.
Wentworth, had for instance, condemned a man named Esmond
in Dublin; Esmond died soon after, and some of Wentworth's

HENRIETTA MARIA
by *Anthony Van Dyck*

enemies put it about that he died from the after-effects of a blow
struck by Wentworth's own vice-regal hand. To crush this
libel Wentworth prosecuted the scandalmongers in the Star
Chamber. The malicious or ill-informed at once suspected that
the Court of Star Chamber was being used to cover the tyrannies
committed in Dublin.

The worst characteristic of the prerogative courts was that
they encouraged informers and were by no means always
competent to distinguish between false information and true;
the innocent might be wrecked in the Star Chamber as well as
the guilty. Certainly of late years high words at the village
pump or a quarrel in an alehouse could, through the malice of
an informer, bring a frightened victim before the Star Chamber:
Will Brown heard Tom Smith say, " Let the King be hanged "
but Tom Smith says he said, " You be hanged," and no word
concerning the King's Majesty. And so on and so forth, until
a sensible justice at Ipswich reporting the case of Ann Dixon,
aged fourteen, accused of treasonous words by a neighbour,
remarked that if informers continued at this rate every scold's
quarrel in the land would come up before the King's council.[11]

Another recent development aroused criticism both in lay
and legal circles. The ecclesiastical Court of High Commission
had begun to act in very close co-operation with the Court of
Star Chamber; they sometimes appeared to function as the
spiritual and temporal arms of the same fierce justice. When
Dr. Alexander Leighton wrote a virulent attack on the bishops,
the Court of High Commission unfrocked him, but the Court
of Star Chamber had him flogged and imprisoned for life.

In an age when branding and whipping were common
punishments, the prerogative courts had no monopoly of
cruelty, but public opinion distinguished very clearly between
permissible and impermissible barbarity in criminal sentences:
in that steadfastly hierarchic society much depended on the social
position of the victim. It was strongly felt that lawyers, physicians and clergymen, persons of university education, who wore
black gowns, clean linen, hats, cloaks and gloves, and wrote

"gent" after their names, ought not to be subjected to the physical punishments reserved for screeching harlots or drunken vagabonds. The Court of Star Chamber, occasionally, passed such inappropriate sentences and half a dozen of them over as many years were enough thoroughly to perturb the conventional. When the public executioner, making ready to apply the lash, politely addressed his victim as " Sir," it was evident that a very singular situation had arisen.

The prerogative courts had one other sinister peculiarity. In England torture was unknown to the Common Law; its application was the King's prerogative. As the distinguished lawyer John Selden reflectively remarked: " The rack is nowhere used as in England. In other countries 'tis used in judicature, when there is a *semiplena probatio*, a half-proof against a man: then, to see if they can make it full, they rack him if he will not confess. But here in England they take a man and rack him, I do not know why nor when: not in time of judicature, but when somebody bids." " Somebody" was one of the King's councillors, using the royal authority to apply the torture. King James had used it several times, King Charles once only—unfortunately on an innocent man.[12]

Had the King made the prerogative courts the object of respect, had he asserted a watchful control over the justices of the peace, he would have gone a long way towards making his vision of authority into a reality. But he lacked concentration of purpose. He was too often deflected by immediate considerations of convenience or profit. He had been on the throne twelve years, seven of them without either Parliaments or wars to distract him, yet it was evident to any perceptive observer that he had neither won popular favour for his government nor built up enough strength for himself to make that favour unnecessary.

The reason for this mismanagement—or, more exactly, this absence of management—was to be found at the centre of the administration. To help him to realise his vision, the King had need of such ministers as Elizabeth had had—wise, wary, judicious and vigilant, single-minded in their devotion to the task of government. But the very core of King Charles's government, his own council, was feeble, factious and corrupt.

The central government of England was discharged by the King's council, chiefly by an inner group with no official title although it was sometimes referred to as the Junto or the Cabinet. At moments of crisis, or on special occasions—when the Lord Deputy of Ireland came to report on his government— the King presided; at ordinary times he rarely attended. As the council consisted of men who were constantly about the court or held important offices in the Royal Household, it was easy for him to consult with individual advisers at any convenient moment, and since ultimate decisions rested with him alone, the most important were often taken in private.

The council was essentially a council of courtiers. Little attempt was made to find the most experienced man for any special task or to make use of his ability; the King preferred to choose from his friends and servants those who were most congenial to him, in the ill-grounded belief that he would find in them the knowledge and technical skill that was wanted. The principal members of this almost fortuitous group of noblemen and court officials were few of them remarkable. There was William Cecil, Earl of Salisbury; one of the least distinguished men of a distinguished family, he had a reputation for caution and parsimony and for having no will of his own. There was Philip Herbert, Earl of Pembroke, who concealed his natural craftiness under a mask of buffoonery; he was a bad-tempered, overbearing man who swore " God damn me " and boasted of being illiterate—a singular figure in that cultured society; he retained the King's favour partly because he could offer him the best hunting in England, partly because his eccentric pose appealed to Charles's slow-moving sense of humour, and chiefly because as a youth he had been a favourite of the late King James. Charles was always good to those whom his father had loved. Another of his councillors, who had risen in the same way, was Henry Rich, Earl of Holland, whose flashing dark eyes and glossy black hair had earned him the nickname of *El Conde*. Vapid, vain and silly, his thoughts were mostly of dress and of past and future conquests in the lists of love, but under a surface charm he was stubborn, arrogant and vindictive. Holland was younger brother to the Earl of Warwick, the Puritan pirate and the most prominent of the lords in opposition to the Court. Although he resembled his energetic and capable brother in very little, he was known to further his brother's interests whenever he could, which did not make him a disinterested counsellor for the King. By comparison with these three the Earl of Northumberland stands out for his intelligence; his letters show him to have been a man of reasonably shrewd observation and judgment, and he had enough knowledge of naval affairs to acquit himself creditably in the office of Lord High Admiral.

Two Scots also sat on this English council, the Marquis of Hamilton and the Duke of Lennox. Hamilton, a favourite with the King from boyhood, had a kind of slow-witted cunning and more confidence in his own judgment than it deserved. The character of Lennox can be read from Anthony Van Dyck's different versions of his fair, aristocratic, equine features: he was a good young man, loyal, sweet-natured and simple-hearted, but not clever.

The Treasurer was William Juxon, Bishop of London, an urbane prelate and a very upright man. The Chancellor of the Exchequer was Francis, Lord Cottington, an irresponsible, irrepressible good fellow, with a shrewd head, a witty tongue and few moral scruples; a man whom everybody liked and no one altogether trusted. There were two secretaries of state; plodding old John Coke, honest, painstaking and slow, but quite incapable of checking the corruption of his clerks,[13] and the lively Francis Windebanke, with a finger in every intrigue and a family of up-and-coming sons to place in the world. As makeweight there was the Comptroller of the Household, Sir Harry Vane, a jaunty little man bursting with personal ambition and his own importance.

Holland, Hamilton, Cottington, Windebanke and Vane were all, by taste and temperament, schemers who used their influence to get profitable places for themselves, their families and friends. The Queen, whose busy and gay nature overflowed easily into such petty conspiracies, encouraged them, and they found other willing friends in the many idle courtiers. Lord Northumberland was not himself a natural plotter, but he had for brother and sister a pair of notable intriguers, Harry Percy, and the beautiful Countess of Carlisle, the Queen's closest friend. The King had friends no less dangerous: his two most trusted Gentlemen of the Bedchamber, Will Murray and Endymion Porter were inveterate wire-pullers. Through these people and their like, the council became the heart and centre of Court intrigues rather than the heart and centre of government.

The King's council in England had its exact parallels in Scotland and Ireland. In Ireland it was under the control of the King's Viceroy, the Lord Deputy, who being a strong man and an energetic ruler guided it pretty well as he pleased. Scotland had no Viceroy; the King governed his native country direct from England, but he governed it personally with no reference to his English council which, naturally, had no right to meddle in the affairs of the other nation. The King's Council for Scotland was too far away for the King to be able to discuss matters with them in any effective manner. The connecting link was the Secretary of State for Scotland, Lord Stirling, who followed the Court and communicated the royal wishes to the council at Edinburgh. Their task was mainly to carry out those wishes. King James had developed this peculiar form of government. "Here I sit and govern Scotland with my pen," he had remarked with satisfaction, but he had been able to do so only because by twenty years of astute intrigue and policy he had reduced Scotland to a state of unprecedented docility. In his son's time this was no longer so. What counted in Scottish administration was the authority of Highland chiefs and southern nobles and lairds; early in the century the English system of justices of the peace had been introduced, but it had done no more than confirm the authority already wielded by these men. What counted in Scottish Law was the opinion and influence of the judges, the Lords of Session. King James's Council had represented their interests, made use of their opinions and commanded their respect.

King Charles's Council did none of these things. In the attempt to make it more amenable to his will he had eliminated the Lords of Session altogether from the board and when vacancies were to be filled, he would pass over the great and powerful nobles and place on the Council instead lesser men, in the belief that they would serve him more obediently. It was only a matter of time until he should discover that the authority he exercised through his Council in Scotland had ceased to be any authority at all.

The Scottish Councillors had fewer opportunities for corruption and intrigue than their English counterparts, though they used all that they had, and Lord Traquair the Treasurer was generally regarded as having made a fair part of his fortune out of his office.

The councillors in both countries were open to a certain moral corruption not wholly of their own seeking. Conciliar government in their time was midway between modern cabinet government and the personal system of the Tudors. A modern minister who finds himself in disagreement with government policy resigns his place. A Tudor minister who persistently disagreed with the sovereign's policy would not long have remained in his (or her) confidence. The position of several of King Charles's ministers, both in Scotland and in England, was not only unprecedented but unique in the history of the British Isles. Their advice and opinions were systematically overruled or disregarded by the King, but he kept them in his council and expected them loyally to support and carry out his policy. They could not resign because resignation from the King's Council would have been tantamount to self-inflicted political disgrace. Men like Northumberland in England and Lord Lorne in Scotland were therefore compelled to serve, although it grew yearly more difficult for them to serve with sincerity, honour or loyalty.

The King's two most intelligent ministers, the Archbishop of Canterbury and the Lord Deputy of Ireland, stand out head and shoulders above their corrupt or feeble colleagues and were single-minded in their devotion to the King's ideals. But Charles was as much inclined to pass over their advice as he was that of lesser men.

He supported his Archbishop in his plans for the Church but in most other spheres he resented his interference. Laud was greatly disliked by the Queen and, as if to make up to his wife for his partiality to the Archbishop's views on the Anglican Church, the King opposed him on almost all other matters. He went clean against his advice, for instance, in the favour he showed to Roman Catholics, and was disposed to be irritable when Laud drew his attention to the more difficult and problematical aspects of his home policy. After one discouraging effort to explain to his master certain worrying aspects of the political situation, Laud lamented to his friend the Deputy of Ireland, "The King is more willing *not* to hear than to hear." [14]

The Lord Deputy of Ireland, the King's only other outstanding adviser, owed his position largely to the Archbishop's judgment. It was probably Laud who had persuaded Charles to offer a seat on the council and a title to one of the most troublesome members of the House of Commons in the Parliament of 1628. Laud had seen that the fervour which moved Thomas Wentworth to oppose the King was a fervour for strong government rather than a factious resentment of royal authority. The offer had been accepted, and the leader of an angry House of Commons had been transformed into the most zealous of the King's servants. Wentworth was a tall, spare, formidable Yorkshireman, with a notoriously bad temper and no personal charm. His dictatorial manner, which reflected his sense of his own position, generally inspired dislike and his ostentatious display of the wealth he had acquired in the course of his career provoked envy. But he had strong and tender affections and depths of simple loyalty and gratitude in his nature which made him truly beloved by those who knew him best. As a practical administrator he had done well in the North of England, and more than well in Ireland. He was efficient and fearless, and he worked with a violent methodical energy at every task he took in hand. Like the King, like Laud, he believed in the establishment of unquestioned authority as the foundation of good government.

Charles, Laud and Wentworth had each of them the desire, and, acting together would have had the skill, to make a reality of that ideal vision of authoritarian government pictured by Rubens or set forth in the masques at Whitehall. But the King wanted the thing to be done without the strenuous effort of doing it; he deflected the energy and discouraged the efforts of his two best ministers, and believed that he had mastered the problems of the political situation when he had done no more than postpone their solution. He was encouraged in this delusion by optimistic, flattering or ignorant voices at Court, and he became, as each peaceful year went by, ever more willing to be deceived.

The friendship of Laud and Wentworth was cemented by their common frustration. Both were deeply loyal to the King but critical of his behaviour. In their lengthy correspondence each detailed to the other his views on the events of the day and deplored the intrigues of Court and Council. These letters reveal in both Laud and Wentworth a grasp of essentials, an analytical sense of the situation and a sharpness of judgment which are impressive. The alliance of the two, had it ever become effective, would have given to the King's government the strength it so gravely needed. But Charles, following an old, sly, unwise maxim of his father's, did not care to encourage men who were stronger than he.

The King was serious-minded, but he was not industrious. His gravity of manner, and the solemn character of many of his pleasures, have done much to conceal the disarmingly simple truth that he was lazy in all matters of government. His casual attitude to his council, his unwillingness to listen to disturbing information, his hunting three or four times a week, the long hours spent in pursuit or enjoyment of works of art, or in theological discussion—all tell the same tale: he was not interested in practical administration. He idled away the opportunities of his reign, while his two ablest ministers—Laud confined to Church matters only and Wentworth virtually in exile—exchanged their troubled letters, and the rest of his ill-chosen councillors concealed from him anything likely to disturb his equanimity [15] and played at pitch-and-toss with the reputation and resources of the Crown.

The reputation of the Crown was deeply involved with its resources because the measures taken to increase the royal revenues were a principal reason for the dwindling respect in which the government was held. A constant need for money hampered and deformed the King's policy, and the methods he chose to raise it were unpopular and corrupt.

Charles was not himself responsible for the financial difficulties of the Crown. He was by nature careful but he had certain costly obligations—the help he gave to his sister—and he had at least one very expensive taste, his collection of works of art. It was no fault of his that the value of money had declined while the demands made on the Crown had grown. Out of dwindling revenues he had to meet the expenses of the central government, and the efficiency with which that government was carried out depended on the amount of money forthcoming.

The lands from which, in the Middle Ages, the Crown had derived its chief revenue had some of them been sold in the last century to raise ready money. The rents from those which were left were still considerable, but the cost of collecting them tended to rise; these rents formed the most calculable part of the royal income, and were therefore often mortgaged in advance. The net revenue from land, after payment of all expenses and of the assignments which annually accumulated against it, was by King Charles's reign only about £25,000; in the early part of his father's reign it had been three times as much. The steep drop was symptomatic of the rate at which rents had been alienated for ready money and of the accumulating demands made on the remainder.

The bulk of the King's income was derived from import taxes levied on various commodities. The amount of these taxes, collectively known as Tonnage and Poundage, was fixed by Parliament at the beginning of each reign. But the first Parliament of Charles I had taken the unprecedented step of refusing to fix the rate of Tonnage and Poundage for more than a year at a time. From the King's point of view, this was unpardonable and insulting conduct for which the laws and customs of the realm gave no authority. From the point of view of the House of Commons, it was a justifiable attempt to exert control over the royal policy, justifiable because the Commons distrusted both the policy and the advisers of the King. Failing to come to a satisfactory agreement with any of his Parliaments, the King had in the end fixed Tonnage and Poundage at a rate that he considered reasonable. Although some defiant merchants had refused to pay and been imprisoned by order of the royal council, the bulk of his people had yielded rather than dislocate the trade on which they and the country depended.

The collection of taxes had grown more complicated with the extension of commerce and the increase of the King's demands. A central office, the Exchequer, existed through which the royal revenues were supposed to pass, but there was no government organisation for the collection itself, or at least none large and effective enough. Taxes were therefore farmed to courtiers and financiers; they bought a lease of the tax for a period of years, paid an agreed sum to the King, and organised the collection to allow a reasonable profit for themselves. The King, in straits for ready money, complicated the situation further by anticipating the returns on the taxes and making grants on them in advance. He also borrowed from the tax farmers, creating double and treble confusion. The receiving officers of his Exchequer complained that these assignments and anticipations meant that less than half the King's supposed revenues passed through the Exchequer. The debts contracted on the yield of the taxes were often paid out direct by the tax farmers, and this by-passing of the Exchequer made it impossible to keep track of the King's money. It might well be that some grants of money or debts were paid twice over.[16]

Besides these two major sources of revenue, the Court of Wards provided a discreditable third source. For a gentleman to leave a minor as his heir was often a real disaster; the administration of the estate fell to the Crown which sold it back to a guardian of its own choosing. Admittedly the Crown usually chose the nearest kinsman, but even so the charges connected with wardship and with the final freeing of the estate when the heir came of age were heavy, and by the time the Crown and the guardian had each made a profit the estate was often, in the expressive contemporary idiom, " tottering." The wardship of some great heir or heiress might yield fat returns to the guardian who administered the estate largely for his own profit during the child's minority, and he could sell the hand of his ward, male or female, for a high price in the marriage market. The guardianship of a wealthy lunatic was also profitable, and to " beg a fool " of the Crown was an accepted procedure among grasping courtiers. The King intended well by the wards of the Crown, but he needed the revenues brought in by the Court of Wards too much to work any reform in its organisation. The Court was at the moment under the control of the cheerfully unscrupulous Cottington who had immensely increased its yield, to his own advantage and the King's. In the year 1637 it brought £61,972 to the royal coffers, an increase of more than £25,000 since the beginning of the reign.[17]

The King's financial advisers, like those of his father before him, were indefatigable in their efforts to find new sources of income. Two principal methods were employed: the revival of obsolete medieval practices, and the exploitation of the expanding world of industry and trade. In both of these the King's principal adviser for several years was the ingenious old lawyer, William Noy. An anagram of his name—" I moyl in law "—fitly described his activities: his moylings unearthed a number of interesting possibilities, for many of which the King found immediate use.

In feudal England every landowner of a certain standing had been required to do a knight's service for the King in war, or to compound in money if he could not. This practice, to the acute annoyance of the gentry, was now revived and all those who came within the prescribed income limit were required to receive—or, as they put it, to "endure"—knighthood, paying the necessary fee to exempt them from military service. Those who refused the unwanted title were still liable for the fee.

More profitable still was Noy's revival of the old Forest Laws. When the King had in very truth depended on the game that he killed in the hunting season to feed himself and his retinue, it had been an offence to enclose or encroach on the great stretches of royal forest which were scattered over the kingdom. Gradually, as the King's need for game grew less urgent, much of what had once been royal forest had been brought under tillage or pasture and had passed into private hands. This made it possible for the King suddenly to institute an inquiry into enclosures of forests within the last fifty years. Those who had offended were fined large sums—or at least they were condemned to pay large sums, although the King often subsequently reduced the fines. The reduction rarely consoled the victim for the inconvenience, interference and fright to which he had been subjected.

Noy's next revival was the Elizabethan tax of Ship-Money, a contribution levied on seaports and coastal regions for the building and maintenance of the navy. The sums were fixed by the King's council, collected by the justices of the peace and sheriffs, and paid direct to the treasurer for the navy. This was in many ways the best managed and most economical of the King's plans, for relatively little of the money leaked away in the expense of collection and the tax went direct to the purpose for which it was intended.

Noy's masterpiece was his evasion of the legislation against monopoly. Queen Elizabeth had made the happy discovery that the Crown could raise money by granting the sole right of trade in certain commodities, or the sole right of manufacture, to some rich and favoured person. The abuse of such monopolies and the source of extra-Parliamentary revenue that they gave the Crown, had caused the House of Commons to attack them, and the Parliament of 1624 had finally made them, one and all, illegal.

William Noy found a legal way out of the difficulty. In future, monopolies were granted only to those who had found and wished to develop some new form of manufacture: in order that invention and valuable new processes might be given every encouragement, it was only fair that such people should enjoy special favour and protection. The word *monopoly* was replaced by *patent*. The King granted patents to the *projectors* who wanted sole rights of manufacturing beaver hats or copper pins because they had a specially efficient method which stood in need of protection from competition until it should be established. Some patents were justly given for interesting experiments; the majority were given on the most trivial pretexts. Monopolies, expelled by Parliament, came back fourfold in this transparent disguise. A further ingenious plan was to grant, not the sole right of manufacture, but the sole right of transport of some particular kind of goods. Occasionally the complications went even further, and the King would sell to one projector rights of manufacture and transport, and to another the right to grant, for a consideration, licences to individuals to infringe the privileges of the first projector.

Besides patents, and licences to evade patents, the King also made money out of the so-called incorporations. For a sum of money, he was willing to incorporate new companies of craftsmen—the leather-workers, for instance, the beaver-makers and others—granting them the right to organise their own industry. The inspiration for patents and incorporations was chiefly financial, but there was an element of policy behind these expedients. The granting of patents could be used to bring certain industries very closely under the supervision of the Crown, thus creating a primitive nationalisation of manufacture. The incorporations arose from a genuine economic grievance and did something to alleviate it. Many of the older companies had ceased to be corporations of craftsmen and become corporations of merchants: they merely *sold* the goods which were made by others. Already the social revolution had turned its quarter-circle; craftsmen were being driven down, by the united pressure of these companies of merchants, into the position of mere suppliers, whence it might be a short step to being hired labourers. The independent craftsmen therefore strove to band themselves together into companies which could negotiate on equal terms with the tradesmen who bought and marketed their wares. Charles's grants of incorporation were a reasonable attempt to improve the conditions of the craftsmen, to stem or alter the course of economic and social changes, and to create a firm attachment between the Crown and the artisan, against possible exploitation from entrenched companies of middlemen.

Charles's policy provided the ground-plan of a politico-economic programme which foreshadows that of Colbert in France fifty years later and which, had it been firmly pursued, might have established the Crown in the affections of the artisan population and set England on the road to an enlightened *étatisme*.

But long-term and constructive economic plans were in pawn to the King's immediate needs. The exaction of fines, not the protection of the poor man's rights from the wealthy encroacher, was the first consideration in applying the forest laws. The somewhat wider laws originally intended to prevent depopulation, and enforced against those who enclosed common and waste land, were used with the same financial purpose and social inconsistency. The King himself enclosed common land and encouraged enclosure when it seemed profitable to do so; he supported the great drainage and enclosure schemes for the fens, and he turned over to tenant farmers a part of the once common land on the royal estates near Berkhampstead.[18]

In the same way, the money that flowed into the treasury, and not the intrinsic merit of patents or of commercial schemes, governed the grants to projectors, and if there was money to be made out of the struggle between a new incorporation and an ancient company, as there often was, the King was prepared to let the quarrel fester, with a concession now to one side, now to another. Four patentees shared the right to trade wholesale in tobacco in the county of Durham; one, the most powerful, took proceedings against the retailers, mostly alehouse keepers, who were buying from the others. Small men were harried, accused and persecuted about twopenny screws of tobacco, and, whoever was to blame, the affair did not make the King popular in Durham.[19]

The King's ingenious bullying of the London Vintners' Company had aroused some ill-feeling in the City. He had demanded from them payment of £4 on every tun of wine. When they refused the Star Chamber issued a decree forbidding Vintners to cook and serve meat to customers. As most of the Vintners had long practised this auxiliary trade the prohibition hit them hard. They paid £6,000 to the King in the belief that he would proceed no further with the decree. Soon however prosecutions began again and the Vintners learnt that these would be stopped only if they agreed to pay 1d. to the King on every quart of wine sold. Some of them were for resisting and letting the matter go before the Star Chamber, but the Master of the Company, Alderman Abell, was rather a man of business than a man of principle. He saved the Company from further trouble by negotiating a deal through the King's Master of the Horse, the Marquis of Hamilton. The Company would pay £30,000 a year (£4,000 of it to Hamilton) for the privilege of serving meals as well as selling wine.[20]

The King, inspired by a salt shortage early in his reign, had considered making salt into a royal monopoly, as it was in France, thus taxing at the source a prime necessity of life and securing a steady income. The need for immediate funds caused him to grant not one, but two, patents for the production of salt. The two patentees naturally came into collision; with the Crown behind them, they also collided with the people of Yarmouth when they tried to set up salt pans on what was time-honoured common land, and they annoyed fishermen and fish merchants throughout the country by interfering with the pro-duction and distribution of that absolutely essential commodity, saltfish. Not content with the working of the rival patents, Charles next revived an old tax on salt in order to farm it for a substantial sum; the monopolists claimed exemption and Charles prosecuted them in the interests of the tax farmer; but the tax farmer complained that, as everyone now used Scottish salt, he had lost on the transaction. The Scots added a contradic-tory note, by claiming that the English monopoly had ruined their trade. Not all the complaints can have been true, but this much at least was true: that the Crown was very little richer and a great deal less liked for the whole business.[21]

More absurd and quite as irritating as the salt business was the trouble over soap. In 1631 the King granted to a group of projectors, several of whom were Roman Catholics, the exclusive right to make soap of vegetable oil for fourteen years. They agreed to pay the King £4 a ton and to make five thousand tons a year at 3d. a pound; they were permitted, in view of the supposed superiority of their soap, to examine all other manu-factured soap and impound or destroy any that they thought below standard. At a test held in private in London, their soap was certified better than that of the London soap-makers. It did not fare so well at Bristol where a tavern maid and a laundress lathered away in public at some soiled linen napkins with the projectors' soap and with soap made by the Bristol soap-makers; they demonstrated that the Bristol soap washed whiter and more economically than the projectors' soap. In spite of this the King ordered the closing down of seven out of Bristol's eleven soap-boiling workshops.

In London the struggle went on with unabated venom. The King's projectors prevailed on the King to prohibit the use of fish oil in soap altogether; on the strength of this they

THOMAS, VISCOUNT WENTWORTH
by Anthony Van Dyck

seized the stock of the London soap-makers and prosecuted them in the Star Chamber, following this up by an offer to buy them out of business. The London soap-makers refused the bait and some of them were imprisoned. Murmurs were now rising on all sides. While fishing companies were affected by the prohibition on whale oil, the people in general declared that the projectors' soap was bad. The projectors mobilised the Queen's ladies to write testimonials to the excellence of their soap but laundresses and—more important—cloth-workers throughout the country continued to condemn it. In response the King prohibited the private making of soap altogether and gave the projectors the right to enter and search any private house. All in vain. By the summer of 1634 illicit soap was being sold at a shilling the pound or six times its original price, so low was the general opinion of the projectors' soap. At this point the projectors gave up their plan of using only vegetable oil and took to using the fish oil, which they had made illegal for everyone else. In a final effort to drive their rivals out of business the King put a tax of £4 a ton on Bristol soap. The Bristol soap-boilers refused to pay, and fourteen of them followed the London soap-makers to prison. The farce could not continue much longer and in 1637 the King wound up the project and bought in the projectors' rights for £40,000 of which he made the London soap-makers contribute half. He then allowed the London men to go back to their interrupted manufacture on payment of a tax of £8 a ton to the Crown.[22]

The intermittent bullying and imprisonment angered and injured a minority. It was, in the long run, the constant prying interference arising from the King's financial projects which alienated the majority, an interference so marked that quite innocent strangers who asked questions would suddenly find themselves the object of insulting hostility, because they had been taken for government spies.[23]

The salt trouble and the soap trouble had irritated the Scots as much as the English. The poorer nation felt and feared the effect of the King's financial tamperings more than the richer one. England had already a well-established position in the economy of Europe. Scotland was struggling for a place and what was in England an irritation might in Scotland be a disaster. Salt was, after plaiding, the principal export of Scotland, and although the King's planned salt monopoly had in truth done little, if any, damage, it had caused grave anxiety while it lasted. The soap business was more serious, because by restricting the use of whale oil for soap the King had injured the Arctic fishery interests of the Scots. Further injury was done to Scottish trade by doubling the export duty on their coal, in spite of energetic protests;[24] worst of all was the scandal of the copper coinage.

Scotland, where the people still resorted to barter in many transactions, was perpetually short of small coin. The King had therefore granted to the Earl of Stirling the right to mint copper tokens. This patent was to serve a double purpose: the coins were to solve the problem of small change in Scotland and the profits made by Stirling were to be written off against a considerable debt which Charles had incurred towards him. Stirling was suspect in his native land because he belonged to the large group of courtier Scots who had followed their King southward and associated their fortunes with his, to the neglect of their own country. A poet, a scholar and nothing of a financier, he so managed the copper coinage as to create a noticeable inflation, to bring the quality of the King's money into disrepute and yet not to cover his own debts. The King, who had no other means of paying him off, remained deaf to repeated protestations from the Scots, and left Stirling, year after year, to bedevil the currency of Scotland.

William Noy had died in 1634, leaving his taxation schemes for others to operate. He had claimed to be a lawyer rather than a financier, and it is possible that if the King had had a Treasurer who was also something of a statesman and an administrator, Noy's ingenuity might have become the basis of an effective policy. A man who controlled and organised the collection of taxes so that the maximum came in to the King, and kept the scheming and corruption of Court speculators within bounds, could have given the King's government a steady income. A man who could develop the elements of policy embedded in the King's financial plans might have saved the King's government. No lack in the King's Council was more disastrous than the lack of a clever man at the Treasury.

The lack was the more regrettable because it was unnecessary. When the King's first Treasurer, the adroit and dishonest Portland, died in 1635, Archbishop Laud had used all his endeavours to have Wentworth appointed to the place—a man of ability and statesmanship, with a marked gift for financial administration. But he would have severely checked the courtiers who filled their pockets at the King's expense, and they, knowing this very well, had combined to oppose the appointment. The King did not wish to be surrounded by reproachful and indignant faces, which he must certainly expect if he placed Wentworth at the Treasury; he kept him in Ireland instead. Let the reproachful and indignant faces, which Wentworth's methods invariably created, be out of his sight, in Dublin. First he put the Treasury into commission between several councillors, which greatly increased the chances of delay, loss, confusion and corruption; then he gave the post to the Bishop of London. William Juxon was honest and careful as far as his eyes and hands could reach: he did his best. But he could not attack the trouble at the root, expose the corrupt, control the projectors and licensees, buy out the tax-farmers, and institute thorough-going reform. He had been appointed to the task because it was known that he would not do or want to do such troublesome things.

Wentworth, exiled from the Treasury for which he had hoped, set himself to improve the King's finances in the way still left open to him. He determined to make Ireland a valuable source of revenue to the Crown by making it prosperous and developing its resources. Prosperity could come by encouraging the Irish to work hard and—as even Wentworth anticipated difficulties in that plan—by bringing over industrious settlers in large numbers. He set his face resolutely against any short-term policy that would prevent the realisation of his plans; because it would have damaged Irish trade in saltfish, he opposed the King's attempt to extend the salt monopoly to Ireland, and he argued as firmly against the imposition of vexatious taxes on settlers who had not yet established themselves. "The Kingdom is growing apace," he wrote, "and a thousand pities it were, by bringing new burdens upon them, to discourage those that daily come over . . . especially when, but by a short forbearance, till they have taken a good sound root, his Majesty may at after gather five times as much from them without doing any hurt, where a little pulled from them at first breaks off their fruit in the very bud." [25]

He had to argue unceasingly with the King, who, when he was not expecting quick returns from taxes, was granting away Irish land for ready money. This, too, Wentworth strove hard to prevent by pointing out that only the right kind of settler could make Ireland permanently prosperous and a permanent asset to the Crown. In the meantime he did for the Irish taxes what he had longed to do in England: he bought out the tax-farmers and, refusing all outside requests for a share in the booty, farmed the principal taxes himself. He made his own profit on them and needed it, because he considered that the King's dignity ought to be fitly maintained by his Deputy in Ireland; he bought land, built hunting boxes and gave fine entertainments in Dublin castle, which he had greatly enlarged. His enemies —all those whose grants of land he had stopped or whose profits in the taxes he had curtailed—declared that he grew " monstrous rich " and hinted to the King that Wentworth enriched himself and not the Crown. But the King's revenue from Ireland rose from year to year, and the growing prosperity of the country promised even better things for the Treasury. The King, rightly, trusted Wentworth, although he deplored his capacity for annoying people. The disquieting energies of the York-shireman had been diverted to Ireland, but they overflowed none the less. Whitehall and St. James's were soon full of irritated courtiers whose hopes for profitable grants of Irish land had been dashed.

In this summer of 1637 the King and Wentworth were corresponding chiefly about the great affair of the Londonderry Plantation. About twenty-five years earlier, the City of London had entered into a contract with the Crown to farm and develop an indefinite area of northern Ireland in the region of Derry. There had probably been *bona fide* errors in the original charter, and ambiguities deliberate or accidental. The acreage of the land taken over by London was nearer 400,000 acres than the 40,000 mentioned in the charter. King James, before long, felt he had given away too much, and surveys set on foot by the Crown had shown that the City was failing to fulfil its obligations under the Charter. Early in 1635, the City was finally tried before the Star Chamber for wilful neglect; they pleaded that they had been faithful to the spirit and intentions of the charter but lost their case. Justice, of a kind, was probably done in this matter but its purity was suspect because it was evident from the first that the Crown intended to revoke the City's charter and resume control of the land.

Following the usual procedure, the Star Chamber not only deprived the City of all its lands, but added a fine of £70,000. "Londonderry hath almost undone London," it was said, but the City did not accept this without a struggle, and after two years of argument and numerous counter-propositions the fine was reduced to £12,000.

Wentworth, who had worked out the potential value of the land and the actual value of its excellent fisheries, was anxious to retain it all as a part of the royal possessions, and suggested it should be settled on the little Duke of York, the King's second son. To Wentworth's profound annoyance the King seemed more inclined to snatch at immediate profit by leasing it away.[26] Whatever he did with the land it was questionable whether either the King or Wentworth had done wisely to alienate the richest and most influential city in the three Kingdoms for £12,000 and the lands and fisheries of Derry.

The King's ambition was so to organise and develop his resources that he would never again be under the necessity of calling Parliament in England. Although he naturally made no public declaration of this purpose, it was unmistakably implied and was well known to foreign ambassadors as well as to the King's own councillors, who took care, as far as possible, not to mention even the possibility of a future Parliament.[27] He recognised that patents and fines were no permanent solution, but he felt, not without reason, that a permanent solution was within his grasp. He had enforced Tonnage and Poundage after Parliament's dissolution in spite of their refusal to grant it and, after the initial outcry, his subjects had accepted the situation. In the year 1636 by the issue of a new Book of Rates compiled by his authority alone he adjusted in the interests of the revenue all the customs duties payable in the Kingdom. This too went through without undue clamour. The King had thus arrogated to himself the right to settle this very important part of his income without having recourse to Parliament.

If he could also exercise and enforce the right to impose new taxes on his subjects without recourse to Parliament, he would have finally and effectively emancipated the Crown. It was therefore with a double purpose, political and financial, that he adopted Noy's suggestion of reimposing the Elizabethan tax known as Ship-money. This was a levy on the coastal counties and seaports of the realm for the express purpose of strengthening the navy. The tax was well-selected for the King's purpose because the expansion of sea-power was usually popular with the English, and the raids of Barbary corsairs on the south coast and of Dunkirk pirates in the Channel fully justified an increase in the navy. The tax, unlike so many of the King's financial plans, was in itself profitable and economical: the money was collected direct by justices of the peace and delivered to the sheriffs of counties who paid it over at once to the Admiralty. Very little leaked away in the process.

The revival of the Elizabethan impost was calmly received, and in the following year the King tried the critical experiment of extending the tax to the inland counties. This was an innovation, and at once—as he had expected—the critics of the government began to argue that he should have consulted Parliament first. Lord Danby gave the King a written protest, asking that Parliament might at once be called. The King had accepted the paper and begun to read it before he saw what it was. He went pale and paced the room angrily and in silence. For the next week he gave up his usual hunting expeditions and spent long hours in council. As a result he strengthened his policy against the Dutch, grew more insistent in his demands that the herring treaty be respected, and officially republished a book called *Mare Clausum* by John Selden, which claimed that the English had exclusive rights in the Narrow Sea. He hoped by this demonstration to stimulate enthusiasm for the navy and willingness to pay Ship-money. But although Selden, whose book was thus singled out, was a popular and influential man in the very party which most opposed the King, the demonstration had almost no effect. Spanish rivalry, and the poor figure cut by their country in the struggle for colonial power and the Protestant cause, interested English seamen more than this lesser dispute with the Calvinist Dutch. The Earl of Warwick, making one of his rare appearances at Court, told the King, openly and in public, that he would not raise a finger to make his tenants pay Ship-money against their consciences, but that if Charles would call a Parliament he would find his subjects ready, nay eager, to grant all he wanted for a war on Spain and Austria in the interests of the Elector Palatine. The King listened with an absent smile until Warwick had finished and then, brushing all he had said into oblivion, told him that he hoped he would set an example to all by his own obedience and promptitude in meeting the tax.[28]

All the same the King took the precaution of propounding a critical question to the judges. In time of national peril and imminent danger, he asked, could the King demand, without further ado, financial or other help from his subjects? All except two of the judges, Sir George Croke and Sir Richard Hutton, agreed that the King had such a right, and was furthermore " sole judge both of the danger, and when and how the same is to be prevented and avoided." [29] In the belief that they were bound to yield to the majority, the two dissident judges signed the general statement. The King thenceforward considered that he had a unanimous judicial ruling in favour of Ship-money.

Notwithstanding the ruling of the judges some of his subjects refused to pay. Sometimes resistance became violent; high words and cudgel blows were exchanged between Thomas Cartwright, the squire of Aynhoe in Northamptonshire, and the sheriff's men. Much of the resistance was, noticeably, in the districts where the leading opposition peers were powerful. The Earl of Warwick had said that he would not compel his people to pay; he went further for he strenuously encouraged them not to do so. It was clear to the King and his Council that those who openly refused were hoping to be prosecuted. Prosecutions for non-payment would provide the King's opponents and their lawyers with a chance to argue the constitutional merits of their case in public. Next to a debate in Parliament, this would be the most effective method of attacking the policy and actions of the Crown.

The King saw the danger and at first evaded it. To the undisguised annoyance of Lord Saye and Seal, he took no notice of the crafty peer's repeated and rude defiance of the sheriff's demands for money. The constable was sent to distrain his goods, and drove off some cattle that the rich old man could well spare; Lord Saye, drawing attention to himself again, brought an action against the constable. The King, disregarding the Ship-money business, retaliated by prosecuting him for infringing the forest laws—proceedings which gave Lord Saye and his lawyers no chance to open their mouths about Parliament or taxation.

The defiance of subjects could not with safety be tolerated, and although the King was determined not to gratify Lord Saye by prosecuting him, he had to find means of settling effectively with his opponents. In the summer of 1637 the case of Rex *v.* Hampden came up in the Exchequer Court. John Hampden of Great Missenden in the county of Buckinghamshire was only one of many who had refused to pay Ship-money on principle. At this time about forty-three years of age, a man of high intelligence and great charm, he was an influential landowner, a shareholder both in the Providence and the New England Companies, and a friend of the Lords Warwick, Brooke and Saye, and of John Pym.

English law ran its course with due deliberation. Hampden was not cited before the Exchequer Court until May 1637 to show cause why he should not pay an assessment of 20s. on his lands at Stoke Mandeville. What with preliminaries and delays, it was evident that the case would not be tried until after Michaelmas.

In the summer of 1637 King Charles had projects and problems in plenty: the Hampden case, the reform of the Scottish Church, the prosecution of the Bishop of Lincoln in the Star Chamber, not to mention Prynne, Burton and Bastwicke, the rebuilding of St. Paul's, the extension of the fleet, the draining of the fens, the development of the Welsh mines, the improvement and colonisation of Ireland, the purchase of new pictures for his collection, the enlargement of his deer park at Richmond. Although anxieties were inseparable from the office of a King he viewed most of his projects with hope and confidence. He spoke with a deep and grateful sincerity when he described himself to his nephew the Elector Palatine as "the happiest King in Christendom."

The Elector, young in years but already old in disillusion, had seen and heard enough during his sojourn in the country to make him doubt his uncle's judgment. The present happiness of King Charles, like the painted ceiling of his banqueting house at Whitehall, bore no relation whatever to the political reality.

BOOK I CHAPTER III REFERENCES

1. David Jenkins, *Lex Terrae*, 1647.
2. Fulbecke, *A Parallel or Conference of the Civil Law, Canon Law and Common Law* London, 1602.

3. Holdsworth, *History of English Law*, London, 1922, v, p. 353.
4. Fulbecke, *op. cit.*
5. *Anecdotes and Traditions.* ed. W. J. Thomas. *Camden Society.* 1839. p. 53.
6. *Records of the Honourable Society of Lincoln's Inn*, London, 1897, II, p. 326–7.
7. See *Hudibras*, Cant. III, Part III, ll. 760–5.
8. *Cal. S.P. Ven*, 1636–9, p. 165. The very great emphasis put by Shakespeare in *The Merchant of Venice* in the trial scene on the incorruptibility of Venetian justice is interesting in this context; the idea needed to be hammered home to an English audience.
9. Spelman, *History of Sacrilege*, London, 1698, p. 233; for a full account of the Court of Wards see H. E. Bell, *Court of Wards and Liveries*, Cambridge University Press, 1953.
10. Skeel, *Council of the marches of Wales*, London, 1904, p. 151.
11. *C.S.P.D.*, 1637, pp. 417, 463–4; 1637–8, p. 140.
12. Selden, *Table Talk*; Jardine, *A Reading on Torture*, London, 1837, pp. 53–4, 108.
13. *C.S.P.D.*, 1639, p. 181.
14. *Strafford MSS.*, X, Laud to Wentworth, December 19th, 1637.
15. *C.S.P. Ven*, 1636–9, p. 125.
16. *C.S.P.D.*, 1639–40, p. 61; see also Dietz, *English Public Finance*, New York, 1932.
17. H. E. Bell, *Court of Wards*, Appendix.
18. *C.S.P.D.*, 1639–40, p. 71.
19. *Ibid.*, pp. 89–90.
20. Rushworth, III, p. 277; Knowler, I, p. 507.
21. Hughes, *Studies in Administration and Finance*, Manchester, 1934, pp. 88–115 *passim*; Hist. MSS. Comm. *Rep. XIII*, *App. IV*, p. 206–7.
22. *A True relation of the State of the Business of Soap*, London 1643; H. E. Matthews, *Company of Soapmakers*, Bristol Record Society Publications X, Bristol, 1940, pp. 122, 194–5, 207–10.
23. *Short Survey of 26 Counties*, pp. 8–9; *Carriers' Cosmography*, Preface.
24. *Register P.C. Scot.*, 1633–5, pp. 223–4, 258–60.
25. Knowler, II, p. 89.
26. See T. W. Moody, *The Londonderry Plantation*, Belfast, 1939, for the details of this complicated case; Knowler, II, 91.
27. *C.S.P. Ven*, 1636–9, p. 124.
28. *Ibid.*, pp. 110, 124–5.
29. Rushworth, II, 608.

BOOK TWO

CHALLENGE FROM SCOTLAND
June 1637 - July 1639

Subjects ought with solicitous eyes to watch over the prerogative of a crown. The authority of a King is the keystone which closeth up the arch of order and government, which, once shaken, all the frame falls together in a confused heap of foundation and battlement.

THOMAS WENTWORTH

Let God, by whom Kings reign, have His own place and prerogative.

ALEXANDER HENDERSON

CHAPTER ONE

THE COVENANT

June 1637 – February 1638

A FAVOURABLE decision in the Hampden case and the imposition of the new Prayer Book on Scotland would carry the King a long way towards realising two of his ambitions: the financial independence of the Crown, and uniformity of religion in his dominions. In the meantime the Court of Star Chamber dealt drastically with the three men who had written and preached against the bishops in general and Bishop Wren in particular. Prynne, Burton and Bastwicke were small fry but their punishment was of importance in the royal scheme of things. "The intention of these men," Laud declared justly enough at their trial, "was and is to raise a sedition, being as great incendiaries in the State as they have ever been in the Church." [1] Lord Chief Justice Finch, the principal pillar of the King's judicial system as Laud was of the Church, fully concurred in this view. He led the councillors in imposing a sentence of extreme severity. All three men were sentenced to pay fines which amounted to more than all that they possessed; all three were to be confined for the rest of their lives in the remotest parts of the King's dominions. Before they disappeared for ever from public view they were to stand in the pillory and lose their ears. Prynne was also to be branded.

On June 30th, 1637, a hot bright day, the victims were led out to suffer in Palace Yard, Westminster. Sympathetic crowds had gathered to watch. Rosemary and sweet herbs were scattered before the martyrs' feet, and cups of wine and *aqua vitae* were offered to refresh and strengthen them. When they were uncomfortably wedged in two pillories, Mrs. Burton climbed on a stool and kissed her husband. The crowd cheered. Burton was in his best clothes, with new white gloves and a little nosegay in his hand, on which a curious bee alighted; the incident inspired him to utter a short sermon. The sufferers stood in their awkward pulpits for two hours, in the glare of a hot sun, and had plenty of time to preach, Prynne speaking loudest and longest. When the executioner approached to cut off their ears, Bastwicke, the doctor, produced a surgeon's knife and instructed him how to perform his task. The man, none the less, treated Prynne very roughly because—so the Court said afterwards—Prynne had undertipped him, only half a crown and all in sixpences.

The crowd surged about the victims, and relic-hunters strove to dip handkerchiefs in their blood; Burton, who was over sixty, fainted for lack of air and it was almost impossible for a surgeon to get through the press to attend to their wounds. Prynne, meanwhile, with astonishing fortitude, repeated a Latin epigram which he had composed on the subject of the letters (S.L. for Seditious Libeller) with which his face had been branded. Someone in the crowd drew a growl of agreement by remarking that if these three men had been Papists no harm would have come to them.[2]

The Archbishop's annoyance when he heard of the demonstration was mixed with anxiety which he confided to Wentworth. Both of them recognised the dangerous force which lay behind this outburst of enthusiasm for the fanatics. Such feelings were not confined to the Londoners. On their way to prison the three were followed and helped by crowds of sympathisers. Prynne especially was warmly welcomed at Chester, given dinner by the mayor and presented with a set of hangings for his prison room at Carnarvon Castle. With praiseworthy resignation to his fate, he had procured a Welsh Bible and was studying the language.

The Star Chamber had one more important case to decide before the summer recess. On July 15th, 1637, Laud's antagonist, John Williams, Bishop of Lincoln, was sentenced for perjury. Williams's guilt in this unhappy and extremely complicated case is not in serious doubt. But his reputation as a conciliator and an opponent of Laud was well known, and the popular belief that he was being deliberately victimised was not quite groundless. His crimes provided a means towards his ruin which was extremely welcome to the King and the Archbishop.

The Star Chamber and the High Commission worked hand in hand over this significant prosecution. The Star Chamber condemned Williams to pay a fine of £10,000, deprived him of all his ecclesiastical revenues, and sent him to the Tower during the King's pleasure, and the High Commission suspended him from the exercise of all episcopal functions. Perjury and bribery were not offences for which Williams could be deprived of his various preferments. An unashamed pluralist, he held both the bishopric of Lincoln and the deanery of Westminster. Laud hoped that, discredited as he now was, he would humbly buy his release from the Tower by resigning both and creeping away to whatever desolate small diocese in Ireland or Wales was pityingly assigned to him.

John Williams was no fanatic martyr for religion's sake, nor was he an innocent man deeply wronged; he was a politician of irrepressible tenacity and optimism, convinced that his judgment in Church matters was right and that Laud's was wrong. He had no intention of relinquishing two key positions in the Church merely because of a conviction for perjury. Laud had assumed jurisdiction in the see of Lincoln, but as long as Williams refused to resign, some turn of fortune might always restore his power; he held out, waiting for the change of affairs which should undo Laud. Harried by threats of further prosecutions, deprived of almost all his means, reduced to a single square meal a day—at which, however, he often entertained guests—he continued in the Tower, voluble, obstinate and unafraid.[3]

One or two lesser matters marked the end of the summer.

The Attorney-General, John Bankes, considered what should be done about a pamphlet with the offensive title "A Breviate of the Prelates' Usurpation" which had been slipped into his hand together with a reproachful personal letter declaring that it was a pity to see "a religious and godly gentleman" like Bankes associating himself with the persecutors. Bankes was in truth one of the milder of the King's legal advisers and he disadvised a Star Chamber prosecution in this case.[4] Meanwhile the King's Council reprimanded two unruly young noblemen who had come to blows in a narrow street, and reversed the action of a London jury which had acquitted a couple of draymen who, after colliding with a nobleman's coach in a traffic block, had used abusive language to him. The saucy fellows were flogged and sent to Bridewell by direct order of the Council, which severe and high-handed action in defence of the social order called forth no protest from anyone.[5]

Vacation silence had descended on the law courts, and King Charles was enjoying the season's sport at his favourite country house of Oatlands, when, in the first week of August 1637, unwelcome news reached him from Edinburgh.

His council in Scotland had fixed Sunday, July 28th, for the introduction of the new Prayer Book throughout the country and announced that they themselves would mark the occasion by going in procession to St. Giles' Cathedral for the morning service. One councillor, Lord Traquair, who was never afterwards able to explain his conduct satisfactorily to the King, remembered a pressing engagement on the other side of the kingdom; his more astute colleague, Lord Lorne, had a sudden indisposition. For the rest, the councillors attended.

As soon as the Dean, Dr. Hannah, began the service, the crowd at the back of the church set up a shout and followed their words by hurling clasp Bibles and folding stools at the Dean and councillors. The rioters were with some difficulty put outside by the guards, but a great crowd round about the cathedral battered the doors and pelted the windows for the rest of the service. Demonstrations of the same kind had taken place in other churches that day, and in the afternoon roving gangs in the Edinburgh streets set on some of the King's supporters to the peril of their lives.

The demonstration had been premeditated. For the past three months the principal ministers, gentry, citizens, and lords who objected to the Book had been considering what to do when the crisis came. The religious fervour of the populace was genuine; they had only to give it guidance. The King's councillors, knowing both the zeal of the populace and the intelligence of those who were directing it, realised how great was the threat to the King's authority in Scotland, but they also realised the peril in which they themselves stood. Consequently, although they declared the rioters guilty of treason and worthy of death, they also suspended the Service Book, and removed the seat of their session from the heart of incensed Edinburgh to the defensible seclusion of Holyrood. By their words they proclaimed the King's unshaken authority, but by their acts they revealed themselves unable, and perhaps unwilling to support it.[6]

This was the news which reached the King at Oatlands. He was coldly and fiercely angry, as much at the cowardice of his Scottish council as at the insolence of the rabble. He sent a peremptory command that the use of the Book be immediately resumed and the principal rioters forthwith arrested and sentenced for their crime.[7] He acted with majestic indifference to common reality. Rebellion was still to him no more than a painted hydra, something not yet experienced in the rough and personal manner known to his councillors as they apprehensively traversed the narrow streets of Edinburgh.

They could not carry out the King's orders because they had not the strength to do so. Even the ministers willing to use the Book could do so only if their congregations allowed them. William Annand, a Glasgow minister, who boldly continued with the new service, was all but torn in pieces by a crowd of women, and the Bishop of Brechin, tough and formidable, who glared at his congregation over a pair of loaded pistols while he conducted the service, barely escaped the rabble which lay in wait for him afterwards.[8]

Petitions against the Book poured in from all the southern parts of Scotland. Crowds from Fife and the Lothians began to gather in Edinburgh. The first outbreak was followed and sustained by burghers, by men of learning, by lairds and noblemen from all the south. National as well as religious fervour fed their anger. Thirty-five years of resentment lay behind this movement; the King was paying for his own and his father's neglect, for the long absence in England, for the attempt, once too often, to govern Scotland from Whitehall with a stroke of the pen.

In England meanwhile the King attended the wedding of his cousin the Duke of Lennox to the only daughter of his one-time favourite, the murdered Duke of Buckingham. The young people, who were thought to be much in love, were married by the Archbishop at Lambeth Palace on a thundery wet day in August, the King coming in person to give away the bride. A reception at the house of the bridegroom's aunt was the occasion of much innocent mirth and the presentation of splendid gifts, including a white satin purse containing five thousand pounds in gold.[9] The King and Queen left late and called again on the following morning, early. They were genuinely attached to Lennox and his lady and wished to see them happy before leaving London for another visit to Oatlands. Both husband and wife were their personal attendants, but had leave of absence from Court for a brief honeymoon.

The honeymoon was shorter than had been intended, for just at this time the Duke's mother died in Scotland and he had to hurry north to attend her funeral and settle her affairs. Lennox was little acquainted with politics, but he was the King's cousin and a chief nobleman of Scotland, and it was natural for Charles to expect from him a personal report on the situation in the troublesome North.

He reached Edinburgh about the third week in September 1637 and the Council courteously asked him to be present at their session of the 20th of that month. Lennox, as he walked through the streets to his appointment, was impressed and disquieted by the great crowd of people who lined his path, with suppliant, expectant gestures, "saluting very low."[10] Both the populace and the Council hoped much from Lennox: he was the King's nearest kinsman of the Stewart family; he was thought to have influence, and he had the reputation of a good-natured, honest, conciliatory gentleman.

As witness to the deliberations of the Council at this critical time, the King's cousin got no very happy impression. On the council board lay a handful of typical petitions against the new form of worship, and the lengthy text of a Supplication, drawn up and signed by a great body of the clergy supported by some of the nobility. "This new Book of Common Prayer," so ran the Supplication, "is introduced and urged in a way which this Kirk hath never been acquainted with, and containeth many very material points contrary to the Acts of our National Assemblies, his Majesty's laws of this Kingdom and to the religion and form of worship established and universally practised to the great comfort of all God's people, His Majesty's subjects since the Reformation . . ." The Council asked only one thing of Lennox: that he would explain the pressing danger of the situation to the King and take with him two or three of the more violent petitions to prove that they were telling only the truth when they humbly entreated His Majesty to believe that they could proceed no further with the Book.[11]

On his return to England Lennox found the King in no mood to yield to insolent rebellion, and had not himself the firmness of character to change his master's set opinions. The King's plans for improvement at home and abroad, in small things and in great, still appeared to make steady progress. He had just peremptorily prohibited corporations and city companies from voting by ballot at their meetings, a secretive process, introduced from Venice some years earlier, of which his father also had strongly disapproved.[12] His attention was drawn, at the same time, to a new silver mine in Wales. It would produce, it was estimated, three hundred pounds worth of the precious ore every week, and the King had granted its enterprising exploiter, Thomas Bushell, the right to set up an additional mint for this bullion at Aberystwyth.[13] Among the schemes for reclaiming land, a hopeful project for the draining of Romney Marsh was under discussion.[14] The usual plans of projectors for raising money for themselves or for the Crown were canvassed at Court, foremost of these, Sir William Courtine's new East India Company, a competitor which the London East India merchants viewed with indignation. Sir Thomas Roe's West Indies Company, an enterprise which was still a vision of the future, caused some speculation and already gave its founder as much pleasure " as if by his industry the Indies were already conquered." [15]

The new ship, the *Sovereign of the Seas*, had been successfully launched at Deptford. The Earl of Northumberland had thought of the name for this splendid giant of the ocean, two hundred and fifty-four feet long and armed with a hundred and forty-four guns. The name, with its implied reference to his own sovereignty of the seas, delighted King Charles and, while Lennox was in Scotland, the whole court had gone to see the launch. The occasion had been a disappointment, for the tide did not rise high enough and the *Sovereign* in the end slid into the water in the presence of a less distinguished company some weeks later.

From Ireland the King received, month by month, from his efficient Deputy, reports which showed that the royal authority and the royal revenues had never been in better state. Wentworth had concluded a busy summer with a progress into the southern provinces where he intended to develop the country on a great scale. Looking upon the land with the eyes of a practical, hard-working Yorkshireman, he saw that it was good. " The province of Munster is by much the best that I have yet seen amongst them," he reported to Cottington, " yet I dare confidently assure you if there were seven times as many people, there would be room sufficient for them all and make it a much

better country for the dweller." The Irish were unworthy of
their opportunities: here for instance was Limerick, "the
bravest place for trade that ever I saw, seated in a rich country
. . . and the goodliest river doubtless in Christendom running
under the walls." The water was so deep and the harbour so
good that a ship of four hundred ton might " come with safety
and lay her nose upon the quay." Yet owing to the miserable
Irish sloth there was " not one ship of above a hundred ton
belonging to the town." The pen in the Yorkshireman's hand
quivered with indignation; it did not occur to him that the
Irish themselves had any right to be consulted in the treatment
of their neglected land. In his opinion they should have been
glad to throw themselves on the King's mercy for their property.
It was preferable to remaining, as they had for the past generation, a prey to the arbitrary seizures of unscrupulous English
speculators, or to their own " petty but imperious " lords.
Throughout the south he was received with a great show of
enthusiasm and loyal addresses of welcome, " three at Kilkenny, two very deadly long ones at Clonmel, four not of
the shortest here at Limerick." Limerick was gay with triumphal arches, including a tableau of " the seven planets in a
very special and heavenly motion," with the sun in the midst
of them squirting rose water on the Deputy out of an object
which looked suspiciously like a doctor's syringe. [16]More
remarkable than this joyous entry was the fact that in Ormonde, Clare and Limerick the local landowners, without
further question, acknowledged the King's right to dispose of
their land.

Wentworth had a plan for restoring Christ Church Cathedral, Dublin, not unlike Laud's plan for restoring St. Paul's. It
would cost £30,000 but this could be extracted from the
obedient Irish Parliament; the only obstacle was the behaviour
of Archbishop Ussher who disapproved of vain expense on
building, having as Wentworth complained, " a more domestic
way of serving God Almighty than I like of, or David thought
of when he purposed the building of a temple." [17]

While things went forward so favourably in Ireland, the King heard with equal satisfaction that the commission sent to investigate the illegal engrossing of forest land in Northampton-shire had imposed fines amounting to more than fifty thousand pounds, the Earl of Salisbury heading the list with the crippling liability of £20,000. The rich were not the only people to be disciplined for contravening the laws of the realm. An Eliza-bethan act had made it unlawful for any cottage to be built and occupied unless it had four acres of ground for cultivation and pasture. This regulation had often been ignored, usually by poor labourers and small yeomen's sons who could not find land but must needs have a roof to cover them. Fines now rained upon these people's heads, as well as on the richer landlords; but it was generally felt that the government should have something better to do than to " vex the poor people." [18]

Ship-money, on the contrary, seemed to be justifying itself, practically if not legally, for the coasts badly needed protection. The Barbary pirates that summer had made at least one successful raid in the south-west and carried away more than thirty captives, but in September an English squadron, which had sailed under Captain Rainborough to the west coast of Africa, dropped anchor in the Thames estuary and set on shore more than three hundred English men, women and children, released from Moorish thraldom. Rainborough also brought back with him an ambassador from the Moors, to discuss with the King of England the future prevention of piracy. When the Moorish envoy, a Portuguese eunuch with a very fine presence, rode in procession through the streets of London, with the released captives, all in white, following behind him, and four noble Barbary horses in glittering caparison to offer to the King, it seemed that the factious voices of Hampden and his friends had received an answer.[19] What did the legality of Ship-money matter, since it had proved its usefulness?

Worries and distractions interrupted the interests and plea-sures of the Court. A scandal occurred in the autumn when Lady Newport, on her way home from the play in Drury Lane, slipped into the Queen's Chapel at Somerset House and was received into the Roman Catholic Church. Her husband protested; the Queen denied all participation in the matter, but Archbishop Laud declared that the priests who enjoyed her favour abused it to make conversions. The Queen retaliated by refusing to speak to the Archbishop for two months, but her favourites, Wat Montagu and Toby Mathew, thought it politic to vanish from Court for a while.[20] Charles himself, although distressed at Lady Newport's change of faith, spoke sternly to her husband for persecuting his wife for conscience' sake—a rebuke which may have had repercussions in the Puritan circles in which Newport moved.[21]

With so much else on his mind, the King had little time to spare for Scotland, although early in October he commanded his Scots council to take effective measures to disperse the multitudes of petitioners still in Edinburgh. The Council's half-hearted attempt to comply with this order provoked a riot in which the Bishop of Galloway was frightened out of his wits and Lord Traquair lost his hat and cloak in coming to his rescue; after that, the council made no further effort. " The Lord give this business a fair end for it has a fair beginning," wrote a Presbyterian lawyer, Archibald Johnston of Warriston, in his diary on the night of this savage tumult.[22]

The fair beginning was not essentially or exclusively the Lord's work; the King's supporters and the bishops were well aware that resistance was being encouraged and organised by a group of nobles, lawyers and ministers. The riots were frequently led by women, that breed of resolute harridans whose voices may still be heard uplifted in argument in the back streets of southern Scotland. Neither these women, nor the men and boys who joined them in bishop-baiting, would have acted so appositely had there been no guiding power to hold them together, keep their anger alive and unloose their rage at the proper moment, but the fanatic emotion which made them terrible was all their own. The religious and national feeling of the great majority in the lowlands of Scotland was guided by a sagacious and experienced few who saw how best to use it, but the feeling itself was deep, widespread and by no means irrational. As for the leaders of the party—nobles, ministers and men of law— they were not less sincere in their religion because they were also capable of political strategy and worldly calculation.

The nobleman who, ever since the beginning of the King's reign had been the foremost opponent of his Church policy for Scotland, was John Leslie, Earl of Rothes. The immediate and natural leader in the present crisis, he was a man approaching forty, tough, independent and well-experienced in politics. His lands were scattered, some in Fife, some in the region of Elgin, and his influence, though it was not to be compared with that of such great nobles and clan chiefs as Huntly or Argyll, was singularly widespread. He was a reasonably devout Presbyterian, but the political aspects of the cause had always been more important to him than the spiritual: as a Scot he resented and suspected the attempt to bring the Kirk into line with England, and as a nobleman whose ancestors had had their share of pillage at the Reformation he objected to the re-establishment of the bishops and the royal attempt to restore their ancient endowments.

With him were associated a number of other Scots lords mostly from the Lowlands—Balmerino, Lothian, Lindsay, Loudoun, Cassilis. It was not until the middle of October that a young man of stronger personality than any of these associated himself with the party and became, next after Rothes, the moving spirit of their actions. James Graham, Earl of Montrose, was twenty-five years old, newly returned from a tour of Europe, cultivated, witty and gallant. The news that he had signed the Supplication against the Prayer Book caused dismay among the bishops, for he was personally known to several of them and had always seemed friendly; it had been assumed, from his tastes, his friends, his travels—he had stayed long in Italy, studied in Padua, and visited Rome—that he would be a King's man. But Montrose, for all his European polish, was a believing Calvinist and had a fierce pride in the independence of his nation. These were the reasons which made him join his fortune with the opposition, not as some preferred to argue, his annoyance at the cold reception accorded him by the King when he had visited London.[23] He was a valuable recruit to the party because his easy grace and gay good looks made him an attractive leader.

A young man of a different social background, different gifts, and harshly different character was Montrose's contemporary, Archibald Johnston, Laird of Warriston. He came of a border family of small gentry, but his father had prospered in trade and Warriston inherited a shrewd business head. On the mother's side he had ancestors distinguished in the law and he himself had chosen that profession. Well under thirty, he was already one of the leading advocates at the Edinburgh bar. Warriston was not simply a religious fanatic; the spiritual diary which he kept reveals a man walking on the dizzy verge of madness. His exceptional gifts of logic, of memory, of concentration and calculation, were supported by no broadening wisdom and no human understanding. He could analyse a legal text or extract every particle of verbal meaning from a passage of Scripture, but he was lacking in ordinary powers of criticism; he was credulous to the point of silliness, intolerant from a rabid ignorance, unable fairly to examine his own heart or motives. For so narrow and hard a mind the long hours of prayer common to the Presbyterians meant a daily exercise in self-deception. " For the space of two or three hours I got an exceeding great liberty, freedom and familiarity with my God," he would write; and again, " the Lord all this time was powerfully, sensibly, speaking in me and to me, praying in me and answering to me." In a cold sweat of terror and devotion he learnt that " I was appointed for eternal salvation and my name written in the Book of Life " and was inexpressibly uplifted by the conviction that he would not only be glorified after death, which was "too little favour and common to all His saints and chosen, but He would even in this life glorify Himself visibly and sensibly in my life and death." He knew, no less, that unworthy as he was, he was God's chief instrument for the "welfare of His Church, Satan's overthrow, Antichrist's ruin, and comfort of the godly." The dazzling revelation of his mission made him reel "like a man drunken."[24] His intoxication lasted a melancholy and bitter lifetime.

Reflections such as these occupied the thoughts of Warriston in the intervals of applying his formidable intellect to the problems before the rebellious party in Scotland. He was at this time minutely studying the Confession of Faith of 1580, the document, deeply sworn, by which the Scots had once tried to stabilise the Church of Knox.

The principal leader of the clergy was Alexander Henderson, minister of Leuchars in Fife. He was an older man than the secular leaders, well on into his fifties, and with a patience and human understanding acquired during more than thirty years as the conscientious minister of a large parish. His abilities had long since marked him out for some more important charge, but his known opposition to the bishops had prevented his preferment to Edinburgh or Stirling. He had from the beginning of the present troubles taken a leading part in refusing the new Service Book and petitioning against it. Henderson stands out among his contemporaries for honesty and largeness of heart. He was firm in his devotion to the doctrine and worship of the Kirk, but he respected sincerity in others and was capable of tolerance, though not of yielding. He was a good diplomatist because he had the imagination to understand points of view other than his own and could meet them with argument rather than anger. A certain irascibility was occasionally apparent in his words, but it added to, rather than diminished, his authority.

These were the open leaders of the party. Two other men, who could not yet proclaim their sympathy, were already in private agreement with the rebels: Archibald Campbell, Lord Lorne, and Sir Thomas Hope, both members of the King's council.[25] Lord Lorne, eldest son to the Earl of Argyll, was already possessed of his father's lands and was, in effect, the head of a noble house and the chief of the largest clan in the Highlands.

The circumstances were unusual. His father, a treacherous old ruffian who had built up a formidable position in the Western Highlands by suppressing the disorderly clans whose territories abutted on those of his own people, had fled the country twenty years before on account of his creditors. Later, becoming a Roman Catholic in Flanders and entering the service of the King of Spain, he had forfeited his estates, and his son, at twenty-one, had become Earl of Argyll in all but name.

Lord Lorne, in the years during which he had controlled the great estates of his father, had restored order to the disordered finances of the house of Argyll. He had also suppressed the plundering MacGregors by land and the piratical Macdonalds by land and sea. He was an admirable organiser with a shrewd eye to advantage and, as he got the better of piracy, he had built up small fishing fleets and a petty coastal trade from the many villages on the indented seaboard of his land. By this time he was the wealthiest as well as the most powerful nobleman in Scotland.

He lacked nevertheless many of the personal characteristics useful to the chief of a clan and a great nobleman. He was small and unprepossessing, had neither a good presence nor a powerful voice, and his florid, rather undistinguished face was marred by a disfiguring cast in his pale blue eyes. With these physical drawbacks went a cautious and secretive manner; he had no charm. Yet his concentration of purpose and his profound gravity were impressive, and his exceptional intellectual powers were apparent to anyone who had any dealings with him. His colleagues held him in respect and his clan was greatly, and rightly, in awe of him.

Lorne was a convinced and devout Presbyterian, although as a member of the King's Council he had had to give official support to the royal policy. Sir Thomas Hope of Craighall, Lord Advocate of Scotland, was in the same embarrassing position. A scholar and practitioner of the law with more than forty years' experience at the bar, Hope was approaching his seventieth year and was generally acknowledged to be the finest legal mind of his time in Scotland. His mother, Jaqueline de Tott, came of a Dutch family, and Hope, a wealthy man with commercial interests both in Scotland and the Netherlands, stood foremost among those who kept the economic and religious interests of their country in close touch with the Amsterdam Exchange and the pulpits of Leyden and Dordrecht.

His judgment was exact, his intellect profound, his temper irritable, and his character cautious but firm; his honesty was strictly measured by what did, and what did not, hold good in law. The founder of a great fortune and prolific dynasty, he practised a certain shrewd self-interest, yet he could be obstinate in what he believed to be right, either by God's law or Scotland's, and, for all his worldly wisdom and commonsense, he had, at his prayers, heard the voice of the Lord offering him personal encouragement.[26]

As winter drew on, the crowds in Edinburgh gradually dispersed at the bidding of their leaders, but first they chose representatives of the three principal classes—nobles, ministers and burgesses—to remain in the city and act on their behalf. These small elected groups who, as time went on, were to wield extraordinary power, were familiarly known as the Tables.

The Tables, led by Rothes and Montrose, had audience with the council early in December when the Earl of Roxburgh, recently returned from London as the messenger of His Majesty's extreme displeasure, tried once more to hector them into obedience. They were so little impressed that Alexander Henderson took it upon himself to reprove the King's spokesman " for his oft swearing." [27] Deadlock had been reached: the rebels demanded that the King read and answer their Supplication, and the King, from the safe distance of London, resolutely refused to do so.

Throughout the winter the situation in Scotland grew steadily more dangerous. Some of the King's friends made attempts, neither well-sustained nor successful, to divide the ranks of the opposition by setting the citizens against the nobles and the gentry against the ministers. The manœuvre was too apparent, and the opposition only closed its ranks the more firmly. At least once in the darkness of the winter evenings, Lord Lorne came privily down from his eminence as a Councillor and consulted long and thoughtfully with the fanatic Warriston. He cancelled his usual winter visit to his castle at Inveraray and stayed through the drear season in the capital "to see the event of these matters " [28]—to see it from both sides.

The unhappy Council in Edinburgh sent off Lord Treasurer Traquair once again to London to face the royal displeasure and to try to explain the situation to the obstinate, incredulous King. Traquair was a lowland gentleman who had risen to a peerage and his present place in the Council by a small talent for intrigue and by courting the right people. He was shrewd enough to realise that, as the King's present policy could not succeed, unquestioning loyalty would pay him no dividend. With far less excuse, for his religion was negligible, he had also, like Lorne and Hope, entered into private communication with the rebels.

In England at the centre of the King's government, diplomatic relations with foreign powers were causing some anxiety. The King's neutrality in the European war was still the object of criticism at home and attack abroad. The King's nephews, Charles Louis and Rupert, on their return to The Hague where their mother lived in a house provided for her by the Prince of Orange, had taken service for the autumn in the Dutch armies engaged at that time in besieging the town of Breda, the frontier fortress which the Spaniards had captured twelve years before. The siege, long drawn out and full of incident, was the principal foreign news in England for several weeks. Many English volunteers fought in the Dutch forces, with the two Palatine princes, for the Protestant Cause against Spain. Several distinguished gentlemen were wounded; others behaved with conspicuous gallantry, and the Court at home hummed with their praises—wild Harry Wilmot dangerously wounded, gallant George Goring shot in the leg, brave Charles Lucas, first into the breach. The King thus faced increasing pressure to declare official war, and not leave it to individual Englishmen to redeem their nation's honour. The French ambassador, Bellièvre, who presented his credentials in the autumn, had come to complete the process by drawing England into offensive and defensive alliance with France and the Dutch against Spain. The French enjoyed the tacit support of the Vatican and the influence of Fr. George Con, the Papal agent at Court, would be exerted to help Bellièvre.

All this was watched with anxiety by Wentworth from Ireland, by Laud and Cottington in London. They knew the value of the King's agreement with Spain for the transport of bullion. Without the welcome silver from the Peruvian mines his finances would be hard to balance. Furthermore, peace alone could give his royal government the opportunities to establish itself beyond question. Wentworth was particularly anxious to avoid a war with Spain which would wreck his plans for the smooth and peaceful development of government in Ireland and at home. "God set us well over this brig o' dread," he wrote to the Archbishop. He meant the dread of a French alliance, not the dread of trouble in Scotland.

Lesser matters from time to time engaged the King's attention. He was perturbed at the wastefulness of his household; too many hangers-on, whole families of them, lived and ate free on the bounty of Whitehall. A Commission must be set up to inquire into this abuse. Then there were the Christmas masques in preparation; the one to be presented by the Queen and her ladies was to be exceptionally rich and beautiful. A large, temporary hall of fir-wood was being hastily erected to accommodate it; the King feared the smoke of candles for the new Rubens ceiling in the banqueting house.[29]

As to graver questions, the King was seriously distressed by the spread of Roman Catholicism and authorised the Archbishop to draft a proclamation forbidding his subjects to attend public mass at the chapels of foreign ambassadors. Partly as a result of Lady Newport's recent conversion, he set on foot a plan by which the eldest sons of Roman Catholic Lords were to be removed from their homes and educated under his eye at Court, thus preparing them for conversion to Anglican or, as he held, true Catholic doctrine. The scheme caused so much distress to many of his own and the Queen's friends that it was very soon abandoned. The Queen, indeed, regardless of caution or policy, arranged for her little flock of Court converts to take the sacrament together in her chapel at Christmas so that her friends could see how richly her efforts and her influence had worked.

The appearance at about this time of a book defending Anglican against Roman Catholic doctrine by a young Oxford scholar named Chillingworth, who had himself fallen at one time into the Roman error, gave great satisfaction to the King, who marked out its author for preferment.[30] Chillingworth's book, *The Religion of Protestants*, merited high favour for its serene and philosophic tolerance. On paper and in the minds of its best men the Anglican Church did indeed aim at a nobler and broader view of doctrine than that of any existing Church of the time, but broadness of doctrine which attacks the fanatic and narrow-minded with such zeal and relentlessness as that used by the King and the Archbishop is itself a tyranny. Chillingworth's noble words—" I seek not to offend any man, but for truth only "—sounded oddly against the background of silenced ministers, pilloried critics and resentful Scots.

The postponed Ship-money case was now before the Exchequer Court. Hampden and his friends had chosen their friend and colleague, the legal adviser of the Providence Company, Oliver St. John, to argue their case. St. John was a man of about forty who had been practising at the bar for a dozen years without attracting any particular notice. He had devoted much attention to constitutional law, and those who briefed him must have had occasion to admire his depth of knowledge in the political discussions which no doubt often followed the Company's meetings. The rest of the world was unprepared for the closely argued display of reason and erudition with which St. John opened his client's case. He developed two principal arguments, one general and one particular. The first was that if the King claimed the right to levy taxes on his subjects at will, the foundation of property itself was attacked and no man could possess anything but " at the goodness and mercy of the King " —a proposition evidently at variance with the accepted principles and practice of English law. His second argument referred back to the ruling of the judges that the King, in case of imminent peril to his subjects, could raise money without recourse to Parliament. But, as St. John with nice legal precision pointed out, there was no unusual peril when the Ship-money writ went out, and no pretence or excuse of it had been so much as hinted. " It appears not by anything in the writ that any war at all was proclaimed against any state." St. John's arguments, supported by whole batteries of precedents and quotations from statutes, lasted for two days. This might seem long enough, but Solicitor-General Littleton took four days to put the case for the Crown. Hampden's other lawyer, Holborne, then argued his client's case for six consecutive days. Attorney-General Bankes wound up for the King, taking three days to complete his arguments, in which he subtly combined his points of law with examples of the dangers already suffered and yet to be endured from the pirates who infested the seas. There could be grave dangers, he pointed out in answer to St. John's argument, without any such thing as a national war. This was true, but he did not explain why pirates, who were always a threat to English shipping, suddenly in 1636 had to be dealt with as an emergency.

The English passion for law enabled the audience to find these interminable arguments not only interesting but absorbing. Almost the whole of English history had been reviewed before the four of them had done; they cited statutes of all the Henries and Edwards, dredging up from the wreckage of the Hundred Years War, or the baronial struggles, this or that pearl of information about the levying of taxes; Bankes even cast back to the reign of King Egbert. There was very little in these arguments respecting broad principles, nothing whatever about right and wrong; no moral, no political indignation. The four honest, painful, learned men resembled for the greater part of the time nothing so much as a group of earnest archæologists, sieving with assiduity and without passion the dust of the past and selecting this or that recognisable fragment to prove their point. December was half spent before the arguments ended in the Exchequer Court. They continued with fervour in the eating houses of Westminster and the chambers and private dwellings of barristers and their friends. Politics apart, the Hampden case had raised a problem of fascinating complexity and interest. Certainly political passions were not silent; from Ireland the Lord Deputy Wentworth wrote in exasperation that he wished Hampden and his like could be " whipped home into their right senses." But political feeling about the case was at this time much more violent among the King's supporters than anywhere else. With the majority the Hampden case aroused not so much political indignation, as a vigorous concern about the proper interpretation of the law.

The four barons of the Exchequer, as the judges of that Court were called, were thoroughly perplexed. St. John and Holborne had produced precedents which troubled them—not morally, not politically, but legally. Whatever they felt on the broad principle of the King's rights, the technical aspects of the Ship-money writ, and of Hampden's case in particular, were far from clear. Littleton and Bankes had not been able to allay every doubt raised by Hampden's lawyers. This was a question that required consultation with all the judges. Judgment was postponed until the ensuing term; the case was transferred from the Exchequer to the special Court of Exchequer Chamber, and the judges of the King's Bench and the Common Pleas were required to consider and deliver their opinions upon it.

There may have been—probably was—a political motive in this decision. Lord Chief Baron Davenport, the principal Exchequer judge, was in an embarrassing position. He was a strong King's man and firmly believed in Charles's legal right to levy Ship-money. But the arguments for the defence had revealed to him a technical error in the writ directed to Hampden; he would therefore have felt compelled to pronounce in Hampden's favour. From discussions with his three colleagues he must have gathered that one of them, Denham, not only agreed on the technical question but was wavering altogether on the legality of Ship-money. The other two, Trevor and Weston, were strong King's men. This meant at best a division of the Exchequer judges two against two, with the Chief Baron giving judgment for Hampden—in effect a defeat for the Crown. It was very probably to avoid this that Davenport arranged for postponement and laid the Hampden case before all twelve judges.

Anxieties over this and other matters prevented the King from giving much attention that winter to the plan suggested to him by Captain Rainborough for ridding the Mediterranean entirely of pirates by using the English fleet to blockade Algiers. Rainborough's triumph on the Moroccan coasts in the summer was likely to remain a solitary success as the navy, in spite of recent expansion, was conspicuously failing to hold its own even in territorial waters. French and Spanish ships insulted English vessels at sea,[31] while Dutch shipmasters of Calvinist opinions successfully eluded the watch kept for them and unloaded parcels of forbidden religious literature on lonely parts of the Essex coast.[32] A Star Chamber decree prohibiting the printing and sale of unlicensed books made little difference to the dissemination of religious pamphlets. Some were secretly printed in England, more were printed in the Low Countries and smuggled over. A youth named John Lilburne, arrested on a charge of importing Bastwicke's pernicious book from Holland, was in prison awaiting his trial by the Star Chamber. He was the unlucky victim of whom an example was to be made, but he was only one of the many who had distributed forbidden books and were still doing so.

Newspapers from abroad had been prohibited early in the King's reign; no newspapers were authorised in England and the printing of news from Scotland was naturally forbidden. But the bolder Puritan booksellers circulated manuscript sheets containing the latest information about the Scottish dispute,[33] and sympathetic Londoners probably knew better what was going on in the north than did the King's English councillors, from whom he had so far concealed all details. Something more threatening to the King than the general sympathy of Puritan English for Calvinist Scots already existed. The dissident Scots had their agents and friends in England, while in the Low Countries exiled or visiting ministers, soldiers and merchants of both nations had for the last ten years drawn ever closer together, encouraged in this by the Dutch.

Only gradually did Charles come to admit that the Scottish business presented real difficulties in itself and was likely to become dangerously associated with the widespread Puritan opposition in England. In the circumstances, both the King and the Archbishop believed that severity alone would serve their purpose. The royal and episcopal authority must be exerted and examples must be made in both countries. The young Lilburne would be one; another whom Laud had in view was the headmaster of Westminster School, Dr. Lambert Osbaldeston, who had been indiscreet enough to correspond with the Bishop of Lincoln, the condemned and imprisoned Williams, and unlucky enough to have his letters found. In one of them he referred to " the little meddling hocus pocus," a person all too clearly identifiable as the Archbishop. Osbaldeston, on Christmas Eve, was still protesting that he could and would explain, but Laud was for making it a Star Chamber case and a serious one.[34]

In this atmosphere of righteous severity Lord Treasurer Traquair on his arrival with messages from the King's council in Scotland met with a cool reception. His clumsy efforts to blame the Scots bishops for provoking the crisis by hurrying matters too much greatly annoyed the King. So did the whole conduct of his council in Scotland. "We do no way approve the same," he wrote, "because your course herein hath been more derogatory to our authority than conducive to the true quiet of the country, for we can never conceive that the country is truly quiet when regal authority is infringed." He added to this reprimand a proclamation which the council was forthwith to issue. In this, the King declared that all those nobles who had dared to protest against the Service Book were worthy of his highest censure. If, however, they would immediately conform he would overlook their conduct, ascribing it rather to a " preposterous zeal " than to treasonable intent. But they must understand that in complete submission lay their only hope of mercy.[35]

The judges had begun at fortnightly intervals to give their opinions on the Hampden case; the first three spoke out strongly in the King's favour. Of these Robert Berkeley, on February 10th, 1638, was particularly eloquent. " The subjects of England," he declared, " are free men and not slaves "; but he went on to show that their freedom rested on the law, and that the law was, in its ultimate essence, the expression of the King's benevolent will. No conflict between King and law was imaginable. " Rex is lex," he said, " lex loquens, a living, a speaking, an acting law." [36] Seldom had the King's own view of his office been better expressed; he was the law, he was guardian and judge of his people's freedom. Berkeley's dictum matched well with the proclamation of mercy and the demand for unconditional surrender which the King had, in the same month, sent out to Scotland.

The King now dismissed his cares temporarily from his mind and went to Newmarket for a hunting holiday. He was displeased to find other people's dogs trespassing on his preserves, but an order for the destruction of all greyhounds or mongrels within ten miles of his Court set matters to rights. He had taken with him his giant, Muckle John, and his dwarf, Jeffrey Hudson, besides a large and cheerful retinue. After the days in the open air, the long evenings were passed pleasantly, with good food, good wine, chess and dice.[37]

These royal gaieties were unseasonable. For in Scotland, towards the latter end of that raw February of 1638 was celebrated " the great marriage day of the nation with God." To that wedding feast, so huge with consequences, King Charles was not invited.

Traquair's return to Scotland with the King's orders was the signal for which the opposition had been waiting. On February 20th, 1638, the council met, at Stirling, in miserable spirits, to issue the King's proclamation. Sir Thomas Hope dissociated himself from the action; Lord Lorne was conspicuously absent; nearly all the bishops sent excuses, fearing, not without cause, the angry crowds which had gathered in Stirling.[38]

In theory the contents of the proclamation and the council's intention to publish it at Stirling were kept secret to lessen the chance of an organised demonstration. But the opposition were well-informed, possibly by Traquair. Their leaders with about a thousand followers faced the King's herald at Stirling when he read out the proclamation and protested instantly. The council could think of no more dignified action than to send for the principal leaders, Rothes and Montrose, and implore them to disperse the crowd before a riot could break out. They could hardly have revealed more clearly their own weakness and the strength of their opponents.[39]

Rothes and Montrose, quietly triumphant, dispersed the demonstrators and transferred their attention from Stirling to Edinburgh where, forty-eight hours later, the farce of reading the King's proclamation was again enacted. This time the opposition lords had gathered an even larger crowd, and formal protests were accompanied by stirring speeches from the leaders. Montrose, to be seen and heard the better, climbed on top of an empty barrel. "Jamie," said Rothes, "ye will never be at rest till ye be lifted up there above the rest in three fathom of rope."[40]

In the troubled years since the Reformation the Scots had known many protests and popular demonstrations. Deeply imbued with tradition and by nature legal-minded, they did not act, in February 1638, without seeking for a precedent. They had found it—Warriston and others—in the year 1580. In that year the nobility and ministers had compelled the boy King

James VI to subscribe a Confession of Faith which ought to have established Calvinist worship and Calvinist organisation in Scotland for good. The cry in February 1638 was not for new things, but for a return to 1580.

Warriston had pondered the Confession for the past four months. He was joined in his deliberations by Alexander Henderson and another able minister, the narrow and arrogant David Dickson. These three seem to have been chiefly responsible for the document which became the manifesto and foundation of the party, the National Covenant. In effect it was a restatement of the Confession of 1580 buttressed by a protest against all that had since been done to alter true religion in Scotland. The closing paragraph was a defiant vow to maintain the faith.

" From the knowledge and conscience of our duty to God, to our King and country, without any worldly respect or inducement, we promise and swear by the great name of the Lord our God to continue in the profession and obedience of the aforesaid religion; that we shall defend the same and resist all those contrary errors and corruptions according to our vocation, and to the utmost of that power that God hath put into our hands, all the days of our life."

Six days after the scene at the Mercat Cross, on Wednesday, February 28th, 1638, the principal leaders of the revolt met in Greyfriars Kirk; Henderson preached a sermon, Warriston read out the lengthy document and the congregation of lords and gentlemen, led by the Earl of Sutherland, filed up to set their hands to it. On Thursday the gentry and the ministers were still signing; on Friday it was the turn of the Edinburgh citizens. They crowded in, overflowing the little church, gathering without in the churchyard.[41]

In the next weeks copies of the Covenant were carried over all Scotland, and in one kirk after another, in burgh and hamlet, through all the southern parts of the land, men set their hands to the sacred bond. " I have seen more than a thousand all at once lifting up their hands, and the tears falling down from their

eyes," wrote a thankful minister.[42] In Warriston's words,
" this spiritual plague of Aegyptian darkness covering the light
of the Gospel " had lifted at last and the Scots celebrated " the
great marriage day of this nation with God." [43]

Archbishop Spottiswoode fled: " All that we have done
these thirty years past is thrown down at once," the poor old
man lamented as he journeyed to London and an exile's grave in
Westminster Abbey.[44] The council at Stirling, in a despatch so
sulkily conceived as to be almost in itself a new revolt against
the King, declared themselves powerless to mitigate the storm
provoked by his ill-considered policy.[45] " The fearful wrath of
God " had come upon the land.

BOOK II CHAPTER I REFERENCES

1. Laud, *Works*, VI, i, 42.
2. *Harleian Miscellany*, IV, pp. 17–22; C.S.P.D. 1637, p.287.
3. The almost indecipherable complexity of the case against Williams is well summarised in B. Dew Roberts: *Mitre and Musket*, London, 1938; for his condition
   in the Tower *see* Knowler, II, 167, and Hacket, *Scrinia Reserata*.
4. *Bankes MSS.*, 63/62, 63.
5. *C.S.P.D.*, 1637, p. 299.
6. *Register of the Privy Council of Scotland*, 1637, pp. 483, 484, 490.
7. *Ibid.*, p. 509.
8. Baillie, *Letters, Bannatyne Club*, Edinburgh, 1841, I, pp. 21, 41.
9. Laud, *Works*, III, p. 229; *C.S.P.D.*, 637, p. 355.
10. Rothes, *Affairs of the Kirk of Scotland, Bannatyne Club*, Edinburgh, 1830, pp. 8–9.
11. *Register P.C. Scot.*, 1637, pp. 529, 699.
12. *C.S.P.D.*, 1637, p. 420.
13. *Ibid.*, p. 301.
14. *H.M.C.*, XII, iv, p. 204.
15. *Strafford MSS.*, X, folio 251.
16. *Ibid.*, Vol. III, Wentworth to Cottington, August 28th, 1637; Vol. X, Wentworth
    to Cottington, August 21st; *C.S.P. Ireland*, 1633–47, p. 169.
17. *Strafford MSS.*, VII, Wentworth to Laud, October 18th, 1637.
18. Knowler, II, 117.
19. *H.M.C. Report, XII*, ii, p. 161; *Report, X*, iii, p. 166; *C.S.P.D.*, 1637, p. 431;
    Knowler, II, pp. 118, 129.
20. Knowler, II, 128.
21. *Gordon Albion*, p. 213.
22. *Register P.C. Scot.*, 1637, pp. 537 ff.; Rothes, p. 20; *Ancram and Lothian Letters*, ed.

Laing, Edinburgh, 1875, I, pp. 94–5; Gordon of Rothiemay, *History of Scottish Affairs*, *Spalding Club*, Aberdeen, 1841, p. 23; Warriston, *Diary*, *Scottish History Society*, Edinburgh, 1911, I, p. 271.

23. Guthry, p. 31; Wilson, p. 12; Burnet, *History*, p. 47; the *Scottish Historical Review* XXII. pp. 24 ff. gives the text of a protest to the Council dated October 18th 1637, and signed among others by Montrose. This is the first time that his name occurs and is a few weeks earlier than the date usually given for his joining the party.

24. Warriston. *Diary*. pp. 355, 357, 362.

25. Hope's *Diary*, and Warriston's *Diary* for these months make the opinions and sympathies of Lorne and Hope clear beyond doubt.

26. Hope, *Diary*, *Bannatyne Club*, Edinburgh, 1843, p. 89.

27. Rothes, p. 44.

28. Warriston, *Diary*, p. 289; *Breadalbane MSS.*, *Letters*, 1636–9, Nos. 703, 706, 709.

29. *C.S.P.D.*, 1637; Knowler, II, pp. 130, 140–1; *C.S.P. Ven*, 1636–9, p. 374.

30. Knowler, II, pp. 133, 147.

31. *Strafford MSS.*, Vol XVII, Northumberland to Wentworth, January 26th, 1638.

32. *C.S.P.D.*, 1637–8, pp. 365-6.

33. *C.S.P.D.*, 1637–8, p. 27.

34. *Ibid.*, p. 377.

35. *Register P.C. Scot.*, 1638, pp. 4, 15, 16.

36. *State Trials*, ed. Cobbett, London, 1809, III, p. 1098.

37. *H.M.C.*, XII, ii, p. 176; *Portland MSS.*, III, p. 52.

38. Rothes, 65; *Register of P.C. Scot.*, 1638, pp. 3–4.

39. Rothes, *loc cit.*; Guthry, p. 33.

40. Rothes, 66–7; Gordon of Rothiemay, 33.

41. All contemporary accounts agree that the Covenant was signed inside the Church, but the venerable Edinburgh tradition that it was signed on a tombstone in the churchyard may perhaps derive from memories of the waiting crowds outside.

42. Livingstone, *Life*, ed. Tweedie, *Wodrow Society*, Edinburgh, 1845, p. 102.

43. Warriston, *Diary*, pp. 265, 322–3.

44. Guthry, p. 35.

45. *Register P.C. Scot.*, 1638, pp. 9–12.

CHAPTER TWO

SHIP-MONEY

March – June 1638

IN England, spring came early that year, bringing the hedgerows out in a rush; tulips, even in northern gardens, were in flower before the end of March and " apricocks and plum trees . . . full of blossom." [1]   In this mild season the King became unwillingly aware of the disquieting turn that his fortunes had so suddenly taken.

The Covenanters—the name sprang into being within a few weeks of the Covenant—acted fast. The text of the Covenant, carried to London by an active young minister, was known to the King's opponents sooner than it was known to the King. Accounts of the Scots revolt spread rapidly to its many sympathisers. As for the Covenant, " the written copies are in all men's hands in London," complained Laud to Wentworth. [2] Even in the precincts of Whitehall there were those who sided with the rebels. The jester, Archie Armstrong, growing indiscreet in drink, called Archbishop Laud a " monk, rogue and traitor." He was packed off to gaol, and proceedings in the Star Chamber were contemplated, but abandoned at Laud's own request. [3]

The minuscule revolt of a tipsy jester was something that the King could suppress but he suspected that Archie had been encouraged by those of greater importance at Court or in London. Defiance of the royal authority was everywhere growing bolder. Petitions against the collection of Ship-money had reached the King from Lincolnshire, Northamptonshire

and the borders of Wales; the sheriffs reported that the difficulties of collecting the tax were almost insuperable in Somerset,
Hampshire, Surrey, Berkshire, Huntingdon, Norfolk, Worcester,
Derby, Nottingham, Northumberland, and in central Wales.
In Norfolk the resistance was exceptionally ingenious: when the
sheriff tried to distrain the cattle of those who would not pay,
their neighbours took the beasts into their own herds and made it
impossible for the sheriff's men to identify them. Even if the
sheriff's men managed to seize a few head of cattle they could
raise no money on them, for no one would buy property which
had been seized in this way.[4]

This obstinate and widespread defiance of the King's authority in England and Wales was as dangerous as anything that
had happened in Scotland. Rhymes and pasquinades against the
King and his policy and the most outspoken criticism were heard
everywhere in London. That the rebels of both nations were
likely to be in sympathy with each other was clear to any dispassionate observer; the King, the Venetian agent in London
reported home to his government, would never be able to put
down the revolt in Scotland with the help of his English subjects,
more than half of whom were themselves Calvinists.[5]

The directors of the Providence Company, using the half-
permission the King had given them to assert themselves against
Spanish attack, had been discussing the future of their depressed
and precarious settlements in the Caribbean. They had inter-
viewed a Scottish soldier of fortune, Lord Forbes, a rough
adventurer who had seen service by sea and land on the Baltic
shores with the Kings of Denmark and Sweden. But the
Providence Company had not at the moment the funds to employ
him about their business with Spain.[6]

Another Scottish soldier of fortune, Alexander Leslie, also
passed through London at this time. He was on his way home
from the German wars where he was a marshal in the armies of
the Queen of Sweden. An officer of so high a rank may well
have had friends and business in London on his way to Scotland.
Who and what they were is uncertain, but news of some kind he

brought with him from England when, at the end of March, he regained his native land. He saw much of the Covenanters, especially Rothes, who contemplated marrying his daughter to him. England and Scotland vibrated already with rumours of war.[7]

The feeling in the South and West of Scotland grew more violent with the advancing year. No one in those parts dared open his mouth to say a word in favour of the bishops or the King, for the people " possessed with a bloody devil," as one of their more temperate ministers put it, would set upon anyone who did so, and one Anglican clergyman, innocently travelling in Galloway, had all his clothes and baggage " torn in fritters " and barely escaped alive. Most of the bishops fled the country, not without cause; Sydserf, one of the most hated who was alleged to wear a crucifix round his neck, was three times stoned by an angry crowd. Known sympathisers were dogged in the streets of Edinburgh with angry mutterings and swords half drawn. The more extreme Covenanters were already clamouring for the expulsion from the Kingdom of all who refused to sign. There was to be no " banding, minching and carving by halves in God's cause."[8]

An indignant royalist who had seen the crowds signing the Covenant, copies of which were now in constant motion throughout the kingdom, declared that children of ten and beggarly rascals were allowed to set their hands to it; and certainly by this time many signed out of fear rather than conviction. Greater opposition existed in some men's hearts than appeared on the surface, but in general the tide of religious fervour ran strong and deep. With true gratitude hundreds attended Greyfriars' Kirk for the celebration of the Lord's Supper " purely", after twenty years during which the idolatrous habit of kneeling had been insisted on. The minister, though gravely hampered by a heavy cold, preached at great length on the text " When the Lord turned again the captivity of Sion." " Ye will find a very near parallel betwixt Israel and this Church," mused Warriston, " the only two sworn nations to the Lord."[9]

The King had sent for Traquair, Roxburgh and Lorne to report to him in England, but he confided in none save the Archbishop, and his interviews with these Scottish councillors were matters for speculation only. Lord Lorne, whose own tenants were said to be most "forward and hearty" for the Covenant, was believed to have expressed himself very freely to the King, who was evidently displeased with him.[10] Lorne's friends, kinsmen and clansmen, with touching faith in his influence and wisdom, cherished for some weeks the illusion that, by speaking plainly, their chief had made the King see that he could not with peace and safety compel the Scots to accept the Prayer Book and had induced him to change his policy. The truth was far otherwise; Charles had even considered placing Lorne under arrest. The old Earl of Argyll was credited with having told the King that unless his son were put under lock and key he would "wind him a pirn."

Lorne and his fellow councillors were allowed to go home. In England Charles had other troubles. Owing to his attempt to sell to Newcastle the monopoly in coal transport, a monopoly resisted by the London shipowners, the people of the South had had a chilly winter, short of their favourite fuel; the lifting of the monopoly in the warm spring did not at once mollify them.[12] Sectaries and fanatics or the merely demented continued to give trouble; a religious tailor in Hosier Lane denounced the King as guilty of blood and the bishops as false prophets and was led away protesting by a scandalised parish constable.[13]

In April eight ships carrying emigrants to New England were forbidden to sail; after a week's delay and discussion, the King withdrew his prohibition for this particular fleet but soon after gave out a proclamation that all further sailings were to be by special licence only. Sir Ferdinando Gorges, veteran survivor of the Elizabethan age and president of the New England Company, petitioned the King in eloquent protest; did not the Romans, Spanish and Dutch grow great by colonies, and should not England do the like? Lord Cottington, the Chancellor of the Exchequer, dismissed the petition in a contemptuous minute:

" Romans, Spanish and Dutch did and do conquer, not plant tobacco and Puritanism only, like fools." His opinion tersely summarised that of the King, who not long after was rating Lord Dorset because of rumours of Puritan practices among the settlements he had financed in Bermuda.[14]

Englishmen overseas and foreigners at home—both gave trouble, and the Walloon congregation in Norwich were again an object of attention that spring. Bishop Wren, in accordance with Laud's policy for the suppression of these communities, had turned them out of the episcopal chapel which they had used for many years. Sympathisers in Norwich had come to the rescue of the homeless congregation by giving them the use of a little church in the city. The Bishop now presented them with a bill, for alleged damage done to his chapel during their occupation, which their funds could hardly cover.[15] The small, persistent persecution went on.

The spring's most serious event for the King was the pronouncement in April of two more of the judges on the Hampden case; both gave judgment against the King. It cannot have been wholly unexpected, for these two, Sir George Croke and Sir Richard Hutton, had always doubted the legality of Ship-money, but the King and Court had probably not anticipated statements quite so decisive. The venerable Croke with great emphasis accepted the arguments put forward by Oliver St. John. " Royal power," he said, " is to be used in cases of necessity and imminent danger, when ordinary courses will not avail ... but in a time of peace and no extreme necessity, legal courses must be used and not royal power." Hutton, elaborating the same arguments a fortnight later, asserted that, except in the emergency of war, subjects cannot by law be made to part with what is their own merely on a demand from the King.[16] This was as much as to say that *Rex* in Croke and Hutton's opinion was not *lex*, whatever Sir Robert Berkeley might have averred to the contrary.

Midway through April, before the pronouncement of Hutton but after that of Croke, while the Inns of Court laughed over someone's inevitable pun (" The King has Ship-money by hook but not by Croke "), the young Lilburne had been punished for distributing forbidden religious literature and had been the object of a new popular demonstration. He was a great deal younger than Prynne, Burton and Bastwicke, came of a respectable yeoman family in the North and had little or no learning. He had neat, unimpressive features, distinguished by fine eyes; was small, excitable, evidently delicate; talkative rather than eloquent. There was nothing gloomy about Lilburne's Puritan fanaticism; his manner was lively, and his clothes (within the limits of his humble purse) were trim and sparkish.

The Star Chamber imposed a savage sentence, and on April 18th, 1638, he was whipped from the Fleet to Westminster, where he was to stand in the pillory. The crowds which gathered round him during this painful procession were sympathetic, although some of those closest to him unreasonably asked him for a speech, a testimony of the Lord, as he staggered along. He told them with difficulty, for he was breathless and suffering greatly, that he would speak in the pillory. The promise, rumoured through the crowds, reached Westminster, where the Court of Star Chamber was in session, some minutes ahead of Lilburne himself. Judging by the size of the crowd in Palace Yard that another demonstration, like that for Prynne, Burton and Bastwicke, might take place, the councillors assembled in the Star Chamber took an unusual step. They sent a messenger to parley with Lilburne. A merciful convention allowed him a few minutes to recover before he was put in the pillory; during this interval while he sat, caked with dust and blood, trying to get his breath, a gentleman approached him from the Star Chamber telling him that he would be spared the pillory if he would humbly confess his fault. Lilburne by this time had got his breath again; he refused the offer, at some length.

The King's councillors, looking down on the scene in Palace Yard, saw with indignation that he not only addressed the people, but with acrobatic ingenuity distributed three copies of the offending book which he had secreted about his person.

They sent down to have him gagged but by that time the harm had been done.

When Lilburne reached the Fleet again he found that the Council had given orders that no one might have access to him. He was himself penniless; without the help of friends, he was deprived of medical care and forced to rely on the food which the gaoler provided. Bedding and fresh water had, of course, to be paid for and were therefore not for such as he. After a month of this, when hunger and discomfort were assumed to have lowered his spirits, he was sent for and questioned on the speech he had made. Attorney-General Bankes, who conducted the inquiry, was a humane man and did not bully or shout at the hungry, feverish, unshaven prisoner before him. Lilburne faced him—he would have faced anyone—with undiminished fire. The Lord, so far from deserting him, had marvellously comforted him in all his sufferings. He repeated the substance of his pillory speech with pride, refused to retract a word, and when the interrogation was handed to him to sign, he grasped the pen and, leaning heavily upon it, wrote—"This I will seal with my dearest blood by me John Lilburne." [17]

While Lilburne suffered and the Hampden judgments continued to be the talk of Westminster a remarkable event took place in Ireland. The King's Deputy in Dublin had the Lord Chancellor of Ireland arrested. Here was another conflict between *Rex* and *lex*, but Wentworth's friends felt that he might have waited until the Scottish storm had subsided before stirring up new trouble in Ireland. Lord Chancellor Loftus had powerful friends in England; why make more enemies for the King's government when its need was for friends, especially among lawyers? [18]

Wentworth saw the matter with different eyes. No time, he thought, was so right as the present for a demonstration of royal authority, attacked as it was both in Scotland and in England. Hutton's judgment in the Hampden case distressed him the more because the judge was a Yorkshireman and an old friend, to whose son Wentworth had given one of his sisters in marriage. He argued with him by letter, courteously but firmly. It was no part of a subject's duty, he said, to think out "curious questions" or brood on "vain flatteries of imaginary liberty." The King's ordinance, he said, outdoing even Sir Robert Berkeley's *Rex lex*, is "no other than the ordinance of God." [19] Something like this he must have had in mind when in April 1638, by his attack on the Lord Chancellor of Ireland, he set out to win a resounding victory for the King's prerogative and redeem in one of Charles's three kingdoms the losses it had sustained in the other two.

The Lord Chancellor, Adam Loftus, had in his own and his friends' interests, shamefully abused his position, for the last twenty years. He had at first been cautious with the keen-eyed Deputy, but had soon reverted to his earlier evil practices, such as trying cases in which he was personally concerned *in camera*, and evading the Deputy's and the King's authority whenever it suited him to do so. One of his victims, a farmer, John Fitzgerald, whom he had dispossessed and wrongfully imprisoned, appealed direct to the Deputy for justice. Wentworth, by taking his case over into the prerogative Court of Castle Chamber, of which he himself was President, precipitated a crisis which he had seen coming for a long time. Wentworth had two strong reasons for his act; the more important was the assertion of the King's right to override other courts, the less important was to get justice for Fitzgerald. Loftus also had two reasons for opposing Wentworth: as an experienced lawyer he believed it his duty to combat the encroachments of the prerogative courts; and, he did not want the facts about the Fitzgerald case brought to light.

When he was called upon to answer to Fitzgerald's accusation before the Court of Castle Chamber, Loftus tried to laugh it off. At a stormy meeting of the council Wentworth pressed the point, Loftus grew noisily rude and Wentworth ordered him out of the room. While he fumed in a neighbouring corridor, the council unanimously suspended him for contempt of court—an unusual offence with which to charge a Lord Chancellor. Wentworth, always too stubborn in small details, insisted that he should hear his sentence kneeling; "I will die first," said Loftus. Weeks of wrangling ensued during which the furious old gentleman held up the business of the realm by hiding the Great Seal, saying that he would give it up to no one but the King.[20]

Wentworth took no notice of one irrelevant but dangerous weapon which Loftus might use against him. The Chancellor cordially disliked his own son and had tried to defraud his daughter-in-law of her marriage settlement; this daughter-in-law, a beautiful and intelligent woman, enjoyed the Deputy's indiscreet but innocent admiration. It was, therefore, easy to start a scandal by hinting that the Lord Chancellor had been overthrown to please his wicked daughter-in-law and to serve the private ends of the adulterous Wentworth.

The tittle-tattlers at Whitehall preferred this version of the story and it was soon widely accepted. The King, while far from suspecting any such motive, was worried at the prospect of the duel between the Sovereign and the Chancellor to which Wentworth had committed him; although he supported his Deputy, it was with evident hesitation. He did, however, command Loftus to hand over the Great Seal to the Deputy and at the royal summons the Chancellor obeyed, formally, on his knees;[21] he had decided to abandon his defiant pose for that of a broken old man wrongfully oppressed by a ruthless tyrant.

Wentworth had triumphed in Dublin so effectively that he treated himself to one of his brief holidays and went off, that warm Whitsuntide, for a few days deer-hunting at his new park at Coshaw where he greatly enjoyed himself, although the midges were troublesome.[22]

The larger midges at Whitehall were also swarming and biting. The King's eldest son would be eight years old at the end of May and his father had decided to create him Prince of Wales and give him an establishment of his own. A place at Court was a coveted reward, and Charles intended that the little Prince's household should give honourable satisfaction to a number of the nobility and gentry. Unfortunately, the appointments were so widely canvassed for so long that in the end more hopes were dashed than gratified. The Scottish business had decided the King against any great expense, and the new household was planned in a disappointingly cautious manner. Charles showed his keen displeasure with the entire Scottish nation by appointing only Englishmen to attend his son. This hurt the feelings of the loyal Scots at Court and still left too few places to satisfy all the English claimants. Even the Earl of Newcastle, the Prince's new governor, was not content when he found that he had to share his kitchen and table with the Prince's tutor, the amiable but humbly born Bishop of Chichester, Dr. Brian Duppa.[23] The sallow, lively little Prince alone set a good example by accepting everything and everyone with the gayest good humour.

Other public and Court appointments caused envy or criticism. Lord Holland, who had absurdly hoped to be made Lord High Admiral, retired from Whitehall with a diplomatic illness to nurse his chagrin when the Earl of Northumberland was—very properly—preferred to him.[24] The valuable post of secretary to the Queen, eagerly coveted because of the indirect patronage its owner could wield, went unexpectedly to a man almost unknown at Court. Sir John Winter, nephew to the Earl of Worcester, was a Roman Catholic, which made him doubly welcome to the Queen, but caused inevitable criticism elsewhere. It did not escape public notice that he was of the same family as one of the principal conspirators in the Gunpowder Plot.[25]

The true reason for the appointment was not religious. Winter was one of the richest men in the country and had already made generous advances to the King. His lands in the Forest of Dean were rich in iron and coal, both well exploited. In bringing this powerful industrialist into the innermost circle of the Court the King was obliquely pursuing his policy of drawing the principal industries of the country into the orbit of the Crown.

Something of the same plan was in his mind when he embarked this summer in pursuit of one more mirage. For several years now, the Earl of Bedford and a company of shareholders had been attempting to reclaim the fens round Ely. The resentment of the fenlanders had found expression earlier in the year in petitions to the King, and in the summer rioting broke out. Untimely rain and the interference of the fenmen badly damaged the drainage works, and the whole scheme looked like coming to a standstill. The King who had long regretted the lease of the fen country to a private company, now stepped in and, as if in response to the outcry of the fenmen, took over the scheme himself. His intention was not to yield to the fenmen but to complete the profitable scheme. He was encouraged by the engineer Vermuyden to believe that soon there would be a fruitful plain where now were only reeds and waters, and in the midst of it a new town to be called Charlemont.[26]

This was the last of the King's happy dreams. Reality was fast catching up with him, although he did his best to shut it out by keeping the deplorable affairs of Scotland as secret as possible. He consulted with none of his council except Laud, and his discontented advisers went about the Court shrugging their shoulders in open annoyance at their exclusion and declaring that they washed their hands of the royal policy.[27] Although the Archbishop was at least admitted to the King's confidence, his advice was not taken, for when Charles decided to send a Commissioner into Scotland with powers to deal with the Covenanters, his choice fell on the Marquis of Hamilton, an appointment the wisdom of which the Archbishop gravely doubted.[28]

Hamilton was a bad choice but he was the only possible candidate for the task. No Englishman would have been able to handle the Scots at that time without increasing their antagonism. A Scotsman therefore had to be chosen, and one loyal to the King and possessed of enough prestige and power in his own right to impress his troublesome countrymen. Lord Lorne, the most powerful man on the Privy Council in Scotland, was ruled out because he had already shown his antagonism to the new Service Book; the only devoted loyalists on that dubious and divided body were lesser nobility who lacked the needful authority. The bare truth was that only three men could be considered: the Marquis of Huntly, the Duke of Lennox and the Marquis of Hamilton. Huntly, the greatest man in the north-east and the head of the Gordon clan, stood haughtily aloof from the Covenant and was in theory a devoted King's man. " You may take my head from my shoulders," he was to say a few months later, " but not my heart from my sovereign." He was good at a phrase. What else he was good at, no one well knew. He had spent much of his life in France as Captain of the French King's famous Scots Guard and had returned to Scotland only two years before on his father's death. His father had been a Roman Catholic; his mother, who was still alive, also practised that religion, as did many of his clan. He himself appears to have belonged to no very well-defined faith and, although his wife and children were Protestant, he gave countenance and protection to the old religion throughout his territories. His wife was a sister of Lorne, and Huntly had mortgaged a great part of his estates to his brother-in-law, without fully extricating himself from the quicksands of debt. Had he been appointed King's Commissioner it would have been difficult for him to set foot in Edinburgh where his creditors abounded. His embarrassments made him a figure of contempt in spite of his ancient name and handsome presence. " Three parts of his name is decayed," Rothes had sneered, " I would not give a salt citron for him." [29]

Next came young Lennox. The King trusted him and knew him well, and he had qualities which might have served better than Hamilton's, although his experience was small and his intellect unremarkable. But, like Huntly, he had too many ties with the Roman Catholics; one brother was a priest, another had just married a Roman Catholic bride, and rumour at this moment credited Lennox himself with being a secret convert. [30] That left only Hamilton; with a kind of accidental inevitability, this most disastrous of all King Charles's friends took up his position. This blundering, ambitious, complicated and stupid man was neither as bad nor as powerful as his contemporaries thought him. Opportunity made a fool and accident made a villain of him, as little by little in the next eleven years, he became, in popular opinion, the arch-traitor:

> He that three Kingdoms made one flame,
> Blasted their beauty, burnt their frame—
> Rather than he his ends would miss
> Betray'd his master with a kiss,
> And buried in one common fate
> The glory of our Church and State . . .[31]

The fierce indictments of contemporary opinion have long since lost their force. Bishop Burnet, in an accomplished apologia,[32] written many years later, covered the naked failure of Hamilton with a cloak of decency. Traditional history has, to a great extent, forgotten him. Other figures, in Scotland and England, tower above him—Argyll, Montrose, Strafford, Rupert, Hyde, the King himself. It is easy to forget and startling to rediscover in the voluble writings of contemporaries for how long, like a Colossus, Hamilton bestrode the political scene.

At this time he was in his early thirties, a rather fine-looking man, with a stately manner and ponderous way of speech which impressed and amused the King. He had been Charles's page as a boy, had been something of a favourite and had been married into the all-powerful Buckingham connection. He was restless and ambitious but with a native caution which held him back from dangerous ventures; he would have liked to play a heroic part and had once raised and led troops to assist the Protestant Cause in Germany, but he never got them to any scene of action, and his Swedish and German allies had complained of his incompetence so loudly that he had had to be withdrawn. Hamilton, undiscouraged, still believed himself to be an excellent soldier and the King shared his opinion, for

Charles was truly attached to him, with that rare, deep, tenacious friendship of his, blind to faults.

Hamilton not only believed himself a soldier; he believed himself a diplomatist. His mind had a purposeless subtlety; he concealed from his left hand what his right hand was doing, though there was usually no reason whatever why he should. The ingenuity and scope of his political schemes would have done credit to Machiavelli had any master-plan given them coherence. There was no plan; beyond his personal prejudices and his conviction of his own importance, he had neither guidance nor goal. Some negative and some positive virtues even his enemies allowed him. He was good-tempered, he was not cruel; his dependants thought him " one of the best masters to vassals and servants that our kingdoms afforded," [33] and he was consistently civil to his inferiors, an unusual virtue at that time. Hamilton was appointed on May 8th and on the same day both Charles and he sent letters into Scotland. The King wrote to his council there to meet at Dalkeith on June 8th to receive his Commissioner. Hamilton wrote to his friends and tenants in Scotland to meet him on June 5th at Haddington: he would show the Covenanting leaders that the King's Commissioner could command as large a following as they.[34]

Hamilton's preparations for his northern journey were interrupted by the sudden death of his wife. He had married her as a very young man much against his will, and the indifference with which the Court appears to have taken her death suggests that there was little pretence of love between them. Burnet asserts that he learnt to value her too late and was remorseful for his past neglect. It seems possible, for although several marriages were later proposed to him, he took no second wife. One other enigma presents itself in the study of this strange man. At the time of his wife's death he had three little sons, as well as two daughters. In the course of the next two years, and in the midst of Hamilton's political troubles, his three sons died, one after another. These deaths, like that of his wife, aroused little contemporary comment. What lies behind this reticence we do not know but if Hamilton can never be a tragic figure, he might be, on closer knowledge, a pathetic one.

When Hamilton was chosen to go to Scotland as Commissioner he had sense enough to feel dismayed and, with forethought for his own future, asked the King to give him his personal assurance that, whatever the outcome, he would not in any way suffer in his favour.[35] This point once settled, he spent a week in his master's company, discussing the policy to be pursued. The King's instructions were clear. Only one concession was to be made; Charles would permit the temporary suspension of his order to use the new Prayer Book, and he would receive petitions from his subjects about it, but in return he commanded that the Covenant be utterly repudiated and all copies surrendered at once. Hamilton had his authority to dismiss unsatisfactory or disloyal members of the council, to arrest any of the King's subjects who made public protestations, to bribe the Covenanters one against another if necessary, and to disperse the crowds by force. In the last resort he could proclaim the rebellious lords to be traitors. "You shall declare," so ran the King's instructions, "that if there be not sufficient strength within the Kingdom to force the refractory to obedience, power shall come from England, and that myself will come in person with them, being resolved to hazard my life rather than to suffer authority to be contemned." [36]

The threat of force could hardly, as things stood, be implemented, but as Hamilton travelled northward in the stormy wet weather which had succeeded the too early spring he summoned the sheriffs of the English counties and ordered them, to see that the local trained bands throughout the summer assembled for military exercises at least twice a week.[37] It was a first move to furnish the royal authority with essential force.

In London the law term drew to a close, not without events of some significance for the King. The ill-timed zeal of his supporters could be as troublesome to the King as the insolences of his opponents. A crack-brained clergyman, Thomas Harrison, marched into the Court of Common Pleas when Hutton was presiding and "suddenly and very abruptly said with a loud voice 'I accuse Mr. Justice Hutton of High Treason.'" The incident made something of a stir but it chiefly drew attention to Hutton's pronouncement against Ship-money which the King would rather have forgotten. Poor Mr. Harrison kept Whitsuntide in the Fleet to punish him for his indiscretion.[38]

Harrison's offence in accusing one of the judges was in effect an insult to the King's Majesty, and whatever Charles felt about Hutton's views on Ship-money, it was necessary to take action against Harrison. His case came up in the Star Chamber at the same time as that of a baronet, Sir Richard Wiseman, who had accused the Lord Keeper of bribery. The Star Chamber condemned Harrison to a fine of £5,000 and a public apology. Wiseman, whose offence was considerably more serious, received a much heavier sentence; he lost his baronet's title and was condemned to stand in the pillory and to pay a fine of £10,000.[39]

Both sentences, and especially Wiseman's, were intended to vindicate the reputation of the King's justice, but neither of them particularly interested the London populace or the Inns of Court. Harrison's views were not popular and Wiseman, who had presumably been driven a little crazy by unsuccessful litigation, had long been a familiar nuisance round the Courts, with his real or illusory troubles and wild accusations. The Lord Keeper, Coventry, who was the object of the slanders for which he suffered, was an old, quiet, respectable figure, who had risen under the late King James, had held office since the beginning of the reign, and had exercised on the whole a moderating influence on the King's policy.

One other Star Chamber sentence of some importance concluded the session. Christopher Pickering, a Roman Catholic, had boasted that the King was a secret convert, with other damaging allegations, which his unkindly neighbours had reported to higher authority. His follies, or rather the report of them, came at a timely moment, for they gave the Court of Star Chamber an opportunity to demonstrate that Puritans were not the only objects of its attentions. The hapless Pickering was condemned to suffer in his single person all the rigours that had been inflicted on Prynne and Lilburne separately; in this way Londoners were to have ocular demonstration that Roman Catholic subjects who libelled the King were no more spared than any others.[40] This piece of policy failed of its purpose. The illogical Londoners took very little notice of Pickering and what befell him, while the fate of Prynne and his fellows remained lodged in their biased memories.

Before the courts rose, the last of the judges gave their opinions on Ship-money. Nothing so effective as the pronouncements of Croke and Hutton was to be hoped or feared from the others. Denham was too ill to appear in court but sent a written opinion in favour of Hampden. Davenport and Bramston both made it clear that they upheld the legality of Ship-money but had to pronounce for Hampden in this particular case because the writ issued to him had a technical defect. Jones pronounced for the King and so, naturally, did Finch at tedious length.

The King had won by a majority of seven to five. The judgment pronounced by Davenport and Bramston showed that the majority for the legality of Ship-money itself—as distinct from the legality of the particular writ to Hampden—was nine to three. The Court might have regarded this as a victory but they were not quite so blind as to do so. The arguments of Oliver St. John on his client's behalf and the measured, emphatic pronouncements of two highly respected judges far outweighed the simple arithmetic of the King's majority. In June, Attorney-General Bankes announced the official result of Rex *v.* Hampden: the King had won, the legality of Ship-money was established. Bankes knew very well, as did every thinking lawyer of the King's party, that the supposed victory was a disastrous defeat.

How far the King himself recognised the truth of what had happened remains doubtful, but his customary calm was ruffled. He looked anxious and preoccupied, was hunting less often than usual and had almost entirely given up his other summer pastimes, tennis and pell-mell.[41] But his royal spirit recoiled from any policy of conciliation and he resented pessimism in his advisers. His natural desire was to assert his authority the more emphatically, to challenge where he was challenged, and to overthrow. He had already decided on that course for Scotland. On June 11th, two days after Finch had made his pronouncement on Ship-money, Charles was writing to Hamilton in Scotland: "I expect not anything can reduce that people but only force . . . I give you leave to flatter them with what hopes you please . . . till I be ready to suppress them . . . I will rather die than yield to these impertinent and damnable demands." Ten days later his preparations had gone further; he informed Hamilton of forty cannon in readiness, and of an order he had placed in Holland for arms for two thousand horse and fourteen thousand foot, to make a timely end of "those traitors the Covenanters."[42]

He had not yet officially spoken to his English council of these bold plans, but he had sounded Cottington and Juxon on the state of the Exchequer and the Treasury, and had managed to understand from answers which must have been more tactful than truthful that he had at least two hundred thousand pounds at his disposal. A letter from Lord Deputy Wentworth in the same month, announcing an increase in the Irish revenues, may have further strengthened his belief that he had the means to reduce the Scots by war.[43]

On the last day of June he issued a proclamation to the lords lieutenants of the six northern counties to muster the trained bands, and on Sunday, July 1st, at a full meeting of his English council he gave them officially to know for the first time that a rebellion had occurred in Scotland which, in the event of further resistance, he intended to put down by force.

Of his English councillors, the Archbishop saw most clearly that the King's decisions did not match with reality. The royal authority was as much an article of faith with him as with the King but he did not believe that it could be held upright by faith alone. "My misgiving soul is deeply apprehensive of no small evils coming on," he wrote to Wentworth. "I can see no cure without a miracle and I fear that will not be showed." [44]

BOOK II CHAPTER II REFERENCES

1. *Strafford MSS.*, X, folio 192.
2. Livingstone, pp. 101–2; Laud, *Works*, VII, p. 427.
3. Knowler, II, 154; *Bankes MSS.*, 18/24, 42/30, 65/19.
4. *C.S.P.D.*, 1637–8, pp. 289, 293, 320 ff.
5. *C.S.P. Ven.* 1636–9, pp. 376–7, 387.
6. *C.S.P. Col.*, 1574–1600, pp. 263, 272.
7. *Breadalbane MSS., Letters*, 1636–9, Nos. 718, 720; *C.S.P. Ven.*, 1636–9, p. 373.
8. *Breadalbane MSS., loc. cit.*; Baillie, I, 16, 23, 51; *Strafford MSS., VII*, Wentworth to Laud, July, 1638; Warriston, *Diary*, p. 340.
9. *Breadalbane MSS., loc. cit.*; Warriston, 334–5, 344.
10. *Breadalbane MSS., Letters*, 1636–9, No. 721.
11. *Ibid.*, No. 725; Baillie, I, 75–6.
12. *C.S.P.D.*, 1637–8, p. 295.
13. *C.S.P.D.*, 1637–8, pp. 295, 259.
14. *C.S.P. Col.*, I, p. 276; *Acts of P.C. Col.*, I, pp. 228–9, 241–2.
15. *C.S.P.D.*, 1637–8, p. 356.
16. *State Trials*, III, pp. 1162, 1201.
17. Lilburne, *A Worke of the Beast*, London, 1641; *Bankes MSS.*, 13/12, 18/31. The weight with which Lilburne leaned on his pen is evident from the firmness and heaviness of his signature. *See also* M. A. Gibb, *John Lilburne*, London, 1947.
18. *Strafford MSS.*, X, Letters of May 1638 *passim*.
19. Knowler, II, 389.
20. *Strafford MSS., XI*, folios 57–66.
21. *Ibid.*, XI, Wentworth to Croke, May 26, 1638
22. Knowler, II, p. 173.
23. *Ibid.*, 167.
24. *Ibid.*, 156.
25. *Ibid.*, 166.
26. *C.S.P.D.*, 1637–8, pp. 493–4, 503–6; 1638–9, pp. 301–2.
27. *C.S.P. Ven.* 1636–9, pp. 392–3.
28. *Strafford MSS.*, X, Laud to Wentworth, May 14th, 1638.
29. Rothes, pp. 62–3.
30. Baillie, I, 74.
31. Nedham, *Digitus Dei*, London, 1649.
32. Burnet, *Lives and Actions of the Dukes of Hamilton*, London, 1677.
33. Turner, *Memoirs, Bannatyne Club*, Edinburgh, 1829, p. 84.
34. *Register P.C. Scot.*, 1638, p. 19; Burnet, *Lives*, p. 43.
35. Burnet, *Lives*, p. 49.

36. *Ibid.*, pp. 50–1.
37. Baillie, I, 80.
38. Knowler, II, pp. 167, 170, 177.
39. *Ibid.*, p. 180.
40. *C.S.P.D.*, 1637–8, p. 474; Rushworth, *Appendix*, pp. 156–8.
41. *C.S.P. Ven.* 1636–9, p. 436.
42. Burnet, *op. cit.*, pp. 55–6, 59.
43. *Ibid.*, p. 59; Knowler, II, p. 175.
44. Laud, *Works*, VII, 456.

THE GLASGOW ASSEMBLY

June – December 1638

"NOT anything can reduce that people but only force," Charles wrote from Greenwich on June 11th, 1638. Before he received the letter Hamilton had evidence that this was true.

Thirty peers and gentlemen and six hundred ministers of the Covenanting party met him in Edinburgh, before a huge, attentive crowd. Mr. William Livingstone, "the strongest voice and the austerest in countenance" of all the preachers, appealed to him, in what was rather a sermon than a speech, to give peace to the land.[1]

No one expected peace: Hamilton's tenants had been unable to gather in Clydesdale in obedience to his commands, for fear of provoking armed resistance from the tenants and followers of Covenanting lords. Edinburgh castle was closely watched by Covenanting patrols lest Hamilton should try to strengthen it for the King. A new gunpowder plot to destroy the Covenanting leaders was rumoured, and they were already, like the King, buying arms in the Low Countries and north Germany against all eventualities.[2]

The eloquence of the ministers kept spiritual fervour at its height. "Not a man is known to fall from their number," wrote a spectator, "but daily coming in. There was never at any time such plenty of preaching and prayer as is now in Edinburgh. All the most able ministers are set a-work, preach every day in many places, and on the Lord's day three sermons in each church ordinarily, and so in all the halls and other great houses."[3]

In these circumstances Hamilton found all attempts to flatter Rothes into submission useless and was further embarrassed by the sulky and unhelpful behaviour of the Council. Sir Thomas Hope, from the depth of his legal knowledge, flatly contradicted him on several points of law and refused to admit that there was anything in the Covenant contrary to the laws of Scotland. " He is no fit man to serve you," wrote Hamilton helplessly to the King, " but the time is not proper for his removal." [4]

If the King's Advocate refused to condemn the document, Hamilton could not very well proclaim its signatories traitors, and the principal weapon with which the King had armed him fell to the ground. He went ahead, as best he could, with the first part of his plan and ordered the proclamation at the Mercat Cross of the royal pardon to all Covenanters who unconditionally submitted. This only gave the leaders a new occasion to justify themselves; Warriston answered the herald's words by reading out a Protestation which condemned the King's policy in unequivocal terms and demanded the calling of Parliament and of an Assembly of the Church. A few bold, anonymous royalists shouted " Rebels " from the windows of neighbouring houses, but their cries were soon drowned by the applause of the crowd. The Council that very afternoon dissociated themselves from Hamilton's action and insisted that their consent to it, which he had gained the day before, be erased from the minutes of the meeting.[5]

The motives of the King's councillors in undermining the royal policy are easily determined. A majority of them were either in sympathy with the Covenanters or afraid of them. Hamilton's motives for his next move are altogether obscure. He had been " stately and harsh " in his official interviews with the Covenanting leaders, but on the day of the Protestation he drew some of them privately aside and assured them " as a kindly Scotsman, if you go on with courage and resolution you will carry what you please; but if you faint or give ground in the

least you are undone. A word is enough to wise men." [6] The
incident remains unexplained. Hamilton alone in Scotland was
in a position to know with absolute certainty that the King had
no intention of yielding. He may conceivably have hoped to
make a moral advantage for his master by advising the Covenanters to courses which would justify Charles in waging the
war on which he had already decided.

By this time there was real as well as imaginary evidence of
military preparation on both sides. Hamilton's own mother,
a formidable dowager who seems to have thoroughly disapproved of her son, was alleged to have bought up in the Covenanting interest all the gunpowder in Edinburgh. General Leslie
on his visit in the early spring had planned the organisation of
a Covenanting army, before returning to Germany to offer the
Covenant for signature to Scottish professional soldiers in the
Protestant armies. From the beginning, some of the leading
Covenanting lords had gone about with bodyguards of armed
followers—a not uncommon habit in Scotland—and rumour
soon credited the party with forty thousand men under arms. It
was common report that the King was negotiating for the use
of Spanish regiments from Flanders, and that the Archbishop
and Lord Deputy Wentworth had a scheme for bringing over
an Irish army to suppress the Covenant.[7]

Rumour deformed the truth, for the Deputy had no such
plan, although such a plan was part of the King's policy. Already
in the summer of 1638 the conflict between the King in England
and the Calvinist majority in Scotland was linked to the confused
and dangerous problems of Ireland.

The lowland Scots in Ulster were thrifty settlers, but their
religious obstinacy and the behaviour of some of their ministers
had already brought them into collision with the government
and Church of Ireland and into contact with the Covenanters.
Their womenfolk especially were " stark mad against the ceremonies of the Church," and as early as Easter 1638 the Bishop
of Down reported that many of them were conspicuously absent
when he administered the Sacrament. In the late summer copies

of the Covenant reached them from Scotland and they began to sign it with pious enthusiasm, in spite of Wentworth's efforts to " crush that cockatrice in the egg." [8]

The lowland Scots were not the only inhabitants of Ulster. Besides several thousand English settlers in and around Derry an incalculable number of the native Irish, chiefly O'Neills and Macdonnells, worked and lived among the settlers or gathered on the lands of the remaining native chiefs and gentry. The Macdonnells were not confined to the Irish mainland; over long centuries they had flourished in the Western Isles and Western Highlands. Proud, prolific, warlike, they embraced, in an ancient, indissoluble tradition of loyalty and kinship, the whole of this coastal and island region, Scots or Irish, and made it unsafe by their disorders and marauding on sea and land. It was against them that Lorne, from his strategically placed lands in the south western Highlands, had waged successful war, building up at the same time greater security for trade and fishing and greater power for himself and his Campbells.

The Macdonnells were mostly of the old religion and had suffered, at the Reformation and after, both in Scotland and in Ireland. In Ulster they had been forced out of the better country by the licensed encroachment of the new Protestant settlers, and in Scotland they had been expelled from the best of their lands by the Protestant clan Campbell. The process of extinction might have continued but for an odd accident. The principal chief of the Irish clan, Randall Macdonnell, Earl of Antrim, had been taken away from Ireland as a child and carefully brought up under the eyes of the King and Court. He grew up frivolous, irresponsible and very good-looking; Archbishop Laud thought him delightful, so did the middle-aged widow of the great Duke of Buckingham. He married her and thereafter with teasing fondness called her " my old Duchess." They were in the heart of the Court circle, to which Antrim's feckless, voluble Irish charm was an unusual experience. Both the King and Queen found it irresistible. He was poor; his remaining lands were in confusion and his debts were enormous. To help him, the King granted him the Scottish peninsula of Kintire. It was one of the unwisest grants that Charles ever made, for Kintire, however just the Macdonnell right to it, had been taken over in the last thirty years by the Campbells.

Antrim pranced about the Court, boasting in his delightful brogue how he would land with a great host upon Kintire and make mince-meat of the Campbells. It was hardly surprising that Lorne complained of the matter privately to Hamilton, saying that if Antrim attacked him he would certainly defend himself. On this hint Hamilton merely wrote to the King advising him to make all the use he could of Antrim to harass Lorne. Antrim's wild boastings immediately flared up into extravagant projects. He appealed, both personally and with the support of the King, to the Lord Deputy of Ireland to help him to raise and arm the Macdonnells of Ulster for an attack on Scotland, and to establish an arsenal at Coleraine stocked from the stores in Dublin. Wentworth, unlike his English colleagues, had learnt in the last five years what value to attach to fluent Irish promises. He refused help to Antrim for three excellent reasons. In his opinion the Macdonnells were a race of smugglers and brigands, to be disarmed rather than armed. He had no intention of sending military stores to Coleraine, where the Ulster Scots were strong and " might chance to borrow those weapons for another purpose than his lordship would find cause to thank them for." Finally—and conclusively—he thought Antrim's offers absurd: as for leading thousands into Scotland, " he is as well able to do it as I to take upon me the Cross with so many for the Holy Land." [9]

The foolish business contained in little all the dangers that the shrewd Wentworth most feared. It gave gratuitous offence to Lorne whose doubtful loyalty should have been strengthened, not undermined; it encouraged the Catholic Irish whose endemic disorders needed, in Wentworth's view, to be kept under control; by favouring the Catholics it gave colour to the rumour that Charles was seeking help from the Spaniards and that they in response were about to send over the Irish regiments in their pay under the leadership of the long-exiled chief of the O'Neills; it gave the Scots settlers legitimate reason to arm themselves against possible attacks from the Macdonnells; and even had the scheme been wise, Antrim was wholly incompetent to execute it. There, in little, were the misjudgments and misapprehensions which at every turn weakened the King's policy. So much Wentworth could see. He could not see that Antrim's extravaganza was the beginning of the greatest single disaster in the King's reign: it was the first forewarning of the Irish Rebellion.

The King in his encouragement of Antrim showed clearly, for the first time, that mistaken and reckless cunning which, in the latter part of his reign, was to be so marked a feature of his policy. Like many hesitative and cautious men, he had moments of an abandoned rashness. This was becoming evident in his handling of the Scottish situation. His decision to make war was the outcome of an unjustified optimism about his prospects. He had great faith in his navy, which had already given chase to and seized several Scottish vessels laden with arms. He was planning to fortify the north of England, to seize Leith from the sea, and to blockade the Scots into submission, with, presumably, the additional compulsion of Antrim's invasion in the west. His warships were already patrolling the east coast of Scotland. He had recovered his spirits, and a general gaiety once again prevailed at Court where the troubles of Scotland " neither hinder seeing of plays or hunting." [10]

This cheerfulness was shared neither by the Archbishop nor by the Lord High Admiral, Northumberland. The latter declared, in a querulous letter to Wentworth, that the Exchequer was empty and the total expectation in revenue little more than £100,000. " The King's magazines are totally unfurnished of arms and all sorts of ammunition," he wrote, " and commanders we have none either for advice or execution; the people through all England are generally so discontented by reason of the multitude of projects daily imposed upon them, as I think there is reason to fear that a great part of them will be readier to join with the Scots than to draw their swords in the King's service." [11]

Northumberland was partly right in regarding the King's incessant interference with trade and manufacture as a chief source of annoyance, and Charles himself that summer, in a politic attempt to regain popularity, called in a number of patents. The principal grievance was, and remained, Ship-money. The King's defeated victory in the Hampden case had stimulated resistance throughout the country. In Northampton-shire the chief constable went about openly saying that the English, like the Scots, should rebel when their rights were infringed, and opinions of the same sort were uttered by respons-ible officials in Norfolk.[12] Ship-money and the religious question were now so freely and generally discussed that the university of Oxford put forward the legality of Ship-money and the new Scots liturgy as suitable themes for dialectical argument. The Archbishop, who was Chancellor of Oxford, instantly ordered these dangerous topics to be withdrawn.[13]

In the North, preparations for war had begun. The Earl of Arundel, Earl Marshal of the Kingdom, advised the re-arming of the fierce borderers on the English side with their traditional old-fashioned weapons, bows and spears, and sent for cannon and muskets for the projected garrisons at Berwick and Newcastle. Two professional soldiers, Jacob Astley and Will Legge, were reporting on the defences of Hull and Newcastle. But the mustering in the northern counties, ordered by Hamilton on his way through, was not progressing satisfactorily. Sir Edward Osborne, Vice-President of the Council of the North, found the local gentry obstructive and was troubled by the lack of profes-sional soldiers to train the levies and of any but the most anti-quated weapons with which to arm them.[14]

The King, while still confident of his ultimate victory, recognised that he would have to postpone the use of force until he had adequate force to use. The war could not take place before next summer, and the immediate problem, therefore, was to " play " the Scots rebels until he was ready to attack. This was the mood in which he received Hamilton who returned in late July to report his mission and to consult on further action.

Charles instructed him to yield to two of the Covenanters' demands. Let the Service Book be temporarily suspended (as it had been forcibly suspended anyway this made little difference) and let an Assembly of the Church be called, provided only that the bishops took their proper place in it.

When Hamilton again reached Edinburgh on August 10th he found that the situation had further deteriorated during his absence. The Covenanters, fearing trouble from the Roman Catholic and Episcopalian region round Aberdeen, where the influence of the Marquis of Huntly was predominant, had despatched the energetic Montrose to whip up support for the Covenant in the district. Great enthusiasm was not to be expected in this stronghold of Royalism, but Montrose, who had been granted the freedom of Aberdeen a few years before, was locally popular and had a most persuasive tongue. By inserting a mitigating clause in the Covenant to allay their doubts he obtained a larger number of signatures than the Aberdonian royalists were ever afterwards willing to admit. A total triumph it was not, but neither was it a rebuff and in the circumstances that amounted almost to victory.[15]

While the royalists of the north-east argued and wavered, the Covenanters were mustering and drilling their troops in all the country round Edinburgh. Lorne, understandably in view of the Antrim affair, was arming his people and had placed a competent soldier, Duncan Campbell of Auchinbreck, in charge of their training. Watching his movements from Ireland the Lord Deputy Wentworth reported that he was fortifying " those isles which are within three hours sail from the north of this kingdom. There are, as is reported, brought thither sixteen pieces of ordnance well provided and mounted in places of best advantage for the defence of his country, and the people taught the use of their weapons." The purpose of all this Lorne himself rather vaguely stated was " to do His Majesty service." [16]

In Edinburgh itself the people were active. They stormed and broke up Holyrood Chapel but the organ, unholy purveyor of Popish music, was saved intact and carried away by the

regrettably frivolous Montrose.[17] More serious politically was
the signing of the Covenant during the summer by the leading
advocates in Scotland; the adoption of the Covenanting cause
and the desertion of the King by most of the Lords of Session
was as grave a blow to the prestige of the Crown in Scotland
as the division of the judges over Ship-money had been in
England.[18]

But the nine days' wonder was the solemn reconciliation
with the reformed religion, in Greyfriars Kirk, of the Jesuit
priest, Thomas Abernethy. The renegade marked his conversion
by supplying the names of nearly a score of Roman Catholic
priests who were secretly working in Scotland. He averred
with equal conviction, although he could not give their names,
that six thousand priests were active in England and upwards of
three hundred masses were read in London of a Sunday. The
Pope of Rome, he concluded, had seen and approved the King's
new Service Book for Scotland.[19]

Hamilton, who perceived that events were now moving so
fast that the Covenanters themselves might resort to war before
the King was ready for them, stayed only a fortnight in Scotland,
made no immediate offer of an Assembly but cast about instead
for some means of weakening and dividing the Covenanters. He
consulted principally with Traquair, whose very considerable
ingenuity could be relied on, although his loyalty could not.
Between them they concocted a plan to checkmate the Covenanters. The Covenant was based on a Confession of Faith sworn
by King James VI in 1580; although he had sworn under compulsion, he had never in so many words repudiated the Confession. In spirit it was Calvinist but it was less explicit than the
new Covenant, and its wording could be reconciled with the
support of episcopacy; it said nothing specific to the contrary.
So at least Hamilton thought on examining the document.

The Covenanters themselves spoke freely of the Confession
of 1580 as the foundation of their faith. Should the King therefore re-issue the Confession of 1580 as his royal answer to the
Covenant and call on his friends to subscribe to it, the Coven-

anters would have difficulty in preventing the desertion of their own cause for another which looked almost exactly like it. If they objected to the Confession of 1580 after all that they had previously said about it, they would inevitably put themselves in the wrong.

Hamilton hurried back to England and spent a week at Oatlands with the King, persuading him of the wisdom of this action. Charles, who intensely disliked the Confession of 1580 and knew that his father had disliked it, was at first very unwilling to use it. He gave in because it was, after all, only a temporary pretext. He was shipping six cannon and nine hundred muskets to Newcastle that month, and Hull too was being armed.[20] By the following spring he would be in a position to enforce his will and until then he needed only to maintain his position and weaken that of the Covenanters. By re-issuing the Confession of 1580 he would cut the ground from under their feet at the same moment as he offered them the Assembly of the Church for which they had asked; in this way he might so divide their ranks as to prevent them from commanding a majority in the Assembly. It was to meet in Glasgow, in the heart of the country where Hamilton's influence was supreme, and that fact also might be turned to account.

Hamilton's return with this new offer took the Covenanters aback. Even their friends on the Council were momentarily defeated. Neither Sir Thomas Hope nor Lorne could think of any sufficient reason why the King should not revive the Confession of 1580 and call upon all loyal subjects to sign it in preference to the Covenant, but they saw very well that by doing so he would make fools of the Covenanters. Much against their wills, Lorne and Hope had to join with the rest of the Council in signing the renewed Confession. Immediately afterwards they consulted Warriston.[21]

Warriston perceived at once the cunning of the King's move and had at first no legal argument to oppose to it, although he bitterly upbraided Hope for having been so weak as to sign at Hamilton's bidding. He was enough of a respecter of persons not to upbraid Lorne. But in truth Hope's concession was far more serious than Lorne's, for his legal opinion on any subject carried more weight than that of anyone else in the kingdom. Warriston could expect to find no legal flaws where Hope had failed and he fell back on mere railing. The King's new move was, he said, " the devil taking the Lord's bow in his hand to outshoot him therein," and the revived Confession of 1580 was " the horriblest atheism, perjury and mockage of God." [22] If no legal flaw could be found in the King's offer, the Covenanters could only contest it by vilification, and at this they were already expert. When the King's herald, on Hamilton's command, at the Mercat Cross called on all loyal subjects to abandon the Covenant and re-affirm the Confession of 1580, the usual crowd had gathered and already knew what to do. " Away with any Covenant but our own! " they shouted, and when they grew quieter, Warriston in the by now familiar fashion read a formal protest. He was followed by Montrose, the most popular of the Covenanting leaders, who spoke with a genial eloquence which brought the signatories hurrying in—not to the King's Confession, but to the protest against it.[23]

The few moderate men left in southern Scotland were shocked at the out-of-hand rejection of the first conciliatory gesture which the King had made,[24] but in general it was assumed that the anti-Covenant, as it was offensively labelled, was a trick. The behaviour of the Covenanters was unreasonable but their suspicions were just. They received accidental confirmation from the sudden appearance in their midst of a prophetess. A minister's daughter, one Margaret Mitchelson, fell into trances, was powerfully moved of the Lord, spoke strangely of " Covenanting Jesus " and declared that the Covenant had been made in Heaven and that the King's document was damned. As she lay raving, the devout and curious thronged round her chamber door, and Warriston was so deeply impressed that he took her into his household. Here she frequently prophesied for many hours at a time before audiences which included such distinguished devotees as Rothes and Lorne.[25]

The King's Council, to crown all, found means to betray the royal policy. They refused to condemn the new Protestation of the Covenanters and, in sending out copies of the King's anti-Covenant to the various regions of Scotland for signature, they appointed the leading Covenanters to organise its acceptance. When Hamilton objected to this extraordinary conduct, they argued first that these men were the local great ones on whom public duties naturally fell—which was true—and secondly that they ought to be given a chance of showing their loyalty—which was absurd. Lorne, who of all the Council had the most lands and the greatest power, excused himself from pressing the signature of the 1580 Confession in his own country because, he said, it would confuse the people to offer new ideas to them so short a time before the Church Assembly was to meet.[26]

In the upshot the King's anti-Covenant was subscribed almost exclusively in the Gordon country and especially at Aberdeen. Huntly saw to this, indignant at the light-hearted incursion of Montrose earlier in the summer into what he regarded as his especial sphere of influence. He now made solemn entry into Aberdeen, flanked by his family of handsome sons, and required the citizens to show their loyalty by accepting the King's Confession of Faith. The Aberdonians for the most part obeyed, but Huntly was deeply mortified to find his summons rejected when he commanded the same obedience in Banff and Inverness. He achieved, all told, the respectable total of twelve thousand signatures among his friends, allies and dependants.[27]

Huntly's supporters notwithstanding, the King's anti-Covenant as a stroke of policy had failed. In spite of Sir Thomas Hope's initial acceptance of it, the majority of the Lords of Session withheld their support,[28] and after six weeks of cogitation Sir Thomas himself uttered an opinion which effectively killed the moribund document. He told Hamilton that on reconsidering the Confession of 1580 he had no doubt that it committed its signatories to an absolute repudiation of episcopacy.[29]

If this were true, and Hope's opinion was enough to make it so, the document was useless and dangerous to the King's cause and should never have been resuscitated. Hamilton abandoned it forthwith and devoted all his efforts to organising a majority for the King in the Assembly which was to meet in November at Glasgow.

He was both too late in starting this policy and too half-hearted in pursuing it. The Covenanters had begun to organise their supporters the moment the date was fixed, and they had settled the representation of the greater part of Scotland before Hamilton began to think about it. Their representatives were by no means always reputable and their methods of securing their election even less so. Blackmail and intimidation were by now common; the gangs of retainers who followed the Covenanting Lords kept all their opponents in dread of violence. Hamilton complained repeatedly that his life was in danger, and although his particular fears were exaggerated the entire episcopalian contingent from Aberdeen, who would have been the King's strongest supporters in the Assembly, were, justifiably, too frightened to venture on the journey.[30] But Samuel Rutherford, an eloquent minister who had been silenced some years before and exiled to Aberdeen, made the journey safely enough and prepared to take part in the Assembly. The hapless bishops who had dared to remain in Scotland were almost prisoners in Glasgow castle, living on the bounty and under the protection of Hamilton. Pending the Assembly they were targets for continual abuse. They were accused, naturally, of Popish leanings, of worldliness, arrogance and pride, but also of sabbath-breaking, gluttony, drunkenness and whoring. A loose woman who wandered up and down with a baby which she claimed to be the bastard of the Bishop of Brechin received a great deal of unseemly encouragement.[31]

The bishops would have preferred to abandon the attempt to hold an Assembly, being already certain that it could only do harm to their cause. Hamilton had another plan for them. He intended to challenge the legality of the Assembly unless the

Covenanters would allow the bishops to take their places. If this was refused he would dissolve the meeting as unconstitutional, and claim that the King's intention to convene a free Assembly of the Church had been wilfully obstructed by the Covenanters.[32]

The idea was good, but once again the Covenanters circumvented him. They organised a popular petition, to be placed before the Assembly, that the " pretended bishops " be tried for their manifold crimes. This move had a twofold purpose: as accused or suspected persons the bishops could legally be forbidden to take their seats in the Assembly until they had cleared themselves. The petition also served as propaganda, because it mainly consisted of a list of their supposed crimes. Hamilton heard—late on a Saturday night—that the petition was to be read from every pulpit in Edinburgh on the following morning. He hurriedly forbade this, but his action served only to show how low the authority of the Crown had fallen, for the indictment was generally read.[33]

The pretence of a desire for peace had by this time been almost altogether abandoned by both sides. General Leslie, who had slipped through the King's blockade in a small fishing boat, was again in Scotland, frequently in the company of Rothes, and openly organising an army. He was said to have boasted, when told that the King was fortifying Berwick and Newcastle, that Charles would do better to fortify the Cinque Ports lest the Protestant armies of Europe came to the help of their Scottish brethren by invading the King in his own country. The King at Whitehall had set up a Committee of the Privy Council to act as a Council of War, and had sent to Wentworth in Ireland to ship him over five hundred men under an able commander to garrison Carlisle. Meanwhile Hamilton had offered the constable of Edinburgh castle two thousand pounds sterling to hand it over to him.[34]

In this atmosphere of hostility and tension the Covenanting lords assembled at Glasgow, bringing with them, in defiance of the royal command " great bands and troops of men . . . with guns and pistols." Hamilton, whose power in the district was, or should have been, predominant, avoided open clashes by keeping his own people strictly on the defensive. But few religious conferences can have opened in a less religious atmosphere than did this on November 21st, 1638. The ceremony lacked something in solemnity because the crowds were so thick about the doors that the participants could only get to their seats with " such delay of time and thrumbling through as did grieve and offend us." When they were at last in their places nothing happened except an inaudible sermon; the preacher, a Dr. Bell, selected by Hamilton, was probably wise to make it so, for no sermon would have satisfied both the King's Commissioner and the Covenanting majority in the Assembly.[35]

On the next day the struggle between Hamilton and the Covenanters began in earnest. The Assembly did not consist only of ministers; these were a minority. Each presbytery was also represented by lay elders, and, in this peculiar character, almost every nobleman of the Covenanting party was present. As a result laymen outnumbered the clergy and far outweighed them in influence. The principle of admitting lay elders at all was open to question, and many of the elections had been shamelessly procured. On both these issues Hamilton intended to challenge the legality of the Assembly. Furthermore, when the bishops, as accused persons, had not been permitted to take their seats they had by letter denied the right of the Covenanters to bring charges against them and declared that the Assembly could not legally meet without them. This gave Hamilton another reason to pronounce the Assembly illegal at the outset. Unhappily for him, he could not rely on the support or co-operation of the King's Council. Hope was frankly and almost insolently, opposed to him and Lord Lorne, who had just by his father's death become Earl of Argyll, was deep, dark, and doubtful in his intentions.

Since the Aberdonians had not come and the bishops were excluded, the Commissioner was almost without any representative of the episcopalian party among the clergy. One man he had, Dr. Balcanquhall, who was fortunately tough, resolute and intelligent enough to be willing and able to defend the King's policy single-handed.

The first full day's work began with the frugal decision to have one session only each day, from ten in the morning to five in the afternoon. Participants, fortified by a good breakfast, would work through to an early supper and avoid the expense of mid-day dinner.[36] The rest of the day's debate was more controversial. Hamilton's attempt to challenge the legality of the Assembly failed because the majority voted that the election of a Moderator and a clerk should precede all other business, and the King's Commissioner had perforce to sit still while the principal minister of the Covenanters, Henderson, was elected into the chair, supported by the redoubtable Warriston as clerk. Warriston improved the occasion by uttering a short extempore prayer that the prerogative of King Jesus should triumph over all earthly prerogatives.[37] The two key positions had thus immediately been won by the Covenanters.

After this grave tactical defeat, Hamilton walked into an ambush. The Assemblies which, in the days of Knox, had been the architects of Calvinism in Scotland, had at a later date fallen under the sway of an organised King's party. It had been suggested that the old register books of these Assemblies be consulted for precedents as to how to proceed on the present occasion. Only those from 1590 had been officially kept, and these Hamilton now produced. He had hardly made the official announcement when Warriston rose to state that he had, during the last few months, succeeded in tracing the lost registers of the earlier Assemblies—the Assemblies which had not been under the King's influence. Hamilton immediately questioned their authenticity and for several sessions, on and off, there was heated argument and comparison of handwritings. But it was difficult to disprove their authenticity and impossible to shake the faith of the Covenanters in documents which Henderson had welcomed on the first day as the *Magna Carta* of the Kirk.

Hamilton made one last effort to outwit the hostile Assembly by requiring them to answer the official protest of the excluded bishops. The majority postponed the reading of the bishops' letter, not wishing to have any documents which impugned their legality put on record. The King's Commissioner had now only the faint remaining hope that he might be able to question the elections of some of the Covenanting elders when the returns were officially checked, and in this way get rid of a few of his more troublesome opponents. Even here he failed, for although heated argument broke out over a number of the elections, his questions were persistently overruled by the majority.

The end of the first week found Hamilton at his wits' end, with the Covenanters in full command of the situation and ready at any moment to proceed to the trial of the bishops. Nothing remained therefore but to dissolve the Assembly by any means before it could do more harm. On the morning of November 28th Hamilton called the King's Council and told them of his intention. Argyll asked if he was seeking their advice but Hamilton curtly replied that he had already decided on the dissolution and was asking only for the Council's support in his action.[38]

The rumour of a dissolution reached the Covenanters even before the matter was brought up in the Privy Council,[39] and they entered the hall prepared for a crisis. One of them took the precaution of locking the door and concealing the key. The question under debate was the Assembly's right to call the bishops to judgment. Dr. Balcanquhall, Hamilton's only effective spokesman among the clergy, delivered a formidable attack on the pretensions of the Assembly in spite of two or three snubbing interventions from the Moderator and the rumbling anger of his colleagues on the benches. His arguments were, naturally, of no avail against the determination of the majority, who as soon as he sat down voted the Assembly capable of proceeding to judgment on the bishops. Hamilton had waited only for this moment. In eloquent anger—and Hamilton could be impressively eloquent—he told them that they were unworthy of the great concessions that the King had made to them. " You have called for a free General Assembly; His Majesty hath granted you one, most free on his part . . . but as you have handled and marred the matter, let God and the World judge whether the least shadow or footstep of freedom can be discerned in this Assembly." [40]

Hamilton's accusation was just enough, but whatever the force and pressure used by the Covenanters to obtain their majority, Hamilton's right to object was corrupted at the source because he was acting in the name and on the instructions of a King who had never intended the Assembly to do other than pass the time until he should be ready to make war.

Alexander Henderson answered the attack with a dignified defence of the Assembly's procedure and its rights. He was far from questioning the King's rights, he said, " but let God by whom Kings reign have his own place and prerogative."

" Sir," said Hamilton, " ye have spoken as a good Christian and doubtful subject." He allowed Henderson sincerity of religion at least but now, to reveal the base intrigues of the Covenanting lords, he suddenly produced papers which he declared were the secret instructions issued by some of them showing the devious ways in which the elders had been elected. This was the strongest move Hamilton had yet made and was unexpected, for Rothes and Loudoun, two who had been busiest in the matter, sprang up to deny the authenticity of the documents with an alacrity that betrayed their alarm. Above the din of argument which ensued Hamilton's voice rose once more in denunciation. " By what law or practice," he demanded, " was it ever heard that young noblemen or gentlemen or others, should be rulers of the Church? " What kind of freedom was this which, in effect, delivered over the clergy to " the tyranny of lay elders who would . . . prove not only ruling, but overruling elders " unless timely checked? Let this Assembly disperse as a corrupt and illegal thing, and the King would then permit them to call another.

After the excitement of challenge and response a quietness seems to have fallen, for the voice of Argyll was now heard, speaking low and fast. Argyll had no right to speak, for he was not a member of the gathering, but his words carried weight

because of his position on the King's council. " I have not striven
to blow the bellows. But studied to keep matters in as soft a
temper as I could, and now I desire to make it known to you
that I take you all for members of a lawful Assembly and my
honest countrymen."

Hamilton called on Henderson to dissolve the gathering.
The Moderator, confused for a moment by the authority in his
gesture, hesitated, but the Covenanting lords were all on their
feet shouting to him to disregard the order. Hamilton had only
one course left. He rose and made to withdraw, thus taking
away the King's authority by which alone the Assembly sat.
The dignity of his exit was marred by the unexpected discovery
that the door was locked; he had to wait several minutes, in an
attitude of righteous repudiation, while his servants forced it
for him.[41] This awkward interim was filled by Henderson with
extempore pulpit eloquence. Some, he said, were zealous to
obey the commands of an earthly master: " Have we not also
good reason to be zealous towards our Lord and to maintain
the liberties and privileges of His Kingdom? " On his example,
other ministers rose in their places to elaborate this noble theme,
and the departing Hamilton left the room to the accompaniment
of triumphant and sonorous preaching.

The councillors, all but Argyll, followed Hamilton out and
reassembled with him that afternoon in Glasgow castle. His first
care was to ask them to sign a statement declaring that " never
servant did with more industry, care, judgment and patience go
about the discharge of so great a trust, and albeit the success
has not answered his desires . . . yet his deservings herein merit
to be remembered to posterity." After securing this testimonial,
he issued a proclamation declaring all members of the Assembly
traitors should they continue longer in session. Both Argyll
and Hope refused to sign this, and its publication had no terrors
for the Covenanters.[42]

The Assembly sat on, and with it sat Argyll. " The Earl
resolves not to wrong his conscience for any earthly respect," [43]
wrote a loyal clansman, although others made question whether

conscience alone dictated his behaviour. No lord in the Covenanting party had half the power of Argyll; from the moment he
cast in his lot with them he was bound to be their leader.[44] He
was so great indeed that his right to speak and sit in the Assembly
was granted by common consent, although he had not been
elected and had no official right to be there once the King's
Council had withdrawn. No one even drew attention to the
fact that he had not signed the Covenant and made no move to
do so, although other late converts to the cause were daily
setting their hands to it with tears and prayers.[45]

The Assembly sat on for a busy three weeks after Hamilton
had proclaimed the dissolution. They abjured ceremonies and
vestments; they abolished episcopacy; they deposed and excommunicated, individually, all the bishops in Scotland, and to
maintain the purity of this new reformation they set up a permanent commission to examine into all reported abuses and to
inflict penances, expulsions and excommunications on recalcitrant
ministers or parishioners.

The powers of intimidation which this commission wielded
were of a kind to impose political and religious agreement with
the Covenanters on all but the boldest, both clergy and laity.
Any ministers with episcopal sympathies would naturally be
thrust out as " impure corbies " from God's ark and their places
filled by those whom the Covenanters chose. Laymen, and
especially the Covenanting lords, played a dominating part in
this examination, rejection and replacement of ministers. The
Glasgow Assembly brought into being a powerful instrument of
secular policy and the mechanism by which something like a
dictatorship could in due course be established.

On the day on which the Assembly abolished episcopacy in
Glasgow, the King in London issued a massive proclamation
annulling every act, made or to be made, by this gathering of
traitors. He also repeated and enlarged his instructions to all
the lords lieutenants of the northern and midland counties of
England to look to the arming and drilling of the local trained
bands of horse and foot, and to follow the advice of the exper-

JAMES, MARQUIS OF HAMILTON
by Anthony Van Dyck

ienced Colonel Astley whom he had sent on a tour of the north expressly to help them in their task.[46]

The situation which had arisen was, from the King's point of view, both confusing and grotesque. Not only had he no power to control or punish his enemies in Scotland but he had no power even to control his own Council. Argyll, now in everything but name the leader of the Covenanters, continued to exercise his rights and functions as a councillor. Sir Thomas Hope refused to speak to the Bishop of Brechin because he had been excommunicated by the Assembly; the Bishop protested that, as a Privy Councillor, Hope was bound to repudiate the Assembly,[47] but Hope, like Argyll, had his own opinions on the matter. The King's own councillors thus openly opposed the royal policy and disregarded the proclamation which the Council had been responsible for publishing.

In the midst of these confusions Hamilton, who had hitherto been merely incompetent, seems to have made the first of those deviations into half-treachery which marked his later career. Lord Deputy Wentworth, watching from Ireland, believed that he was fomenting trouble among the Ulster Scots with perhaps some idea of unsettling the country so as to procure a large grant of land there for himself.[48] Whatever his relations may have been with the troublesome Ulster Scots, Hamilton's conduct in Glasgow disappointed those of the King's followers who had hoped that he would disperse the Assembly by calling up his tenantry to drive them out. He was incomparably the most powerful landowner in that region, but he had a sound excuse for inaction; it would have been folly to risk beginning a war until the King himself was ready.

Hamilton's behaviour to Argyll was less explicable, for he conferred with him privately and parted from him with the greatest cordiality.[49] Hamilton may have had no more in mind than a legitimate desire to acquaint himself with Argyll's intentions, or to dissuade him from continuing in rebellion, but his conduct puzzled the King's loyal friends, and later, when the intimate alliance between Argyll and Hamilton became an accepted element in Scottish affairs, men remembered and speculated on their unaccountable *rapprochement* at the close of the Glasgow Assembly.

Conduct which puzzled the King's friends may have been less puzzling to the King. On the day on which he failed to dissolve the Assembly, Hamilton had written to the King a highly confidential and very strange dispatch. In this he had frankly blamed the stupidity and arrogance of the bishops for the disasters which had occurred and he had strongly advised the King to do all in his power to cultivate and win over Argyll of whom—almost alone of the Scots lords—he spoke with real respect. With one hand Hamilton was trying, clumsily, to act as a peacemaker while, with the other, he carried out the King's war policy. The King, who seems to have approved of the manœuvre was by no means always aware of how far Hamilton had carried it.[50]

By Christmas 1638 all hope of peace had gone. The actions of the Glasgow Assembly in repudiating the policy of Scotland's lawful sovereign and defying his Commissioner were tantamount to a declaration of war. Christmas festivities at Whitehall were curtailed under the excuse of Court mourning, because the Queen's brother-in-law, the Duke of Savoy, whom she had never met, had recently died. The talk was all of war; Arundel and Northumberland persistently offered advice on its conduct, while Colonel Astley and Captain Legge assisted the preparations in the north parts. Wentworth, from Ireland, urged the King to send for the three principal rebels to London—Argyll, Rothes, Montrose. If they came they were to be arrested; if they refused to come they were to be proclaimed traitors. In this way the King could demonstrate what punishment awaited those who further defied him and perhaps break up the Covenanting party by threats and fear.[51]

The Covenanters talked less and did more. The Lords, headed by Argyll, Rothes and Montrose, drew up minute instructions which were circulated throughout the country, allotting to each shire its quota of regiments and distributing the responsibility for raising, arming and training the men between the various presbyteries.[52]

The King's friends in Scotland, intimidated in the south and bewildered in the north, did nothing. Huntly contented himself with a religious demonstration: on the Sunday before Christmas, accompanied as usual by two tall sons, the Lords Gordon and Aboyne, he received the sacrament in Aberdeen cathedral from the hands of the Bishop whom the Assembly had excommunicated.[53]

Before leaving the country, Hamilton had the King's plate and tapestry removed from Holyrood and shipped to England. His own departure was held up by a brief illness, the result, Burnet asserts, of anxiety and overwork, although Archbishop Laud at the time described the indisposition scornfully as a bilious attack.[54] Early in the New Year of 1639 he returned to Whitehall whence he communicated the King's orders to the Privy Council of Scotland. His Majesty's intention was to be at his principal northern city and second capital, York, not later than Eastertide.[55] There he would expect his Scottish councillors to meet him and learn his will. It meant in effect that the King was coming with all his power against the rebels of Scotland.

BOOK II CHAPTER III REFERENCES

1. Rothes, p. 115; Baillie, I, p. 83; Balfour, II, p. 265.
2. Burnet, *Lives*, pp. 52–3; Baillie, I, 81.
3. *C.S.P.D.*, 1637–8, p. 529.
4. Burnet, *op. cit.*, p. 53; *Hamilton Papers, Camden Society*, 1880, p. 8.
5. Balfour, II, p. 276; Burnet, *op. cit.*, p. 64; Baillie, I, 91.
6. Guthry, p. 41.
7. Baillie, I, p. 81; *C.S.P.D.*, 1636–8, pp. 533–5; Rushworth, II, 811.
8. Knowler, II, p. 196; *Strafford MSS.*, VII, Wentworth to Laud, April 26th, 1638, and September 1638 *passim*.
9. Baillie, I, p. 93; Knowler, II, p. 187; *Strafford MSS.*, VII, Wentworth to Laud, August 7th, 1638; *Hamilton Papers*, pp. 12–13.
10. *Strafford MSS.*, X, Conway to Wentworth, August 3rd, 1638.
11. Knowler, II, 186.

12. *C.S.P.D.*, 1637–8, pp. 493–4, 503–4, 506.
13. *Ibid.*, pp. 560–1, 597.
14. *C.S.P.D.*, 1637–8, pp. 584, 590; *H.M.C. XII, App. II*, p. 189; Knowler, II, p. 218; *Strafford MSS.*, X, folio 199.
15. Spalding, *Memorials of the troubles, Spalding Club*, Aberdeen, 1850, I, pp. 92–3; Gordon of Rothiemay, pp. 82–6; Row, *History of the Kirk, Wodrow Society*, Edinburgh, 1842, pp. 494–5; Baillie, I, p. 97.
16. *C.S.P.D.*, 1637–8, pp. 595, 603; *Breadalbane MSS., Letters*, 1636–9, Nos. 736, 738; Knowler, II, 225–6.
17. Spalding, I, 97; Gordon of Rothiemay, II, p. 212.
18. *Breadalbane MSS., Letters*, 1636–9, No. 738.
19. Baillie, I, 108; Forbes-Leith, pp. 202–3.
20. Burnet, *op. cit.*, pp. 72–4, 79; Balfour, II, 286; *C.S.P.D.*, 1638–9, p. 18.
21. Warriston, *Diary*, pp. 391–3.
22. *Ibid.*, pp. 392–3.
23. Balfour, II, p. 293; Guthry, p. 43; *Large Declaration, concerning the late tumults in Scotland*, London, 1639, pp. 157–73.
24. Guthry, p. 44.
25. Burnet, *op. cit.*, p. 83; Warriston, *Diary*, pp. 393, 395, 397; *Large Declaration*, pp. 226–8.
26. Burnet, pp. 81, 87; *Register P.C. Scot.*, 1638, pp. 95–7.
27. Spalding, I, 112–14; Burnet, *op. cit.*, p. 86.
28. *Scottish Historical Review*, XIV, pp. 62–6.
29. Hope, *Diary*, p. 78.
30. Burnet, *Lives*, p. 84.
31. Baillie, I, p. 105.
32. Burnet, *op. cit.*, pp. 87–8; *Hamilton Papers*, pp. 46–9.
33. Burnet, p. 88; Balfour, II, 297–8.
34. Baillie, I, 111; *C.S.P.D.*, 1638–9, pp. 108, 120, 152; Knowler, II, pp. 228, 274; Burnet, *op. cit.*, pp. 88–90.
35. Baillie, I, 128; Warriston, *Diary*, p. 401.
36. Baillie, I, 128.
37. Warriston, *Diary*, p. 401.
38. Burnet, *op. cit.*, p. 101; *Hamilton Papers*, pp. 62–3.
39. Baillie, I, p. 138.
40. Burnet, *op. cit.*, p. 101.
41. *Large Declaration*, pp. 286–7; Gordon of Rothiemay, I, pp. 184–92; Peterkin, *Records of the Kirk of Scotland*, Edinburgh, 1843, pp. 129 ff.
42. *Register P.C. Scot.*, pp. 91–4; *Hamilton Papers* p. 63.
43. *Breadalbane MSS., Letters* 1636–9, Archibald Campbell to Glenorchy, December 7th, 1638.
44. Laud, VII, p. 517.
45. He apparently signed the Covenant for the first time in the ensuing April. *Breadalbane MSS., Letters*, 1636–9, No. 763.
46. *Register P.C. Scot.*, 1638–9, pp. 96–102; *C.S.P.D.*, 1638–9, p. 155.
47. Hope, *Diary*, p. 83.

48. *Strafford MSS*, VII, Wentworth to Laud, Nov.–Dec. 1638 *passim*.
49. Spalding, I, p. 120; *Breadalbane MSS*., *Letters*, 1636–9, Archibald Campbell to Glenorchy, December 31st, 1638.
50. *Hardwicke State Papers*, London, 1778, II, p. 113.
51. Knowler, II, 261.
52. *C.S.P.D.*, 1638–9, pp. 405–10.
53. Spalding, I, p. 126.
54. Spalding, I, p. 127; Burnet, *op. cit.*, p. 111; Knowler, II, p. 265.
55. Burnet, *op. cit.*, p. 112; *Register P.C. Scot.*, 1639, p. 106.

CHAPTER FOUR

THE FIRST SCOTS WAR

December 1638–July 1639

THE autumn in England had been marked by a number of public and private disasters. Widecombe Church was struck by lightning during evening service one Sunday and three of the congregation were killed; this was generally agreed to be a judgment, though whether on England's wickedness or Widecombe's remained in doubt.[1] A few days later an equally lamentable accident occurred at the other end of the kingdom; the chimney of the Lord President's house in York crashed through the roof and killed Sir Edward Osborne's eldest son. Osborne, Vice-President of the North and the King's most loyal and prominent servant in Yorkshire, was for some time prostrated with grief, to the hindrance of military preparations in those parts.[2]

The worst news came from Germany. The King's nephew, the Elector Palatine, who had been urged to fend for himself, had enlisted Dutch help to put a small army in the field. Marching to join the Swedes, he was cut off and routed by the imperial forces at Vlotho on the Weser; the Elector saved himself by precipitate flight, but his brother, Rupert, last seen charging to the rescue of a captured standard, was missing after the fight. Various rumours reached London, that he had been killed, or had died of wounds, before the truth emerged. He was alive and unhurt but prisoner in a remote Austrian fortress. The sad news provoked more Puritan criticism of the King's policy.

Instead of concentrating his interest and his energy on attacking their brethren of Scotland, he should have given more effective help to his Protestant nephews in their struggle for the Cause in Germany.

The Queen was the object of particular malice, for she had, it was argued, diverted her husband's attention from the forlorn plight of his sister. A recent arrival in England, the Duchesse de Chevreuse, added to the Queen's unpopularity; expelled from France for her incessant intrigues and believed to be in the pay of Spain, this beautiful, mischievous creature became the self-invited guest of the Court. " She spends as if our treasure were infinite," complained Laud.[3] But he could do nothing to stop her, for the Queen was attached to her and the King gave way. In the meantime she got the Court a bad name by flaunting her religion in the face of the Londoners and conducting an indiscreet love affair with the susceptible Lord Holland.

That same autumn of 1638 the King received another unwelcome visitor. His wife's factious and foolish mother, Marie de Medici, who, like Madame de Chevreuse, was well known to be in the pay of Spain, had fled from the Court of her son, Louis XIII, to take refuge in the Spanish Netherlands. She now invited herself to England. The arrival of this Italian, Roman Catholic princess, with a suite of six hundred attendants, could hardly have been worse timed, the more so that Marie de Medici had never been famed for tact. Her formal entry to London made a pleasing show for the populace and ensured her a temporary welcome, but soon her haughty behaviour to visitors, the extravagance of her household and the open establishment of yet another centre of Popish worship at her chapel, had made her cordially disliked not only by the censorious Londoners but by most of the Court as well.[4]

In the simplified popular version of political affairs, the Popish Queen's Popish mother living in state on English money was contrasted with the King's Protestant sister, the exiled Queen of Bohemia, living in poverty abroad, her eldest son defeated for lack of help and her second son a prisoner in Austrian hands.

The King, forgetful of his own flesh and blood, made ready for war against his Protestant subjects of Scotland instead of fighting his own and his sister's Popish foes. . . . So, in broad and displeasing outline, the picture presented itself to average Protestant Englishmen; it was not necessary to be far gone in Puritanism to see it in this way. The subtleties of European politics that were clear to a Laud or a Wentworth or to the King himself, eluded them completely, but in some ways they were not far wrong. The European intervention for which they yearned might not have been so much to their liking or their interest as they thought, but the Scots war on which the King was bent was to nobody's liking and nobody's interest at all.

Furthermore, the King's attempts to raise arms, money, and even troops in the Spanish Netherlands were unkindly taken by the Dutch, who suspected that his dubious neutrality was about to end in open alliance with Spain. The Protestant-Catholic animosities which had so long divided Europe seemed to them to be echoed in this new war in the British Isles. Indeed the whole course of events in Scotland bore, to them, a very striking resemblance to the course of their own revolt against Philip II seventy years before.[5] The same fear of a still closer Anglo-Spanish alliance also troubled the French and the Venetians, whose agents in London were instructed to inquire into the matter and keep a close watch on events. When informed European diplomatists entertained such suspicions, it was natural that the King's own subjects should do the same. In attacking the Calvinist Scots, Charles seemed to be taking up a definite position at last in the religious conflict of Europe, and to be taking it up on the wrong side.

The wildest stories circulated in London, coming sometimes from the lips of Scotsmen visiting friends in the South: for instance, that the Scots were about to proclaim an independent republic and could count on the help of the French, the Swedes and the Dutch.[6] Such rumours sprang from the belief that the King, after seeking Spanish help would enter the European war, on that side. In that event the Protestant powers and the enemies of Spain would defend their own interests by assisting the Scots, and the European turmoil would be extended to Great Britain.

The King's preparations went forward with a great show of seriousness. Sir Jacob Astley sent detailed reports of the fortifications of Hull, Newcastle and Berwick, with plans for projected gun-sites and trenches, lists of the arms in readiness and reports of what was needed and what most easily to be had. The King's Council of War at Whitehall placed large orders for arms in the Netherlands and worked out a plan of campaign which looked very convincing on paper.[7] Scotland was to be the object of a fourfold attack: the King, with the principal army, would cross the border while Hamilton and the fleet landed five thousand men at Aberdeen, Wentworth sent a contingent of the Irish army to Dumbarton, and Antrim with his Macdonnells invaded Kintire. The fleet, when not engaged in these landing operations, was to blockade the east coast of Scotland. The Lowlands, where the Covenanters were strongest, would thus be held between the King's army in the south and Hamilton's contingent, reinforced by Huntly and the loyal Gordons, in the north. Argyll would be fully occupied in defending himself from the Irish, and foreign help would be cut off by the vigilance of the fleet.

The plan belonged to the King's imaginary world of order and good organisation. He spoke in Council as though his projected army of six thousand cavalry and twenty-four thousand infantry was already in being; he answered no questions and gave no hint of knowing where the money was to be found to pay it. He had made a few personal economies, such as reducing the prices to be paid to Sir Anthony Van Dyck for a number of commissioned works, but he rejected any suggestion that Parliament should be called to vote him a subsidy, although Cottington, his chief financial expert, who in the last two years had increased the profits of the Court of Wards by another £20,000, suddenly declared that there was no money at all in the Exchequer.[8] Even the navy, object of so much care and forethought, was not large enough for the variety of tasks which the King's plan imposed upon it. Confident in the justice of his cause, the King relied on the support of his loyal subjects, a very few of whom justified his faith. The Earl of Worcester freely gave fifteen hundred pounds, and the Marquis of Winchester a thousand. It did not escape comment that both these generous givers were Roman Catholics. Lord Strange, eldest son to the Earl of Derby, and Lord Lieutenant of Lancashire, zealously performed his duties in raising the Lancashire levies and in equipping his own tenants. For the King's misfortune, Lancashire was a bitterly divided county and Lord Strange exceptionally unpopular with the Puritans.

The peers of England in general were called upon to perform their antique feudal duty to the King either by leading troops into the field at their own charge or by compounding for a sum of money to the Exchequer. A great number of them made excuses, announcing that they were too old, or—by the mouth of a guardian—too young, or too poor; the wealthy Lord Clare pleaded that he had seven daughters yet to marry and must save all for their dowries.[9] It was rumoured that the Lords Saye, Brooke and Mandeville might even refuse altogether. Mandeville was heir to pious old Lord Manchester, whose sons were a constant source of anxiety to him. First his younger boy Wat Montague, became a Roman Catholic and got into disgrace for making conversions at Court, and now his eldest was a notorious Puritan. Manchester, to conceal the shortcomings of his family, busied himself vigorously to put his own quota of men into as smart a shape as possible for the King's service.[10]

In the Court circle at least, especially among the younger men, a number offered to raise and equip small bodies of cavalry —Lord Carnarvon, Lord Goring's eldest son George, and Lord Wilmot's son Harry, who had both newly returned from the Low Countries, carrying honourable scars from the siege of Breda. Cottington put up the money for fifty horse, and Secretary Windebanke's eldest boy, a popular young spark known to his friends as " Signior Tomaso," was prominent among the courtiers who assumed the insignia and duties of cavalry officers. Most noticeable was Sir John Suckling, the gamester and poet, who poured what remained of his credit and all his effervescent energy into equipping a troop that should outshine all others. The unkind said that he had supplied his men with cockades and then his means had given out. This was not true; his men were complete with plumes, swords, armour, battle-axes and fringed scarves—everything except training.[11]

A few gifts of money came from prominent lawyers and rich citizens, but the Inns of Court refused to make any joint offering,[12] and the City of London, when approached for a loan or a gift, was equally obdurate. Sir Paul Pindar, jeweller and Turkey merchant, on whose riches the King had drawn before to pay for works of art, generously advanced a hundred thousand pounds [13] and placed the King's affairs on a more solid footing. How long they would remain so was more doubtful. The Lord Deputy of Ireland complained that some of the King's servants —he mentioned Arundel, Holland and Hamilton—thought themselves privileged " to take out by handfuls and scatter abroad at their pleasure." [14] In the circumstances it seemed unlikely that Astley's efficient schemes for strengthening Hull and Newcastle would be put into practice. The two cities had been instructed to proceed with them at once at their own expense, an order which was altogether too heavy a strain on their purses and their loyalty.[15]

In January the King decided on the principal army appointments. So great were the jealousies at Court that no decision could have given general content, and Charles had to balance the claims of ancient lineage against military skill. Arundel, whose knowledge of war was as antique as his hereditary title of Earl-Marshal, was nominally appointed commander-in-chief. Next under him was a competent professional soldier, the Earl of Essex; this choice was made with an eye on the Protestant critics of the Court,[16] for Essex was friend and close kin to the dissident peers, had fought for the Dutch abroad and was respected by the Puritans. This was a good appointment but the

King spoilt its effect by yielding to his wife's plea on behalf of one of her favourites.

The Queen, always precious to him, became more so when on January 20th she all but died in giving birth to her seventh child. Princess Katherine lived only to receive her name at the font.

> " Ah, wert thou born for this, only to call
> The King and Queen guests to your burial?
> To bid good-night, your day not yet begun,
> And show us a setting, ere a rising sun? "

wrote Richard Lovelace, and fifty more lines to the same effect.

Under the shadow of the Queen's pain and their joint loss, the King would give her anything and she begged the generalship of the cavalry for the Earl of Holland.[17] This appointment was equally insulting to Arundel and Essex because to command an army without commanding the cavalry was to have only the semblance of authority. The cavalry consisted chiefly of troops raised, equipped and officered by the principal nobility and courtiers in answer to the King's feudal appeal; these felt no great enthusiasm for serving under the notoriously frivolous, haughty and incompetent Holland. The appointment caused annoyance to the King's friends and aroused the derision of his opponents; Leslie contemptuously commented that he would make " my Lord of Holland rise without his periwig." [18]

The King completed his list by placing Hamilton in command of the fleet. It was reasonable to entrust the principal venture by sea—that of making a landing at Aberdeen—to a Scot, but Hamilton himself protested that he knew nothing about the management of ships,[19] and bitter offence was caused to the Earl of Northumberland who was Lord High Admiral of the fleet and saw no reason why his experience and knowledge should be set on one side.

Confusion reigned in other spheres. The King had prohibited all armourers from working except at his direct command.

This prohibition made it impossible for lords and gentlemen, who had undertaken to arm their own companies, to get what they wanted or to get it in time.[20] The arms ordered in the Low Countries proved on arrival to be very bad. Of two thousand pikes none were good, and nearly three hundred were downright useless; more than a third of the swords were defective; the belts and hangers were of poor quality or used leather, and some of the bandoliers were found to be made of brown paper.[21] The troops which gradually came together from the counties were indifferent and ill-equipped. Desertion was very common, mutiny less so, although it occurred. Some Herefordshire men set upon and wounded an officer before dispersing home again to their villages. Most of them grumbled bitterly when they found how far from home they were to march, and made up for the inconveniences to which they were subjected by plundering the strange and, to them, foreign parts of England through which they passed.[22]

From the north, Sir Jacob Astley reported that the borderers were tough, broad-shouldered men, used to fighting, who would do well in plundering expeditions against the Scots, but they must be armed with muskets; the bows and arrows with which Arundel had diligently supplied them in the previous year hardly answered to the needs of modern war. He asked also for artillery and suggested that the Durham pit-ponies be commandeered for drawing cannon. The armour hitherto supplied for the use of the northern troops was inadequate and a whole consignment of pikes had been too short for practical use. He reported disquieting tales of the mustering of the Scots in large numbers on the farther side of the border.[23]

In Yorkshire, the Vice-President of the North, the gentle Sir Edward Osborne, still grief-stricken over the accident which had cost him his son, had failed to bring the obstructive gentry under control; some complained of the cost of equipping the men; others went to the Netherlands for a time to avoid their duties. The decision to organise heavy-armed cavalry had to be reversed because the horses available were suitable for light cavalry only; all arrangements had to be altered and the equipment cancelled and changed. The man-power of York-shire was considerable, but too few professional soldiers could be found to train the recruits, and the shortage of armourers or gunsmiths in the north was frustrating. The most forward recruits were unfortunately the tenants of the Roman Catholic gentry, and these, who had long been prohibited the use of arms by law, came to the rendezvous with hardly a sword or pike between them.[24] The King's growing doubt of the strength he could raise in England was reflected in the direct negotiations which he opened with the Spanish government in Brussels to release troops for his use in Scotland.[25]

The hostile muttering of public opinion made an uncomfortable accompaniment to the King's preparations. To demonstrate that Archbishop Laud had no sympathy with the Papists, the famous dialogue in which he had long ago confuted Fisher, the Jesuit, was republished, but trenchant as were Laud's theological arguments against the Roman doctrine, they did not divert the attention of the Puritans from the continued stream of prosecutions in the Courts of High Commission and Star Chamber. A Lincolnshire curate, who refused to wear a surplice, was imprisoned and fined £1,000 for having preached a sermon against sabbath-breaking and the King's publication of the Book of Sports. No doubt his behaviour had been uncanonical; he had assaulted a wandering piper who had played on the village green for his parishioners to dance on a Sunday afternoon.[26] Bishop Williams, still obstinate, was now answering to another libel charge, together with the headmaster of Westminster School, Lambert Osbaldeston, for their outspoken exchange of letters about " the little meddling hocus pocus." Osbaldeston was sentenced to the loss of his ears and to stand in the pillory in front of his own school. With characteristic inefficiency, the officers of the court did not notice him slipping quietly away while sentence was being pronounced. The hue and cry raised for him revealed nothing, save some charred papers in his study and a derisive note left on his desk, " If the Archbishop inquire

after me, tell him I am gone beyond Canterbury." Literal-
minded, his pursuers sought him at the Kentish ports, but he
was well hidden in London, beyond the clutches of the Archbishop.[27]

A new headmaster had to be found for Westminster School,
and Laud, seeking for a divine of unimpeachable views, sent for
Dr. Richard Busby from Oxford, thus in the midst of his
gathering troubles, making the wisest and most beneficial
appointment of his career.

Lesser voices all over the country were raised against the
Archbishop. Conventicles in London, in Shropshire, in Northamptonshire, on the borders, were discovered and broken up,
but Astley, the practical soldier, implored the King to leave the
Puritans alone, at least while he was trying to raise troops. In
February the Scots had issued an appeal to the people of England,
for religion's sake, and this document, in print and in manuscript, ran from hand to hand all over the country. A chapman
whose cloak-bag was crammed with copies was seized at Penrith;
another was reported to be distributing them in the region of
Manchester, and a clergyman in Bedfordshire was put in the
pillory for handing out a manuscript version.[28] Daring rhyme-
sters dropped abusive doggerel in market places, pinned it on
doors, even threw it down within the precincts of the King's
palaces. "Desiring Your Highness to pardon my pen," concluded one of these anonymous critics, to the King—"carry
Laud to the Scots, and hang up Bishop Wren."[29] Whenever
two or three are gathered together, went the common tale, two
of them will be exclaiming against the government; the health
of the gallant Scots with destruction to Laud "the Pope of
Lambeth" was proposed by those whom drink made bold in
alehouses.[30]

A raid on the Postmaster's office, carried out on Secretary
Windebanke's instructions, proved only what was already
suspected, that the Scots were in friendly correspondence with
some of the most influential men in England. Lord Brooke, a
leader among the Puritan nobility, was seriously incriminated,

but the King, in a rare access of caution, decided to leave him unmolested for fear of revealing too broadly the strength of the opposition.[31]

As spring came on, the streets of London were disturbed by the Puritan prophetess Lady Eleanor Davies, wild-eyed and loud-voiced, foretelling the total destruction of the city before Easter.[32]

The Archbishop was harassed with misgivings which pursued him even into his sleep. He dreamed that the King desired to marry a minister's widow and asked him to perform the ceremony, but he looked in vain through his Prayer Book without being able to find the Order for Marriage.[33] Waking, he could at least turn from the espousals of King Charles and the Scottish Kirk to less distressing topics. He continued his campaign against the Walloon congregation in Canterbury [34] whose resistance, though dogged, gave him no such cause for anxiety as did that of the Scots.

Other happier interests still from time to time cheered him. He had been corresponding with Edward Pocock, the Oxford Professor of Arabic, whom he had sent to Constantinople in quest of Greek manuscripts and whom he advised to visit Mount Athos. Disposing of the treasures in his own possession he presented this year to the university of Oxford five hundred and seventy-six volumes in Hebrew, Arabic and Persian. In his home town of Reading he was busy endowing a fund for the relief of the deserving poor.[35]

The King in his natural optimism still believed that a silent majority in Scotland were in his favour and " only wanted a head and arms " to rise against the Covenanters.[36] This belief was not quite groundless. Some of those who had been indifferent at first had been provoked by the aggression of the Covenanters into belated resistance; unexpected trouble broke out even in the Campbell country, and Glenorchy who, after Argyll, was the principal Campbell chieftain, found difficulty in getting the Covenant subscribed in his lands; at one point a mutiny against the Covenant seemed likely to break out even

ARCHIBALD CAMPBELL, MARQUIS OF ARGYLL
by an Unknown Artist

in Argyll's own forces in the Western Highlands. The resistance was speedily crushed and the Covenant enforced under threats of dire punishment.[37]

Eastwards from the Campbell country, along the fringe of the highlands, lay Lord Ogilvy's lands. He and his people were staunch Royalists, but they were neither strong enough nor in a strategic position good enough to effect anything. The most important Royalist in Scotland was the Marquis of Huntly with his Gordons, representing a fighting force of at least two thousand men. Furthermore, the highlanders in general did not love the lowlanders and might prove dangerous. But to most of these Gaelic-speaking, hunting, fighting, cattle-herding people, the King's policy mattered far less than the ancient enmities or friendships of their chiefs. Many of them had, out of rivalry or dislike of the Gordons, subscribed the Covenant. A leader had not yet arisen who could inspire them to make common cause; and the Covenanters rightly trusted in their bitter divisions.[38] They held an equally contemptuous view of the Irish troops which the Lord Deputy was to send to the King's help; Rothes had confidently threatened to " dight their doublets." [39]

Alexander Leslie, the Covenanting commander-in-chief, was not an outstanding military genius but he was an experienced organiser. The Scots army had no troops so glorious as the plumed cavalry on which Sir John Suckling had lavished his money and his taste, but officers and men had the cause at heart and those who could not fight helped to the best of their ability. " I furnished to half a dozen of good fellows muskets and pickets, and to my boy a broad sword," recorded Dr. Baillie, the earnest and kindly minister who was, until the wars came, professor of philosophy at Glasgow, but who now found himself the chaplain of a regiment.[40] The problems of inadequate pikes, brown-paper bandoliers, infantry without arms, and cavalry without horses did not afflict the Scots. Professional soldiers, who had come home from Germany in great numbers to assist in the Holy War at home, were distributed throughout the country to teach the young men how to handle pike and musket. The patriarchal system of society made recruiting easier than in England. Apart from Argyll, no major highland chief with a clan at his call was a Covenanter, but over all the lowlands ties of kindred and traditional obedience brought the soldiers in as soon as the heads of families gave the word. The traditional and professional experience of a people with whom war, until the last generation, had been endemic served the Scots well. Equipment, commissariat and transport were smoothly organised; the building of wagons, the casting of bullets were planned well in advance; it was known how much powder and match each musketeer should have, what arms were to be issued, in default of muskets, what was essential, and what could be dispensed with.[41]

The principal difficulty was money to bring the men together from the remoter parts and to keep them in the necessities of life. "Our soldiers were all lusty and full of courage," wrote Baillie, "most of them stout young ploughmen: the only difficulty was to get them dollars for their voyage from home ... for among our yeomen money at any time, let be then, uses to be very scarce; but once having entered on the common pay, their sixpence a day, they were galliard." The citizens of Edinburgh contributed generously because their ministers in fervid sermons "moved them to shake out their purses." Supplies of wheat for the army were built up by the simple process of raiding the garners of those who had not signed the Covenant.[42] But the enthusiasm for the Covenanting cause in Edinburgh and round about was for the most part unfeigned, and travellers out of Scotland reported that the women of Edinburgh and Leith helped the men to fortify the cities, carrying earth for the ramparts in baskets and aprons.[43]

Argyll, who was principally engaged in defending the west against invasion from Ireland, commanded his tenants and friends on the long, vulnerable coast to build boats for patrolling the seas. He had fairly ousted Rothes as the foremost man in the party, and was gradually assuming a new grandeur. In future he planned to have twelve or sixteen young gentlemen of his kin to attend always upon his person as a guard of honour.[44]

The young Montrose, who had some academic knowledge of warfare learnt at a military school in France, was acquiring practical knowledge from Leslie with astonishing speed. The first, bloodless, action of the war was his. In the second week of February 1639 he heard, at Perth, that Huntly had called a gathering of his clan at Turriff in the heart of the Gordon country. Montrose, with a picked band of musketeers, marched swiftly through the Grampian passes and occupied Turriff at daybreak, an hour or two before Huntly and his clansmen arrived. Huntly lacking instructions from England and uncertain what consequences might follow should he begin the war, looked askance at the intruders in his country but thought it wiser not to challenge them. He sent his clansmen home again.[45]

While the King's Scottish champion withdrew, baffled, the offers of his Irish champion resounded through Dublin. The Earl of Antrim, after contemptuously refusing a passage on the regular packet boat and demanding the use of the royal frigate *Swallow*, had landed in Dublin and proclaimed to all that he would raise ten thousand foot and three hundred horse, and transport them all to Scotland in a fleet of his own building. Wentworth, who knew that Antrim could not raise a loan of £300 from any merchant in Dublin, so poor was his credit, paid no serious attention to these " vast, vain, and child-like propositions." The young man vapoured, complained, outlined his plans with energy to the Deputy's council, asked for supplies of powder and shot from the royal arsenal, hurried to his country estate and began assiduously felling trees for the ships, discovered that his workmen could not make masts, sent measurements to the Deputy for some from the King's shipyards (the measurements were wrong: the masts did not fit), reappeared in Dublin with a boon companion who was to assist in the conquest of Scotland and asked the Deputy to knight them both for the great services soon to be rendered. That, at least, seemed a harmless vanity and Wentworth, having " much ado to forbear smiling," bestowed the accolade on the two sillies. Antrim's companion had an unusual, Irish name, Phelim O'Neill.[46]

Anxiety underlay Wentworth's laughter. Contrary winds delayed the dispatches from London to Dublin, and his information was scarce and worrying: the Queen was interfering in the army appointments, the Puritans were rebellious, the King's preparations were inadequate. He put together a gloomy, accurate picture from the many hints. For his own part he had sent over a garrison of five hundred men to strengthen Carlisle; he wished he could believe the King's other garrisons were as good. Ireland stirred uneasily; the O'Byrnes were suddenly on the move, raiding and burning in the Wicklow hills. Other raiders broke out in Donegal; the Scots in Ulster grew insolent and he compelled them to take an oath of loyalty to the King. Since the removal of nearly all the King's fleet from the Irish coasts to blockade the east coast of Scotland and prevent trade with the Continent, the fishing boats and merchant vessels of the Ulstermen defied the customs officers and communicated with the Covenanters. A pirate from Dunkirk entered Dublin harbour in broad daylight and towed away a Dutch merchantman. This kind of thing brought the royal authority into contempt. Wentworth saw very well, but saw too late, that his master was taking too great a risk. On March 21st he wrote imploring the King to reconsider his plan and postpone the war by any means.[47]

The letter cannot have reached Whitehall before the King himself had left. After distributing Easter gifts of venison to the Lord Mayor and all the ambassadors resident in his capital, he began his journey to York to join his army on March 27th, 1639. Hamilton at the same time proceeded to Yarmouth to embark the troops for Aberdeen. The Earl of Northumberland, to console him for being passed over as Admiral and General, was left behind to look after the King's most precious possession. He was made responsible for the safety of the Queen: " She is my jewel," said Charles.[48]

On March 30th when the King reached York the war was already lost. In the previous fortnight the Covenanters in a series of swift, concerted moves had consolidated their position.

On March 20th the only important Royalist on the Scottish side of the border, the Earl of Douglas, fled, allowing his castle and his pregnant wife to fall into the hands of the Covenanters.[49] A Roman Catholic by conversion, he had been wholly unable to hold his Protestant tenants in check.

On March 21st, between four and five in the afternoon, Alexander Leslie with some " choice companies " of musketeers rushed Edinburgh Castle. " In half an hour that strong place is won without a stroke," marvelled Dr. Robert Baillie, but it was no great marvel, for the garrison was almost without arms.[50] Immediately after, a band of Covenanters under Rothes appeared before the castle of Dalkeith, the King's chief arsenal, where the Crown Jewels of Scotland were kept and Traquair was in command. He refused the keys but hinted that experienced soldiers might effect an entry by other ways. The Covenanters scrambled in by the unguarded windows, and Traquair stood by while they carried away the arms, the powder, and the Crown Jewels in triumph to Edinburgh.[51]

On Sunday, March 23rd, at Dumbarton—the seaport on the south-west coast where the King's Irish troops were to land—the provost with forty armed men met the Royalist governor of the castle with his lady as he came out of kirk and asked him home to dine. When the governor refused, he was forced into the provost's house and compelled to give up the keys. The Covenanters occupied the castle, of which the garrison, to a man, came over to their side. What had possessed the King to leave in Dumbarton a garrison rotten with disaffection—lamented the Lord Deputy of Ireland—when it could easily have been garrisoned effectively from Ireland had the King but given leave? Now it was gone and with it all hope of landing Irish troops in Scotland.[52]

Huntly all this time was busy about Aberdeen, but he had been strictly charged not to begin the war until Hamilton and the fleet arrived—the fleet which was still in Yarmouth roads waiting for the troops to embark. Huntly, who had gathered together about three thousand followers, did what he thought best: he sent a flattering embassy to Montrose, who was mustering his troops within his own territory, suggesting a gentleman's agreement that neither should enter the other's country. The messengers found Montrose busy issuing his troops with lengths of blue ribbon to make themselves cockades (" one of Montrose's whimsies " said his critics sourly), and he showed little interest in Huntly's offer. He was, he said, the servant of the Covenant and had orders to occupy Aberdeen, which, with or without Huntly's permission, he intended to do in as orderly and peaceable a manner as possible. Huntly's messengers went disconsolately home again, noticing the evil omen of an angry sunset as they went—the sky seemed as if fresh blood had been " poured into a bright silver basin." [53]

Three days later in high, windy, brilliant, weather Leslie and Montrose marched on Aberdeen, with horse and foot, drums and trumpets, and banners flaunting to the sun the legend, " For God, Covenant and Country." Huntly had already withdrawn, and the port and stronghold, on which the King had built his highest hopes, received the conquerors in helpless dismay.[54]

On March 30th in the afternoon the King made his official entry into York, driving in a coach, with Lennox and Holland in attendance. The Yorkshire trained bands lined the way, and Arundel, accompanied by the mayor of York, came out to meet him. At about the same hour the Covenanters were entering Aberdeen, but he did not know of this until five days later. It was the worst news out of Scotland since he started on his journey.[55]

He was still convinced of his ultimate victory, and although he sent to instruct Hamilton to blockade Leith and abandon the project for Aberdeen, he gave more time to considering the punishments to be inflicted on the rebels when they were conquered than to the means of conquering them. The proclamation with which he intended to enter Scotland, at the head of his army, promised his loyal subjects peace and a Parliament, but added a long list of traitors exempted from pardon either of life or estates. It included the names of Argyll, Rothes, Montrose and Warriston. The double-faced Traquair, who had presented himself at York with specious excuses for his conduct at Dalkeith, was already under arrest.[56] For once, however, he had followed the advice often given by Laud and Wentworth, and bestowed rewards on the loyal. At York he raised the loyalist Lord Ogilvy to the dignity of Earl of Airlie and created another faithful Scot, Robert Dalzell, a soldier of some reputation, Earl of Carnwath.

The first military necessity seemed to be the security of Berwick, and the King began to denude his other garrisons in order to strengthen it. There was big talk, rather late in the day, of improving its fortifications; Astley, always practical, was for a dry ditch—like that at Bergen-op-Zoom—rather than the complicated engineering of a moat. The King's mind wandered to a happier future. When the war was over Berwick must be suitably rewarded; it was dreadfully poor, something must be done to restore its dwindling trade. Even the best church in the place—the King spoke with shocked recollection of a previous visit—was so dilapidated that he would have been loth to stable a horse in it.[57]

York provided plentiful entertainment for the King and his followers. Charles and his chief officers lodged at the King's House, the magnificent residence enlarged by Wentworth as the seat of the Lord President of the North. Sir Arthur Ingram's noble mansion, with its famous Italian garden, served for other members of his suite. Officers and gentry in general found good but expensive accommodation at the *Talbot* and the *Dragon*, and cheaper lodging at the *Bell*.[58] In the friendly atmosphere of the city confidence rose again, and Charles was disposed to disregard the gloomy letter which the Lord Deputy of Ireland had sent urging him to postpone the invasion of Scotland for another year or at least until his prospects of success were greater. Charles responded by ordering Wentworth to give full support to the Earl of Antrim in his proposed attack on Kintire by himself leading the Irish army in person against Argyll. How this was to be done when the navy was wholly occupied elsewhere and the principal port in western Scotland had already been lost, he did not explain.[59]

Charles meanwhile watched his "cavaliers on their brave horses" perform before him in the "ings," the meadows by the city, a sight as merry as "the recreations in Hyde Park." A day or two later he reviewed the rest of his cavalry, including Sir John Suckling's resplendent troop, at Selby. Afterwards he visited the Abbey and admired its fine East window.[60]

Soon after his return to York an astonishing rumour reached him that Huntly had not only abandoned Aberdeen but had signed the Covenant. To his indignation he found that some of his own following dared to defend the document. To stop this creeping rot he tendered to the lords gathered at York a new oath of loyalty and obedience in the coming war. Lord Saye and Lord Brooke both refused it, Lord Saye asserting that, since the union of the crowns, he could not hold it lawful to kill a Scot. Charles lost his temper: "My Lord," he cried, "there be as good men as you that will not refuse to take it, but I find you averse to all my proceedings." Saye continued in his refusal and Charles placed him and Lord Brooke under arrest.[61]

Five days later with a gesture of generosity he released them, but Saye left York immediately, taking his entire contingent of troops with him, because, he argued, they were his personal attendants, not the King's soldiers.[62] The sly peer was well nicknamed "Old Subtility," for his last statement was a pointed criticism of the King. If Charles revived the obsolete feudal practice of calling on his lords for military duties, why should not they, in their turn, revive other obsolete feudal practices, such as maintaining a personal armed retinue as in the Wars of the Roses?

Essex, the King's General of the Infantry, had meanwhile received an appeal from the Covenanting leaders to use his best endeavours to prevent a war. With scrupulous correctness he at once handed the letter to the King, a fact which did not prevent Lord Holland, his associate in command of the army, from

informing some of his particular friends that in his opinion
Essex was a traitor. This disagreement between the respective
generals of the King's cavalry and the King's infantry was speedily
reflected in brawls and disorders among their men.[63]

The news from the south was not of the best. Hamilton
had had difficulty in embarking the levies raised in East Anglia;
they were very unwilling to fight the Scots.[64] In London, the
players of the Fortune Theatre had been reprimanded by the
council for making a mock of Laudian ritual on the stage to the
high delight of the vulgar audience. Trade in London was
almost at a standstill because of the interruption of the war and
doubt of its results; the utterly irrepressible Lilburne, from his
prison, managed to issue a paper calling on the apprentices to rise
against the government.

To alleviate this dangerous situation, Charles, from York,
suddenly sent word that licences, projects and restrictions touching twenty-seven different commodities, from hatbands to
seaweed, from iron to red herrings, were to be withdrawn.
The idea was good, but it came too late and its sole effect for
that summer was to flood his inadequate secretariat in London
with extra work. Secretary Windebanke's office, manned
largely by his relations, already felt itself to be overworked with
the occasional raiding of suspect Puritan households and the
examination of their tedious papers. Robert Reade, the Secretary's nephew and right-hand man, wrote peevishly to his cousin
" Signior Tomaso " that he scarcely had time to undertake the
wooing by proxy of the latter's bride; a charge which had been
entrusted to him when Tomaso marched north with the King.[65]

More energy was displayed by the Queen and her friends.
She set on foot a collection for the expenses of the war from the
ladies of her attendance; each was asked to forego some desired
finery and offer to His Majesty's cause a suitable proportion of
her dress allowance. Far larger sums, it was thought, could be
raised from the King's Roman Catholic subjects, grateful for the
reliefs he had given them. This second collection was organised
by the Papal agent, George Con. He was helped by an active

committee of prominent Catholics, the Queen's secretary Sir John Winter, Wat Montagu of course, Sir Basil Brooke and Sir Kenelm Digby. But the comings and goings between the committee and the Queen gave rise to rumour of a Popish Plot.[66]

The suspicions which his policy aroused were again brought home to the King by the Earl of Leicester, his ambassador to Paris, who reported to him at York in the course of April. He made it more than ever clear to Charles that the rebel Scots had considerable hope of assistance from France, or indeed from any European power opposed to the Spanish interest. A few weeks later when the King's negotiations for troops in Brussels began to ripen, and a contingent of four thousand men was offered to him by the Cardinal Infante, governor of the Spanish Netherlands, Charles had come to the conclusion that it would not be safe for him to accept. Too many of those English lords and gentry who had obeyed his summons to bring troops against the Scots were now openly criticising his policy. Here were two armies, English and Scots, about to fight one another when either or both would far more gladly put their arms at the service of the King's nephew, the Elector Palatine, and the Protestant Cause in Europe. So ran the dangerous, irrepressible current of criticism.[67]

All the while the King's financial position deteriorated. The Hampden trial had virtually ended his hopes of raising any substantial sums by extra-Parliamentary taxation. His monopoly policy had been deliberately abandoned in the vain attempt to regain popularity, and all the expected revenues of the Crown had been pledged for the next five years.[68]

In the shadow of these anxieties the King marched to Durham. On the way the Comptroller of his Household Sir Harry Vane, who was becoming ever more favoured as a confidential adviser, splendidly entertained him at his country seat, Raby Castle. On Sunday, May 5th, the Bishop, preaching before him in Durham Cathedral, recently so much restored and beautified by John Cosin, expounded the duties of obedience to the King, taking the text: " Let every soul be subject unto the higher powers." The King later ordered this excellent homily to be printed and distributed. The citizens of Durham notwithstanding continued to receive and entertain travellers from Scotland and some of them got into trouble for drinking a health to the Covenant.[69]

At Newcastle the King was received on May 6th with ringing of bells and firing of cannon. Again he reviewed his troops and again listened to rumours, delusive or dismaying, from Scotland: reliable news was harder to come by, although Scots came and went at will in the town, in spite of the sentries, sat and drank in the taverns and freely talked sedition to the inhabitants. A Scots courtier, Lord Roxburgh's son, suddenly deserted to the Covenanters, whereupon the King arrested his father. The only result was another desertion, that of the hitherto loyal Lord Southesk who was, justifiably, afraid lest he should suffer Roxburgh's fate because his eldest and youngest daughters were married respectively to Traquair and Montrose.[70]

The principal excitement was the arrival of the fugitive Lord Aboyne, Huntly's second and favourite son, a spirited boy of eighteen, who gave the King the first clear account of what had happened in the north. After the fall of Aberdeen Montrose had sought out Huntly and persuaded him to sign a modified version of the Covenant. A few days later, acting apparently in the belief that Montrose had guaranteed his safety, Huntly entered Aberdeen with his two sons, where, on Easter eve he was to his great indignation, compelled to go to Edinburgh virtually as a prisoner. Since one breach of faith justified another, he got permission for his younger and favourite son, Aboyne, to return home on parole to fetch him money and necessaries. Parole was granted and Aboyne, on his father's instructions, escaped to join the King.[71]

Aboyne believed, rightly, that the Gordons would rise to avenge the capture of their chief. While he was with the King at Newcastle they had already, in a sudden onrush, broken through Montrose's outpost at Turriff, and driven the Covenanters out of Aberdeen although only for a few days. Aboyne now asked the King for ships and men to assist his clansmen from the sea, and Charles dispatched him with a commendation to Hamilton.

He found Hamilton out of humour with the war. He had sailed from Yarmouth with eight warships and about thirty Newcastle colliers used as transports. He had aboard five thousand men, supposedly infantry, although barely two hundred understood the use of a musket. As he approached the Firth of Forth beacons flared up on every hill; the fisherfolk were watchful against him all along the coast; his landing parties in search of water were repelled. He had to fetch all his supplies from the nearest friendly base, which was Holy Island. Small-pox broke out among his troops. To crown all, his mother, emerging from her widow's retirement to fight the battles of the Covenant, announced that she would shoot him with her own hand if he tried to land his army.

This was the first great venture of the King's Ship-money fleet, the warships which were to have been his glory and pride. Cruising ineffectively between the Firth of Forth and Holy Island, it cut a lamentable figure. The polished cannon on the decks fired only once and that was in error. Hamilton had with some difficulty managed to convey ashore the King's proclamation of pardon to those who laid down their arms; he believed that it would be obediently read at the Mercat Cross of Edinburgh and timed a full salute of his guns to mark the moment. The salute was fired, but the proclamation was not read then, or at any time in Edinburgh.

Hamilton himself at first refused, then agreed, to parley with the Covenanting lords. His conduct aroused suspicion and it was widely said that he had conferred for two hours in secret with them at night in a deserted part of the links of Barnbougall. Probably he was the victim of slander and an accident; he had gone prospecting for water with a landing party, the boat had run aground and he had been for a time stranded among the dunes.

To Hamilton, in this baffled state, suddenly appeared the

zealous Aboyne with the King's letter of recommendation. Hamilton was usually jealous of young noblemen who had gained the King's attention and he at once disliked and disapproved of Aboyne.[72] An admiral less sour might have felt the same, for Aboyne was only eighteen and he asked for a couple of warships. Grudgingly Hamilton yielded in part to the King's command, supplied Aboyne with a ship, men and guns and let him go his way. He sailed north, came close inshore at Aberdeen and trained his guns on the town.

Montrose, who had been patrolling the restive Gordon country, hurried back to Aberdeen. Leslie and the bulk of the army had long since gone southward taking the artillery with them, and he saw that he would have difficulty in holding the town against an attack from the sea and a rising of the countryside, especially as the citizens would probably welcome the invaders. He decided to evacuate the town, gather reinforcements and guns at his Perth headquarters, and retake it; better a retreat and return than a rash and possibly disastrous defence. Aboyne, therefore, was able to make an undisputed entry into Aberdeen in the first week of June.

The King meanwhile had left Newcastle after knighting the Mayor, reviewing his troops and ordering the removal of the unsightly wooden galleries which defaced the principal churches of the town.[73]

The weather, which had been unseasonably cold, wet and windy, had suddenly turned to a sweltering heat, darkened and made oppressive by an ominous eclipse of the sun. The heavily dressed infantry slogged their way from Newcastle to Alnwick, mutinously realising, as the thirsty, shadeless march continued, that no adequate arrangements had been made for food, drink or shelter. The lack of water was the worst. At night they slept where they could, the officers disputing for places in the mud-floored rooms of wretched alehouses, and buying up all the poultry they could find, the men grumbling over the dryness of the bread ration as they pitched their tents. Alnwick Castle, through long disuse, was so dilapidated that no decent lodging for the King could be found there; he slept in the adjoining abbey.[74]

Discomfort and disorder increased as they advanced to Berwick where they were joined by some of the men from Hamilton's ships, a reinforcement which only temporarily raised their spirits. The border town, sullenly in sympathy with the Covenanters, was too small to lodge the whole of the King's army. They camped outside, south of the Tweed, in the open ground called the Birks. Charles lived under canvas with his men, in his well-appointed royal tent, round which the formal order of the Court was maintained. Windebanke's son "Signior Tomaso" complained (but not, of course, to the King) that he found his duties of mounting guard tedious and exacting, but Charles, busied as always with letters and proclamations to be considered and revised, imposed heavier burdens on his secretaries than on his soldiers; it was, as one of them grumbled, to " play Pyramus and Thisbe and the Lion too," before all was done.[75]

Astley had rightly complained that the King's lines of communication were too long drawn out, and indeed the centre of the army organisation was still partly in London. The royal secretariat there was responsible for much that had gone wrong; it had planned wagons for transport and portable ovens in great numbers for the baking of bread, but while the secretaries in London proclaimed the excellence of their arrangements, those in the north received nothing they wanted. "It is not as you and your colleagues conclude in your committee, but as we find and feel," [76] they grumbled.

The King did not spare himself. While the camp was being organised he tired out two horses, riding from one part to another, inspecting and encouraging. His conscientiousness could not make up for his lack of military experience, but the troops although wet, hungry and discontented, were momentarily impressed by his activity and received him with ephemeral enthusiasm, which he took for a sign that their hearts were in the war. It was not so: the rising tide of discontent was now swelled by an undercurrent of fear. Rumours of Scottish strength were ever more persistent and a sinister silence on the far side of the border added to the growing uneasiness.[77]

On June 1st Lord Arundel, with the splendid attendance and caparison of the Earl Marshal of England, crossed the Tweed into the rebel kingdom of Scotland. In the first village he read out King Charles's proclamation, calling his subjects back to their obedience, to an audience of barefoot women and gaping children. There was hardly a man to be seen. When the ceremony was over the women offered their eggs and milk for sale, and Arundel's men after buying some of the eggs marched home again.[78]

Next day, Whit Sunday, Charles heard a sermon in his tent. Towards evening news came that the Scots forces under Leslie were a day's march off at Kelso. The time for action had come. A thousand of the splendid cavalry, under Lord Holland, set out towards Kelso at first light on the following morning. Their marching order had been the occasion of an angry scene between the Earls of Holland and Newcastle. Newcastle, as governor of the Prince of Wales, rode at the head of the so-called Prince's troop, who had the honour to carry his arms on their colours. Holland assigned them a place in the rear; Newcastle claimed a place in the van. Holland insisted, whereupon Newcastle had the Prince's colours furled rather than see them so dishonoured. In this order they left Berwick, Newcastle pondering on the challenge which he would send to Holland as soon as the fighting was over.[79]

The cavalry were accompanied at the start by three thousand infantry, but as Holland made no allowance for the different pace of their marching, they were out of sight, reach and hearing by the time he approached Kelso. This was unfortunate, for late in the summer afternoon, out of the deceptively peaceful landscape whose rolling hills and leafy copses gave abundant cover, Holland perceived a huge body of Scottish infantry—eight thousand, he reckoned—closing in upon his column in a well-ordered half-moon. He halted his men. The Scots also halted.

They eyed each other suspiciously in the blazing sun. The Scots had only a handful of cavalry but the highly professional appearance of their infantry was as intimidating as their number. Holland sent a trumpeter to request them to withdraw. The trumpeter came back with a counter-request from Leslie that Holland should withdraw. Holland having no other suggestion to put forward, accepted the hint. His cavalry wheeled about and fled, pursued by derisive shouts from the Scots.

The news of their discomfiture spread fast over the country-side. Two of the King's officers, leaning over the parapet of Berwick bridge that evening and speculating on the fortunes of the cavalry, were rudely interrupted by a passing Scotsman with news of Holland's flight. The account was speedily confirmed by the arrival of Lord Holland himself and all his men. To cover their ignominy, the cavalry started a rumour that the scoutmaster who had permitted them to ride straight into the jaws of the Scots was alone to blame. He was a local man, appointed by the Earl of Arundel, and as ill-fortune would have it, a Roman Catholic. It was not very logical to suspect a Roman Catholic of betraying them to the Covenanters, but the King's cavalry were in no mood for logic. Arundel indignantly defended the scoutmaster on the grounds that he had done good work against the Scots in the time of Queen Elizabeth.[80]

The King meanwhile had received a personal message from the Lord Deputy of Ireland. Wentworth, increasingly worried by all that he heard of the conduct of affairs, was anxious that his master should avoid anything so fatal as a military defeat at the hands of rebel subjects. He sent an active and highly intelligent Scotsman, John Leslie, Bishop of Raphoe in Ulster; this energetic, devoted and trustworthy cleric frankly implored the King to put off all idea of invading Scotland that summer.[81] Charles was still hesitant when the Covenanters' army appeared in force on the opposite bank of the Tweed. With speed and efficiency they made themselves a camp partly of tents and partly of turf and wood huts. The King carefully examined their activities through a perspective glass, and refused to be perturbed either by their nearness or their numbers.

Although the local farmers yielded to the temptation of selling their produce only to the English who were paying scarcity prices, the commissariat of the Scots had been too well organised for this to be of any great consequence. Alexander Leslie managed all with an authority astonishing in that little, gnarled, misshapen body; his manner, homely, friendly yet firm, worked well with the notoriously difficult Scots lords, of whom he had a dozen or more as colonels under him. The remarkable unity and good order of the Scots camp were largely his doing, but he owed something also to the ministers, mostly chosen from the younger men, who not only preached and prayed with fervour but carried arms like the soldiers and worked beside them on trenches and fortifications.[82]

Every company had its standard, stamped in letters of gold, " For Christ's Crown and Covenant," and most also had a piper or a fiddler to keep up their spirits. A tougher race than the English, used to exposure in toil and sport, following the plough or following the deer, they hardly noticed the weather which alternated between heavy thunderstorms and steamy heat and was a constant trial to the English forces. " None of our gentlemen," boasted Dr. Baillie, " was anything worse of lying some weeks together in their cloak and boots on the ground, or standing all night in arms in the greatest storm." [83]

In spite of the dross that the Covenanting party had collected to itself during eighteen months of triumphant progress, the inspiration which moved them to war was still profoundly religious. Even Sir Thomas Hope, the shrewd, calculating, ambitious lawyer, fancied that he caught a whisper from the Lord in answer to his prayers: *I will preserve and save my people.* Simpler men, with no stake in the matter but their consciences, believed in all sincerity that the Lord was with them. Night and morning in the Scots camp, psalms were sung, Scriptures expounded, loud and vehement extempore prayers raised to Heaven. The honest admitted that brawling and swearing also occurred but with so many thousands it was hardly to be avoided.[84]

In the King's quarters a different atmosphere reigned. In the King's mind, when he was at prayer, quietly, in his tent, the war seemed a war for religion and for the authority which was a part of that religion. But it was not a war of religion for the Lords Holland and Newcastle, venomously preparing to fight a duel in the fashionable French manner, three a side; nor for Windebanke's son, sulkily regretting the expensive pleasures of London; nor for Sir Edmund Verney, the King's standard-bearer, who had always thought the war unnecessary; nor for the hedgers and ditchers, the herdsmen and farm-hands who from Herefordshire and Suffolk, Lincoln and Lancashire, had been marched against their will to the border and who were wondering how their families fared, or what stay-at-homes made love to their girls in the June hayfields. Unlike the Scots, they had no ministers to inspire and instruct them. Only the most deplorable off-scourings of the Anglican Church had been routed out to play the part of chaplains. The better of them assumed fastidious airs which annoyed the troops, and the worse chewed tobacco and drank with the men in a way most unfitting to their cloth.[85]

In a camp demoralised with doubt and irritation, Charles called a council to his tent. Although the hostile Lords Brooke and Saye had left him at York, a spirit of obstruction persisted among many of the lords who remained. Lord Bristol, who had never been in the King's favour and had nothing to lose, spoke for several others when he flatly told the King that he must call Parliament before proceeding any further in the religious policy which had driven the Scots to revolt. The disheartened King, unwilling to discuss his policy further in public, gave Bristol a private audience which lasted for nearly two hours.[86] Charles did not agree with him, but he saw clearly from the discussion that he could not, in the face of so much opposition, successfully complete his war on the Scots that summer. In the course of the next few days, after a last vain appeal to London for a loan, he decided to abandon the campaign. He deliberately postponed the achievement of his plans, but he did not change his policy. He would enforce his will on the Scots when he had power to do so; until that time he would put them off with temporary concessions and promises.

Peace negotiations opened, in the English camp, on June 11th and were concluded a week later. The chief spokesmen for the Covenanters were Rothes, Henderson and Warriston with others in attendance. The King's manner, haughty at first, softened later, and he made on some of them—notably on Henderson and Baillie—a very agreeable impression. The King had much of the argumentative and legal-minded Scot in him and his attitude was not unattractive to his fellow Scotsmen; they respected and understood the depth of his religious feelings, while they disagreed with his doctrines. The King was feeling his way, not without subtlety and intelligence, with these men whom he intended in the final event to divide and outwit. It amused him to compel them into embarrassing admissions. When they spoke of the powers of excommunication which they claimed for the Assembly, Charles asked Rothes whether it had power to excommunicate him, the King of Scots. Rothes side-stepped: " Sir," he said, " you are so good a King as you will not deserve; but if I were King and should offend, I think the Church of Scotland might excommunicate me." [87] The King did not appear unduly displeased by this answer.

A few days later when the Earl of Argyll made his appearance, Charles gave him a long audience and permitted him to kiss his hand.[88] Not two months ago, he had wished to proclaim Argyll and Rothes traitors, exempt from all pardon. If in their hearts they did not fully trust his new graciousness, they were not to blame. But they preserved the conventions that the King himself laid down for them, and replied with courtesy when courtesy was offered. Not so Warriston; his trenchant language embarrassed his colleagues, especially Henderson, who was shocked to hear him openly express his distrust of the King's offers. When Charles promised the Scots another Assembly and Parliament to discuss the future of their Church, Warriston declared his belief that the King was playing for time, with the intention of ultimately overruling by force whatever the Assembly might decide. Charles turned on him in royal wrath; " The Devil himself," he declared, " could not make a more uncharitable construction." [89] The King's indignation was genuine because in his anger at such insolence he had probably forgotten that this devilish interpretation of his actions was unquestionably correct.

Warriston spoke out what others only thought. Rothes and Argyll were not deceived, although Henderson and some of the milder ministers—the warm-hearted, voluble Baillie of course—were convinced that the war was over, the King their friend and the Kirk safe. The Covenanters had little to lose by the postponement of the struggle and possibly much to gain. In that, the calculations of their ablest men were wiser than the King's. They were gaining sympathy every day in England, and they had friends abroad. Charles's attempts to borrow troops from the Cardinal Infante to use against Scotland were known and abhorred in Holland, which had suffered much from the King's intervention in their war; a Dutch warship in English territorial waters had recently held up an English merchantman transporting fifteen hundred Spanish soldiers to the Netherlands. This kind of thing made the Dutch sympathetic to any and all opponents of King Charles.[90] France, deeply involved in a war with Spain, might be drawn into sympathy with Scotland on the same pretext. In the meantime an Assembly and a Parliament in Scotland could only build up more strongly the constitutional position of the Covenanters.

With such mental reservations on both sides the Pacification of Berwick was signed in Lord Arundel's tent on June 19th, 1639. Both armies were to disband. The King undertook to come in person to Scotland for the meeting of Parliament and for the Assembly of the Kirk to be called in the early autumn. On the following day many of the English lords were entertained by Leslie at dinner and conducted round the Scottish camp, where the soldiers received them with friendly enthusiasm and the pious wish " God bless His Majesty and the Devil confound the Bishops." [91]

On the border, temporary peace had come. But on the same day, outside Aberdeen, the first battle of the long civil wars was being fought out between Aboyne's Gordons and Montrose's Covenanters. They had not heard of the Treaty.

Montrose had returned with reinforcements and some cannon, the latter in charge of two artillery officers from the German wars, Middleton and Henderson. The first attempt to assault the town on its western side was repelled by the counter-attack of the Gordons, but towards evening a second attack was mounted from the south, across the narrow approach known as Brig o' Dee. On the early morning of the second day, June 19th, Montrose had his batteries moved close against the bridge and, in a day-long continuous cannonade, battered down part of the city gates and the morale of the defenders. The Gordons withdrew leaving the citizens to surrender and Montrose for the third time entered Aberdeen as a conqueror, and for the third time resisted the pleas of some of his officers and of the more vindictive ministers for a general sack of the town.

The fame of the great cannonade re-echoed through Scotland, carrying the names of Montrose's two artillery officers into ballad fame.

> His name was Major Middleton,
> That manned the Brig o' Dee;
> His name was Colonel Henderson;
> That let the cannons flee.[92]

It was on June 24th that Hamilton, still in his character of King's Commissioner, had peace officially proclaimed at Edinburgh and received the keys of the Castle for the King. Already, between the signing and the proclamation, doubt and suspicion had grown, for Charles had publicly announced that the calling of a new Parliament and Assembly must be held to annul the acts of the "pretended" General Assembly of Glasgow. This the Covenanters declared was contrary to the spirit of the Treaty, and Hamilton, making his solemn entry to Edinburgh, was accordingly greeted with cries of "Traitor" or pious exhortations to "Stand by Jesus Christ." [93] The King's use of that insulting phrase—the "pretended" Assembly—added to the mounting unrest and when, on the evening of July 1st, the new Assembly was officially proclaimed by the luckless Traquair, and the bishops were summoned to sit in it, Edinburgh broke into riot. Traquair was rescued from the rabble only by the intervention of some of the better-behaved Covenanting gentlemen who gave him their protection.[94] He hurried back to Berwick to consult with the King.

He found that the King's mood had already hardened. No sooner had the Scots army disbanded than the wilder sparks among the King's officers began to boast that they could have eaten them alive had the King but risked a battle. Huntly, newly released from Edinburgh Castle, had reached Berwick to fall on his knees before his royal master in a blaze of indignation, frustrated loyalty and fatherly pride in the exploits of his favourite son, Aboyne. The King bestowed a number of knighthoods on his gallant officers to console them for not having been able to show their mettle. He also wrote to Attorney-General Bankes and Solicitor-General Littleton to inform him by what means they could compel obstructive sheriffs to collect Ship-money.[95] While they, far off in London, considered the best means of prosecuting these offenders, the King, assisted by Hamilton (who slept nightly in his room),[96] worked out his further policy against the men with whom, a fortnight before, he had signed a treaty of peace.

Traquair now slyly advised the King that no act passed by an incomplete Parliament, one for instance from which the clergy were absent, would be good in law. He therefore advised Charles not to summon the bishops either to the new Assembly or the new Parliament because he would the more easily be able to annul the proceedings of an incomplete Parliament.[97] Charles agreed to this disingenuous plan, and Traquair returned to Edinburgh, with full powers as the King's Commissioner, in succession to Hamilton, to call and conduct the coming Parliament.

For Hamilton himself the King had other plans and he had been freed of the difficult responsibility of acting officially for the King in order that he might act, unofficially, with greater freedom. On July 17th the King issued to him a secret warrant to approach at his own discretion any members of the Covenanting party he chose and to pretend sympathy for their point of view if by that means he could better serve the King. Half spy, half conciliator, and wholly confused, Hamilton was by his dubious, but authorised, machinations to bring only fresh trouble on his master.[98]

The unreality of the peace settlement was already clear. When Charles summoned the Covenanting Lords to wait on him at Berwick several of them, but principally Argyll, failed to appear. The King received those who had come, led by Rothes and Montrose, with a coldness markedly different from his manner at the signing of the Treaty. He objected strongly to what he described as breaches of the agreement on their side—the Edinburgh riots, the continuation of inflammatory preaching, the persecution of those who had remained loyal to him. He declared himself above all unsatisfied with so small a deputation from their party and commanded them to go back and fetch Argyll, Henderson and the provosts of Edinburgh and Stirling.

The lords withdrew, well aware of a rumour raised all round the Court that the King intended to seize Argyll, and very probably the rest of the deputation, as soon as they came back.[99] Had such a stroke seriously been intended and had it succeeded, it would have crippled their party; it was not surprising, therefore, that none of them returned to Berwick. A week later three others appeared bearing their excuses and those of Argyll and hinting that they feared to fall into a trap. The message gave the King the excuse he needed to end all pretences. He curtly informed the messengers that if the Covenanters trusted him so little, he trusted them even less; he would not come to

Edinburgh for their Parliament but would return to London forthwith.

Before he left Berwick, the King sent for Wentworth's emissary the Bishop of Raphoe. He spoke fully and privately to this discreet messenger on the evening of July 27th, saying all that he wished the Lord Deputy of Ireland to know but would not trust to paper. What he wrote was the brief and significant request to Wentworth: " Come when you will, you shall be welcome———" [100]

A year too late, the King was turning for help to the ablest of all his councillors. The Lord Deputy of Ireland was to come home at last.

BOOK II CHAPTER IV REFERENCES

1. *C.S.P.D.*, 1638–9, p. 97; *Harleian Miscellany*, III, 211.
2. Knowler, II, pp. 232–3.
3. Laud, *Works*, VII, p. 425.
4. *C.S.P.D.*, 1636–9, p. 471.
5. The resemblance between the events of the Low Countries in the 1560's and those of Scotland in the 1630's is so close that it is surprising that it should so long have escaped comment. The part played by the nobles (for Rothes read Brederode, for Argyll read William of Orange) is very similar, and the means chosen is the same. Supplications were presented to the government, the mob was encouraged to demonstrate, etc. Much of the similarity was natural, the same causes producing the same effects. But some of it may perhaps have been imitative. There is room for a thorough study of Dutch-Scottish relations during the century of the Reformation.
6. *Bankes MSS.*, 62/28b.
7. *C.S.P.D.*, 1638–9, January 1639 *passim*.
8. *H.M.C. Buccleuch MSS.*, Vol. I, pp. 278, 282–3; *C.S.P.D.*, 1638–9, p. 196; Knowler, II, 246.
9. *C.S.P.D.*, 1638–9.
10. *H.M.C. Buccleuch MSS.*, I, pp. 278, 282–3.
11. *Ibid.*, p. 278; Knowler, II, 287.
12. *Buccleuch MSS.*, I, p. 277.
13. *C.S.P.D.*, 1639, p. 3.
14. *Strafford MSS.*, VII, Wentworth to Laud, February 7th, 1639.
15. *C.S.P.D.*, 1638–9, p. 372.
16. *C.S.P. Ven.*, 1636–9, p. 497.
17. *C.S.P.D.*, 1638–9, pp. 362, 378.

18. *C.S.P.D.*, 1639, p. 234.
19. Burnet, *Lives*, p. 113.
20. *Buccleuch MSS.*, I, p. 282.
21. *C.S.P.D.*, 1638–9, p. 184.
22. *C.S.P.D.*, 1639, pp. 19–20, 49–50, 59, 95.
23. *C.S.P.D.*, 1638–9, pp. 357, 385–6, 437, 505, 564.
24. *Strafford MSS.*, X, Osborne to Wentworth, *circa* Dec. 1638; *C.S.P.D.*, 1638–9, pp. 291–2, 311, 328, 445.
25. *Clarendon State Papers*, II, pp. 19–24.
26. *C.S.P.D.*, 1638–9, p. 362.
27. Rushworth, II, pp. 803–17.
28. *Ibid.*, pp. 512, 555; *H.M.C.*, XII, App. II, p. 216–17; *C.S.P.D.*, 1638–9, pp. 417, 437, 588.
29. *C.S.P.D.*, 1638–9, p. 633.
30. *Ibid.*, p. 90; 1639, p. 300; *Bankes MSS.*, 42/78.
31. *C.S.P.D.*, 1638–9, p. 518.
32. *Ibid.*, p. 620.
33. Laud, *Works*, III, p. 231.
34. Bulteel, *Relation of the Troubles of the Foreign Churches*, London, 1645, pp. 48–51.
35. Laud, *Works*, VI, ii, p. 521; V, i, p. 177; III, p. 233.
36. *Strafford MSS*, X, folio 312.
37. *Breadalbane MSS.*, *Letters*, 1636–9, Nos. 759, 761.
38. Baillie, I, pp. 82–3.
39. Knowler, II, 272.
40. Baillie, I, p. 211.
41. Numerous letters in *Breadalbane MSS.*, *Letters*, 1639–59, refer to the organisation and raising of this army.
42. Baillie, I, p. 213.
43. *H.M.C.*, XII, App. IV, p. 503.
44. *Breadalbane MSS.*, *Letters*, 1639–59, Argyll to Glenorchy, April 6th, 1639.
45. Gordon of Rothiemay, II, 212; Spalding, I, 93–4.
46. *Strafford MSS.*, VII, April 10th, 1639; X, Dec. 10th, 1638, Feb. 10th and 26th, April 19th, June 3rd, 1639; Knowler, II, 300–7, 318 ff.
47. *Strafford MSS.*, X, May 30th, 1639; XI, October 30th, 1638, June 20th, 1639.
48. *C.S.P.D.*, 1638–9, pp. 506, 607, 622.
49. *C.S.P.D.*, 1639, p. 4; Balfour, II, p. 323; Burnet, p. 115.
50. Baillie, I, 195; Row, p. 511; Balfour, II, p. 301.
51. *C.S.P.D.*, 1639, p. 198.
52. Balfour, II, p. 323; Baillie, I, 195–6; *Strafford MSS*, X, Wentworth to Northumberland, 19th April, 1639.
53. Gordon of Rothiemay, II, 220–4.
54. *Ibid.*, 226–7; Spalding, I, p. 108.
55. *H.M.C.*, XII, *Appendix* IV, p. 504.
56. *C.S.P.D.*, 1639, pp. 41, 80–1.
57. *H.M.C.*, XII, *Appendix* IV, pp. 504–5.
58. Aston, *Diary*, Surtees Society, Durham, 1910, pp. 4–5.

59. Knowler, II, 313, 318.
60. *Ibid.*, p. 507; Aston, *Diary*, p. 5.
61. *C.S.P.D.*, 1639, pp. 59, 139; *H.M.C.*, *XII*, App. IV, pp. 507 f.
62. *Ibid.*, p. 509.
63. *H.M.C.*, *XII*, App. IV, p. 508; Aston, p. 6.
64. *C.S.P.D.*, 1639, p. 74; Rushworth, II, ii, p. 1327.
65. Knowler, II, p. 351; *C.S.P.D.*, 1639, pp. 96, 140; Rushworth, II, ii, p. 916.
66. *C.S.P.D.*, 1639, p. 74; Rushworth, II, ii, p. 1327.
67. *C.S.P. Ven.*, 1636–9, p. 545; *C.S.P.D.*, 1639, p. 180.
68. *C.S.P. Ven.*, 1636–9, p. 545.
69. Rushworth, II, ii, 923; Aston, *Diary*, p. 8.
70. Aston, *Diary*, pp. 9–10; *C.S.P.D.*, 1639, pp. 144–5, 155, 167, 173.
71. Spalding, I, pp. 160, 165, 169–71.
72. *C.S.P.D.*, 1639, pp. 126, 127, 146, 331; Guthry, 56–7; Burnet, *Lives*, pp. 121–2, 124, 137–9.
73. *Archaeologia Aeliana*, N.S. XXI, p. 101.
74. Aston, *Diary*, pp. 12–13; *C.S.P.D.*, 1639, p. 368.
75. *Ibid.*, pp. 267, 272; Aston, *Diary*, p. 21.
76. *C.S.P.D.*, 1638–9, pp. 566, 593–4; 1639, p. 270.
77. Aston, *Diary*, p. 14; *C.S.P.D.*, 1639, p. 243.
78. *Ibid.*, p. 272.
79. *Ibid.*, p. 267, 283; *H.M.C.* XII, Appendix IV, p. 517.
80. *C.S.P.D.*, 1639, pp. 272, 281–3; Rushworth, II, ii, pp. 937–8.
81. *C.S.P.D.*, 1639, p. 273.
82. Baillie, I, pp. 210–14.
83. *Loc. cit.*
84. *Loc. cit.*; Hope, *Diary*, p. 89.
85. *Correspondence of Jane, Lady Cornwallis*, London, 1842, p. 292; *C.S.P.D.*, 1639, pp. 294, 330.
86. *Ibid.*, p. 294.
87. *Ibid.*, p. 319.
88. Breadalbane MSS., *Letters*, 1639–59, Letter of June 22nd, 1639.
89. Warriston, *Diary*, p. 8.
90. *C.S.P.D.*, June 1639, *passim.*
91. Rushworth, II, ii, p. 960 f; *H.M.C.*, XII, *App.* IV, p. 514.
92. Maidment, *Ballads*, Edinburgh 1871, I, p. 290; Gordon of Rothiemay, II, pp. 276–?.
93. Burnet, *op. cit.*, p. 144; *C.S.P.D.*, 1639, p. 355.
94. *C.S.P.D.*, 1639, p. 370.
95. *Ibid.*, pp. 341–2, 348; *Bankes MSS.*, 5/40 and 41.
96. C.S.P.D., 1639, p. 409.
97. Burnet, *op. cit.*, p. 149.
98. *Hardwicke State Papers*, II, pp. 141–2.
99. *C.S.P.D.*, 1639, p. 407.
100. Knowler, II, p. 374.

BOOK THREE

AN ARMY IN IRELAND
August 1639 - November 1641

———————————————————————

CHAPTER ONE

THE RETURN OF THE LORD DEPUTY

August–December 1639

THE Bishop of Raphoe made the journey from the Scottish border to Ireland in nine days, and on August 5th, 1639, put the King's letter into the hands of Wentworth at his hunting-box in the green wooded country near the Naas. Here for some years past the Deputy had been building a stately red brick mansion as a country residence for future governors of Ireland. He studied the architectural maxims of Vitruvius and superintended the design with critical care. The strongly vaulted cellars for supplies of wine and grain were already completed and the walls with their straight, symmetrical, handsome windows had risen as high as the second storey; when the house was ready he hoped to have the honour of entertaining the King there. The urbane and solid structure among the pastures and deer forests was a manifestation of the new Ireland which he had been striving for the last six years to create and of which he had often spoken, with enthusiasm and honest self-praise, to the Archbishop and the King.

Although he had watched the events of the last year with irritation and anxiety, he faced the future without misgiving, for he was accustomed to succeeding in what he himself undertook and did not doubt his ability to solve the English and the Scottish problems as he had solved the Irish. He was confident that he could redeem the past errors of the King's policy and rebuild his shaken authority on a firm foundation. He believed that the motives of the Covenanters and of the English Puritans were political, not religious. They aimed not at bishops and ceremonies, but at monarchy itself " which they would have circumscribed and brought under the government of their narrow and shrivelled-up hearts." [1] He was right in perceiving that their religious views had significant political consequences, but he was wrong in believing them to be for that reason hypocritical and contemptible. For him it stood out, simple and clear, that the " strait bond of allegiance " was man's first earthly duty and that his heavenly duty was a purely private matter. In his own active and devoted career he was sustained by profound belief, but he was—strangely for so vehement a spirit—of a contemplative mind. He found peace in private meditation and regarded the ceremonies and organisation of the Church as things to be obediently endured because authority imposed them; he lacked the imagination to understand that for others the problem was not so simple, and, when he did not understand, Wentworth's dictatorial temperament led him to condemn.[2]

He received, a few days after the summons from the King, a letter of welcome from his old friend Northumberland, who had with relief and joy heard the news of his impending return. This quiet, proud, efficient nobleman was still unshaken in his loyalty to the King, although the appointment of Hamilton to command the fleet and of Holland to command the army had been a double disappointment to him. The summoning of Wentworth heralded, he hoped, a thorough reform in Charles's executive policy.

Northumberland had been the confidant of Wentworth's personal views on the Scots revolt some months earlier. Nothing would serve in Scotland, Wentworth had then said, but a downright demonstration of the King's power and justice—such a demonstration as his own firm government had given in Ireland. The Scots must first be defeated in war, which would not be difficult if the King's forces were efficiently used; next the King must appoint a strong governor to crush the pretensions of the nobility and reorganise the revenues of the country for the benefit of the Crown. The governor of conquered Scotland must be an Englishman.[3] Wentworth may have meant no more by this emphasis than that he did not wish to see Hamilton appointed, but he had confidence in his own powers, and he may have hoped for the opportunity to prove them in Scotland as he had done in Ireland.

It remained for him now only to settle his public and private affairs in Ireland before rejoining the King in London. Lord Chancellor Loftus, after a long wrangling year spent under arrest in his house in Dublin, was permitted to leave for England to answer before the Star Chamber for some of his misdemeanours. With his fall, the more dishonest speculators at the Council Table in Dublin had been reduced to obsequious silence. The composition of the Council was far from perfect, in Wentworth's opinion, while any of them remained on it, but at least they were balanced by the men of his own choosing or training—more especially his three devoted supporters, Christopher Wandesford, George Radcliffe and Philip Mainwaring, whom he had brought from England with him six years before. Of those with longer experience of Ireland, the most important was the young Earl of Ormonde, of a Norman-Irish family, whom Wentworth had encouraged and put forward, seeing in him an unusual mixture of conscience, ability and traditional knowledge. Before leaving for England, Wentworth initiated in the Court of Castle Chamber a series of prosecutions designed to quell any further rebellion from the Ulster Scots and to profit the Crown. Scottish landowners who had signed the Covenant were brought before the Court on charges of treason and sentenced to the forfeiture of all their lands.[4]

Answering the King's letter, Wentworth assured him of the loyalty and peace of Ireland but urged him to fortify Berwick and Carlisle before withdrawing his troops from the north. "The higher these incendiaries cast their smoke and flame, the higher duties may your Majesty justly call from us your faithful and obedient servants, to the performance whereof I shall cheerfully pass along through all the periods of this life, it being a very narrow and contemptible prospect for me to look upon myself, or anything that is mine, where your Majesty's honour and Crown are so deeply and so importantly concerned." [5]

He arranged for his two little daughters to spend the winter in England with their grandmother. "Nan, they tell me, danceth prettily," he wrote, but he believed that Arabella's French accent was not good. Both girls, he assured her, were well provided for and dowries of ten thousand pounds a-piece would be paid on their marriages. So, from his writing-desk, looking out on the serene summer landscape, with his only son sitting beside him, he set his affairs in order.[6] Neither then, nor for some months afterwards, did he feel any real anxiety as to his master's future or his own.

The same false optimism reigned at Court where the events of the past months were freely misinterpreted. The Scots, with infinitely superior forces, had not fought: therefore the Scots, though stubborn and rebellious, were not strong. The achievement of the eighteen-year-old Aboyne in taking Aberdeen was cried up to prove the power of the King's friends in Scotland. The humiliation of the royal army at Berwick was forgotten, then transformed, until defeat became triumph in disguise, and the poet Cowley could welcome the King with lyrical delight:

> Others by war their conquests gain,
> You, like a God, your ends obtain,
> Who, when rude chaos for His help did call,
> Spoke but the word and sweetly ordered all.[7]

The idea that the King had " sweetly ordered all " was not confined to poets and the Court; for a very short time and for different reasons it was shared by some of the English Puritans and by the Londoners, who received the King on his journey southwards with unusual enthusiasm in the belief that his behaviour to the Scots meant that he had changed his religious policy. The same illusion cheered the King's sister, the Queen of Bohemia, who from her exile in The Hague had followed the course of his policy with increasing anxiety; his renewed friend-

ship with the Spaniards, his unwillingness to help her eldest son
to regain his lands and his inability to secure the release of her
younger son from captivity in Austria had given her infinite
distress. But with sisterly loyalty she attributed his actions to the
evil advice of others, fixing her especial animosity on Archbishop
Laud. The news of the Pacification of Berwick gave the Queen
her first real happiness in many years. She believed that her
brother had truly given the hand of friendship to his fellow
Scotsmen and might even authorise General Leslie and some of
the Covenanting forces to fight for her son in Germany. "My
dear brother did all himself," she wrote of the peace which had
been made, "in spite of papists and clergy who did all they
could to disturb it. Leslie doth offer to go with his troops to
the Prince Elector." [8]

In the same month occurred another event to raise her own
and her son's hopes. Bernard of Saxe-Weimar, the greatest
soldier of fortune then fighting in the European conflict, died
suddenly at Breisach on the Rhine. Bernard, in alliance with
France and in French pay, had seized Breisach from the Spaniards
some months earlier, thereby blocking the vital line of communication from the Habsburg dominions in South Germany to
the Spanish Netherlands. The French had assumed that Bernard
would obediently place Breisach under their authority. Bernard,
aware of the immense power that this fortress gave him in the
strategy and politics of Europe, made no haste to do so. Its
future was still undecided when he died. He left his army, by
testament, to his second in command, the capable Swiss mercenary Erlach, who was thus enabled to offer his services (and
with them the immediate possession of Breisach) to the highest
bidder.

If money alone counted, the French would evidently gain
Erlach and all that he possessed. But a wild hope entered into
the usually cautious mind of the Elector Palatine: the army was
largely a German army, Breisach was a German town. As a
Rhinelander himself and a German, gravely wronged by the
House of Austria, he believed he could make an appeal to the

heart and honour of these German soldiers, who were known to be restive in the service of the French. If he could put himself at the head of this army, if with its help he could reconquer his own lands on the Rhine, he would become within a few months a prince to be reckoned with in European politics. The prospect was dazzling, and his chances of success were the greater now that his uncle, King Charles, had made peace with the Scots, and might support his enterprise with the promise of an army from Scotland.

The Elector lost no time. Hardly waiting to assemble his formal suite or charter suitable shipping, he put himself on the first boat he could find and hurried to join his uncle at Berwick to procure his consent to the hopeful plan. He missed Charles at Berwick but caught up with him at Durham and accompanied him to London, divulging his scheme as he went. On the journey, all the hopes that he and his mother had built on the recent peace with the Scots were laid in dismal ruin. Everything pointed to the continuance and intensification of his uncle's policy in the old direction.

The Spaniards, unable since the fall of Breisach to send troops to the Netherlands by the overland way of the Rhine, had, with the King's permission, secured the use of neutral English shipping for men as well as money, and while Charles was treaty-making at Berwick the Dutch stopped three English ships in the Channel on suspicion of carrying men from Spain to Flanders. The challenge was justified for there were fifteen hundred soldiers on board, of whom the Dutch took off the greater number, although one ship escaped and put into Portsmouth. Hence the Spanish officers, leaving their men in billets, made their way to London where they strolled between the Spanish embassy and Whitehall, haughtily complaining of the cowardice and perfidy of the English captains for yielding to the Dutch in their own waters. In due course they were allowed to march their men across England, by way of London, to Dover, where shipping was officially supplied to them for the Spanish Netherlands.[9]

Charles, on returning to London, immediately gave orders for the account of the Berwick negotiations which the Covenanters had published to be formally burnt by the common hangman, as unauthorised and seditious.[10] Two days later he assured the Scottish bishops that they need fear nothing from the forthcoming Assembly which he had called in Scotland: "though perhaps we may give way for the present to that which will be prejudicial both to the Church and our own government, yet we shall not leave thinking in time how to remedy both." [11]

Archbishop Laud, perturbed at the way in which the Scots revolt had encouraged the English Puritans, was considering stronger action against their excesses. An unusually large number of conventicles had been detected in various parts of the country during the past year. The worst case was that of a Dover stonemason named Trendall; he could not read, but on Sundays he would expound the Scriptures from seven in the morning until six at night with only an hour's interval for dinner. He declared that the Anglican hierarchy was unpleasing to God, and his audience of cobblers, fishermen and shipwrights with their wives and daughters found great comfort in all that he said.

The examples of Prynne, Burton, Bastwicke and Lilburne had evidently not been effective and Laud cogitated more terrible punishments. As a young man he had assisted with advice at the trial of Edward Wightman, the last English heretic to be burnt alive. Seeing some parallel between Wightman's aberrations and those of Trendall, he wrote to the aged Archbishop of York, Richard Neile, who had presided at the trial, for confirmation of certain details. Neile, a frail, kindly old man who disapproved of flogging in schools felt quite differently about heresy and obediently supplied the details.[12] Happily for Trendall, more pressing problems were to divert attention from him before the horrible precedent could be applied.

Before the end of August the Queen formally received a new emissary from the Pope, an attractive young Florentine nobleman, Count Rossetti. Although Rossetti, like Con before him, had no official standing at Court, being merely a private envoy to the Queen, the King was present when he had his first audience with Henrietta Maria, a circumstance which greatly stimulated the usual hostile rumours. The departing Con was, moreover, given an official escort from the royal navy as far as the French coast.[13]

While honour and consideration were accorded to the Spaniards and the Pope, the Elector Palatine can hardly have failed to observe the suspicion with which his uncle treated those who had fought for the Protestant cause. A group of Scottish officers who had served in the previous year in his own ill-fated army had come back from Germany in the course of the summer. They arrived at Newcastle after the war was over and asserted, on being questioned, that they had come to volunteer for the King. Charles suspected that they had intended to join the Covenanters and, in spite of their past record in his nephew's service, threw them all into prison where they remained for several months.[14]

In Scotland, meanwhile, on August 12th, Lord Traquair had opened a new Assembly of the Kirk in the King's name. On Traquair's right hand walked the King's principal supporter, the Marquis of Huntly, but such lustre as his splendid person shed upon the royal cause was tarnished for those who knew that he was able to appear in public in Edinburgh only because he had been granted special immunity from arrest by his creditors.[15] The episcopal party was badly served at the outset by George Graham, Bishop of Orkney, who, on the day of the Assembly's opening, publicly repudiated both his office and the erroneous belief in episcopacy which had led him to accept it.[16]

The Assembly next proceeded to repeat all that had been done at Glasgow in the previous autumn. Their actions showed that they were pursuing a constitutional as well as a religious reform. The King, by placing churchmen in positions of trust, had curtailed or evaded the influence of the nobles. In Scotland the old medieval struggle, never fully resolved, between the

King and the barons, had taken on a new form shaped by the ideas of the seventeenth century. By making the cause of Kirk and conscience their own, the Scots lords had found the surest way of weakening the power of the Crown by attacking the Crown's instruments, the bishops and the episcopal clergy. In the confusion of religious fervour and political calculation which characterised the Covenanting movement, politics had gained the upper hand. The acts of the Edinburgh Assembly made this very clear. They asserted a right to hold annual Assemblies, which would exercise a regular scrutiny over the King's religious policy. They not only abolished Episcopacy and declared that no churchman might hold any place of civil power, but declared that the appointment of bishops had always been wrong and contrary to God's law. Thus they ensured their own position for the future by retrospectively condemning the entire royal policy for the past forty years.

The King, hearing of this procedure, fully realised the distinction between a reversal of his religious policy and a total repudiation of it. He had been willing to yield to the abolition of episcopacy, having every intention of reimposing it afterwards. It was another matter to agree that it should be proclaimed, from all time, illegal and contrary to God. That he could not allow, and he wrote peremptorily to Traquair to refuse to accept any such resolution.[17]

He wrote too late. Traquair was unable to quell the pretensions of the Assembly who were now planning to impose the political and religious tenets of their party on all Scotland by forcing the entire adult male population to subscribe the Covenant. To make it possible for the King's supporters to do so, the additional clause which Montrose had added for Huntly's benefit earlier in the summer was incorporated in the Covenant, but this merely consisted of a reaffirmation in very general terms of loyalty to the Crown and meant as much or as little as circumstances dictated.

Traquair, faced by a deputation from the Assembly, led as usual by Rothes and Montrose, flanked by Henderson and

Warriston, was either too frightened or too stupid to comply with the King's latest commands, but after a little protest and hesitation accepted the Assembly's resolutions in the King's name.[18] It only remained for the Scottish Parliament, which he opened, also in the King's name, on August 31st, to give to the resolutions of the Assembly the force of laws.

Parliament in Scotland was more commonly called, in the European fashion, " the Estates," namely: nobility, clergy, barons (smaller gentry) and burghers. Neither in its structure nor in its procedure did it at all closely resemble the Parliament of England with its simpler division into Lords and Commons. In practice and tradition the King had used the bishops to control the nobles. The Reformation, by destroying the power of the bishops, had shattered a principal weapon in the King's hand. For this reason James VI had fought and won the struggle to bring back the bishops; for this reason he had coined his catch phrase " No Bishop, no King." Because of this the King, Wentworth and Laud, as well as the King's friends in Scotland, believed that the cause of the present rebellion was not the religious fervour of the people but the political ambitions of the nobility.

The superficial ingenuity which had inspired Traquair to argue at Berwick that the King could the more easily disallow the action of Parliament if it met in an incomplete form, without the bishops, was misapplied. The absence of the bishops in the Parliament of 1639 gave the Covenanting lords the opportunity for which they had been waiting to gain control of the government of Scotland. Once they had established themselves in power, all the King's horses and all the King's men would never again dislodge them.

The Scottish Parliament was in the habit of choosing a small committee known as the Lords of the Articles. This body was the intermediary between the Council, or the King, and Parliament. It acted as a committee on all proposed legislation, and the recommendations which it made to Parliament were usually accepted as tantamount to commands; on occasion the voting rights of the Estates were delegated to it. It was difficult to keep a full Parliament in session for more than a few weeks at a time in a country as sparsely populated as Scotland; the country's day-to-day affairs could hardly be carried on with all its principal citizens away from home. Parliament was therefore adjourned, often for very long periods. During the adjournments, the Lords of the Articles exercised the authority of the whole body. To control this committee was therefore to control Parliament, and successive Kings had, with greater or lesser effect, striven to do so. The Lords of the Articles were selected from each of the Estates, and the manner of their election had varied greatly over the centuries. Of late years the nobles and clergy had come to have the chief say in the matter, and the King had relied on the clergy to see that his own supporters were well represented.

In the Parliament of 1639, with no clergy, the question immediately arose: how were the Lords of the Articles to be chosen? The nobility asserted their right to decide on the new procedure and debated the matter behind closed doors for nearly five hours.

In this lengthy debate Argyll and the Covenanters had the best of it and nominated a majority of their own men for all three Estates. But it was evident to the far-sighted Argyll that he might not always be able to count on a victory of this kind if the nomination of the Lords became the exclusive concern of the nobles. He suggested therefore that in future each Estate should make its own nominations. This apparently democratic suggestion was based on the knowledge that the Covenanters could make and control a majority in the lesser Estates, the barons and burgesses, and this would stand them in good stead if the King were to create for himself a faction among the nobles.[19]

The Covenanters now controlled this particular Parliament and this Parliament might easily come to control the future destinies of Scotland. Once it had made the acts of the Assembly into laws, confirmed the abolition of Episcopacy and the exclusion of the clergy from secular office, the Lords of the Articles could arrange for the best positions in the King's government, forcibly vacated by his episcopal councillors, to fall into their own hands. With the Lords of the Articles well entrenched, with two of the King's own council—Argyll and Hope—working wholly in the interests of the Covenanters, the King's government in Scotland by the early autumn of 1639 was no more than a beleaguered fortress of which the Covenanters had blocked every strategic outlet and seduced a number of the garrison. Such was the consequence of the King's concessions at Berwick and the misplaced ingenuity of Traquair.

The naked emergence of the political motives of the Covenanters and the increasing influence of Argyll caused anxiety to some members of their own party, foremost among them the young Montrose. He was the hero of the war, he alone had had to face effective armed opposition and he alone had come to Edinburgh fresh from military victory at Brig o' Dee. He alone of the Covenanting nobles—the matter was worthy of notice—had the manners and appearance of a popular leader. His value to the party was therefore considerable and his influence important. He had naturally been appointed one of the Lords of the Articles; but he did not stand with Argyll and Rothes in striving to retain the choice within the control of their party. On the contrary he supported the Royalist Marquis of Huntly in asking that the King be given the right and the opportunity of confirming the appointment of the Lords of the Articles.[20]

This was the first clash between Argyll and Montrose. Their rivalry, which was later to be a dominating element in Scottish politics, arose from differences of character and tradition. Argyll was a Highland chief, born to lead and to govern, nurtured in the knowledge that he would one day exercise powers of life and death over thousands of clansmen, and that his first duty was to protect the land and lives of his people and destroy or subdue their enemies. Intense, concentrated and sincere religious feelings enabled him to accept these inherited traditions as sacred duties which God authorised for him anew every day at his prayers. He was not a small man, reaching for political power

—like Rothes, like Traquair; he was a man naturally born to greatness whose sense of religious mission, whose duties and responsibilities, impelled him to make full use of his abilities. His abilities, at least in organisation and the management of men and affairs, were incomparably greater than those of any other man in Scotland. The extension of his power was therefore, to him, natural, just and God-directed. At times, the Lord greatly blessed his endeavours, which proved to Argyll that they were pleasing in His sight.

The tradition of Montrose was different. He was not a Highlander and although he and some of his forebears occasionally styled themselves, or allowed themselves to be styled, chiefs, they enjoyed in practice no more rights over their fellow Grahams than were commonly exercised by the heads of families in southern Scotland. Their authority was respected by their kin, but it was not, as Argyll's and Huntly's was, the only effective law in a great region of land. Montrose and his ancestors belonged to a small, important group of noblemen whose lands lay along the foothills of the Highlands and whose traditional task had been alternately to defend the low-lying country from Highland raiders and to conciliate and tranquillise the land. The royal policy of successive Scots Kings had made these men by tradition respecters of the law and servants of the Crown. While Argyll's heritage was one of leadership and command, Montrose had been bred to an ideal of service and devotion. He had also travelled widely, had studied both in France and in Italy, had been on easy terms with men of many faiths and nations. He wore his Calvinism with a difference, did not confuse the personal wishes of the Almighty with his own, nor believe that every man who opposed Kirk or Covenant was necessarily damned.

Differences of tradition were accentuated by differences of character. Montrose was of a frank, impetuous character with the unsuspecting nature and cheerful over-confidence of one who had from childhood easily inspired affection and commanded admiration. Argyll, of a more secretive and complex temperament, whose youth had been crossed by family quarrels and jealousies, lacked that generosity of spirit which, in Montrose, made up for many faults. He had no great faith in the goodness of the world or of his fellow men and was vindictive and suspicious.

Both Montrose and Argyll had qualities of mind which raised them above such men as Traquair, Rothes, Huntly or Hamilton. Both men had vision; both worked for something greater than the mere winning of the next trick. Each in his different fashion sought the general good: for Argyll this meant the patriarchal government of Scotland by himself and his friends with the co-operation of the Kirk; for Montrose it meant the maintenance of the King's authority against the sectional ambitions of the few, together with the establishment of such checks on that authority as would guarantee the purity and independence of the Kirk. Of the two, Argyll's idea was to prove the easier of achievement.

In the autumn of 1639 time had not fully revealed these differences. But Montrose's defence of the King's rights was inconvenient: the Covenanters' seizure of political power had been bold enough to provoke criticism. It was essential therefore to maintain unity in their ranks and to stimulate the uncritical support of the people until they were abundantly sure of victory. If the King marched against Scotland again, as they well knew that he would, their chances of defeating him depended on their unanimity.

For this reason an inspired rumour about Montrose was at once circulated in Edinburgh. It was succinctly summarised in a tag fixed to the door of his lodging: *Invictus armis, verbis vincitur.* " Unconquered in arms, he was conquered by words." The tale went round that the fearless champion of the Covenant had been talked over by the King in private at Berwick and was no longer to be trusted.[21]

The arguments between the Covenanters and the King's friends in the Scottish Parliament were accompanied by disquieting rumours from England. The stream of Spanish troops and money continued to pass through the country; five more shiploads had been disembarked at Plymouth, to pass overland to Dover and thence get the advantage of the shorter passage to the Low Countries. The King remained deaf to the protests of the Dutch ambassador.[22]

An Armada of seventy-five vessels, with an army intended for the Netherlands, sailed up the Channel in mid-September. A Dutch fleet, less than half the size, attacked it, but the Spanish commander, relying on the neutrality, and hoping for the assistance, of the English Government, took refuge in the Downs. The Dutch admiral, Maerten Tromp, who was reinforced within a few days by supplies of ammunition from France, blockaded him. Week after week the two great armaments rode at anchor under the English coast while a third fleet, the King's Ship-money fleet, with the famous *Sovereign of the Seas* among them, watched from a safe distance. The situation was grave enough to embarrass even the King, for the Spanish Admiral instantly invoked the treaty of alliance and asked him to order the Dutch away. Charles, who knew that the Dutch would not relinquish their prey so easily, did not intend to involve himself, or his cherished fleet, in a clash with their navy. He attempted to pacify the Spanish ambassador by selling the Spanish fleet gunpowder at a very high price and assisting a few smaller vessels to run the blockade. Then he went to Windsor and postponed further action while the more indiscreet Roman Catholics, at Court and in the country, declared that the English fleet would certainly be ordered to the help of the Spaniards in the event of a fight. Among the King's Protestant subjects, from the Kentish coast to the Scottish lowlands, ugly rumours multiplied. The King's recent negotiations for help from the Spanish Netherlands against the Scots caused a general belief that the army on board the Spanish fleet had never been intended for the Netherlands but had come to assist the King against his rebellious subjects. Charles unintentionally encouraged these damaging speculations by making arrangements for billeting Spanish troops at Dover and Deal in case bad weather or the hostile Dutch should force the Spanish ships inshore.[23]

At about the same time he sent a party of courtier soldiers to inspect the fortifications of the Isle of Wight. They did little good, for with the cheerful assistance of the governor of Cowes Castle they shot off all the powder in the place firing salutes " in a frolic, at drinking of healths." Later one of their number, the high-spirited George Goring, delighted his companions by scrambling up the ladder to the public gibbet in the main square of Newport, pushing his head realistically through the dangling noose, and calling upon all who heard him to take warning from his untimely end and shun bad company.[24] The royal inspection of the kingdom's southern defences, however ineffective, only added to the general suspicion. Clearly the King was not himself fortifying these places against attack: was he therefore arranging to receive foreign troops to man them, and if foreign, presumably Spanish?

The King had no such intentions. While the Dutch fleet watched the Spanish in the Downs, and the English fleet watched both, the King, receiving representations from the Spanish and the Dutch envoys, pondered on the financial advantages to be gained from both or either. The deadlock was unbroken when the Elector Palatine took his leave, still meaning to place himself at the head of Bernard of Saxe-Weimar's troops, even though he had abandoned the hope of any help from his uncle for this enterprise. As his ship put out to cross the Channel all three fleets, competing in an empty courtesy to the King's nephew, saluted him with a salvo of guns.[25]

A week after the Elector's departure, Admiral Tromp, tired of waiting, opened fire on the Spaniards. What resulted was not so much a sea battle as the massacre of the helpless Armada. Under the onslaught of Dutch artillery and fire-ships, more than twenty Spanish ships ran ashore between Walmer and Deal: fourteen surrendered; several were burnt to the waterline. About a dozen escaped. The Spanish disaster was watched by crowds of joyful spectators from the English cliffs and beaches.

Sir John Pennington, the English admiral, had orders to prevent the fighting, which meant, if it meant anything, that he must command the Dutch to cease fire and close with them if they refused. He knew that to order his men to protect the Spaniards was to invite mutiny and, thanking God for a slight fog and a contrary breeze which excused his inaction, he spent the day in his cabin writing dispatches. When Admiral Tromp had completed the destruction of the Spanish fleet in English territorial waters, he courteously acknowledged King Charles's sovereignty over the seas by striking sail and firing a salute of nineteen guns.

From the south coast to the Scottish lowlands a sigh of relief and joy went up from the King's subjects; in Edinburgh they praised the wonderful mercies of the Lord which had delivered them from the greatest danger of the time; in London and along the south and eastern coasts they thanked God for deliverance from a second Armada; the Walloon pastor of Canterbury, heartened in his losing struggle with Archbishop Laud, composed a lengthy hymn in French to mark the great deliverance:

> Près de Folkestone, Hythe, Dovre et Diel
> Ce combat a esté cruel,
> Horrible et redoubtable. . . .

Spanish soldiers and mariners seeking shelter in the billets which had been ordered for them, were received, if at all, with angry looks and unwilling hands. Their wrecked ships, though the King's Council fulminated from a distance, were plundered by the Kentish fishermen.[26] In spite of this demonstration of popular feeling, some Roman Catholics at Court were indiscreet enough to complain of Sir John Pennington's culpable neglect in abandoning the Spaniards to their fate. At one moment it was even rumoured that proceedings would be taken against him.[27]

Charles was still battling with the aftermath of the great fight in the Downs when he received news—soon after known throughout the country—that his nephew, the Elector Palatine, was a prisoner. Cardinal Richelieu had almost brought negotiations for control of Breisach and the Saxe-Weimar troops to a happy conclusion for France and had no intention of permitting any last-minute attempt by the Elector to disturb his plans. He had him seized and shut up in a royal prison. While the mortified Prince fumed behind bolts and bars at Vincennes, his uncle of England, through his ambassador in Paris, lodged a dignified and useless protest.

In tavern and dinner-table talk among the King's Protestant subjects, the fate of the Elector Palatine provided more grounds for criticism. His two eldest nephews were now both prisoners, the younger, Rupert, in Austria, the elder in France; this was a fine way for the King of Great Britain to look after his sister and her orphan children!

To do him justice King Charles sincerely strove to relieve his nephews, and negotiations were almost continuously on foot for the release of both. But he was mistaken in dismissing the persistent misinterpretation and attack on his policy as groundless and insignificant because the first essential, if he wished to reduce the Covenanters and silence his critics in England, was to regain public confidence.

Lord Deputy Wentworth, who had arrived from Ireland in the midst of these events, made the same error. Convinced that firmness and a strong hand would be enough, he failed to realise that in a country where administration depended in the last resort on the goodwill and co-operation of the gentry, the King could be strong only if he had their support.

Wentworth, in spite of his ability and energy, brought with him indeed the burden of his own unpopularity to increase the dislike and suspicion of the royal policy. He was already known to the foreign ambassadors resident in London, and was soon known to the public, as wholly devoted to the Spanish interest in foreign policy. His conduct in Ireland had made him enemies in England: the City of London detested him for the part he had played in rejecting their offers for the renewal of their grant of lands in Derry. Lord Chancellor Loftus (now in England) and his friends had made his name odious in legal circles by emphasising the high-handed way in which he had used the prerogative to overrule the other Irish courts. Astonishing stories of his arrogance and cruelty were current in London, many of them groundless or greatly exaggerated. Earlier that year, a number of people had been before the Star Chamber on a charge of slandering him, by saying that he had caused the death of a poor prisoner in Dublin Castle by striking him with his cane. They were found guilty of deliberately inventing and spreading this libel,[28] but the case did Wentworth only harm. All London now knew the story and there were many who distrusted the Star Chamber verdict and pitied the slanderers as victims of Wentworth's wrath.

Wentworth's reputation was bad, not only in London; he had provoked the antagonism of all those in the north of England and especially in his native Yorkshire who had, for whatever motives, opposed the patriarchal despotism which he exercised as Lord President of the North. It was the King's singular ill-fortune that his ablest, strongest and most devoted servant had a facility for making enemies and for giving an ugly outward appearance to almost all innocent actions.

The immediate outcome of his arrival was a stiffening of policy towards the Scots. Traquair had been too weak to obey the King's orders to withstand the demands of the Assembly, but now, in the midst of his troubles with the Scottish Parliament, he received renewed instructions from the King couched in much more emphatic terms. Charles told him to refuse altogether to allow Parliament to abolish Episcopacy as " unlawful ": that word was on no account to be tolerated. The King declared himself perfectly willing to quarrel altogether with his Scottish Parliament provided that the quarrel could be made on a political, and not a religious question.

Traquair, thus encouraged, decided to gain time by an adjournment. Two of the Covenanting lords, without his permission, immediately went to London to protest against this interference with the session. Charles, advised it was thought by Wentworth, refused to see them and commanded them to leave London within six hours. This was on November 7th, 1639. On the following day the King dispatched to Traquair an order to prorogue Parliament until the following summer. Traquair did so with little success on November 14th, for the Lords of the Articles claimed the right to remain in session, thus maintaining in Edinburgh a body which exercised a great number of the powers of Parliament, and which continued to protest vigorously against the high-handed closing of the session before any legislation could be passed.[29] Traquair, knowing how ill he had advised the King, hurried to London and in a lengthy exculpation before the King's inner council—Hamilton, Wentworth and Laud—denounced the wickedness of the Covenanters and urged the King to make a second war.

Later, this weathercock politician was accused of having fatally influenced the King's decision. But Traquair only confirmed Charles in an opinion that he had not ceased to hold since he left Berwick. His preparations for next summer's campaign had begun several weeks before Traquair reached Whitehall and he had already sent out, for the fourth year in succession, demands for full payment of that famous temporary emergency tax, Ship-money. Orders for arms had been placed at Hamburg and the English arsenals were hard at work at the King's command; the fortification of Berwick, Carlisle, Hull and the Tower of London went on apace. To the great relief of the King, the party favourable to him in the divided city of London had got their candidate, Alderman Henry Garraway, chosen as Lord Mayor. With Wentworth's efficiency, with money from the City—a loan of £100,000 was hoped for—the King was confident he could subdue the rebel Scots.

Laud, Hamilton and Wentworth united to urge upon him one more measure to ensure success. Wentworth owed his success in Ireland partly to the dexterity with which he had overpersuaded and controlled the Irish Parliament. He believed that, with reasonable planning, the same thing could be done in England. His voice was therefore the strongest in urging Charles to abandon his stubborn resentment of Parliaments and summon in England a Parliament which could be organised into voting him adequate subsidies to quell the outrageous Scots. In the

ALGERNON PERCY, EARL OF NORTHUMBERLAND
by Anthony Van Dyck

interim he called upon the King's councillors to show their devotion to their royal master by freely lending to him. Wentworth knew very well, after ten years in the service of King Charles, that almost all the men round the Council table —and he himself not least—had made huge profits through the King's direct grants or the exploitation of his financial schemes. The moment had come for them to make some repayment. They could, he argued, easily raise three hundred thousand pounds between them, and he himself put down twenty thousand pounds for a beginning.[10]

BOOK III CHAPTER I REFERENCES

1. Knowler, II, pp. 372, 382; *Strafford MSS.*, X, Wentworth to Charles Price, Dec. 8th, 1638.

2. In a MS. account of his life among the Strafford MSS. possibly written by his tutor and chaplain Charles Greenwood, occurs the following: " He was bred up in Calvin's opinions wherein he was afterwards more moderate preferring piety before contention, labouring to be well grounded in fundamental truths rather than to trouble himself with disputes, and he chose rather to be devout than to make show of it . . . for many of his last years in his devotions he used Gerard's *Meditations and Exercitium Cotidianum.*" As a young man he bought *Le Jardin Sacré de l'Ame Solitaire* by Antoine de Nervèze, in which he wrote the inscription *Qui nimis notus omnibus ignotus moritur sibi.* The picture built up by these and other hints is of an essentially meditative and private type of religious belief, not very usual among his contemporaries in the political world. It casts an interesting light on his tragic career and flawed yet noble mind.

3. *Strafford MSS.*, X, Wentworth to Northumberland, August 28th, 1638.

4. *Ibid.*, Wentworth to the Council, July 18th, 1639; *C.S.P. Ireland*, 1633–47, pp. 223, 251.

5. Knowler, II, 376–7.

6. Knowler, II, 376, 378–9.

7. Cowley, *Poems*, Cambridge, 1905, p. 22.

8. *C.S.P. Ven.*, 1636–9, p. 551; *The Letters of Elizabeth Queen of Bohemia*, transcribed by L. M. Baker, London, 1953, p. 133.

9. *C.S.P.D.*, 1639, June, *passim*; *C.S.P. Ven.*, 1636–9, pp. 553, 555, 560.

10. Rushworth, II, ii, pp. 965–6.

11. Burnet, *Lives*, p. 154.

12. *C.S.P.D.*, 1639, p. 421; 1639–40, pp. 80–5.

13. *C.S.P. Ven.*, 1636–9, p. 570; *C.S.P.D.*, 1639, p. 463.

14. *C.S.P.D.*, 1639–40, pp. 263–6.
15. *Register P.C. Scot.*, 1639, p. 122.
16. Rushworth, II, ii, p. 957.
17. Burnet, *op. cit.*, pp. 156–7.
18. *Register P.C. Scot.*, 1639, *pp.* 131–2.
19. *Breadalbane MSS, Letters,* 1636–9, Letter 786; *Acts of Parliament of Scotland.* v. pp.252-5
20. *Ibid.*, Letter, 789.
21. Guthry, p. 65.
22. *C.S.P. Ven.*, 1636–9, p. 574.
23. *C.S.P.D.*, 1639–40, pp. 18, 22–3, 41; *Breadalbane MSS, Letters,* 1639–59, Letters of September 25th and 30th, 1639; *C.S.P. Ven.*, 1636–9, pp. 573, 575, 577.
24. Rushworth, II, ii, p. 969; Oglander, p. 98–9.
25. *C.S.P.D.*, 1639–40, pp. 22, 24–7, 32–40.
26. *C.S.P.D.*, 1639–40, pp. 33, 35, 45; 1640–1, p. 19; *Breadalbane MSS, Letters,* 1639–59, Letter of October 18th, 1639; Cross, *History of the Walloon Church*, London, 1898, pp. 97–8; *Clarendon State Papers*, II, pp. 72–9.
27. *C.S.P.D.*, 1639–40, p. 37. For this great sea battle see also C. R. Boxer's article on Tromp in *The Mariner's Mirror*, XL, (1954) and his edition of Tromp's journal for 1639.
28. *C.S.P. Ireland*, 1633–47, p. 113; *C.S.P. Ven.*, 1636–9, p. 595.
29. *Register P.C. Scot.*, 1639, p. 142; Burnet, *op. cit*, p. 160.
30. *C.S.P.D.*, 1639–40, pp. 149, 158; Laud, *Works*, III, p. 233.

THE SHORT PARLIAMENT

December 1639–May 1640

THE explanation of Wentworth's confident belief that he could manage a Parliament was to be found in his own experience. Not only had he managed an Irish Parliament, he had very nearly managed the last English Parliament. In those days he had been one of the principal Parliamentary leaders in opposition to the Crown but his aim had been to achieve an understanding with the King in the interests of Parliament. He had failed to do so because the King and Court had blankly refused to co-operate; owing to their intransigence the leadership of the House had been taken out of Wentworth's hands by the more extreme Sir John Eliot.

Eliot was now dead and Wentworth knew, or thought he knew, from his own past experience the calibre of the surviving Parliamentary leaders—John Pym, William Strode, John Hampden, Denzil Holles. He knew that managing a Parliament depended on the intelligent co-operation of the King (or his Deputy as in Ireland) with those in the Commons who understood Parliamentary strategy and were working in the King's interest. He believed that it would be possible to organise a vocal Court party in the House which, if it could count on an intelligent response from the King's council, would be able to outmanœuvre the old opposition. With his own intimate knowledge of the moods and reactions of the House of Commons, he did not doubt his ability to supply that co-operation. In this confidence he awaited the assembling of the English Parliament in April. With the King's permission he also summoned the Irish Parliament for March so that its obedient behaviour, on which he could count, would provide an example to England. In the meantime all his efforts were bent on making effective preparations for war on the Scots.

A small Council of War was appointed to decide on the necessary measures and this time the King seemed willing to employ those who had the most knowledge of military and naval matters. Northumberland was appointed General of the future army and Secretary Windebanke had the delicate task of telling the last commander-in-chief Lord Arundel that he was not merely superseded but excluded from the Council of War.[1]

Windebanke seems to have acquitted himself tolerably of this duty. The little man's hands were, that winter, inordinately full of business, for the King had dismissed the other Secretary of State, Sir John Coke. Coke was seventy-five years old and had always been slow, old-fashioned in his ideas and rather obstinate. He was suspected, perhaps unjustly, of taking bribes from the Dutch, as Cottington probably did from the Spaniards and Windebanke from everyone, but his going left a valuable appointment vacant and stirred up a chatter of intrigue.

Windebanke was too busy to act as secretary to the Council of War and, before a new Secretary of State was chosen, it was essential to put at least some competent clerk into this post. The place was one of trust rather than of profit, and choice fell on Edward Nicholas, an unassuming man who had already spent half a lifetime serving the Court in various secretarial capacities. One of the King's few happy chances in that evil time made him decide on this honest, painstaking, faithful servant, who was to become the unrewarded, unreproachful general factotum of the Royalist cause through twenty disastrous years.

The Council of War, with Wentworth dominating and Nicholas taking notes, met regularly three times a week throughout the winter, the King himself being frequently present. On paper, the Council did well. The defences of the Tower were set in order, and those of Berwick made rapid progress. Hull was to be garrisoned with troops from Ireland. In spite of a stormy winter, with destructive gales, heavy snow and floods in Essex and the fens, preparations at these strong points seemed to be satisfactory. In the very heart of the Covenanting country, the King held Edinburgh Castle, the only remaining fruit of the Pacification of Berwick. His garrison there was commanded by the tough old soldier Patrick Ruthven. Before the supposed peace with his Scots subjects broke down he had managed to send men and supplies to stand a six months' siege if necessary, and more ammunition was from time to time smuggled in, disguised as barrels of beer.

Plans were made for the manufacture of swords in England at the rate of 1,000 a month, and for a corresponding supply of muskets, light cannon, powder and shot; others were to be bought abroad, the whole to serve an army of 35,000 foot and 3,000 horse. Portable bread ovens and flour mills were arranged for, and the usual inventors who put forward ingenious plans, such as that by which a single man could fire two hundred muskets simultaneously, were briskly dealt with. Measures were also taken to prevent the exploitation of so-called " dead pays " by officers who made false musters. For this offence the death penalty was decreed, but in order to remove the temptation the pay of the officers was to be exceptionally liberal and—of course—prompt.[2] The lack of good officers having been a principal weakness of his army in the previous summer, Charles was full of gifts and promises to distinguished Scottish and English soldiers serving abroad, some of whom accepted his offers. He was also in treaty with the government of the Spanish Netherlands for arms and men, and a little later he opened similar hopeful negotiations with the King of Denmark. His diplomatic soundings were not exclusively military. His daughters, Mary and Elizabeth, were nine and five years old, and he appears, in the course of the winter, to have made tentative and very secret offers of the elder to the King of Spain for

the Infante Don Balthasar Carlos and of the younger to the Prince
of Orange for his son.

The winter was thus on the whole profitably occupied,
although the Court did not unlearn its habits of frivolity and
intrigue. Wentworth, had he more carefully considered the
men and motives which he despised, would have been aware
that to work a thorough reform in the royal administration
he needed more than his own and the Archbishop's energy,
Northumberland's solid ability and the honest care of Edward
Nicholas.

From November onwards the King was daily rehearsing the
masque which was to be given at the Christmas revels; this, one
of the most elaborate ever to be mounted, may have served
a lesser purpose in keeping some idle hands out of mischief.
Although the King and—rather surprisingly—the Master of the
Ordnance, Lord Newport, found time to take part in it, the
performers were mostly drawn from the smaller fry of Whitehall.
Davenant had supplied the words, Inigo Jones the decor, and
the subject was yet another variation on the King's favourite
theme: it represented the furies of disorder and rebellion stilled
by " the great and wise Philogenes "—the King who loved his
people.

Two fashionable marriages varied the Court's routine, the
King giving away the brides in person and the Queen helping in
the ceremony of putting them to bed. These successive events,
and a third which was intended to follow, represented policy
as well as pleasure. The bridegrooms were the sons of the Earl
of Cork, the most successful of all the entrepeneurs in Ireland
and still so rich, even after a brush or two with Wentworth,
that the King thought it wise to flatter him in hopes of a loan.
Giving three well-born and well-dowered girls to three of his
sons was an act of royal forethought, but the bridegrooms were
very young and the second bride babbled so indignantly to her
girl friends of her disappointment on the wedding night that
the third intended bride drew back and even appeared in public
on the arm of a previous admirer. The third intended bride-

groom, a formidable young tough, who took after his father, instantly challenged the rival to a duel. All this pleasingly diverted the Court from more serious business, but did not, in the end, much profit the King. The Earl of Cork had kept the careful habits of his humble origin; he made the same pair of expensive shoes serve each bridegroom in turn, and, when the weddings were over, he packed his pretty daughters-in-law into a hired coach and drove to Court with them to tell the King that he could not, with so many family responsibilities, spare any money for a loan.[4]

There was frequent speculation at Court on the appointment of a new Secretary of State to replace Coke. Wentworth was in favour of the Earl of Leicester for the post; he was brother-in-law to Northumberland and represented the same moderate and intelligent point of view. The King, however, was entirely averse to this choice, and Hamilton, later supported by the Queen, strongly urged the claims of the pushful Sir Harry Vane, the Comptroller of the Household. A professional courtier, and a man of the world, Vane, for all his ambition, did not think himself ideal for the post; he wrote slowly and lacked method, two embarrassing drawbacks since he would be expected to take full notes at council meetings.

Wentworth neither liked nor trusted Vane and, with that harsh indifference to other men's feelings which was his greatest failing, chose this moment to offend him by an act of astonishing tactlessness. The King had decided to gratify Wentworth's own yearning for worldly greatness by raising him from a Viscounty to an Earldom. Wentworth chose for title the name of the region in Yorkshire where his lands were chiefly situated, Strafford. But he wished also to have a courtesy title for his only son. At some remote period of the Wentworth family history they had been associated with Raby Castle, the present seat of Sir Harry Vane. The new Earl of Strafford asked the King to make his son Viscount Raby. Vane was justifiably indignant and his indignation was fully shared by all his friends and by all Strafford's enemies. For a few weeks, while the outrage was news, the Court was tacitly divided into two camps on the rights and wrongs of Vane and Strafford.[5] It was unfortunate that Strafford should have exercised his talent for making enemies at a time when he most needed friends, but an error which might have been trivial in its consequences became serious when, on February 3rd, 1640, the Queen and Hamilton got their way and Vane, much to his surprise, was appointed Secretary of State.

This was not the only new appointment that winter. The old Earl of Stirling, the unpopular and ineffective Secretary of State for Scotland, conveniently died. The broad hints of Traquair, who had long had his eye on the place, were disregarded by the King, who appointed instead Hamilton's brother, the twenty-four-year-old Earl of Lanark, a reserved, melancholic young man, obedient to his brother's commands.

The most important change was caused by the death of Lord Keeper Coventry. This distinguished, traditional and moderate man was an old friend of Strafford's. Although he had steadfastly supported the King's policy from the beginning of his reign and had upheld the legality of Ship-money, he was a respected and respectable figure. Within ten days of his death the King appointed as his successor the truculent and highly unpopular Finch, who took over his new honours and responsibilities with " such a clatter " of self-importance as to irritate and annoy his subordinates and his fellow councillors.[6] Instead therefore of having the co-operation of men whom he trusted, Strafford had seen no fewer than three posts of influence in the State and at Court fall into what he could only regard as the wrong hands.

An air of confident gaiety prevailed at Court. The Queen was pregnant, always a cause for congratulation and rejoicing, and the King was in the highest good humour. He sat late at cards while Windebanke's assistants waited impatiently to all hours of the night with letters for his signature.[7] From Mortlake he ordered new sets of tapestries which, before spring came, were " all ready finished upon the looms." [8] The masque, assiduously rehearsed for nearly three months, was pronounced with complacency by Inigo Jones to be the finest he had ever staged. The Queen's mother, the royal children and a distinguished throng of courtiers and ambassadors were edified by the sight of the King, in silvery blue, and the Queen, attired as an Amazon, descending from the clouds to vanquish the furies of rebellion.[9]

Some days after this performance another delegation from the Covenanters reached the Court, on February 20th, 1640. It was again led by Lord Loudoun, a dour, intelligent lawyer who had risen to prominence in the party during the last year as a principal henchman of his cousin Argyll. This time the King agreed to see them, though without any intention of granting or even receiving their requests. They still obstinately demanded, " on the knees of their hearts " as they rather oddly put it, that he should accept the legislation put forward by the Scottish Parliament as well as the new method of choosing the Lords of the Articles.[10]

The Scots, on the way to London, had distributed copies of their own account of the Pacification of Berwick, the account which the King had had burnt in the previous August. In open conversation they had compared the King to a truant schoolboy who had promised them everything when his schoolmaster Laud was not by, and had taken it all back again when the Archbishop resumed his sway.[11]

In the circumstances the King received them with asperity [12] and rejected their demands. They had expected some help from his Council, especially Pembroke and Salisbury, both of whom were suspected with some justice of having assisted in the distribution of Covenanting propaganda. But in this the Scots were disappointed, for when Pembroke was confronted, in the King's presence, with a letter which Rothes had sent asking for his good offices on behalf of the Scots, he thought it wiser to reject it with indignation.[13] The time had not come for him to show his hand.

While the King coldly argued with Loudoun and his fellows,

he wrote privately to the Royalist commander of Edinburgh Castle, instructing him to be in readiness to fire on the town as soon as he should think it necessary.[14] Charles had no intention of coming to any peaceful agreement with the Scots, but he held their commissioners in England with delays, questions and arguments for another reason. Some time during the winter Traquair had sought to regain his favour by placing in his hands a copy of a letter which the leading Covenanters had written to the King of France. This rhetorical composition implored Louis XIII to show his ancient friendship for Scotland by mediating for them with his brother of England. They had nothing to conceal, the Covenanters declared, and were willing that all their acts should be illuminated as with a ray of sunlight. The malicious asserted that there had been some trouble about this phrase between Montrose, whose poetic inspiration it was, and Maitland who had asserted that the word " rai " meant not a sunbeam but a vulgar kind of fish.[15]

This letter, in the King's opinion, was evidence enough to put all its signatories at the mercy of the law. They were the best known of the leaders—among others, Rothes, Montrose, and Loudoun himself; Argyll had as usual avoided incrimination. If it could be released at the moment when Parliament met, the King thought it would demonstrate that the Covenanters were shameless traitors seeking the intervention of a foreign power in the affairs of Great Britain. It might well be the means of rallying the English against the Scots, and if one of the traitors, Loudoun, could be confronted in person with his crime and arrested for it, the dramatic effect of the revelation on Parliament assembled at Westminster would be all the stronger.

Charles's natural faith in his own government contributed as much as the possession of this letter to the confidence with which he awaited the assembling of Parliament. Manifestations of popular discontent continued without materially disturbing his optimism. He believed, and the over-confident Strafford ministered to that belief, that all opposition, whether secular or religious, was the work of a minority.

The vicar and people of the suburban parish of St. Giles'-in-the-Fields urgently complained to the Privy Council of three Catholic priests who were openly conducting missionary work. They had already twenty-one conversions to their credit so that—the vicar palpably exaggerated—there would soon be no Protestant parishioners left.[16] The Council took no action in response to the complaint.   Meanwhile, quarrels between the Laudian clergy and their parishioners continued.   One or two obstinate men, lamented the vicar of St. Ives in Huntingdon, could disturb a whole parish: his entire flock, once amenable, had refused to come to the altar rails to receive the sacrament, because two recalcitrant Puritans had set a bad example. The significant thing, overlooked by the vicar of St. Ives and the King of England, was not that *two* began the trouble, but that all the rest joined in.[17]

Puritanism mingled with local resentments to cause scenes of violence. The mayor of Sudbury insolently shut up a government official in a cage used for criminals, where the people pelted him with mud and stones in spite of the joint efforts of the vicar and parish constable to rescue him. In Herefordshire one of the bishop's secretaries who attempted to establish the episcopal right to some common land was killed by a rabble of poor folk. More significant were the proceedings at Lewes Quarter Sessions when a group of Sussex justices, led by Anthony Stapley, registered a formal protest against the alterations and innovations recently made in some of the neighbouring churches. These things, they proclaimed, were contrary to the will, and insulting to the glory, of God.[18] In Northumberland, and more especially at Newcastle, the Puritans gave trouble of a more instantly dangerous kind. Scots known to be Covenanters were freely entertained and allowed to roam about the borders, spying out the King's military preparations. The mayor of Newcastle, accused of having allowed two of them to make a thorough inspection of the city walls, replied coolly that he had taken them for merchants travelling on business. The northern churches meanwhile were said to be half-empty while Puritan meetings were so full and so frequent as to defy all attempts at suppression.[19] In London at the Middle Temple Edward Bagshaw, an influential and popular reader, announced a course for the coming term to show that by an ancient law—25 Edward III Cap. 7—the clergy were not entitled to any say in Parliament either in civil or religious matters. Lord Keeper Finch ordered him instantly to alter his subject. Bagshaw, feigning the astonishment of innocence, argued that the subject was a most interesting one in law. Finch conceded that it was, but at the present time " unseasonable," and Bagshaw capitulated.[20]

Resistance to the collection of Ship-money was by this time almost nation-wide; even the county of Devon with its powerful seafaring tradition was as sullen as inland Bedfordshire. The Sheriff of Yorkshire encouraged the gentry to refuse to pay, and the Sheriff of Northamptonshire reported that he could not assess the county because the Grand Jury, going flatly against the majority decision in the Hampden case, had declared Ship-money illegal.[21] Finch roundly told the judges before they rode on circuit, to insist on the legality of Ship-money and the duty of paying it. " I know not how it comes about," he complained, " that there is not alacrity and cheerfulness given to the obedience of His Majesty's writs for Ship-money."

In London the Royalist Lord Mayor Garraway and the aldermen whose interests in Spanish trade bound them to the King were in a minority against their discontented colleagues. Apart from the Londonderry business, still bitterly resented, an ill-timed quarrel broke out between the powerful Merchant Adventurers and the Duke of Lennox. Charles had recently granted to his young cousin the exclusive rights of levying the dues on the shipment of raw wool from London. In theory these dues were intended to curtail the export of material which could be worked up in England. The profitable trade of the Merchant Adventurers Company was at the cost of the English weavers and knitters, and the King's attempt to check a process which was altering the structure of English economy and causing widespread distress had been prompted in the first place by anxiety at the growth of unemployment in the wool-working districts. The idea behind the intervention was benevolent but its implementation was, as usual, defective. The inspectors and collectors employed by Lennox had no responsibility except to bring in enough money to satisfy the Duke's stewards and to help themselves to a few pickings by the way. The inevitable trouble between the Duke's men and the merchants reached a peak during the spring of 1640 when Lennox, asserting his rights with the co-operation of the King's navy, impounded all ships with cargoes of wool in ports throughout the kingdom.[23]

The King and his friends accidentally stimulated the opposition while their deliberate efforts to placate their critics were few and misconceived. The recalling in the previous year of more than twenty different monopolies, patents and other forms of interference with trade and manufacture had not been wholly successful and the King found it necessary to abolish a number of the same monopolies over again,[24] which suggests that the previous ordinance had been disregarded.

To show his goodwill he ordered the release from prison of two members of the 1629 Parliament who, partly owing to their own obstinacy, had remained under constraint for the whole of the intervening eleven years. William Strode and Benjamin Valentine might, at any time, have bought their way out by paying the fines imposed on them for their opposition to the King's will in the House of Commons, but as they denied the justice of their condemnation they had preferred to stay in prison. Neither of them on his release showed any gratitude to the King and each went down into the country to organise his own re-election to the coming Parliament.

The election cast its shadow far before it. Lord Keeper Finch, when he instructed the judges in their special duties before they rode on circuit, had touched on other questions beside Ship-money. "There are some," he said, "that affect popularity, diving into the people's hearts with kisses, offerings and fawnings." The judges were to keep a sharp watch for any signs of this reprehensible behaviour among sheriffs and magistrates and were to prevent the neglect of justice, law and order which might arise from it.[25]

This "diving into the people's hearts" was suspect because those who did it had ulterior motives, and although Finch may have had habitual corruptions or deflections of justice in mind, it is more likely that he was thinking of the forthcoming Parliament. "Kisses, offerings and fawnings" by local great ones within two months of a projected Parliament would be mainly directed to securing the suffrage of the freeholders for candidates of their own choosing.

In theory Members of Parliament were elected in the county by freeholders and in the towns by burgesses of a certain standing. In practice, elections frequently degenerated into contests between rival landowners or rival families to get their friends and dependants chosen. Sometimes, to make certain of a seat, the same man would be a candidate in more than one borough. Should he be elected for both, he could make his choice between them afterwards. At other times a bewildered sheriff or mayor, caught between rival factions and anxious to offend no one, would make a double return and leave it to the House of Commons themselves to decide at Westminster which candidate had been truly elected. Bribery, intimidation, flattering promises or dishonest counting of votes were common. But in spite of this disorder something like a representation of local and national interests was obtained. The promises made, and sometimes implemented, were truly related to local needs; the men returned to Parliament were rarely professional politicians—a breed unknown outside the close circle of the Court and government—and they almost always bore some relation to the places they represented, having interests or lands or kinsfolk in the neighbourhood. A great number were lawyers, some were local squires, some the sons, and some the secretaries or stewards, of noblemen.

Party organisation as such hardly yet existed, although the Court, for the past hundred years, had been in the habit of securing seats in Parliament for the principal advisers and officials of the Crown. This was an accepted procedure, but when the critics of the Crown showed signs of attempting the same thing so as to ensure coherent representation in the Commons, the Court looked upon it as an outrageous conspiracy. In 1640 the critics of the King had what they had never had before: in the directors of the Providence Company, that largely Puritan group of influential men, they had an executive body which could to some extent unite and organise the efforts of their friends.

The King's Council on the one hand and the Providence Company on the other may be said faintly to foreshadow, in their relation to the forthcoming election, the executive committees of the party in power and of the opposition party. But in this peculiar and somewhat fortuitous political development the heads had come into existence without bodies. Neither the Council nor the lords and gentlemen of the Providence Company could count on the support of anything that resembled a political party. For the last seventy years a " Court " party and a " Country " party had been vaguely spoken of, but the terms meant nothing definite. No programme and no defined principles held these " parties " together. The greater number of the Commons were governed by family loyalties, by personal obligations and by the local interests of their boroughs, and might be swayed now one way, now another.

When it came to an election, the Court had to depend in the last resort not on those who supported its policy and principles but on the intelligence and zeal with which courtiers could exploit local rivalries and influence to get their friends returned to Parliament. The same was true of the opponents of the Court, whose leaders were now, almost for the first time, acting as a co-ordinated group.

There was in truth little to choose between the methods employed by the Court and by its opponents in striving for the upper hand in counties and boroughs. Lord Saye busily organising the return of his two sons to swell the opposition was neither more nor less reprehensible than the royalist lords who mobilised their families and dependants in the interests of the

Court. The courtiers, finding local sympathies aroused and marshalled against them in more regions than usual, cried out indignantly on all this " bandying for places." Their own clergy were encouraged to preach political sermons on obedience, but when Puritan preachers were found to be preaching political sermons too, that was a monstrous interference with the election. Both sides, of course, behaved with primitive dishonesty and each was shocked at the behaviour of the other. When Edward Nicholas, the Court candidate, failed to be returned for Sandwich because of a lying tale circulated in the town that he was a Papist, the King's supporters had legitimate reason to complain. But so had the opposition, when the royalist mayor of Hastings, overruling the will of the majority, returned the Court nominee, Windebanke's nephew.[26]

Early in March, while the elections in England were still incomplete, Strafford left for Ireland carrying the King's authority to raise the Irish army to nine thousand men and to obtain subsidies from the Irish Parliament. Not doubting his success, the Court already counted with confidence on this fiery and loyal force to destroy the Scots.[27] Strafford himself, more realist and less light of heart, punctuated his journey to Chester, where he was to take shipping, with the dispatch of salutary advice. He was irritated to hear that the Yorkshire gentry were making trouble about Ship-money, and urged that they be firmly reprimanded, but he did not doubt that one single, resounding victory, such as that which Charles would shortly win against the Scots, would establish his authority for good.[28] An untimely attack of gout delayed his crossing to Ireland: " that God should give me so good a heart only to take my legs from me in such a conjuncture of His Majesty's affairs as this is," he lamented, between mockery and earnest, to Laud, and when he managed to reach the sea, the winds were contrary. Parliament had been in session for two days before he reached Dublin and formally communicated to it the King's commands.

The Irish, Lords and Commons alike, received him with deferential enthusiasm. Publicly thanking the King for having

JOHN PYM
from an engraving by John Glover

bestowed on them "so just, wise, vigilant and profitable a governor," they voted the necessary subsidies and cheerfully agreed to enlarge the army, during the next two months, to a total of eight thousand foot and a thousand horse. Pending the collection of the subsidies, Strafford wrote to Cottington to hold up all the rents of the Londoners' forfeited estates in Derry to pay the Irish troops. At the same time the episcopal clergy of Ireland, gathered in Convocation, added their contribution to the moneys already voted in Parliament. In little more than a week Strafford had achieved all that was necessary in Dublin and could set sail for England again in a ship well named the *Confidence*. The English Parliament had but to follow the example of Ireland, he wrote triumphantly, " and His Majesty will have the Earl of Argyll and the rest of them very good cheap." [29]

The Court, in the quiet interlude between the elections and the meeting of Parliament, prepared for Easter. In Holy Week, Laud had the pleasure of presenting to the King young Nicholas Ferrar, a shy but welcome visitor from the Anglican retreat at Little Gidding. He had come to present to the Prince of Wales a sumptuous illustrated Bible that the ladies of the Ferrar household had arranged and bound for him. The King had time for a long interview with the devout young man and a long, admiring contemplation of his beautiful books, about the arrangement and composition of which he asked many questions. He sympathised with Master Ferrar's misfortune in being afflicted with a stammer, and discussed its cure. Singing, he said, was a help; it was also important to form every sentence complete in the head before uttering it. Determination alone was not enough and pebbles in the mouth were quite useless; he knew, for he had tried.

After his audience at Court, Ferrar carried the book to the Prince at Richmond in time for Easter. Young Charles unfastened the satin ribbons that secured the bright volume with exclamations of joy—" Here's a gallant outside! " Opening it, and finding it was the Bible—" Better and better! " cried the tactful child as he eagerly turned the pages, while the little Duke of York asked if the ladies of the Ferrar family would make him, too, a Bible the equal of his brother's.[30]

All this while, from the four points of the compass, several hundred gentlemen were travelling to London for the opening of Parliament. It took place on April 13th, 1640. The King, whose impediment prevented him from making a long speech, left it to Lord Keeper Finch to make his policy known. Finch was well known to all as the subservient Lord Chief Justice who had supported all the King's measures both on the bench and in the Star Chamber; he was remembered, too, for his unscrupulous enforcement of the forest laws in Essex, and as Speaker of the last Parliament, he had been manhandled by some of the Commons for serving the interests of the King and not of the House. He was for all these reasons the last man to persuade a suspicious House of Commons to support the King, and he also lacked the gift of handling a delicate situation. Ten years of uninterrupted authority, during which his every petty ambition had been gratified, had swelled his self-conceit. His speech to Parliament was patronising and arrogant; he made no attempt to persuade, to conciliate or to disarm potential critics.

Never, proclaimed Finch, had a country been blessed with so good a King, so virtuous a Queen, so hopeful a band of royal progeny. The Scots, out of unspeakable wickedness, had rebelled. It therefore behoved the English to grant generous subsidies that the rebels might speedily be crushed. This done, the King would graciously listen to any grievances that they wished to make known. He added that they must repair the insolencies of previous Parliaments by immediately passing a retroactive Bill, prepared for them by the royal councillors, granting the King Tonnage and Poundage for the whole reign: they were in fact to confirm the customs duties which Charles had levied on his own authority for the past ten years at the increased rates to which he had recently raised them. As Finch concluded his address, Charles dramatically handed to him the Covenanters' letter to the King of France. But this revelation of treason, which was expected to rally all loyal Englishmen against the Scots, failed of its effect. The contents of the letter neither convinced nor interested the Commons, while the tone of Finch's speech irritated them considerably.

In the first week of the session petitions complaining of Ship-money and the King's church policy came in from six different counties, and the attempts of the King's supporters to keep the Scots' treasonous letter before the House were frustrated by John Pym, the member for Tavistock. The secretary of the Providence Company had served in six previous Parliaments and was able to apply his practical organiser's mind to his knowledge of Parliamentary procedure. He was tacitly accepted as their leader by the King's opponents whose opinions he summarised in a long, clear analytical attack on the royal policy. His friends followed him up and neither Speaker Glanville, nor the two Secretaries of State, nor the various Court nominees and supporters, could force the debate back into the narrow channel mapped out for it in the King's interest by Lord Keeper Finch. The arrest of Lord Loudoun as a traitor for his participation in the Scottish letter to France and Windebanke's report of his preliminary examination before the Privy Council were treated by the Commons with as much indifference as if they were events in the moon.

On the sixth day of the session, the King's critics passed from complaint to action. They moved the re-investigation of the Hampden case; they called for an inquiry into the imprisonment of Strode, Valentine, Holles, and the late Sir John Eliot after the conclusion of the last Parliament; and they accused Finch of having committed a breach of privilege ten years before when, as their Speaker, he had tried to break up the session against their will. They thus implied that the King's judges had broken the law, and that the man he had appointed Chancellor was himself a delinquent.

This was the situation at the end of the first week, when Strafford, who had been delayed at Chester by another untimely attack of gout, at length arrived in London. The second week was spent in the concentrated efforts of the King's party to regain the initiative in the Commons. Convocation, which had met at the same time as Parliament, had virtuously voted a subsidy to the King, but it proved useless to hold up Convocation as an example to the Commons. On April 23rd, St. George's Day, Secretary Windebanke in a flight of eloquence appealed for a glorious gift to honour the glorious day, but the Commons, unmoved, continued to ask for redress of grievances before they voted supplies. The list of these was formidable—Ship-money, the exaction of coat-and-conduct money for the troops of the previous summer, monopolies and the whole variety of economic nuisances, intermission of Parliaments, breach of privilege and, of course, religion.

Strafford, still hopeful, saw in the intransigence of the Commons a strong possibility that they would give offence to the Lords and hoped that, by winning the Upper House, Charles could coerce the Lower House. In pursuance of this new strategy the King in person appealed to the Lords, offering to intermit the raising of Ship-money if they would vote supplies. Strafford, with great eloquence and a more compelling personality than Windebanke, secured a majority in the Upper House to condemn the resolution of the Commons to take grievances before supply. Following up this advantage, Finch, at a general meeting of both Houses, solemnly announced that while they delayed the war had already begun. The rebel Scots had fired on the King's garrison in Edinburgh.

So ended the second week. On Monday, April 27th, as soon as they met again, the Commons declared that the conduct of the Lords in discussing supply was a breach of their privileges and demanded a consultation between both Houses. Strafford believed that an open quarrel between the two Houses was now at hand, but he was thinking of the old assertive leadership of the Commons in the past. John Pym was determined that there should be no quarrel and he had several friends in the House of Lords—Warwick, Saye and Brooke—who were as resolute as he to prevent a breach. The fire that Strafford had tried to kindle was stamped out in two hours' talking. Further news from Edinburgh reached London in the course of the week: not the Scots, it seemed, but the King's garrison had fired the opening shot of the war.

In the Westminster taverns there was wild talk that the populace would burn Lambeth Palace over the Archbishop's head rather than let him make his unholy Bishops' War on Protestant Scotland. Strafford still obstinately believed that, with moderation and dexterity, the King could get his way with the Commons. The effective opposition was the work of a handful of members; the King's spokesmen—Vane, Windebanke and a dozen more—with help from Speaker Glanville could surely wrest the initiative from Pym. He suggested that the Secretaries of State be instructed to reduce the King's demands, to ask for six subsidies only, not twelve as heretofore, and to offer in return, and only after the subsidies had been voted, the grace which had already been offered in the House of Lords—the discontinuation of the present levy of Ship-money.

But the King would not sink his demands lower than eight subsidies, Secretary Vane handled the matter ineptly in the House, and Speaker Glanville, in an effort to conciliate the Commons, hinted at a doubt as to the legality of Ship-money. This, from a notorious King's man, greatly heartened the opposition, and an impertinent message was sent to Whitehall, that the Commons wished to hear Counsel's opinion on Ship-money before they further considered the propositions which had been laid before them.

Vane, whether on his own initiative or not, suddenly tried to break the deadlock. He told the House of Commons that if they would raise the subsidies to twelve and vote them instantly, Ship-money would be abolished. Pym and his friends took this, rightly, as the index of the King's distress. So far from accepting the bribe, they redoubled their demands that grievances, *all* grievances, be settled first.

Strafford believed that something might yet be done to control, cajole or compel this intractable Parliament, but the majority of the King's advisers were against him. The King himself was both angered and agitated by the business-like way in which Pym and his friends had appointed special committees to collect and examine popular complaints against the royal policy. Graver still, it was rumoured that the opposition leaders were in touch with the Scots and intended to bring up the religious grievances of Scotland as well as their own in the House, thus completely reversing the purpose for which Parliament had been called and exposing the King to a fundamental attack on his policy. Faced with this threat the Council met early in the morning on May 5th; Strafford, who came late owing to some mistake about the time, found himself unable to stand out against the majority who, with the King, were strongly for a dissolution. At eleven o'clock that day the King, in a speech of reproof and disappointment, dissolved the fourth unmanageable Parliament of his reign, and the last that he was ever able to dissolve.[31]

BOOK III   CHAPTER II   REFERENCES

1. *C.S.P.D.*, 1636-40, pp. 193-4.
2. *Ibid.*, pp. 224, 228, 296, 327-40, 398-9, 455, 468; Balfour, II, p. 373; *H.M.C.*, X, i, p. 48.
3. *C.S.P.D.*, 1639-40, pp. 109-11, 368, 420, 434; *C.S.P. Ven.*, 1640-2, p. 62; *Clarendon State Papers*, II, p. 83; Groen van Prinsterer, *Archives de la Maison d'Orange-Nassau*, 2nd Series, The Hague, 1858, III, pp. 159, 169.
4. *Ibid.*, pp. 297, 365; *Lismore Papers, First Series*, V, pp. 112, 118, 119, 148.
5. *C.S.P.D.*, 1639-40, January, *passim.*
6. *Ibid.*, p. 436.
7. *Ibid.*, p. 474.
8. *H.M.C.*, XV, II, p. 296.
9. *Ibid.*, p. 365; the text of the masque *Salmacida Spolia* is to be found in Davenant's *Works* and some designs for the dresses, drop scenes and effects have survived among the drawings of Inigo Jones.
10. *C.S.P.D.*, 1639-40, p. 472.
11. *Ibid.*, pp. 446-7, 557.
12. *C.S.P. Ven.*, 1640-2, p. 23.
13. Rushworth, II, ii, p. 984; Burnet, *Lives*, p. 165.
14. *C.S.P.D.*, 1639-40, p. 558.
15. Rushworth, II, ii, p. 956; Burnet, *op. cit.*, p. 161. In defence of Montrose's French as well as Maitland's it is fitting to record that Cotgrave's *Dictionary* gives " rai "

as another form of " rayon " for ray or sunbeam; he also gives the fish now commonly called " raie," as " rai."

16. *Commons Journals*, p. 41.

17. *C.S.P.D.*, 1639–40, pp. 444–5, 456.

18. *Ibid.*, pp. 260–1, 386; Brilliana Harley, *Letters, Camden Society*, London, 1854, p. 67.

19. *C.S.P.D.*, 1639–40, pp. 321–2, 345, 346, 401, 429, 469, 515 f.

20. *Ibid.*, pp. 522–4; Rushworth, II, ii, p. 990.

21. Rushworth, II, ii, p. 991.

22. *Ibid.*, 987.

23. *C.S.P.D.*, 1639–40, January–March, *passim*.

24. Rushworth, II, ii, p. 1203.

25. Rushworth, II, ii, p. 987.

26. *C.S.P.D.*, 1639–40, pp. 561, 564–5, 580–3, 587.

27. *C.S.P. Ven.*, 1640–2, p. 21.

28. Knowler, II, 393–4.

29. *Ibid.*, 394–403; *C.S.P. Ireland*, 1633–47, p. 239.

30. *Nicholas Ferrar: Two Lives*, ed. J. E. B. Mayor, Cambridge, 1855, pp. 126–37.

31. *Lords & Commons Journals;* Rushworth, II, ii, pp. 1114–20, 1131–7, 1154–5; *C.S.P.D.*, 1640, pp. 33, 39, 61, 64, 76–9, 108–10, 144–5; Whitaker, *Life of Sir George Radcliffe*, London, 1810, pp. 233–5.

CHAPTER THREE

THE SECOND SCOTS WAR

May–November 1640

THE dissolution of Parliament left the King no choice but to proceed with a firm hand. Strafford, in whose strength he trusted, still believed that resolution and efficient management could prevail. At the Council meeting on the day of the dissolution, he brushed aside the doubts of the realist Northumberland, and stirred his more cheerful and more irresponsible colleagues to some measure of activity.

Ireland—he asserted—was the King's to command, and in Ireland an army of 8,000 would be ready in a few weeks to be landed in the Western Highlands, or wherever else seemed best. If the English were slow to help their sovereign to subdue the rebel Scots "You have an army in Ireland you may employ here to reduce this kingdom." That phrase, or something like it, fell from his lips and was scribbled by Secretary Vane into his remarkably incoherent notes.[1] Whether Hamilton made any comments on this project, does not appear from Vane's notes. But Hamilton must have known that of all actions likely to inflame the Scots, and especially the lowland Scots and the Campbells, against the King, this of bringing Irish forces to fight them would be the worst. It could only appear to them as though the King had given the royal authority and arms to the savage forces which for centuries they had tried to check.

After the strenuous Council meeting of the morning, Strafford spent the afternoon of May 5th at his own house in a long session with the Spanish ambassadors. Three envoys to the

Court of King Charles, two from Spain and one from the Spanish Netherlands, now represented the Habsburg interest in England. Since the Spanish fleet had been shattered and the Rhine valley barred by the French occupation of Breisach, the co-operation of King Charles was more than ever essential for the transportation of the necessary troops from Spain to the battlefront in Flanders. The traffic had been quietly increasing for the last year and transports containing three thousand Spanish soldiers had been convoyed from the Downs to the Flemish coast while Parliament was still sitting. But the Spanish and Flemish governments needed a regular, reliable arrangement and were prepared, in their present straits, to pay handsomely for it.

The propositions discussed at Strafford's house on the afternoon of May 5th were dazzling: the Spaniards offered four million ducats in return for a permanent guard of thirty-five English warships to convoy their transports through the Channel.[2] Four million ducats would make King Charles master in his own house again, if he could fulfil his side of the bargain, but the Spaniards would want something more than mere promises before they paid over the money. The King had a fleet fully capable of performing the task if he could find enough sea captains to carry out his orders but, as the Spaniards had discovered during the disastrous battle in the Downs of the previous autumn, the King's power to command his navy was less than his will to do so. In spite of this the Spaniards were still prepared to give the King the benefit of the doubt; they still believed —partly because they wished to believe—that he could and would help them. The King of Spain had even indicated that he would be willing to discuss the possibility of a marriage alliance between his only son and Charles's eldest daughter.

With four million ducats in prospect the King felt strong enough to assert his authority with vigour against those who had opposed and embarrassed him in the last Parliament. Within twenty-four hours of the dissolution three leading men in the Lords and three in the Commons were arrested and their lodgings ransacked for evidence of correspondence with the Scots. They were the Earl of Warwick, Lord Brooke, Lord Saye, John Pym, John Hampden and Sir Walter Earle. The next day, four more members of the House of Commons had to answer before the Council for having questioned in Parliament the King's right to exact money for the equipment and transport of the levies. Another member of the House, John Crew, was peremptorily required to hand over his notes of the complaints reported to him as chairman of the committee chosen to inquire into religious grievances. Crew refused, on the grounds that the information was confidential and privileged; he followed the seven others to prison.[3]

Garraway the Royalist Lord Mayor, was summoned and told that the King must now double his previous demand for a loan of £100,000 from the City; he was requested to submit a list of citizens capable of advancing sufficient sums by Sunday at latest or the demand would be raised to £300,000 and be fully enforced. Garraway did his best, but on Sunday four of the aldermen who should have supplied the names of the richest citizens refused to give any information; for this offence they were at once arrested, but they remained stubborn.[4]

The rumbling discontent of London, the great, angry, Protestant seaport, suddenly burst into a roar of rage. Apprentices, effervescent with May Day humour joined the mariners and dock hands, a whole angry, young, vehement population, indignant that their merchant ships were held up, their trade hampered, their once glorious fleet an object of scorn, their favourite preachers imprisoned, Papists and Spaniards encouraged everywhere, Parliament turned out of doors because it had complained of their grievances, and the old sea-dog Warwick, whom the mariners loved, shut up in the Tower.

They came together on the south bank, from Southwark and Blackfriars: someone beat a drum to attract more. In their hundreds they poured westward, making for Laud's palace at Lambeth. Laud fled and his servants stood on their guard while the rabble surged round the walls and a young seaman tried to break in the door with a crowbar. The ringleaders were arrested but the apprentices smashed into the gaol and let them out. "God bless them all, God speed them all!" cried an excited Londoner as he fought back the constables who were trying to recapture the prisoners; later when he was informed against and questioned for these exuberant exclamations he declared that he had been praying for the King and his Council, not for the rioters at all. New crowds began to assemble at Southwark and Blackheath; Charles ordered the Lord Mayor to call out the trained bands against them when, with the suddenness of a summer storm, they dispersed.[5]

Charles, still unable to believe that anything in his government could have provoked such a demonstration, was sure that his ill-wishers had set the people on. Using the royal prerogative for the purpose for the second time in his reign, he had the man who had beaten the drum put to the torture, but the victim said nothing, having nothing to say. The seaman who had wielded a crowbar against the Archbishop's door was charged with high treason, the law being somewhat stretched for the purpose. He was hanged and quartered and his head spiked on London Bridge. His name was Thomas Bensted and he was only nineteen years old; for some time afterwards he was remembered on the London quaysides as a martyr whose innocent blood was on the guilty hands of Archbishop Laud.[6]

The May Day riots of London were echoed later that month by Whitsuntide riots at Colchester. A fantastic rumour went round among the ignorant poor of this Puritan district that Laud and the hated Matthew Wren, Bishop of Ely, were plotting mischief together at the house of a prominent Roman Catholic in the neighbourhood, which was said to be stuffed with arms. Gunpowder plots always found ready believers, and the mayor of Colchester, who was a sensible man, was confronted with angry crowds asserting that their town was in danger. Some of them claimed to have seen two villainous Irishmen slinking about the walls evidently intent on starting a fire. In order to quiet them the mayor had to call out the trained bands.[7]

While such grotesque suspicions went about, Convocation was still in session at Westminster, protected by an armed guard against the hostility of the populace. The legal position was doubtful as Convocation usually met only when Parliament was sitting and the King's critics were not slow to complain that the Anglican clergy continued undisturbed in their debates while the King's lay advisers, the Parliament of England, were silenced.[8]

The Archbishop agreed with Strafford that the best hope for the future lay in dauntless resolution: no concessions and no retreat. Convocation in May 1640 proclaimed the official triumph of the Laudian reforms in a series of new Canons. These set forth in unequivocal terms the doctrine of the Divine Right of Kings and decreed that it should be expounded by the clergy to their parishioners at least once a quarter. Twice a year they were to preach sermons on the importance of conformity to established doctrine. The hierarchy of the Church was confirmed and the placing of the Communion table in the East was made compulsory. Following the example set by Strafford in Ireland in the previous year, Convocation imposed an oath on all members of learned professions. They were to swear never wittingly to subvert " the government of this Church by Archbishops, Bishops, deans and archdeacons, &c. as it stands now established." Of all these defiant Canons, this provoked the loudest outcry. Were men to endanger their immortal souls, asked the Puritans, by swearing loyalty to an *etcetera*, a cipher, a monster, a mask which might conceal the Mass, the Pope, the Church of Rome?[9]

The Etcetera Oath—it soon had no other name—was the instant target of all abuse. " &c " to the Puritans became " the curl'd lock of Antichrist."[10] Insolent and jeering opposition broke out, showing how little reverence was felt for the King's or the bishops' authority. When the Bishop of London's Chancellor, with a huge mace borne before him, entered one church to exact the oath, the verger barred his way crying, " I care nothing for you, nor for your artichoke," and the jeering congregation took up his mockery.

An additional complication shadowed the passing of these unfortunate Canons. The Bishop of Gloucester, Godfrey Goodman, had warned Laud beforehand that he could not subscribe them. This woolly-minded, kind-hearted old scholar, once chaplain to the King's mother, had been elevated to a bishopric early in King Charles's reign and had been an exasperation to Laud ever since. He was an unabashed pluralist—like many of his colleagues—and his financial confusion and his debts were as openly criticised as was his ritualism in his Puritan-ridden diocese. In religion he was one of those who hoped that the unity of Catholic Christendom might yet be restored, and a means of reconciliation with Rome be found. The Canons of 1640 were too secular for him; by attaching the Anglican Church firmly to the King and the State they seemed to him to deepen and perpetuate the cruel gash in the spiritual unity of the Church made at the Reformation. He was neither a Roman Catholic nor an English Catholic; he believed, with the Creed, in one Holy Catholic Church and, as he pathetically told Laud, he would sooner be torn in pieces by wild horses than agree to Canons which appeared to accept and confirm the separation of Christendom.[11]

When it came to the point, Goodman tried to evade the issue by refusing to subscribe the Canons on the ground that they ought not to be passed unless Parliament was sitting. That a man whose opposition was based on Catholic principles should at the last minute take refuge behind a Puritan argument was too much for Laud. He suspended him from his bishopric and confined him in the Gatehouse.[12]

While the problem of Bishop Goodman was yet unsolved, a new Ship-money case, not brought by the Crown, had come before the courts. A London citizen, who had had his goods distrained because he refused to pay, brought an action against the sheriff for unlawful seizure. His case provided a public platform on which Ship-money was again discussed with no advantage to the Crown.[13]

These incidental troubles would have mattered little had

Strafford achieved the Spanish alliance with its promise of four
million ducats. But Strafford, within a week of the dissolution
of Parliament, fell gravely ill and during the interval of nearly
a month when he could not attend to business, the French and
the Dutch between them prevented the implementation of an
Anglo-Spanish treaty. Cardinal Richelieu, perceiving that the
King was no longer master in his own country, saw no purpose
in wasting an ambassador on him. Accordingly, he withdrew
the French envoy and left no one except a secretary—Montreuil,
a very good observer—to attend to French interests in England.

At about the same time, and with almost equal contempt,
Richelieu released the King's nephew the Elector Palatine. The
young man wished to come to England but was prevented by an
agitated letter from Secretary Vane, telling him that his uncle
could not receive him at present.[14] The arrival of his dispossessed
Protestant nephew would be calculated to agitate the Puritan
opposition and would moreover be extremely inconvenient
when the King was wooing the Spaniards.

The Spaniards in England no doubt drew conclusions un-
flattering to King Charles from the contemptuous indifference
of Richelieu. The behaviour of the Dutch envoy, the Baron de
Heenvliet, caused the breakdown of the negotiations altogether.
For France, a great power, English assistance to Spain would
have been hampering and inconvenient; but to the Dutch it
might be a matter of life and death. Heenvliet therefore spared
no pains to prevent the agreement. He made it clear that if
English ships assisted Spaniards in the transportation of their
troops, the Dutch would no longer treat them as neutrals; in
fact, that Charles could not become the ally of Spain on the
terms at present offered without involving himself in a war with
Holland. At the same time he sought out the leading merchants
of the East India Company whose ships, more frequently than
any others, were hired for the Spanish traffic. The East India
Company had no love for the Dutch, their principal rivals in
the trade with Asia, and for that reason they had willingly lent
themselves to the unpopular transport of men and money to

help in the war against them. But the East India merchants were Protestant, none the less; their ships were each provided with Foxe's *Book of Martyrs* as well as the Bible for the leisure reading of the crew.[15] Heenvliet played on the religious question while at the same time offering substantial concessions from the Dutch East India Company. Within a very few weeks, he had thrown difficulties in the way of the Spanish treaty which would, at the very least, take months to resolve, if indeed they could be resolved at all.[16] Strafford's vision of rebuilding royal authority on a foundation of Spanish gold faded into a remote future. Meanwhile the Scots war had to be fought.

In his desperate need for money the King permitted the Queen to sound the Pope's emissary, Count Rossetti, on the possibility of a loan from the Vatican. The Privy Council having for the most part subscribed handsomely to his funds (Hamilton gave £8,000) the King assessed all the Court officials and mulcted them in suitable forced gifts. Reviving his monopoly policy, he sold to another group of courtiers, among whom were his favourite attendant Endymion Porter and several of Windebanke's relations, the sole right to manufacture white writing-paper for the next fifty-seven years.[17]

On a sudden inspiration, late one Saturday afternoon, he seized the bullion deposited in the mint by London merchants and confronted them on the following Monday with an offer of 8 per cent interest on this unintentional loan to the Crown. The loyal Garraway, who was striving hard as Lord Mayor to raise loans and troops in the City, was startled by this unforeseen action and shocked still more when the King announced his intention of debasing the value of all coins below a shilling. The City revolted at this, imploring the King not to resort to measures so harmful to trade; rather than run the risk of any more royal experiments in finance, they agreed to advance the £200,000 he had asked of them some weeks before.[18] Having bought him off with this promise, they did not in fact keep it.

While the King and his Council wrestled with the money problem—Strafford grimly resolute, Cottington cheerfully fatalistic and Northumberland in glum despondency—the problem of raising the local levies troubled the nation at large.

English administration, and therefore the responsibility for bringing the troops together, rested on the gentry and the King had now reached the limit of his unpopularity with them. The breakdown in contact and understanding between the Crown and the men whose duty it was to execute its policy was almost total. After ten years in which they had submitted to persistent interference, to the irritation of knighthood fines, of petty prosecutions for enclosure, of prohibitions, licences and regulations affecting their closest interests, they saw themselves faced with the heavy trouble and not inconsiderable expense of making the largest levy of troops within the memory of man. And for what? For a war on their Protestant neighbours and fellow-subjects, provoked by the Archbishop.

So few were the gentry who fully supported the King in this dismal season that when his ministers had arranged for the return to Parliament of those favourable to his policy, they had done so at the expense of local administration. Sir Edward Osborne, the devoted Vice-President of the North, wrote despairingly to Strafford that every loyal gentleman in Yorkshire had been required in Parliament and, during their absence, the obstructionists had hindered all levying of troops and preparation for war.[19] This experience was not peculiar to the North. From the Home Counties, the Midlands, the Welsh marches, and the West came news of truculent and mutinous levies, and gentry either unwilling or unable to set them in better order. The long tradition of a decent obedience to the Crown made the gentry go through the business of getting the troops together but they were slack and dilatory and very bitterly resented the heavy charge for coat-and-conduct money, for clothing and transporting the men, which had to come out of their own pockets. A single vocal obstructionist could easily persuade his indifferent and unwilling colleagues to neglect a task that none of them liked. Examples of hindrance, even of downright refusal, sometimes came from the highest; sheriffs and deputy sheriffs, Lords Lieutenant and their deputies hesitated to send out the necessary warrants, argued and protested. The King's Council reprimanded some, summoned a few to London, even placed some under arrest: useless demonstrations in the face of hostility so deep and wide.

This evil brought another in its train. The King seemed doomed to involve himself ever more deeply in misunderstandings, for the only group in the country which strongly supported him were the old Roman Catholic gentry. They could not help him to raise the troops because they were excluded from the administration, but they provided the officers of the army as it came into being. This was inevitable. While the sons of the Protestant squires were mostly unwilling to go, the sons of the recusant gentry were eager to serve a King who had been generous to them. Many of them were, in any case, trained soldiers. The wars abroad had for two generations provided one of the few careers open to the younger sons of Catholic landowners, excluded by their religion from the professions. Far more professional soldiers therefore were to be found among English Catholics than among English Protestants. Although English Protestant adventurers fought in the armies of the Dutch and Swedes, by far the larger number of English soldiers serving abroad were Roman Catholic volunteers in the Spanish and Austrian forces. Many of these young men, feeling a genuine gratitude to a King who had protected their religion, and a genuine distaste for the opinions of the rebel Scots, had thrown up their foreign commissions and come home to help in the religious war.

The number of Roman Catholic officers in the army was therefore relatively high, although not as high as rumour made it. Nothing that the King did could stifle the continuous whispering of the old story that he was in some way selling England to Spain. In Scotland, for instance, it was stated that "His Majesty has absolutely taken the King of Spain by the hand" and in return for men and money had ceded him the Cinque Ports and a part of Ireland.[20] These tales were partly the echo of the alliance which had not materialised, and partly the outcome of the shocking situation on the English coasts. The Ship-money fleet, languishing for lack of funds, was involved in preparations for the Scots war, and the Channel guard was consequently so weakened that the Barbary pirates were again active and had recently carried off sixty men and women in the neighbourhood of Penzance. A fleet of twenty-four Dunkirkers —privateers who operated in unofficial alliance with Spain— were systematically landing and pillaging the Kent and Sussex shores, the navy being forbidden to meddle with them for fear of extinguishing for ever the King's hope of an alliance with Spain. As a result the Dunkirkers boldly spread to the Irish Sea and before the end of the summer had established a useful base on Islay where they co-operated with wilder Gaelic sea rovers from Ulster and the Hebrides.[21]

All these things naturally added to the discontent and anxiety of the King's subjects, the majority of whom made their living by the sea, and gave ground for the rumours which spread dangerously among the newly levied troops. Among those who were being assembled at the ports to be taken to Scotland by sea wholesale desertion began because they had heard—and believed—a story that they were to be carried off to Barbados for slaves.[22]

In other parts of the country the discontented levies broke into disorder and set themselves to levelling all unpopular enclosures. The Deputy Lieutenants of Staffordshire, having got the recalcitrant levies together and marched them into Uttoxeter, were called up from the supper table by the dismaying news that the men had left their billets and were throwing down and burning the fences round some newly enclosed forest land. In Derbyshire the troops tore down Sir John Coke's palings and set fire to his mill; later they killed the deer in Lord Huntingdon's park and released the prisoners from the county gaol. Riot, mutiny, robbery and violence were reported from Leominster, Hereford, Marlborough, Warwick, Oxford and Cambridge. The prisoners in the house of correction at Wakefield were set free by passing troops. In the fens, where the dismally wet spring had made the floods worse than usual, the perpetual outcry against the drainage project found expression in new riots. Since the King had officially taken over the scheme the fenlanders' resentment became easily fused with bitter feelings against his Church and his war. On a rumour that Laud's most efficient henchman, Matthew Wren, was at a meeting in Wisbech Church, a gang of angry soldiers battered on doors and windows shouting, " Give us the damned Bishop of Ely." All over the eastern counties, recruits burst into the churches, tore out and made bonfires of the Communion rails, usually with the approval of the inhabitants.[23]

If the men suspected an officer of Popery they sometimes refused obedience until they were satisfied that he would take the sacrament with them. Secretary Windebanke's second son, following in the footsteps of his elder brother " Signior Tomaso " as a wag and a character, nonplussed his men by affecting a fanatic Protestantism, kneeling down, praying loudly, and quoting the Scriptures on all occasions. Wisely, he also distributed free drinks and tobacco.[24]

The situation was less often a jesting matter. The Somerset levies murdered a Catholic officer before deserting homewards. The Dorset levies, who had marched very unwillingly as far as Faringdon in Berkshire, flared into violence at the supposed injustice of a martinet lieutenant, he too a Catholic. They stormed his lodging, and when the wretched man tried to save himself by scrambling out of the window along the iron strut which supported the inn sign, they pelted him down with stones, and later dragged him through the streets and clamped his lifeless body in the pillory.[25]

The disorders of the troops, violent and dangerous as they often were, menaced the royal government less than the open and secret protests of the professional classes. A dozen law students of Lincoln's Inn displayed their sympathies at the Three Cranes Tavern one evening by holding under the pump a hanger-on of the Court until he agreed to drink confusion to

Archbishop Laud. More sober and more serious were meetings like that which took place at Kettering during the summer when twenty-seven clergymen and some local worthies, including a justice of the peace, solemnly approved the cause of the Scots and pledged themselves in no circumstances to take the monstrous "Etcetera oath." [26]

While disaster approached, the King, who had replenished his stables at some expense in the spring, was hunting at Oatlands, from time to time riding in to Whitehall to see what progress his plans were making. At his pretty country palace early in July the Queen gave birth, with less difficulty than usual, to her eighth child, a healthy boy. To celebrate the occasion Charles ordered the release of all Catholic priests. A fortnight later the Archbishop came out from Lambeth to christen Prince Henry, who was carried to the font by a procession of brothers and sisters. His father created him Duke of Gloucester, but in the old medieval way he came to be known by the place of his birth and to the family he was always "Henry of Oatlands." Sometime in early childhood, in the palace gardens, he planted a cedar. The great tree is to-day the only surviving memorial of the once happy, gay and graceful Court brought there summer after summer by King Charles and his Queen. [27]

The birth of his youngest son and certain illusory hopes from Scotland greatly cheered the King. He believed that his enemies were ill-provided and quarrelling among themselves. He was wrong on the first point. The army of the Covenanters was incomparably better than his own. Parishes loyally provided their quota of men and arms, and the many professional soldiers still in Scotland, with others who had come home too late for last year's campaign, saw to their training. France had sent no help after all, but regular shiploads of arms came in from Holland, and the King's navy showed itself quite incompetent to check this traffic. The good wives of Edinburgh sacrificed three thousand pairs of sheets to make tents for the men. A gloomy informant of the King's in Edinburgh reported that three times as many men were in arms as in the previous year, better equipped, with more artillery. Charles preferred to trust in the cheerful reports of Lord Conway, his general at Newcastle, who persistently assured him that the Scots had no army worth speaking of and that all their talk of great forces was an empty vaunt.[28]

The King hoped with more reason that the Covenanting party was itself disintegrating. Montrose had been restive since the autumn and had exchanged letters with the King and with friends at Court. Uninformed as to the King's true intentions, puzzled and wounded by the reckless proceedings of some of his colleagues, he tried to be at one and the same time loyal to the Covenant and to the Crown. When the Scottish Estates met again in June, with no Royal Commissioner in the chair, and defied the King's order that they should immediately prorogue their meeting, Montrose protested against this flouting of the King's authority. He was overruled. The Estates confirmed the legislation of the previous autumn and resolved on November for their next meeting, all without the agreement of the King or of his representative. They had thus set up a precedent for meeting, legislating, and organising their future sessions without the help or consent of the Crown: a silent and profound altera- tion [29] which made the effective government of Scotland inde- pendent of the King.

A few weeks later occurred the first open quarrel between Montrose and Argyll. The Stewarts of Atholl and their neigh- bours the Ogilvys were rumoured to be stirring on the King's behalf. Late in June, Argyll, armed with a commission from the Estates, led a picked body of Campbells into the braes of Atholl to disarm the Stewarts. When their principal men came to his tent under a safe conduct, he arrested them and, deprived of leadership, the royalist movement in Atholl collapsed. Argyll improved the occasion by explaining the constitutional position to the misguided gentry of Atholl; some of them understood him to say that the conduct of the King in bringing an army against Scotland rendered him liable to deposition. Certainly from the time of that campaign in Atholl rumours began to circulate in Scotland that Argyll was for dethroning the King.[30]

The Atholl campaign at an end, Argyll transferred his attention from the Stewarts to the Ogilvys. Their chief's principal seat, Airlie Castle, had been occupied by an officer under Montrose's orders several weeks earlier. The occupation had been conducted with courtesy and restraint because Lord Airlie was next neighbour and first cousin to Montrose. Argyll trusted neither Montrose nor the measures he had taken. Disregarding his assertion that the Ogilvys had been rendered harmless, he marched on Airlie Castle with his clansmen, ordered Montrose's small garrison out, plundered and set fire to the place. The Earl of Airlie and his son were both in London with the King; in the castle was only the young Lady Ogilvy who was shortly expecting to lie in. Whatever military justification Argyll might plead, his harsh behaviour to a defenceless woman has remained from that day to this embedded in the ballad history of Scotland.

> Lady Ogilvy looks o'er her bower window,
> And O but she looks warely!
> And there she spied the great Argyll,
> Come to plunder the bonnie house of Airlie. . . .

When Argyll's men had taken all they wanted, the Ogilvys had not left in all their land so much as "a cock to crow day." There were those among the Covenanters, Montrose the chief of them, who bitterly blamed Argyll for this unnecessary violence. These quarrels echoed across the Border and news of them reached England in an exaggerated form; some said Montrose and Argyll had had a personal quarrel, and Argyll had accused Montrose of conniving at the escape of Lady Ogilvy and her unborn child.[31]

While the Campbells dealt with the Stewarts and Ogilvys, another detachment of Covenanters under Robert Monro, a professional trained in Germany, had attacked the Gordons, laid waste the regions of Banff and Strathbogie and carried off hostages from Aberdeen.[32]

The violence of these proceedings as well as the conduct of the Estates caused anxiety to others beside Montrose. They feared that their country was to become, as it had been in the past, a prey to the violence and ambition of those who exploited the political situation for their own ends. Their fears were confirmed when an extraordinary proposition was laid before the leaders of the Covenanting forces. It was suggested that in the present emergency Scotland should be divided into two regions—north of the Forth and south of the Forth—each to be under the military command of a single great lord. Argyll was to be in charge of the north, Hamilton of the south. Opposition to this scheme among the officers of the Covenanting army caused it to be abandoned almost at once; it is indeed hard to understand why Argyll thought that it had any chance of acceptance. For what were the soldiers to make of it? Hamilton, to whom overriding power was offered on the south side of Forth was the *King's* commander. The implication was that some private understanding existed between him and Argyll. The ordinary straightforward man could only assume that one or other of them was playing false. Montrose was not alone in assuming that both these great lords, whose private relations with each other had been the subject of speculation since the Glasgow Assembly, were concerned to gain some high advantage for themselves rather than to serve either King or Covenant.

The scheme was allowed to drop, but it was not surprising that Montrose and a party of friends gathered together soon after at the house of one of his kinsmen at Cumbernauld and there, at Montrose's instigation, drew up a secret agreement directed against Argyll, known as the Cumbernauld Bond. It was a statement of loyalty both to the Covenant and to the Crown, to which they added a joint undertaking to defend its true principles against " the particular and indirect practising of a few." [33]

Montrose no doubt saw a double purpose in creating this inner alliance of like-minded men within the ranks of the Covenanters. He intended to prevent the peculiar machinations of Argyll and Hamilton, whatever they were, and at the same time to reaffirm what he believed to be the honest intentions of true Covenanters towards the Crown.

He remained wholly sincere in his attachment to what he believed to be the original and authentic purpose of the Covenant —the freedom of the Scots Kirk. His doubts of Argyll notwithstanding, he was ready to take his place in the field against the forces which the King was preparing in England. Within a few days of signing the Cumbernauld Bond he brought his regiments, well equipped and in good order, to the rendezvous of the Covenanting army near Coldstream.

While the Scots forces gathered together in strength, Lord Conway at Newcastle, still astonishingly ill-informed, declared that they had not the power to invade. A week later, perturbed at evidence of their increasing numbers, he reported that they must either invade or disband: their army was too large to remain for long in that poor country. He seemed to think the latter course the more probable. But the Scots army among the border hills continued to grow. Suddenly, on August 16th, the King's Council in London, who had been fed all that summer with contemptuous and confident dispatches from Lord Conway, received the shocking announcement that he expected the Scots to cross the border in force at any moment and that, in the face of the odds, he could not hold Newcastle.[34]

In a crisis the King's natural courage gave him resolution. He immediately announced that he would go north to place himself at the head of his threatened and invaded people. The dissuasions of his advisers, who doubted the effect his presence would have, retarded him for a few days only and on Thursday, August 20th, he left for York.[35]

Early in the following week Strafford followed him. He had, until a few days before, intended to return to Dublin to embark the Irish army for which hitherto Hamilton had sent no shipping. An unforeseen disaster prevented him. Northumberland, the commander-in-chief, had fallen ill. Some said his illness was diplomatic. The kinder modern word is psycho-somatic; Northumberland tended to succumb to illness when he could no longer face his responsibilities. Once the admirer of Strafford, Northumberland had, all this year, failed to respond to the over-confident energy of his friend. Since the early spring he had predicted that the King would not be able to raise money enough to wage a successful war, and his reiteration of this comment at the council table, with a kind of gloomy relish, had long been his chief contribution to discussions of royal policy.[36] Northumberland, unlike Strafford, did not look upon an impossible task as a challenge to be taken up with defiant energy. He thought it foolish to attempt the impossible and no part of his duty to encourage the King in such a policy. His bad health, neither for the first nor the last time, was remarkably convenient.

Strafford's ill-health was his misfortune; at forty-seven he was already worn out with pain, knotted with gout and tor-mented by the stone. But he did not shirk the task before him. Taking up the burden cast down by Northumberland, he hurried northward to command the unruly rabble which had by this time come together from all parts of the kingdom in his native Yorkshire. Sir Jacob Astley was doing his best to equip them: "I am to receive all the arch-knaves of this Kingdom and arm them at Selby," he said, with an old soldier's humorous resignation.[37]

Strafford's confidence seemed unshaken. He had soundly rated Conway for his cowardly dispatch, refusing to believe that the situation could be so desperate and urging him to behave with more soldierly resolution.[38] In Huntingdon, at dusk, at the end of his first day's journey, he received news that the Scots were over the Border. Even in this he claimed to see cause for rejoicing: the English would surely not endure to let their ancient enemy triumph on their own soil and would rise in wrath to defend it.[39] Cheered by this illusion, he continued his painful journey northward.

On August 20th the Scots at Coldstream crossed the Tweed

into England. After the wet summer, the river was very full, and Montrose, to encourage his men, waded through on foot, the first of the whole army. Some attributed the act to the young man's desire for public notice and his wish to contradict the growing suspicion " that in his heart he was turned royalist."[40] But Montrose was a man of action, without so much guile; a natural leader in the field, he had done what time and the hour demanded.

While the Scots advanced without opposition from the Tweed to the Tyne, the King reached York. The discontented gentry of the county had petitioned him a fortnight earlier against the expense of raising troops, complaining that the disturbed summer had injured both trade and the harvest, and asking insistently for a new Parliament. In a long interview with these petitioners, Charles enlarged persuasively on the danger which now threatened their native county, and won so much upon them that they agreed to raise more forces which, with their King in person to command them, would hold the Tees, as a second line of defence against the invaders.[41]

The King, like Strafford, still believed that he could rally support for his war and was considering a new means of doing so, by calling the nobility of the realm to an emergency council at York.[42] He had not forgotten his intention of placing himself as soon as possible in the front line of his people's defences, and on August 27th he led an army out of York for the relief of Newcastle; he had got as far as Northallerton before he realised that he was already too late.[43]

The Scots had advanced in business-like fashion across the Northumbrian hills, sometimes encouraged by the music of the pipes and sometimes by the singing of psalms. The people made no move against them, although a woman shouted at Leslie, " Will Jesus Christ not come to England without twenty thousand men at his back? "[44] At Wooler they easily brushed off a skirmishing party sent against them from Berwick. Lord Conway at Newcastle, among the unfinished fortifications, declared that the Tyne must be held at all costs and added, " but there goes more to it than to bid it to be done." [45] He placed four cannon, two thousand foot and a thousand horse, the best part of his forces, at the most vulnerable place, the ford of Newburn, a few miles west of Newcastle. They were still hurriedly throwing up a breastwork when the Scots army appeared in the village on the farther bank. The English forces opened fire but with little effect. Leslie dismantled one of his light cannon and had it carried to the top of Newburn Church tower; from this dominating position the cannon balls that he sent "bowling in among the English" caused considerable alarm.

Under cover of the bombardment, he started the crossing. The honour of leading the way fell to the volunteers from the Edinburgh bar, led by a younger son of Lord Advocate Hope. This intellectual contingent meeting with stiff resistance from the English musketeers, a second party plunged into the water to their help and, supported by firing from the batteries, advanced on the English position. At this the English foot soldiers, who were mostly pressed men, abandoned the breastwork. The first line of the English defences being down, the Scots poured across the ford to take possession of the undefended river bank. Harry Wilmot, an intelligent young professional, in command of the English cavalry, tried to charge them as they landed; but their discipline was too good; their musketeers had instantly taken command of the ground, and against their steady firing the raw English cavalry was helpless. They fled in panic, trampling down and scattering what was left of their own infantry. The personal courage of a few cavalry officers and, it was said, of one artillery officer named George Monck, alone redeemed the honour of England at that "infamous, irreparable rout of Newburn." [46]

The Scots had begun to cross at four in the afternoon. At half-past five the incoming tide made the ford impassable for the rest of the daylight, so that the invading army passed the night divided by the river. No English were left to take advantage of their dislocation. The fleeing troops had meanwhile reached Newcastle with the news that the Scots were over the Tyne.[47]

All that summer forethought and energy had been spent on the fortification of Berwick, and not until the last few days had it entered Lord Conway's mind that the Scots would be so astute as to outflank Berwick, which was ready for them, and come in upon Newcastle, which was not. The town was fairly well-provided: cheese and biscuit were plentiful; good store of powder and muskets had been laid in and some heavy artillery; cannon balls and bullets had unaccountably been overlooked. But the true reason why neither Conway nor any experienced soldier contemplated holding the city was that its outer defences had been neglected. It was not defensible against siege and could not be held once the Tyne had been crossed. Conway evacuated the major part of the troops and the heavy artillery by road to Durham; he had the powder-barrels loaded on shipboard and hurried away on that same tide which was even then hampering the Scots crossing at Newburn.[48]

On the following day when the advancing Scots reached Gateshead they were astounded to learn that Newcastle had been abandoned. On Sunday, August 30th, Leslie entered the city at the head of his army. "Never so many ran from so few," lamented the stunned English, and Leslie, incredulous of so immediate a success and suspecting a more deadly line of defence farther back, made himself strong at Newcastle and sent to Edinburgh for more troops.[49]

The King fell back to York while Strafford, who had joined him, exchanged angry messages with Conway. Anger kindled hope and neither the King nor his chief minister accepted the first defeat as final. Strafford's formidable presence intimidated the disaffected gentry and put fresh heart into the loyal. The troops were drilled and disciplined; laxity and disorder were severely punished. The rabble began to assume the outward semblance of an army,[50] and again the King's delusive expectations rose. In theory the fleet, under Hamilton, would soon land forces from Ireland in the West of Scotland and make an effective

348

diversion in Leslie's rear. Meanwhile the first rumours of Newburn were contradicted by others: the battle, it was alleged, had cost the Scots very heavy losses, and several people claimed to have slain the Earl of Montrose in person. Some grains of encouraging truth were mixed with the chaff of consoling lies; an explosion in the powder magazine at Dunglass, behind the Scots lines, killed several of their chief officers, destroyed important stores, and started new rumours of treachery in their own ranks. The Scots forces in Newcastle, at first welcomed as liberators, soon annoyed the inhabitants by glorying in the discomfiture of the English. This arrogance and the disorders which inevitably went with a military occupation would, the King believed, arouse the long-delayed surge of national feeling against the invaders.[51]

His Queen and his councillors in the South were far less cheerful. The Scots had issued a printed manifesto justifying their action, and this, in spite of all prohibitions, was popular reading in London. The temper of the Londoners and the machinations of the King's principal opponents were alike to be feared. Released from the Tower, Warwick, Brooke, Saye, Pym and Hampden had remained in London and were known to meet frequently for consultation. The Earls of Bedford and Essex joined them. Their excuses for the consultations were the affairs of Providence Island and the New England colonies but, as the Court well knew, they spent more time discussing the affairs of their native land. That Pym was on friendly terms with Secretary Vane's eldest son was a detail the significance of which seems to have eluded the Court, at least for the moment.

After the outburst of May, London was restless and full of rumours; Cottington, who had been made Lieutenant of the Tower, had orders to keep the city quiet by whatever means seemed best. But there was nothing tangible to attack, only an atmosphere of hostility and suspicion, and occasional placards and scrawled papers calling on the apprentices to defend the reformed religion. At the time of the May riots, the King had found, and shattered with his own hand, a scratched message on a window-pane: "God save the King, confound the Queen and her children and send the Palsgrave to reign over us." Hatred of Popery, hatred of the Queen and her friends, vague murmurings for a Protestant succession continued. A woman named Anne Hussey declared that she knew of an Irish-Popish plot to overwhelm the country. She may have been encouraged by those anxious to provoke a crisis—the secretly-consulting peers and commoners at Lord Warwick's house. Nothing can be proved. It is as likely that her hysterical intervention was spontaneous, since it was common knowledge that Spanish troops and bullion had been conveyed through England.

All that summer the Court had openly bragged of the strength of Strafford's Irish army which was to deal with the Scots, and all the previous summer Lord Antrim had broadcast his intention of sending his wild Macdonalds into Scotland to eat the Covenanters alive; such things gave fuel enough to the underground fires of rumour about Irish-Popish-Spanish enterprises. Now the flames flickered everywhere. Ships and mariners going to and coming from the Netherlands discharged and brought back, with other cargo, the international political speculations of the quaysides. At one moment the Dutch were regaled with a story that King Charles had been deposed and his sister, the exiled Elizabeth of Bohemia, proclaimed the new Protestant Sovereign amid wild scenes of rejoicing. Not to be outdone, the Dutch themselves generated a story of a gigantic plot, contrived between the rebel Scots and the King's Popish subjects to destroy the Church and murder the King. The English consul in Holland thought it better to communicate this fantastic tale to Archbishop Laud, who passed it on to the King in the North, but neither of them appears to have known what to make of it. The King's Council in London at least took the precaution of preventing public demonstrations by closing all playhouses, bear-gardens and places of common resort.

Harassed by doubts and rumours the Queen would have liked the King to come home, having a wifely but unjustified confidence in his ability to deal with the trouble. She sent to him the one piece of information distilled from these doubts: Warwick and his friends were planning to present him with a remonstrance for which they were gathering the signatures of many other peers.[52] The King was not wholly unprepared for this development which may even have been welcome to him. He seems to have thought it possible that he could outwit the opposition peers by rallying to his support the rest of his lords, if he could make them see that their position and authority, logically dependent on his own, were threatened when his were threatened. Strafford's skill had almost created a breach between the Commons and the Lords when the peers had thought their rights infringed during the last Parliament. The Short Parliament had eluded his control for two reasons—because Pym had been clever enough to close the gap between Lords and Commons, and because the Protestant and irritable atmosphere of London had encouraged the King's critics and discouraged his friends. A half-Parliament, a Parliament of peers alone, called at York, far from the pressure of London's angry mariners and bold apprentices, might be won to the King's support. The support of the peers of the realm might—indeed could—save the situation. Their influence, direct and indirect, over county administration was very large; their financial interests in trade and industry were extensive. Much of the wealth and power of the Kingdom was concentrated in their hands. By calling a Council of Peers at York the King hoped to form against his critics a party large enough to serve him in the present and, if it should be essential to call Parliament again, powerful enough to divide and weaken the Commons.

The King therefore received with equanimity the remonstrance drawn up by the cabal of his critics in London. It had been drafted by John Pym with the help of Oliver St. John. The Providence Company peers—Warwick, Saye and Brooke—had brought a number of others to set their hands to it: Essex and his brother-in-law Hertford, the austerely pious Lord Mandeville, Lord Howard of Escrick who was powerful in the North. The grievances stated were those which the Short Parliament had raised: innovations in religion, favour to Roman Catholics, monopolies, Ship-money. Another more specific protest was added: the peers implored the King not to transport any troops out of Ireland.[53] The fear that the wild Irish—this formidable, alien, Popish people, this ancient and hostile force—might be unleashed against them by the King, or by Strafford in the King's name, came increasingly to overshadow the minds of the English.

Charles answered this remonstrance by sending out writs calling his peers to a Great Council, to meet at York on September 24th. The writs were signed on September 7th; on the 10th the King reviewed his army. The two thousand horse and sixteen thousand foot, smartened up by Sir Jacob Astley's drilling and Strafford's discipline, looked very well to the unpractised eyes of civilian observers. Secretary Vane ventured the opinion that Gustavus Adolphus had never had better. With these, and Strafford's boasted army from Ireland, the Scots were as good as dead men. At Court, the plan was still to play for time in which to rouse the English against the invaders, to win the support of the peers, to raise money with their help, to land the Irish in Galloway or on the west coast, and to smother with a show of force and a new enthusiasm for the war the factious criticism of opponents.[54]

These hopes were founded on a series of misapprehensions. The Scots army was in good heart, had suffered no serious loss at Newburn and had quickly recovered from the accident at Dunglass. The English, even in the north, grumbled a little but showed no sign of rising to expel the invaders. The Irish army remained in Ulster for lack of shipping. Hamilton, in charge of the fleet, had provided none, acting out of a kind of crafty loyalty: he did not believe that the King could win the war, and knowing the fanatic anger and suspicion aroused among the Covenanters by the mere idea of an Irish army, he thought it better that no Irish army should set foot on the Scottish mainland. Admittedly, since Dumbarton had once more been seized by the Covenanters, a landing could now only be made from the Solway Firth where Carlaverock Castle was loyally held for the King by the Catholic Lord Nithsdale. But if Hamilton intended not even to attempt to bring the Irish over, he would have done better to say so instead of allowing the plan to be agreed on, but failing in his own part in it.

The King's optimism continued for some days longer. To demonstrate that his calling of a Great Council betokened no change of policy, he showed every mark of open favour to Strafford and on September 13th bestowed upon him the Order of the Garter. The ceremony was splendidly performed and the new Knight was formally escorted to the steps of the throne by the Marquis of Hamilton and the Earl of Holland. Strafford disliked, despised and distrusted them both; his elevation to the noblest and most coveted honour in the Kingdom, at such a time and with such support, was as substantial in meaning and permanence as a Court masque.

He no longer shared the optimism of the King but understood very clearly the strength of the Scots, the feebleness of the English army, the disaffection of the countryside, and the delays and dishonesties of his fellow ministers. While he maintained an outward air of hectoring confidence, all his hopes had perished. He admitted the truth to his old friend George Radcliffe: "Never came man to so lost a business." [55]

The King's hopes, on the other hand, still continued to rise. On September 18th a party of marauding Scots crossed the Tees. This incursion was reported to a young professional soldier, Captain John Smith, who was stationed not far off with a troop of horse. Descending rapidly on the careless raiders, he beat them back, helter-skelter, to their own lines. It was the first—and the last—successful action by an English officer in the war. Charles, who mistook this solitary action for the dawn of a new spirit in his army, was uplifted. When he heard, at about the same time, that the citizens of London were preparing a petition for a new Parliament, he resolved to place the petitioners under arrest as soon as they arrived in York. As for calling another Parliament, he was wholly opposed to it.[56]

Four days later he changed his mind. Ruthven, the governor of Edinburgh Castle who had defied the Covenanters since the spring, capitulated on September 15th. For the past nine weeks, since a cannon shot from the town rendered their well unusable, the garrison had had no fresh water; many had died, all were ill, Ruthven himself had lost most of his teeth, gone very deaf and was horribly afflicted with scurvy.[57] Carlaverock Castle fell at the same time. As for the new spirit of the army at York, there was no such thing. A few honest professionals applauded Captain Smith, but the rank and file were unmoved or resentful, and civilians who obstinately regarded the Scots as liberators condemned John Smith as a bloody-minded incendiary. He was—like most of the King's best officers—a Roman Catholic.

Even Charles was now aware that he could hope for no spontaneous change in the temper of his people, and that he stood to gain most by conciliation. As in the previous summer at Berwick, so now at York, he played for time. When the deputation from London appeared on September 22nd with their petition for Parliament, he received them without resentment, and he allowed it to be rumoured, before the Council of Peers was opened, that he was willing to call a Parliament.[58]

When the Great Council met on September 24th the King's strategy was not what had first been planned. He did not try to win support from the peers for the present war but sought instead to conciliate them so that he might have them on his side in the coming Parliament. He permitted, even encouraged, plain speaking, and listened with patience to the attack on his policy eloquently put forward by the Earl of Bristol. He promised a Parliament: he agreed to the appointment of Commissioners to treat with the Scots and allowed a group of lords to be chosen, among whom scarcely one was favourable to his policy. These concessions made, he sent a deputation of peers to London to ask for a new loan.[59]

All this looked like a change of policy and was meant so to look. The King who, a fortnight before, had elevated Strafford to the highest honour in the realm, now exposed him to attack without coming to his defence, and allowed him to be harried and questioned about his part in advocating the war. Not only in the Great Council, but in private also, the King sustained this pretence of having abandoned his chief minister. Lord Clanricarde, an Irish peer, who had long disputed with Strafford over a grant of land, argued his point before the King, who compelled Strafford to yield. Clanricarde, on the father's side, was Norman-Irish, and in religion a Catholic; but he gained his point for a different reason. On his mother's side he was half-brother to one of the principal opposition peers, the Earl of Essex.[60] By supporting him against Strafford, the King was only extending into private matters the policy of conciliating his opponents before Parliament met.

The subsequent course of events has made the Great Council at York appear as the natural forerunner of the Long Parliament and the first in the long series of political defeats which the King sustained at the hands of his enemies. It fits more truly into the sequence of meaningless concessions which had marked his policy towards Scotland over the last eighteen months. He now extended that policy to England and once again conceded everything to win time in order that he might divide his opponents, make a party for himself and regain all.

When the Council broke up in the last week of October an armistice had been signed with the Scots, writs had gone out for a new Parliament, and the City of London had offered a loan. The Covenanting forces were to occupy the six northern counties and to be paid the sum of £860 a day until peace was concluded. The Commissioners of both parties, who had hitherto assembled at Ripon, were to transfer their discussions to London, so that Parliament could be consulted as to the final terms of the peace treaty.[61] This transference of the treaty to London was an astute stroke on the part of the King's opponents, for it enabled them to work in the closest possible co-operation with the Calvinist Scots and thus to have the weight of both nations behind the Parliamentary attack on the King.

The King's second war against the Scots, in which victory had been essential, if his authority was to survive, had come to dismal defeat. But it had not ended. The armistice might lead on to a firm peace and the victory of the Covenanters—as the King's opponents in both countries believed; but it might equally break down into a renewed war, with the King's party strengthened in England and the Covenanters divided in Scotland. Much depended on the events of the next months, and Charles was not without hope.

His friends were working hard to place as many supporters as possible in the new Parliament. Even before the end of September Lord Northampton, a simple, devoted loyalist, had written from York to his wife in Warwickshire to busy herself in finding suitable people for the various boroughs where his family was powerful; he had also peremptorily summoned home from an educational tour on the Continent his eldest son, whom he hoped to make one of the knights of the shire.[62]

The internal divisions of the Covenanting party, temporarily closed at the moment of invasion, had opened again. Montrose at Newcastle had criticised Argyll in the most indiscreet manner and early in October he and some of his friends raised an angry complaint that all the affairs of Scotland were "contrived and carried on by a few." The young man and his growing party were effectively stifled by the damaging revelation, made within the next few days, that he had entered into private correspondence with the King. Montrose, with the ingenuousness of a spoilt child, who had always done as he liked without question, protested that he saw nothing wrong in his action. But it made a bad impression and for the moment discredited him as a possible leader of a moderate or middle party. The Covenanting ranks, momentarily weakened, closed again.[63]

Montrose was not the King's only hope in Scotland. Indeed, he rather distrusted the young man on account of his previous record as an active rebel. Hamilton had with the King's knowledge been in private correspondence with the Covenanters ever since the Glasgow Assembly. He still believed that he could best serve the King by working out some kind of agreement or co-operation with Argyll. His behaviour was clumsy and disingenuous; it was not wholly bad. As a lowland Scot, he was far more acutely aware than any of the King's other advisers of the harm that had been done by the Antrim project in the first Scots war and the more serious Irish project of the second. He believed that he could do better for the King secretly than he could openly, at least as long as Strafford, the author of the Irish scheme, was still the chief minister.[64]

While plans for managing Parliament and dividing the Scots occupied the King's mind, he was not neglecting possibilities of foreign aid. He had been disappointed in help from his uncle the King of Denmark, whose envoys had paid a brief visit to him at York but had not been sufficiently impressed by his prospects to entertain talk of a treaty. The Spanish alliance had broken down and the King of Spain, who now had a Portuguese and a Catalan revolt simultaneously on his hands, was unable to spare money for Charles's assistance. Charles therefore turned for help from Spain to Spain's enemies. Very privately he renewed the offer of his younger daughter, Princess Elizabeth, to the only son of the Prince of Orange. The Prince of Orange was among the richest noblemen of Europe and by election the effective ruler of the Netherlands, so that the alliance promised to be of the greatest financial profit. The King was extremely anxious that his sister, the Queen of Bohemia—who lived in The Hague within a stone's throw of the Prince of Orange—should not come to hear of the matter; he knew that she had hopes of his daughters as brides for her sons and he wished to confront her, therefore, with a *fait accompli* lest she should attempt to stop the betrothal.[65]

Three promising projects were thus before King Charles; at the best, the winter of 1640 might see a Parliament controlled and managed, the Scots rebels divided, and the House of Orange ready to pour the much-needed money into his coffers. The further presence of Strafford, generally detested as he was, was not necessary and might be harmful to the King's cause. Charles had allowed him to face the attack on the royal policy almost unaided throughout the Council of Peers, and when the Council rose, Hamilton, who may well have had the royal warrant for what he did, urged Strafford to leave the country. Hamilton, most of all, must have wanted him to go, because, while he stayed, the King's intentions for the Irish army must remain ever present to men's minds.

The minister's immense personal unpopularity, as well as the Irish complication, were dangerous to the King his master, and had he gone it is possible that Charles would have faced Parliament in a clearer atmosphere. But everything depended on the ability of the King and his Council to manipulate the coming Parliament, and, with Strafford away, there would be no minister at Charles's command who could undertake so difficult a task. Strafford's continued help and advice was therefore of the first importance. In a sense also the violent hatred that he aroused might be turned to account. He might, at the worst, be made a scapegoat as he already had been from time to time during the Great Council. Either as adviser, or as a chosen victim, or as both at once, he could still be useful. All these things were evident both to him and to the King, but Charles rightly felt that he must give his faithful servant the chance of escaping, if he wished to do so. Strafford preferred to stay. Before the King left York for London he had a long private consultation with him: what was said, but for one detail, rests on conjecture only. The King knew that Strafford would be in danger both from the populace and from the House of Commons, and that his removal stood high among the demands of the Covenanters. But he still believed that this new Parliament would be better managed than the last, and the outward sign of his confidence was the promise that he gave to Strafford: on the word of a King, he said, he should not suffer in life or fortune, whatever turn events might take in London.

Strafford, who for the last thirteen months had seen every hopeful project of the King's or his own wrecked by misjudgment in the execution, set little store on this promise. But he

could not abandon the work for which he had unceasingly
striven. His hopes and beliefs were alike bound up with the
monarchy as was also a great part of his personal fortune. For
his master's and for his own sake he must try to save the King's
government. Therefore he obeyed the King's command, only
taking the precaution to visit his house in Yorkshire and set
some order in his private affairs before taking horse for London.
Weighing the hopes and dangers in his clear and resolute mind
he did not quite despair. " I am to-morrow to London," he
wrote to Sir George Radcliffe, a friend from whom he concealed nothing, " with more danger beset, I believe, than ever
man went with out of Yorkshire; yet my heart is good and I find
nothing cold within me. . . . All will be well, and every hour
gives more hope than other."[66]

BOOK III CHAPTER III REFERENCES

1. *C.S.P.D.*, 1640, pp. 112–13.
2. *C.S.P. Ven.*, 1640–2, pp. 44–5.
3. *C.S.P.D.*, 1640, p. 156.
4. *Ibid.*, pp. 154–6.
5. *Ibid.*, pp. 167, 221–2.
6. *Canterburie's Amazement*, London, 1641.
7. *C.S.P.D.*, 1640, pp. 342–3.
8. *Portland MSS.*, III, p. 63.
9. Cardwell, I, pp. 389 ff.
10. Cleveland, *Poems*, London, 1642, p. 26; Bray, *Anatomy of Etcetera*, London, 1641.
11. See Soden *Godfrey Goodman* Chapter XXVI for a careful account of this rather complicated incident.
12. Laud, *Works*, III, p. 287 f.
13. *C.S.P.D.*, 1640, pp. 307–8.
14. *Ibid.*, p. 162.
15. Louis B. Wright, *Religion and Empire*, Chapel Hill, 1943, p. 71.
16. *C.S.P. Ven.*, 1640–2, pp. 50, 53.
17. *C.S.P. Ven.*, 1640–2, pp. 26, 52; *C.S.P.D.*, 1640, p. 226; *C.S.P.D.*, 1639–40, pp. 493, 525, 546; Burnet, *Lives*, p. 166.
18. *C.S.P.D.*, 1640, pp. 451, 491, 500, 521–2; *C.S.P. Ven.*, 1640–2, p. 59.
19. *Ibid.*, p. 10.
20. *Breadalbane MSS., Letters*, 1639–59, Glencarradale to Glenorchy, June 2nd, 1640.
21. *C.S.P.D.*, 1640, pp. 124–5, 450; *C.S.P. Ven.*, 1640–2, p. 55.
22. *Ibid.*, p. 509.
23. For the attitude of the gentry and the various mutinies of the troops, see *C.S.P.D.*, 1640, May–July, *passim*; see also Rushworth, II, ii, pp. 1191–4; *H.M.C., XII*, iv.

pp. 520–2; *William Salt Society Collections*, XV, p. 205, *Yorkshire Archaeological Society, Record Series*, LIV, p. 230.

24. *C.S.P.D.*, 1640, p. 492.

25. *Ibid.*, pp. 316, 333.

26. *Ibid.*, pp. 487, 636–7.

27. Albion, p. 339; Laud, *Works*, III, p. 236; *C.S.P.D.*, 1640, p. 495; *C.S.P. Ven.*, 1640–2 p. 62; the tree, known by long tradition as Prince Henry's, flourishes at the time of writing (1953) in the beautiful garden of the Oatlands Court Hotel Weybridge.

28. *C.S.P.D.*, 1639–40, pp. 382–3; 1640, pp. 99–100, 215–16; Warriston, *Diary*, p. 97.

29. Balfour, II, pp. 373–9; Rushworth, II, ii, p. 1044.

30. *Breadalbane MSS., Letters*, 1639–59, Glencarradale to Glenorchy, May 25th; Napier, *Memorials of Montrose*, Edinburgh, 1848, I, pp. 258, 259, 266–7.

31. Napier, I, pp. 264–5; *C.S.P.D.*, 1640–1, p. 53.

32. Balfour, II, p. 381; *C.S.P.D.*, 1640–1, p. 53.

33. Napier, I, 154–5.

34. *C.S.P.D.*, 1640, pp. 516, 563, 571, 587–8.

35. *Ibid.*, pp. 590–1, 609; *Hardwicke State Papers*, II, p. 147.

36. Knowler, II, p. 401; *C.S.P.D.*, 1640, pp. 112–13, 179, 514, 591.

37. *Ibid.*, p. 462.

38. *Ibid.*, p. 600.

39. *Ibid.*, p. 627.

40. Guthry, p. 32.

41. *C.S.P.D.*, 1640, pp. 595–7, 625, 630.

42. *Ibid.*, p. 640.

43. *Ibid.*, p. 645.

44. Livingstone, p. 106.

45. *C.S.P.D.*, 1640, pp. 616, 626, 632–3.

46. Maidment, *Analecta Scotica*, Edinburgh 1834, I, pp. 383–5; *Breadalbane MSS., Letters*, 1640–69, 813; Gumble, *Life of General Monck*, London, 1671, p. 10.

47. *H.M.C. Various*, II, pp. 256–8.

48. *Loc. cit.*; *C.S.P.D.*, 1640, p. 658; 1641, pp. 38–9; Balfour, II, p. 388.

49. *H.M.C., XII, App. IV*, p. 523; Balfour, II, pp. 388, 390.

50. *H.M.C. Egmont MSS*, I, I, p. 120.

51. *C.S.P.D.*, 1640–1, pp. 23–4, 28–9.

52. *Ibid.*, p. 652; 1640–1, pp. 46, 53; *C.S.P. Ven.*, 1640–2, pp. 74, 76–7; Rushworth, II, ii, pp. 1310–3, 1321, 1266–7.

53. *C.S.P.D.*, 1640–1, p. 23.

54. *Ibid.*, pp. 47, 63.

55. Whitaker, p. 203.

56. Walsingham, *Brittanicae virtutis imago*, Oxford, 1644; *C.S.P.D.*, 1640–1, pp. 74, 84.

57. Balfour, II, p. 403; *C.S.P.D.*, 1640–1, p. 111.

58. *Ibid.*, p. 84–5.

59. *H.M.C. XII, App. IV*, p. 524; *C.S.P.D.*, 1640–1, pp. 92–7; Rushworth, II, ii, pp. 1275 ff.

60. *C.S.P.D.*, 1640–1, p. 197; his mother was Frances Walsingham, wife first of Sir

Philip Sydney, then of Elizabeth's favourite Essex. After the execution of Essex she married the Irish Catholic peer, Ulic Burke, Earl of Clanricarde.

61. Rushworth, II, II, pp. 1295–6, 1302–4.
62. *C.S.P.D.*, 1640–**1**, p. 113.
63. Napier, I, pp. 302–5; Guthry, p. 87; Burnet, *op. cit.*, p. 179; *Breadalbane MSS.*. Letters 1639–59, Glencarradale to Glenorchy, October 6th, 1640.
64. Clarendon, Book II; Burnet, *op. cit.*, pp. 179 ff.
65. *C.S.P.D.*, 1640–1, pp. 278–9.
66. Whitaker, pp. 214 ff.

CHAPTER FOUR

PARLIAMENT AND THE CROWN

November 1640–March 1641

THE King reached Westminster to find his prospects for controlling Parliament sadly clouded. The High Commission Court, in session in St. Paul's Cathedral, had been broken up a week before by a rabble shouting "No Bishop." A few days later, Archbishop Laud, going into his study to examine a further batch of rare manuscripts which he was presenting to Oxford, stopped short on the threshold: flat on its face on the floor lay the great portrait which Van Dyck had painted of him. "I am not superstitious," Laud would boldly write in his diary as he recorded every dream that disturbed his rest. He was not superstitious about the fall of a picture but—"God grant this be no omen."[1]

In the City of London the King's friends lost ground. All the efforts of the Lord Mayor, Sir Henry Garraway, of Alderman Abel of the Vintners' Company, of Reynardson of the Merchant Taylors, of Alderman Gurney and other loyal supporters, failed to secure the election of a King's man for the next Lord Mayor. The effective control of the City passed for the time being to the opposite party, who immediately postponed the payment to the King of the promised loan until such time as Parliament should meet; they had no intention of making the King financially independent of the Commons. At the Parliamentary election meanwhile they had rejected their own recorder, the Royalist Sir Thomas Gardiner, and chosen four notorious opponents of the Court, one of whom, Samuel Vassell, had been in prison for several years for refusing to pay the King's unparliamentary taxes.

The failure of the King's friends to secure Gardiner's election was serious, because Charles had counted on him for Speaker, and it was not easy to think of another man who would be at once acceptable to the Commons and not hostile to the Crown. After anxious consultation with his friends, the King decided on William Lenthall, a respectable lawyer, in whom he thought he saw the makings of a good servant. His choice was unfortunate for his own party; Lenthall was a timid man, prone to follow the majority, and it was not Charles whom he served during his many years in the Speaker's chair.

With misplaced economy the King decided to eliminate the solemn procession which was usually a feature of the opening of Parliament. This disappointed the populace, who always resented the curtailment of any public display, and left an impression of doubt and foreboding, at a time when a show of boldness was needed.[2] The truncated ceremony took place on the afternoon of Tuesday, November 3rd, 1640; this time the King himself made the opening speech and although his manner seemed nervous because of his difficulties of utterance, his matter was bold enough. Twice over he referred to the Scots as rebels and told Parliament that their first duty was to provide money to keep the English army in being.

The King's speech was coolly received and the Commons proceeded to their own chamber to pursue a policy independent of it: a policy inspired and directed by John Pym. John Pym had had his rehearsal as leader of the House in the spring; all the summer he had been in the inner councils of the opposition peers. His abilities marked him out as the principal man of the Commons, whilst his relations with the Lords Warwick, Saye, Brooke, Mandeville and the rest linked him to the King's critics in the Upper House. The secretary of the Providence Company, by virtue of his business training and his business associates, occupied a stronger position than any political leader in the

Commons had done before. He had the necessary connections with the City, the navy and the peerage, and he had the clear mind, the cool judgment, the comprehensive grasp of an administrator of genius. Other men in the House of Commons, among his friends and associates, could supply the qualities he lacked: John Hampden diplomacy and charm, Oliver St. John expert legal knowledge, William Strode and Denzil Holles fiery eloquence, Arthur Haslerig and young Harry Vane (the Secretary's Puritan son) the reckless drive of fanaticism. But these things were brought together, organised, directed, almost, in the theatrical sense, *produced* by the skill of John Pym.

John Pym was the principal architect of the constitutional revolution of the next eighteen months, and therefore one of the most significant single figures and one of the most remarkable intellects in the constitutional history of England. A West country man, born in 1584, he was a child of the Elizabethan age, reared in hatred of Spain, in strong Protestant beliefs, and in the faith that God intended the English to establish his Gospel by sea-power and settlement over the face of the earth. Like most prosperous country gentlemen, he had been educated at the University and the Inns of Court—Pembroke College, Oxford, and the Middle Temple. At one time he had held a post in the Exchequer Office but he had gained the greater part of his experience in business as the secretary of the Providence Company and in the management of overseas enterprises. A regular member of Parliament, at first for Calne in Wiltshire and later for Tavistock, he had a high reputation among the King's opponents as a forceful and well-informed speaker, but he had never—like the fiercer Strode and Holles—acted with violence or on impulse. He was a man of clear perceptions and patient resolution whose eloquence consisted in the application of his well-arranged knowledge to enforce his point of view. In his youth he had been married, but had long been a widower; his immediate family consisted of two grown-up sons of whom little is known. He was one of those men to whom personal and emotional ties are of no great strength and it was natural to him to live for and in his work. Sober in his habits and strenuous in his duty, he was capable of rising at three in the morning and working steadily—but for an hour or so for his devotions—until the following midnight. The only surviving likeness of him taken in his lifetime shows him as a broad-browed heavy-jowled man, with small alert eyes, a straight nose, and a full-lipped mouth framed by the typical curled moustache and pointed beard of the epoch. He wears his hair brushed straight back from the forehead and long enough to conceal his ears. His dress is the respectable black of a professional man, set off by a plain linen collar.

The first task of the House of Commons was to disentangle the confusions of a singularly troublesome election. The strenuous efforts of the Court and its opponents to get their friends and dependants into Parliament had many of them continued beyond the contest at the polls. Three or four members claimed to have been duly returned for boroughs which had a right to only two; half a dozen such cases were not unusual in an average House of Commons. In November 1640 there were nearly thirty of them, the House would in the next weeks hear a great deal about how many votes had been procured by canvassing in alehouses, and how " fourteen pounds was laid out on beer and tobacco " by the candidate's friends.[3]

The Committee of Privileges, for settling disputed elections, was selected on the first day. It was always a large Committee, with a maximum of forty members. This time, by some miscounting, forty-seven members were elected to it, but nothing was done to alter the error for fear that the Court party should be left in a majority. Of the forty-seven, half at least were within the orbit and influence of Pym and his friends. For the next week or two they expeditiously solved the problem of the disputed returns by declaring the men they wanted to be truly elected and disallowing the elections of their rivals. It can only be said, in extenuation of this conduct, that had the Court party been in control of the Committee of Privileges—as it had hitherto usually contrived to be—it would have acted in the same way.

The Court party, in spite of all efforts, was more poorly represented than in April. Neither Edward Nicholas nor Windebanke's nephew and right-hand man, Robert Read, had managed to secure a seat. The irritation and distrust which had shown itself throughout the summer in the obstructive conduct of the gentry had only to be voiced by a few in the House of Commons for the overwhelming majority to join in. Those whose feelings varied from irritation to anger at the King's taxes, monopolies and wars, and from a vague disquiet to real distress at his neglect of the Protestant Cause and favour to his Catholic subjects, were not for the most part bent on reforms either in religion or the constitution. They spoke and thought in the old-fashioned way of grievances and abuses; their concern was to make life, and possibly their consciences, more easy. They wished to stop the unceasing demands for Ship-money, for coat-and-conduct money, for unwanted knighthoods, the petty fines for petty enclosure offences, the small blackmailing requests for subscriptions to the rebuilding of St. Paul's Cathedral. They wished to prevent the interruption of honest labour and the lawful occupations of town and country for a third year in succession by an expensive and unnecessary levy of troops. Almost every member of the House of Commons, in that autumn of 1640, excepting only the King's servants and courtiers, thought that the King's policy was wrong and his government bad. They were concerned to get rid of the ministers responsible—Archbishop Laud who had oppressed the Protestants and made the Scots revolt, and Strafford who had thrust the second war upon them and supported the alliance with Spain.

So far this attitude was traditional. But Bedford, Saye, Brooke and others among the Lords, Pym, Hampden, St. John and their like among the Commons, were thinking of changes more far-reaching than the removal of the King's "evil coun-sellors." That phrase was time-honoured, medieval; critics, parties, factions of one kind and another had been attacking and removing the King's "evil counsellors" since the days of

King John. What they wanted was something more: the transference of effective power from the King's hands into that of the High Court of Parliament. Therein lay the only permanent safeguard against the increase of royal power at the expense of their own. They believed themselves to be preserving the ancient balance of the constitution but the plain truth was that the law, as they practised and understood it, and the local administration of England, had made the ordinary life of the country depend at every point upon them, and hardly at all upon the Crown. The entire machine—law-courts, parishes, poor law, city and country—could run very well without the King; but it could not run without the gentry. In other words, the gentry were essential to the power of the King, but he was not essential to theirs. Neither Bedford, Pym nor any of them harboured a thought so shocking as the removal of the King; but they did envisage of a policy by which his theoretical power and his actual power should be brought into line with each other and properly defined. Otherwise they might risk the continuance of the present intolerable situation in which the King directed policy without power to execute it, and they, with power to prevent and obstruct policy, had none to direct it. It was a natural outcome of all this, so natural that few people at first noticed or commented upon it, that the House of Commons within a few weeks of its assembling, assumed the practice of sending out its own orders and instructions on public affairs to justices of the peace throughout the realm.[4]

Early in the session the Scottish Commissioners had arrived in London to consider, with the English Parliament, the terms of the treaty which was to end the war. The Committee of Estates in Edinburgh had given them instructions, some of which reflected precisely the same constitutional policy which inspired Pym and his associates; for instance, they suggested that the forthcoming treaty should provide for the calling of Parliaments in both countries at regular intervals of from two to three years.

The Scots were well received in London and were given Saint Antholin's Church, always a well-known Puritan centre, for their services. Here their preachers, principally the impressive Henderson, commanded congregations so large that late-comers thought no shame to haul themselves up to the windows and catch what they could from the outside. Thirty years of derisive jokes at the broad speech of " our brethren of Scotland " stopped overnight; all was now friendship and admiration.[5]

The King therefore faced from the beginning a formidable and intelligent alliance between his critics in Parliament and the Scots. In the circumstances it was unfortunate that Lord Keeper Finch, on the first day of the session, had tried to justify the summer's war by declaring that the King had undertaken it not at the advice of one or two ministers only, but at that of his entire council. By this speech he put all the King's servants under the same cloud and so prevented the King from making use in Parliament even of those who enjoyed some personal popularity.

Strafford, enjoying the last tranquillity he was ever to know in his own home in Yorkshire, condemned the folly of what Finch had said.[6] The condemnation is interesting because it reveals something of what was going on in his mind. He had a clear idea of Pym's ability and less sanguine expectations of the present Parliament than the King. His disapproval of what Finch had said shows that he sincerely hoped to draw the anger of the King's critics as much as possible upon himself. The Archbishop would hardly escape it, but Strafford had been the more prominent of the two during the last year, and it was his belief that the Commons would almost certainly impeach him first. He had seen in his youth three Parliaments in turn waste their fury in attacks on the King's favourite Buckingham; the same situation was now about to arise in his own case. But the outcome would be different. The King had never allowed Buckingham to be put on trial, so that the favourite's guilt had been left in permanent doubt. But if this Parliament were allowed to impeach and try Strafford they would have to abandon general vilification for sober charges which could be sustained in law, and would have to prove them to the satisfaction of the House of Lords. It was one thing to call a man " the source of all evils," as they had Buckingham, or " Black Tom Tyrant ", as they now called Strafford. It was another to prove treason against him, article by article, more especially as he had committed none.

This then was Strafford's intention and his hope. He would stand out as the man frankly responsible for the King's policy, and face whatever charges John Pym and the Commons brought against him: *and he would refute them.* He knew the law of England as well as any lawyer in the land and better than John Pym; he knew by past experience the temper and complexity of Parliaments and he knew that a good half of those discontented, disturbed and angry gentlemen, whose resentments were now fixed upon him as the author of their evils, would be perturbed and shaken when they saw the weakness of the legal case and heard the arguments that he himself could so eloquently urge. In all Pym's calculations he knew that there could be no room for an impeachment that failed. Once let impeachment be tried and fail, and the Commons would be divided from the Lords and divided among themselves. Then let the King use well and quickly their moment of weakness; he could redeem much, perhaps all. This idea, or something like it, must have been in Strafford's mind when he set out from Yorkshire, feeling, as he had said, " nothing cold within me."

In plain truth he did not much miscalculate, and the match he was to play with John Pym was a close one. Had he been as intelligently supported by King and Court as Pym was in Parliament, he might have succeeded; more than once between the dark November of 1640 when the contest opened and the bright May of 1641 when it ended, it seemed almost as though he had won.

John Pym was wary from the start. He avoided the traps. Parliament opened on November 3rd and, to the surprise of many, not a word was said about Strafford for more than a week. For the first days every other kind of complaint was aired and encouraged: this was good strategy, for it established so many different complaints and grievances against the King's government that Pym could later choose which to press and which to abandon, as the mood of the House shifted.

In the Short Parliament the King's critics had contrived to organise half a dozen petitions from the counties complaining of their grievances. In the first week of the Long Parliament about twenty petitions had already come in, mostly from counties and towns, some from individuals; these were directed against Ship-money, innovations in religion, Star Chamber sentences, monopolies and exactions. Mrs. Burton and Mrs. Bastwicke petitioned for the release of their husbands, a servant of Prynne brought a petition from his master, and Oliver Cromwell, the member for Cambridge, raised the case of Lilburne. The petitions were inspired by the more active critics of the King, who had bestirred themselves to get them drawn up and signed. Popular feeling does not manifest itself spontaneously in writing; it manifests itself in argument in alehouses and church porches, in parlours and studies, in the market place or hunting field. But the petitions, in this autumn of a disturbed and unhappy year, were a very fair representation, only a little heightened and organised, of what a great number of the King's subjects were thinking.

Pym wove them together with his habitual skill into a cogent speech against the government at the end of Parliament's first week. Their grievances were, he said, of three kinds. The ancient privileges of Parliament had been attacked by long intermission of the assembly and by the arrest of members merely for speaking their minds; true religion had been persecuted while such clergy only were preferred who " pretended Divine Authority and Absolute Power in the King to do what he will with us "; the liberty of the subject had been invaded by illegal taxes, the revival of obsolete laws and the advantages granted to projectors and monopolists. The Star Chamber, once the defence of the poor against oppression, had become merely " an instrument of erecting and defending monopolies, to set a face of public good on things pernicious." The King's subjects had even been threatened with invasion by foreign and Irish troops. Modestly, after this deep and wide attack, he claimed for Parliament no more than the right and duty of " declaring the law where it is doubtful and providing for the execution of the law where it is clear." [7]

On November 10th George Digby, presenting the complaints from Dorset, showed himself to be a speaker of persuasive fervour and charm. He was eldest son to the Earl of Bristol and son-in-law to the Earl of Bedford and belonged to the group of discontented nobility who shunned the Court. He himself, a talented and attractive young man, and a dilettante of the sciences, had wished to shine at Court but had been reprimanded by the King for a high-spirited quarrel and had retired in mortification. This new recruit to Pym's forces distinguished himself by the suggestion that the House draw up a Remonstrance against the ministers responsible for the King's policy. The idea was well received and a committee was at once appointed to collect the necessary material.[8]

Other speakers, on this and the succeeding day, took up and enlarged the grievances outlined by Pym. Sir John Colepeper, presenting a petition from Kent, denounced Ship-money, monopolies and the expensive levying of troops. Sir Edward Dering, scholar and antiquary, who represented the county of Kent along with John Colepeper, was smarting from a recent interview with the Archbishop, who had curtly refused his plea on behalf of a Puritan minister. He was the first to name Laud in person. " Our manifold griefs do fill a mighty and vast circumference," he eloquently proclaimed, " yet so that from every point our lines of sorrow do lead unto him and point at him, the centre from whence our miseries do flow."[9] Few voices were raised in defence of the royal government and when William Widderington, recently sheriff of Northumberland and now its representative in Parliament, spoke, like a loyal Borderer, of the invading Scots as rebels, Denzil Holles, the hot-tempered member for Dorchester, compelled him to withdraw the offensive phrase.[10]

On Wednesday, November 11th, the attention of the

Commons was divided between the misdeeds of monopolists and the suspicious behaviour of Secretary Windebanke (who had been returned to Parliament for Corfe, a constituency controlled by Attorney-General Bankes). Windebanke, it seemed, had slightingly dismissed the hysterical Mrs. Hussey when she had come to him earlier that summer with her tale of seven thousand Irish Papists hidden about London and only waiting to cut all good Protestant throats.[11] This ridiculous affair was being hotly pursued, when at about eleven in the morning, Sir John Clotworthy, the member for Maldon, acting presumably on a hint from Pym, made a violent and incoherent speech against Strafford. This was the opening move in the well-planned attack that Pym had been holding back until the time was ripe.

His decision to open the attack this day and hour was the outcome of news which he seems at that moment to have received. Strafford, who had reached London the previous night, had just taken his seat in the House of Lords. Pym respected the skill of his adversary too highly to give him so much as a day's grace to plan a counter-stroke; as soon as he knew that Strafford was at Westminster he could risk no more delay. He was, of course, ready with a roughly drafted general accusation, and the feeling against Strafford was so strong that, to command enthusiastic support from all quarters of the House, he had only to rise and outline the case for his impeachment. George Digby in a high flight of eloquence denounced Strafford, whom he hardly knew, as " that grand Apostate to the Commonwealth," and only Lord Falkland, who sat next to his friend Edward Hyde, and represented Newport in the Isle of Wight, raised a philosopher's gentle voice to warn the House against the danger of proceeding too fast on undigested evidence. The danger of proceeding too slowly was, in Pym's opinion, far greater. By the close of an extended morning session he was able to carry up the accusation to the House of Lords.[12]

Strafford was no longer present. Knowing what was afoot in the Commons—for one of the Court members must surely have got word to him—he had slipped away to Whitehall for a last-minute consultation with the King. What, if anything, was decided at that interview, is unknown, but Strafford miscalculated the speed of Pym's action and mistimed his return. When he reached the portals of the House of Lords, Pym with a delegation from the Commons had already laid the impeachment before them. He was compelled to withdraw, and was taken that afternoon to honourable confinement in the house of Maxwell, Gentleman Usher of the Black Rod. He bore all with an air of haughty unconcern, although some of his fellow peers openly rejoiced in his discomfiture. The mighty had indeed fallen, and Dr. Baillie, who with the Scots Commissioners saw it all, recorded gravely in his diary that the evil man had been taken away " all gazing, no man capping to him, before whom that morning the greatest of England would have stood discovered." [13]

Returned to the House of Commons, Pym, still maintaining the attack on all fronts, switched the attention of his colleagues back to the reprehensible behaviour of Secretary Windebanke, and they were upon this fruitful subject when a messenger from the Upper House informed them that their lordships had sequestered the Earl of Strafford and placed him in custody. For this the Commons returned suitable thanks.[14]

During the next weeks the committee appointed to draw up the charges against Strafford worked hard, fetched witnesses out of Ireland and the North, sifted and examined innumerable allegations. From time to time the committee reported and the charges were discussed in the House. Lest the impeachment should fail for lack of strict legal proof, Pym also investigated the possibility of having a Bill of Attainder introduced to dispatch Strafford. A Bill of Attainder—a Parliamentary Bill which simply *decreed* a man guilty of treason—did not need to rest on precise points of law: a general presumption of guilt, or more crudely a general hatred of the victim, was enough. This ruthless form of action had been evolved in the Wars of the Roses, but discontinued since.

The preparations went forward for Strafford's trial, but they did not occupy the House of Commons to the exclusion of all other matters. Pym deliberately prevented the impeachment of Strafford from becoming at this stage the "Great Business," the only business which could fill and inspire the House, and the days of the Commons were fully occupied with grievances of other kinds. Religion was the foremost. The attack on the King's religious policy was directed against favours to Roman Catholics, and the Romanising tendencies of the Archbishop. The Commons had refused to take the Communion at St. Margaret's, Westminster, until the altar rails had been removed and the Table brought down into the nave. But no one had yet spoken against the organisation of the Church or said anything against bishops in general. Sympathy for the Scots did not necessarily argue a slavish desire to copy their conduct in all things, and although a minority in the House of Commons was opposed to episcopacy itself, Pym knew them to be a minority and did not at this stage encourage them lest their inconsiderate fervour should provoke a breach among his supporters.

Laud's cleverest opponent within the Church itself, John Williams, Bishop of Lincoln, took his seat in the House of Lords amid considerable popular rejoicing, on November 16th. He had been in the Tower for over three years, except for a few weeks when he had offered bail that he might attend the Short Parliament but had been prevented from doing so. Williams, the moderate churchman, who had always feared the consequences of Laud's emphasis on ritual, enjoyed at the moment the popularity of a martyr, and was well aware of the strength of his position. His friends in both Houses were, in the main, Pym's friends: Bedford, Saye, Hampden. He was clever, diplomatic, with Welsh vitality and charm; he was also ambitious and, after his long eclipse, saw himself as the new architect and statesman of the Church who would redeem the fatal errors of Archbishop Laud, find for the Church a middle way, and rebuild a Protestant Episcopate on the love of the people and the support of the lords and gentry.

Larger crowds than those that had cheered Bishop Williams

on his progress from the Tower to the House of Lords lined the streets of London a fortnight afterwards for the triumphal entry of Prynne and Burton on November 28th and of Bastwicke a few days later. Their more distinguished sympathisers followed them in coaches and rode behind, wearing sprigs of rosemary [15] —rosemary for remembrance, rosemary, the grey-green sea-colour which was to become in the next ten years the insignia of the extremists, of those who thought all men free and equal before God—grey-green for liberty and the reign of King Jesus.

Animosity against Roman Catholics had re-doubled. Count Rossetti, the papal envoy, was rudely knocked up at one in the morning by some city magistrates with an angry crowd at their back demanding to search his house. Imperturbably dignified and amiable, he asked the justices in and courteously showed them his pictures and works of art. They retired, apologetic and embarrassed. A few weeks later, none the less, Rossetti yielded to the Queen's entreaty, gave up his house and agreed to live under guard in the house allotted to the Queen's mother.[16]

The King, late in the day, tried to disarm criticism by dismissing all Roman Catholics from Court except the Queen's personal servants. Little old Toby Mathew's brief summer was at an end; he slipped away to pursue philosophic speculation and make his cups of chocolate among the friendly people of Ghent. Wat Montagu held out longer, relying on the protection of his father, the aged and pious Earl of Manchester, and his brother Lord Mandeville, one of the most eminent Puritans in the House of Lords.

Of those who had helped the King in protecting the Catholic minority in England, the first to be sacrificed was Secretary Windebanke. Windebanke's own religion was unobtrusive; his interest in life had been in acquiring and retaining a position at Court, building up a fortune the foundation of which had been laid by his father and grandfather, also servants of the Crown. As to taking money from Spain, issuing licences to exempt recusants from paying fines and prohibiting the prosecution of Roman Catholic priests, these things were part of his work; he was a little man who obeyed orders and enriched himself, within reason, on the side. Suddenly, in the heartless cold of an early winter, he found that he was a solitary hare running for dear life before the whole pack of Commons. John Glynne, an able barrister of strongly Calvinist views, reported from the committee on religion that sixty-four priests had been released from prison in the last year on Windebanke's order, that more than seventy letters of grace signed by him had been issued to Papists throughout the Kingdom; finally—most damning of all—that the total sum in recusants' fines collected by him in the last thirteen years was only just over four thousand pounds. Recusants were supposed to pay a shilling a Sunday to the poor. A simple calculation showed that if Windebanke's figures were right only about a hundred and forty-six Catholics in the whole of England could have been mulcted.[17] Windebanke, hearing of these accusations, hurried home and hid under the bedclothes. Messengers from the Commons, sent to seek him, were told by his servants that he had been up late the previous night and must have his sleep out. In the House his nephew and right-hand man, Robert Read, vainly attempted to justify his uncle, then rejoined him and under cover of darkness rode to the coast. The weather was foggy and the wind sluggish, but they bribed a man to put them across the Channel in a rowing boat.[18] When the Commons sent for Windebanke again he was out of reach in France. He was safe but was never to be happy again; the French Court were good to him and he was not in want. He was invited to fashionable masques and to the wedding of Richelieu's niece. But he remained inconsolable, asking, always in vain, why his master the King did not exonerate him before Parliament by declaring the simple truth that he had only obeyed orders. Windebanke was not born to carry the dangerous responsibilities of office or to sacrifice himself with uncomplaining loyalty, and he remained to the end a querulous, reproachful victim.[19]

But he respected his master's confidence, however unfair he felt his punishment to be. His colleague, Secretary Vane, was less scrupulous; he also had a son, young Harry, to whom he seems to have been genuinely attached, who followed with deep conviction the most extravagant religious sects and held extremist views on God and politics. Old Vane was indiscreet and selfimportant and he hated Strafford. Possibly, indeed probably, he had hinted and babbled at home of things said and done at the council table. Probably Windebanke did the same with his wife and family—but none of them were Puritans, still less fanatics. Old Vane, moreover, if his son was to be believed, left his notes of council meetings scattered about among his private papers. Here young Vane, searching with his father's permission for a family document, had in the course of the previous summer come upon and read the notes of the meeting held on May 5th, 1640; from these he had learnt that Strafford had suggested bringing over the Irish army to reduce "this Kingdom." Young Vane smelt the importance of the document and, after a brief tussle between filial loyalty and his sense of public duty, copied it for Pym. John Pym, to spare young Vane's feelings as far as possible, copied it again himself so that the source of the betrayal would be less apparent.[20]

It was common knowledge that Strafford had planned to bring over the Irish army to attack the Scots in the rear. But this conduct, however bitter the resentment it had aroused, could not easily be construed as treason because at the time the Scots had been in arms, and Strafford as the King's minister was bound to consider the means to put them down. His peers, however much they might condemn his policy against the Scots, could hardly in logic say that it was treasonous.

But the note taken at the council meeting and now in Pym's hands was capable of a far more dangerous interpretation. "An army in Ireland you may employ here to reduce this kingdom..." Which kingdom? The notes gave no indication. Had Strafford, in anger at the behaviour of the Short Parliament and impatience at English resistance to the royal policy, meant not Scotland but England? Had he suggested bringing over Irish troops to subdue not the rebel Scots who were in arms but the recalcitrant English who were not?

The sentence could bear that interpretation. It is possible that John Pym sincerely believed that it did. The known ruthlessness of Strafford's methods, no less than the widespread belief that the King had negotiated for military help from the Spanish Netherlands, made this interpretation perfectly credible. If it was indeed a possible and a credible interpretation of the words, then Strafford had committed an act from whose treasonous implications there was no escape: he had advised the King to make war on his own peaceful subjects and had offered the means to do it.

This was the awful value of the evidence which young Vane had produced. But how could it be used? Young Vane was not very willing that his intrusions into his father's private papers should be revealed; it would be better if old Vane himself could be inveigled into incriminating Strafford. The House of Commons accordingly sent a message to the King for permission to examine Privy Councillors on oath on what had passed in council. The request put the King in a quandary; a more outrageous intrusion into the inner sanctum of government could hardly be thought of, but if the King refused to allow it, his refusal would imply that he doubted Strafford's innocence or had something to hide. Of two evils he may have chosen the lesser when, on December 4th, he gave the House permission to question his own councillors. The Venetian ambassador, wise in the cunning statecraft of the Republic, recorded this demand of the Commons as the most serious attack yet made on the sovereignty of the King and his yielding to it as infinitely unwise. Certainly this decision, coming as it did on top of the tacit repudiation of Windebanke, made the King's remaining councillors very unwilling to put their loyalty to their master before their own interests or to give him any advice which might possibly be quoted later to their disadvantage.[21]

With the flight of Secretary Windebanke the King lost his most important representative in the Commons. An order that no monopolist might occupy a seat in the House excluded several more. When, on December 7th, the Commons proclaimed

Ship-money an illegal tax, it was evident that any members who injudiciously supported the King might be expelled or suspended on the grounds that, in one way or another, they had been concerned in collecting Ship-money; most loyal gentlemen had at one time or another in the past few years, been involved in assessing their neighbours or assisting the sheriff in the pursuance of his duties. The chief offenders in the Ship-money business were the King's own judges, and Lord Falkland, in words of unusual forcefulness now directed the batteries of the House of Commons against the judicial Bench and the Lord Keeper himself.

The judges, by their monstrous dictum, said Falkland, had "allowed to the King the sole power in necessity, the sole judgment of necessity, and by that enabled him to take from us what he would, when he would, and how he would." He hinted at corruption. "I doubt not," he went on, "we shall find when we examine them, with what hopes they have been tempted, by what fears they have been essay'd, and by what and by whose importunity they have been pursued before they consented to what they did." Among them all none was more culpable or more worthy to be removed than Lord Keeper Finch; "he who hath prostituted his own conscience hath the keeping of the King's." After so powerful an accusation the impeachment of Finch was only a matter of time.[22]

A diversion postponed the formal accusation of Finch for some days yet. On December 11th one of the members for London, Alderman Isaac Pennington, presented a petition with fifteen hundred signatures for the abolition of the ungodly institution of bishops, "root and branch." This move by Pennington and the fiercer Puritan spirits in London was not from Pym's point of view happily timed, because any action that might be taken on the Root and Branch petition was likely to divide the House. Pym managed to have it referred to the committee for religion, and to satisfy the Londoners, while disregarding their petition, he managed to direct the main force of the religious attack on to Laud's Canons and Laud himself.

The principal spokesmen were Sir Walter Strickland and Sir Edward Dering. Dering had already planted some good phrases in debate by declaring that if Laud did not aim to be Pope of Rome, he certainly aimed to be Patriarch of Lambeth, and complaining that wicked Popish books were licensed while good sound doctrine was prohibited " by the supercilious pen of my Lord's young chaplain." Now he proceeded in an impressively learned oration to condemn the Laudian Canons passed by Convocation in the spring.[23] From this it was a short step to the impeachment of Laud and his principal lieutenant Matthew Wren on December 18th. Wren was allowed to remain at liberty on giving bail of £10,000, but Laud, on whom the Scots Commissioners had demanded justice as a principal incendiary in the late war, was to be secluded immediately in the house of the serjeant-at-arms. He asked leave of the Lords to go home to Lambeth to fetch some necessaries and a few books; this, with a movement of mercy towards the broken old man, they granted him. He spent the short day collecting his papers at Lambeth, and was permitted, for the last time, to attend evensong with his household in his own chapel. It was December 18th, Friday, a week before Christmas, and he found marvellous comfort in the lesson, the fiftieth Chapter of Isaiah, and the psalms for the day.

> The floods are risen, O Lord, the floods have lift up their voice. . . . Blessed is the man whom thou chastenest, O Lord . . . that thou mayest give him patience in time of adversity: until the pit be digged up for the ungodly. . . . They gather them together against the soul of the righteous: and condemn the innocent blood.
>
> But the Lord is my refuge. . . .

He had asked that he might make his departure from Lambeth after dark " to avoid the gazing of the people." But a kindly surprise awaited him; as he passed down to the river to his barge " hundreds of my poor neighbours stood there, and prayed for my safety and return to my house. For which I bless God and them." [24]

The attack on the institution of episcopacy had been for the moment diverted into a personal attack on Laud and Wren, and it was possible for Pym to turn the attention of the House again to the less controversial question of Lord Keeper Finch. On December 21st, three days after the Archbishop had been removed to prison, the man whose office it was to sit in black and gold robes on the Woolsack and preside over the sessions of the peers, appeared before the Commons, bare-headed, to answer the accusations unanimously made against him: not one voice had been raised in protest. He was not, like Strafford and Laud, hated with violence and venom, but he was perhaps more universally disliked than any man in England. In this, his last public appearance as Lord Keeper, he behaved with unexpected restraint and dignity, calmly repudiated Falkland's suggestion that he had been bribed to pronounce Ship-money legal and affirmed his conviction that he had interpreted the law faithfully as he understood it. He had, however, made his preparations and before the House reassembled on the morning of December 22nd he had got himself aboard a ship in the cold and dark and was on his way to the Netherlands. [25] Windebanke at Paris, Toby Mathew at Ghent, Finch in The Hague—they were only the first of the flock of English refugees who in the next twenty years were to become a familiar, pathetic and finally boring spectacle in the little towns of the Netherlands, Paris and the French provinces, even in Venice, Madrid and Rome; keeping up their English customs and their conventions of gentility in reduced circumstances, talking of a past which grew in retrospect ever more rich and glorious, and believing in a future when they and the King would enjoy their own again. Finch was one of the fortunate: he survived. At the age of seventy-six he would totter triumphantly back to a seat in the House of Lords.

The Commons continued with the impeachment of Finch even after his flight, for it was essential to prove, beyond question, the abuses of the law which had been permitted under the King's authority by the men of his own appointment. As Falkland, who continued to direct this impeachment, very aptly put it: " He used the law against itself, making it, as I may say, *Felo de se.*" [26] This kind of argument sustained the claim of the House of Commons made in Pym's opening speech to do no more than " declare the law where it was doubtful and provide for the execution of the law where it was clear." Falkland, of all those who in these months supported Pym's policy, had the deepest views on political theory; he was more philosopher and theorist than practical man, or he might have seen more clearly that an onslaught on the Chancellor and the judges, with whatever justice and moderation it was conducted, was bound to have a revolutionary rather than a steadying and restorative effect on the legal structure of the state.

His friend, Edward Hyde, a working barrister and a more practical man of affairs, came in the end to see very clearly that the tendencies of the dominating group in the House of Commons had been revolutionary from the beginning. But in the winter of 1640-41 he was as eloquent and as forward as Falkland for the destruction of the powers which the King had tried to gather to himself. While the subservient Bench was Falkland's target, Hyde was the principal speaker against the prerogative courts, the abolition of which the House now began most insistently to demand.

Before the close of the year it had become clear that the demands and behaviour of this Parliament were different from those of its predecessors. They had attacked the King's policy; this Parliament was attacking the King's position. Even a document like the Petition of Right, forced through by the 1628 Parliament, had been an attempt only to stop the enforcement by the King of an unpopular policy; it prevented him from exploiting his powers of raising and billeting troops in such a way as to punish or control those who objected to his policy. It had not fundamentally altered his position or curtailed his sovereignty in any crucial point.

But the Long Parliament (as it came to be called) attacked the roots of sovereignty. This was not done by pompous statements of political theory; it was done in a direct, business-like, Pym-like manner, by fastening systematically in turn upon every vital place. By asserting their right to inquire into the levying of Ship-money and of coat-and-conduct money for the troops, the Commons had tacitly implied that all the administrative officers of the Kingdom were answerable, not to the King, but to Parliament. It was an extension of this principle to assert, tentatively and in one single instance at first, Parliament's right to know what went on in the King's inmost councils and to question those who advised him on how and why they spoke. If the King's lesser officials were answerable to Parliament, why not his ministers? Why not the King? By accusing the judges, Parliament implied that it alone could decide the validity of laws: that Parliament, and not the King, was the fountain of justice. It followed logically from this that the prerogative courts must go; if the King was not, in his proper person, the fountain of justice, no court could function by his authority alone. The High Court of Parliament remained; it could indeed prosecute and try men—as it would shortly do Strafford—because it embodied the King's justice. King-in-Parliament was the source of law, not the King alone.

Two pillars supporting the monarchy remained: the revenues and the armed forces. Before the end of the year the House, pursuing the question of monopolies, tax-farming and other alleged abuses, had asked to examine the officers responsible for collecting the royal revenue and their books. The King conceded the request, again for fear of seeming to conceal anything upon which a dangerous construction could be put. The outcome was an order of the House of Commons soon after Christmas that the officers of the customs were to pay no more money into the royal coffers except for the daily expenses of the household.[27] To this unprecedented impertinence the King had no choice but to submit. The sums of money which had to be officially paid to the Scots pending the conclusion of a treaty, together with such other expenses as paying the remnant of the

English army, now passed through Parliament only. Parliament, not the King, had taken over and renewed the loan made by the City.

The question of the army remained in abeyance. The local levies had gone home, but the cavalry and some of the infantry which had been raised by the King's supporters remained in being; with the six northern counties occupied by the Scots forces and the treaty not yet signed, it was only reasonable to keep some kind of an English army in existence, although notoriously Roman Catholic officers—the gallant John Smith among them—had been asked to resign. With Strafford's impeachment the chief command fell vacant, and the King had bestowed it once more on the Earl of Essex, who was trusted by Parliament, very well liked of the men, and not openly hostile to the King. There, in a kind of neutrality, the matter rested.

Parliament, under Pym's guidance, had taken order for everything except the control of the army and their own future. The King could still dissolve Parliament when he chose and was not bound to call it except when he pleased. To curtail this latter right, the Parliamentary lawyers had dug up an old, never implemented, Bill of the time of Edward III for the annual holding of Parliaments. This, in a modernised form, was debated in the House before the end of December. In two months, therefore, the beginnings of a constitutional revolution had been made at every vital place and there was as yet no sign of the King taking any counter-measures. Even if Strafford achieved what he—and the King—hoped, and triumphantly disproved the accusations made by the Commons, the Commons had made themselves so strong in other ways that it would be hard to force them back from the position they had gained.

In the circumstances gloom and depression should have prevailed at Court, but the Venetian envoy reported with faint disapproval in December that the King and his friends were cheerful. The loss of a daughter, the four-year-old Princess Anne, early in the month, probably went nearer to the Queen than it did to the King; her health responded all too quickly to anxiety and strain, and during these crucial months she lost weight and sleep, became excitable to the point of hysteria, and gave way to tears at the least frustration. The King was physically and emotionally of different stuff. His nerves were good and his health excellent. The regularity and order of his personal life continued, he prayed, ate and slept regularly, and was sustained by his unalterable conviction that God might chasten him for a time but would not desert a righteous King. He did not doubt that he would in the end overthrow his enemies.

His hopes in the winter of 1640–41 were fixed on the help of the House of Orange. The Baron de Heenvliet, the diplomatic Dutch nobleman who in the previous summer had undermined the King's Spanish alliance, had busied himself to some purpose, though very secretly, with this new project. By the middle of December it was generally known at Court that the only son of the Prince of Orange was to marry one of the King's daughters. The Prince of Orange, a rich and powerful nobleman in his own right, was by election the commander-in-chief and the virtual head of the government of the Protestant Netherlands. The position of the House of Orange in relation to the Dutch was unique; three princes of that house, William the Silent and his two sons, Maurice and Frederick Henry, had with ability and devotion guided the politics of the northern Netherlands during the seventy years of their war of liberation from Spain. The government of the Dutch provinces was republican and, inevitably, as the danger of Spanish victory faded, good republicans in Holland grew suspicious of the quasi-hereditary power of the House of Orange. The position of Frederick Henry was however still nearly as secure as that of a ruling sovereign—far more so than that of King Charles—and the private resources of the family were unquestionable.

The Prince of Orange, while careful not to offend Dutch susceptibilities, was very willing to establish his family on an equality with the reigning houses of Europe; late in life he had married the beautiful Amalia von Solms, maid-of-honour to Elizabeth of Bohemia, and his wife's ambition for their only son helped in persuading this otherwise sage statesman to involve himself with the difficult fortunes of the Stewart dynasty. He offered to advance £100,000 to King Charles immediately and asked that the princess who was to be his son's bride should be sent to Holland to complete her education. In the earlier stages of the negotiation he had looked no higher than the King's second daughter, the five-year-old Princess Elizabeth, and things had gone far enough with this little girl for her intended bridegroom to send her a jewel worth a thousand pounds.[28] The match was almost made before the Princess of Orange took it upon herself to confide in the Queen of Bohemia from whom the matter had hitherto been carefully concealed. The poor Queen expressed outward pleasure at this piece of family news, but was deeply mortified at her brother's secretive behaviour. She justly suspected, from the embarrassment of her former maid-of-honour, that something else was being kept back, and guessed, with anguish, what that something was. For years she had trusted in a tacit understanding with her brother that he would give his eldest daughter to her eldest son. She wrote at once to a faithful friend at the English Court, imploring him to use all his influence to prevent the ambitious Prince and Princess of Orange from stealing her son's bride.[29] Her suspicions were correct: as it became clear to Heenvliet that King Charles was desperate for the alliance and the immediate financial relief that it would bring, he shifted the demand from the younger to the elder daughter, and by the middle of January 1641 had secured Princess Mary, nine years old and very pretty, for the twelve-year-old Prince William.

With this foreign alliance and financial help secured, the King's confidence grew. He began to marshal such forces as he had for the counter-attack. The flight of Finch, leaving the Woolsack vacant, had opened the way for new appointments. The King made Sir Edward Littleton Lord Keeper in his room, moved Sir John Bankes, hitherto Attorney-General, to Littleton's place as Chief Justice of the Common Pleas, and promoted Sir Edward Herbert to Attorney-General instead of Bankes.

All these men were strongly loyal to the Crown and had supported Ship-money, but as if to cover these appointments with an act of conciliation, the King gave to Oliver St. John, who had conducted Hampden's defence, the lucrative post of Solicitor-General. The massing and arrangement of his legal strength was of great importance, because the conflict between him and Parliament was essentially an argument over the interpretation of the law. In theory neither side admitted to making or desiring the least innovation: the King claimed that his view of the laws —interpreted by Finch, by Strafford, by Bankes, by the late ingenious Noy—was the correct one. Pym and his friends —supported by barristers of weight and learning like Maynard, Selden, Hyde, and by the writings and dicta of the late Sir Edward Coke—contended that the interpretations of the King's advisers were subversive and their own correct. Neither denied that the law, in some absolute sense and meaning, already existed; it needed only to be restored and made manifest in action.

In this theory of law subverted or law interpreted the coming impeachment of Strafford played an important part. If he could shake the legal contentions of his prosecutors as to the manner in which he had exercised his office as the King's Deputy, he would go far to undermine the widespread belief among the law-conscious English, from barristers to country justices, that the King had, in his personal role, acted against the law. Once this belief, the outcome of the last years' inconveniences and interferences, began to weaken, it might be possible for the King to show that impeachment had a double edge, and that his Attorney-General could bring charges against his opponents quite as effectively as they could bring charges against his ministers. This policy would need patience and the right men in the right places at the right time. The King's choice of men for preferment in the legal offices of the Kingdom during his personal rule had, unfortunately, given him no very great reserves on which to draw. The lawyers of brilliance, daring and strength were nearly all on the opposing side. Finch had already shown himself unequal to the crisis, and his departure removed a man who was by this time a liability to the King's cause. Littleton and Herbert, both good, solid, helpful, honest men and the best appointments that could be made in the circumstances, lacked the courage and vision essential for the task before them.

These appointments revealed something of the King's intended policy. He sought to win over his less violent critics among the peers, those whose opposition was not so much fundamental as incidental—men who objected to the mismanagement of the Scots war but whose traditions and past relations with the Court made them essentially the servants of the Crown rather than its opponents: men who, although Protestant in feeling, were neither Puritan nor Presbyterian in their religious sympathies. The King had already gone far to win Lord Bristol, who had been the spokesman of the opposition peers at York. He aimed also at Bedford and at the moderate Hertford, believing rightly that these men could be detached from intransigents like the troublesome Saye and Brooke, the dark and dangerous Warwick. The same process, if well begun in the Lords, could be extended to the Commons. The fears of those who had been disturbed by what appeared new and overbearing in the King's last years of government were to be systematically allayed by the moderation of his present conduct, while their suspicions of the extremists among his critics were gradually aroused. The majority in Lords, Commons and the country at large were conventional: they feared any kind of " overturning "—the word was frequently on their tongues. They had disliked Ship-money, patents, monopolies, licences, because these things overturned or threatened to overturn conventional ideas about property rights. But the attitude of some of Pym's more extreme followers, especially in religion, threatened to " overturn " other things equally important to them: the relation of Church and State or the social hierarchy itself. It could only be a matter of time and forbearance on the King's part before the feelings, so strong against his government at the end of the year 1640, should begin to rise against the opposing party.

This was the dominant theme in King Charles's policy during the next months, but it was not the only theme. He felt the necessity—and the Queen felt it still more acutely—to have more deadly alternatives in reserve in case his long-term policy did not work fast enough. He still controlled the army, and although he had made the Earl of Essex commander-in-chief he knew that a number of army officers drawn from the Court circle were devoted either to him or to the Queen, or, at any rate, much opposed to John Pym, Puritans and Covenanters. Many of the Roman Catholic officers had had to withdraw, but the King kept in touch with the best of them: to Captain John Smith he offered a baronetcy gratis which the sensible young soldier refused on the grounds that his fortune was too slender to support so high a rank.[30] He was naturally on good terms with the young noblemen who officered his personal guards and who, all that winter, lent a decorative martial air to his Court: Harry Jermyn, the Queen's Master of the Horse, George Goring, governor of Portsmouth and son of Lord Goring a principal courtier and favourite with the Queen, Harry Percy, brother of Northumberland, John Suckling and William Davenant, poets and courtiers turned soldiers, Hugh Pollard, John Berkeley, John Ashburnham, more soldiers than courtiers, and Harry Wilmot who had distinguished himself, if anyone could be said to have done so, at Newburn. There was also an Irish officer, Daniel O'Neill. Protestant by conversion and well known at Court, he was by birth the nephew of the Red O'Neill, the exiled Earl of Tyrone and the tacitly acknowledged leader of Catholic Ireland.

These men and others were much about the Court in the early months of 1641; several of them combined their unexacting military tasks with Parliamentary duties, being among the small number of King's men who had successfully procured seats in the Commons. They formed a group, or several groups, who moved in and out of each other's lodgings of an evening to take sack and tobacco, met in the Westminster taverns, and attended —some of them—the Queen's drawing-room. Their business in politics and at Court had nothing to do with the King's policy of moderation and patient waiting. They represented the beginnings of a new striking force, a new extremism of which the Queen was the moving spirit.

Pym, who took care to be well-informed, was not unaware of the growth of the military *junto* about the Queen, but he was, rightly, more anxious in the opening weeks of 1641 to prevent any split in the House of Commons which could assist the King in forming a body of moderate-minded supporters. For the first eight weeks of Parliament the Commons had been so carried away with the questions they had to debate that they had not even noticed the physical discomfort of their meeting-place. In the long intermission, many windows had been broken; this had not mattered greatly in the Short Parliament of the spring, but in an exceptionally cold and wet December, icy rain whistled through broken panes while they debated the affairs of the nation. Not until January 4th did they take action to have the windows reglazed.[31]

This attention to their personal comfort indicated a slackening in tension which might have been dangerous to Pym, especially as the Puritans, both in the House of Commons and the City, encouraged by the Scots, were becoming very hard to control. In Pym's judgment this was not the moment to listen to the clamour for the removal of bishops, an " overturning " of accepted institutions which was bound to dismay the majority of moderate men. He strove, with patient skill, to confine Puritan enthusiasm within safer channels. Let them attack Roman Catholics, let them complain of inefficient clergy, of whom there were plenty; let there by all means be an inquiry into the number of English livings recently bestowed on the episcopal Scottish clergy who had had to flee from their own country; let there be an inquiry into the number of idolatrous images to be found in English churches, and let Dr. Cosin who had introduced some at Durham be impeached. Let a vote of censure be passed against the clergy who had preached against the Scots or the behaviour of the Short Parliament; let the Vice-

Chancellor of Oxford, Dr. Christopher Potter, Provost of Queen's College and chaplain to the King, be compelled to ask the House's pardon on his knees because he had suspended Dr. Henry Wilkinson of Magdalen Hall for preaching a godly sermon.[32] But in spite of the London Root and Branch petition and in spite of a Kentish petition which came in to support it in January—Pym would not allow the question of the bishops to be taken up yet.

With the bishops, the Prayer Book was also protected from the full blast of Puritan rigour. Both Houses still officially advocated its general use throughout England, and conventicles were, in theory at least, discouraged. The Prayer Book, and compulsory attendance at the parish church on Sunday, had been confirmed by Act of Parliament under Queen Elizabeth; since the Commons insisted that they were preserving the law, they were not at this stage prepared to overrule an Elizabethan Act to please a minority, however clamourous.[33]

The situation was not easy for Pym. While the Scots pressed hotly for the reform of the English Church, he was urging on the Commons the importance of placing before the King as soon as possible the Bill for the frequent calling of Parliaments. An interval of three years, instead of the one year of the old Bill of Edward III's time, was now the longest to which they would consent. The proposed measure, commonly referred to as the Triennial Bill, had its third reading on January 20th, 1641. It had barely passed from the Commons to the Lords for their consent when the agitation against the bishops began again, this time in the form of a petition from numerous godly ministers asking for a thorough reform of the Church and complaining in particular of the secular offices which bishops now so frequently occupied.

The King himself at this juncture caused a diversion. At the last assizes in London one of the priests, who had long officiated in and about the City, had been tried under the law of Elizabeth which made it a felony for a priest of the Church of Rome to enter the country. His name was John Goodman and he was a kinsman of the unfortunate Bishop of Gloucester, although not, as was commonly reported at the time, a brother.[34] Father Goodman had been trained at Douai for the English mission and was steeled to martyrdom if it should come. He was the first to be tried under this law for many years and he hoped, reasonably enough, that a saving hand would be extended to him from the King's majesty. He did not hope in vain. Charles, at the request of the Queen reprieved Goodman on January 22nd. The instant outcry in London for a time diverted attention from other matters and the City refused to pay any further instalments of the promised loan until Goodman went to the gallows. So far all instalments of the City loan had gone to satisfy the Scottish army of occupation; the next payment was intended to cover some of the arrears due to the English army, and although the money would go through Parliament to the forces, the King was none the less anxious that the troops should get it because of the hopes he was beginning to build on the army's loyalty.

For the next ten days the life of Father Goodman brought the King and the Houses of Parliament together in a series of unsatisfactory interviews in the banqueting house at Whitehall. The King, deprived of almost all the councillors on whose eloquence he had relied, conducted these interviews himself with dignified tenacity. The first was chiefly devoted to the Church question; here Charles said with firmness that he would permit reform but not alteration, and desired that everything might be as it had been under Queen Elizabeth. He did well to cite Queen Elizabeth, the accepted norm for the laws of the realm. More than half the members would, in the long run, want nothing more in the Church than the abandonment of controversial ceremonies, the retirement of the bishops from secular power and an end to visitations and inquisitions. Pym, who knew this very well, but knew also the uncontrollable zeal of the extremists, cannot have been happy about this evident appeal of the King to the moderate men of both Houses. For him it was fortunate when the excitement about Goodman communicated itself to the Houses, who once again waited upon the King in person, this time with a general remonstrance about papists, and a particular request that the law might take its course. Charles, still admirably patient, conceded to both Houses of Parliament the right to make the final decision on Goodman, but reminded them that if a priest were hanged in England they might justly fear reprisals on English merchants and mariners in the dominions of Catholic sovereigns.[35] They went away to think this over, returning five days later with a new remonstrance against the continued presence of Roman Catholics at Court, and more especially that of Rossetti whom they took to be a Papal nuncio. The King, still exercising patience, informed them that Count Rossetti was not in any sense a nuncio but came on a private mission to the Queen, who was permitted by her marriage treaty to receive a personal envoy from the Vatican. He reminded them that he had himself expelled Roman Catholics from the Court, had enforced the penal laws during the previous year and had on numerous occasions put it beyond doubt that he was utterly opposed to the Church of Rome.[36] On the following day he sent to the House of Lords a petition which he had just received from Father Goodman; in this the devoted priest declared that he would far sooner die than be a cause of ill-feeling between the King and his people. With this moving document before them, the Lords revolted against the vindictive Commons. Goodman's death was indefinitely postponed.

In the midst of the agitation over the fate of Father Goodman, and the repeated audiences of the two Houses at Whitehall, during the short January days of the least brilliant winter King Charles's Court had yet seen, one gay social evening became memorable. It happened at " a house with stairs," as Sir John Suckling casually describes it, near Haymarket: the house was that of the younger brother of the Duke of Lennox, the dashing Lord d'Aubigny who had made a runaway match not long before with the high-spirited beauty Lady Catherine Howard. She it was who now provided the marriage feast for her sister's wedding to Lord Broghill, one of the numerous sons of Lord

Cork—he a nineteen-year-old gallant with a duel or two to his credit, she one of the prettiest brides in English poetry:

> Her feet beneath her petticoat,
> Like little mice, stole in and out,
>   As if they feared the light:
> But O she dances such a way
> No sun upon an Easter day
>   Is half so fine a sight.

The cates were plentiful, the company good, the usual jests were made, the usual healths drunk—

> On the sudden up they rise and dance
> Then sit again and sigh, and glance:
>   Then dance again and kiss:
> Thus several ways the time did pass,
> Whilst ev'ry woman wished her place,
>   And ev'ry man wished his.

So the time passed for those who were young and happy on Wednesday evening, January 27th, 1641, while Strafford lay in the Tower and Father Goodman at Newgate, and the King at Whitehall wondered what next to do, and the Queen wept over her frustrated hopes, and the Londoners muttered about Papists and Bishops.

> Such sights again cannot be found
> In any place on English ground. . . .

So John Suckling wrote in his "Ballad upon a Wedding" to Richard Lovelace who had missed it. Within two years the handsome bridegroom would be fighting a savage war in Munster, Lord d'Aubigny killed on the slope of Edgehill, his widow planning, not a wedding party, but a *coup d'état*, and the poet himself dead in exile.

On January 30th the Commons had at last completed the case against Strafford and he was brought from the Tower to the House of Lords to hear the accusation. The charge, containing nine general accusations of subverting the laws, and twenty-eight individual cases of alleged injustice, took a considerable time to read. When he had heard them he asked for some days to prepare an answer, and with that was escorted back to the Tower. He wrote tenderly to his wife that night, and in a more business-like manner to the Earl of Ormonde, a trusted friend in Ireland. In both letters he used the same phrase: there was, he thanked God, "nothing capital" in the charges against him. The Commons, in his opinion, had failed to make out their case for high treason and he saw the way towards acquittal opening out before him.[37]

While Strafford optimistically examined the articles of his impeachment in the Tower, Pym was still with difficulty holding back the attack on the bishops for which the extremists in the Commons were spoiling. In a debate on Church government, arising out of the recent petitions, George Digby proved helpful; he strongly argued that the Triennial Bill, which was even then awaiting the King's signature, would, by ensuring frequent Parliaments, prevent the growth of abuses in the Church.[38] The question of the Church was accordingly referred to a committee where the extremists could inveigh against the bishops without causing further difficulty in the House. To satisfy the Scots and maintain their friendship while postponing the alterations in the Church for which they hoped, a further sum of £300,000 was voted towards the expenses of their army. In the course of the debate on this question the member for Grimsby, Gervase Holles, whose political opinions were the opposite of those of his cousin Denzil, spoke sharply of the Scots' rebellion, words for which Speaker Lenthall suspended him until the end of the session.[39] Another Royalist had been conveniently silenced, and the alliance of the Scots and the House of Commons effectively confirmed.

By this time Edward Hyde and his committee had prepared

the accusations against the judges who had supported Ship-money, and on February 12th the first of five impeachments was launched. Sir Robert Berkeley, while presiding in the Court of King's Bench, was peremptorily summoned to appear before the House of Commons; he had no choice but to obey. Four days later the King, perceiving that no money would be voted for the English army unless he gave in to the Commons over the Triennial Bill, consented to this measure. Both Houses discussed the propriety of ringing bells and lighting bonfires to mark their triumph, but the King in a well-phrased speech reminded them that in three months they had taken his government to pieces like a watch that needed repairs. He suggested that the time had come when the watch should be put together again and made to go.[40] City loans, generously passed on to the Scots, were well enough, but what of his revenues, what of the legitimate needs of the state?

With this reminder he left them, but all was now moving rapidly towards the trial of Strafford. At the end of the month he appeared once again in the House of Lords to make a formal answer to the charges. The King had intimated that he wished to be present but he did more than merely attend on this occasion; he came down to the House of Lords before Strafford was brought in, and had some minutes of private conversation with him before the hearing began. During the subsequent proceedings the King, so far from maintaining a judicially dispassionate air, honoured the prisoner at the bar with friendly salutations. All this must have been deliberate, possibly even pre-arranged with Strafford. He intended to show, and thought it safe to show, that he was satisfied with the way in which the minister had refuted the charges brought against him. Since this was a mere preliminary to the trial itself, the open demonstration by the King that he had pre-judged the issue was very ill-received by Parliament.[41] But it was not a mistaken action in itself, because it was evidently a matter of some importance in the presentation of Strafford's defence that the King, whom he had served, should not seem to doubt his capacity to justify all that he had done.

So far Pym had done no more than organise the preliminary strategy of the struggle. Much was claimed, much attempted, much begun. The destruction of royal power, the abolition of the prerogative courts, the impeachment of the judges: the attack had been mounted but it had not yet been carried through. The King had given his consent, so far, only to the Triennial Bill, and the other projected constitutional changes might never come to fulfilment. The whole widespread attack depended on Pym's ability to retain public confidence and the support of the House, and on the King's inability to win back either. If Strafford out-argued and defeated his accusers, he would go far to reverse the situation in Charles's favour, and his hopes that he would do so were well founded. Pym's principal anxiety was still the maintenance of good relations between the Commons and the Covenanters. If the attack on Strafford was to be successful, it was essential that the Scots War should appear unprovoked and unjustified. It was therefore unfortunate that a memorandum privately drawn up by Henderson, on the reform of the English Church, should by an accident become public at this moment. The Covenanters now appeared as aggressors, determined to force their form of worship on England and the storm which Pym had long dreaded broke over the House of Commons. Honest churchmen and patriotic Englishmen fiercely attacked the Scots; and Pym only with great difficulty managed to get the matter talked out and so, once again, temporarily shelved.[42]

The King meanwhile had publicly announced the betrothal of his daughter to the Prince of Orange's son, diplomatically representing it as a change of foreign policy. The principal object of this treaty, he declared to the House of Lords, was to help his dear sister the Queen of Bohemia and her orphan children. The new alliance was certainly a Protestant one, and as such an improvement on the Spanish friendship of the past, but the King was not to be successful in the pretence that it was intended for his sister's benefit because his nephew, the Elector Palatine, refused to enter into the deception. Disregarding a message from the King forbidding his journey, he arrived in

England on March 2nd, received a hollow, embarrassed welcome from his uncle and aunt, and, with calculated indiscretion, let it be known that he had come to claim his promised bride, the Princess Mary, and to appeal to Parliament for the help his uncle had never given him.[43]

The romantic popularity of his mother inspired the Londoners with sympathetic feelings for the young German prince, but he had not himself the qualities which inspire devotion; otherwise he would have been not merely an exasperation but a danger to his uncle. As it was, he did little, after making his dramatic arrival, except press in vain for a clause in the marriage treaty promising him—in return for relinquishing his own claim on the bride—financial help and possession of a fortress in Holland.[44] Failing to get this, he remained as a sulky, uninvited and expensive guest at the palace of Whitehall, for he was not above taking free board and lodging when he got the chance.

Three weeks after the Elector's arrival the trial of Strafford opened on March 22nd, 1641, in Westminster Hall.

BOOK III CHAPTER IV REFERENCES

1. Laud, *Works*, III, pp. 237–8; H.M.C., XII, II, p. 262.
2. *C.S.P. Ven.*, 1640–2, p. 93; Clarendon, III, I.
3. Verney, *Notes on the Long Parliament, Camden Society*, 1854, pp. 2–3.
4. Twysden, *Journal, Transactions of the Kent Archaeological Society*, I, 1858, pp. 188–9.
5. *C.S.P.D.*, 1640–1, pp. 244–6; Rushworth, III, i, pp. 12–16.
6. Whitaker, p. 220.
7. Rushworth, III, i, pp. 21–4; D'Ewes, *Journal*, ed. Notestein, Yale, 1923, pp. 7–11.
8. Rushworth, III, i, pp. 30–5, 37; D'Ewes, ed. Notestein, p. 20 n.
9. Rushworth, III, i, pp. 39–40; Dering, *Speeches*, London, 1641.
10. *Commons Journals*; Balfour, II, p. 425; D'Ewes, ed. Notestein, p. 20.
11. See Book III, chapter iii, p. 350.
12. Clarendon, III, 3–4; D'Ewes, ed. Notestein, pp. 25–9.
13. *Lords Journals*; Baillie, I, pp. 271 f.
14. *Commons Journals*.
15. Lady Brilliana Harley, *Letters*, p. 104.
16. Albion, pp. 341, 347.
17. *Commons Journals*.
18. *H.M.C.*, II, I, p. 267.

19. *C.S.P.D.*, 1640–1, pp. 297–9, 314–15, 437. Robert Read's letters to Windebanke's sons, written from Paris and scattered through the State Papers Domestic for many months give a very clear idea of the Secretary's last days.

20. *Commons Journals*, II, p. 118; Verney, p. 37; Clarendon, III, 135–7.

21. *C.S.P. Ven.*, 1640–2, p. 105.

22. Rushworth, III, I, pp. 86–7.

23. *Ibid.*, pp. 55, 101–4; D'Ewes, ed. Notestein, pp. 146–9.

24. Laud, *Works*, III, p. 239.

25. *Commons* and *Lords Journals*; Rushworth, III, i, pp. 124–8.

26. *Ibid.*, IV, i, p. 140.

27. *Commons Journals*.

28. *C.S.P.D.*, 1640–1, pp. 278–9, 291.

29. *C.S.P. Ven.*, 1640–2, pp. 113, 117.

30. *Brittanicae Virtutis Imago.*

31. *Commons Journals*, 63.

32. *Commons Journals*, 64, 72; Rushworth, III, ii, p. 1327.

33. *Lords Journals*; Rushworth, III, i, p. 144.

34. Soden, *Godfrey Goodman*, pp. 311–2.

35. Rushworth, II, ii, p. 1334; III, i, pp. 158–60.

36. *Ibid.*, pp. 165–6.

37. Knowler, II, p. 415; Carte, *Ormonde*, Oxford, 1851, V, p. 245.

38. Rushworth, III, i, pp. 170–4; D'Ewes, ed. Notestein, p. 263.

39. *Commons Journals*.

40. *C.S.P.D.*, 1640–1, pp. 460–1.

41. *C.S.P. Ven.*, 1640–2, p. 128.

42. Baillie, I, p. 306; D'Ewes, ed. Notestein, p. 417.

43. *C.S.P. Ven.*, 1640–2, pp. 130, 133.

44. *C.S.P.D.*, 1640–1, pp. 493–4.

CHAPTER FIVE

THE END OF STRAFFORD

March–May 1641

THE destruction of Strafford was the key to the political strategy of John Pym. The success of his attack on the King's position and the permanence of his achievement depended on victory in this crucial conflict over the guilt and the life of the Lord Lieutenant of Ireland. Therefore the whole of Strafford's Irish policy became for Pym no more than the material for his impeachment; the politics and personalities of Ireland had no significance for him except as they contributed to this end.

But the politics of the three kingdoms—England, Ireland, Scotland—could not cease to act upon each other merely because it had become a political necessity in England to destroy the work of Strafford in Ireland. While John Pym understood very well what he was doing at Westminster and what effect Strafford's fall would have on the power of Parliament and the government of the country, he did not understand what he was doing to Ireland, what the effect would be or what the ultimate consequences to all three kingdoms.

Sixteen of the twenty-eight articles of the impeachment were directed at Strafford's Irish policy. He was attacked principally for two things—for increasing the direct power of the King through the judicial use of the Court of Castle Chamber, and for interfering with Irish manufacture, produce and customs duties. These two things—the use of the prerogative courts and the interference with trade—were the elements in the King's policy most unpopular in England; to prosecute Strafford for his use of them in Ireland was to cast by implication an even blacker shadow on Charles's proceedings in England. In English politics and in Pym's policy the whole picture fitted together.

But in Irish politics Strafford's actions had a different face, and in attacking him on these two issues Pym was in effect taking the part of the most unscrupulous of the recent settlers in Ireland, whose tactics of exploitation Strafford had consistently fought.

These men were well represented in the English Parliament and several had seats in person; others had sons, sons-in-law, cousins, friends or dependents who were willing to act for them. In the Irish Parliament, still in session at Dublin, this same group of people, quiescent in the previous session while Strafford's influence was dominant, became active as soon as his fall appeared imminent and his influence waned. Strafford had left as his deputy in Ireland, when the King called him to England, his close friend and right-hand man, Christopher Wandesford, but Wandesford, a conscientious second-in-command, was of too mild a nature to deal strongly with an opposition which had been held in check only by fear of Strafford himself.

For different reasons the majority of the Irish Parliament had now turned against Strafford and, with few exceptions, Protestant settlers and Catholic Irish united to repudiate their past obedience. The blockading of the Scottish ports during the war had damaged Irish trade and almost all the Protestant settlers of northern Ireland, whether Englishmen or Scots, sympathised with the Covenanters and resented Strafford's past enforcement of an oath of loyalty to the King. The Irish army, kept expensively in being by money voted in their Parliament, was not liked by the majority of the settlers, who feared and suspected Strafford for thus arming and training the warlike native population. The repressive measures taken against those of Covenanting sympathies in Ulster by the Bishops of Down and Derry aroused bitter feelings against the Church.

While the more recent settlers and all the more vehement Protestants hated him, the Catholic Irish gentry had supported him only so long as they felt confidence in his strength. They had been driven to accept his plan for the redistribution of land in the belief that his final settlement would make an end of the uncertainty and constant fear of expropriation in which they had lived for the past generation. With Strafford impeached in England and the land question broken off before the re-organisation of tenure was completed, their state was worse than before. No love was lost on the man who, by making promises for the future which he was now in no position to perform, had compelled them to put their estates at the mercy of the King. The suspicions of the Irish gentry were increased by the last important appointment that Strafford made in Ireland. He had replaced Chancellor Loftus by Sir Richard Bolton, chief baron of the Irish Exchequer, a man of unspotted reputation who had spent half his lifetime of seventy years in the Irish courts and had published legal works which established him as the principal authority on Irish law: an upright man, a man whose knowledge of the laws was un-surpassed—but an extreme and austere Protestant. No doubt his religion was a private matter for him, as it was for Strafford himself. His political affiliations were not with the restive Protes-tant settlers and his loyalty to the Crown was sincere and strong. But the Catholic Irish only saw in his appointment another reason to doubt Strafford's good faith with them.

The unfortunate Wandesford was powerless to control the angry outbreak against Strafford from almost all quarters of the assembly when the Irish Parliament met for its second session. Both sides of the House were ready to add their accusations to those which were being made in England against the minister. Sir George Radcliffe, Strafford's chief personal adviser and friend, was shouted down when he suggested that they ought to in-vestigate the wild charges now being flung against the Lord Lieutenant before they believed them. He was himself impeached a few days later. So, in turn, were all Strafford's friends and assistants, the Bishop of Derry who had carried out the Laudian policy in the north, and the blameless Chancellor Bolton.[1]

In the midst of disaster the Lord Deputy Wandesford lay down and died. He was only forty-eight and there does not seem to have been much wrong with him except a winter chill and anxiety too great for him to bear. Ireland was now without any deputy of the King in Dublin. Strafford, from his imprisonment, suggested to Charles two men to fill the gap—Lord Dillon who was almost instantly rejected by the King on account of his Roman Catholic connections, and the Earl of Ormonde.

James Butler, twelfth Earl of Ormonde, was the most distinguished and powerful of the Norman-Irish lords. Brought up in England, he was a Protestant and an Episcopalian. His background, his education, above all his energetic and intelligent mind, had secured him friends and connections in every party in Ireland. Probably no man was more widely liked and trusted, as far as any man in Ireland could be trusted. He was now thirty years old, a tall vigorous handsome young man, with a certain nobility of thought and action and a singular grace of manner.

His relations with Strafford had begun seven years earlier in a young man's quarrel about his right to wear a sword in Parliament. Soon, however, Ormonde had recognised Strafford's quality as Strafford had recognised his. Since then he had been one of those to whom Strafford principally looked to carry out his plans for the better government of Ireland.

Ormonde had shown both loyalty and political skill when the Irish Parliament turned on Strafford. With great dexterity he had held off the attack in the House of Lords for several days by dragging the red herring of a point of privilege across the trail.[2]

Had the King dared to take Strafford's advice and put Ormonde into the Deputy's place left vacant by Wandesford, the collapse of Strafford's policy in Ireland might have been averted. But Charles was still convinced of the wisdom of playing for time and conciliating the most dangerous forces of the opposition, and he felt that the appointment of a Norman-Irish peer and a known friend of Strafford to the post of Lord

Deputy would alienate the dangerous faction of powerful settlers led by the Earl of Cork. For the time being he left the Deputy's place vacant and appointed two Lords Justices to carry on the government of Ireland in his name. The men on whom he fixed, Sir John Borlase and Sir William Parsons, were between sixty and seventy years old, strongly Protestant and in the main devoted to the settlers' interests.

Strafford himself, while he was anxiously aware of the consequences which his fall might entail for Ireland, was, still principally concerned to redeem his position, and with it the King's policy, at the forthcoming trial before the peers at Westminster. He saw with relief, on examining the charges, that he could disprove most and shake all of them. But he underestimated the effect that the mere making of such charges might have on the minds of his peers or the state of feeling in London. Pym was indeed relying on the effect made by the reiteration of Strafford's crimes to build up a resistance to any evidence that might be brought to disprove them. Three weeks before the trial the Commons, following the example set them by the industrious propaganda made by the Covenanters through the printed word, published the charge against Strafford, which was thus, by the time the trial opened, as familiar to all as the latest horrid murder on a broadsheet.

The Lords took exception to this impermissible act on the part of the Commons against one of their number but Strafford's enemies in the Upper House managed to prevent a breach. Two more events in the House of Lords darkened his prospects; Littleton, the new Lord Keeper, a personal friend, fell ill, so that he could not preside at the trial, and Lord Arundel, as Earl Marshal, became therefore in some sort the arbiter of the trial's progress and arrangement. Arundel, a haughty conservative under suspicion of Catholic sympathies, ought to have been the King's loyal servant, but his pride had been deeply wounded by his loss of the military command in the previous year on—he presumed—Strafford's advice. Throughout the trial he was markedly hostile to the prisoner.

One great hope of acquittal lay with the Bishops. It was to be expected that all their votes in the House of Lords would be exercised in Strafford's favour, and Pym, knowing how far this would endanger the success of the impeachment, had encouraged in the House of Commons a Bill against the exercise of temporal or judicial power by bishops or clergy, this being held incompatible with their spiritual function. The effect of the Bill was forestalled by the dexterous action of Bishop Williams in the House of Lords. He suavely suggested that the impeachment of their noble colleague the Earl of Strafford, being a matter of life and death and therefore a *causa sanguinis*, was not fit to be meddled with by men of their cloth; the bishops, he said, might therefore, of their own choice, waive their undoubted right to speak and vote on the case.[3] Most of them, in a legitimate anxiety to preserve the Church and therefore not to give any cause of anger to the Commons or the people, were thankful to accept this means of escape.

The trial opened in Westminster Hall on March 22nd. From then, for seven weeks, the affairs of the nation were at a stand: everything waited upon the outcome of this central event. No other business engaged the law courts; no other talk or news filled London and Westminster. Great crowds assembled outside the Hall and all who could contrive to get themselves a seat on the public benches did so. They came early, prepared to sit it out, however long the sessions, bringing bread and cheese and onions and bottles of ale against the pangs of hunger. Other needs they also relieved without moving from their places. The ladies and gentlemen in the galleries reserved for the Court thought this behaviour ill-mannered and lacking in reverence to the King.

Strafford himself was not the dread figure that many of them had expected to see. Weakened by anxiety and illness, crippled by recurring attacks of gout, he no longer looked like the overbearing tyrant who had declared—according to the indictment—that he would make " the little finger of the King heavier than the loins of the law." Instead of an upright, dominating vigorous man, the crowds in Westminster Hall saw a stooping grey-beard, his head sunk between his shoulders, well wrapped in a warm cloak, and wearing—by permission of his peers—a close-fitting fur-lined cap to shield him against the draughts. The appearance of Strafford did not fit with the idea of him that Pym and his supporters had been at pains to create, and it was not surprising that within a few days the more suggestible of the spectators were exclaiming "Alas, poor soul!" shaking their heads with pity, and murmuring that there might be two sides to the question.

This appeal to pity was accidental; it was not in Strafford's character deliberately to try to evoke such a sentiment. But the impression added to the effect of his defence as, worn, bent and weary, he fought on day by day with steady wits and an unfaltering voice.

The first week of the trial went badly for the Commons. John Pym opened the case and was ably supported by two of the best lawyers in the House, John Glyn and John Maynard. All three developed much the same argument. They urged the Lords to look upon the indictment as a whole. Although the charges individually might not seem to go so far as treason, yet the tendency of the whole was unmistakable. "It is a habit, a trade, a mystery of treason exercised by this great lord," said Maynard. In support of this general attack a remonstrance from the Irish Parliament was read in Court as though it had been evidence instead of a series of unproved accusations.

Strafford's defence was a masterpiece of precision. Disregarding the wider aspects of the indictment and refusing at this stage to be drawn into any general statement, he held tenaciously to the factual charges made against him and repeatedly demonstrated discrepancies of time and place or cast doubt on the competence and honesty of the witnesses. By the end of the first week Strafford was rapidly gaining the advantage over his opponents.[4] The King would have done well to leave it to his resourceful minister to work out his salvation in the teeth of his accusers while he, for his part, built up support among moderate men, ready for the moment when the failure of the impeachment would give him the chance of winning the initiative from Pym.

Things were moving smoothly in this direction. He had gained the support of the influential Bedford who had come so far towards the King's orbit as to consider marrying his daughter to the Marquis of Hamilton. Hamilton himself, pursuing his private policy of conciliation in Scotland, had offered his own daughter to Argyll's son.[5] These projected family connections suggested a new framework of councillors and friendships around the throne, an alliance of which Hamilton would be the pivot, between the moderates in England and the leading Covenanting nobles in Scotland. This would break down the connection between the extremists in the House of Commons and the Scots and give to the monarchy a new, broad and solid foundation. Charles had gone so far as to raise to the rank of Privy Councillor —although without admitting them to his inner cabinet— almost all his critics in the House of Lords: Bedford, Bristol and Essex, Hertford and Savile, even the incorrigible Puritans Saye and Mandeville. But he knew that their firm alliance was not to be obtained except by concessions which he still hoped to avoid, and he hankered after an alternative solution.

The Covenanting army, in occupation of the northern counties, was openly the ally of the House of Commons. In these unprecedented circumstances, it was reasonable for the King also to seek some kind of military support in case of need. He had hitherto successfully resisted the requests of the House of Commons that Strafford's Irish army should be disbanded, and he was resolute to keep it in being until the Scots withdrew theirs. He had also been told by Harry Percy that the English army officers were resentful of their treatment by Parliament and might support him in a crisis.[6]

Percy and his principal supporters, Wilmot, Ashburnham and Pollard, by drawing together a group of like-minded men and indicating their sympathy to the King had not generated a plan for a military counterstroke but they had provided the material out of which, at some future date, a military counter-stroke might be contrived.

The Queen's Master of the Horse, Harry Jermyn, would have liked to see things move at a greater pace, and somewhat contrary to Percy's judgment, encouraged the two poets, Suckling and Davenant, both irresponsibles, to consider more immediate and drastic military action for which a leader could be found in the governor of Portsmouth, Colonel George Goring. This young officer, a soldier by profession with five or six years' experience, was the feckless eldest son of one of the Queen's favourite servants, Lord Goring. As a young man he had caused his family almost as much anxiety, though for different reasons, as Harry Vane had caused his father the Secretary. Young George, the antithesis of young Harry, had never been troubled with religion; gaming and women were his undoing. His father had hoped that on his marriage to one of Lord Cork's daughters he would settle down and perhaps make a career in Ireland, but the young man took neither to his wife nor his father-in-law and very soon outraged the family by departing without notice on the best horse in the stable. He was later sent to the wars in the Nether-lands to make good. Surprisingly, he did so; he had audacity, physical endurance, a quick judgment and the power to inspire his men. He had also an insinuating charm which he used to some purpose when he thought it worth his while, because, with all his wildness, he was ambitious. In the two mismanaged campaigns against the Scots he had suffered the mortification of seeing his talents wasted and his ambitions checked by the incom-petence of the high command. Since then, discontented with his post as governor of Portsmouth, he had intrigued to be made Lieutenant-General in the North where, should war again break out with Scotland, he believed he could conduct it with success. Popular with the Queen and her friends, Goring was suspect to his more experienced seniors in the army; they distrusted his ambitions and knew that although he was an inspiring leader in battle he was at other times careless and irre-sponsible. Both Sir John Conyers at Berwick and Sir Jacob

Astley at York were strongly opposed to his appointment in the north.[7]   For other reasons, it suited the King and Queen better to keep him at Portsmouth.   The Queen cherished baseless hopes of help from France, so that the necessity of keeping a royalist commander in the Portsmouth garrison was evident.

Goring, reckless, ambitious and disappointed in his hope of the northern command, went far beyond the modest and tentative suggestions of Percy and his friends.   He was for occupying London and seizing the Tower.[8]   The difference between the two plans, the moderate and the immoderate, was still one of words, for neither Percy nor Goring had taken any steps to translate their ideas into action.

Discretion is rarely a virtue of amateur conspirators, and the courtier-officers, many of them wits and poets, were not by nature discreet, nor were the circumstances in which they evolved their plans favourable to secrecy.   Oaths of silence had of course been taken, by some, if not all, of them; Goring, in Percy's lodging at Westminster, over tobacco after supper had put his hand on a Bible and sworn to reveal nothing.[9]   But the important looks, the sidelong glances, the hurryings in and out of the Queen's apartments, advertised that something was afoot.   Some time in April George Goring, dubious about the success of the enterprise, the wisdom of his associates and the advantages to himself decided to put himself right with Parliament by betraying the plot.   He sought out Lord Newport and warned him of the growing conspiracy.   Newport passed the information on to the Earl of Bedford, who appears to have under-valued its significance, and to Lord Mandeville, Pym's principal friend and associate in the Lords, who passed it on to Pym.   Goring meanwhile went quietly back to Portsmouth and awaited the outcome.[10]

Pym made no immediate use of his knowledge, knowing that its value hinged on the time at which he chose to make it public.   Article twenty-three of Strafford's impeachment had yet to be heard, and much depended on the success or failure of the Commons to prove his intention of bringing in an Irish army against the King's English subjects. The exposure of a conspiracy among the King's soldiers to seize the Tower and overawe London might come in at an apposite moment to confirm the suspicions aroused by article twenty-three. Pym held it in reserve.

On Monday, April 5th, the prosecution called Secretary Vane to give evidence of what Strafford had said at the Council eleven months before, when the Short Parliament was dissolved. Vane must have been aware that his son had provided the information on which article twenty-three was based, although he may not have known precisely what shape that information had taken. It should have been his function, as a servant of the Court, to deny the imputation that Strafford had offered the Irish army for the reduction of England; as Secretary of State he was in a position to know that no such offer had been made, that the Irish army had always been intended for Scotland. He disliked Strafford, but an ambitious man will hardly jeopardise his position for dislike alone, and to give evidence against Strafford was to endanger his future as the Queen's courtier or the King's Secretary of State. Vane, therefore, must have known that the Commons had, or thought they had, stronger means of proving article twenty-three than his words alone, and that it might be safest for him and his family, in this disastrous turn of affairs, to please the winning side.

Whatever his motives, Vane proved an unshakable witness. He declared that Strafford had advised the King to remember that he had an army in Ireland which could be used " here to reduce *this* kingdom." In cross-examination he refused to bate a syllable from the fatal phrase although its interpretation was a matter that must necessarily be left to the hearers. In his defence Strafford called three other councillors who had been present on that day, Hamilton, Cottington and the Bishop of London, all of whom categorically denied that he had advised using the Irish army against England. After a session of nearly ten hours, with battering assertion and counter-assertion, impassioned speeches from Glyn and Maynard for the prosecution, and a persuasive appeal from Strafford to their lordships to distrust mere verbal evidence " for words pass and may be easily mis-taken," the critical hearing closed. No one could say with certainty whether the prosecution or the defence had the better of it, but at the next session, on April 7th, Strafford was clearly winning his case. The prosecution, leaving aside article twenty-three, turned their attention to the charges connected with his tyrannical conduct during the second Scots war, and Strafford was able conclusively to disprove, or at least to cast grave doubt on, the truth of the assertions on which their accusations were based.

All in all he had now disposed of a good number of the specific charges made against him, had created a certain sympathy for his predicament and a growing distrust of the prosecution. Neither he nor anyone else can have hoped for a violent popular reaction in his favour, but the bitter, unreasoning general hatred felt for him had given way, among Lords and Commons and among those who followed the trial, to a much more uncertain feeling. The legal arguments he had used and the weight of evidence he had been able to produce in his own defence had made the inevitable impression. The legal-minded English, knowledgeable in the law and respectful of it, did not like the idea of condemning a man to death for high treason on charges as dubious as those against Strafford had been shown to be. Broadcast in print without comment they had served well as propaganda, but argued out in the hearing of thousands they were very weak.

Pym was alive to the gravity of the situation and fully aware that article twenty-three alone gave unquestionable grounds for the charge of treason—if article twenty-three were accepted as proven, which was far from being the case. Something had to be done to strengthen the evidence of Secretary Vane. So far, it depended on nothing but his personal recollection of what had been said, and Strafford's witnesses had impugned the accuracy of his memory by giving different accounts of the incident. Pym and the committee for the prosecution therefore decided that they must buttress this inadequate evidence by producing the written copy of Vane's notes on which, in the first place, the charge had been based. All that they now possessed was a copy in Pym's handwriting of a copy made by young Vane from his father's original and since destroyed. This was poor enough but it might serve their turn.

On April 10th when the Court reassembled Glyn opened the proceedings by informing the peers that he had new evidence to submit on article twenty-three. Strafford immediately asked for a like permission to call new witnesses, not only in respect of article twenty-three but of other articles if necessary. The Lords, after some consideration, gave way to his request, a concession which reflected the doubts that most of them now felt as to the wisdom and justice of the prosecution.

This concession threw out the strategy of the prosecution who wished to reopen only article twenty-three, and were anxious to prevent the prisoner from reopening any other, lest he gain further advantages against them. Glyn, with a rash conviction that Strafford was bluffing, went forward none the less and rose to call the new witness for article twenty-three. Strafford, on the instant, announced that he had additional evidence on four earlier articles of the indictment which should be heard first.

Amid a tumult of shouting from Pym's party, Glyn offered to forego the new evidence altogether, and the Earl of Arundel, who stood the Commons' friend throughout, with remarkable acumen adjourned the Court. Strafford watched their embarrassed retreat from the hall with a sardonic smile, and the King, remote in his box, was seen to be laughing.[11] Both of them, in that moment, believed that the hour of danger was over, and the game once more in their own hands. The impeachment had failed.

John Pym had not foreseen the defeat of the impeachment, the moment at which it would crumble or the form that the defeat would take; but he had always been prepared for the possibility. On the morning of April 10th, 1641, his first attack on Strafford, doggedly prosecuted since the autumn, came to a sudden end. On the afternoon of the same day he mounted the second attack for which he had long had everything in readiness.

His spokesman in this was Sir Arthur Haselrig who that afternoon introduced into the House of Commons a Bill of Attainder against the Earl of Strafford.[12] The Bill was nothing more than a restatement of the charges put forward in the impeachment but the difference in procedure was all-important. The purpose of the impeachment was to convince a majority in the House of Lords that Strafford was by English law guilty of certain crimes for which the punishment was death. The purpose of a Bill of Attainder was to declare by Act of Parliament that Strafford's death was necessary to the safety of the state. The impeachment could succeed only if legal proofs of Strafford's guilt were forthcoming, but a Bill of Attainder could be passed as long as the majority felt that the presumption of guilt was strong enough. This change of tactics brought in once again to Pym's support those who believed Strafford guilty of an intention of treason, but were troubled at the difficulty of proving it, and did not wish to countenance an undue stretching of the law. To such men as the conscientious and logical Falkland or the learned, meticulous Selden, the Bill of Attainder provided the perfect solution.

It was possible, in support of the Bill in the House of Commons that afternoon, to introduce the written evidence for article twenty-three which had been abandoned in Westminster Hall that morning—Pym's copy of young Vane's copy of his father's notes. The occasion caused a painful outburst from Secretary Vane, who, with an air of astonishment and horror, rose in his place and denounced the treachery and deceit of his son in making copies of his papers for Pym's benefit.[13]

The elder Vane must have known that Pym had had access to his notes; the wording of article twenty-three, and the way in which he had been handled as a witness, suggests as much. His exact repetition, when supposedly answering from memory, of the phrase which appeared in the written version betrays something like co-operation with the prosecution. The inference is that the elder Vane had been prepared to let the evidence be used in drawing the charges, and to support it, in the witness-box, apparently from memory. But he had not been willing that the carelessness which had enabled his son to procure the evidence should become a matter of public knowledge.

Although the Bill of Attainder had been introduced, the process of impeachment was not fully concluded. Strafford was to speak in his own defence on April 13th. That speech, in the existing circumstances, would be an appeal to the Lords to reject the Bill which the Commons were preparing against him. Pym, in a conference with the Upper House, laid before them the copy of Vane's notes on the day before they were to hear Strafford's defence; he was thus at least certain that they had taken notice of the whole of the evidence for the prosecution before being exposed to the persuasive eloquence of the accused. The fight was still a very close one and, although Pym was fairly sure of getting the Bill of Attainder through the Commons, he was by no means sure of the Lords. A well-judged appeal from Strafford to their sense of justice and their political wisdom might easily prevent its passing.

Pym's fears were fully realised when, on April 13th, he and the other managers of the prosecution listened for two hours to Strafford's speech in his own defence. First he took the charges against him one by one and demonstrated their malice and inaccuracy, emphasising the points which had told in his favour during the trial. From this he turned to the more general aspects of the impeachment. His crime, as he saw it, was to have defended the King's prerogative with too much vigour. In the last months the mere word " prerogative " had been made to stink in the Commons as though any act committed under that shield was of itself evil. Against this dangerous exaggeration he now protested. The safety of the Commonweal, he argued, depended neither on the destruction of the prerogative nor on the excessive use of it, but on the harmony and balance between the King's authority and the subject's liberty.

" The prerogative of the Crown and the propriety of the

subject have such mutual relations that this took protection from that, that foundation and nourishment from this; and as on the lute if anything be too high or too low wound up, you have lost the harmony, so here the excess of a prerogative is oppression, of a pretended liberty in the subject disorder and anarchy. The prerogative must be used as God doth his omnipotency, at extraordinary occasions; the laws . . . must have place at all other times, and yet there must be a prerogative if there must be extraordinary occasions."

These were unexceptionable sentiments, intended to counteract the suspicion of the prerogative which Pym had sedulously encouraged during the last months. Politically, this was the heart and centre of Strafford's defence, the belief from which his career and actions as a statesman had arisen. This was the theory that he left as legacy to those who, after him, would have to support and defend the policy of the King, and stop, if they could, the overturning acts of Pym and the extremists. But it was not the principal argument on which he depended to save his own life.

Knowing his own countrymen, he defended himself in the last resort by a direct appeal to the laws of the land. Nothing capital had been proved against him; in all their charges the Commons had failed to prove against him anything that by any existing law could be called treason. " My Lords," he pleaded, " do we not live by laws and must we be punishable by them ere they be made? " It went against every principle of English justice to create a new law in order, retrospectively, to punish a man who had offended against it. " These gentlemen tell me they speak in defence of the Commonweal against my arbitrary laws," he said, indicating the Commons. " Give me leave to say that I speak in the defence of the Commonweal against their arbitrary treason." [14]

Throughout his speech Strafford had been careful to appeal from the Commons to the Lords, to make it apparent that he trusted in the wisdom and dignity of the Upper House who were themselves, as he hinted, endangered by the arbitrary accusations made by the Commons against one of their number. He strove to arouse the jealousy of the Lords and he partly succeeded. Already, he knew, a considerable party among them were for saving his life, not out of any love for him, but because they did not wish to see a dangerous reversal of the normal order of things. For a minister and a peer of the realm to be executed at the instance of the Commons and against the known will of the King, was something new and dangerous in politics. As the full implications of the question became clear to them, the Lords as a body were drawing back from that alliance with the Commons which had marked the first months of the Parliament. The leaders in this movement were the Earls of Bristol and Bedford whose influence was now wholly bent towards the formation of a middle party and a new moderate government in which the House of Lords, and more especially their friends in it, would hold an even balance between the claims of King and Commons.

Bristol apparently did not know of, and Bedford did not seriously consider, the mysterious confederacy of the young army officers. They believed the King to be ready to extricate himself from his unhappy predicament and to buy Strafford's life by accepting their help and advice and placing them, in due course, in the foremost offices of state.

Bristol's son, George Digby, hitherto one of Pym's most reliable supporters, suddenly changed his tactics in the House of Commons. He was not the only member to have been dissatisfied with the evidence in support of article twenty-three but it seems likely that his decision to denounce it was taken in consultation with his father Lord Bristol, and his father-in-law Lord Bedford. The timing was extremely apposite. But no amount of pre-arrangement with his friends in the Lords can take away from Digby the credit for his courage in speaking out. His argument, put with all the fervour of a young and consciously eloquent speaker, was strictly legal: two witnesses were, by statute, essential before a man could be condemned for treason, but so far only one witness had been found to support article twenty-three. Sir Harry Vane's personal account of what had happened, given in evidence, and a copy, at two removes, of what Sir Harry Vane had written down about it at the time were not by any stretch of imagination *two* witnesses: there was still one witness only to article twenty-three and that did not satisfy the law. To condemn a man on such evidence was not justice but murder. " Before God," declared George Digby, " my vote goes not to the taking of the Earl of Strafford's life." [15]

Digby was a moving speaker but too much the young nobleman to make a deep impression in the House of Commons, who knew his affiliations in the Lords and were suspicious and jealous of them. It was Digby's misfortune throughout life that, although he could inspire affection and admiration, he rarely inspired confidence. The harm that his speech might do to the Bill of Attainder now before the Commons was more than counter-balanced by the thoughtful support given to it by the persuasive Lord Falkland. Falkland was one of those men who carry in their faces and manner the unmistakable marks of extreme conscientiousness. When Falkland spoke, it was not from impulse but conviction, not from any hope of gain or consideration of friendship, but from a sense of duty even, as now, of painful duty. Falkland was not vindictive; he disapproved of Strafford in the negative manner dictated by a naturally moderate temperament and a tolerant and liberal political philosophy. He may, in some other compartment of his well-regulated mind, have disliked him personally, for Strafford's predecessor in Ireland had been Falkland's father, and Strafford was inclined to think—and say aloud—that his predecessor had been incompetent. But political disapproval and private dislike would not have moved Falkland to seek the death of Strafford had his conscience not been satisfied that his death was lawful. Any legal doubts that he had were removed by the new procedure by Bill of Attainder. It was possible, he argued, to recognise treason without knowing precisely how it came to be treason, as it was possible to know a tall man from a short man without precisely knowing how many hairs' breadths made the difference between them.[16]   These things depended not on exactitude of detailed measurements, but on a clear general impression. With the argument placed before them in this fashion, the majority in the House of Commons on April 19th resolved that an intention to subvert the laws was tantamount to treason,[17] and that such an intention was clear in Strafford's case. Whether the House of Lords would accept this view, or yield to Strafford's appeal that a man could not be retrospectively condemned for offences invented afterwards, depended much on the skill and management of Bedford and Bristol.

The King was reasonably confident; he had both his moderate party in the Lords and the support of his army to sustain him. If his army friends were to be ready for a possible crisis they must be at their posts, and therefore, towards the middle of April, the loyalist officers who had long been about Whitehall were ordered to their various stations. Half a dozen of them were also members of Parliament and could not abandon their duties in the Commons without permission. Commissary General Wilmot, member for Tamworth, asked leave for them all;[18] it was quietly granted, but Pym, who still waited his time to reveal what he had learnt from Goring of their intentions, did not fail to notice this forewarning move.

The only son of the Prince of Orange, magnificently accompanied by a suite of four hundred servants, had meanwhile arrived in London. On April 20th he made his first visit to Whitehall to see his bride. It was the children's hour; the twelve-year-old bridegroom, a beautiful child in gorgeous clothes, was received on the stairs of Whitehall by his future brothers-in-law, the Prince of Wales and the Duke of York, the elder nearly eleven, the younger seven and a half. They led him to the King, Queen and Princess, but although the scene was one of indulgent smiles and prettiness, Henrietta Maria did not kiss her future son-in-law and the nine-year-old bride offered only her hand and not her cheek. The French friends of the Queen still elected to despise the House of Orange, and Henrietta Maria, although herself the daughter of a Medici whom her father had called " ma grosse banquière," encouraged her daughter to resent the inferior match that circumstances forced upon her. The little girl may have heard the wounding exclamations of the French at Court—" *Jesu-Marie, la fille d'une fille de France!* " [19]

Some said the Prince of Orange had sent over 200,000 ducats in gold to assure his son a warm welcome. Whether this was true or not, the bride allowed herself to be kissed a few days later and was reconciled to her fate by the end of the week.[20] Sir Anthony Van Dyck painted the wedding portrait, the Prince in scarlet satin and gold, the Princess in cloth of silver, a pretty pair, well brushed, well curled, demure, and holding hands.

On April 19th Charles had ordered his loyal officers to their posts. On April 20th he received his little son-in-law. On April 21st the House of Commons voted on the Bill of Attainder; two hundred and four voted for the Bill and fifty-nine against it. Of the two hundred and four who voted Strafford to death, one at least did so in the conviction that the Lords would certainly stop the Bill.[21]

On April 23rd, Good Friday, King Charles wrote to Strafford in the intervals of the day's devotions, solemnly reiterating his earlier promise. He should not suffer in life, honour, or fortune, wrote the King, and added with deep feeling—" a very mean reward from a master to so faithful and able a servant." [22]

On April 23rd, therefore, the King was quietly confident that he could save Strafford's life. On the 24th, the Saturday, Pym again sent forward to the King the urgent request of the Commons and a petition from the citizens of London that he should disband the Irish army and dismiss—once and for all— every Roman Catholic from his Court. On the 25th, Easter Day, rioters tried to break into the Spanish ambassador's house during Mass; crowds began to gather on the waterfront and about the Tower. Rumours went round: it was said that the King intended to dissolve Parliament by force, that the English army was on the verge of mutiny because Parliament had so far failed to pay it, that Pym was to be offered a place on the King's Council as Chancellor of the Exchequer.[23]   The contradictory and inconsistent character of these rumours reflects the indiscreet talking of all parties rather than deliberate rumour-mongering on the part of any one of them. Trade was depressed and there was considerable unemployment among mariners; May Day, always the moment for riots, was fast approaching.

In this atmosphere the King continued to pursue his two plans simultaneously. The Earl of Bedford, with practical good sense, had outlined a scheme by which Charles could ensure the financial stability of his government in future by the imposition of a general excise on exported goods, a tax already in use in the Low Countries. To avoid the confusion and corruption of the past, he suggested that Pym, whose business abilities were transcendent, should be made Chancellor of the Exchequer to organise the excise and set the finances of the Crown at last on a firm foundation.[24] In return for this support and assistance Charles would naturally adopt a more moderate policy in religion, following the suggestions of Bishop Williams. He would eliminate the more unpopular members of his Council and draw about him, in positions of trust, such men as Bristol, Essex, Warwick, Hertford, possibly even Lord Saye. Strafford, whose life and fortune would be spared, must retire for ever from public life.

On the face of it this looked like a workable and satisfactory programme, but everything depended on the King's good faith, and Pym, differing in this from Bedford and Bristol, was unwilling to believe in it. For him, the Irish army was the touchstone of the King's sincerity. He may or may not have believed that Strafford had seriously advocated using that army against the English. But he certainly believed that the King could only disprove such an intention on his own part by disbanding the Irish army. He knew of the intrigues in the King's favour in the English army. He knew therefore that the King was not acting frankly with the Earl of Bedford and the moderates. If the King should also refuse to disband Strafford's army in Ireland, that could mean only that the King intended sooner or later to appeal to force. On April 28th Charles again returned a negative answer to a request to disband the Irish army and Pym dissociated himself from the Bedford plan.[25]

At the same time Charles made another move. He attempted to reinforce the garrison in the Tower with a hundred men under the command of an officer of his own selection. Rumours of a plot among the officers of the English army were now all over London and Edward Hyde reported to the House of Lords a prevalent belief that Strafford was about to escape.[26] The Lords took notice of it, but did nothing. Lord Newport, Warwick's half-brother and Constable of the Tower, was one of Strafford's most virulent enemies: while he remained at his post it was impossible for the King's friends to gain control of the Tower and unlikely that Strafford could escape.

Charles continued his double manipulation. On Saturday, May 1st, he fell in with a suggestion of Bedford's that he should address a personal appeal to the Lords to reject the Bill of Attainder. Bedford no doubt intended the King to elaborate the argument which Strafford himself had used and to emphasise in the strongest terms to the Lords the danger of agreeing to a measure so offensive to justice and the laws of England. In Bedford's conception the King's new position was to be built solidly upon the laws of the land; but at this critical juncture Bedford was suddenly taken ill.

Lacking the intelligent guidance of Bedford, King Charles informed the House of Lords on Saturday, May 1st, that he was not himself satisfied in his conscience of Strafford's guilt and could therefore in no circumstances agree to pass the Bill against his life.[27] A singleness of purpose, a noble blindness inspired the King's action; he knew the laws of the land and understood the legal objections to the Bill, but in the last resort, and in spite of all his communings with Bedford and Bristol, he believed that no higher law than his kingly conscience could be cited to protect the Earl of Strafford. He could have cited nothing worse, for this placing of his conscience before all earthly respects sounded to most of his hearers like a defiance rather than an appeal. Moreover, it relieved the Upper House from further responsibility.

If the King intended in no circumstances to consent to the Bill of Attainder, what did it matter if the Lords gave way to it?

Pym, in the House of Commons, was busy strengthening the position of the present Parliament against eventual attack. He had a Bill put forward to guard it against sudden dissolution. This Parliament, by a special act, was to be dissolved only by its own consent. The scrambled, emergency measure, patched up to guard against violence or against a desperate move to save Strafford's life, was to confuse the politics of England for eighteen years to come.

At Whitehall on May 2nd the King and Queen saw their daughter married, very quietly, in an atmosphere of anxiety and strain. The Elector Palatine was conspicuously absent from the family gathering. It was Sunday and popular Puritan preachers were thundering from their pulpits for the death of Strafford. Roving bands of apprentices and seamen set upon the servants of Roman Catholic ambassadors and demonstrated outside their chapels. At almost any moment now most of the foreign diplomats in London expected the King's counterstroke and feared civil war.[28]

No counterstroke came. The King had tried and failed to put troops into the Tower; he had sent his loyal officers to their action stations. But as Secretary Vane was to say, " the design has been ill-carried whatsoever it has been." [29] What had it been? In the end, nothing but talk and bragging and indiscretion, of no avail to the King but of great value to Pym.

On Monday, May 3rd, Pym acted at last on the hints that Goring had given nearly a month before. A committee was appointed to examine the now widespread rumours of unrest in the army. The unrest was genuine enough, and on the same day the Commons instructed Speaker Lenthall to write to Sir John Conyers in the North assuring him that the English army would be paid in full and all its wrongs and grievances be carefully considered.[30] Ever since the King's attempt to send troops to the Tower in the previous week, rumours of a plot had been growing in London. A plot to save Strafford, a Popish Plot, a

Gunpowder Plot—plots were meat and drink to the Londoners in the merry month of May. All shops were closed and the crowds flooded westwards to the Parliament house, crying for "Justice," asking for news of the plot, inventing news of the plot. This thronging to Parliament went on for the best part of two days while, within doors, the Commons drew up a declaration that they would live and die for the true Protestant religion, the liberties and rights of subjects and the power and privilege of Parliaments. This Protestation, as it came to be called, was tendered to all their number for signature, and on May 4th sent to the Lords for theirs.[31]

In the midst of the excitement the ordinary business of the House continued; on this flurried May 4th the committee appointed to inquire into John Lilburne's case reported that the sentence pronounced against him in the Star Chamber was "illegal and against the liberty of the subject, bloody, wicked, cruel, barbarous and tyrannical." The young man himself had on that very day again got himself arrested for shouting too loudly and prominently among the crowds outside the House. He was set free after questioning but "free-born John" was never long out of trouble.[32]

Strafford from the Tower watched the situation deteriorate and was powerless to prevent it. Some faint knowledge of the King's army plans he must have had, for when Charles tried to introduce the new troops into the Tower he had himself offered a bribe of £20,000 to Sir William Balfour, Newport's lieutenant at the Tower, to assist him to escape.[33] He would hardly have done this without a hint from the Court that his escape would be welcome to the King. The scheme had failed.

The House of Lords, irritated and offended by the King, was now surrounded by a shouting crowd of Londoners. The chances of their rejecting the Bill of Attainder were small. For the first time, perhaps, in the long months since his arrest, Strafford saw death very near. He had no fear of death in itself but he feared the consequences for the King. If the Bill could not be stopped in the Lords, would the King have the resolution, in the face of popular clamour, to stop it with his sole veto? If he failed to do so, having openly declared it a matter of conscience, could the Crown ever recover from so disastrous a surrender? Strafford fought for something more than his own life. He fought to save the King from irreparable defeat.

For the second time that year Charles was defending the life of one man against the will of Parliament and the angry people. In January he had reprieved Goodman, the priest; during the crisis of the ensuing days, Goodman's life had been saved not so much by the King's action as by his own generous rejection of the King's reprieve.[34] Goodman's fine act had placed him at the mercy of the Lords as arbiters of his fate and they had been unwilling, in the circumstances, to be less noble-minded than their victim.

Knowledge of this may have suggested to Strafford the course he now took. He released the King from a promise he could no longer keep.

"May it please your Sacred Majesty," he wrote from the Tower, "I understand the minds of men are more and more incensed against me, notwithstanding your Majesty hath declared that, in your princely opinion, I am not guilty of treason, and that you are not satisfied in your conscience to pass the bill. This bringeth me in a very great strait; there is before me the ruin of my children and family, hitherto untouched with any foul crime: here are before me the many ills, which may befall your Sacred Person and the whole Kingdom should yourself and Parliament part less satisfied one with the other than is necessary for the preservation both of King and people; there are before me the things most valued, most feared by mortal men, Life and Death.

"To say, Sir, that there hath not been strife in me, were to make me less man than God knows my infirmities make me and to call a destruction upon myself and my young children will find no easy consent from flesh and blood. To set Your Majesty's conscience at liberty, I do most humbly beseech Your Majesty (for preventing of evils which may happen by your refusal) to pass this bill. . . ." [35]

The Christian, the politician, the faithful servant—each had his part in this letter. Facing an almost inevitable end, Strafford was prompted by his religious faith and his personal devotion to free the conscience of the King; but in so far as the end was not yet quite inevitable, he had a faint hope left that this deliberate release of the King's conscience might, by casting the responsibility for his life or death back upon the Lords, work the King's and his own salvation.

He wrote on the evening of May 4th. On the morning of May 5th the committee for inquiry into the Army Plot, as it was now generally called, made their first report to the House and sent for various officers whom they believed to be concerned in it. During the next twenty-four hours most of those whom they wished to question fled the country or otherwise vanished from public view.[36] Only Colonel Goring remained quietly at Portsmouth. The Queen's friends could hardly have done worse: their flight seemed to prove their guilt and to justify the wildest speculations.

On 7th and 8th May the crowds were thick at Westminster. The ports had been closed and the London quays were idle. While the Commons took measures for securing the principal seaports, especially Hull, Portsmouth, and the coast of Kent, the people in the streets of Westminster talked of invasion; some said French forces had been seen in the Channel, some Spanish, some Irish.[37] When the Lords drove up in their coaches for the debate on the Bill of Attainder, they could hardly make their way through the throng furiously crying out for "Justice."

Bedford had died at the week-end. Lord Bristol had no longer any control of the House. The bishops were not voting. The King had not understood the use he might have made of Strafford's letter. Only forty-eight lords were in their seats when the Bill of Attainder was put to the vote: eleven of them, with useless courage, gave their voices against it.[38]

On Sunday, May 9th, the Bill was before the King at Whitehall, and the crowds, transferring their attentions from the Houses of Parliament, now wrapped in sabbath silence, congregated about the precincts of the palace. The King remained unmoved; he was without fear. The Queen, irritable, anxious and as deeply mortified as she was disappointed by the flight of her friends and the disintegration of the Army Plot, gave way by turns to anger and tearful despair.[39] She had never fully understood the constitutional issues at stake in Strafford's trial, had never liked him personally, and was not at this time able or willing to strengthen the King's resolution to save him.

In painful anxiety the King sent for the judges to advise him on the state of the law in Strafford's case. When they had gone his doubts were still unresolved. He sought spiritual guidance. How could he consent to the Bill when it was against his conscience to do so? Strafford's letter might release him from an obligation to Strafford: it did not release him from an obligation to God. On this point and no other he called in those in whose spiritual gifts he trusted. He sent for the Primate of Ireland, Archbishop Ussher, then on a visit to London. Ussher, who received the message in the pulpit of St. Paul's, Covent Garden, sent to say that he could wait on His Majesty only when he had done his duty to God. It was the kind of answer which pleased Charles. But Ussher, when he arrived later in the day, gave it as his opinion categorically that the King should in no circumstances perform an act against his conscience. William Juxon, Bishop of London, resolved the moral problem in the same way and with the same firmness.[40]

Bishop Williams spoke round and about in a very different manner. He pointed out to the King the evils that might ensue from his refusal to gratify his people. He discoursed learnedly of the dual character of kingship, showing how the King, as a private man, may think and act in one way, but, as a King, is bound to think and act differently. The King in his private conscience could not condemn Strafford, but what of the King's public conscience? Could he load it with the fearful responsibility of bloodshed? He must go against the dictates of conscience either as a man, or as a King, whichever decision he took; as a King, was he not more answerable than as a man to God from whom his power came? [41] The argument was subtle and well urged. It moved the King. What had been a crime against his conscience appeared to him in a new light—as a duty: with tears in his eyes he gave his consent to the Bill of Attainder. " My Lord of Strafford's condition," he said, " is happier than mine." [42]

Another Bill had been presented to him at the same time as the Attainder. It was Pym's hurried Bill prohibiting the dissolution of the present Parliament without its own consent. He passed that too.

The King gave his consent to the Act of Attainder against the greatest of his servants on the afternoon of May 10th. Strafford's execution was fixed for noon on May 12th. The interval allowed little time for second thoughts, but the King had them. On the 11th he sent the Prince of Wales, whose youth he thought might touch the peers, to appeal to the Lords for mercy.[43] It was in vain. In vain too his gnawing regret, his bitter, growing certitude that the conscience of the King and the conscience of the man were one and indivisible. He had done wrong; he had failed in his sacred trust; he never forgave himself.

The tragedy was for Charles a moral one; he never fully realised the enormity of the political mistake, or the cruelty of the personal betrayal. He had valued Strafford as a servant but never loved him as a friend, and he had not adequately understood the significance of Strafford's fate in the conflict between him and his Parliament. Towards the lonely and awful end of his own life the King was to say, more than once, that all his sufferings had come upon him as a just punishment for his sin in letting Strafford die. He never said, and perhaps never realised, that they were also the logical outcome of the political error.

Archbishop Laud, miserably alone in the Tower, perceived it, and confided with bitterness to his diary that the King whom he and Strafford had served had not been worth serving—" he knew not how to be or be made great." [44] He saw, once more before he died, the great colleague whom he had loved and trusted, with whom he had shared his hopes and fears during that time—now so remote—when they had strenuously worked together to realise a great vision. The two prisoners were allowed no private farewell, but Laud stood at the window of his room in the Tower, as Strafford, sombre in black, went out to his death, and with trembling hands gave him a last, speechless blessing.[45]

On the scaffold itself, in the mild May sunshine, before the dense crowds who had come to rejoice in his death, Strafford spoke for the last time, saying with simplicity what he believed to be the truth:

" In all the honour I had to serve His Majesty, I had not any intention in my heart but what did aim at the joint and individual prosperity of the King and his people. . . ." [46]

The words echoed another speech, made twelve years before when he first assumed high office under the Crown:

" To the joint individual well-being of sovereignty and subjection do I here vow all my cares and diligence through the whole course of this my ministry." [47]

He had not been selfless in his exercise of power. He had used his office to aggrandise himself and his family. Yet according to his large abilities and his narrow judgment had not swerved from his ideal. In other circumstances, with a different master, he might have done good service and might be remembered in history for what he had achieved in power, not merely for the tragedy of his end.

BOOK III CHAPTER V REFERENCES

1. *C.S.P. Ireland*, 1633–47, pp. 252, 261–5; Rushworth, III, i, p. 214.
2. *H.M.C.Ormonde MSS.*, New Series, II, p. 352.
3. *Harleian MSS.*, 6424, folio 13.
4. *C.S.P. Ven.*, 1640–2, p. 138.
5. *Breadalbane MSS., Letters*, 1639–59. Glencarradale to Glenorchy, March 9th, 1641.

6. *Portland MSS.*, I, p. 15.

7. *C.S.P.D.*, 1640–1, pp. 532, 535.

8. Rushworth, III, I, pp. 255–7.

9. *Portland MSS.*, I, pp. 16–17.

10. Nalson, II, pp. 272–3.

11. *C.S.P.D.*, 1641, p. 539.

12. *Commons Journals*, p. 118.

13. Verney, p. 37; Clarendon, III, 135–7.

14. The details about Strafford's Trial are from Rushworth's volume devoted to it; the above speech is also given at greater length in *C.S.P.D.*, 1641, pp. 540 ff.

15. Rushworth, III, I, pp. 227–8.

16. Rushworth.

17. *Commons Journals*, II, p. 123.

18. *Ibid., loc. cit.*

19. *C.S.P. Ven.*, 1640–2, pp. 142, 145; *C.S.P.D.*, 1640–1, pp. 554, 560.

20. *C.S.P. Ven.*, 1640–2, p. 145.

21. Knowler, II, p. 432.

22. *Ibid.*, p. 416.

23. *C.S.P.D.*, 1640–1, p. 560; *H.M.C. Egmont MSS*, I, I, p. 133.

24. *C.S.P.D.*, 1640–1, p. 560.

25. *Commons Journals*, II, 127, 131.

26. Rushworth, III, I, pp. 238, 254.

27. *Ibid.*, III, I, p. 239; *C.S.P.D.*, 1640–1, p. 567.

28. *Portland MSS.*, I, p. 12; *C.S.P. Ven.*, 1640–2, pp. 141–2, 147, 149.

29. *C.S.P.D.*, 1640–1, p. 571.

30. *Ibid.*, p. 569.

31. Baillie, I, p. 352; Rushworth, III, I, p. 241–2

32. *Commons Journals*, II, p. 134.

33. *Portland MSS.*, I, p. 719.

34. Rushworth, III, i, p. 166.

35. Rushworth, *Trial of Strafford*, p. 743 f.

36. *Commons Journals*, II, pp. 135, 137; *C.S.P.D.*, 1640–1, p. 571.

37. *Egmont MSS.*, I, i, p. 134.

38. *Lords Journals*, IV, p. 239.

39. *Egmont MSS.*, I, I, p. 134.

40. Hacket, *Scrinia Reserata*; N. Bernard, *Life of Usher*, p. 96.

41. *Scrinia Reserata.*

42. *Hist. MSS. Commission*, II, p. 99; XII, ii, p. 281.

43. *Lords Journals*, IV, p. 245.

44. Laud, III, p. 443.

45. *Ibid.*, p. 445; Heylin, *Cyprianus Anglicus*, p. 480.

46. Rushworth, III, I, pp. 267 f.

47. The speech, first printed in *The Academy*, June 1875, has been reprinted in whole or in part in every subsequent life of Strafford.

CHAPTER SIX

THE KING AND JOHN PYM

Summer 1641

STRAFFORD made his last solemn declaration of political faith on the scaffold on May 12th, 1641. The same day, the House of Commons authorised the publication of the late Sir Edward Coke's exposition of an opposing creed. The generation of lawyers then present in the House of Commons had grown to maturity under the powerful influence of Coke's mind and character. He had been silenced twelve years before by Charles I; his papers had been seized and the commentaries on the laws of England through which he had defended the Common Law against the Prerogative had been forcibly interrupted. The House now gave orders for the printing of Coke's *Second Part of the Institutes of the Laws of England*, which contained his commentary on *Magna Charta*.

Coke, with irresistible logic, had applied the general terms of chapter twenty-nine of *Magna Charta* to the particular instances of his own epoch. The medieval King had sworn in the following terms to his barons:

> " No freeman shall be taken, or imprisoned, or be disseised of his freehold, or liberties, or free customs, or be outlawed or exiled, or any otherwise destroyed; nor will we not pass upon him, nor condemn him, but by lawful judgment of his peers, or by the law of the land. We will sell to no man, we will not deny or defer to any man either justice or right."

Coke found in these words a depth and breadth of meaning very much to the purpose. The vagueness of the royal undertaking not to "destroy" any freeman, he invested with a clear and comprehensive significance:

> "Every oppression against law," wrote Coke, "by colour of an usurped authority, is a kind of destruction . . . and it is the worst oppression that is done by colour of justice."

Imprisonment at the King's pleasure, or sending men abroad on the King's service against their will, were both shown to offend against the Charter, a point which had been confirmed under Coke's influence when King Charles had been compelled to pass the Petition of Right in 1628. By a wide, inclusive gesture, Coke managed also to cite the Charter against restrictions of trade and manufacture:

> "Generally all monopolies are against this great charter, because they are against the liberty and freedom of the subject and against the law of the land."

Such phrases as "the law of the land" and "justice or right" depended for their meaning entirely on the experience and intelligence of lawyers. Therein lay the danger to the Crown, once the legal opinion of the country was, for whatever reason, at variance with that of the King. The King had promised not to "deny or defer to any man either justice or right." This meant, so Coke averred, that the King must concede not only justice to his people but *right*, which in this case, he argued, meant *law* because law was the accepted means by which justice was to be given. The King had therefore admitted himself to be bound by the law and to the law. Coke did not add—but he certainly implied—that, given the practice of England, this meant that the King was bound not by an abstract, disembodied law, but by the opinions of lawyers. His interpretation of Magna Charta utterly contradicted Lord Chief Justice Berkeley's ruling in the Ship-money case, that *Rex* is *Lex*. It made a recent statement of Lord Keeper Finch, that it behoved not the Chancellor to do anything other than the King's bidding, look like an ignorant surrender of established principles.

In conclusion, Coke broke into eloquence:

"As the gold finer will not, out of the dust, threads and shreds of gold, let pass the least crumb, in respect of the excellency of the metal, so ought not the learned reader to let pass any syllable of this law, in respect of the excellency of the matter."

In concentrating his energies on the destruction of Strafford, John Pym had not lost his hold upon other questions of more far-reaching significance than the removal of a single minister. His well-planned attack on the power of the Crown had achieved almost complete success by the early summer of 1641. In the seven months since Parliament met, almost all the supports of the throne had been cut away. Strafford was dead, Laud in the Tower, Finch in exile; six of the judges were under threat of impeachment. The King's rich friends, in the City and elsewhere, were being harried and intimidated as projectors and monopolists. His customs revenue and the men responsible for collecting it were the subject of question and scrutiny. His Postmaster-General had been accused of abusing the public service in the interests of the Crown. The most intimate part of the administration had been damaged by the threatened proceedings against Windebanke and his flight. The Triennial Parliaments Bill was already law, and the King had consented to the Act perpetuating the existing Parliament on the same day as he consented to the Attainder of Strafford. Bills for the abolition of the Prerogative Courts—in Wales and in the North as well as the Star Chamber—were passing smoothly through the Commons, along with the Bill against the High Commission. Since the appointment of the Puritan Warwick to be Lord High Admiral even the navy appointments were out of the King's hands.

WILLIAM OF ORANGE AND PRINCESS MARY
by Anthony Van Dyck

By his policy of the last six months Pym had brought the Crown under the control of Parliament and achieved political changes in England more far-reaching than those achieved in the previous year by the Estates in Scotland.

He did not advertise his achievement as a revolution and it did not appear so to him. He believed that he was restoring the ancient balance between the sovereign and the people glorified under Queen Elizabeth. Antiquarians, like Sir Symonds d'Ewes the member for Sudbury, thought they could trace the elements of this balanced government in the institutions of the Anglo-Saxons, and Sir Edward Coke's exposition of Magna Charta seemed to show that the Plantagenet kings had set their seal upon it four hundred years before.

In this revolution, which at first appeared to many as the restoration of a more authentic order, the House of Commons, except for the King's own friends and servants, had willingly supported Pym. But if few of King Charles's subjects shared his exalted view of the royal authority, fewer still wished to see that authority wholly overthrown. Once the " evil counsellors " had disappeared and the worst of them had lost his head on Tower Hill, they felt the time had come to let the King alone. The English gentry liked to exercise freely their right to grumble as much and as loudly as they pleased at the King's government but they meant no disrespect to the King's person. While they thought it best for him to govern with the help of Parliament, they regarded him as the undoubted head of the State, the fountain of justice, the apex of society and, next after God, the object of awe and veneration. The idea of the King compelled by a vulgar rabble to give his consent to a Parliamentary Bill was, in retrospect, disquieting—even to members of Parliament and Londoners when the crisis was over. It was a violation of the social order, an overturning of the accepted conventions. This terror of " overturning "—immensely strong in England's hierarchic society of social climbers—was the impulse behind the now growing opposition to Pym in the House.

With the coming of the spring and the Lent Assizes the

subsidies voted in Parliament had to be assessed and in due course collected throughout the country. But instead of being paid as usual into the Royal Exchequer they were to be forwarded by order of Parliament direct to the Guildhall to meet the debt incurred to the City of London for paying the Scots indemnity. This perturbed the gentry who doubted whether money which had been voted to the King ought to go into coffers other than his. Whatever financial follies might have been committed by the royal officials, they had no higher regard for the honesty of those into whose hands the money would fall at the Guildhall. There was at least something traditional and respectable in paying money into the Royal Exchequer, but to pay money into the hands of subjects like themselves was a disturbing innovation.[1]

Pym's anxieties had not lessened with the death of Strafford and the achievement of the political revolution. He knew the King would not accept defeat, that he had made concessions merely to gain time until he should be strong enough for a counter-attack. For the next months, therefore, Pym's policy was to safeguard the position he had won and forestall any move the King might make against it.

For his own purposes, Pym had greatly exaggerated the plot between the Court and the discontented officers of the English army; but he had not invented it. There had been a plot. In a desperate situation the King was bound to find desperate remedies. Force was in the end his only answer and force was what Pym feared. The words for which Strafford had died, that ambigious phrase of " an army in Ireland you may employ here to reduce this kingdom," had been stretched at his trial to convey a threat to England. In the summer of 1640 when Strafford spoke them, the Irish army had been intended only for Scotland; but now, in the spring of 1641 this Irish army of eight thousand men, seven thousand of them Roman Catholics, was still in existence, and Charles was very unwilling to disband it. Pym had some legitimate cause for anxiety there. To these fears of army plots in England and Ireland, a third was added.

Charles might so conduct affairs as to break the friendship between Parliament and the Covenanters: Hamilton was still pursuing his laborious policy of trying to win the friendship of Argyll, first for himself, and then for the King. Charles himself was working on the envious Rothes who, distrustful and jealous of Argyll had promised the King to use his influence to make a party for him in Scotland, and claimed that he had already gained Loudoun.[2]

Fears of this kind were never far from the minds of Pym and his chief supporters in the summer of 1641, but the most immediate and serious danger that he had to face was the resurgence of sympathy for the King and the opinion, sincerely held by the growing body of " moderates " in the House of Commons, that Charles had changed his convictions and was now ready to be respectfully guided along the path of Parliamentary government.

The King himself assiduously encouraged those who held this view by a further display of moderation. He relinquished suspect advisers without pressure from Parliament, withdrew Cottington from the Exchequer and the Court of Wards and bestowed the latter, with all its opportunities for private profit on Lord Saye. Sometime also in the course of the summer he made approaches to Edward Hyde, the able and eloquent lawyer who had been directly responsible for the bill against the Prerogative Courts. In foreign policy he became cool to his Spanish friends, arranged to send his wife's troublesome mother out of the country, and received an ambassador from the Portuguese, now in revolt against Spain.

The Queen of Bohemia heard with relief of this change of policy and of the favour that the King was now showing to her son, the Elector Palatine. Charles's more friendly attitude to his nephew was made possible by the departure of the young Prince of Orange, three weeks after his marriage to Princess Mary and a fortnight after Strafford's death; while the bridegroom was still at Court the King had found it necessary, in accordance with etiquette, to mortify his grown-up nephew by

compelling him to take second place to his child son-in-law.[3]
But as soon as the bridegroom had gone home, the Elector found
himself the object of flattering attention. Unlike his mother,
he was not deceived. The King spoke of raising troops in
England and Scotland (or using those already raised) to help him
to regain his German lands; the Elector accepted the suggestion
without enthusiasm. He believed that the King wanted the
troops for his own purposes and was using his name and the
Protestant Cause merely as a cover. He could not, of course,
voice his doubts in public, but he saw no reason why he should
assist his uncle in the deception. Although for the next months
he was repeatedly made to appear at his uncle's side when
appeals were being made on his behalf, he said little or nothing
on these occasions and maintained a stubborn air of boredom.
He had his own spies and informers about the Court,[4] had a
shrewd idea of the Queen's influence and the King's plans, and
maintained discreetly his own relations with individual members of the House of Commons.

It was of the first importance to the King to have troops at
his disposal. He might gain this end by encouraging a Royalist
faction in the English army, by retaining Strafford's Irish army,
by winning over all the Covenanters under Argyll, or half of
them under Rothes, or by a levy in favour of the Elector
Palatine; he tried to do it—in his usual diffused manner—in all
five ways at once. While the Queen encouraged the Royalism
of the English officers and stimulated the fears and hopes of the
Irish, the King soothed the moderate-minded men in the House
of Commons, courted the friendship of Argyll through Hamilton,
promised favours to Rothes if he would overthrow Argyll and
entered into a correspondence with Montrose behind the backs
of both. His policy was of an elaborate complexity, but poorly
co-ordinated.

It imposed, all the same, a heavy task on Pym who had, at
one and the same time, to hold together his majority in the
House of Commons—which depended on the support of the
moderate men—and to outbid the King for the continued

friendship of the Covenanters. The two things were incompatible; he could outbid the King with the Covenanters only by hastening legislation for the reform of the English Church on the Presbyterian model, but such drastic action, while encouraging an extremist minority, would alienate the Protestant but conservative majority in the House of Commons.

The summer of 1641 was therefore a time of play-acting and changes of mood. The King assumed the outward appearance of moderation, forbearance and devotion to the Protestant Cause while Pym tried to shake this pose without alienating those moderate men in the Commons who believed in it. Charles and Pym, men unlike in almost every respect, had in common an intense political fanaticism. The King believed that, under God, his authority was sacred and must be restored by force if necessary; Pym believed that, under God, the King was answerable to his subjects (meaning the House of Commons) and must be kept so. Both men were prepared to use any means to secure what they conceived to be right.

Immediately after Strafford's death, Pym moved to strengthen the Scottish alliance by allowing the Presbyterians in the Commons to go forward with their Bills for reorganising the Church by the abolition of episcopacy and the secularisation of colleges and cathedrals. These projects shook the intellectual centres of the land, startled ancient scholars of Oxford and Cambridge, troubled many lawyers and all conservatives. Both the universities petitioned the House against the secularisation of cathedral chapters lest the learning and dignity of the clergy should suffer by it.

The universities, except for such islands of Puritanism as Emmanuel College, Cambridge, had been deeply penetrated by fashionable Anglican theology; if Puritanism gained the upper hand, they would be more in need of help themselves than able to give it to others. Laud's beloved Oxford was in the greatest danger and, at about this time, he wrote from the Tower of London to resign the Chancellorship. " The university," he wrote, " hath great need of friends, great and daily need ... if you had another Chancellor you could not want the help which now you do." His withdrawal was an act of true devotion. "If there be any good which I ought to have done to that place and have not done it, it proceeded from want of understanding or ability, not will or affection," he wrote.[5] Long after his death, his manuscripts in the Bodleian library, the fellowships he had endowed, and the tranquil colonnades of St. John's College would be his monuments in the place which had the most of his heart and the best of his service.

The attack on the organised Church brought with it, for Pym, a tangle of political problems. On May 24th the Lords rejected the Bill for excluding the bishops from their House; this opened still further the breach between the two Houses which Strafford had tried hard to make and which the King encouraged. The Presbyterians in the Commons at once introduced the more far-reaching Root and Branch Bill for removing the bishops altogether. The more violent became the actions of the religious extremists in the Commons, the more essential was it for Pym to undermine confidence in the apparent moderation of the King. In May, to precipitate the crisis which had cost Strafford his life, he had revealed the information given by Goring about the Army Plot. In June, to divert attention from the violent religious policy of his colleagues, he maintained interest in the Plot by frequent reports from the committee which had been set up to investigate it.

On June 8th, Nathaniel Fiennes, Lord Saye's son, reported some startling details. Sir William Balfour, lieutenant of the Tower, had deponed that, at the time of the Plot, five weeks ago, Strafford had offered him £20,000 to connive at his escape. At the same time, Colonel Goring, governor of Portsmouth, had admitted attempts on the part of the Court to secure the governorship of Portsmouth for Jermyn, presumably to receive French ships and troops into the town. He hinted that Commissary-General Wilmot was deeply involved. At these revelations from the committee, Wilmot himself and George Digby rose to protest that the accusations were groundless. They demanded more proof than Goring's bare word. Other members shouted them down. Lenthall, an ineffective Speaker in a rowdy House, strove in vain to bring order out of the hubbub, but could not make himself heard. Dusk was thickening and he could scarcely see who was standing, who trying to catch his eye. Someone moved for candles. Others cried " No," for already all possibility of serious debate was at an end. Two members, none the less, brought them in unbidden. This unorthodox behaviour restored the Commons to a sense of their own dignity; the majority voted the candle-bringers to the Tower for a breach of order, and the Speaker adjourned the House.[6]

The desired crisis had arisen, and the revived rumour of an Army Plot hampered the King's new policy as much as Pym had intended that it should. To satisfy the extremists, debates in the House on the Root and Branch Bill went on, and Sir Symonds d'Ewes argued eloquently from an early Greek manuscript, preserved in the King's own Library, that St. Paul had addressed neither Titus nor Timothy with the title of bishop, the word being an impertinent interpolation of a later date.[7] But the focus of interest was elsewhere; the assertions and counter-assertions of Goring, Wilmot and Digby held all attention. Digby was by far the ablest in debate, but in action he was impulsive and indiscreet. Perhaps from vanity, in which he was not lacking, but more probably as propaganda against Pym's party, he chose this moment to publish the admirable speech he had made against the Attainder of Strafford. Incontrovertibly, to do such a thing without permission of the House was a breach of privilege and Digby might have found himself in the Tower had not the King instantly elevated him to the peerage. Pym would not permit an attack on a peer for his past misdeeds lest he should further widen the breach with the Lords.

The crisis was not over. On June 14th, the King was unexpectedly betrayed by the Earl of Northumberland. The earl had been Strafford's friend, and it is possible that angry contempt of the King for his desertion of a good servant, added to the many slights he had himself endured, had finally turned him against the Court. Family and personal ties perhaps hastened his decision. He may truly have felt, as he himself said, that a brother's honour was at stake and must be vindicated. His brother, Harry Percy, accused when news of the Army Plot first came out a month before, had escaped abroad. Northumberland now placed before Parliament the letter he had received from him, in which the story of the Plot was set forth in detail. Percy proclaimed his own and Wilmot's innocence of any evil intent; he had merely informed the King that his army was loyal and would serve him. Goring, on the other hand, with Suckling, Iermyn, Davenant and the young Lord Carnarvon, had urged on the King a plan for seizing the Tower and occupying the City of London. This, said Percy, the King had very properly rejected.[8]

The effect of this letter was all that Pym could wish. In a sense, of course, it exonerated the King, and Wilmot's steadfast assertion under examination, that it was the exact truth, should have had the same effect. But the niceties of the King's position among the interlocking plots were not exactly studied and the general impression created was that violence and mischief had been planned at Court. Goring delicately enhanced this impression, by admitting the existence of the second and more violent plot but denying his own participation.[9]

In the midst of the excitement, on June 16th, a sinister paper from Scotland was laid before the Commons by their Scottish allies. A messenger carrying a letter from the King to Montrose had been intercepted on the Border. The letter was harmless, but with it was an inexplicable series of notes, presumably a code, about an elephant, a dromedary and a serpent. These " dark memorials," it was alleged, concerned a plot, suggested by Montrose to the King, for gaining control of the government of Scotland.[10]

The King took this strange happening calmly and returned a soft answer to an insolent challenge from Argyll about his correspondence with Montrose. He did not deny the letter: " I do avow it as fit for me to write, both for the matter and the person to whom it was written."[11] But of dromedaries, elephants and serpents he denied all knowledge. The zoological incursion remained unexplained, but otherwise Charles's correspondence with Montrose had been singularly innocent and high-minded. In Scotland, as in England, a moderate party was coming into existence; Montrose had himself almost originated that party by his criticisms of the actions of the Scots Estates and his association with a few like-minded friends in the secret Cumbernauld Bond, of the previous year, to preserve the true Covenant " against the indirect practising of a few."

But Montrose had not been included in the more cautious plans of Rothes for overthrowing Argyll. He was too indiscreet and impulsive, and was left therefore to his own free-lance devices. He had got into trouble for criticising Argyll and writing letters to the King during the treaty negotiations at Ripon; reproved but forgiven by the Covenanters, he had got into trouble again when the existence of the Cumbernauld Bond leaked out a few months later. Once again he was let off with a reproof, but he had become a marked man and deeply suspect. He went boldly on his way and soon after wrote the King a budget of unsolicited advice on how to govern Scotland. The advice was unexceptionable: he strongly advocated " the temperate government," and the maintenance of the Presbyterian religion.[12]

Charles was within his rights in answering this letter with courteous thanks, and the Covenanters were most certainly stepping beyond theirs when they intercepted the answer. They had acted under the pressure of a crisis which, unknown to Charles, had been suddenly sprung upon them by the irrepressible Montrose. Towards the end of May, Mr. John Graham, minister of Auchterarder, the town which lay at the gates of Montrose's chief castle of Kincardine, had said in an Edinburgh tavern that Argyll intended to depose the King. Summoned before the Committee of Estates for this dangerous slander, he gave

Montrose as the source of it. Montrose did not deny it; he had had it from John Stewart, Commissary of Dunkeld, who had reported to him a speech made by Argyll in the previous July when he entered Atholl to subdue the royalists. Argyll (according to Stewart) had said that if the King levied war on his own people he should be deposed. A few days later John Stewart himself, before the committee, confirmed the words, whereat Argyll " broke out into a passion and with great oaths denied the whole." [13]

Argyll soon recovered himself and a few days later John Stewart admitted after long cross-examination that he had not thought Argyll was speaking of King Charles, but only of kings in general. Later, when he discussed it with Montrose, the special application to King Charles had been suggested to him. In this way the evidence against Argyll was turned back against Montrose and he now stood under suspicion of having deliberately spread false rumours about Argyll. The interception of his correspondence with the King and the peculiar notes about the dromedary—of which he denied all knowledge—were enough to justify his arrest on suspicion of conspiracy against the government. On June 11th he was sent to Edinburgh Castle by order of the Committee of Estates, and held *incommunicado*. [14]

The news of Montrose's arrest and the discovery of his correspondence with the King, reaching London at the same time as the revelations of the Army Plot, set rumours flying. The King had already announced his intention of opening the next session of the Scottish Parliament in Edinburgh and it was soon a current belief in London that he planned, on his journey northward, first to place himself at the head of the discontented English army in these parts, then to join with the Scots conspirators and so to overthrow all his enemies. [15] This rumour was a natural consequence of the double revelation—the Army Plot and the correspondence with Montrose. Fears and speculation both in London and the country were increased, as usual, by the persistent belief in a possible Popish Plot. Justices of the peace, by ordinance of Parliament, were ordered to make sure that no recusants had arms, and the resultant questioning and searching stimulated anxiety among the Protestant population and gave it new rumours to feed on. There was little or no logic in rumours that credited the King with plotting both with Catholics and Covenanters, but there was a half-truth in both beliefs, and Pym, who knew better than anyone that the King's plans were neither so complete nor so elaborate, made the rising panic an excuse to request him to postpone his visit to Scotland for a fortnight, or until the English army in the north should be disbanded and the Scots forces have gone home.[16]

Rumour gave to the plots more definite shape than they had, and Pym was willing enough to stimulate rumour and to exaggerate the importance of the revelations that had been made. All the same, certain things were happening in Ireland which justified his suspicions. The King had yielded to pressure about the Irish army, but it had been disbanded rather in name than in fact. Officers and men had been permitted to re-enlist in foreign service if they wished to do so; large companies therefore stayed together waiting for shipping to France or Spain, and the country was full of scattered bands of troops, attached to their own officers, but no longer owning any higher authority.

A situation which would have been dangerous anywhere was doubly so in Ireland where the resentment and uncertainty of the populace, after the collapse of the Strafford administration, might at any moment break into violence.

The Lords Justices, who ineffectively presided at the head of the government in Dublin, contemplated the future with apprehension.[17] Since the winter, priests had been working among the people and more landed daily from Europe. They rode about the country speaking to the disbanded troops, telling them not to go abroad to seek wars, for God would soon have work for them in Ireland. The Catholic Archbishop of Tuam, Malachi O'Queely, held meetings openly. A gathering of Catholic clergy was said to have met for consultation with the Irish gentry as near to Dublin as " the wood of Maynooth."[18] These stirrings alarmed the two elderly Lords Justices and the divided, unguided, quarrelsome council in Dublin; but they did nothing.

Rumours of these things reached England but the fear of an Irish rising, though it must have been present to Pym's mind, was overshadowed by what seemed to him more immediate dangers. His first aim was to make sure that the English army in the north was disbanded and the Scots on their way home before the King started on his journey to Edinburgh. Before the end of June the negotiations with the Scots Commissioners, which had begun at Ripon in the previous October and continued in London since Parliament met, were brought to an end and the terms of the peace treaty settled. The Covenanters and the English House of Commons seemed, in these terms, to present a united front and the King yielded with little protest. He undertook to withdraw all declarations made at any time against the Covenanters, to ratify the legislation put forward by the Scottish Parliament in the previous year, to withdraw the garrisons from Berwick and Carlisle, to indemnify the Scots for ships and goods captured by his navy, to place Edinburgh Castle henceforward in the control of the Estates, and to allow the victorious party in Scotland to proceed against whom they pleased for having provoked the war. The Scots furthermore demanded the reformation of the English Church, for which joint consultations were in due course to be held, and the exclusion of all Roman Catholics from places about the King and his eldest son. For damages sustained in the war they required a payment of £300,000, of which the first instalment was to be paid before they would evacuate England.[19]

For the next weeks the King worked hard to allay the suspicion raised by the further revelations about the Army Plot. He dismissed the Marquis of Newcastle from his post as governor of the Prince of Wales because his name had been mentioned among those thought to be sympathetic to the conspiracy. In his place he appointed the Earl of Hertford, a known moderate and brother-in-law to the Earl of Essex. He even changed the Prince's tutor, Dr. Duppa, lest he should be thought too Laudian.

The new tutor, John Earle, rector of a Wiltshire parish and fellow of Merton College, was an innocuous, open-minded theologian, chiefly famous for having published as a young man his *Microcosmographie*, a pleasing collection of " characters " which has enduring fame as a minor work of literature.

These concessions were not enough to please Pym, or to satisfy him as to the King's future intentions. In a conference with the House of Lords he gained their support for a singularly bold demand, namely that in future all appointments to the household of the Queen or her children should be made only with consent of Parliament. At the same time he pressed once more for the dismissal of all Roman Catholics and the expulsion of Rossetti.[20] The King who had already permitted the Queen's confessor, Father Philip, to be questioned before Parliament on the Army Plot, continued his gracious policy by agreeing to the departure of Rossetti. The Pope's agent did not leave in disgrace; both King and Queen bade him an affectionate farewell and he was escorted to his ship by the Venetian ambassador and his servants to protect him from any impertinences of the people.[21] All the same, he had left. It was, or seemed, a triumph for the Protestant Cause to which official expression was given some days later in a Parliamentary manifesto authorised by the King proclaiming his intention to restore the Elector Palatine to his rightful heritage.[22]

Early in July, the Bill for the abolition of the prerogative courts came up for the King's consent. He persisted for forty-eight hours, no doubt testing the state of opinion in Parliament and London, but on this issue the majority in both Houses was strong and included nearly all the moderates. On the third day he passed the Bill and made an end of the direct judicial powers of the Crown.

The Army Plot excitement was flagging although Pym spun out all through July the examinations of the officers who had been involved, so that neither the Commons nor the Londoners would be able to forget the supposed menace. A new French ambassador had arrived and been welcomed by both King and

Queen. They had given him four hours of private talk, a circumstance which provoked comment.[23] The Queen announced an intention of going to Spa for her health, perhaps accompanied by her mother, whose departure, repeatedly postponed, was planned for August at latest. The House of Commons objected and insisted on questioning the Queen's doctor. Even to this unprecedented impertinence the King gave in, and Sir Theodore de Mayerne satisfied the vulgar curiosity of the House about the Queen's morning tears, her spinal curvature and the rash on her upper lip.[24] The Commons were not reassured; they asked next about her household accounts and the safety of her jewellery which they did not wish her to take abroad. On this the Queen reversed her decision since she found it the cause of so much anxiety to her husband's subjects.[25] She had meant, naturally, to take jewellery with her to raise a loan, and the journey lost its point if she had to go empty-handed.

The frenzy against the Roman Catholics continued to rise in London. One of the Douai priests, Father William Ward, was tracked down and brought to trial. Another, Father Cuthbert Greene, attendant on the Venetian ambassador, was rudely dragged from this diplomatic protection, and both were sentenced to be hanged, drawn and quartered. The Venetian ambassador, resolute that no one should infringe the diplomatic rights of the Serene Republic, managed to save Father Greene, in spite of the offensive behaviour of Secretary Vane, who took it upon himself to lecture the King at a public audience on the wickedness of granting a reprieve to a priest on whatever grounds. Vane, who had forfeited all hope of royal favour, had become the servant and mouthpiece of his friends in the Commons and was making the most of the King's inability, as things stood, to dismiss him. Father Ward had no one to protect him, for the King could not risk a second intervention after the trouble over Father Goodman six months before. He was an old man and was offered a mitigation of a horrible death if he would abjure the Roman error. He remained constant and died with a fortitude which impressed even the Londoners.[26] But it did not soften for long their vindictive mood; a week later, two English priests from the household of the Portuguese ambassador were arrested. They were rescued by the French ambassador's servants after a street fight.[27]

The King continued his policy of conciliation. When the bad-tempered Earl of Pembroke, the Lord Chamberlain, slapped the foolish face of Lord Maltravers during an argument, the King made it an excuse for dismissing him and elevated to his place the Puritan Earl of Essex.[28] This appointment was another move to win the support of all moderate men. By the late summer the King had, in some quarters, so far disarmed criticism that he was credited, or allowed himself to be credited, with the intention of raising not only the Lords Saye and Brooke, but Pym, Hampden and Holles to his inner council.[29]

On Scotland the King's immediate hopes were fixed. Hamilton for the last nine months had been ingratiating himself with Argyll: something must surely come of that when Charles reached Edinburgh in person. Rothes, although in the last weeks he had become alarmingly ill and had had to seek rest and health in the country air of Richmond, believed that he had built a party for the King. All in all the possibility of getting help in Scotland from one group or another smiled on Charles. He even entertained the idea of uniting the Scots forces in the north with his English troops there, to form an effective army for his service. With this in view he had sent two officers, William Legge and Daniel O'Neill, secretly to test the loyalty and intentions of the principal officers in the north.

Pym, for his part, was holding to the Scottish alliance with difficulty. "Our brethren of Scotland," who had been so friendly in the winter, had grown cooler in their love, and Pym, weighing one danger against another, felt that whatever the risk of weakening his majority in Parliament, he must try to restore the old friendship by a further demonstration against the bishops. Early in August thirteen of them were impeached for having countenanced the sittings of Convocation after the Short Parliament had been dissolved.[30] The gesture might do something to restore confidence between Commons and Covenanters; unfortunately it also angered the House of Lords, a majority among whom increasingly resented the pretensions of Pym's party in the Commons. The task of holding together the whole of his disparate alliance against the King—Lords, Commons, Covenanters, and English Protestants—was becoming more problematical with every new development in the complex situation. Charles, who watched the divisions between Lords and Commons with pleasure, was meanwhile buying support and raising money simultaneously by the creation of new honours. The price of baronetcies sank in the month of July from £400 to £350 apiece. Nineteen new baronets were created in July, twenty-four in the first fortnight of August. Favours, at a comparatively low rate, rained on those who might be useful. The King overwhelmed by the variety of business, was sometimes a little confused, and on one occasion, seeing a petitioner kneeling in his path, embarrassed him considerably by bestowing an unwanted knighthood on him.[31]

All this activity perturbed Pym. He made a last-minute attempt to stop the King's journey, now finally fixed for August 10th. A small crowd gathered in the precincts of Westminster when, on the morning of that day, he came down to the House to give his consent to a further group of Bills. They clustered round the King's horse imploring him to stay, but he shook them off, saying only, with a touch of irony, that he was glad to find himself so much desired in both his kingdoms.[32]

At noon that day he began his journey to Scotland, taking with him the Elector Palatine, in whose interests he intended to ask the Scots Parliament to grant him the authority to raise and control an army. He left the Queen at Oatlands, privately giving her authority to instruct and organise his friends in and out of Parliament for a new attack on Pym in the next session. He was full of hope that the autumn would see a change in his fortunes. His own difficulties, although heavy, were at least no more serious than they had been a year before—less so, for Strafford's death and the peace with Scotland had removed two

THE HOUSE OF COMMONS
from an engraving by John Glover

of the causes of quarrel between him and his subjects. The King hoped in the next months to win the Covenanters to his own side, to widen and deepen the breach between Commons and Lords in England and to gain for himself—from Ireland, England or Scotland—an armed striking force to have in reserve against his enemies if they tried again to raise tumults in the City.

To achieve the first of these ends, Charles relied on his own skill and judgment in dealing with his countrymen in Edinburgh. For the second and third he relied at least in part on the Queen; she was to use her influence and charm with those members of the House of Lords who might be brought to help her husband, and she was to see to it that the light-hearted young nobles, who had not hitherto taken their political duties too earnestly, made it a point of honour to attend Parliament in its next session, to defend the dignity of their House against the Commons and serve the policy of their King.

The Queen's political intervention was not to end with this salutary encouragement of the too frivolous royalist lords. She was also to keep in touch with the loyal officers in the King's army—now in process of disbandment—and hold together the framework of armed support for the King which might still be needful.

With so many strands of policy to control and so much that must of necessity be kept secret, the King recognised the need to have trustworthy servants about him. He was under the unfortunate necessity of taking Secretary Vane with him to Scotland but he instructed those who wished to communicate with him privately to do so through his cousin Lennox, whom he now created Duke of Richmond. In England he gave his special trust—and this time also justly—to Edward Nicholas. During the last eighteen months, since he had become secretary to the Council of War in the spring of 1640, Nicholas had shown himself a careful and entirely devoted servant. To him therefore in these critical weeks of absence, Charles entrusted the task of watching the actions of his enemies and reporting at length upon them, with any advice that Nicholas deemed fit.

These dispositions made, the King journeyed to Scotland. In hot, restless, plague-ridden London, Parliament sat for a few weeks longer, and Pym anxiously looked for means to hold his crumbling alliance together and above all to prevent the defection of the Covenanters. One weapon, offered months before by George Digby and since put by, was now taken up again. This was a Remonstrance which should set forth in detail all the errors of King Charles's rule. When Digby had suggested this he had been, with his father, Lord Bristol, among the critics of the King; he had now joined those who believed that all necessary reform was accomplished and complete. By an irony of fate, John Pym took up this half-forgotten idea when its author wished it buried. A Remonstrance which recalled every unpopular act, every attack on liberty in religion, every imprisoned merchant or minister over the last sixteen years, would be the best way to destroy again the confidence in the King which he and his friends had newly built up.

While the Remonstrance was discussed in a half-empty House, six Commissioners, two from the Lords, four from the Commons, were chosen to follow the King to Scotland and keep in touch with what went forward there. At Westminster Pym concluded the session with a further concession to Scots opinion. The House of Commons—much depleted because many members had gone home for the harvest or fled the plague—passed an ordinance on sabbath-keeping and idolatry. They decreed that no games were to be played on Sunday, that all images were to be removed from churches, that the Communion table was once again to be shifted from its Popish position in the East and set in the middle of the church, and that all bowing at the name of Jesus was henceforward to cease.

This ordinance, well pleasing to the Scots and to English Puritans, gravely embittered the feeling between Lords and Commons. Only a minority in the Lords were truly in its favour and even among those who were not personally out of sympathy with the ordinance there was angry resentment that the Commons should take it upon themselves to send out orders without the concurrence of the Lords.

With this quarrel in the air, Parliament adjourned for the recess. But Pym had one more innovation to make. Imitating the practice of the Scots Estates, Parliament elected a committee of fifty to look after the business of the nation during the recess.[33] They met officially at Westminster; unofficially they met at Pym's lodging in Chelsea or at the more spacious house of Lord Mandeville in the same village.

Mandeville, the eldest son of the Earl of Manchester and elder brother to the Queen's Catholic favourite, the convert Wat Montagu, had in the course of the last months emerged as the most astute and active of the Puritan lords. He sat in the Upper House during his father's lifetime by right of his own barony of Kimbolton, although he preferred to be known by his courtesy title of Mandeville. He was a heavy, humourless man, deeply and narrowly religious, without much inspiration or fire, but with something of Pym's organising ability and judgment of political advantage. Lord Saye, the Earl of Warwick, the Earl of Newport, might carry more weight in the Lords as personalities and as speakers, but Mandeville had become the organising brain of the Puritan party. The meetings between the Puritan leaders at his house—even more than at John Pym's—attracted the attention and provoked the anxiety of Edward Nicholas as, like a faithful watchdog, he tried to guard his master's house during his master's absence in Scotland. Some plot, some re-arrangement of political forces against the next session of Parliament and the King's return was evidently being perfected. Something was afoot: Nicholas did not know what. But Charles answered him almost merrily from Scotland; if Pym and Mandeville could plot a campaign so could his clever wife, and Nicholas must consult with the Queen.[34] So both sides, each working in half darkness, made their plans against the autumn.

BOOK III CHAPTER VI REFERENCES

1. Twysden, *Journal*, pp. 191 ff.
2. Rothes, p. 225.
3. *C.S.P.D.*, 1640–1, pp. 549–50, 589; 1641–3, pp. 5, 16.
4. *Ibid.*, 1640–1, p. 121.
5. Laud, *Works*, VI, i, p. 301.
6. Rushworth, III, i, pp. 282–3; *Commons Journals*; Symonds d'Ewes, *Correspondence*, Camden Society, XXIX, p. 169; *C.S.P.D.*, 1641–3, p. 6.
7. Rushworth, III, i, pp. 283–4.
8. *Ibid.*, pp. 255–7; Collins, *Historical Collection*, p. 109.
9. *Portland MSS.*, I, pp. 15–22.
10. Rushworth, III, I, p. 291; Napier, I, pp. 286, 292.
11. *Letters of Argyll*, ed. Macdonald, p. 36.
12. Napier, pp. 273 ff.
13. *Ibid.*, p. 279; Guthry, pp. 92–3.
14. *Ibid.*, p. 96; Napier, pp. 296–301.
15. *C.S.P. Ven.*, 1641–3, pp. 166, 171.
16. Rushworth, III, i, p. 291; Carte, *Ormonde*, V, pp. 248–9; *C.S.P. Ireland*, 1633–47, p. 295.
17. *Ibid.*, pp. 298–9, 302–3.
18. *Ibid.*, pp. 307–9.
19. Rushworth, III, i, pp. 264–70.
20. *Ibid.*, pp. 298–301.
21. *C.S.P.D.*, 1641–3, p. 127; *C.S.P. Ven.*, 1641–2, p. 175.
22. *Lords Journals*, July 5th, 1641.
23. *C.S.P. Ven.*, 1641–3, pp. 175–6.
24. Verney, *Notes on Long Parliament*, pp. 106–7; Norman Moore, *History of the Study of Medicine*, London, 1908, p. 176.
25. Rushworth, III, i, pp. 349–50; *C.S.P. Ven.*, 1641–2, p. 187.
26. *C.S.P. Ven.*, 1641–2, pp. 191–2; *C.S.P.D.*, 1641–3, p. 63.
27. *C.S.P. Ven.*, 1641–2, p. 198.
28. *C.S.P.D.*, 1641–3, pp. 59, 62.
29. *Ibid.*, p. 63.
30. Rushworth, III, i, p. 359; *Commons Journals*.
31. *C.S.P.D.*, 1641–3, pp. 38, 53, 82.
32. *C.S.P. Ven.*, 1641–2, p. 201.
33. *Commons Journals*.
34. *Nicholas Correspondence* in Volume IV of *The Diary of John Evelyn*, ed. Bray, London, 1859, p. 76.

CHAPTER SEVEN

SCOTLAND AND IRELAND

August–November 1641

WHILE the King travelled to Scotland, Members of Parliament, released for the recess after the heavy session of ten months, went back to their ordinary business or their ancestral acres, to their families, neighbours and servants. They had leisure, far from the quarrel and bustle of Westminster, to enlarge their doubts or sharpen their convictions in the light of local politics and local interests.

The country was restless. Soldiers, disbanded after more than a year in arms, brought home the disorderly manners of the camp. Some remained together in groups and fell to robbery. In Lincolnshire rioters pulled up the fences of new enclosures and burnt the barns of the enclosers. An organised band of poachers, nearly a hundred strong, broke into Windsor Great Park and made free with the King's deer. They had to be reasoned with, argued and bought off because they were too strong for the ordinary procedure of the law.[1] The abolition of the prerogative courts left those who administered the judicial system with a sense of incompleteness, of lack of control. The destruction of the ecclesiastical courts removed the power which had enforced the moral sanctions of society. Lawyers were having to revise their ideas of what moves were possible and what impossible in the skilful chess of the English law; no longer could one angry gentleman clinch an argument by shouting at another " I will make a Star-Chamber matter of it "; and the threat of a High

Commission prosecution could never again be held over the head of a dissolute priest, a faithless husband, or a neglectful father. No great change had yet taken place in the daily pattern of local life, with its accepted authorities, rules and customs, but the new legislation at Westminster had opened possibilities which were dimly and apprehensively discerned.

The only visible sign of Parliamentary ordinances over the last months was the removal or obliteration of all remnants of Popery from parish churches. This went forward rapidly in the more Puritan districts, but in others was neglected, and in a few was already a matter of angry dispute between justices of the peace holding different views about it. Whitewash covered over the Saint Christophers, the Dooms, the Archangels, the Patriarchs, whose painted images had survived on the walls of churches—or even been repainted—since the Reformation. Stone saints were shattered from reredos and tomb, village crosses overturned, stained glass broken. Secular ornaments were respected—the crusader and his lady, the blackened brasses, the stiff, recumbent gentlemen in gowns and ruffs and armour, couched by their wives in farthingales and canopied by armorial bearings. Nothing idolatrous could be urged against them, and besides they were often related to the squire.

These removals and destructions perturbed responsible men much less than the prevailing atmosphere of doubt and change. The monarchy, which had now for a hundred and fifty years remained stable against all shocks, had become so abject that the King had consented to the disgrace and death of ministers whom he trusted, to the reversal of his acts of justice and the destruction of his own power. Educated men could refer to history and note with interest or dismay that nothing like this had happened since the Wars of the Roses. The less educated felt that the society and especially the law that they knew was being very roughly handled. This was not what they had anticipated a year ago when they complained of Ship-money, objected to restraints and licenses, muttered over surplices, Communion rails and popery, or wished Strafford at the devil. They had wanted to go back, to reject the changes they believed the King was making. They had not anticipated that greater changes would be made under pretence of returning to their ancient rights.

The more convinced Puritan Members of Parliament, returning to their homes, were concerned to answer, or to overrule, the doubts of their neighbours. Sir Robert Harley of Brampton Bryan, who represented the county of Hereford, did not fail on his return home to espy and to order the removal of a crucifix, a wall painting and a window of stained glass at Leominster church. But the strong-minded were a minority; the greater number of the members found only reasons to deepen their doubts during the recess. Looking back on the last months, now that they had time to do so, they saw and they resented the way in which John Pym and a few others had managed affairs, had indeed managed *them*.[2]

Meanwhile the King, in reviving spirits, reviewed the Scots army at Newcastle and entertained Leslie at dinner. He spared no pains to please the Covenanting commander on whom, he broadly hinted, he would shortly bestow an earldom.[3] After the disbanding of the Covenanting army a force of four thousand was to be retained for emergencies: of this four thousand and of General Leslie the King had hopes. At six o'clock on August 14th he made his formal entry into Edinburgh, escorted by the Elector Palatine, his cousin Richmond, and Hamilton. On the 17th he came in procession to the Parliament House, with Hamilton bearing the crown and Argyll the sceptre before him. The solemnity was disturbed by the Laird of Langton who quarrelled with the Earl of Wigton for the place of usher. Charles, who was still master in details of etiquette, withdrew in anger to an inner chamber, whence he issued a warrant for Langton's arrest. The intruder thus disposed of, he entered Parliament and took his seat on the throne; his nephew the Elector occupied a small embroidered stool on his left hand but Richmond, Hamilton and the Earl of Morton, who had not yet signed the Covenant, had to be left outside.[4]

The King in a short and gracious speech asked his loyal

subjects to give what help in money or arms they could to restore his wronged nephew to his German lands.[5] The request was well received and the King's behaviour during the next days seemed to show a change of heart; he attended worship according to the Scottish fashion, allowed Alexander Henderson constant access to his person, listened to him in private and to many other ministers in public, with the greatest civility, and sat attentive while bishops and evil counsellors were denounced from the pulpit. He allowed his cousin Lennox to subscribe the Covenant; he received Argyll with warmth and looked graciously even on Lord Balmerino—whom he had sentenced to death a few years earlier, and who had been chosen by the Covenanters to preside in Parliament. He gave no favours and little attention to any of those who had in the past two years openly served him against the rebels. The bold Montrose, shut up in the castle, clamoured in vain for an open trial: " What I have done is known to a great many and what I have done amiss is unknown to myself," he challenged the Estates. " As truth does not seek corners, it needeth no favour . . . My resolution is to carry along fidelity and honour to the grave."[6] The splendid phrases fell on deaf ears; neither the King nor the Estates would agree to an open trial, in which Montrose might well accuse Argyll of treason and upset the King's present austere honeymoon with the Covenanters.

On August 28th Charles solemnly ratified the legislation of the previous year; he had now, in two of his three Kingdoms, pronounced his *fiat* upon acts which limited his authority and ran directly counter to his belief in the sanctity and inviolability of his office. To celebrate and conclude his surrender he welcomed his new friends and masters to a feast at Holyrood.[7]

The King congratulated himself on the happy impression he had made on his fellow-Scotsmen during the first fortnight of his visit, and the Commissioners dispatched by Parliament —spies, Charles privately called them [8]—felt no slight anxiety when they reached Edinburgh. The party consisted of two from the House of Lords and four from the Commons—the new

Lord Bedford and Lord Howard of Escrick, both consistent supporters of the Scots, Nathaniel Fiennes, who was the son and mouthpiece of Lord Saye, the persuasive John Hampden, Sir Philip Stapleton, a scrawny Calvinist Yorkshireman, and Sir William Armin who, like Hampden, had fought the King on every vital issue since the impeachment of Buckingham.

The fears of the English Commissioners were partly allayed by their first official meeting with the Committee of Estates, which took place privately at Argyll's house.[9] Appearances were deceptive; the Covenanters had eaten and drunk with the King in apparent friendship, but their friendship depended on his acquiescence in their purposes. They were not willing to be used by him and were as alert as Pym and his associates to the probable intentions behind the King's apparent change of policy. Their occasional disagreements with the English House of Commons were essentially the disagreements of allies; their present friendship with the King was a cautious, diplomatic truce with an enemy.

The doubts of the Covenanters as to Charles's true intentions were shared by European observers, and the King's attempt to raise forces in Scotland, ostensibly for the Elector Palatine, was soon checked by reports reaching Edinburgh from the imperial Diet at Ratisbon. Sir Thomas Roe, veteran diplomatist and indefatigable servant of the Protestant Cause and the Elizabethan tradition, had been sent earlier that summer to attend on the Diet and persuade the representatives of Spain and Austria that his master would go to war with them unless they would agree to restore the lands and dignities of the Elector Palatine. Roe was distressed rather than surprised when he found that he could make no converts to this view of King Charles's intentions. The experienced diplomats who represented the European powers at Ratisbon saw very well what had happened. The King of Great Britain, with his subjects in revolt and a Parliament he could not control, was doing as any other European king would have done in his situation; he was making a bid for popularity. It was evident to them that the only use King Charles could reasonably have for an army, if he could get one, would be against his own people. This they put to Sir Thomas with an almost contemptuous frankness.[10] The unwillingness of European diplomatists to take the King's intentions seriously heightened the suspicions of his own subjects, and on September 4th the Scots Parliament refused to countenance the use of their remaining army or the levying of any more troops for the Elector until they should have further news of the negotiations at Ratisbon.[11]

This was the first serious check to the King's hopes. A graver one soon followed. He had hoped for the support and help of Rothes in establishing an agreement with the Covenanters, but Rothes, left behind in England and gravely ill at the time, died at the end of August. Charles could therefore depend only on the friendship which Hamilton had, in the last months, built up with Argyll. How far this had gone—with the usual talk of the widower Hamilton marrying Argyll's eldest daughter —no one quite knew. The two noblemen certainly appeared to be on cordial terms but some of the King's friends doubted whether Hamilton could, or would, use his influence to forward the King's plans.

The King was shortly to place before the Estates the list of the new officers of State chosen to replace those dead, exiled or excluded since the troubles started. He made his list cautiously; he retained Sir Thomas Hope, the principal adviser of the Covenanters, as Lord Advocate and he elevated Argyll's kinsman Loudoun to the important place of Treasurer. As Secretary of State he proposed to retain Hamilton's brother Lanark. But the vital place of Chancellor, left vacant by the flight and death of Archbishop Spottiswoode, he was determined to keep under his own influence. He selected for it the Earl of Morton, an ageing, moderate loyalist on whom he could rely; he anticipated no real difficulty in securing his will because Morton, whatever his politics, was the father of Argyll's wife, and family ties are strong in Scotland.

The King miscalculated. Argyll was not a man to care for

appearances when God's cause was at stake. At the name of Morton he rose to his feet in the Parliament House and denounced his father-in-law as a man crippled by age and debt and under suspicion of worse crimes. Morton replied with dignity that he was unaware what offence he had given to Argyll whom he had had the honour to know from his childhood and had partly brought up. The appeal to natural affection seemed to stir a greater bitterness in Argyll, who had not had a happy childhood. He reminded Morton that he would not have been able to attend Parliament at all but for his own intervention; he had satisfied the creditors who would otherwise have laid his father-in-law by the heels on his arrival in Edinburgh. Morton, in painful distress, asked the King to withdraw his name, but Charles would not accept defeat. He called on Parliament to vote on the list as a whole, not name by name. This suggestion fell upon an obstinate silence, broken at last by Morton's renewed entreaty to the King to withdraw his name rather than make him a cause for misunderstanding.

A prolonged deadlock followed this inauspicious beginning; agreement could not be reached and the leading Covenanters, at all hours, pressed the King with their arguments. "There was never King so much insulted," a faithful royalist reported. "It would pity any man's heart to see how he looks, for he is never at quiet amongst them, and glad he is when he sees any man that he thinks loves him." [12]

The King's disappointment and the bullying of his opponents provoked more than pity among some of those in Edinburgh. He had brought with him a number of professional soldiers or gentlemen volunteers who were to have posts in the army he hoped to raise. Several of these were from the disbanded Irish army and one at least, Lord Crawford, from the Spanish service. Their first loyalty was to the King, and they, with others of the King's servants, had become friendly with such of the Covenanting officers as they believed would also, in the last resort, serve the interests of the King, chief among them Colonels Cochrane and Urry, both veteran professional soldiers, who were critical of the growing influence of Argyll.

The King pursued his usual technique of hedging against defeat by developing a second and different policy alongside his plan for conciliating the Covenanters. He loitered on the outer edge of this Scottish Army Plot much as he had done in similar circumstances in England, and left backstairs meetings and whispering in corners of Holyroodhouse to his favoured Groom of the bedchamber, Will Murray. Once he had a private talk with Cochrane which Murray arranged but did not hear. The King knew probably no more than it was safe for him to know, but he was certainly aware of something. He was also, as his letters to Edward Nicholas in England showed, still extremely confident, announcing with satisfaction at about this time that Pym and his party " will not have such great cause for joy " when he came home again.[13]

He was however for the first time in his life, disillusioned about Hamilton's diplomatic skill and doubtful even if he had been fully loyal to him in his dealings with the Covenanters. He remarked with some asperity to Lanark that his brother " had been very active in his own preservation." [14] The King's criticism of his once most trusted servant was quickly known among the fiery young men and ambitious soldiers he was now encouraging.

In the midst of the King's wrangle with the Estates, on September 29th, news burst upon Edinburgh that Lord Ker, Roxburgh's son, had called Hamilton a traitor and sent a challenge to him by the hand of Lord Crawford. The Estates immediately summoned Ker to answer for his ill conduct; he came obediently, but was escorted through the streets by several hundred of his father's armed tenantry. He apologised to Hamilton and shook hands. The King on the same day, to conciliate the Covenanters, confirmed as Chancellor of Scotland, Argyll's clansman, Lord Loudoun.[15]

But the Covenanters had been thoroughly aroused. Ker was the first royalist who had boldly followed their own custom and brought armed retainers into Edinburgh. That royalist plots were afoot about the Court and even in their own army, they already suspected; Ker's action made them fear riot and treachery in their ranks beyond their control.

On Friday, October 8th, Colonel Cochrane came down to Musselburgh where his regiment was stationed, stood drinks to his officers and promised to make all their fortunes if they would stand by him. Most of his officers were professionals from the German wars and recognised this procedure, if not from experience, then at least from report. The professional soldier, about to change his allegiance from one General to another, or from one Crown to another, habitually sought to buy and flatter his subordinates to come with him, knowing that his value to his new masters depended on how large a force he could offer them. The great drinking parties, the persuasions, the oaths offered by the imperial general Wallenstein to his staff, when he tried to lead an army of twenty thousand men from the imperial into the Swedish camp, was but one gigantic and famous instance of a manœuvre which, in a more humble manner, was often practised by ambitious mercenary colonels in the European wars.

' The example of Wallenstein, who had been murdered by officers loyal to the Emperor (an Irishman, an Englishman and a Scot) was a recent event in the memory of veteran professionals. They had their code and their honour, but although some were willing to believe that a soldier's only loyalty was to his paymaster, others admitted a higher morality. Not every man could be won by drink and promises.

Robert Home, Cochrane's lieutenant-colonel, was one of these. When Cochrane, drawing him aside, dropped hints of Court favour and spoke of some private understanding with Will Murray of the Bedchamber, Home stiffened. He told his colonel that he wished to hear no more. Cochrane, only a little discouraged, returned to Edinburgh, joined company with Lord Crawford and others and drank destruction to the King's enemies far into the night.

On the morning of Monday, October 11th, Colonel Urry

461

and Captain William Stewart were strolling down the street when Colonel Alexander Stewart asked them to step into his lodging for a drink. Urry excused himself, but his companion accepted, only to rejoin him a little later in great agitation. Colonel Stewart had appalled him by telling him of a plot to kidnap Argyll and Hamilton out of the King's own rooms at Holyrood that night, with the assistance of Will Murray who would admit the plotters by the back stairs. He had come in all haste to warn Colonel Urry, because he knew him to be dining with Lord Crawford and the principal conspirators that day and believed that they would compel him to join them.

John Urry, an intelligent, unscrupulous professional soldier, had already heard something of the plot. He saw—as Goring had seen in the same situation in England—that the conspiracy, whatever it was, was likely to be found out, since the conspirators had made the error of trying to draw into it those who did not want to come. It was safer to be the betrayer than the betrayed: John Urry, before dinner on Monday, October 11th, told General Leslie all he knew. Together, they found Hamilton and communicated the story to him and Argyll who, according to Urry, told him to keep his appointment at dinner-time with Lord Crawford and see if he could learn more. In this Urry was disappointed, for all Crawford did was to ask him to call next day, bringing three or four " good fellows " whom he could trust. Crawford hinted that, by means unspecified, he would make the fortunes of all of them.

That afternoon, the weather being fine, Hamilton attended the King as he walked on the lawns of Holyroodhouse; he was, as often happened, to sleep in the King's room that night, but for reasons obscurely expressed, " in a philosophical and para-bolical way," he asked leave of absence and, on being pressed, hinted that there were those about the King who did not love him and whose actions he feared. Charles, puzzled and annoyed, refused him leave of absence. Hamilton disregarded the King's refusal. That night he withdrew with his younger brother, Lanark, and Argyll, to his house at Kinneil about twenty miles away; hence, on the following day, Argyll gave out that there was a conspiracy against their lives, of which he implied the King himself was not ignorant.

The muddled plot misconceived between the intriguer Will Murray and some mischievous, ambitious soldiers, usually the worse for drink, had—like the Army Plot before it—turned into a valuable weapon for the King's enemies. Charles was probably innocent of any design against Argyll and Hamilton, but he had, as before in England, by silence, by hints, by granting secret audiences to Cochrane, by encouraging Lord Roxburgh, Lord Ker and Lord Crawford, prepared the way for the disaster, and he had given his trusted servant Will Murray enough rope to hang them all.

The news of the Incident—as this affair came to be called— spread quickly to the excitable people of Edinburgh. Charles came up to the Parliament House with Roxburgh's retainers as a guard against the people. This necessary precaution gave Hamilton and Argyll the opportunity to proclaim, with an air of suffering virtue, that they would not come back to the capital for fear of untoward incidents between their servants and the King's armed followers.

The popularity that Charles had briefly enjoyed vanished overnight. In vain he declared his innocence to the assembled Estates and, almost with tears, taxed the absent Hamilton with ingratitude for allowing himself to believe so horrible a falsehood as that his life or liberty was unsafe in the King's own bed-chamber. He demanded an immediate and public examination of the whole scandalous business. His opponents in the Estates, knowing that uncertainty and rumour worked for them and not for the King, hung back. The King's wild friends continued their indiscretions; the scandal multiplied. Lord Carnwath, another loud-voiced, wooden-headed warrior, was reported to have babbled of three Kings in Scotland, Argyll, Hamilton and King Charles, and to have said that the first two would be better without their heads. This childish rubbish linked well with the speeches said to have been made by Montrose's friends in May, for which Montrose was still awaiting trial in the castle. A Royalist campaign to blacken the character of the godly Argyll, and perhaps to murder him, seemed credible to many and was believed.

On October 15th, Sir Thomas Hope strongly advised the Estates to conduct the inquiry in secret because in privacy alone would men disclose all that they knew. The King protested: " If men were so charitable as not to believe false rumours, Sir Thomas, I would be of your mind," he said, " but since I see the contrary, you must give me leave to think otherwise. . . . I must see myself get fair play." The rumours in Edinburgh increased; four days later the King was stung to yet stronger words before the assembled Estates. " By God," he cried—and when the King used his Creator's name it was an invocation and not an oath—" it behoved Parliament to clear his honour." But the Estates saw no reason to clear his honour and his opponents won the day; the inquiry was held in private.

Colonel Urry and Captain William Stewart, who had between them revealed the plot, were questioned on October 12th; so was Cochrane's lieutenant-colonel, Robert Home. All three of their stories pointed to Will Murray as a central figure in the plot, and therefore most damningly to the King.

Crawford and Cochrane, with soldierly bluster, denied any plot; they had, admittedly, looked upon the alliance of Hamilton and Argyll with suspicion, and had talked—but only in theory— of what might be done to overpower them should they be found to be disloyal. This too was the substance of Colonel Alexander Stewart's account. He claimed that Captain William Stewart had misunderstood him, when they talked over their drinks, on the morning of Monday, October 11th; he had spoken of no actual plot, but only of a possible method of procedure, should Hamilton and Argyll be proved traitors.

Will Murray, examined three times, appeared as a confident man of the world—very ready to help and not in the least embarrassed. He admitted that he had arranged a private interview for Cochrane with the King but had no idea what had been said;

Cochrane had stood close by the King's bed, His Majesty having retired for the night, and the bed curtains had been drawn round them both for greater privacy. He steadfastly denied the existence of any plot and laughed off the suggestion that he had intended the kidnapping of Hamilton and Argyll from the King's rooms at Holyroodhouse. But with a quiet, insistent subtlety he emphasised a new element in the story. Crawford had muttered something about a letter from Montrose to the King. Will Murray elaborated this: he said that Montrose had managed to convey not one but three letters to the King, that the King had not shown much interest in the first two, but that the third, received on October 11th in the morning, had contained statements on which he had intended to question Montrose, had not the Incident intervened. This third letter was produced—the two others were not, and may well have been imaginary; what Montrose had written was a request that he might have leave " to acquaint His Majesty with a business which not only did concern his honour in a high degree, but the standing and falling of his Crown likewise."

The meaning of this letter is clear enough when Montrose's position during the last three months is brought to mind. He had been shut up in the castle, out of touch with current events. He knew nothing of Crawford, Cochrane and Ker, but was still brooding on the accusation that he had sought, and failed, to bring home to Argyll in May. He had once or twice been cursorily examined, he had never been tried, and a thorough search through his private papers had revealed no additional evidence on which he could be arraigned. The Committee of Estates had taken the precaution of hanging his principal witness against Argyll, the unfortunate John Stewart. Montrose was therefore desperate to see the King and to explain to him the dangers of which he believed him ignorant. His letter had no bearing on the Incident; it belonged to another, and an earlier, sequence of events.

That had not prevented Will Murray from quoting ambiguous phrases from it to encourage the military plotters. He now used it with equal skill to direct attention from himself and his friends and canalise suspicion against Montrose.

It was round Edinburgh in a flash that Montrose had offered to cut the throats of Argyll and Hamilton, seize Edinburgh Castle for the King and establish his authority in Scotland by force of arms. The palpable absurdity of this story was disregarded, not only by the King's enemies, but also by his friends. The idea of Montrose offering bloody deeds to his sovereign suited the Covenanters very well in their desire to discredit the Royalists. But once his name had been brought in, he served as a scapegoat for those Royalists who had actually done the mischief. Cochrane, Crawford, Will Murray became in the popular view, mere satellites and unimportant figures in the Incident of which the revealed architect was Montrose.

This transference of responsibility saved the conspirators from the worst consequences of their folly, but did not restore to the King the possibility of forming a Royalist party in Scotland. Moderate-minded men, who distrusted the Covenanters, now saw good reason for distrusting the King also. "It behoves you to clear my honour," Charles had declared to the Estates, but the Covenanters preferred to leave his honour under the cloud his mischievous friends had brought upon it.[16]

The cloud hung upon him as heavily in England as in Scotland. From Westminster the faithful Nicholas, appalled at the shocking versions of the Incident now current in England, implored the King to send him some clear information, to issue some official statement that could be put out to stop the mouths of the slanderers.[17] But Charles sent him no such explanation, having none to send. The Queen's little Court at Oatlands was all this time closely watched by Pym and his associates. Since August they had tried to gauge her husband's hopes and fears from her changing moods, often with confusing results. The Standing Committee of the House of Commons had at first received with equanimity the news that the Covenanters were retaining four thousand men under arms, but when they learnt that the Queen was also delighted their faces lengthened and they suspected a secret understanding between the King and Leslie.[18] They became more cheerful again as the little Queen's momentary joy evaporated; she drooped when she heard of her husband's defeat over the Chancellor's appointment and became tearful and distraught at the news of the Incident.

She had good reason for anxiety; whatever conspiracies she had encouraged or was still encouraging in her husband's name, she was herself the object of conspiracy. Lord Newport, who as Constable of the Tower had, in April, announced his intention of cutting off Strafford's head on his own authority, had since then increased the Tower garrison and uttered another fierce indiscretion. Dining in Kensington with Lord Holland, he remarked that, in the event of the King making any dangerous move, the Queen and her children should at once be seized as hostages.[19]

The attention of the King's enemies was for the moment fixed on him in Scotland or on his wife in England. They had temporarily forgotten about the unquiet state of Ireland. They trusted to the strong and confident men, the powerful Anglo-Irish who had helped them to destroy Strafford, to control any disturbances and they failed to realise the magnitude of the forces which the death of Strafford and their subsequent policy was stirring into action. They made no allowance for two things: first, that Strafford's army, even disbanded, was still a danger because seven or eight thousand discontented men cast loose upon so small a country necessarily constituted a danger; second, that Strafford's army was not the only potential force in Ireland.

Strafford, who believed with passion in law and order, had in 1639 skilfully repressed the dangerous offer of the Earl of Antrim to raise the Irish Macdonnells for the King against the Covenanters. He had strengthened and increased the Irish army because it gave him an opportunity to keep these wild forces under discipline and draw off some of them into authorised and honourable employment. This army, disbanded, scattered throughout the country a leaven of trained troops who could impart their knowledge, and distribute their equipment, to their fellow-Irishmen. Strafford's army, in its disintegration, did precisely what he had created it to prevent: it gave arms, encouragement and military knowledge to the "wild Irish."

The Earl of Antrim's plan had been ridiculous because he was himself ridiculous. But his people were not. Acting in small bands, under lesser chieftains, the Macdonnells were determined fighters. So were their neighbours in Ulster the O'Neills; so were the O'Byrnes in Wicklow, the O'Reillies in Cavan, the O'Gradies in Clare and the rest of those throughout the country whom Strafford had contemptuously called "the O's and Mac's." Their raiding had been held in check for the last forty years, but it had not ceased. Bound together by the Catholic religion, by the Irish language and by a deep sense of wrong, these scattered, disinherited people were potentially very dangerous.

The King had always hankered after Antrim's scheme and had not forgotten it. He was in touch, this summer of 1641, with Sir Phelim O'Neill, the young Irish chieftain whom Antrim had planned to have for his second in command. Phelim O'Neill that summer held at his house several meetings of the Irish gentry of Ulster. Other Irish lords of the north, MacMahon and M'Guire, were busy recruiting. The troops they raised were, they said, for Spain.[20] Messages of some kind had been exchanged between the King and O'Neill. But this Irish business was on the King's part only one of his many attempts to win allies for the rebuilding of his broken power. If Parliament knew and understood scandalously little about Ireland, Charles knew and understood even less. John Pym for his part had only studied the politics of Ireland in so far as he had had to use them to destroy Strafford. For Charles, Ireland had never been anything but a potential source of revenue and now a potential source of troops. Neither saw that the Irish were a people brought to the edge of despair who, if they once appealed to arms, would not soon lay them down again.

When Strafford fell, and Wandesford died, a government

came to an end which, although alien and exacting, had been at least reliable and, within defined limits, scrupulous and just to the Irish. The party in power in England, which had destroyed Strafford, had thus in Ireland confirmed the triumph of the adventurers, English and Scots, who were insatiable in their greed for Irish land and who recognised no rights of the Irish or the Norman-Irish which stood in their way. Strafford had tried vainly to get the King to appoint for his successor a man who had some understanding of the Irish problem and some respect for the rights—however limited—of the Irish themselves. It is significant that both his suggestions were Norman-Irish lords—Lord Dillon and the Earl of Ormonde. The King had not been able to follow his advice. Instead the two Lords Justices Sir John Borlase and Sir William Parsons, appointed with Parliamentary approval to govern for the time being, were themselves prominent men among the recent adventurers, in sympathy only with their practical and ruthless point of view.

The dominance of the Puritan party in the English Parliament, and the reassertion by the English Parliament of its power over the Irish Parliament, meant that extreme Protestantism might at any moment be rigidly enforced on Ireland with all the penal laws against Catholics and the total extinction of their religion.

To a threat of this magnitude to their land, their religion, their very lives, only one answer was possible from a people still warlike, still unsubdued, and still in a majority over the newcomers. Nothing and no one in the autumn of 1641 could have prevented the rising in Ireland. It was like no other rebellion the King had known; it was not, like the rising in Scotland, subject to political control and exploitation. It was disordered, elemental, desperate, a movement over which no single leader at any moment in its ten years' course had complete control.

In Dublin, on the night of October 22nd, one Owen O'Conolly, not altogether sober, knocked up Sir William Parsons at the castle. He declared that on the morrow, Saturday and market day, a party of Irish under the Lords MacMahon and M'Guire would seize Dublin. Parsons had MacMahon arrested in his lodging that night but M'Guire, forewarned, fled and was discovered early next morning crouching among the fowls in a henhouse in the suburbs. The city gates were closed, the market cancelled; all day and far into the night Parsons and the council questioned the prisoners. The two boisterous young chiefs were airily defiant; knowing that the seizure of Dublin was but a part of a wider plan they waited in confidence for the news the evening would bring. It came at midnight, while the anxious council was still in session; Lord Blaney, an old Welsh soldier, commander of the garrison at Monaghan, rode stumbling up the castle hill on a tired horse. The O'Neills had risen in force, had rushed his town of Carrickmacross at daybreak, had surrounded Castle Blaney with his wife and children in it, and laid siege to Monaghan. He was the first of many frantic messengers who in the next days filled Dublin with horror and dismay. In eastern Ulster the insurgents, burning farms and scattering the terrified settlers, carried all before them; they seized Newry; they threatened Belfast. From hill to hill their beacons spread news of the rising and summoned their clansmen to arms. While the government hesitated and the settlers fled, the O'Neills gathered strength. A horde, wildly estimated at twenty thousand, plunged towards Drogheda. Belfast was already cut off.[21]

The King was playing his customary round of golf on the links at Leith when, on October 27th, the first news from Ireland was put into his hand. Like Sir Francis Drake on a different occasion, he finished the game. Later that day he reported the matter with becoming gravity to the Scottish Parliament.

The news created a kind of breathless uncertainty. But no one yet perceived that this was something more than another incident in the struggle for power between the King and his subjects. Argyll knew of the King's one-time agreement with Antrim; it was he who had defended the south-west coasts of Scotland from that projected Irish invasion which Charles, two years before, had countenanced and encouraged. He can hardly have doubted that Charles knew something of this present rising. The English Parliamentary Commissioners entertained the same fear: six months earlier they had had constantly in their minds that dubious threat of Strafford's "Your Majesty has an army in Ireland." Would this Irish rebellion turn out to be simply a rising of the King's friends? It was one thing to suspect, another to act. The King's conduct was correct; he deplored the rising; he asked for help in restoring peace to Ireland. What action then could safely be taken by those who agreed with his expressed intentions but gravely doubted what lay behind them? The English Commissioners asked him to come back to Westminster to consult with Parliament, and the Scottish Estates, playing for time, appointed a committee to consider the matter of Ireland, but postponed further action till they should know the intentions of the English Parliament.

The Elector Palatine in a private letter to a friend in the House of Commons immediately passed on this decision,[22] which thus reached Westminster earlier than it could have done in the report of the Commissioners. The Elector made no comment but his anxiety that the strong alliance between the Scots and the English Parliaments should not break down shows how far he disagreed with his uncle's private policy and how much he too wondered what was really happening in Ireland. News must by this time have reached Edinburgh—although it passed without comment in the general excitement—that his younger brother Rupert had at last been released. The terms of the prince's release, settled by the English ambassador at Ratisbon, were that he would never again fight against the Emperor. But Rupert was a professional soldier; if he could not fight against the Emperor, where would he fight? There was more than a hint in the air of some employment for him in King Charles's service and this the Elector was determined to prevent.

As for the King himself, he had written to Nicholas with his usual optimism: "I hope these ill news from Ireland may hinder some of these follies in England."[23] The rebellion in Ireland seemed to him primarily an event that could be turned to account in the renewed struggle for power with his English Parliament.

The House of Commons had reassembled at Westminster on October 20th but its ranks were thin. Plague was still bad in the City and Members were in no hurry to come back. The disbanded troops seemed dangerous, and vicious words, scrawled on walls or scattered in public places, threatened Pym and Parliament. Some ill-wishing person sent him a filthy rag said to have been infected with the plague. The London trained bands under the Earl of Essex guarded the House against possible violence. The fear of violence dominated the debates. The Incident and its possible connection with the Army Plot were discussed and Pym laid before the House evidence he had obtained during the recess of the King's attempts to win the northern army wholly to his interests.[24]

News of the rebellion in Ireland was officially communicated to Parliament by Lord Keeper Littleton on November 1st. Pym immediately focused attention on the Court by putting forward a request for a list of all the Queen's servants. Her confessor, Father Philip, later in the day refused to answer questions put to him in Parliament on the ingenious excuse that he could not swear on a Protestant translation of the Bible. In sober truth, Father Philip knew nothing about the Irish rebellion but was afraid lest questioning should expose another awkward secret —the Queen's continued friendly communications with the Vatican.

The Commons, in the hope of detecting foreign machinations behind the Irish trouble, intercepted all letters from Dublin to the envoys of Catholic powers in London and broke open the despatches of the Spanish ambassador.[25] But the danger of foreign intervention in the Irish rising was less immediately serious than its possible effect on politics at home. John Pym, like the King, saw that he must use this new event in the struggle to maintain the power of Parliament against the King, and he saw at the same time the way in which the King was likely to use it. Armed forces would have to be raised to put down the

Irish revolt. The King's principal need in the struggle had been just that—the control of armed forces. It was evident to Pym that the King would not use any armed forces which were placed under his authority exclusively to put down the Irish revolt—if indeed he used them in that way at all. A year ago the King had certainly intended to use an Irish army against the Scots and—so the impeachment of Strafford implied—may have entertained a desire to use an Irish army against the English. That Irish army, disbanded, was now in alliance with the rebels; some of its officers were among the leaders of the Irish revolt. Who could say with certainty that the King had no further connection with these men? They themselves asserted that they were in rebellion not against him but only against his enemies. Early in November the news reached London that the Irish rebels claimed that the King was to land on the coast of Ulster and put himself at their head.

On November 5th the Commons celebrated their usual thanksgiving for their deliverance from the Gunpowder Treason, the Popish Plot of 1605. In the mood which this ceremony engendered Pym solemnly addressed the House on the message that they were drawing up to send to the King in Scotland about the measures to be taken against the Irish rebels. No offers or plans of theirs, no raising of loans in the City or gathering of arms and troops would be of any avail to quell the revolt, he argued, unless the King would once and for all rid himself of all "evil counsellors." He must agree to have only such men in his service and among his advisers as Parliament should choose. The demand was astonishing, so astonishing that Edward Hyde, until this time a supporter of Pym on every legal issue, rose to object. But Pym was never in theory an innovator and he had taken good advice on this question. He could cite a precedent for the request of such respectable antiquity as the reign of Edward III.[26]

Edward III notwithstanding, Pym knew he was on dangerous ground. The Lords were bound to object to attaching so outrageous a demand to the message sent to Scotland about the

Irish revolt. The King from a distance, and the Queen from closer at hand, had done their work well in the Lords. Bristol and his son Lord Digby were well instructed and well prepared to fight this new attack, and the younger royalist peers were being rounded up from their country houses by the Queen's letters.[27]

Pym in the Commons continued methodically to build up the attack as he had done the year before. Then he had had to remove Strafford and destroy the legal strength of the royal position by pulling down the prerogative courts. Now he had only one problem left but that the hardest: he must destroy the King's authority over the armed forces in time of emergency. He must get the army, once and for all, under the direct control of Parliament. The renewed attack on evil councillors was only a necessary move in that scheme. On November 6th one of his principal henchmen, Oliver Cromwell, the Member for Cambridge, a man of heavy, uninspiring presence but considerable eloquence, moved that the Commons join with the Lords in asking that the Earl of Essex, whom all trusted, should be given the command of all the trained bands in the south.[28] This was the quiet opening move in the campaign to have all military appointments placed under the control of Parliament.

Pym knew that he could only win in this last struggle if he systematically undermined all trust and faith in the King. For this reason his party went ahead day after day with drafting that Remonstrance, first suggested by Digby a year before and taken up again a little before the recess. This was to blast the King's reputation by recalling, act by act, everything in his reign that had given offence to his subjects.

Terribly aware of the danger of this Remonstrance, the Queen and Nicholas wrote repeatedly to Charles in Scotland. They implored him to return before Pym could marshal all his forces against him and get his deadly Remonstrance through the Commons. Charles, miscalculating the speed of Pym's action and the number of his supporters, wrote to Nicholas instructing him to tell all his trusted friends in Parliament that " by all means" they contrive to stop the Remonstrance.[29]   He was himself on his way home to confront and, as he hoped, to outwit his enemies.

In the interim he had concluded his business in Scotland. He had worked hard to pacify the Covenanters and make them his allies when it should come—as soon it must—to an open breach with the English Commons. After making Lord Loudoun, Argyll's clansman, Chancellor he had put the Treasury into commission with Argyll as a principal commissioner, and confirmed Sir Thomas Hope as Lord Advocate. He elevated to his Council the Lords Balmerino, Cassilis and Maitland, thus entrusting the government of Scotland, in his absence, exclusively to his enemies. Of his Council at least half had been, during the last ten years, either accused or under suspicion of treason; not one of them had, since then, altered his opinions. This extraordinary conduct, which dismayed the loyalists and the sad remnant of the episcopal party in Scotland, reflected Charles's prevailing mood of optimism. He was confident that he had gained these men for his friends although he had secured nothing in return for his favours but the unconditional release of the Incident plotters, Crawford and Cochrane, and the release on bail of Montrose.

To seal these new friendships he made Argyll a Marquis and General Leslie Earl of Leven. Hamilton, who had come back to Holyrood and been restored to favour, was probably the architect of this alliance. With his usual over-confidence, he may truly have believed that these new friendships would last, and so have persuaded the King, always too easily convinced of good news, that he could henceforward count on the friendship of the Covenanters against his English Parliament.

Superficial appearances easily deceived the King; in his native land, his voice, his manner, his addiction to golf and natural fondness for Scots servants and Scots jokes, gave him a spurious feeling that he was at home again and this, in spite of disagreements, convinced him that his fellow-countrymen would, in the last resort, be staunch to him. At his Court at Holyrood, the

English Parliamentary Commissioners, with their thin southern voices and their stiff English manners—so different from the rugged fervour of the Scots—had seemed foreign, mistrustful and mistrusted. For the second time in two years, the King gambled on the strength of national prejudice. In 1640 he had been sure the English would rise for him against the Scots; in 1641 he was convinced the Scots would stand by him against the English.

He was mistaken. John Hampden, Philip Stapleton and the rest might not understand Scots jokes, might indeed barely understand Scots English; but the community of interest between them and the Covenanters went deep. The community of interest between the King and the Covenanters did not exist at all. No one knew this better than Argyll and no one knew better than Argyll how to accept and make use of each change and turn in the King's erratic policy. He got from him on this occasion the royal commission to defend the Highlands and Islands against possible attack from the Irish rebels, a commission which was to prove very useful to him in years to come.

On November 17th in cheerful spirits the King adjourned the Estates. Sir Thomas Hope pronounced congratulatory words: "a contented King is to depart from a contented country."[30] That evening Charles feasted his lords at Holyrood and the castle cannon fired joyful salvoes. Early next day he rode away from his capital city of Edinburgh to face with equanimity the problems which awaited him at Westminster.

On this first day of his journey he received a letter from Nicholas warning him at length about the Remonstrance, but Charles was confident that his friends in the House of Commons could prevent its passing. He was confident of everything. He believed that the worst of his dangers were over, that he had won the Scots and was half-way to defeating Pym. While he had heard from Nicholas of his enemies' manœuvres, he had also heard of their difficulties. The citizens of London were growing tired of the pretensions and claims of the Commons and were displeased at the activities of the extremer Puritans. For most of them, the Protestant religion was a form of social discipline as well as a spiritual belief. They saw with grave annoyance the congregations which now gathered round self-appointed prophets who, free from the fear of prosecution in the ecclesiastical courts, stalked the streets expounding the Scriptures. Many of the preachers were humble folk—a cobbler, a hawker of pots and pipkins familiar in Cheapside, a zealous button-maker, some were even women.[31] Being moved of the Lord, they frequently scorned the appointed order of society and exhorted their betters to repent. In the face of these uncomfortable manifestations the fervour of the City for religious reformation cooled. The Puritans lost ground. At the election of the new Lord Mayor the decision hung in the balance and the King's friends among the City men, led by one of the sheriffs, secured the election of the royalist alderman Henry Gurney by a hurried, tumultuous demonstration.

Against this royalist reaction Pym fought with the double weapon of rumour and slander. He encouraged every tale of plot and conspiracy that could be used to discredit the King's friends and link them with the Popish-Irish danger. Thomas Beale, a tailor, regaled the House for several days with the details of a plot which he swore he had overheard, for the massacre of all the Parliament-men.

Sir Walter Earle, the Member for Hampshire, reported from his county that letters were passing very frequently between the Queen at Oatlands and Colonel Goring, the governor of Portsmouth. Goring, it was said locally, had mounted cannon to overawe the town but had put up no defences on the seaward side, as though he expected and would welcome a foreign landing. "The Papists and jovial clergymen" of the district were said to be "merrier than ever."[32] But Earle's report of these suspicious circumstances failed of its purpose, for Goring, alone among the conspirators whom the Queen encouraged, was a liar of such bland confidence that he could outface any accusation. He appeared in the House of Commons and made so clear and convincing an explanation of all his actions that they

477

let him go again with the good thanks of the House for his loyalty to them.

Far more damaging to the King's prestige were the revelations made a little later in the month, concerning the whole mysterious business of the King's plan to use the northern army against Parliament in the previous summer. Sir John Conyers had clearly stated on examination by a Committee of the House of Commons, that Major Daniel O'Neill—the significance of his surname was missed by no one—had come to him from the King very secretly in the summer, and tried by persuasion and by veiled threats to get him to agree to a plan for marching on London to overawe the Parliament.[33]

Meanwhile the King approached, travelling down the Great North Road by Northallerton, York and Doncaster. On his journey he kept his forty-first birthday on November 19th; but he was travelling too fast to spare time for much ceremony. In the fruitful, peaceful land through which he travelled, he was well received. News from Ireland had hardly penetrated to it. But west of the Pennines, on the Lancashire coast, in Wales, in the region of Watling Street, the direct road from Chester to London, and farther south in Devon and Somerset, the news spread fast. The first fugitives, wives of wealthy settlers and Dublin officials, cumbered with trunks of household goods and tearful with tales of horror, had already landed at Chester and Bristol. Mariners from the southern Irish ports coming back to Gloucester, Barnstaple, Minehead, brought news which ran fast up the Severn valley, and over Devon and Somerset. From Chester, tidings from Dublin were carried over the Midlands and the Welsh marches. Ships from Belfast and Londonderry gave the lamentable story to Liverpool and Whitehaven, thence to Carlisle; to Ayr and Irvine and Dumbarton and over all the Scottish Lowlands.

The Popish-Irish-Spanish plot expanded in the telling. North Wales shuddered at a supposed conspiracy to seize Conway Castle. Near Hereford Lady Brilliana Harley, at her husband's express orders, fortified his castle of Brampton Bryan in dread of siege. Messengers from Kidderminster warned the hill-town of Bridgnorth that invasion was hourly expected and Bridgnorth, as in the Armada days, lit the alarm beacon, with a prodigious expenditure in coal and beer.[34]

All this was vague, alarmist—the uninformed reactions of doubt and fear. At Westminster they had more definite news in a stream of letters from the government in Dublin. They wanted ten thousand men, money, arms . . . . O'Neill was sweeping south; he was closing in on Drogheda. Farther west and north the M'Guires had risen and were driving all before them towards Londonderry. The O'Byrnes were out in Wicklow, the O'Reillies in Cavan. Peaceable Irish gentry gave them shelter and arms, turned suddenly on their English neighbours. . . . Gradually the council in Dublin came to understand that they were facing a co-ordinated revolt.

In Munster it had come like a thunderclap, sending Lord Cork and his four elder sons helter-skelter to raise arms and men for the defence of their ill-got possessions. For once the Boyle family had been caught unprepared. Wickedly triumphant over Strafford's fall, the old Earl of Cork could not seriously believe that a revolt of the native Irish would come to trouble him in his last days. He heard the news from Ulster while he sat at table at Castle Lyons feasting his favourite son, Lord Broghill, the Haymarket bridegroom of the previous winter who had that week brought home his bride. The fearful messenger from Dublin broke in on them with news of what had happened in Ulster. He added a further warning: he had seen armed men gathering in the villages, and gangs on the roads as he passed. He had heard strange threats and caught the glint of arms and what looked like banners.[35]

Among Lord Cork's guests was an Irishman, Lord Muskerry. He laughed the messenger to scorn; some men were cowards enough to be frightened by the sight of peasants going to market. . . . The Boyles, well pleased to enjoy their false security a little longer, accepted this view, which was precisely as Muskerry had hoped; he was himself the chief of the rebels when a few days later the revolt flared up over Munster.

The Lord President of Munster, the veteran soldier Sir William St. Leger, tried to make light of the matter. " A company of naked rogues," he wrote angrily to Dublin; if they would send him a regiment of cavalry he would dispose of the rebels before they could interfere with the hunting.[36] The Lords Justices in Dublin sent no cavalry; they hardly even sent news. The roads between Dublin and the South were cut by the insurgents. The settlers, abandoning their farms, fled in terror to Kilkenny. Each region, each man, fought for himself. The government had no troops to send, while the officers and men of Strafford's disbanded army joined with the rebels.

While the Lords Justices in Dublin wailed for help to their friends in the English Parliament, the Norman-Irish landowners, the Lords of the Pale who had once been the bulwark between the English settlements and the Irish of the south and west, behaved in suspicious fashion. For the past fifty years the aggressive new English settlers had driven these Norman-Irish Roman Catholic nobility into closer friendship with the Irish. Now the testing time had come, and if they did not immediately join with the rebels, they showed a dreadful slowness to assist the government. While Ulster farmsteads went up in flames and triumphant robber bands drove off the cattle and burnt the barns everywhere, the Lords of the Pale sent a letter to the King asking him for some security in future for the lands of the Irish, that they might not be, to all time, subject to the " quirks and quiddities " of English law.[37] It was a very sound request, but it did not suggest to the Justices in Dublin or to Parliament in England that the Lords of the Pale were making ready to defend law, order and the existing government against the insurgents.

In the North Sir Phelim O'Neill boasted and bragged to his men and to English prisoners as his forces thrust on towards Drogheda. He was no rebel but the King's true knight and faithful servant who had risen in arms to liberate His Majesty from the oppression of his enemies and those who dared to set limits upon his sacred authority.

In support of this contention he showed, to prisoners in his camp at Newry, a commission under the King's Great Seal. His supporters, up and down the land, had copies of it; by the middle of November it had reached Dublin and a priest in Bull Tavern on Merchants' Quay displayed a copy, showing how the King had given order to O'Neill to seize the castles, houses and property of Protestant settlers—" witness Ourself at Edinburgh the first day of October, in the seventeenth year of our reign." [38] That the document was, in whole or in part, a forgery should have been apparent to any dispassionate eye. Whatever Charles had done to encourage the rebels, he would hardly have authorised their actions in such terms. But the rights and wrongs of the matter were less important than the effect it made.

Before King Charles approached his capital for his second great encounter with Pym in the battle for authority, his name and fame had been entangled once and for all with the cause of the Irish rebels.

In the fear rather than the knowledge of what was happening in Ireland, the House of Commons continued to debate their Grand Remonstrance against the King's past government.

Charles had sent word of his return to his Queen and to Sir Edward Nicholas. Henrietta Maria in a flutter of happy anticipation made ready to drive out to meet him at Theobalds with the three eldest children. The loyal gentlemen of Hertford planned a reception for him at Ware. Nicholas sent word of the royal time-table to the Lord Mayor so that the City of London, under Henry Gurney's genial persuasion, should receive the King with a demonstration of loyal enthusiasm, dissociating themselves from all base suspicions of the King spread abroad by the Puritan faction. Nicholas, writing to Charles, permitted himself a word of respectful advice: if His Majesty could perhaps smile at those who received him, and " speak a few good words to them. . . ." [39]

The King was expected in London by November 24th. On

November 22nd Pym's Remonstrance was again before the House. The debate opened at midday. Edward Hyde, the Member for Saltash, asked that messengers should be sent to call in Members strolling in Westminster Hall and a handful of errant royalists were rounded up for the debate. Hyde, who had supported Pym in the attack on the prerogative courts and had been until this time a principal architect of the constitutional changes of the last year, was now to measure himself against Pym in organising the Commons. A fortnight earlier he had been startled by Pym's claim to control the appointment of the councillors round the King, and he rightly saw in the Remonstrance the opening of a more far-reaching attack on the royal power than any he had anticipated. Henceforward, he was never again Pym's man.

On this 22nd November he stood, with his friend Lord Falkland beside him, as the advocate of a moderate policy and an enemy to the Remonstrance. Hyde's attack was well conceived. He had learnt in the last year a great deal about political strategy from Pym, and his experience as a barrister had given him training in the special strategy of debate. He was careful not to oppose the Remonstrance in principle. On the contrary, he declared himself very willing that a short statement, touching only the events of the present Parliament, should be made to the King. But, he argued, it was a grave error of judgment to put forth a long, injurious catalogue of complaints covering the entire reign. This could only anger the King and alienate the House of Lords, perhaps even provoke them to issue a counter-Remonstrance.

Lord Falkland persuasively enlarged on the theme set forth by Hyde. What would people think of the Commons, he asked, if they persistently, and for no good cause, raked over events of the past better consigned to oblivion? The King had come far to meet them in the last year; they had asked nothing that he had not conceded. To receive the King on his homecoming with revived accusations of past misdeeds was to do grave injury to their cause.

Sir John Colepeper took up and developed the criticisms made by Falkland and Hyde. The clauses of the Remonstrance which attacked the King's religious policy were, he argued, bound to cause a breach with the Lords, already angry at the religious ordinances of the Commons. More serious, in his view, was the unconstitutional character of the Remonstrance—it masqueraded as a document for the attention of the King, but it was in truth addressed to the people: it was a public statement by the Commons accusing the King, a procedure as yet unheard of in the annals of England.

The irrepressible Sir Edward Dering felt no less strongly on this point. " When I first heard of a Remonstrance," he said, " I presently imagined that like faithful councillors we should hold up a glass to His Majesty . . . I did not dream that we should remonstrate downward and tell stories to the people."

The criticisms made by Hyde and Falkland and enlarged by Colepeper and Dering drew the moderate men of the Commons together and linked them with the more active royalists against the Remonstrance.

Pym, who fully apprehended the growing strength and improved organisation of his opponents, answered their criticism with an overriding argument: the necessity of the times. He was willing to drop a clause of the Remonstrance here and modify one there, but the Remonstrance as a whole must go through. He reiterated his belief that a malignant party still existed and was still strong round the King. In the last month every conspiracy and every violent design had been, in Pym's words, " thrust home to the Court." While such counsels prevailed there, the religion and liberty of the subject were in perpetual danger. " It is time to speak plain English," he said, " lest posterity shall say that England was lost and no man durst speak truth."

The debate outlasted the winter afternoon and went on by candlelight. At midnight, Edward Nicholas went wearily home; he wrote to the King that the opponents of the Remonstrance were making head against Pym but for his own part he could sit up no longer.

At one o'clock the House divided. Three hundred and seven Members had sat it out so long. The division, in the flickering light, seemed almost even. It must have been with infinite relief that Pym heard Lenthall announce the numbers: a hundred and forty-eight against the Remonstrance, a hundred and fifty-nine in its favour. He had won by eleven votes.

More than eighty sleepy Members now pushed out of the House, but the night's work was not over. Geoffrey Palmer, the Member for Stamford, a strong King's man, rose to announce that the minority wished to enter a protest against the Remonstrance. Confusion broke out. The Royalists shouted their support of Palmer, Pym's following were as noisy in objection. Members sprang to their feet, tweaked each other's hair and tore ill-temperedly at each other's collars. Some rattled their swords or banged their scabbarded points menacingly on the ground. Lenthall was unable to restore peace but John Hampden, dominating the clamour with his fine resonant voice, urged that nothing further be done that night. The tumult subsided. The Speaker adjourned the House and two hundred tired men came muttering and yawning, into the empty streets of Westminster "just when the clock struck two."[40]

The King slept that night within two days' ride of London. Behind him lay his kingdom of Scotland, deceptively tranquil, deceptively content. Before him lay his great City of London, decked and prepared to do him honour, and his angry, divided House of Commons, John Pym with his Remonstrance, that declaration of distrust, Oliver Cromwell with his demand that Parliament choose the commanders of the armed forces. Far to the west lay Ireland where the fires of camp and beacon and burning homestead lit the cold November night.

It was not five years since these three kingdoms had seemed the most tranquil in Europe and their sovereign the happiest King in Christendom. The tranquillity of the kingdoms, the happiness and the power of their King had proved to be illusions.

In Scotland a formidable faction, controlling and directing the fervour of the Kirk, had bereft the King of all but the semblance of sovereignty. In Ireland the imposed framework of government had been shattered by the popular rising. In England the King had pledged himself not to dissolve a Parliament which had destroyed his judicial powers, taken over the management of his finances, and awaited his return with an indictment such as had never before been presented to a reigning English sovereign.

The crucial conflict had begun between the King and John Pym—the conflict for the ultimate source of all authority, the power of the sword.

Early on the morning of November 23rd, 1641, while the Members of the House of Commons slept off the effects of their late night, the King and his following were once more upon the road, a distinguished, orderly, elegant cavalcade, moving towards London.

BOOK III CHAPTER VII REFERENCES

1. *Nicholas Correspondence*, p. 60; *C.S.P.D.*, 1641–3, p. 117.
2. *H.M.C. Portland MSS.*, III, p. 81; *C.S.P. Ven*, 1640–2, pp. 206, 222.
3. Guthry, p. 98; *C.S.P. Ven*, 1640–2, p. 205.
4. Balfour, II, pp. 40, 44.
5. Rushworth, III, i, pp. 382–3.
6. Balfour, III, pp. 46 ff.; Napier, I, 311–16; *Wigton Papers*, p. 429; *C.S.P.D.*, 1641–3, pp. 101, 110.
7. Balfour, III, p. 54; *C.S.P.D.*, 1641–3, p. 110.
8. *Ibid.*, p. 84.
9. Balfour, II, 56.
10. *C.S.P.D.*, 1641–3, p. 70.
11. Balfour, III, p. 57.
12. Carte, *Letters*, I, p. 4.
13. *Nicholas Correspondence*, p. 79.
14. *Hardwicke State Papers*, II, p. 299.
15. Carte, *Letters*, I, p. 7; Balfour, III, pp. 82–5.
16. The incident is described in Balfour, III, pp. 95 ff; also in *C.S.P.D.*, 1641–3, pp. 137–9, 143; *Hardwicke State Papers*, II, pp. 299–300. The evidence given by those involved is in *Hist. MSS. Commission*, IV, pp. 163–70. Few accounts tally and many mysteries remain unsolved; my own view is different from earlier versions because I am disposed to regard Montrose as wholly unconcerned in the

business. Clarendon accepted the contemporary story of his dominant part in the Incident and it was taken over by later historians until further examination of the facts and documents proved it substantially untenable. Gardiner, however, accepts Will Murray's evidence of Montrose's stream of letters to the King without difficulty and presumes some connection with the plot. Montrose's name is not mentioned in evidence until Crawford brought it in on October 23rd. Thereafter he figures ever more largely, especially in Murray's evidence. From this, and from a careful examination of the chronological sequence of events, it seemed to me reasonable to deduce that the Royalists were thankful to find a scapegoat.

17. *Nicholas Correspondence*, p. 92.
18. *C.S.P. Ven.*, 1640–2, pp. 213, 215.
19. *Ibid.*, p. 272. Newport later denied the words, but he could hardly have acknowledged them; they are typical enough of the man and the situation to sound plausible.
20. Carte, *Ormonde*, V, p. 254–5.
21. *H.M.C. Ormonde MSS.*, N.S. II, pp. 1–5; *C.S.P. Ireland*, pp. 342, 344.
22. D'Ewes, *Journal*, ed. Coates, Yale, 1942, p. 77.
23. *Nicholas Correspondence*, p. 97.
24. *C.S.P.D.*, 1641–3, pp. 141, 147; Rushworth, III, i, pp. 392, 394; *Harleian MSS.*, 6424; D'Ewes, ed. Coates, pp. 18, 21, 58, 60.
25. *C.S.P.D.*, 1641–3, pp. 162, 168; *C.S.P. Ven.*, 1640–2, pp. 241, 244.
26. D'Ewes, ed. Coates, pp. 94–5, 94 n.
27. *Nicholas Correspondence*, pp. 115, 124.
28. D'Ewes, ed. Coates, pp. 97–8.
29. *Nicholas Correspondence*, p. 117.
30. Balfour, III, pp. 139–40, 162–5.
31. John Taylor, *Swarm of Sectaries*, London, 1642.
32. D'Ewes, ed. Coates, pp. 169, 170.
33. *Ibid.*, pp. 155–7.
34. *H.M.C. Portland MSS.*, III, pp. 81–2; *H.M.C. X*, IV, pp. 433–4; *C.S.P.D.*, 1641–3, pp. 170, 270; *C.S.P. Ireland*, p. 345.
35. *Egmont MSS.*, I, i, p. 152; Carte, *Ormonde*, V, p. 259.
36. *C.S.P. Ireland*, pp. 345–6.
37. Rushworth, III, i, p. 400.
38. Bowle, *Mystery of Iniquity*, London, 1643, pp. 34–6.
39. *Nicholas Correspondence*, p. 127.
40. D'Ewes, ed. Coates, pp. 183–7.

BIBLIOGRAPHICAL NOTE

THE REFERENCES given at the end of each chapter indicate the sources from which information has been directly drawn. I have followed the usual practice of giving the full name and the date of publication of any book the first time it is cited and citing it thereafter by an abbreviated title, or simply by the name of the author.

The sources cited in the references represent only a proportion of the works consulted. The material for the seventeenth century is limitless and each further advance into it only serves to show the historian how much unexplored territory lies beyond. The literature of the epoch is moreover very fruitful in historical evidence and many of my impressions and deductions are as much the outcome of leisure reading, more especially in seventeenth-century poetry and drama, as of research proper.

I have made use of two important MS. sources which have recently become available to historians. The Strafford Papers, now housed by the courtesy of the owner Lord Fitzwilliam in the Sheffield Central Library, are of the greatest value for the period of King Charles's absolute rule. The other source of which I have made great use is the Breadalbane MSS. preserved at the General Register House, Edinburgh. I am particularly grateful to the Keeper of the Records for Scotland, Sir James Fergusson, for drawing my attention to the great importance of this collection for the early Covenanting period, as also to other relatively unexplored sources in the Register House, of which I hope to make use for succeeding volumes.

The Bankes MSS. which I have occasionally cited are the papers of Sir John Bankes recently deposited at the Bodleian Library, Oxford, by Lord Bledisloe.

Harleian MSS. 6424, to which one or two references are made, is a Diary of the House of Lords during the Long Parliament, compiled by an unidentified bishop.

I am indebted to more modern scholars than I can here name either for the impersonal assistance of their writings or for personal kindness and help, or for both. The exhaustive bibliography of the epoch compiled by Professor Godfrey Davies has been my bedside book for twelve years. For the economic background I owe much to the second volume of Dr. E. Lipson's incomparable *Economic History of England* and to his comprehensive and authoritative *History of the Woollen and Worsted Industries*. Professor John Nef's *Rise of the British Coal Industry* is—appositely—a mine of information on seventeenth-century methods and administration, as well as on the coal trade itself. Dr. Mildred Campbell's *English Yeoman* is rich in suggestions.

For Parliamentary affairs all workers in this field are indebted to Professor Notestein. I would like also to record my gratitude to Professor Willson Coates for much help and for kindly lending me his transcript of part of D'Ewes Journal. Professor J. H. Hexter's *Reign of King Pym* (Yale, 1942) is extremely interesting on the management of the Long Parliament. *The Members of the Long Parliament* (London, 1954) by D. H. Pennington and the late Douglas Brunton—which appeared while this book was in the press—bears out in detail the general conviction that I had myself formed when working many years ago on the seventeenth-century section of the *History of Parliament*—that political divisions in the House of Commons did not follow any clearly defined lines of class, property or social interest. Professor J. E. Neale's great work on the Elizabethan Parliaments does much to explain, to the student of the succeeding epoch, how Parliament came to be so firmly entrenched.

For the atmosphere, moral, social and religious, of the epoch, I owe many ideas and suggestions both to the writings and the conversation of Dr. David Mathew, of Dr. Margaret Judson author of *The Crisis of the Constitution* (Rutgers, 1949) of Miss

Mary Coate, Miss Gladys Scott Thomson, and of the late Dr. W. Schenk. I would like to thank Dr. Agnes Mure Mackenzie for helping me towards a more sympathetic understanding of the episcopal position in Scotland. Sir George Clark's great work on *The Seventeenth Century* first guided my footsteps into this incomparable epoch.

The twentieth-century controversy on the economic interpretation of history is almost as fierce as the religious controversy of the seventeenth. I have learnt much from the broad vision of Professor R. H. Tawney, from the writings of Mr. Hugh Trevor-Roper and Mr. Christopher Hill, if sometimes by the stimulus of disagreement.

Finally Dr. B. H. G. Wormald's *Clarendon: Politics, History, Religion* (Cambridge, 1951) is of fundamental importance not only for the better understanding of Clarendon's work and career but for the better understanding of the key epoch 1641-3. The political developments of that critical period are but faintly foreshadowed in the present volume; they will be treated at length in the succeeding one.

Any writer dealing with the first half of the seventeenth century must take up a position in relation to the late Samuel Rawson Gardiner. Gardiner wrote in an epoch when moral certainty was not only possible but natural; we live in an epoch when it is extremely difficult either to reach or to maintain certainty about moral issues in politics. This seems to me a much more fundamental difference between Gardiner and ourselves than anything brought about by changing fashions and emphasis in research, or changing historical judgments. For him the seventeenth century was a time of confusion and distress compared to his own. For us it cannot seem so. But we are not wiser because we are more disillusioned. Gardiner was certain he knew which side was right in the Civil War and was therefore on that side, although he tried to be fair to the characters of the men on the other side—which is more than can be said for writers of the neo-Royalist school. His prejudices and his point of view are so evident that any intelligent reader should be able to detect and make allowances for them. His scholarship, on those subjects which interested him and for which the sources were available, has not its equal to-day.

INDEX

THE POLISH PEASANT
IN EUROPE AND AMERICA

THE POLISH PEASANT

IN

EUROPE AND AMERICA

BY

WILLIAM I. THOMAS

AND

FLORIAN ZNANIECKI

DOVER PUBLICATIONS, INC.
NEW YORK • NEW YORK

This new Dover edition first published in 1958
is an unabridged and unaltered republication
of the second edition.

Manufactured in the United States of America

Dover Publications, Inc.
920 Broadway
New York 10, N. Y.

GRATEFULLY DEDICATED

TO

HELEN CULVER

PREFACE TO FIRST EDITION

Among the questions included in the as yet relatively unformulated field of social science (without reference to logical order) are: immigration; racial prejudice; cultural assimilation; the comparative mental and moral worth of races and nationalities; crime, alcoholism, vagabondage, and other forms of anti-social behavior; nationalism and internationalism; democracy and class-hierarchization; efficiency and happiness, particularly as functions of the relation of the individual to the social framework containing his activities; the rate of individualization possible without disorganization; the difference between unreflective social cohesion brought about by tradition, and reflective social co-operation brought about by rational selection of common ends and means; the introduction of new and desirable attitudes and values without recourse to the way of revolution; and, more generally, the determination of the most general and particular laws of social reality, preliminary to the introduction of a social control as satisfactory, or as increasingly satisfactory, as is our control of the material world, resulting from the study of the laws of physical reality.

Now we are ourselves primarily interested in these problems, but we are convinced of the necessity of approaching these and other social problems by isolating given societies and studying them, first, in the totality of their objective complexity, and then comparatively. The present study was not, in fact, undertaken exclusively or even primarily as an expression of interest in the Polish peasant (although our selection of this society was influenced by the question of immigration and by other considerations named below, pp. 74 ff.), but the Polish peasant was selected rather as a convenient object for the exemplification of a standpoint and method outlined in the methodological note forming the first pages of the present volume. The scope of our study will be best appreciated by having this fact in mind.

The work consists of five volumes, largely documentary in their character. Volumes I and II comprise a study of the organization of the peasant primary groups (family and community), and of the partial evolution of this system of organization under the influence of the new industrial system and of immigration to America and Germany. Volume III is the autobiography (with critical treatment) of an immigrant of peasant origin but belonging by occupation to the lower city class, and illustrates the tendency to disorganization of the individual under the conditions involved in a rapid transition from one type of social organization to another. Volume IV treats the dissolution of the primary group and the social and political reorganization and unification of peasant communities in Poland on the new ground of rational co-operation. Volume V is based on studies of the Polish immigrant in America and shows the degrees and forms of disorganization associated with a too-rapid and inadequately mediated individualization, with a sketch of the beginnings of reorganization.

We are unable to record here in a detailed way our recognition of the generous assistance we have received from many sources, but wish to express a particular appreciation to the following individuals, societies, periodicals, courts, etc.:

Professor Fr. Bujak, University of Cracow; Professor Stefan Surzycki, University of Cracow; Dr. S. Hupka, Cracow; Mr. Roman Dmowski, Warsaw; Mr. Władysław Grabski, Warsaw; Mr. Jerzy Gościcki, Warsaw; Priest Jan

Gralewski, Starawieś; Mr. A. Kulikowski, Vilna; Mrs. Eileen Znaniecka, Chicago.

The Emigrants' Protective Association of Warsaw (*Towarzystwo Opieki nad Wychodźcami*); the Cracow Academy of Sciences (*Akademia Umiejętności w Krakowie*); the Society for the Knowledge of the Country (*Towarzystwo Krajoznawcze*); the Society of United Women Land-Residents (*Towarzystwo Zjednoczonych Ziemianek*); *Amerika Institut* (Berlin: Dr. R. W. Drechsler, Dr. Karl O. Bertling).

Gazeta Świąteczna (Warsaw: Tadeusz Prószyński, Mrs. Burtnowska); *Zaranie* (Mr. M. M. Malinowski, Miss Stanisława Malinowska, Miss Irene Kosmowska); *Tygodnik Polski* (Warsaw: Gustaw Simon); *Naród* (Warsaw: Mr. A. S. Gołębiowski); *Zorza* (Mr. Stanisław Rutkowski, Mr. Stanisław Domański); *Poradnik Gospodarski* (Posen: Mr. K. Brownsford); *Dziennik Poznański* (Posen); *Zgoda* (Chicago); *Dziennik Chicagoski* (Chicago).

Chief Justice Harry Olson, the Municipal Court of Chicago; Judge Merritt W. Pinckney, Judge Victor P. Arnold, Judge Mary Bartelme, Chief Probation Officer Joel D. Hunter, and the probation officers and keepers of the probation records of the Juvenile Court of Cook County; the officials of the United Charities of Chicago, particularly of the Northwest District; the officials of the Legal Aid Society of Chicago; the keepers of the records of the Cook County Criminal Court; the keepers of the records of the Cook County Coroner's Office.

W. I. T.
F. Z.

PREFACE TO SECOND EDITION

This edition is not abridged in any way and remains unaltered except for the correction of a few textual errors, the repagination, the transposition of what was originally Volume III (the autobiography) to the end of Volume II, and the addition of an index.

W. I. T.
F. Z.

CONTENTS

VOLUME ONE

PART I: PRIMARY GROUP ORGANIZATION

CONTENTS

PART I

PRIMARY-GROUP ORGANIZATION

METHODOLOGICAL NOTE

One of the most significant features of social evolution is the growing importance which a conscious and rational technique tends to assume in social life. We are less and less ready to let any social processes go on without our active interference and we feel more and more dissatisfied with any active interference based upon a mere whim of an individual or a social body, or upon preconceived philosophical, religious, or moral generalizations.

The marvelous results attained by a rational technique in the sphere of material reality invite us to apply some analogous procedure to social reality. Our success in controlling nature gives us confidence that we shall eventually be able to control the social world in the same measure. Our actual inefficiency in this line is due, not to any fundamental limitation of our reason, but simply to the historical fact that the objective attitude toward social reality is a recent acquisition.

While our realization that nature can be controlled only by treating it as independent of any immediate act of our will or reason is four centuries old, our confidence in "legislation" and in "moral suasion" shows that this idea is not yet generally realized with regard to the social world. But the tendency to rational control is growing in this field also and constitutes at present an insistent demand on the social sciences.

This demand for a rational control results from the increasing rapidity of social evolution. The old forms of control were based upon the assumption of an essential stability of the whole social framework and were effective only in so far as this stability was real. In a stable social organization there is time enough to develop in a purely empirical way, through innumerable experiments and failures, approximately sufficient means of control with regard to the ordinary and frequent social phenomena, while the errors made in treating the uncommon and rare phenomena seldom affect social life in such a manner as to imperil the existence of the group; if they do, then the catastrophe is accepted as incomprehensible and inevitable. Thus—to take an example—the Polish peasant community has developed during many centuries complicated systems of beliefs and rules of behavior sufficient to control social life under ordinary circumstances, and the cohesion of the group and the persistence of its membership are strong enough to withstand passively the influence of eventual extraordinary occurrences, although there is no adequate method of meeting them. And if the crisis is too serious and the old unity or prosperity of the group breaks down, this is usually treated at first as a result of superior forces against which no fight is possible.

But when, owing to the breakdown of the isolation of the group and its contact with a more complex and fluid world, the social evolution becomes more rapid and the crises more frequent and varied, there is no time for the same gradual, empirical, unmethodical elaboration of approximately adequate means of control, and no crisis can be passively borne, but every one must be met in a more or less adequate way, for they are too various and frequent not to imperil social life unless controlled in time. The substitution of a conscious technique for a half-conscious routine has become, therefore, a social necessity, though it is evident that the development of this technique could be only gradual, and that even now we find in it many implicit or explicit ideas and methods corresponding to stages of human thought passed hundreds or even thousands of years ago.

The oldest but most persistent form of social technique is that of "ordering-and-forbidding"—that is, meeting a crisis by an arbitrary act of will decreeing the disappearance of the undesirable or the appearance of the desirable phenomena, and using arbitrary physical action to enforce the decree. This method corresponds exactly to the magical phase of natural technique. In both, the essential means of bringing a determined effect is more or less consciously thought to reside in the act of will itself by which the effect is decreed as desirable and of which the action is merely an indispensable vehicle or instrument; in both, the process by which the cause (act of will and physical action) is supposed to bring its effect to realization remains out of reach of investigation; in both, finally, if the result is not attained, some new act of will with new material accessories is introduced, instead of trying to find and remove the perturbing causes. A good instance of this in the social field is the typical legislative procedure of today.

It frequently happens both in magic and in the ordering-and-forbidding technique that the means by which the act of will is helped are really effective, and thus the result is attained, but, as the process of causation, being unknown, cannot be controlled, the success is always more or less accidental and dependent upon the stability of general conditions; when these are changed, the intended effect fails to appear, the subject is unable to account for the reasons of the failure and can only try by guesswork some other means. And even more frequent than this accidental success is the result that the action brings some effect, but not the desired one.

There is, indeed, one difference between the ordering-and-forbidding technique and magic. In social life an expressed act of will may be sometimes a real cause, when the person or body from which it emanates has a particular

authority in the eyes of those to whom the order or prohibition applies. But this does not change the nature of
the technique as such. The prestige of rulers, ecclesiastics,
and legislators was a condition making an act of will an
efficient cause under the old régimes, but it loses its value
in the modern partly or completely republican organizations.

A more effective technique, based upon "common sense"
and represented by "practical" sociology, has naturally
originated in those lines of social action in which there was
either no place for legislative measures or in which the *hoc
volo, sic jubeo* proved too evidently inefficient—in business,
in charity and philanthropy, in diplomacy, in personal
association, etc. Here, indeed, the act of will having been
recognized as inefficient in directing the causal process, real
causes are sought for every phenomenon, and an endeavor
is made to control the effects by acting upon the causes,
and, though it is often partly successful, many fallacies are
implicitly involved in this technique; it has still many
characters of a planless empiricism, trying to get at the
real cause by a rather haphazard selection of various
possibilities, directed only by a rough and popular reflection,
and its deficiencies have to be shown and removed if a new
and more efficient method of action is to be introduced.

The first of these fallacies has often been exposed. It
is the latent or manifest supposition that we know social
reality because we live in it, and that we can assume things
and relations as certain on the basis of our empirical
acquaintance with them. The attitude is here about the
same as in the ancient assumption that we know the physical
world because we live and act in it, and that therefore we
have the right of generalizing without a special and thorough
investigation, on the mere basis of "common sense." The
history of physical science gives us many good examples
of the results to which common sense can lead, such as the

geocentric system of astronomy and the mediaeval ideas about motion. And it is easy to show that not even the widest individual acquaintance with social reality, not even the most evident success of individual adaptation to this reality, can offer any serious guaranty of the validity of the common-sense generalizations.

Indeed, the individual's sphere of practical acquaintance with social reality, however vast it may be as compared with that of others, is always limited and constitutes only a small part of the whole complexity of social facts. It usually extends over only one society, often over only one class of this society; this we may call the exterior limitation. In addition there is an interior limitation, still more important, due to the fact that among all the experiences which the individual meets within the sphere of his social life a large, perhaps the larger, part is left unheeded, never becoming a basis of common-sense generalizations. This selection of experiences is the result of individual temperament on the one hand and of individual interest on the other. In any case, whether temperamental inclinations or practical considerations operate, the selection is subjective—that is, valid only for this particular individual in this particular social position—and thereby it is quite different from, and incommensurable with, the selection which a scientist would make in face of the same body of data from an objective, impersonal viewpoint.

Nor is the practical success of the individual within his sphere of activity a guaranty of his knowledge of the relations between the social phenomena which he is able to control. Of course there must be some objective validity in his schemes of social facts—otherwise he could not live in society—but the truth of these schemes is always only a rough approximation and is mixed with an enormous amount of error. When we assume that a successful adaptation of the individual to his environment is a proof that he knows this environment thoroughly, we forget that there are degrees of success, that the standard of success is to a large extent subjective, and that all the standards of success applied in human society may be—and really are—very low, because they make allowance for a very large number of partial failures, each of which denotes one or many errors. Two elements are found in varying proportions in every adaptation; one is the actual control exercised over the environment; the other is the claims which this control serves to satisfy. The adaptation may be perfect, either because of particularly successful and wide control or because of particularly limited claims. Whenever the control within the given range of claims proves insufficient, the individual or the group can either develop a better control or limit the claims. And, in fact, in every activity the second method, of adaptation by failures, plays a very important rôle. Thus the individual's knowledge of his environment can be considered as real only in the particular matters in which he does actually control it; his schemes can be true only in so far as they are perfectly, absolutely successful. And if we remember how much of practical success is due to mere chance and luck, even this limited number of truths becomes doubtful. Finally, the truths that stand the test of individual practice are always schemes of the concrete and singular, as are the situations in which the individual finds himself.

In this way the acquaintance with social data and the knowledge of social relations which we acquire in practice are always more or less subjective, limited both in number and in generality. Thence comes the well-known fact that the really valuable part of practical wisdom acquired by the individual during his life is incommunicable—cannot be stated in general terms; everyone must acquire it afresh by a kind of apprenticeship to life—that is, by learning to select experiences according to the demands of his own personality and to construct for his own use particular schemes of the concrete situations which he encounters. Thus, all the generalizations constituting the common-sense social theory and based on individual experience are both insignificant and subject to innumerable exceptions. A sociology that accepts them necessarily condemns itself to remain in the same methodological stage, and a practice based upon them must be as insecure and as full of failures as is the activity of every individual.

Whenever, now, this "practical" sociology makes an effort to get above the level of popular generalizations by the study of social reality instead of relying upon individual experience, it still preserves the same method as the individual in his personal reflection; investigation always goes on with an immediate reference to practical aims, and the standards of the desirable and undesirable are the ground upon which theoretic problems are approached. This is the second fallacy of the practical sociology, and the results of work from this standpoint are quite disproportionate to the enormous efforts that have recently been put forth in the collection and elaboration of materials preparatory to social reforms. The example of physical science and material technique should have shown long ago that only a scientific investigation, which is quite free from any dependence on practice, can become practically useful in its applications. Of course this does not mean that the scientist should not select for investigation problems whose solution has actual practical importance; the sociologist may study crime or war as the chemist studies dyestuffs. But from the method of the study itself all practical considerations must be excluded if we want the results to be valid. And this has not yet been realized by practical sociology.

The usual standpoint here is that of an explicit or implicit norm with which reality should comply. The norm may be intrinsic to the reality, as when it is presumed that the actually prevailing traditional or customary state of things is normal; or it may be extrinsic, as when moral, religious, or aesthetic standards are applied to social reality and the prevailing state of things is found in disaccord with the norm, and in so far abnormal. But this difference has no essential importance. In both cases the normal, agreeing with the norm, is supposed to be known either by practical acquaintance or by some particular kind of rational or irrational evidence; the problem is supposed to lie in the abnormal, the disharmony with the norm. In the first case the abnormal is the exceptional, in the second case it is the usual, while the normal constitutes an exception, but the general method of investigation remains the same.

There is no doubt that the application of norms to reality had a historical merit; investigation was provoked in this way and the "abnormal" became the first object of empirical studies. It is the morally indignant observer of vice and crime and the political idealist-reformer who start positive investigations. But as soon as the investigation is started both indignation and idealism should be put aside. For in treating a certain body of material as representing the normal, another body of material as standing for the abnormal, we introduce at once a division that is necessarily artificial; for if these terms have a meaning it can be determined only on the basis of investigation, and the criterion of normality must be such as to allow us to include in the normal, not only a certain determined stage of social life and a limited class of facts, but also the whole series of different stages through which social life passes, and the whole variety of social phenomena. The definition a priori of a group of facts that we are going to investigate as abnormal has two immediate consequences. First, our attention is turned to such facts as seem the most important practically, as being most conspicuously contrary to the norm and calling most insistently for reform. But the things that are practically important may be quite insignificant theoretically and, on the contrary, those which seem to have no importance from the practical point of view may be the source of important scientific discoveries. The scientific value of a fact depends on its connection with other facts, and in this connection the most commonplace facts are often precisely the most valuable ones, while a fact that strikes the imagination or stirs the moral feeling may be really either isolated or exceptional, or so simple as to involve hardly any problems. Again, by separating the abnormal from the normal we deprive ourselves of the opportunity of studying them in their connection with each other, while only in this connection can their study be fully fruitful. There is no break in continuity between the normal and the abnormal in concrete life that would permit any exact separation of the corresponding bodies of material, and the nature of the normal and the abnormal as determined by theoretic abstraction can be perfectly understood only with the help of comparison.

But there are other consequences of this fallacy. When the norm is not a result but a starting-point of the investigation, as it is in this case, every practical custom or habit, every moral, political, religious view, claims to be *the* norm and to treat as abnormal whatever does not agree with it. The result is harmful both in practice and in theory. In practice, as history shows and as we see at every moment, a social technique based upon pre-existing norms tends to suppress all the social energies which seem to act in a way contrary to the demands of the norm, and to ignore all the social energies not included in the sphere embraced by the norm. This limits still more the practical importance of the technique and often makes it simply harmful instead of useful. In theory, a sociology using norms as its basis deprives itself of the possibility of understanding and controlling any important facts of social evolution. Indeed, every social process of real importance always includes a change of the norms themselves, not alone of the activity embraced by the norms. Traditions and customs, morality and religion, undergo an evolution that is more and more rapid, and it is evident that a sociology proceeding on the assumption that a certain norm is valid and that whatever does not comply with it is abnormal finds itself absolutely helpless when it suddenly realizes that this norm has lost all social significance and that some other norm has appeared in its place. This helplessness is particularly striking in moments of great social crisis when the evolution of norms becomes exceptionally rapid. We notice it, for example, with particular vividness during the present war, when the whole individualistic system of norms elaborated during the last two centuries begins to retreat before a quite different system, which may be a state socialism or something quite new.

The third fallacy of the common-sense sociology is the implicit assumption that any group of social facts can be treated theoretically and practically in an arbitrary isolation from the rest of the life of the given society. This assumption is perhaps unconsciously drawn from the general form of social organization, in which the real isolation of certain groups of facts is a result of the demands of practical life. In any line of organized human activity only actions of a certain kind are used, and it is assumed that only such individuals will take part in this particular organization as are able and willing to perform these actions, and that they will not bring into this sphere of activity any tendencies that may destroy the organization. The factory and the army corps are typical examples of such organizations. The isolation of a group of facts from the rest of social life is here really and practically performed. But exactly in so far as such a system functions in a perfect manner there is no place at all for social science or social practice; the only thing required is a material division and organization of these isolated human actions. The task of social theory and social technique lies outside of these systems; it begins, for example, whenever external tendencies not harmonizing with the organized activities are introduced into the system, when the workmen in the factory start a strike or the soldiers of the army corps a mutiny. Then the isolation disappears; the system enters, through the individuals who are its members, into relation with the whole complexity of social life. And this lack of real isolation, which characterizes a system of organized activity only at moments of crisis, is a permanent feature of all the artificial, abstractly formed groups of facts such as "prostitution," "crime," "education," "war," etc. Every single fact included under these generalizations is connected by innumerable ties with an indefinite number of other facts belonging to various groups, and these relations give to every fact a different character. If we start to study these facts as a whole, without heeding their connection with the rest of the social world, we must necessarily come to quite arbitrary generalizations. If we start to act upon these facts in a uniform way simply because their abstract essence seems to be the same, we must necessarily produce quite different results, varying with the relations of every particular case to the rest of the social world. This does not mean that it is not possible to isolate such groups of facts for theoretic investigation or practical activity, but simply that the isolation must come, not a priori, but a posteriori, in the same way as the distinction between the normal and the abnormal. The facts must first be taken in connection with the whole to which they belong, and the question of a later isolation is a methodological problem which we shall treat in a later part of this note.

There are two other fallacies involved to a certain extent in social practice, although practical sociology has already repudiated them. The reason for their persistence in practice is that, even if the erroneousness of the old assumptions has been recognized, no new working ideas have been put in their place. These assumptions are: (1) that men react in the same way to the same influences regardless of their individual or social past, and that therefore it is possible to provoke identical behavior in various individuals by identical means; (2) that men develop spontaneously, without external influence, tendencies which enable them to profit in a full and uniform way from given conditions, and that therefore it is sufficient to create favorable or remove unfavorable conditions in order to give birth to or suppress given tendencies.

The assumption of identical reactions to identical influences is found in the most various lines of traditional social activity; the examples of legal practice and of education are sufficient to illustrate it. In the former all the assumptions about the "motives" of the behavior of the parties, all the rules and forms of investigation and examination, all the decisions of the courts, are essentially based upon this principle. Considerations of the variety of traditions, habits, temperaments, etc., enter only incidentally and secondarily, and usually in doubtful cases, by the initiative of the lawyers; they are the result of common-sense psychological observations, but find little if any place in the objective system of laws and rules. And where, as in the American juvenile courts, an attempt is made to base legal practice upon these considerations, all legal apparatus is properly waived, and the whole procedure rests upon the personal qualifications of the judge. In education the same principle is exhibited in the identity of curricula, and is even carried so far as to require identical work from students in connection with the courses they follow, instead of leaving to everyone as much field as possible for personal initiative. Here again the fallaciousness of the principle is corrected only by the efforts of those individual teachers who try to adapt their methods to the personalities of the pupils, using practical tact and individual acquaintance. But as yet no objective principles have been generally substituted for the traditional uniformity.

The assumption of the spontaneous development of tendencies if the material conditions are given is found in the exaggerated importance ascribed by social reformers to changes of material environment and in the easy conclusions drawn from material conditions on the mentality and character of individuals and groups. For example, it is assumed that good housing conditions will create a good family life, that the abolition of saloons will stop drinking, that the organization of a well-endowed institution is all that is necessary to make the public realize its value in practice. To be sure, material conditions do help or hinder to a large extent the development of corresponding lines of behavior, but only if the tendency is already there, for the way in which they will be used depends on the people who use them. The normal way of social action would be to develop the tendency and to create the condition simultaneously, and, if this is impossible, attention should be paid rather to the development of tendencies than to the change of the conditions, because a strong social tendency will always find its expression by modifying the conditions, while the contrary is not true. For example, a perfect family life may exist in a Polish peasant community in conditions which would probably be considered in America as a necessary breeding-place of crime and pauperism, while uncommonly favorable external conditions in the Polish aristocratic class do not hinder a decay of family life. In Southern France and Northern Italy there is less drunkenness with the saloon than in the prohibition states of America. In Russian Poland alone, without a Polish university and with only a private philosophical association, more than twice as much original philosophical literature has been published recently as in Russia with her eleven endowed universities. And innumerable examples could be cited from all departments of social life. But it is easy to understand that in the absence of a science of behavior social reformers pay more attention to the material conditions of the people than to the psychology of the people who live in these conditions; for the conditions are concrete and tangible, and we know how to grasp them and to conceive and realize almost perfect plans of material improvements, while in the absence of a science the reformer has no objective principles on which he can rely, and unconsciously tends to ascribe a preponderating importance to the material side of social life.

And these fallacies of the common-sense sociology are not always due to a lack of theoretic ability or of a serious scientific attitude on the part of the men who do the work. They are the unavoidable consequence of the necessity of meeting actual situations at once. Social life goes on without interruption and has to be controlled at every moment. The business man or politician, the educator or charity-worker, finds himself continually confronted by new social problems which he must solve, however imperfect and provisional he knows his solutions to be, for the stream of evolution does not wait for him. He must have immediate results, and it is a merit on his part if he tries to reconcile the claims of actuality with those of scientific objectivity, as far as they can be reconciled, and endeavors to understand the social reality as well as he can before acting. Certainly social life is improved by even such a control as common-sense sociology is able to give; certainly no effort should be discouraged, for the ultimate balance proves usually favorable. But in social activity, even more than in material activity, the common-sense method is the most wasteful method, and to replace it gradually by a more efficient one will be a good investment.

While, then, there is no doubt that actual situations must be handled immediately, we see that they cannot be solved adequately as long as theoretical reflection has their immediate solution in view. But there is evidently one issue from this dilemma, and it is the same as in material technique and physical science. We must be able to foresee future situations and prepare for them, and we must have in stock a large body of secure and objective knowledge capable of being applied to any situation, whether foreseen or unexpected. This means that we must have an empirical and exact social science ready for eventual application. And such a science can be constituted only if we treat it as an end in itself, not as a means to something else, and if we give it time and opportunity to develop along all the lines of investigation possible, even if we do not see what may be the eventual applications of one or another of its results. The example of physical science and its applications show that the only practically economical way of creating an efficient technique is to create a science independent of any technical limitations and then to take every one of its results and try where and in what way they can be practically applied. The contrary attitude, the refusal to recognize any science that does not work to solve practical problems, in addition to leading to that inefficiency of both science and practice which we have analyzed above, shows a curious narrowness of mental horizon. We do not know what the future science will be before it is constituted and what may be the applications of its discoveries before they are applied; we do not know what will be the future of society and what social problems may arise demanding solution. The only practically justifiable attitude toward science is absolute liberty and disinterested help.

Of course this does not mean that the actual social technique should wait until the science is constituted; such as it is, it is incomparably better than none. But, just as in material technique, as soon as a scientific discovery is at hand an effort should be made to find for it a practical application, and if it can be applied in some particular field a new technique should take the place of the old in this field.

But if no practical aims should be introduced beforehand into scientific investigation, social practice has, nevertheless, the right to demand from social theory that at least some of its results shall be applicable at once, and that the number and importance of such results shall continually increase. As one of the pragmatists has expressed it, practical life can and must give credit to science, but sooner or later science must pay her debts, and the longer the delay the greater the interest required. This demand of ultimate practical applicability is as important for science itself as for practice; it is a test, not only of the practical, but of the theoretical, value of the science. A science whose results can be applied proves thereby that it is really based upon experience, that it is able to grasp a great variety of problems, that its method is really exact—that it is valid. The test of applicability is a salutary responsibility which science must assume in her own interest.

If we attempt now to determine what should be the object-matter and the method of a social theory that would be able to satisfy the demands of modern social practice, it is evident that its main object should be the actual civilized society in its full development and with all its complexity of situations, for it is the control of the actual civilized society that is sought in most endeavors of rational practice. But here, as in every other science, a determined body of material assumes its full significance only if we can use comparison freely, in order to distinguish the essential from the accidental, the simple from the complex, the primary from the derived. And fortunately social life gives us favorable conditions for comparative studies, particularly at the present stage of evolution, in the coexistence of a certain number of civilized societies sufficiently alike in their fundamental cultural problems to make comparison possible, and differing sufficiently in their traditions, customs, and general national spirit to make comparison fruitful. And from the list of these civilized societies we should by no means exclude those non-white societies, like the Chinese, whose organization and attitudes differ profoundly from our own, but which interest us both as social experiments and as situations with which we have to reconcile our own future.

In contrast with this study of the various present civilized societies, the lines along which most of the purely scientific sociological work has been done up to the present —that is, ethnography of primitive societies and social history—have a secondary, though by no means a negligible, importance. Their relation to social practice is only mediate; they can help the practitioner to solve actual cultural problems only to the degree that they help the scientist to understand actual cultural life; they are auxiliary, and their own scientific value will increase with the

progress of the main sphere of studies.   In all the endeavors
to understand and interpret the past and the savage we
must use, consciously or not, our knowledge of our civilized
present life, which remains always a basis of comparison,
whether the past and the primitive are conceived as analogous with, or as different from, the present and the civilized.
The less objective and critical our knowledge of the present,
the more subjective and unmethodical is our interpretation
of the past and the primitive; unable to see the relative
and limited character of the culture within which we live,
we unconsciously bend every unfamiliar phenomenon to the
limitations of our own social personality.   A really objective
understanding of history and ethnography can therefore
be expected only as a result of a methodical knowledge of
present cultural societies.

Another point to be emphasized with regard to the
question of the object-matter of social theory is the necessity
of taking into account the whole life of a given society
instead of arbitrarily selecting and isolating beforehand
certain particular groups of facts.   We have seen already
that the contrary procedure constitutes one of the fallacies
of the common-sense sociology.   It is also a fallacy usually
committed by the observers of their own or of other societies—litterateurs, journalists, travelers, popular psycholo-
gists, etc.   In describing a given society they pick out the
most prominent situations, the most evident problems,
thinking to characterize thereby the life of the given group.
Still more harmful for the development of science is this
fallacy when used in the comparative sociology which
studies an institution, an idea, a myth, a legal or moral
norm, a form of art, etc., by simply comparing its content
in various societies without studying it in the whole meaning
which it has in a particular society and then comparing this
with the whole meaning which it has in the various societies.

We are all more or less guilty of this fault, but it pleases us to attribute it mainly to Herbert Spencer.

In order to avoid arbitrary limitations and subjective interpretations there are only two possible courses open. We can study monographically whole concrete societies with the total complexity of problems and situations which constitute their cultural life; or we can work on special social problems, following the problem in a certain limited number of concrete social groups and studying it in every group with regard to the particular form which it assumes under the influence of the conditions prevailing in this society, taking into account the complex meaning which a concrete cultural phenomenon has in a determined cultural environment. In studying the society we go from the whole social context to the problem, and in studying the problem we go from the problem to the whole social context. And in both types of work the only safe method is to start with the assumption that we know absolutely nothing about the group or the problem we are to investigate except such purely formal criteria as enable us to distinguish materials belonging to our sphere of interest from those which do not belong there. But this attitude of indiscriminate receptivity toward any concrete data should mark only the first stage of investigation—that of limiting the field. As soon as we become acquainted with the materials we begin to select them with the help of criteria which involve certain methodological generalizations and scientific hypotheses. This must be done, since the whole empirical concreteness cannot be introduced into science, cannot be described or explained. We have to limit ourselves to certain theoretically important data, but we must know how to distinguish the data which are important. And every further step of the investigation will bring with it new methodological problems—analysis of the complete concrete data into elements, systematization of these elements, definition of social facts, establishing of social laws. All these stages of scientific procedure must be exactly and carefully defined if social theory is to become a science conscious of its own methods and able to apply them with precision, as is the case with the more mature and advanced physical and biological sciences. And it is always the question of an ultimate practical applicability which, according to our previous discussion, will constitute the criterion—the only secure and intrinsic criterion—of a science.

Now there are two fundamental practical problems which have constituted the center of attention of reflective social practice in all times. These are (1) the problem of the dependence of the individual upon social organization and culture, and (2) the problem of the dependence of social organization and culture upon the individual. Practically, the first problem is expressed in the question, How shall we produce with the help of the existing social organization and culture the desirable mental and moral characteristics in the individuals constituting the social group? And the second problem means in practice, How shall we produce, with the help of the existing mental and moral characteristics of the individual members of the group, the desirable type of social organization and culture?[1]

If social theory is to become the basis of social technique and to solve these problems really, it is evident that it must include both kinds of data involved in them—namely, the objective cultural elements of social life and the subjective characteristics of the members of the social group—and that the two kinds of data must be taken as correlated.

---

[1] Of course a concrete practical task may include both problems, as when we attempt, by appealing to the existing attitudes, to establish educational institutions which will be so organized as to produce or generalize certain desirable attitudes.

For these data we shall use now and in the future the terms "social values" (or simply "values") and "attitudes."

By a social value we understand any datum having an empirical content accessible to the members of some social group and a meaning with regard to which it is or may be an object of activity. Thus, a foodstuff, an instrument, a coin, a piece of poetry, a university, a myth, a scientific theory, are social values. Each of them has a content that is sensual in the case of the foodstuff, the instrument, the coin; partly sensual, partly imaginary in the piece of poetry, whose content is constituted, not only by the written or spoken words, but also by the images which they evoke, and in the case of the university, whose content is the whole complex of men, buildings, material accessories, and images representing its activity; or, finally, only imaginary in the case of a mythical personality or a scientific theory. The meaning of these values becomes explicit when we take them in connection with human actions. The meaning of the foodstuff is its reference to its eventual consumption; that of an instrument, its reference to the work for which it is designed; that of a coin, the possibilities of buying and selling or the pleasures of spending which it involves; that of the piece of poetry, the sentimental and intellectual reactions which it arouses; that of the university, the social activities which it performs; that of the mythical personality, the cult of which it is the object and the actions of which it is supposed to be the author; that of the scientific theory, the possibilities of control of experience by idea or action that it permits. The social value is thus opposed to the natural thing, which has a content but, as a part of nature, has no meaning for human activity, is treated as "valueless"; when the natural thing assumes a meaning, it becomes thereby a social value. And naturally a social value may have many meanings, for it may refer to many different kinds of activity.

By attitude we understand a process of individual consciousness which determines real or possible activity of the individual in the social world. Thus, hunger that compels the consumption of the foodstuff; the workman's decision to use the tool; the tendency of the spendthrift to spend the coin; the poet's feelings and ideas expressed in the poem and the reader's sympathy and admiration; the needs which the institution tries to satisfy and the response it provokes; the fear and devotion manifested in the cult of the divinity; the interest in creating, understanding, or applying a scientific theory and the ways of thinking implied in it —all these are attitudes. The attitude is thus the individual counterpart of the social value; activity, in whatever form, is the bond between them. By its reference to activity and thereby to individual consciousness the value is distinguished from the natural thing. By its reference to activity and thereby to the social world the attitude is distinguished from the psychical state. In the examples quoted above we were obliged to use with reference to ideas and volitions words that have become terms of individual psychology by being abstracted from the objective social reality to which they apply, but originally they were designed to express attitudes, not psychological processes. A psychological process is an attitude treated as an object in itself, isolated by a reflective act of attention, and taken first of all in connection with other states of the same individual. An attitude is a psychological process treated as primarily manifested in its reference to the social world and taken first of all in connection with some social value. Individual psychology may later re-establish the connection between the psychological process and the objective reality which has been severed by reflection; it may study psychological processes as conditioned by the facts going on in the objective world. In the same way social theory may later connect various attitudes of an individual and determine his social character. But it is the original (usually unconsciously occupied) standpoints which determine at once the subsequent methods of these two sciences. The psychological process remains always fundamentally a *state of somebody;* the attitude remains always fundamentally an attitude *toward something.*

Taking this fundamental distinction of standpoint into account, we may continue to use for different classes of attitudes the same terms which individual psychology has used for psychological processes, since these terms constitute the common property of all reflection about conscious life. The exact meaning of all these terms from the standpoint of social theory must be established during the process of investigation, so that every term shall be defined in view of its application and its methodological validity tested in actual use. It would be therefore impractical to attempt to establish in advance the whole terminology of attitudes.

But when we say that the data of social theory are attitudes and values, this is not yet a sufficient determination of the object of this science, for the field thus defined would embrace the whole of human culture and include the object-matter of philology and economics, theory of art, theory of science, etc. A more exact definition is therefore necessary in order to distinguish social theory from these sciences, established long ago and having their own methods and their own aims.

This limitation of the field of social theory arises quite naturally from the necessity of choosing between attitudes or values as fundamental data—that is, as data whose characters will serve as a basis for scientific generalization. There are numerous values corresponding to every attitude, and numerous attitudes corresponding to every value; if, therefore, we compare different actions with regard to the attitudes manifested in them and form, for example, the general concept of the attitude of solidarity, this means that we have neglected the whole variety of values which are produced by these actions and which may be political or economical, religious or scientific, etc. If, on the contrary, we compare the values produced by different actions and form, for example, the general concepts of economic or religious values, this means that we have neglected the whole variety of attitudes which are manifested in these actions. Scientific generalization must always base itself upon such characters of its data as can be considered essential to its purposes, and the essential characters of human actions are completely different when we treat them from the standpoint of attitudes and when we are interested in them as values. There is therefore no possibility of giving to attitudes and values the same importance in a methodical scientific investigation; either attitudes must be subordinated to values or the contrary.

Now in all the sciences which deal with separate domains of human culture like language, art, science, economics, it is the attitudes which are subordinated to values—a standpoint which results necessarily from the very specialization of these sciences in the study of certain classes of cultural values. For a theorician of art or an economist an attitude is important and is taken into consideration only in so far as it manifests itself in changes introduced into the sphere of aesthetic or economic values, and is defined exclusively by these changes—that is, by the pre-existing complex of objective data upon which it acted and by the objective results of this activity. But unless there is a special class of cultural values which are not the object-matter of any other science, and unless there are special reasons for assigning this class to social theory—a problem which we shall discuss presently—the latter cannot take the same standpoint and subordinate attitudes to values, for this would mean a useless duplication of existing sciences. There may be, as we shall see, some doubts whether such groups of phenomena as religion or morality should be for special reasons included in the field of social theory or should constitute the object-matter of distinct sciences; but there is no doubt that language and literature, art and science, economics and technique, are already more or less adequately treated by the respective disciplines and, while needing perhaps some internal reforms, do not call for a supplementary treatment by sociology or "folk-psychology" (Wundt).

But there is also no doubt that a study of the social world from the opposite standpoint—that is, taking attitudes as special object-matter and subordinating values to them—is necessary, and that an exact methodology of such a study is lacking. Ethics, psychology, ethnology, sociology, have an interest in this field and each has occupied it in a fragmentary and unmethodical way. But in ethics the study of attitudes has been subordinated to the problem of ideal norms of behavior, not treated as an end in itself, and under these conditions no adequate method of a purely theoretic investigation can be worked out. Ethnology has contributed valuable data for the study of attitudes and values as found in the various social groups, particularly the "lower" races, but its work is mainly descriptive. Of the sociological method in the exact sense of the term we shall speak presently. Psychology is, however, the science which has been definitely identified with the study of consciousness, and the main question at this point is how far psychology has covered or is capable of covering the field of attitudes.

As we have indicated above, the attitude is not a psychological datum in the sense given to this term by individual

psychology, and this is true regardless of the differences between psychological schools. Concretely speaking, any
method of research which takes the individual as a distinct
entity and isolates him from his social environment, whether
in order to determine by introspective analysis the content
and form of his conscious processes, or in order to investigate
the organic facts accompanying these processes, or, finally,
in order to study experimentally his behavior as reaction to
certain stimuli, finds necessarily only psychical, physical, or
biological facts essentially and indissolubly connected with
the individual as a psychical, physical, or generally biological reality.   In order to reach scientific generalizations, such
a method must work on the assumption of the universal
permanence and identity of human nature as far as expressed
in these facts; that is, its fundamental concepts must be
such as to apply to all human beings, some of them even to
all conscious beings, and individual differences must be
reconstructed with the help of these concepts as variations
of the same fundamental background, due to varying inten-
sities, qualities, and combinations of essentially the same
universal processes.   Indeed, as every psychological fact is
a state of the individual as fundamental reality, the uniformity of these facts depends on the permanence and uniformity
of such individual realities.   The central field of individual
psychology is therefore constituted by the most elementary
conscious phenomena, which are the only ones that can be
adequately treated as essentially identical in all conscious
beings; phenomena which are limited to a certain number of
individuals either must be treated as complex and analyzed
into elementary and universal elements, or, if this cannot be
done, then their content, varying with the variation of social
milieu, must be omitted and only the *form* of their occurrence
reconstructed as presumably the same wherever and whenever they happen.

But psychology is not exclusively individual psychology. We find numerous monographs listed as psychological, but studying conscious phenomena which are not supposed to have their source in "human nature" in general, but in special social conditions, which can vary with the variation of these conditions and still be common to all individuals in the same conditions, and which are therefore treated, not as mere states of individual beings, but as self-sufficient data to be studied without any necessary assumptions about the psychological, physiological, or biological constitution of the individuals composing the group. To this sphere of psychology belong all investigations that concern conscious phenomena particular to races, nationalities, religious, political, professional groups, corresponding to special occupations and interests, provoked by special influences of a social milieu, developed by educational activities and legal measures, etc. The term "social psychology" has become current for this type of investigations. The distinction of social from individual psychology and the methodological unity of social psychology as a separate science have not been sufficiently discussed, but we shall attempt to show that social psychology is precisely the science of attitudes and that, while its methods are essentially different from the methods of individual psychology, its field is as wide as conscious life.

Indeed, every manifestation of conscious life, however simple or complex, general or particular, can be treated as an attitude, because every one involves a tendency to action, whether this action is a process of mechanical activity producing physical changes in the material world, or an attempt to influence the attitudes of others by speech and gesture, or a mental activity which does not at the given moment find a social expression, or even a mere process of sensual apperception. And all the objects of these actions can be treated as *social* values, for they all have some content which is or may be accessible to other individuals—even a personal "idea" can be communicated to others—and a meaning by which they may become the objects of the activity of others. And thus social psychology, when it undertakes to study the conscious phenomena found in a given social group, has no reasons a priori which force it to limit itself to a certain class of such phenomena to the exclusion of others; any manifestation of the conscious life of any member of the group is an attitude when taken in connection with the values which constitute the sphere of experience of this group, and this sphere includes data of the natural environment as well as artistic works or religious beliefs, technical products and economic relations as well as scientific theories. If, therefore, monographs in social psychology limit themselves to such special problems as, for example, the study of general conscious phenomena produced in a social group by certain physical, biological, economic, political influences, by common occupation, common religious beliefs, etc., the limitation may be justified by the social importance of these phenomena or even by only a particular interest of the author, but it is not necessitated by the nature of social psychology, which can study among the conscious phenomena occurring within the given social group, not only such as are peculiar to this group as a whole, but also, on the one hand, such as individual psychology assumes to be common to all conscious beings, and, on the other hand, such as may be peculiar to only one individual member of the group.

But of course not all the attitudes found in the conscious life of a social group have the same importance for the purposes of social psychology at a given moment, or even for its general purposes as a science of the social world. On the one hand, the task of every science in describing and generalizing the data is to reduce as far as possible the limitless complexity of experience to a limited number of concepts, and therefore those elements of reality are the most important which are most generally found in that part of experience which constitutes the object-matter of a science. And thus for social psychology the importance of an attitude is proportionate to the number and variety of actions in which this attitude is manifested. The more generally an attitude is shared by the members of the given social group and the greater the part which it plays in the life of every member, the stronger the interest which it provokes in the social psychologist, while attitudes which are either peculiar to a few members of the group or which manifest themselves only on rare occasions have as such a relatively secondary significance, but may become significant through some connection with more general and fundamental attitudes.[1]

On the other hand, scientific generalizations are productive and valuable only in so far as they help to discover certain relations between various classes of the generalized data and to establish a systematic classification by a logical subordination and co-ordination of concepts; a generalization which bears no relation to others is useless. Now, as the main body of the materials of social psychology is constituted by *cultural* attitudes, corresponding to variable and multiform *cultural* values, such elementary *natural* attitudes as correspond to stable and uniform *physical* conditions— for example, attitudes manifested in sensual perception or in the action of eating—in spite of their generality and practical importance for the human race, can be usefully investigated within the limits of this science only if a connection

[1] In connection, indeed, with the problems of both the creation and the destruction of social values, the most exceptional and divergent attitudes may prove the most important ones, because they may introduce a crisis and an element of disorder. And to the social theorist and technician the disorderly individual is of peculiar interest as a destroyer of values, as in the case of the anti-social individual, and as a creator of values, as in the case of the man of genius.

can be found between them and the cultural attitudes—if, for example, it can be shown that sensual perception or the organic attitude of disgust varies within certain limits with the variation of social conditions. As long as there is no possibility of an actual subordination or co-ordination as between the cultural and the natural attitudes, the natural attitudes have no immediate interest for social psychology, and their investigation remains a task of individual psychology. In other words, those conscious phenomena corresponding to the physical world can be introduced into social psychology only if it can be shown that they are not purely "natural"—independent of social conditions— but also in some measure cultural—influenced by social values.

Thus, the field of social psychology practically comprises first of all the attitudes which are more or less generally found among the members of a social group, have a real importance in the life-organization of the individuals who have developed them, and manifest themselves in social activities of these individuals. This field can be indefinitely enlarged in two directions if the concrete problems of social psychology demand it. It may include attitudes which are particular to certain members of the social group or appear in the group only on rare occasions, as soon as they acquire for some reason a social importance; thus, some personal sexual idiosyncrasy will interest social psychology only if it becomes an object of imitation or of indignation to other members of the group or if it helps to an understanding of more general sexual attitudes. On the other hand, the field of social psychology may be extended to such attitudes as manifest themselves with regard, not to the social, but to the physical, environment of the individual, as soon as they show themselves affected by social culture; for example, the perception of colors would become a socio-psychological problem if it proved to have evolved during the cultural evolution under the influence of decorative arts.

Social psychology has thus to perform the part of a general science of the subjective side of social culture which we have heretofore usually ascribed to individual psychology or to "psychology in general." It may claim to be *the* science of consciousness as manifested in culture, and its function is to render service, as a general auxiliary science, to all the special sciences dealing with various spheres of social values. This does not mean that social psychology can ever supplant individual psychology; the methods and standpoints of these two sciences are too different to permit either of them to fulfil the function of the other, and, if it were not for the traditional use of the term "psychology" for both types of research, it would be even advisable to emphasize this difference by a distinct terminology.

But when we study the life of a concrete social group we find a certain very important side of this life which social psychology cannot adequately take into account, which none of the special sciences of culture treats as its proper object-matter, and which during the last fifty years has constituted the central sphere of interest of the various researches called *sociology*. Among the attitudes prevailing within a group some express themselves only in individual actions—uniform or multiform, isolated or combined—but only in actions. But there are other attitudes—usually, though not always, the most general ones—which, besides expressing themselves directly, like the first, in actions, find also an indirect manifestation in more or less explicit and formal *rules* of behavior by which the group tends to maintain, to regulate, and to make more general and more frequent the corresponding type of actions among its members. These rules—customs and rituals, legal and educational norms, obligatory beliefs and aims, etc.—arouse a twofold

interest. We may treat them, like actions, as manifestations of attitudes, as indices showing that, since the group
demands a certain kind of actions, the attitude which is
supposed to manifest itself in these actions is shared by all
those who uphold the rule.   But, on the other hand, the very
existence of a rule shows that there are some, even if only
weak and isolated, attitudes which do not fully harmonize
with the one expressed in the rule, and that the group feels
the necessity of preventing these attitudes from passing into
action.   Precisely as far as the rule is consciously realized
as binding by individual members of the group from whom
it demands a certain adaptation, it has for every individual
a certain content and a certain meaning and is a value.
Furthermore, the action of an individual viewed by the
group, by another individual, or even by himself in reflection, with regard to this action's agreement or disagreement
with the rule, becomes also a value to which a certain attitude of appreciation or depreciation is attached in various
forms.   In this way rules and actions, taken, not with regard
to the attitudes *expressed* in them, but with regard to the
attitudes *provoked* by them, are quite analogous to any other
values—economic, artistic, scientific, religious, etc.   There
may be many various attitudes corresponding to a rule or
action as objects of individual reflection and appreciation,
and a certain attitude—such as, for example, the desire for
personal freedom or the feeling of social righteousness—may
bear positively or negatively upon many rules and actions,
varying from group to group and from individual to individual.   These values cannot, therefore, be the object-
matter of social psychology; they constitute a special group
of objective cultural data alongside the special domains of
other cultural sciences like economics, theory of art, philology, etc.   The rules of behavior, and the actions viewed
as conforming or not conforming with these rules, constitute

with regard to their objective significance a certain number of more or less connected and harmonious systems which can be generally called *social institutions,* and the totality of institutions found in a concrete social group constitutes the *social organization* of this group. And when studying the social organization as such we must subordinate attitudes to values as we do in other special cultural sciences; that is, attitudes count for us only as influencing and modifying rules of behavior and social institutions.

Sociology, as theory of social organization, is thus a special science of culture like economics or philology, and is in so far opposed to social psychology as the general science of the subjective side of culture. But at the same time it has this in common with social psychology: that the values which it studies draw all their reality, all their power to influence human life, from the social attitudes which are expressed or supposedly expressed in them; if the individual in his behavior is so largely determined by the rules prevailing in his social group, it is certainly due neither to the rationality of these rules nor to the physical consequences which their following or breaking may have, but to his consciousness that these rules represent attitudes of his group and to his realization of the *social* consequences which will ensue for him if he follows or breaks the rules. And therefore both social psychology and sociology can be embraced under the general term of social theory, as they are both concerned with the relation between the individual and the concrete social group, though their standpoints on this common ground are quite opposite, and though their fields are not equally wide, social psychology comprising the attitudes of the individual toward *all* cultural values of the given social group, while sociology can study only one type of these values—social rules—in their relation to individual attitudes.

We have seen that social psychology has a central field of interest including the most general and fundamental cultural attitudes found within concrete societies. In the same manner there is a certain domain which constitutes the methodological center of sociological interest. It includes those rules of behavior which concern more especially the active relations between individual members of the group and between each member and the group as a whole. It is these rules, indeed, manifested as mores, laws, and group-ideals and systematized in such institutions as the family, the tribe, the community, the free association, the state, etc., which constitute the central part of social organization and provide through this organization the essential conditions of the existence of a group as a distinct cultural entity and not a mere agglomeration of individuals; and hence all other rules which a given group may develop and treat as obligatory have a secondary sociological importance as compared with these. But this does not mean that sociology should not extend its field of investigation beyond this methodological center of interest. Every social group, particularly on lower stages of cultural evolution, is inclined to control all individual activities, not alone those which attain directly its fundamental institutions. Thus we find social regulations of economic, religious, scientific, artistic activities, even of technique and speech, and the break of these regulations is often treated as affecting the very existence of the group. And we must concede that, though the effect of these regulations on cultural productivity is often more than doubtful, they do contribute as long as they last to the unity of the group, while, on the other hand, the close association which has been formed between these rules and the fundamental social institutions without which the group cannot exist has often the consequence that cultural evolution which destroys the influence of these secondary regulations may actually disorganize the group. Precisely as far as these social rules concerning special cultural activities are in the above-determined way connected with the rules which bear on social relations they acquire an interest for sociology. Of course it can be determined only a posteriori how far the field of sociology should be extended beyond the investigation of fundamental social institutions, and the situation varies from group to group and from period to period. In all civilized societies some part of every cultural activity—religious, economic, scientific, artistic, etc.—is left outside of social regulation, and another, perhaps even larger, part, though still subjected to social rules, is no longer supposed to affect directly the existence or coherence of society and actually does not affect it. It is therefore a grave methodological error to attempt to include generally in the field of sociology such cultural domains as religion or economics on the ground that in certain social groups religious or economic norms are considered—and in some measure even really are—a part of social organization, for even there the respective values have a content which cannot be completely reduced to social rules of behavior, and their importance for social organization may be very small or even none in other societies or at other periods of evolution.

The fundamental distinction between social psychology and sociology appears clearly when we undertake the comparative study of special problems in various societies, for these problems naturally divide themselves into two classes. We may attempt to explain certain attitudes by tracing their origin and trying to determine the laws of their appearance under various social circumstances, as, for example, when we investigate sexual love or feeling of group-solidarity, bashfulness or showing off, the mystical emotion or the aesthetic amateur attitude, etc. Or we may attempt to give an explanation of social institutions and try to subject to laws their appearance under various socio-psychological conditions, as when our object-matter is marriage or family, criminal legislation or censorship of scientific opinions, militarism or parliamentarism, etc. But when we study monographically a concrete social group with all its fundamental attitudes and values, it is difficult to make a thoroughgoing separation of socio-psychological and sociological problems, for any concrete body of material contains both. Consequently, since the present work, and particularly its first two volumes, is precisely a monograph of a concrete social group, we cannot go into a detailed analysis of methodological questions concerning exclusively the socio-psychological or sociological investigation in particular, but must limit ourselves to such general methodological indications as concern both. Later, in connection with problems treated in subsequent volumes, more special methodological discussions may be necessary and will be introduced in their proper place.

The chief problems of modern science are problems of causal explanation. The determination and systematization of data is only the first step in scientific investigation. If a science wishes to lay the foundation of a technique, it must attempt to understand and to control the process of *becoming*. Social theory cannot avoid this task, and there is only one way of fulfilling it. Social becoming, like natural becoming, must be analyzed into a plurality of facts, each of which represents a succession of cause and effect. The idea of social theory is the analysis of the totality of social becoming into such causal processes and a systematization permitting us to understand the connections between these processes. No arguments a priori trying to demonstrate the impossibility of application of the principle of causality to conscious human life in general can or should halt social theory in tending to this idea, whatever difficulties there may be in the way, because as a matter of fact we continually do apply the principle of causality to the social world in our activity and in our thought, and we shall always do this as long as we try to control social becoming in any form. So, instead of fruitlessly discussing the justification of this application in the abstract, social theory must simply strive to make it more methodical and perfect in the concrete—by the actual process of investigation.

But if the general philosophical problem of free will and determinism is negligible, the particular problem of the best possible method of causal explanation is very real. Indeed, its solution is the fundamental and inevitable introductory task of a science which, like social theory, is still in the period of formation. The great and most usual illusion of the scientist is that he simply takes the facts as they are, without any methodological prepossessions, and gets his explanation entirely a posteriori from pure experience. A fact by itself is already an abstraction; we isolate a certain limited aspect of the concrete process of becoming, rejecting, at least provisionally, all its indefinite complexity. The question is only whether we perform this abstraction methodically or not, whether we know what and why we accept and reject, or simply take uncritically the old abstractions of "common sense." If we want to reach scientific explanations, we must keep in mind that our facts must be determined in such a way as to permit of their subordination to general laws. A fact which cannot be treated as a manifestation of one or several laws is inexplicable causally. When, for example, the historian speaks of the causes of the present war, he must assume that the war is a combination of the effects of many causes, each of which may repeat itself many times in history and must have always the same effect, although such a combination of these causes as has produced the present war may never happen again. And only if social theory succeeds in determining causal laws can it become a basis of social technique, for technique demands the possibility of foreseeing and calculating the effects of given causes, and this demand is realizable only if we know that certain causes will always and everywhere produce certain effects.

Now, the chief error of both social practice and social theory has been that they determined, consciously or unconsciously, social facts in a way which excluded in advance the possibility of their subordination to any laws. The implicit or explicit assumption was that a social fact is composed of two elements, a cause which is either a social phenomenon or an individual act, and an effect which is either an individual act or a social phenomenon. Following uncritically the example of the physical sciences, which always tend to find the one determined phenomenon which is the necessary and sufficient condition of another phenomenon, social theory and social practice have forgotten to take into account one essential difference between physical and social reality, which is that, while the effect of a physical phenomenon depends exclusively on the objective nature of this phenomenon and can be calculated on the ground of the latter's empirical content, the effect of a social phenomenon depends in addition on the subjective standpoint taken by the individual or the group toward this phenomenon and can be calculated only if we know, not only the objective content of the assumed cause, but also the meaning which it has at the given moment for the given conscious beings. This simple consideration should have shown to the social theorist or technician that a social cause cannot be simple, like a physical cause, but is compound, and must include both an objective and a subjective element, a value *and* an attitude. Otherwise the effect will appear accidental and incalculable, because we shall have to search in every particular case for the reasons why this particular individual or this particular society reacted to the given phenomenon in this way and not in any other way.

In fact, a social value, acting upon individual members of the group, produces a more or less different effect on every one of them; even when acting upon the same individual at various moments it does not influence him uniformly. The influence of a work of art is a typical example. And such uniformities as exist here are quite irrelevant, for they are not absolute. If we once suppose that a social phenomenon is the cause—which means a necessary and sufficient cause, for there are no "insufficient" causes—of an individual reaction, then our statement of this causal dependence has the logical claim of being a scientific law from which there can be no exceptions; that is, every seeming exception must be explained by the action of some other cause, an action whose formulation becomes another scientific law. But to explain why in a concrete case a work of art or a legal prescription which, according to our supposed law, should provoke in the individual a certain reaction A provokes instead a reaction B, we should have to investigate the whole past of this individual and repeat this investigation in every case, with regard to every individual whose reaction is not A, without hoping ever to subordinate those exceptions to a new law, for the life-history of every individual is different. Consequently social theory tries to avoid this methodological absurdity by closing its eyes to the problem itself. It is either satisfied with statements of causal influences which hold true "on the average," "in the majority of cases"—a flat self-contradiction, for, if something *is a cause*, it must have by its very definition, always and necessarily *the same effect*, otherwise it is not a cause at all. Or it tries to analyze phenomena acting upon individuals and individual reactions to them into simpler elements, hoping thus to find simple facts, while the trouble is not with the complexity of data, but with the complexity of the context on which these data act or in which they are embodied—that is, of the human personality. Thus, as far as the complexity of social data is concerned, the principle of gravitation and the smile of Mona Lisa are simple in their objective content, while their influence on human attitudes has been indefinitely varied; the complex system of a graphomaniac or the elaborate picture of a talentless and skilless man provokes much more uniform reactions. And, on the individual side, the simple attitude of anger can be provoked by an indefinite variety of social phenomena, while the very complicated attitude of militant patriotism appears usually only in very definite social conditions.

But more than this. Far from obviating the problem of individual variations, such uniformities of reaction to social influences as can be found constitute a problem in themselves. For with the exception of the elementary reactions to purely physical stimuli, which may be treated as identical because of the identity of "human nature" and as such belong to individual psychology, all uniformities with which social psychology has to deal are the product of social conditions. If the members of a certain group react in an identical way to certain values, it is because they have been socially trained to react thus, because the traditional rules of behavior predominant in the given group impose upon every member certain ways of defining and solving the practical situations which he meets in his life. But the very success of this social training, the very fact that individual members do accept such definitions and act in accordance with them, is no less a problem than the opposite fact—the frequent insuccess of the training, the growing assertion of the personality, the growing variation of reaction to social rules, the search for personal definitions—which characterizes civilized societies. And thus, even if we find that all the members of a social group react in the same way to a certain value, still we cannot assume that this value alone is the cause of this reaction, for the latter is also conditioned by the uniformity of attitudes prevailing in the group; and this uniformity itself cannot be taken as granted and omitted—as we omit the uniformity of environing conditions in a physical fact—because it is the particular effect of certain social rules acting upon the members of the group who, because of certain predispositions, have accepted these rules, and this effect may be at any moment counterbalanced by the action of different causes, and is in fact counterbalanced more and more frequently with the progress of civilization.

In short, when social theory assumes that a certain social value is of itself the cause of a certain individual reaction, it is then forced to ask: "But why did this value produce this particular effect when acting on this particular individual or group at this particular moment?" Certainly no scientific answer to such a question is possible, since in order to explain this "why" we should have to know the whole past of the individual, of the society, and of the universe.

Analogous methodological difficulties arise when social theory attempts to explain a change in social organization as a result of the activity of the members of the group. If we treat individual activity as a *cause* of social changes, every change appears as inexplicable, particularly when it is "original," presents many new features. Necessarily this point is one of degree, for every product of individual activity is in a sense a new value and in so far original as it has not existed before this activity, but in certain cases the importance of the change brought by the individual makes its incalculable and inexplicable character particularly striking. We have therefore almost despaired of extending consistently the principle of causality to the activities of "great men," while it still seems to us that we do understand the everyday productive activity of the average human individual or of the "masses." From the methodological standpoint, however, it is neither more nor less difficult to explain the greatest changes brought into the social world by a Charles the Great, a Napoleon, a Marx, or a Bismarck than to explain a small change brought by a peasant who starts a lawsuit against his relatives or buys a piece of land to increase his farm. The work of the great man, like that of the ordinary man, is the result of his tendency to modify the existing conditions, of his attitude toward his social environment which makes him reject certain existing values and produce certain new values. The difference is in the values which are the object of the activity, in the nature, importance, complexity, of the social problems put and solved. The change in social organization produced by a great man may be thus equivalent to an accumulation of small changes brought by millions of ordinary men, but the idea that a creative process is more explicable when it lasts for several generations than when it is performed in a few months or days, or that by dividing a creative process into a million small parts we destroy its irrationality, is equivalent to the conception that by a proper combination of mechanical elements in a machine we can produce a *perpetuum mobile*.

The simple and well-known fact is that the social results of individual activity depend, not only on the action itself, but also on the social conditions in which it is performed; and therefore the cause of a social change must include both individual and social elements. By ignoring this, social theory faces an infinite task whenever it wants to explain the simplest social change. For the same action in diffcrent social conditions produces quite different results. It is true that if social conditions are sufficiently stable the results of certain individual actions are more or less determinable, at least in a sufficient majority of cases to permit an approximate practical calculation. We know that the result of the activity of a factory-workman will be a certain technical product, that the result of the peasant's starting a lawsuit against a member of his family will be a dissolution of family bonds between him and this member, that the result of a judge's activity in a criminal case will be the condemnation and incarceration of the offender if he is convicted. But all this holds true only if social conditions remain stable. In case of a strike i the factory, the workman will not be allowed to finish his product; assuming that the idea of family solidarity has ceased to prevail in a peasant group, the lawsuit will not provoke moral indignation; if the action upon which the judge has to pronounce this verdict ceases to be treated as a crime because of a change of political conditions or of public opinion, the offender, even if convicted, will be set free. A method which permits us to determine only cases of stereotyped activity and leaves us helpless in face of changed conditions is not a scientific method at all, and becomes even less and less practically useful with the continual increase of fluidity in modern social life.

Moreover, social theory forgets also that the uniformity of results of certain actions is itself a problem and demands explanation exactly as much as do the variations. For the stability of social conditions upon which the uniformity of results of individual activity depends is itself a product of former activities, not an original natural status which might be assumed as granted. Both its character and its degree vary from group to group and from epoch to epoch. A certain action may have indeed determined and calculable effects in a certain society and at a certain period, but will have completely different effects in other societies and at other periods.

And thus social theory is again confronted by a scientifically absurd question. Assuming that individual activity in itself is the cause of social effects, it must then ask: "Why does a certain action produce this particular effect at this particular moment in this particular society?" The answer to this question would demand a complete explanation of the whole status of the given society at the given moment, and thus force us to investigate the entire past of the universe.

The fundamental methodological principle of both social psychology and sociology—the principle without which they can never reach scientific explanation—is therefore the following one:

The cause of a social or individual phenomenon is never another social or individual phenomenon alone, but always a combination of a social and an individual phenomenon.

Or, in more exact terms:

The cause of a value or of an attitude is never an attitude or a value alone, but always a combination of an attitude and a value.[1]

It is only by the application of this principle that we can remove the difficulties with which social theory and social practice have struggled. If we wish to explain the appearance of a new attitude—whether in one individual or in a whole group—we know that this attitude appeared as a consequence of the influence of a social value upon the individual or the group, but we know also that this influence itself

[1] It may be objected that we have neglected to criticize the conception according to which the cause of a social phenomenon is to be sought, not in an individual, but exclusively in another social phenomenon (Durkheim). But a criticism of this conception is implied in the previous discussion of the data of social theory. As these data are both values and attitudes, a fact must include both, and a succession of values alone cannot constitute a fact. Of course much depends also on what we call a "social" phenomenon. An attitude may be treated as a social phenomenon as opposed to the "state of consciousness" of individual psychology; but it is individual, even if common to all members of a group, when we oppose it to a value.

would have been impossible unless there had been some pre-existing attitude, some wish, emotional habit, or intellectual tendency, to which this value has in some way appealed, favoring it, contradicting it, giving it a new direction, or stabilizing its hesitating expressions. Our problem is therefore to find both the value and the pre-existing attitude upon which it has acted and get in their combination the necessary and sufficient cause of the new attitude. We shall not be forced then to ask: "Why did this value provoke in this case such a reaction?" because the answer will be included in the fact—in the pre-existing attitude to which this value appealed. Our fact will bear its explanation in itself, just as the physical fact of the movement of an elastic body B when struck by another elastic moving body A bears its explanation in itself. We may, if we wish, ask for a more detailed explanation, not only of the appearance of the new attitude, but also for certain specific characters of this attitude, in the same way as we may ask for an explanation, not only of the movement of the body B in general, but also of the rapidity and direction of this movement; but the problem always remains limited, and the explanation is within the fact, in the character of the pre-existing attitude and of the influencing value, or in the masses of the bodies A and B and the rapidity and direction of their movements previous to their meeting. We can indeed pass from the given fact to the new one—ask, for example, "How did it happen that this attitude to which the value appealed was there?" or, "How did it happen that the body A moved toward B until they met?" But this question again will find its limited and definite answer if we search in the same way for the cause of the pre-existing attitude in some other attitude and value, or of the movement in some other movement.

Let us take some examples from the following volumes. Two individuals, under the influence of a tyrannical behavior in their fathers, develop completely different attitudes. One shows submission, the other secret revolt and resentment. If the father's tyranny is supposed to be the cause of these opposite attitudes, we must know the whole character of these individuals and their whole past in order to explain the difference of effect. But if we realize that the tyranny is not the sole cause of both facts, but only a common element which enters into the composition of two different causes, our simple task will be to find the other elements of these causes. We can find them, if our materials are sufficient, in certain persisting attitudes of these individuals as expressed in words or actions. We form hypotheses which acquire more and more certainty as we compare many similar cases. We thus reach the conclusion that the other element of the cause is, in the first case, the attitude of familial solidarity, in the second case, the individualistic tendency to assert one's own personal desires. We have thus two completely different facts, and we do not need to search farther. The difference of effects is obviously explained by the difference of causes and is necessarily what it is. The cause of the attitude of submission is the attitude of familial solidarity plus the tyranny of the father; the cause of the attitude of revolt is the tendency to self-assertion plus the tyranny of the father.

As another example—this time a mass-phenomenon—we take the case of the Polish peasants from certain western communities who go to Germany for season-work and show there uniformly a desire to do as much piece-work as possible and work as hard as they can in order to increase their earnings, while peasants of these same communities and even the same individual peasants when they stay at home and work during the season on the Polish estates accept only day-work and refuse piece-work under the most ridiculous pretexts. We should be inclined to ascribe this difference of attitudes to the difference of conditions, and in fact both the peasants and the Polish estate-owners give this explanation, though they differ as to the nature of causes. The peasants say that the conditions of piece-work are less favorable in Poland than in Germany; the estate-owners claim that the peasants in Germany are more laborious because intimidated by the despotism of German estate-owners and farm-managers. Both contentions are wrong. The conditions of piece-work as compared with day-work are certainly not less favorable in Poland than in Germany, and the peasants are more laborious in Germany on their own account, regardless of the very real despotism which they find there. To be sure, the conditions are different; the whole social environment differs. The environment, however, is not the sufficient cause of the attitudes. The point is that the peasant who goes to Germany is led there by the desire of economic advance, and this attitude predominates during the whole period of season-work, not on account of the conditions themselves, but through the feeling of being in definite new conditions, and produces the desire to earn more by piece-work. On the contrary, the peasant who stays at home preserves for the time being his old attitude toward work as a "necessary evil," and this attitude, under the influence of traditional ideas about the conditions of work on an estate, produces the unwillingness to accept piece-work. Here both components of the cause—pre-existing attitude and value-idea—differ, and evidently the effects must be different.

If now we have to explain the appearance of a social value, we know that this value is a product of the activity of an individual or a number of individuals, and in so far dependent on the attitude of which this activity is the expression. But we know also that this result is inexplicable unless we take into consideration the value (or complex of values) which was the starting-point and the social material of activity and which has conditioned the result as much as did the attitude itself. The new value is the result of the solution of a problem set by the pre-existing value and the active attitude together; it is the common effect of both of them. The product of an activity—even of a mechanical activity, such as a manufactured thing—acquires its full social reality only when it enters into social life, becomes the object of the attitudes of the group, is socially valued. And we can understand this meaning, which is an essential part of the effect, only if we know what was the social situation when the activity started, what was the social value upon which the individual (or individuals) specially acted and which might have been quite different from the one upon which he intended to act and imagined that he acted. If we once introduce this pre-existing value into the fact as the necessary component of the cause, the effect—the new value—will be completely explicable and we shall not be forced to ask: "Why is it that this activity has brought in these conditions this particular effect instead of the effect it was intended to bring?" any more than physics is forced to ask: "Why is it that an elastic body struck by another elastic body changes the direction and rapidity of its movement instead of changing merely its rapidity or merely its direction?"

To take some further examples, the American social institutions try, by a continuous supervision and interference, to develop a strong marriage-group organization among the Polish immigrants who begin to show certain signs of decay of family life or among whom the relation between husband and wife and children does not come up to the American standards in certain respects. The results of this activity are quite baffling. Far from being constructive of new values, the interference proves rather destructive in a great majority of cases, in spite of the best efforts of the most intelligent social workers. In a few cases it does not seem to affect much the existing state of things; sometimes, indeed, though very seldom, it does bring good results. This very variation makes the problem still more complicated and difficult. To explain the effects, the social workers try to take into consideration the whole life-history and character of the individuals with whom they deal, but without progressing much in their efforts. The whole misunderstanding comes from the lack of realization that the Polish immigrants here, though scattered and losing most of their social coherence, are still not entirely devoid of this coherence and constitute vague and changing but as yet, in some measure, real communities, and that these communities have brought from the old country several social institutions, among which the most important is the family institution. In new conditions these institutions gradually dissolve, and we shall study this process in later volumes. But the dissolution is not sudden or universal, and thus the American social worker in his activity meets, without realizing it, a set of social values which are completely strange to him, and which his activity directly affects without his knowing it. As far as the family organization is concerned, any interference of external powers—political or social authorities—must act dissolvingly upon it, because it affects the fundamental principle of the family as a social institution—the principle of solidarity. An individual who accepts external interference in his favor against a family member sins against this principle, and a break of family relations must be thus the natural consequence of the well-intentioned but insufficiently enlightened external activities. The effect is brought, not by these activities alone, but by the combination of these activities and the pre-existing peasant family organization. Of course, if the family organization is different—if, for example, in a given case the marriage-group has already taken the place of the large family—the effect will be different because the total cause is different. Or, if instead of the protective and for the peasant incomprehensible attitude of the social worker or court officer a different attitude is brought into action—if, for example, the family is surrounded by a strong and solidary community of equals who, from the standpoint of communal solidarity, interfere with family relations, just as they do in the old country—again the effect will be different because the other component of the cause—the attitude as expressed in action—is no longer the same.

Another interesting example is the result of the national persecution of the Poles in Prussia, the aim of which was to destroy Polish national cohesion. Following all the efforts which the powerful Prussian state could bring against the Poles, national cohesion has in a very large measure increased, and the national organization has included such elements as were before the persecution quite indifferent to national problems—the majority of the peasants and of the lower city classes. The Prussian government had not realized the existence and strength of the communal solidarity principle in the lower classes of Polish society, and by attacking certain vital interests of these classes, religious and economic, it contributed more than the positive efforts of the intelligent Polish class could have done to the development of this principle and to its extension over the whole Polish society in Posen, Silesia, and West Prussia.

These examples of the result of the violation of our methodological rule could be multiplied indefinitely from the field of social reform. The common tendency of reformers is to construct a rational scheme of the social institution they wish to see produced or abolished, and then to formulate an ideal plan of social activities which would perhaps lead to a realization of their scheme if social life were merely a sum of individual actions, every one of them starting afresh without any regard for tradition, every one having its source exclusively in the psychological nature of the individual and capable of being completely directed, by well-selected motives, toward definite social aims. But as social reality contains, not only individual acts, but also social institutions, not only attitudes, but also values fixed by tradition and conditioning the attitudes, these values co-operate in the production of the final effect quite independently, and often in spite of the intentions of the social reformer. Thus the socialist, if he presupposes that a solidary and well-directed action of the masses will realize the scheme of a perfect socialistic organization, ignores completely the influence of the whole existing social organization which will co-operate with the revolutionary attitudes of the masses in producing the new organization, and this, not only because of the opposition of those who will hold to the traditional values, but also because many of those values, as socially sanctioned rules for defining situations, will continue to condition many attitudes of the masses themselves and will thus be an integral part of the causes of the final effect.

Of course we do not assert that the proper way of formulating social facts is never used by social theory or reflective social practice. On the contrary, we very frequently find it applied in the study of particular cases, and it is naïvely used in everyday business and personal relations. We use it in all cases involving argument and persuasion. The business man, the shopkeeper, and the politician use it very subtly. We have been compelled in the case of our juvenile delinquents to allow the judges to waive the formal and incorrect conception of social facts and to substitute in the case of the child the proper formula. But the point is that this formula has never been applied with any consistency and systematic development, while the wrong formula has been used very thoroughly and has led to such imposing systems as, in reflective practice, the whole enormous and continually growing complexity of positive law, and in social theory to the more recent and limited, but rapidly growing, accumulation of works on political science, philosophy of law, ethics, and sociology. At every step we try to enforce certain attitudes upon other individuals without stopping to consider what are their dominant attitudes in general or their prevailing attitudes at the given moment; at every step we try to produce certain social values without taking into account the values which are already there and upon which the result of our efforts will depend as much as upon our intention and persistence.

The chief source of this great methodological mistake, whose various consequences we have shown in the first part of this note, lay probably in the fact that social theory and reflective practice started with problems of political and legal organization. Having thus to deal with the relatively uniform attitudes and relatively permanent conditions which characterized civilized societies several thousand years ago, and relying besides upon physical force as a supposedly infallible instrument for the production of social uniformity and stability whenever the desirable attitudes were absent, social theory and reflective practice have been capable of holding and of developing, without remarking its absurdity, a standpoint which would be scientifically and technically justifiable only if human attitudes were absolutely and universally uniform and social conditions absolutely and universally stable.

A systematic application and development of the methodological rules stated above would necessarily lead in a completely different direction. Its final result would not be a system of definitions, like law and special parts of political science, nor a system of the philosophical determination of the essence of certain data, like philosophy of law, the general part of political science, ethics, and many sociological works, nor a general outline of social evolution, like the sociology of the Spencerian school or the philosophies of history, but a system of laws of social becoming, in which definitions, philosophical determinations of essence, and outlines of evolution would play the same part as they do in physical science—that is, would constitute either instruments helping to analyze reality and to find laws, or conclusions helping to understand the general scientific meaning and the connection of laws.

It is evident that such a result can be attained only by a long and persistent co-operation of social theoricians. It took almost four centuries to constitute physical science in its present form, and, though the work of the social scientist is incalculably facilitated by the long training in scientific thinking in general which has been acquired by mankind since the period of the renaissance, it is on the other hand made more difficult by certain characters of the social world as compared with the natural world. We do not include among these difficulties the complexity of the social world which has been so often and unreflectively emphasized. Complexity is a relative characteristic; it depends on the method and the purpose of analysis. Neither the social nor the natural world presents any ready and absolutely simple elements, and in this sense they are both equally complex, because they are both infinitely complex. But this complexity is a metaphysical, not a scientific, problem. In science we treat any datum as a simple element if it behaves as such in all the combinations in which we find it, and any fact is a simple fact which can indefinitely repeat itself— that is, in which the relation between cause and effect can be assumed to be permanent and necessary. And in this respect it is still a problem whether the social world will not prove much less complex than the natural world if only we analyze its data and determine its facts by proper methods. The prepossession of complexity is due to the naturalistic way of treating the social reality. If it is maintained that the social world has to be treated as an expression or a product of the psychological, physiological, or biological nature of human beings, then, of course, it appears as incomparably more complex than the natural world, because to the already inexhaustibly complex conscious human organism as a part of nature is added the fact that in a social group there are numerous and various human beings interacting in the most various ways. But if we study the social world, without any naturalistic prepossessions, simply as a plurality of specific data, causally interconnected in a process of becoming, the question of complexity is no more baffling for social theory, and may even prove less so, than it is for physical science.

The search for laws does not actually present any special difficulties if our facts have been adequately determined. When we have found that a certain effect is produced by a certain cause, the formulation of this causal dependence has in itself the character of a law; that is, we assume that whenever this cause repeats itself the effect will necessarily follow. The further need is to explain apparent exceptions. But this need of explanation, which is the stumbling-block of a theory that has defined its facts inadequately, becomes, on the contrary, a factor of progress when the proper method is employed. For when we know that a certain cause can have only one determined effect, when we have assumed, for example, that the attitude A plus the value B is the cause of the attitude C, then if the presumed cause $A+B$ is there and the expected effect C does not appear, this means either that we have been mistaken in assuming that $A+B$ was the cause of C, or that the action of $A+B$ was interfered with by the action of some other cause $A+Y$ or $X+B$ or $X+Y$. In the first case the exception gives us the possibility of correcting our error; in the second case it permits us to extend our knowledge by finding a new causal connection, by determining the partly or totally unknown cause $A+Y$ or $X+B$ or $X+Y$ which has interfered with the action of our known case $A+B$ and brought a complex effect $D=C+Z$, instead of the expected C. And thus the exception from a law becomes the starting-point for the discovery of a new law.

This explanation of apparent exceptions being the only logical demand that can be put upon a law, it is evident that the difference between particular and general laws is only a difference of the field of application, not one of logical validity. Suppose we find in the present work some laws concerning the social life of Polish peasants showing that whenever there is a pre-existing attitude A and the influence of a value B, another attitude C appears, or whenever there is a value D and an activity directed by an attitude E, a new value F is the effect. If the causes $A+B$ and $D+E$ are found only in the social life of the Polish peasants and nowhere else, because some of their components—the attitudes or values involved—are peculiar to the Polish peasants, then, of course, the laws $A+B=C$ and $D+E=F$ will be particular laws applicable only to the Polish peasant society, but within these limits as objectively valid as others which social theory may eventually find of applicability to humanity in general. We cannot extend them beyond these limits and do not need to extend them. But the situation will be different if the attitudes A and E and the values B and D are not peculiar to the Polish peasant society, and thus the causes $A+B$ and $D+E$ can be found also in other societies. Then the laws $A+B=C$ and $D+E=F$, based on facts discovered among Polish peasants, will have quite a different meaning. But we cannot be sure whether they are valid for other societies until we have found that in other societies the causes $A+B$ and $D+E$ produce the same respective effects C and F. And since we cannot know whether these values and attitudes will be found or not in other societies until we have investigated these societies, the character of our laws must remain until then undetermined; we cannot say definitely whether they are absolutely valid though applicable only to the Polish peasants or only hypothetically valid although applicable to all societies.

The problem of laws being the most important one of methodology, we shall illustrate it in detail from two concrete examples. Of course we do not really assert that the supposed laws which we use in these illustrations are already established; some of them are still hypotheses, others even mere fictions. The purpose is to give an insight into the mechanism of the research.

Let us take as the first example the evolution of the economic life of the Polish peasant as described in the introduction to the first and second volumes of this work. We find there, first, a system of familial economic organization with a thoroughly social and qualitative character of economic social values, succeeded by an individualistic system with a quantification of the values. This succession as such does not determine any social fact; we obtain the formula of facts only if we find the attitude that constructs the second system out of the first. Now, this attitude is the tendency to economic advance, and thus our empirical facts are subsumed to the formula: familial system—tendency to advance—individualistic system. The same facts being found generally among Polish peasants of various localities, we can assume that this formula expresses a law, but whether it is a law applicable only to the Polish peasants or to all societies depends on whether such a familial economic organization associated with a tendency to advance results always and everywhere in an individualistic system. We may further determine that if we find the familial system, but instead of the tendency to economic advance another attitude—for example, the desire to concentrate political power in the family—the result will be different—for example, the feudal system of hereditary estate. Or we may find that if the tendency to economic advance acts upon a different system—for example, a fully developed economic individualism—it will also lead to a different social formation—for example, to the constitution of trusts. These other classes of facts may become in turn the bases of social hypotheses if they prove sufficiently general and uniform. But certainly, whether the law is particular or general, we must always be able to explain every seeming exception. For example, we find the familial system and the tendency to advance in a Polish peasant family group, but no formation of the individualistic system—the family tends to advance as a whole. In this case we must suppose that the evolution has been hindered by some factors which change the expected results. There may be, for example, a very strong attitude of family pride developed traditionally in all the members, as in families of peasant nobility who had particular privileges during the period of Poland's independence. In this case familial pride co-operating with the tendency to advance will produce a mixed system of economic organization, with quantification of values but without individualism. And if our law does not stand all these tests we have to drop it. But even then we may still suppose that its formulation was too general, that within the range of facts covered by these concepts a more limited and particular law could be discovered—for example, that the system of "work for living," under the influence of the tendency to advance, becomes a system of "work for wages."

As another type of example we select a particular case of legal practice and attempt to show what assumptions are implicitly involved in it, what social laws are uncritically assumed, and try to indicate in what way the assumptions of common sense could be verified, modified, complemented, or rejected, so as to make them objectively valid. For, if science is only developed, systematized, and perfected common sense, the work required to rectify common sense before it becomes science is incomparably greater than is usually supposed.

The case is simple. A Polish woman (K) has loaned to another (T) $300 at various times. After some years she claims her money back; the other refuses to pay. K goes to court. Both bring witnesses. The witnesses are examined. First assumption of legal practice, which we may put into the form of a social law, is: "A witness who has sworn to tell the truth will tell the truth, unless there are reasons for exception."[1] But according to our definition there can be no such law where only two elements are given. There might be a law if we had (1) the oath (a social value); (2) an individual attitude x, still to be determined; (3) a true testimony. But here the second element is lacking; nobody has determined the attitude which, in connection with the oath, results in a true testimony, and therefore, of course, nobody knows how to produce such an attitude. It is supposed that the necessary attitude—whatever it is—

---

[1] It is the formal side of this assumption, not the sphere of its application, that is important. Whether we admit few or many exceptions, whether we say, "The witness often [or sometimes] tells the truth," has not the slightest bearing on the problem of method. There is a general statement and a limitation of this statement, and both statement and limitation are groundless—cannot be explained causally.

appears automatically when the oath is taken. Naturally in many, if not in the majority of cases, the supposition proves false, and if it proves true, nobody knows why. In our case it proved mainly false. Not only the witnesses of the defense, but some of the witnesses of the plaintiff, were lying. What explanation is possible? We could, of course, if we knew what attitude is necessary for true testimony, determine why it was not there or what were the influences that hindered its action. But, not knowing it, we have simply to use some other common-sense generalization, such as: "If the witnesses are lying in spite of the oath, there is some interest involved—personal, familial, friendly." And this was the generalization admitted in this case, and it has no validity whatever because it cannot be converted into a law; we cannot say that interest is the cause making people lie, but we must have again the *tertium quid*—the attitude upon which the interest must act in order to produce a lie. And, on the other hand, a lie can be the result of other factors acting upon certain pre-existing attitudes, and this was precisely the case in the example we are discussing. The Polish peasants lie in court because they bring into court a fighting attitude. Once the suit is started, it becomes a fight where considerations of honesty or altruism are no longer of any weight, and the only problem is—not to be beaten. Here we have, indeed, a formula that may become, if sufficiently verified, a sociological law—the lawsuit and a radical fighting attitude result in false testimonies. Apparent exceptions will then be explained by influences changing either the situation of the lawsuit or the attitude. Thus, in the actual case, the essence of most testimonies for the plaintiff was true, namely, the claim was real. But the claim preceded the lawsuit; the peasant woman would probably not have started the lawsuit without a just claim, for as long as the suit was not started considerations of communal solidarity were accepted as binding, and a false claim would have been considered the worst possible offense. The situation preceding the suit was, in short: law permitting the recovery of money that the debtor refused to pay—creditor's feeling of being wronged and desire of redress—legal complaint. There was no cause making a false claim possible, for the law, subjectively for the peasant, can be here only a means of redress, not a means of illicit wrong, since he does not master it sufficiently to use it in a wrong way, and the desire of redress is the only attitude not offset by the feeling of communal solidarity.

It would lead us too far if we analyzed all the assumptions made by legal practice in this particular case, but we mention one other. The attorney for the defense treated as absurd the claim of the plaintiff that she had loaned money without any determined interest, while she could have invested it at good interest and in a more secure way. The assumption was that, being given various possibilities of investing money, the subject will always select the one that is most economically profitable. We see here again the formal error of stating a law of two terms. The law can be binding only if the third missing term is inserted, namely, an attitude of the subject which we can express approximately: desire to increase fortune or income. Now, in the actual case, this attitude, if existing at all, was offset by the attitude of communal solidarity, and among the various possibilities of investing money, not the one that was economically profitable, but the one that gave satisfaction to the attitude of solidarity was selected.

The form of legal generalization is typical for all generalizations which assume only one datum instead of two as sufficient to determine the effect. It then becomes necessary to add as many new generalizations of the same type as the current practice requires in order to explain the exceptions. These new generalizations limit the fundamental one without increasing positively the store of our knowledge, and the task is inexhaustible. Thus, we may enumerate indefinitely the possible reasons for a witness not telling the truth in spite of the oath, and still this will not help us to understand why he tells the truth when he tells it. And with any one of these reasons of exception the case is the same. If we say that the witness does not tell the truth when it is contrary to his interest, we must again add indefinitely reasons of exception from this rule without learning why the witness lies when the truth is not contrary to his interest if he does. And so on. If in practice this process of accounting for exceptions, then for exceptions from these exceptions, etc., does not go on indefinitely, it is simply because, in a given situation, we can stop at a certain point with sufficient approximation to make our error not too harmful practically.

It is evident that the only way of verifying, correcting, and complementing the generalizations of common sense is to add in every case the missing third element. We cannot, of course, say in advance how much will remain of these generalizations after such a conversion into exact sociological laws; probably, as far as social theory is concerned, it will be more economical to disregard almost completely the results of common sense and to investigate along quite new and independent lines. But for the sake of an immediate improvement of social practice it may sometimes prove useful to take different domains of practical activity and subject them to criticism.

In view of the prevalent tendency of common-sense generalizations to neglect the differences of values and attitudes prevailing in various social groups—a tendency well manifested in the foregoing example—the chief danger of sociology in searching for laws is rather to overestimate than to underestimate the generality of the laws which it may discover. We must therefore remember that there is less risk in assuming that a certain law applies exclusively in the given social conditions than in supposing that it may be extended over all societies.

The ideal of social theory, as of every other nomothetic science, is to interpret as many facts as possible by as few laws as possible, that is, not only to explain causally the life of particular societies at particular periods, but to subordinate these particular laws to general laws applicable to all societies at all times—taking into account the historical evolution of mankind which continually brings new data and new facts and thus forces us to search for new laws in addition to those already discovered. But the fact that social theory as such cannot test its results by the laboratory method, but must rely entirely on the logical perfection of its abstract analysis and synthesis, makes the problem of control of the validity of its generalizations particularly important. The insufficient realization of the character of this control has been the chief reason why so many sociological works bear a character of compositions, intermediary between philosophy and science and fulfilling the demands of neither.

We have mentioned above the fact that social theory as nomothetic science must be clearly distinguished from any philosophy of social life which attempts to determine the essence of social reality or to outline the unique process of social evolution. This distinction becomes particularly marked when we reach the problem of testing the generalizations. Every scientific law bears upon the empirical facts themselves in their whole variety, not upon their underlying common essence, and hence every new discovery in the domain which it embraces affects it directly and immediately, either by corroborating it or by invalidating it. And, as scientific laws concern facts which repeat themselves, they automatically apply to the future as well as to the past, and new happenings in the domain embraced by the law must be taken into consideration as either justifying or contradicting the generalization based upon past happenings, or demanding that this generalization be supplemented by a new one.

And thus the essential criterion of social science as against social philosophy is the direct dependence of its generalizations on new discoveries and new happenings. If a social generalization is not permanently qualified by the assumption that at any moment a single new experience may contradict it, forcing us either to reject it or to supplement it by other generalizations, it is not scientific and has no place in social theory, unless as a general principle helping to systematize the properly scientific generalizations. The physicist, the chemist, and the biologist have learned by the use of experiment that their generalizations are scientifically fruitful only if they are subject to the check of a possible experimental failure, and thus the use of experiment has helped them to pass from the mediaeval *philosophia naturalis* to the modern natural science. The social theorician must follow their example and methodically search only for such generalizations as are subject to the check of a possible contradiction by new facts and should leave the empirically unapproachable essences and meanings where they properly belong, and where they have a real though different importance and validity—in philosophy.

The ultimate test of social theory, as we have emphasized throughout the present note, will be its application in practice, and thus its generalizations will be also subject in the last resort to the check of a possible failure. However, practical application is not experimentation. The results of the physical sciences are also ultimately tested by their application in industry, but this does not alter the fact that the test is made on the basis of laboratory experiments. The difference between experiment and application is twofold: (1) The problems themselves usually differ in complexity. The experiment by which we test a scientific law is artificially simplified in view of the special theoretic problem, whereas in applying scientific results to attain a practical purpose we have a much more complex situation to deal with, necessitating the use of several scientific laws and the calculation of their interference. This is a question with which we shall deal presently. (2) In laboratory experiments the question of the immediate practical value of success or failure is essentially excluded for the sake of their theoretical value. Whether the chemist in trying a new combination will spoil his materials and have to buy a new supply, whether the new combination will be worth more or less money than the elements used, are from the standpoint of science completely irrelevant questions; and even a failure if it puts the scientist on the trail of a new law will be more valuable than a success if it merely corroborates once more an old and well-established law. But in applying scientific results in practice we have essentially the practical value of success or failure in view. It is unthinkable that a chemist asked to direct the production of a new kind of soap in a factory should test his theory by direct application and risk the destruction of a hundred thousand dollars worth of material, instead of testing it previously on a small scale by laboratory experiments. Now in all so-called social experiments, on however small a scale, the question of practical value is involved, because the objects of these experiments are men; the social scientist cannot exclude the question of the bearing of his "experiments" on the future of those who are affected by them. He is therefore seldom or never justified in risking a failure for the sake of testing his theory. Of course he does and can take risks, not as a scientist, but as a practical man; that is, he is justified in taking the risk of bringing some harm if there are more chances of benefit than of harm to those on whom he operates. His risk is then the practical risk involved in every application of an idea, not the special theoretic risk involved in the mere testing of the idea. And, in order to diminish this practical risk, he must try to make his theory as certain and applicable as possible before trying to apply it in fact, and he can secure this result and hand over to the social practitioner generalizations at least approximately as applicable as those of physical science, only if he uses the check of contradiction by new experience. This means that besides using only such generalizations as can be contradicted by new experiences he must not wait till new experiences impose themselves on him by accident, but must search for them, must institute a systematic method of *observation*. And, while it is only natural that a scientist in order to form a hypothesis and to give it some amount of probability has to search first of all for such experiences as may corroborate it, his hypothesis cannot be considered fully tested until he has made subsequently a systematic search for such experiences as may contradict it, and proved those contradictions to be only seeming, explicable by the interference of definite factors.

Assuming now that social theory fulfils its task satisfactorily and goes on discovering new laws which can be applied to regulate social becoming, what will be the effect of this on social practice? First of all, the limitations with which social practice has struggled up to the present will be gradually removed. Since it is theoretically possible to find what social influences should be applied to certain already existing attitudes in order to produce certain new attitudes, and what attitudes should be developed with regard to certain already existing social values in order to make the individual or the group produce certain new social values, there is not a single phenomenon within the whole sphere of human life that conscious control cannot reach sooner or later. There are no objective obstacles in the nature of the social world or in the nature of the human mind which would essentially prevent social practice from attaining gradually the same degree of efficiency as that of industrial practice. The only obstacles are of a subjective kind.

There is, first, the traditional appreciation of social activity as meritorious in itself, for the sake of its intentions alone. There must, indeed, be some results in order to make the good intentions count, but, since anything done is regarded as meritorious, the standards by which the results are appreciated are astonishingly low. Social practice must cease to be a matter of merit and be treated as a necessity. If the theorician is asked to be sure of his generalizations before trying to apply them in practice, it is at least strange that persons of merely good will are permitted to try out on society indefinitely and irresponsibly their vague and perhaps sentimental ideas.

The second obstacle to the development of a perfect social practice is the well-known unwillingness of the common-sense man to accept the control of scientific technique. Against this unwillingness there is only one weapon—success. This is what the history of industrial technique shows. There is perhaps not a single case where the first application of science to any field of practice held by common sense and tradition did not provoke the opposition of the practitioner. It is still within the memory of man that the old farmer with his common-sense methods laughed at the idea that the city chap could teach him anything about farming, and was more than skeptical about the application of the results of soil-analysis to the growing of crops. The fear of new things is still strong even among cultivated persons, and the social technician has to expect that he will meet at almost every step this old typical hostility of common sense to science. He can only accept it and interpret it as a demand to show the superiority of his methods by their results.

But the most important difficulty which social practice has to overcome before reaching a level of efficiency comparable to that of industrial practice lies in the difficulty of applying scientific generalizations. The laws of science are abstract, while the practical situations are concrete, and it requires a special intellectual activity to find what are the practical questions which a given law may help to solve, or what are the scientific laws which may be used to solve a given practical question. In the physical sphere this intellectual activity has been embodied in technology, and it is only since the technologist has intervened between the scientist and the practitioner that material practice has acquired definitely the character of a self-conscious and planfully developing technique and ceased to be dependent on irrational and often unreasonable traditional rules. And if material practice needs a technology in spite of the fact that the generalizations which physical science hands over to it have been already experimentally tested, this need is much more urgent in social practice where the application of scientific generalizations is their first and only experimental test.

We cannot enter here into detailed indications of what social technology should be, but we must take into account the chief point of its method—the general form which every concrete problem of social technique assumes. Whatever may be the aim of social practice—modification of individual attitudes or of social institutions—in trying to attain this aim we never find the elements which we want to use or to modify isolated and passively waiting for our activity, but always embodied in active practical *situations*, which have been formed independently of us and with which our activity has to comply.

The situation is the set of values and attitudes with which the individual or the group has to deal in a process of activity and with regard to which this activity is planned and its results appreciated. Every concrete activity is the solution of a situation. The situation involves three kinds of data: (1) The objective conditions under which the individual or society has to act, that is, the totality of values—economic, social, religious, intellectual, etc.—which at the given moment affect directly or indirectly the conscious status of the individual or the group. (2) The pre-existing attitudes of the individual or the group which at the given moment have an actual influence upon his behavior. (3) The definition of the situation, that is, the more or less clear conception of the conditions and conscious-ness of the attitudes. And the definition of the situation is a necessary preliminary to any act of the will, for in given conditions and with a given set of attitudes an indefinite plurality of actions is possible, and one definite action can appear only if these conditions are selected, interpreted, and combined in a determined way and if a certain systematiza-tion of these attitudes is reached, so that one of them becomes predominant and subordinates the others. It happens, indeed, that a certain value imposes itself imme-diately and unreflectively and leads at once to action, or that an attitude as soon as it appears excludes the others and expresses itself unhesitatingly in an active process. In these cases, whose most radical examples are found in reflex and instinctive actions, the definition is already given to the individual by external conditions or by his own tendencies. But usually there is a process of reflection, after which either a ready social definition is applied or a new personal definition worked out.

Let us take a typical example out of the fifth volume of the present work, concerning the family life of the immigrants in America. A husband, learning of his wife's infidelity, deserts her. The objective conditions were: (1) the social institution of marriage with all the rules involved; (2) the wife, the other man, the children, the neighbors, and in general all the individuals constituting the habitual environment of the husband and, in a sense, given to him as values; (3) certain economic conditions; (4) the fact of the wife's infidelity. Toward all these values the husband had certain attitudes, some of them traditional, others recently developed. Now, perhaps under the influence of the discovery of his wife's infidelity, perhaps after having developed some new attitude toward the sexual or economic side of marriage, perhaps simply influenced by the advice of a friend in the form of a rudimentary scheme of the situation helping him to "see the point," he defines the situation for himself. He takes certain conditions into account, ignores or neglects others, or gives them a certain interpretation in view of some chief value, which may be his wife's infidelity, or the economic burdens of family life of which this infidelity gives him the pretext to rid himself, or perhaps some other woman, or the half-ironical pity of his neighbors, etc. And in this definition some one attitude—sexual jealousy, or desire for economic freedom, or love for the other woman, or offended desire for recognition—or a complex of these attitudes, or a new attitude (hate, disgust) subordinates to itself the others and manifests itself chiefly in the subsequent action, which is evidently a solution of the situation, and fully determined both in its social and in its individual components by the whole set of values, attitudes, and reflective schemes which the situation included. When a situation is solved, the result of the activity becomes an element of a new situation, and this is most clearly evidenced in cases where the activity brings a change of a social institution whose unsatisfactory functioning was the chief element of the first situation.

Now, while the task of science is to analyze by a comparative study the whole process of activity into elementary facts, and it must therefore ignore the variety of concrete situations in order to be able to find laws of causal dependence of abstractly isolated attitudes or values on other attitudes and values, the task of technique is to provide the means of a rational control of concrete situations. The situation can evidently be controlled either by a change of conditions or by a change of attitudes, or by both, and in this respect the rôle of technique as application of science is easily characterized. By comparing situations of a certain type, the social technician must find what are the predominant values or the predominant attitudes which determine the situation more than others, and then the question is to modify these values or these attitudes in the desired way by using the knowledge of social causation given by social theory. Thus, we may find that some of the situations among the Polish immigrants in America resulting in the husband's desertion are chiefly determined by the wife's infidelity, others by her quarrelsomeness, others by bad economic conditions, still others by the husband's desire for freedom, etc. And, if in a given case we know what influences to apply in order to modify these dominating factors, we can modify the situation accordingly, and ideally we can provoke in the individual a behavior in conformity with any given scheme of attitudes and values.

To be sure, it may happen that, in spite of an adequate scientific knowledge of the social laws permitting the modification of those factors which we want to change, our efforts will fail to influence the situation or will produce a situation more undesirable than the one we wished to avoid. The fault is then with our technical knowledge. That is, either we have failed in determining the relative importance of the various factors, or we have failed to foresee the influence of other causes which, interfering with our activity, produce a quite unexpected and undesired effect. And since it is impossible to expect from every practitioner a complete scientific training and still more impossible to have him work out a scientifically justified and detailed plan of action for every concrete case in particular, the special task of the social technician is to prepare, with the help of both science and practical observation, thorough schemes and plans of action for all the various *types* of situations which may be found in a given line of social activity, and leave to the practitioner the subordination of the given concrete situation to its proper type. This is actually the rôle which all the organizers of social institutions have played, but the technique itself must become more conscious and methodically perfect, and every field of social activity should have its professional technicians. The evolution of social life makes necessary continual modifications and developments of social technique, and we can hope that the evolution of social theory will continually put new and useful scientific generalizations within the reach of the social technician; the latter must therefore remain in permanent touch with both social life and social theory, and this requires a more far-going specialization than we actually find.

But, however efficient this type of social technique may become, its application will always have certain limits beyond which a different type of technique will be more useful. Indeed, the form of social control outlined above presupposes that the individual—or the group—is treated as a passive object of our activity and that we change the situations for him, from case to case, in accordance with our plans and intentions. But the application of this method becomes more and more difficult as the situations grow more complex, more new and unexpected from case to case, and more influenced by the individual's own reflection. And, indeed, from both the moral and the hedonistic standpoints and also from the standpoint of the level of efficiency of the individual and of the group, it is desirable to develop in the individuals the ability to control spontaneously their own activities by conscious reflection. To use a biological comparison, the type of control where the practitioner prescribes for the individual a scheme of activity appropriate to every crisis as it arises corresponds to the tropic or reflex type of control in animal life, where the activity of the individual is controlled mechanically by stimulations from without, while the reflective and individualistic control corresponds to the type of activity characteristic of the higher conscious organism, where the control is exercised from within by the selective mechanism of the nervous system. While, in the early tribal, communal, kinship, and religious groups, and to a large extent in the historic state, the society itself provided a rigoristic and particularistic set of definitions in the form of "customs" or "mores," the tendency to advance is associated with the liberty of the individual to make his own definitions.

We have assumed throughout this argument that if an adequate technique is developed it is possible to produce any desirable attitudes and values, but this assumption is practically justified only if we find in the individual attitudes which cannot avoid response to the class of stimulations which society is able to apply to him. And apparently we do find this disposition. Every individual has a vast variety of wishes which can be satisfied only by his incorporation in a society. Among his general patterns of wishes we may enumerate: (1) the desire for new experience, for fresh stimulations; (2) the desire for recognition, including, for example, sexual response and general social appreciation, and secured by devices ranging from the display of ornament to the demonstration of worth through scientific attainment; (3) the desire for mastery, or the "will to power," exemplified by ownership, domestic tyranny, political despotism, based on the instinct of hate, but capable of being sublimated to laudable ambition; (4) the desire for security, based on the instinct of fear and exemplified negatively by the wretchedness of the individual in perpetual solitude or under social taboo. Society is, indeed, an agent for the repression of many of the wishes in the individual; it demands that he shall be moral by repressing at least the wishes which are irreconcilable with the welfare of the group, but nevertheless it provides the only medium within which any of his schemes or wishes can be gratified. And it would be superfluous to point out by examples the degree to which society has in the past been able to impose its schemes of attitudes and values on the individual. Professor Sumner's volume, *Folkways*, is practically a collection of such examples, and, far from discouraging us as they discourage Professor Sumner, they should be regarded as proofs of the ability of the individual to conform to any definition, to accept any attitude, provided it is an expression of the public will or represents the appreciation of even a limited group. To take a single example from the present, to be a bastard or the mother of a bastard has been regarded heretofore as anything but desirable, but we have at this moment reports that one of the warring European nations is officially impregnating its unmarried women and girls and even married women whose husbands are at the front. If this is true (which we do not assume) we have a new definition and a new evaluation of motherhood arising from the struggle of this society against death, and we may anticipate a new attitude—that the resulting children and their mothers will be the objects of extraordinary social appreciation. And even if we find that the attitudes are not so tractable as we have assumed, that it is not possible to provoke all the desirable ones, we shall still be in the same situation as, let us say, physics and mechanics: we shall have the problem of securing the highest degree of control possible in view of the nature of our materials.

As to the present work, it evidently cannot in any sense pretend to establish social theory on a definitely scientific basis. It is clear from the preceding discussion that many workers and much time will be needed before we free ourselves from the traditional ways of thinking, develop a completely efficient and exact working method, and reach a system of scientifically correct generalizations. Our present very limited task is the preparation of a certain body of materials, even if we occasionally go beyond it and attempt to reach some generalizations.

Our object-matter is one class of a modern society in the whole concrete complexity of its life. The selection of the Polish peasant society, motivated at first by somewhat incidental reasons, such as the intensity of the Polish immigration and the facility of getting materials concerning the Polish peasant, has proved during the investigation to be a fortunate one. The Polish peasant finds himself now in a period of transition from the old forms of social organization that had been in force, with only insignificant changes, for many centuries, to a modern form of life. He has preserved enough of the old attitudes to make their sociological reconstruction possible, and he is sufficiently advanced upon the new way to make a study of the development of modern attitudes particularly fruitful. He has been invited by the upper classes to collaborate in the construction of Polish national life, and in certain lines his development is due to the conscious educational efforts of his leaders—the nobility, the clergy, the middle class. In this respect he has the value of an experiment in social technique; the successes, as well as the failures, of this educational activity of the upper classes are very significant for social work. These efforts of the upper classes themselves have a particular sociological importance in view of the conditions in which Polish society has lived during the last century. As a society without a state, divided among three states and constantly hampered in all its efforts to preserve and develop a distinct and unique cultural life, it faced a dilemma—either to disappear or to create such substitutes for a state organization as would enable it to resist the destructive action of the oppressing states; or, more generally, to exist without the framework of a state. These substitutes were created, and they are interesting in two respects. First, they show, in an exceptionally intensified and to a large extent isolated form, the action of certain factors of social unity which exist in every society but in normal conditions are subordinated to the state organization and seldom sufficiently accounted for in sociological reflection. Secondly, the lack of permanence of every social institution and the insecurity of every social value in general, resulting from the destructive tendencies of the dominating foreign states, bring with them a necessity of developing and keeping constantly alive all the activities needed to reconstruct again and again every value that had been destroyed. The whole mechanism of social creation is therefore here particularly transparent and easy to understand, and in general the rôle of human attitudes in social life becomes much more evident than in a society not living under the same strain, but able to rely to a large extent upon the inherited formal organization for the preservation of its culture and unity.

We use in this work the inductive method in a form which gives the least possible place for any arbitrary statements. The basis of the work is concrete materials, and only in the selection of these materials some necessary discrimination has been used. But even here we have tried to proceed in the most cautious way possible. The private letters constituting the first two volumes have needed relatively little selection, particularly as they are arranged in family series. Our task has been limited to the exclusion of such letters from among the whole collection as contained nothing but a repetition of situations and attitudes more completely represented in the materials which we publish here. In later volumes the selection can be more severe, as far as the conclusions of the preceding volumes can be used for guidance.

The analysis of the attitudes and characters given in notes to particular letters and in introductions to particular series contains nothing not essentially contained in the materials themselves; its task is only to isolate single attitudes, to show their analogies and dependences, and to interpret them in relation to the social background upon which they appear. Our acquaintance with the Polish society simply helps us in noting data and relations which would perhaps not be noticed so easily by one not immediately acquainted with the life of the group.

Finally, the synthesis constituting the introductions to particular volumes is also based upon the materials, with a few exceptions where it was thought necessary to draw some data from Polish ethnological publications or systematic studies. The sources are always quoted.

The general character of the work is mainly that of a systematization and classification of attitudes and values prevailing in a concrete group. Every attitude and every value, as we have said above, can be really understood only in connection with the whole social life of which it is an element, and therefore this method is the only one that gives us a full and systematic acquaintance with all the complexity of social life. But it is evident that this monograph must be followed by many others if we want our acquaintance with social reality to be complete. Other Slavic groups, particularly the Russians; the French and the Germans, as representing different types of more efficient societies; the Americans, as the most conspicuous experiment in individualism; the Jews, as representing particular social adaptations under peculiar social pressures; the Oriental, with his widely divergent attitudes and values; the Negro, with his lower cultural level and unique social position—these and other social groups should be included in a series of monographs, which in its totality will give for the first time a wide and secure basis for any sociological generalizations whatever. Naturally the value of every monograph will increase with the development of the work, for not only will the method continually improve, but every social group will help to understand every other.

In selecting the monographic method for the present work and in urging the desirability of the further preparation of large bodies of materials representing the total life of different social groups, we do not ignore the other method of approaching a scientific social theory and practice—the study of special problems, of isolated aspects of social life. And we are not obliged even to wait until all the societies have been studied monographically, in their whole concrete reality, before beginning the comparative study of particular problems. Indeed, the study of a single society, as we have undertaken it here, is often enough to show what rôle is played by a particular class of phenomena in the total life of a group and to give us in this way sufficient indications for the isolation of this class from its social context without omitting any important interaction that may exist between phenomena of this class and others, and we can then use these indications in taking the corresponding kinds of phenomena in other societies as objects of comparative research.

By way of examples, we point out here certain problems suggested to us by the study of the Polish peasants for which this study affords a good starting-point:[1]

1. *The problem of individualization.*—How far is individualization compatible with social cohesion? What are the forms of individualization that can be considered socially useful or socially harmful? What are the forms of social organization that allow for the greatest amount of individualism?

We have been led to the suppositions that, generally speaking, individualization is the intermediary stage between one form of social organization and another; that its social usefulness depends on its more or less constructive character —that is, upon the question whether it does really lead to a new organization and whether the latter makes the social group more capable of resisting disintegrating influences; and that, finally, an organization based upon a conscious co-operation in view of a common aim is the most compatible with individualism. The verification of these suppositions and their application to concrete problems of such a society as the American would constitute a grateful work.

2. *The problem of efficiency.*—Relation between individual and social efficiency. Dependence of efficiency upon various

---

[1] Points 2 and 8 following are more directly connected with materials on the middle and upper classes of Polish society which do not appear in the present work.

individual attitudes and upon various forms of social organization.

The Polish society shows in most lines of activity a particularly large range of variation of individual efficiency with a relatively low scale of social efficiency. We have come to the conclusion that both phenomena are due to the lack of a sufficiently persistent and detailed frame of social organization, resulting from the loss of state-independence. Under these conditions individual efficiency depends upon individual attitudes much more than upon social conditions. An individual may be very efficient because there is little to hinder his activity in any line he selects, but he may also be very inefficient because there is little to push him or to help him. The total social result of individual activities under these conditions is relatively small, because social efficiency depends, not only on the average efficiency of the individuals that constitute the group, but also on the more or less perfect organization of individual efforts. Here, again, the application of these conclusions to other societies can open the way to important discoveries in this particular sphere by showing what is the way of conciliating the highest individual with the highest social efficiency.

3. *The problem of abnormality—crime, vagabondage, prostitution, alcoholism, etc.*—How far is abnormality the unavoidable manifestation of inborn tendencies of the individual, and how far is it due to social conditions?

The priests in Poland have a theory with regard to their peasant parishioners that there are no incorrigible individuals, provided that the influence exercised upon them is skilful and steady and draws into play all of the social factors—familial solidarity, social opinion of the community, religion and magic, economic and intellectual motives, etc. And in his recent book on *The Individual Delinquent*, Dr. William Healy touches the problem on the same side in the following remark: "Frequently one wonders what might have been accomplished with this or that individual if he had received a more adequate discipline during his childhood." By our investigation of abnormal attitudes in connection with normal attitudes instead of treating them isolately, and by the recognition that the individual can be fully understood and controlled only if all the influences of his environment are properly taken into account, we could hardly avoid the suggestion that abnormality is mainly, if not exclusively, a matter of deficient social organization. There is hardly any human attitude which, if properly controlled and directed, could not be used in a socially productive way. Of course there must always remain a quantitative difference of efficiency between individuals, often a very far-going one, but we can see no reason for a permanent qualitative difference between socially normal and antisocial actions. And from this standpoint the question of the antisocial individual assumes no longer the form of the right of society to protection, but that of the right of the antisocial individual to be made useful.

4. *The occupational problem.*—The modern division and organization of labor brings an enormous and continually growing quantitative prevalence of occupations which are almost completely devoid of stimulation and therefore present little interest for the workman. This fact necessarily affects human happiness profoundly, and, if only for this reason, the restoration of stimulation to labor is among the most important problems confronting society. The present industrial organization tends also to develop a type of human being as abnormal in its way as the opposite type of individual who gets the full amount of occupational stimulation by taking a line of interest destructive of social order—the criminal or vagabond. If the latter type of

abnormality is immediately dangerous for the present state of society, the former is more menacing for the future, as leading to a gradual but certain degeneration of the human type—whether we regard this degeneration as congenital or acquired.

The analysis of this problem discloses very profound and general causes of the evil, but also the way of an eventual remedy. It is a fact too well known to be emphasized that modern organization of labor is based on an almost absolute prevalence of economic interests—more exactly, on the tendency to produce or acquire the highest possible amount of economic values—either because these interests are actually so universal and predominant or because they express themselves in social organization more easily than others—a point to be investigated. The moralist complains of the materialization of men and expects a change of the social organization to be brought about by moral or religious preaching; the economic determinist considers the whole social organization as conditioned fundamentally and necessarily by economic factors and expects an improvement exclusively from a possible historically necessary modification of the economic organization itself. From the sociological viewpoint the problem looks much more serious and objective than the moralist conceives it, but much less limited and determined than it appears to the economic determinist. The economic interests are only one class of human attitudes among others, and every attitude can be modified by an adequate social technique. The interest in the nature of work is frequently as strong as, or stronger than, the interest in the economic results of the work, and often finds an objective expression in spite of the fact that actual social organization has little place for it. The protests, in fact, represented by William Morris mean that a certain class of work has visibly passed from the stage where it was stimulating to a stage where it is not—that the handicrafts formerly expressed an interest in the work itself rather than in the economic returns from the work. Since every attitude tends to influence social institutions, we may expect that, with the help of social technique, an organization and a division of labor based on occupational interests may gradually replace the present organization based on demands of economic productivity. In other words, with the appropriate change of attitudes and values all work may become artistic work.

5. *The relation of the sexes.*—Among the many problems falling under this head two seem to us of fundamental importance, the first mainly socio-psychological, the second mainly sociological: (1) In the relation between the sexes how can a maximum of reciprocal response be obtained with the minimum of interference with personal interests? (2) How is the general social efficiency of a group affected by the various systems of relations between man and woman?

We do not advance at this point any definite theories. A number of interesting concrete points will appear in the later volumes of our materials. But a few suggestions of a general character arise in connection with the study of a concrete society. In matters of reciprocal response we find among the Polish peasants the sexes equally dependent on each other, though their demands are of a rather limited and unromantic character, while at the same time this response is secured at the cost of a complete subordination of their personalities to a common sphere of group-interests. When the development of personal interests begins, this original harmony is disturbed, and the disharmony is particularly marked among the immigrants in America, where it often leads to a complete and radical disorganization of family life. There does not seem to be as yet any real solution in view. In this respect the situation of the Polish peasants may throw an interesting light upon the general situation of the cultivated classes of modern society. The difference between these two situations lies in the fact that among the peasants both man and woman begin almost simultaneously to develop personal claims, whereas in the cultivated classes the personal claims of the man have been developed and in a large measure satisfied long ago, and the present problem is almost exclusively limited to the woman. The situations are analogous, however, in so far as the difficulty of solution is concerned.

With regard to social efficiency, our Polish materials tend to show that, under conditions in which the activities of the woman can attain an objective importance more or less equal to those of the man, the greatest social efficiency is attained by a systematic collaboration of man and woman in external fields rather than by a division of tasks which limits the woman to "home and children." The line along which the peasant class of Polish society is particularly efficient is economic development and co-operation; and precisely in this line the collaboration of women has been particularly wide and successful. As far as a division of labor based upon differences of the sexes is concerned, there seems to be at least one point at which a certain differentiation of tasks would be at present in accordance with the demands of social efficiency. The woman shows a particular aptitude of mediation between the formalism, uniformity, and permanence of social organization and the concrete, various, and changing individualities. And, whether this ability of the woman is congenital or produced by cultural conditions, it could certainly be made socially very useful, for it is precisely the ability required to diminish the innumerable and continually growing frictions resulting from the misadaptations of individual attitudes to social organization, and to avoid the incalculable waste of human energy which contrasts so deplorably in our modern society with our increasingly efficient use of natural energies.

6. *The problem of social happiness.*—With regard to this problem we can hardly make any positive suggestions. It is certain that both the relation of the sexes and the economic situation are among the fundamental conditions of human happiness, in the sense of making it and of spoiling it. But the striking point is that, aside from abstract philosophical discussion and some popular psychological analysis, the problem of happiness has never been seriously studied since the epoch of Greek hedonism, and of course the conclusions reached by the Greeks, even if they were more scientific than they really are, could hardly be applied to the present time, with its completely changed social conditions. Has this problem been so much neglected because of its difficulty or because, under the influence of certain tendencies immanent in Christianity, happiness is still half-instinctively regarded as more or less sinful, and pain as meritorious? However that may be, the fact is that no things of real significance have been said up to the present about happiness, particularly if we compare them with the enormous material that has been collected and the innumerable important ideas that have been expressed concerning unhappiness. Moreover, we believe that the problem merits a very particular consideration, both from the theoretical and from the practical point of view, and that the sociological method outlined above gives the most reliable way of studying it.

7. *The problem of the fight of races (nationalities) and cultures.*—Probably in this respect no study of any other society can give so interesting sociological indications as the study of the Poles. Surrounded by peoples of various degrees of cultural development—Germans, Austrians, Bohemians, Ruthenians, Russians, Lithuanians—having

on her own territory the highest percentage of the most unassimilable of races, the Jews, Poland is fighting at every moment for the preservation of her racial and cultural status. Moreover, the fight assumes the most various forms: self-defense against oppressive measures promulgated by Russia and Germany in the interest of their respective races and cultures; self-defense against the peaceful intrusion of the Austrian culture in Galicia; the problem of the assimilation of foreign colonists—German or Russian; the political fight against the Ruthenians in Eastern Galicia; peaceful propaganda and efforts to maintain the supremacy of Polish culture on the vast territory between the Baltic and the Black seas (populated mainly by Lithuanians, White Ruthenians, and Ukrainians), where the Poles constitute the cultivated minority of estate-owners and intellectual bourgeoisie; various methods of dealing with the Jews—passive toleration, efforts to assimilate them nationally (not religiously), social and economic boycott. All these ways of fighting develop the greatest possible variety of attitudes.

And the problem itself assumes a particular actual importance if we remember that the present war is a fight of races and cultures, which has assumed the form of war because races and cultures have expressed themselves in the modern state-organization. The fight of races and cultures is the predominant fact of modern historical life, and it must assume the form of war when it uses the present form of state-organization as its means. To stop wars one must either stop the fight of races and cultures by the introduction of new schemes of attitudes and values or substitute for the isolated national state as instrument of cultural expansion some other type of organization.

8. Closely connected with the foregoing is *the problem of an ideal organization of culture*. This is the widest and

oldest sociological problem, lying on the border between theory and practice. Is there one perfect form of organization that would unify the widest individualism and the strongest social cohesion, that would exclude any abnormality by making use of all human tendencies, that would harmonize the highest efficiency with the greatest happiness? And, if one and only one such organization is possible, will it come automatically, as a result of the fight between cultures and as an expression of the law of the survival of the fittest, so that finally "the world's history will prove the world's tribunal"? Or must such an organization be brought about by a conscious and rational social technique modifying the historical conditions and subordinating all the cultural differences to one perfect system? Or is there, on the contrary, no such unique ideal possible? Perhaps there are many forms of a perfect organization of society, and, the differentiation of national cultures being impossible to overcome, every nation should simply try to bring its own system to the greatest possible perfection, profiting by the experiences of others, but not imitating them. In this case the fight of races and cultures could be stopped, not by the destruction of historical differences, but by the recognition of their value for the world and by a growing reciprocal acquaintance and estimation. Whatever may be the ultimate solution of this problem, it is evident that the systematic sociological study of various cultures, as outlined in this note and exemplified in its beginnings in the main body of the work, is the only way to solve it.

INTRODUCTION TO PART I

THE PEASANT FAMILY

The Polish peasant family, in the primary and larger sense of the word, is a social group including all the blood- and law-relatives up to a certain variable limit—usually the fourth degree. The family in the narrower sense, including only the married pair with their children, may be termed the "marriage-group." These two conceptions, family-group and marriage-group, are indispensable to an understanding of the familial life.

The family cannot be represented by a genealogical tree because it includes law-relationship and because it is a strictly social, concrete, living group—not a religious, mythical, heraldic, or economic formation. The cult of ancestors is completely lacking; the religious attention to the dead is practically the same whoever the dead family member—whether father, brother, husband, or son. We find, indeed, certain legends connected with family names, especially if many persons of the same name live in one locality, but these have little influence on the family life. Heraldic considerations have some place among the peasant nobility and in certain villages where the peasants were granted various privileges in earlier times, but the social connection based upon these considerations is not only looser than the real familial connection, but of a different type. We shall speak again of this type of organization in connection with class-distinctions and the class-problem. Finally, there seems to be a certain economic basis of familial continuity in the idea of ancestral land; but we shall see that the importance of this idea is derived partly from the familial organization itself, partly from communal life.

In short, the idea of common origin does not determine the unity of the familial group, but the concrete unity of the group does determine how far the common origin will be traced. Common descent determines, indeed, the unity of the group, but only by virtue of associational ties established within each new generation. And if we find examples in which common origin is invoked as a reason for keeping or establishing a connection, it is a sign that the primitive unity is in decay, while the sentiments corresponding with this unity still persist in certain individuals who attempt to reconstruct consciously the former state of things and use the idea of community of origin as an argument, just as it has been used as an explanation in the theories of family and for the same reason—because it is the simplest rational scheme of the familial relation. But, as we shall see, it is too simple an explanation.

The adequate scheme would represent the family as a plurality of nuclei, each of them constituted by a marriage-group and relations radiating from each of them toward other marriage-groups and single members, up, down, and on both sides, and toward older, younger, and collateral generations of both husband and wife. But it must be kept in mind that these nuclei are neither equally consistent within themselves nor equally important with regard to their connection with others at any given moment, and that they are not static, but evolving (in a normal family) toward greater consistency and greater importance. The nucleus only begins to constitute itself at the moment of marriage, for then the relations between husband and wife are less close than those uniting each of them to the corresponding nuclei of which they were members; the nucleus has the greatest relative consistency and importance when it is the oldest living married couple with the greatest number of children and grandchildren. Each nucleus is a center around which a circle may be drawn including all the relatives on both sides up to, let us say, the fourth degree. Abstractly speaking, any marriage-group may be thus selected as center of the family, and the composition of the latter will of course vary accordingly; we shall have as many partly interfering, partly different families as there are marriage-groups. But actually among all these family-groups some are socially more real than others, as is shown by the fact that they behave more consistently as units with regard to the rest of the community. For example, from the standpoint of a newly married couple the relatives of the wife in the fourth degree may belong to the family, but they do not belong to it from the standpoint of the husband's parents, and it is the latter standpoint which is socially more important and the one assumed by the community, so long at least as the parents are alive. After their death, and when the married couple grows old, its standpoint becomes dominant and is adopted by the community. But at the same time the husband usually has brothers and sisters who, when married, constitute also secondary centers, and these centers become also primary in the course of time, and thus the family slowly divides and re-forms itself.

The family is thus a very complex group, with limits only approximately determined and with very various kinds and degrees of relationship between its members. But the fundamental familial connection is one and irreducible; it cannot be converted into any other type of group-relationship nor reduced to a personal relation between otherwise isolated individuals. It may be termed *familial solidarity*, and it manifests itself both in assistance rendered to, and in control exerted over, any member of the group by any other member representing the group as a whole. It is totally different from territorial, religious, economic, or national solidarity, though evidently these are additional bonds promoting familial solidarity, and we shall see presently that any dissolution of them certainly exerts a dissolving influence upon the family. And again, the familial solidarity and the degree of assistance and of control involved should not depend upon the personal character of the members, but only upon the kind and degree of their relationship; the familial relation between two members admits no gradation, as does love or friendship.

In this light all the familial relations in their ideal form, that is, as they would be if there were no progressive disintegration of the family, become perfectly plain.

The relation of husband and wife is controlled by both the united families, and husband and wife are not individuals more or less closely connected according to their personal sentiments, but group-members connected absolutely in a single way. Therefore the marriage norm is not love, but "respect," as the relation which can be controlled and reinforced by the family, and which corresponds also exactly to the situation of the other party as member of a group and representing the dignity of that group. The norm of respect from wife to husband includes obedience, fidelity, care for the husband's comfort and health; from husband to wife, good treatment, fidelity, not letting the wife do hired work if it is not indispensable. In general, neither husband nor wife ought to do anything which could lower the social standing of the other, since this would lead to a lowering of the social standing of the other's family. Affection is not explicitly included in the norm of respect, but is desirable. As to sexual love, it is a purely personal matter, is not and ought not to be socialized in any form; the family purposely ignores it, and the slightest indecency or indiscreetness with regard to sexual relations in marriage is viewed with disgust and is morally condemned.

The familial assistance to the young married people is given in the form of the dowry, which they both receive. Though the parents usually give the dowry, a grandfather or grandmother, brother, or uncle may just as well endow the boy or the girl or help to do so. This shows the familial character of the institution, and this character is still more manifest if we recognize that the dowry is not in the full sense the property of the married couple. It remains a part of the general familial property to the extent that the married couple remains a part of the family. The fact that, not the future husband and wife, but their families, represented by their parents and by the matchmakers, come to an understanding on this point is another proof of this relative community of property. The assistance must assume the form of dowry simply because the married couple, composed of members of two different families, must to some extent isolate itself from one or the other of these families; but the isolation is not an individualization, it is only an addition of some new familial ties to the old ones, a beginning of a new nucleus.

The relation of parents to children is also determined by the familial organization. The parental authority is complex. It is, first, the right of control which they exercise as members of the group over other members, but naturally the control is unusually strong in this case because of the particularly intimate relationship. But it is more than this. The parents are privileged representatives of the group as a whole, backed by every other member in the exertion of their authority, but also responsible before the group for their actions. The power of this authority is really great; a rebellious child finds nowhere any help, not even in the younger generation, for every member of the family will side with the child's parents if he considers them right, and everyone will feel the familial will behind him and will play the part of a representative of the group. On the other hand, the responsibility of the parents to the familial group is very clear in every case of undue severity or of too great leniency on their part. And in two cases the family always assumes active control—when a stepchild is mistreated or when a mother is left alone with boys, whom she is assumed to be unable to educate suitably. When the children grow up the family controls the attitude of the parents in economic matters and in the problem of marriage. The parents are morally obliged to endow their children as well as they can, simply because they are not full and exclusive proprietors but rather managers of their inherited property. This property has been constituted mainly by the father's and mother's dowries, which are still parts of the respective familial properties, and the rest of the family retains a right of control. Even if the fortune has been earned individually by the father, the traditional familial form applies to it more or less. Finally, being a manager rather than a proprietor, the father naturally has to retire when his son (usually the oldest) becomes more able than he to manage the main bulk of the property—the farm. The custom of retiring is therefore rooted in the familial organization, and the opinion of the familial group obliges the old people to retire even if they hesitate. In the matter of marriage the parents, while usually selecting their child's partner, must take into consideration, not only the child's will, but also the opinion of other members of the family. The consideration of the child's will results, not from a respect for the individual, but from the fact that the child is a member whose importance in the family will continually grow after his marriage. Regard for the opinion of other members of the family is clearly indispensable, since through marriage a new member will be brought into the family and through his agency a connection will be established with another family.

On the other hand, the attitude of the children toward the parents is also to be explained only on the ground of a larger familial group of which they are all members. The child comes to exercise a control over the parents, not conditioned by any individual achievements on his part, but merely by the growth of his importance within the family-group. In this respect the boy's position is always more important than the girl's, because the boy will be the head of a future marriage-group and because he is the presumptive manager of a part of the familial fortune. Thence his greater independence, or rather his greater right to control his parents. In a boy's life there are four (in the girl's life usually only three) periods of gradually increasing familial importance: early childhood, before the beginning of man's work; after the beginning of man's work until marriage; after marriage until the parents' retirement; after the parents' retirement. In the first period the boy has no right of control at all; the control is exerted on his behalf by the family. In the second period he cannot dispose of the money which he earns (it is not a matter of property, but of management) and is obliged to give it to his father to manage, but he has the right to control his father in this management and to appeal, if necessary, to the rest of the family. In the third period he manages his part of the fortune under the familial control and has the right to control his father's management of the remainder; he is almost equal to his father. In the last period (which the woman does not attain) he takes the father's place as head manager. And the management of property is only the clearest manifestation of a general independence. Thus, in questions of marriage the choice is free at a later age, and becomes almost completely free in the second marriage. But evidently by freedom we mean only independence of the special control of the parents as representatives of the group, not freedom from a general control of the group or of any of its members.

As the parents are obliged to assist the children in proportion to their right to exert authority, so the children's duty of assistance is proportional to their right of control. Helping in housework and turning over to the family money earned is not assistance, but the duty of keeping and increasing the familial fortune. Assistance may begin indeed at the second stage (the boy doing man's work), but then it is expressly stated that a given sum of money, for example, is destined to cover personal expenses of the parents, and in this case it is difficult to determine whether we have still the primitive familial organization or a certain individualization of relations. In short, at this stage simple familial communism in economic matters and familial assistance are not sufficiently differentiated. But the differentiation is complete in the third stage, after marriage. If the married son or daughter is in a better position than the parents, help is perfectly natural, and it is plainly help, not communism, to the degree that the division of property is real. In the last stage, when the parents have retired, assistance becomes the fundamental attitude; and it is now a consciously moral duty powerfully reinforced by the opinion of the familial group.

In all the relations between parents and children the familial organization leaves no place for merely personal affection. Certainly this affection exists, but it cannot express itself in socially sanctioned acts. The behavior of the parents toward the children and the contrary must be determined exclusively by their situations as family members, not by individual merits or preferences. The only justification at least, on either side, of any behavior not determined by the familial situation is a preceding break of the familial principle by one of the members in question.

Thus, the parents usually prefer one child to the others, but this preference should be based upon a familial superiority. The preferred child is usually the one who for some reason is to take the parental farm (the oldest son in Central Poland; the youngest son in the mountainous districts of the south; any son who stays at home while others emigrate), or it is the child who is most likely to raise by his personal qualities the social standing of the family. And, on the contrary, a voluntary isolation from the family life, any harm brought to the family-group, a break of familial solidarity, are sufficient reasons, and the only sufficient ones, for treating a child worse than others and even, in extreme cases, for disowning it. In the same way the children are justified in neglecting the bonds of solidarity which unite them with their parents only if the latter sin against the familial spirit, for example, if a widower (or widow) contracts a new marriage in old age and in such a way that, instead of assimilating his wife to his own family, he becomes assimilated to hers.

The relation between brothers and sisters assumes a different form after the death of the parents. As long as the parents are alive the solidarity between children is rather mediate; the connection between parents and children is much closer than the connection between brothers and sisters, because neither relation is merely personal, and the parents represent the familial idea. In a normal familial organization, therefore, in any struggle between parents and child other children side with the parents, particularly older children, who understand fully the familial solidarity, unless, of course, the parents have broken this solidarity first. But if the parents are dead, the relation between brothers and sisters becomes much closer; indeed, it is the closest familial relation which then remains. Thus the nucleus, constituted by the marriage-group, does not dissolve after the death of the married couple; the group remains, and as a group it resists as far as possible any dissolving influences. It is true that the guardians take the place of the parents as representatives of the familial authority, but they remain outside the nucleus, while the parents were within it. This is one more proof that the familial organization is not patriarchal, or else the patriarchal organization would dissolve and assimilate this parentless group. And this phenomenon cannot be interpreted as a sign of solidarity of the young against the old, for among the brothers and sisters the older assume an attitude of authority, and in this case, as well as during the life of the parents, any member of the older generation has a right of control over all the members of the younger generation.

These general principles of control and of assistance within the narrower marriage-group and within the larger family, and from any member to any member, are reinforced, not only by the opinion of the family itself, but also by the opinion of the community (village, commune, parish, and loose-acquaintance milieu) within which the family lives. The reality of the familial ties once admitted, every member of the family evidently feels responsible for, and is held responsible for, the behavior and welfare of every other member, because, in peasant thinking, judgments upon the group as a whole are constantly made on the basis of the behavior of members of the family, and vice versa. On this account also between any two relatives, wherever found, an immediate nearness is assumed which normally leads to friendship.

In this connection it is noticeable that in primitive peasant life all the attitudes of social pride are primarily familial and only secondarily individual. When a family has lived from time immemorial in the same locality, when all its members for three or four generations are known or remembered, every individual is classified first of all as belonging to the family, and appreciated according to the appreciation which the family enjoys, while on the other hand the social standing of the family is influenced by the social standing of its members, and no individual can rise or fall without drawing to some extent the group with him. And at the same time no individual can so rise or fall as to remove himself from the familial background upon which social opinion always puts him. In doing this social opinion presupposes the familial solidarity, but at the same time it helps to preserve and develop it.

As to the personal relations based upon familial connection, it can be said that the ideal of the familial organization would be a state of things in which all the members of the family were personal friends and had no friends outside of the family. This ideal is expressed even in the terminology of some localities, where the term "friend" is reserved for relatives. This does not mean that personal friendship or even acquaintance is necessary to the reality of the familial connection. On the contrary, when a personal relation is thought to be the condition of active solidarity, we have a sign of the disintegration of familial life.

An interesting point in the familial organization is the attitude of the woman. Generally speaking, the woman has the familial group-feelings much less developed than the man and tends unconsciously to substitute for them, wherever possible, personal feelings, adapted to the individuality of the family members. She wants her husband more exclusively for herself and is often jealous of his family; she has less consideration for the importance of the familial group as a whole and more sympathy with individual needs of its members; she often divides her love among her children without regard for their value to the family; she chooses her friends more under the influence of personal factors. But this is only a matter of degree; the familial ideal is nowhere perfectly realized, and on the other hand no woman is devoid of familial group-feelings. Nevertheless, in the evolution of the family these traits of the woman certainly exert a disintegrating influence, both by helping to isolate smaller groups and by assisting family members in the process of individualization.

The organization here sketched is the general traditional basis of familial life, but actually we find it hardly anywhere in its full force. The familial life as given in the present materials is undergoing a profound disintegration along certain lines and under the influence of various factors. The main tendencies of this disintegration are: isolation of the marriage-group, and personal individualization. Although these processes sometimes follow each other and sometimes interact, they may also go on independently, and it is therefore better to consider them separately. There are, however, some common factors which, by leading simply to a disintegration of the traditional organization, leave the new form of familial life undetermined, and these may be treated first of all.

The traditional form of the Polish peasant family can evidently subsist only in an agricultural community, settled at least for four or five generations in the same locality and admitting no important changes of class, religion, nationality, or profession. As soon as these changes appear, a disintegration is imminent. The marriage-group or the individual enters into a community different from that in which the rest of the family lives, and sooner or later the old bonds must be weakened or broken. The last fifty years have brought many such social changes into the peasant life. Emigration into Polish cities, to America, and to Germany scatters the family. The same thing results from the progressive proletarization of the inhabitants of the country, which obliges many farmers' sons and daughters to go to service or to buy "colonies" outside of their own district. The industrial development of the country leads to changes of profession. And, finally, there is a very rapid evolution of the Polish class-organization, and, thanks to this, peasants may pass into the new middle or at least lower middle class within one generation, thus effecting an almost complete break with the rest of the family. Changes of religion or nationality are indeed very rare, but, whenever they appear, their result is most radical and immediate.

In analyzing the effect of these changes we must take into consideration the problem of adaptation to the new conditions. Two points are here important: the facility of adaptation and the scale of adaptation. For example, the adaptation of a peasant moving to a Polish city as a workman is relatively easy, but its scale is small, while by emigrating to America or by rising in the social hierarchy he confronts a more difficult problem of adaptation, but the possible scale is incomparably wider.

The effect of these differences on family life is felt independently of the nature of the new forms of familial organization which the individual (or the marriage-group) may find in his new environment. Indeed, the adaptation seldom goes so far as to imitate the familial life of the new milieu, unless the individual marries within this milieu and is thus completely assimilated. The only familial organization imitated by the peasant who rises above his class is the agnatic organization of the Polish nobility. Except for these rare cases, the evolution of the family is due, not to the positive influence of any other forms of familial life, but merely to the isolation of marriage-groups and individuals and to the accompanying changes of attitude and personality in the presence of a new external world.

If this process is difficult or unsuccessful, the isolated individual or marriage-group will have a strong tendency to return to the old milieu and will particularly appreciate the familial solidarity through which, in spite of its imperfections, the struggle for existence is facilitated, though in a limited way. We say in a limited way, because familial solidarity is a help mainly for the weak, whom the family does not allow to fall below a certain minimal standard of life, while it becomes rather a burden for the strong. The result of an unsuccessful or difficult adaptation will therefore tend to be a conscious revival of familial feelings and even a certain idealization of familial relations. We find this attitude in many marriage-groups in South America and Siberia, among soldiers serving in the Russian army, and among a few unsuccessful workmen in America, in Western Europe, and even in Polish industrial centers.

If the process of adaptation is easy but limited—that is, if the scale of control which the individual can attain is narrow but easily attained (as is usually the case with workmen in Polish cities)—the result is more complicated. There is still the longing for the old conditions of life, but not so strong as to make the organization of life in the new conditions unbearable. The familial feelings still exist in their old strength, for the extra-familial social life does not give full satisfaction to the sociable tendencies of the individual, but the object of these familial feelings is reduced to the single marriage-group. When territorially isolated the marriage-group is also isolated from the traditional set of rules, valuations, and sentiments of the old community and family, and with the disappearance of these traditions the family becomes merely a natural organization based on personal connections between its members, and these connections are sufficient only to keep together a marriage-group, including perhaps occasionally a few near relatives—

the parents, brothers, or sisters of husband or wife. Under these circumstances, and with economic conditions sufficient to live but hardly to progress, we meet in towns and cities an exclusiveness and egotism in the marriage-group never found in the country. In the Polish towns the bourgeois type of familial organization tends to prevail among the lower classes—single, closed marriage-groups behaving toward the rest of society as indissoluble units, egotistic, often even mutually hostile. And, as we see from our materials, the constitution of such groups is favored and helped by the women. The woman appears as clearly hostile to any social relations of her husband in the new milieu, and thus tends to isolate the marriage-group from it; of the old familial relations she keeps only those based upon personal affection, and thus helps to eliminate the traditional element. Through her typical feeling of economic insecurity, resulting from her insufficient adaptation to the modern conditions of industrial life, she develops more than her husband the egotism of the marriage-group.

The third form of adaptation—an adaptation relatively easy and successful—gives birth to a particular kind of individualization, found among the bulk of young immigrants of both sexes in America and among many season-immigrants in Germany. The success of this adaptation—which should of course be measured by the standard of the immigrant, not of the country to which he comes—consists mainly in economic development and the growth of social influence. In both America and Germany this is due, in the first place, to the higher wages, but in democratic America the Polish social life gives the immigrant also a feeling of importance which in Polish communal life is the privilege of a few influential farmers. There is indeed no such field for the development of self-consciousness in Germany, but the emigrant returns every year with new experience and new money to his native village, and thereby his social rôle is naturally enlarged. Formerly the individual counted mainly as member of a family; now he counts by himself, and still more than formerly. The family ceases to be necessary at all. It is not needed for assistance, because the individual gets on alone. It is not needed for the satisfaction of sociable tendencies, because these tendencies can be satisfied among friends and companions. A community of experience and a similarity of attitudes create a feeling of solidarity among the young generation as against the old generation, without regard to family connections. The social interests and the familial interests no longer coincide, but cross each other. Externally this stage is easily observable in Polish colonies in America and in Polish districts which have an old emigration. Young people keep constantly together, apart from the old, and "good company" becomes the main attraction, inducing the isolated emigrant to join his group in America or return to it at home, but at the same time drawing the boy or the girl from the home to the street.

The familial feelings do not indeed disappear entirely; the change which the individual undergoes is not profound enough for this. But the character of their manifestation changes. There is no longer an attitude of dependence on the family-group, and with the disappearance of this attitude the obligatory character of familial solidarity disappears also; but at the same time a new feeling of self-importance tends to manifest itself in an attitude of superiority with regard to other members of the group, and this superiority demands an active expression. The result is a curious, sometimes very far-going, sometimes whimsical, generosity which the individual shows toward single family members regardless of the validity of the claim which this member could put forward under the traditional familial organization. This generosity is usually completely disinterested from the economic point of view; no return is expected. It is essentially an expression of personality, a satisfaction at once of personal affection and personal vanity. It is shown only toward persons whom ties of affection unite with the giver, sometimes toward friends who do not even belong to the family. Pity is a motive which strengthens it and sometimes is even sufficient in itself. Any allusion to obligation offends it. Often it is displayed in an unexpected way or at an unexpected moment, with the evident desire to provoke astonishment. It is the symptom of an expanding personality.

On the other hand, the unequal rate at which the process of individualization and the modification of traditional attitudes takes place in different family members leads often to disintegration of both the familial and the personal life. This is seen particularly in the relations of parents and children as it appears in emigration. When the boy leaves his family in Poland and comes to America, he at first raises no questions about the nature of his duties to his parents and family at home. He plans to send home all the money possible; he lives in the cheapest way and works the longest hours. He writes: "Dear Parents: I send you 300 roubles, and I will always send you as much as I can earn." He does not even feel this behavior as moral; and it is not moral, in the sense that it involves no reflection and no inhibition. It is unreflective social behavior. But if in the course of time he has established new and individualistic attitudes and desires, he writes: "Dear Parents: I will send money; only you ask too much." (See in this connection Butkowski series.)

But the most complete break between parents and children—one presenting itself every day in our juvenile courts—comes with the emigration of the family as a whole to America. The children brought with the family or added to it in America do not acquire the traditional attitude of familial solidarity, but rather the American individualistic ideals, while the parents remain unchanged, and there frequently results a complete and painful antagonism between children and parents. This has various expressions, but perhaps the most definite one is economic—the demand of the parents for all the earnings of the child, and eventually as complete an avoidance as possible of the parents by the child. The mutual hate, the hardness, unreasonableness, and brutality of the parents, the contempt and ridicule of the child—ridicule of the speech and old-country habits and views of the parents—become almost incredible. The parents, for example, resort to the juvenile court, not as a means of reform, but as an instrument of vengeance; they will swear away the character of their girl, call her a "whore" and a "thief," when there is not the slightest ground for it. It is the same situation we shall note elsewhere when the peasant is unable to adjust his difficulties with his neighbors by social means and resorts to the courts as a pure expression of enmity, and with a total disregard of right or wrong. A case was recently brought before the juvenile court in Chicago which illustrates typically how completely the father may be unable to occupy any other standpoint than that of familial solidarity. The girl had left home and was on the streets. When appealed to by the court for suggestions and co-operation, the father always replied in terms of the wages of the girl—she had not been bringing her earnings home. And when it appeared that he could not completely control her in this respect, he said: "Do what you please with her. She ain't no use to me."

The last type of adaptation—one requiring much change, but giving also much control—is typically represented by the climbing tendency of the peasant and is always connected with an intellectual development. This adaptation brings also the greatest changes in the familial sentiments. Individualization is the natural result of rising above the primitive group and becoming practically independent of it. But at the same time, unlike the preceding type, this form of adaptation leads to qualitative changes in the concept of the family. Indeed, the individual rises, not only above the family, but also above the community, and drops most of the traditional elements, and in this respect the result is analogous to that of the second type of adaptation. On the other hand he meets on this higher cultural level those more universal and conscious traditions which constitute the common content of Christian morality. The Christian elements were embodied in the system of peasant traditions, but they constituted only a part of the rich traditional stock, and their influence in peasant life was essentially different from that which the church as well as the popular Christian reflection wished it to be. Their power in peasant life was a power of social *custom*, while on a higher level of intellectual development and individualization they claim to be *rational norms*, directing the conscious individual morality. Thus, the familial attitudes of a peasant rising above his class undergo a double evolution: they are simplified, and they pass from the sphere of custom to that of conscious, reflective morality. Only a few fundamental obligations are acknowledged, and in the sphere of these obligations the "moral" family coincides neither with the "traditional" family nor with the "natural" family—the marriage-group. In its typical form it includes husband or wife, parents, children, brothers, and sisters. Its nucleus is no longer a group, but an individual. The husband has, for example, particular moral obligations toward his own parents, sisters, and brothers, but not toward the family of his wife. The moral obligations toward the members of the latter do not differ from those toward any friends or acquaint-ances, are not particularly familial obligations. And the consistency of this moral family does not depend any longer upon social factors, but merely upon the moral development of the individual—assuming, of course, that the element of custom has been completely eliminated, which is seldom the case. We find individuals who feel the obligation as a heavy burden and try to drop it as soon as possible; we find others who accept it readily and treat the family as an object of moral obligation even after it has lost its social reality.

In distinguishing these four formal types of evolution of familial life we have of course abstractly isolated each of them and studied it in its fullest and most radical expres-sion. In reality, however, we find innumerable interme-diary and incomplete forms, and we must take this fact into consideration when examining the concrete materials.[1]

MARRIAGE

The Polish peasant family, as we have seen, is organized as a plurality of interrelated marriage-groups which are so many nuclei of fami ial life and whose importance is various

[1] The Polish terminology for familial relationship corroborates our definition of the family. We must distinguish, first of all, the use of familial names when speaking *to* a relative and *about* a relative to *strangers*. In the latter case the proper term is used, while in the first there is a tendency to substitute for it another term, indicating a much closer degree of relationship. When one is speaking *about* a relative *within* the family, both usages are possible.

The proper terms, i.e., those used when one is speaking about a relative to strangers, are of three kinds:

a) Terms which define a unique relation, such as *mąż* ("husband"), and *żona* ("wife"), *teść* ('father-in-law"), *ojciec* ("father"). Only the terms "husband" and "wife" remain unique when one is addressing a member of the family, while terms for blood-parents and blood-children are usually substituted for those which indicate a step- or law-relation of descent.

b) Terms which essentially define a unique relation, but can be extended to any relation of a certain degree. Such are, for example, *brat* ("brother"), *szwagier* ("brother-in-law"), *dziadek* ("grandfather"), *wuj* ("maternal uncle"), *stryj* ("paternal uncle"). Their original meaning is the same as that of the correspond-ing English terms, but they are applied also to remoter degrees of relationship. If exactness is required, they are defined by special adjectives, but habitually, up and changing. The process of constitution and evolution of these nuclei is therefore the essential phenomenon of familial life. But at the same time there culminate in marriage many other interests of the peasant life, and we must take the rôle of these into consideration.

1. *Marriage from the familial standpoint.*—The whole familial system of attitudes involves absolutely the postulate of marriage for every member of the young generation. The family is a dynamic organization, and changes brought by birth, growth, marriage, and death have nothing of the incidental or unexpected, but are included as normal in the organization itself, continually accounted for and foreseen, and the whole practical life of the family is adapted to them. A person who does not marry within a certain time, as well as an old man who does not die at a certain age, provokes in the family-group an attitude of unfavorable astonishment; they seem to have stopped in the midst of a continuous movement, and they are passed by and left alone. There are, indeed, exceptions. A boy (or girl) with some physical or intellectual defect is not supposed to marry,

to the third and sometimes the fourth degree, no adjectives are required. Thus, a cousin of second degree is *stryjeczny, wujeczny,* or *cioteczny brat* ("brother through the paternal uncle, maternal uncle, or aunt"), or simply *brat;* a father's paternal uncle is *stryjeczny dziadek* ("grandfather through the paternal uncle"), or simply *dziadek,* and so on. A wife's or husband's relative may be determined in the same way, with the addition "of my wife" or "of my husband." But if no particular exactness is necessary, this qualification is also omitted, except for collateral members (of the same generation), where law-relationship is indicated by particular terms (*szwagier* instead of *brat*). In addressing a member, not only all the qualifications are omitted, but even for collateral members the terms "brother" and "sister" are often substituted for the special terms indicating law-relationship of any degree.

c) Terms which are merely class-names. Of these there are only two: *krewny* and *powinowaty,* "blood-" and "law-relative." They are never used in addressing a person, and in general their usage is limited to cases where the degree and kind of relationship is forgotten or when the speaker does not desire to initiate the stranger more exactly. The intelligent classes sometimes use the French word *cousin* (Polonized, *kuzyn*), but this custom has reached as yet only the lower middle class, not the peasant.

and in his early childhood a corresponding attitude is adopted by the family and a place for him is provided beforehand. His eventual marriage will then provoke the same unfavorable astonishment as the bachelorship of others.

The condemnation attached to not marrying is not so strong as that incurred by the omission of some elementary moral or religious duty, and with the growing complexity of social conditions cases are more and more frequent where a person remains unmarried through no fault of his own, and so the condemnation is becoming less and less. But the standard binds the parents of the marriageable person even more than the latter, and we see in many letters that the parents do not dare to put any obstacles in the way of the marriage of their child even if they foresee bad results for themselves from this marriage (estrangement of the child, or economic losses), and they persuade the child to marry even against their own interest. The contrary behavior (see Sekowski series) incurs immediate and strong social condemnation. The only limitation of this principle is the question of the choice of the partner. But even this limitation disappears when the parents have no certainty that a better match than the one proposed will be arranged. It is better to make a bad marriage than not to marry at all.

The traditional familial factor ceases to exert any influence upon the *second* marriage; no determined line of conduct is prescribed in this case by the familial organization except that marriage is viewed unfavorably after a certain age.

The family not only requires its members to be married, but directs their choice. This is neither tyranny nor self-interest on the part of the parents nor solicitude for the future of the child, but a logical consequence of the individual's situation in the familial group. The individual is a match only as member of the group and owing to the social standing of the family within the community and to the protection and help in social and economic matters given by the family. He has therefore corresponding responsibilities; in marrying he must take, not only his own, but also the family's interests into consideration. These latter interests condition the choice of the partner in three respects:

a) The partner in marriage is an outsider who through marriage becomes a member of the family. The family therefore requires in this individual a personality which will fit easily into the group and be assimilated to the group with as little effort as possible. Not only a good character, but a set of habits similar to those prevailing in the family to be entered, is important. Sometimes the prospective partner is unknown to the family, sometimes even unknown to the marrying member of the family, and in this case social guaranties are demanded. The boy or girl ought to come at least from a good family, belonging to the same class as the family to be entered, and settled if possible in the same district, since customs and habits differ from locality to locality. The occupation of a boy ought to be of such a kind as not to develop any undesirable, that is, unassimilable, traits. A girl should have lived at home and should not have done hired work habitually. A man should never have an occupation against which a prejudice exists in the community. In this matter there is still another motive of selection, that is, vanity. Finally, a widow or a widower is an undesirable partner, because more difficult to assimilate than a young girl or boy. If not only the future partner, but even his family, is unknown, the parents, or someone in their place, will try to get acquainted personally with some of his relatives, in order to inspect the general type of their character and behavior. Thence comes the frequent custom of arranging marriages through friends and relatives. This form of matchmaking is intermediary between the one in which the starting-point is personal acquaintance and the other in which the connection with a certain family is sought first through the *swaty* (professional matchmaker) and personal acquaintance comes later. In this intermediary form the starting-point is the friendship with relatives of the boy or the girl. It is supposed that the future partner resembles his relatives in character, and at the same time that the family to which those relatives belong is worth being connected with. But this leads us to the second aspect of the familial control of marriage.

b) The candidate for marriage belongs himself to a family, which through marriage will become connected with that of his wife. The familial group therefore assumes the right to control the choice of its member, not only with regard to the personal qualities of the future partner, but also with regard to the nature of the group with which it will be allied. The standing of the group within the community is here the basis of selection. This standing itself is conditioned by various factors—wealth, morality, intelligence, instruction, religiousness, political and social influence, connection with higher classes, solidarity between the family members, kind of occupation, numerousness of the family, its more or less ancient residence in the locality, etc. Every family naturally tries to make the best possible alliance; at the same time it tries not to lower its own dignity by risking a refusal or by accepting at once even the best match and thereby showing too great eagerness. Thence the long selection and hesitation, real or pretended, on both sides, while the problem is not to discourage any possible match, for the range of possibilities open to an individual is a proof of the high standing of the family. Thence also such institutions as that of the matchmaker, whose task is to shorten the ceremonial of choosing without apparently lowering the dignity of the families involved. The relative freedom given to the individuals themselves, the apparent yielding to individual love, has in many cases its source in the desire to shorten the process of selection by shifting the responsibility from the group to the individual. In the traditional formal *swaty* is embodied this familial control of marriage. The young man, accompanied by the match-maker, visits the families with which his family has judged it desirable to be allied, and only among these can he select a girl. He is received by the parents of the girl, who first learn everything about him and his family and then encourage him to call further or reject him at once. And the girl can select a suitor only among those encouraged by her family.

(*c*) A particular situation is created when widow or widower with children from the first marriage is involved. Here assimilation is very difficult, because no longer an individual, but a part of a strange marriage-group, has to be assimilated. At the same time the connection with the widow's or widower's family will be incomplete, because the family of the first husband or wife also has some claims. Therefore such a marriage is not viewed favorably, and there must be some real social superiority of the future partner and his or her family in order to counterbalance the inferiority caused by the peculiar familial situation. A second marriage is thus usually one which, if it were the first, would be a mesalliance.

With the disintegration of the familial life there must come, of course, a certain liberation from the familial claims in matters of marriage. But this liberation itself may assume various forms. With regard to the personal qualities of his future wife, the man may neglect to consult his family and still apply the same principles of appreciation which his family would apply—select a person whose character and habits resemble the type prevailing in his own family, a person whose relatives he knows, who comes perhaps from the same locality, etc. Therefore, for example, immigrants in America whose individualization has only begun always try to marry boys or girls fresh from the old country, if possible from their own native village.

A second degree of individualization manifests itself in a more reasoned selection of such qualities as the individual wishes his future mate to possess in view of his own personal happiness and regardless of the family's desire. This type of selection prevails, for example, in most of the second marriages, when the individual has become fully conscious of what he desires from his eventual partner and when the feeling of his own importance, increasing with age, teaches him to neglect the possible protests of his family. It is also a frequent type in towns, where the individual associates with persons of various origins and habits. The typical and universal argument opposed here against any familial protests has the content: "I shall live with this person, not you, so it is none of your business."

Finally, the highest form of individualization is found in the real love-marriage. While a reasoned determination of the qualities which the individual wishes to find in his future mate permits of some discussion, some familial control, and some influence of tradition, in the love-marriage every possibility of control is rejected a priori. Here, under the influence of the moment, the largest opportunity is given for matches between individuals whose social determinism differs most widely, though this difference is after all usually not very great, since the feeling of love requires a certain community of social traditions.

2. *Marriage from the standpoint of other social groups: territorial (community), national, religious, professional.*—

The claims which the community has upon the individual in matters of marriage corroborate those of the family-group to the extent that every individual (except a future priest) is required to marry, if he is not hindered by a physical or an intellectual defect. The community demands from its members a steadiness of life which is necessary for its interior harmony; but a peasant individual can acquire this steadiness only after his marriage. The life of an unmarried man or woman bears essentially an unfixed character. A single person, as we know, cannot remain indefinitely with his family, for the latter is organized in view of the marriage of all of its members. He cannot carry on normal occupational activity alone—cannot farm or keep a small shop—he can be either only a hired laborer, living with strangers, or a servant. In both cases the sphere of his interests is much narrower than that of a married couple and his life has less fixity. A single person does not take an equal share with married couples in the life of the community; there is little opportunity for a reciprocity of services, still less for co-operation. He cannot even keep a house, receive, give entertainments, etc. He has nobody to provide for, no reason to economize. All these features of single life tend to develop either a spirit of revelry, vagabondage, and pauperism, or an egotistic isolation within a circle of personal interests—both opposed to the fundamental set of peasant attitudes and undesirable for the group.

Accordingly, the community gives a positive sanction to the marriage of its members. This is done in three ways: (1) Each wedding is a social event in itself, not limited to the families who intermarry, but participated in by the community, and the pleasure of being for some days the center of interest of the community is a strong motive in favor of marriage. (2) The community gives a higher social standing to its married members: after marriage they are addressed as "you" instead of "thou," they begin to play an active part in the commune, in the parish, in associations, etc. Unmarried individuals have a certain kind of social standing as members of families and prospective matches, but this kind of a standing decreases with age. (3) The private life of married couples is much less controlled by the community than that of unmarried persons. The control of the family in normal conditions is thought perfectly sufficient for the first; the community interferes only in extraordinary cases of important familial misunderstandings. But an individual who does not marry in due time is supposed not to be sufficiently controlled by the family, and the community allows him no privacy.

But the community, as a territorial group, assumes also a right to control the choice of its members whenever the question is raised of taking a partner from a different territorial group. The same right is claimed by the professional, the national, the religious groups, which usually do not interfere with the celibacy of their members nor with their marriage so long as this remains endogamous. In this respect the claims of these groups are different from the claims of the family, and may even be contradictory.

First of all, an individual can belong at once to two families, but not normally to two territorial, professional, national, or religious groups. This leads to important differences of standpoint.

Let us take first the case of a member of a social group who, by marriage, passes into a different group—moves to another locality, takes a new profession, changes his nationality or his religion. For the family such a fact may be more or less unpleasant, but only on account of the divergence of attitudes which thus arises between its members; but the individual who has passed into another social group is not necessarily lost; he may remain (if there are no other factors of disintegration) a real, solidary member of the family. On the contrary, for a territorial, professional, national, or religious group such an individual is lost, and, since no group likes to lose its members, every kind of exogamy which involves a passage into another group incurs a social condemnation. This condemnation is particularly strong if the individual, by passing into another group, renounces the essential values of his first group—customs, traditions, ideals. Formerly, when the differences of custom and tradition between communities and professions were much greater than now, the marriage outside of a community or professional group was condemned very strongly; we find many traces of this stage in folklore. At present a change of locality incurs a relatively slight condemnation; a change of group professionally (as, for example, when a peasant girl marries a handworker) is only ridiculed; but a change of nationality or religion is still an almost unpardonable offense, the latter even a crime. And, of course, the family is influenced by the larger social group to which it belongs; the national and religious groups usually require that the family shall disown a renegade member, and the family in general complies with this demand and rejects such an individual, even if he wishes to keep the familial solidarity.

The other side of the case is presented when a new member is brought through marriage into a social group. For the family, as we know, two questions are here involved: what is the social standing of the new member's family within the larger group to which it belongs, and what is the character of the new member. But for the social group the first question does not exist. The family indeed becomes connected through marriage with the new partner's family;

and to it the social standing of the latter is important. But the community at large does not enter into any particular relation with another group by the mere fact of receiving a member from it, and it cares little for the other group's standing. Therefore the family may occasionally acquiesce in the fact that its member marries a girl who will be assimilated with difficulty, if the family of this girl has a particularly high social standing—is very rich, instructed, of good origin, or influential. The benefit of being connected with such a family may be greater than the displeasure of having an unadaptable new member. But for the community those reasons cannot overshadow the only point which counts for it, namely, how will the new member be assimilated? This depends, of course, upon the nature of social customs and traditions which he brought with him, and the more they differ from those which prevail in the given group the greater is the social condemnation of exogamy. This condemnation is usually strengthened by the jealousy of the marriageable members of the group, their parents and relatives. The exogamous member is judged to lack the feeling of solidarity and to inflict a humiliation upon the group by selecting a stranger. Sometimes the attitude of the group is rather mixed, as when a person of a different nationality or religion, in marrying into the group, accepts its national or religious ideals; there usually remains enough difference of traditions and habits to provoke a certain unreceptivity in the group, but the spirit of proselytism is flattered. And so it happens, for example, that a converted Jew is laughed at within the Christian community, but defended against his former co-religionists.

As the new member is not backed by his old group, his position is usually rather helpless. No particular social norm arises from this intermarriage analogous to the norm of respect between husband and wife, which has its source in the fact that both belong still to their respective family-groups. Only a complete assimilation neutralizes the lack of cordiality of the social group toward the new member.

3. *Marriage from the economic point of view.*—In order to understand the economic side of marriage we must remember (1) that marriage is not a mere relation of individuals but the constitution of a new social unit, the marriage-group, in which two familial groups intersect, while each of these preserves to a degree its own integrity, and (2) that the question of property, particularly of property in land, is not in peasant life a merely economic, but a social, question; the meaning of property is determined by social traditions.

From these points results the general principle that both families are obliged to contribute to the economic existence of the newly married couple by giving dowries corresponding to their own situation. A family which does not give a sufficient dowry to a boy or girl proves either that it is poor or that it lacks solidarity, and in general lowers its own social standing.

Fundamentally the aim of the dowry is not merely to help the married couple to get a living, but to enable them to keep on the same social level as that of their families—to avoid being outclassed. As long as the boy and girl live with their parents they belong to the latter's class, even if they have then nothing of their own; but if they had no property to manage when starting their own household, they would pass into the class of hired laborers. The economic form in which this tendency to avoid being out-classed expresses itself is always the establishing for or by the newly married couple of a business of their own; and this principle applies indeed to all the old social classes—handworkers, bourgeoisie, nobility—for up to fifty years ago the difference between hired work and independent work constituted a social as well as an economic difference; and to a certain extent this remains true today. Among the peasants property in land is evidently the basis of this difference, and therefore the practice of dowry is adapted to the solution of the problem of making every young married couple own a farm. It is clear also that in most cases this problem can be solved only by a contribution from both families. Usually these contributions are so arranged that the family of the boy gives land, the family of the girl money, because land means more than money and a husband settling on his wife's land loses some of his dignity as head of the marriage-group, and is usually looked down upon by other farmers.

The peasant practice of inheritance is to leave the undivided farm to one son, who has then the obligation of paying off his brothers and sisters, and for this purpose he must have a large dowry in cash from his wife. The father is seldom able to put aside money enough to give the other children their parts, and mortgaging the farm, in view of the half-sacred character of land property, is hated by the peasant, aside from the fact that it often means ruin. The division of the farm is, as far as possible, limited by tradition; below a certain size even by law. The sale of the farm is avoided even after the death of the parents, and is never possible during their life. Sale, division, or mortgaging of the farm means a lowering of the social standing of the family. The head of the family, who has worked during his whole life upon the farm, wants his work to be continued by his son on the same scale. In short, it is a familial duty of one son at least to marry rich.

But even if the farm were divided or sold, each son would hardly be able to farm without getting some dowry, and the family of the wife would never allow her to live in very poor conditions if it could prevent it. The same is true of the sons who are paid off by their brother; they seldom get money enough to buy a farm sufficient for living, especially since the son who takes the farm is usually favored in the settlement.

There are of course cases when there is no necessity of taking a dowry. For example, the only son of a sufficiently rich farmer is free to marry without money. But as the dowry has not only a practical value, but is also an expression of the family's importance and solidarity, the custom is usually kept up unless the family of the poor girl has for some reason a relatively high social standing in spite of poverty.

Exactly the same social and economic reasons oblige a girl who has some dowry to marry a boy with property. The dowry is seldom sufficient to buy a farm and thus to keep the social level which the girl had in her family; and even if it should be large enough, the girl's family will seldom allow her to marry a poor boy, because it would be considered a proof that the girl had no suitors of a higher social standing, and therefore that she had some personal defect.

There are many exceptions to this general rule, but they admit of special explanations. A boy or girl who is already declassed or whose family did not belong originally to the class of farmers (or masters of handicraft) is not socially obliged to marry with dowry. It is customary for the young couple to have money or goods enough to furnish the house, and both families are obliged to help them as far as possible. The familial solidarity is still strong; but since property which has not the form of an independent business does not determine the social standing of the family as does land or a master-workman's position, the consideration of dowry plays a quite subordinate rôle in the selection of a mate. A boy who has money enough to furnish the house may marry freely a girl who has nothing except her personal clothing and household linen, and a girl with some money may marry a completely poor boy; there is no real inequality in either case. If the question of dowry is often raised, it is rather a remnant of the traditional attitude, or an imitation of the owning classes, not an actual social or economic problem.

A real marriage for money, that is, one in which a poor boy or girl selects intentionally a partner with some fortune, always incurs a social condemnation or at least ridicule. In the case of a craftsman who needs a dowry in order to establish his own shop the condemnation is very slight. He ought not, indeed, to count exclusively upon the dowry, but since acquired handicraft was equivalent to capital in the old guild tradition, and a journeyman was often pushed into the master-class by his wife's family, dowry under these circumstances has lost its social disapproval. But social opinion knows no justification for a poor country boy or girl who by making a rich match passes into the farmer-class; the members of the latter consider it the worst kind of climbing. And it is still worse if the unskilled city workman marries a rich girl. He cannot use the dowry productively in any line of handicraft, and so is supposed to make the rich marriage only for the sake of being lazy and enjoying pleasure at his wife's expense. In the two latter cases the condemnation is perhaps strengthened by the fact that in such matches the richer party is usually either much older, or personally unattractive, or with some moral stain, etc., since otherwise he or she could have made a better choice. Thus a marriage which is most evidently made for the sake of money is most clearly considered abnormal. Even if there are no personal disadvantages on the side of the richer party, the match is almost certainly concluded against the will of his or her family and incurs condemnation from this reason also. And, generally speaking, the economic relation of the parties in marriage is subjected to a *moral* appreciation, only if it appears as a *personal*, not a familial, arrangement, on one side or on both.

From the economic point of view a second marriage presents a particular problem. In the case of a widow or widower the normal control of the family is greatly diminished, since these have more importance within the family-group than the bachelor or girl, and their private life has acquired through marriage more independence. The problem of keeping the same social standing is also involved, but usually there is less danger of losing it, for the widow or widower already has property. In this case the personal help of the second husband or wife in keeping the farm and household going is normally a sufficient economic contribution, and no capital is needed. If there are children from the first marriage, the situation is more complicated, for the family of their parent has an interest in them and in the maintenance of their social position, especially in view of the eventual children from the second marriage. The lot of these children must also be considered, and a dowry is therefore sometimes required even in a second marriage. But it is much more difficult to get. Indeed, since the widow's or widower's marriage-value is much lower than that of a maid or a bachelor, a claim of this kind on the basis of social, and therefore also of economic, equality would be unjustified.

There is a double evolution of the economic side of marriage, influenced on the one hand by the dissolution of the old class-hierarchy and substitution of a new class-organization, and on the other by the process of economic individualization.

The old social classes are becoming mingled and intermarriage is more and more frequent. At the same time new criteria of social superiority appear in place of the old ones, or along with them, and an equilibration of different advantages becomes possible. The old advantages of fortune or good birth may be offset by instruction or off-set each other. Within the economic sphere itself the stand-point of income begins to compete with that of property; hired work loses its socially depreciative character, etc. Thus marriages are more and more frequent in which some other social superiority is put forward by one side as against the property brought by the other party, and such mating becomes more and more normal in social opinion and more and more easily acknowledged by families on either side.

At the same time economically unequilibrated matches become gradually more possible because of the liberation of the individual from the pressure of the family and com-munity. Still it is clear that the possibility of showing a real disinterestedness depends upon the economic conditions set by the environment. We must remember that in the Polish country life of the lower classes the possibility of economic advance is very small, as compared even with that of the Polish city life, and quite insignificant in comparison with that of American life. On the contrary, there are numerous possibilities of retrogression as the population increases. Thus a married couple does well if it succeeds in keeping to the end the economic ·standard of life with which it started, and it is natural for them to try to start with as high a standard as possible. Disinterestedness would be a luxury for which the children as well as the parents would pay. Marriages quite free from economic considerations become, therefore, practically possible only in some parts of the country where season-emigration is practiced, to some extent in Polish industrial cities, and particularly in America, where they are, indeed, almost the rule.

4. *Marriage from the sexual point of view.*—The sexual factor, as a mere necessity of sexual satisfaction, aside from the question of individualized love, must play of course an important rôle as a motive of marriage in general, although it is somewhat difficult to determine to what extent the want of sexual satisfaction is consciously conceived as a reason for marriage. Certainly the popular songs and jokes of young people show that sexual tendencies are developed before any actual sexual intercourse. Both sexes mix frequently together in work and play, and sexual desires must arise. But, on the other hand, their development depends upon marriage as a social institution. Indeed, the social activities which are most favorable to their development have all, mediately or immediately, marriage in view. There is a stock of sexual information and attitudes acquired before puberty, and this is not conditioned by the idea of marriage. But after puberty the boy and the girl always look upon each other as possible matches, and social intercourse between the sexes is always arranged with marriage in view. All the entertainments which are not merely ceremonial have this aim. An interesting fact shows how the sexual side of this preliminary intercourse is institutional and socially controlled. No indecent allusions are ever allowed in a private conversation between boy and girl, but any indecent allusion can be made publicly, in the form of a song or joke, at a gathering where young people of both sexes are present.

And marriage is the only form in which sexual satisfaction can be obtained. Illegal relations before marriage are relatively rare, not so much because of any particular moral self-restraint as, once more, because of the familial control, reinforced by the control of social opinion and exerted in view of the future marriage. Sexual intercourse before marriage is normally and immediately treated by the boy, the girl, the family, and the community as an illicit extension of the sexual preliminaries of marriage, but anticipatory of marriage, and it leads almost universally to marriage, even when, under the influence of disintegrating factors, it becomes frequent. The idea of sexual intercourse *per se*, without relation to marriage, plays hardly any part in the primitive peasant organization of life. Therefore the main reason for the prohibition of sexual intercourse before marriage is to be sought in the familial form of marriage itself. The boy and girl who begin sexual relations before marriage begin also in fact the marriage-relation, thus avoiding the familial control and trifling with the social sanction expressed in the whole series of marriage-ceremonies. This must evidently lead to a disorganization of the whole marriage system. Even if a match arranged in this way is one agreeable to the respective families, still in form it is a rebellion against the familial authority and a neglect of the community.

After marriage sexual intercourse ceases almost completely to be a social problem; it is intentionally ignored by society. Conjugal infidelity in normal conditions is not assumed to exist; it is very seldom even spoken of, and, if it occurs, is unconditionally condemned, equally in man and woman. But even the legal sexual relation between man and wife is the object of a very far-going discretion. It is never mentioned when one is talking about marriage; even by the married couple itself, in private conversation or letters, sexual allusions are scrupulously avoided. In a few cases where we find them they are accompanied by apologies. It seems as if the whole sexual question were felt, not so much as impure, as incongruous with the normal and socially sanctioned conjugal relation, which, for the social consciousness, is fundamentally a familial relation, belonging to the same type as other relations between members of a family. Conjugal sexual life is not institutionalized, as is courtship, nor morally regulated, as is family life, but is reduced to a minimum and left out of consideration. It is a curious fact that in spite of ten centuries of Christian influence there is a disharmony between the peasant attitude and the standpoint of the church. The latter conceives marriage as precisely a regulation and institutionalization of sexual intercourse and, far from avoiding allusions to sexual matters, subjects them to an analysis and valuation which, though mainly negative, is very detailed. Frequent misunderstandings therefore arise between the priest and his parishioners, particularly if the former is not of peasant origin.

Sexual life in general is thus completely subordinated to marriage, is regulated in view of marriage before the ceremony and denied any independent value after the ceremony. In a later volume we shall treat the process which leads to a development of sexual life outside and independent of marriage. Here we can only indicate that the sexual factor is beginning to play a more important rôle in marriage by determining more and more its selection.

In a perfect familial and social organization the individual can choose his partner within the limits indicated above, but this free choice is itself not exclusively determined by sexual love, because the development of sexual love is dependent upon the whole system of courtship. Not only is the individual prohibited from selecting outside of the relatively narrow circle of socially possible matches, but even within this circle his possibilities of choice are further restrained by all the formalities which make the exclusiveness of sexual love a matter of the gradual elimination of all matches but one. An immediate falling in love, leading directly to engagement, is psychologically impossible. In most cases it is not only true that all the possible partners are known from childhood—which is evidently an important obstacle to a rapid infatuation—but indecision, careful selecting, taking of all possibilities into account, are traditional attitudes, originating in familial considerations, but transferred to matters of love.   This indecision is reinforced by the limitations of speech mentioned above; expressions of love containing even the faintest sexual allusion are socially sanctioned only when publicly made and consequently impersonal or half-impersonal; private declarations are very limited.   For the normal young boy or girl, therefore, there are a certain number of persons of the other sex more or less pleasing, and all of them are sexually acceptable.   The ultimate choice is then made under the influence of the family, or for various reasons all these possibilities fall away one by one and the decision settles upon the one remaining.   The only case when this "liking" of one person among others can ripen into love before marriage is when for some reason the two individuals have more opportunity to meet each other than anyone else. After the engagement, and particularly after marriage, exclusiveness is attained, but precisely then the love-relation changes into the respect-relation.   Of course, there is often love shortly before and after the wedding, but it is gradually submerged by familial and economic interests.

The first stage of the liberation of the factor of sexual love is actually the illegal sexual intercourse before marriage. We call it the first stage, because it exists at the very beginning of individualization, if external conditions are favorable.   Thus, among the young season-emigrants to Germany, and even among wandering season-laborers on Polish estates, who are isolated from their families and communities for from seven to ten months and have the opportunity to meet privately, almost 50 per cent have sexual intercourse and then marry after coming home, or even send money to their priest during the season, asking for the publication of their banns. Here the mere "liking" grows into sexual love, thanks to the actual sexual intercourse, and may become strong enough to cause the young people to take upon themselves the whole responsibility for their marriage, though usually the permission of the parents is obtained before the priest is asked to publish the banns.

The second form of the liberation of sexual love is more normal, because it requires no exceptional conditions and does not break the traditional sexual morality; but on the other hand it shows a higher stage of individualization. We find it particularly often in America, but also in Polish cities. It consists in the reduction of all the complicated process of selection and courtship to an offhand proposal to a girl who "pleases" after a relatively short personal acquaintance. If the girl rejects the proposal, the boy tries to find another whom he "likes" and repeats the performance. This way of concluding a marriage shows a very important evolution of the traditional attitudes. It is possible only when all the familial, social, or economic motives have lost their influence and the indecision, the hesitation among many possibilities, is no longer artificially maintained. The boy or girl desires to marry in general, and in this mood, after the liberation from all social pressure, the slight "liking" (which under the old conditions would only suffice to put the person liked among those from whom a closer selection would be made) becomes a sufficient impulse to start the decisive action.

Finally, the last stage is attained when this "liking," under the influence of a general cultural progress, and particularly of a development of imagination and feeling made independent of practical activity, grows into a typical "romantic" love, in which the sexual element is neither stifled, as in the traditional conditions, nor given in its crude form, as in sexual intercourse before marriage, but exalted and idealized, and the exclusiveness results neither from institutional reasons nor from habit, but from a rich complexity of feelings and ideas connected with the given person.

THE CLASS-SYSTEM IN POLISH SOCIETY.

In the present state of Polish society there is a general revaluation of social distinctions, a breaking down of the old social hierarchy and an establishment of a new one. This process is going on more rapidly in certain parts of the country (it is the slowest in Galicia), but everywhere it includes also the peasants and the lower city classes and exerts a great influence upon the psychology of the younger generation in particular.

The old class-organization presents two independent and partly parallel social hierarchies—that of the country and that of the town population. The first is fundamental, the second additional.

The highest rank in the first hierarchy (and completely dominating the second as well) was occupied by a few families of great nobility. At the time of Poland's independence they occupied the highest official posts, kept their own armies, directed politics, etc. After Poland's partition their political influence disappeared. At present fortune, tradition, and in most cases title (there were no recognized titles in Poland before the partition, except for a few Lithuanian and Ruthenian princes) are all that distinguish these forty or fifty families from the rest of the nobility. The numerous middle nobility constitutes the second stratum. Then comes the peasant nobility, distinguished from the middle nobility by the lack of fortune and culture, from the peasant, formerly by its rights, now only by tradition.[1] Then come the peasant farmers, formerly classified into crown peasants (almost completely free, but having no political rights), church peasants, and private serfs. Finally comes the landless peasants. It was in fact not possible during Poland's independence to draw an absolute line between any two contiguous classes; particularly the gradation of noble families on one side, the gradation of peasant families on the other, was continuous, and between the lowest noble and the highest peasant families the distinction was political, not social. But the position of each family was very exactly determined; rising and falling were possible, but very seldom within a single generation. And as far as the social organization still persists, the same is true at present.

On the other hand, the town population was also hierarchized, mainly upon the basis of fortune, secondarily upon that of culture and birth. The highest place was occupied in every large town by some wealthy trades-families; then came the intellectual workers and the craftsmen; then the petty merchants and unskilled workers. Politically the rights of the old bourgeoisie, except in town administration, were lower than those of the nobility in general; socially the position of old and rich bourgeois families ranked with that

[1] "Peasant nobility" is a class found only in Poland and called in Polish *szlachta zaściankowa*, "village nobility," *szlachta zagonowa*, "bed-nobility" (referring to their small beds of land), and *szlachta szaraczkowa*, "gray nobility." They had almost full political rights, and coats-of-arms like the rest of the nobility. Usually one large family of the same name occupied a whole village and even several villages. They were quite independent economically, but as they had no serfs they were in the same economic condition as the peasants. Their origin dates back mainly to the fourteenth and fifteenth centuries. They were usually the descendants of warriors endowed with land by the dukes, and sank to their low economic and social level as a consequence of their numerical increase and the division of land. They were and are still particularly numerous in the ancient duchy of Mazovia (unified with the kingdom of Poland in 1525–27); thence large numbers of them emigrated to, and organized large settlements in, Lithuania and Ruthenia. At the end of the eighteenth century they outnumbered the middle nobility—400,000 as against 300,000.

of the middle nobility. Outside of both hierarchies, and in fact, with rare exceptions, outside of Polish social life in general, was the Jew.

As early as the end of the eighteenth century many factors began to contribute to a gradual dissolution of this system, and the process of dissolution reached the lower classes some thirty or forty years ago. The "Constitution of May 3" (1791) gave political rights to the bourgeoisie, but the later loss of independence made all political privileges illusory. The process of personal and economic liberation of the peasants, begun before the second partition and carried on by private initiative and legal acts, was completed in 1864. The development of industry, the ruin of many noble families after each revolution through confiscation of their fortunes, the agricultural crisis caused by foreign importation, the spread of instruction and democratic ideas, are all factors destroying the content of old distinctions while leaving the form. The process is still going on, and the actual situation may be stated in the following way.

First, there are still the old classes, wherever the conditions permit a certain isolation and the development of a strong class-consciousness—that is, wherever the class is at the same time a social group with real intercourse and common interests. The factors which keep the old class-consciousness strong are mainly territorial vicinity and identity of occupation. Thus, the old families of middle nobility settled in some district or province, the old bourgeois families in large towns, the peasant families or the peasant nobility settled in the same village or parish from immemorial time—these have still a class-feeling strong enough to resist any external influences. They do not admit anybody from a lower class, and they do not try to get into a higher class. But these scattered groups have among themselves a feeling of congeniality and of equality; and intermarriage creates among them new links of solidarity.

But these groups, without being exactly dissolved, are diminishing through a process whose mechanism is determined by the nature of their own constitution as well as by the changes which the economic and political evolution of the country brings with it. The economic form corresponding to the social system expressed in these groups is that of familial property, that is, property, parts of which are under the management, not in the complete ownership, of the individual. In this form of economic organization the class can subsist as a real social group because through it territorial vicinity and identity of occupation can be preserved through a series of generations, and class-consciousness can persist even if it has no longer any real basis in the political organization. Under these conditions, if an individual is unable to maintain his part of the family fortune the family helps him and controls him, and as far as possible hinders his ruin. But this control and help are of course limited. The family may be unable to help, it may be unwilling to help, or the individual may be unwilling to accept any control, if for some reason the attitude of solidarity is weakened or the strain is too great. And the economic changes of the last century make the preservation of the old forms of property more and more difficult, particularly since the lack of political independence did not permit the development of any adequate social mechanism to facilitate the modernization of the ancient economy in agriculture, handiwork, and commerce. Thus the cases in which the family cannot save the individual from ruin, or even where the whole family is ruined, are very frequent. And when the modernization of economy is finally attained, it usually proves that greater individualization of property is required, the familial solidarity is thus weakened, and the individual is left more or less to his own resources.

But any member of the class-group who ceases to be a proprietor is declassed. He cannot maintain the old social relations on a basis of equality; he must usually leave his territorial group in search of work; he loses community of interest with his class, and, above all, he has to do hired work—he becomes dependent. Now there is hardly another economic distinction so profoundly rooted in Polish consciousness as that between independent work on the person's own property and hired work. The occasion of this, as is shown by our analysis of the economic attitudes, is threefold: (1) hired work, before the development of industry, meant almost always "service," including personal dependence of the employee on the employer; (2) hired work in whatever form has the character of compulsory work as opposed to free work; (3) hired work is more individual than independent work, and bears no direct relation to the familial organization. (Of course professional work, based on fee, not on wages, must be distinguished from hired work.)

The loss of class is seldom complete in the first generation. The individual still keeps the attitudes of his class-group and personal connection with its members. Even in the second, sometimes in the third, generation some attitudes remain, personal relations are not completely severed, the familial tradition is kept up, and the question of birth plays a rôle.

In this way, during the last century and particularly during the last fifty years, there has been a continually growing number of those who have lost class, derived from all the social classes of the old complicated hierarchy. But while a hundred years ago these outclassed individuals hung about their old class in some subordinate position, the industrial and commercial development of the country has opened for them new lines of activity and new fields of interest, while the progress of instruction and of modern social ideology has helped to construct new principles of social distinction, class-solidarity, and class-hierarchy. The result is that along with the declining, but still strong, old social organization there exists in growing strength a new organization, based upon quite different principles and tending gradually to absorb the first.

An interesting feature of this new organization, distinguishing it from parallel social structures in France, Germany, or Italy, is that the principle of hierarchization is in the first place intellectual achievement, and only in the second place wealth, in its modern forms of capital and income. This is due mainly to two factors. First, while in other societies the rich bourgeoisie, by becoming the capitalistic class in the modern sense, constituted the nucleus of the new hierarchization, in Poland the old Polish bourgeoisie was too weak to play the same rôle; its number was small, its wealth limited. Not only was the town life less developed in Poland than in the West, but the Polish bourgeoisie had to share its rôle of capitalistic class with the Jews, who, being themselves outside of Polish society, could not impose the capitalistic principle of social distinction. On the contrary, the fact that the Jews were to a large extent representatives of the capitalistic economy has certainly helped to maintain, almost up to the present time, a certain contempt toward "money-making" and the attitudes of business in general. At the same time, after the fall of Poland the conditions were not favorable for the constitution of a bureaucracy, except, to a certain extent, in Galicia. The "intellectual aristocracy" was therefore almost unrivaled, and succeeded in imposing its standard of values upon the whole new system. The second factor which helped the intellectual aristocracy to do this was the loss of political independence and the subsequent efforts to keep the Polish culture in spite of political oppression. Every intellectual achievement appeared in this light as bearing a general national value. When later the capitalistic class grew in power, it had to accept, more or less, either the standard of the new intellectual class or that of the old aristocracy, and it still hesitates between the two, but with a marked inclination toward the first. Its wealth gives it an additional superiority over the intellectual, not over the birth, aristocracy, and it is easier to satisfy the intellectualistic standard than that of birth. Thus, the new hierarchy gains in extension, while at the same time the intellectual criterion becomes complicated by that of wealth. And those criteria go down to the lowest strata of society.

There is, of course, a continual passage of individuals from the old hierarchy to the new, and on the other hand a growing infiltration of individuals and families of the new class into the old class-groups through marriage and property. But the old bourgeoisie is already largely amalgamated with the new class-organization; the middle nobility began to amalgamate with it some thirty or forty years ago, and the process is going on, although rather slowly; the amalgamation of the peasant began in the present generation. Only the highest aristocracy and the peasant nobility remain still isolated in their class-groups, though losing members continually.

Finally, the individually Polonized Jews and foreigners, when they settle in Poland and become assimilated, are received into the new organization. The same can be said of the bureaucrats.

In this new hierarchy we can distinguish four classes. The highest class is constituted by those who, besides a sufficient degree of instruction (university) and an indispensable social refinement, have some particular superiority in any line—wealth, talent, very good birth, high political, bureaucratic, or social position. The middle class—the essential part of this hierarchy—is composed of professionals: lawyers, physicians, professors, higher technicians, literary men, tradesmen of middle fortune, higher employees. University instruction and a certain minimum of good manners are, generally speaking, the criteria delimiting this class from the lower middle class. The latter is the most important for us in the present connection, because it is the usual medium through which the peasant rises above his own class, for in the old social hierarchy he could not do this. His old social position corresponds, in fact, somewhat to one between the lower middle class and the workman class, and he may now rise to the one or fall to the other.

In the city the lower middle class is composed of shop-keepers, craftsmen, lower post and governmental officials, railway officials, private clerks and salesmen, etc. To this class in the country belong manor officials (farm-managers, stewards, clerks, distillers, foresters); commune secretaries, teachers, organists; rich shopkeepers and mill-owners, etc. But we must remember that the criterion is not so much the position itself as the degree of instruction which this requires and the average cultural level of the men who occupy it, and that a man of good birth, good manners, and higher instruction, even if filling an inferior position, does not fall below the middle class. On the other hand, lack of instruction and bad manners hardly permit even a relatively rich man to rise to the middle-class level. Thus it may happen that a clerk belongs to a higher social *niveau* than his employer and is received in circles which are closed to the latter.

In the city the lower middle class is connected by imperceptible gradations with the working class and in the country with that of manor servants; the differences become smaller the lower the social level. While education still retains its value, the kind of occupation, money, dress, are beginning to play a more important rôle. The criteria which usually exclude a man definitely from the lower middle class and place him in that of the workman are unskilled labor and illiteracy, though the contrary does not hold good; that is, an occupation requiring some special skill or reading and writing does not place a man above the working class.

Of course all kinds of pauperism and vice declass a man definitely, put him outside of both the old and the new hierarchy. Beggars, tramps, criminals, prostitutes, have no place in the class-hierarchy. The same holds true of Jews, except those who are Polonized, and to some extent of Polish servants in Jewish houses. In Russian and German Poland the officials and the army are outside of Polish social life.

This system of social distinctions is even more complicated than we have here described it; the distinctions become sometimes almost imperceptible, but they are very real, and their influence in the new hierarchy is even greater than in the old, because in the former they stimulate uncommonly the climbing tendency. Under the old system progress in social standing requires the collaboration of the greater part of the family-group, is necessarily slow, and no showing-off can make the individual appear as belonging to a higher class than his family, for where his family is known, his social standing is determined, and where it is not known, he has no real social standing. Particularly since the old class is a plurality of class-groups, unified by territorial and professional solidarity, and connected from group to group by a feeling of identical traditions and interests (sometimes by intermarriage), social advance is essentially not passing into a higher class, but rising within the given class-group. The factors which permit a family to rise are the development of property along the line of the occupations of the class (land in the country, buildings and trade in the town), practical intelligence, moral integrity, and, in general, all the qualities which assure an influence upon the class-group, such as good marriages within the class-group, familial solidarity.

On the contrary, in the new social organization an individual (or marriage-group) can rise alone and rapidly. He is easily tempted to show off, to adopt the external distinctions of the superior class in order to appear as belonging to it, and, if he is clever enough, this showing-off helps him to rise. And the rise itself is here essentially a passing into the higher class, facilitated by the fact that the criteria are so complicated that the territorial or professional groups in this organization have not the importance of real class-groups, and that no groups can have the stability and impenetrability which the old groups possessed before the dropping of the familial principle. The factors of climbing are here instruction, economic development— rather as an increase of income than as an acquisition of property—wit, tact, a certain refinement of manners, and, in general, qualities which assure, not the influence upon a given social environment, but the adaptation to a new social environment, including marriage above one's own class and breaking of familial solidarity.

It is easy to understand how this new, fluid, individual-istic class-hierarchy, opening so many possibilities of social progress, must be attractive to the members of a society in which the question of social standing and class-distinction always played an exceptionally important rôle. It has enough of democracy to permit anyone to rise and enough of aristocracy to make the rise real. Particularly among peasants its influence must be felt more and more, as with the dismembering of land and growing proletarization of the country inhabitants the possibility of rising within the peasant community is closed for a large part of the young generation.

Since passing into the new organization and rising within it involve a far-going modification of the traditional attitudes, there arises an estrangement, and sometimes a struggle, between the old and new generations, and of this we have numerous examples in this and the following volumes.

In general, the attitude of the members of the traditional class-groups toward the old and the new class-hierarchy is very characteristic. All the old classes, from the highest aristocracy down to the peasant, are based, as we have seen, upon the same general principles, and to this extent they understand each other's attitudes. This understanding is particularly close between country classes, where an identity of occupation creates a common universe of discourse; but it is not lacking either between the town and country population, wherever they meet. And, more than this, even the Jew, although outside of the Polish society, is understood by the noble and the peasant and understands them. This understanding between the old classes does not exclude antagonism, hostility, and mistrust whenever whole groups are concerned, whenever the peasant, the noble, the Jew, the handworker, meet upon the ground of antagonistic class-interests. But it makes possible a curious closeness of relations between individuals wherever class-antagonisms are for a shorter or longer time out of the question. And in spite of all antagonisms and hostilities, a member of any class-group wants the members of any other class to be true and perfect representatives of their class-spirit, to incorporate fully all the traditional attitudes of the class, including even those which are the basis of class antagonisms. Thus, the peasant wants the noble to be a lord in the full sense of the word, proud but humane and just, living luxuriously, unconcerned about money, but a good farmer; not easily cheated or robbed by his servants or even by his peasant neighbors, but consciously generous, conservative, religious, etc.—in a word, to have those features which, while putting him at an inaccessible distance above the peasant, still make him familiar and possible to understand.

On the contrary, the members of the old class-groups do not understand at all the new men. There is no class-antagonism; on the contrary, in many cases there is a solidarity of interests which may be even acknowledged. In spite of this, individual relations between members of the old and the new hierarchy can hardly ever be very close, except, of course, in so far as a member of a new social class still keeps some attitudes of the old one, or a member of some old class-group becomes modernized. Nor is it merely a matter of different occupations. A professional who buys an estate, a city worker who buys a peasant farm, can hardly ever become quite intimate with any of the old inhabitants. All this manifests itself curiously, for example, with regard to the Jews. The Jewish boycott of the two years preceding the war extended only with great difficulty to the country population, because in many localities the peasant, sometimes even the old-type noble, understood better, and felt himself nearer to, the Jewish merchant of the old type than to the more honest and enlightened Polish merchant of the new class. But let a rich, instructed, even christened, Jew, belonging essentially to the new middle class, buy an estate and he will feel incomparably more isolated from the Polish nobility and the Polish peasant than some little old crass Jewish merchant from the neigh-boring town.

We shall see in our later volumes many and important manifestations of the class-evolution in communal and national life.

SOCIAL ENVIRONMENT

The family is practically the only organized social group to which the peasant primarily belongs as an *active* member. Outside of the family his social milieu can be divided into two distinct and dissociated parts: (1) a political and social organization in which he does not play an active rôle and of which he does not feel a member; and (2) a community of which he is an active member, but which is constituted by a certain number of groups whose internal unity is due merely to actual social intercourse and to an identity of attitudes. This dissociation is an essential feature of the original peasant social life; its progressive removal, the constitution of organized groups of which the peasant becomes an active member, is the main characteristic of the evolution of social life which we shall study in a later volume.

1. The complete lack of political rights until the end of the eighteenth century made the peasant only an object, not a subject, of political activity. In the process of gradual liberation he has acquired some political rights—communal self-government, participation in elections. But at the beginning he was unprepared to use them and was always governed as before, and even since he has begun to participate actively in political life this participation, except in Galicia, has been limited up to the present, for the peasant as for the other Polish classes, by the political oppression of the country. The society developed some equivalent of an independent state-organization, as we shall see later, but only in German Poland is the peasant a fully active element of this organization, while in Russian Poland he is only on the way to it. And since in Russian Poland political rights

have always been more limited than anywhere else, the old attitude toward the state is there preserved in the most typical form. This attitude can perhaps be best compared with the attitude toward the natural order on one hand, and toward the divine order on the other; it is intermediary between the two. The political order appears to a certain extent as an impersonal and a moral power, absolutely mysterious, whose manifestations can possibly be foreseen, but whose nature and laws cannot be changed by human interference. But this order has also another side, more comprehensible but more unforeseen, with some moral character, that is, capable of being just or unjust and of being influenced; in this respect it is the exact parallel of the divine world. The bearers of political power whom the peasant meets are men, and their executive activity can be directed within certain limits by gifts or supplication, or they can be moved to intercede before those higher ones whom the peasant seldom meets, who are more powerful and more mysterious, but still in some measure human and accessible. Above them all is the emperor, less human than divine, capable of being moved but seldom, if ever, directly accessible, all-powerful but not all-knowing. This whole system, this combination of impersonal power and half-religious hierarchy, evidently permits a certain explanation of everything, but excludes absolutely any idea of political activity. The peasant can accept only passively whatever happens and rejoice or grieve. He does not always even feel able to praise or to blame, for a given fact may be the expression of the impersonal power as well as of the personalities, and even in the latter case he does not know whom to praise or to blame. Usually he tries to interpret everything more favorably for the higher, less favorably for the lower, personalities, because this always leaves some way out of pessimism; the higher personalities may not have known the situation; when they know it, they will change the oppressive measures or show themselves the peasant's benefactors. The unlimited power ascribed to the state and the mystery with which its leaders are surrounded in the peasant's imagination make him cherish often the most absurd hopes or give way sometimes to the most absurd fears. For even if the leaders are accessible to such motives as the peasant understands, they have besides an unlimited sphere of unknown motives and plans, exactly as it is with God. Therefore in the state as viewed by the peasant there is a self-contradictory combination of an impersonal regularity, incorporated in the habitual functions, and of almost whimsical change. Being a superhuman order, it is at the same time a source of unlimited possibilities.

All this explains the traditional loyalty of the peasant and makes us understand at the same time in what ways this loyalty disappears. The first step is usually connected with a change of the habitual valuations. The source of evil is placed higher and higher, until finally, as often in Russian Poland, the tsar is conceived as being practically parallel with, and similar to, Satan. The unlimited possibilities included in the state become fundamentally possibilities of evil; the good comes only incidentally, as a consequence of an imperfect realization of the evil, due to the fact that the lower personalities in the state-hierarchy are more human. Their human character acquires a positive value; it is still weakness, but weakness in evil, resulting from an accessibility to the motives of ordinary interest (as in accepting bribes), and sometimes even to good feelings. Then comes the second step—the development of a half-mystical faith that this empire of evil can be broken and a new and perfect organization established in its place, not indeed with the ordinary human forces alone, but with the supernatural help of God or by the half-supernatural powers of other states, of "the people," of "the proletariat," etc. This is the typical psychological path of revolution in the lower classes.

The other way is that of a progressive growth of the peasant's positive or negative part in the state—participation in state-activities and organized struggle with the government within legal limits. A real understanding of the state-organization, sufficient for practical purposes, dissolves the mystical attitudes, while at the same time the development of a national consciousness makes loyalty to an oppressive state appear as national treason. This evolution has begun in Russian Poland and is nearly completed in German Poland.

Besides the state, the two other organized social groups of which the peasant is a member are the commune and the parish. In both he was passive for a long time. Although the commune is based upon the principle of self-government, its freedom is often limited by administrative measures of the state, and in the beginning the peasant was hardly able to use his liberty even within these limits. The commune was in fact governed by the secretary, who knew the formal side of administration, and in many communes this situation lasts up to the present. As to the parish, the priest was all-powerful, not only in fact, but to a great extent also in form, and up to the present in many parishes the peasants can hardly get an account of the money which they give. It is not so much dishonesty on the part of the priests, many of whom are really disinterested, as the expression of the principle of patriarchal government, the influence of the idea that any control would be harmful to the priest's authority. The struggle for active participation in the commune and the parish organization is one of the important points in the actual evolution of the peasant's social life, particularly in Russian Poland.

Finally, the same passivity characterized the peasant's part in economic life. Well adapted to the old conditions of the local farming economy, he stood powerless, ignorant and isolated in face of the great economic phenomena of the external world, and even in face of the small and informal Jewish economic organizations of the neighboring town. In this line his present evolution is most rapid and is particularly important in its psychological consequences.

2. The social environment to which the peasant is primarily adapted, within which he is active and lives his everyday life, is the partly coincident primary groups—the village, the parish, and the commune. These are here treated, not as organized administrative units, but as collectivities, loosely unified by personal interrelations among their members, by a certain identity of interests which does not as a rule give birth to common activities, by periodical meetings, through which the particular kind of solidarity developed for a short time in a mob is perpetuated as a psychological deposit. To this environment we must add the neighboring town, a part of whose inhabitants the peasant knows mainly through business relations, and the neighboring parishes and communes, whose inhabitants he occasionally meets at fairs and parish festivals. The Polish popular term corresponding to this undetermined environment, with which the individual or the family has close or remote, but always immediate, relations, is *okolica*, "the country around," both in the topographic and in the social sense. In the latter sense we shall use the term "community."

Of course the circle of the community widens with the facilities of communication and the frequency of social intercourse, but there is always a criterion which enables us to determine its farthest limits: It reaches as far as the *social opinion* about the individual or the family reaches.

Social opinion is the common factor which holds the community together, besides and above all the particularities which unify various parts of the community, individuals, or smaller groups with each other, and it is the only indispensable factor. Occasionally there may arise a local interest which provokes some common, more or less organized, action, usually of an economic nature. But this faculty of common action shows that the old community has already risen to a new level, and is again one of the marked points of the present social evolution of the peasant. The peasant community subsisted for centuries independent of common action and lacked any organization, even a transitory one.

The manner in which social opinion holds the community together is easily analyzed. Any extraordinary occurrence becomes for a certain time the focus of attention of all the members of the community, an identical attitude toward this is developed, and each member of the community is conscious that he shares the general attitude or that his attitude is shared by the rest of the community. These are the three original elements of the mechanism of social opinion: the phenomenon, the identity of attitude, and the consciousness of this identity.

First of all, the social unity of the community depends upon the frequency with which social opinion has the opportunity to manifest itself. This is inversely proportional to the size of the group and directly proportional to the number of relatively important phenomena occurring in it. In the community the number of phenomena sufficiently important to occupy the social opinion is, of course, much more limited than in the parish or commune, in the parish more limited than in the village. But in any given group the number increases with the increase of the sphere of interests of the members. When, for example, in some village an agricultural association has bought a new machine, or a milk association has had an exceptionally large amount of milk, the whole community learns of it and talks about it. The awakening of national and political interests has the same effect, as many phenomena occurring within the community assume a new importance from those points of view. Finally, a very important factor is added by the press. Through it phenomena from the external world—first only those which have or seem to have some relation with the interests prevailing among the members of the community, then also those which arouse a purely intellectual interest— are brought into the focus of social opinion, are talked about, more or less identical attitudes are developed with regard to them, etc.

But with the introduction of these new phenomena, particularly the external ones, social opinion loses a character that it possessed eminently in more primitive conditions— its reliability.   In a primary group, with steady components, with a form of life relatively simple and changing very slowly, with a close connection between its members, mistakes in the perception or interpretation of an interesting fact are relatively rare, and gossip is usually as well motivated as it can be.   The peasant is a keen observer within the sphere of his normal environment, for good observation is there a condition of practical success, and he knows his environment well enough to interpret exactly the observed data.   So those who start a piece of gossip are usually sure of their fact, and those who hear it know enough to be critical, to distinguish between the probable and the improbable.   And deliberately false gossip incurs a strong censure of social opinion.   Of course interpretation and criticism are exerted from the standpoint of tradition, and nothing can prevent errors resulting from false traditional beliefs; accusations of magic are a classical example.   From our point of view, therefore, many expressions of the peasant's social opinion are partly false. But they prove true as soon as the tradition of the peasant community is taken into account; for example, in normal conditions only those are accused of magic who really try to exert it. The error lies in the whole system of beliefs, not in the interpretation of a particular fact from the standpoint of this system.

But when a phenomenon of a new and hitherto unknown kind appears in the focus of social attention, the old mechanism fails at once. Observation becomes incomplete, the fact distorted by old mental habits; interpretation is hazardous and real criticism impossible, because there is no ready criterion of the probable and improbable. And particularly if such a new fact occurs, and the gossip originates outside of the community, the disorientation of social opinion is complete. Any absurdity may circulate and be generally accepted.[1] Of course this is due, not only to the impossibility of tracing the gossip to its source and the difficulty of verification, but also to the general mental attitude of the peasant who, once outside of his normal conditions, faces the world as an unlimited sphere of incalculable possibilities.[2]

We have spoken of an identity of attitudes, developed by the members of a community with regard to the socially interesting phenomenon. In fact, this identity is a necessary condition of social opinion and it becomes more perfect when social opinion is once formed, in view of the pressure which this exerts on the individual. Were it not for this

---

[1] Thus, during the emigration to Paraná in 1910–12, in many eastern isolated communities the legend was circulated that Paraná up to that time was covered with mist, and nobody knew of its existence. But the Virgin Mary, seeing the misery of Polish peasants, dispelled the mist and told them to come and settle. Or a variant: When the mist was raised, all the kings and emperors of the earth came together and drew lots to decide who should take the new land. Three times they drew, and always the Pope won. Then the Pope, at the instigation of the Virgin Mary, gave the land to the Polish peasants.

[2] See *Religious Attitudes* and *Theoretic and Esthetic Interests*.

pressure, unanimity of social appreciation could hardly be
attained as often as it is, in view of the frequent divergence
of individual and familial interests in a given case. The
main factor in establishing this uniformity and in enforcing
it in spite of individual disagreement is tradition. The
attitude to be taken with regard to any phenomenon of a
definite class is predetermined by tradition, and an individual
who took a different attitude would be a rebel against
tradition and in this character would himself become a
socially interesting phenomenon, an object instead of a
subject of social opinion, and in fact an object of the
most unfavorable criticism. But there comes eventually a
progressive dissolution of tradition, and at the same time
an increase in the number of phenomena which cannot be
included in any of traditional categories, either because they
are quite new or because the new interests which have arisen
in the community throw a new light upon old classes of
phenomena. And the result is a dissociation of attitudes
within the community, a formation of opposite camps, more
or less durable, sometimes even a struggle, usually leading
to some crude beginnings of organization. If the divergent
attitudes assume steady directions, if they remain divergent
with regard to many new phenomena and thus point back
to certain profound social changes going on within the
community, the latter may split into two or more parties,
which may in turn join some larger organizations. But all
this does not mean that the community is dissolved. As
long as the same phenomena arouse social interest, it is
a proof that behind a diversity of, or even opposition in,
details there is an identity of general attitudes, and it is
with regard to this identity that the community still
remains one group; only its unity is weakened, because the
stock of common traditions is poorer and the unanimity
incomplete. A complete division of the community would

occur only if every identity of interests disappeared, if its members belonged to completely different social organizations, which would respectively absorb and satisfy all their social tendencies. This state of things is approximately realized where different nationalities live together—Poles with Russians or Germans, much less so with Jews.[1]

The third element of social opinion—the consciousness of the attitudes of others—is mainly kept up by all kinds of social meetings. While individual conversation and the communication of news favor the development of identical attitudes, its action is neither strong nor rapid enough when taken alone to make the social opinion self-conscious. The meeting not only shortens the process of communication, but, thanks to the immediate influence of the group upon the individual, is the most powerful medium through which social tradition is applied to each case and an identical attitude elaborated and enforced upon the members. Through frequent meetings a village can develop a certain (of course limited) originality of attitudes which gives it a particular social physiognomy. Through meetings also a village may be much more closely connected with some distant village belonging to the same parish than with a near one which belongs to another parish, even if individual intercourse with the second is more animated than with the first. The commune, before it became a real social organization, had incomparably less unity than the parish, because general meetings were rare and included only a part of the population (men farmers). The connection with people of other parishes and communes is mainly due to meetings—fairs, parish festivals, etc.

Among the more intelligent the popular press plays the same part as the meeting; the correspondence or the article

---

[1] The latter case presents this particularity, that Jewish social opinion is much more concerned with phenomena going on among the Poles than reciprocally—evidently because of the economic interests of the Jews.

permits the communication of the event and of the attitude toward it, and the printed word has the same influence as the expressed opinion of the group, because it is implicitly assumed to be the expression of social opinion. There are certainly essential differences between the meeting and the paper with regard to the mechanism by which social opinion is elaborated; the relation between the individual and the group is immediate in the first case, mediate in the second, and through the paper the individual as well as the community enters into relation with the external world. But the function of the Polish popular paper, which we shall study in the fourth volume, can be clearly understood only if we take it in connection with the social opinion of the community.

The nature of the influence of social opinion upon the individual who is its object is rather complicated. First of all, it seems that for the Polish peasant in general it is rather pleasant to be the focus of public attention, apart from the cause of it; even if this cause is indifferent from the standpoint of personal value and public attention involves no admiration, it still brings a pleasant excitement. This would explain to a great extent, for example, the usual vehement display of grief, even if we recognize the traditional element in it. The excitement of departure to military service or to America contains certainly some of this pleasure; still more the excitement of return with anticipation of public admiration. But certainly this pleasure never goes so far as to neutralize the feeling of shame at being the object of intense public blame, as it sometimes does in city criminals. On the contrary, the negative influence of public blame in criminal matters goes so far that suspicion of crime, just or unjust, is one of the most important causes of suicide. Another intensely felt public disgrace is that which follows ruin and the declassing

which accompanies it.   Not less intense is the shame brought
to a girl by the discovery of her misconduct.   But if
this misconduct consists, not in actual sexual intercourse
(particularly if followed by the birth of a child), but in a
far-going flirtation with many boys, the distress of incurring
public blame is neutralized by the pleasure of having much
success with the boys.   Finally, there is one matter in which
the peasant universally dislikes publicity in whatever form;
it is the matter of conjugal relations.   But, generally
speaking, the desire of showing off is a much more powerful
factor in the peasant's behavior than the fear of shame.
People who, by rising above, or falling below, the normal
level of the community, have learned to disregard public
blame still show themselves very susceptible to public
appreciation.   The peasant's vanity does not require for
its satisfaction explicit public praise; the general pleasure
of attracting attention is adequate.   It may even adjust
itself to a moderate amount of blame, for which the peasant
has a ready explanation: they calumniate because they
envy.   And certainly this explanation is often true.   In a
community where everybody wants more or less to be the
object of general attention anybody who succeeds in this
aim becomes in so far an object of envy.   We may add that
envy of notoriety is probably much stronger than envy of
economic well-being, and success in any line is appreciated
at least as much for the public admiration which it attracts
as for itself.

Behind this actual machinery of the action of public
opinion there may perhaps still remain some profound,
unconscious vestiges of forgotten motives, consisting in the
belief in an immediate, useful or harmful influence of the
appreciation expressed in words.   But we have no data
which would clearly require the use of this magical explanation.

The influence of social opinion upon the single individual is only one side of the question; we must also take into consideration its effects upon a smaller group within the community. Here the problem is more complicated.

The starting-point is the internal and what we may call the external solidarity of every social group, in the face of the opinion of its social environment. The internal solidarity consists in the fact that every member feels affected by the opinion expressed about his group, and the group is affected by the opinion expressed about any one of its members. The external solidarity—that is, the solidarity enforced from without—is manifested in the tendency of every community to generalize the opinion about an individual by applying it to the narrower social group of which this individual is a member, and to particularize the opinion about a social group by applying it to every member of this group.

It is quite natural that in all matters involving social blame the external solidarity imposed by the environment is usually the condition of the internal solidarity of the group itself. The opinion of the environment often makes the group responsible for its members even if there is feeble unity in this group, and practically obliges it to become solidary, either by reacting together against the environment or by enforcing upon every member compliance with the environment's demand. Thus, when in a village some people begin to develop a certain vice, the rest of the inhabitants cannot throw the responsibility upon the guilty members alone, for the opinion of the community will always accuse the whole group without discrimination. So they have either to interfere with the guilty members or to accept the judgment and make the best of it. The latter course is sometimes taken, and the result may be that the vice becomes general in the village. There are, for example,

villages notorious for theft, drinking, card-playing, etc.
Besides imitation, there has been in such cases also a passive
resignation and acceptance of the *vox populi*, after a vain
struggle, and a subsequent adaptation to the bad opinion.
The priests know very well how to deal with such cases.
When a vice is only beginning to develop in a village, they
proclaim it publicly from the chancel and brand the whole
village, without discrimination. In this way they get the
collaboration of the greater part of the inhabitants in their
struggle against the vice. But if a village has long been
notorious for some vice, the priest proclaims publicly the
slightest improvement in order to show the possibility of
changing the bad name.

The unorganized social group usually lacks, of course,
the most efficient arms against the members who bring
shame upon it, namely, exclusion. In some cases this is
attempted, more or less successfully, but then the group
organizes itself temporarily in view of this particular end.
It is possible for the individual to disclaim solidarity with
an ill-famed unorganized group by leaving it, but this
again does not happen frequently, because the individual,
supported by his narrower group, feels less strongly the
blame of the wider community. This process of enforcing
solidarity upon the group by the social environment is
frequently repeated, on a larger scale, when a community
is blamed in the newspapers for the acts of some of its
members. We find it, also, in a somewhat different form,
when in some intellectually isolated community on the
ethnographical limits of Poland national solidarity is
awakened by the blame of foreigners, for example, in German
Poland.

The contrary process, when the group acquires solidarity
in the eyes of the larger community by enforcing its own
claims to this solidarity, is, of course, found only in matters

involving social praise; the group wants recognition on account of the social prominence of its members, the individual wants recognition as member of a social prominent group. This is the well-known mechanism of familial, local, national, pride. We have to distinguish this mechanism, which is possible also in an organized group but does not require organization, from the other, by which the organized group demands recognition on account of its social function, as a whole; we shall meet this problem later on.

How does the individual free himself from the influence of social opinion? As we have already noted, the Polish peasant rids himself more easily of the dread of social blame than of the attraction of social praise. But, making allowance for this difference, we find that there is already in the primitive peasant psychology a germ of independence of social opinion which, under favorable circumstances, can develop. We have seen that originally conjugal life is, at least in part, out of the reach of public intrusion. There is, in general, a tendency, particularly among men, to resent intrusions of the community into family matters; this tendency increases usually with the growing importance of the man within the family-group and reaches its highest stage in old heads of the family before their resignation. Besides this, the peasant frequently likes to keep secret all those personal matters which would not attract a particularly favorable attention of the community. And the same is often done under the influence of his desire for publicity; he likes to prepare carefully his effects in order to make them unexpected and as striking as possible. This aiming at great effects makes him often disregard or even encourage social blame for some time and to some extent in order to make the contrast stronger; he may even be dissatisfied with social praise if it comes before his own chosen moment and spoils his effect. In this way his ambition itself teaches

him to disregard to some extent public opinion and helps
to find a particular pleasure in the contrast between his
own economic, moral, intellectual value and the erroneous
appreciation of social opinion. Back of this all the while
is the idea that a day will come when he will show his real
value and astonish the community.

These psychological features make easier the real process
of liberation, which usually comes when the peasant becomes
a member of some group whose opinion differs more or less
from that of the community. Sharing the views of this new
group and feeling more or less backed by it, he learns to rise
above the community and to disregard the traditions. This
process is facilitated by his leaving the community, going
to a city or to America. But it goes on also among those
who stay within the traditional group. In fact, all the
recent changes of the peasants' views are taking this direction. When once a small circle of "enlightened" peasants
is formed in a community, the further movement becomes
much easier. The social workers in the country understand this necessity of opposing a group to the group-
influence and always try to organize a "progressive circle,"
even the smallest one. When reading is developed, it often
suffices for the individual to communicate by letters or by
print with some group outside of his community in order to
feel strong enough to oppose the prevailing opinion. Some
popular papers have therefore organized loose associations
of the adherents of some movement, who communicate with
one another through the paper. But, even in the cases of
an almost perfect liberation from the pressure of the immediate environment, there is a latent hope that some day
the community will acknowledge the value of the new ideas
and of their bearers.

At present the unorganized social environment of
the peasant is itself undergoing a profound evolution, in

connection with a modification of the traditional class-hierarchy. The constitution, the criteria, the interests of public opinion, are changing very rapidly, and the reaction of the individual to the influence of this changing environment, without being necessarily either weakened or strengthened, is changing qualitatively, in connection with the formation of new social classes.

ECONOMIC LIFE[1]

Among the Polish peasants we find three coexisting stages of economic development with their accompanying mental attitudes: (1) the survival of the old family economy, in which economic values are still to a large extent qualitative, not yet subordinated to the idea of quantity, and the dominant attitude is the interest in getting a good living, not the tendency to get rich; (2) the spontaneously developed stage of individual economy, marked by a quantification of economic values and a corresponding tendency to make a fortune or to increase it; (3) the stage of co-operation, developing mainly under external influences, in which economic values and attitudes are subordinated to the moral point of view.

To be sure, these types are seldom realized in their pure form in concrete groups or individuals; some attitudes of a lower stage may persist on a higher level. It happens that social individualism develops under influences other than economic, while the economic attitudes logically corresponding to it are not yet realized. Or the familial attitude may

[1] In addition to first-hand materials, including a report on season-emigration made by one of the authors at the request of the Central Agricultural Association of the Kingdom of Poland to the Russian Minister of Agriculture, some data from the following works have been used in writing this chapter: Władysław Grabski, *Materyały w sprawie włościanskiej;* Franciszek Bujak, *Żmiąca* (a particularly important monograph of a village), and *Limanowa;* Jan Słomka, *Pamiętniki włościanina.*

be kept.by men or groups who in economic life adapt themselves to individualistic attitudes and valuations while their
family-group behaves economically like an individual or a
marriage-group. We have thus many mixed forms, some
of which will be found in our present materials. But their
distinctive feature is their instability; the discrepant elements which they contain lead soon to their disappearance.
They are interesting only as showing the way in which
evolution goes on.

1. In the first stage all the categories of economic life
have a distinctly sociological character. The economic
generalization based upon the principle of quantitative
equivalence has not been consistently elaborated, and we
therefore find distinctions between phenomena of this class
which are economically meaningless but have a real social
meaning. The same lack of quantitative generalization
leads to another result—a lack of calculation, which has
sometimes the appearance of stupidity, but is in fact only
an application of the sociological instead of the economic
type of reasoning to phenomena which are social in the eyes
of the peasant even if they are merely economic when viewed
from the standpoint of the business man or the economist.

There are three classes of property, none of which exactly
corresponds to any classical definition: land, durable
products of human activity (including farm-stock), and
money. Natural powers and raw materials, not elaborated
by human activity, cannot be included in any economic
category; things which can be used only once (food, fuel,
work—animal or human) belong, as we shall see, rather to
the class of income than to that of property, although sometimes a distinction is made between their simple consumption and their productive use.

In taking land property into consideration we must
remember that for centuries the peasant was not the legal

owner of his land, and that therefore the legal. side of property plays up to the present a secondary rôle, although there has necessarily been a far-going adaptation to legal ideas since the abolition of serfdom. The difficulty of this adaptation is shown by the innumerable, often absurd, lawsuits about land, of which mainly Galicia, but also Russian Poland, has been the scene. The modern legal categories are incommensurable with the traditional social forms, and therefore the peasants either try to settle land questions without using the legal scheme at all, or, when the matter is once brought before the court or even only before the notary, they cannot reconcile their old concepts with the new ones imposed by the law, and a situation which would be simple if viewed exclusively from the traditional or the legal standpoint becomes complicated and undetermined when the two standpoints are mixed.

But the influence of serfdom upon land property ought not to be overestimated. It seems to have been rather negative than positive; it hindered the development of the legal side of property, but hardly developed any particular features. Indeed, the main characteristics of the peasant land property are found among the higher classes, although perhaps they are more distinct in the peasant class. The system of serfdom has simply adapted itself to pre-existing forms of economic life whose ultimate origin is lost in the past.

Land property is essentially familial; the individual is its temporary manager. Who manages it is therefore not essential provided he does it well; it may be the father, the oldest son, the youngest son, the son-in-law. We have seen that it is usual for all the members of the family to marry and to establish separate households, but if a member of the family is unlikely to marry (being a cripple, sick, or otherwise abnormal), or if, exceptionally, a member does not wish to marry, he can live with his brother or sister, working as much as he is able, not working if he is not able, but in any case getting his living and nothing but his living. No amount of work entitles him to anything like wages, no inability to work can diminish his right to be supported on the familial farm.   The same principle is manifested in the attitude toward grown-up children living with their parents. They have the right to live away from the farm, but they have the obligation to work for the farm; and if, later on, they go to work outside, the money they earn is not their own, because the work which they gave for this money was not their own—it was due to the family-farm and diverted from its natural destination. Of course the collateral branches of the family lose to some extent the connection with the farm, but the connection is only weakened, never absolutely severed.   Its existence was very well manifested in some localities under serfdom.   If a serf managed his farm badly, the lord could give it to someone else, but absolutely to the nearest possible relative who gave a sufficient guaranty of a better management.

This familial character of the farm should not be interpreted as if the family were an association holding a common property.   The members of the family have essentially no economic share in the farm; they share only the social character of members of the group, and from this result their social right to be supported by the group and their social obligation to contribute to the existence of the group. The farm is the material basis of this social relation, the expression of the unity of the group in the economic world. The rights and obligations of the members with regard to it do not depend upon any individual claims on property, but upon the nearness of their social relation to the group. It was therefore only with the greatest difficulty that the idea could be accepted that the land left after the death of the head of the family should be treated together with other kinds of property as belonging in common to the heirs and eventually to be divided among them.

The first form of providing separately for the members of the family, other than the one who was to take the farm, was certainly a payment in cash or farm-stock, made during the life of the head of the family—the member managing the farm. This is not the acknowledgment of their rights to the farm, but simply an expression of familial solidarity, a help, whose individualistic form is necessitated by modern economic conditions. With the progress of individualism the old principle begins to yield, and we find the first sign in the sometimes almost purely nominal shares which after the death of the head of the family the principal heir, or rather the new manager, has to pay to his brothers and sisters. Then, these shares, by which already the principal heir acknowledges some rights of the other heirs to the land as such, begin to increase, but they never become equal to the share of the member who holds the land. Finally when in rare cases the farm itself is divided (usually only after a premature death of the head of the family) it is seldom divided among all the heirs; usually most of them are "paid off." And we see the older generation endeavoring by all means to prevent the division. A curious stratagem is, for example, the bequeathing of the farm to one son, and mortgaging it nominally and above its value for the benefit of other heirs. A legal division then becomes, of course, practically impossible.

The indivisibility of the farm has nothing to do with the question of its territorial unity. Most of the farms are composed of fragments, sometimes over a hundred of them, disseminated over the whole area of a village neighborhood. And changes of territorial arrangement—the exchange of separate fragments between neighbors or the modern integration of farms—do not seem to have a dissolving effect upon the social unity of the farm. Nevertheless, not every farm is equally adapted to playing the part of familial property. A farm upon which many generations of the same family have worked is quite naturally associated with this particular family and often even bears its name, while a new farm is devoid of such associations. But the old land may lose, and the new land may assume, the function of familial property; the principle of indivisibility remains in force even if the object to which it is applied is not the same as before. This explains how the idea of familial property has been kept up in spite of colonization and emigration from province to province, and is still exerting its influence even among Polish colonists in Brazil.

The land being thus a social rather than an economic value—the material condition of the existence of a group as a whole—other characters of land property can be deduced from this fundamental fact.

No land communism is acceptable to the Polish peasant. When the Russian government colonized Siberia, constituting villages according to the communistic principle prevailing among the Russian peasants, almost the only Polish colonists attracted there were factory workmen, who had forgotten the peasant attitude. And it is evident that communism would destroy the very essence of the social value represented by the land; the latter would cease to express the unique familial group. A comparison may illustrate this attitude: communism of land from the standpoint of familial property would mean something more or less like a communism of objects of personal use from the standpoint of individual property.

Land should never be mortgaged, except to a member of the family. Mortgaging to a stranger, and particularly to an institution or government, not only involves the danger of losing the land, but it destroys the quality of property. Mortgaged land is no longer owned by the nominal proprietor. "The land is not ours, it belongs to the bank," says the peasant who has bought a farm with the help of a bank. This attitude leads to a particularly irrational behavior in matters of loans. The conditions on which the state bank lends money on land are particularly favorable. The debt is paid back in from forty to sixty years, and the yearly payment with interest is from 2 per cent to 3 per cent less than the interest on any average investment. The peasant knows this very well, but, in spite of it, as soon as he has any money he tries first of all to pay the mortgage. A private mortgage is preferred, even if the interest is higher and no partial payments possible. The peasant prefers above all a personal debt, even at high interest and for a short term. And this again results from the social character of the land; mortgaged property becomes a purely economic category and loses its whole symbolical value. The situation is here analogous to that which we find in every profanation; the profaned object passes into a different class and loses its exceptional character of sanctity.

Finally, land property is evidently the main condition of the social standing of the family. Without land, the family can still keep its internal solidarity, but it cannot act as a unit with regard to the rest of the community; it ceases to count as a social power. Its members become socially and economically dependent upon strangers, and often scatter about the country or abroad; the family ceases to play any part in the affairs of the commune, its young generation can hardly be taken into account in matters of marriage, it cannot give large ceremonial receptions, etc. The greater the amount of land, the greater the possibility of social expression. Of course all this gradually changes on the higher levels of economic development.

Land has also an exceptional value from other points of view—as an object of work, as an object of magical rites and religious beliefs, and later as a basis of national cohesion. But all these questions will be considered in other contexts.

The second class of property—products of human activity—shows a partial, but only a partial, independence of the familial idea. These products are not destined for the use of the family as a whole, and in this sense they are individual, but not personal, property. Members of the family own them, but for every member in particular this ownership is, so to speak, accidental. The head of the family owns the farm-stock, can sell it or give it, but only as long as he is the manager of the farm. House furniture is owned by those who hold the house, but again only as long as they hold it. Even valuable pieces of clothing, particularly home-made, often passing from generation to generation, are owned really, but only temporarily. Things bought or made by the individual himself are no exception to this rule. The function of this class of property is precisely to complete the function of land property in assuring the material existence of the group, wherever this requires individual ownership, and the right of every member of the family to own something individually depends upon this fundamental aim and is determined by the position which he occupies in the group. The head of the family owns the farm-stock because this is necessary for his management of the farm, and he and his wife are the general distributors of these goods; they have to give everyone what he needs as member of the group. To a member who stays at home they give the only individual property which he needs to live—clothes; he has no other function in the group except being a member. To those who marry and establish a new household the goods are distributed which are necessary, not only to live personally, but also to fulfil the function of householders—besides clothes, some house and bed furniture, some farm-stock and farming implements. And every member of the family should be ready to give to any other member things which the other needs and which he can spare himself, taking the particular position of both into account. Thus, an unmarried member who has the opportunity to get from without any household or farm goods should give them to a married or marrying one. Dividing the inheritance means primitively only dividing this class of goods, for no others are inherited in the proper sense of the word, and the division is regulated by the same principle: to everyone according to his needs, as far as those needs result from his function in the family-group, not from his personal desires. And under no pretext should any goods of this class, as long as they have any value, be given away to strangers, or sold as long as anybody in the family needs them.

Money is a relatively new kind of property which has adapted itself to the pre-existing organization and whose importance grows as the modern economic life penetrates the peasant community and makes that pre-existing organization insufficient. For the peasant, money property has originally not the character of capital, but of an immediate and provisional substitute for other kinds of property. He does not at first even think of making money produce; he simply keeps it at home. And if he lends it privately, the mediaeval principle of no interest prevails, or at most, as we shall see later, a reward in money or products is taken for the service. Even now interest on private loans from peasant to peasant is very low. Putting money into the bank comes still later, and, last of all, using it on enterprises. Being a provisional substitute for other kinds of property, money is individualized according to its source and destination. A sum received from selling a cow is qualitatively different from a sum received as dowry, and both are different from a sum earned outside. The distinction goes still further. The money which the husband gets for the cow is qualitatively different from that which his wife puts aside by selling eggs and milk, not because either belongs personally to husband or wife, but because each represents the equivalent of a different sort of value; the first is property, the second is income. We shall consider the latter presently. The qualitative difference between various sums of money equivalent to property was originally expressed in the fact that they were kept separately. And to the difference of origin corresponded a difference of destination. Money received as dowry could be used only to buy land, and the same was, of course, true of money received from the sale of land. Money so derived had the character of familial property and it could never be diverted to any individual end or any enterprise, not even for a time, but had to wait for an opportunity to buy land. Money from the sale of cattle, horses, hogs, or poultry was to be put aside in order to meet all the individual difficulties of the members of the family arising from the complication of modern life and the beginning economic individualization, particularly to help newly married couples, or, later, to help the principal heir in "paying off" other heirs. It was the equivalent of the second class of property. Money earned outside, if it was not mere income but acquired the character of property, was usually assimilated to the same second class. But there was a general tendency to make money pass from a lower into a higher economic class— from the class of income into that of property, from that of individually controlled into that of familial property. Actual economic evolution tends to abolish all these distinctions and to make money more and more fluid. But the tendency to individualize money was so strong that up to the present time a peasant who has a sum put aside for a determined end, and needs a little money temporarily, prefers to borrow it, even under very difficult conditions, rather than touch that sum.

At this stage of evolution property, not income, is exclusively the measure of the economic situation of the family or the individual. And evidently it must be so, since the economic situation is socially important only in view of the social standing which it gives and since it is property which expresses the social side of economic life. A larger but badly managed farm is therefore more valued than a well-managed but smaller one, even if their real economic values are inversely proportional. And there is a curiously mixed attitude of envy and commiseration toward town people or manor employees who have an income much larger than the peasant, but no property.

The concept of income itself which we use here is originally strange to the peasant. We can apply this category to the yearly products of the farm, but we must remember that the peasant does not apply it. The products of the farm are not destined to be sold and not evaluated quantitatively. Their destination is simply to give a living to the family and to keep farming going on—nothing more. And the original system of farming (one-third winter crops, i.e., wheat and rye; one-third summer crops, i.e., barley, oats, potatoes, etc.; one-third fallow), with an average low level of agricultural practice, really does not leave much to sell from a farm of the average size of ten to thirty acres. Below ten acres a farm gives hardly enough to feed the family and the stock; and if the peasant cannot earn some money outside he must in the spring either borrow grain from a rich neighbor or sell his pig, cow, or even horse in order to get a living until the new harvest. And if his situation is good, he will think rather of increasing his stock than of selling any products. There are also in this case greater claims to be satisfied—servants to be fed, old parents or collateral members of the family to be supported, neighbors to be helped, guests to be received. For, unlike the property which should never pass outside of the family, the farm income (products) has to be shared as far as possible with poor members of the community, guests, wanderers, beggars, etc. Its essence is to support human or animal life. To waste the smallest part of it is a sin, almost a crime. To sell it is not a sin, but perhaps even here we may find in the background of the peasant's psychology the half-conscious conviction that it is not quite fair. There is another way of using what remains after the satisfaction of the needs of the family and of the duties toward the community: the income in products can be turned into property by increasing the farm-stock, improving the buildings, buying new farm implements, all of which is property. The attitude of the village or commune toward pastures and forests belonging to it is almost the same. They are not common property in the real sense of the word, for the peasant does not consider, as we have seen, raw materials as the property of anyone. They are simply a source from which every member of the village or commune can draw materials which he needs in addition to the farm products in order to support his family, to feed his stock, and to keep up his farm buildings, without getting into trouble with the law. Only with regard to the relation to other villages or communes these goods assume the secondary character of property. In this line there has been also an evolution during the last period.

This attitude toward the natural products of the farm explains why the agricultural progress of the Polish peasant was so slow up to twenty or thirty years ago. There were no sufficient motives to increase the productivity of the land. The standard of living simply adapted itself to the natural income, and the question of increasing the farm equipment was hardly important enough to justify agricultural studies, harder work, more trouble in running a complicated system of farming, etc.   If we take the passive clinging to tradition into account, we shall hardly wonder at the slowness of the progress.   And precisely in the only case where the motive could be strong enough—when the farm income was not sufficient to give a living to the family —there were no resources for making improvements.

When the general conditions began to change, the peasant found at first additional sources of income which allowed him to solve the new situations.   The growth of the large cities, the development of the means of communication, of national and international commerce, gave him the possibility of selling secondary products of his farming— butter, eggs, vegetables, fruit, etc.   Home industry, which had existed from time immemorial, although it was never very much developed, found new markets, thanks to the sudden interest which it awakened in the higher classes of Polish society.   But the main source of additional income was hired season-work, at first only in the neighborhood, then also in more distant parts of the country and in Germany, and finally work in America.

The first use of this income was to cover such new expenses as were not accounted for in the old economy; it had to supply the deficiencies of the old system of living in the same way that money property supplied the deficiency of the old system of property.   Taxes increased and had to be paid in cash, whereas they were formerly paid mainly in natural products.   The multiplication of the family obliged the purchase, whenever possible, of new land, and this could be done usually only by contracting debts, on which interest had to be paid in cash.   New needs arose among the members of the younger generation, needs of city products, city pleasures, learning;   individualization progressed, and the older generation had to yield, sometimes after a hard struggle. Finally, when the products of the farm were not sufficient to feed the family, food began to be bought instead of being borrowed. This is the latest stage of evolution.

But even in this evolution the principle of qualification of economic values held good. Every sum of money, additionally earned, had a particular end and could be used on nothing else, not even partially and temporarily. And there was always a tendency to let as much of it as possible pass from the class of income into that of property, whenever the sum was large enough to make a marked addition to the latter. If a sum was once set aside to increase in some particular way the property, the necessity of spending it on some actual need was felt as a misfortune. We have here the explanation of the stinginess of the peasant, which remains his characteristic feature even as an immigrant. Traditionally all the elementary needs of food, shelter, clothing, fuel, were satisfied by the natural products of the land, and there was and is still an aversion to spending money on them. Even when natural products were sold, the money was not used for living, but for other needs. We therefore find the seemingly paradoxical situation that an increase of income in cash usually means for a time a lowering of the standard of living. In localities where they find an easy market for their products the peasants often live worse than in more remote villages. But they usually spend more money on city pleasures and objects of luxury, because with regard to expenses of this kind the inhibition is not traditional and has to be acquired. In the same way the peasant in America tries to limit his living expenses even more than his extraordinary expenses, particularly if he comes directly from the country. And when he has a plan for the use of a sum of money which he has earned, nothing except final misery and the impossibility of earning or borrowing can compel him to spend this sum on his living.

The third kind of income known at this stage of economic life is wages.   But here again the principle is not the modern one.   Primarily there seems to be no idea of an economic equivalent of the work done, of an exchange of values. There is rather a collaboration, entitling the collaborator to a living.   The servant or employee, by co-operating with his employer, is assimilated to his family.   His position is evidently inferior to that of his employer, because the latter is the manager of the property and the distributor of the income; but it is inferior only to that of other members of the employer's family in the fact that these members may become managers themselves.   There can also be other reasons of inferiority.   The family of the employer has usually a higher social standing than that of the employee. But when the employer is a peasant, the position of an employee or farm servant, a *parobek*, involves as such no social inferiority.   In the case of manor servants the element of class-distinction enters and can never be obviated, and the employee's work includes also always some element of personal service essentially different from collaboration, and involving a real personal inferiority.   But in this case also the employee is assimilated to the employer's family to the degree that the relation involves collaboration.   To be sure, this assimilation resulting from collaboration led only to an internal solidarity of the family-group with reference to work and living, not to a solidarity of external reactions toward other family-groups.   The latter solidarity is acquired only through a long life in common.

The manifestation of this attitude toward dependent work is that the salary of the servant was always originally given in natural products.   The single servant received his board and a determined or undetermined amount of clothing;

the married servant in manors had lodging, fuel, grain (called *ordynarya*), a field for potatoes, the permission to keep one or two cows, etc.—in short, everything included in the peasant idea of living. Later on the same economic evolution which obliged the peasant farmer to seek for an additional income obliged the employer to pay a little money to his employee. But that this money is considered as only an addition, an equivalent for products which cannot be furnished, is shown by the fact that the wages in cash paid to manor servants amount even now on the average to only 10 per cent of the wages in natural products. Another modification, parallel with the hired season- or day-work of the farmer's family, is the custom by which the manor servant keeps a boy or girl to do day-work on the manorial farm. Originally based on the fact that the larger children of a servant worked with him, the custom was made obligatory by manor-owners, who need cheap hands for light work. A manor servant who has no large children must therefore hire a boy or girl (called *posyłka*). But here also the old principle is retained as far as possible; the servant receives for his *posyłka* an additional remuneration in natural products besides the daily pay, which is therefore lower than that of occasional workers, and the hired *posyłka* is treated by the manor servant in the same way as the *parobek*, the farm servant, by the farmer, that is, he receives his living and a small addition in cash.

Naturally this situation excludes any idea and any possibility of changing income into property, of economizing for the future. As a consequence of the principle of a living instead of a regular wage, the servant can never become an owner, except by inheritance from some member of his family, or incidentally by marriage. The problem of living in old age was solved on the familial principle. A disabled worker was to be supported by his own family, or, if he had served in one place long enough to become closely connected with the family of his employer, the latter was socially obliged to support him until his death—an obligation which was always respected.

Another interesting consequence of this state of things was the type of moral regulation of the relation between employer and employee. The attitude required was essentially identical on both sides, in spite of the difference of positions and spheres of activity. Its basis was "goodness," consisting on either side in the care for the interests and welfare of the other side—including the families. The employer had to be "just," that is, to reciprocate the goodness of his employee; the employee was to be "true," that is, to reciprocate the goodness of the employer. The moral regulation did not touch at all the matter of proportion between work and remuneration. And even now, when the peasant speaks of a "just" master or a "just" pay, he means a master who cares well for good servants, a pay which shows the intention of the employer to provide well for his employees.

One of the reasons why the relation between work and wages is not taken into account is certainly the attitude of the Polish peasant toward work. While among handworkers a long tradition of guild life developed an appreciation of craftmanship and efficiency, or, more generally speaking, attracted the attention to the results of the work, the peasant is fundamentally interested, positively or negatively, principally in the process of work. Many factors collaborated to develop this attitude. First of all, the compulsory work under the system of serfdom could hardly awaken any interest in the results. What did the serf care whether his work for the lord was efficient or not? On the contrary, the process of compulsory work evoked a strong interest—a negative one, of course, because of the hardship and loss of time which it involved, and because of its compulsory character. But, under continual oversight, the peasant had to work, willingly or not, and a certain obligatory character has been acquired in the course of time by the process of work as such. It was strengthened by religion: "Man has to work, it is his curse, but also his duty; the process of working is meritorious, laziness is bad, independent of any results." And up to the present this attitude is retained, even if other interests and other motives have been added.

We should expect a different attitude from the peasant toward the work done on his own farm. But even this work was often half-compulsory. The peasant had to keep his farm in good condition in order to be able to meet his obligations to the lord. And even when this work was free, as it was sometimes even under the serfage system, another factor hindered the development of an appreciation of efficiency. The ultimate result of farm-work does not depend exclusively upon the worker himself; his best efforts can be frustrated by unforeseen circumstances, and in a particularly good year even negligent work may be well repaid. On a rich background of religious and magical beliefs this incalculable element gives birth to a particular kind of fatalism. It is not the proverbial oriental fatalism, based upon divine predestination and, if consistent, making work essentially an unimportant element of life, but a limited kind of fatalism, based upon the uncertainty of the future. The essential point is to get the help of God, the distributor of good, against the indifferent forces of.nature and the intentionally harmful magical forces of hostile men and of the devil. Now, in addition to religious magic, the process of work itself is a means of influencing God favorably; it is even the most indispensable condition of assuring God's help, for without it no religious magic will do any good. We cannot solve here the problem, whether the process of work has assumed this importance only under the influence of the Christian ideology or whether there is a more primitive and fundamental religious character belonging to it. The fact is that when the peasant has been working steadily, and has fulfilled the religious and magical ceremonies which tradition requires, he "leaves the rest to God" and waits for the ultimate results to come; the question of more or less skill and efficiency of work has very little importance. The attitude is somewhat different with regard to work whose results are immediate—carpenter's, blacksmith's, spinner's, weaver's work. But even here it is not so much the skill as the conscientiousness of work that counts, and the thing made "will hold if God allows it"— an attitude very different from that of a city handworker.

When hired work begins to develop, there gradually enters a new motive—that of wages. But the essential attitude is not changed. It is for the process, not for the results of his work, that the servant gets his living; it is for the process of work that later the employee, the hired laborer, even the factory workman, considers himself to be paid. Even when later the idea of wages as remuneration for the results of the work is accepted, often eagerly accepted, it is applied less willingly to work at home than abroad. The most absurd explanations are given by the peasants who reject piece-work in Poland and ask for it in Germany; the irrationality of this attitude shows that its source lies in the old habits.

The stress put on the process of work rather than on its results explains also the importance which the kind of work and its external conditions have for the peasant. The motives of pleasure and displeasure connected with this process are at the first stage more important than the profits. The main factors of pleasure are freedom, variety, facility, companionship. Independent work is more pleasant than dependent, farm-work incomparably more pleasant—or rather less unpleasant—than factory-work, and the only case in which the pleasure of the process of work outweighs always and everywhere its hardship is when all the neighbors come together to help one of their number to gather his crops. This kind of help, always disinterested, is almost equivalent to a pleasure party. It is becoming rare since the new appreciation of work for its results has developed and the old communal life has lost its primary character.

Up to the present we have spoken of the economic attitudes which concern a single family or individual—for even the employment relation belongs to these. We now pass to those which determine economic relations between various members of a peasant community. These relations may be classed under the following seven concepts: giving, lending for temporary use, crediting, renting, exchanging, selling, stealing. There is no possibility of reducing these to a more limited number of purely economic categories, but all of them are modifications of one fundamental relation— of an occasional solidarity between the members of a community, in the same way as all the relations between members of a family in matters of property are modifications of a permanent solidarity within the family.

The gift is the most elementary form in which solidarity is expressed, because it is the simplest form of help. We must distinguish a real gift, when the object given has a material value, from a symbolical gift, when the value of the object is essentially moral. The real gift between strangers can be only an object of consumption, belonging to the category of income, not to that of property, because, as we have said, property cannot go out of the family. A symbolical gift is usually a religious object (medal, cross, image, wafer, scapular, etc.), sometimes an object of adornment, a trifle made by the person himself, etc. It is in itself property, but its material value is so insignificant that it does not diminish the stock of property of the giver and does not increase the wealth of the receiver. Its moral value consists in the social attitudes which it symbolizes and which constitute its meaning. Now, the common meaning of all the symbolical gifts is that they establish between the giver and the receiver a spiritual bond, analogous to the familial bond, precisely because they formally bear the character of gifts reserved for the familial relation; the receiver is conventionally incorporated into the giver's family. In the case of a religious or magical object the latter has still another meaning in itself which heightens the moral importance of the gift; the bond between the giver and the receiver is sanctified, so to speak. By gradations of the material value of the gift and of the sanctity which it imparts to the relation between the giver and the receiver we pass from a conventional to a real familial relation. Thus, the boy offers to the girl whom he intends to marry gifts of real value, which increase as the marriage becomes more probable, and the betrothal and wedding rings have a particularly sanctifying function, because they have been specially blessed for the occasion.

If the symbolical gift establishes a new relation, the real gift is the result and the acknowledgment of the pre-existing relation of communal solidarity. It has thus a double function, the primitive one of help in emergency and the derived one of manifesting solidarity. It assumes the latter on particular occasions and is then ritualized. Food, offered at all ceremonial meetings, has certainly this character. The ceremonial meetings occur on all the important familial occasions—christening, betrothal, wedding, funeral —and even on secondary ones, such as the arrival of a member of the family, the name-day of the head of the family. By inviting members of other families and offering them food the family manifests that it wants the event to be considered a social, not a private affair, and that in spite of any change in its life or composition it remains solidary with the community. Moreover, this is not a mere question of the good will of the family; the community requires such a manifestation. This explains the enormous proportions which all these ceremonial meetings assume with regard to the number of people invited, the treatment offered, and the time the meeting lasts. Theoretically, the whole community ought to be invited, and the treatment must be a real, not a symbolical gift; that is, every guest ought to be really fed for a certain time, a day, two, three, originally often more. The motive of showing off, using the ceremonial entertainment as a sign of the standing of the family, has certainly developed later on, as a consequence of the attitude of the community toward that manifestation of solidarity.

But on some of those occasions the community had also to manifest its solidarity with the family by a real, effective help. The idea was to assist the family in procuring a living for a new member (at christening) or for a new marriage-group (at the wedding). Every person invited had to offer something for the child or the new couple. At present the gifts are made in money, but we have vestiges showing that, at least in the case of marriage, they were made in farm products—food, fuel, linen, cloth, etc. The family helped the new couple mainly, though not exclusively, in matters of property; the community helped it to get a living during the first months. That those gifts were not intended as a reciprocity for the entertainment (as sometimes seems the case now, when the custom has degenerated) is proved by the fact that no gifts were offered on other occasions, when there was no actual increase of the family— at death or betrothal, for instance.

The gift does not involve necessarily any relation of superiority or inferiority of the giver to the receiver. In the precarious conditions of peasant life everybody may need help occasionally. Of course non-ceremonial gifts are usually made by a richer to a poorer person, and the giver is usually superior to the receiver, but this superiority does not result from the fact of giving. Even habitual living at the expense of others, as, for example, beggary, is not humiliating in itself; the humiliation lies in the circumstances which cause this necessity—in the loss of fortune, or in the lack of solidarity in the family of the beggar which permits him to lead such a life. The situation is different if the gift is one of property, because such gifts are not in use among peasants and anybody who accepts them from a stranger acknowledges thereby the class-superiority of the latter.

Closely connected with the gift, although never ritualized, is lending of mobile property (property of the second class) for a temporary use. This is a form of help quite obligatory in many circumstances; and if the object is used immediately for purposes of living, the situation contains nothing essentially new in comparison with giving. But if the object is used for productive purposes, if, thanks to it, the person who borrowed it gets some income, or, in other terms, if the relation of the object to the purposes of living is indirect, then a new moment is added: the person who borrowed the object is morally obliged to offer a part of the product to the owner. Thus, for example, a horse and a cart borrowed in order to go on a visit, instruments borrowed to repair the house, lead to no obligation. But the same horse and cart borrowed in order to bring the crops into the barn, or instruments used in hired work, are considered productive, and the owner should get something for his good service. The remuneration grows with the importance of the results obtained (even by chance), and not with the importance of the sacrifice of the owner, although a marked deterioration of the object should be made good. The distinction is not very precise in detail, but the principle is clear. The act of lending is a social service, not an economic enterprise, and the remuneration is not an equivalent of any profits lost by the owner, for this loss is accounted for and accepted in lending as well as in giving, but an expression of gratitude and reciprocal help on the side of the person who borrowed the object proportionate to the increase of the resources of this person.

The primitive attitude toward money-lending is exactly the same, since money is at first only the equivalent of mobile property. The debtor in paying the money back adds a certain sum, not as interest, but as reciprocation of social solidarity proportionate to the subjective importance of the service rendered. Up to the present, even after the introduction of interest, the custom is sometimes observed that, if the debtor has been particularly successful, thanks to the money borrowed, he will add a free gift to the determined interest, as a sign of benevolence toward the creditor.

But a quite different principle prevails in the matter of rent. Land—the first object of rent—is the basis of the existence of the family; therefore, when it is rented, it ought to bring income, that is, it ought to enable the family to live, as when it is cultivated. And, indeed, the form of rent which we can consider primitive is in perfect accordance with this principle. Usually a farmer who has enough farm equipment rents the land of another who cannot cultivate it himself, either because he has not the necessary strength or because he cannot buy or keep the equipment. The products are then divided. In this way the relation of tenant and owner is already an exchange of services, but it is regulated by the idea of living. But, in general, renting is not primitively a frequent fact among peasants, for as long as familial solidarity exists and the whole family is not ruined or dispersed, some collateral member, assuming the rôle of head of the family, usually undertakes the cultivation of the land which the owner cannot cultivate. This was regularly the case with the land of widows and orphans.   Renting of land for money appears as a rule only in the temporary absence of the owner.

As to the rent for buildings, an evolution seems to have occurred. Temporary lodging in a house was originally equivalent to any gift of things which serve for living.   It was involved in hospitality and was always only occasional among strangers, since almost everyone except beggars had a steady lodging, if not in his own house, then at least with his family, with his actual or former employer, in some cabin lent by the estate-owner, etc.   But at the same time a barn or a stable could be lent on the same principle as any mobile property for productive purposes; that is, the person who used someone's barn to house his crops remunerated the owner by giving him a part of these crops.   In short, there was no renting, but lending of buildings, and this was perfectly logical, for the buildings belonged to the class of mobile, manufactured property, as against land.   Later on there developed the class of *komorniks*, that is, people who had no houses and lived from day labor, lodging in other people's houses, and the principle of remuneration, applying originally to farm buildings, was extended to houses and rooms permanently used.   There was simultaneously a process of regulation of the remuneration, about which we shall speak later.   Finally, in some cases, when buildings were rented together with land, the principle of land rent seems to have been partly extended to them, although this last phase is uncertain.

Naturally all the arrangements described above, being based upon social solidarity, are changed as soon as solidarity begins to weaken, and many modifications in the peasant's economic life are due, not to the development of a new economic attitude, but only to this weakening of solidarity. The result of this process is the substitution of the principle of exchange for the principle of help along the whole line of economic relations, except in those which have been ritualized. The reciprocity of help, at first undetermined as to its value and time, becomes determined in both respects; an equivalence of services is required. This means that a relation of things is substituted for a relation of persons, or that, more exactly, the relation of persons is determined by the relation of things. The solidarity within the primary group is a connection between concrete personalities, and every economic act, as well as every other social act, is merely one moment of this solidarity, one of its results, expressions, and factors; its full meaning does not lie in itself, but in the whole personal relation which it involves. An act of social help therefore does not create an expectation of a particular and determined reciprocal service, but simply strengthens and actualizes the habitual expectation of a general attitude of benevolent solidarity from the other person, which may find its expression at any time in any act of reciprocal help. But when this concrete personal solidarity is weakened, the act of help assumes an independent importance in and of itself; the economic value of the service rendered becomes essential, instead of its social value.

When the change begins, the expectation of reciprocity is justified by the amount of the sacrifice made by the giver, and no longer by the efficiency of the help which the receiver got. There must be a reciprocal service to remunerate the giver for this sacrifice, and it must be proportionate to the sacrifice itself, given at the right moment and in the right way. This is only an intermediary stage between social help and objectively determined exchange, but we find the corresponding attitude very frequently. Grain lent in the spring has to be given back with a very large interest, because that is the time when it is most needed by the creditor himself. Money is often lent on the condition that it will be given back whenever the creditor needs it, and the latter refuses to accept it at any other moment. Night and Sunday work is valued by the worker exceptionally highly because of the sacrifice which it involves; but the same man may do it disinterestedly when he applies to it the principle of solidarity and is asked for it as for a help. In selling or exchanging some object the peasant adds to its economic value the subjective value which the object has for him on account of personal or familial associations. And many other illustrations can be found.

But of course when once the egotistic attitude is introduced into economic relations, these relations have to be objectively regulated. And thus ultimately the principle of economic equivalence of services is introduced and becomes fundamental, while there still remains always some place beside it for the old valuation based upon the efficiency of the help and for the transitory valuation based upon the subjective sacrifice. This may be said to be the actual state of things in the average peasant community. The objective equivalence of values is the usual norm, but its action is modified by social considerations. The principle of equivalence requires that natural products lent for living shall be given back at a determined time without interest, but it may be modified in two ways. If the debtor is in a bad condition and the creditor rich, the latter ought to postpone the payment of the debt; but if their conditions are more or less equal and the debt was contracted in a period of scarcity and paid back in a moment of abundance, an interest should be added which is measured by the difference of subjective value of the product at these moments of time, and can therefore be objectively very high.

On the principle of equivalence any mobile property or money lent should be given back with a determined remuneration, representing the resultant of the three factors: deterioration of the object, sacrifice of the creditor as temporarily deprived of its use, benefit derived by the debtor. The remuneration is determined beforehand; but if any of those three factors proves different from what was expected, the idea of social solidarity requires a corresponding modification of the agreement. And the idea of solidarity requires that if the debtor is unable to pay any debt whatever in the same form in which he contracted it he shall be allowed to pay it, as far as possible, by working for the creditor. Nevertheless, this principle became a source of exploitation of debtors by creditors. Finally, the idea of exchange has modified the essence of rent; the owner now allows the tenant to profit from a determined quantity of land in return for a determined remuneration. But if a year proves exceptionally bad the owner should as far as possible remit the rent, or at least allow it to be paid the next year, and if the year is exceptionally good the tenant ought to offer the owner more than was agreed.

Applied to work, the idea of exchange becomes the source of the modern principle of wages as remuneration for the result, although here it is particularly difficult to get away from the personal relation. It is therefore almost exclusively in hired work (day- or piece-work) and not in employment or service that this principle is active.

The only case in which equivalence tends to be perfect is in the simple exchange of objects. The idea is that the objects must be really equivalent from the economic point of view, independent of subjective factors. To be sure, a person may ascribe to an object a special subjective value, or, on the contrary, give it voluntarily for a less valuable one. But neither of these attitudes has any social sanction attached to it. Only cheating is forbidden; the cheater becomes an object of social condemnation; the cheated, of ridicule.

The idea of exchange of equivalent services prepares the second, individualistic stage of economic life, because it introduces economic quantification, at least into the relations between members of a community. Nevertheless, it still belongs rather to the first stage, because it can co-exist with a strong familial organization (it is not applied at first to the members of the same family) and because it does not harmonize with the tendency of economic advance which, as we shall see, characterizes the second, individualistic stage of evolution. It expresses an egotistic economic organization of a community which rises very slowly and gradually, remaining still solidary in so far as it permits nobody to profit too much at the expense of others. No individual fortune can be made in such a community, and in fact no individual fortune is made within the peasant community (except by socially condemned usury); for this the individual must enter into relations with the external world.

And this is illustrated by a curious fact. There was originally no commerce between members of a community, no buying and selling at all. It was hardly necessary in the primitive conditions, and it would not have been in accordance with the idea of solidarity as we have outlined it. Therefore the attitudes in buying and selling developed exclusively under the influence of and in contact with people from outside—Jews, foreign peddlers, town merchants. Thence the necessity and importance of the fairs, where almost all the buying or selling was done. And later, by a sort of half-conscious convention, the fair became a place where everybody could be treated as an outsider, and a money transaction could be concluded, not only with somebody of a different community, but even with a neighbor. It happened and may happen still that when a farmer has a horse which his neighbor wants to buy they both go to the fair, and there, after the first has pretended to wait for a buyer and the second to search for a horse, they meet and conclude the transaction. Of course neither of them acknowledges that he intended to make the transaction beforehand. Actually the custom is almost broken down, but the peasant still does not like to buy from or sell to his neighbor, because he feels morally bound by the principle of economic equivalence and cannot hope to do a particularly good piece of business.

This development of buying or selling in exclusive contact with outsiders accounts for the fact that none of the principles dominating the economic relations within the community is applied to money transactions. Here we find the typical business tendency in its pure form: buy as cheap, sell as dear, as possible; no limitations of honesty, no personal or social considerations. But the peasant had to be taught this purely economic attitude. He had to learn, first, that goods brought to the market acquire a new character—that of being subjected to a common quantitative standard of value, in spite of any qualitative distinctions which they may possess as social values within the community. Everything can be bought from, or sold to, outsiders. And it was not easy to learn this. Up to the present many peasants do not apply the economic standard to some of their goods and are disgusted and offended if someone else does it. This happens most often with regard to land, but sometimes also horses or cattle which have been used on the farm are sold unwillingly, the peasant preferring to sell the young ones. As we have seen, there was probably an unwillingness to apply the economic point of view to farm products which served for living, and up to the present, except in localities near large cities, the peasant will not sell bread. There is, of course, no such limitation in buying, although the fact that every individual sum of money has a particular destination, can be used only to buy objects of a particular class, shows that there is still, independently of the question of needs, a remnant of some qualitative, social classification.

After learning to apply the economic standard the peasant had to learn also that it is possible and desirable to sell very dear and to buy very cheap. This did not come at once either; the idea of equivalence, applied to exchange within the community, hindered the development of the spirit of business, and in a few remote localities hinders it even now. The peasant will not take more nor give less than he thinks is right; and if accidentally he makes a better bargain than he expected, either he reproaches himself for having cheated the other man or he feels gratitude toward him. The Jews, whose method of business is adapted to the average psychology of the people with whom they deal and is consequently traditional and often correspondent with disappearing attitudes, use in bargaining the appeal: "Do you want to wrong a poor Jew?" This introduces at once the idea of equivalence and the personal element, and the transaction becomes assimilated to an exchange between members of the community. But of course the necessity of making such an appeal indicates the partial formation of the business attitude. This attitude now prevails, with few exceptions, in all relations with outsiders. It assumes often the most extreme forms. In buying, the peasant bargains up to the last, and he does not like to buy if he cannot bargain, because he wants to be persuaded that he has bought the cheapest possible. In selling, he often demands the most exorbitant prices, particularly if he has some reason to think that the buyer needs his goods very much. As his business attitude is displayed only within a limited part of his economic life, however, it is not systematically organized. The quantitative side of economic value is, in his eyes, only one among its other qualities, brought forward at particular moments, among particular circumstances, with regard to particular people. Each act of buying or selling is a single, isolated action, not connected with other actions of the same class. The principle of cheap buying and dear selling is therefore not limited by any idea of the future, by any endeavor to get a class of steady customers. The peasant at this stage avoids any contracts of delivery which are proposed to him; he makes no calculations for a longer time, but tries simply to get as much as possible at the given moment. He will break any contract of work and go to another place with higher pay, even if he loses more in the long run than he wins. This was for many years the practice of season-emigrants in Germany. The number of contracts broken was enormous. This was due in large part to bad treatment, but partly also to a lack of organization of the business attitudes, which frequently had their first application to work in contact with foreigners. This whole situation left, of course, no place for any spirit of enterprise along commercial or industrial lines.

Finally, we must take into consideration the question of theft, as it corroborates our previous conclusions. There is absolutely no theft in "taking" any raw material which is not in any way the product of human activity; trees, grass, minerals, game, fish, wild berries, and mushrooms are, as we have said, everybody's property. This attitude remains unchanged up to the present, because of the *servituts*, that is, the right which the former serfs and their descendents have to use to a limited extent the forests and pastures of the manorial estate. "Taking" the products which serve to maintain the life of man or animal may be unfair, but unless the products are taken for sale it is not theft. "Taking" prepared food to satisfy immediate hunger is hardly even unfair, except that it would be better to ask for permission. When clothes are stolen and worn, the act is on the dividing line between "taking" and theft. But as soon as any product is stolen for sale, there is no justification; it is theft in the full sense of the word. Even here we find a gradation. The stealing of goods which belong to the class of income is incomparably less heinous than the stealing of farm-stock, particularly horses and cows. Since money draws its character from the objects for which it is the substitute, a condemnation of money theft varies with the amount stolen, simply because a small sum can represent only a part of the natural income, a medium one an object of individual property, a large one land. And the condemnation, on any level, increases if the proprietor is poor and if the thief belongs to the same community; it decreases if the thief is in real need and if the proprietor is a member of another community or, particularly, of another class.[1] There can be no theft between members of the same family.

2. After the definite liberation of the peasants and their endowment with land their condition was at first no better, sometimes it was even worse, than before. They were indeed free of duties and charges to the lord, but had heavy taxes to pay; they could not rely on the lord's help in case of emergency and were often insufficiently prepared materi-

---

[1] We find often also the contrary reasoning: stealing in another village is worse than stealing in one's own village, because it gives rise to a bad opinion of the thief's village.

ally and morally to manage their farms independently. But gradually they adapted themselves to the new conditions, and sometimes in the first generation, usually in the second and the third, there awoke a powerful tendency to economic advance, a "force which pushes you forward" as one peasant expresses it. This tendency, which, as we shall see, was the main factor breaking down the old forms and creating new ones, found its expression in connection with the general crisis which the country underwent at this epoch. The progress of industry opened new fields for labor, while at the same time the rapid growth of country population, by increasing the number of landless peasants, made this progress of industry particularly welcome. The improvement of communication drew the peasant communities out of their isolation and put each particular member in a direct and continuous relation with the external world. The growth of cities and the increase of international commerce introduced more money even into the most distant communities and helped to disseminate the quantification of economic values and the business attitude. Emigration opened new horizons, made the peasant acquainted with higher standards of work, of wages, of living. The evolution of the class-hierarchy, while to a certain extent conditioned by the economic evolution, influenced it in turn, because the new system gave a new motive for economic advance by opening the way to social ambition. Finally, instruction was popularized and helped to a better understanding of the natural and social environment.

About half a century was required for the full development of the attitudes involved in the tendency to economic advance, and even now they are neither universal nor perfectly consistent. This is quite as we should expect, for the tendency to advance took at first the line of least resistance; the climbing individual either adapted himself to the traditional conditions and morals of his immediate environment or simply moved to another environment where he found conditions awaiting him which required no particular adjustment. Only gradually the more independent forms of advance could appear—the effort to modify the old environment or to climb within the new environment.

Land-hunger and emigration are the phenomena corresponding to the lower forms of economic advance, while the higher forms are expressed in agricultural, industrial, and commercial enterprise at home and in the active adaptation to a higher milieu in towns and abroad. For those who remain in the community, increasing or acquiring property in land is the form of advance, satisfying at once the traditional idea of fortune, the desire of social standing, and, to a smaller extent, the desire for a better standard of living. The first two factors are fundamental. The proportions which land-hunger assumed in the second half of the last century are the best proof of the power of the new tendency to advance. But at the same time the lack of economic calculation in buying land proves that the old attitudes remain in force at least with regard to the qualitative character of land property. In the consciousness of the peasant who pays absurd prices for a piece of land there is no equivalence possible between land and any other economic value; they are incommensurable with each other. Land is a unique value, and no sum of money can be too large to pay for it; if there is bargaining and hesitation, it is only because the buyer hopes to get elsewhere or at another moment more land for the same money, not because he would rather turn the money to something else. And if later the interest on his capital is hardly 1 per cent to 2 per cent, he does not complain if only his general income, that is, the interest and his work, is sufficient to give him a living. He does not count his work, or rather he does not dissociate the interest on his capital and the product of his work, because his work is due to the land, and he is glad that he can work on his own land, not elsewhere. How strong and one-sided the land-hunger can be is proved by some examples of emigration to Brazil. Peasants who had twenty morgs of cultivated land sold it and emigrated, because they were to get there, at a cheap price, forty morgs of land, although not cultivated. So the mere difference of size between their actual and their future farm was a sufficient motive to overcome the attachment to their country and the fear of the unknown, to lead them to undertake a journey of two months and incalculable hardship afterward. This was the attitude of many a rich farmer, while the poor and landless naturally looked upon this opportunity to get land as an undreamed-of piece of luck. There was a real fever of emigration. Whole villages moved at once, and this emigration, in 1911–12, was centered in the most isolated and backward part of the country, in the eastern parts of the provinces of Siedlce and Lublin, and precisely where the tendency to advance had still the elementary form of land-hunger.

A phenomenon essentially different from this emigration of colonists with their families in search of land is the emigration of single individuals in search of work. We shall speak of it in detail later on. Here we mention it only in connection with the tendency to economic advance. Of course there are many in the community—and their number increases every year—who cannot hope to advance if they stay in the country. Most of them, indeed, can live as hired laborers, servants, or proprietors of small pieces of land, and earning some money in addition by outside work. Their living is on the average even better than that of their fathers and grandfathers under similar conditions, but they are no longer satisfied with such an existence; they want a better future, "if not for ourselves, at least for our children," as they express it.   This is the essential change of attitude which accounts for the simultaneous appearance and enormous development both of emigration and of land-hunger. Moreover, emigration to cities, from this standpoint, belongs to the same category as emigration abroad.   When a peasant emigrates, it is usually with the desire to earn ready money and return home and buy land.   He goes where he can find a ready market for work involving no technical or intellectual preparation, and he is at first satisfied with the wages he can secure for his unskilled labor.   Astonishment and regret are often expressed that the peasant shows no decided inclination to become a farmer in America, but undertakes in mines, on railroads, and in steel works forms of labor to which he is totally unaccustomed.   But it will be found that the peasant has selected precisely the work which suits his purpose, namely, a quick and sure accumulation of cash.

Usually it is the second generation which begins to rise above the economic level of the parents by other means than the accumulation of land, for at a certain point this means ceases to be effective.   The increase of landed property is always limited by the contrary process of division among the children, and there are already many localities where no land can be bought at all owing to the fact that the larger estates have already been parceled.   Under these circumstances the only remaining possibility of advance lies along the other line—increase of income through skilful farming and through industrial and commercial undertakings. A notable progress has already been accomplished along the first line.   As a typical example, four sons divided among themselves their father's land, and now each of them has more income from his portion than the father had from the whole.   Industrial undertakings develop more slowly.   The most important are mills, brick factories, the production of butter and cheese. The development of commerce is still slower. It is largely limited to trade in hogs, poultry, and fruit, and to petty shopkeeping in villages.

Among those who have left the country the second generation tends to higher wages, better instruction, and usually tries to rise above the ordinary working-class. The new milieu usually gives more opportunity, but requires more personal effort in order to rise, and it is therefore here that we find the greatest changes of attitudes.

Finally, education and imitation tend to create in the country another form of economic progress. The parents who cannot give their children land try to prepare them for higher positions by giving them a general and technical instruction instead of sending them to industrial centers, to Germany or America, as unskilled laborers.

During this evolution the economic attitudes become gradually adapted to the fundamental problem of economic advance. The result of this adaptation is that they cease to be social and become almost purely economic; they quantify all the material values and tend to increase the quantity. The economically progressive individual becomes approximately the classical "economic man"; that is, the economic side of his life is almost completely detached from the social side and systematized in itself, even if it continues to react to social influences. Or, in more exact terms, the general tendency to advance in the material conditions of existence effects in the peasant an analysis of his social life, and the result of this analysis is the constitution of a systematic body of new attitudes, social in their ultimate nature, but concerning merely material values and viewed with regard to the greatest possible increase of their enjoyment by the subject.

The evolution of property in this direction shows two phases: individualization and capitalization. As soon as the problem of advance takes the place of the problem of living, the rôle of the individual in matters of property increases more and more at the cost of the family. When a certain amount of property was assumed and the question was merely how to live from it, the individual had no claim to the property at all; it was there beforehand, he was not concerned in any way with its origin and essence, but only with its exploitation. The basis of his existence was in the group, and he could only help to maintain this basis. But the situation was totally changed when he became an active factor in the modification of this basis. To be sure, to a certain extent even here the family could act as a unit without distinguishing the part played by individuals in this modification. The property often increased under the familial régime, and up to the present we find many examples of families behaving with solidarity in matters of advance as they behaved formerly in matters of living. But the tendency to advance has necessarily a dissociating element which the old type of solidarity cannot resist very long; only in modern co-operation has the problem of harmonizing economic advance and social solidarity been solved, as we shall see in a later volume. On the one hand, the part played by individual members of the family in the increase of property was not equal, and, when the social and moral side of familial solidarity began to weaken, those who were the most efficient began to feel the familial communism as an injustice. Still more important is the fact that the family as a whole could advance only slowly, and the progress made by one generation was followed by a regression in the next generation when the number of marriage-groups increased. Consequently the members in whom the tendency to advance was particularly strong and impatient began to consider the family group as no longer a help but a burden. And even those who, as heads of the family, represented the familial principle assumed when they were particularly efficient an attitude of despotism which was in itself a step toward individualization and provoked also individualistic reactions from other members of the group. The more intense the desire to advance and the more rapid the progress itself, the more difficult it was to retain the familial form of property. The individuals began by claiming the products of their own activity; then the principle of individual ownership became extended to the hereditary familial land, and the last stage of this evolution is the quantitative division of the whole property—land, farmstock, house furniture, and money—among individual members of the family. The only vestige of the old solidarity in such cases is the desire to keep the land, even if divided, as far as possible in the family. The same members, therefore, never receive cash and land, but these are apportioned separately, and there remains a tendency to favor those who take the land, in order to preserve this as far as possible intact. But this is only one side of the process. The familial property was the highest form of economic value, the ultimate aim of any economic change. Other forms of property could pass into it, but it could not pass into them. And property in general was an incomparably higher economic category than income; it was an end in itself, and its use as a means of existence was a secondary matter. It resulted from the nature of property that it could be used as a basis of living, but its value did not consist merely in the living which could be got out of it; the living was always an individual matter, while property corresponded to the group. The fact that the idea of property could never be subordinated to the idea of income made impossible the treatment of property as productive capital. All this was changed as soon as property became individual, but even then, indeed, its nature was not completely exhausted by its being the source of an income, since it continued to stretch by heredity over more than one generation. Still this became its essential character and led to a revaluation of the various forms of property upon a new basis. The new valuation of every particular form of property on the basis of its productivity, of the amount and durability of the income which it brings, has two results: it gives a common measure of all the various forms of property, in spite of their qualitative differences, and it gives a greater fluidity to all forms of property—makes the change of one form into another relatively frequent and easy. The peasant in the country seldom reaches this complete capitalization of property, but he approaches it more and more. He already begins to think of individual fortune in terms of money, without enumerating separately land, farm-stock, money, and objects of private use; he compares goods with regard to their productivity, tries to increase this productivity by selling and buying, tries to change less productive for more productive goods of the same class (land for land, farm-stock for farm-stock), puts, not only his work, but also his money, in improvements, even such as require long waiting for the results. But even the most advanced peasant will not yet sell his land in order to start with this money a more productive business of a different nature unless he is already settled in a city or abroad, particularly in America. He will resign all property, sell his land, and emigrate in order to live elsewhere as a hired workman if his farm is too small to keep him and his family, but he seldom tries to exchange land for something else. The economic equivalence of land and other forms of property is not yet fully established.

The attitude with regard to income is undergoing a somewhat similar evolution. The individual effort to raise the income makes of this also an individual matter;

nobody has any longer the right to claim a part in its enjoyment, neither the community nor even the family. At the same time the qualitative distinctions between various sorts of income become meaningless under the influence of a new idea which we may term the standard of living. In a certain narrow sense the idea was not totally absent from the old economy. There was a social standard of living, adapted to the average economic level of the community and modified in each particular case with regard to the fortune of the family. There was in matters of food, clothing, lodging, and receptions a certain norm, and each family limited its scale of living both below and above, permitted it to be neither too modest nor too fastidious. The standard of living in the modern peasant economy, however, is very different. First, it is personal; the individual sets it himself, and he does not like any prescription of norms in this respect from either community or family. Again, it is virtual rather than actual; its essence lies in the power which the individual has over his economic environment by virtue of his income. Moreover, this power must express itself; but its expression is free, there is no particular line along which the income has to be spent. It may be spent mainly in acquiring property, or in acts of generosity, or in good eating, fine dressing, and lodging, or in amusements, or in all these together. The ways of spending may be varied as much as the individual pleases; stinginess along some lines may be equilibrated by lavishness along others. And, finally, the standard of living so conceived always concerns the future, not the present, because its meaning lies more in the possibility of spending than in spending itself; the individual sets a standard of what he can and will do. Such a standard therefore involves advance. The individual usually takes into account any foreseen increase of his economic power. The economic standard of life becomes thus an economic ideal of life. And of necessity the relative fluidity of this standard, the postulated possibility of passing from one expression of power to another, requires the translation of every form of income into terms of money.

This attitude has been particularly developed among Polish immigrants in America, but it exists also in Poland among those who have succeeded in rising above the economic level of the preceding generation. It often becomes one of the sources of the general feeling of self-importance typical of successful climbers, and is one of which we find many examples in the present materials. It has an important influence upon various social attitudes, particularly in matters of marriage and in relations with the family and the community. We shall point out these consequences presently.

As increase of fortune and income is mainly effected through individual work, the attitude toward work becomes also essentially changed. Work was always a necessary condition of living, but living was not unequivocally determined by work; there were other factors complicating the relation—good or bad will of men, God's help, and the devil's harmful activity. And even when occasionally, as in hired daily labor, the relation between work and living was simple, the process, not the result of work, was regulated by it, and the duration and intensity of this process were limited by the actual needs of which the peasant was conscious; he worked only in order to satisfy a determined want. The search for better work which we find at a later period was at first merely an endeavor to get more pay for the same limited amount of activity. But all this was changed when advance, instead of living, became the end of work. There are no predetermined and steady limits of advance. In the tendency to rise the needs grow continually. The peasant begins to search, not only for the best possible remuneration for a given amount of work, but for the opportunity to do as much work as possible. No efforts are spared, no sacrifice is too great, when the absolute amount of income can be increased. The peasant at this stage is therefore so eager to get piece-work. It is well known in Germany that good Polish workers can be secured only if a large proportion of piece-work is offered them. And during the period when piece-work lasts (harvesting) the peasants often sleep and eat in the field, and work from sixteen to twenty hours a day. And as wages in Germany are about 50 per cent higher than at home, all the best workers prefer to go there rather than work on a Polish estate, though the work is much harder and treatment worse. They take the hardship and bad treatment into account, but accept them as an inevitable condition of higher income. When they come back, they take an absolute rest for two or three months and are not to be moved to do the slightest work, proving that work is still highly undesirable in itself and desirable only for the income which it brings. Another consequence of this new attitude is that instead of changing work if there is a slightest hope of immediate improvement, and without regard to the future (as expressed in contract-breaking and wandering from place to place), the peasant now begins to appreciate more and more the importance of a steady job, particularly in America.

But the evolution does not end here. When the relation of the results of work to wages has been once established through the medium of piece-work, a further step brings to the attention the difference of results and of wages between skilled and unskilled labor. The mere increase of the quantity of work proves more limited and less effective than the improvement of quality. While this difference was abstractly known before, it acquires now a concrete, practical importance, since social evolution has opened new possibilities for the unskilled worker to pass into the skilled class, and the tendency to advance becomes sufficiently strong to overcome the old passivity and lack of initiative of the peasant. The problem of skilful and efficient work therefore begins to dominate the situation. At first the skill is valued only with regard to the income which it brings; but slowly and unconsciously the standpoint is shifted, and finally the skilled or half-skilled workman attains the level of the old guild hand-worker, is able to evaluate the results of his work and to be proud of his skill even without immediate reference to the remuneration. This reference changes its character. The question of earning a certain amount for some particular piece of work becomes secondary as compared with the general earning power of the individual. The ultimate level reached here is parallel with that which we found at the culmination of progress in matters of income. There the tendency to rise expressed itself finally in an ideal incorporating the highest possible buying power at a given stage. Here an increase in the general earning power is the object, and it finds its expression in a corresponding ideal which gives direction to the efforts to acquire a higher technical ability. Necessarily, these two ideals are closely connected, and we should expect that finally the question of buying-power would become secondary to that of earning-power; but the peasant does not seem to have reached this stage of systematization of the economic attitudes except in a few cases in America. The attitude of perfect security and independence with regard to the actual income can be acquired only by a man who has the consciousness of his own earning-power along the line of independent business and who is, moreover, not limited to a single specialty. But the Polish peasant, in the great majority of cases, had not had time enough to develop the spirit of initiative and the rapid adaptability which characterize, for example, the native American. This explains, among other facts, why no Polish peasant has succeeded up to the present in making a really big fortune, either in America or at home. The fear of failure, resulting from a feeling of insufficient adaptation to the complexity of modern economic life, necessarily hinders the undertaking of great enterprises.

The economic attitudes expressed in the relations to other men undergo a parallel evolution. The economic importance of the family and the community diminishes very rapidly as the relations of the individual with the external world become more various and durable. It may happen indeed that an individual who in his habitual economic life is almost a modern business man still behaves occasionally in the traditional way in his relations with some member of the traditional groups. But this occurs only if those relations are few and rare and if the old attitudes do not hinder the individual's advance. Thus, for example, an emigrant who has been for many years in America and has become relatively rich will occasionally show an unexpected generosity toward some poor relative, often even without regard to the degree of familial connection—which is of course quite contrary to tradition. And it is quite typical that a peasant settled in a city or abroad will receive his fellow-countryman with particular hospitality, and when he visits for a short time his native village will treat all of his old friends and acquaintances in an ostentatious way. This occasional display of the old attitudes has in it, of course, much of showing off. The attitudes of solidarity may be in reality very weak, but they get strength from the desire to manifest the importance of the individual's own personality in a way which is sure to bring recognition in his old milieu.

But if the individual still lives among his family or in his community, the old economic attitudes are dropped as hindering advance. Usually the attitudes which were formerly applied to the community are now transferred to the family. The obligation of help is acknowledged only in matters of living, not of property, and to a limited extent. For example, a member of the family can enjoy the hospitality of another member, but only for a time not exceeding a few months, or varying in individual cases. After that time he has to pay for his living. In matters of property the attitude of help may still exist in the form of lending, but not of gift. The dominant principle is that of exchange of equivalent goods. The attitude formerly employed toward strangers may be extended in some measure to the community, though a real exploitation of the members of the community, as in the not infrequent case of usury, is condemned. Even the ritualized attitudes—for example, ceremonial receptions and gifts,—do not escape the influence of the general egotism; reciprocity begins to be expected and lack of reciprocity provokes contempt. Only in matters of marriage does the new evolution lead to a greater disinterestedness, because the possibilities of individual advance make marriages without dowry possible, and because the marriage-group, isolated from both families, behaves in economic matters as a single individual.

The new attitudes are thus to be sought in the individual's relation to the world outside of his community, which is now his real economic milieu. Here the dominant feature of economic advance is, as we have seen, a progressive adaptation to a higher and more complex economic organization, and every economic act takes the form of business; it is an investment with the expectation of a profit. The individual always wants to get from others more than he gives. In this way his behavior corresponds to the classical economic type. His business acts are organized with regard to the future and constitute a practical system, a life-business. And as far as the individual meets others who have aims which interfere with his own, competition arises. The business attitudes are too well known to require analysis here. The point is that they did not exist at the beginning in the peasant's economic life, but appeared as the result of a long and complicated evolution.

3. In the second half of the past century, particularly after the unsuccessful revolution of 1863, there originated among the intelligent classes of the three parts of Poland a movement to enlighten and to organize the peasants in order to prepare them for a future participation in some new effort to recover national independence. The movement began in a different way in each part of Poland. In Galicia the starting-point was political organization, in Posen economic organization, in Russian Poland instruction. But gradually the problem of organization along all lines of social activity assumed an importance by itself, not alone with regard to a future revolution; and as the advance of modern militarism proved more and more the hopelessness of any endeavor to recover independence by arms, the idea of a national revolution almost lost its hold except in connection with the idea of social revolution or a European war. At present the social organization of the peasants is immediately connected with the problem of constituting a strong national unity of the social type as a substitute for national unity of the political type (the state), and economic organization is the most important part of this problem. All the traditional and modern economic attitudes, solidarity as well as individualism, are used to construct a new form of economic life based on co-operation. There is an imitation, of course, of the western peasant associations and labor

organizations, and the most self-conscious tendency in this line has been the importation of the English form of co-operation, but the whole movement has an original character through its connection with certain traditional attitudes on one hand and with the national ideal on the other. We shall study this movement in detail in our fourth volume.

The economic evolution of the Polish peasant gives us thus an exceptional opportunity to study the process of development of economic rationalism, since, in consequence of particular circumstances, the process has been very rapid, and all of its stages coexist at the present moment, as vestiges, as actual reality, or as the beginning of the future. We see that in the first stage economic life was completely subordinated to, and indissolubly connected with, social organization, that any methodological abstraction which constructs a system of economic attitudes as isolated from other social attitudes, and any theory which tries to deduce social organization from economic life, must fail. Then out of this first stage we see a new state of things developing— a historical status which corresponds practically with the classical economic theory. The economic life becomes abstracted in fact from the rest of social life; economic attitudes are elaborated which can be of themselves motives of human behavior. These are connected among themselves so as to constitute a rational practical system which is isolated in the consciousness of the individual from other spheres of interest, although occasionally interfering with them. But this is not a general law of economic life, only a particular historical status, due to the appearance of the tendency to economic advance. Finally, the third status, as we shall see in detail later on, realizes historically, in part, the socialistic doctrine of dependence of social organization upon economic life. The economic organization becomes in fact one of the fundamental conditions of a social organization, of the social national unity. But this is effected only through particular historical conditions and under the influence of particular social and moral ideals.

We do not assert that the evolution of the Polish peasant gives us a general law of economic evolution. It did not go on independently of external influences, and the action of those influences cannot as yet be methodologically excluded. A study of other societies in different conditions is indispensable, because only by comparison will it be possible to determine what in the process of economic evolution of the Polish peasant is fundamental and what accidental.

RELIGIOUS AND MAGICAL ATTITUDES[1]

The religious and magical life of the Polish peasant contains elements of various origin. There is still the old pagan background, about which we know very little and which was probably itself not completely homogeneous; there is Christianity, introduced in the tenth century, and gradually disseminated, partly absorbing, partly absorbed by, the old stock of beliefs; there are some other oriental elements, brought later by the Jews, the gipsies, infiltrated from Russia, Turkey, etc.; there are German elements, brought by the colonists; finally, much is due to the gradual popularization of the contents of classical literature and of mediaeval learning. It would be an impossible and useless

[1] In the following volumes we do not give a particular place to magic and religion as concrete data, partly because they do not possess for us relatively so great an importance, and partly because this is a field in which the data of peasant experience have been collected on a relatively complete and extensive scale—though these data have never been given a systematic sociological treatment. But on this account we offer here a relatively full treatment of the magical and religious elements in order to establish their proper importance in the peasant's scheme of attitudes and values. We have drawn freely as to details (but not as to theory) from Oskar Kolberg's great work, *Lud* ["The People"], and from the ethnographical materials published by the Cracow Academy of Sciences (*Materyały antropologiczno-archeologiczne i etnograficzne*).

undertaking to attempt a historical analysis of this complex. What we seek at this point is a determination of the fundamental attitudes shown by the peasant in his religious and magical life, aside from the question of the origin of these attitudes and of the beliefs and rites in which they express themselves. And of these we find four partially independent types: (1) general animation of natural objects, but no spirits distinct from the objects themselves; solidarity of life in nature; no distinction possible between religion and magic; (2) belief in a world of spirits, partly useful, partly harmful, and distinct from natural objects; the beliefs are religious, the practice is magical; (3) absolute distinction of good and evil spirits; the relation with the good spirits is religious and expressed in social ceremonies, the relation with bad spirits is magical and established individually. (4) Introduction of mysticism, tendency to self-perfection and salvation; personal relation with the divinity.

Although it is possible that these types of attitude represent as many necessary stages in the development of religious life, this cannot be affirmed with certainty without comparative studies. And in a concrete religion like Catholicism we naturally find mixed elements representing various stages of religious evolution, and a concrete group or individual shows a combination, often a very illogical one, of attitudes belonging to various types.

1. All the natural beings—animals, plants, minerals, the heavenly bodies, and the earth—are objects of the peasant's interest and sympathy. His motives are not consciously utilitarian, although, as we shall see, natural objects are always in some way related to the man's life and welfare. We may perhaps assume that it is this general interest which causes the man to invent a direct utilitarian connection between himself and some natural object (a connection which in fact does not exist) when he wishes to justify his

interest rationally.[1] This point will become clearer when we determine the essence of the relation between man and nature.

But the fact that natural objects are related to man's welfare at all distinguishes this interest from the purely aesthetic one whose origin we shall analyze elsewhere. The common feature in both is the tendency to individualize. The individualization goes far. Not only all the domestic animals, but even the wild ones, are always, as far as possible, identified, which act sometimes (with domestic animals always) expresses itself in name-giving. Every tree, every large stone, every pit, meadow, field, has an individuality of its own and often a name. The same tendency shows itself in the individualization, often even anthropomorphization, of periods of time. At least one-third of the days of the year are individually distinguished, and the peasant never uses numbers for these dates, but always individual names. The Christian consecration of every day to a saint is very helpful in this respect, and the peasant usually substitutes (for example, in his innumerable proverbs) the saint for the day.[2] Tales in which months or days are anthropomorphized are frequent. The anthropomorphization itself is not serious, but it is a sign of the tendency to individualization. Thanks to this tendency, time becomes a part of nature, and individualized periods of time become natural objects. There is little trace of an analogous individualization of space, except the usual distinction of the six cardinal directions—objective: east, west, south,

---

[1] It is forbidden, for example, to touch a swallow's nest or even to observe the swallow too persistently when it is flying in and out of it. The rationalistic justification of this attitude is that the swallow may become angry and drop her excrement into the man's eye, causing blindness.

[2] For example: "When St. Martin comes upon a white horse, the winter will be sharp." Or: "St. Matthew either destroys the winter or makes it wealthy." Or: "If Johnny begins to cry and God's Mother does not calm him, he will cry till St. Ursula."

north, up, down; subjective: right, left, before, behind, up, down.

When individualization is impossible, as, for example, with regard to many wild animal species, there is at least a tendency to invent an imaginary individual which becomes then the representative and the head of the whole species. Thus we find everywhere the legend of a king of the serpents, whose crown in some tales a peasant succeeds in stealing; the wolves, deer, boars, hawks, owls, etc., have particularly old and powerful individuals whom they obey; in many tales there appear various individual animals and birds endowed with exceptional qualities and knowledge to whom their species has to listen, and even if in some cases these animals prove to be metamorphosed men, this is not essential at all, and even such changes, as we shall see, can be explained without any appeal to extra- or supra-natural powers.

For the interesting point in all this individualization of natural objects is that, while there are no spirits in or behind the objects, the latter are always animated, often conscious and even reasonable. To be sure, we find also spirits attached to objects in the peasant's belief, but these cases belong to a quite different religious system. In the system we are now considering we find only living beings whose life is not at all distinguished from its material manifestation— no opposition of spirit and body. The animals, the plants, the heavenly bodies, the earth, the water, the fire, all of them live and all of them think and know in varying degrees. Even individualized fields and meadows, even days and times of the year, have some kind of independent existence, life, and knowledge. The same characters belong in various degrees to manufactured objects and to words. In short, anything which is thought as individually existent is at the same time animated and endowed with some consciousness; the "animated and conscious thing" seems to be a category of the peasant's thinking in the same sense that the mere "thing" or "substance" is a category of scientific reasoning. Or, more exactly, when a scientist isolates an object in thought in order to study it, his act is purely formal; the object does not (or rather, it should not) acquire in the eyes of the scientist any new property by being thought, except that of becoming the subject of a judgment. But the peasant, at least at the stage of intellectual culture which we study here in its vestiges, cannot isolate an object in thought without ascribing to it (unintentionally, of course) an independent existence as an animated and more or less conscious being.

We find innumerable examples of this attitude. If we take only one manifestation of nature's consciousness—her conscious reaction to man's activity—we see that up to the highest forms of animal life and down to the manufactured thing or to the animated abstraction of a time-period man's action is understood and intentionally reacted upon. An animal not only feels gratitude for good treatment and indignation at bad treatment, not only tries to reward or to avenge, but even understands human motives and takes them into account. This is not only shown in all the animal tales, but is manifested in everyday life. A peasant in whom this belief is still strong will never intentionally mistreat an animal, and tries to explain or to cause the animal to forget a mistreatment due to accident or anger. After the death of the farmer his heir has to inform the domestic animals of the death and to tell them that he is now the master. Some animals understand and condemn immoral actions of man even if these do not affect themselves. The bees will never stay with a thief, the stork and the swallow leave a farm where some evil deed has been committed; the same was formerly true of the house snake. As to the plants, if fruit trees grow well and bear fruit, if crops succeed, it is not merely a result of a mechanical or magical influence of the man's activity; the plants are conscious of being well treated and show their gratitude. This must be taken literally, not metaphorically. We find the same belief dignified in the tales, where, for example, an apple tree bends its branches and gives its best fruit to a girl who cleaned its trunk from moss, and refuses anything to another who did not do this. The same literal sense is contained in a saying about the gratitude of the earth, which consciously rewards the laborer's well-intentioned and sincere work. Every field knows its real owner and refuses to yield to a usurper. The earth is indignant at any crime committed upon its face; it was crystalline before Cain killed Abel and became black after this. It sometimes refuses to cover a self-murderer, particularly one who has hanged himself. The sun sees and knows everything that happens during the day. If something is said against it, it punishes the offender, while it is no less susceptible to thanks and blessings. Prayers are still addressed on some occasions to the moon, and evil doings are to be performed rather when the moon does not see them. The stars understand the man who knows how to ask them, and give an answer literally and immediately in the form of inspiration, not mediately, through the calculation of their positions, as in astrology. The water should not be dirtied or dried up. Nothing bad should be done or said near it, because it knows and can betray. In the tales a pit shows the same gratitude for being cleaned as the apple tree. Fire is perhaps still more animated and conscious, and there is a peculiar respect shown toward it. The children who play with the fire are told: "Don't play with the fire. It is not your brother." The fire should be kept with the greatest care and cleanliness, blessed when lighted in the morning, blessed when covered with ashes at night. Once a year (on St. Laurentius' Day) the old fire is extinguished and a new one lighted, both ceremonies being accompanied with thanks and blessings. Fire should never be lent, either from respect or because it is particularly connected with the family. There is a tale of two fires meeting; one of them praised its hostess for treating it well, the other complained that its hostess mistreated it, kept it carelessly, and never blessed it. Then the first fire advised the second to avenge itself, and on the following night the second burned the house of its hostess. Nothing offensive should be said against any natural phenomenon—wind, thunderstorm, hail, rain, cold—or against a season of the year; vengeance may follow. Again, we have tales in which anthropomorphized natural phenomena (e.g., frost, wind) prove grateful for good and revengeful for bad treatment. A peculiar attitude can be noticed with regard to the days of the year. Each day, in view of its individuality, is particularly fit for determined action,[1] or, more exactly, reacts favorably upon some actions, unfavorably upon others. But, more than this, each day returns the next year and can then avenge a bad action or reward a good action committed last year. Thence comes mainly the importance of anniversaries. The same is true of week-days and months, and we find here also the exaggeration of the normal attitude in tales, where days and months are anthropomorphized. Traces of the same (but here only half-conscious) belief that things understand are found in the peasant's unwillingness to change the pronunciation of words or to play with them; the pun is seldom if ever used by the peasant as a mere joke. Nor should words ever be misused, great words applied to petty things, etc. Finally,

[1] There is scarcely any relation between this belief and astrology. Of all the mediaeval magical doctrines astrology was the last to reach the peasant, when he already knew how to read almanacs; like all other book-doctrines, it reached him in disconnected fragments, while the belief stated in the text is systematically applied to the whole year.

the power of blessings and curses depends in a certain measure upon the immanent life of the words. It seems natural to explain this respect for words by a magical connection between the word as a symbol and the thing symbolized, because for us the word is nothing but a symbol, and we have difficulty in imagining how a word can have life and power in itself independently of any relation to something else. But for the peasant the word is not only a symbol, it is a self-existent thing. We find also, as will be shown, magical power ascribed to the word, but then we are in a different system of beliefs. The attitude toward the word as an independent being exists. This fact we must fully recognize, and only then can we raise the further question whether there is any direct genetic relation between this attitude and the magical one.

In connection with the objects made by man the animating tendency is expressed perhaps less clearly than in connection with natural objects, but it is essentially the same. No object should be hurt, destroyed, soiled, neglected, or even moved without necessity and this not because of utilitarian considerations alone nor because of the fear of magical consequences, although those reasons are also active. The object has an individuality of its own, and, even if it is not alive and conscious in the proper sense, it has a certain tendency to maintain its existence. There are cases of an almost intelligent vengeance taken by man-made objects, and in tales they are also often endowed with consciousness and speech. The animation decreases in the case of objects whose process of manufacture has been observed, and disappears sometimes (but not always) almost completely in the case of those which the individual has made himself. And the latter are also the only ones which the individual has sometimes implicitly the moral right to destroy, if he does so immediately after having made them. By existing for a certain time they acquire immunity.

The intelligence of natural objects, particularly of animals, manifests itself, not only in the conscious reaction upon human activity, but also in other lines. While the animal does not know everything man knows, every animal has knowledge about some matters which remain hidden from man. The properties of wild plants and of minerals have been mainly learned by man from the animals, and he has yet much to learn. For example, swallows and lizards know herbs which can resuscitate the dead; the turtle know an herb which destroys every fence and wall, breaks every lock, etc. The snakes and the wild birds are the most knowing, but the quadrupeds, even the domestic ones, understand some things better than man. Another knowledge which all the animals possess to some degree is the prevision of future events, particularly changes of weather and deaths. If man carefully watches their behavior, he can avoid many mistakes, and he would be still wiser if he understood their language. The plants, heavenly bodies, earth, water, and fire have the same knowledge of one another's properties and the same prevision of the future, but in varying degrees.

Nevertheless, except in tales, where all the anthropomorphic properties of natural objects are exaggerated, we can hardly say that in point of knowledge man is generally inferior to his environment. In some matters he knows less, but in others more. There is no contrast of any kind between man and nature. Man is a being of the same class as any natural object, although men understand one another better and are more closely connected with one another than with the animals or plants. In saying that man is a being of the same class we mean also that he has no spirit distinct from the body, leaving it temporarily in dreams and forever in death. As to dreams, there is no trace of the belief that a part of the personality, a soul in any sense whatever, leaves the body and visits other places.

This explanation exists, but in connection with another system of beliefs. The fact of seeing everything in dreams seems to call for no explanation at all, because it is simply assimilated to the fact of imagining things in the waking state; it is too naturally accepted to be a problem. The problem appears only in connection with prophetic dreams, explicit or symbolical, but here again it is not distinct from other facts of prophecy or second sight found in the waking state, and the explanation is made, not on a theory of the soul, but, as we shall see presently, on the basis of the whole conception of the natural world. As to death, there is certainly a "spirit" which leaves the body, but it is only "vapor" or "air" which dissolves itself in the environment. The body simply loses the part of its vital power of which the "air" or "vapor" is a condition, in the same way as it loses in sleep the power of voluntary movement, seeing, and hearing. And even then the body is not really dead; it is never quite dead as long as it exists, for under certain influences it may come to full life again. It may awake periodically at certain moments, or, if it has a particularly strong vitality, it may live indefinitely in the tomb, coming out every night to eat. This is the case with the vampire. A man who will be a vampire can be distinguished even during his life by the redness of his cheeks, his strength, his big teeth. And all of this has nothing to do with the question of a returning soul.

This, however, is only a partial life. To have a real second life the body must be destroyed, and then the man is regenerated and lives again, in this world or in some other. The regeneration is nothing particular. Every year the whole of nature is regenerated from death. There are cases of men who, without waiting for natural death, let their bodies be destroyed and arose again, young and powerful. In other cases the regeneration in this world took place in the form of a tree, a lily, an animal, etc. Thus regeneration in another world is a fact classed with many other perfectly natural facts. The only difference is that the man usually lives his second life somewhere else, out of reach of his friends, though sometimes mystical communication is possible. The instrument of destruction and regeneration can be either fire or earth. The purificatory properties of fire make it particularly fit for destruction, the fecundity of the earth for regeneration. Both cremation and burial were used in funerals at different epochs, and agriculture gave analogies of regeneration by both means. In primitive agriculture the forest was burned and the soil acquired a particular fertility. The branch of the willow placed in the earth grows into a tree.

Now this whole world of animated and more or less conscious beings is connected by a general solidarity which has certainly a mystical character, because the ways of its action are usually not completely accessible to observation and cannot be rationally determined, but whose manifestations express the same moral principle as the solidarity of the family and of the community. Even in the reaction of nature upon man's activity which we have indicated in the examples enumerated above, this solidarity is manifested. But we find still more explicit proofs. There is a solidarity between certain plants and certain animals. When the animal (for example, a cow) is sick, the peasant finds the proper plant, bends it down, and fastens its top to the ground with a stone, saying: "I will release you when you make my cow well." The same evening the cow will recover. Then the man must go and release the plant, or else on the next day the cow will fall sick again and die. Similarly animals are interested in plants and can influence them. Hence the numerous ways of assuring good crops or the successful growth of fruit trees through the help of animals. A stork nesting upon the barn makes a full barn. A furrow drawn around a field by a pair of twin oxen insures it against hail, and the same means is used against the pest, with the addition that twin brothers must lead the oxen. Sparrows should be allowed to eat cherries in summer and grain in winter, and pigeons should be allowed to eat peas, because these birds are allies and companions of man, and for their share in the crops help them to grow. If there are many maybugs in spring, it means that millet will be good. The cuckoo can call only till the crops have ceased to blossom, because then they fall asleep and the bird ought not to wake them.

There is also a relation of solidarity between the earth (also the sun) and all living beings, which is strikingly expressed in such beliefs as the following: The earth can communicate its fecundity to an animal (for example, to a sterile cow), and, on the other hand, the fecundity of animals or women can be communicated to a sterile field. The sun should not look upon dead animals, because it is disturbed, sets in blood, and may send hail and rain. Fires lighted on the eve of St. John (June 24), in some localities before Easter, make the crops succeed—an old pagan custom. There is also solidarity between the fire and all living beings. It is used in many mystical actions whose aim is to increase life, and it should never be fed with anything dead (remnants of dead animals; straw from the mattress of a dead man, or even remnants of wood left after the making of a coffin), unless of course the aim is the regeneration of the dead object.[1] The same is true, although perhaps in a lesser degree, of water.[2]

---

[1] A particular solidarity exists between the fern and the fire; therefore nobody should plant the fern near his house, or else the house will burn. In general, the fern is a privileged plant. Whoever finds its flower (it is supposed to blossom at midnight, June 24) sees all the treasure under the earth and all the things which were lost or stolen.

[2] We shall speak later of the magical use of fire and water as symbols of mystical powers; here their influence results from their own nature and their solidarity with other beings.

But between beings of the same class the principle of solidarity is still more evident. Plants are solidary and sympathetic with one another. Therefore the success of some of them results in the success of others, and, on the contrary, the destruction of any kind of plants never goes alone, but influences the lot of others. Predictions can be made about crops from the observation of wild plants, and this can hardly be interpreted as a rational inference based upon the knowledge that these plants need the same atmospheric conditions. No such explanation is in fact attempted, even when the peasant is asked for the reason of his belief. Among animals the solidarity is still greater. The house snake is solidary with the cattle and poultry; if it is well treated all the domestic animals thrive, but if it is killed they will certainly die. The same kind of sympathy exists between the goat (also the magpie) and the horses. If a swallow's nest is destroyed or a swallow killed, the cows give bloody milk. The cow is also related by some mysterious link with the weasel; whenever a cow dies some weasel must die, and reciprocally. When there is danger the animals warn one another. In autumn the redbreast rises high in the clouds and watches; when the first snowflake falls upon his breast he comes down and informs everybody, calling: "Snow, snow!" (*śnieg*). Again, night animals are more closely connected with one another than with others. But animals of the same species are naturally more solidary than those of different species, and their solidarity is less mysterious, because more often observable empirically and more easily interpreted by analogy with the human solidarity. An animal, particularly a wild one, can always call all its mates to its rescue if attacked or wounded, and there is always some danger in hunting even the apparently most inoffensive animals.

The knowledge ascribed to natural objects is also as much a sign of solidarity as of intelligence, because it is always a knowledge about other natural objects, either a result or a cause of the mystical affinity between them. We cannot omit here the analogy between social life and nature. In social life solidarity reaches as far as the sphere of the peasant community, that is, as far as people know one another or about one another, and only secondarily and accidentally, under the influence of the belief that a guest may be the bearer of some unknown power, is it applied to the stranger. Nature is also a primary group, and man belongs to this group as a member, perhaps somewhat privileged, but not a "king of creation." The attitude of natural beings toward him, as well as his attitude toward them, is that of sympathetic help and respect. Nature is actively interested in man's welfare. The sun gives him warmth and light (in tales it considers this to be its moral duty), the earth gives him crops, fruit trees give fruit, springs and rivers give water. Domestic animals give him milk, eggs, wool, the dog watches his house, the cat keeps the mice away from his food, the bees give honey and wax, the stork, snake, swallow, and mole give him general happiness, the magpie brings him guests, the fire prepares food for them. The cuckoo makes him rich or poor for the year, according to the amount of money (or some other possession) he has in his hand when hearing its voice for the first time. And all this is not a metaphor; the "giving" is to be understood really, as a voluntary act. Other animals, particularly birds, advise him what to do. The lark, the quail, the landrail, the pigeon, the sparrow, the frog, etc., tell him when to begin some particular farm-work, their calls being interpreted as indistinctly pronounced phrases. And at every moment he is warned by some intentional sign against misfortune. If a hare or a squirrel runs across his way, it is an advice to return. The horse foretells a good or bad end of the journey; the dog foresees fire, pest, war, and warns his master by howling; the owl foretells death or birth, etc. The mice help the children to get good teeth if the child's tooth is thrown to them and they are asked to give a better one. Any sickness which befalls the man or his farm-stock is healed by the help of animals and plants, for this is the essence of medicine in the system of beliefs which we are now analyzing. We find an enormous number of remedies against sickness, and among the oldest of them some which contain not the slightest trace of magical symbolism and also are not based upon the concept of purely physical action, but can be explained only by the idea of sympathetic help. We have seen that plants by being bent are compelled to help the domestic animals; there are plants which act remedially by the mere act of growing in the garden; others which destroy sickness when brought home on Easter or Pentecost (ancient pagan spring holidays, symbolizing the awakening of nature), St. John's Eve (midsummer holiday), or on Mary's Day (August 15, and harvest-home holiday). And probably many of the plants used internally or applied to the body owe their power to the mystical solidarity, not to the magical or mechanical influence. There is no doubt that the same attitude prevails with regard to animals, at least when the help of the animal is asked, though in the use of various parts of the dead animal we find mainly the magical attitude, and this is quite the contrary of the attitude of mystical solidarity. Thus, while from the latter standpoint the killing of a snake is a crime, we find in the magical system of beliefs that the ointment made from a snake killed and boiled (or boiled alive) in oil is among the most efficient remedies.[1]

---

[1] The use of stones seems to be mainly magical. There is, for example, a small stone which, as the peasant believes, comes from sand melted by lightning, and this is particularly efficient, because it has a symbolical relation to the power of the lightning. But in some cases a stone helps by its own immanent power, and these stones are usually found by birds and reptiles, and their use is learned from them.

Plants and animals have also the power of provoking toward a given person favorable feelings in others, and of promoting in general the social solidarity among men. In addition to magical love-charms we find also some plants which when sown and cared for by a girl help her to succeed with boys, without any magical ceremony. The stork, the snake, and the swallow, among other functions, keep harmony in the human family with which they live.

Finally, even with regard to the beings whose relation toward man is not determined (spiders, moths, flies) or which may even seem harmful (bugs, mosquitoes, fleas, etc.) the normal attitude is expressed in the words: "We don't know what they are for, but they must have some use." And, as most of the old beliefs are interpreted now from the Christian standpoint, a peasant says to a boy who wants to kill a frog: "Don't do it. This creature also praises our Lord Jesus." Christian legends are indeed connected with most of the natural beings who have a mystical value. Healing properties of certain plants brought in on the midsummer day are explained by the legend that the head of St. John when it was cut off fell among these plants. The lark, which soars so high, is the favorite bird of the angels; during a storm they hold it in their hands, and when, with every lightning-flash, the heaven opens, it is allowed to look in. The nightingale leads the choir of birds which sing to the Virgin Mary on her assumption day, etc.

Although the belief in the solidarity of nature is most evidently manifested in connection with isolated and somewhat extraordinary occurrences, we see that it pervades, in fact, the whole sphere of the peasant's interests.

The solidarity of nature, in the peasant's life, is neither a matter of theoretical curiosity nor an object of purely aesthetic or mystical feelings aroused on special occasions.

It has a fundamental practical importance for his everyday life; it is a vital condition of his existence. If he has food and clothing and shelter, if he can defend himself against evil and organize his social life successfully, it is because he is a member of the larger, natural community, which cares for him, as for every other member, and makes for him some voluntary sacrifices whose meaning we shall investigate presently. Even the simplest act of using nature's gifts assumes, therefore, a religious character. The beginning and the end of the harvest, storing and threshing the crops, grinding the grain, milking the cow, taking eggs from the hen, shearing the sheep, collecting honey and wax, spinning, weaving, and sewing, the cutting of lumber and collecting of firewood, the building of the house, the preparation and eating of the food—all the acts involving a consumption of natural products were or are still accompanied by religious ceremonies, thanksgivings, blessings and expiatory actions. And here we meet a curious fact. Usually when a tradition degenerates the rite persists longer than the attitude which was expressed in it. But here the old rites have often been forgotten, more often still changed into Christian ceremonies (religious or magical), while the attitude persists unchanged. This is an evident sign that the essence of the old belief is still preserved. Christianity has been able to destroy the rite but not the attitude. There is a particular seriousness and elation about every one of those acts, a gratitude which only by second thought is applied to the divinity and first of all turns to nature, a peculiar respect, expressing itself, for example, in the fear of letting the smallest particle of food be wasted, and a curious pride, when nature favors the man (with a corresponding humiliation in the contrary case), quite independent of any question of successful efforts, and reminding us of the pride which a man feels when he is favored by his human community.

And man must in turn show himself a good member of the natural community, be as far as possible helpful to other members. Many old tales express explicitly this idea. The hero and heroine are asked for help by animals, plants, mountains, water, fire, etc., in distress, and they give it out of the feeling of sympathy, often without any idea of reciprocity, although some reciprocal service usually follows. These extraordinary cases give, as usually, only a more evident and striking expression of a habitual attitude. But every work done in order to increase and to protect life assumes the character of an act of solidarity and has a religious value. Work is sacred, whenever its immediate aim is help. Plowing the field, sowing, sheltering and feeding the domestic animals, digging ditches and wells, are actions of this kind. They have, of necessity, human interest in view, but this would not be enough to make them sacred. They consist mainly in a mere preparation of conditions in which the immanent solidarity of nature can work better.

On the other hand, any break of solidarity is immediately punished. Some examples have been given, but there is an innumerable quantity of them. Cutting a fruit tree means sure death to the criminal. Killing a stork is a crime which can never be pardoned. In old times a man who killed a house snake ceased to be a member of the human community, probably because he was no longer a member of the natural community. A man who kills a dog or a cat is up to the present avoided by everybody unless indeed he shoots these animals, for curiously enough this is tolerated. Even lack of solidarity among men is avenged by nature. We have already seen that the stork leaves a house where some evil deed has been committed. If someone refuses a pregnant woman anything which she asks for, mice will destroy his clothes. The destructive forces of nature (about which we shall speak presently) usually abide, when personified, upon the ridges between fields, because those places are desecrated by human quarrels and hate. The bees give testimony to the purity of the girl and the honesty of the boy by not stinging them. And so on.

In this system of attitudes the relation between bad work and bad results in agriculture is not that of a purely physical causality, but that of a moral sanction. If nature does not yield anything to a lazy and negligent man, it is to avenge his neglect of the duties of solidarity. And the sanction may be expressed in a quite unexpected way, on a different line from that of the offense. A neglect of the duties of solidarity toward some animals or insects may be punished by bad crops; careless behavior with regard to fire or water may result in some unsuccess with domestic animals, etc.

But there is always a certain amount of destruction necessary for man to live; all actions cannot be helpful and productive. And in nature itself there are hostilities and struggles, not solidarity alone. How is this to be reconciled with the beliefs stated above?

In order to understand these partly apparent, partly real breaks of solidarity we must know what is the general meaning, the aim of this solidarity itself. It cannot be a struggle with the external world, for the solidarity embraces the whole world; nor a struggle with any evil principle, because there seems to be no evil principle in nature; nor yet the struggle against bad and harmful beings, for there are no beings essentially bad and harmful. The only reason for nature's solidarity is a common struggle against death, or rather against every process of decay, of which death is the most absolute and typical form. Sickness, destruction, misery, winter, night, are the main phenomena correlated with death.

It is really difficult to say how far this essentially negative idea of death is interpreted as meaning a positive entity, because the peasant's attitude toward it seems not to be quite consistent. On the one hand, indeed, death with all the connected evils has no place within the community of nature. It is neither a natural being nor a natural force, for there are no forces distinct from individual things, there is no trace of a philosophical abstraction to which any kind of reality could be ascribed. There is therefore only a plurality of phenomena of decay, each of which separately seems to be nothing but a result of the immanent weakness of the decaying thing itself—everything "has to die," is "mortal"—or of a harmful influence of some exterior natural things which make a break in solidarity or punish such a break. But, on the other hand, death as an objectified concept is an animated thing and can be anthropomorphically represented, like other phenomena of decay. We know by tradition of two usual shapes which death assumes —that of a nebulous woman in white and that of a skeleton. The latter seems to be derived from Christian paintings. But it can change its shapes and appear in the form of an animal, plant, or any other natural object; it may also be, as in some tales, shut up by man in a cask, buried in the earth, etc. It likes also to stay on ridges between fields and about hedges. In short, it has no exclusive form or abode and differs therefore from natural beings, while there is an evident analogy between it and the spirits. The same is true of diseases (pest, fever) and sometimes of "misery." Winter has a little more of the character of a natural being. We find here a hesitation between attitudes and a type of belief intermediary between naturalism and spiritualism, resulting from the fact that for death, diseases, misery (poverty), etc., as independent beings there is no place in the community of nature and therefore they must, if anthropo-

morphized at all, stay outside. But precisely for this
reason this is the only case where objectification and animation have no essential importance. The activity of every
natural object and its relation with others result, as we have
seen, from its character as an animated and conscious
being. But it is not so with death. It is impossible to
interpret all the actual facts of death in nature by the
activity of the death-spirit, and such interpretation is
never attempted. We find at most the fact of human death
explained in this way. This limitation of the activity of
the death-spirit to the human world is still more evident
with regard to the "bad air" or "black death," that is, the
pest, which is more distinctly represented as a woman, sometimes flying on bat-wings, sometimes waving a red kerchief
above villages and towns; but this "black death," whose
essence is quite inexplicable for the peasant, is afraid of many
natural beings—of water, fire, reptiles. In short, as soon as
death is conceived as a being, its power is limited; and it is
not at all identical with a general principle of natural decay.
Such a conception seems, therefore, to be a late result of evolution, going on with a separation between the human and
the natural world. The more determined the image of
death (as well as of disease, misery, etc.), the farther we are
from the primitive naturalistic system. It is probable,
therefore, that originally death, more or less vaguely identified with disease, misery, winter, meant an undetermined
"something," "it," or "the evil"—rather a species than a
unique entity, having just enough reality to provoke a mixed
and characteristic attitude of dread, hate, and disgust which
the peasant manifests in the presence of anything connected
with death.

This attitude is found in the aversion which the peasant
always shows to talking about death, passing near a cemetery or near a place where someone died, staying with a

dead body, etc.   It is bad luck to meet a coffin containing a dead body, and particularly to look after it.   The straw from the last bed and the splinters left from the coffin should not be left in the house, because somebody else may die in the house.   (We have seen that they should not be burned out of respect for the fire.)   For the same reason no one should look into a mirror which hung in the dead person's room during death, and no member of the family should throw earth upon the coffin when it is sunk into the grave.   All these beliefs are magical, but they show how fundamental is the dread of death.   And anyone who by his occupation has some connection with death is more or less feared, hated, and despised—the executioner, the gravedigger, even the women who wash and dress the body.   A person who cuts down the body of a hanged man, even with the best intentions, is particularly shunned.   This attitude prevails with regard also to animal death.   Those who have something to do with killing animals and preparing their bodies are avoided almost as much as the executioner.   Among these are the dog-catchers, tanners and skin-dealers, butchers (if they kill), etc.   All these functions were therefore usually performed by Jews, or by men who had little to lose.   Up to the present, in Russian Poland the dog-catchers are often men who at the bidding of the authorities act as the executioners of political offenders, and most of the butchers and skin-dealers are still Jews.   But hunting does not provoke this attitude, perhaps because in old times it was indispensable to defend the crops and the domestic animals.

The same attitude, as we have already seen in some examples, is ascribed to other natural beings.   The sun hates the sight of death; animals and plants foresee it for themselves and for the man; they avoid and despise anybody who brings death, they will not abide in a place soiled with death, etc.   Only earth, water, and fire, while they should never be profaned uselessly by anything connected with death, are still, in a sense, above the dread, because they have a power over death.

Sickness (except pest), misery, and winter do not provoke the attitude of dread and hate to the same extent because, although they are varieties of the same evil, their influence is weaker, they are more easily avoided, and their effect is more easily repaired.

But this dread of death never rises to a tragical pitch, never leads to a pessimistic view of existence or to fatalism. The tragic attitude comes only with Christianity, with sin, the devil, and hell. In the naturalistic religious system life is always ultimately victorious over death, thanks to the solidarity of living beings. Within certain limits, death. total or partial (for example, sickness, misery), can be avoided through reciprocal help, and when it comes it is always followed by regeneration. And this explains at the same time the necessity of sacrifice, required from all the natural beings by the natural solidarity, and the possibility of sacrifice, since no sacrifice is ultimate in view of the future regeneration.

The life of every natural being can be maintained only by willing gifts of other beings, which may go as far as a voluntary gift of life. In many tales we find animals consciously sacrificing their life for the sake of man or of one another, even if this sacrifice proves usually only temporary, because the animal is regenerated in the human form, which was its primitive form. In some legends animals and plants sacrifice themselves for the Virgin Mary, or for Jesus during his human life. A reward usually follows. In everyday life there is no explicit acknowledgment of the readiness or natural beings to sacrifice themselves, but implicitly this readiness is assumed; while, as we know, any useless destruction of life is a crime because a break of solidarity, a destruction which is necessary to maintain the life of other beings, is permitted. This applies indifferently to man and nature. We find the story of a girl, the ward of a village elder, whom the latter buried alive during the pest, making thus an expiatory sacrifice in order to save the life of the rest of the inhabitants. Man is justified in killing animals for food, but never more than he actually needs and not for sale, although, sophistically enough, he may sell the living animal knowing that it will be killed. He can cut trees to build a house or a barn, but it is not fair to cut them for sale. Dry wood should be used as firewood, and only when none can be found is it licit to fell some tree; old or poorly growing trees should be selected for this purpose, even if the forest belongs to the state or to a manor, and therefore no utilitarian considerations prevail. The only case in which it is permitted to cut, sell, or burn any trees is when the land is to be turned to agricultural purposes, because here destruction will be expiated by production. The man may destroy the insects which damage his crops or the rats in his barn, but it is always better to drive them away by some means—to frighten them, for instance, by catching and maltreating one of their number. The wolf is justified in eating other animals, but man is also justified in slaying him. In short, every living being has the right to get its living and to defend itself against death or decay in any form, and other beings have to acknowledge this right; but every destruction beyond the necessary is a crime, and then retaliation is just. And there is, in this respect, no essential difference of value between man and animal which would justify destroying life for his purposes. We have an interesting story which shows this very plainly. A lark complains to a hungry wolf that a mole threatens to destroy her nest with her young ones—an unnecessary act of destruction, since the mole should take the trouble to pass around the nest. The wolf helps her and kills the mole, but on the condition that the lark will procure him food, drink, and amusement. The lark does this, but at the cost of a human life, and this situation is morally all right.

The idea that natural things may be destroyed only if there is an immediate relation between them and actual needs of living beings explains the peasant's aversion toward the industrial exploitation of nature on a large scale. Indeed in this exploitation the relation between the act of destruction and the need to be satisfied becomes so remote and mediate, and the needs themselves are so abstract when viewed from the standpoint of the traditional industrial activity, that the peasant fails to see any adequate reason for destruction, and the latter seems a crime against natural solidarity. Such is always the first reaction of the peasant when a sawmill, a brewery, or a sugar factory is set up, a railway built, or a mine dug; perhaps even the use of agricultural machines is disliked partly because through them the relation of man toward nature becomes impersonal and devoid of warmth and respect.

But the sacrifice of life necessary to support the life of others is, as we have said, never ultimate. Regeneration always comes unless death was a punishment for a break of solidarity. The ideal is a regeneration of the same individual in the same form, that is, resurrection. This ideal is depicted in tales. We find it in the pagan funeral ceremonies, where the dead man was burned with his horse, his dog, his agricultural instruments, arms, etc. In Christian legends actual present resurrection, not a future life in heaven, is the favorite theme, and traces of this belief are found also in the tales of today. The annual return of leaves and fruits to the trees, the recovery from a sickness, the melting of ice on the rivers, the phases of the moon, eclipses, the growing heat of the sun in spring, the lighting of a fire which was kept under the ashes, and other analogous phenomena are conceived as partial resurrections after a partial death. And whenever resurrection cannot be admitted attention is turned at least to the continuity of successive generations, and the connection between generation and regeneration in the peasant's mind is thus very close. The familial attitude, the continuity of the family in spite of the death of its members, the lack of purely individual interests, certainly gave a particular strength to this partial identification of the resurrection of the individual with the regeneration of life in new individuals. The appreciation of home-bred domestic animals above those purchased, the unwillingness to change seeds, manifested even now in many localities, may have their background also in the same attitude.

Even when the continuity of generations is lacking, however, the idea of regeneration is not absent. The dead may appear in a different form, or a different individual may appear in his place. Between these two ideas the distinction is not sharply drawn, and sometimes we do not know what the real idea is. The changing of men, animals, and plants into one another—a particularly frequent subject of tales and legends—gives us definitely the first idea; the individual is the same throughout the process of regeneration, in spite of a different form, and may assume sometimes his preceding form. The change, we must remember, is quite real and should never be interpreted as a mere assuming by a spirit of different bodily appearances. The second idea, that of new individuals appearing in the place of the old ones, is found when, after the burning of a forest, crops grow upon the same soil, when a new fruit tree is planted upon the spot where another grew, when worms are "born from" a dead body. But in such examples as the following: a willow growing upon the grave of a girl and betraying her sister as her murderer; lilies growing upon the grave of a murdered husband and betraying the wife, we cannot tell whether it is the same living being or another. And it is easy to understand that in view of the general solidarity of nature this question has not a very great importance. As the familial attitude helps to obliterate the distinction between individual regeneration and generation, so the close solidarity of communal life and the corresponding social attitude make the difference between change of form and change of individual a secondary one. Death is regarded both from the individual standpoint and from that of the group; and while from the first it is of great importance whether the same individual or another is regenerated, for the group it signifies relatively little, so long as the number and value of the individuals are not diminished. Death is dreaded in general for the human or natural group, but the dread is much weaker when only the death of a particular individual, even of the subject himself, is in question. The peasant is able to prepare himself calmly for his own death or for that of his dearest ones, but he grows almost insane with fear when a calamity menaces the whole community. The memory of pest and war has lived for two centuries in some localities.

Of course, the easier the regeneration, the less importance ascribed to death and to acts of destruction. In general therefore, man is freer to use plants than animals, though the question of a higher degree of consciousness and individualization and of a greater similitude with man plays a part here. Among plants, again, those are more freely used which are regenerated every year. When the forests in Poland were large, the inhibitions with regard to trees (except fruit trees) were much weaker than they are now; the forest seemed to restore itself easily and spontaneously. Among the animals, aside from the question of economic value, the more productive ones are less appreciated individually—more readily sold or killed, etc.

The religious system which we have sketched does not require any magician, priest, or mediator of any kind between the layman whose everyday occupations keep him within the sphere of profanity and the sacred powers which are too dangerous to be approached without a special preparation. Here every man in his practical life is continually in touch with the religious reality, is supported and surrounded by it, is an integrate part of the religious world. The opposition of sacred and profane has no meaning in this system; if sometimes it appears later, it is only when the religious attitude toward nature encounters an irreligious one.

But there is another practical problem connected with the present system which makes a religious specialist necessary. In order to prosper within the community of nature, the peasant must know the relations which exist among the members of this community. He must know his own rights and duties; he must know how to make good an offense against the group of which he is a part, how to avoid vengeance, how to conciliate the good-will of, and to get help from, his fellow-members. The relations in the natural society are still more various and complicated than in the human society, and it is indispensable to know the degree and the kind of solidarity between any and all natural beings in order to act upon one through another. Last but not least, only a man who knows nature and understands the warnings and signs which other beings give to him can foresee future events and direct his activity according to this foresight. But it is evident that the ordinary man has among his occupations no time to acquire all this knowledge, even if he is sufficiently intelligent. Thence comes the necessity of a specialist, of a "person who knows." A man who "knows" is usually called *wróż* or *wiedzący*, "prophet" (augur) or "knower"; a woman *mądra*, "the wise one." Both should be strictly distinguished from the magician and witch on the one hand, the priest on the other, although actually they often degenerate individually into magicians and witches. The *wróż* is often recruited from among those who have to deal much with nature and have leisure enough to learn what they need to know—bee-keepers, shepherds, sometimes foresters, but seldom hunters or fishermen, whose occupation requires killing. Woman's activity in peasant life is less specialized, and therefore any woman, but usually one who has not many children, can become a *mądra*. There are somewhat more wise women than men, probably because the woman's usual occupations involve a closer relation with plants and domestic animals, and because the woman finds more easily the necessary leisure; but this numerical difference is not even approximately so great as that between magicians and witches, and this shows that the sex as such has no importance in matters of "knowing," while it has much in magic.

The fundamental functions of the wise man or woman are to preserve from generation to generation the store of naturalistic-religious "knowledge," including the legends and tales, and to give practical advice and help. They are paid for their advice, but they never try to harm anyone as the witches do, and can be moved by no reward to do this, because they are afraid of incurring the vengeance of the natural community. Their usual answer in such cases is, "I am not allowed to do this." With regard to the Christian religion they behave rather indifferently. They go to church, perform the rites, use Christian formulae in their conjurations, but they do it rather in order to get credit among the people and not to be identified with witches and magicians than from true Christian feeling. On the other hand, they never use Christian sacred objects in a perverted sense, and sacrilege has no value for them as it has for the witches and magicians. In fact, not only are there no magical elements in their practice, but they are able to destroy magic. They recognize magical influences easily; they know at once a magician or a witch and show a curious attitude of hate and contempt for them. Their main means of destroying magic is conjuration, in which they address themselves to the spirit in the bewitched object with entreaties and threats, and call for help to good spirits and to natural objects.[1] Nature in general is regarded as hostile to harmful magic, and natural beings help one another against magical influences and harmful spirits and collaborate also with useful spirits. The same plants and animals which bring good luck to man can defend him against evil forces. Flowers and plants which while growing are helpful immediately to men and animals keep the witches away when cut and buried under the threshold, and when burned disclose the presence of a witch. In one of the tales the bluebell defends a woman against water spirits; the magpie when killed and hung above the stable hinders the bewitching of the horses, etc. It is easy to understand that magic appears as a disturber of the natural harmony, but the faith in nature, as long as it remains alive, permits man to hope that the community of natural beings has power enough to defend its members against this unnatural evil as well as against the natural evil—death. It is only when the faith in nature is partly lost that this hope is shaken and man appeals to supernatural powers—that is, to good magic—in order to defend himself against the harm brought by evil magical influences.

2. We have now to examine the second system of religious beliefs and attitudes, based upon the admission of a

[1] The concept of "spirits" is of course here borrowed from the second religious system, treated below, in which we find the properly magical action developed.

world of spirits within, beside or above natural objects. We point out that no historical connection can be established in the present state of historical knowledge between this system and the one just examined, and perhaps it will never be possible to establish it with certainty, since Christianity has destroyed as much as it could of the vestiges of the pagan past. Most of the spirits and magical practices of the present were introduced with the Christian religion, but in the pagan period a system of spirits coexisted with the naturalistic system. It is even possible that the two were more closely connected at that time than later and that Christianity had the effect of dissociating them. It brought a world of spirits in which the pagan spirits but not the pagan naturalism found a place. Two examples will illustrate this supposition. The lightning or thunderstroke (*piorun*) was at the same time a natural being (fire) and a divinity or the expression of a divinity; probably the two meanings were not quite distinguished. Its second character was assimilated to the Christian mythology, but not the first. We find, therefore, two contradictory beliefs. The lightning is the instrument of punishment in the hands of God or a weapon of the angels in their fight against the devils; a man struck by lightning must be a great sinner. But there is also a belief that a man struck by lightning is without sin and goes immediately to heaven, because fire in the naturalistic system is the purifactory instrument of regeneration.[1] Another example is the snake. The snake was a powerful natural being, and at the same time it was consecrated to a divinity. In the Christian system it became a symbol of the devil, but its first character was

---

[1] A mixture of both elements is found in another belief—that lightning is turned mainly against the souls of children who die without christening. There is present the idea of punishment and also of regeneration. The souls are persecuted for not being Christian, but at the same time the fire seems to be an equivalent of baptismal water.

left unheeded, and thus we find the curious contradiction that the snake is sometimes considered a benefactor and its killing is a crime, and sometimes again it is the incarnation of the evil spirit and should always be destroyed.

The existence of mythological beings is not in itself always sufficient to constitute a religious system different from naturalism, for these beings may be conceived as natural beings and included in the system of natural solidarity. Thus, when we find legends of giants and dwarfs who live more or less like men within nature, helped by, and helpful to, animals, plants, or men, and who, like all nature, fight against death and destruction; or when there are mythical home-, field-, and forest-beings who need human offerings of food and drink in order to live, and prove their gratitude by protecting the house and the crops, who avenge a breach of solidarity, and who run away if not cared for, we have nothing but an imaginary extension of the natural world, not a supernatural structure outside of this world. The attitudes which man shows toward these beings and which he ascribes to them are not different from those which characterize the whole natural community. And we can easily understand why such an extension of nature is necessary and what its rôle is. In any given stage of knowledge about nature extraordinary and unexpected phenomena cannot always be derived from the assumed properties of the known natural beings, and then two ways are opened. Man may either suppose that his knowledge is false, that the natural beings have other properties than those which he ascribed to them, or he can imagine that the inexplicable phenomena are caused by some beings which up to the present he had no opportunity of knowing. The second explanation requires, certainly, less intellectual effort and has been used in the history of human thought more frequently than the first. We do not know how far the mythological beings of the naturalistic religious system were spontaneously invented and how far brought from elsewhere; but their function in either case is clear: they have to account for the extraordinary and unexpected, to fill eventual gaps in the system. Their rôle is therefore limited; they are only one class of natural beings among others and share with others the peasant's religious attention at certain moments and in certain circumstances.

The new religious system is found only when behind all the natural events, ordinary as well as extraordinary, supernatural powers are supposed to reside and to act, where there is a dissociation between the visible, material thing and process on the one hand and the invisible, immaterial being and action on the other. No such dissociation is found in the naturalistic system. The things themselves have a conscious, spiritual principle indissolubly united with their outward material appearance, and the mystical, invisible influence of one natural being upon another imperceptibly mediates a visible material action. When these elements are dissociated, the invisible, immaterial principle is a *spirit* in the proper sense of the word, as opposed to the material objects and distinct from them, even if it should manifest itself, not only by acting upon these objects from outside, but by entering into an object or dwelling permanently in it. And the invisible, immaterial process of action of one thing upon another becomes *magical* as against the visible process of material action, even if it should be exerted, not only by a spirit upon a material object or reciprocally, but by one material object upon another.

There are many categories of spirits, differing by the nature of their relation to material objects. Some of them are scarcely more than naturalistic mythological beings; their spiritual nature manifests itself only indirectly by the fact that man's attitude toward them is the same as toward other spirits and differs from that toward natural beings. Here belong, for example, water spirits, *boginki*, who have human bodies but can become invisible at will, who can be heard washing their linen at night or at midday, and who bear children. They often try to exchange their children for human ones, usually only so long as the latter are not yet baptized. Like real spirits they can assume the form of any woman, and it even happens that under the aspect of friends and relatives they entice a woman after childbirth from her home into the forests and marshes and mistreat her there, while one of them steals the child, puts her own in its place, and remains in the house in the form of the abducted woman. A changed child can be recognized from its bad temper, its growing ugliness, and its enormous appetite. The *boginka* who took the place of the real woman is also bad-tempered, capricious, and evil. In order to force the *boginka* to give the child back, a naturalistic means is often used. The *boginka's* child must be mistreated and beaten. Then the *boginka* brings the real child back and takes her own away, but she tries to avenge herself by biting off, for example, a finger of the real child, or by making it as bad-tempered as her own. With the exception of this means of getting the real child back (which shows that the *boginka* is still very much a mythological pagan being), the other means are mainly magical and the same as against the devil—the sign of the cross, Christian amulets, exorcisms. The priest can free the woman from the hands of the *boginka*, but he must wear all his ceremonial clothes turned wrong side out.

Another kind of beings, intermediary between mythological natural beings and spirits, are the *topczyki*—children born of illegal relations and drowned secretly without baptism. Except for the last point, in which the analogy with real spirits of the dead is evident, the *topczyk* is a natural being. He has a body, which he may, indeed, sometimes change. He grows in water. His action is physical, not magical. He spoils the hay, draws by mere strength animals and men into the water, etc. Magical rites have no particular power against him. The best way is simply to avoid him. The naturalistic tendency in the representation of the *topczyki* is shown in a legend in which two of them are drawn by fishermen out of a pond. One was hunchbacked from having been shut up in a pot for seven years; the other was covered with hair like an animal. They were taken to a human house and christened, but they died soon after.

Skrzat, the house-being, and *leśny*, the wood-being, have lost the importance they had in pagan times. The first was beneficent, the second brought little harm except by making men lose their way. The last vestige of a field-being is probably preserved in the *południca*, midday-woman, who strangles anybody who sleeps at noon in the field, particularly upon the ridge between fields. Will-o'-the-wisps (compare below) are beings who live in marshes and meadows; they have little of a spiritual character, have very small bodies, warm themselves around a fire, etc. They viciously mislead drunken people, but do no other harm unless aroused by some tactless action. Religious magic is only partly efficient against them.

The belief in cloud-beings, *planetniki* or *latawce*, is very indeterminate and hesitant. Sometimes they are mythological natural beings dwelling in the clouds; sometimes spirits directing the clouds, bringing rain, hail, thunderstorm; sometimes spirits of children who died without baptism (often represented as persecuted by the clouds and lightnings); sometimes even living men and women, magicians or witches. The means of attracting or dispelling clouds are sometimes based, therefore, upon natural solidarity—against lightning, the stork and swallow; against hail, plowing around the field with oxen, particularly twins, planting certain trees, etc.—and sometimes again magical, as we shall see presently.

Another being is the *kania*, which appears in the form of a beautiful woman and steals children, who are never seen any more. The *jedza* is a horrid old woman who eats children; the *wił*, a being who comes in the night, terrifies children, and hinders people from sleeping ("It stands always where you look"). The nightmare, *zmora*, has two meanings: it is sometimes a soul, as we shall see later, but sometimes also a distinct, half-spiritual being which strangles sleeping men and rides at night upon horses. All these beings have the same intermediary character between natural objects and spirits; they are more or less materialistically conceived, but they are acted upon mainly by magical means, not by appeals to natural solidarity.

The probable origin of their intermediary character can be traced. They were primitively nothing but natural beings, requiring some help from man and harmful only if this help was refused. But Christianity tried to assimilate them to the devil and to fight against them by magical means. Thus they assumed gradually the features of beings against which man had to fight, and which consequently were essentially harmful, and some of the spiritual character of the devil was transferred to them. We find facts, in the past and even in the present, proving that the peasant for a long time hesitated between the two attitudes. Officially he used the magic of the church against them, treated them as harmful, and tried to drive them away; but privately and secretly he kept the old duties of solidarity toward them, sought to excuse himself for using the church magic against them, and tried to win their help. Even if accepting their help was as sinful in the eyes of the church as accepting the help of the devil and led to damnation, the peasant could hardly be moved to believe this. And he did not even believe in the complete efficiency of church magic against them. Up to the present magic remains only partly efficient, and it is easier to get rid of the devil than of these intermediary beings.

A particularly interesting gradation of beliefs is found with regard to the human soul. There are at least six varieties of beings corresponding to the concept of soul— the ordinary vampire, the man-nightmare, the Christian vampire-spirit, the specter, the soul doing penance on earth, the soul coming from purgatory, hell, or, occasionally, paradise. The relative degree to which these spirits are detached from the body and lead an independent existence is the reason for this diversity.

The ordinary vampire, mentioned in the preceding section, is scarcely a spirit at all. It is a living body, even if less alive than before death and devoid of some of the human ideas and feelings. It can be touched, even grappled with, and killed for the second time, after which it does not appear again. Sometimes it continues to occupy itself at night with farm- or housework, and the male vampire can even have sexual intercourse with his wife and bring forth children, but they are always weak and die soon—of course because the father has less life. The only spiritual characters of the vampire are relative independence of physical conditions (ability to pass through the smallest opening, to disappear and to appear suddenly, etc.), which was acquired only after death, and the possibility of being influenced to a certain extent by religious magic—sign of the cross, prayer, amulets—again a character not possessed by the man during his life. But the most effective means of getting rid of the vampire are the well-known natural actions—

cutting off the head, passing of an aspen pole through the heart, binding of the feet with particular plants, etc.

The human nightmare is already a soul, detaching itself from the living body during sleep and embracing, strangling, sucking the blood of men and animals or the sap of plants. During its absence the body lies as dead, and real death may follow if someone turns it, because then the soul cannot find the way back. The soul is of course half-material, since it exerts immediate material action, can be wounded (the scar is then seen upon the body), can be physically grasped. But it is also spiritual, because it can be detached from the body, assume various forms—animal, plant, even inanimate object—can pass where a material being could not pass, and finally because the really efficient means against it are magical (Christian amulets), not natural.

The Christian vampire is also a soul, of the same nature as the nightmare, but walking after the man's death, and thus still more dissociated from the body. It is not even referred to any particular body. We call it "Christian" because it originated from the primitive, bodily vampire under the evident influence of the Christian theory of the soul and of Christian rites. On the one hand, a christened soul must be detached from the body after death; the old bodily vampire theory is therefore not in accordance with the Christian system of beliefs. But, on the other hand, the christened soul cannot be a spirit-vampire, unless damned, and then it belongs to a different class of spirits. The contradiction was solved by a theory, to which the Catholic rites themselves gave birth, that there are two souls, one of which becomes Christian through baptism, the other through confirmation. The second soul of the unconfirmed lives on earth and becomes a vampire. According to a different legend, there was a time when vampires were frightfully numerous, and the people appealed to the pope for help. The pope advised them to give two names at baptism, in order to christen also the second soul. Since that time the vampires have almost disappeared.

The specter is a very undetermined kind of spirit. It is always some soul, but seldom identified, and its aim is unknown. It is neither harmful nor useful. It appears in a visible form at night, walking near a cemetery or a church, sometimes in the church. It is thus not anti-Christian, not afraid of church magic. There is a story of a specter frightening men who planned a sacrilegious use of church objects. It is an intermediary being between the souls which are still partly connected with the system of nature and those which are already quite supernatural.

The souls doing penance upon earth belong to the latter group. Their origin seems purely Christian, as the idea of penance itself. Spirits of this class are very numerous. They manifest their existence mainly by noises, but sometimes they talk, sometimes they appear in any form. The bodies which they assume can often not be touched, even when, as sometimes happens, they enter into real bodies, human, animal, or plant. To this group belong unchristened people (some of them, as we have seen, still naturalistically conceived), those who died suddenly, without penitence, and those who have sinned only in some particular line. The penance which they do has a magical character; it is always analogous to the sin and has thus the aim of destroying the sinfulness. Children who died without baptism try to attract attention by various noises—cracking in the fire, rapping on the furniture and walls, moaning in the wind, etc.—in order to be baptized; the man who hears them should throw some water and baptize them, giving them always two names, Adam and Eve, for the sex of the dead is unknown. Not only unbaptized children, but also men who were wrongly baptized, wander after their death. For instance, there are in one locality many graves of Russians killed in a battle against the Poles in the eighteenth century, and their souls find no rest anywhere, for they were christened according to the rites of the Greek church. They cannot be helped, and must await the last judgment. Those who died a sudden death always haunt the place where they died. They want to confess their sins, and it happens sometimes that they succeed and are saved, if only they find a courageous priest to absolve them. Any sudden death has something uncanny for the peasant and is supposed to be sent, not by God, but by the devil—whether with God's permission or not is not always clear. Finally, people whose sin was not, as in the previous cases, a lack of religious purification, but some particular evil deeds, often try in vain to undo the harm which they wrought. Thus a man who was a miser during his life, wronged the poor, or refused gifts to the church, and particularly one who buried or in any way hid his money, hovers about his collected wealth, wants to show the living where it is or to compel his heir to divide it with the poor and the church; but the devil usually hinders the living from understanding or fulfilling his bidding. The soul of a surveyor who measured falsely during his life wanders in the form of a will-o'-the-wisp, looks over his wrong measurements, and wishes in vain to correct them. The soul of a woman who did not respect the food and threw the remnants into the pail with the dishwater is heard at night dabbling in the pail in search of remnants in order to still her hunger. A man who once slapped his father wanders at night, in human but indistinct form, and compels his own living son to give him a blow. Two *kums* who quarreled during their life cannot find rest until somebody brings them together and reconciles them. A man who hunted on Sunday during the mass wanders after his death and hinders people from hunting. Another who swore by the devil and never said his prayer on *Angelus* shows himself at noon in the form of a dog which devils, in the form of crows, chase about. And so on.

These souls still dwell in their old world, though they are spirits, completely detached from material bodies, which they assume only in order to carry out their particular end, and absolutely dependent on magic, not at all on natural actions.

The last class of souls, while always more or less interested in their old environment, dwell elsewhere—in purgatory, hell, or paradise, as distinguished from heaven. Those places are sometimes thought to be beyond, sometimes upon, the earth, in remote localities. In one myth they are beyond Rome, and from one of the Roman churches the funnels of hell can be seen. The souls come occasionally to their old residence, to warn or to help the living, to ask them for prayers or good deeds; those from purgatory come every year on All Souls' Day, and listen to a mass which the soul of some dead priest celebrates. From paradise they come relatively seldom and only on some altruistic mission. Whenever a soul manifests in some way its appearance (this concerns also, to some extent, the previous category of souls), it should be addressed with the words: "Every spirit praises God." If it answers: "I praise him also," the living person should ask: "What do you want, soul?" Whatever it begs for, prayer or good deed in its favor, ought to be granted. But if the soul answers nothing to the first greeting, the living person should make the sign of the cross and say, "Here is the cross of God; fly away, contrary sides." For it is a damned soul and can no longer be saved.

The devil is not regarded as a unique character. First, of course, there are many devils, though only a few of them have distinct names. The devil is not an essentially evil being, although often malicious, harmful, or disgusting. The proverb: "The devil is not so terrible as he is painted," is very popular, as well as the other: "Who lives near hell, asks the devil to be his *kum*." In dealing with men the devil is often cheated, not only because he is not particularly clever, but also because he usually shows more honesty in keeping agreement than men show. Often the term "devil" is simply substituted for some other mythological being whose old character and name are forgotten. With regard to the devils we therefore find also a gradation of spirituality. But all the devils are more spiritual, more detached from the natural world, than the mythological beings of the first category and than most of the souls, so that the substitution of the devil for the *boginka*, the nightmare, the vampire, etc., means an evolution from the naturalistic toward the spiritualistic religious system.

The least spiritual are the local devils, who are more or less attached to particular places—ruins, marshes, old trees, crossroads, etc. They are usually invisible, but can show themselves at will either in the form of animals (usually owls, cats, bats, reptiles, but also black dogs, rams, horses, etc.) or in a human or half-human body. Although popular imagination has naturally been influenced by the traditional mediaeval pictures of the devil and orthodoxly conceives them as representing the devil in his real form, still it has constructed for itself representations more adequate to the popular sense. The devil is represented as a little man in "German clothes" (fashion of the second half of the eighteenth century) with a small "goat's beard," small horns hidden under his hat; sometimes he has a tail and one horse- or goat-leg, as in the paintings. The local devil has nothing to do with the questions of temptation and salvation; he does not try to get any souls, but is a mischievous being who frightens the living and gets them into trouble.

often merely in the way of a joke. Sometimes he has indeed a serious function to perform, for example, watching buried treasures, lest the living should get them; there is a real danger of life in searching for treasures, or for the fern flower which opens the eyes of the possessor and enables him to see the treasures under the earth. It is believed that these devils purify the treasures once a year with fire, and do it as long as the soul of the man who buried them does penance; after this, the devil ceases to watch the treasure and it can be found by the living. In this tale the local devil is already associated with the purgatory devil.

The second class of devils are those who possess the living beings, men or animals. Possession is quite different from the assumption of a visible form. In the latter case we have to do with an apparition, but in the first with a natural thing in which the devil, himself invisible, dwells. The natural thing can be explicitly thought to have a soul besides the devil, or the matter of the soul may be left out of consideration. The devils who take possession of a person may be many—three, five, seven. Not all of them are harmful; some are good and useful to the possessed person as well as to others. And if we note that sometimes a wise woman is identified with a possessed one, we must conclude that the idea of possession, originating in the Christian mythology, was simply applied at a later time to phenomena which had a different meaning under the system of naturalism.

The third kind of devils are those who, while leading an independent existence outside of the natural world, are still mainly interested in matters of this world. According to the orthodox tradition their only aim ought to be tempting men in order to get them damned, but the peasant sometimes makes them play also the part of spirits with whom simple co-operation on the basis of reciprocity is possible, without involving damnation.   They have supernatural powers, but they lack natural achievements, and this makes a co-operation fruitful for both sides.   Thus, a devil may become the apprentice of a blacksmith or a miller and learn the trade while teaching his master supernatural tricks.   In connection with the witches, the devil wants to learn what is going on in the human community (for he is not all-knowing) while he bestows some of his own magical powers upon the witch.   Or he gives the witch the means of getting an exceptional quantity of milk, while she must bring him, for his unknown purposes, butter and cheese.   Or he sows the field in company with a man, for he does not know agriculture, but he can make the crops grow better, or he gives the man some money out of a hidden treasury.   This is the type of devil with whom witches have sexual relations or who receives his friends at a weekly (sometimes monthly or yearly) banquet on the top of the Łysa Góra.[1]   Of course the motive of damnation is very popular and important, but its moral value is sometimes doubtful.   The devil, according to an explicit or tacit agreement, takes the soul of a man as his own reward for some service, in the same way as in relations among men a poor peasant may become a servant of his rich neighbor for a certain time to pay a debt which he cannot pay in another way; there is often scarcely any idea of moral punishment.   A man may even promise his child to the devil before the child is born.   And it is here that the devil is most often cheated, for at the last moment the man frequently gets rid of him by magical means.   The idea of temptation, in this system of beliefs, does not mean "temptation to commit a sin," but temptation to do business.   And if the sin as such leads to hell, it is because of its magical influence, of the break of the magical

---

[1] "Bald Mountain," proper name applied now mainly to a mountain in the province of Kielce, but used also in other provinces in relation to local hills.

solidarity with the heavenly powers and the establishment of a magical solidarity with the devil. The only sins to which the devil really instigates his followers are those which have immediately this magical consequence—sacrilege, denial of the heavenly powers, recognition of the devil, and rites whose effect is to establish a magical affinity with him. On the other hand, we find also attitudes which prevail in the naturalistic system transferred to the spiritualistic one; the devil often appears on earth as well as in hell as an avenger of breaks of solidarity between men, or even between men and nature. He performs vicariously the functions which human society or nature are for some reasons unable to perform.

The last class of devils are those who dwell permanently in hell and have almost no relation with nature or living men, except sometimes taking souls from the earth to hell. They torture the souls and endure punishment themselves for their revolt against God.

The category of heavenly beings—God, Jesus, the Holy Spirit, the Virgin Mary, the saints, and the angels—are completely spiritualized. Any connection between them and actually existing natural beings, if it ever existed, has been forgotten. For example, heaven is identical with the skies and is God's dwelling-place, the thunder and lightning are manifestations of God's activity, etc., but there is not the slightest trace of any identity of God with those natural phenomena.

Naturally the theological problem of the Trinity seldom attracts the peasant's attention. The Holy Spirit has little importance, and is individualized only through the liturgical and popular prayers addressed to him and through his symbolization by the dove. God and Jesus are certainly, in this system, dissociated beings, owing to the earthly life of Jesus. The names are often mixed, but the functions are sufficiently distinguished to allow us to consider God and Jesus as separate divinities in the eyes of the peasant.

God's main attribute is magical power over things. This power is not limited by the nature of the things themselves, and in this sense God may be called all-powerful; but it is limited by the magical power of the devil and even of man, although it is certainly greater. It may be used at any moment and with regard to any object, but it is not so used in fact; many phenomena go on without any divine influence. God directs the world when he wishes, but does not support it. The idea of creation is rather undetermined and does not play an important part in the peasant's mythology; it is usually assimilated to workmanship.

The divine power can be used for beneficent or harmful purposes without regard to properly moral reasons. It is qualitatively but not morally antagonistic to the devil's power. There is, of course, a certain principle in the harmful or beneficent activity of God; an explanation can be given of every manifestation of God's benevolence or malevolence. But this explanation has a magical, not a moral, character, even if it is expressed in religious and moral terms. God's attitude toward man (and toward nature as well) depends upon the magical relation which man by his acts establishes between God and himself. If the magical side of human activity or of natural things harmonizes with the tendencies of divine activity, the latter is necessarily beneficent, and it is necessarily harmful in the contrary case, that is, whenever the acts of things are in harmony with the intentions of the devil. The main sins, therefore, are those against religious rites—that is, all kinds of sacrilege—and every other sin is termed as "offense of God," that is, assimilated to sacrilege. Therefore also magical church rites can destroy every sin, and it is enough to establish a relation of magical harmony with God in order to keep one's self and one's property safe from any incidental harm. But from this it results also that the consequences of the sin reach much farther than they should if the idea of just retribution were dominant; the magical estrangement from God extends itself over the whole future situation of the man and thus leads to eternal damnation if not made good by some contrary act, and it may also extend itself over the man's milieu and bring calamities to his family, community, farmstock, and even to his purely natural environment.

Jesus, in this religious system, has the somewhat subordinated position of a magical mediator between the divine power and man. He is the founder and keeper of the magical rites by which man is put into a relation of harmony with God or defended against the devil. Accordingly it is Jesus who judges men's actions and personalities as harmonizing or not with God, and upon whom the lot of the soul after death mainly depends. He is somewhat more personalized than God, but he is also not a moral divinity; in his eyes the magical, not the moral, value of the act is always important.

The Virgin Mary is more particularly a beneficent divinity, helping always and everybody by the way of miracles. In fact, she is the only divinity working miracles even now. For, although the whole activity of God and Jesus is supernatural, it does not break the normal order of things, because this normal order includes material as well as magical phenomena, or, more exactly, there are two coexisting orders, the material and the magical. The real miracle is therefore one that breaks both orders. Healing a sick person is only a magical action when sickness is a result of natural causes or of some spontaneous action of the devil or the witch, but it is a miracle when the sickness is a necessary consequence of sin, of a dissolution of the magical harmony between man and God. This is precisely the kind of miracles, besides simple magical actions, ascribed commonly to the Virgin Mary. She disturbs in favor of men the divine magical order itself; she saves men from the consequences of their sins in this world and even in the other.

The saints have a more limited sphere of activity. Every saint has a special line along which he acts, usually beneficently, by modifying, through a supernatural influence, natural phenomena. Some saints, as, for instance, St. Franciscus, give also magical help against the devil, but this is less frequent than help in natural difficulties. Thus, St. Anthony helps to find a lost article, St. Agatha to extinguish a fire, etc. Every man's patron saint saves him in danger. Every parish has a patron saint who averts calamities from it; the day of this saint is a parish festival. There are patron saints of corporations, fraternities, cities, provinces. St. Stanislaus is the patron of Poland; St. Casimir, of Lithuania.

The functions of the angels are rather undetermined. They have to fight against the devils, to praise God, to take human souls to paradise from the earth or from purgatory, to fulfil, according to their original meaning, errands of God. The guardian angel of every man watches over him, to keep him from natural and magical dangers, and defends his soul against the devil immediately after death.

If we omit now all the intermediary stages between natural beings and spirits, and take the spiritual world in its pure form as distinguished from the material world, we notice that there are two antagonistic spiritual communities —divine and devilish. To the first belong also once and forever the souls of the saved, to the second the souls of the damned. Souls in purgatory are on the way between the two. These communities are connected, each separately, by a particular kind of solidarity which we can call magical, and they are opposed to each other also by a magical contrariety. The living men belong partly to one, partly to the other community, and they pass from one to another according to the magical bearing of their acts. All other natural beings, animated or not, can also acquire a divine or a devilish magical character, but they are without exception passive, objects, not subjects, of magical activity, although a spirit can enter into them and act through them. In this respect their rôle differs completely from the active one which they play in the naturalistic system.

In order to understand this spiritual solidarity, we must analyze more closely the magical attitude, for this does not originate in the belief in spirits, but both have a common root from which they grow simultaneously.

The common feature of the physical and the magical fact is that in both there is an action of one object upon another. Without this external influence the object is supposed not to change; and if change is already included in its nature, its formula remains the same.[1] Thus, when a body at rest is suddenly set in motion, physics and magic alike will explain it by the action of external forces. Even if it is an animated being, the movement will be explained either psychologically, by a motive which is ultimately referred to the external world, or physiológically, by an irritation of physiological elements whose ultimate source is also in the external world or by a magical influence. The system of magical interpretation is less complete and more immediately practical. It is applied to phenomena whose practical importance is perceived at once, consequently to those which, being to a certain extent more than ordinary, require some change in the habitual course of life. For example, puberty, sickness, and death require a magical explanation more insistently than the ordinary physiological functions,

---

[1] Magic applies this principle even more rigidly than physical science, for it seldom includes change in the definition of the object.

sexual life more insistently than eating, eating more insistently than breathing. The phenomenon of snow is hardly explained magically by the Polish peasant, while hail and thunderstorm are very frequently referred to magical activities.

But this is only a difference of degree between the magical and the physical systems. The difference of nature lies elsewhere. Magical action differs essentially from physical action in that the process by which one object influences another is given and can be analyzed in physical action, while in magical action it is not given and avoids analysis. There is a continuity between physical cause and physical effect; there is an immediate passage, without intermediary stages, between magical cause and magical effect. Thus, when a woman comes by night to her neighbor's stable and milks the cow; when a man in a fight strikes another a blow; when wind drives hail-clouds away; when crops rot in the field because of too much rain—in all these cases the process of action of one thing upon another is known, or supposedly known, the cause and effect are connected with each other without any break of continuity, and we can analyze the process into as many stages as we wish. But when a witch, by milking a stick in her own house, draws the milk of her neighbor's cow into her own milk-pot; when by saying some formulae and burning some plants she causes headache to her distant enemy; when the first chapters of the Four Gospels, written down and buried at the four corners of a field, avert hail-clouds; when peas, sown during the new moon, never ripen, but blossom again every month until winter—here between the cause and effect continuity is broken, the influence is immediate, we do not know anything about the process of action and we cannot analyze the passage between the state of one object and the state of another. Therefore we can, of course, *modify* in many ways a physical process, *direct* it by introducing various additional causes; but we can only *abolish* the magical influence, *destroy* it, by introducing some determined contrary factors.

This character of the magical relation explains the fact that most of those relations are, or rather appear to us to be, symbolical. This symbolism can assume different forms. Sometimes it is analogy between the supposed cause and the desired effect, as in the example of the witch milking a stick, or in the very general case when two bones of the bat, resembling respectively a rake and a fork, are used, the first to attract something desirable, the second to push away something undesirable. Sometimes, again, it is a part representing the whole, as when some hairs or finger-nail parings of a man are used to harm or to heal through them the whole body, or when a rite performed upon a few grains taken from a field is supposed to affect the whole crop. Or an action performed upon some object is presumed to exert an influence upon another object which is or was in spatial proximity with the first, as when an object taken from the house or some sand from under the threshold is used to influence magically the house or its inmates. Succession in time, particularly if repeated, becomes often a basis of a magical connection; this is the source of many beliefs in lucky or unlucky phenomena. The connection between the word and the thing symbolized by it is, as we know, particularly often exploited for magical purposes. The words exert an immediate influence upon reality, have a magical creative power. The relation of property is also assumed to be a vehicle of magical action; the owner is hit by magic exerted upon some object which belongs to him, and, reciprocally, by bewitching the owner it is possible to affect his property. Things often connected by some natural causality can be easily connected by a magical causality; food can be spoiled by bewitching the fire upon which it is cooked, the miller can arouse the wind by imitating its effect, that is, by turning the wings of the mill. The last example gives us a combination of two kinds of symbolism: by analogy and by the relation of (natural) cause to effect. Such combinations are very frequent in the more complicated kinds of magic, as when a witch, by sitting upon goose eggs, brings hail as big as those eggs, or when a consecrated host is put into a beehive in order to make the bees prosper. This last is a triple magical relation: the words of the priest change the host into the flesh of Jesus; the particle represents the whole divinity; the supposed effect of religious perfection which the host exerts upon the soul of the man is transferred by analogy to the insects.

Now in all these cases magical relation is supposed to exist among objects which are in some way already connected in human consciousness, so that one of them points in some way to the other, reminds one of it, symbolizes it. And we can easily understand that this is a necessary condition, without which it would be hardly possible to imagine the existence of a magical relation between two given objects. Indeed in physical causality we can follow the process of causation, and therefore (except in cases of error of observation or reasoning) we know what effect a cause has or what is the cause of a given effect. But in magical causality the process is hidden, and there would therefore be no reason to think of a given fact A as being the cause or effect of a determined fact B rather than of any of the innumerable other facts which happen about this time if A and B had not been connected previously in the mind. Sometimes the facts are connected traditionally and the reason for this connection can no longer be determined, but whenever we see the reason it is always a symbolical relation of some of the types enumerated above.

If, now, the magical causality existed alone, it would probably be considered natural, not supernatural. But it coexists, in the peasant's experience, with a multitude of cases of purely physical causality, including most of the common material phenomena, and it becomes supernatural by antithesis to these, exactly as spirits become supernatural by antithesis to material beings.[1] And certainly the fact that most of the magic came to the peasant with Christianity and was already connected with spirits must have helped to develop this opposition between natural and supernatural causality.

But the connection of magic with the spiritual beings is not merely the result of their common opposition to the material world. Magic contains in itself elements which, at a certain stage, make this connection necessary. Indeed, magical causality is by no means an instrument of theoretical explanation but of practice; only such relations as are supposed to help to attain a desirable end or to avoid a danger are taken into consideration. Every magical relation is therefore connected in some way more or less closely with the idea of the conscious intention of somebody who acts, who wants to apply it to a certain end. In many cases, even in a relatively primitive magic, intention is a necessary condition of causality. The witch who milks a stick must think at the same time of the woman whose cow she wants to deprive of milk, and it is her intention which directs the magical effect. It is also indispensable in all endeavors to convey sickness to direct the attention to the person whom one desires to harm. In searching for a hidden treasure harmful magical powers are neutralized if the digger has at this moment the intention (provisionally

[1] The antithesis is particularly evident when the same object exerts a natural and a magical effect. Thus, water naturally washes physical stains, but consecrated water magically purifies an object from the devilish magical power.

assumed) of giving the treasure to a church.   And we know
that in religious magic the use of consecrated objects can
have its whole influence only if exerted with a determined
intention and belief in its efficiency.   There are certainly
many cases in which the effect of a magical cause is presumed to come mechanically, when the intention is not
necessary to produce it.   This happens when an object,
amulet or talisman, has a permanent property of magical
action, or when a magical effect is brought about inadvert-
ently.   But usually we find some intentional action in the
beginning.   Most of the amulets and talismans (when their
action does not result from their own natural power, that is,
when they are not members of the first, naturalistic, religious system) have been at some moment intentionally
endowed with magical powers; such are all the consecrated
objects and many of those which the magicians and witches
prepare.   Most of the inadvertent actions have a magical
influence because they are actions of conscious beings who,
even if they have no explicit intention at the given moment,
have a latent power of will, are capable of intentional influence.   By the usual association the inadvertent action is
supposed to exert the same influence as the intentional
action which it resembles, because the spiritual power, non-
directed, takes the habitual channel.   And even when there
is no conscious action in the beginning, the peasant tends to
suppose, more or less definitely, some kind of intention in
every case of imprevisible good or bad luck which happens
to him.   In short, in every magical causation there is *more
or less* of the conscious element completing the mechanical
magical relation between cause and effect; there is always
behind it somebody, man or spirit, and the object through
which the action is exerted is here merely an instrument,
not a spontaneously acting being, as in the naturalistic
system.

But there is a curious gradation of the part which consciousness plays in magical causality, which is also the basis of distinction between human and spiritual magic. In the ordinary ritualistic magic the intention is only one component of the magical action, more or less necessary, but subordinated to the objective causal relation between visible phenomena—the more so, the more complicated the rite. Its rôle is increased in the action by words, particularly when the words are not traditional formulae (to a great extent efficient by their mere sound and arrangement), but spontaneous expressions of an actual feeling or desire. The blessing or curse is efficient whatever its form, which proves that it is the intention, not the expression, which is essential. In the evil eye sometimes the visible act counts more, sometimes the intention. In any case there is a marked disproportion between the physical act, trifling in itself, and its consequences. Evidently the "evil eye" has a magical influence only because it is a conscious being which looks, because in the eye spiritual powers are concentrated. But man can never exert a magical influence by consciousness alone, without the help of visible means. This is the privilege of the spirits who, when completely detached from nature, can act immediately by the magic of their will. Those who are intermediary between spirits and natural beings may sometimes need the help of visible rites. The devil who keeps hidden treasures cleans them with fire; local spirits and some of the lower devils can get a man into their power by holding any part of his body or his clothing, etc. But the more spiritualized and powerful devils and the heavenly spirits do not need anything for their magical action. And of course the whole practical importance of supernatural beings depends upon their ability to exert a direct magical influence by their mere will. If they were unable to do this, they would not count at all, for, being detached from nature, they cannot act through material objects. In other words, the dissociation of mythological beings from the material world is possible only on the condition that those beings can influence this world by the magic of their will, and thus the magic of consciousness is the condition of the existence of spirits. For spirits without practical influence cannot exist in the popular mythology; their power is the measure of their reality.

This magical power, which, among the spirits, God possesses in the highest degree and of which the spirits in general have more than men, is nothing but the *faculty* of producing magical effects. It is quite parallel with the "energy" of physics. The spirits and certain living men possess it from the beginning. Its manifestations can be directed and often checked at will. This is the case among higher beings, but among men it happens that the magical power tends to manifest itself even in opposition to the present conscious act of will. The case is exactly analogous to that of an "inborn" tendency to evil; the permanent direction of the will is stronger than an actual motive; the individual's nature is so bent upon exercising magical influence upon all objects which come within his sphere of action that he can only with difficulty refrain from exercising it upon some particular object. Thus, many persons who have the evil eye do harm even when they do not wish it and must use particular means in order to neutralize their power, for example, look upon their own nails before looking upon any object which may be harmed. Of the witches, in many localities the opinion prevails that they are more unhappy than guilty, that their magical power is either inherited or communicated to them by a curse of God (a curse, since their power is contrary to the divine power), and cases are even quoted in which a witch, unable or unwilling to harm her neighbors, exerted her influence aimlessly upon inanimate objects, or even bewitched herself. But a person whose magic is of a higher quality, as, for example, a priest or a wise person who uses magical power only for good purposes, can use it or not, at will.

This magical power can be communicated to men or things, and we can suppose that, as magical causation involves some degree of intention, all the magical powers of things are communicated to them by men or spirits, as they are in the Christian system. There is always some kind of consecration, actually performed or presupposed, explicitly or implicitly. Obviously we do not mean to say that the idea of consecration was in fact the historical origin of the magical powers ascribed to things, but only that in the magical system of the Polish peasant the magical power of things is *actually believed* to have originated always in some kind of a consecration. For example, there are innumerable legends in which the beneficent or maleficent magical powers of animals, plants, or stones are ascribed to a blessing or curse of God, Jesus, the Virgin Mary, the saints. If some animals are connected with the devil, it is not only because the devil used to appear in their form, but also because he is supposed to have endowed them with magical power; such are the snake, the cat, the owl, the peacock, the rat, black dogs, black goats, etc. In the same way it is the devil who communicates magical properties to the localities in which he resides, to many instruments which the witches use, to money, etc., and all the witches who are not born such are consecrated by the devil, or sometimes by other more powerful witches. The consecration is, moreover, the more efficient the more powerful the consecrating man or spirit. The power of Christian amulets depends upon the position in the church hierarchy of the priest who consecrated them (ordinary priest, bishop, pope); the consecration of the witch by the devil is worth more than by another witch.

The curse of a saint is more influential than that of an ordinary person. Thus, nobody in or from the town Gniezno can ever make a fortune since St. Adalbert cursed the town more than nine centuries ago. Numerous are the legends of towns, churches, castles which sank into the earth, of men turned into stone when cursed by priests, hermits, etc.

But the magical power of spiritual beings when acting upon material objects must adapt itself to the immanent laws of magical causality in the same way as human technique must adapt itself to the laws of physical causality. The idea of consecration is used to explain magical powers of objects only within the limits of the symbolism of which we have spoken above. Thus, not every object can be consecrated to every use, but each one by consecration acquires only a particular and determined power of action. For example, in Loreto consecrated bells are particularly adapted to avert thunderstorm, salt consecrated on the day of St. Agatha extinguishes fire, determined plants, when consecrated, acquire a magical power against determined diseases, etc. Nowhere perhaps is this adaptation of spirits to the immanent laws of magical causality so evident as in the use of water. As we have said above, because water washes away material dirt, consecrated water, by an evident symbolism, purifies magically, that is, destroys the stamp which the devil put upon the objects, consecrating them to his own use. Hence water becomes the universal and dominant purificatory medium, as against fire in the naturalistic system.[1] Another good example of adaptation of the spirits to the laws of magic is found in the curse. The father's or mother's curse is particularly powerful because of the relation between parents and children; God *must* fulfil it. A priest has communicated to us that an old

[1] The use of fire in hell and, secondarily, in purgatory has a completely different meaning; in hell, fire tortures without purifying.

peasant confessed the cursing of his son as the most heinous sin of his whole life. The son went to the army and was killed, and in his confession the peasant said: "Why did I interfere with the business of God?" He felt that God was *obliged* to see to it that the son was killed.

We have already met more than once the problem of magical dualism. The belief in magical causation leads necessarily to the standpoint of a duality of contrary influences. Indeed, whenever a magical action does not bring the intended result, the agent can only either deny the efficacy of the means used or suppose that the influence of the magical cause was neutralized by a contrary influence, the causation destroyed by an opposite causation. In physical explanation a process of causation cannot be destroyed, but only combined with another process, because we can follow both in their development and their combination; but in magical explanation, as we have seen, the process of causation is not given, and when the effect does not come the causal relation must be assumed to be annihilated.

Of course this opposition of contrary magical influences does not involve any absolute appreciation. From the standpoint of the subject who desires to attain a certain effect a magical influence favorable to this aim will be valued positively, an influence which destroys the first, negatively. But the appreciation changes with the change of the standpoint, and no magic can be termed good or evil in itself. There are, indeed, actions which bring harm and actions which bring benefit to other individuals or to the community as a whole, but in order to make this a basis of classification of magical actions the moral viewpoint must be introduced into magic and religion, and this is done only in the third religious system, which we shall analyze presently. Before this moralization of religion, actions performed with the help of magic can be useful or harmful, the person who performs them can be virtuous or wicked, but the magical power is neither good nor bad in itself. This is particularly evident if we remember that the same magical influence can be, according to circumstances, useful or harmful to the community or to the individual. The bringing or stopping of rain is a good example. Even directly harmful influences, such as those which bring sickness or death upon a man, can sometimes be useful to the community, when the harm is a punishment for a breach of solidarity. And if this is true of actions which have a determined result, it is the more true of magical powers which spirits, men, or things may possess, for these powers can be used for very different actions.

We understand, therefore, that not even Christianity, in spite of its absolute opposition of God and devil, heaven and hell, was able to introduce at once the idea that there is a good magic and an evil magic, and that the magic of heavenly beings and of priests was good, all other magic evil. We do not raise here the question how consistently this idea was developed in Christianity itself. The peasant, standing on practical, empirical ground, could frequently not avoid the conclusion that the effects of divine magic can be disastrous as well as beneficial, and that the devilish magic does not bring harm always, but may often be very useful. The ideas of reward and punishment in future life were hardly ever strong enough with the peasant to influence his choice in a decisive way, the less so as it was always possible to cheat God during life and the devil at the moment of death by accepting any good which might come from both sources as long as it was possible and by turning to God when nothing good could any longer be expected from the devil. This is the attitude which persists in most of the tales and in real life, in spite of some incidental, evidently imitated and formal, moralization. If God were alone against the devil, the influence of religion upon peasant life would be very equivocal. But the factor which, in spite of all this, makes the religious magical system so powerful as to direct the peasant's attitudes in all the important events of his life is the above-mentioned magical solidarity of all the divine beings, on the one hand, and all the devilish beings, on the other. This solidarity consists, not in an essential opposition between the two magics as such, but in the fact that the magical action of any divine being always supports and corroborates the magical action of all the other divine beings and is always opposed to the magical action of any devilish being; the same is true of the devilish community. On this basis, when a man acts in harmony with the divine community he is assured of the protection of this whole community, because he becomes its member, while by a single action supporting the tendencies of the devilish community, he becomes indeed a member of the latter, but makes all the divine beings his enemies.

The choice between these communities will depend upon three factors: First, the number and the concreteness of the divinities belonging to them respectively. In this regard the devilish community had a decided superiority in the beginning, when the church itself put all the pagan mythological beings, numerous and concrete, into the same class with the devils; the influence of this rich and plastic world must have been, and was indeed for a long time, stronger than that of the poorer and relatively pale community of heavenly beings. This, more than anything else, accounts for the long persistence of the devilish mythology and rites. But gradually the heavenly pantheon increased in number and concreteness; many local saints were added to it, legends grew up about them, their graves preserved a magical power, churches consecrated to them perpetuated their memory and made them familiar and plastic divinities. With the development of reading, lives of the saints became a favorite topic; and before this their lives were related by priests, amulet-peddlers, pilgrims, etc. In this way many foreign saints became known and worshiped. The Virgin Mary, whose cult came down from the higher classes to the peasant, became through the many churches, miracles, and legends one of the most powerful divinities. Particular legends connected God, Jesus, Mary, the saints, and the angels with the familiar environment of the peasant, and most of them were adapted to Polish life and nature and bear thus a distinctly local character. Finally, art in all its forms—painting, sculpture, music, architecture, poetry—contributed in an incalculable measure to make all the beings of the heavenly pantheon concrete and alive. Of course the hell-pantheon grew also, but its growth was less extensive and was decreased by a loss in number and concreteness of the pagan mythological beings.

The second reason for choosing the divine rather than the devilish community is that of their relative power. In this respect the church has also done very much to increase the power of the heavenly world as against hell, even if the latter is not too much minimized, in view of other considerations of which we shall speak presently. We notice, for example, that the pagan mythological beings assimilated to the devil have a rather limited sphere of activity. The most important natural phenomena—sunshine and thunder, summer and winter, birth and death, extraordinary cataclysms and extraordinarily good crops, war and peace, etc.—are as far as possible ascribed to God. We have already spoken of the power of Mary as manifested in her miracles, and of the patron saints to whom most of the more usual phenomena of social and individual life are subordinated. Jesus, whose main function is to attract men to the divine community, to defend them against the devil—and to give them up to him if they are stubborn—is always shown as a more powerful magician than the devil. The angels are always depicted as victorious against the devils in direct struggle. Finally, the decision of the lot of the human soul after death belongs mainly to the heavenly community, because Jesus, if he wishes, can always take the soul away from the devil on the basis of a single good deed, and after paying its due to the devil in purgatory the soul can reach paradise, while the devil cannot take a saved soul into hell.

But another tendency of the church in the same line did not succeed quite so well. The objects to which divine magical powers were communicated by consecration and which were to help man to attain influence over the spirits and over nature ought to belong also exclusively to the divine order, ought to bear such a magical character as would make them by themselves useful only to the members of the divine community and harmful to the devil. Here belong, for example, the localities and instruments of divine service, amulets, holy water, consecrated wafers, etc. But this idea implies the distinction between good and evil magical powers, and therefore the endeavor of the church failed. The use of objects consecrated by the church could be made in the favor of the devilish as well as of the divine community, according to the intention of the person who used them. Sometimes it was necessary, indeed, to use them in a perverse way in order to attain results favorable to the devilish community, especially in cases where the long use for divine ends had evidently imparted to these objects a certain incompatibility with the world of the devil. We find this attitude in such facts as the saying of prayers backward, crossing with the left hand and in the contrary direction, etc. But very often consecrated objects can be used at once for devilish purposes. Every witch or magician tries to get hosts, church candles, consecrated earth, water, oil, or salt, fringes from church banners, etc., for magical purposes; sometimes even the devil asks them to get such objects. A candle put before the altar with certain rites and a determined intention had the same magical effect as a waxen image of the person whom the witch wanted to kill; the person was consumed with sickness and died while the candle was gradually burned away during divine service. A piece of clothing put upon the organ caused insufferable pains to the person to whom it belonged, whenever the organ was played. The churches, cemeteries, crosses, and chapels erected upon the roads or in the fields are places near which devilish forces are supposed to reside; one of the means of calling the devil is to walk, with ceremonies, nine times around a cross or chapel.

But of course the fact itself that the church was in actual possession of so many objects endowed with magical power increased enormously, not only its influence, but the influence of the divine community of which it was a part and which it represented. The political supremacy of the church made it impossible for the devilish community to have as many magical things at its service. One of the meanings of sacrilege, which all the witches and magicians feel morally obliged to perform whenever they can, is to destroy the magical power of consecrated objects and to weaken in this way the church and the divine community.

In trying thus to increase the divine powers at the expense of the devil the church went still farther and tried to introduce the idea that whatever the devil does he does only by God's permission, that God leaves to him voluntarily a certain sphere of activity. But this idea seems to have been assimilated by the peasant rather late and only in connection with the religious system which we next treat, for the church itself apparently contradicted it by making all possible efforts to ascribe useful phenomena to the effects of divine magic, all harmful phenomena to the devil. This last distinction, the beneficent character of the divine as against the maleficent character of the devilish community, became the third great factor helping to the victory of the divine community in the consciousness of the peasant. But to the unsophisticated peasant mind it seems evident that the devil must have some power of his own in order to do as much harm as the church tries to lay upon him if God is to be conceived as an essentially beneficent being. The omnipotence of God had to be sacrificed to save his goodness, though the latter was as yet only practical, not moral, goodness. And, even so, it was impossible to establish at once on the magical ground an absolute opposition between God as source of *all* good and the devil as source of *all* evil; the contrast could be only relative. As we have seen, harm and benefit brought by magical actions are relative to the subject and to the circumstances. The first and indispensable limitation of the principle was necessitated by the duality of the religious world itself; only those who belonged to the divine community could be favored by the good effects of divine magic, or else there would be no particular reason for belonging to this community. But in that case the good which "the servants of the devil" experienced must have come from the devil, not from God. And some of the evil which befell the members of the divine community must have come from God, or else, if it came only from the devil, many men would be moved rather by the fear of the devil's vengeance than by the attraction of the divine gifts. All this was admitted, but the Christian teaching succeeded in partly overcoming the difficulty with the help of the contention that the good which the devil offered to his believers was not a real good and the evil which God sent down upon his servants was not a real evil. The good given by the devil turned ultimately to evil, sometimes only in the next world but often even in the present one. And the evil sent by God, if man did not lose his faith and did not turn to the devil, was sooner or later rewarded by a greater good. In short, the heavenly community proved true with regard to its human members, while in the hell community they were cheated. An interesting expression of this belief is found in many tales. In these it is the theatrical contrast between appearance and reality which suddenly discloses itself to men in their relations with the divine as well as with the devilish world. Any trash given to a man by some member of the first turns into gold; apparent calamities sent by heaven prove to be a source of happiness; divinities in human form behave apparently in the most absurd or cruel way and disclose afterward the wisdom and benevolence of their acts. On the contrary, devilish gold becomes trash, devilish food, seemingly the finest possible, is in reality composed of the most disgusting substances, the splendor and beauty with which the devil or his servants appear to men change into the utmost poverty and ugliness. Even if this tendency to lower the value of the hell community is not completely successful, it is not without its influence. The great resource of the church in inculcating the belief that the devil is ultimately harmful was, of course, the conception of future life. All the pictures of future life in hell, without exception, represent the devil as torturing the souls. The Christian teaching had probably no contrary ideas to combat or to assimilate in the sphere of the representations of the human soul's existence after death, since in the naturalistic system there were no souls.

The whole evolution of the divine community, the growth of the number, concreteness, power, and benevolence of the heavenly beings, resulted finally in an actual state of things in which the importance of divine magic is incomparably greater in practice than that of devilish magic. While the first still pervades the whole life of the peasant, is an indispensable component of all his practical activity, the second is mostly degraded to an "old women's stuff," not disbelieved, but unworthy of a real man's occupation; it is used only incidentally, except for a few individuals, and is more a matter of credulous curiosity than a part of the business of life. It still exerts an attraction, but this attraction itself is due to its abnormal character, and evidently when an attitude comes to be considered as abnormal it is no longer socially vital.

This concerns of course only the intentional magical activity of men; it is the voluntary alliance with the devil which is rare. But the magical importance of the devil himself within the whole magical system still remains great enough to make the question of belonging to the community of God or of the devil the main religious problem. Indeed it is not only by voluntary and conscious choice that men can become members of the devil's community; every act which is as such contrary to the divine solidarity, every "sin," if not expiated, causes a temporary or durable exclusion of the man from the community of heaven and automatically makes him a member of the community of hell. The man passes many times during his life from one community to the other, not because he does not want to be a member of the divine world, but because the limitations and the duties which this membership imposes upon him are numerous and difficult to keep.

The devilish community, in this magical religious system, is an indispensable condition of the existence of the divine solidarity itself. In the naturalistic system the aim of the solidarity of natural beings was the struggle against death. Here the magical solidarity of the heavenly world has its only reason in the fight against the world of hell. The aim of the whole heavenly community, from God down to the humblest saved soul, is to attract as many new members as possible from among the living and to own as much as possible of the material world. But as the hell community wants the same for itself, the struggle goes on. At the same time both communities, exactly like any human community, want only true members, such as do not destroy the harmony of the whole; they therefore exclude those who are not solidary. The heavenly community is more difficult in this respect, probably because it does not need new members as much as hell; but neither does the devilish community accept new members without selection. In tales and legends there are cases in which the devils drive away untrue members. In magical pacts with the devil the man must be consistent, and, for example, any mention of Jesus or the saints may lead to a terrible punishment. There are men whom neither heaven nor hell wants. Purgatory is not a mere place of punishment, but also a preparatory stage for heaven, making the souls eager and likely to be true members of the heavenly group.

The material world is also an object of contest. The heavenly beings as well as the devils want to appropriate, in the name of their respective groups, as many material objects as they can. We may say that the material world, with regard to the magical communities, plays the same part as property with regard to the family. It is perhaps not the basis, but at any rate one condition of the existence, of the group. It gives a dwelling-place, and we must remember that in this respect the devil was wronged at the beginning. It gives, as we have seen, the means of extending the power of the community among men who can act magically only with the help of material objects, and it is therefore important to give into the hands of the living adherents as many magical instruments as they can handle. Finally—and this point is not very clear—the spirits, at least the souls, seem to need natural food and clothing; it is difficult to say whether this conception is only a vestige of the belief of regeneration after death or belongs to the magical religious system itself.

The character of the priest and the witch (or magician) within this system can be easily determined from what has been said. They are persons who by divine or devilish consecration have acquired a magical power superior to that of ordinary men, or sometimes they became priest or witch because they originally possessed this power in a higher degree. At the same time they have a knowledge of the world of spirits and of the means of magical action which was communicated to them partly by the spirits themselves, partly by other priests or witches. The priest "knows all the things, present, past or future"; the witch has perhaps a less extensive knowledge, but with regard to the devil and devilish magic she knows even more than the priest. With regard to their knowledge the functions of the priest and of the witch do not differ much from those of the *wróż* or *mądra*, except that there the object of knowledge was nature, here it is the supernatural world. But from the superior magical power of the priest and the witch result new functions. As technically trained and efficient specialists, they take the place of the ordinary men wherever strong magical action is necessary; their own power is added to the power of the magical instruments and they can attain with the latter more important results than the layman. At the same time they are intermediaries between the profane, natural life and the magical, supernatural powers. The magical power as such is undetermined; it may have any incalculable effect, and for anybody who has not power enough himself it is dangerous to manipulate objects and rites endowed with power, because he cannot efficiently *direct* their action. The priest and the witch can do this because their will, their intention, has more magical influence by itself than the will of ordinary men, devoid of the same power.

Finally, the priest and the witch are permanent members of the respective communities (the priest can scarcely ever go to hell, the witch to heaven), and in this character they are intermediaries between the layman and the community which they represent. But this function is not necessarily limited to the official representatives of heaven or hell; a holy man, without being a priest, a possessed person, without being a witch, can play the same part. It consists in helping the respective communities to get new members or in rejecting those who are harmful, and in helping laymen to become active members of the magical groups.

The influence of this whole magical religious system upon the peasant's life-attitudes was very durable and of a great, mainly negative, importance. The belief in immediate, magical causality, inculcated for nine centuries by those whom the peasant always regarded as his intellectual superiors and applied to all the important matters of human existence, developed a particular kind of credulity with regard to the effects which may be expected from any incidents, things, or men outside of the ordinary course of life. Anything may happen or not happen; there is no continuity, consequently no proportion, between cause and effect. Out of this a feeling of helplessness develops. The peasant feels that he lacks any control of the world, while he has been accustomed to think that others have this control to an almost unlimited degree. He has no consciousness of the limitations of power of those who are his intellectual superiors and whom he does not understand, and he ascribes to somebody the responsibility for anything that happens. His only weapon in these conditions is cunning—apparent resignation to everything, universal mistrust, deriving all the benefit possible from any fact or person that happens to come under his control.

3. The third type of religious system is purely Christian, contains no pagan elements except ceremonies which the church has assimilated and christened. It has attained its full development recently, and certain of its consequences began to manifest themselves only a few years ago. Its basis is the idea of a moral unity of the human society, under the leadership of the priest, with a view to the glory of God and to the benefit of men, in conformity with the divine law and with the help of the divine world. The mythological beings are nominally the same as in the preceding system, but the attitudes are completely different, often contrary, and this obliges us to treat this system as a different religion.

In practice the corresponding attitudes of the peasant have originated mainly in the parish life, and of course the church is their initiator. The parish is a kind of great family whose members are united by a community of moral interests. The church building and the cemetery (originally always surrounding the church) are the visible symbol and the material instrument of this unity. It is the moral property of the parish as a whole, managed by the priest. We say "moral property," because economically it does not belong, in the eyes of the peasant, to any human individual or group; it is first God's, then the saint's to whom it is dedicated. The priest manages it economically also, not as a representative of the parish, however, but only as appointed by God. This explains why in America the Poles so easily agreed in earlier times to have their churches registered as property of priests or bishops, not of the congregations who had built them. It was not a question of ownership, but a mere formality concerning management. Gradually, however, they became accustomed to the idea that churches can be treated as economic property, but up to the present certain consequences of the American stand-point, such as the sale of a church, appear in some measure as sacrilege. The claim of the parish to the church as moral property consists in the right of the group to guard the religious destination of the church. The latter cannot be used for any other ends than those which are involved in the religious life of the group—meetings, parish festivals, dispensation of sacraments, burials, etc. Any use of the church building and its surroundings for any profane ends whatever is not only contrary to the magical character of these objects, but is a profanation of their social sacredness, an injury done to the parish-group. On the other hand, it is a moral duty of the latter to make the church as fit as possible for its religious and social purposes, and no sacrifice is spared in order to fulfil this duty. There is a striking contrast between the poverty of the peasants' private houses and the magnificence of many a country church. Building and adorning the church is one of the manifestations and the most evident symbol of the solidary activity of the parish for the glory of God. At the same time a beautiful church satisfies the aesthetic tendencies of the peasant, gives an impressive frame for religious meetings, and strengthens the feeling of awe and the exaltation which all the religious ceremonies provoke.

The moral rights and duties of the parish with regard to the church originate thus exclusively in the functions which are performed in the church. The most important events of individual, familial, and communal life occur there, at least partly; all the essential changes which happen within the parish-group are sanctioned there; the relations of the group with the highest powers are identified with this place; moral teaching, exhortation, condemnation, are received in the church. In short, the most intense feelings are connected with the place, which is therefore surrounded with a nimbus of holiness, is an object of awe and love. Its sacred and familiar character is still stronger because it was in the same sense a center and symbol of moral unity with the preceding generations, since, as far as the peasant's tradition reaches, his fathers and forefathers had met in the same place, their bodies had been buried around it, their souls might return there on All-Souls' Day and celebrate divine service. And after the present generation their children and grandchildren will meet there also "up to the end of the world," with the same feelings toward those now living as the latter have toward the preceding generations. We understand, therefore, what the peasant loses when he emigrates, why he moves unwillingly from one parish to another and always dreams of going back in his old age and being buried in the land of his fathers. We understand also why the matters concerning the parish church are so important and so often mentioned in letters.

The divine service, at which all the parishioners meet, is the main factor in the moral unity of the group. We have already mentioned, when speaking of the peasant's social environment, the importance of meetings for the primary unorganized group. At this stage it is almost the only way for a group to have consciousness of its unity. Now in the religious meeting, during the divine service, the group is unified, not only by the mere fact of its presence in one place, but also by the community of interests and attitudes, and this community itself has particular features which distinguish it from any other form in which the solidarity and self-consciousness of the group are elaborated. When a primary group meets incidentally, it is not determined beforehand what interests among all those which its members have in common will become the center of attention, and what attitudes among all those which are the same in all or in most of its members will be unanimously expressed. Even if the meeting is arranged with regard to a determined practical problem, and if thus a certain common interest is presupposed, the attitude which the members will take with regard to the problem is not formally predetermined, even if it may be foreseen. The conscious unity of the group is therefore mostly produced anew during every meeting—does not antedate the meeting itself. But the religious unity of the parish—not its administrative unity, of which we do not now speak—depends upon the meetings; the conscious community of interests and attitudes is kept alive only by the common assistance at the religious service. And for each particular meeting this community is predetermined; the center of interest is known beforehand, and the attitudes can be only of a definite kind and direction. This is made possible by the *ceremonial*. Every ceremony performed by the priest before the congregation has not only a magical meaning (through which it belongs to the preceding magical religious system) but also a social and moral tendency; it symbolizes a certain religious idea of a type which we shall analyze presently, and it makes this idea the center of interest of the present group. The response of the latter is also embodied in ceremonial acts—in gestures, songs, schematized prayers —and those acts symbolize and provoke definite attitudes common to all the members. This goes so far that even the sermons, with their varying contents, and the process of listening to a sermon are objects of a certain ceremonial, to some extent spontaneously evolved, non-liturgical. The gestures and intonations of the priest are performed according to an unwritten code. The congregation reacts to them in a determined way by gestures, sighs, sometimes even exclamations. A priest who does not know how to use this unofficial ritual can never be an influential preacher. Thus, through a series of successive meetings, the ceremonial maintains a continuity of group interests and attitudes, which without it could be attained only by a perfect organization.

Besides the general meetings of the whole parish on Sundays and holidays there are partial meetings of an undetermined number of members on other occasions— mass on week days; evening prayers and singing on holiday eves; service during May in honor of Mary; service during December, preparatory to Christmas; prayers and songs during Lent commemorating the sufferings of Jesus and inciting to contrition; common preparation for the Easter confession; adoration of the Holy Sacrament during the week after Corpus Christi Day, etc. Whoever lives near enough and has leisure tries to assist at these meetings. In more remote villages small groups of people gather on winter evenings and sing in common half-popular, half-liturgical songs on religious subjects. The after-Christmas songs are called *Kolenda* and concern the coming of Christ; those during Lent are called *Gorzkie żale*, "bitter regrets," in remembrance of the Passion. In almost every parish there are religious associations and fraternities whose aim is a particular kind of worship, such as the adoration of the Holy Sacrament, the worship of Mary or some saint, common recital or singing of the rosary. They have a determined part to perform during each solemn divine service; they cultivate religious song and music. Some of them have also humanitarian and practical ends—the care of the sick and poor, help to widows and orphans, funeral and dowry insurance. These last functions are performed mainly by fraternities in towns; in the country, where familial and communal solidarity is stronger, the necessity for philan-thropy and organized mutual help is less felt. All of these meetings and associations, composed mainly, but not exclusively, of women and elderly men, are under the direction and control of the priest, even if he does not always actually preside.

It is easy to understand how powerfully this intense religious life operates in developing the unity of the parish. On other, more extraordinary, occasions the members of the parish get into an immediate touch with other religious congregations. Such occasions are festivals, celebrated once a year in every parish, where all the people from the neighborhood gather; religious revivals, organized usually by monks; visitation by the bishop; festivals during the consecration of a new church, an image, etc.; priest jubilees; pilgrimages to miraculous places. The last assume a great importance in the peasant's life when they are made collectively, often by hundreds of people, under the leadership of the priest. Hundreds of such "companies" come every year to such places as Częstochowa, Vilno (Ostra Brama), and many localities of minor importance. Some people take part in pilgrimages to Rome, Lourdes, even Jerusalem; many a man or woman economizes for many years in order to be able to make such a pilgrimage.

In cases of extraordinary calamities which befall the parish (drought, long rains, epidemics) the priest organizes a special divine service with solemn processions, carrying the Holy Sacrament through or around the parish, etc.

But even individual or familial occurrences give an opportunity for religious meetings. Every christening, wedding, or funeral is attended by numerous members of the community, and the occasion itself, as well as the corresponding ceremonial, arouses in all the assistants the consciousness of an identity of interests and attitudes.

The meetings are the most powerful factor of the moral unity of the parish, but not the only one. All the members of the group in their individual religious and moral life, as far as this life is regulated by the church, are also obliged to manifest the same interests and attitudes. They must, all alike, go to confession and communion, perform the same duties with regard to the church, behave more or less identically in their relations with the priest; they ask for his advice, listen to his remonstrances; they say the same prayers on the same occasions, use the same consecrated objects, perform the same traditional ceremonies in the familial circles, greet one another by the same religious formulae, read the same religious books, etc. In short, they have in common a vast sphere of attitudes imposed by the church, and they are conscious of this community even outside of religious meetings—in their personal relations of every day. This makes the unity of the parish still closer and more persistent. At the same time this unity is distinguished from that which is due merely to social opinion by the fact that its form and content are equally fixed and imposed by the superior power of the church. To be sure, any phenomenon belonging to the religious sphere can also, at any moment, become the object of social opinion; the religious sphere is a part of the peasant's social environment, but it is its most fixed part. The parish in the religious sense of the term is, indeed, not an organized group like a commune or an association; it does not function as a unique group within the social world in a steady and determined way; we cannot speak of the functions of a parish. But the attitudes of its members which constitute its unity are relatively independent of the fluctuations of social opinion and are embodied in stable symbols, and in this sense this part of the peasant's social environment rises above the level of the primitive community and popular tradition, is an intermediary stage between the community and the higher, organized group of the church.

The central object of the religious attitudes of the parish is the glorification of God and the saints by acts of worship.

God becomes for the religious consciousness of the peasant the supreme lord and master of the human community; the saints, its guardians, intercessors, and models of perfection. The difference between this conception and the one which we find in the preceding system is quite essential. There the function of the spirits is magical; here it is moral and social. There man, by the magical bearing of his acts, becomes a member of a spiritual community; here the spirit, by the moral character which is ascribed to it, becomes incorporated into the human community, and social worship is the form which this incorporation assumes. A characteristic expression of this difference is found in the fact that, while in the magical system Jesus is subordinated to God, in the moral system he takes the place of God. The name of Jesus is incomparably more frequently used as that of the spiritual head of human society than the name of God. This is of course the result of the half-human personality of Jesus, which makes his incorporation into the human community much more easy and natural.

As the mythology is almost identical in both systems, the difference is evidently based upon practical attitudes. It is not a pre-existent theoretical conception of the magical nature of the spiritual world which makes the man use magic in his religious life, but the use of magic which causes the spiritual world to be conceived as a magical community. In the same way the source of worship is not a theoretical conception of the divinity as spiritual leader of the community, but the practice of worship, gradually elaborated and fixed in the complex ceremonial, is the origin of the social and moral functions of the divinity.

We have seen that in the magical system the magical bearing of human acts has been extended from those which are intentionally performed to produce a determined magical effect to the whole sphere of human activity, so that there is hardly any action which is magically indifferent. The same happens in the moral system. The idea of worship does not remain limited to the ceremonial practices, but is extended to all human actions which have a moral value in the eyes of the community. God (Jesus) as the lord of the community is interested in its harmony, and thus every act which helps to preserve the harmony becomes at the same time an act of worship. Altruistic help, pedagogical and medical activity, maintaining of concord in the community, spreading general and religious instruction, become religiously meritorious. By a further extension every contribution to the material welfare of men by licit means is willed by God (Jesus), even the good management of one's own property. Further still, Jesus is glorified also by anything which helps to maintain a teleological and aesthetic order in the natural environment of men—agricultural work, raising and feeding domestic animals, adornment of houses, establishment of orchards and flower gardens, etc. Partly perhaps under the influence of the church, but more probably in a spontaneous way, thanks to the old idea of the natural solidarity and animation of natural objects, the idea arose that the whole of nature, even the meanest natural beings, glorify God by their life as men do. Unnecessary destruction is therefore forbidden in this system as well as in the naturalistic one, although the subordination of nature to human ends is incomparably greater since only man glorifies God in the prescribed way, only man has an immortal soul, and it is for man that Christ died.

As against this moral organization of the human community under the spiritual leadership of Jesus and the saints, the devil and devil-worship assume for the first time a distinctly evil character; they are not only harmful but immoral. The reason for this is evident. There is no human community which would enter into the same relation with the devil that the parish enters into with God; the relation with the devil is individual and lacks social sanction and social ceremonial. The opposition between the divine and the devilish world is thus associated with the opposition between social and individual religious life, and both oppositions acquire through this association a new character and a new strength. The divine world becomes socially acknowledged, a positive social value; the devilish world is socially despised, a negative social value. The worship of God is meritorious, official, and organized; the worship of the devil illicit, secret, and incidental. A man who serves God is a good member of the community, trying to be in harmony with his group; a man who serves the devil is a rebel, trying to harm his fellow-citizens. Since every socially moral action is subordinated to the glorification of God, and since there is an essential opposition between God and the devil, every socially immoral action is conceived as serving the devil.[1]

It is only in the latter sphere, in things subordinated to the devil, that magical action keeps most of its old character, precisely because this sphere, becoming secret and individual, did not undergo the same evolution as the sphere of divine things. In the latter, actions whose meaning in the magical system consisted in bringing immediately and mechanically a determined effect become now acts of worship, and their old effect is now conceived as a divine reward, as conscious action of the divinity moved by human worship. It is no

---

[1] Naturally the devil, thrown out of social life, has lost still more of his old importance. Whatever he does, he does it by God's permission; God allows him to tempt men in order to give them the merit of victory. But even temptation becomes rare. The peasants have a curious explanation of this fact. God does not allow the devils to tempt men as much as they did before, because men have grown so evil themselves that if the devil could use all his power no man could be saved. The women are a little better, and therefore they are more subject to temptation and see the devil more frequently.

longer the letter, but the meaning of the prayer and the religious feeling which accompanies it that influence God or the saint; it is the confidence in, and the love of, God, manifested by the use of consecrated objects, that compel God to grant the men what they need when they are using those objects.

Only human magic, however, has changed its significance. The magical power of God remains the same. God's action still exerts an immediate influence upon the material world. But now he is supposed to exert his power with a view to the moral order which he wishes to maintain in the world, not in the interests of the heavenly community; his activity becomes altruistic, while in the magical system it was egoistic.

The rôle of the priest is modified in the same way. From a magician he becomes a father of the parish, a representative of God (Jesus) by maintaining the moral order, a representative of the parish by leading the acts of common worship. From his representation of Jesus results his superior morality, implicitly assumed wherever he acts, not as a private individual, but in his religious, official character. Therefore also his teaching, his advice, his praise or blame, whenever expressed in the church, from the chancel, or in the confessional, are listened to as words of Jesus, seldom if ever doubted, and obeyed more readily than orders from any secular power. This influence is extended beyond the church and manifests itself in the whole social activity of the priest, though there it loses some of its power, since it is not quite certainly established by the peasants whether the priest outside of the church is still in the same sense a representative of Jesus. On the other hand, from the fact that the priest is the representative of the parish in acts of worship it results that all his religious actions are supposed to be performed in the name of the community, and he is socially bound to perform them conscientiously and regularly.   In general, the greater the rôle of the priest, the greater is his responsibility and the more required from him in the line of moral and religious perfection.   In later volumes we shall have the opportunity of studying more in detail the rôle which the priest plays in peasant society because of his place in the moral-religious system.   For this system is now decidedly the dominating one.   Naturalism survives only in fragmentary beliefs and practices and in a general attitude toward nature, whose real meaning is already in a large measure forgotten.   The magical system is still strong, and the influence which it has exerted upon the peasant psychology can hardly be overestimated.   But it is no longer developing, no new elements are added to it, and in fact it is rapidly declining.

The fourth system, that of individual mysticism, which we shall presently define, is still rare among the peasants and does not seem to be on the way to an immediate and strong development.   But the moral-religious system not only retains almost all of its traditional power, except in some limited circles, but is still growing as new conditions of communal life arise and the old principle is applied to new problems.   We already see in these first volumes of letters that most of the religious interests explicitly expressed belong to this system, and we shall see it still more clearly in other volumes.

4. Religion as a mystical connection of the individual with God expressed by the attitudes of love, personal subordination, desire of personal perfection and of eternal life with God, etc., is, as we have said, not very much developed among the peasants.   The peasant is a practical man; religion remains interwoven with his practical interests, while mysticism requires precisely a liberation from those interests, a concentration of thoughts and feelings upon beings and problems having little relation with everyday life.

A sign of the lack of mysticism is the absolute orthodoxy of the peasant; unless by ignorance, he never dares to imagine any religious attitude different from the teaching of the church, because outside of the church he never imagines himself in any direct relation with the divinity. He is in this respect radically different from the Russian peasant. Still there are cases in which a mystical attitude develops during extraordinary religious meetings—revivals, pilgrimages—when the usual environment and the usual interests are for a while forgotten, and the individual is aroused from his normal state by the example of the devotion of others and by the influence of the mob of which he is a part. But these occasional outbreaks of mysticism in determined social conditions belong as much to the preceding religious system as to the properly mystical one. The way upon which the peasant can really pass into a new form of religious life leads through the problem of death. When death ceases to be a natural phenomenon preceding regeneration and becomes a passage into a new supernatural world, brooding upon the problem of death must lead to a certain detachment from the practical problems and open the way to mysticism. But this brooding upon death is possible only when the individual ceases to look upon his own death or that of his dear ones from the traditional social standpoint, from which the isolated death of a member of the group is a more or less normal event, particularly at a certain age; he must begin to view death only as a fact of individual life, for only then it has extraordinary, abnormal importance which can give birth to mystical reflections and attitudes. And this requires again more individualization than the average peasant shows, more realization of the uniqueness of the individual. We find indeed mystical attitudes always during calamities which threaten the existence of the whole community—pest or war. But single individuals develop such attitudes only when more or less isolated from their communities (e.g., servants in large cities) or when exceptionally cultivated.

In Part II we shall have the opportunity of studying the peasant's theoretic and aesthetic interests in their full development under the influence of the culture of the superior classes.   As these interests were, however, apparently never lacking, and are manifested in Part I, it will be useful to determine their place within the traditional peasant life and their relation to the practical attitudes. We shall then be able to understand how they have sometimes succeeded in occupying within a single generation the center of attention of individuals and of whole groups.

1. There are three primary forms in which theoretic interests are manifested in the peasant—the schematism of practical life, interest in new facts, and interest in religious explanations of the world.

The first is completely original.   It arises out of the peasant's spontaneous reflection on his activity and its conditions, on his human and natural environment.   It constitutes the peasant's "wisdom," and is very clearly distinguished by public opinion from practical ability in itself.   A man may be very wise, have valuable generalizations concerning practice, and still be unpractical through lack of energy, of presence of mind, etc.   This distinction assumes a satirical meaning in the tales having as their subject three brothers, two wise and one stupid.   The last is always practically successful, while the first two, with all their wisdom, behave like fools.

For a man accustomed to live in action the task of reflection is not an easy one.   We see how the peasant prepares for it, tries to find free time and a solitary place, and then spends occasionally many hours in thinking. Even when he wants to write a letter which requires reflection, he treats it as a difficult and long business. A proof of the importance of reflection in his eyes is seen in the fact that he remembers for many years every act of reflection which he performed (cf. the case of Wladek in Part IV). But precisely on that account the process of reflection, artificially isolated from the process of activity, assumes a somewhat independent interest; the peasant enjoys the solution of a problem as such. The numerous riddles which we find in the Polish folklore are also a proof of this.

The results of such individual acts of reflection, accumulated through generations, constitute a rich stock of popular wisdom. A part of it is expressed in proverbs; but with the growing complexity of economic and social life and growing rapidity of change the new reflections have no time to crystallize themselves into proverbs, but tend to formulate themselves in changing abstract schemes of life communicated gradually by the peasants to one another.

We may divide this practical philosophy into two classes —schemes of things and schemes of people. The first concerns agriculture, handicraft, trade, medicine, etc. It is of course impossible to study here the whole content of the respective beliefs; we can only note certain of their general characters. First, they proceed always from the particular to the general, by induction, and their systematization, the subordination of details to a general view, seems very slow. We have already noticed this with regard to economic concepts; the extension of the quantitative viewpoint to farm goods comes very late. Another very general example is the slowness of imitation. It may come from many other reasons, but a frequent reason is also the lack of generalization. The peasant who sees an estate-owner apply some new technical invention with good results does not imitate him, simply because he does not see the identity of their respective positions as farmers. His usual argument is: "It is all right for you, who are a rich and instructed man, but not for a poor, stupid peasant like me." The difference in social position as a whole hinders him from noticing that in this particular respect he can do the same as his superior. For the same reason the peasant brings relatively little agricultural learning from season-emigration. In Germany he usually finds an agricultural level even higher than that on the estate of his neighbor, and the difference between his own farming and that of the large German estates is so great that he does not dare to generalize and to apply at home what he learned abroad. On the other hand, we find him making most hasty and superficial generalizations; proverbs and sayings concerning farmwork and weather in connection with the days of the year are based mostly upon a few disconnected observations; a new object is often classified upon the basis of a quite superficial analogy with known objects. Both the slowness and the incidental superficiality and hastiness of generalization result from the way in which the process of reflection occurs. When the peasant begins to think, the result depends upon the material which at this moment is present in the sphere of his consciousness. If the material happens to be well selected and sufficient, the generalization is valid; if not, it is false. But valid or false it will be accepted by the author himself and often by others until a time of reflection again comes and some new generalization is made in accordance with, or contrary to, the first. Because reflection requires so much effort its results are seldom verified in experience, seldom criticized. This explains the many evident absurdities and contradictory statements current among the peasants; once created they live, and they have even a useful function because they help to equilibrate one-sided views of others.

The peasant seldom uses dialectic in criticizing any view and can hardly be persuaded by dialectic. He simply opposes his opinion to another; and the more effort the elaboration of this opinion has cost him, the less willing is he to exchange it for another. He may even acknowledge that the contrary opinion is right, but he holds that his own is also right, and he feels no necessity of solving the apparent contradiction unless the problem is important enough to compel him to do some more thinking and to elaborate a third, intermediary opinion. He is so accustomed to live among partial and one-sided generalizations that he likes to collect all the opinions on some important issue, listens with seeming approval to every one, and finally either does what he intended to do at first or sets about reflecting and elaborates his own view. If he selects the opinion of anybody else, he is led, not by the intrinsic merit of the opinion, but by his appreciation of the man. If only he has confidence in the man's sincerity and intelligence, he supposes that the man's advice was the result of a sufficient process of thinking and considers it useless to repeat this thinking himself in order to appreciate the advice on its merits.

His ideas about other people are equally schematic, either appropriated from the traditional store or independently elaborated at some moment of intense thinking and afterward used without any new reflection. The peasant's general prepossession about people is that everybody is moved only either by his egotistic interest or by solidarity with his group; if neither can be detected, then evidently the man is clever enough to keep his motives hidden. If, nevertheless, a person's activity, particularly that of a stranger, is manifestly disinterested, the peasant supposes first stupidity, and recurs to altruism only as the last explanation. The only exception is the priest, who has to be altruistic ex officio; here egotistic interest is usually the last, more or less forced, explanation. The willingness of the peasant to do business with a given person and particularly to be persuaded by him depends upon the degree to which he understands or thinks that he understands the motives of this person. He will show confidence more readily in a man whose motives he knows to be not only interested but even dishonest than in one whom he does not understand, because in the first case he can take the motives into account, while in the second he does not know how to limit the possibilities and does not know what to expect. Accordingly he has a summary and egocentric classification ready and applies it in any given case. Those of the first class are the members of his family, whose behavior ought to be determined by the familial relations themselves and from whom solidarity can be expected. Then come the members of the community, classified again according to their nearer or more remote neighborhood, their fortune, character, etc. Then come all the other, unknown peasants, whose interests are supposed to be the same as those of the known ones. The priest, the noble, the Jew, are people of different classes, but still supposedly known. The priest's official character has already been determined, and, of course, the peasant understands the usual weaknesses of the country priest—money, wine, and his housekeeper. Every noble is supposed to desire in his heart the reintroduction of serfdom; but besides this he is a farmer, a man who has innumerable common traditions with the peasant. There may be hostility between him and his peasant neighbors, but there is always more or less of reciprocal understanding. The Jew is classed once and forever as a merchant and cheater, and no other motive than money is ascribed to him; but this makes his schematization relatively easy in spite of the fact that the peasant knows little, if anything, about his familial and religious life. In this connection, however, the Jew often cheats the peasant by putting forward a smaller or pretended interest to fit the scheme and keeping the larger and real interest in the background. Political agitators sometimes do the same. There is also a scheme corresponding to the lower officials in small towns and to the handworkers. But the peasant does not understand at all the instructed city fellows. Those who came to the country with idealistic purposes had no success at all for many years; only lately, thanks to a few eminent men, a favorable schematization has been formed of those who want to raise the peasant intellectually and economically, and the peasant has begun to understand this kind of interest.

If now it accidentally happens that one of these pre-established schemes fails in a particular or general case, the peasant loses his head. Every exception from the admitted rule assumes in his eyes unlimited proportions. A member of the family who shows no solidarity, a member of the community who does not reciprocate a service, provokes an astonishment which the peasant cannot forget for a long time. A bad, "unworthy" priest or a noble who acts against the traditions arouses the most profound indignation; and if, on the other hand, a noble (particularly a woman) proves really well disposed and democratic, without being too familiar, the peasant's attitude in the course of time comes near to adoration. And when some of the city men succeeded in breaking down the peasants' mistrust and becoming political or social leaders, the confidence of the peasants in them became unlimited, absurd. Finally, when the peasant finds himself among strangers, as upon emigration, and sees that none of his schemes can be applied to the people around him, he is for a very long time absolutely unable to control his social environment, because it takes so long to elaborate a new scheme. In the beginning, therefore, he simply must settle among people from his own country in order to learn from them at least a few elementary generalizations, unless, indeed, as seldom happens, he has some time free to observe and to reflect. The fault is here again insufficient generalization; the peasant has schemes of particular classes of people, but not of man in general.

The interest in new facts is always strong, even if not supported by practical motives. We are here very much reminded of the curiosity of a child, without the child's restlessness. The intensity of social life in an unorganized community naturally depends upon this interest. Anything that happens within the community attracts attention, even if only the most striking of these facts become the center of attention of the whole community. Each fact provokes some kind of a reaction, and, as we have seen in a previous chapter, common attitudes are elaborated and become factors of social unity. In this way the interest in facts happening within the community has a social importance. But the peasant is not conscious of the social consequences of his curiosity; he just naïvely wants to know. And he knows and remembers everything about his environment. This is of course also useful to him personally, for it enables him to construct practical schemes; this is a consequence, however, not a motive. He does not try to know in order to build schemes, but he builds schemes when, among all the facts that he has learned, one strikes him as practically important. Consequently the sphere of his concrete knowledge is incomparably larger than the sphere of his practical schemes, and one of the most important sides of his latest intellectual development is the learning of the practical significance of things with which he was acquainted long ago.

This independence of curiosity from practical problems enables the peasant to show a lively interest in things that can have no practical importance for him. In older times the main bulk of such information was supplied by returning soldiers, emigrants, pilgrims, travelers, beggars. Happenings in the political and religious world, extraordinary social events outside of the community, marvels of nature and industry, the variety of human mores, were and are still the main objects of interest. Fiction stories also are gladly listened to, but the interest in them seems to be in general much less lively. They are treated as history, as true, but concerning facts that were past long ago, and are therefore less interesting than those which are still real in themselves or in their consequences. When the imagination is disclosed as such, even this interest is usually lost. The peasant wants to know only about reality.

When reading developed, the interest for facts got a new food. As we shall see later, the popular newspapers have to give many descriptions of concrete facts in order to be read, and the promotion of practical and intellectual progress must to a large extent take this concrete curiosity into account. Even on a higher intellectual level this character of theoretic interests is preserved. Descriptive works on geography, ethnography, technology, zoölogy, botany, etc., have the greatest popularity; historical books are on the second plane; fiction comes last, unless its subjects are taken from the life of other classes and other nations or, in general, unless it informs about things that the peasant did not know. As a result some of the popular papers have dropped completely the old custom of publishing novels and short stories.

The situation is quite different among city workers and the lower middle class, where fiction-reading assumes enormous proportions and a powerfully developed interest for plot has favored the recent success of sensational literature. This difference of interest between the country and city population is certainly due to a difference in social conditions. The city inhabitants have not as keen an interest in new facts as we find in the country because city life gives them a superabundance of new facts and the receptivity is deadened, and because the additional excitement which the peasant gets by sharing the news with his community is here almost lacking. The relatively unsettled character of the life of a city inhabitant as compared with that of the peasant, the uncertainty and the relatively numerous possibilities of the future, give more food for imagination, make it easier for the reader to put himself in the place of the hero of the novel and thus enjoy the plot. But, on the other hand, the numerous social and political problems raised by modern industrial life find a more ready reception among city workers than among peasants, and open the way to the development of an intense and serious intellectual life. Hence it may be said that with regard to intellectual activities the lower city class can be divided into fiction-readers without social interests and non-fiction readers with social interests.

There is indeed one kind of fiction that always finds a strong interest among the peasants; it is religious fiction— legends, lives of saints, etc. This, however, is quite a different kind of interest, based on the general theoretic and practical value which the peasant ascribes to the religious conceptions. The peculiarities of this attitude compel us to notice it here as a distinct class of theoretic interest. Here of course, the theoretic interest is not primarily independent of other kinds of interests, but is only a part of the general religious interest which contains also practical and aesthetic elements. But while in the whole complicated machinery of the cult these elements are indissolubly connected, in the myth the theoretic element predominates and becomes frequently quite isolated from the others. The relation to practice is then only mediate.

It is useful, indeed, to know everything about nature, or spirits, or magic, in order to control eventually the religious reality; but this control is exerted by the peasant himself to only a small extent, since there are specialists who not only know more than the peasant does about the nature of this world but have particular means and particular powers. Except by prayer and a few simple ceremonies, the peasant does not try to turn his knowledge directly into control, but appeals to the specialist. As soon as the latter intrudes between religious theory and religious practice the interest in theory loses its relation to practical aims. Myth then becomes for the layman chiefly a theoretic *explanation*, but, on the other hand, the interest in mythology remains for a long time the most popular form in which the peasant's desire for explanations manifests itself. The reality of this desire is shown by the fact that Christian mythology, particularly its part concerning the origin of things and of their qualities, has grown considerably, and many old myths, such as those of Genesis, have been greatly changed, systematized, and completed. Lately the explanatory sciences—physics, chemistry, biology, geology—have begun to take the place of religion.

To these three spheres of theoretic interest—schemes built in view of practice, concrete facts, genetic explanations—correspond three different types of specialists. We find, first of all, the wise and experienced old peasant who plays in the village or in the community the rôle of an adviser in troubles and is the real intellectual leader at all the meetings having some practical situation in view. He has usually a good material position; his success is a guaranty of his wisdom. He must be well known for his honesty, otherwise people would not listen to him. He must have traveled more or less and met many different people, for this gives assurance that he will be able to grasp any new situation. He is prudent, conservative, mistrusting. He talks with deliberation, slowly, weighing carefully every word. His arguments seldom fail to persuade, because they express ideas which his listeners had more or less clearly realized themselves. He usually selects only some of the many ready schemes; his main function is their systematization and adaptation to the given practical problem. These "advisers," as we may call them, are frequently the greatest obstacle to all the efforts to enlighten and organize the peasants; but if once such an intellectual leader is won, the community follows him rapidly and easily. Such men are often elected mayors of the commune. In extraordinary epochs of rapid social change (as during the revolutionary period of 1904-6) the old adviser may be provisionally supplanted by a popular agitator whose influence is based, not upon personal authority and not upon a selection of arguments which the community implicitly approves, but upon an ability to provoke favorable feelings. Then the peasant himself finds among his various schemes the necessary arguments.

The second type may be called the "narrator." He may be old or young; formerly he should have traveled much, now he may simply read much. He is the source of information about facts. His importance is not even approximately as great as that of the adviser. He is seldom if ever asked for advice in important matters. He may have no social position at all; he may be a daily worker, a hired servant, or even a parasite. He has inherited the function of the ancient beggar or pilgrim. A solid social position is even hardly compatible with this function if the latter is steadily performed, for naturally much time is needed to learn new facts. Insignificant in times of work and serious business, the narrator becomes a personality at moments free from practical care, on winter evenings when the family and the neighbors gather in the big room of some rich peasant—men smoking, women doing some light handiwork—and listen to the narration. Lately, since reading has developed, the narrator is being gradually supplanted by the reader.

The function of "explaining" was traditionally performed by the "wise" man or woman, and by the priest, often by the organist. Since religious explanations have begun to give place to scientific explanations there is an evident need for a new kind of specialist. Indeed, this is the moment for the appearance of the "philosopher" in the ancient Greek sense, for the modern scientist with his specialization cannot satisfy the peasant's many-sided desire for explanation. Hence this type also is beginning to develop. It is the self-taught man, reading every book he can get, always prepared to discuss any subject and eager to explain everything. He writes elaborate letters to the papers, wants to contribute to the solution of every scientific problem about which he hears, is eager to correspond with scientists whose fame reaches him, and is continually thinking about abstract matters. · As this type is recent in the country his position in the peasant community is not yet sufficiently determined. But since he is the natural antagonist of the priest, it is probable that he will become an intellectual leader of the anti-religious movement when this movement develops in the country. Among the lower classes of the town population he already plays a part in this movement.

The social prestige attached to the functions of the adviser, the narrator, and the philosopher, even if often mixed in the beginning with a particular kind of condescension with regard to the two latter types, is a strong factor in instruction. Reciprocally, when instruction develops, the prestige of these functions grows. We shall see how the movement of "enlightenment" uses this circumstance for its ends.

In general, the rapid intellectual progress of the peasant during the last thirty years, as well as the progress of social organization, are made possible only through certain pre-existing features of the peasant's intellectual and social life. The men who lead the peasants have succeeded in exploiting those features for the sake of a higher cultural development, and this is their merit.

2. The aesthetic interests of the peasant have two main sources—religion and amusement.

We have already noticed the frequent analogy between religious and aesthetic fantasy; both tend to individualize their object, both find a particular meaning in the empirical data which goes beyond the sensual content. However, while in religion this super-sensual side of the world is taken quite seriously as a perfect reality and referred to practice, from the standpoint of the aesthetic interest its existence is not believed and its rôle is only to give more significance to the sensual world itself. Hence religious beliefs whose seriousness is lost or whose real sense is forgotten become aesthetic attitudes. We find innumerable examples in the peasant life. Old tales in which naturalistic religious beliefs are still plainly noticeable and many of the spirit stories are now merely matters of entertainment; the narrator often changes, shortens, develops, combines them, giving free play to his imagination. Most of the patterns, forms, and combinations of colors in popular architecture, furniture, dress, and ornament had a magical value.[1] The magical significance is mainly forgotten, but the traditional models still determine the taste. Old ceremonies whose original religious meaning can be easily recognized even now often remain only aesthetically valuable for the peasant,

[1] Cf. M. Wawrzeniecki, *Nowe naukowe stanowisko pojmowania i wyjaśniania niektórych przejawów w dziedzinie ludoznawstwa* (Warsaw, 1910).

who has a very keen sense for the picturesque, theatrical side of ceremonial groups and collective or individual performances. Often while the religious attitude is still vital it is so mixed with the aesthetic feeling that it is impossible to determine which is more important. Many religious songs are sung at home for the sake of aesthetic enjoyment, and it happens that a religious melody is used with worldly words, or vice versa. Images of saints are frequently treated simply as pictures. When the church is adorned with flowers or when girls dressed in white throw flowers before the priest during the Corpus Christi procession, the religious attitude is evidently dominant. But we cannot say this with certainty when houses are adorned at Pentecost with green and flowers or when the Christmas-tree is dressed. In short, we not only see the results of the degeneration of old religions into aesthetic attitudes, but at every moment and in innumerable details we see the process still going on.

From social amusements arise many of the aesthetic interests of the peasant. Popular music and poetry in particular have their main source here. Most of the music is developed from dance music, as the rhythm shows. All the popular poems are songs. At present it is still the custom in many localities when boys and girls meet, with or without dancing, to sing alternately old songs and invent new ones, either seriously or jokingly. Sometimes long poems are composed and repeated in this way, one stanza by a boy, another by a girl. Love is usually the more or less serious subject of the poems sung in a mixed society, while others sung by boys or girls alone have a great variety of subjects, embracing the whole sphere of peasant life.

A type of poetry whose source is undetermined is ceremonial songs and speeches in verse sung or recited at weddings, funerals, christenings, the end of harvest, and at other familial and social festivals.   Many of them are very old and in all probability originally had a religious significance.   Sometimes they are modified to suit the occasion. Others are more recent, sometimes composed for the occasion, and their aim is evidently social—to entertain the persons present, to give advice and warning, to express feelings of familial or communal solidarity, to ask for gifts, to extend thanks for hospitality, etc.

More recently an intense aesthetic movement has manifested itself among the peasants, particularly along literary lines, and while this is developed upon the traditional background it tends increasingly to come under the influence of the models presented by the upper classes.   There are probably few, if any, among the half-educated peasants who do not try to become poets.   We shall examine this movement in a later volume.

FORM AND FUNCTION OF THE PEASANT LETTER

The Polish peasant, as the present collection shows, writes many and long letters. This is particularly striking, since the business of writing or even of reading letters is at best very difficult for him. It requires a rather painful effort of reflection and sacrifice of time. Letter-writing is for him a social duty of a ceremonial character, and the traditional, fixed form of peasant letters is a sign of their social function.

All the peasant letters can be considered as variations of one fundamental type, whose form results from its function and remains always essentially the same, even if it eventually degenerates. We call this type the "bowing letter."

The bowing letter is normally written by or to a member of the family who is absent for a certain time. Its function is to manifest the persistence of familial solidarity in spite of the separation. Such an expression became necessary only when members of the family began to leave their native locality; as long as the family stayed in the same community, the solidarity was implicitly and permanently assumed. The whole group manifested its unity at periodical and extraordinary meetings, but no single member in particular was obliged to manifest his own familial feelings more than other members, unless on some extraordinary occasions, e.g., at the time of his or her marriage. But the individual who leaves his family finds himself in a distinctive situation as compared with that of other members, and the bowing letter is the product of this situation. There is nothing corresponding to it in personal, immediate familial relations.

In accordance with its function, the bowing letter has an exactly determined composition. It begins with the religious greeting: "Praised be Jesus Christus," to which the reader is supposed to answer, "In centuries of centuries. Amen." The greeting has both a magical and a moral significance. Magically it averts evil, morally it shows that the writer and the reader are members of the same religious community, and from the standpoint of the moral-religious system every community is religious. A common subordination to God may also be otherwise expressed throughout the entire letter, but the greeting is the most indispensable expression. There follows the information that the writer, with God's help, is in good health and is succeeding, and wishes the same for the reader and the rest of the family. We know that health (struggle against death) and living constitute the reason of natural and human solidarity (only spiritual solidarity aims at power). Finally come greetings, "bows," for all the members of the family, or from all the members of the family if the letter is written to the absent member. The enumeration should be complete, embracing at least all the members who still live in the same locality, if the family is already scattered, as often happens today.

These elements remain in every letter, even when the function of the letter becomes more complicated; every letter, in other words, whatever else it may be, is a bowing letter, a manifestation of solidarity. Various elements may be schematized; the words "bows for the whole family" may, for example, be substituted for the long enumeration, but the principle remains unchanged in all the familial letters.

The bowing letter is the only one which has an original function. The functions of all the other types of familial letters are vicarious; the letter merely takes the place of a personal, immediate communication. It has to perform these vicarious functions when the absence of the member of the family becomes so long that it is impossible to wait for his arrival.

According to the nature of these vicarious functions, we can distinguish five types of family letters, each of which is also and fundamentally a bowing letter.

1. *Ceremonial letters.*—These are sent on such familial occurrences as normally require the presence of all the members of the family—weddings, christenings, funerals, name-days of older members of the group; Christmas, New Year, Easter. These letters are substitutes for ceremonial speeches. The absent member sends the speech written instead of saying it himself. The function of such a letter is the same as the function of meeting and speech, namely, the revival of the familial feeling on a determined occasion which concerns the whole group.

2. *Informing letters.*—The bowing letter leaves the detailed narration of the life of the absent member or of the family-group for a future personal meeting. But if the meeting is not likely to occur soon, the letter has to perform this function vicariously and provisionally. In this way a community of interests is maintained in the family, however long the separation may be.

3. *Sentimental letters.*—If the primitive, half-instinctive familial solidarity weakens as a consequence of the separation, the sentimental letter has the task of reviving the feelings in the individual, independently of any ceremonial occasion.

4. *Literary letters.*—We have seen that during informal meetings as well as during ceremonies the aesthetic interests of the peasant find their most usual expression in the form of music, songs, and recital of poems. The absent member who cannot take a personal part in the entertainments

of his group often sends a letter in verse instead, and is sometimes answered in the same way. It is an amusement which has an element of vanity in it, since the letter is destined to be read in public. The literary letters certainly play an important part in the evolution through which the primitive aesthetic interests, manifested during the meetings of the primary group, change into literary interests whose satisfaction depends upon print.

5. *Business letters.*—The vicarious function of these is quite plain. As far as possible the peasant does all his business in person, and resorts to a business letter only when the separation is long and the distance too great for a special meeting.

Up to the present we have spoken of family letters, for the original function of the letter was to keep members of a family in touch with one another. Letters to strangers can perform all the functions of a family letter, but the essential one of maintaining solidarity exists only in so far as the solidarity itself is assumed. Correspondence with a stranger can also help to establish a connection which did not exist before—a function which the family letter has only when a new member is added to the family through marriage, i.e., when a stranger becomes assimilated.

We must mention also the question of the relation of expression to thought in the peasant letters. The peasant language, as can be noticed even in translation, has many traditional current phrases used in determined circumstances for determined attitudes. They are not, like proverbs, results of a general reflection about life, but merely socially fixed ways of speaking or writing. The peasant uses them, not only for traditional attitudes, but also in some measure to express attitudes which already diverge from the tradition, if this divergence is not felt clearly to necessitate a new expression. And when he gets outside of the usual form of expression and tries to find new words and new phrases, then, of course, it is difficult for him to keep the exact proportion, particularly when he uses the literary language. He sometimes uses great words to express trifles, or, more frequently, he expresses profound and strong feelings in phrases which to an intelligent reader seem weak and commonplace, but which seem strong and adequate to the writer, who is less familiar with them. But when the peasant, instead of trying to imitate the literary language, finds for his new attitudes words in his own philological stock, his style has often a freshness and accuracy impossible to render in translation.

Further, society always tends to ritualize social intercourse to some extent, and every modification of a ritual produces disturbances more profound than could reasonably be anticipated. We have, for example, ritualized remarks on the weather in connections where social intercourse is limited to casual meetings and greetings, and if on these occasions a man remarked habitually, "Fine trees," in the place of "Fine weather," this would lead to speculations on his sanity. With the peasant, as with the savage, the whole of social intercourse, including language, is more rigorously ritualized than with ourselves, and so long as the peasant remains within the sphere of traditional language the slightest shading of the expression is significant. We notice in this connection that in our material there is very little profanity or abuse between acquaintances or family members in personal intercourse. For the outsider and the absent person there are indeed adequate forms of abuse, but between those nearly related the maximum effect can be produced by the minimum divergence from the usual language norms. See Raczkowski series, Nos. 404, 429.

SPECIMEN PEASANT LETTERS

The following letters, or portions of letters, are printed here to illustrate the elements, as enumerated above, that enter into a letter. It will be understood that these specimens are intended to represent the more primitive and elemental types, into which little of the informing and business elements enters. Specimens of informing and business letters are not reproduced at this point, as they are the dominant type in the later series. See, for examples, Wróblewski series and Kowalski series.

No. 1 below is an almost pure type of bowing letter.

No. 2 is of the same type, written to a priest who took special interest in teaching peasants to write informing letters—not very successfully in this case.

No. 3 is sentimental, designed to "warm the frozen blood" of an absent brother.

No. 4 is the ceremonial-congratulatory portion of a letter.

No. 5 is interesting as containing all the norms of a peasant letter, and also as an example of how proper and charming a letter may be within the traditional norms. The letter was written on "Palmer House" paper, but the writer was either a scrub-girl or a chambermaid. She is barely literate, as shown by the orthography and the absence of punctuation and capitalization. The girl to whom the letter was addressed could not write at all.

No. 6 is from a girl in Poland to her brother-in-law in America, and shows in its most naïve form the character of literary effort. It contains indications that the brother-in-law also was attempting literary achievement.

No. 7 is the beginning of his reply to Magdusia.

No. 8 is the rhymed and versified portion of a ceremonial letter to the writer of No. 7. As poetry it is very bad, and toward the end the versification and rhyme break down.

Generally speaking, every literate peasant tries at some time in his life to write poetry, but the tendency expresses itself in profusion only when he begins to write for the newspapers, and this situation we treat in Volume IV.

1   PERTH AMBOY, N.Y., August 11, 1911

In the first words of my letter, beloved parents, we address you with these words of God: "Praised be Jesus Christus," and we hope that you will answer, "For centuries of centuries. Amen."

And now I inform you about my health and success, that by the favor of God we are well, and we wish you the same. We wish you this, beloved parents, from our whole hearts. We inform you further that we received your letter, which found us in good health, which we wish to you. And now we ask how is the weather in the [old] country, because we have such heat that the sun is 110 degrees warm and many people fell dead from the sun during the summer of this year. Now, beloved father and beloved mother, I kiss your hands and legs. I end my conversation with you. Remain with God. Let God help you with good health and [permit me] to meet with you, beloved parents.

So now I bow to you, beloved sister, and to you, beloved brother-in-law, and I wish you happiness and health and good success—what you yourselves wish from God this same I, with my husband, wish you. So now I bow to Aunt Doruta, and to brother Aleksander, and to Józef, and to you, my grandmother, and I wish you health and good success; what you yourself wish from God the same I wish to you, beloved grandmother, and to you, beloved sister, together with you, beloved brother. Now I bow to brother-in-law Moscenski and to sister Adela, and we wish them all kinds of success; what they wish from God the same we wish them. Now we send the lowest bow to the Doborkoskis, to brother-in-law and to sister and to their children, and we wish happiness, health, good success. What they wish from God the same we wish to them. Goodbye.

Now I, Stanisław Pienczkowski, send a bow to my [wife's] parents, and I inform you, beloved parents, about my health, and that by the favor of God I am well, and the same I wish to you, beloved parents, and I ask you, beloved parents, why you do not write a letter, because I sent [a letter] to the Nowickis a week later, and they received it, and I cannot wait long enough [cannot endure the waiting] to get a letter. Therefore I ask you, beloved parents, to write me back a letter quicker.   [No signature]

2   GERIGSWALDE

I, Leon Wesoły, writing April 28, 1912. "Praised be Jesus Christus." First of all, I lay down low bows to you, Canon Priest, as to my shepherd, and I inform you, Ecclesiastical Father, about our work and health. Thanks to God and the Holiest Mother, I am well. The work that I have is to arrange the bricks for burning. Also I inform you, Canon Priest, that there was a solar eclipse on the 1st of April from 1 to 2 o'clock, but it happened so indecently that even shivers were catching a man. I do not have more to write, only I lay down sincere low bows from everybody with whom I work and live in this [despicable] Germany. Also I send a low bow to my wife, Rozalja. I do not have more to write. May God grant it. Amen. Praised be Jesus Christus. Address the same.

                                                          LEON WESOŁY

3   WARSAW, April 29, 1914
"Praised be Jesus Christus."

DEAR BROTHER: [Greetings; health]. Although we write little to each other, almost not at all, and I don't know why such coldness prevails between us, still I write this letter from fraternal feeling, not from principle. I was with our parents for the holidays of the Resurrection of Our Lord. I read your letters, the one and the other. Our parents grieve that we live only for our own selves, like egotists. So it is my duty to take the pen into my hand and with God's help to write you a few words. At first, I thank you, dear brother Jan, for your kind memory of our parents—for not forgetting them. Don't forget them in the future. Our father still looks sound and gay. Mother has grown old already, but she does not look bad, either. I have seen our whole brother-in-law [all of him]. I don't know whether you are acquainted with him. Such an [ordinary] boy! Not even ugly, only too small and with a white head. But our sister Marya looks very sickly. I could not recognize her. Stefa is in good health, but she "lacks the fifth stave" [is crazy]. And Franciszka is sick of consumption. I don't know whether it will be possible to save her, because she has been ill for the whole winter and looks like a shadow. And she is our pride, endowed with knowledge and a clever mind. What faculties she possesses for learning and for everything! So, dear brother, we ought to make the greatest efforts to keep alive a sister whom we love exceedingly and who loves us. This is the result of my inquiries in the parental home. I write today letters to our parents also and to our aunt in Zambrów. Write to them also. I send them my photograph. Send yours also. I send my photograph also to you. Send me yours. . . . . You know the address of our aunt . . . . and I beg you, dear brother, [write to her]. She loves us so much though she never sees us. Be so good and God will reward you. This will be her whole comfort, because who can comfort her? She prays God for our health and good success. Don't forget her. I kiss you and shake your hand. Your loving brother forever.

STANISŁAW NUCZKOWSKI

May this letter warm your frozen blood! Let us live in love and concord, and God will help us.

4   PORĘBY WOLSKIE, January 30, 1910

"Praised be Jesus Christus."

DEAREST CHILDREN, AND PARTICULARLY YOU, DAUGHTER-IN-LAW: We write you the third letter and we have no answer from you. [Greetings; health; wishes.] We hope that this letter will come to you for February 16, and on February 16 is the day of St. Julianna, patron of our daughter-in-law. Well, we congratulate you, dear daughter-in-law, because it is your name-day. We wish you health and happiness and long life. May you never have any sorrow; may you love one another and live in concord and love; may our Lord God make you happy in human friendship; may you be happy and gay; may our Lord God supply all your wants; may you lack nothing; may our Lord God defend you against every evil accident and keep you in his protection and grant you his gifts, the heavenly dew and the earthly fat. May our Lord God give you every sweetness, make you happy, and save you from evil. This your father and mother wish you from their whole heart . . . . .

JAN AND EWA STELMACH

5   28, 1912

I am beginning this letter with the words: "Praised be Jesus Christus," and I hope that you will answer: "For centuries of centuries. Amen."

DEAREST OLEJNICZKA: I greet you from my heart, and wish you health and happiness. God grant that this little letter reaches you well, and as happy as the birdies in May.   This I wish you from my heart, dear Olejniczka.

> The rain is falling; it falls beneath my slipping feet.
> I do not mind; the post-office is near.
> When I write my little letter,
> I will flit with it there,
> And then, dearest Olejniczka,
> My heart will be light [from giving you a pleasure].
> In no grove do the birds sing so sweetly
> As my heart, dearest Olejniczka, for you.

Go, little letter, across the broad sea, for I cannot come to you. When I arose in the morning, I looked up to the heavens and thought to myself that to you, dearest Olejniczka, a little letter I must send.

Dearest Olejniczka, I left papa, I left sister and brother and you, to start out in the wide world, and today I am yearning and fading away like the world without the sun.   If I shall ever see you again, then, like a little child, of great joy I shall cry.   To your feet I shall bow low, and your hands I shall kiss.   Then you shall know how I love you, dearest Olejniczka.   I went up on a high hill and looked in that far direction, but I see you not, but I see you not, and I hear you not.

Dear Olejniczka, only a few words will I write.   As many sand-grains as there are in the field, as many drops of water in the sea, so many sweet years of life I, Walercia, wish you for the Easter holidays. I wish you all good, a hundred years of life, health, and happiness. And loveliness I wish you.   I greet you through the white lilies, I think of you every night, dearest Olejniczka.

Are you not in Bielice any more, or what?   Answer, as I sent you a letter and there is no answer.   Is there no one to write for you?

And now I write you how I am getting along.   I am getting along well, very well.   I have worked in a factory and I am now working in a hotel.   I receive 18 (in our money 32) dollars a month, and that is very good.   If you would like it, we could bring Wladzio over some day.   We eat here every day what we get only for Easter in our country.   We are bringing over Helena and brother now.   I had $120 and I sent back $90.

I have no more to write, only we greet you from our heart, dearest Olejniczka.   And the Olejniks and their children; and Władysław we greet;   and the Szases with their children;   and the Zwolyneks with their children; and the Grotas with their children, and the Gyrlas with their children; and all our acquaintances we greet.

My address: North America [etc.]

Goodbye.   For the present, sweet goodbye.

6   WÓLKA SOKOŁOWSKA, April 22

> I sit down at a table
> In a painted room.
> My table shakes.
> I write a letter to you, dear sister and
>   brother-in-law.
> A lily blossomed
> And it was the Virgin Mary.
> I dreamed thus
> That my heart was near yours.
> First we shall greet each other,
> But not with hands,
> Only with those godly words,
> The words "Praised be Jesus Christus."

I inform you now that it is cold here, hard to plant or to sow anything.   I beg you, don't be angry with me for not having answered you [for] so long, but I had no time.

Now I am writing to you, dear brother-in-law, with a smile, for when I read your letter, I laughed very much and I thought that you must have been in a good school since you knew so [well] how to compose that letter.   But all this [that you write] is nothing [cannot come to pass], for is there any boy quite ready to come [and to marry me]?

Now, dear sister Ulis, I inform you that Jasiek went to you and I remained at home, for we could not both go together.   And then, perhaps [sister] Hanka will get married, so there would be nobody to work.   Perhaps there will be a wedding [Hanka's] when everything is planted.   Now I beg you, dear brother-in-law, and you, Ulis, send me a few cents, for when I am a best maid, I should like to treat my . . . . [illegible word], and I have no money, for at home nothing can be earned.   And I think that you don't need much money yet, for you have no children.   Now I thank our Lord God that I have got such a good and funny brother-in-law, that we know how to speak to

each other in such a funny way in our letters.   When I am marrying
I will invite you to be my best man.   Now there won't be any war.
Now there is nothing more interesting at home, only we are in good
health, all of us, and we wish you the same.   Our cattle are healthy,
thanks to God.   There is nothing more to write.   When Hanusia is
married they will write for you [to come] and invite you. . . . .
[Greetings.]

[MAGDUSIA]

Now, dear [cousin] Jaguś, I write to you.   When father was once
in your mother's house, your mother talked much against you, for
when Makar was coming back to our country Józef [your husband]
wanted to give [send] trousers and a blouse, but you did not give
[them].   So your mother is angry with you.

7   April 6, 1914

Go, little letter, by railway
But don't go to the tavern, where people drink beer,
For if you went there, you would get drunk.
And you would never find the way to my sister,
Go, little letter, through fields and meadows
And when you reach Magdusia, kiss her hand.

And now "Praised be Jesus Christus" and Mary, his mother, for
she is worthy of it. . . . .

[JÓZEF DYBIEC]

8   BRANNAU, December 11, 1910

. . . . And now, beloved brother and dear brother-in-law,
On the solemn day of Christmas and New Year
I send wishes to your home,
And I beg you, beloved brother-in-law and sister and dear
brother,
Accept my wishes,
For I am of the same blood as you.
On this solemn day I am also rejoicing.
And if I live and come back, I shall wish you by words.
I think that I shall live to come back to you,
And I wish you to live until then,
And to congratulate together one another.

For the day of New Year I wish you everything;
May the Lord God bless you from His high heaven.
I wish you happiness and every good luck,
And, after death, in heaven a heavenly joy.
As many sands as there are in the sea, as many fishes in the
    rivers,
Even so much health and money I wish you.
As many drops as fall into the sea,
Even so much happiness may God grant you.
And now I wish you happy holidays
And a happy "Hey, kolenda, kolenda!"[1]
And may you live until a gay and happy New Year.
And may God grant you health and strength for work,
And may you earn much money.
And I wish you a fine and merry amusement
On Christmas day at the supper.
I will not write you more in verses,
For I have to write in other words [i.e., in prose].

. . . .

STANISŁAW DYBIEC

[1] Refrain of a Christmas song.

CORRESPONDENCE BETWEEN MEMBERS OF FAMILY-GROUPS

In addition to the exhibition of various attitudes these letters show the primitive familial organization in its relation to the problems which confront the group in the various situations of life. These situations are conditioned either by normal internal and external processes and events to which the familial organization was originally adapted—birth, growth, marriage, death of members of the group, normal economic conditions, traditional social environment, traditional religious life—or by new tendencies and new external influences to which the familial organization was not originally adapted, such as the increase of instruction and the dissemination of new ideas, economic and social advance, change of occupation, change of social environment through emigration to cities, to America, and to Germany, and contact with neighboring nationalities, mainly the Russian and German.

Materials of this character do not lend themselves to a strictly systematic arrangement, but the letters are arranged as far as possible with reference to the presentation of two questions: the dominant situation in which the group or its member finds itself, and the progressive disintegration of the family-group.

BOREK SERIES

We place first a short series of letters written by children. The girl, Bronisława, is about seventeen years old, the boy, Józef, thirteen or fourteen. The business part of the letters is evidently written at the request of the parents. The Polish of the letters is very interesting, typically peasant, without the slightest influence of the literary language; even many phonetic peculiarities find their expression in the spelling. This proves that the writers, particularly the girl, who is the principal author, are untouched by new cultural influences. And indeed for a Polish reader Bronisława appears as a perfect type of a plain peasant girl in all her attitudes and interests. And this is the more noticeable because in the same village and vicinity live families who, particularly in the younger generation, are to a great extent outside and partly above the traditional peasant set of attitudes. This proves how individualized and variable is the influence of modern life upon the peasant milieu; we meet wide variations even within a single family.

The particular freshness and vividness of interest toward all the elementary problems of communal, familial, and personal life shown in this series—typical for the peasant, though in the case of Bronisława due in part to the fact that the girl is passing from childhood to womanhood—may be compared both with the Markiewicz series (Nos. 142 ff.), where many interests have been developed under the influence of instruction, and with the Kanikuła series where the lack of interest in the communal life results in an intellectual dulness which hinders the persons from becoming interested in the variety of situations which even the simplest life involves.

Another point of special interest in this series is the early fixation of attitudes in the peasant child. In a "primary" group like the peasant community the schematization of life in its main outlines is relatively fixed and simple, and the attitudes and values involved are universally and uncritically accepted. The child, as we may note in these letters, participates freely in the interests of the family and the community and acquires at a tender age the elements of a very stubborn conservatism.

9–16, FROM BRONISŁAWA AND JÓZEF BOREK IN POLAND TO THEIR BROTHER IN AMERICA

9   DOBRZYKÓW, October 9, 1913, month 10th

DEAR BROTHER: [Usual greetings and wishes; letters received and sent.] As to this Alliance, you can inscribe yourself [become a member], for you may be in danger of life.[1] Moreover, you will receive a paper, you will have something to read. In our whole parish there is no news. The priest is building a barn and is calling for money. The organist is already consecrated as priest. He was here in Dobrzyków. In Gombin they are building the basement of the church. In Dobrzyków they sing very beautifully [in the choir]. They want to build schools in the commune of Dobrzyków,[2] but people don't want to agree, because it would be very expensive for every morg [taxes being paid in proportion to land]. Nothing good happened here. It rains more than in any year. [Crops and farm-work.] We should have harvested everything, but we had to work back [pay back with work] for the horses which they [our neighbors] lent us to plow. When we were digging [potatoes], an accident happened. Our hog broke his leg. And, in general, times are sad, it is autumn, it rains continually, and everything is very sad. My

---

[1] The Polish National Alliance in America insures its members. But the plan of life insurance is little known among the peasants, and in this case the girl seems to assume that the insurance of life would protect from death.

[2] The result of a new law permitting every commune to have as many schools as it determined, and assuring certain governmental help. This led to an agitation among the peasants by the intelligent classes for the development of public instruction. (See Vol. IV.)

dear brother, I am also weary [with staying] at home. And now, we beg you, send us as soon as possible any money which you can, for we need it very much. . . . . And now you have a new suit, so send us your photograph, for I am curious to see. . . . . Grodny's [daughter] Ewka is going to America, also to Chicago. She boasted that she is going to a sweetheart. She told it only to me, but people are also talking about it. Amen.   [BRONISŁAWA]

10   October 26, 1913

. . . . DEAR BROTHER: . . . . We received the money, 100 roubles, for which we thank you heartily. . . . . With [sister] Michalina it is as it was. She has no wish to marry this one, she waits for another. And now we inform you what we did with this money. We gave the Markiewiczs those 50 roubles back with interest, and to the [commune] office a payment and interest. You asked for our advice, dear brother, whether you ought to inscribe yourself in the alliance. [Repeats the advice of the preceding letter.] When you send money, now, it will be for Michalina [i.e., dowry]. We are very satisfied that our Lord God helps you, so that people even envy you. What are the wages for girls? What could I earn? Although you work much, yet at least you earn well.

I [Józef] have an accordeon, and I assist at the holy Mass. Mother bought me a surplice. Bronisława goes to the choir and sings. Now it is sad here, because autumn came.

I, Bronisława, and I, Józef, beg you, dear brother, with our whole heart, send us 10 roubles for a gramophone. Now I inform you, dear brother, that I long very much for you, because I never see you. I have tears in my eyes always whenever I remember you.[1]

                                [BRONISŁAWA]

11   December 23, 1913, month 12th

. . . . DEAR BROTHER: . . . . We received your letter. . . . . We were very sad, particularly Brońcia [Bronisława] and I, Józef, that you did not write for so long a time. . . . . We have now not so much work. . . . . We have holidays. It will be very merry for us,

---

[1] Certainly the longing is sincere, but it is here naïvely used to make the brother more favorable to the request. We see in it the germ of the policy of Kozłowska. (Cf. that series.)

for now they [the season-workers] have come from Prussia, so there are many people in our village. We have no horse, for we don't need it any more. Our young cow will calve soon. After Christmas we shall thresh the rest of the rye. We killed the pig for ourselves. . . . . There is no news now. . . . . In carnival perhaps there will be more news. [Marriages enumerated.]

There is a blacksmith who wants to buy the forge. . . . . Do you order us to sell it or not, for he is waiting. . . . . We ask you, dear brother, whether you write letters to Bugel's daughter, for Bugel boasted to our father that she intends to wait for you. Władysława Jarosińska boasts also [that you write to her]. Bronka [Bronisława] is curious what work she will do in America and what weather is there now. We thank you for this gift which you intend to send us. When you send it, address it to Bronka's name, or else they [the parents] will take it. Now I, Józef, know already how to assist very nicely at the Mass in Latin. And the singers [women] sing beautiful Christmas songs. Our priest built a very nice barn. And in Gombin they built a barn for people [to worship], because only the basement of the church is ready. And Walenty Ostroski began to go [to the church] and to sing, but he had no voice.

And I, Bronisława, will probably visit you in the spring, for we don't know with certainty whether Michalina will get married or not. I, Bronisława, I could marry if I wanted to take the first man, but I won't marry just anybody. Szymański's son wants to marry me, and perhaps it would be well for me, because he will take me to Warsaw, to [set up] a shop or restaurant. But I don't want him, for he is crippled. I have another who turns my head, but only when he comes back from the army. If Michalina marries, I will also marry. But I am not in a hurry to get married. Did I merit with God nobody more than him [the cripple]? Our Lord God will help me to get somebody else. I hide myself from him, but he comes to me nevertheless, and brings with him more boys from the mills. We ask you whether Witkowski has children in America, or some additional wife? . . . . Alina Krajeska brought a small Prussian for herself [had an illegal child in Prussia]. We inform you, brother, what a good father we have. He lives like a king, and we all—you know how it was before? Well, now it is still worse. It is hard, much to complain of on all sides. . . . .

I, BRONISŁAWA and JÓZEF BOREK

12   February 10, 1914

. . . . I, Bronisława, received 10 roubles and 1 copeck, for which I thank you heartily, dear brother. Now we inform you that the wedding [of Michalina] has been celebrated already on the day of Our Lady of the Thunder-Candles,[1] at 5 o'clock in the afternoon. Very few guests were in our house, only 60. There were 4 musicians. The music was very beautiful. The musicians were strangers, from Wyków. There were 8 best men and 8 best girls. . . . . The wedding was very merry, so that even grandmother and grandfather danced. [Enumerates other weddings.] We were at the *poprawiny* [supplementary dancing; literally, "repairing"; a festival to compelte a former one] in Trosin, in the house of the parents of our brother-in-law. He is a great success for us. Their fortune is big enough. . . . . If you did not send those 100 roubles, don't send them now, only together [with the next] in March, because we don't need them now. Don't be afraid, you can send this money, we won't waste it, we shall lend it at interest. We have nothing more to write, only we salute you. Brother-in-law and Michalina salute you. And now we will write you who was with us at the wedding. [Enumerates.] And others also, but we won't express [name] any more. The family of our brother-in-law is orderly and full of character and agreeable and good. The brother-in-law's brother has an accordeon of one and a half tunes [octaves?], worth 40 roubles. He plays and sings very nicely. Michalina is greatly respected, all his brothers kiss her hand. . . . .

[BRONISŁAWA and JÓZEF]

13   February 26, 1914

. . . . DEAR BROTHER: . . . . Our young cow calved on February 18. Grandfather and grandmother promise to will their land to Michalina, from April 1. They are to live in the grandparents' house, to give them to eat and 1 rouble every week. Our young cow calved, had a she-calf. We shall keep her. And you, Władzio, don't be afraid that we shall lose this money; we won't waste it, we won't spend it on drinking; when you come back, you will have this money. . . . . Michalina collected 25 roubles for her caul.

And I, Michalina Jasińska, thank you for the forge which you gave me for my caul, and also for those 100 roubles which you intend

---

[1] So called because of the ceremony of the consecration of candles supposed to avert thunder-stroke.

to send me for the wedding, although you did not send them. . . . .
We borrowed 100 roubles from Markiewicz, but this money we paid
back to K. . . . . With the money which I collected for my caul I
bought for myself a feather-cover, 3 pillows, and I paid 2 roubles to
the cook. There were gaps enough which I had to stop. Only 10
roubles were left, and they want me to give even them, grandfather
for a horse, and father for flour. Well, I got married, it is true, but
I am neither upon water nor upon ice [not settled]. . . . .

And now I write, Bronisława B. . . . . In our choir there are
few girls left, for the others got married. [Enumerates these.] On the
last day of carnival we were in Trosinek [with the parents of the
brother-in-law]—our brother-in-law, Michalina, grandfather and I.
His brothers respect me much. His brother played the accordeon, and
I played also. They were at our house on Sunday. People envy us
very much because of this luck. Now our brother-in-law is in our
house, and later perhaps he will be in grandfather's house, for grandfather cannot work. And perhaps he will will him [his farm], for he
pleased grandfather much. And I, Bronka, shall be at home, for
you write, dear brother, that in America it is bad. Don't grieve, dear
brother, about me, I shall get married even in our country, since
Michalina is already married.[1] But I will wait until you come from
America, for I desire either you, dear brother, to be at my wedding,
or myself to be at yours. Either I will be best girl at your wedding
or you shall be best man at mine.

We are very satisfied that Michalina got married, only we were
very sorry that you were not at the wedding. His brothers are so
agreeable that nobody could be ashamed of them. They greet us
while they are still far from us. The youngest of them is 20 years old.
From this money I, Bronka, bought myself stuff for a dress, and I,
Józef, a suit, and we gave mother the rest. Michalina had a white
dress at her wedding. Three carriages went to the wedding. I greet
you, I, Bronisława, and I, Józef.

14 May 19, 1914

. . . . We thank you, dear brother, for your photograph, and
father asks you for money—to send some to us. If you cannot send
more, send at least 100 roubles for the Markiewiczs, and if you can

---

[1] The younger daughter customarily waits for the marriage of the older, and
parents usually refuse to let the younger daughter be married first.

send more, send more. We should lend it . . . . in a very sure place. . . . . Markiewicz [Stanisław] from Zazdzierz came on May 15 [from America], and gave us money, 2 roubles. . . . . I, Józef, thank you for these 2 roubles. . . . . Our brother-in-law got acquainted with Michalina as boys usually do with girls, as you did with Buglówna. Dear Władzio, Bugiel boasts that Staśka is to wait for you. But she is sick with consumption. . . . . If our Lord God allows you to come back, you could marry where Wiktor Markiewicz did. He wishes you to marry there [his wife's sister]. And of those singers none sings any more, because they quarrelled with the organist and the priest, and now others are learning. I go to sing whenever I have time, and later perhaps I shall go weeding. . . . . I shall earn at least enough to buy slippers.　　　　BRONISŁAWA

15　　　　　　　　　　　　　　　　　June 5, 1914

DEAR BROTHER: . . . . We received money, 500 roubles, for which we thank you heartily. . . . . Michalina and our brother-in-law are leaving us. They will rent a lodging, because the old ones [grandparents] won't take her yet. Now we inform you what was the news at Pentecost: a merry-go-round, a theater, 12 crosses [processions], many of them from far away.　　　　[JÓZEF]

I, Bronisława Borek, write to you a few words, dear brother. About money I shall write later on, where we lend it, for now we don't know yet. And so, my dear brother, our father cannot come to an understanding with our brother-in-law. I am very ashamed and pained, and I don't know how it will be further. I will write you more, for I have nobody to whom to complain. I will go soon to work, for 4 weeks. . . . . Władysław Żabka writes me letters from the army. He wants to marry me when he comes in autumn from the army, but I don't want to. I should prefer some craftsman, and I will wait until I get some craftsman. . . . .[1]　　　　[BRONISŁAWA]

16　　　　　　　　　　　　　　　　　July 23, 1914

DEAR BROTHER: . . . . Your money is lent. Jan Gołębiewski borrowed 100 roubles and Jan Switkowski 300 roubles. We have notes. . . . . Now we inform you about our farm-stock. We have

---

[1] Because she wants to go to the city.

2 cows and one she-calf from the young cow. Father bought a cow for Michalina . . . . and they were to go and rent a lodging, but they sold the cow and took the money and don't go anywhere. . . . . Michalina does not want to buy a cow for herself, but they began to trade in pigs and orchards. For me, Józef, they [the parents] bought nice shoes, but only a cotton-suit, for there was not enough left for a cloth-suit. Father hardly could calculate. . . . .

[Józef]

And now I, Bronisława, write you a few words, dear brother. . . . . We inform you what father did with these 100 roubles. He bought a cow for Michalina, a horse [for himself] and made the payment in the [communal-bank] office. We gave Michalina a cow once, but we won't give her one a second time. You have sent us already 600 and 12 roubles. Dear brother, we thank you very much for the money which you sent. People marvel much, that our Lord God helps you so, and they envy. Don't grieve that a single grosz will be lost. When you return, all this will be given back to you. . . . . I intended to send you wishes for your name-day, but I was not at home, I was working on the other side of the Vistula. I have worked for 5 weeks. I earned enough to buy a nice velvet dress and slippers, and I have also a watch. Perhaps later I will send you a photograph of my person. I am not going to sing any more, for I have no time. . . . . Although I am tired with work and burned with the sun, at least I have something to dress myself in. . . . . Michalina is with us, but for the winter we want her to go away, because it is too difficult to live all together. . . . .[1] Dear brother, I would ask you, I, Bronisława, be so kind and add some money for a sewing-machine for me. . . . . I will now go to work, I will work for some weeks, and if you offer me anything I could buy one. . . . . But if you offer me anything, send it to my name, because those 10 roubles our parents took. . . . .

[Bronisława]

[1] Michalina's grandfather was evidently expected to retire and will her the farm, but he declined to do this and her father, counting on the grandfather's help, had failed to provide her with a sufficient dowry. So the young people find themselves in a difficult situation. We see here, as elsewhere, that the retirement of the old people is a necessary link in the familial organization.

WRÓBLEWSKI SERIES

The Wróblewskis live in the northeastern part of ethnographical Poland, in a relatively poor province. The family (whose real name we do not use) belongs to the peasant nobility and is relatively well instructed. It has lived in the same village since at least the fifteenth century. Twelve neighboring villages are chiefly occupied by descendants of the same ancestors, though their names have been partly diversified. The community of origin has probably been in a large measure forgotten.

The main figure of the series is Walery Wróblewski, the author of most of the letters. His letters belong almost exclusively to the informing and relating type; their function is to keep up the familial connection between Walery and his brothers by sustaining and developing a common "universe of discourse" and a sphere of common interests. Thanks to this, the letters become particularly valuable for us. They give us, indeed, a full account of the fundamental life-interests of Walery, who in this respect represents very well the normal Polish peasant.

The essential interest is clearly that of work, particularly of personal work. The salaried labor (as gardener at the governmental railway-station) plays in Walery's life a purely additional part and is done merely for the sake of money, while his life-business is farm-work. It is the same with the average Polish peasant, with whom even the difference between farm-work and salaried work is frequently expressed in a separation of economic aims: the farm has to give *living* for the whole family (lodging, board, fuel), better or worse according to its size, the value of the soil, etc., while any *cash* needed for clothes, pleasures, ceremonies, etc., has to be earned outside, by salaried work, either on a neighboring estate or through season-emigration. A peasant who does not need additional income from his own or his children's paid labor is above the normal; a peasant who needs additional income for living is on the edge between the farmer-class and the country proletariat.[1]

But the curious point in the present case is that the interest in work as such is already independent of its economic purpose, and that this independent interest is shown only with regard to the farm-work. Walery puts his whole life into farming, house-building, etc., and does not care much about his salaried work, in spite of the fact that the farm is not his own, while the money which he earns is his personal property. He complains continually about his insecure situation, and still he works for the pleasure of work. The interest is objectified. The same objectification is shown in his eagerness to learn everything about the farming of his brothers in America.

The second fundamental set of interests is that of the family. It happens that we find here most of the possible familial situations:

1. Walery's relation to his father and brothers on the ground of the problem of inheritance. In this relation Walery, the oldest brother, as against the father and partly against Feliks, represents the old principles of familial solidarity—according to which the family should act harmoniously as a whole, and the father should pursue the interests of this whole, not his own egotistic ends—and of justice—according to which the economic problems should be settled upon a moral as against a merely legal basis. This relation is expanded and complicated by the new marriage of the father. The stepmother is not an isolated individual, but the member of another family, and the

[1] Cf. Introduction: "Economic Attitudes."

antagonism of interests prevents absolutely her assimilation to her husband's family. On the contrary, as no harmonious coexistence of the two families is possible, it is the husband, Walery's father, who loses all connection with his own family and becomes assimilated to his wife's family.

2. Purely sentimental and intellectual relation between Walery and Antoni.

3. Walery's relation to his first wife through her sickness and death. (See notes.)

4. Walery's relation to his stepdaughter Olcia—an economic and sentimental problem. (See notes.)

5. Walery's relation to his children, and the evolution which goes on under the influence of changes in the economic situation and of the progressive manifestation of the character of the children. He continues to work on the farm for their sake and out of interest in work; but his feelings change. As long as his first wife lives his paternal attitude is perfectly normal; he is the head and representative of the family. After her death he becomes merely a guardian, and his security and authority are shaken. But the children are small, and they may be as poor as he, for half of the farm belongs to Olcia, and thus a feeling of pity keeps his paternal attitude definite and strong. After the death of Olcia his children are the only rightful proprietors of the farm. But as they become older his personal situation isolates itself in his mind from that of his children, and a slight antagonism appears between himself and the oldest son, though he still hopes that the latter will eventually take the farm and care for him in his old age. Finally he marries again, new children appear, it becomes evident that his son cannot be expected to take him and his new wife and children, and his interests become almost completely dissociated from those of the children of his first wife. The

sentimental connection is the only one left and even this seems weakened in the last letters.

6. Walery's relation to his second wife. (See notes.)

7. Walery's relation to his sister-in-law, Feliks' wife. This is only sketched, but in very distinct lines. There is a marked mutual hostility whose immediate cause is certainly economic antagonism, but it is prepared by the total estrangement resulting from the long separation and the quite different conditions in which Feliks and his family have lived. These facts illustrate two very general phenomena: (1) As we see in many letters, even a normal relation through marriage (to say nothing of an abnormal one like that resulting from the third marriage of Walery's father) is ceasing more and more to produce a connection between the persons thus allied; acquaintance and friendship, if not community of interest, are necessary to consolidate the relation. In other words, the assimilation of a new member has become more difficult and longer since the old type of peasant family began to disintegrate. (2) The estrangement brought by emigration to Russia is much more profound than that resulting from emigration to America. This difference, it seems, is due to the fact that emigration to America has become a more normal and ordinary course, always with the expectation of return, and that the emigrant is more or less identified in America with strong and numerous Polish communities. At any rate, the Russian life, with its weaker familial organization, exerts a more disorganizing influence on the emigrant. Another good example of this is found in the Raczkowski series, letters of Ludwik Wolski.

With regard to the religious interests, Walery's attitude is also the typical attitude of the modern peasant. His religious life, while very strong, has mainly a social form. The individual relation to the Divinity, as expressed in prayer, vision, ecstacy, feeling of subordination, etc., is quite secondary as compared with the social side of religious reality—meetings, public service, church-building, priest-hood, etc. We find the former attitude only once clearly expressed (No. 37). There are but slight traces of the old naturalistic religious system and little interest in the magical system.

The social interests of Walery are limited practically to his relations with neighbors and acquaintances. He does not seem to play any active part in the political organization and activity of his commune—the only political group in which a peasant can be active. But he is interested as an observer in general social and political phenomena, upon which he can exert not the slightest influence. The form of this inter-est is also typical for the peasant of the present time; it marks the transition from a total lack of such interests to the effort to influence practically the political and social organization, as we already find it among the city workers and to some extent among the peasants, and expressed in socialistic, nationalistic, and economic associations.

The interest in plays and amusements is not strong in Walery, and is never so in peasants of his age, burdened by the heavy task of life. Social entertainments are, in fact, the only form of recreation which a peasant knows—besides drinking and card-playing, which may be regarded also as forms of social entertainment, and in this character (not as independent amusements) are morally permitted. The variety of amusements is much greater among city workers. Nevertheless in the case of Walery we find a relatively new amusement—photography.

Walery's purely theoretic interests are turned toward natural, particularly cosmic, facts. It may be noted that in general popular books on natural sciences are the favorite reading of the peasants.

We notice an absolute lack of one interest which prevails in many other series—the one which we may term the "climbing" tendency. Walery does not try to get into a higher class, although the fact that he is a skilled workman (gardener) and the relative degree of his instruction would enable him to do this more easily than could many others.

The lack of this tendency may be explained by the exceptional social conservatism prevailing among the peasant nobility of this province. Living for centuries in analogous conditions, with very few opportunities to rise to the level of the middle nobility, particularly since a political career was closed after Poland's partition, and economic advance hindered by overpopulation, poor soil, and lack of industry in this province, lacking the incentive to advance which was given to the peasants proper by liberation and later by endowment with land, the peasant nobility is more stabilized in its class-isolation than any other of the old classes. And there is little to achieve within the community by climbing. Walery tries perhaps to be the first of his village, but rather by personal qualities than by social or economic influence.

He has some pride in his work, in his house, and his garden-products, but no vanity. And in general, the problem of social hierarchy seems hardly to exist for him. No determined attitude toward the higher classes is ever expressed.

The only other type more or less definitely outlined in these letters is that of the father. His fundamental feature, by which his whole behavior is explained, is the powerful desire to live a personal life up to the end, in spite of the tradition which requires the father to be the bearer of the familial idea and to resign his claims on the control of economic and general familial matters when he is partly invalided by age and unable to manage those matters for the greatest benefit of the family.[1] In his struggle against this tradition, the old Wróblewski finally has no course other than to resign completely his place in his own family. In fact he becomes a stranger, and can thus live an unimpeded personal life. By marriage he gets, it is true, into another family, but the latter has no claims upon him.

The other characters, as far as determined in the material, seem perfectly clear.

THE FAMILY WRÓBLEWSKI

Wróblewski, a farmer
His second wife
"Klimusia," his third wife
Walery, his son
Józef, his son
Antoni (Antoś), his son (lives in America)
Konstanty (Kostuś), his son (lives in America)
Feliks, his son (lives in Russia)
Walery's first wife
Anna P., Walery's second wife
Feliks' wife
Józef's wife _____

Olcia (Aleksandra), daughter of Walery's first wife

Edward
Wacław } Walery's children by his first wife
Józia
Michał

17–57, FROM WALERY AND JÓZEF WRÓBLEWSKI IN POLAND, TO THEIR BROTHERS IN AMERICA: 17–54, FROM WALERY; 55–57, FROM JÓZEF.

17   ŁAPY, January 2, 1906

. . . . DEAR BROTHERS: [Usual greetings and generalities about health.] Your letter of October 29 I received on December 30. It traveled for about 2 months, and perhaps it lay in the post-offices,

[1] In this regard there is a striking likeness between himself and Franciszka Kozłowska (cf. that series), with this difference, that Kozłowska, as a woman, was never called upon to be the representative of the familial idea.

because there has been a strike.   All the trains stopped for more than a week, and afterward in the post and telegraph service there was a strike for 3 weeks.   "Strike" means in our language "bezrobocie" and in Russian "zabastowka" ["stopping of work"].   It happens now very often among us, particularly in factories.   Workmen put forward their demands.   They want higher pay and a shorter working-day; they refuse to work more than 8 hours a day.   Now everything has become terribly dear, particularly with shoemakers and tailors. . . . . Even now there is no order in the country, the whole time tumults about liberty are going on, because on October 30 the Highest Manifesto was proclaimed concerning personal inviolability, liberty of the press, etc.   In a word, by favor of the monarch we have more liberty, because we are citizens of the country, not as formerly, when we were only subjects; now we are all equal in the country.   Papers are published without censure, so they now write more truth, only all this is not yet fixed.   The liberty of speech has also been given by the Highest Manifesto, and for this reason different songs are sung, as "Boże, coś Polskę. . . . . "   In short, thanks to God, conditions would not be bad, but still much trouble can happen, because there is no peace in the land, and even terrible things happen, as in Moscow and many other towns. . . . . [1]

[1] The revolution of 1905–6 contributed greatly to the development of social consciousness and interest in political problems among the peasants.   Up to this time those interests in Russian Poland were developed artificially, by patriotic agitation from the intelligent classes.   Indeed, the relative simplicity and isolation of peasant life, together with the bureaucratic organization of the Russian state made it hardly possible for the peasant to understand that there was any relation between the real interests of his life and the more general political problems.   The communal self-government allowed, within certain limits, the settlement of most of the problems of everyday life, but outside of the commune the peasant had no influence upon social and political life, and thus all the phenomena whose source lay in the state and in the economic organization—law, military service, taxes, school-organization, official language, means of communication, prices of natural and manufactured products—appeared to him as regulated once and forever by a superior and undetermined force.   His attitude toward them was more or less like his attitude toward the weather—fundamentally passive resignation, with some-times an attempt to influence with prayer or gift the powers in their treatment of the individual's own sphere of interests.   (Cf. Introduction: "Social Environment".) The revolution of 1905–6 showed the peasant that this assumed order is modifiable and may be influenced directly and in its organization by human will; it showed at the same time unknown and unsuspected relations between many apparently abstract problems and the facts of everyday life.

At last I received your letter which I awaited so impatiently. . . . . It is not right not to write for so long a time; for more than half a year we had no news from you. We don't ask you to send us money, because we still live as we can, but we request you to send letters more often; other people send them every month or even more often. Although they don't know how to write themselves, still they give news and ask for information about what is going on at home. I believe that you are interested to know, particularly now. . . . . Józef was somewhat offended by your letter. It was impossible to avoid it. I had to give him the letter to read; if I had not, he would have said that we have a secret, and this ought not to be among us.[1] As to your coming, do as you wish, only reflect about it and write us positively this or that, because the farm cannot remain as it is now. If you don't intend to come, Feliks will agree to return, but I believe that he is too weak for farm-work. Nevertheless there seems to be no other way, because it will be difficult to repair the losses. I intend also to leave my position soon and to stay at home, because it is very difficult [to be employed and to farm together]. It will be worse at home for some years, I know it surely, but later on perhaps it will get better, if our Lord God helps, because "It is better to be in a sheep-skin with God than in a fur-cloak without God," and "As Kuba behaves toward God, so God behaves toward Kuba."[2] I sold the oxen in the fall and I bought one cow. I intend to buy one more in order to have 4. I intend to sell one horse and to buy another, because this one is bad for plowing, and I intend to plow with horses. I will keep two cows for myself and sell the milk of the two others. I bought also 7 geese; I don't know how they will breed. I intend also to carry out my plan of building a house.

[1] This is the last, reasoned explanation of the original and unreasoned fact that the letter is not individual but familial property. In this fact is to be found the fundamental function of the peasant letter in general—retaining or re-establishing the connection of the individual with the family-group when this connection has been weakened by separation.

[2] The confidence in God as shown in the belief that God will interfere practically in human business is naturally more developed in isolated communities with little practical energy and a slow rate of life, and decreases near the industrial centers and in active and evolving communities. It is of interest that Walery, himself a very active person, still retains the attitude of religious fatalism perfectly adapted to the low intensity of the practical life of his environment but unadapted to his own character.

Edward is going this year to school in Łapy; I pay now for his learning 50 copecks monthly, but when I leave my position [as gardner of the governmental railway-station] probably they will demand more. Both my horses had the strangles, and now they look bad. The winter up to Christmas was light. Now, since New Year, the weather is colder; it is already possible to go on sledges. . . . . I don't remember whether I have written about building a church in Łapy. They intend to build first a chapel, and later on, when they have money, a church. . . . . In our mill we grind corn, father for himself and I for myself, when the one or the other has time. Now I send you a salutation from us, and the children salute you—Aleksandra, Waclawa, Edward, Józefa and Michal. We wish you every good. May God grant it.

W. WRÓBLEWSKI

18
February 8, 1906

DEAR BROTHERS ANTOŚ AND KOSTUŚ: . . . . Now I inform you, that I will probably remain at my post, although I am not very glad because I don't know when I shall be able to do something for myself [build the house]. Every year I hope to do it and I cannot. Now also I was sure that I should remain at home, and a week ago I thanked for [resigned] my place. They gave me one day for reflection, and after this they were to say something to me. One day, then another, then a week passed and they said nothing. I was sure that they were trying to find somebody else. I was sure because last year it seemed as if they intended to change me, although when I thanked them they said that they were satisfied with me. After more than a week, when I went to the office for a ticket to go to Warsaw, the chief asked me whether I intended to remain or not. I said that I could remain on different conditions, but I did not hope to obtain them. I asked for some improvements in the service, and moreover for fuel. The chief said that he was willing to grant it. If so, I will remain, but I am not sure, because meanwhile it is only a promise; if they don't fulfil it, I will not serve.

Everything else is unchanged. Father still provides for himself at home. He has threshed all his grain, but he has not yet brought the hay from the riverside, and now it is impossible to get through to the riverside, and I don't know how it will be, because now we have successively two days of frost and three days of rain. But when summer comes I don't know how we shall do. I don't know whether Feliks will come or not, and father probably won't be able to keep the farm alone. If Feliks does not come, I don't know what will result, because father does not promise to work any longer on the farm. Perhaps he will finally sell it, although he could take somebody to help him, because he has money enough, but he does not intend to do it. . . . . On my farm there is also nobody to work. I thought that I should do it myself, but now nothing is certain; on the other hand, I want very much this little money which I can earn. . . . . Now the church in Płonka has been robbed. . . . . The thief stole into the church in the evening, was shut in there, took the money and fled through the window. . . . . We have no weddings here, although it is carnival. . . . .

W. Wróblewski

19 April 2, 1906

Dear Brothers: . . . . We will divide with you in thought at least the consecrated food [święcone]. It is a pity that you will probably have no święcone, because you are surely far away from the church. Well, it cannot be helped; you will probably only remember our country and nothing more.[1] But perhaps our Lord God will allow you to return happily; then we shall rejoice. . . . .

As to the money, when I receive it I will do as you wrote; I will give 10 roubles to father and will keep by me the remaining 240, or I will put it somewhere until you come back. Meanwhile my children thank their uncle for the remembrance and the promise. Spring approaches, but although it is already April, weather is bad, it snows every day. Some people have seen storks already; they must be wretched, walking upon white [snow].[2] As I wrote, I have sold the oxen and bought a cow; I wanted also to buy another, but there has been no opportunity, because cows are bad and very dear. I have sold also the horse which you bought, for 62 roubles, and I have

---

[1] The Easter wishes, dividing the "święcone" with the thought of absent relatives, are evidently means of preserving the family connection in spite of separation, and in the particular form which this connection assumes in group-festivals.

[2] An example of the sympathy of the peasant with animals. The peasant stories show that this sympathy developed to a very high degree. Spontaneous to some degree, it is also a vestige of the naturalistic religious system.

bought another for 64 roubles. He is 4 years old, of the same color as the other; it would even be difficult to distinguish them, because the movement is also the same, only the other had white fetlocks on his hind legs, and this one is a little longer. I intend to plow with him and the two-year-old. Adam Drop from Pluśniaki promises to plow. I bought this horse in Skwarki in the neighborhood where Frania Perkoska, the daughter of Wojciech, is now with her husband. I don't know whether I have written you, she married Kleofas Gołaszewski. When you go from us to Sokoły, you have to turn near their barn, at the left, on the corner. . . . .[1] The wedding was in the last days of carnival and we were there at dinner. During the dinner I played on the phonograph of Józik; he lent me it for that time. He bought it in Warsaw and he has a score of different songs and marches.

Now I don't know whether I have written you about the misfortune from which only our Lord God kept our father. At the end of the carnival thieves came to steal horses, and father slept in the barn near the granary. He heard something tapping and got up and stepped out of the door. He saw something black under the wall and called, "Who is there?" The man shot with a revolver, but happily he missed. They ran. There were two of them. On the next day people found the bullet in the door. Father made a noise, and came to us and awoke us and other people, but they were not to be found. They went to Płonka, stole a horse and a wagon of grain and disappeared. So the misfortune ended. At present there are terrible thefts and robberies in our country. Highwaymen attack people on the roads and rob them, and in towns robbers come to houses, kill or threaten with revolvers, take whatever they can and usually disappear without any trace. And all this goes on since the strikes of the last year. Many factories stopped, workmen were turned out, and that is the cause of the present robberies.[2]

[1] This kind of detailed information reminding the absent member of the family of the environment in which the family lives has evidently the function of keeping up the old common "universe of discourse" and thus maintaining the familial connection.

[2] The real cause was evidently different. Although lack of work may have played a certain rôle in recruiting the bands of robbers, the fundamental reason was the disorganization of social and moral life brought by the new ideals, which for the mass of the people were not equivalent to the traditional social constraint in organizing practical life. (Cf. notes to Jasiński series, Nos. 757 ff.)

After the holidays brother Feliks is coming to the farm, but mainly because he has no church there and nowhere to teach the children. But I believe that it will be too difficult for him to work on a farm. Well, but he cannot remain there either, because of what I have said.

Now I inform you that in our holy Roman Catholic faith a new sect, heresy or falling-off has arisen, and the priests themselves produce it. The papers write that there are 50 to 70 such priests who call themselves "Maryawitas," and the people have nicknamed them "Mankietniks." They regard some girl, a "tertiary," as a saint, She dictates to them her different visions, and they believe her; they won't listen to their bishops, and they proclaim a doctrine about her— that she was immaculately conceived. They have drawn some parishes to their side; people believe their erroneous teaching. This happens in the neighborhood of Płock, on the other side of Warsaw from us. Those priests say three masses every day. The bishop sent priests to close and seal these churches, but the Maryawitas beat the true priests and did not allow them to close [the churches]. All this is going on at present. It is a she-devil, as a bishop writes, a certain Felicia Kozłowska, seamstress of priest-clothes, and therefore it is clear that young priests favor her. It is a horror to read in papers what is going on there; perhaps the end of the world is not far away.[1]

I wrote you what I could about our country, although in short, for if I wanted to write in detail, I should need many sheets of paper. Now, please, write us about the mines. How are the passages to them made under the earth? Are there any props? What happens when coal is dug out—whether they [the passages] fall in or stand? In short, whatever may be new for us. . . . .[2]

W. WRÓBLEWSKI

[1] The sect of the "Maryawitas" represented the first heresy in which the peasants had taken part for centuries. We shall have more details of this in Part II. The "end of the world" is assumed whenever any great and general demoralization is noticed. It is of course dependent upon the eschatological Christian ideas.

[2] Here, as in many other similar questions, it seems as if the interest of the writer were purely objective, i.e., not determined by the fact that the conditions about which he asks are those in which his relatives live. But the *effect* is evidently the constitution of a new common field of intellectual life and thus the maintenance of the group-connection, whether this was the conscious aim or not.

20   April 25, 1906

DEAR BROTHERS: . . . . I have remained in service. Here we have full spring; people sow in the field oats, peas and potatoes, trees blossom, storks, swallows and other birds have come back. I am waiting now for brother Feliks. He has already thanked for [resigned] his place and is waiting only for his pay and tickets for the journey. They will come very soon   Father looks for help every day. Now I send you some photographs made [by myself] at Easter. [Description of the photographs.] We know from the papers that a terrible misfortune has happened in California, in the city San Francisco. May God keep us and you from this! [Salutations.]

W. WRÓBLEWSKI

21   May 12, 1906

DEAR BROTHER: . . . . I don't wonder that you wrote so [being ill], but I don't know why Kostuś . . . . presented me to you in such a manner, as if I had done some mischief to him. He ought to understand that you, being sick, could not bear all this; in other conditions [you would look upon it] as a trifle. But in human life the road is not always strewn with flowers; there are many different thorns upon it.[1]

Now you know, probably, that I remain at home on my farm. Work is going on in the field, we are planting potatoes, and when we finish planting, we will set to building the house. I cannot buy that field from Tomasz Pal. After a long reflection he said finally, that he would sell it, but only if I gave him 150 roubles for the field near the garden. I offered him 80 roubles, but he does not agree. Later I heard from his servant that he would part with it for 100 roubles, but I am not in a hurry, because it would be too expensive. I could pay so much only if I had as much money as he has.

Now I inform you that Jan Głuchy came back from America and intends to build his house in the garden near Staś. Before he came back, his wife wanted to build some sort of shack, but Filuś did not want to give her a lot. He proposed the lot near my garden. . . . . but it was too small for her. She was set on having father sell her an [adjacent] bed, but I did not wish to have such a neighbor so near and

---

[1] Allusion to some incidents which we cannot determine, as we have only the letters written to Antoni, not those to Kostuś.

I asked father not to sell; I was ready to pay it myself. But father has planted it himself. Later Filuś proposed to give her the lot near the pond, but this was also too small for her, because there also she would be my neighbor. At last, after much begging, he gave them the lot near Staś Łaba, and there they will build their house. Now, as people say, they hang dogs upon me [abuse me], especially Filuś, because Jan got the best of it in getting that lot.[1]

Now as to the marriage of Józef, our brother. I went with Olcia to the wedding, and after dinner I returned home. It was a week before the end of the carnival. Now, as I wrote already, he lives with his wife in the house of Staś Gembiak, and our father took a small boy from Kozły and is still farming himself. Józef is planting potatoes for himself upon a part of father's land. I have now a dispute with Feliks Gembiak; he crawled into my garden behind my house and plowed the part of the garden up to the fence. I will write you later how this ends.

Spring is late this year, trees blossom only now, and last year they blossomed at St. Wojciech [St. Adalbert's day]. Now I have nothing more of interest to write, only I inform you, that our Michałek began to walk on the first day of Easter, and he says that Little God ordered him to walk, because He rose from the dead. Now he walks well enough, and he would like to walk the whole day in the yard. . . . .

W. Wróblewski

22   June 30, 1906

. . . . Dear Brothers: . . . . First I inform you, that here in Płonka the basement for the new church has been made already; in a week, on Sunday, the consecration of the headstone will be celebrated. Now everybody is bringing offerings, whatever he can. If it is not very difficult for you, I beg you to send a little money. The priest proclaims every Sunday who gave and what the offering was.[2] In Łapy divine service is celebrated in the chapel as in every church. They will also build a church.

[1] Most of the quarrels of neighbors are the result of the system according to which all the old villages are built, and which makes any increase of the area occupied by the single farm-yard impossible except by buying from a neighbor an adjacent lot behind the yard. (Cf. Nos. 26, 39, 40.)

[2] It is a question of family pride. By sending an offering the brothers in America would prove that they still consider themselves members of the family and community and at the same time that they are in good circumstances.

Now, on Corpus Christi day in Białystok there was a pogrom of the Jews. Two processions walked around the city, one ours, the other [Greek] orthodox. Some persons began to fire from a house with revolvers on the orthodox procession.[1] Panic arose among the people, but it is said that nobody was killed by these shots. The army was called and fired at the windows; whoever looked at the street [was shot at]. Other robbers rushed to Jewish shops; they broke and stole whatever they could and killed Jews. About 600 Jews were killed and many wounded. Along some streets all the shops were ruined. Next day in Łapy local vagabonds destroyed a few shops, but they are sitting now in prison. The Jews fled wherever they could, and so it ended. Now we have a state of war; the army is stationed everywhere.

Yesterday we had a storm with lightning; rain poured down, and the hay is upon marshes. People began to mow grass although water stood upon the meadows, but now the hay will float. In the river water is also high, and it is impossible to mow. Probably there will be no hay this year, but in the fields everything is growing beautifully. In a week, if we have fine weather, people will begin to harvest rye. This year the spring has been warm, and the harvest will be early. I intend to go to Częstochowa [on a pilgrimage] with my wife and Edward about this time, but I don't know how soon the tickets will come. . . . .

Now I inform you how farming is going on at home. Well, it turns out that Feliks cannot get along with the old people. Although he *does* work, he plows and carts manure, in short, he does everything necessary in farming, yet under the management of the old man it is impossible to work. He must dress himself and his children, and live, but the old man does not give any money; he keeps everything himself. He does not even give possible food. He wants to drive them away in this way the soonest possible, and that will probably happen very soon, and the old man will again sell [parts of his land] and gratify himself and the old woman. It will be enough for them both [the land will last as long as they last]. And now the quarreling is incessant. "Why did they come?" But he wanted them to come, because he said, "I sell the ground because there is nobody to work."

[1] It is known that these shots were a provocation from Russian hooligans, preparatory to the *pogrom*. They were directed at the Russian procession in order to assure the sympathy or at least the passivity of the Russian authorities.

And now, "Do as you please and get your living where you please!" So Feliks will be obliged to seek a job, and father will farm on in the old way, until there will not be a single lot of land left. If he lives long, then finally a bag and a stick only will remain from this farming, and that will be our only inheritance, because there is no possibility of getting along with father. . . . .

W. WRÓBLEWSKI

23 July 5, 1906

DEAR BROTHER: . . . . I mentioned about brother Feliks, how they are farming at home. Now I will write you still more. As I wrote already, father gave him the farm to manage, but this lasted perhaps for two days; then father took it again into his hands. And then began the misery and quarreling. Feliks complains that he was wronged, that he lost his employment, and now father gives him nothing. He was angry with me, because I wrote him that father intended to give him [the management of the farm] and now he does not give it, or rather he gave it, but took it away. I began also to claim for their sake, that father was acting badly—first so, then otherwise. Then father said, "If it is my fault, I will will them Kopciowizna [some part of the farm]. Let them work and help me to the end, then they will have this as a reward." I did not oppose this strongly, only I said that I could not decide alone, but that I must write to you and ask what you say, and meanwhile wait. So I wrote, but I have no answer yet, and they did not wait. At home they quarrel continually; Feliks complains about his misery, that he has enough work but not enough to eat—that father gives them nothing to eat. Feliksowa [wife of Feliks] comes to me several times a day, and every time with a new complaint. Things went so far that Feliks and father took knives and axes. And she runs frequently to me, saying once that father wants to beat them, then again that he wants to drive them away from his home with hunger. Evidently, I did not praise father for all this. But whatever I said against father, Feliksowa reported it so to father that I [seem to] incite her against him, and she complained to father against me. At last all their knavery and meanness appeared clearly. . . . . When brother Józef came, he told me that when they quarreled with father, father gave the whole secret up and confessed it himself. He said, "I wronged the other [children] and willed you Kopciowizna, and this is

your gratitude?"[1]   Up to this time all was done secretly; we did not
know anything about it, neither I nor Józef.   Then I understood the
whole thing in a different way, and I told Feliks everything about their
meanness.   I brought their anger upon me; they were provoked
with me for telling them, "You have robbed us all, because you have
done it secretly."[2]   He said that father had forbidden them to tell.
They circumvented father in some way during the fair in Sokoły, and
father willed [the land] to them in such a way, that now he will own
this up to his death, and after his death it will be theirs, as a gift from
father, the remainder of the farm to be divided equally.   After that
they quit boarding with father and yesterday they moved over to
Józef Pilat, and live there.   What happens later I will inform you
in due time.   I hear that they plan a law-suit against father and me
for indemnity for their pretended wrongs.   They will try to prove by
my letter that I wrote them to come, that father intended to give
them the farm to manage, and now he refuses, that he gave it, but
took it away, etc., and so they are wronged.   But I wrote him, "If
you have to come, reflect well about it."   He answered, "I must move
to my country because of my children."   Well, and he came, making
a good move!   I told him that he can now lie lazy for two years, since
he has already [in the bequest] earned his full wages; he need not
search for an employment. . . . .   Please write us your opinion about
this affair.   Perhaps this letter will find itself among the documents
of Feliks?   [Perhaps you will concert with Feliks against me and
send him this letter.]   But I don't believe it.

   I remain respectfully yours, but writing always the truth

                                              W. WRÓBLEWSKI

24   July 27, 1906

   DEAR BROTHER: . . . .   On July 23—a day which will remain
forever memorable for us—I was with my wife and Edward in Częstochowa.   It is worth seeing.   I don't know whether I shall have such

---

   [1] This act of the old man was evidently done with the intention of assuring
himself of the alliance of at least one son against the others and of getting rid of
his control without making him an enemy.   It proves that the old man did not
feel his position very strong morally, although he had legally full right to do as
he pleased with his farm.

   [2] The secrecy is particularly bad, because to the economic wrong is added a
social wrong—destruction of the familial solidarity.

an opportunity again; it was the first time, and probably also the last, for it is far enough from us. But it would be worth seeing once more. Well, it will be as it pleases our Lord God, whether He will grant us the opportunity to be in a locality so renowned by its miracles, or not. Thanks be to God that we visited it at least once in our life.

Now I inform you about Jan Głuchy. He is in New York and sends money for his wife. Not long ago he sent to my address 210 roubles; I received it for her. Smaller sums he sends directly to her, and wants to send everything through me, but I don't wish to have trouble about other people's money. . . . .[1] Now I send you one photograph, although a bad one, of the church of Płonka, taken on the day of the consecration of the basement. . . . . On the same day a new cemetery was consecrated. [Description of the cemetery.] Now I inform you that we have already harvested the rye. The weather now is good, dry, even too dry. Only now we have begun to mow summer grain and hay. . . . . The crops are mediocre, the potatoes won't be so good as last year. . . . .

Now I inform you about home and the conflict with Feliks. If you received my letter, you know already how it was about the willing of Kopciowizna—how they did it secretly with father, then how they quarreled with father, how he moved to the house of Józef Pilat. Now she remains here with her children, and he went to the old place in search of employment. He does not write me anything, because we are angry with each other. I told him that such things ought not to be done by cunning, but that he could have done all this so that everybody might know. He excuses himself, on the ground that father forbade him to mention anything to us about his having willed [the land] to them. But even now I don't know whether there is in this will any mention about the mill; probably not, and then I must move it away from that lot. Father is farming as he did formerly; he hires harvesters and drives the crops from the field, but I don't know how long this will last. When the old man goes to bed I don't know how he will do the farming. Feliks has received his part already, and if the old man does not change it, he will still receive an equal part with us. What ought we to do? I ask you beforehand, how are we

[1] Głuchy evidently distrusts the ability of his wife to manage the money. In such cases the man in America attempts to exert a control over the wife through the medium of relatives and friends.

to act? In my opinion he ought to have only this lot and nothing more, and father ought to divide the remainder among us. Judge yourself. . . . .

W. W.

25   August 27, 1906

DEAR BROTHER: . . . . Józef told me that he also received a letter from you. Whether he answered I don't know, but he says that he is unwilling to go to America, because he has it here well enough. Now you ask me for advice, whether you ought to remain in the mines, or to return home, or to search for other work in America. Well I leave the decision with you, but in my opinion it would be dangerous to throw your work away just now, but rather [I advise you] to search first for other work in America and then to come back about spring, or to remain where you are meanwhile and then to come back. But don't take my advice. Whatever you do will be well, because I fear it may be as with Feluś, though I don't believe that you could be so mean as he.[1] He curses me now ceaselessly for his own meanness. I wrote to him also: "If you are to come, first think it over thoroughly lest you regret it later." (And he [answered]: "I must move to my country for my children's sake.") And what has resulted? He robbed us all, and he continually slanders me and father. The old man is somewhat guilty in not having given him what he promised; but he rewarded him, even more than is right, in the will. And what does he want from me? I have heard that he abuses me also in the letters which he writes to her [his wife], saying that he suffers misery by my fault. And why does he abuse me? Because I said the truth openly, that it is unfair to act in such a thievish manner; everybody ought to know what you intend to do. This pricked him, my telling him his fault to his eyes. But even if father gave him the whole fortune, still he would not get on so well as he did there. But whose fault is it? Did he not know farm-work? He ought to have known what work there is on a farm and what a life, and if he risked it he ought not to slander others now without any

---

[1] The responsibility of an adviser for the consequences of his advice is particularly great when the personal influence of the adviser is great, because, as we have pointed out (Introduction: "Theoretic and Esthetic Interests"), the peasant gives to the advice a consideration proportionate to the prestige of the adviser rather than the intrinsic value of the advice. In the present case the advice of Walery is the more weighty because he is the oldest brother.

cause. I loved him like all my brothers, but now I hate him for his action, for such meanness; even a stranger would not do this, and he is a brother. Well, enough of this, let him bark what he pleases. But now, dear brother, I am even afraid to write my opinion. It seems to me that it would be the best to do as I wrote you above, because it seems to me that even if you had much money, but if the earth were to cover you, you would rather prefer to look once more upon your native country, even without a penny. And if you had some money in your pocket it would be still better.

Now I inform you that summer has been dry this year. I walk with Edward through the marsh in shoes, to fetch horses from the pasture; the water has dried up everywhere. Edward rides also on the young horse; he drives him home. Now he will soon begin to go to school again in Łapy. I send you herewith their photograph. As you see they have all grown pretty well, only Michalek, your foster-son, is not there. He does not walk; he is somewhat ill; but perhaps he will get better.

The crops are mediocre this year; on the Transfiguration of Our Lord there was no more summer-grain in the fields; everything had been harvested, because the weather was favorable. We are already digging potatoes. They are not so bad for such a dry season. In some places they even grew big. Yesterday Wacława with Edward dug a whole wagon-load from the small ravine near father's enclosure. Wacława tended geese during the summer, but there were not many of them. The 6 geese brought 23 young ones, for which we got 23 roubles, and besides some worse ones walk about, which did not grow big enough. It would be well to make a road now to the pasture fields, because it is dry; but in our village people don't unite. Nobody went to make it. I worked alone for some mornings, making the beginning, but I was the only one so stupid; all the others are so clever, and nobody goes to work, although it is difficult to get a better time. Why, laziness, stupidity and darkness will never make anything good!

Now, since the Japanese war, there is much news in the country, but I won't relate it here, because whole newspapers would be necessary to describe all that is going on here. If you read papers, surely you know. You ought to subscribe at least to Gazeta Świąteczna, for now all the papers write more truth, because they are published without censure.

Up to the present father is farming alone, and I don't hear him complain that it is hard to work. He plows, he carts manure, and the work goes on. But how long will this last?

Last Sunday in Sokoły the basement of the new church was consecrated and I was there with my children. On the same day I photographed them in my house, or rather before my house. . . . .

W. WRÓBLEWSKI

26   October 29, 1906

DEAR BROTHER: . . . . I received your second letter also, from which I learned about your misfortune, the bruising of your arms.

Now I inform you first, that I intend to remain at home this year, unless any unforeseen circumstances happen. I do nothing but plan about my house. I bought this year more than 5 kop [5×60] flower-pots for my garden. As to the field from Tomaszek, I have not bought it yet. Although I am somewhat short of money, the thing could be done in some way or other, if he wanted to sell it. But what can I do? Last year I went often expressly to him, asking him to sell it, but he declined under some pretext or other. He is willing to exchange, but I have nowhere [to give him a corresponding lot]. If I could only buy somewhere for him; but nobody wants to sell. And it would be very useful to me [to have this lot] near the garden, because Łapy is growing continuously. Now we have a chapel in Łapy, I send you its photograph. They are building now a small tower upon it. It is very convenient now with the churches. One can go where one wishes, either to Łapy or to Płonka; it is near in both directions. When returning from my work I enter the chapel to say the rosary, because now in the evening rosary-service is celebrated by candle-light, and this looks very pretty.

Now I inform you that Roch came home some weeks ago. I have not spoken with him yet, but people say that he was captured when crossing the frontier and was sent home by etapes [with criminals]. Now, as to the horse, father sold it in the summer for 60 roubles, and today perhaps he will buy something in Suraz, if horses are not too expensive, because there is a small fair today. Feliksowa has left again and went there to him [Feliks], having sold her things to Józef Pilat. She sold the cow also which father gave them, because she lived in Pilat's house. She went like a swine, because she called neither on me nor on father before leaving for those forests. That is just where she ought to live, with bears, not with men. She was something of an ape before, and there she became altogether an ape. No honest person would have done as they did. Whose fault is it? And how much they have cursed me, and father! May God not punish them for it. They think only about a fortune and money and don't want anything else; they don't regard church-going and fasting, if only they can live comfortably in this world.[1]

Now, as to Michałek, he is already better and begins to walk by himself. Edward has been sick recently with small-pox. Now he is getting better slowly. . . . . We had a dry summer, and the autumn is also dry. There is lack of water in the wells, and the cold is not far away. If it goes on like this we shall have no water in the winter.

Now in our country disorders still go on, sometimes robberies, sometimes killing with bombs or revolvers. Not long ago there was a pogrom in Siedlce, where the army even fired with guns for 3 days, as the papers write. Now we have a state of war; the general governor of Warsaw proclaimed that whoever does not come at the call to military service, his parents will be condemned for 3 months to prison or 300 roubles fine, and the head-minister added that in localities where the state of war exists whoever does not come is subject to court-martial. And what a court-martial is you know probably, and I won't describe it. . . . .

It would be well if Kostuś thought sometimes about his native country and wrote something, at least about his health and success. Roch brought the news that he is married. Perhaps on that account he has changed and does not write.[2]

[W. WRÓBLEWSKI]

27
February 24, 1907

. . . . DEAR BROTHER: I learned about the misfortune which happened to you. . . . . This news dismayed us all very much, and we are very sad that such a misfortune happened to you. I got also a letter from Kostuś today . . . . and I learned that you are somewhat

---

[1] Typical expression of the peasant's idealism, which is always latent in all the practical attitudes. There is a marked difference in this respect between a peasant like Walery and a handworker like Wladek. For the character of the latter, see Vol. III.

[2] There is a proverb, "Whoever gets married gets changed," which is justified in the sense that the individual is determined to a large extent by his family-group, and by marrying he comes under the influence of an additional group.

better, and I learned also from him that a little miner came to him; only, please, let him send us a photograph of his family. I received also your other letter of February 4, in which you tell about your misfortune and write that I caused you a great displeasure by my letter—that I gave you the last blow.[1] Believe me, if I had known that it would reach you when you were in such a condition, I would have chosen not to mention anything, but who could have expected anything like this? . . . . If I made some reproaches, your own letter induced me to do it. You wrote that you keep company in which you cannot get along for a single day without beer or whisky. Then I wanted to draw you back from it, and therefore I made some remarks —that this money would be useful here, and for whom [it would be useful].[2] I had also had no idea, that you had any difficulties in sending money. I know only this, that if somebody has money and wants to send it, and has anybody to whom he may send it, he does send it, and does not write that it is difficult, unless he has none. But what happened between us is quite ridiculous. Well, never mind, let it be as you do it. Today, in your present condition, I don't want anything from you. But you were wrong in writing that you did not take any property with you.[3] I have none either, and it is possible that nobody among us will have any. I don't get any benefit out of it. If I want a bushel of corn, and if I take it from father, I pay him like any other neighbor. And what can yet happen with father's farm, nobody knows. As I said, it is possible that no one among us will get anything. . . . . We might perhaps be able to prevent it, but we should think about it all together, because it is high time. . . . . I cannot prevent it alone, and perhaps you would not like it; so it is necessary to deliberate as soon as we can about father and the farm.

Now, as to Józef, he got married during last carnival. He does not want to live with father, but he rented a lodging in the new house of Staś Gembiak, where he moved with his wife. He is serving as before. I have left my employment already, and since the first day of Lent I am home and will think about building my house. . . . .

W. Wróblewski

[1] The letter referred to is lacking.

[2] Walery probably asked for the payment of some money which Antoni owed him. Cf. No. 29.

[3] Wrong because it looked like a hint that Walery was profiting from the common family property.

28 August 15, 1907

. . . . DEAR BROTHER: [Greetings. News about crops.] Now I inform you . . . . that there is news. On August 7, after the Transfiguration of Our Lord, grandmother, or rather our stepmother, died. She had put aside some money, but had given it to the priests for the building of the church,[1] and different rags [dresses, etc.] which remained were stolen by her family even before her death, so that when she died there was not a single rag left; everything was empty. Even a hen disappeared during the funeral. Father asked a priest to come to lead the burial-procession, but without a speech, and so it was decided. But Mrs. Malinowska [some relative of the dead] did not like it and she requested the priest to thank [the dead] before the grave. Evidently she had some reasons to thank; the dead must have been good to her. Now we don't know how father will act; perhaps he will get married even for the third time. It would be very undesirable for us, perhaps even a great calamity. But what can be done, since father does not say anything about the future. He could very well live with me and Józef, or divide the farm between us, and we would give him his living. We don't know how it will be. But if he gets married once more, we are totally lost. I ask your advice, how to prevent it?

Now, as to the building of my house, probably this year only the basement will be ready. I have no time to carry the building further, because I have enough to do alone on my farm. I lacked stones and I paid 8 roubles for half a cube which they brought me. There will not be enough lime, and other material will be needed. Meanwhile my money is almost out and my geese have died, and my pigs also. In short, it is going on very badly. Moreover, I have been already 3 times in Markowszczyzna to fetch bricks for the church, and that is not the end of it. And I have still other work to do. Now, some boys from Kozły, who are in America, sent 110 roubles for the building of the church. The priest announced their names. Some lady from

---

[1] Walery is evidently provoked that she gave her money to the church and her clothes to her own family, so that nothing was left for her husband's family. The money was given by her to the church in order to assure her soul's salvation. In this respect the peasant women show the most profound and reckless egotism. We have met a woman who has about 2,000 roubles and is still earning as a cook. She has a widowed daughter with small children, but never helps her and says openly that all her money will eventually go to the church to secure masses for her soul.

Białystok sent also 100 roubles. In a word, offerings flow, but the parishioners are not in a hurry about bringing bricks, otherwise the church could be covered before winter.

Now I ask you, dear brother, how about your leg? Is there any hope that you will recover? How do you live there? Why does Kostuś never mention himself or us? Does he care no more for our father and for our country? He could perhaps remember once that he has a father and brothers. . . . .

W. Wróblewski

29   October 7, 1907

. . . . Now, as to that debt, please don't make yourself any trouble about it. Although it would now be useful to me, it is true, yet since you are in such a situation, you need it also. In the last necessity I can ask father to give me at least the interest, either in food-stuffs or in a field to sow, since he sells now and then piece after piece to strange people. But as yet I defend myself against poverty as best I can. Now as to my building, the work advances only since St. Michael. It would be very well to do it now, because the weather is favorable, but I must often stop and go to other work. Józef has helped me also more than once by preparing mortar. If the weather were good and the walls dried rapidly, the work would progress; and if there were somebody preparing mortar. . . . .

Now, I learned in Łapy that brother Feliks came here for some weeks, but he evidently does not want to show his eyes among us any more, because he went directly from Łapy by the Narew railway to Sokoły and thence to Jabłonowo. Somebody asked him there why he did not go to Ziencinki. He said there was nothing to go for. And he came for a church-festival with his whole family [to Jabłonowo]. That is nice, what he is doing! It is human to sin, but it is devilish not to repent and not to amend his faults. Because it is said, "If you want to offer a gift to God and you remember that your brother has anything against you, put your offering down near the altar and go and make peace with your brother," or in general with whomever it may be. But he forgot this for he does not want to see, not only his brother, but even his father. Perhaps he will yet change his mind, but I doubt it, because in his letters to Jabłonowo he wrote only curses against father and against me.

Now as to our father, you wrote that Kostuś advises him to come to America, where he could quietly spend the rest of his age with him.

This won't be. Although I have not spoken with father about it, I know that he would not go. And why should he? If he did not want to work himself on his farm, we could give him support but how can he part with his farm, leave the barn, etc.?[1] And Kostuś deserves praise for having taken care of you, but he might work himself in as dangerous a place, and if—God forbid!—any accident happened to him, with father in America, what then? It would be very unwise. And we could then give no effective help, because if we sent 10 roubles, you would receive there only 5, and moreover it is so difficult to get money here, while from America, when you send 5, we receive here 10, and that is a different thing. . . . .

                                          W. WRÓBLEWSKI

30   November 10, 1907

. . . . DEAR BROTHERS: . . . . Now I inform you about my building. I have raised it up to the windows and I end here my work for this year, because winter is near, and there is yet plowing in the field to be done before winter, and some arrangements to be made around the house for winter. The autumn is clear and dry. . . . .

Now I pass to the news. I inform you that our dear father [ironical] got married for the third time. He took for wife that Klimusia, or rather Franciszkowa [widow of Franciszek] Pilat, that bitch, so to speak, because she came in order to rob us. Her children did not drive her away from their home, but she wants to profit out of our fortune. When father gave [money] for the banns, he did not mention anything to us, but did it secretly. When we heard the banns of our father, we went directly to him with Józef, and we tried to persuade him in different ways not to marry. But he refused to listen, he wanted only to marry. We tried also to persuade her not to marry our father. About this time somebody broke her windows on All Saints' Day, and she throws the suspicion upon me; she had the policeman come and drew up a verbal process, and there will be a law-suit. I will write you how this ends; but she has no witnesses to testify who broke her windows.[2] I also begged our priest to dissuade father from marrying her, but even this did not help, because the old man stubbornly stood upon marrying her. On Wednesday, November 6, the wedding was performed. We did not know anything about

---

[1] Ironical, meaning that he is too avaricious and egotistic to leave his property.

[2] Certainly the writer or his children did it.

it, but I saw the old man coming back from the church, and I guessed it.   On the very next day we went with Józef to say good morning to the new couple and we greeted them so that it went to their heels [proverbial: They felt it deeply.].   The old man saw that he could not evade and promised to give us the small lots to cultivate, and to leave for himself the riverside and Uskowizna.   So he got rid of us for this time, but "Promise is a child's toy"; we won't be satisfied with it, we will insist as strongly as we can that he do it black upon white [in writing], for us and for you also.   We care not only about ourselves, but also about you, lest Klimusia get it.   She is a cunning [avaricious] old woman, since she dared to go to marriage almost in the face of violence.   I will tell you everything that happens.   We want father to will us all, everything, and to keep to it, but we don't know how it will turn out.   Of course, we except Feliks, because he has his part already.   I wrote you that he was in Jabłonowo with his family and did not show his eyes among us.   He was there for 4 days and went back, although I know that he had leave for 2 weeks.   That is also a meanness.   What is the matter with our family, that they keep things secret from one another, like thieves? . . . .[1]

W. Wróblewski

31   March 25, 1908

DEAR BROTHERS: . . . . I did not write, as I was waiting for the news which I expected from our father.   We have called upon him more than once, with Józef, asking him to make some division of the farm, but he got stubborn and refuses to do anything for us; only to his Klimusia he refuses nothing.   We called upon him with the priest, then alone, then with people; nothing helps.[2]   Once he took an ax to us and tried to frighten us; he jumped around wildly, like a mad-. man.   He gives us in words the field in Szalajdy to sow, but Józef refuses to take it without a [written] will.   I intend myself to harvest what I have sown, but I don't know how it will be later.   Józef

---

[1] Expression of the feeling that the family is disintegrating. "Keeping things secret" is clearly a proof that there is no real solidarity.   In the primitive peasant family no member can have any secret from other members; there are no purely personal matters.

[2] Calling with the priest and with people proves that in the general opinion the father is morally wrong in his behavior, that he ought to occupy the familial, not the personal standpoint.

advises me not to do even this, but it seems to me that would be bad, for father will justify himself afterwards saying that he gave, but we would not take, and he will sell more readily. We also drove the Trusie [the stepmother's family] away from father's house, for they had settled their whole family already. Now at least they only call often. There would be much to write, whole newspapers would be necessary; in this letter the rest cannot be described. I spit upon all this, so to speak; if he is determined to waste all this, let him waste it; if his own children are not dear to him, only strange children, for everything there is free to strangers.

At the end of the carnival Józef Łaba got his daughter married to the son of Fortus from Łynki. We were not at the wedding, but father with his Klimusia was there, and he got so drunk that he lay under the hedge. The next day he invited perhaps half the people from Goździki, but we were left out. Although I never overlooked father [in my invitations], he always keeps away from us, as from enemies. Well, I end it, because I loathe all this.

[News about weather.] Now, a terrible thing happened. On March 23 in the village Somachy a score of robbers came in the evening to the Porowskis. They found the whole family at home. They attacked Porowski and killed him with a blow on the head and revolver-shots, they wounded and bound the other members of the family, they took all the money they could find and fled, nobody knows where. This terrible incident frightened everybody. The next day I drove lumber from the forest of Kruszewo . . . . and I saw [mourning] banners on the house of Porowski, and I learned about this accident after coming to Matyski. . . . .

I made window frames during the winter, and in the spring, if God grants health, we will set to work in the field and near the house. The walls of the house have been spoiled a little by the cold. Work approaches, and there is nobody to help. Although Michałek [3 years old] promises to help, still I don't believe in the efficiency of his help. I will tell you something more about him. Mother laid upon him the duty of helping the poor. He asked why she let him give a grosz to a beggar. She answered, "In order that he may pray our Lord God to let your foster-father in America recover."[1] Now he

---

[1] The beggar is a religious personality, and giving of alms a religious act. In tales most of the beggars are either personifications of God or of the saints, or good magicians—bearers of a beneficent divine power—or at least instruments of the

asks very often, "Has my foster-father recovered yet?" He is in good health, himself and Józefa as well. The latter can read a book pretty well already. Edward goes to school in Łapy. . . . .

W. WRÓBLEWSKI

32   May 8, 1908

. . . . DEAR BROTHERS: As always, I inform you also today first about our health, that we are all in good health, thanks to our Lord God the Highest, and we wish you the same. Only my wife is in rather bad health; for more than a year she has not been able to work much. She cannot eat much either; therefore she has no strength to work. She coughs incessantly and no medicine can help her much, neither doctor nor home-medicine. Probably it will end badly. [Remarks about letters received and sent.]

We have spring already. All the birds are here—larks, lapwings, storks, swallows, cuckoos, nightingales—in short, all of them. But

---

divinity. The function of the beggar is to pray, and not only his prayer, but also almsgiving has a magical importance, compels the divinity. This religious character of beggary is shown also by the fact that beggars in towns stay around churches, that in the country the parish festivals are the meeting-dates and -places of beggars, that "miraculous" places like Częstochowa are the main centers of beggary. This may be accounted for partly by the fact that in these places and on these dates the largest crowds gather, but this does not explain it completely. The peasant gives alms more frequently to the beggar before the church than to the beggar upon the street; more frequently during a parish festival than on an ordinary day, more frequently in a miraculous locality than in an ordinary church. This is evidently because the religious character of the beggar, the value of his prayers and of his mediation before God and the saints, increase in proportion to the sacredness of the time and the place. The principle is exactly the same as that which determines the value of a mass. A mass said on Sunday is more valuable than one on a week day, during a parish festival more valuable than on an ordinary Sunday, in a miraculous locality more valuable than in an ordinary locality. Further, the religious character of the beggar is proved by the conditions required for the acknowledgment of his occupation. Only the old man or the cripple can be a proper beggar, not because of any consideration of social utility, but because more or less consciously these features are considered the marks by which God destined them to this function. The proof that no utilitarian reflections play here any rôle is, that women, though less able to work, do not enjoy so full an acknowledgment of their begging function as the men. The woman, indeed, can be a member of the congregation or a divinity (saint), but not a priest, an intermediary between both. The women beggars are, on the contrary, often the bearers of a mischievous, magical character—witches. The religious character of the beggar is perfectly expressed in the popular stories. (Cf. No. 261. note.)

the spring does not progress favorably.   We have St. Stanislaus [day] today, and the trees are still black and don't think of blossoming. Some years ago the orchards had blossomed already at St. Wojciech. Cold wind blows from all sides.   I wasted all the food from my barns in feeding my stock; everything is empty.   There was no hay. Moreover water flooded the potatoes in early spring . . . . and afterward they froze in the barns.   Everything goes on unfavorably. Now my fields are already sown and I expect soon to begin building . . . . but my capital is exhausted, I must now ask father [for the debt], because . . . . otherwise I can do nothing.   If God helps me to move to the new house perhaps it will go on better, for now I can change nothing, because so many things are commenced.   I could return even today to my old employment, but I cannot because of this building; . . . . and if I could keep a garden at home, I should have a good bargain; people come themselves from Łapy, if I only had something to sell.   These few hot-beds—what do they amount to?

As to our father—our fortune runs out in different ways; one feels oppressed inside at seeing how the care of us all [what we have worked for] is wasted in vain.   But what can be done, since there is nobody among us to look after this, strange people benefit now. . . . .

W. WRÓBLEWSKI

33   June 29, 1908

DEAR BROTHERS: . . . . My wife is unwell all the time, and I don't know whether she will recover.   Although much money has been spent, no improvement can be seen. . . . .

Now I inform you that I got from father the money which I needed so much, but after much bargaining.   When I mentioned it, he talked without end; he told me to bring a law-suit.   At last he saw that he could not extricate himself by shifts and he paid it back. But what happened then?   Instead of the 100 roubles he sold the riverside near Bociany to Roszkowski, from Ziencinki, for 300 roubles, because Marcinek [Roszkowski's son] came from America and brought money.   That is the way it goes on with us.   And he could have paid the debt without selling anything, for not long ago he got 100 roubles from Staś Łaba which the latter had borrowed from him.   But this money surely fell into the claws of Klimusia.   Finally, he could have borrowed, if he had no money, or by giving a mortgage on the meadow, he would also have got 100 roubles; or he could have sold somewhere a lot for 100 roubles, but not so big a one for 300. Everybody says that the riverside is worth about 400. In this way our dear father gets rid of land and rids us of it at the same time. Józef went to remonstrate with father, for wasting the fortune so. They almost fought. Father jumped upon Józef with a yoke [for carrying buckets] and Józef took a pole. The old man brandished his yoke so that he broke the pole. At last Józef sprang forward and wrested the wood from him, and so they separated. I was not there at that time, but Józef came back and told how it was. The old man said that we are bad. "Why did I ask for the 100 roubles?" Does he think I am going to give him my work for the benefit of my enemies, that they may have more and live better? He does not give us his fortune, which justly belongs to us after him, and he wants us not to claim this [our own money] until he wastes everything and there is nothing left from which to recover [the debt]. He said that you had sent money as if for a joke [so little]. But I told him that it was lucky, for now our dear father would not care even if you were dying there from hunger. Why do other people not act in this way? What shall we do now? Perhaps it would be best to help him to finish it the soonest possible! Let there be no more of this grief and this sorrow! One cannot bear it, seeing how strange people profit from us and grow rich from the fruit of our labor. [Sends a photograph of the house which he is building and of his family; describes the photograph.]

W. WRÓBLEWSKI and A. A. W. E. J. M.,

[initials of other members of the family] also Wróblewskis

34   November 22, 1908

DEAR BROTHERS: . . . . First I inform you about the building of my house, that it is covered already with a roof, but inside there is still much to do; nothing yet is finished. [News about weather.] In the spring I intend to move the granary. . . . . The worst is that I have spent all my money; but if God grants us health, with some pains everything will be done. People praise my house; many have said already, that I have adorned all Ziencinki with it. . . . . The granary and barn must be moved, because it will be very inconvenient if they remain. There will be much work in moving them. Now I know how much work it costs to build a house and to do everything with one's own hands, but perhaps our Lord God will yet help me to do this also [transfer the barn]. Now I don't know what to do with that unlucky mill. I cannot take it down alone without breaking it. I pay about 4 roubles taxes yearly for it, and I drive my grain to grind to strange mills, because it is not worth grinding in it—only loss of time and repairs. Father drew out long ago; he refuses to help in paying the tax and in repairing. If I found an amateur [one who wanted it] I would sell it, and if not, I must demolish it the best I can for it is impossible to pay so much and to have no benefit. At least there will be some fuel. It cost money enough, and there is no use from it. [Description of the last summer and autumn.] Now I inform you that Feluś Łaba is dead . . . . and his son has got married. . . . . Brother Józef received your letter about the accordeon, and certainly he will attend to it when he has money. . . . .

My wife is always the same, she cannot work at all. She does not lie down continually, but there is no help from her. It is a great damage for me. The girls do everything alone. Edward goes to school in Łapy. After this year he will have still two years to learn in order to finish the school. Józefa is learning already to read Russian. Michałek is at least in good health; he calls for bread as soon as he wakes. . . . .

W. WRÓBLEWSKI

35   December 22, 1908

DEAR BROTHERS: . . . . I inform you that last Friday I received from the post-office in Łapy 80 roubles through a money-order in which there is no mention from whom it comes. . . . . Surely it is from you, and surely for the purchase about which you wrote in the previous letter. . . . . I will wait for word from you.

Now I inform you that my wife is already very ill; when you read this letter, dear brother, probably she will be no more among the living in this world, and if God grants you to come again to our country, dear brother, you will see your sister-in-law no more. We are sad, and we shall have sad Christmas holidays, although they will come in a few days. But nobody knows what will happen. Not long ago we brought the priest to her. There was no hope of her living up to the present. Like this candle which is burned almost to the end and is already going out, so is her life; it will soon go out, and we shall remain in deep sorrow.

As I wrote you already, I am now in a very bad situation. I have spent all my money and shall be obliged to borrow about 100 roubles when the funeral and the moving of the barns come.[1] So, dear brothers, perhaps you could do it for me, and lend me [this money]. I beg you, if you can. But probably it is difficult for you now. In that case I shall be obliged to ask for a loan in the communal bank. I should not like to let people know that I lack money, though I hope soon to get rid of this debt. But I must borrow somewhere now, because the moving of the barns cannot wait until I have cash. . . . .

W. WRÓBLEWSKI

36   February 2, 1909

DEAR BROTHERS: . . . . I received the letter in which you wrote how to use those 80 roubles and we acted according to it. Józef had a suit made for which he paid 32 roubles, but it will probably be somewhat difficult to send it. Probably somebody going to America will take it and send it to you. We gave for the holy mass which was celebrated on January 18 at which we were—I, Olcia and Józef. Now I thank you very much for that money which you sent to buy gifts for my children . . . . because it was very useful to us at that time. If God permits, we shall be able perhaps to prove our gratitude in some way. Meanwhile we remain indebted to you and we all thank you once more.

Now I inform you that my wife is still alive, although before Christmas we did not expect her to live through the holidays. And we don't know how long it will last; but she will never more have health. If we could only move from here to the new house [before she dies].

[1] This anticipation of the funeral expenses while his wife is still alive, and in general the calm foresight in speaking of her imminent death are not a proof of any coarseness of feeling. It is the normal, traditional attitude of the peasant toward death. Death is a perfectly *normal* phenomenon for the peasant, normal not only in the naturalistic, but in the sentimental sense. It has a perfectly established and predetermined social and religious meaning, so that the individual reaction toward it has a very narrow field of unexpected possibilities open within the range of the traditional attitudes. And the practical anticipation of death belongs precisely to the sphere of these traditional attitudes. Moreover, the practical side of life has nothing base in the peasant's eyes which would make a connection of death and money-affairs unsuitable. (Cf. Introduction: "Religious Attitudes," and note to Osiński series, No. 69.)

Spring will come, and during spring I have a great task to accomplish. I want to clear everything out of this place before the sowing-season, in order that nothing except the ground may be left here. I want to move the barns, to sell the house to somebody who will take it away, to transplant different shrubs which are good and to destroy these which are not good, and all this will require much work. The new house is not ready either; there are neither ceilings nor floors, and the middle-walls are also not quite ready. But if I can prepare at least one room for summer, we can move, and then before winter we shall finish the rest. . . . . And I have still threshing enough up to the end of the carnival. . . . . There will be much work and many expenses from now on. But if God allows us to win, then perhaps we shall be able to arrange everything better about the home, being rid at last of this detestable neighborhood, with this street and [adjacent] barns and everything, that I cannot enumerate here, but of which I have had enough. . . . . The winter is steady, cold and good sledge-road, but there are neither weddings nor visits, and probably there will be none, because the end of the carnival is approaching. And even if there were some, we could not amuse ourselves. [Meaning not clear: "It would not be suitable," or, "We should not be able."]

W. W.

37   March 21, 1909

DEAR BROTHERS: . . . . First I inform you, dear brother Kostuś, that I received both your sad letters, for which I thank you. I went on Sunday to the post-office for the paper and I received the two letters at once and I knew by the writing that they were from you, and I had at once a bad foreboding. . . . . I was not mistaken for . . . . I found such terrible news about the breaking of the legs of Antoś. What misfortunes came one after the other! Evidently God is putting us to the test. For, as it is said, "Whom God loves, He gives him crosses, and who bears them meekly, becomes happy." And perhaps God punishes us for our sins or for the sins of other people? Still we must submit to the will of God, because it is said: "Oh Lord, here cut me, here burn me, but in eternity pardon me." And you know that our Lord God inflicted upon St. Job such a terrible calamity, that being rich he became a lazar, and yet he said: "The Lord gave, the Lord took away, blessed be His name." For what have we of our own? Nothing. Fortune and health, everything is from our Lord God.[1] And the worst misery for man is if God takes the latter [health] away from him.

I have still another great sorrow besides our brother's misfortune. Hardly did our brother get out of one misery when another, one worse still, befell him. In the same way it goes on in my home. My wife has been ill for two years, and now since autumn she has not risen from her bed. She has dried up like a skeleton, and we look only for the time when she will close her eyes. Twice already we brought the priest with our Lord God, and we thought that she would be in the tomb long ago. But now there remains only a short time to live, we think a few days perhaps. Therefore I am very sad, and now from two sides. But what can I do? I owe money already to brother Antoni, and now I must contract a still greater debt for my needs, and if it is necessary, I must try to send him [money]. Write about this, for . . . . I am very badly off for money now, with this building and the sickness of my wife. Surely I shall have to bury her soon. . . . .

I am planning now to move the barns to where the new house stands. It will require work and workmen, because I cannot do it alone. And this makes me sorrowful, for I build everything as if upon ice, as people say, because what do I own here? Everything is my children's property. But it is difficult to do nothing. Perhaps [my reward will be] that I shall live my last years I don't know how and where [my children will perhaps drive me away], but I cannot leave them now and go somewhere else. [News about weather.]

W. WRÓBLEWSKI

38   March 31, 1909

"Praised be Jesus Christus!"

DEAR BROTHERS: "The world will rejoice, and you will weep," so said Christ our Lord to his disciples. And so it happened with me, because everything in the world rejoices at the coming of spring, and I remain in a heavy sorrow after the death of a person so dear to me.

---

[1] This is the only clear example in this series of a mystical subordination to the will of God. There are a few examples in other series, e.g., Cugowski series, No. 314.

On March 31 died Anna Wróblewska, born Gonsowska, having lived 46 years, after a long illness, provided with the holy sacraments.[1]

I send you today the sad news of the leaving of this world by my wife. I am still more grieved about the misfortune which befell you, brother.[2] God puts us indeed to a heavy test, but let us be true to him unto our death, and He will give us the crown of eternal life.

Dear brother Kostuś, write me as you can, what is the condition of Antoni, how is his health, whether there is a hope that he will live. And when he gets out of this misery, let him not grieve about his further life. Perhaps our Lord God will grant us that if we are in good health he will find some support with us. It is true that I am now left as if upon ice, ... because everything there is belongs to the children, but with the children I can live in some way, and if God grants them not to be bad, we could perhaps keep our brother also. Now, although we are in such a difficult situation, I begin the work of moving the barns. I will now end with my children what was before intended with my wife.[3] When we do this, with God's help, it will be perhaps somewhat better. We shall be able to do something with the garden and this will give us a better possibility of living.

Now I refer to our father, how well disposed he is toward us all. When my wife was sick neither he nor his Klimusia showed themselves, although the priest passed by twice with our Lord God. All the people from the village called upon us, but they did not call. And they did not come either for funeral and burial, although I asked [him]. That is a good father! He has disowned us, but he has renounced God also, because he would not come to honor Him in the

[1] The form of this announcement is evidently imitated. The first part reminds us of the beginning of a funeral speech, the second part is a typical official death notice. The man keeps in his whole correspondence about his wife's death within the strict limits of the socially sanctioned attitude, with sometimes a slight individual sentiment. (Cf. No. 35, note.)

[2] With the strong familial feeling of the Polish peasant, an attachment to brother or sister greater than that to husband or wife is not an exception. It would probably be much more frequent, were it not for the fact that marriage creates an active community of interests which strengthens the mere sentimental and sexual attachment. This explains the fact that whenever the husband or wife comes to live with the family of the other, i.e., when no separate household is constituted, his or her position is very difficult, because the old familial connection of the other remains stronger than the new marriage connection.

[3] This hint of a personal sentiment and one in No. 43 are the only ones made by Walery with reference to his wife.

most Holy Sacrament. He said that he did not know. But who can believe it? The whole village knew, he alone did not know. I told him that perhaps he saw at least the [mourning] banner when the wind waved it for almost two days. He muttered something, and so it ended. . . . .[1]

I cannot even send you wishes for the approaching merry holidays of our Lord's Resurrection, because I know that they will not be merry for either you or me. . . . .

W. WRÓBLEWSKI

39 May 16, 1909

DEAR BROTHERS: . . . . In the Green Holidays [Pentecost] we intend to move to the new house . . . . because here the house stands alone and on a bare place; everything is cleared away, the barns moved there; we live here still only until the chimney and stoves are built in the new house. . . . . Although there are no ceilings and floors we shall move, ... and finish the rest before winter. My farm buildings look very good now; I put both barns on the side of the road and between them I made a gate-way. . . . . The sties are on the edge of the field. . . . . If I have the opportunity to make a photograph of the house, I will send it to you. . . . . My brothers-in-law helped me for some days, only brother Józef could not make up his mind to come and help; . . . . he did not refuse, but before he came we had done everything. Now we shall have a dispute with Kazimierz Płaksa. He has here now too much and too little room at once, for he will have no way to drive behind the barns if I make a fence from the road-side. He bought a strip near us from Piotr Pilat for 70 roubles, in the hope that we shall cross it and then he will have the whole road, his own and ours, but I don't know whether I will cross it . . . . at any rate not at once. . . . .

W. WRÓBLEWSKI

40 June 13, 1909

DEAR BROTHERS: . . . . Now I inform you that I had some bad luck also. Before Pentecost I was invited by the priest in Płonka to plant flowers in his garden. I did not refuse, although I had enough

[1] This is a proof that the father in fact no longer considers himself a member of the family. For a relative not to assist at a funeral is unheard of.

work of my own. When I had finished the work the priest's coach-
man was going to Łapy to bring the priest's sister, and he took me
home. Suddenly the mare ran away and . . . . overturned us with
the carriage. I got a terrible blow upon my leg. Three weeks have
passed . . . . and I cannot walk without pain. May God grant
me to recover before the hay-harvest, or else it will be bad. . . . .
We are living in the new house. . . . . Upon the old place there is
nothing more, no trace left. . . . . I sold the house for 56 roubles
and I gave them directly back, because I had borrowed exactly as
much from brother-in-law Feliks for the funeral and for the moving
of the buildings. Well, after long bargaining, I exchanged with
Kazimierz Płaksa some land for the road. Though he barked enough
he had to give what I wanted. He had said that the road would be his
without anything, because it is common. Well, for this "common"
road he had to give me the hillside opposite the old gate . . . . and
I gave him my road up to his house. . . . . He had bought from
Piotr Pilat a bed near my garden with the idea that I would cross it
[with the road] and then he would have the road. He had paid 70
roubles for it—rather expensive. But I did not want it, because there
are minors who have a part [in Pilat's property; therefore, the
proposed combination was not to be considered quite secure]; let
him rather keep what he bought. It looks ridiculous; he had bought
it for me and I did not want it. I shall now have much to do still
before I have everything in proper order, but people are already
praising me and saying that I live as in a small manor. The house
does not look bad and the barns look good also. The fruit trees have
grown well enough; they blossomed this year; a few bee-hives—all
this together looks pretty good. I send you a photograph of my
house, although a very bad one. It is the front-wall, 3 windows in it;
a fourth and fifth in the side-wall, near the door; before the door a
sort of a veranda; upon the roof two vanes turned by the wind, in the
other side-wall two windows and in the rear also two windows. Altogether 7 ordinary windows and 2 big ones near the door. . . . . [News
about weather.]

W. W.

[Two letters, dated May 16, and June 13, relate the moving into the
new house, the transfer of the barns, an exchange of land with Płaksa,
minute description of new house, etc.]

41 September 29, 1909

DEAR BROTHERS: . . . . I received from you the letter for which I had waited so long, and I learned the curious news that brother Kostuś has bought such a big farm. This pleased me very much. I am almost carried away. Could I have such a fortune, or even the half of it! There are probably about 60 morgs, and I have 7, and these are in more than 40 places; and even with these 7 morgs I don't know how it will be, because Olcia can take half of them. People are already instigating her. If it happens so, I don't know what I shall do with the other children. And surely she won't be long with us, because people want to extort this small bit of land as soon as possible. Envy does not sleep. My late wife foresaw it and told me before her death that when I built the new house and everything looked better there would be terrible envy. And so it is. If she had lived, it would be only half a misery [not so bad], but now I don't know how it will be. To remain alone with the children would be bad. To go anywhere into the world would also be impossible. How could I leave these little ones alone? There will be nothing to farm upon; if it were at least as it is now, one could live along, though not without difficulty. (People have often talked of my marrying Olcia, that it is possible. I asked the priest about it. He told me that there have been such situations and people have asked for permission, but that it is not possible in any way. Although different difficulties about property have been exposed, it has been refused.) Here I stop [writing] about this.

Now I want to ask about this farm which Kostuś bought, in what country it lies, whether there is a town near it, whether there can be a good sale of agricultural products? Still I believe that if he found his way before and could gather money enough to buy such a farm, he surely will know how to manage further and pay the rest. And if the garden is in a good state and the town is not far away, it can give a good income. And also it is necessary to cultivate those plants which can be sold most easily.[1]

W. WRÓBLEWSKI

[1] The fact that Kostuś has bought a farm creates between the brothers a new community of interests and strengthens the familial connection. All the following letters are full of agricultural details, advice, information, experiments (mainly omitted here). In spite of the passage of time, the correspondence remains as animated as it was at the beginning of their separation.

[Two letters, November 14, 1909, and January 1, 1910, contain advice about farming and gardening. Writes that his house has been reproduced in Gazeta Świąteczna. Complains that he cannot get along alone with the children.]

42   February 22, 1910

DEAR BROTHERS: [Weather, early spring, larks and bees have appeared, farm-work.] Thanks to God, we have not so much trouble as last year. This has been a very hard year for us after the loss of a wife and mother. . . . .

Now you asked me, dear brother, to write about our father. I can say that, although we don't live far from each other, I don't know anything about him, for he never comes to us and we never go to him. Why should we go, since he has disowned us. He said that he did not want our tutorship, that he will get on pretty well. It is true that he gets on pretty well, because from time to time we hear that he has sold some gully or patch. He keeps Klimusia and her children; they are all there continually, so we have no reason to go there. It is sad. But what can be done? I am happy only when I don't remember him; then my heart does not pain me. But whenever I recall it all I am very sad. If he were a father loving his own children and not those of others surely we should all be better off now. It is all right when strange brats ["bachory," contemptful word for "children"] creep upon him from all sides like vermin, but he refused to live with his own children. I am not of his age today [it is natural for *old* people to live dependent on their children] but I live with my children upon their fortune, and still I don't weep. I commend myself to God's care and I live along. For me in my actual situation it is very bad that he did so, but may God's will be done. [Asks about the exact place of the brothers' farm upon the map, about the corn, vegetables, trees which grow there.] In our village and neighborhood a great deal is changed, it would seem strange to you now. And as to Feliks, I don't know for certain his address, because he does not write to us at all. . . . .   W. W.

43   March 8, 1910

DEAR BROTHERS: . . . . I thank you for your letter; I learned much from it about what grows there and how things are paid. I understood everything. Now I describe to you my farm-stock. I have two horses, one 6 and the other 3 years old, two cows, both have calved now; for the milk which I send to Łapy I get 6 roubles monthly, ... for 2 calves I got $7\frac{1}{2}$ roubles, ... I have 2 old sheep and 3 young ones, 2 pigs, 4 hens, a dog and a pair of turtle-doves, and that is all my farm-stock. [Describes prices, probable crops, farm-work, weather, new churches in Łapy and Płonka.]

Now there are many changes in our village; Józef Łaba built a new house, Bolesław a new one, Staś Gembiak a new one, Roch a new one, Jan Głuchy a new one. Głuchy has gone now for the third time to America, and Roch is in America again. I moved to the new place. Where it was there is nothing, and where there was nothing, there it is. Now I have it nice and comfortable, everybody says that it looks like a manor, only it is a pity that mine [my wife] is not there and that I still have a few roubles of debt. But the latter would be a trifle if she lived. Now there can be a bad misfortune for me with the children, especially with such a difference of age. Now all of them would like to learn, but there is nobody to work for them. . . . . [Advises them to keep bees; sends wishes for Easter.]

W. WRÓBLEWSKI

44   April 23, 1910

. . . . DEAR BROTHERS: . . . . I received your letter with the picture-patterns for [Easter] eggs, for which we thank you; we have no such yet. America is always the first to invent anything. [Weather, farm-work, crops.] The seeds called "pop-corn" which you sent me sprang up, but the cotton has not yet come up, though it was sown long ago.

Now I inform you more about my condition. In the introduction I wrote that we are in good health, but not all of us, for Olcia coughs too much since carnival.[1] She does different things but all this does not help. I went with her to a doctor, he gave a medicine and advises her to work in the fresh air. He said to me, "May it not be with her as with her mother!" He says that her left lung is weak. Now there is almost no work from her, she stops to rest every moment. At home lack and disorder are growing. I don't know what will come of it. There is work enough for women at home, and there is nobody

---

[1] An instance of the purely formal nature of the introductory news about health, prosperity, etc.

to work; everything is torn and worn, and there is nobody to make anything. I hope I may be not obliged to look for some woman [as wife], for I am not very willing to do it.[1] As long as this one was in good health, we were going on more or less, although with difficulty; but now it is indeed a misery; there is nobody either to govern or to work at home. I give directions and leave the house; when I come back, nothing is done. The one cannot, the other [the boy] is too lazy. They are quarreling continually. [Sends vegetable seeds to be tried in America.]

W. WRÓBLEWSKI

45   May 1, 1910

DEAR BROTHERS: . . . . I thank you for your letter. Now it is somewhat clearer to me about America. I learned much from your letters, what grows there, what are the prices, and in what locality you are settled. [Weather, crops, prices, farm-work.] We have this year enough to eat and work enough, but too little money. Thanks to God, at least I am gradually getting rid of my debts. It is bad that at home there is nobody to keep the house. Too much trouble for me.

[1] It would be interesting to know why he does not wish to remarry. He is certainly not deterred by the remembrance of his first wife, as such sentiments are absolutely strange to the peasant's traditional attitude. There are only two possible reasons—his attachment to Olcia, or his unwillingness to introduce an incalculable element of change into his life. But the latter supposition is less probable, because he does not hesitate to marry after Olcia's death, and because, as far as we see, there is no example of any fear of remarriage among peasants. His attachment to Olcia does not express itself openly, because of the unlawfulness of such a feeling. Still, it can be inferred. He mentions that Olcia sometimes accompanied him to entertainments, ceremonies, fairs, etc., and he had the idea of marrying her. Even if this idea was mainly determined by economic considerations, the sentimental and sexual elements were hardly absolutely lacking; these are almost always present in peasant marriages, even in men of a rather low level of intellectual and moral development, while Walery is certainly a peasant a little above the average. Finally, even if the love-element was originally absent, this idea of marrying Olcia made the man look upon her in a new way, as upon a woman, and some degree of love must have developed, particularly if we remember what an influence the conscious idea and its expression in words have upon the feelings of the peasant.

Some indications can be found also in letter 48. Walery writes there of Olcia's death in a much more informal personal way than that of the death of his wife. He mentions also that Olcia wished to will to him her part of the inheritance, but this may have been caused only by the usual familial attachment. At any rate, it is probable that his feeling for Olcia was only half-conscious.

But what else can be done? If mine [my wife] were living everything would be well, and so even all this rejoices me not much, although the farm is in a better order and the buildings nice. . . . .

Now I mention what you wrote about the comet of Halley. Among us people also know it, and different wicked speculators spread various rumors. There is nothing true in it. Our editor of Gazeta Świąteczna explains, that there is nothing to be feared from it, because the moon moves 50,000 miles from the earth and the one does no harm to the other; what damage then can the one bring to the other when the comet of Halley moves 3,000,000 miles away from the earth? I don't know where it is now; in March after sunset we saw it above the western sky, but now we don't see it any more. Perhaps you see it in America? . . . . Now what you wrote about the sun, if we live next year I will do so here at the appointed time, and so we shall learn who of us is nearer the equator. You had a very good idea, but now it cannot be done, for during this time the sun has turned much off from the earth, or rather the earth from the sun, and a second trial ought to be made.[1]

Now as to the machines which you bought and which are so expensive—don't they know scythes and sickles there? With these tools you can do much during the summer. But you ought not to lose hope, even if one year disappoints you; perhaps the next year will be better. One always works more willingly upon his own [land] and has more pleasure in everything and particularly it makes a difference in old age; you can live more easily to the end on your own [land] . . . . .

W. WRÓBLEWSKI

[Letter of June 19, entirely filled with questions of agriculture at home and in America; one of August 5, with news of the visit of bishop, confirmation of Edward and Józefa, arrest and imprisonment of brother Józef, by mistake; one of December 1, filled again with news and advice about farming and gardening.]

46   January 8, 1911

DEAR BROTHERS: [Usual beginning.] The holidays passed, we decorated the [Christmas] pine-tree and the children had great joy. [Difficult to bring in the hay.] Now I answer your questions. The

---

[1] Their idea is probably to measure the length of a shadow. It does not occur to them to consult a map, because of the total lack of any tradition about the use of books of reference. When information was needed it was always sought either by asking someone or, whenever possible, by observation and experiment.

village-elder is Kazimierz Płaksa; he is ending his third year. The shop in Łapy under the name "Consumers Association in Łapy" exists, but the income scarcely covers the expenses. It would prosper pretty well, if it were not for our darkness [lack of instruction]. What can be done, if people prefer to go to the Jews? They are afraid of making the Jews angry. Perkowski Roman opened a shop in his house also . . . . and it is not going badly. In the autumn I gave him a pumpkin for his shop which weighed more than 2 poods, and upon which was written: "Village-gardener W. W."

Now as to the autonomy of the Kingdom of Poland, it will probably be no sooner than pears grow upon a willow [Proverb]. [News about farm-work, crops, prices.] If it were always so [as this year], it would be only half a misery, but I don't know how it will be in the future with this farm. Perhaps it will soon fall into pieces, and then neither here nor elsewhere. I like to work, but only if there is something to work upon. I think that for you it is also agreeable to work upon a farm, and the more so upon such a farm. If our Lord God helps you to pay [the mortgage], it is the most sure piece of bread. . . . . If I had so much of my own land I believe that I should feel fine, but I commend myself to the will of God. . . . . I am in a bad situation. Even if it came to paying [the stepdaughter's part of inheritance in cash, instead of giving her land, in the case of her marriage], it would be difficult to find a loan, because I don't know myself what and upon what I am [what is my position, as the father of the heirs]. The worst is that my hands are tied, so that I cannot manage the affairs freely. Even now I do much, for I don't know what another man would do in my situation [probably less]. Now I think it a pity that I did not go earlier to America; at present it is too difficult. . . . .

WALERY WRÓBLEWSKI

The stork's nest fell down last summer; it was rotten with rains. Now there is none.

47   March 15, 1911

DEAR BROTHERS: [More than half the letter filled with farm and weather news.] Now as to the fast in our country, the Holy Father, or the Pope, gave an exemption for 7 years. On all the days of the whole year except the eve of the day of God's Mother, December 8, and Good Friday, we can eat milk. On all Saturdays of the year, if it does not happen to be the eve of some holiday or quarterly fast-day, we can eat meat. On all the Sundays during Lent, we can eat meat, even more than once. On all the Mondays, Tuesdays, Thursdays in Lent, except Good Thursdays, we can eat meat once a day. The Holy Father gave an exemption for the Kingdom of Poland for 7 years, commuting the fast for other good deeds. He did it last year, in April. The papers published it at once. The priests did not publish it; only when the whole people learned it and it was impossible to keep it secret they proclaimed it. Nevertheless we keep the old habit about meat, only in Lent we eat milk on Sundays, Mondays, Tuesdays and Thursdays, and on the other days we fast. . . . .[1]

W. WRÓBLEWSKI

48   March 16, 1912

"Praised be Jesus Christus!"

DEAR BROTHERS: I announce to you today sad and painful news. Today, March 16, at 4 o'clock in the morning, our Olcia ended her temporal life, and moved to eternity, toward which we also are going. It is sad and sorrowful news. For the second time I bear such a painful blow. What is left to me? Even this one who has been instead of a mother to these younger ones bade us farewell, not for a day, not for a week, but for eternity. She went often to church, but she came back, and now she will never come back. Oh, how sad it is to think of it! And the house is empty without her.

The spring comes, and there will be much work. Who will do this? Now I can do almost nothing at home, I must do my work, because, thanks to it, we can more easily drive poverty away, the more so as this funeral will cost more than 60 roubles. . . . . And moreover, there are rumors that the Stalugis from Barwiki and Feliks . . . . Łaba intend to claim the inheritance after her, but I believe that they will receive from us as much as the Stalugis formerly received from my late wife [nothing]. . . . . Olcia wanted to bequeath it to me, but it was not possible, because she was not full 21 years old.

---

[1] The persistence of old customs among peasants is very well shown in the matter of fasting. The example of Wróblewski, who fasts in spite of the exemption, is typical. The whole modern evolution in the church's attitude toward fasting remained without any influence upon the isolated peasant communities. This shows also the relative independence of religion *as custom* from the sanction of the church.

But as far as I have asked, her part belongs by the right of inheritance to the younger half-brothers and half-sisters. . . . .

W. W.

49 May 14, 1912

DEAR BROTHERS: . . . . Now I inform you that I have already a new housewife at home. I took her from Płonka. She is Miss Anna Perkowska, from the house where Horko formerly lived. She is the daughter of Horko's son-in-law, and 30 years old. Moreover, she is a good seamstress, because others learn from her. Although she does not look pretty, for me it is more than enough, for I am no longer the same as I was long ago. Now I have two sewing-machines; one can even be sold. Her stock of clothing is substantial enough— no need to buy her new dresses soon. And the order at home is becoming different, and I am glad of it, because up to the present there has been a terrible confusion in the house. Now, if only good harmony prevails at home, it will be better, I hope. . . . . I have nothing more of interest to write. I mention only that our marriage was performed on May 7, on the eve of St. Stanisław, and there was a good enough, although not a big wedding-feast. . . . .[1]

W. WRÓBLEWSKI

50 August 2, 1912

DEAR BROTHERS: [Weather, farm-work, crops.] Now I have had no letter from you for a long time. I wrote in May that a change had happened with me, that I had taken a new wife. . . . . Now at least the order at home is somewhat better, because up to this time it has been very bad; and a little money is more easily found when necessary, since I took my position again. Although my occupations are more numerous, at least there is some result. Now it will be more easily possible to go somewhere and to see something. It would not be bad, only Edward is somewhat lazy. Perhaps he will improve when he grows up. . . . .

W. WRÓBLEWSKI

[1] Less ceremonial and less social importance are always attached to second marriages, but the lack of any touch of romance and of any wedding announcements marks this as an unusually matter-of-fact arrangement.

51   October 21, 1912

DEAR BROTHERS: [Weather, crops, prices; news about acquaintances.] Now in Płonka we have a new church . . . . it will be consecrated next year. Our village gathered 150 roubles for one window of the new church; other villages give money also, but we have shown ourselves munificent as compared with the others, for which we have been praised more than once from the chancel by the priest. Now, at home it does not go badly. My present housekeeper, or rather wife, keeps good order at home and also with the children; they are all cleaner than before, and my Józia says that she never had such a chemise as she has now. . . . . Well, the service is not bad; I get 30 [roubles] every month. She earns for herself by sewing . . . . and I do not have to pay for the weeding, harvesting, digging, etc. . . . . [More farm-news.]

                                                    W. WRÓBLEWSKI

52   March 7, 1913

. . . . DEAR BROTHERS: . . . . We live still in the old way, but perhaps soon there will be something new [war]. Everything here is as you wrote. We expected bad times very soon. Now it seems that for the present there will be peace, but it seems that, as the papers write, this misery is unavoidable sooner or later. Where shall we go then? We shall all perish probably in some awful way, if we live long enough to see it come. . . . . Although even now we don't enjoy any delights, then a terrible misery awaits us, and we shall be separated from you, not singly, but all together, and we shall give no news about ourselves and get none from you. . . . .

These 30 roubles which I earn monthly are still not enough for such expenses. And as my son is moreover a lazy boy, the farming is bad at home. Even now I have been obliged to kill a cow; she could neither rise nor calve. Only two are left. And then everybody must be clothed and shod, and I must count well in order to get our living. I got entangled in this misery so that there is no way out of it. I became the slave of my own family. If I saw that my son would be a farmer and that, if God allowed me to live until old age, I could spend it with him, then it would be possible to bear it. But I don't see it, for he is lazy in every line, careless. Wherever he goes, he will have hard times. Now when I am not at home he becomes still more idle. I cannot decide about this property, and he will be no farmer, as it seems. So if I live so long that I am unable to work myself—what then? [Weather; Easter-wishes.]

WALERY WRÓBLEWSKI

53 October 10, 1913

DEAR BROTHERS: . . . . I am always very interested in how you live there in the foreign country. It is a pity that you have worse luck this year, but this happens always and everywhere. Do you hope at least to keep this farm? Will there be no failure? Now I inform you that there is a change with me. My chief went away and a new one came. I don't know whether it will be possible to serve under him; it seems that he will be very particular. I should be glad to remain at least for the winter. . . . .

Now I inform you that we shall surely have colonies [commassation of land], because all the villages of the commune Łapy agree; and not a great agreement is needed, because it is enough if more than half of the village wants it; then the others must agree. . . . . Everybody will sit upon a single spot, the pasture will be common, and the fields and meadows will be measured anew. I am very curious what will come of it.[1]

Now, on August 24 was the consecration of the new church in Płonka. Now we are already going to the new church. It is a pleasure to see, how beautiful it is. . . . . Michał is now going to school, and the youngest boy Wacław [son of the new wife] is growing very well. . . . .

W. WRÓBLEWSKI

54 April 4, 1914

DEAR BROTHERS: . . . . Now I remain in the same employment. My chief will go away again and a new one will come. It is not very good to have to get accustomed to a new one so often. There is now work enough for me . . . . and there is always something for the work [some money], but there is one misfortune. My

---

[1] Under the old system the peasant had his land in small pieces (Wróblewski, as he says, had his seven morgs—nine and one-half acres—in forty spots), and with as many neighbors as he had plots of land the peasant was in constant disputes over questions of trespass and the like. The new system has resulted in incomparably fewer quarrels and lawsuits.

Edward every year sees the stork for the first time standing or lying, and I, on the contrary, see him always flying. Yesterday also I saw the first stork this year flying; surely he will bring something this year. Such is my luck.[1]

My youngest Wacław is a strong boy and keeps well. Perhaps he will have more energy, because these older ones have been bad and miserable since childhood, and even now there is little energy in them; and there is work enough, if not at home, then elsewhere, if one is not a lazy fellow. . . . .[2]

W. WRÓBLEWSKI

55 Tuesday, December 10, 1907

DEAR BROTHER: . . . . I thank you for your letter, which pleased and grieved me at the same time. It pleased me because I learned something about you from your own hand, and grieved me because you described truly your situation. I knew about it long ago, it is true, but up to the last moment I could not believe that the danger was so imminent. How can I help you? I may only say that if you are unhappy (in this life), think that perhaps there are others, a hundred times more unhappy than you; and even those who at first sight seem to succeed well enough, if we looked nearer, and if we could discover the mysteries of their life, we should know that the life of every one of them is one series of sufferings. And if a man could see all his sufferings at once, he would certainly try to shorten them voluntarily.

But let us not talk about other people, only about ourselves. Let us begin with the oldest. Is Walery happy? Is everything with him going on as he wishes? At first it would seem we could say yes. It is but enough to look at the health of his wife and his children, particularly in their first years, in order to have an idea of his success.

[1] We have here an instance of a very general belief that the good or bad omen is a real factor causing the foretold phenomenon to appear. This belief is the background of the magical hygiene of the peasants. There is a whole code of prescriptions—as to what and how omens are to be avoided.

[2] The laziness of which he complains is certainly a result of heredity. The children have inherited a weak organism from their consumptive mother. But this interpretation is never very clearly realized by a peasant. The attitude toward hereditary physical weakness is usually one of moral condemnation, unless there is a definite defect which puts the given person a priori outside of any social competition.

Further, was Marysia, in the flower of her age, happy? Certainly not. About Feliks I don't know much. But if somebody ordered me to be in his skin, a scapegoat, then I should be glad if there were ten Americas. You think probably that I make suppositions—true or not—about his wife. Then come you, I and Konstanty. We know about you. As to me, we can shrug our shoulders. To live alone seemed to me no business. I considered marriage a difficult duty, but nobody who has not experienced it can have any idea about it. It is not because I have made a bad choice, but because with marriage are connected the most painful and irritating questions. I don't say that my condition is the worst, but it is far from being good, and the skies, instead of brightening, get clouded. Let us mention only one, the least important question. Every beast has its lair, the dog has his kennel, while we must wander about strange corners and depend upon the landlord's caprice, and we cannot even dream about our own kennel. And it is useless to speak about the rest. There remains Konstanty. I don't know how he succeeds. You write that he does very well, but I cannot believe that a man condemned to live far away from his native country could feel really happy.[1]

I was astonished in reading in your last letter the question, whether I had not forgotten you. In my opinion to forget for a long time one's brothers and sisters would be equal to forgetting for a long time to eat. Particularly now, when our father has disowned us, when our own father tries to harm us in every possible way—as you know probably from our brother's letters—we ought to be, all of us, near one another, "one for all and all for one." And if we cannot unify ourselves materially, then at least let us be united spiritually as closely as possible, and then it will be easier to bear the burden of life, and our Lord God will help us.[2]

[Józef Wróblewski]

[1] The letter is full of meaning as showing the nature of the peasant's pessimism. Whenever theoretical reflection takes the place of action the practical optimism of the peasant changes into a theoretical pessimism; the less of active energy we find in an individual or a group, the more pessimism prevails. (Cf. Osiński series, No. 78, note.) But religion, where the practical rather than the theoretical attitudes are expressed, is optimistic, as far as uninfluenced by the Christian terrors of God's wrath.

[2] A good expression of the peasant's own conception of familial solidarity.

56   [No date, probably 1908]

DEAR BROTHERS: I wrote in my preceding letter that I would
write another soon, and I am doing it now.   It does not cost me much,
and to you it is probably the same, for if you pay for a box yearly
a smaller or larger number of letters makes no difference.   I promise
my wife that if I go to America, I shall write her letters regularly
every week, but I don't know myself whether it will be true, for
sometimes something may change or some impediment may come.
Is it not true? . . . .

Jan Laba, from our village, is going to America for the second time.
He says it is the best to go there for winter, because it is not hot and
is easier to work.   Last Wednesday we had the autumnal *odpust*
[parish-festival][1] in Płonka, on St. Michael's day.   During the day
the weather was nice, but in the morning it rained and therefore
people from farther districts did not come.   I, Franciszek and Ignacy
came together—for now we seldom come together—and we talked of
course about "old times."   Franciszek related how, about 12 years
ago, he came back from the same parish-festival when the people
were driving the cattle into the fields.   Evidently, there can be no
question of that now, for his dear wife would arrange for him upon
earth, or even simply in their home, a "Dante's hell," and he would
merit it in fact.[2]   And thus having talked and complained about bad
luck, after the end of the divine service we went back at once, each
his own way.

In general now it is sad in Płonka, for nobody comes there from
Łapy, because they have their own chapel and soon they will begin
to build a church.   But we shall have time enough to talk about it
when I come to you.   And now I renew my request to Kostuś.   If
he can and if both of you believe that it is worth while, let him send

[1] "Odpust" means literally "indulgence," that is, partial or total remission
of punishment for sins to be suffered on earth or in purgatory.   During the parish
festival full indulgence is granted to those who confess and commune and perform
certain good deeds.   Hence the identification of "indulgence" and "festival."

[2] The peasant conscience excludes conjugal infidelity absolutely.   (Cf. the
last letters of Stasia in the Piotrowski series.)   Besides murder and wronging of
the helpless, it is the only sin which he never excuses.   Even in the tales, in which
almost all sins occasionally find pardon, there is no remission of infidelity.   In this
respect the conscience of townspeople, particularly of handworkers, is much more
lax.   The relation of the master's wife with the journeyman is not always condemned.

me a ship-ticket, for here people say that if one goes without a ship-ticket, he must have 200 roubles, for if he does not show 50 roubles when leaving the ship he will be sent back. And if it is true, I could hardly gather 200 roubles, unless by selling all my household effects at auction, and I should not like that at all. And then, I should leave a few roubles for my wife and my son. But first I ask you for advice, whether it is worth going, for if I don't earn $1½ a day, it would not be worth thinking about America. . . . . It is a pity that Kostuś is no longer in the mines, for I should like to have piece-work, for work is never too hard. . . . .

Józef Wróblewski

57   December 13, 1909

DEAR BROTHERS: The man was not stupid who made the proverb: "Man shoots and aims, but the Lord God directs the bullets." The same proved true with me. At the moment when I had a real intention of going to you, and when I received your letter, then a "something," as we call it usually, got me, but such a "something" that while I could still think of America it was only of the America from which nobody ever comes back. I was not actually laid up, but worse still, for with a man who is lying in bed things are soon decided in one way or another. As to me, I am sick in my lungs, coughing, catarrh, sore throat, headache. In a word, like a broken pot. . . . . Now I am better than in the beginning, but far from being fully recovered. . . . . I don't know now myself when I shall be able to visit you, and whether I shall be able at all, for to feel something bad about one's self and to go beyond the sea in search of bread would be very silly. . . . . To tell the truth, day-work does not attract me much, for during 10 years I have become unaccustomed to anybody's controlling my work. Even if I worked the best possible, I should always have the impression that the boss considered it insufficient. Piece-work is quite another matter. I want it still and always. Perhaps I could find it.[1]

As to the news, there is a sad piece. Wincenty K. (from whom our father bought the mill-wheel), became half-insane because of money troubles and a few days ago cut his throat with a razor. He walked after this about a verst, and died under a fence near his home.

---

[1] On piece-work see Introduction: "Economic Attitudes."

And it is a pity, for he was such an honest man. There is also gay news. Stefka G. married a boy from Szolajdy. . . . . The wedding was on the last Sunday before Advent. But God pity us! What marriage-festivals there are now! It began at 10 o'clock in the morning, and at 10 in the evening there was not a strange soul left, except of course the groom, who was not so stupid as to leave his beloved. Thus the whole festival did not last even 12 hours.[1] There were only 5 bottles of brandy for 60 persons. To tell the truth, it would be better in general if there had been none. There was more beer, but people got sick, for even without beer it was cold enough. . . . .

Józef Wróblewski

[1] We find in many letters the statement that the marriage-festivals are becoming shorter and less ceremonial. It is an immediate sign that marriage is losing more and more its social character; mediately it shows the progressive individualization of peasant life in general.

STELMACH SERIES

Jan Stelmach, the old man who writes these letters, is a perfect type of Galician peasant farmer, with some instruction, indeed, but without any climbing tendencies and with a definite class-consciousness.   Except for the usual troubles of country life, he seems to be perfectly satisfied with his position.   In this respect the Galician peasant differs from the peasants in Russian and German Poland. Perhaps owing to greater national freedom and because of the relatively insignificant industrial progress of Galicia, the peasant there developed a particular pride and a strong class-feeling.   Even when he gets a higher instruction, becomes a priest, a teacher, an official, he is seldom ashamed of his origin, remains and wants to remain a peasant.   From the advice which old Stelmach gives to his son and daughter-in-law it is evident that he considers, consciously and after reflection, the peasant form of life the most normal and sound, physically and morally.

There is also an interesting variety of the family problem. We see that the Stelmach family, except for some slight misunderstandings, remains harmonious—much more so than the Wróblewskis or even the Osińskis.   But this does not mean that the old solidarity and community are preserved.   On the contrary, there is already a far-going individualization, as shown, for example, in the question of marriage and in economic matters (real division of the property; independence of the son in America).   But the individualization goes on without any struggle.   The old man, for instance, voluntarily resigns any active control of his son, and limits himself to giving advice.   He welcomes with joy his unknown daughter-in-law, although the way in which the marriage was performed was contrary to all the traditions. He never asks his son for money, although he knows that the latter is well off; he has a sufficient understanding of the desire of the other children to get better individual positions in America, and not only does not protest against their plan of emigration, but asks the oldest son to help them. In short, in this matter there seems to be also a more rational and self-conscious attitude in the Stelmach family than in many others. Instead of a stubborn holding to tradition, we find an acknowledgment of the inevitable limitation of its power. Perhaps familiarity with the phenomena of emigration (of which we find a proof in Stelmach's knowledge of the American conditions) has helped to develop this attitude.

THE FAMILY STELMACH

Jan Stelmach, a farmer
Ewa, his wife

Józef
Jędrzej
Michał } his sons
Piotr
Wojtek (Wojciech)

Kaśka
Jadwiga } his daughters

Sobek, the husband of Kaśka
Julianna (Julcia, Julka, Ulis), the wife of Józef
Julianna's parents
Makar, Julianna's brother

Magdusia
Hanka } Julianna's sisters

Krzysztof Żak, uncle of Ewa Stelmach

Rózia Stefańska
Jagusia Sasielska (Wojtkowa) } his daughters
Zośka (Zosia)

58   PORĘBY WOLSKIE, March 1, 1909

Praised be Jesus Christus and the Holiest Virgin Mary, His Mother!

DEAREST CHILDREN: . . . . I wanted to send wishes for the name-day of Julianna, and I saw in the yearly almanac that St. Julianna is on March 20, so I intended to send my wishes to you both. But I did not succeed, because I ascertained finally that St. Julianna is on February 16, and so I have erred through this yearly almanac. So now I will send my wishes only to you, dear son. To you, dear daughter-in-law, I will send wishes for your name-day next year, if I live so long, because now I know already that the day of your patron is February 16.

Well, dear son, a year has passed away, and the day of March 19, your name-day, approaches. Your mother and I want to offer you various wishes, dear child. We wish you health, happiness, good success, an honored name, every good luck, indissoluble love in your marriage. May you love each other and never know any sorrow, may you never know misery, may you have bread and money enough! May our Lord God illuminate you with his mercy, that you may always know what to do and what to avoid. May our Lord God send you happiness and blessing, that you may have everything, want nothing, live happily and praise God. May our Lord God grant you every sweet thing! This wish you your father and mother. Vivat our son Józef! May he live a hundred years, may our Lord God weave health and happiness, health and fortune into his life!![1]

Now I describe to you our condition. Your aunt wrote to us and sent us a dollar in the letter. We received the letter but the dollar was not there, because somebody had stolen it. I wrote to the aunt never to send money again in a letter, not even in a registered one, because many dollars have already been lost from letters. Poor aunt, she has so little herself and she wants to help us! May our Lord God give her whatever is the best, because she wants to help us as she can, but some wicked man has swallowed $6 already. . . . . And don't you send money in a letter either, because a letter can be opened easily. You have only to moisten it with spittle where it is

---

[1] The whole paragraph (half in verse) is a typical *speech*, such as would be said during a family festival. The function of ceremonial wishes is here made as plain as possible. (See Forms and Functions of the Peasant Letter.)

glued and put it under your arm. When it becomes warm, the glue loosens up and it is easy to open it with a needle, to read it, then to moisten and to glue it up, adjusting carefully the borders of the seal. If it won't hold, you need only rub it with a potato and it will stick up, and nobody will know it. . . . . So don't dare to send it in a letter, because it is nowhere difficult to find a thief.[1]

We are all in good health, but our condition is meanwhile a little sad because, as you know, when there is one thing another thing is lacking. So we lacked milk during the carnival, and our cow was to calve at the end of February, and we were watching whether she would not calve. On the night of February 26 to 27 I went to the stable to see whether the cow was not calving, and I found the cow strangled. . . . . The other young cow had torn herself loose and had pushed her with her horns. The cow had pulled the chain, but the chain was strong and could not be broken, and the cow was strangled. So we had a sorrow in those days, but God gave it, God took it away, may He have honor and glory; he afflicted us, but he will also comfort us. . . . .[2]

Aunt Walkowa Stelmaszka [wife of the paternal uncle, Walek Stelmach] intends to send her daughter Agnieszka to America to Borek [probably her brother]. You write that Borek did not answer you. It was because many fellow-countrymen tumbled upon him there, and he was afraid that you had no work and he thought that if you came to him, he would be obliged to support you.[3] But if you

[1] The old man has evidently used this means of opening and reading letters, but it must be remembered that there is no strong feeling of privacy about letters among peasants. The letter is always at least family-property, and all the members of the family have the right to read it independently of the will of the person by whom it is written or to whom addressed. To some, often to a very large, extent the whole village claims the right to read a private letter, particularly if there are greetings for many neighbors, or if the news interests the community. This was e.g., the case with letters from Brazil during the craze for emigration to that region. The refusal to give a letter to read is considered almost an offense. The more isolated the community from the external world, the rarer the news, the less the feeling of privacy is developed.

[2] The formula is exactly the same after the death of a child.

[3] According to the principle of solidarity Borek should have received his relative. But there are too many claims, and the situation is abnormal. Normally the relation of solidarity exists first of all between the individual and the group, and only secondarily among individual members of the group. The individual has duties toward the group as a whole and the group as a whole has duties toward every individual; but an individual has duties toward another

don't wish to go to a farm you don't need to write to him. We won't write you more, only we greet you very warmly. May our Lord God make you happy and bless you, our dear children!

Your parents,

Jan and Ewa Stelmach

And we also, your brothers and sisters, greet you, brother and sister-in-law, very warmly.

I, your aunt Wojtkowa [wife of Wojtek] Sasielska, greet you, my nephew Józwa [Joseph] and my niece Julka [Julianna]. As I happened to be here when your letter came and as they answer you while I am here, so I greet you and wish you health and happiness for your new household.

59   September 27, 1909

. . . . Dear Son: We wrote before to you and to your aunt, and now we write again to you and to your aunt. We wrote before to your aunt that her sisters are to pay her 50 crowns each, and now I have written her that the sisters calculate that either Rózia will give them [this money], or it will be lost [to her], because she won't come here to our country for these 100 crowns. And I wrote to your aunt that if she wants to collect these 100 crowns herself, let her do it, but if she were to give [this money] to them, let her not give it to them, but let her rather give it to us, i.e., to your mother. If your aunt gives it to us, let her send us a power of attorney certified by the consul. But the consul won't certify it without money, so we beg you very nicely, beg your aunt in our name to do it, and pay whatever it costs. If your aunt will collect [this money] for herself, let her collect it, but instead of giving it to her sisters and your aunts, let her rather give it to us. So when you receive the letter, do your best, because we

---

individual only because and as far as both are members of the same group, not because they are immediately connected with each other. Therefore, when the individuals are isolated from their groups, as happens on emigration, their reciprocal duties cease to be real, just in the measure in which they are cut off from the common basis. A personal, variable, voluntary, relation takes the place of the social norm. Claims on help are, as a matter of fact, much less exacting at home than abroad. At home a single individual who needs help finds many who can help him, each one a little; abroad a single individual who is able to help has often to bear the burden of supporting many who are in a difficult condition. (Cf. Raczkowski series, the situation of Adam after his marriage.)

send a letter to you and another to your aunt. We beg you, do your best, that your aunt may give this money to us, and not to Jagusia and Zosia. . . . .[1]

[JAN and EWA STELMACH]

60

November 5, 1909

. . . . DEAR CHILDREN: . . . . We gathered from the field what our Lord God gave us. He did not take it away in our village, but on other sides of the country hail has beaten [the crops]. Wola was left free from [God's] punishment, but we have gathered less than last year. . . . .[2]

We are very glad that you are in good health and that you speak to us. May God make you happy and bless you and save you from any evil. Here Urbanowa [wife of Urban] Chudzicka, our relative, is dead and Urban married at once in the house of Łukaszek Maruta [the daughter of L. M.], that Rózia who worked in Wola, and now he has a young wife. Krzysztof Zak is also dead. Aunt Stefańska wrote to us asking who will pay her part of the inheritance [who is the main heir, taking the land and paying the other heirs in cash]. But I did not answer her directly, because the government ordered this money of the heirs to be put in the bank, and I thought that they would put it there. But the other aunts won't put it, because your grandfather had at first left the field near the forest to Rózia [Stefańska], but finally he willed it to Jagusia and Zoška [other sisters], and they are to pay to Rózia 25 gulden each. They will give together 50 gulden, i.e., 100 crowns. They would be glad if Stefańska gave them these 100 crowns as a gift, and your mother intended also to write Rózia asking her to give these 100 crowns to your mother, but she did not dare, because Aunt Rózia received too small a part of the

[1] The grandfather evidently thought that Aunt Rózia, being in America, needed no money. He wanted, in fact, to relieve the heirs who took the land from a heavy payment. A hundred crowns is a trifle in comparison with the probable value of the land, and leaving the sum to her at all was certainly nothing but a formality; the grandfather did not wish to omit her completely in the will, as this would mean a disavowal of the daughter. That it was a formality is proved by the request of the sisters to give this money to them. And this explains old Stelmach's similar request. He would hardly have asked his sister-in-law to cede her rights to his wife if her inheritance were *real*, e.g., a piece of land.

[2] The aleatory element in economic life. For the consequences of this element, see Introduction: "Economic Life"; "Religious and Magical Attitudes."

inheritance.[1] You will ask perhaps what she will do, whether she will let them [the two other aunts] send her these 100 crowns, or will give them to one of them. But they . . . . [illegible word; perhaps "have slandered" or "have wronged"] the aunt, so she ought not give this money to them.

Michał [son] wrote to us that you had answered him. If you think it good, you could let him come there, but not until spring. . . . . You say that [workmen] are striking; well, that is funny! Not long ago they had no work, and now already they don't want to work, but require a higher pay! We have now repaired the stable; we made two stables, one for the horses, another for the cows. People say that in that town where you are there is a big stench, the whole town is covered with smoke as with clouds. . . . .

JAN and EWA STELMACH

[The first paragraph of the following letter is of the ceremonial type (similar to the first part of No. 58) and is printed as No. 4 among the specimens of peasant letters.]

61   January 30, 1910

. . . . In the last letter I asked you to advise me whether I should send Michał and Wojtek to Prussia or to America. You did not even answer me. If you think that it is good there and if you have a little money, you may send a ship-ticket at least to one of them, so at least one shall go. You never say to them any word of praise, that it is well there, so they are afraid to go to America, and here at home you know yourself how it has been. They quarrel with each other. Sometimes one succeeds in Prussia and sometimes not, and then the summer is passed in vain. If he came there to you he could work back for the ship-ticket, in the same way as you worked back for the ticket which your aunt sent you. It would be well if you sent [tickets] for both of them. . . . . So now you understand it to be better, on that side praise it [praise, in writing to them, the course which you consider the best], because people think it strange, that you don't take either

[1] The situation has an additional interest from the fact, that Jagusia and Zosia are the own sisters of Aunt Rózia, while the writer's wife Ewa is only her cousin. The Stelmachs' claim is therefore based not upon family-relationship, but upon the nearness of personal relations.

of them.[1] If you had taken Kaśka also, it would have been easier for us, and perhaps better for her, because we contracted debts for her sake and she does not get on well. The sister and brother of Sobek [son-in-law, husband of Kaśka] require the debt to be paid, and if not, then interest to be paid, and the interest on twelve hundred is 72 gulden. Think how it is necessary to work in our country in order to live and to put 72 gulden aside. This makes her sad. But you never wrote her "Sister, come here, you will earn, and you will get on well." But this is past. Now you can only advise your brothers so that everything may be well. [Greetings from the whole family.]

JAN and EWA STELMACH

Gud Baj [goodbye; probably imitates the son who adds this in his letters].

62

November 31, 1910

.... DEAR CHILDREN: .... We wrote to you in August but you did not answer, and so now we risk writing to you, because we think that you have moved somewhere and our letter did not reach you. .... Our condition is not pleasant, because winter tumbled upon us, snows have been falling since November 22, and it is difficult to go out anywhere. The boys did not come from Prussia, they wrote that they will come only for Christmas. The cold annoys them, because they must rise at dawn to work and labor long in the evening. Dear children, we send you consecrated wafers. Although there are also wafers [there], yet you are entered in the registers of this parish, so we send you them from here, because you are Christians.[2] Many people forget there that they are Christians, but

---

[1] It is explicitly stated here that the sending of ship-tickets to one's relatives is not a mere act of kindness, but a familial duty—more so than the sending of money home, for that question is never raised in this series. A certain individualization of familial relations seems to be manifested by this distinction. Indeed, by sending money home the emigrant helps his family immediately as a whole, while by taking one family-member to America he evidently helps this member immediately and the rest of the family only mediately.

[2] This connection between religious valuation and local patriotism is very frequent. Not only the wafer from one's own parish has more value than one from anywhere else, but the same is true of any other object of religious or magical significance. A particular importance in this respect was attached to earth. It was an old custom of emigrants and wanderers to carry a little earth of their

don't you forget that you are Christians and that you believe in one God.   As long as you speak to your parents, it is evident that you believe in our Lord God, but when you disown your parents, it is evident from this that you don't believe in our Lord God.[1]   I asked you to answer us and to give the address of the Stefańskis . . . . and your mother wanted you absolutely to answer at once and to write why you wanted to go to the mines, whether you had no work where you are.   People say that there in Pittsburgh it would need a dragon to hold out.   They say that even in fine weather no sun is to be seen. . . . . If it is true, move rather to another city. . . . .

Jan and Ewa Stelmach

63   March 28, 1911

. . . . Dear Children: . . . . When you did not write for so long a time we thought different things about you.   I asked a peasant from Wólka how Wojciech Maksyn was getting on.   He said that he [Maksyn] was selling his horse and asked me how I knew about him. I said that my son married his daughter.   And this peasant said, "One son-in-law ran away from his daughter."   Then I thought that you had run away and therefore don't write to us, and I intended to write to Maksyn in Wólka [to learn] which of his sons-in-law had run

---

ancestors' land with them which played the rôle of a talisman and was to be put under their heads in the grave in case they died and were buried far from their native village.

[1] The very real psychological unity of the traditional set of attitudes is here evidently exaggerated, since various attitudes *may* be dropped or changed separately.   But this exaggeration itself is significant, for it must exert a real influence upon the evolution of the subject himself and upon the attitude of the environment toward him.   A man who has dropped one traditional attitude will drop the others more easily, because in his own conscious reasoning they seem more connected than they are in reality.   This will happen particularly if, as is often the case, intellectual factors in general tend to influence strongly individual life while the level of instruction is rather low.   Thus, among the socialists of the lower classes many traditions are rejected without any real necessity and against the man's own feeling, simply because they are *believed* connected with others which were logically rejected as incompatible with the socialistic ideals.   On the other hand, the behavior of the social environment toward an individual who has dropped some traditions is usually determined by the prepossession that he must have dropped all traditional attitudes—precisely as Stelmach explicitly states here.   Sometimes a very trifling change is sufficient to arouse this prepossession, e.g., a change of dress, of the old way of farming, the dropping of magical beliefs, etc.

away and from which of his daughters. But now you have written to us and we already know that it is not you who left your wife. We pity you very much that you have no health there now, and I wrote you already to move away from that Pittsburgh. . . . . I would advise you to move with your wife to Trenton, N.J. There in Trenton are people from our neighborhood, and they are in good health and they earn well enough. Kuba Chudzik from Brzyski is now there and intends to come home. If he does not leave before this letter reaches you, you could write to him; so you might succeed him in his work when he comes home. He works in an iron-factory and has good wages. [Gives addresses of other people in Trenton.] But you must try to get information, so as not to lose the work which you have . . . . before you find anything in Trenton. . . . . Even if you wanted to come back to our country there is no goodness here, because, as you know, those who were with you returned to our country and then went to America again, because it is strait here.

And you, Julka, don't grieve, for you are sick from grief; you will get a nervous illness, when you are so you are neither healthy nor sick, and no doctor can help against a nervous illness. So don't worry. Commend yourself to the will of God and work as much as you can; then you will have no time to grieve. And don't lace too tightly, for there the women lace their corsets so much that they look squeezed up like wasps, and when they bind themselves up so tightly, the blood is checked and the body is ill. And don't grieve either that your little son is dead. The Lord gave, the Lord took away, praised be His name. . . . .

There in Pittsburgh, people say, the dear sun never shines brightly, the air is saturated with stench and gas. The most healthy life is on farms, but if you have no intention of going on a farm, then at least move where the air is better. . . . .

JAN and EWA STELMACH

64   [May, 1911]

. . . . DEAR CHILDREN: [Thanks for the wishes which were sent for his name-day.] We had a little sorrow because in one week three lay sick with measles, Jadwisia, Marcin and Wojtek. . . . . Wojtek was to go to Prussia, but he remained, and therefore he was more sick than the smaller ones, and so the summer will pass. But he could be useful even at home, because our stable is ruined and it is necessary to repair it and to build another for the horse. . . . . We had another sorrow, because a mare of Kaśka died. She was worth 100 gulden. This has pained us also, because, dear children, if anything pains you, it pains us also, because we love you all as ourselves. If you write that you are getting on well and your little wife, our daughter-in-law, also, then we are glad, even if misery oppresses ourselves, because we see that although we have misery, yet at least our children have good success.

This year seems not to be bad here, but from the past one everybody is thin, because the winter was big. The cattle are standing at home up to the middle of May, and we were obliged to mix the chopped straw with flour and potatoes, and now men are lacking food. The prices are as high as in America. . . . .

You write that you have a small lodging. Have you then nobody to live with you and to help you pay the rent? Julka does not go to work now, so if she has no occupation whatever in her hands she is tired. If you had people boarding, she would have distraction and she would even be more healthy, because when a man works, he is healthy, but when he loafs around in vain he gets weaker and weaker. It is said that therefore many people have no good health in America. As long as a girl goes to work she is healthy, but when she gets married she does not go to work and she stretches herself [lies idle] so that blood cannot run in her veins, fresh air does not reach her because she sits continually in her lodgings. Even if she goes out into the world petticoats drag behind her and air does not reach her [because she is too heavily dressed], and she has no health. And she goes to her country, and then from her country again to America, and so they lose money on ship-tickets. Let them dress as easily as at home. Don't sit in vain [idle] don't eat much meat, and thus you will all be healthy. . . . .

JAN and EWA STELMACH

You write that Michał wrote to you that he wanted to go to America, but he is too weak for America. He got thin in serving, particularly with Pełka. You were there and you saw how it was. Wojtek is younger, but stronger than Michał. Jędrzej would find his way in America, but he is afraid of America, he cannot be persuaded. . . . .

65   February 23, 1913

. . . . DEAR CHILDREN: . . . . We are very glad that you keep so much poultry and a pig; it is as if you had a farm. When you learn to keep poultry and pigs, and when your children grow up, then you will go to a farm. . . . .[1]

I thought that only in our country people talk about war, but I see that even in America they write about war and insurrection. But there they speak about war lightly, and here among us they are so afraid of war that they weep. The reservists called in autumn have been kept up to the present. In the beginning of March there is to be a military call; 206,065 soldiers are to be taken to the army. The Sokols are waiting for war even in our country, but the people in villages are so afraid that they tremble from fear.[2]

From your aunt Stefańska also we received a letter and a photograph of her two daughters. She wrote that formerly you called upon them often but now you do not come to them, and her children ask, "When will Józef come to us?" She said that she sends her two boys to work, and she said that they are getting on well. You write that [it would be well] if one [of your brothers] went to America. Well, I want absolutely to send one of them, or later even two; then you would not be homesick. Here it may be better perhaps only after the war. But who knows who will be left after the war? . . . . If I were stronger and if my leg did not pain me so much I would go to Wólka to your brother-in-law, and I would send you as a gift at least a few cheeses through him. But who knows whether he will go, and I cannot walk far. I asked about Julcia's father. I was told that he is getting on pretty well and has one daughter [married] rich, and the dowry cost him little. One man told me that he farms at home with his son, another said that he farms

---

[1] The people at home like to have their relatives in America become farmers. It is perhaps because of the analogy of interests. And this in spite of the fact that an emigrant who becomes a farmer in America will never return. (Cf. in this respect Wróblewski series.)

[2] The fear of war, so general among the peasants, is based upon old, only half-reasoned tradition rather than upon experience. Particularly the Galician peasants had had no experience of war since 1866, and then not a trying one. War is enumerated among the calamities which the peasants pray God every Sunday to avert, and there is an undetermined but on that account more awe-inspiring tradition of the horrors of war.

alone, and that he intends to have one daughter come from America, but he did not know which one. . . . .

[JAN and EWA STELMACH]

[Letter of May 3, 1913, regrets that his sons in America do not make greater efforts to meet in America certain relatives and acquaintances from Poland. Describes efforts to build new church.]

66   April 1, 1914

. . . . DEAR CHILDREN: . . . . I received the papers from you, four copies, I shall have an amusement for the holidays. Piotr and Wojtek went to [season-work in] Prussia on March 19; I wrote it to you, but I don't know whether you received my letter. I wrote you to send a ship-ticket for Piotr, but in leaving he said that he won't go from Prussia [to America], but later on from home. His address is: . . . . Write to them, don't begrudge the five cents, and they would answer you, and you would speak with one another, like brothers. I wrote you to send me "żmijecznik," a medicine which is called "żmijecznik," if anybody from Wólka or from Turza comes home . . . . because your mother has no good health, now as before.[1] I have been healthy, but now my leg aches, and people say that it won't be healed, and if it is healed, they say that I shall be sick. . . . .[2] [Weather.]

Dear son, your mother would be glad to see you before she dies, but it is difficult, because here in our country it gets worse and worse. Now many people get separated, although they have land. Many husbands leave their wives and go in search of work, some of them go to America, others to Prussia. The wife of Wawrzek Sidor fled to Prussia, and many others did so, because misery creeps into the houses and drives people away into the world.[3] [Complains about cost of

[1] "Żmijecznik" is a magical remedy.

[2] It is a very frequent belief that if some particular disease, painful but not dangerous, is healed, the patient will become seriously sick, or will die within a certain time. The background of this belief is evidently magical. If the "evil principle" manifests itself through one of those diseases, it means that it has taken possession of the patient and that it cannot be driven out of him. If hindered in doing the smaller harm it will express itself in a greater harm.

[3] This is the only case in our materials where we find bad economic conditions expressly stated as the cause of a wife's running away from home. Other cases have been recorded by the Emigrants' Protective Association in Warsaw, but it

living.]   Dear children, work and economize as much as you can, that you may have some help for the black hour [for any misfortune], because man is imperfect in this world and always lacks something. If man insisted on always having what he needs to be satisfied he would waste millions.   It is best to live modestly, in order that it may suffice, because even counts have wasted their manors when they wanted to satisfy all their wishes.   So live as you can.   May our Lord God grant you health and happiness, the best possible. . . . .

JAN and EWA STELMACH

67

[Beginning lacking.]   You ask whether Jędrzej married in the house of that Ludwik who had the [son] Kuba who called upon Dawik [visited the Dawik girls].   Yes, he married in the house of that Ludwik, but both the Ludwiks died, and Kuba married that Jadwiga who is the ablest among all the girls of Dawik.   The others are like grandmothers.   That Zośka who was in America got married to [a man from] Korowiska, and she is always sick.   She has two children, but she did nothing more than bear them; she does not nurse them, only she had to buy a kind of a bottle and milks a cow and with this she feeds her children.   The man who married her got little comfort from her.   Dawik gave her only the money which she earned in America, and keeps until his death the field which she had after her mother; only when he dies, Zośka will have the field.

When Jędrzej got married, we had to make a will.   We had to make a will because I am so as if I were ill, and your mother has also weak health.   So your mother willed him that field near Pełka's [farm], and this one where we sit, and two morgs in Zrąbki, and these small buildings [contemptuously], and he is to keep us to the end and pay 1,000 crowns to you, 1,000 crowns to Piotr and 1,000 crowns to Michał.   To Jadwiga we willed the field behind Urban's [farm], to Wojtek 3 morgs in Zrąbki.   If we are not well [do not get along well] remaining with Jędrzej, then we have the right to harvest ⅓ of the field and to have a place in the buildings.   There are still 600 crowns of debt, so we are to work together and to pay this debt.   Perhaps you

---

always proved that the husband was a drunkard or a good-for-nothing.   If external conditions are the cause of hard times husbands and wives may separate provisionally but in good understanding.

think, the sum which is to be paid to you is too small; but he [Jędrzej] even complained that he won't be able to pay so much. So, dear son, don't be angry with us, because what can we do, when it is difficult to throw the misery away; very seldom food is on hand, always we must buy more. . . . . The prices are as high here as in America, or perhaps even worse, because meat is brought from South America to our country, i.e., from Argentine. You write that you have killed the pig for yourself, and we did not kill, but we buy bacon for seasoning food.[1] [Enumerates prices.] So, dear children, work and economize as much as you can for your old age, because old people suffer misery. May our Lord God make you happy and bless you with your children; and don't forget us, but speak to us as long as we are alive.[2] Even so Walek Maryla and his wife envy us, because they have two sons in America, and they don't know whether they are even alive; they never write to them. . . . . I won't write you more until the next time, because here nothing is changed, nobody among the family died, everybody is alive but got older. . . . . [Greetings from the whole family.]

JAN and EWA STELMACH

[1] This complaint of high prices from a relatively rich peasant, the fact of buying food and the division of land, are signs of the growing difficulty of continuing the old forms of economic life, particularly in Galicia. Until industrial development restores the equilibrium emigration seems a necessity.

[2] This phrase and the whole form of the letter disclose the profound importance which giving up the farm to the children has for the old peasants. The phrase could be used by one entering a cloister; it expresses a feeling of having broken all the real connections with other people, so that nothing but a sentimental connection remains. The old man ceases to be an active member of the real family-group, and becomes an *individual* whose only relations with the family are sentimental and blood relations. The obligations toward him, as well as his obligations toward the rest of the family, cease to be *social*, and become only *moral*.

OSIŃSKI SERIES

In the present series we find a very full and typical image of the life of an average modern peasant family—one neither above nor below the normal level, and whose sphere of interests contains nothing particular. The life of the peasant woman is particularly well represented because most of the letters are written or dictated by women. The letters of the men are not without interest, but less complete.

Of course this is not a primitive peasant family, and we should not expect to find the old forms of familial and communal life untouched by modern life. The family lives near the German frontier, some thirty or forty miles from Thorn, in a locality in which season-emigration to Germany and emigration to America have existed for many years, and, naturally the disintegrating and modifying influence of this is strongly felt. But this is precisely the normal situation. Communities, families, and individuals preserving perfectly the old forms of life today are exceptions. Where emigration has not reached, the influence of Polish industrial and cultural centers is manifest, and, taking everything into account, this influence is incomparably more powerful and profound than that of emigration.

The most important personality is the mother Wiktorya Osińska. The first forty letters are dictated by her, in her own and her husband's name. She is the real proprietor of the farm, which was probably left to her by her parents, who died when she was four years old. But, of course, under the system of familial community, this question is never raised; probably her present husband brought also some land or money, but in any case the property is now simply common. Wiktorya married first Baranowski and, after his death, her present husband, Osiński. She is a woman of the old type, very laborious, very religious, with a strong affection for her children—stronger probably than for her husband. Her son from the first marriage seems to be the one preferred, though this preference does not hinder her from occupying the standpoint of general familial solidarity and from agreeing with her husband in economic matters. She mediates between her sons, her daughter, her husband, trying to avoid any quarrels and to keep harmony within the family (see particularly No. 103). She has not been taught how to write, but she is interested in intellectual matters and appreciates instruction highly.

Her husband Antoni seems to be just an average peasant, with a strong familial, rather patriarchal, attitude; with a tendency to despotism but without sufficient power of will to be really despotic; much less egotistic than his sons or than some other fathers (cf. for example, Markiewicz series).

His two sons show egotism in a very high degree. Perhaps it is a result of the partial dissolution of the traditional solidarity. Michał is really interested in nothing except his personal life; he is an egotist in a passive way; he does not claim much (cf. Wiktorya's letter, No. 103) but neither does he give much; he barely writes home. He has real friendship for Jan, but no familial feelings. He has departed further from the traditional peasant attitudes than anyone else in the family—probably under the influence of his early life as groom in a manor house, and his early emigration. Aleksander has preserved much more of the old attitudes— love for land and farming, attachment to his country, traditional conception of marriage, interest in the family. But the real feeling of solidarity and community of familial life is weakened, and all these traditional attitudes take a new form, are directed in practice toward egotistic ends.

This is a very frequent type of partial disintegration of solidarity; the individual is still attached to the group and wants to live within it, but he develops purely personal tendencies and refuses to make any sacrifice for the group.

Jan Baranowski seems to be a rather unequilibrated man. He certainly gives proofs of true generosity, not only with regard to his own family—his mother praises his good heart —but also toward the family of his wife. (He married the daughter of Franciszka Kozłowska. See that series.) It seems that his friends have even exploited his generosity (cf. No. 72). On the other hand, he shows occasionally a lack of consideration, as, for instance, in his attitude toward Frania's marriage, and some avarice, as in his haste to get his part of the inheritance, his dissatisfaction with his share, and his effort to get as much money as possible from us for his letters. Although this avarice in matters of inheritance has nothing very prejudicial from the individualistic point of view, it is contrary to the familial spirit. His attitude toward Frania, on the other hand, is to be understood only from the familial standpoint. It seems in general that in Jan contradictory elements coexist—a broad basis of familial attitudes, and some individualistic tendencies, acquired during his solitary struggle for existence, but not interacting with the first; at different moments different sets of attitudes prevail in his behavior. This is, of course, one of the typical forms which a partial disintegration of the old psychology assumes.

Frania, the daughter, is, on the contrary, a rather harmonious character. Her psychology is determined in its main outlines by her familial functions, first as daughter, then as wife. But the (still rather low) degree of instruction which she received, and the individualistic tendencies which influenced her, as well as every other member of the community, make her perform her functions more consciously, without the passivity which a peasant girl would have shown fifty years ago and sometimes still shows in more isolated groups. She is in particularly good relations with her mother, whose situation and feelings she understands better than anyone else. If she sides with her parents against her brothers in all the misunderstandings between them, it is not because of a mere subjection to authority, but out of real familial feelings. Even in writing letters under her mother's dictation she shows an effort to express exactly what her mother wants her to express, contrasting with the negligence of Aleksander. For the sake of economic and familial considerations she has to make a sacrifice and makes it, even postponing her marriage for three years. She finally marries from real love the man who waited for her, refusing another brilliant match. Later she is a loving wife and mother while keeping always the same attitude toward her parents.

We know little about the other members of the family. Adam, Frania's husband, is evidently a nice and relatively cultivated peasant, as is shown by his attitude toward Frania and by the fact that he has been elected to a post of confidence in a peasant association. The wives of Jan and Aleksander seem to be rather insignificant; there is not a trace of their influence upon the family life. The other branch of the family, the Smentkowskis, is also very little characterized. Their situation is more or less the same as that of the Osińskis.

Now, the Osiński situation is very typical for the present moment. The whole of the old organization of life is proving unadapted to the solution of new problems, and the result is a tragedy for the individuals who are unable to change their attitudes. Thirty or forty years ago the course of life of the family would have been very different. Each son would have lived at home until his call to military service; he would have helped the parents, perhaps worked in addition as a hired laborer in the neighborhood. Having served his term, he would have returned and married, in the same village or in the neighborhood; he would have received money or land from his parents, taken some dowry with his wife, and settled upon a farm. One of them would have taken the parents' farm, as Aleksander did, others would have bought land. Of course, in spite of the dowries, each of them would have been poorer than the parents were, and only perhaps after many years, much work, and great parsimony would have attained almost the same level. But this problem was not particularly important as long as the fundamental economic idea was that of living, not of advance. If only each member of the family had enough to live on his own farm, the situation was all right.

But now comes the new tendency—that of advance. It is evident that the old organization gave no opportunity to advance. At best the next generation could attain the level of the preceding generation, and even this was more and more difficult. And it is also evident that a new organization is required to meet the new problem based no longer upon mere familial arrangements but upon the idea of improvement of personal economic aptitudes. Actually, a spirit of enterprise and a higher technical instruction in various lines should be developed in the young genera-tion, enabling each member to rise independently, without further help from the group. But instead of this we find only partial and insufficient changes brought into the old organization. Jan, having spent his time unproductively until his twenty-sixth year, first at home, then in the army, has to increase his fortune instead of marrying and settling, according to the tradition. But no way other than emigra-tion is left to him. Michał is sent to serve, in order to spare the cost of his living; in the manor he develops a different psychology, but acquires no useful technical knowledge, and so his only recourse is also America. But he calculates rationally that since he is to emigrate he may as well do it before his military service and not waste his time unproductively. Later, the Russo-Japanese war breaks out, and after this neither he nor Jan, classed as deserters, can return. When they finally get their shares of the familial property these shares are certainly of very little productive utility to them in America. On the other hand, Frania gets a little technical instruction, but not enough to be of any real use, and she must be provided for in the old way, by a dowry. Thus the result of these inconsistent and partial changes of the old organization is that the family, whose task is really to provide for its members and which it would do more or less for all the members under the old system, is able to provide for only two—Frania and Aleksander. The two others get no serious help from the group, or get it too late. They become and have to remain isolated from the group and from their country. The parents are separated once and forever from two of their children; even if they went to America to live, against all their habits and traditions, the situation would not be better. In this way, through mis-adaptation the family loses all its real functions, and until a new and more perfect adaptation is elaborated its dis-integration is a social necessity.

THE FAMILY OSIŃSKI

Antoni Osiński, a farmer
Wiktorya Osińska (by first marriage Baranowska) his wife
Jan (Janek) Baranowski, Wiktorya's son by her first husband
Michał (Michałek) ⎫
Aleksander (Aloś) ⎬ sons of Antoni and Wiktorya
Frania (Franciszka), daughter of Antoni and Wiktorya
Adam (Adaś) B., Frania's husband
Marysia Kozłowska, Jan's wife

Julka (Julcia), Aleksander's wife
Uncle and Aunt Smentkowski, probably cousins of Antoni or
    Wiktorya
Antoni, their son
Anneczka (Anna, Anusia)⎫
Frania   ⎬ their daughters

[68–138. Nos. 68–69 are to the authors from Jan Baranowski, in America, to whom most of the letters of the series are addressed. Nos. 70–106 are from Wiktorya Osińska in Poland to her sons in America. They are dictated to her daughter Frania, except as indicated in the notes. The name of the husband is associated with the mother's in signing, and he occasionally dictated a passage. Nos. 107–24 are from Frania. Their brevity and informality are due to her youth and to the fact that until her marriage she inclosed them with the letters dictated to her by her mother. Nos. 125–28 are from Michał; Nos. 129–38 from Aleksander.]

68   November 23, 1914

RESPECTED SIR: I, signed below, found in the *Dziennik Związ-kowy* your advertisement that whoever has letters from the old country should send them to your address to demonstrate the nature of the Polish people. I have more than 100 letters from my parents and my wife's parents and from my dear brother who has perhaps already given his spirit to God or lies wounded in some hospital or is a prisoner. But I ask you whether it is true that, as your advertisement says, I shall receive 10 to 20 cents for each letter and that these letters will be returned. For they have a value for myself to keep, because when this unhappy war is over, I have money to get or this farm to take. . . . . So I beg you for a written answer and for better information: (1) Shall I receive the reward as advertised and how much? (2) Shall I get the letters back? I beg you to send me a guaranty, for should I lose these letters, I should prefer not to have this reward at 20 cents each. . . . .

                                                     JAN BARANOWSKI

69   December 7, 1914

RESPECTED SIR: I received your letter, ... and after reading it I commit myself to your generosity. . . . . I send you the letters which I have. . . . . These letters from my parents are very good and detailed with regard to your demand. Most of them are from the time of the Japanese war and during the bloody troubles until two years before the actual bloody tragedy which no pen can describe and no reason embrace. What my dear fatherland, and my parents and sister and brother are suffering! My brother is perhaps already murdered, and even perhaps my dear parents who longed so much for me and wanted to see me once more. When I prepared these letters to be sent to you, I read a few of them and I wept bitter tears and thought thus: "Perhaps they are the last." So I beg you very much to send them back to me in totality, for I want to keep them in remembrance. And also, as I wrote you in my preceding letter, I have an inheritance [in cash] or a farm to get, if this accursed war is calmed. . . . .[1]

JAN BARANOWSKI

70 September 9, 1901

"Praised be Jesus Christus."

DEAR SON: I received your letter . . . . and I am glad that you are healthy and that you got happily through. As to Antoni, we learned two weeks ago that he was stopped in Otloczyn [as having trachoma]. First his mother learned it and came to me crying and said that they would surely spoil his eyes [in trying to cure them] or he would die.[2] But I persuaded her that there are surely more [patients], and their eyes don't get spoiled, so his won't be either.

Now I inform you, dear son, about our health. Your father was ill, he had some pains inside, and I had to manage the harvesting alone. I hired 3 men to reap and 4 women to rake, and 3 more men to build. As to the building, dear son, it was so: When you left, the

---

[1] The letters are to be used as evidence of his claims. The connection of sentiment and business is not felt to be improper and does not hinder the reality of the sentiment. In the same way, death of a member of the family hardly interrupts the usual home occupations of the other members. The material side of life has originally nothing of the "low" character which it acquires later by antithesis to the higher moral, religious, intellectual, aesthetic, interests. For the peasant it is a part of the essential human task to support life and to fight against death. The most trifling practical affairs may assume in this light a character of solemnity, almost sanctity. Cf. Introduction: "Religious and Magical Attitudes."

[2] The peasant occupies the habitudinal standpoint, and everything seems possible to him outside of his normal conditions and known environment. The lack of continuity and proportion between cause and effect in general does not permit the prevision and limitation of the effects of a given cause. This attitude is particularly strong with regard to the government. Cf. Introduction: "Social Environment"; "Religious and Magical Attitudes."

building stopped for 2 weeks. I could not sit in this [new] house at all from sorrow,[1] as if half of the people in the village were dead and you were dead also. In the 3d week the carpenter worked alone with your father for 2 days. . . . . And in the fourth week the carpenter worked 3 days with Adam. And in the fifth and sixth weeks the carpenter, the mason and 4 men worked. Your father's work was such [of as little worth] as when you were here. I finished the work with these men on the last day of August. This whole work, harvest and building, cost us 25 roubles, besides the carpenters and yourself, dear son. . . . . And all this building, as we calculated, will cost us about 700, and still it won't be finished before next year, for we don't wish to make big debts. We sold the horse for 34 roubles, and father sold the pigs for 50 roubles and now we must also sell the cow and the calf.[2] Now, dear son, I don't know what to do with your clothes, whether I shall keep them or give them to your father to wear.[3] You wrote me, dear son, to hire somebody to dig the potatoes, and you would pay for it. May God reward you for your promise! I cannot thank you [reward you] in any other way, except by these words. Michałek gave me also a rouble for my dress. May our Lord Jesus grant you health and pay you with Heaven for your good heart. . . . .

[WIKTORYA OSIŃSKA]

71   November 12, 1901

. . . . DEAR SON: . . . . The carpenter finished his work on the day before St. Michael, and your father drove him to the town and we moved into the house with our beds and our cooking. The remaining furniture is still left in the barn. . . . . All is now finished except the white-washing and the stairs. . . . . It cost us 1,000 roubles in all. [Weather; acquaintances.]

---

[1] Because the son had worked at the building of the house.

[2] It would seem quite simple to give a mortgage and in this way cover the cost of the house. But for the peasant this is logically impossible. The house belongs to the class of movable property, like the horse, the pig, or the cow, as against land property. It is an inferior kind of property. And mortgage would destroy the social value of land, the highest class of property. To give a mortgage in order to build a house would be, in the peasant's eyes, an action like that of selling a valuable horse or cow in order to have good time on the money.

[3] Clothes do not constitute property in the proper sense, but, like food, belong to the objects of consumption owned primarily by the family, only secondarily by the individual. Cf. Introduction: "Economic Attitudes."

Now I thank you heartily for the shoes which you bought me [before going away]. They are so comfortable that I can walk as far as I need without feeling that I have anything on my feet. Whenever I put them on I always remember you with tears. . . . .[1] I am very glad that everybody acknowledges that you are very good. May our Lord God grant you not to be spoiled in America! May you always be good, first toward God and toward God's Mother, then toward us, your parents, and toward all men, as you have been up to the present. Amen.[2]

WIKTORYA OSIŃSKA

72   December 22, 1901

. . . . DEAR, BELOVED SON: . . . . We were glad on receiving your letter, but we were not glad that, although you know how to write, you describe very little of your condition. You did not even write why you could not come back to our country if you married her. But probably they considered you a good man [appreciated you] only as long as they did not profit from your work.[3] So I thought myself, and when Michał came and read this letter, he said the same, that you would have a good Christmas-gift [in the woman]! We said to each other, I and Michał, that you were in the army and you did not write us the truth even then [how ill he felt], but although you did not write us the truth, still we guessed it. Certainly now you don't write us the truth either. It would be much better if you earned a little money, came back to our country and got married here. We [Michał and I] spoke so before parting. And moreover, we advise you, we your parents, if you have any money earned, send it to us, for here it won't be lost; we will put it in the savings-bank. But if you

[1] She is probably not accustomed to wearing shoes regularly. The habit of going barefoot is very persistent, mainly for economy. Shoes are in many localities worn only on Sunday. And often when going to church or to a fair the peasants (particularly women) carry their shoes and put them on only when approaching the church or town.

[2] The original obligatory familial and communal solidarity is here already treated as moral goodness and put into relation with the religious idea. This is the state of things which we have studied in the Introduction: "Religious and Magical Attitudes."

[3] The girl's parents probably first agreed to give her to him unconditionally because they wanted to borrow money from him. When they got it, they made the condition that he should not take her from America. Wiktorya supposes that in general they have changed their behavior toward him after having got money.

keep it with you you will always find friends who will want to borrow it from you and will want to get you married. Moreover, they could steal it from you, as [was done] in the army. [Greetings and New-Year wishes.]

WIKTORYA OSIŃSKA

73 January 3, 1902

DEAR SON: . . . . We thank you nicely for the 10 roubles. You wrote us, dear son, that we might make [from this money] a better Christmas tree [instead of the word "tree" a tree is roughly drawn by the sister who writes this letter] and make ourselves merry during the holidays. I should be much merrier if you came here. . . . . This money has been of use to us, for we were owing 8 roubles to the carpenter, so your father gave them back at once. He brought 2 roubles home. Of these two we gave 8 złoty [1 rouble, 20 copecks] for a holy mass, and the rest we took for our Christmas festival. Father says so [to you]: "Economize as much as you can so that no one [of your creditors] may drum at your windows when you come back." If our Lord Jesus allows us to get rid of our debts, we shall remember you, for our debts amount to 70 roubles. If God grants us health in this New Year we hope to pay them back, for last year there were only expenses, and no income at all.

Now inform us whether you are near a church, and whether you have already been in it a few times, and how is the divine service celebrated, whether there are sermons and teachings like those in our country. And inform me how do you like America, whether you like it as much as our country. Describe everything, for it is difficult for me [to write you long letters], since I cannot write myself to you. [Wishes for the New Year.] Now I admonish you, dear son, live in this New Year honestly and religiously, for I pray our Lord Jesus for you every day, when going to bed and rising. . . . .[1]

WIKTORYA OSIŃSKA

The candle burned down, the ink is out, the pen broke, the letter is ended. [Pleasantry by Frania.]

---

[1] The mother's prayers are a reason for the son's living honestly and religiously, because by those prayers she helps him to become a member of the divine community and he ought not to break the harmony which she has established between him and God. Cf. Introduction: "Religious and Magical Attitudes."

DEAR SON: . . . . Your last letter grieved us very much, when we learned that you were sick. Particularly I, as your mother, wept, thinking who cared for you in this illness, you orphan! When we are ill, we nurse one another, while you are always alone in the wide world. But I remembered and I sighed at once [in prayer], that you had still a Father in Heaven and a Mother who guards orphans.

Now I inform you, dear son, that I was also sick with colic for two weeks. For the first week I could do nothing, so that your father had the organist come and he applied 12 cupping-glasses. Then I felt somewhat better, but still for a week I could not work. And during my sickness Legoski came for money, for he was going to America. . . . . But not only we had no money, there was not even anyone to prepare a good dinner for him, a suitable one. We had 10 roubles, for we got 30 for the cow and we paid Radomski 20 back. So we gave him these 10 roubles. Your father would have gone and borrowed more, but he did not wish it . . . . and he said that perhaps you would send some for Easter, then your father would give it back to his wife. . . . . Then we sold the calf and got 12½ which we paid to your aunt Smentkowska. Then we sold the pig and gave Skunieczny 10 and Szymańska 5. We left 5 for the tax and for Easter. We are still owing 12 to your uncle, 6 to Pazik, 6 to Mr. Krajewski; these are the debts which we still have. And then we lack many things for the house, which we reckon as about 30 roubles. And you know, dear son, that this year is bad, you have seen yourself that the crops were not abundant, so we can sell no grain.

Here your father speaks to you: "If our Lord God grants you health, economize as much as you can and send [your debt] back, that they [your creditors] may not come to us so often. Were it not for the building and for our own debts we should have paid this debt for you."

You asked who died. . . . . In Trombin the organist's wife [or widow?] whom you knew, is dead. . . . . There are 8 children left and the ninth [girl] is in America. When these orphans began to weep at the churchyard during the funeral, all the people began to weep and even the priest wept and could not make the speech. [Information about marriages, weather.]

You ask about Michał. He has a strong wish to go to America, but father won't let him go before the military service, for he has only 2 years to wait and he will be called during the third [and if he does not go when called, he will never be able to return to his country]. . . . .

And now I beg you, dear son, if you intend to enter into such a state as Antoni did [get married], don't look at her dresses, but esteem only whether she loves our Lord Jesus. Then she will respect you also. . . . .[1] On the same day when I received this letter from you the parents of Antoni's girl came to his parents . . . . and there was joy such as if all of you came back from America. But they visited us also and are very agreeable people, particularly her mother. They invited his parents and they invited us for the holidays, so on Sunday after Easter they [the uncle and aunt, Antoni's parents] will go, and your father is to go with them, but I probably shan't go, for there is nobody to take my place at home in my household. . . . .[2]

WIKTORYA OSIŃSKA

75   May 25, 1902

DEAR SON: . . . . You asked me to send you one *gomółka* [small home-made cheese]. When they read it to me, I laughed. It is true that I had none when she left [a cousin going to America], but if she would have taken it, I would have found one. So instead of cheese I send you a godly image—you will have a token—and from every member of the family I send you a small medal. When you receive this image, kiss it, that it may bless you in your work and your health and guard you against a mortal sin. . . . .[3] Michał sends you a package of tobacco and Aleksander a package of cigarettes. . . . .

You wrote to your father asking, what he would send you. Well, he sends you these words: "Remember always the presence of God,

[1] The expression of the norm of respect instead of love as fundamental in marriage-relations, and at the same time the connection between religious life and family life.

[2] The invitation for the holidays is a proof that the relation between the writer and her husband on one side, the parents of their nephew's wife on the other, is a familial relation, although it is a mixed blood- and law-relation of the fourth and fifth degree.

[3] Both the image and the medals are consecrated; if therefore the first has a particular magical value, while the medals are treated merely as family-tokens, it is evidently because of the particular *intention and desire* of the mother to let the image have a magical influence. Cf. Introduction: "Religious and Magical Attitudes."

and when we shall stand before the last judgment you will calmly wait for the holiest sentence." Now I send you other words: "Work and economize as much as you can; I won't take [the fortune] into the grave with me. When you are not able to work longer [in America], then I will divide [the fortune] among you. And God guard us against a sudden death. Amen."[1]

I can send you nothing more, dear son except my heart. If I could take it away from my breast and divide it into four parts, as you are four whom our Lord Jesus keeps for me still [besides those who are dead], I would give a part to every one, from love. . . . . [Wishes and greetings.]

[WIKTORYA and ANTONI OSIŃSKI]

76 July 29, 1902

DEAR SON: . . . . I inform you now that on July 1, there was a terrible storm. The lightning struck in 3 places in our village, but, thanks to God, without damage, for only in trees and in the stream. But do you know Betlejeski in Lasoty? Well, lightning struck him dead and burned his house, and beyond Rypin a man was killed. This storm lasted for 3 hours; it lightened continually.

The crops are good this year, but it is difficult to harvest them, for it rains often. . . . . We ask you now, dear son, to inform us how long do you intend to be in America, for about America bad rumors are spreading, that it is to sink in, and even priests order us to pray for those who are in America. [Referring to the eruption in Martinique.] Now I inform you, dear son, what accidents happen in our country. Two men were going away to America; one of them had money and was to pay for the other and for himself, but the one who had no money killed him. They were even brothers-in-law and *kums*. And in Ostrowite also a man killed another.[2] May this be a lesson for you, my dear son, not to believe too much and not to be overconfident in friendship. . . . .

[WIKTORYA]

---

[1] Perfectly typical father's harangue. Cf. the address of the mother immediately following. As to the familial standpoint of the father and the more personal standpoint of the mother, cf. Introduction: "The Family."

[2] The spirit of the letter is like that of the mediaeval chronicles. The news is evidently derived from verbal rumors.

77

October 27, 1902

DEAR SON: . . . . As to your wish, we agree with it, if you think that your lot will be better. You cannot always live so lonely, so we, as your parents, permit you [to marry] and give you our parental blessing. May our Lord God, God's Mother and all the Saints bless you! We beg Him most heartily that He will grant you, your dear wife, her parents and all of us health and His blessing.[1] This we wish you with our parental heart.

And we inform the parents of your wife that they can be willing, for you have been always very good to us, obedient in everything that can be expected from a child, so we guarantee that it will be so later on. And not only we, but all the people of the whole village, can gladly testify that you are from a good house[2] and of good conduct.

WIKTORYA and ANTONI OSIŃSKI

78

July 29, 1903

. . . . DEAR SON: . . . . We are late with the answer but on Sunday I was with Aleksander at the parish festival in Obory, for he joined the Scapulary Fraternity,[3] and on week-days we had no time, for we harvested. We received the money in June and at once father paid the debts. . . . . You wrote us, dear son, to take a maid-servant,

[1] The future wife and her parents are thus taken at once into the family-group by making them share the expected effects of the blessing, whose object is the family.

[2] The presupposition that the origin of a man is a guaranty of his character. The same presupposition which allows a man in America to bring over a girl whom he does not know but whose family he knows.

[3] Religious fraternities are a very old institution; we find them in the earliest mediaeval traditions. They are of two types—with and without a social end. The first exists mainly in towns, and develops mutual insurance (sickness, burial expenses, dowry, widowhood) and philanthropic activity (help to the poor, nursing in hospitals). In the country the merely religious form prevails, as there is less occasion for mutual insurance, and philanthropic activity remains familial or individual. The members gather periodically for common prayers and adoration, and perform determined functions during solemn divine services. At a solemn mass they kneel in the middle of the church with burning candles; at a procession they carry feretories [moving altars], standards, candles; they do the same during the funeral of a member. Most of them develop choral singing. They are named according to their particular religious purpose, object, and means of their adoration—fraternities of the Holiest Sacrament, Rosary fraternities, Scapulary fraternities, and those of particular saints.

but the worst is that there is none to be found; they all go to America. Probably we shall manage alone until you come back. Aleksander can already help me in the heaviest work, he can already reach the sheaves to the cart and then pull them back [into the barn], and Frania also works as she can. So instead of sending money for the servant, if you have any, send them a little for *okrężne*.[1] Then they will be still more willing to work, and when you come back we shall give you whatever we can. . . . . Father was ill for a week; now he has already recovered. . . . . I was so grieved, for father lay ill, and Michałek was on the journey—such is my luck, that I am always at work and in grief. Such my life has been and such it will probably be up to the end.[2]

As to Michał, we tried by all means to persuade him not to go, particularly I told him about his journey, how it would be, and that he would be obliged to work heavily. But he always answered that he is ready to work, but he wants to get to America and to be with you. Now I beg you, dear son, if he is in grief [homesick], comfort him as much as you can and care for him. You wrote me, dear son, not to grieve about you, but my heart is always in pain that we are not all together or at least all in our country, that we might visit one another. . . . . You asked us how many years there are since we

[1] Festival after the harvest. In some localities called "dożynki." It is one of the oldest pagan traditions. The word is used sometimes, as here, for the extra ward which the proprietor gives after a successful harvest.

[2] The pessimistic view expressed here and in many other letters, is particularly frequent whenever the peasant begins to *reflect* upon his life. On the contrary, in *practice* he is usually very optimistic, he expects that in some undetermined way his action will have the desired effect even if rationally there seem to be no sufficient natural causes to produce this effect. Both the pessimism of reflection and the optimism of practice are rooted in the same attitude as the magical beliefs; the peasant does not give sufficient attention to the continuity between cause and effect. In his opinion a determined fact may produce another fact even if he does not see in what way this is possible, provided only those facts seem in some way connected with each other. So long as he is acting, he is inclined to hope against all probability; when he begins to reflect, the same insufficient analysis of the process of causation makes him fear also against all probability. (Cf. Introduction: "Religious and Magical Attitudes," and note to No. 70.) There is also another reason why the old-type peasants tend to emphasize unconsciously in their reflection the evil as against the good; it is the lack of any idea of advance. The modern type of peasant, with his strong tendency to climbing, is much more optimistic. Finally, as we shall see later, the peasant often complains insincerely. But here the attitude is evidently sincere.

were married.   Well, only the 24th year is going, since Janu...
[Greetings.]   And care for Michałek.

[WIKTORYA

79   November 20, 1903

DEAR SON: . . . . We received your letter . . . . but we were
not very glad, first because you wrote that Michał had been ill without
saying with what, and second, because you wrote that we don't care
for you at all.   You err much in saying so. . . . . We could not send
you the photograph for your name-day, because father was ill.   We
promised to send it on St. Michael's day, but we had no time, for the
harvest lasted up to autumn, for first the weather was bad, and then
in autumn it was fair; then we dug the potatoes.   Afterward father
brought fuel and plowed what was necessary for winter, and Aleksander went to earn for his winter suit and boots, and we both [mother
and daughter] worked industriously, and kept the stock.   [Stock
sold; debts paid; no money left.]   It is easy for you to say that we
don't care for you or begrudge a few złoty for this photograph!   In
America nobody comes to you and calls: "Lend me money, for I
have nothing to live," or, "Give me my money back."   You wrote
that you did not work for 7 weeks.   But we must always work, like
worms.   [Greetings, Christmas wishes.]

WIKTORYA OSIŃSKA

[Inclosed with the preceding letter.] . . . . Now I, your sister,
did not forget you yet.   I send you this flower as a token for these
solemn holidays of Christmas, and I divide the wafer with you.
[Wishes].   As to mother, don't write it ever again, that mother does
not care about you for we can never reward mother for all these tears
which she sheds. . . . . More than once I have tried to comfort her,
when mother weeps that you are not in this country. . . . .

[FRANIA]

80   May 17, 1904

DEAR CHILDREN: . . . . We received your letter . . . . together
with the photograph.   We were very glad, so that we even wept from
joy.   You wrote, dear son, that you had a sad Easter, for you did
not see your parents.   I had also [sad holidays].[1]   When I arranged

---

[1] Holidays are always occasions on which there is a revival of familial feelings,
and traditionally the whole family ought to meet.

the *święcone*,[1] I sat at the stove, and thought that there was nobody to make a *święcone* for you, and I wept. You wondered, dear children, why I look so sickly [in the photograph]. But you also look sickly and sad. Not only we say so, but all those who have seen you. Everybody wonders particularly about Janek, who looked fatter and merrier on the other photograph. Some people envy us that you write so often and that on every holiday you send something, either money or a photograph—that you don't forget about your parents. . . . .

Now we inform you about our farming. We had 4 horses; we sold one of them and got 50 roubles, for they were sick. We have 2 cows, 2 calves and a young cow, one year old, and more than 20 bee-hives. Father has sowed rape for them, and now it blossoms; and there is such a humming as if somebody were playing an accordeon. Now I inform you about the crops. Rye is nice up to the present; summer grains are nice above, but it has been too wet below, for it rains often. This year is like the last one; up to the present some people have not planted the potatoes, for they cannot plow, but we planted and sowed everything, thanks to God and to God's Mother. . . . .

[WIKTORYA]

81   June 26, 1904

. . . . Now I inform you about the misfortune which befell your aunt and uncle Smentkowski. On June 25 lightning struck Anneczka [their daughter] and killed her and the Zwoleński child. At 4 o'clock in the afternoon she was sitting near the kitchen stove and your aunt was standing near holding the child. The lightning came in through the chimney and went out through both windows, but thanks to God, it did not burn the house. So we beg you, and they also, for the love of God inform their whole family [the children in America] about it, and ask them, that someone among the four of them come. They are old and cannot work. Moreover, your aunt is often sick, and

---

[1] On Easter all kinds of food which the peasant uses during the year are consecrated by the priest. The consecration, by a magical symbolism, is supposed to sanctify and purify any food of the same kind which the family will eat till the following Easter. The custom is connected with the old pagan spring festival. Easter eggs are also consecrated and form an indispensable part of the *święcone*. At the same time, there is a connection with fasting: Lent ends on Easter, and the first meat, dairy, and alcoholic drink after the fasting must be consecrated before being consumed.

what will now happen after such a misfortune! . . . . Your aunt could not write from grief, and we can write no more, for tears drown our eyes. . . . .

[Osińskis]

If I wrote you badly, excuse me, for my hands trembled from all this.

[Frania]

82 July 21, 1904

Dear Children: . . . . Now we inform you in what way the Zwoleński child was killed. It was so. The Smenkowskis came from the field and the uncle remained in the garden, while the aunt and Andzia [Anneczka] came back home and brought firewood. The aunt took Zwoleńska's child for it wanted to go to her. Zwoleńska wished later to take it, but it did not want to go to her, so your aunt took it and they went into their house, and Zwoleńska into her house. Your aunt sat down near the table with the child, and Anneczka sat down near the stove, and when the lightning struck, it killed both Anneczka and the child. Your aunt alone remained alive and called to Anneczka, telling her to go away, or she would be burned. Immediately your uncle ran into the room and people gathered. They took Anneczka and the child and dug them into the earth, but they did not awaken. And now I explain to you in what a manner the Zwoleńskis were there [the Z's were manor-servants, and had to live in manorial buildings]. They lived first in the *ośmioraki* [long house for 8 families]; there they could not come to an understanding with their neighbors, and got a lodging in the *czworaki* [house for 4 families]. They had lived there hardly a week when the *czworaki* burned down; but they did not lose many things, for people came and saved them. . . . . Thence they moved to the same house where the Smenkowskis live. And I inform you about the burial, how uncle had her buried. It cost him 20 roubles [to the priest]. The priest went to meet the procession, boys brought her to the church, and there she stood upon a catafalque during the whole holy mass. Thence the priest led and church-servants brought her to the cemetery. There were many people, for she was in a [religious] fraternity and bore the flag [during processions]. Everybody wept, for she was liked and respected. But your uncle did not regret any expenses, saying that this was her dowry. . . . .

You asked whether Antoni would be exempted from military service as a guardian [of his old parents]. Now, during the war, no exemption is valid. Your uncle would be glad to see them [Antoni and wife] if they came to work, for he is already weak; but should Antoni come back and go again to another country [to the Japanese war], they would be still more grieved.

Whoever of them is to come let him come the soonest possible, for now there is continuous work. And perhaps the aunt would sooner forget Anusia [if she had another child with her]. . . . .

[OSIŃSKIS]

[Letter of July 21 contains further details about the death and funeral of Anneczka and the child.]

83   September 24, 1904

. . . . DEAR SON: . . . . We are very glad that you are in good health and that you succeed well, so that you even want to take us to America. But for us, your parents, it seems that there is no better America than in this country. Your father says that he is too weak and sickens too often. I should be glad to see you, but it is impossible to separate ourselves in our old age. I have also no health; particularly my arms are bad . . . . and you wrote that in America one must work hard, and often cannot get work even if he wants it, while here we have always work and we can hire somebody to do the heavy labor. You wrote me, dear son, that you will send me a gift. I was very glad, not so much because of the gift as because of your good heart. . . . .

Dear son, when I learned from your letter and from Frania [Smentkowska] that you love reading, I was gladder than if you had sent me a hundred roubles.[1] May our Lord God bless you further, may God's Mother of Częstochowa cover you with her mantle from every evil and every misfortune.

Now, dear sons, I inform you that I want to let Frania learn dress-making, for she respects her parents and is obedient, and secondly,

[1] Interesting appreciation for seemingly devoid of any idea of the practical application of learning which is so emphasized in the movement for instruction carried on by the newspapers. Back of this appreciation is probably the idea that reading keeps one away from mischief and denotes a seriousness of character.

because she is too weak for heavy work.   Although it will cost us, yet
if we live, we must leave her at least such a token. . . . .[1]

Your aunt and uncle and Frania [Smentkowska's cousin] greet
you, and they greet their own children.   Auntie says that Antosia
ought to remember her mother's old age and send her [money] for a
warm dress for winter. . . . .

WIKTORYA OSIŃSKA

84   November 8, 1904

. . . . DEAR SON: . . . . You wrote about a church-certificate,
but we don't know which one you wanted.   Father got your birth-
certificate.   Is it good or not?   And as to my family, about which you
wanted to learn, our priest says that in his records there is nothing,
but we must go to the mayor of the commune.   Your father will do
it when he finds time.   Dear son, you say that it is well if everybody
knows about his family for many years [past].   But only those people
can know whose parents live long, while I was 4 years old when my
parents died.   How can I know anything about my family?[2]   I
asked your aunt, but she does not know either.   She says only that
some years ago a paper from Prussia came, that some money there
was owed to us, some family-inheritance.   But there was nobody to
go for it, and your uncle did not wish to go, for he said that perhaps
it was not worth going for.

You wrote, dear son, that probably we shall not see one another
any more.   We were very grieved, and particularly I was.   But we

[1] This desire to give the girl technical instruction already involves a modification of the primitive economic attitudes; the individual is no longer conceived as
exclusively dependent upon the family, familial property ceases to be the only basis
of individual existence, and there is a tendency to advance along the line of an
improvement of work and income, not merely of an increase of property.   (Cf.
Introduction: "Economic Attitudes.")   But the whole attitude is still evidently
new, for the technical instruction is conceived as a gift, justified by exceptional
circumstances.

[2] We have here a good proof that the peasant family is essentially only an
actual social group, and does not depend upon the remembrance of the preceding
generations, as does the noble European family (heraldic continuity) or the ancient
Roman family (cult of the spirits of the ancestors).   The ancestry is traced only as
far as the actual, real connection between the living members requires.   (Cf. Introduction: "The Family.")   In the present case the son's demand is clearly felt
as strange; he is influenced either by the idea of the noble family (probably drawn
from his reading), or by economic considerations—the hope of getting some
unexpected inheritance.

should grieve still worse if you had to go to this bloodshedding. And perhaps we shall see one another yet, if they annoy us further [for we shall go to America]. Already they have raised the taxes, and now it is said that they will take the cows; whoever has four will have only one left. . . . .[1] You wrote, dear son, that you and Michał listen much to each other. I am very glad. Nothing could make me so glad as this. . . . .

[OSIŃSKIS]

As to Michałek, we don't write to him, for he does not write to us either, as if he had forgotten us.

85   December 18, 1905

. . . . DEAR SON: . . . . You ask about Frania, how much her learning and living will cost. When we sent her there, we agreed upon 55 roubles, but now she only dines there, and buys breakfast and supper herself, so we don't know how much we shall pay. She learns with the daughter of Brunkowski, who was manager of the estate of Gulbiny 30 years ago and lives now in Dobrzyń. . . . .

And Frania, how clever and cunning she is! When I persuaded her that [her learning] would cost us much, and that I did not learn, she said that I had no parents, while she has and she wants to have some token from them.

Now I advise you to marry, so perhaps you will be happier, as Antoni and other people are. . . . .[2]

[WIKTORYA]

86   February 6, 1906

. . . . DEAR SON [Michał]: . . . . We received the money today . . . . and we thank you kindly and heartily for this money, we your parents, your brother, and also I your sister, for most of it is destined for me [Frania]. . . . .

I came to our parents on February 2, and I learned that many young men come, but the girls don't seem to want them, and probably there will be no marriage this year.[3] Cousin Frania [Smentkowska]

[1] Anything may be expected of the government. Cf. note to No. 70, and Introduction: "Social Environment."

[2] He evidently did not marry the girl mentioned in No. 77.

[3] Marrying assumes often an epidemical character in a village or parish. There comes a year when, without any apparent reason, the number of weddings assumes an astonishingly high proportion; then again, as in the present case, the

says that she won't marry until you come back. And I inform you, dear brother, that I am learning embroidery, and it goes on pretty well. Now I have no time to write more for I must go back to Dobrzyń. . . . .

[FRANIA]

87   February 18, 1906

. . . . DEAR CHILDREN: . . . . You write us to sell [our property] and to go to you. We should be very glad to see you, if even only a few days before our death, but perhaps you heard yourself how difficult it is now to be admitted, particularly for old people. It is true that here we must work heavily, and [get cash] only for taxes and fuel, and even this is difficult to get. But your father persuades us that if we sold it and then were not admitted [to America], we should then have no place to go. Then we say that, if even only two of us went [one of the parents with one child], the two remaining would not be able to do all the work and the longing would be still greater. . . . .

[OSIŃSKIS]

[Letter of one page, March 6, requests the children "not to travel so much about America, as it is a spending of money and some accident might happen." Also that they receive the newspaper Gazeta Swiąteczna at home and preserve the copies.]

88   May 24, 1906

. . . . DEAR SON: You wrote us that you intend to marry and you asked us for our blessing. We send it to you. May our Lord God help you, and God's Mother of Częstochowa, and all the saints. It is very sad for us that we cannot be at your wedding, but let God's will be done. But we are anxious whether you have met a good girl, for it happened already that one man from Gulbiny wrote how he got married [in America]. He lived for only a year with her, for she stole his whole fortune and went, nobody knows where. I thank you for your flowers; we adorned half the house with them, and when I come into the room and look at them, I shed tears.

[WIKTORYA]

Now, dear brother, I send you a little tobacco. I had no time to send it to your wedding, so at least I want it to come to your name-

---

marriage season (December–February) passes without a single wedding. The reason seems to be imitation, or rather a certain common attitude developed among the boys or girls during a given period—a kind of fashion.

day. And I beg you, send me the watch, for you don't need it now any more.

[ALEKSANDER]

89 October 29, 1906

. . . . DEAR SON [Michał]: . . . . We received your letter. . . . . We are glad that you are in good health for we thought that you all were dead [allusion to their not writing]. You had written, dear son, that you would write us something curious, so we waited impatiently thinking that perhaps you were already journeying home. . . . . So now when we read this letter of yours we were very much grieved, for we remember you ten times a day and it is very painful to us that you evidently forget us. Dear son, since you did not come, surely we shan't see one another in this world, for this year a penalty was established, that if anybody who belongs to the army [who is of the age to be called] went away, his father must pay big money for him, and when he comes back after some years, he must serve his whole time in the disciplinary battalion. This is a still greater penalty than for these reservists who went away before the war, for these have only 2 months of prison or 300 roubles to pay. The punishment is not so severe, for Cieszeński [a reservist who did not come from America until after the war] has even earned 7 roubles during this time [of prison].[1]

Dear son, you write that you are getting on well enough. Thanks to God for this, but we beg you, we your parents, not to forget about God, then God won't forget about you. It is very hard for us that we cannot see you. More than once we shed bitter tears that we have brought you up and now we cannot be with you. . . . . May we at least merit to be in heaven together. . . . .

[OSIŃSKIS]

[1] Prison for offenses against the state, for violation of police ordinances, and in general for offenses which do not imply the condemnation of social opinion is not considered a serious punishment except for the loss of time. Prison for slight administrative offenses can usually be converted into fine, but the peasant always chooses prison. A curious incident characterizing the peasant's attitude toward the Russian state occurred four years ago in a commune of the province of Piotrków. When the district chief of that commune proposed to the peasants to contribute a certain sum toward the expenses involved in the celebration of the jubilee of the imperial family, there was some hesitation. Finally an old peasant, after some talk with the others, stepped forward and said, "Could we not sit instead?"

90 April 26, 1908

DEAR CHILDREN: . . . . We received your letter and the post-notification on Good Friday evening when we came back from the passion [service commemorating the sufferings of Jesus]. So we read only about your health, for we were very tired for it rained the whole week, even on Sunday morning. So we read your letter only on the first day of Easter, after the divine service, and only then we learned the rest.[1] At once Aleksander went on the third day for the tokens [holy images, etc.] and got them. We thank you heartily. May our Lord God reward you. We are glad, dear children, that you remember about God. Thank you once more for these tokens and for your letter so nicely written.

Dear children, you write that you think about taking Aleksander to America. But we and our work, for whom would it be left? You would all be there and we here. While if he goes to the army for 3 years and God keeps him and brings him happily back, he would help us as he does now. Well, perhaps Frania could remain upon this [the farm]; but even so we could see him no more [forever, if he escaped military service]. Moreover, now whole throngs of people are coming back from America . . . . and the papers write that it won't be better, but worse. And about this army [service] we don't know yet how it will be, for it is intended to have a communal decision—when the chief of the district asks. So if the Gulbinaks answer that Michałek is not there and does not write, he [Aleksander] could perhaps be exempted. But it people say that sometimes he [Michałek] sends news of himself, then nothing can be done, for though he does not write himself, Ulecka wrote to your uncle that he was there, and your uncle does not give the letters to us at home to read but goes to Lisiecki, so that everybody learns at once. . . . .[2]

[OSIŃSKIS]

[1] The fact shows how difficult and important a matter are the reading and writing of letters with the peasant. This must be kept in mind if we are to appreciate how much familial attachment is implied in frequent letter-writing, and how the peasants themselves consider the frequency and length of letters a sign of this attachment.

[2] As in Russia the number of recruits needed is less than the number of young men of eligible age, there are different kinds of exemption. A man is exempted when he is an only son, or when he is the oldest son and his father is at an age when he is supposed not to be able to support his family. A certain number is also exempted because of defective health, and out of the remainder a number, fixed for

91   November 15, 1908

DEAR CHILDREN: . . . . We are late with our answer, for we
have waited [to see] what will become of Aleksander. Now it is
decided that he must serve. On December 1, they will go away.
Father could do nothing, for the officials with whom he tried to settle
the matter went away and others came, and now there is another
mayor, and when the decision was made at the communal meeting
the Gulbinaks [inhabitants of Gulbiny] said that Michałek is alive
and writes. Particularly your uncle Smentkowski said it. Then no
exemption was possible; it would cost big money and even so it would
not be certain. It will be very hard for us without him, for you know,
dear children, that we are no longer young. It will be very painful
for us to be alone, but we cannot help it. At least we are glad that
you succeed well enough, as you inform us. We beg you heartily,
don't forget about us, but write as often as you can, for it is particularly painful for me and I shed tears more than once. I have had so
many troubles with you, I bred you, and now in my old age, when I
can work no more, you left me, all of you. . . . .

[WIKTORYA]

92   March 9, 1909

. . . . DEAR CHILDREN: You write us that you are very much
pained at our being alone, and that Janek intends to come to us. We
should be very glad, but we don't wish you to have any losses through
us, and we should grieve still more about Michałek if he remained
there alone. Now you are two, so if—God forbid!—some sickness
or accident happens, you can help each other. During this year we
shall still manage alone, if our Lord God grants us health and life, for
Frania will leave her sewing and will help, and Stanisław Ochocki, for
whom your father carried bricks when he built his house, will help us
also. As to the rest, we shall hire somebody from time to time, for
a servant must now be paid much, and even so it is difficult to get

---

each community beforehand, is selected by drawing lots. Thus in the place of
each man exempted because of the family situation or health some other member
of the commune must serve. And as the commune must certify that a young man
ought to be exempted because of his family situation, evidently the members of
the commune are not eager to exempt anyone without real reasons. Therefore
the efforts to exempt Aleksander fail, for the commune knows that the old man has
another son.

any, for everybody goes either to America, or to Prussia for season-work. And so we shall live this year alone, for we don't wish to get Frania married this year, although some [boys] have called on her already and begged [to be allowed to court her]. We are too sad now after Aleksander left us. Perhaps next year, if some good party appears, we won't oppose her marrying, lest she might complain about us later on. Then, if we cannot get on alone, and if it is impossible to find a good servant, we hope that you will help us [and come]. But now, if the work is better, earn for yourselves, and may our Lord God help you and bless you, and God's Mother of Częstochowa, our dear children!

Dear son Michałek, we are very glad that you have begun to occupy yourself with farming [literally: country-housekeeping] and that you succeed pretty well, since you keep so many young ones [poultry? rabbits?]. Frania envied your having so many and she had none. I was obliged to find some, and she will receive them as a gift from a man from Rypin. . . . .

[Osińskis]

93   August 23, 1909

. . . . Dear Children: . . . . When we read your letters, we were very much grieved, but nothing can be done. We must submit to fortune. If you cannot come back to us we must find another way. Although it is painful, we must be pained for some time, if our Lord God allows us to live longer. We should not like to scatter our old bones about the world. Here we have worked for so many years, so we should be glad to rest here, on our fathers' soil.[1] And you work and find your own way as well as you can. May our Lord God help you, since, alas! we cannot be together, dear children. [Crops; weather.] You wrote us to send you tobacco and honey through Bendykowski. If he goes and if he will take it, we will send you some. Zygmunt K. from Trąbin took your address, but now it is impossible to believe everybody. Perhaps he will do as Zieleniak did.

[Osińskis]

[1] Typical arguments of old people against emigration. This attitude, how-ever, gave way completely during the emigration fever to Brazil. People of seventy were seen going with their children and even inciting them to go. Two reasons may explain this difference. The emigrants were to settle in Brazil upon *land*, and, as it seems, almost all of these old emigrants to Brazil were manor-servants or parents of manor-servants, not farmers. In the same way the old Sękowskis (see that series) do not hesitate to go to America.

94   September 28, 1909

. . . . DEAR CHILDREN: We wrote to you, but you would not
come, so father is trying to get Aleksander back. It is hard for us
to work, but we shall be obliged to get on as well as we can. But this
is worse, that if he ends his military service, afterward he will be often
called to the commune, and still further [to drill]. And there are
rumors about a possible war, and Aleksander begs us to get him back,
if we can. So father went to that official and told him that there is no
news of Michał at all for some years. He told father to get a certificate, confirmed by the consul, that Michał was lost somewhere.
So I, your father, wanted to ask your advice, dear children, and
particularly yours, dear son Janek, for you have been more in the
world. Advise me, whether you could not get there such a certificate,
for it would be very useful, for without any big cost he would be set
free. I beg you very much, dear children, try to get it, if you can.
And Michałek, if he wants to come back some day, could take a
passport as an American. . . . .

                                              [OSIŃSKIS]

95   December 9, 1909

. . . . DEAR SON: You write us that it is dangerous [the arrangement to get Aleksander out of the army]. When we reflected about
the matter, we acknowledge that you are right and we thank you for
your advice. Nothing can be done, such is evidently the will of God,
for we can by no means have him exempted. Probably he must suffer
his whole appointed time. If only Lord Jesus grants health to us and
to him, perhaps we shall still live up to his return and he will help us.
Could we only get a servant now! It is really hard for us to work
alone. When your father walks a few steps he complains of his legs,
and I have also pain in my arms and legs, and we must always work
in the soil. [Crops; weather.]

Now, dear children, come the solemn holidays of Christmas. We
are here, three of us, while you are there in distant foreign countries.
But there is the same God, our best Father. So we commit you, dear
children, and ourselves to His care, we are confident in his holiest will,
and we hope that this Jesus born [on this day] will not desert you and
will bless you, if you only love him. And we, on the occasion of this
solemn commemoration, send you this wafer and we divide it with
you, wishing you every good, and health. Dear children, spend

merrily these holidays and during this solemnity remember kindly your parents and your sister who longs for you. Oh, if we could see one another once more! May God grant it, Amen. [Typical Christmas wishes; less formal than usual.]

[OSIŃSKIS]

96 January 10, 1910

. . . . DEAR CHILDREN: I, your father, write to you these few words. First, I inform you that Frania intends to marry after Easter, and on this occasion I ask you, whether you will also require your parts or any money. I suppose that you are somewhat better off, for you economized, i.e., earned some money, so perhaps you will bequeath it [your parts of the inheritance] to them, i.e., to Frania and Aloś [Aleksander]. For if it came to sending this to you, it would not be worth while, for in American money it would be only a half. So I beg you very much, dear children, reflect and answer me, for I should like to have peace with you all before I die, that you might not disturb me [my will] later on, as it often happens. I am now weaker and weaker, I often fall sick, so I should like to die in peace, when this last hour comes. Now I inform you that I still try to get Aleksander free, but I don't know whether our Lord God will allow me to succeed in getting him out of this jaw. Now, dear children, we beg you once more, we your parents, inform us as soon as possible how you decide there. Then we would also know how do you advise Frania to do, for she had already some opportunities [to marry], rather good ones, but she knows how we despair about you, dear children, that we educated you and now we have none with us, so she lingered, wishing to be longer with us. . . . .[1]

[OSIŃSKIS]

[1] The letter is important for the understanding of the relation of family-life and the economic situation. The dominant factor in the father's attitude is the wish to assure the integrity of the farm after his death. In this wish a complex of various feelings is involved—the love of the farm as the object of his work; the complicated, not exclusively economic, but partly social idea of property; the idea of family as a continuity of generations, and the wish that his family may have in the future a standing in the village and community. (Cf. Cugowski series.) The situation is complicated by the fact that the farm is really the wife's property and that one son (Jan) is the old man's stepson, having therefore a particular moral right to the inheritance.

97   February 28, 1910

.... Dear Children: .... You ask us whether we could not send you about 2,000 roubles.[1] But it is true, dear children, that we have not so much money of our own, for you know yourselves that it is not so long ago since we built the house, and then we spent all our money and even made some debts. Later we economized [earned] some money but we built a barn, as we wrote you, and this cost also enough. Why, from 12 morgs there is not such a big income, and the expenses are different and many—taxes and fuel and various others. This year a priest's house and two schools will be built in our commune, so money will be continually required. We have still some money, but we are trying to get Aleksander free, and this year we have hired a servant, whom we must pay 30 roubles [a year]. He is 17 years old, but nevertheless it will be much easier for us. So we can send you nothing from our own money. We could perhaps get some money by borrowing, but at interest, and then if we could not pay it back they would sell our farm, as often happens. Moreover, you would receive only, so to speak, half the sum [in dollars], so it is not worth while. Therefore you must find your own way, dear children, as you can, for if you were here in our country, we would share our last copeck with you.[2] We thought, dear children, that you had paid everything, and we are very much pained that you still have trouble with your debts. And we cannot help you at all. You must forgive us this time, for it is already too difficult for us, old people. [Acquaintances; weather.]

Now we inform you that in our country a greater and greater movement spreads out. Everywhere shops [consumers' associations]

[1] The sum is the probable share of inheritance which the sons in America, both together, would have if the property were equally divided, as a good farm of twelve morgs is worth about 4,000 roubles.

[2] All the excuses are trifling. The expenses enumerated except the house, which was built nine years before, are really small. Borrowing money by mortgage is easy, on a very long term, and the difficulty of paying the interest is hardly real in peasant life. The old man wishes to preserve the familial property intact, and feels that in separating themselves from the family interests they have separated themselves from the right of participation in its property also. This shows that the mere sentimental connection between individuals, without an active group-organization, could never explain the family in its whole social reality. On the contrary, this sentimental connection is only a secondary effect of the group-solidarity, and remains after the group has disintegrated.

are set up, and agricultural circles.   Well, and if somebody comes in a few years into our village he won't be able to recognize it.   There is this brick-factory, so in one place they dig holes, in another again they cover holes, so that it is difficult to get to the lake where the mill was, and the forge is falling down, for they have dug under it. Mr. Piwnicki [the manor-owner] has now such a beautiful environment near his palace!   The factory has been rented by the *dziedzic* [heir; estate-owner.   Half-honorific title] from Trombin, and he established a telephone from Trombin to Gulbiny.   Now a common store is set up, and they intend to build also a common bakery.   Soon everything will be like in a town.   Many people from our country intend to go to America.   And another bit of news: a star with a tail, or a so-called comet, appeared in the sky, on the western side.[1]

Now we have nothing more of interest to write, only we wish you health and happiness. . . . . Remember, dear children, God and our holy faith and our beloved fatherland, then our Lord God will not leave you and will help you. . . . .

[OSIŃSKIS]

98   August 2, 1910

. . . . DEAR SON [JAN]: We thank you for having written us so much news.   It is a pleasure for us that you at least don't forget us and inform us that you are alive, for as to Michałek [if we depended on him], we should never know anything about you.   It is very painful for us that a year has passed since he wrote us a few words with his own hand.   Does he want to forget about us altogether?   [Health, weather; harvest.]

And so everything is going on in the usual way.   As to the news of the world, you know more than we do, dear children, though we also keep a paper and read different books.   You write, dear son, that you long for your fatherland and would be glad to see it.   Why, dear son, you can come back!   Michałek cannot any more, but many such as you came back and nothing bad befel them.   We should be glad also, dear children, to see you, but for us old people it is more difficult to drag our old bones about the world.   So we ask you, dear children, if you intend to remain in America for many years still, you could visit us this winter.   Many people come here for some time and then

---

[1] This news is evidently added to weaken the impression of the refusal to send money.

go back. We beg you heartily, dear children, come to us if you can, but don't wait till winter for now it is nicer here than in winter, and it would be merry for us. May God grant it to be accomplished!

[OSIŃSKIS]

99 December 5, 1910

. . . . DEAR CHILDREN: We inform you that now we are alone, father and I [because Frania is married], and I am very sad and I don't care any more for this farm and household. Were it not for that water I would go at once into the world after you. I did not expect, dear children, that in my old age I should have to live alone in our house. I look at the walls around, I see you [pictures] which Frania hung there—but what! I cannot speak with you. I could still see Janek at any time, but I shan't probably see Michał in this world. . . . .

Now, dear children, we inform you about Frania. It is very painful for us to be without her. When he took her away, we all wept. But still they visit us and come to us often, and he is up to the present very polite to us. They wonder, for they sent you their photograph and have no answer yet. [Weather; Christmas wishes; greetings.]

[WIKTORYA]

100 January 7, 1911

DEAR CHILDREN: We thank you for your letter with the wafer. We pray to God that he may keep you in His guardianship, and since by His holiest will we must be separated far from one another, may He grant us to be again together, if not in this world, then to be happy in the other world.

I am very glad, dear children, that you are so well-disposed to one another. When Janek was in the army and wrote for money, Michałek always spoke for him, that we must send him some, and now Janek got easy work for him, and you agree also with one another. This rejoices us very much. And we beg you, inform us whether you have still much to pay for your house, and how are you getting on with your farming [probably only gardening and poultry-keeping]. . . . .

Now we inform you that together with your letter we got also a letter from Aloś. He comforts us [by saying] that he will be free in

October. May God grant us to live up to this time. [Weather.]
We have spent the holidays alone.   On the star-evening [Christmas
eve] Frania and Adaś [the son-in-law] were with us, and then your
mother went with them to the pastoral service [night-service on
Christmas, called so in commemoration of the legendary shepherds].
When we are at church, we always visit them and they also visit us
on Sunday afternoon, but on week-days we are alone, and we long for
you and we remember you often. . . . .

Your loving parents,

[Osińskis]

[Letter of May 10, 1911, explaining again why they cannot go to
America.]

101
June 17, 1911

. . . . Dear Children: We did not answer you at once, for we
waited for the Radomski boy to come to us [from America].   But
we have not seen him yet.   I saw only Radomski, his father, who said
that he had sore feet.   But I learned almost nothing from his father,
and it is difficult for me to be there, for we are now alone.   Even our
servant went to America, and now in the summer it is difficult to get
another.   Only Frania and Adaś visit us sometimes, and help us a
little.   So we did not learn anything, only Radomski mentioned
something I was pained at, as he said Janek has learned to swear
and does not respect his wife much.   I don't know whether I ought
to believe it, but if it is so, then, dear son, it is not very pleasant for
me, your mother. . . . .

[Wiktorya]

102
February 17, 1912

The first words of our letter to you, dear children: "Praised be
Jesus Christus."   Then we inform you that we received your letter
which found us in good health and success, and from which we learned
about your dear health.   This rejoiced us the most, dear children,
when our Lord God gives you health.   And it rejoiced us, dear son,
that you wrote at such length in your letter about your success.   May
our Lord God help you the best possible and bless you for your further
life.   This we wish you, we your parents.   And also Frania with her
husband and little son sends you greetings and good wishes, and in

general all your relatives and acquaintances. May God grant it.
Amen.[1]   [OSIŃSKIS]

103   February 6, 1913

DEAR SON [JAN] AND DAUGHTER-IN-LAW: . . . . I received your
letter and I am very glad that you are in good health, but it is very
disagreeable to me that you wrote such a complaining letter. My dear
son, I beg you don't send me such letters, for happily I learned about
this letter, got it myself and had it read, and I did not show this one
sheet at all at home, for if they had received this letter, I should have
much displeasure to bear from them, for your father and Aleksander
would be very much pained. We received a letter also from Michałek,
but he did not write wrongly and did not quarrel as you did, only he
thanked and asked father to send him this money when he was able,
and did not require more than that. Dear son, you say so [that it is
too little?], and you count so dear this farm, but if you knew what
expenses are now, larger and larger. Formerly it was possible to
save much more money, for everything was not so expensive, and
such large taxes were not collected. Now a priest's house, then a
school was built, and for all, this money is collected from us, the
farmers. Dear son, Aleksander must give us living and covering
[clothes] and fuel costs 30 roubles a year . . . . and with his wife
he did not get any big money either. He got what God helped
him to, so now he must also spare in order to be able to exist. So
don't imagine at all, dear children, that you have too small payments,
for if you were here, dear son, you would know how great the expenses
are, and you would not envy at all, for there is nothing to envy.

Now I beg you, don't answer this letter at all, for I wrote it only
from myself; they don't even know it at all. When father sends you
a letter, answer only then. . . . .

                                        Your mother,
                                  WIKTORYA OSIŃSKA

Don't be angry, dear children, for my sending you this letter
without stamp, but I had no money for it.

[1] An empty and perfunctory letter written by Aleksander in the name of
his parents. The greetings at the beginning and end are greatly abridged in
comparison with those in the letters written by Frania. For example, the latter
always enumerated the "relatives and acquaintances" who sent greetings. This
and two other letters written by the son and here omitted show how the form and
content of the letter depend on the person who acts as secretary.

104 March 12, 1913

. . . . DEAR CHILDREN: . . . . We inform you about our success. We succeed well enough, thanks to God. The weather does not annoy us too much. We think already about work in the field. When our Lord God grants the soil to get dry, we will go at once to work, for in the barn we have threshed everything. This only is bad, that grain is exceedingly cheap, so all this remains in the barn. Write us what is the news there about our country, for you know more than we do [because of the censure]. We inform you only, that industry and commerce develop more and more in our country, common [co-operative] shops are set up, they wish to kill the Jewish trade, but we don't know whether it will succeed. Now, as to your inheritance, which you asked us to send you, it would be well, but the money is in the savings-bank, and when I wanted to take it, they refused to give any interest until the money has remained a whole year. So I reflect, let it remain till the end of the year; only then will I send it to you. Why should we give them these roubles for nothing?[1] I ask you moreover, advise me, for you are more in the world. I intend to go to you after the swarming of the bees, so write me whether it is better to go with a [prepaid] ship-ticket or for ready money, and whether I can yet come to you. Answer me, and after swarming I will prepare myself to visit you, for you cannot come, and I would be glad to see you before my death. . . . .

After reading this letter give it to Janek, for it does not pay to write separate letters to you both, so I wrote it upon a single sheet.

[Your father,

ANTONI OSIŃSKI]

105 September 3, 1913

. . . . DEAR CHILDREN: . . . . We wait for your letter, but we hear nothing. We don't know what happened to you. Perhaps you are angry with us for not having sent the money to you?

Now we inform you that here is a farm to sell after Szczepan B. ['s death]. Janek remembers it certainly. We write it because Janek promised to come back to our country. So if he wanted to settle upon a farm we could buy it with your money and Janek could pay

---

[1] This is only a pretext. The real reason is given in the following letter.

his part to Michałek there, and here he would have this farm. There are 9 morgs of land, good buildings. The proprietor wants 2,000 roubles for it. So speak with one another. If Janek wants to come back upon a piece of land, answer us.[1] He [the proprietor] asks you to answer in any case, whether so or not. And inform us how you succeed. Then we shall write you more news in another letter. Now we end our few words and wish you health and every good.

Your loving parents

Also Adam, Frania, Zygmuś and Walcia greet you. Also Aloś and Julka wish you every good.

Now I, your mother, must also send you a few words. You have always spoken in favor of Aloś, that he might remain with us, and your father also wanted him [to take the farm]. But he does not know now how to be grateful to us. He is not very good to us, and our daughter-in-law sees how he does and does not respect us either. She told me to go to my half of the house. Now it is still worse for me than it was while I was alone. Then I knew that I had nobody, but now I have a son and a daughter-in-law, and it is not good enough for them to speak to us. And I am so sad now. It is difficult for me to go to Frania, and she has children and cannot visit me often either. Dear children, if you don't intend to come back to our country forever, could you perhaps visit us for some time? Please inform Janek also about it, and when you answer me, I beg you, dear children, send the letter to Frania's address. . . . .

Your loving mother,
[WIKTORYA]

106　　　　　　　　　　　　　　　　　　　November 4, 1913

. . . . DEAR CHILDREN: . . . . This year we shall still remain with Aleksander, as we have lived up to the present, but next year we shall probably live and board separately, for we don't wish to importune [burden] them too much.

Then, dear son, as to this money, I write you from myself, that I have spoken to father for your sake, asking him to send you the

---

[1] As soon as the possibility of the son's returning and settling in his native village appears all the reasons quoted by the father for not paying at once his part of the inheritance disappear; the father is ready to spend all the money immediately in buying land for him. Of course the reason is that the son by returning would become again a member of the family-group.

money now, but father told me, that we don't know how long we have still to live, and he is afraid to remain without money at all, for there is no money stipulated from Aleksander [only natural products]. Father counted that you are rather well off there and that you won't require your dues at once, and for a few years still we shall be able to get the interest from this sum. So I beg you, my dear children, don't be angry and don't grieve. That which is yours won't be lost to you; even if we don't add anything, nothing will be missing. I will look after it myself [literally: I shall be in it]. And now manage as you can, my dear children. It is very painful for me, not to be able to help you, but really at present I can do nothing.

Now, dear children, remember me at least, your mother, who have bred you! God alone knows how many tears I have shed that, for all my suffering and troubles about you when you were small children, I have now nobody to comfort me, nobody to speak merrily with. If I could, I would fly to you, but surely I shan't have now any opportunity to see you in this world, for I feel by my bones that everything is more or less diseased. So I beg you once more, speak to us at least through paper. May I not have this disappointment, at least. . . . .

[WIKTORYA]

107   [GULBINY, September 9, 1901]

I, your sister Franciszka, write to you also that I am in good health. . . . . Don't be angry with me for not having written to you nicely or much [in letter for mother of same date]. . . . . I beg you, dear brothers, inform me what is the news in your country, for in our country there are frequent misfortunes and accidents. Karpiński was nearly killed by his horses. He lies as if he were without a soul. In Upielsk half the village is burned down. . . . . In Bożomin the miller mounted upon the windmill to cover it. He fell down and was killed, and so on, continually. . . . .[1]

[FRANIA]

[1] The first of Frania's letters show a characteristic interest in any extraordinary happenings in the community and neighborhood. With this anecdotic interest in the neighbors' life the peasant child gets its first introduction into the life of the community. The town child lacks in general this interest in the doings of grown-up people, except those of its parents and teachers. Cf. also Borek series.

108 November 12, 1901

I, Franciszka, your sister, greet you and inform you about my success, that I was digging [potatoes] for 4 days—and I earned 4 złoty [60 copecks]. I hoped that I should earn at least for a second skirt for myself and for mother.[1] But it rains and there are cold winds, and they [the parents] have still potatoes to dig, for a week at least [so I cannot go to work elsewhere, where I am paid]. Now I inform you who was taken to the army. [Enumeration.]

[FRANIA]

109 December 3, 1901

I, your sister, dear brother Jan, thank you heartily for your gift and for your noble heart. You sent me a token which, keeping it with care, I can have for my whole life. But, dear brother, Aleksander [younger brother] when he learned, that there was nothing for him, began to cry. He was grieved, that Michałek promised him a watch and sent him none.

I inform you, dear Janek, that I was with a procession in Płonne at a parish festival. The festival was very beautiful. I was at confession. When the priest began to preach people wept as if they were going to death. . . . .[2] Now I inform you about Michał that he remained in Długie [as the Count P.'s groom] for a year more. Michał was here on the day when I wrote you this letter, and mother wept that while Michał sometimes comes, and will be here at Christmas, you cannot. . . . . [Christmas wishes.] Amen.

F[RANIA]

[1] The money earned at hired work, as additional income, has always some particular destination. See Introduction: "Economic Attitudes."

[2] The children are taken very early to the church; it depends only upon their having holiday-clothes. The powerful influence of church-ceremonies upon the peasant begins thus in childhood. And the child is not excluded from any manifestation of religious life, except sacraments; there is a gradually growing understanding of the ceremonies, but no particular initiation. The only process which has some character of initiation is the preparation for the first communion, but, as the child has taken a part in the religious life of the community before this, the first communion has not the same importance for the peasant children as for the children of intelligent classes, who, even if admitted to ceremonies, are not initiated into the personal religious life of grown-up people. Here, as well as in other spheres of social life, the peasant child shares much earlier the interests of the community than a child of a higher class.

110   May 25, 1902

Now I, Franciszka, your sister, speak to you. . . . . I inform you that I send you a small cross through [our cousin], for you wrote, dear brother, that I would be the first [to send you a token]. I should be glad to give you something more, with my whole heart, but I have nothing except this divine sign. May it help you in everything. I have a small bottle of honey but our cousin did not wish to take it. . . . . Now I inform you about Aleksander's stock, for he has no time to write. He has 3 rabbits and 4 pigeons. [Greetings and wishes.]

[FRANIA]

111   July 29, 1903

DEAR BROTHER [JAN]: You say that I don't write well; but it only seems to you so. I write characterfully. But you, dear brother, try also to write better. I remain with respect.

F.

Appreciate my writing!

Dear brother Michał, I, your sister, inform you that Stefka Jabłonianka gave me no peace, but asked always for your address, and I had to give it to her. She always says that she will be my sister-in-law, but God forbid!

If I wrote anything bad[ly] pardon me.

[FRANIA]

112   September 24, 1904

. . . . Now I inform you, dear brother, that in our country fires continually break out. Not long ago Strzygi was on fire; half the village was burned. In Guńsk the whole village and the chapel are burned; only 5 houses are left. In Bożomin, a few days ago the whole courtyard [all the farm-buildings] burned down, and there is no village where something has not been burned. . . . . And I inform you, dear brother, about the air. It is very dry, and our parents say they don't remember such a year in their whole life. . . . .

You asked me, dear brother, about Frania's [Smentkowska] journey. We sent you a letter, but evidently you did not receive it. . . . . Her health was good. . . . . She was sent to Aleksandrowo, so before she got to the commune it cost her 14 roubles [bribing Russian police, for she had no passport]. . . . . When she came, we did not know what to give her and where to seat her [we were so glad and honored her so]. But still we cannot forget the other one [the one killed, whose place this cousin came to fill].

Now, dear brothers, I thank you kindly and heartily for your gift. I have nothing to send you, except these words: "God reward." I shall be thankful to you during my whole life. I will pray God and God's Mother to give you happiness and blessing and that we may see one another, if not here, then in heaven. . . . .

Now, dear brothers, I inform you about Aleksander. When I read him this letter of yours, he said so: "Let them not jest about me, I will write them a letter yet. But I don't mind it at all, and may they only come. I will give them a dinner of my pigeons and a supper of my rabbits, buy a keg of beer for them, and bake wheat-bread." . . . .

[FRANIA]

113   May 17, 1904

. . . . Now I, your sister, write to you, dear Michałek, a few words. I inform you that the strawberries passed the winter well. I weeded them and I hope that they will bring fruit. If our Lord God grants you life and health, you will also try them. . . . . Before the house I made small round flower-beds and sowed the flower-seeds which you brought me from Długie. . . . . Only I need a fence, for the poultry spoil my work. But our parents say that before this we shall build a new barn, for the old one wants to fall down. So this year we shall bring material, and next year we shall build. Then, if some money is left, we shall make the hedge. Now I inform you that in Długie [where M. was a groom] they are already selling the small things, and the Count will go away in July. Mr. Bożewski's brother will live there. . . . .

[FRANIA]

114   January 18, 1905

. . . . DEAR BROTHER: . . . . We received two letters from you, which found us in good health . . . . but we could not understand much of them, for they were written upon such dark paper that it was difficult for me to see what was written. And as to what you wrote in your first letter, that mother should inform you about her parents and family, mother tells you, don't turn her head [worry her] for the mayor is not in the village, and mother walked enough when you were in the army.   Now she hardly walks about the house.

Now I inform you, dear brother, that I write this letter myself, from myself, even our parents don't know about it.   Father told me not to write, for Michał Zieleniak went to America and took the address of Michałek.   He will inform you about everything. . . . . I and brother sent you small gifts, brother 10 cigarettes, 5 for each of you, and I a handkerchief for each of you.   You won't be perhaps satisfied with this token, but I can send you nothing more. . . . . In our village nobody is dead and nobody married, for all went to the army.

Pardon me for sending you such a letter [without stamp], but I have no money at all. . . . .

F[RANIA]

On the same day when I wrote this letter, the priest went through our village on a visitation [*kolenda*].[1]

115   February 18, 1906

. . . . Now I, your sister, thank you heartily for your gift, dear brother. . . . . Dear brother and sister-in-law, I would gladly go to you in a single hour [at once], but when I say to mother that I will go, mother weeps directly, that she bred us up and now, when she is old, we all want to leave her.   And I could not earn for my living in that country, for now, although I have much work and must sit the whole day, in the evening I get scarcely 30 copecks. . . . .

[FRANIA]

116   January 24, 1907

DEAR BROTHER [JAN]: . . . . Pardon me for not having answered at once, but I was in a hurry with wedding-dresses for Stanisława Czechoska . . . . and then I had to be at the wedding. . . . . Here, thanks to God, is no news except weddings.   On one Sunday there were 13 banns in our parish. . . . .[2]   I was asked to every wedding but I was only at that of Czechoska, for if I went everywhere, I

---

[1] *Kolenda:* (1) Christmas wish, song, gift; many Christmas songs have this word as refrain; (2) visitation of the priest after Christmas (originally probably during or before Christmas), during which the priest inspects the parish, examines the parishioners on religious matters, and gets gifts from them.

[2] There were no weddings at all the preceding year.   Cf. No. 86, note.

should have no money left for clothes, for now at weddings everybody pays largely [to the bride's collection].   I have indeed work enough, but in the country the prices of living are very low, so that my work is very ill paid.   Dear brother Michał, your betrothed pleases me very much, but I should like to be at your wedding.   Dear brother, if I see that it is not worth working here and if Aleksander gets married, so that mother has help, I would go to you, but I don't know when. . . . .

[FRANIA]

117   April 25, 1909

DEAR BROTHER: You write me not to marry until Michałek comes here with his fiddle.   But so it could easily happen that I should remain an old girl.   But never mind, if at least one of you were with me.   As it is, I live as in a prison.   I must weep almost every day.   If it lasts longer, I shall consume myself with grief, so I think. I have nobody even to speak with.   Our parents are old and go to sleep early, and I think often that my head will burst, I must weep so, and I long for you, for I am alone like an orphan.   If I did not pity our parents, I should go at once to you, for with this needle I can earn little, and money is needed for everything.   Now I won't even sew, for there will be work enough at the farm.   But is it possible to leave our parents to the mercy of fortune, while they have raised us? Well, I will bear it as I can and pray to God that he will bring here at least one of you, for I long terribly.   Goodbye, and don't be angry with me for writing this, for I have nobody to whom I can complain.

Your sister,

FRANCISZKA

118   February 28, 1910

Now, dear brothers, I also pen a few words to you. . . . . I intended to marry, but you write that it would be better if Alos remained on the farm, so I shall probably come now . . . . to you, for I won't marry a man who has to pass from one manor to another [as manor-servant].   Even if he were a craftsman,[1] and if he wanted to

[1] Marrying a manor-servant would be a step downward for a farmer's daughter. But the wandering life of the servant, not his dependence, is put forward by the girl in a contemptuous way.   And it is not an economic matter, for a craftsman in a manor (blacksmith or carpenter) usually lives better than a small farmer.   Two

settle upon a good farm, at least 2,000 are needed. But, as I wrote you, there is not so much money now; our parents have only enough for their expenses. So perhaps when brother Aloś comes back, with God's help, he will pay us what will be the suitable part to everybody. If he gets more dowry with his wife, he will be able to pay more to us.[1] Meanwhile I shall probably leave our parents as you did[2] and will go to earn a little for myself, for here I have a bad income, for when I am at home I must always do something else. Moreover, mother complains often now, for she is no longer young, so I must busy myself with the household. And father also would not like to pay me anything, for he pays the servant, while I always need a little money besides everything else. Now, if you have no money you cannot show yourself anywhere, particularly a young person. Lastly I am always so alone, you are all scattered about the world, so it is very sad for me. Therefore I must find some other way. . . . .

[FRANIA]

119 August 2, 1910

DEAR BROTHER AND SISTER-IN-LAW: I beg you also, be so kind and visit us. Perhaps you will come just for my wedding. You would cause me a great joy, for to have 3 brothers and to have none at the wedding, this is something very painful. My wedding was to be in August, but the father of my betrothed died, so our affairs got crossed, but we hope that our intentions will be fulfilled and the wedding will be in autumn. I must inform you who is my future husband. He is the miller from Trąbin, schoolmate of Michałek. Michałek knows him for he went to school with him. I invite him,

---

factors determine this appreciation of the stable life of a farmer as against the wandering life of a servant: (1) The social factor; the farmer is a member of a community, with a determined social standing; and (2) the love of land and farmwork.

[1] For this reason the brothers want Aleksander to take the farm. Frania's husband, whoever he may be, will have no cash ready to pay her brothers off, for cash is first of all reserved for girls as dowry, while Aleksander will get a dowry in cash and will be able to pay. Of course the family of Frania's future husband may mortgage its farm and give him the necessary cash; but we know the peasant's hate of debts.

[2] There is bitterness in this phrase and in the whole letter, although no reproaches are made. The letter contrasts with the preceding one (No. 117), which is only sorrowful.

i.e., Michałek, also heartily, for he promised me to play at my wedding-festival, so I remind him and I invite you all together to my wedding.

[FRANIA]

120 September 12, 1910

. . . . DEAR BROTHER [MICHAŁ]: You wrote that I could wait still a year with my wedding. Evidently, as to my years it would not be anything important, but my betrothed is almost obliged to marry, for his mother cannot work heavily any more, and his sister does not want to, but intends to go away as an apprentice. And then, to say the truth, he has been calling upon us for 3 years; it is long enough. I inform you that the first banns were on September 11, but the wedding won't be at once, perhaps not until middle October, for we are waiting for Aloś. He wrote that he would come. If they don't set him free once and forever, he would come at least for a leave. . . . . As to the wedding, it will probably be sad, without music, for even if it were with music it would be also sad for us, because he has no father. I probably shan't have any brother, so indeed it will be painful and sad. But, dear brothers and dear sister-in-law, I invite you to my wedding. If you cannot be there personally, then be at least with thought and spirit, for I will always think that I have dear brothers and a dear sister-in-law, but there somewhere, far away in the world. But nothing can be done. Such is the will of God. I will inform you later when my marriage will be with certainty, for now I don't know at all. . . . .

[FRANIA]

121 November 4, 1910

DEAR BROTHERS: We thank you for the wishes which you sent, for we received them the day before our wedding. . . . . Now we inform you about our wedding. We amused ourselves well enough, only it was painful for us that we could not rejoice together with you. Then we inform you that the wedding was with music, as you wished it. The marriage-ceremony was performed in the evening after the Rosary, and afterward the priest-vicar went ahead in order to receive us with bread and salt, after the old habit, and gave us at the same time his blessing. Our professor [village-teacher] Paprocki came also to our wedding and received us, together with the priest-vicar, with bread and salt. . . . .[1] And our professor wished us progeny, and as a token brought before us a child, enveloped with big kerchiefs, upon his arm, and the child was very small, for it has finished 7 years already! This was a scene! If you had been there you would have seen!

Then we inform you that the festival lasted for a night and a day, without any collection.[2] After the wedding we went to the photographer in order to send you the token in remembrance, which we send you now, wishing you every good.

Yours, loving,

ADAM and FRANCISZKA

122   March 27, 1911

. . . . DEAR BROTHERS AND SISTER-IN-LAW: . . . . We received your letter . . . . and your [wedding] gift. . . . . We thank you heartily for this money, dear brothers and sister-in-law. . . . . We cannot prove to you our gratitude even now for your good heart, except by thanking you once more. And we inform you at the same time that we gave [money] for a holy mass, at which we will beg God to reward you a hundred fold.

[Weather; crops.] There is nothing interesting in our country. There are rumors again that there is to be war. May God the Merciful give peace, for it would be the worst misery to our Aloś. He rejoices that he has only 7. months more to serve. If there were only peace, we should live perhaps till he comes. We inform you also about the trouble which we have with our farm. We have 8 morgs of land and a windmill. We keep some stock, for the income from the mill is not large, because steam mills have been constructed in the country and these took much bread away from the millers. As to the buildings, we have a new barn, a stable which is not bad; only the dwelling-house is not very good—old fashioned. Moreover, we have 250 roubles of debt which we took over from his parents when they willed us the farm. But if only our Lord God grants us health and life, in a few years we hope to make everything all right, with

[1] This, as well as the whole description, shows that the wedding was first rate from the peasant point of view. Evidently both bride and bridegroom had a high standing in the community.

[2] This is not in accordance with the tradition and shows a somewhat advanced attitude. A collection would probably have been felt as a humiliation, but this proves that the real meaning of communal solidarity is already obliterated.

God's help. Our life flows pleasantly, for we love and respect each other, so whatever happens, grief or joy, we share it together in concord. . . . .

[Greetings and wishes.]

A[DAM] and F[RANIA] BRZEZIŃSCY

123   July 7, 1913

DEAR BROTHER AND SISTER [-IN-LAW]: . . . . We did not answer you at once for we had some trouble with our farming. It was going pretty well, we had paid a part of our debt back, and then suddenly in autumn a fine colt died, and then in May a horse died, and this always befalls the best ones. But what can we do? It won't come back. When our Lord God sends a misfortune the man can do nothing. If only God grants us health and life, we shall manage in some way. Our children, up to the present, get on well enough. Zygmunt already explains himself well enough. They are our whole joy. [Weather and crops; greetings and wishes.]

A[DAM] and F[RANIA] B.

124   TROMBIN, November 4, 1913

DEAR BROTHER AND SISTER [-IN-LAW]: . . . . We had this year some misfortune with the horses, as I wrote you already, and then the wings of our windmill fell down. We both had trouble enough, but nothing could be done. We have talked with each other, that our Lord God is trying us, and we commended everything to His will. This alone makes our life sweeter, that we live in good harmony and respect each other,[1] and that up to the present our Lord God has kept our children well. They are lively and grow well. Little Walcia already stands alone. If we could get some more money, we would send you their photograph.

As to the windmill, probably it won't be worth repairing any more, for now steam mills are built in the towns and everybody prefers to take [the grain] there, for they have it at once and more finely ground. Now we inform you that we have a co-operative milkshop in our

[1] Again the attitude of "respect" as a basis of conjugal life. And it is significant that in the first letter "love" is mentioned, while in the second, two years later, there is no such mention. It does not mean that the relation has grown colder, only that the first sexual novelty has disappeared and the sexual relation is subordinated to the respect norm.

village. Adam was even elected treasurer, to pay for the milk. [Weather.] We won't inform you about political questions, for you know more there from your papers than we know from ours. Now I beg you in my own name, dear brother and sister, remember our parents, and particularly mother. Write often and comfort her as you can, for mother despairs much about you.[1] When she comes to me, she only pets Zygmuś and Walcia a little and leaves at once, and there at home she weeps again and there is nobody who knows how to comfort her, for Aloś is somewhat indifferent. . . . .

ADAM and FRANIA

If anything is bad[ly written] forgive me, for now I don't write often, so it does not go well.

125 DŁUGIE, April 27, 1902

. . . . DEAR BROTHER: I received your letter. . . . . I had at the moment urgent work which hindered me from reading it. Whenever I took it in my hand and began to read, I was called away. I looked always for the words "Prepare to come to America," or, "The ship-ticket is on the way," but I read instead that you were sick. When I read this I did not wish to read any further, for my companion is going now, in April, and I thought that I would go with him, but I did not succeed. I don't know whether my wish is right or wrong.

Now, dear brother, I inform you that in the holidays I was at home with our parents. I went there on the last Sunday [before Easter]. I arrived just after the priest [who consecrated the Easter-food] left. They have their [new] house in order; the priest consecrated it, together with the *święcone* [Easter-food] and my favorite sausage, which I settled [ate] in 2 days. But I was not very glad [I did not amuse myself well], for both holidays were cold and rainy. They remembered you continually, particularly mother. I told them always that I would go to America after the holidays, that I had received a letter [from you] and a ship-ticket. Only when I was about to leave, I told the truth. . . . . Now inform me, where do you like the most [to live] among all the places you have been, in our country and abroad. . . . . I don't know whether anybody got married in Gulbiny; I know only that the girl who expected you in vain to marry

---

[1] The mother has lost her practical interest in life since the farm was given to Aleksander. From this probably, more than from Aleksander's coldness, comes the growing longing for her other boys.

her [or "whom you expected in vain to marry"] took some clay-dabber [brick-maker]. . . . .

MICHAŁ O.

126   May 10, 1902

. . . . DEAR BROTHER: . . . . I wish you good health and happiness, that you may as soon as possible get out of this trouble, in which you cannot even "trink ejn glass Bir." . . . . As to my watch, I have it indeed, but I am not much pleased with it, for it has been already treated by a doctor, and now it wants to stop again, ... but when I frighten it perhaps it will know better.

Now I inform you, dear brother, about our spring in our country. Up to the present it has been bad, for it even snows sometimes, and at night it is impossible to go anywhere for—well, for laughing [love-making], for it is so cold that the potatoes in hot-beds are frozen. Now I inform you about our village Długie. It is so spoiled that nothing can be done to improve it—not the village itself, but the people in the village. First, card-playing without any consideration. People come from other villages to ours [to play]. At the same time drinking, fighting—almost every boy with a stick in his hand, a knife in his pocket and a revolver in his bosom. [It assumes] such proportions that a man who returned from America and brought with him more than 400 roubles was killed and the money taken. I don't suspect exactly that these robbers were from Długie, but they were from the neighborhood, at any rate. It is not yet discovered [who did it]. People began to talk about one man, that he was the one, but he went and hanged himself.[1] [Wishes and greetings.]

Only don't do as Antoni did [don't marry] until I see you. . . . . Everybody dissuades me from going to America [saying] that I shall have to work hard and still to die from hunger, and that I should be killed, for there are so many robbers. . . . .

MICHAŁ O.

---

[1] Suspicion, just or unjust, is the most usual cause of peasant suicide. (Cf. Introduction: "Social Environment.") The main factor here is the fear of the dishonor of condemnation, as a man who has been condemned, or even tried, for a criminal offense loses once and forever all social standing. He can never try to exert *any* influence in his community, for he is always reminded of his condemnation, and it is difficult for him to settle in any other community without his past becoming known; the system of "legitimation papers" prevents it. The peasant's suicide seems to indicate that social opinion can become the most powerful element in the peasant farmer-village life.

127   August 1, 1902

. . . . DEAR BROTHER: . . . . I was rejoiced that you were in good health, until I read that you had no work, and this grieved me. But I hope in God that presently you will get better.   I am also very sad that I shan't see you, dear brother, and also that I must now sit at home.   Therefore I asked father to give me a few roubles in order to go to Warsaw, but father said that he wanted to ask you to lend him 50 roubles, and father and mother say that I could go to Warsaw, that they prefer it to my going to America, for it would not pay to go before the military service.   But what can I do in my misery?   If you could, dear brother (I don't dare to beg you, for you complain that you have no work, but I dare only to say, if you could), help me I will give it back to you with thanks, for I hope in God and God's Mother that I shan't always be so badly off.   And I add, dear and beloved brother, that I should gladly remain at home, but father always says that I ought to earn for myself, that he has already fed me long enough.[1]   In some respects he is right, but if I get into the world, I shall perhaps find some way if our Lord God grants me health.   I have a few grosz, but I cannot go as I am.   I must buy clothes and shirts, or stuff for shirts and have them sewed.   There are also many other trifles, and some sort of a valise.   Now, dear brother, don't reject my prayer, and don't delay, if you only can.   You know, when you needed [money] one time or another, although I could give you nothing[2]—yet if I could, I would have shared with you everything, even the blood from my finger.[3]   And so, dear brother, when we see each other, I will give you everything back with thanks. . . . .

Now I have nothing more to write, only I beg you once more, be so kind and don't wait for anything, only help me.   If you cannot, as I wrote you [lend money], to the parents, then help me at least with a few roubles.   I don't require you to send me your money and to

[1] The idea that every member of the family who is not absolutely indispensable at home ought to earn his living outside by hired work is relatively new.   Of course, when the farm is insufficient to feed the whole family additional work of its members is a necessity; but here this is not the case.   It is the substitution of economic advance for mere living as an aim, which leads to the desire to give the most productive use to the work of each member of the family, in the interest of the family as a whole.

[2] Alludes to the fact that he tried to persuade his parents to send money to his brother when the latter was in the army.

[3] Half proverbial, probably originating in the form of blood brotherhood.

live there in misery yourself, for I am not dying with hunger, but I have no luxury either. For you know, dear brother, that I like to work, but only if I know what I am working for. But I cannot dress myself any more now for 30 roubles [a year]. . . . .

Pardon me, dear brother, for having written so badly, but I wrote and thought about something else. [Wishes.] And now I bow low to my beloved Frania [probably cousin, who went recently to America]. Please beg her, if you see her, to pardon me what I said to her on her departure, and to write me something. . . . .

I embrace you and kiss you kindly and heartily, as well and perhaps even better than my sweetheart.

MICHAŁ O.

128   February 21, 1903

. . . . DEAR BROTHER: . . . . I have waited for your letter for days, and weeks, and months. . . . . I don't know what is going on with you, whether you are ill, or whether you got so proud after your marriage. I make different suppositions. Forgive me my joke, dear brother [about the marriage; Jan was ultimately refused by the girl], for perhaps my Zosia S. will also despise [reject] me. I don't mention her name, for she is in America, and you are still a bachelor, so you would be ready perhaps to take her for yourself. . . . .

Now I inform you, dear brother, that my companions and mates leave me and go to America, and I should also prefer to work if I could only follow them. Those who went write well enough. They have no hard work, and even if it were hard, I ought to be able to hold out as others do, for I shall soon be twenty. I should be glad to earn a little before the military service, or if not, then at least to look a little about the world, for if I keep this groom-work longer in my hands it will go out by the top of my head [upset me]. . . . . Father allows me to go. Mother says it would be better if I did not go, but if you send me a ship-ticket and if I beg her, she will allow me to go. . . . .

MICHAŁ O.

129   March 6, 1906

And now I beg you, dear brothers, help me in some way to get there to you, for here I work at home and as a hired laborer, and even so I hardly earn enough for my clothes.[1]   Moreover, all my companions are going, so I want also to visit America.   Dear brothers, send me money or a ship-ticket.   When I come there, I will work it back with thanks. . . . .

ALEKSANDER OSIŃSKI

130   November 15, 1908

Now I, dear brothers, bid you farewell [on going to the army] and greet you kindly and heartily, for I don't know whether our Lord God will allow us to see one another any more.[2]   I beg you, don't forget about our parents and about me, for you know that there is hardly a day when our mother does not shed tears, either about me, what will happen to me, or about you, whether you are healthy and alive, and there will be nobody to comfort our mother. . . . .

[ALEKSANDER]

131   TOWN KANSK [SIBERIA], May 17, 1909

. . . . DEAR BROTHERS: . . . . I learned from your letter that you sent me 20 roubles.   This rejoiced me, for they will be very useful to me.   I don't wait with answering until they come, but I answer you at once and thank you, dear brothers and sister-in-law.   Perhaps our Lord God will allow me to show you my gratitude. . . . .

Now I inform you . . . . about my service.   On May 21, our oath will be taken . . . . and we hope that it will be somewhat

---

[1] The dissatisfaction with working on his parents' account is a typical sign of the beginning disintegration of the family as a unit.   Cf. letters of Stanisław in the Markiewicz series.

[2] We find this farewell also in other letters of peasants going to serve in the Russian army.   The separation is felt as more absolute than any other, certainly not only on account of any possible war (no war was expected in 1908) and not only on account of the length of the separation, or of the distance, since the emigration to America goes on without such tragic farewells.   It seems to be a social custom, and its source is easily traced back to that period in the middle of the nineteenth century, where a peasant taken to the army was to serve seven to fifteen years or more (because every disciplinary punishment brought a prolongation of the term), when communication by letters was above the means of a soldier, who, moreover, usually did not know how to write, and when the discipline of the Russian army was the most severe and unreasonable possible.   At that time going to the army meant often really a separation for life even if there was no war, and the fact had still more meaning because of its relative rareness, as the number of recruits which a community was to furnish was much smaller than now.

better, at least for our legs, for now there is no day without our running like wet dogs. . . . . Now I inform you about the life of the people here, how they live and with what they occupy themselves here in this Siberia. In villages they occupy themselves mainly with agriculture, for there is no lack of land, but they do badly in it, for they are lazy. On Good Friday we went to the town; there they occupy themselves mainly with trade, and there are many who only loaf about and look out whom they can rob, and get drunk. The soil in this country is fertile and everything would grow, but the winter lasts too long and not everything can ripen. There are no fruit trees at all, the fruits are brought from other countries. Now I inform you that in our country beyond Płock the water [Vistula] did much damage, submerged many villages, tore away the railway-bridge in Modlin, and many people remained without living [work] and without a bit of bread. . . . . Dear brother, inform Janek Sz., if he does not long for our country, let him remain in America, for if he gets here [to the army] he will remember it, but it will be too late. . . . .

ALEKSANDER O.

132   KANSK, September 6, 1909

. . . . DEAR BROTHERS: . . . . I was very sad, for I learned that you received none of my letters. I wrote you two and I paid for both, and I don't know whether they did not reach you because they were paid or because of something else. I send you the third unpaid, perhaps this one will reach you sooner. . . . .[1]

I was very grieved on learning that Michałek won't return home any more. I did not expect it at all. I thought that when our Lord God grants me to finish my service and to go back home, he would come at least on a visit and we should rejoice all together under the native roof. For now we are scattered about the world, and whenever I remember it, I can hardly refrain from weeping. Our father must work alone, and I am living here worse than a beast. It will be soon a year since I have seen a church or a priest.[2] And all the people live

---

[1] The argument seems strange, but it corresponds with the facts. The Russian post is very negligent, and many ordinary letters are lost, but for a letter without a stamp the receiver has to pay double, and on this account there are some formalities connected with its forwarding and delivery.

[2] Example of the importance of religion as the main idealistic factor in peasant life, even for a young boy, who is usually the least religious person in a peasant family.

here in the same way.   In the evening all the shutters are closed, and if anybody shows himself on the street he won't return home alive; he will be either shot or butchered with knives.   Many have been killed so.   Once we stood on guard near the prison and we were attacked by day.   They wanted to set the convicts free, but they did not succeed.   We killed one with a bayonet, and the other fled. . . . .

Now I inform you that the harvest is finished here only now, and the air is cold already.   And I beg you, advise me, whether I may go on leave, for they wrote to me twice already from home to come; but it would cost very much, 30 roubles for the journey alone, without the living.   And they would give me leave for 3 months. . . . .

Aleksander O.

133   Siberia, March 28, 1910

Dear Brothers: . . . . On Easter-Sunday after the evening roll-call I had already gone to sleep when a letter from home was brought to me.   When I read it, I learned first that father had already sent to the governor the decision of the commune that you [Michał] had not been [in the country] for so long a time, dear brother, and in 3 weeks the decision will be in the office of the military chief. . . . . So perhaps our Lord God will grant us to see one another soon under the native roof.[1]   If you knew, dear brothers, how sad my holidays were until I got the letter, you would not believe me. . . . . Now, dear brothers, I learned . . . . that Janek intends to go [home] to the wedding [of Frania].   Perhaps our Lord God will grant me to be there also, for our sister will certainly marry Adam Brz. from Trombin, who went with us to school.   I think that Michałek knows him; he is the son of the miller.   On New Year there was also a man from Obory, but she did not want him, although he is rich; he has more than 40 morgs of land.   She did not want him, for it is too far away from home, and he is as old as the Bible. . . . . As to the farm, I think that you advised father well [to give it to me], for Michałek won't come back any more and won't wish to work in the earth, while I have worked from my young years, so I am very accustomed to the earth and I know how to manage it.   Just for that I am so awfully

---

[1] That is, Aleksander will be released from the army as the sole support of his parents.

homesick in the army, for I am away from the soil, I cannot work in it. [Moving-pictures shown the regiment.]

Now, dear brothers, you wrote that you can help me, so I beg you, when you receive this letter, send me a few roubles. Perhaps they will be useful for my journey, or if not, then in the autumn I will go on leave. . . . . I beg you, dear brothers, don't forget me . . . . particularly you, dear Janek, who have served. You know how bad it smells here; particularly during their Lent one almost dies.

ALEKSANDER O.

[Letter of March 17, 1911 shows that the plan to have him released from the army did not succeed. Letter of January, 1912, announces arrival home.]

134   GULBINY, February 17, 1912

. . . . DEAR BROTHER: First I greet you, and also your wife, and I inform you that I got free from this slavery and came to my dear parents. What was my joy, dear brother, I won't describe it to you, for I know that you know it well, because you have also eaten of this Moscovite bread and you know how good it is. Only I inform you that I am treated without end, everybody invites me, and Frania does not want to let me go from her house, she wants me to remain there day and night and to relate about this Siberia, while I need to go somewhere farther in order to find some girl for myself. You all, dear brothers, are married, only I am still alone. Perhaps you have there in America some pretty and rich girl, so when you come here, bring her to me, for here it is difficult to find such. All the prettiest girls are gone to America. So I beg you, dear brother, don't forget this. [The request is half a jest.]

Now I inform you what is the news here. As to the old people about whom you wrote, only the old Jabłońska from the end of the village is dead, and Uncle Sm. is lying very sick. For a whole year he has not been able to eat and to rise . . . . and we don't know, but probably he will soon end his life. And our Mr. Piwnicki [manor-owner] lives so that you would not know him and his estate. I was away for only 3 years and even so I could not recognize it. What a factory they built near the farm-yard! And the mill and that forge which stood near the mill have been pulled down, and they take clay from that spot.[1]   [Weather.]

Now I have nothing more of interest to write. If you can, inform me when you will come back and how much money you can bring with you, I shall perhaps find you somewhere a nice piece of land. . . . .

Your well-wishing brother,

A. O.

135   July 12, 1912

. . . . Dear Brother: I will pen to you a few words, not much at present, for I am not yet married. As soon as I marry, I will write you more. Do you know, dear brother, that up to the present I have ridden in search of a girl, but now I must walk on foot, for I have already worn the horses out! After so many troubles I found two, one named Bronisława C. . . . . and the other also Bronisława, but excuse me, for I forget her name. Probably one of these two will be mine . . . . and I hope that in my next letter I shall invite you to my wedding. . . . .

Your well-wishing brother,

Aleksander O.

[1] Rather an expression of commiseration (cf. corresponding letter of the parents) than of approval. The peasants are ready to appreciate any aesthetic improvement of the manor, as well as any progress in the purely agricultural line, but every industrial undertaking of the manor-owner, particularly the building of a factory, provokes a mixed feeling of satisfaction, because of the new opportunity of work, of admiration for the man's cleverness, and at the same time a half aesthetic, half moral disapproval. The man is slightly despised because for the sake of a greater income he deprives himself of an aesthetic environment and from a traditional country lord becomes an entrepreneur. The same feeling of commiseration accompanies any endeavor to diminish the household expenses, the number of servants, of carriage horses, etc., and in general any conversion of an aesthetic value into a productive value. The country lord, in the peasant's opinion, ought to live according to his social standing, to afford unproductive expenses, to maintain the same standard of life as his father and grandfather before him. He may and should improve his farming but it is not suitable for him to be too eager to make money, "like a Jew." The argument is always "Is he not rich enough to afford this or that?" This attitude is particularly marked when a new proprietor comes and begins to turn into money values which his predecessor used to maintain his standard of life. Such a man, if not known in the country, is immediately classed as a parvenu.

136   September 24, 1912

. . . . DEAR SISTER [-IN-LAW] AND BELOVED BROTHER: You wrote that you had sent two letters and in one of these [our parents say] you asked for money. We were much grieved that you, having been so long in such a free and rich country, cannot get your living, though you are young, but write to us, old people [speaking in the name of the parents] for help.

You know, dear brother, that I came just now from this prison [the army], I had even no time to look around well among the people, and I needed some clothes to be made for me in order not to be the last among other boys, and all this costs very much in our country. I even expected now a few grosz from you, as first help, and you write in quite another manner. We don't even know whether you are in earnest or making jokes at us. You know, dear brother, that you will receive everything, whatever your father destined for you, but not sooner than I get married. Perhaps I shall even come soon to you, for here it is difficult to get a rich and good wife, and instead of taking just anything I would rather come to you soon. That will be quieter [less distracting]. And if you wish you can come to our country and farm, for now I cannot act in a different way. I pity the old parents who will be left alone, but what can I do?

I inform you that on September 29, is the 50th anniversary [of the priesthood] of the old priest F. . . . . who was for so many years in Trombin and is now in Radomin. A company [procession] will go from here to Radomin. [Weather; farm-work.] The worst of it is the digging of the potatoes. It rains almost every day, the potatoes rot, and it is impossible to hire anybody. People want 50 and 60 copecks a day, and afternoon luncheon, and a bottle [of beer] to be put out for them. This is too expensive for us. We must dig alone. . . . .

> Your well-wishing brother,
> ALEKSANDER O.

137   November 16, 1912

"Praised be Jesus Christus!"

DEAR BROTHER: We signed under, invite you, together with your wife, to our marriage-ceremony and to the wedding-feast which will be celebrated on Wednesday, November 27, 1912, in the house of

Mr. Jur., in Bożomin.   I shall describe to you our life more in detail in another letter.[1]

We remain, with respect for you,

ALEKSANDER and JULCIA O.

[Greetings from the parents and sister, and news about the weather on a separate sheet.]

138

January 20, 1913

. . . . DEAR BROTHER AND SISTER-IN-LAW: I pen to you a few words, together with my wife.   First I inform you that health favors us up to the present.   We live merrily on.   Only now I have got full liberty after such a long waiting, and I don't think of moving anywhere, if only our Lord God gives us health.   When I learned from your letter [about some catastrophe] I felt cold, and my Julka reddened and said that she won't let me go anywhere alone.   As to the photograph, we beg very politely your pardon, but we shall send it to you perhaps in another letter, for now we have no opportunity at all. I beg you also, inform us about Michałek, for he wrote us that he would soon work together with his wife [after being married] and now he does not write.   I don't know whether they live in health; perhaps the stork is near.   Then hurrah!   [Weather.]   We bid you goodbye very kindly and heartily.   My wife always tells me that she would be glad to see you and talk with you about America.   Now be healthy, until the pleasure of seeing you.

ALEKSANDER and JULKA O.

---

[1] The invitation is evidently purely formal, as the letter will hardly arrive before the date of the wedding.   Nevertheless not to invite would be considered a great offense.

GOŚCIAK SERIES

The writer is an average Galician peasant.   The relation of the father and the son-in-law is more cordial than that of the father and son.   The son-in-law has evidently at once taken the standpoint of familial solidarity with regard to his wife's family, while the son has become more or less estranged during his stay in America.

139–41, FROM JAKÓB GOŚCIAK, IN GALICIA TO HIS SON-IN-LAW AND SON, IN AMERICA

139   [1913 ?]

"Praised be Jesus Christus."

DEAR SON-IN-LAW AND YOU, DEAR DAUGHTER: [Generalities about health, success, crops.]   Now I inform you, dear son-in-law and dear daughter, that I tried to buy [land] from those old women in Czarnocin . . . . but they say that somebody . . . . gives them a whole 7,000 [crowns], but we don't know whether it is true or not because now they have very beautiful crops and therefore they are so proud, and so we must wait what will be further.   It pleases me well enough . . . . but it does not please your father.   He says that it is possible to find something better to buy, that this is dear, and worth little.

And now I inform you that a young man from America came here who says that Wojtek Wojtusiak broke an arm and Wojtek Leśny broke a leg.   And here people say that it is true, and you don't write to us anything about it, whether it is true or not.   So answer us.   And people say that in America are wars, and you don't write us anything about it.   And now I inform you that our lawsuit with Tomek is ended, and it resulted so that we have to divide the pine grove between ourselves, and the land will be mine.   We lost much [on the lawsuit], but even so it was worth it, for the land alone is worth something, because now land is very dear there.   They ask 1,000 for a morg.   And I write some words.   How does Józek Patoniec behave there?   Answer me about him.

And now I shall write you some words, sincerest truth. Believe me, what I shall write is the very truth, because your mother herself ordered me to write a few words about your father, how he is farming here. It is such a father. When he began to call upon us and to ask us for a loan of some money, in order to buy a calf, we lent him 25 gulden. What did he do? When he seized this money he bought a pig for it. Because when he seized it he went at once with it to Hejmejka, and drank so long until he spent it all, and it did not even suffice. And what did he do when he lacked more money? He went home, took a cart and a mare and drove to [?] and there sold everything to Placiak, Josek and Szymczyk, saying that he would spend everything in drinking. Your mother told me to describe all this to you, and she asks you not to dare to send any money, none of you, for this liquor. . . . .

Jakób Gościak

140   March 10, 1914

I sit down to the table, I take the pen and I greet you, dear son-in-law, and you, my daughter. [Generalities about health and success; letters received and sent.] Probably my letter did not reach you, since you say that I don't know how to write your address; but I write as I know, and so don't be contrary to me [angry]. And now I write you that we have no more snow, but rain pours down and it is wet and there is no spring yet. And now you write us that we did not send you any Christmas token. But how should we have sent you any since you never once wrote to us about it. And now you ask whether my leg is healed. It is healed, thanks to God, but I cannot walk yet in a small shoe, because it gnaws me. And now you ask about those planks whether I hid them. Well, I hid them in the barn, and I had trouble enough with them, because your father wanted to take them and to drive them to Hejmejka because here [he thinks] they are useless, and your father wants money for liquor, because vodka got dearer, 7 szóstkas [1 crown 40 heller] for a liter. I was obliged to insure my buildings, because your father said that he would burn us. And now I wrote you in that other letter about this money. The Bodziunys and Jasiek paid it back long ago, and now what shall I do with it? Whether I have to put it into a savings-bank, or to lend it to anybody in the village, or to let it remain at home? Answer me at once, how I should do with it. And now you write me, dear daughter, about our son Wojtek. Don't be anxious about him, what he is doing there, let him do what he will. As he makes his bed, so he will sleep. We got rich enough through him, with those wages of his which he sent us! And now here people ask us always whether Wojciech Wojtusiak married Kaśka, your sister, so write us about it. . . . .

[JAKÓB GOŚCIAK]

141   [April, 1914?]

[DEAR SON WOJTEK]: . . . . And now you say that we don't write to you and that we are angry with you. But we are not angry, it is you who are angry with us, for you don't remember us, you have forgotten that you have here parents and a brother and sisters. You say so [reproach us], that we wrote you to work and to send money. So I will tell you this: "As you make your bed, so you will sleep." Now you have a better reason [wisdom] already than you had formerly, [irony] for you said formerly that you had no reason, and now you ask us to give you this fortune, which is first God's, then ours. All this may be. But now we must speak, how to do it. First suppose, that I give you it. But you know that you have here a brother Jasiek and sisters. Perhaps you have forgotten them, so I shall remind you who they are. The name of one is Maryna, of the other Kundzia, of the third Ludwisia. And it is thus here [in our village]. Józek Blaszczyk got married . . . . so his father willed him this his farm. But he has another son, and for this one he designated 5 hundred-notes to be paid [by the older] from these three quarters [morgs?] and this hut. The older said that it was too much, but the younger said thus: "If you think it is too much, then [give me the farm and] I will give you 8 hundred-notes."[1]

And now people say here that you want to marry. But how about the call [to military service]? A constable went here about [the village] and wrote down all of you who went to America without having been at the call. They say that you will be driven home as prisoners [from the frontier]. And now all this is still nothing. But if you marry, where will you put this wife, in her hat? Since here women and girls walk in homespun and kerchiefs [szmata] and eat

---

[1] This means that the son cannot get the farm without having money to pay his brother and sisters because land is expensive and it is no longer the custom to favor too much the son who takes the land.

gruel and potatoes and bread.   And it is necessary to work, while your lady won't work, for where will she put her umbrella?   But all this is still nothing.   But how much money have you sent to us?   We are really ashamed, people laugh at us so.   The wise man promises, the stupid man rejoices.   If I had nothing but this which you help me with, it would be enough, for I get on very nicely on the money which you have sent!   So I thank you for it.   And it will be also useful to you, when you want to buy farm-stock!

But enough of this.   And now I shall write you, dear son, a few words.   You went to America for money, for you know that you will need it if I want to give you a lot of land.

And now we greet you nicely. . . . .

JAKÓB GOŚCIAK

MARKIEWICZ SERIES

The Markiewiczs are a family of peasant nobility living in the province of Warsaw, near the Vistula and on the border of the province of Płock, but not like the Wróblewskis in their ancient family nest. This part of the country has almost no industry, but the neighborhood in which the family lives is not isolated from cultural influence, as the town of Płock, lying across the river, is the seat of a rather strong intellectual movement. Life is much faster in their social environment than in that of the Wróblewskis, who come from the same class, and this may explain the difference of attitudes. Unlike Walery Wróblewski, the Markiewiczs are "climbers." The whole familial situation, the difference between the old and the young generation, the individual differences of character and aspirations are much better understood if this fundamental feature is kept in mind. We find analogous situations in other familial series, but nowhere so universally and fully presented in its most interesting stage, i.e., at the moment when the tendency to rise *within* their own class begins to change into a tendency to rise *above* their own class. The situation of the family Markiewicz is thus representative of the general situation of the middle and lower classes of Polish society. It is a family in which the characters of the old society, with its fixed classes of families, and the new society, with its fluid classes of individuals, are mixed together in various proportions. Their only peculiarity is that, thanks to their origin, the tendency to climb within their class can have much more important consequences than with the ordinary peasants and appears therefore as especially justified. For it happened frequently in the past that a branch of a family of peasant nobility, by a gradual advance in wealth and education, rose to the ranks of middle nobility, and even two or three of the highest noble families are reputed to have grown in this way. Even now if the family Markiewicz as a whole made a fortune and acquired education, it would gradually identify itself with middle nobility. But this climbing within the old familial hierarchy would take at least three generations, while climbing within the new individualistic hierarchy could be achieved in one generation and it is doubtful whether the aim of getting into the middle nobility is consciously realized by the family. We must remember that the isolation of the peasant nobility as a class is four centuries old and that the traditional social horizon of its members no longer reaches beyond their class. Thus the two older brothers, Józef and Jan, are typical peasants whose sphere of interests is completely inclosed within the old social group. They do not tend to rise above their class and they do not understand the conscious or unconscious tendencies of their children in this direction. Each of them wants his family to occupy the highest possible place within the community—his family as a whole, not one or another individual in particular, not even his own personality, which he does not dissociate from that of his family. All the efforts of Józef and Jan are concentrated upon this aim. They both economize as much as possible, making little distinction between their own money and that of their children; they both buy land wherever there is any opportunity; they try to profit from every source of income; they neglect any showing-off except in the traditional lines, giving no money to dress their children, but spending large sums on wedding-festivals. They endow their children ver· well, but want them to make good matches. They give their children instruction, but only as far as instruction helps to a.tain a higher standing in the community itself,

and provided it does not lead to ideas contrary to the traditions. They do not understand at first how their sons in
America can have any other aim than to gather as much
money as possible in order to come back and buy good
farms and marry rich peasant girls. When they begin to
understand that their sons' sphere of interests has become
different from their own, the discovery leads either to a
tragic appeal or to a more or less complete estrangement
between father and son.

The two mothers, wives of Józef and Jan, have no
such determined tendency and seem in general to have
no conscious and far-going life-plans. Their ideas turn
generally in the traditional circle, but their familial attitude is not pronounced and their love for their children
individually allows them to understand them and to sympathize better with their individual needs and their new
tendencies.

Each of the children has a somewhat different attitude.
In Jan's family the three sons, Michał, Wiktor, and Maks
present the most perfect gradation from a typical peasant to
a typical middle-class attitude. (The fourth son, Stanisław,
is not sufficiently characterized in his brothers' letters; he
seems to be more or less like Wiktor.) Michał is nothing
but a peasant, without even his father's tendency to advance.
Perhaps he is too young. His whole sphere of interest is
that of a farmer. He hates the army with a truly peasant
hatred, and does not even try, as members of the lower-
middle class usually do, to become a sergeant. He has so
little ambition as to think about becoming an orderly. At
the maneuvers he is interested only in Russian farming;
cities have no interest for him. And his highest dream is
to come back and to take his father's farm. He has particularly strong familial feelings, not only of love but also of
solidarity, and few purely personal claims.

Wiktor is also a peasant, but much less so than his father or his brother. The career which he desires lies in the line of peasant life in the sense that he intends to remain a farmer. But he has already certain points which distinguish him from the peasant. These are (1) much stronger personal claims, which become a source of antagonism between him and his father; (2) a tendency to general instruction, not limited to the necessary minimum; (3) a tendency to get into "better society," to boast about higher relationships (even if they be those with a Russian official, in spite of his hatred for the Russians), and to assume certain forms and manners of the better society. But this will certainly be dropped when after his marriage he settles down upon a farm, and he will become a typical well-to-do farmer.

Maks has little of the peasant even in the beginning of his career in America, and almost nothing after seven years spent in this country. He drops all the peasant ideals one after another—agriculture, property, communal interests, familial solidarity (without losing attachment to individual members of the family)—and while keeping the climbing tendencies of his father, develops them along a new line, in the typical middle-class career.

Still more variety is shown among the children of Józef. Two of them—Alfons and Polcia—have not the smallest interest in anything outside of the peasant life; on the contrary, they want to remain peasants in full consciousness of the fact. But since at the same time they show no climbing tendencies, it seems that the father's attitude toward them is rather contemptuous. The mother shares the contempt toward Alfons, while she rather favors Polcia, who helps her, although she is not proud of her.

Stanisław and Pecia show a mixture of the attitudes of the peasant and the lower-middle class, which results in rather negative features, as only the superficial characters of the lower-middle class have been assimilated, and many valuable peasant characters lost. Stanisław is peculiarly undecided in his life-plans. He hesitates between marrying and remaining a peasant, and going to America. Finally he goes to America, but comes back after a year, and then regrets it. He has much vanity and very strong personal claims; a superficial tendency to instruction, which does not develop either into professional agricultural instruction, as in Alfons, or into professional instruction along the technical line, as in Maks, or even into a serious "sport," as in Wacław. As to Pecia, she seems to have assimilated merely the external distinctions (dress and manners) of the lower-middle class; she is a climber, but without the strong character necessary to climb. She marries a man a little above the peasant level of general culture, but instead of pushing him in the line of a middle-class career, drops with him into the peasant life again, and has not even the qualities required of a farmer's wife. Her laziness and vanity make a peasant career impossible for her.

Wacław and Elżbieta are perhaps psychologically the most interesting types. Intellectually and morally they are completely outside of the peasant class. Their sphere of interests is totally different from that of their parents and environment and they take their new line of life very seriously, particularly instruction and—with Wacław— social activity. But they have developed no new economic basis of life; they have not the energy or self-consciousness to begin a regular middle-class career. Wacław ought to imitate Maks; Elżbieta ought to become a teacher or a business woman. But they do not do it, and thus arises an interior conflict which is perfectly typical at the present moment. They remain in the old class by their familial connections and economic interests, while intellectually and morally they have little in common with it.

The letters of Michał show fully the peasant's attitude toward military service, particularly in the Russian army. This attitude is universal; we find it, a little less strong, in Aleksander Osiński's letters, and stronger still in the letter of J. Wiater, No. 664; and everyone shares or is supposed to share it. That the military service is a great annoyance to the peasant is shown by the fact that so many peasants prefer to leave their country forever rather than to serve— for example, Maks Markiewicz and Michał Osiński. No other manifestation of the authority of the state interferes so much with the peasant's life.

It is not difficult to understand the peasant's hatred of the army. First of all, in Russia he is completely isolated from his family and community and finds himself among foreign people whose language he does not well understand (even if he was taught it in the school), whose faith is different, whose cultural level is lower than his own, and who dislike him. He is driven far into the east of Russia, often to Siberia, for it is a policy of the Russian government to scatter the Polish soldiers over the whole empire, for fear of a revolution. Further, the peasant accustomed to the relative liberty of country life finds himself in the barracks, under a harsh and continual control; all his acts are prescribed; there are innumerable trifles which never permit him to forget his dependence. Instead of farm-work, which is for him full of meaning, which has a great variety and requires no particular precision, he finds drill, with its efforts to attain mechanical precision, not only monotonous but absolutely meaningless. Not only are three or four years of his life lost without any benefit, but there is nothing to compensate for this evil—no patriotism, since the cause which he is serving is the cause of the enemies and oppressors of his country, no idea of military honor, since in Poland this idea was developed only among the nobility, no expectation of a material benefit, since the military service does not prepare him for any future position.

In Germany, and particularly in Austria, the hatred of the army is not so strong; the soldier is less isolated, he can usually go home on leave more than once; the cultural level of his companions is higher; the military authorities know much better how to interest the soldier in his work. In Austria there is still another reason why the peasant looks differently upon military service—the fidelity of the Austrian Poles to the Hapsburgs. But, even there a strong antipathy to military service persists, for some of its reasons remain always the same.

THE FAMILY MARKIEWICZ

Józef Markiewicz
Anna, his wife
Wacław (Wacio, Wacek)
Stanisław (Staś, Stasiek, Stasio) } his sons
Alfons
Elżbieta (Elżbietka, Bicia)
Pecia
Polcia (Apolonia) } his daughters
Zonia (Zosia, Zofia)
Franuś (Franciszek), Pecia's husband
Grandmother (probably Anna's mother)
J. Przanowski, probably Anna's brother
Feliks } probably Anna's brothers; perhaps
Antoni } cousins of herself or husband
Maćkowa, cousin of Józef or Anna
Teosia, daughter of J. Przanowski
Wacek, Teosia's husband
Maks, son of J. Przanowski
Jan Markiewicz, Józef's brother
His wife
Maks (Maksymilian)
Staś (Stasio, Stanisław)
Wiktor (Wiktorek) } his sons
Michał
Ignac

Weronika ⎫
Julka   ⎬ his daughters
Mania   ⎭

Grandmother (probably mother of Jan's wife)
Ziółek (Ziółkowski), her husband
Jan Ziółek, the latter's son by his first marriage
Ziółek's sister

Other relatives in Poland, in America, in Prussia, in Petersburg.

142–225, FROM MEMBERS OF THE MARKIEWICZ FAMILY, MAINLY TO WACŁAW MARKIEWICZ, IN AMERICA. 142–71 ARE FROM THE PARENTS, JÓZEF, AND ANNA; 172–77, FROM STANISŁAW; 178–84, FROM ELZBIETKA; 185–86, FROM POLCIA; 187, FROM ALFONS; 188, FROM JAN; 189–200, FROM WIKTOR; 201–11, FROM MAKS; 212–225, FROM MICHAŁ.

142   ZAZDZIERZ, January 7, 1907

DEAR SON: We received your letter . . . . and we thank God that you are in good health, because I [your mother] have continually felt and even dreamed about you very badly, and I always remembered that dream, and we both were anxious for you. . . . . There is news that Teosia fled to America, to W. Brzezoski, but it is not certain whether the trick will succeed, because your uncle J. P[rzanowski] went in pursuit of her to Bremen. God forbid, what a meeting it will be.[1] As to grinding, there is much of it this year. Thanks to God, we shall earn enough for the household expenses. You asked about the horse. We sold him during the harvest of summer-grain. We got 24 roubles for him. I bought an ass, but I sold it at once, for it was a dog's worth [proverbial]. Now I write you that from Wincentowo there are a dozen [men] going [to America], and they beg for your address. Shall we give it to them or not? . . . . We have in our farmstock 3 nice cows, 3 rather good hogs, 5 geese. Before winter there will be some young ones, and so we push forward our lot and our age. And Elżbietka has boys from time to time. One came as if to the mill. His name is Tokarski, from Rychlin. His sister says that if we

---

[1] Elopement is very rare among the peasants, and, in view of the familial character of marriage, the family is supposed to condemn severely such an attempt to avoid its control.

want [him], he has 400 roubles in a bank and he can show them for greater certainty. She says that he had a shop in Łódż. But we are not in a hurry, we only said to him that he can call upon us. Staś cannot find anything favorable; that about which I wrote you did not please us, nor him either. So he absolutely wants to go to you. How do you think? Is it worth while or not? . . . .

[ANNA MARKIEWICZ]

DEAR BROTHER: Send soon the ship-ticket or money, or else I shall take money from here for the journey. Why, there is so much money with us! But let it rather remain;[1] I would pay you back later on. Answer at once, and write me, what I shall take of clothes, linen, and living [food], because about the middle of March I am going to you. Let me also try America! I would not spend there longer than 2 years. In our windmill there is big grinding, day and night. . . . . Answer at once, because I will leave about the middle of March.

Be healthy, be healthy [goodbye], dear son and dear brother. As to the ship-ticket, wait a little, because I want now to marry [the daughter of] Gasztyka in Topolno. If I succeed, I shan't go to America, and if I don't succeed, then I shall go.

[STANISŁAW M.]

143   February 10, 1907

DEAR SON: . . . . We thank you for not having forgotten our need which it was absolutely necessary to satisfy. Mr. and Mrs. Goszewski moved on January 22. We gave them the money back; they refused to accept any interest, so we only thanked them. We helped them, when they moved, to pack up their baggage. In bidding them farewell, we all wept. Tadek did not want to go to Ojców; he mentioned very often Mr. W[acław] who will bring him a [wooden] horse from America. And now, when [more] money comes from you, we will at once turn it over to Pecia, and so we shall have peace once for all with these debts. . . . .

And now I write to you about Teosia. Your uncle sent a telegram to Bremen and went himself to Toruń, to your uncle F. F., and they

---

[1] An expression of the old qualification of economic quantities which we have treated in the Introduction: "Economic Attitudes." The peasant is reluctant to touch, even for a short time, money which has been put aside. But in this case it is rather the reluctance of the father than of the son.

sent her photograph, and the police turned the girl back to her father in Toruń. It is said that they wrote a letter to Brzezoski telling him to come, for they give the permission because of the wish of their daughter [and of her behavior]. And Staś cannot find anyone such as he would like to marry. Dear son, send us your photograph. . . . .

[JÓZEF and ANNA MARKIEWICZ]

144   March 10, 1907

DEAR SON: . . . . And now we are very sad, dear son, that you are longing for your family. But I don't marvel, because although I have them all here, I weep [for you] more than once and I pray our Lord God that you may come happily back to your family home. We will now write letters to you oftener, because it won't be so difficult [to get] to Płock, for you know how it is in winter—always snow and cold. We go there seldom, and here we have no post-office.

We received on one day the 100 roubles which you sent and on the next day we gave them to Pecia and Franuś, and 8 roubles of interest.[1] You ordered us to buy for the children [material] for dresses, so I bought it at once, and you made them very glad. They thank you. And now, dear son, when you earn as much as you can without damaging your health, send the money home, and we shall make it safe. Don't think that perhaps we will take it for our household needs; what you send now will be made safe for you once and forever. . . . . You ask about grandmother. She clucks as a hen when all her chickens have been taken away. Walentowa weeps for her boys [who are in America]; Antoniowa does not regret much [her man who went away] because she has another. Everybody whom I meet asks about you, dear son, and wishes you the best possible, and everybody says, "May God grant us to see him happily once more." We bought a good overcoat for Pecia, and in the spring we will also give her a young cow. . . . . Stasio often looks in at Dobrzyków. . . . . Something ties him, some love, nearer to the Vistula. . . . . May our Lord God help you to earn some hundred roubles that you may find your way here. Now bee-keeping is again considered a good business.

---

[1] This money was evidently destined originally for Pecia's dower. It had apparently been advanced to the brother in America, and as Pecia did not receive it promptly on her marriage, interest is added. The giving of interest here indicates the substitution of an economic for a purely social attitude. Under the old system the delay would have formed no reason for the payment of interest.

. . . . Elżbieta's *kum* [god-brother] said that he got 80 roubles for the honey in one year. . . . . So when our Lord God brings you back we shall will you [some land] and you can set up an orchard and bee-hives. . . . .

[ANNA MARKIEWICZ]

145 July 4, 1907

DEAR SON: . . . . We heard about a terrible accident, that Seweryniak who was in America was killed by a train, and it is true, for his brother Franciszek buried him. Dear son, be careful. May God keep you from any accident. . . . . In the autumn Alfons seriously intends going to you, but don't think that it is not a fact.[1] So answer his question. You know his strength. We say that his intention is of no use. The fathers and mothers [of the young men who went to America] and the wife of Mielczarek send you their thanks [for having received and helped the newcomers in America].

Dear son, you write us not to be surprised, that you want to marry. But we don't oppose it at all if she is only a girl with a good education.[2] Consider it well, because the state of marriage is subject to great [many] conditions. But if she pleased you, then very well. May our Lord God bless you, and we wish you with our whole heart everything the best. . . . . In fact I spoke about it myself [wishing] that you might not spend your young years on nothing. So consider it the best you can and marry. If only the girl is orderly and good, we can only rejoice. . . . . If she is from Płock, let her give you her address—if she has parents here, and where they live, so we shall get acquainted with them.

If you don't marry, send your money home, but if you have the intention [to marry], then do not.

Be healthy, be healthy, dear son.

[ANNA MARKIEWICZ]

146 December 5, 1907

DEAR SON: . . . . In our home everybody is healthy enough, only in Pecia's home her youngest daughter died. Stasio and Kocia

---

[1] This phrase is ironical. Alfons is not treated seriously by any one of the family.

[2] Showing how relatively advanced the writers are. In no other series is this question of education raised.

Białecka were the god-parents. She lived only 5 weeks. . . . .
You ask about Teosia. She came home very quietly with her father
and she is at home. Perhaps there somebody told tales like a gypsy,
but don't believe it at all, because all that is untrue.[1] [Weather;
Christmas wishes.] And your father, thanks to God, is not at all the
same as he was [his character has improved]. . . . .

[ANNA MARKIEWICZ]

147   February 24, 1908

DEAR SON: We received your letter. . . . . We wish you to be
healthy in body and soul, because this is the excellence of man. For
the second year is passing already, and you don't mention anything
about religion or church. Remember the admonition of your parents.
For faith is the first thing, and everything else is only additional.
Don't step aside from the true way. Consider it, for you can do harm
to your whole family.[2]

And now I inform you that rye is 7 roubles [a bushel]. Thanks
to God there is work in the windmill; the barn brings also a few
bushels [for space rented ?] and so we try as best we can that there may
be more and more [property] for you [children].

Dear son, reflect well, if you are working beyond the ocean only
for the sake of living [without saving], leave it and come to us.[3] If

[1] Evidently, such an exceptional occurrence as Teosia's flight has stirred up
much gossip. This is one of the reasons why girls and boys avoid any irregularities
in their marriage. Sometimes the smallest irregularity in the wedding ceremony
provokes the most mischievous gossip and most wonderful interpretations.

[2] Probable meaning: "God may punish the whole family for your sins."
Thus, the feeling of familial unity is carried so far as to acknowledge a common
responsibility before God. The attitude is evidently not an isolated fact; common
religious responsibility is still more or less admitted not only for families, but also
for other social units, as villages and parishes. This has clearly nothing to do with
the biblical heredity of sin and punishment: it is merely the manifestation of the
group-solidarity.

[3] The new tendency to advance as against the old interest in mere living is here
expressed as clearly as possible. Fifty years ago it was all right if a young member
of a family, which was too poor to support all its members, earned his living
by servant-work and thus spared the rest of the family his living expenses; there
was not even the idea of his increasing the familial fortune for he had no wages
in cash. Even now, in the Osiński series, we find this attitude, when Michał serves
as a groom, for the father refuses to feed him (although this refusal, in the good
economic condition of the family, is already something new). But here, with re-

you have a few hundred roubles, I will take [add] my money, and I will buy a farm somewhere for you. The inn in Dobrzyków is now for sale, or perhaps something else. . . . .

JÓZEF MARKIEWICZ

148 March 29, 1908

DEAR SON: I received your letter. I rejoiced much that you are in good health, but for another cause you make us sad, for you don't intend to come back to our country. At this moment the paper trembled in my hand or my hand shook in recording it. Why, even birds who fly away from their native place still do come back! How did you dare to pronounce such wretched [mean] words? You ought to hold to the parental exhortations. I never taught you to criticize the clergy. You know that Bonaparte shook the whole of Europe until he broke off with the head of the Church, and later—you know what became of him later! Well, I don't mention that you forgot about religion, i.e., about the greatest jewel, only that after a year you [raise yourself?] above us. What you give to the papers is bad, and it is a pity that you use your learning so, for learning is everywhere useful to man, but [your ideas] are useful to you there, but won't be when you come back. [Whole paragraph obscure and translation conjectural.] And now with us it is as it has been. . . . . As to money, we don't absolutely require you to send any when you cannot, because I try always to have a few hundred roubles on hand. Only don't forget about yourself for your later years. . . . .

I have nothing more to write, only I tell you the news. Wiktor, son of Jan, went to the army to Petersburg and there he found our family. Three sons of my father's brother are there. One of them is a higher railway-conductor, the other a physician, the third a professor. And in Prussia our family also got honors. Stasiek up to the present does not succeed [in marrying] and Elżbietka also sits at home. I end my letter with these words: May you not forget, even as swallows don't forget their native nests.

J. MARKIEWICZ

Dear son, why are you so angry and why do you answer us so severely? The girls wept after reading this letter, so that it was quite

gard to Wacław, the situation of the family is almost brilliant when measured by peasant standards, and still Wacław should increase the fortune. If he cannot do it by working in America he ought to do it by farmer's work. If he does nothing but live on his income he is regarded as losing his time.

gloomy in the house.   And we, the parents, what are we to say ?   You
don't want to come back to us, but I don't think it true.   I believe
in you that you love your parents and your country. . . . .[1]

[YOUR MOTHER]

149   September 7, 1909

DEAR SON: . . . . And as to the letters from you, we had none
except last year in July for my name-day.   Then we answered at once
and we asked you for an answer, but we received no letter until today,
September 7.   Dear son, believe us, there was not a day when we did
not complain about your negligence, and you complain about us!
Neither letter nor postcard, nothing up to the present.   I don't know
what happened.   We have only this letter which you tell us to send
to the editor [of some paper].   As for me, I fall asleep with the thought
about you and I awake with the same thought; I end the day with
tears and I begin it with tears.   I did not understand what happened
to you.   Everybody at home tried to comfort me, but it was hard to
wait.   Your father went to Jan M[arkiewicz] in order that he might
ask Maks.   They said that Maks wrote about your having gone
somewhere without giving any word of yourself, but they did not
allow us to read the letter.

With us everything is as it has been from old; we have a horse,
worth 100 roubles, a new wagon, 3 cows, 2 calves, 4 pigs worth also
about 100 [roubles], etc.   The crops are the average.   Franuś [son-in-
law] is captain [of a Vistula boat].   They bought 6 morgs of land.
We have given them some money already, but we will add some more,
for we must give them at least 500 roubles.   Teosia and Wacek were
with us for a week, but they did not say anything about any loan, so
it is probably a lie.   We heard that they said something to Franuś.
They are all worth the same [little].   Well, God be with them.   I
don't see any blessing of God for them.   They had only her [one
daughter] and even so they came to us asking us for a hundred [roubles]
for her wedding. . . . .[2]

[1] For the meaning of this letter, as showing the contrast between the old and
the young generation, cf. Introduction: "Peasant Family."

[2] We see how success may assume a moral value by being conceived as the
result of God's blessing.   Formally this conception was introduced by the church
in its endeavor to ascribe to God all the good.   But the content is really older.
Prosperity was a sign of a harmony between man and nature.   Cf. Introduction:
"Religious and Magical Attitudes."

Your father was in Włocławek . . . . and called upon Edek. Edek said that he saw you in the spring and that you intend to come back to our country. If you think it good, then come. He said that you are some sort of a boss, and that you earn about $400. Can it be? Or perhaps it is only a slander of your enemies; I don't know. Your grandmother began to reproach us for your education, saying that we have praised you so much, and now you don't write. We grieve ourselves enough. All other people do write, and we don't have any news. How hard and painful it is when anybody asks us [about you]. We were quite ashamed at last. . . . . We keep the shop after Pecia. It brought us also 100 [roubles]. We all work as we can. Elżbieta is in Częstochowa and Polcia in the shop. Answer us the soonest possible. . . . .

[MARKIEWICZS]

150 March 12, 1910

DEAR SON: We received your postcard. On the one hand we are glad that you are in good health, on the other we are pained that you spend your youth in vain, doing nothing. Why, you have your own reason [you know] that it is necessary to provide somewhat in youth for old age. If you have nothing to do there, move to Europe, or, if you think it good, come home. As to the money, if you have not enough, take from Mielczarek, or simply write home and I will send you some to America. And if you borrow from Mielczarek, we will give it back here [to his parents], for some hundred roubles are ready.

What more shall I write you? I can only write you that the winter is here very severe and cold, and at home it is not quite well, because everybody was more or less unwell, particularly Elżbieta. . . . . Your aunt, Antoni's wife, is dead. And except for this, things are not bad in the household, for we have threshed and now we are grinding. And I must tell you that on March 14 is my birthday. I finish 60 years. Perhaps I shall not be able to work for a great while longer, and at least I should like to see all of you again. Your grandmother sits in her house and is farming, but badly. Uncle Feluś was with us for a few days, and your aunt also; they enjoyed our hospitality and danced. As to our country, you know probably the news.

Your father,

JÓZEF MARKIEWICZ

Dear son, we think much about it, for you grieve there perhaps very much that you have no work. But you are not alone [in having no work], so there is nothing to do. Consider it and don't grieve. Our Lord God has more [left] than He has spent. Be healthy, be healthy, dear son. . . . .

[YOUR MOTHER]

151 May 5 [1910]

DEAR SON: . . . . You keep writing always about those 100 roubles. Well, I will send them back, but remember that you don't do harm to me, but to yourself. And with me it is so: I thought that I should increase the fortune, but nothing thrives with my children, neither a good marriage with my daughters nor [a good lot] with any boy. But I return to you once more, I send you these 100 roubles. But why can others send enough money home, while you have not enough even to live or to come back? My whole dream is vain. Come here. Why should you sit there since the star [of fortune] does not shine for you? It is very bad, dear son. If you have not enough for your journey, take from Mielczarek. We will give it back here. Right now land and other property open [for sale], but if you have no money to buy—well, perhaps God will give it.[1]

Your father,

J. MARKIEWICZ

152 June 20 [1910]

DEAR SON: In our home everybody is in good health. As to Staś, it is always the same, ... and as to Elżbieta, she won't marry Janek; she has changed her views already. In our field the rye is average, the peas not very good, the wheat nice, the potatoes nice. Our horse is nice, our cattle as nice as never before, we have 4 cows big with calves and one young cow, we have sold one cow and got 60 roubles, and for the calf 4 roubles; we have pigs, ducks, of all

---

[1] Plainly the fundamental life-interest of the old man is to increase the fortune of the whole family, to arrange rich marriages for his children, to have them all in the neighborhood, prosperous, respected by the community, keeping the traditional attitudes and ideals in harmony with his own, solidarity among themselves, sufficiently instructed to play an active part in communal life, and always obeying the father. The position of head of such a family is the highest one of which an old type of a peasant can dream.

poultry we have more than 100 pieces; there is a nice amount of work. This is not all. We must often help Pecia, because they are building a barn and have made a shack for themselves of the stable. Later on they will build a house, and Pecia has nice rye, potatoes, peas, etc. So in general everything is succeeding well enough with us, only we have the worst trouble with Stasiek, although I did not want to grieve you. When he came from the army he seemed to be healthy for a few days, but then came a continuous cough, and pains in the breast, belly, hands, feet, etc.—everything. After he has been better for a few days, then all this returns. Always nothing but the doctor and the drug-store. I have already proposed to have the doctor and the drug-store move into our house. What can I do? I have grieved and wept enough; it fell upon [settled in] my eyes, which are worse than ever. And now, dear son, don't care about anybody, only mind about yourself. For nowadays people are even too clever when they want to get other people's good, but they keep well their own. . . . .[1] I did not write you for so long a time because I had hoped to write you something new [Elżbieta's marriage], but she says that the lot which she would have now with him may be still had 10 years hence. . . . . You asked what scabs the children had. Very dangerous ones, for it was scarlet fever. Now, thanks to God, they are recovered. . . . . Many different people are visiting us now, as always when there are girls at home. Even sometimes the chief forester [from the manorial forest] of Łąck comes with his wife. Well, you can imagine how it must be [how troublesome and expensive] but all this is done for the children. You know, dear son, often when they amuse themselves, father comes to me and says: "Ah, if Wacek came now, what a joy it would be."

[ANNA MARKIEWICZ]

153   August 8 [1910]

DEAR SON: . . . . As to your marriage about which you wrote, we are very satisfied. If only the girl is as you want her to be, let our Lord God bless you. We all wish you with a single voice:

---

[1] The complaints of old people about the avarice and unreliability of the present generation, which we find in many letters, seem to have a real ground. With the dissolution of the old solidarity the old norms regulating economic relations disappear, while the new norms, corresponding to the individualistic stage of economic life (business-honesty) have not yet developed.

"Whatever is the best in the world, may God grant it to you." But consider well what you intend to do.

[Crops.] Your father went just now with Franek to put the wings on the windmill; it will take some weeks. Stasio is grinding flour, Alfons is mowing peas, Elżbietka is sewing a dress, we all push the work farther on. . . . . You write about Brońcia. She has already got married. She married the baker about whom I wrote you, who wanted our Elżbietka, but she did not want him. . . . . Write us, Wacio, what is your betrothed occupied with and in whose house she lives, for here people say that she went to her uncle. . . . .[1]

[ANNA MARKIEWICZ]

154   [September 13, 1910]

DEAR SON: After returning from that miraculous place [Częstochowa] I am healthy enough, as well as all of us at home, but we are much grieved that you are not in good health. . . . . I begged God's Mother for health and good success for you all. And now, dear son, don't be angry with us about this loan to your aunt [for not having lent her your money], for she has the mouth in the right spot [talks much and knows what to say]. And now we will give Pecia 400 roubles, because they will buy that house from Jakubowski. . . . .

[YOUR MOTHER]

Dear son, mark it well, if your health does not favor you, return home, for why should you do penance there? Here is bread enough in my house. You gave me the order to lend a few hundred of złoty to Maćkowa, but surely you know how I lent 50 roubles to her brother and could not get them back for 10 years. You know that it is easy to let money go away while it is difficult to put it together. An incident like this happened a month ago with Mr. Mroczkowski who lived in our house during the summer. When he left he took 15 roubles from us. Stasiek was too credulous, and now I don't know

---

[1] The letter shows how the control of the family over the individual is lost. There is no mention at all of the girl's dowry, in spite of the father's formerly expressed wishes, and only a discreet attempt (in the last phrase) to learn anything more about her personality and family. The parents agree with their son's wish, and they dare only to advise him "to consider the matter well." The attitude is totally different toward the other son, who stays at home; here the parents show more clearly what are their wishes, and the son could hardly marry a girl who did not please his parents. Compare this letter with No. 145.

when he will get them. I beg you, don't send any more such [orders]. If you need money, I can send it to you. Moreover, I did not forget what Mrs. [ironical] Maćkowa said last year when she met Andzia. . . . . She reproached you for living with her son, saying that you settled in his house and filled your belly with his food—as if you did not pay for boarding! [Crops and weather.]

Y[our] f[ather],

J. MARKIEWICZ

155 November 1 [1910]

DEAR SON: . . . . Walenty in Dobrzyków built a small mill upon his water [in competition with us], but he grinds [only] three quarters of once-ground flour a day. Well, we don't know how it will be later. As to Elżbietka, she has a boy, a butcher from Lubień. I don't know whether she will marry him or not, but she says that this winter she will surely decide. If not this one, then another. I have trouble enough now for my [sins]. Always new guests, always some new fashions, always these new things, so that my income does not suffice.

And you know that [your] father always says so: "When anything is not there, we can do without it." But sometimes it must be had, even if it must be cut out from under the palm of the hand! So, dear son, I beg you very much, if you can, send me a little money, but for my needs. Bicia [Elżbieta] is grown up, Polcia is bigger still, Zonia begins to overtake them, and they all need to be dressed, while it is useless to speak to your father about it. If you can, send it as soon as possible, because if I sell some cow, or hog, or grain, it must be put aside; [your father says that] it cannot be spent. We gave Pecia 100 and 200, but we must still give 200. Bicia also [must have money], so we must put money aside. Well, we have nice hogs, nice cattle, and a nice horse, but I must work conscientiously for all this. Your father just excuses himself with his years and I may work with the children so that my bones crack. He says: "Then don't keep [so much farm-stock], don't work. Do I order you [to do all this]?" But when he wants anything, he requires it. As to the crops, everything is not bad . . . . only we must work so much. Bicia is continually in the shop, she has pupils and sews. Zonia will help her presently, and so we push things further and further. You write us that you won't be the best man [at your sisters' weddings]. It is hard for me to read this and my tears flow. Well, let God's Mother of unceasing Help not forget you. . . . .[1]

Your truly loving mother,

[ANNA MARKIEWICZ]

156   February 6 [1911]

DEAR SON: We received . . . . 50 roubles for which we thank you. . . . . We bought a fur [sheep] coat for Staś for 34 roubles, and for the rest two dresses, one for Bicia and one for Polcia. [Sickness of the children.] As to Elżbieta, there is to be a wedding, but not till after Easter, because he has a brother in America, so they wait until he comes and stays with his family [parents], for it is impossible for her to go there [to her husband's parents]. Let them rather set up a place of their own, when the matter comes to that.[2] And Stasiek is walking and walking [in search of a wife] but I don't know when he will "walk out" anything for himself. . . . . I don't remember whether I wrote you that one of Pecia's children died, a nice little boy, half a year old. [Stock sold and bought, windmill, shop, money received from debtors, farm-work.] We wish you good health, happiness and good success in the new year. Get married, don't mind A. T.,[3] because it is of no use. . . . .

[MARKIEWICZS]

157   June 3 [1911]

DEAR SON: We received your letter . . . . and once 200 roubles, and again 50 roubles. Thanks be to God that He allowed you to earn them. We thank you for this money. We will put it in a safe place. If you can, send even more, it won't be lost. [Health, weather,

---

[1] The difference in the economic attitudes of the man and the woman is here most typically expressed. The man is exclusively interested in the welfare and social standing of the family as a whole; he seems to have very little understanding of the particular, actual needs of any member of the family. The woman, on the contrary, understands the latter very well and sympathizes with the members of the family whenever they lack anything actually and individually, but seems to have no real eagerness to contribute to the fulfilment of her husband's general plans.

[2] It would be bad form if a girl with Elżbieta's social standing went to live with her husband's parents, for it would look as if she had not dowry enough and he could not earn enough to start their own home, even if in this case the real cause were that the boy's parents needed the help of one son.

[3] Evidently a girl, and probably one whom he did not succeed in marrying.

crops.] We have 1 horse, 4 cows, 1 young cow, a young bull of good breed . . . . pigs, 22 geese, turkeys, ducks, chickens; we have more than 100 pieces of poultry in general, because we are preparing for a wedding. Elżbieta will now at last marry that Janek K. She did not want him, but evidently it is God's will for her, for she despised him, but he did his best to please her again. But the wedding won't be sooner than September, because he is as far as Sandomierz, on a government ship. He has not the worst salary. It will be as God grants. We must buy everything for her and give her away; nothing can be done. You ask about Pecia and Franuś. They were sick in the winter, first F., then P., then the children; they spent a nice sum of money! But now, thanks to God, they are in good health. The children loaf about, Pecia rocks the boy to sleep [calls to the others:] "You, don't touch that," "You, put that down." She is always shooing them off. Franuś, since he mounted the boat of Mrs. Jaworska, is sailing up to the present as captain. He does his best. Perhaps our Lord God won't refuse happiness also to that other [son-in-law], for Elżbieta is a good, honest, orderly girl. Nothing is amiss with her. We hoped something else for her. Well, nothing can be done. Polcia is also a good girl, but surely she will soon become a loafer. They sing in the church in the choir, beautifully, it is true, but I have the more to do. Well, let them know that they have a mother. . . . . Stasiek wants to marry, but only if we will him [the farm]. What do you say to this? What shall we do? . . . .

[ANNA MARKIEWICZ]

158 [August–September?] 15, 1911

DEAR SON: We and Elżbieta received your letters. . . . . As to Elżbieta, she postponed all this to future times. Well, you have no idea how great a regret it was for Janek, but she did not care much about it. Well, nothing can be done; she is not for him. She won't despise the man who will be suited to her. Perhaps at last she will choose. We had some expenses, and he also, but nothing can be done. A girl with such a character as Elżbieta's is not easily found, so it is no wonder if she prizes herself much.[1] Even now she was in Płock taking

---

[1] The case of Elżbieta is frequent in the lower classes. In a family which rises above its class the condition of a girl is much worse than that of a boy. The latter has already risen when he has a higher instruction and a better position, and

business lessons, so she profited once more somewhat. Thanks to God, Zosia will be clever also. Well, I work much for them, but what can be done? As to our grinding, we earn poorly now, because such an executioner [accursed big mill] is built in Gąbin as suffices for everybody. [Crops.] Everywhere only work and work, so that the bones lap one over another, but what can be done? But, unhappily my teeth already decline absolutely to work, so I must have some put in, but I have not money enough for it for I have enough other things to spend it on. So if it would not be a great detriment to you, I would beg you for a few roubles for my teeth, but if not, it cannot be helped. Even if I breed anything [and sell], either some clothes must be bought for one child, or another calls for something else, or the boy must be paid who tends the cattle. And your father won't know anything about [have anything to do with] all this. [Greetings from the whole family and for all the relatives who are in America.]

[ANNA MARKIEWICZ]

Maks [Przanowski], send me those 100 roubles back. I think that I have waited long enough. I beg you very much.

[I. M.]

159 November 5, 1911

DEAR SON: In our home everybody is in such health as a worm-eaten nut, but everybody pushes slowly his lot. . . . . It is not well in our home. Stasiek would be glad to marry, but only if somebody gave him bread, a knife, butter, a good sofa to sit upon, etc., but don't speak to him about working: "I am tired," "I don't want to," "I cannot," etc. Don't speak to him about this or that to be done,

---

marriage is for him in this respect a secondary matter. But a girl cannot rise socially, unless by marriage; instruction, relative refinement, do not put her immediately above the level of her class, but only prepare the way to a better marriage, make her fit to rise through marriage. But in a milieu in which the conditions of life are difficult and the tendency to rise is strongly developed such a girl will with difficulty find an opportunity to marry above her class, as the men also prefer to marry above theirs. But a refined girl is not easily reconciled to marriage with a man of her own class, and thus her condition is not enviable. The usual result is that, after waiting for a good match which does not come, she finally resigns, fearing to remain an old maid more than to marry below her aspirations. These aspirations are then transferred to her children.

because he does not care much about anything. Let him be.[1] I don't wish many people what I have [of trouble]. As to Elżbieta, the heart must weep! A pretty, graceful girl, skilful, honest, trained as no other in the family—well, and there is nobody whom it would suit her to marry. So she intends to go to a school. She wants to learn to be a teacher. We don't know how she will succeed, because she is only just now going to make inquiries. I will write you in another letter. If only our Lord God saves us from any accident to the [sick] horse . . . . for it would be [a loss of] 120 roubles. God forbid it!

You ask about your trees. They bore cherries, pears, apples; there were a few olives, and nice wild pears. We sold fruit for a nice score of roubles, as never before, because the summer was very dry and hot. In Pecia's home everybody is in good health. They live on their own land, they made a shack of that stable and live there for the present. Next year they will perhaps build a house. Genia Jaworska is going to marry, but our girls don't even look at such young men. The other who now has Bronka wanted to come to Elżbieta but she refused. Now this one also wanted [to marry her], but she will not even listen. Well, I don't know who will be better off.

You write about your marrying. Decide as you please, provided only that you are happy, and that which is good and nice for you will be that also for us. May our Lord God bless you. . . . .

Zosia is growing, a nice little girl. Soon she will be as big as her mother. She is intelligent enough, she sews not badly. Polcia is not [intelligent], she is only a housekeeper, a scrub-woman, an ironer, a laundress—all of them.

Your sincerely loving parents,

J. [and] ANNA M.

Our horse just died. A horse and 3 pigs! It is a nice comedown! We shall not overtake it soon!

[1] Stasiek is probably demoralized by his military service, and his bad health. But it is very probable that his unwillingness to work is to a great extent due to the loss of family interests and to the lack of personal interests. (Cf. his letters.) The family life is organized by the father upon the old basis of familial unity; each child has to work, not for himself personally, but for the benefit of the whole group. But Stasiek has no longer this attitude, and perhaps his long and fruitless search for a wife is caused by his wish to become independent.

160   January 20, 1912

DEAR SON: We received your letter . . . . for which we thank you heartily, but . . . . don't be such a cause of grief to your family. You know that we all grieve about you [when we have no news]; when anything bad or good happens to you, share it with us, as we do with you. . . . . In our home everybody is healthy enough. There is sufficient grinding, as much as there is wind. Our farm-stock is, 4 cows big with calves, one young cow, 6 pigs which are worth about 100 roubles, geese, ducks, etc. . . . . Our crops are average. . . . . Pecia's children are somewhat ill, because scabs are spread out in our neighborhood. In Tokary, Dobrzyków, many people lie sick with scabs. Walenty's Witek came from the army and has smallpox, Antoni's Maks has smallpox. Antoni has been sick for more than a year. He lies almost continually. She lies sick also, with swelling of the liver. . . . . Bulkoski's wife died just now. In our home up to the present everybody is well enough, but we don't know how it will be later. Stasio is walking here and there [in search of a wife]. Well, I don't know. As to Elżbieta, if anybody wants her she does not want him, so I don't know how it will be, whether she will win or lose. Well, it will be as God grants. She cuts and sews, she sings religious and dancing songs, she has a pupil [in sewing], the girl of Jan Seweryniak, and so she passes her moments. When Sunday comes Andrzej Kusio calls upon them and plays, they dance a little. One and another comes, boys from the manor-farm, and we amuse ourselves. Polcia has grown bigger than Pecia and Elżbieta; when she comes from the kitchen to the room, it [the door] is full of her from the top to the bottom. She works at home and helps Elżbieta. Zonia goes to school and learns. We have a new teacher, but an orthodox [Russian], so we don't have any friendly relations with her. . . . . You ask who got married. [Enumerates 7 marriages.] We had 200 roubles with Fijołek, he paid us the sum and the interest; and Matusiak and everybody paid us back. Write us whether you have any cash. . . . . Everybody who comes to us, asks what you wrote and whether you are in good health, and asks us to greet you: "From me also," "And from me." . . . .

YOUR PARENTS and FAMILY

Dear brother, I am addressing this letter in the home of my betrothed, in Gombin, in the house of Pokorski the tile-maker. Our father and mother are here expressly for the first [preliminary] betrothal. The marriage is to be after Easter, so don't send the ship-ticket.   [Stanisław]

161   March 17, 1912

Dear Son: . . . . I beg you, write letters home oftener, for why should we grieve so much about you? In our house everybody is in good health, but in Pecia's house Feluś has spent the whole winter in getting well, for he caught cold. Well, now he is already sailing upon the ship. And Pecia, you know while she was yet [a girl] at home said: "I must not eat the breakfast, for I shall be thick," or "I must squeeze myself tightly with the corset." Well, and now the results of all this show themselves. Now that she is married, she is sickly. . . . .¹ Jan [Markiewicz] boasts that Maks has already sent some thousand roubles home, that he has there almost 10,000 roubles, that he passed an examination as engineer, and he says: "Your Wacław is also going to this school." And your father answers him: "You are stupid, say 'yes'!" If you intend to send some money, send it; we shall place it here. Don't be afraid, we won't do as your grandparents did. [Incomes and expenses; weather.] And beware of these "engineers" and locksmiths and cabinet-makers, because both sides [the parents here and the sons there] are worth the same. When they [Jan M.] receive a letter, and your father is there, they never give it to him to read, because there are always some secrets from that "engineer.". . . .²

                                        [Anna Markiewicz]

162   October 20 [1912]

Dear Son: We received your last letter . . . . for which we thank you heartily. You pained us [in writing] that your teeth are

¹ Pecia also tried to rise above her class. The purely peasant girl does not resort to lacing and keeping down her weight but uses external ornamentation instead. After her marriage Pecia falls back into the peasant ideals of land-owning and successful farming. Her imitation of town-manners is purely superficial, while Elżbieta tends to acquire an interior culture.

² There is evident rivalry between the two brothers, Józef and Jan, and their families on the score of social standing. Jan's family is more successful, and hence the envy manifested in this letter. The term "engineer," properly applied to a graduate of a higher polytechnical school, is sometimes used by courtesy of graduates of lower technical schools, and hence again the irony and incredulity of the old man.

aching, but that is nothing new, for such is their habit at present. In our home now it is somewhat different, for it was very bad, because I was very sick. I got sick on the way from church on September 10. I was so terribly sick with vomiting and headache on the field of Jankowski that I could not come home alone. Well, they helped me with whatever was possible, but I was in such danger that they had to bring the priest at once, and then the doctor.[1] With the help of a medicine I got a little better, but I lay for two weeks. Now I can walk and I work a little but my head pains me a little still. The money from you has come already; we will get it and put it in the bank. We will add 100 roubles and put 200 together. . . . . We lent 200 roubles to Fijołkowski [Fijołek].[2] . . . . We sold a horse, pigs, a cow and geese, and we got 300 roubles, and these from you will make 400 together. If your health favors you, earn whatever you can and send us; it won't be lost for you here. [Crops.] You ask about your god-son. He is growing, a nice boy, he says always that his god-father will bring him a horse from America. Pecia bore another child, a daughter. We sold more than 8 bushels of pears. Old Seweryniak died. Be healthy.

[ANNA MARKIEWICZ]

Dear son, you need not fear [on account of a possible war], for, everybody here is very calm. The only thing is that you should not return with your hands empty, because, you know, if you want to pay [your brothers and sisters] off, you must have some hundreds of roubles, and if you don't wish [to take my farm], then another farm will be bought, for Franuś has also 400 roubles of cash . . . . [and could take my farm].

JÓZEF MARKIEWICZ

[1] In case of a dangerous sickness it is the habit to bring *first* a priest, and only afterward the doctor; the care for the soul is considered more important than the care for the body, and it would be worse to neglect the opportunity of the patient's making peace with God than to neglect the possibility of his recovery through immediate help. To understand this better, we must remember that the old peasant is not afraid of dying, provided he has religious help and time enough to make his dispositions.

[2] Note the change in the name. In No. 160 the man is called "Fijołek." The old peasant names never ended in "ski" or "cki," which, dating from the fifteenth century, were the endings of the names of the nobility (etymologically adjectives, formed from the names of the estates). Lately the peasants (following the bourgeoisie) have begun to imitate the form by adding these suffixes to their names. But this is not done in Galicia, where class-consciousness is stronger.

163   March 26, 1913

DEAR SONS: We thank God that you saw one another healthy
and happy. Love one another, as you did formerly in school, for we
believe that you love one another sincerely and that you don't wish
one another evil, but good. . . . . Our whole family is in good health,
only in Jan's house one of the girls died, but perhaps there will be
added one more instead, because Maks intends to marry Miss Dobrowolska. [Farm-work.] That man Bużański comes often to Polcia,
and we don't know what to do. Advise us what to do. Fijołkowski
intends to sell the 6 morgs near us. Perhaps we shall take them.

Dear sons, I beg you very much to send me a few roubles for my
teeth, because I must have new ones set in, and I hate to spend money
[which is put aside]. Perhaps you have more, then send me. . . . .

And now, dear Wacio, care for Staś as you cared once for me in
my sickness. May our Lord God reward you for it! . . . .

Your loving mother,

ANNA MARKIEWICZ

164   April 26 [1913]

DEAR SONS: . . . . Alfons sold that old horse and bought a
young one, 3 years old, good for eating and for pulling and for everything; but his hip was somewhat injured. It was so difficult to
notice that at the fair Prussian Jews bought him and did not know it.
Even so, Alfons made a profit of 6 roubles, and the horse's work was
worth 10 roubles. He [the horse] remained 6 weeks with us.

And Andrzej is calling upon us as often as before [courting Polcia].
Surely we must consider it and finish this business. . . . . Our shop is
sold; we gathered in all 100 roubles and there is still a little credited
to people, but there will be always those who won't pay. . . . .
Jankowski moved beyond the Vistula. He had borrowed 100 roubles
more and owed us 200, but when he was to move, he came to us and
calmed us,[1] paid the whole 200 roubles back, and interest, and offered
7 roubles for the sake of good feeling. But we took only 4 roubles in
order that there might always be good feeling between us. . . . .[2]

[1] To "calm the creditors" is an old expression for paying debts.

[2] Survival of the old custom connected with the lending of *naturalia*. When
a natural product borrowed for productive purposes yielded more than was
expected, a return was made greater than the amount agreed upon. This custom
survived in money loans, but is rare. Cf. Introduction: "Economic Attitudes."

I am astonished, how you can write such things, that we don't care for you. Only beyond the grave father and mother [part with] their children. . . . .

[ANNA MARKIEWICZ]

165
July 3 [1913]

DEAR CHILDREN: . . . . I answer only now, because we have such different circumstances. Elżbietka's betrothed was here in the end of June, Edward Topolski, about whom you know. So perhaps now her maidenhood will come to an end. . . . . As to Polcia, she will probably marry this Andrzej, because she won't hear to anybody else, and he waits as if for God's mercy [for our decision]. . . . .

We have a great sorrow, my children, because Alfons bought a mare for 130 roubles which won't pull at all, particularly when going alone, and working double she pulls only badly. Alfons has·now enough to listen to. But he is worth much, for he is clever! [Ironical]. [Farm-stock, farm-work, crops, money loaned.] And now I beg you, my children, economize in order to bring some token [money from America], because my strength decreases. My eyes, hands and feet begin to refuse obedience. . . . .

[ANNA MARKIEWICZ]

166
November 27 [1913]

DEAR SONS: We received the letter and the money from you. Thanks to God that you are in good health, because in our house everybody is in good health and in Pecia's house also. Franuś is still working on the ship. As to money, you [singular] have in the bank 600 roubles and with [loaned to] Pecia 50 roubles, but you told us to give her 10 roubles, so only 40 are left with her. I told her that you wrote me to lend her the whole 100 roubles, but on her note, so she was very much offended and refused. But you are right, quite right, because a note is necessary. Don't think that I am not good to her, but she demands a little too much, for there are others also to take, and only one to give, and it is right to remember them all alike. The news: Władzia, Walenty's daughter, got married. We were at the wedding. She married Guziński of Płock. The Świeckis' windmill is burned. Maks [Przanowski] has not yet paid us the money back. We have 3 stacks of seradella. We have 3 cows big with calves, one bull, one young bull, one chestnut horse, one pig worth about 50 roubles, 12 turkeys, etc. The children have gathered [leaves for] litter. Now they will bring wood. . . . . Wincenty Przanowski died. We have a little grinding, but not much. . . . . As to Polcia, she won't be surely glad [married] before carnival. We wait for Elżbieta [to be married], but probably it will be necessary to give [permission?] to Polcia, because it is difficult for all of them to sit at home.[1] . . . .

Your loving parents and family,

JÓZEF and ANNA MARKIEWICZ

167 December 15 [1913]

DEAR SONS: . . . . We received your letter and 30 roubles, for which I thank you heartily, for we had just been in Radziwi and gave the sheep-skins to line the coat when the postman gave us the money. . . . . I am glad, and Alfons also, for father always says: "Don't make big expenses" . . . . and now we can buy what we need without touching father's money. . . . . You ask me how much money there is in all. In the bank in Gąbin there are 600 roubles of Wacuś [Wacław] and 600 of ours . . . . and Fijołkowski has [borrowed] 200 [ours] and 400 of yours [Stasio] and 50 of Pecia. There is so much in all. . . . . We should have more money but for that trading of Alfons. He lost 100 roubles on the mare, and then we had to give 152 for the horse. Well, but people say that if the horses are so dear in the summer, he will be worth 200. Well, perhaps our Lord God will comfort us. But stealing is developed beyond measure. From Andrzej's brother-in-law they stole horses and a wagon. They did a damage of 500 roubles. . . . . Well, may God avert them. You ask about the Americans. They earned well enough, but . . . . most of them came back. Still, if they had had no work they would not have brought such nice money. . . . . But, dear children, mind your health like the eye in your head. As to Elżbietka, Topolski writes letters. Well, at carnival we shall do [something about it], either to the left or to the right. And with Polcia we will soon make an end [get her married].

[ANNA MARKIEWICZ]

[1] According to a custom almost universal among the Polish peasants, the older daughter should always marry before the younger one. The parents are therefore very unwilling to give the younger daughter away before the older is married, and if such a case happens, they often refuse to give her any dowry before the older has received her part. And the younger daughter considers it a family duty to wait until her older sister is married. In this case the situation is difficult because Elżbieta is too particular in her choice. Therefore Polcia is tired of waiting and angry, and the parents are half-decided to give her away before Elżbieta.

168   January 23 [1914]

DEAR SONS: [Question of getting a passport for Stasio, to cross
the boundary returning.] Rosa's son sent [from America] 650
roubles, and Seweryniak's son 600, etc., but is it true? I did not
count it. And you, Stasio, care for yourself. Dear children, we
have also wept on Christmas and we thought about you and we
talked [wondered] what you are doing there. But Alfons said,
"They are better there than I am here, because these 3 girls [sisters]
beat me and don't even let me cry." Such is the only son whom I
have now. At least when I had you, Stasio, it was possible, but now—
God forbid![1] Andrzej got a basket [the mitten], and there is somebody else in his place. . . . . Elżbietka has a young man from Płock,
a tailor, and his parents have a farm near Bodzanów. He claims he
has 1,000 roubles. He wished [to marry] at once at carnival, but we
postponed it until after Easter, in order not to burn ourselves [be
too hasty]. She has other boys still, and Polcia also. . . . .

[ANNA MARKIEWICZ]

169   April 14 [1914]

[Generalities about health and letter-writing.] Here in our papers
is [written], that in America there has been a very great storm and
terrible rains. We are very anxious what is the news with you.
Write us at once about your being saved, because here everyone
speaks differently. . . . . Please answer, because we don't believe
these gypsy [cheating] papers. We shall probably get Polcia married
to that Andrzej. What do you say to it? [Weather; crops; general
news about friends.]

Your truly loving

[MARKIEWICZS]

---

[1] Alfons evidently loves farming, and particularly horses, and helps at home
and is without any personal claims. There is almost no mention of him in the
letters written before Stanisław went to America. After this, as the only son at
home, he begins to play some part. He is the least loved, as is evident from the
manner in which the mother speaks of him. He is not at all stupid, as is shown by
his letter, but probably is rather unpractical and diffident outside of farming
matters. This may even be the result of the manner in which he is treated at home.
In almost every numerous family there is a child worst treated, least loved, and
most exploited. (Władek and Broniś, in the autobiography forming Part IV
(volume II), are cases of this kind.) Perhaps the source of it is some prepossession on the part of the parents against the child, assumed either because he is
not standard in his traits, or because he was not desired in an already too numerous
family.

170 May 1 [1914]

DEAR SONS: . . . . We are grieved that you have no work, but we are glad that you are in good health, because money is an acquired thing, while health is an important thing. You wrote, Stasio, that you would come; we expected you from day to day, but you did not come. So we don't know whether you have occupation or not. We are very curious, for a man without work has still worse thoughts [sic]. Well, but nothing can be done. There is something for you to come back to, [our] poverty is not yet so great. You can have bread and more than bread, so don't grieve. [Description of the farm-stock and the work.]

[MARKIEWICZS]

171 June 12, [1914]

DEAR SON: We received your 2 letters after the arrival of Stasio. When he arrived, we thought that you would come also, but Stasio himself regrets [leaving] those wages. He says that it is a golden land as long as there is work, but when there is none, then it is worth nothing. Earn, dear son, some hundreds [and come back] to your fatherland. [Conditions bad; dryness; windmill ruined.] You ask, dear son, what your father said about the goods [probably household-goods or clothing]. Well, he rejoiced. He said that Stasio robbed you too much. Still he is satisfied. You ask about this scoundrel [probably Maks Przanowski, who owed them 100 roubles]. He does not even show himself; we must take a complaint [to court]. As to your grandmother, they all arrange this. Grandmother does not think; they write [in her name?]. Well, grandmother wants now to move to us. But your father is honey and sugar, and your grandmother gall and pepper. Whoever has tried it knows the taste. Oh, I have enjoyed during my whole life this honey with this sugar; I have it often under every nail! But what can be done? It is the will of God.

Elżbietka is sewing beyond Bodzanów, for she is bored at home. What she wants, a man that she could love, cannot be found, while she does not want those whom she has a chance to marry. Surely, Polcia will overtake her [marry first]. Stasiek is weighing [his deci-sion] as upon a scale. If he had a ready fortune, he would risk it. But what if he has no health? . . . .

The heat is terrible. . . . . Everything is burned upon the fields and dwindles away while we look. . . . . We just decided today that [Polcia's] wedding will be at the end of August, but I don't know how it will be with your father, because he always says so, "If anything is not there, you can do without it." We cannot do without it, for it must be [a good marriage-feast and bride's outfit], and this year is so heavy for me, and so dry. The last was with water, this one is with heat. . . . . And I must buy many things, since I promised the wedding for the end of August. So if you can, send me a few dollars. But if you have none to spare, don't send them, for we are at home, and you are outside. . . . .

YOUR LOVING MOTHER

172   February 10 [1907]

DEAR BROTHER: Those 50 roubles which you sent have been received, but not yet the 100. Dear brother, I have been everywhere [visited all the girls in the neighborhood], but I don't succeed in finding anyone suitable. Probably I shall come to you in the spring. . . . . Now I want to marry Andzia, Młodziejewski's daughter; you know her. Just today I sent an interceder [match-maker] to him, and in a few days I will go myself. She pleased me very much, and our mother also, only our whole family from Dobrzyków did not like her at all. But you know that Młodziejewski will give 6 morgs to Zych and 12 to Andzia. Only it is said that he does not want her to get married before he builds [new farm-buildings]. So I will now speak with him; if he is willing to get her married in autumn, then I will wait, but if perhaps only in 2 years, then I will go for this time to you. If he willed her these 12 morgs, I would marry her and I would wait even till autumn or even till carnival. You know her very well, so write me what you think about her and how do you like all this. . . . . I was in the last week of the carnival at a wedding in the house of the Białeckis in Dobrzyków, but the wedding was not very good. She [B's daughter] married Józef Kłosiński. I got acquainted with Andzia at this wedding, for I did not know her before. . . . . As to the grinding, I have always grain to grind, sometimes 40 bushels lie in reserve. . . . .

Y[our] b[rother],

STA[NISŁAW] MARKIEWICZ

173   February 24, 1907

DEAR BROTHER: . . . . An awful multitude of people are going from here to America. Uliczny from Wincentowo—you know him—wants to send his boy, but he asks you how it is there. The boy intended to go right now, but his father stopped him and won't allow him to go until the letter comes from you. [Asks about the new conditions of landing in United States.]

Dear brother, I will surely marry, but not until the autumn, that Andzia, as I wrote you in my last letter. . . . .

We gave Pecia her money back, but we have not yet paid the interest. . . . .

The farmers from Zazdzierz say that you were to send 15 roubles for a feast [for them]; but don't do it. . . . .

STANISŁAW MARKIEWICZ

174   [June 4, 1907]

[Following his mother's letter of the same date.]

And I have already left [the girl from] Dobrzyków, I go now to Gostynno, to the house of Mr. and Mrs. Bukowski, to Mania. You know her since you were called to the mobilization with Goszewski. They speak about you, and even now you have a greeting from them. They are all very favorable to me, but I don't know how it will turn out. Our wedding is not to be celebrated until autumn. As you know her, write me anything about her. I was pleased very much with this Maryanna [Mania]. If they only keep their word, then it will be at last the end with my marrying. Write such a letter as I could read to them, and only a [separate] bit about Mania herself. Well, you know yourself how to do. Our crops are average.

This Mania has nationalist ideas like myself, and through this she pleased me much. And how beautifully she plays the accordeon! Every second Sunday she plays to me, and so we spend our time gaily in Gostynno. . . . .   Your brother,

STA[NISŁAW] MARKIEWICZ

175   [September 13, 1910]

DEAR BROTHER: When you notice that the conditions [in America] improve, inform me at once; then I shall go to America. Here nothing succeeds. I have begun now going to Radziwie to a girl, but

I don't know anything, for here, as you know, none of us succeeds in marrying at all, and what can be done? See here, Ignac came from the army in the spring and he marries Andzia, Młodziejewski's daughter, while I don't succeed. I already intended to write you to send me a ship-ticket, but wait still a little. When I learn that there will be no result in Radziwie, then I will write you at once to send me a ship-ticket, and I will work it back.

Sta[nisław] Mar[kiewicz]

176

October 23, 1910

Dear Brother: .... I don't know what to do, because if I were as healthy as formerly I would have asked you for a ship-ticket long ago and I should be there already, but I am afraid because of this rheumatism. Just now I have lain in bed for 3 weeks. Now I am a little better. I went to the doctor. It will be necessary to go more than once, but our father does not want to give me money. He nags me still worse than he did you, but not the other children, only me. He simply drives me away. Since I came from the army and my clothes and overcoat were bought, I have been walking in them up to the present. Now winter is coming and I have no clothes for winter warm enough, on account of my rheumatism. Father said beforehand that he wouldn't buy any, and he drives me away to the factory to earn for a sheep-skin coat while I am still sick. And so often I must go to town for goods. You know that nominally I own the small shop in Wincentowo, though it goes lamely, because they take everything home without counting, so whatever we earn, everything will get into the household. Last year we put 60 roubles into the business, now we have 120 in spite of such a big expense. But I can take nothing from this. When I bought a cap once father told everywhere that I would spend the whole shop-stock for my needs. Every week I sell about 40 roubles of goods. Mostly Elżbietka keeps the shop now. As soon as I recover, I will probably throw everything up. I will draw the money [from the shop], pay my father the debt back and go to America, because I am tired of the life with father.[1] If you only send me a ship-ticket I will most gladly work

---

[1] The letter shows a total lack of understanding between the young and the old generation. The father is not an egotist; he simply does not acknowledge the personal interests of his son as separated from the interests of the family. And the son has totally lost the old feeling of familial solidarity. Only, the father goes too

back whatever I shall owe you. . . . . Why, there is not such misery at home. There are about 600 roubles of cash, we bought a horse for 100 roubles, a cart for 40, we gave 100 roubles to Franuś. Now, indeed, we must give him more, because he has bought 6 morgs in Tokary . . . . at 275 roubles a morg, and without buildings. She lives as she did, and he sails as captain upon the ship of Mrs. Jaworska. He earns 40 roubles a month in summer, and we don't know yet how much in winter. Elżbietka has a suitor. You knew Stasiek. . . . . Well, it is the brother of his wife who is courting Elżbietka. He is a butcher from Lubień; they have a cured-meat shop. They were here on Sunday. Now he intends to come to us next week to buy our hogs. We have 4 worth 120 roubles. . . . . I will go to Lubień and learn what reputation he enjoys. He has two sisters. They want me to take one of them. They are two brothers; one of them is in America. Their father and mother are dead. Their name is Topolski. We know one another already, for his sisters were at our house. The older is a beautiful woman, only there is nothing [no money]. When I recover, I will try, but today I shall write a letter to Miss Plebanek in Jarosław, asking for her hand. If I don't succeed there, I will surely try in Lubień, but if even here nothing [results], then I will write you, "Send me a ticket or money." . . . .

Stanisław Markiewicz

177   December 31, 1912

Dear Brother: You must help me in this, because I must now leave the home, for you know there better than we do what is going on here in our country. Your answer will perhaps find me at home and perhaps not. Father won't give me [money] for the journey, so I must borrow from somebody. This is a shame indeed. Our father, though there are 600 roubles cash at home and 400 lent to people, says that he won't give me anything for the journey. So I beg you, write father to give me from your money, then I will pay you

---

far in his group-attitude, because this attitude is connected in his character with a stronger tendency to make his family rise than that found in an ordinary peasant. And his tyranny is particulary unbearable because he conceives the progress of the family's social standing in the strictly traditional peasant way and does not understand that in the new social and economic conditions in which his children have to live they need more independence than they would have needed forty years ago, in a closed and isolated farmers' community.

back as soon as I get to you.	If you don't, I shall be obliged to borrow money from some stranger, but I must go. . . . . If things don't get more pressing I will wait for your letter, and if not, then I will borrow from anybody and go.	So write to father either to give money to me, or to pay my debt. . . . . As to my marriage, I have now an opportunity, but because of all this I don't know myself what to do and probably I won't marry.[1] . . . .

STA[NISŁAW] MARKIEWICZ

178	May 4, 1908

DEAR WACIO: I inform you that you wounded my heart so much with the word which you wrote in that letter, that I did not know how to comfort myself [probably about his intention to stay in America]. I had never thought that you would write us such a sad word.	So comfort us at least in your second letter.	You ask us how we spent the carnival.	Merrily enough, only we grieved for you. . . . . And now write us how the work is going on, and when will you come back. . . . .

Your loving sister,

E[LŻBIETA] M.

179	[November 4, 1909]

DEAR WACEK: We received your photograph and we are very glad.	We thank you for it and we rejoice that you are in good health and look nice enough.	And now you ask about the rose.	It grows nicely; it blossomed twice during the summer.	None of the fruit trees which you planted bore any fruit.	You asked for a leaf of the rose; I send you it.	The rose put out a wild branch.	I don't know whether I shall cut it or leave it until you come; write me.	As to the plum trees, remind me once more. . . . . I will have it done.	The

---

[1] The boy's search for a wife lasts much beyond the usual time.	It is not because he cannot find a suitable girl, but the girls' parents refuse him.	The reason is perhaps less his personality than economic combinations.	Stanisław, acting here in harmony with his father (or else he would complain about the latter) evidently asks too much dowry, while he cannot himself have a corresponding fortune. Even if his father gave him the farm, it would be impossible for him to pay the brothers' and sisters' parts without mortgaging the farm, unless he got an exceptionally large dowry.	Therefore he would prefer to settle upon his future wife's farm. But in this case his personality begins to play a rôle.	If a farmer agrees to give his farm to his son-in-law, he wants the latter to be strong, healthy, laborious, while Stanisław is the contrary of all these.

nut tree does not grow very well, while the cherry trees grow nicely.[1]
I thank you heartily for the 10 roubles. . . . . As to Stasiek, write
him as [persuasively as] you can, not to leave off this party [girl] in
Gostynno, because they are favorable to him, and he does not wish it
much, but would like rather to go to you.   So write him as you can
and dissuade him from going.   Only let him marry; I think it is time
to finish it.   I have time today and therefore I can write you, while
when our mother wrote the last letter, I was with Pecia, and I was
sad that I could not write a few words.   As to Teosia, no bad news is
to be heard here.   She is sitting modestly after her travels.   Grandmother is in good health.   Write us whether the president has been
elected.   I am very sad in thinking that we cannot see one another
for so long a time, but if you are longing in foreign countries, come
soon to our country. . . . .

Your loving sister,

E[LŻBIETA] MARKIEWICZ

180   [Date undetermined]

DEAR WACIO: I received your letter for which I thank you
heartily, I am healthy enough and I wish you the same.   I am still
a maiden and I feel very happy that I did not marry him [probably
Topolski], for even his companions and my acquaintances approve me
for not having married him.   I thank you also heartily for these few
words of good advice.   I would beg you very much to write me who
told you all this about him.   Indeed I can say that he has a mean
character; just on that account I did not marry him.   In short, he
was not for me and I did not marry him.   And now I don't know; if
I meet somebody according to my mind, I will get married, but if not,
I can remain a maiden for some time still.   I work as before, I have
two girls [apprentices] and Zosia.   We sew, we embroider, and so the
time passes away. . . . .

ELŻBIETA MARKIEWICZ

181   March 26, 1913

DEAR WACIO: I beg you very much, if you think that it might
be better for me, please send me a ship-ticket.   Instead of both
paying for your board, you would have me as housekeeper if I went
there, and I could earn for myself during the free hours.   So, please

---

[1] All planted by the brother; thence their interest for him.

write me what you think about me, because in May some of my acquaintances are to go from here to America, so I could go along with them. . . . .

ELŻBIETA M.

182 March 30, 1913

DEAR BROTHERS: I received your letters. . . . . I wrote you a letter and now I am writing this postcard. . . . . I beg you once more, send me a ship-ticket. We are selling the shop to Kiszkowski, so I have nothing more to do at home, to tell the truth. Why, I have spent here 25 years! I hope it is enough. If you don't send me the ticket, I will go for money. . . . .

ELŻBIETA MARKIEWICZ

183 [Exact date undetermined]

DEAR WACIO: You write us to lend money to Pecia. I tell you truly, as to my brother, that even if we gave her the whole farm and household, it would be not enough for her; even if we worked for her from dawn to night, it would not be enough, because it is a gulf for everything. We told her that you ordered us to lend her money, but that she had to give a note. She is so unreasonable that she got badly offended and said that she prefers to borrow from strangers. It is true that he [Franuś, her husband] is not sure at all [of living?] and in the case of his death you know what she would say. She has become now quite changed. Well, you have Staś there. Ask him. Although it is very bad when one [member of the family] writes against the other, I must do it. I don't write lies; you are my brother as much as she is my sister, but she is a woman without character. . . . .

Dear Stasio, I thank you also for having sent money for the overcoat of Alfons. It is true that money is necessary for more than one thing, while mother is so parsimonious. . . . . But she is so for the sake of us all. . . . .

Your loving sister,

ELŻBIETA

[Wishes and greetings.] And Franuś has got his salary raised by Mrs. J[aworska], but all this is not enough. When you throw anything upon this flowing water [of Pecia's expenses], it floats away at once.

[YOUR MOTHER]

184 January 14, 1914

DEAR BROTHER: [Letters and money received; letters sent; farm-work.] We have now grinding enough, because the windmill of Świecka burned down not long ago. We could have more, but you know how our father grinds, a grain in two parts, and now everybody has a smooth palate. . . . . We work as much as we can, and for this we have every day fresh "choleras" and "thunders" [swearing from the father], as you know. But what can be done? We must bear it, because it is impossible to shorten one's own life or to go a contrary way [*sic?*]. You ask how much money there is in all. [Enumerates the sums in bank, etc.] Maksym. Przanowski has not yet given the money back; he says that it was to be for [building] the church. Probably we shall be obliged to make a complaint [to the court]. Wincenty Przanowski hanged himself. Such is the whole nice species [Przanowski]. Władysława Markiewicz got married. Polcia was to marry that *"cham"* [Ham, the biblical person= ruffian], but it goes on lamely. As to me, I have nothing to write you. The whole road of my life is sown with thorns. . . . . The man [probably, type of man] whom I could marry and even, if necessary, eat my bread in the sweat of my brow, is not in a hurry to marry me, while the kind not worth looking at obtrudes himself on me. And my character is such that instead of marrying and suffering woe I prefer to remain a maiden further. During my whole life I have been the prey of bad fortune, and so my life is being spent.[1]

ELŻBIETA MARKIEWICZ

185 June 28, 1912

DEAR BROTHER: . . . . Elżbietka is to marry in the autumn, and I expect to do the same at carnival, for though I have still time, I am tired of working, for I have worked honestly. And now I beg you, dear Wacio, don't be angry, and send me money for a watch. . . . .

APOLONIA [POLCIA] MARKIEWICZ

[1] The difference between Elżbieta and Polcia (see the letters immediately following) is largely innate, but it must have been greatly increased by *instruction* and by the fact that Elżbieta had probably had better company by working outside of her home. The problem is important in a general way. To what extent is instruction alone able to produce class-distinction? And it may be noticed that in Poland it is more effective in this respect than elsewhere, incomparably more than in the United States. Independently of everything else, wherever instruction is appreciated at all, it creates a class-distinction as profound as birth, and more profound than money.

186   [No date]

DEAR WACIO: I thank you heartily for the postcard, for not having forgotten about me. You ask me whether I have a betrothed or not; yes, indeed, I have one and I had another. The one I wanted, they did not allow me, and the one I don't want, they order me to marry. But I won't marry anybody except a farmer from a village,[1] and now in fact I have 2 of them from Wincentowo. I don't know whether they will allow me to marry one of them, but if they don't allow me now to marry the one I intend to, I won't get married at all, but I intend to go to America in a year. . . . .

APOLONIA MARKIEWICZ

187   April 14 [1914]

DEAR BROTHERS: For the first time I write also a few words to you. . . . . You write, Stasiek, about Elżbietka. So I beg you, forget about it. . . . . I joined the agricultural circle. Now they are arranging a trip to the province Kalisz, to visit the farms in the village Zachowo. This village is the first in all the kingdom of Poland, because not only the peasants there have good order in the fields and at home, but they have in the village even telephones, and electric light in houses and stables. So I want also to go and see it. Ten years ago it was a village of first-rate thieves. The journey will cost 10 roubles; the departure at the end of May. . . . .

[ALFONS MARKIEWICZ]

188   [December 2, 1912]

I think I never yet wrote to you, my Staś. Now before the solemnity of Christmas I will also write to you, for God alone knows whether we shall see each other any more. Do you remember what we spoke once between us when going to Gombin about the mill of Dobrzyków? O my God! I always keep this mill in mind, for it is like family property.[2] I thought that Maks would think about it, but

[1] This single phrase shows how perfectly and consciously Polcia is still a peasant girl and does not want to be anything else. Her mother wrote that it was she who kept the house. Evidently, she loves housework, farm-work, and country life and would not sacrifice these to any career which would bring her outside of the village. The type is frequent.

[2] *Ojcowizna*, land-property handed down from father to son; particularly if kept for some generations in the same family. Considered more valuable from

I cannot rely upon him.   If you think about it, put money aside and send it here.   We will put it in the savings-bank, and perhaps God will help us to buy it.   There, near the church, it is a place the like of which cannot be found in the whole province.   The new priest had the tavern abolished.   Lis of Górki bought it from Kowalska for a joint-stock shop.   They had set up the shop in the stone building of Plebanek, but now they will transfer it here, where the tavern was.[1] . . . .

[Your father],

J[AN] M[ARKIEWICZ]

DEAR BROTHER: I inform you that we are threshing.   When we finish it I shall go to school, but there is no money.   Now I inform you that Maciek J. has beaten Ziółek [the grandmother's husband]. It is not bad, but he must pay 30 roubles and sit 2 weeks in prison. . . . .

IGNACY MARKIEWICZ

189 April 20, 1912

DEAR BROTHERS MAKS AND STAŚ: [Letters written and received.] Then I describe to you the state of grandmother's health.   After Christmas first the right arm and leg began to swell . . . . then the left arm and leg . . . . but grandmother still walks.   She has grown so quarrelsome that it is awful.   And Ziółkowski [her husband] abuses her from time to time: "Why does she groan?"   Well, if he does not come to reason, and if his mouth gets looser we will shut it up.[2]   (At present we live in friendship with him.)   I don't know, my dear brothers, but this swelling of grandmother is probably nothing else than a sign of death.   Ostrowski the carpenter swelled also before his death, and then he died after a little time.   And Cichocki, the

---

the moral point of view than property individually earned or acquired as dowry. Here the appreciation is particularly strong because some of the traditions of the patriarchal noble family are preserved.

[1] This letter characterizes the old man perfectly and is the only one he has ever written to his son.

[2] The grandmother married Ziółkowski at an age when she was no longer supposed to marry.   He cannot be assimilated, and she is also estranged but still a member of the family.   Properly she would retire and leave the management of her property to the family, but her marriage hinders this because Ziółkowski has no property himself, and cannot claim a support from his wife's children.

father of Tomasz, also swelled before his death.   Do you know that Switkoszanka died 8 weeks after her marriage? . . . . Dear Maks . . . . you asked me to get the address of Jadzia Łączanka.   Well, evidently I could not get it otherwise than by asking her good man of a father personally and he, of course, granted my request.   Please, Maks, tell me about your school, whether you are learning in it already or when will you begin to learn.   Nejman Felka's [husband] was in our house on Sunday after Easter.   He praises the writing of your letters highly.   He says that it is evident that you are improving yourself.   It is something very different from what it was.   Send us the form of a note, and the conditions on which you wish to send us those 1,000 roubles. . . . .

Your brother,

WIKTOR MARKIEWICZ

Maks, mother begs you, guard Staś against card-playing and revelry. . . . .

190   August 2, 1912

DEAR BROTHER MAKS: . . . . Pardon me, please, for not sending you your school-certificate for so long, for I see from your last postcard that you need it badly.   I guess that you want it to show it in the school there, do you not?   But I don't know, dear brother, how you will present it, because it is awfully dirty; it is disagreeable to take it into the hand.   Don't think that is the way I took care of it.   It was already in that state when I got it from that Russian hog.[1]   [Relates in 3 pages how he invited a Russian post-official to go hunting, how he treated him and got him drunk, and how he hoped to get permission to keep a gun through this official's influence, because these permissions were very difficult to get.]

I am in a critical position this year.   The orchard is bad, and so I cannot earn money.   The reserve which I had from last year was exhausted on different purchases, such as clothes, shoes, etc.   O my God! how unhappy I am that our father is so indifferent to us in matters of purchases, and particularly when he smells a rouble in your pocket then he won't buy anything, and in that way he draws from you the last grosz. . . . .   Dear brothers Maks and Staś, I don't

---

[1] Either the teacher or some official, to whom Maks may have applied formerly for a position, leaving the school-certificate with him.

doubt that you love me sincerely, as my brothers, and that after receiving this letter you will send me [money] for a nice gun. Well, excuse me and don't be angry. It is only a joke. . . . .

WIKTOR MARKIEWICZ

191   [August 2, 1912]

DEAR STAŚ: I received the papers for which I thank you heartily. Further, to your continual questions about horses I answer that we have sold all the horses except my chestnut mare, and instead father bought one thoroughbred mare, of black color. Father is very well satisfied with this newly bought mare, and he intends to sell my chestnut mare also, because they do not fit together; the chestnut is much smaller and slower. Father received 200 roubles for 3 horses and paid 220 for one. The newly bought mare is $2\frac{1}{2}$ years old. Then I mention, dear Staś, that you sent 100 roubles to the address of our father and you believe probably that the matter is totally settled. Far from this, father has not yet given the money back to grandmother and does not even think of giving it. When I asked him, why he did not give the money to grandmother, he answered: "Your grandmother does not need it; has she not enough already?"[1] Well, what do you say to that? Even grandmother said once to me that it is strange you do not send the money back for so long a time. Probably grandmother guesses that it has been sent back but there is nobody to give it to her. And as to the money which Maks intends to send, it is very well that our father has to send the notes first. Excuse me, dear brother, for not writing carefully; my hand is still awfully tired from mowing barley with a scythe. I will finish it and lie down to sleep, because tomorrow the same work awaits me. . . . .

WIKTOR

[1] Staś has probably borrowed money from his grandmother for his journey to America, the father refusing to lend. The father's unwillingness to give the grandmother her money and his open acknowledgment that he wants to keep it makes his familial attitude still more evident. The same act would be dishonest if performed by any of his sons; it would be simply dishonest of Staś not to send this money back, because he would keep it for his *personal* use. But the father does not consider it dishonest; he does not want it personally for himself, but for the family-fortune. And the grandmother is still so much a member of the family that her interests could be subordinated to those of the family as a whole, while on the other hand she is, through her second marriage, half outside of the family and thus there is a greater temptation to divert a part of her money to familial purposes.

192 December 2, 1912

DEAR BROTHER STAŚ: [Thanks for money sent him.] Further, I inform you that grandmother['s affair] is already settled. She thanks you also most heartily and wishes you every good. [A page about the permission to keep a gun, which has not yet come.] Then, I inform you that mother complains about pains in her right arm, so that she cannot sleep. But don't grieve, perhaps God will grant her to recover slowly. . . . . Michał serves [in the army], as before. In his last letter he writes that he is trying to become an orderly [assigned to the personal service of an officer]. O stupid wretch! He wants to be appointed to keep a Moscovite's backsides clean! I did not answer anything to this.[1] Further, he writes that if he is not appointed an orderly, he will try to get into a hospital [as servant]. Well, you see, he does not try at all to return home [by being pronounced unfit]. My advice is lost. Cieślak's son came back 3 months ago. He says that they tormented him and tried to frighten him, but he did not change his behavior until they let him go. [Probably he pretended or exaggerated some illness.] You see, that is a man. [Marriages; weather, crops, farm-work; wishes for Christmas.]

WIKTOR MARKIEWICZ

I thank you for the poetry "At the Crossway" [probably copied from some book or paper], and I beg you for more like this one.

193 February 15, 1913

DEAR BROTHERS MAKS AND STAŚ: . . . . Three times I began to write letters to you, but I did not send you any of these letters, because I did not want to cause you pain by these letters, informing you about mother's illness, and at the same time about the slight sickness of our *dear little sister Weronika*, to which at the beginning we paid less attention. We waited for mother's health to improve, and God the Merciful granted to our mother better health, so I started to write you a letter. But alas! from the slight weakness of Ś.✝ P. ["*Świętej Pamięci*," "of sainted memory"] our *dear little sister*

---

[1] The conception that personal service is humiliating is never found among the Russian peasants (the position of orderly is much desired in the Russian army) and rarely found among the Polish manor-servants. Among the peasant farmers it is frequent and among the peasant nobility almost universal. The situation is evidently aggravated in this case because the man whom Michał would serve is a Russian.

Weronika, some . . . . stronger illness developed. We called Doctor Grzybowski. He said that inflammation of the lungs had developed, and that there was, alas, no hope of recovery. Nevertheless he did his best to give her health back to our dear sister Weronika, but all this was useless, for the deadly illness grew. On January 31, in the morning we asked the priest from Dobrzyków [to come] with our Lord Jesus. He prepared Ś.✝ P. Weronika, who was conscious, for death. The next day, on February 1, she lost her consciousness. O my dear God, how fortunate it was that the priest, with our Lord Jesus, came in time! From February 1, she raved in fever up to February 3. Then she recovered full consciousness, she ceased to groan, she wanted to rise from her bed, saying so: "Mother, I will get up, dress myself and walk a little, for I am so tired [of lying]." Oh my God, who can imagine our joy in seeing such an improvement in Weronika's health! But our joy did not last longer than until about 8 o'clock in the evening. Then she began to lose consciousness again. She called despairingly "Maks!" "Staś!" "Indiana Harbor" [where both brothers were], then again "Michałek!" and so she called every one of her relatives and acquaintances more than once. So, my dear brothers, we did not expect that before her death Weronika would want to see all of us.[1] About eleven in the evening she ceased to call us, only from time to time she asked for the medicine to drink which the doctor had prescribed. About 1 o'clock after midnight, on February 4, 1913, she ended her life as calmly as if someone extinguished a light, in the presence of us all. The body of Ś.✝ P. our sister *Weronika* was transferred to the church on February 5, at 10 o'clock in the morning, and buried on the same day, after the holy mass. I mention also, dear brothers, that at the funeral there was an extraordinary gathering of people. Then I ask you, did you receive the mourning letters, informing about Weronika's death? And I beg you very much, tell me, did you have any signs or forebodings? For we heard a terrible roar, but it was as long ago as June. I wrote you about it at that time. . . . .[2]

WIKTOR MARKIEWICZ

[1] The familial feeling is always manifested by the peasant at the moment of death. Death is no more a purely individual matter than marriage or birth. In this case we do not know the age of the child, and have a suspicion that the brother reported what should have happened and what would be agreeable to the feelings of the absent relatives.

[2] The expectation of signs foretelling death is a remnant of the old naturalistic religion. Cf. Introduction: "Religious and Magical Attitudes."

Dear Staś, I thank you for those few roubles which I received after Christmas, and I beg you, care for yourself, don't play cards, don't waste the money which you earn by work.   I beg you heartily in God's name.   I am in a terrible sorrow after our beloved Weronika. .   . .

YOUR MOTHER

194   April 8, 1913

DEAR BROTHER STAŚ: [Rumors of war; family has purchased American wheat drill; farming conditions.] You ask me, dear Staś, about this permission to keep a gun.   First I mention to you, may cholera strangle the Moscovites with their laws and their whole shop. As you know, this cholera of a "stupajka" [nickname for a Russian functionary, from the Russian words, "*stupaï-ka,*" "go at once," symbolizing the passive obedience of a subordinate] wrote bad information about me, that in 1905–6 I was interested in political questions.   But they have no proofs at all.   Opas is angry with us for not being a mayor, and he gave such an opinion of me to the constable, and the latter wrote it down.   But I have proofs that it is not true. .   . . Now the whole affair is sent to the minister of the interior . . . . and then the senate will judge it. . . . . If not, we shall write a complaint to the emperor, and I will beg Maks to be so kind as to send it in my name from America.[1]

Grandmother groans, but walks. . . . . With Ziółek we live in good understanding.   Ziółek's sister came to grandmother, to stay with her.   Grandmother is angry, for up to the present she has been groaning alone, and now they will both groan.   She is very brittle already, that Ziółek's sister.

I went to Gostynin on a business matter, and I got acquainted with the girls of Gostynin.   They are nice and rich.   If it doesn't end well with the Kowalczyks I will try to get the favor of one of them.

[WIKTOR]

In order to get *any* governmental permission (to keep a gun as well as to get a passport, to open a business, to teach, to pass an examination, to go to any superior school, etc.) it is always indispensable in Russia to be politically "well-thinking and reliable," and to present a corresponding certificate based upon the opinion of the police and *gendarmerie.*   The certificate may be refused even without stated reasons, on mere suspicion that the individual has ideas which are unfavorable to the "existing order of things," although he may never have acted against the government or even talked against it.

195 April 25 [1913]

Staś! We are very glad that you have such a lively interest in everything. [News about friends, farm-stock, crops, weather.] Frybra built a windmill, but he has nothing to grind. In our mill there is more to grind. Frybra is almost raging; he loafs around and invites the farmers.[1] Opas became a commune-assessor. . . . . Miąckowski is a good mayor up to the present. . . . . The parish of Dobrzyków got another priest, a young and active one. He dislikes liquor immensely, or rather drunkards; he hates them. So Mrs. Kowalska is glad that she has sold the tavern, and the new purchaser is tearing the hair from his head. The peasants keep far away from the tavern, and whoever draws nearer looks toward the church, and most often turns back, because evidently in his ears rings the powerful voice of the priest saying from the chancel: "If I see you—God forbid! —in the tavern, a great displeasure will befall you." And when a peasant passes by the tavern, he only turns and looks at it.

Michał is in Smolensk. I don't know whether he will get off [from the army], because the physician is evidently a scoundrel, and Michał does not know very well how to look out for himself. Well, but it pains him always just the same, and they cannot cure him. Perhaps they will let him go. May God help him! Michał regrets that he did not fly to America, but it is silly. [Because then he could never come back.] (Write your letters to Michał carefully, so as not to betray him, God forbid!) I think so, that if Michał perseveres they will let him go sooner or later. [Sends photograph; describes farmwork.] With Miss Kowalik, or rather with the Kowaliks, nothing is sure as yet, but now within a short time some result will follow. I will inform you at once. Miss Swat is now trying to be very pleasing. After Kowalik, I put Miss Swat in the first line. . . . .

WIKTOR MARKIEWICZ

196 May 24, 1913

DEAR BROTHER STAŚ: . . . . In your last letter you expressed the wish to send to my address 700 roubles which you earned and put aside. I am very glad that you economized such a nice bit of money, and as these American banks are not so secure as the communal savings-bank here, you had really better send it home, and I will give

[1] Inviting customers is considered worthy only of a Jew.

it to the communal bank. . . . .[1] I must add, that here in our country rumors are heard that American money is to be equaled with the Russian money [$1 is to be worth 1 rouble]. Well, if this happened more than one would lose the half of the money he has saved.[2] In view of all this I advise you, dear Staś, sincerely and truly, send your money home. I assure you on my conscience that I won't lose it and won't neglect it, i.e., I will put it into the bank. In case I needed it, I would give you a written evidence, for if I am successful with the Kowalczyks in Czyżew, this money will be a great help to me. It would be necessary to show at least 2,000 there, so if you sent your money, I would be that much bolder, because no stranger would know that it is borrowed money. I say at least 2,000. It would be well to show even more, for although they don't need money themselves, there are [competitors] who have 5,000 cash of their own.[3] I don't know, dear Staś, whether my efforts will bring me happiness or an irretrievable loss. Oh my great God! I implore you to help me. [News about orchards, crops, farm-work; marriages of friends.]

[WIKTOR]

197   [No date]

MY DEAR STAŚ: You ask me for my opinion about marriage, and you ask about Swatówna [daughter of Swat]. My brother, my Staś, I don't know what lot awaits me. About this Swatówna, as you

[1] The distrust in American banks is justified, as many bankers, most of them Jewish, operating among the Polish immigrants have proved dishonest, while the communal savings-bank is under the immediate control of the commune.

[2] Rumors of this kind come from various sources. Sometimes they may come from a misunderstood newspaper article; sometimes from the story of a returning emigrant who, not understanding the conditions abroad and having no standard for distinguishing the possible from the impossible, conceives and believes anything; sometimes the agents or Jewish merchants spread such news intentionally in order to profit by it. Often it is impossible even to guess their source.

[3] This shows that the question of dowry brought by the man or the girl is not exclusively economic. The girl Kowalczyk is rich enough to take a husband without money, or at least not to care for the amount of money which he may bring. And it would not be considered humiliating for a man without fortune to marry such a girl so far as he is *personally* concerned, because he would give his *work*. Nor would it be a humiliation for the girl to marry a man without money, provided he were her equal in education. But since in marriage the man is not an isolated individual but a member of a family, and since fortune has more importance for the social standing of the family than for the social standing of the individual, the man ought to have money, as it is a proof that he comes from a rich family.

know, I tried so hard to gain her favor; I took so many hard steps, and all this brought me nothing. I should have come out all right there, for as this Miss Swatówna told me, she "gave a basket" [the mitten] to Rudkowski because she loved me. But, finally, when I expected to end the business, then they [my family] began to find fault with it, particularly mother. Well, I gave up the game, I stopped calling on her. How they must talk about me there now! Swatówna is still a girl. I don't know what will be the end of the hopes with which I still deceive myself about the Kowalczyks in Czyżew. If God helped me, it would be the best there. All this is in the hands of God. But it is a hard nut to bite, for there is a crowd of various men around, and the Kowalczyks themselves look upon this business from several sides. I hear that they prefer me, but there was a time when things were so bad that I said to myself that I wouldn't go there again. I was there a few times and I never found her. Evidently she hid herself and she hid herself not because she hated [disliked] me, but because different [marriage] brokers laughed at her [for receiving attention from me].[1] Worse still, I noticed that the Kowalczyks began to treat me indifferently, particularly Mrs. K. This observation pained me greatly; but what could I do? I gave up my efforts, though I was sorry. But evidently Kowalczyk did not want to part with me in this way, for he understood my wishes, found some occasion and came to us with his brother Piotr.[2] He pretended to come for quite a different business, but we guess that he wanted also to look at our situation. Well, we tried to treat them as well as we could, and it seems that it pleased them well enough, and

[1] As the peasant is particularly susceptible to ridicule, this is often sufficient to hinder a marriage. A girl will hardly ever marry a man if she suspects that for any reason her choice may be ridiculed. The reasons are various. The most frequent is the inferiority of social position, as in Wiktor's case. The occupation is also very important. There are occupations which make a good marriage impossible for the man. Among these are catching stray dogs in the streets, sterilizing horses and cattle, serving in Jewish houses, and in general occupations having a connection with a Jewish business. (This last prejudice tends to disappear except in connection with personal service.) There are other occupations to which only a slight ridicule is attached, such as shoemaking, tailoring, peddling. Another source of ridicule is a physical defect, however slight. Similar prepossessions are found against girls, but the lack of variety in woman's occupations makes them less pronounced except as against servants in Jewish houses.

[2] It is a bad policy to dismiss an unacceptable suitor too hastily, for the more suitors a girl has the greater her value for each of them, and this influences the social standing of the family. Cf. Introduction: "Marriage."

when I meet them they treat me quite differently.   Well, now I went also to them in the evening, on April 2, and called upon them as if passing by.   They received me well enough, and Miss Mania with such a bashfulness came to the room where I was and we greeted each other very heartily.   However, we spoke little together for her uncle was in a very good humor and tried to treat me well, and moreover it was rather late.   So I have described to you briefly my whole passage. . . . . Now I mention that I met Bańkówna.   She asked me about you, when you will come.   I fibbed and said that you will come after Pentecost.   She told me to greet you politely and begs you to write her a letter.   If you want to, write, but fib cleverly.   [News about marriages and deaths.]

About Jan Ziółek [probably the son of their grandmother's second husband] we don't know anything.   He has not come yet.   And perhaps he went farther inside of America with a whore. . . . .

WIKTOR MARKIEWICZ

198   August 24, 1913

My dear Brother Maks: . . . . In August 14, I was in Warsaw and I asked the editors of *Lud Polski* to send you a few copies of the paper.   They sent it to the College in Cambridge Springs, Pa.   You had asked for *Pan Tadeusz* of Mickiewicz: I bought you the whole collection of his poems. . . . . You wrote a letter to the Kowalczyks [in my favor].   Waste of time and paper. . . . .

WIKTOR MARKIEWICZ

199   Popłacierz, April 13, 1914

Dear Brother Staś: When I was in Grabie father got a letter just then from you in which you complain that you have no news from me.   In my last letter I told about my wedding which was to be, and it was performed on February 18 at 12 o'clock, at noon.[1]   A few days later . . . . I sent a letter to our dear brother Maks . . . . and I expected that you would meet him. . . . . Still, I don't consider myself excused, but I beg you, my dear brother, understand my situation, how many different indispensable affairs are to be settled, and

---

[1] He married neither of the girls mentioned before, but a new acquaintance, an orphan girl living at some distance.   The girl's dowry is very large, as 30 morgs of land are worth at least 6,000 roubles.

they absorb all the time and cause trouble, until one comes to the steps of the altar and gets married.   And do you believe that all this trouble and turning around and hurrying are over when one has performed the wedding-ceremony? Oh no, my dear brother, it was only a beginning of all this.   Now I have whole series of these affairs and troubles before me.   I won't mention to you my important affairs before the wedding, because I am sure that you imagine them; I describe only part of my actual troubles.   On March 28, the family-council turned over to me the whole farm, and I received it in the communal court of Gombin.   I received only 30 morgs of land with the winter grain sown, well, and 15 korcy of potatoes and a part of the barn filled with straw.   Well, how is one to begin farming now, when he has nothing to take into his hand, neither cow nor horse, neither cart nor rope, nothing at all?   The roofs upon the building, dear Staś, are so to speak, in a deplorable state; when rain comes, it rains in the courtyard and it rains in the barn, it rains in the stable and it rains in the cellar—it rains everywhere.   The fences near the house are ruined, for there are none except near the house.   Wherever you look and whatever you look at, you must repair.   In short, it is as tenants usually leave it.   And here even the smallest thing, whether for household or for cultivating the soil, must be bought.   Is my father able to buy me everything, from A to Z, in spite of his sincerest wishes? Already my father has given me in all this more than once the proofs [of his good wishes], and I am and will be grateful to him up to my death.[1]   My small savings were exhausted for my wedding, and only now I understand what it is to begin farming when you have nothing ready. . . . . So, please, don't be angry with me for not writing.

As to the wedding, I mention first, that the weather was splendid on this day. . . . . The ceremony was very nice, the church was beautifully adorned with green and lights; as many people came to look as on Sunday.   In short, it was imposing.   The priest from Radziwie demanded 25 roubles for the wedding, to be paid beforehand, but he did it splendidly, and I am very much satisfied.   We did not

[1] The father's change of attitude toward the son is perfectly clear.   The son's marriage is a familial matter, and thus there is no place for parsimony.   The wedding must be splendid, because of the family's standing; the son must be helped in establishing himself upon his wife's farm, because it is to the family's interest that he should become a prosperous farmer.   This investment of money is productive from the familial standpoint.

make a big feast; my father paid for the whole festival, because it was so agreed. [Enumerates the guests, "only the nearest friends and relatives," about 50 persons.]   The guests were richly entertained and abundantly feasted, so the satisfaction was general.   We did not collect for a caul. . . . .[1]

Now I describe to you, what I have already upon my farm.   A harrow, a plow, a cart, everything new, one cow which my father gave me.   Antosia's [the wife's] grandmother gave her one young cow big with calf, and 10 hens.   My little old grandmother has given me nothing up to the present except one small cheese for the holidays and half a pint of butter.   Well, may God reward little grandmother even for this.[2]   But my father and mother help me the best they can and in whatever they can.   Perhaps our Lord God will help me in the future also, then I will always remember this.   Meanwhile I pray to Him for health and long life for them.   I mention further that with the help of God we shall be able to live here pretty well.   I have many plum and cherry slips, so it will be possible to enlarge the orchard, which is one of the sources of the welfare of a farmer. . . . .   My father and mother are very much satisfied with their daughter-in-law and with all this marriage in general. . . . .

I come to the end of this letter as speedily as I can, because as soon as I put the pen aside I must prepare myself to catch the steamer in order to go to Grabie, to my dear parents, to look once more at the old corners. . . . .

Wiktor M.

200   Grabie Polskie, July 5 [1914]

My very dear Stasieczek [Staś]: . . . . I came today to our parents for business, and on this occasion I write to you. . . . . They complain here at home that it is hard for them to provide for all the work, and there is nobody to help them.   We learn that you also have to work very hard there, and that moreover you have lost your health.   They ask you therefore to come back.   Evidently, if you are getting on badly, come at once; if well, remain still for some time.

---

[1] Old habit of collecting money among the guests for the bride's dresses.   Cf. Introduction: "Marriage."

[2] The grandmother, by her second marriage, has lost the familial feeling and feels no obligation to help Wiktor.

We are about to have a terrible lawsuit with the priest of Dobrzyków and those Hams [ruffians] beyond the range. Oh, thieves, thieves! Those Hams and the priest and the judge are going hand in hand. My brother, what things are going on here!

Your brother,

WIKTOR MARKIEWICZ

201   SOUTH CHICAGO, August 7, 1906

DEAR BROTHER WACŁAW [really cousin]: Fortune arranged it so that unexpectedly we both became pilgrims in America. So I feel my brotherly attachment to you, and that it is so, let it be proved by my letter addressed to you, whose address I got from home.[1] I dare say that perhaps you care less to establish a regular correspondence with me here in America, but it is only a supposition. How it is in reality the future will show.

So I inform you that I came to America, i.e., to New York, on February 13, and then I went to my friends in New Kensington. . . . . There I worked up to May 26. I worked in a glass factory 8 hours a day. The work was not heavy, but hot. I earned $12.50 to $14.00 a week; it depended on how much glass was made.

I left because the factory closed. . . . . I went to Chicago. There I found my acquaintances and my cousin Leonard Król, my mother's uncle's son, with whom I am living up to the present. Since I came to South Chicago, I am working with Polish carpenters 8 hours a day. I am paid 35 c. an hour. And naturally, while it is summer, I am very busy with this work, but in winter it will surely stop. Then I hope to get into a factory . . . . or carshop for the same work. On the 2d of this month I received a letter from home, favorable enough, and at the same time your address. So I want to learn about you, what you are doing, where and with whom you live. And in general inform me about your success. Whatever you ask me, I will gladly inform you about. . . . . I send you hearty wishes of happiness, health and good success, I embrace you and kiss you.

Your brother,

MAKSYMILIAN [MAKS MARKIEWICZ]

---

[1] Typical, disinterested revival of family feelings. It is not the mere result of loneliness, for Maks lives with another cousin.

202 March 27, 1907

DEAR BROTHER: Your letter satisfied me very much, for you have good work. I remember the letter which you wrote to me last summer; I pitied you then, when you described how you worked in a glass factory for $1.50 a day. My hearty advice to you would be to hold steadily to carpenter's work, particularly in carshops, for though they pay better in other works, it is not so steady as in a carshop. Moreover, if you know how to work about cars you can find this work in the whole of America. I intend also in the future to get into a passenger carshop, for not far from me there is a big carshop in which thousands of carpenters are working. It is, I have heard, the main carshop for whole America, called "Pullman." From there come the most splendid cars for all lines. Look carefully, then you will surely see these cars with the inscription, "Pullman."

When Stasio comes, if there is nothing favorable for him where you are, let him come to me, then I will help him as much as I can. But you know that a man who comes fresh from our country can with difficulty, find good work, for he is not acquainted with the American habits and does not understand the language. Therefore I warn you, let Stasio not be very capricious in the beginning. I wish [advise] him also to try carpenter's work. . . . .[1]

MAKSYMILIAN

[1] The problem of work, predominant in this letter and important in all the letters of American Poles plays no such rôle in the life of the Polish peasant-farmer. With him work, that is work for others, is only an additional means of existence, and property is his main interest. There is in the old country no hope of advance through work. It is undertaken only as a means of supplementing an otherwise impossible existence, and is miserably paid. In this respect American emigration, with its many possibilities and its relatively vast range of good and bad chances, effects a profound revolution in the psychology of the peasant, and the problem of work becomes at once the central problem. Interests of the city-workman are added to those of the peasant, without supplanting them, and the result is that the workman of peasant origin differs from the hereditary city-workman in two respects: (1) He has no interest in the work itself but considers it exclusively with regard to the wage; (2) he looks upon his labor, not as a means of organizing his life once and forever, but as upon a provisional state, a means of attaining property, which is for him the only possible basis of a steady life-organization. The good job, particularly in America, is for the peasant nothing but a good chance from which he must get as much as possible, while for a man with a workman's psychology and with the same tendency to rise, the good job will be either an end in itself or a means of getting a still better job. From this results also the apparent stinginess and low standard of life with which the American workman reproaches the Polish immigrant.

203 September 5, 1907

DEAR BROTHER: . . . . I see that you did not receive my last letter . . . . and you probably think that I have forgotten you. But in this respect you are mistaken, dear brother, for I don't intend ever to forget anybody, and particularly you. As to your supposition that some woman turned my head, you almost guessed it. But I know also how to turn women's heads. Only I keep always in mind the severe American laws in this regard.[1] [Was slightly hurt in his left hand; expects to get insurance money.]

MAKSYMILIAN

204 INDIANA HARBOR, April 30, 1908

DEAR BROTHER WACŁAW: . . . . I inform you that I moved from South Chicago to Indiana Harbor, nearer my work, so that now

---

The man with a workman's psychology, considering hired work as his more or less permanent condition, will try to live as comfortably and pleasantly as his means permits, for this life is normal for him. The man with the peasant psychology, considering hired work as a temporary chance, will reduce his actual needs to a minimum, postponing every pleasure of life until the end of his work, for this life is for him provisional and abnormal.

The letters of Maks give us a good example of the evolution of this attitude. In the beginning Maks is an instructed peasant, economizing, putting money aside, thinking of returning and probably of acquiring some property at home. Then he hesitates, and is half-decided not to return; he is not yet decided to remain a workman, but he already makes expenses which only a workman, never a peasant, would make, such as buying a watch for $60. He nevertheless still thinks of property and writes about buying a house. And finally, he does something which is absolutely contrary to peasant psychology; he decides to spend all his money on instruction, and goes to a college. This proves, that no longer property, but hired work has become his life-business, and that his peasant attitude in economic matters has changed into a typical workman's attitude. Cf. Introduction: "Economic Life."

[1] The attitude of Maks toward the problem of love is already to some extent that of the middle class. In the peasant class love is always related to marriage, even if there is much flirting before making the definite choice; in the middle class it becomes an end in itself, a kind of a sport, of which marriage in each given case may be the result, but is not necessarily the acknowledged aim. Of course, as sexual intercourse between unmarried people is normally excluded in the middle class, there must be a sufficient degree of culture in order to make the relation interesting in spite of this limitation and in spite of the lack of an immediate reference to marriage, and it is also usually possible only when the individual is no longer dependent upon the family. Cf. Introduction: "Marriage."

I can go on foot to the factory and I don't need to pay 15 c. a day for the railway-passage.[1]

I was much pleased with your intention to learn English, and even higher [subjects], for if you have some instruction, you will have an assured existence in this country.   I guess that you regret that you did not come to America a few years sooner [before his military service], and did not learn English instead of learning Russian [in the army], you could say today boldly that your existence is secure.[2]

I got a letter also from our country, from father, mother, and brother Wiktor.   When Wiktor was still in Petersburg I wrote him that I intended to marry in America, and that I would therefore never come back to our country.   I asked him to repeat to my parents my decision wholly [as I wrote it], but, instead of sending it by letter, he told it himself to my parents when he came back home.   This is what he wrote me, that he was able to notice: My mother was very much troubled about it and began to cry, longing for me, while my father cared about it very little, and Wiktor noticed that father cared little about it.   Then, my mother begs me much, in her first letter to me, to remove these thoughts from my head, to come back to our country, while my father does not mention a word about my returning home, only informs me with joy, that Wiktor came back healthy from the army.   And when Wiktor was to draw the lot, my father, as I heard, exerted himself [to get him free], and even gave to some official 200 roubles to this effect, so that if the commission in Gostynin exempted Wiktor from the military service, it would cost my father 200 roubles, but if not, then the official would pay the money back. Well, the commission did not exempt him, and my father got the money back.   Therefore he writes me now [when Wiktor, because of bad health, has been sent back from the army], that Wiktor is there and the money is there.   From [in spite of] his joy, as my brother writes me, father would not even buy him clothes for Easter.   In a word, dear brother, I don't see in my father any heart for me, now no more than formerly.[3]   At the same time I got a letter from my

[1] He had lived for a year as described in order to be with a remote cousin.

[2] We find here already a standpoint very different from that of the peasant tradition.   The question of "existence" is put upon a purely individual basis. But this standpoint is not yet definitely accepted, as the following paragraph shows.

[3] Maks evidently had his father sounded with reference to determining what were his chances of receiving the farm or of being established on another if he returned, and the uncordial attitude of his father perhaps had an effect in determining the individualistic sentiments in the earlier part of the letter.

mother, written with her own hand. She weeps for me and she asks me with tears to come back to our country. My heart grieves at the words of my beloved mother, and I am ready to satisfy her wish in the future.

As to the question how I look upon religion and socialism, dear brother, I don't bother myself profoundly with either the first or the second. Not with the former, because I know this much, that I am a Catholic, and I perform the duties of a Catholic as far as I can. I am not devout, for I have no time to pray, because every Sunday I must work, and—I confess it to you alone—I worked even on Easter from 7 until 2. . . . . But nevertheless I desire to remain a Catholic up to my death.

As to politics, I am very little interested in any questions or parties; when I have a little time, I buy a paper for 1 c., I read it, and there it all ends. . . . .[1]   M. MARKIEWICZ

205   September 22, 1908

DEAR BROTHER: . . . . After waiting for 6 months I received at last a letter from my father, with rather favorable news. . . . . They are succeeding pretty well, for my father intends to buy in Dobrzyków the "murowanka" [farm with stone buildings] from Mr. Plebanek for 3,300 roubles, but he has not this whole sum, so he addressed himself to me for some help. I did not refuse him help in this affair, but it seems to me now that perhaps I acted impolitely. I asked my father to send me first notes for 1,000 roubles or more, and promised to send money at once after receiving these. (Tell me your opinion about this question of notes and sending money in general.) I add that if I asked for notes it was because my confidence in my father has been ruined during my stay in America. If you wish, I can tell you about it. . . . .   M. MARKIEWICZ

[1] In comparison with Maks, Wacław remains more of a peasant, in spite of his socialism. Instruction is not for him a means of getting a position on a higher social level. He is enough above the peasant to appreciate instruction in itself independently of its immediate practical application, but not enough to make of it a new basis of life. Economically he is satisfied to belong to the lower class, and wants to rise only socially, like Elżbieta, his sister. Maks, on the contrary, is not interested in instruction and theoretical problems as a matter of distinction, but he gets further from the peasant ideology than Wacław, and is able to make instruction a new life-basis which will allow him to get totally outside of the peasant class, economically as well as socially. Wacław expresses his desire to do the same as Maks, but it does not seem that he fulfilled it.

206   December 14, 1908

DEAR BROTHER: I am very much grieved that you are in so bad a position. I can well imagine your painful situation, and I should be glad to help you, dear brother, and at the same time I would reach the object of my wishes to live together, or near each other in this foreign land. But now it is simply impossible. In the factory where I am working very few men have good work—only the engineers and we three carpenters. As to the ordinary workers in the mill, may God pity them, so bad is their work. . . . . I would not wish it, not only not to my brother, but not even to the Russian [tsar] Nicholas to get it by my protection [assistance]. Perhaps in the future you will have occasion to see it yourself; then you will agree with me that I was right. . . . . As to the carshops, they are not here, but near Chicago, but I hear that even they don't work with full speed, as the papers have drummed it after the election of Taft. If you want money, write to me and I will send you some. . . . .[1] With me everything is good. I am healthy, I work steadily, only I am bored here, because in this small town I am as solitary as in a forest. . . . . Write me what do you think about the Polish National Alliance and the Polish Sokols. . . . .

M. MARKIEWICZ

207   August 16, 1909

DEAR BROTHER WACŁAW: . . . . I received a good letter from my parents, and besides the letter I received beautiful gifts from my parents, brought by Witkowski's brother—a gold watch chain, my monogram sewed with gold and silver threads and six fine handkerchiefs, marked. I am very much pleased with these tokens, and from joy I bought a gold watch for $60.00.[2] I won't write you more, for I intend . . . . to come to you next Sunday. . . . .

MAKSYMILIAN.

208   October 5, 1909

DEAR BROTHER WACŁAW: . . . . I inform you about an offer from which you will perhaps profit. My old boss told me today that he had much work, so perhaps I knew some carpenters, and if so I

---

[1] He kept this promise, but without taking money from the bank.

[2] Cf. No. 202, note.

should send them to him. I told him that I had a brother carpenter (i.e., you) who was working, but if the work would be steady, I could bring him. He answered that he hoped to have steady work. So I advise you to come, dear brother . . . . we would live here in the foreign land together. . . . . We could meet him in South Chicago and speak about the business while drinking a glass of beer. . . . .

MAKS

209 ISLAND CITY, November 18, 1911

DEAR BROTHER: . . . . I am glad to hear that you want to send me your money for keeping. I see that you smother [hoard] it well. So send it and don't ask whether I will accept it. Describe how long the work there can last, what are you building, and how do you live there. I think there are probably colds and snows. . . . . Take care not to catch cold and not to journey thence [into the other world]. Write more about yourself and the country. Are you satisfied with your success? With me there is no news. . . . .

M.

Finally, I shall inform you that I learned something which you supposed I would never learn. You were mistaken. Well, and because of this I have lost in you something forever. First, I confided you this [secret], as to a brother. Then, when I noticed that I had done badly [imprudently] I begged you [not to repeat it, saying] that if it comes through you to the daylight, I should have to pay with my good name. And so it is. But you did not care about anything, and you betrayed me. Be your own judge. I owe it also to the good memory which you have, for you repeated everything very exactly.

MAKS

210 December 1, 1911

DEAR BROTHER WACŁAW: We received today a letter for you from our country and I send it to you. Excuse me please for its being opened, but you know how everybody is curious when anything comes from our country, so we [Stasiek and I] tore the envelope and satisfied our curiosity. Your parents write about a whole series of accidents which they had lately. The most important is the news about that horse. It is a pity to lose such big money as he was worth. Stasiek says that it was a nice horse. We received also a letter from home, but there everything is well.   First, everybody is in good health, and my father bought 5 morgs of land from our neighbor Switek, near ours, for 1,100 roubles.   Further, my brother Wiktor intends to marry during the carnival a Miss Kowalik from Czyżewice.   Stasiek says that it would be a splendid business.   The girl is young, educated well enough, the only daughter, and her parents have a farm worth about 15,000 roubles.   Wiktor hopes that he will reach his goal there, because those people are even some remote relatives of my grand-mother Ziółkowska, and this means something too.   Further, Wiktor asked me to send him about 1,000 roubles, for our father has spent most of his money on that land which he bought.   Probably I ought to help him for some time.   What do you think?

Now, you wished so well to Miss H. G.; but I learned that, as it turns out, she seeks herself the same [danger] against which you warned her.[1]   A proof is the fact, that not long ago she wrote a letter, such a fawning one, to that "priest" [seminarist], and asked him to accompany her [to walk with her] again.   So if she knows everything, how she was betrayed, and dared to address herself to him with such an oration [*sic*], it is enough to give us an idea of her virtue.   But he gave her, I heard, a rather sharp answer, owing to the occupation which she had, that is, she works in a larger sort of a shoemaker shop, just opposite the St. Stanislaus College.   She sews buttons on the shoes, puts laces in, and so on.   With a lady who has such a position he won't have anything to do—so this student answered her.   Enough for the present about this Miss H. G.   At the first opportunity we can speak more. . . . .   I have somewhat important business to speak about, concerning the purchase of a certain house here in Indiana Harbor. . . . .[2]

Your brothers forever,

M[AKS] and S[TANISŁAW] MARKIEWICZ

211   VALPARAISO, August 21, 1912

DEAR WACŁAW: . . . . I shall be in Chicago probably on the 31st of this month.   I must make a few purchases before going to Cam-bridge Springs, Pa.   Among many others, I must buy Webster's Dictionary, which costs $18.00 edited in 1912.   An older edition can

---

[1] Refers probably to the content of his preceding letter.   Wacław probably warned the girl against Maks and told her of some previous love story of his cousin.

[2] A recrudescence of the peasant property interest.

be bought for $12.00. It is an indispensable thing in the school. As to my leaving the school of Valparaiso, it is not an unexpected occurrence, for I planned beforehand to do it. As to the English language, I shall have time enough to learn it in 5 years, and in the school of the Polish National Alliance a year can be spent for $150 while here in Valparaiso it would cost me $300; so it is worth doing, if only for this reason. . . . . Before I come, be so kind and try to learn from somebody about second-hand bookstores, so we can both go and buy this book. . . . .

MAKS

212 SMOLENSK, January 9, 1912

DEAR BROTHERS: "Praised be Jesus Christus!" My pen wrote, and my heart wept that it did not see you for so long a time. [In verse.] Now I send you the sad news that I have been taken to this accursed army. [Describes how he was sent with other recruits to Smolensk.] The physician sent me to the hospital where I am lying the third week already and I don't know how long I shall lie and what will happen to me further. God knows it. In the hospital they give bad food, or rather not so bad as little, but for the work which we have it is enough. There are 23 of us here with ear disease. There are 10 Poles, but they are all from the province of Lublin; I am alone from the province of Warsaw. I am not bored, for I have a good companion who was for a whole year in the agricultural school at Pszczelin. He tells me about this school, and time passes. We have a good physician in the hospital, but only few men are let go, so I don't know what they will do with me. Perhaps only a miracle of God will tear me away from this jaw. . . . .

MICHAŁ MARKIEWICZ

213 May 26, 1912

. . . . DEAR BROTHERS: . . . . I am waiting now for a letter from you, because I received six roubles, sent by you, for which I thank you heartily. They will be very useful for different expenses, for up to the present I had not even money for buying tobacco, because I have not received anything sent from home. And here in Smolensk everything is expensive, average boot-soles cost 3 złoty . . . . a loaf of wheat bread, which in our country can be bought for 3 copecks, here costs 5 copecks.

I never expected that such a bad lot would befall me, as it proves now, for if I had known that I should serve,[1] I should never have come here, to this muddy and dirty Smolensk.   I should have done much better if I had gone to America instead of you, dear brother Stanisław. They plague us, God forbid! We hoped that after the oath [of fidelity] they wouldn't plague us so much, but it is still worse.   Till noon they make us run [exercise] near the barracks.   Afternoon they send us to work. . . . . They expect the tsar to come to Smolensk this year, and they plague us the more for it.   I write home that I am getting on not badly, but if mother knew what conditions I have here, she would shed many tears.[2]   I shall probably expiate for you and for myself.[3]   I am walking like a dead man, for it is so painful to serve. You have extricated yourself, but I shall hardly succeed.   I go often to the medical office, but what is the result? We have a physician who is simply a thief, an old dog.   Whenever I go to him, he seals my ear and writes something. . . . . He says that I am spoiling my ear myself.   He says that he is writing a report and that he is sending me to the court-martial, but there is nothing to this court.   He only tries to frighten me, or the devils know what he thinks. . . . . He did not do anything bad to me up to the present, except that he won't send me to the hospital.   I beg our Lord God and God's Mother for it, because, although in the hospital they gave little to eat, yet it was possible to sleep and to rest enough.   I often see all the men with whom I lay in the hospital. . . . . Only one, from the province of Lublin, has been set quite free. . . . . Another, about whom I know . . . . whose hair fell out and whose head was left as bald as your knee, or as the head of Korzuszek, was not set entirely free, but only sent home for 6 months to recover. [Describes

---

[1] He expected either to draw a high number which would exempt him or to be sent home by the recruiting commission on account of his artificially provoked ear trouble.

[2] This regard for the mother is typical.   It seems somewhat a custom not to complain to one's parents about the military service. Cf. No. 218; also No. 72, and other series containing soldiers' letters.

[3] Stanisław, like Wiktor, was set free on account of sickness, after having served a short time.   Therefore he did not need to go to America in order to avoid military service, and for this reason Michał regrets that he did not go himself instead of his brother. "Expiate" means here "suffer the predestined amount of misery."

weather, exercise and work.] O, God's Mother, deliver me from this Moscovite jaw! . . . .

MICHAŁ MARKIEWICZ

Please don't write home about my "luxurious" life in the army, for mother will grieve.

214 July 14, 1912

DEAR BROTHERS: . . . . As to my illness, I don't go to the medical office now, but I await the winter and the cold. It is true that I am afraid of these dogs the physicians lest they send me to the court-martial, because he decided at once that I had done it intentionally. . . . . Whenever I went there, he always told me not to irritate it, and always put gauze and cotton inside. If he put it loosely, it leaked, but if he put it tightly, so that I was not able to ———, then it did not leak. Now I am waiting for the cold; I will complain of the cold [as irritating my ear] and go often to the medical office. If the physician knew with certainty that it is spoiled [intentionally], he would have sent me to the court-martial, and long ago, because he is a bit of a dog's brother. Now I won't write you more about it . . . . but when you answer, brother Stanisław, do it carefully, that you may not betray me. During June we looked here at the flying of beautiful aeroplanes. . . . . It was like a bird with wings, and when it rose, it twanged like a threshing machine. . . . .

MICHAŁ MARKIEWICZ

215 August 19, 1912

DEAR BROTHERS: . . . . I inform you about my military service, that it is going on slowly, day after day, further and further. We have ended already our duties in the summer camps, amid heat which reached 40° [Reaumur or Centigrade], ... and now the weather has changed; it is cold and it rains every day. They plagued us in the camp, it is true, but it will be still worse, because we are to go to Moscow in a few days for maneuvers which will last for 2 weeks, and then for a week there will be military review by the tsar. It will be hard if it rains then, dear brother. God forbid! To get into this accursed army and to serve—what for? To waste in vain your health and youth! Dear brother Stanisław, I am so weary and home-sick, God forbid! Whenever I remember anything, my heart almost bursts open with grief. Why did I not go instead of you to America? I regret it always, but it is too late. Well, even now I don't lose hope in God. Perhaps our Lord God will grant to me such time and desirable moment, as we both desire, you and I. Meanwhile, I don't go to the medical office, but I plan to get sick during the maneuvers, when we are in Moscow. There perhaps they will leave me in the same hospital where you were, for, as people say . . . . there it is easier to be set quite free. Here in Smolensk it is very difficult; they let only the men go who have been operated, or those who are dying, and even those are not set totally free, but only for some time, until they recover. . . . .

When I had written up to this passage, I was told that I shall be left here . . . . because they consider me unhealthy. . . . . But although I remain here, I shall still have a bad time. Every day I shall be obliged to keep guard at the post. But it will be better than at the maneuvers. It is bad in the army, nothing good ever happens. Dear brothers, you ask me whether I need money. I need it really, because if I wanted to satisfy all my needs I ought to have 10 roubles a month; only then could I be a little free. But when I got those few roubles, they were spent I don't know where. I don't demand of you to send me as much as I ought to have, for you must work for it. You don't receive anything for nothing, but it is easier for you to get a rouble there than for me a copeck here, so be so kind and send me a few roubles. . . . .

Michał Markiewicz

216 January 26, 1913

Dear Brother Stanislaw: . . . . I inform you that I received the money, 9 roubles 72 copecks, long ago, in October, and I thank you very much for so large a help in the military service. . . . . I wrote you then a letter at once. . . . . I had also a letter from home yesterday in which they inform me that everything is good except that our sister Weronika is sick. They write also that a Russo-Austrian war is likely to come. Indeed, people speak much about war, and just because of this they held up the soldiers from the [19]10 year, who ought to have gone on November 1; they don't let them go now. . . . . If the war with Austria began—God forbid! It would be upon our Polish land. It would be dangerous to live in our country. As to me, it would be also bad, because who knows whether I should not be obliged to go to the war. . . . . Up to the present there is nothing terrible, only we hear that Austria held the reserves, as if she were preparing for war, and here the reserves are also held. The whole question is about the Black Sea. But everybody says that there won't be war. . . . . God forbid! If I had to go to the war, dear brother Stanisław, who knows what would happen with us, perhaps we should never see one another again. I regret very much that I did not go to America; there I could live and earn, as you do, dear brother. Well, I beg your pardon, Staś, for writing so. Don't think that I envy you; on the contrary, may our Lord God help you. But I am so worried, and I think that I should have done better in going to America. . . . . They won't let me go. I don't go now to the medical office, because it [ear] won't leak much, but I will go once more. . . . .

Michał Markiewicz

217   March 16, 1913

DEAR BROTHER: . . . . No news is to be heard. I live as in a forest; among this savage Moscovite horde nothing can be learned. [Rumors about the war.] I got a letter also from home, such a one as I saw for the first time in my life, such a terrible mourning letter.[1] I had not even read it and I did not know what had happened at home, and the first look made me terribly afraid, down to the bottom of my soul . . . . . God guard us from more such letters! They wrote me in their last letter that our grandmother is also ill, that her legs are swelling. They wrote that they are overwhelmed with sorrow after the death of our dear sister Weronika. And of the farming they wrote that everything succeeds well, and the grinding is average. . . . . Dear brother Stanisław, you ask me whether our parents are angry with you, that they don't write to you. . . . . God forbid! They never wrote to me anything like that, only the letters don't reach you. . . . .

Michał Markiewicz

218   April 8, 1913

DEAR BROTHER: . . . . I received the money, 6 roubles, for which I thank you heartily. I know, dear brother, that you feel the need which I suffer in the military service, for you know yourself what goodness is in this accursed army. They don't send me money from

---

[1] The letter was a printed death-notice, seldom used among the peasants.

home, because I write them such letters that they may not grieve about me. I write them that I don't feel ill in the army, and they believe that I feel really better in the army than at home. As I don't write for money home they don't guess themselves [my need] and they don't send me any, for they don't know well how it is in the military service.

May God keep even my worst enemy from such a goodness, may not a dog ever serve in the army! [Sends his photograph and asks for photographs.] Now I inform you that the recruits of 1910 have been set free and went away on March 26; even we were more cheerful. . . . . If only time passed more rapidly! . . . .

Michał Markiewicz

219   May 20, 1913

Dear Brother: . . . . We celebrated here the Easter holidays together with the Russians, i.e., on April 27. Here all the holidays, even for free people [civilians], go together with the Russian.[1] We were at the "Resurrection" in the church during the night from Saturday to Sunday. It was celebrated very beautifully. They let off fireworks, shot as if with guns; for the first time in my life I saw such queer fireworks. The holidays have not been bad, as good as they can be in the army. They gave a little of everything, and of beer everybody drank as much as he wanted. And now for 4 days we have been going to Easter confession. It is not very far to the church from here, as far, for example, as from our house to Dobrzyków. The church is not very big, but nice, built of bricks. It has stood only 19 years. I have had no letter from home for a long time. I don't know what is the news at home. A farmer from near Warsaw writes to his son in the army that it is not very well in our country; there was a big frost so that all the oats and barley have frozen. . . . . As to myself, everything is going on slowly. . . . . In these days we are camping. When this summer has passed, less than a half [of the time] will be left. There are rumors that service will be reduced 2 months to the recruits of 1911 and to us, because they kept those of 1910 four months overtime and they will want to get these expenses back. . . . .

Michał Markiewicz

[1] The Catholics in Russia outside of the limits of the so-called "Congress Kingdom of Poland," keep the dates of the old or Julianic calendar, which is official in Russia.

220   June 24, 1913

DEAR BROTHER STANISŁAW: . . . . My service is going on slowly. We went into camp on May 20 . . . . but God forbid to live in these camps! Every day some task, some hard task. It is true that we don't work here, but these tasks [drill] are more annoying than any work. I am worried, I have no wish to do anything, all this because every day it is the same. And if somebody looked from outside it would seem as if it were not so bad in the army. Well, you, dear brother Stanisław, I see that you feel my need the best, for you are the best persuaded how well it is in this accursed Moscovite army. Thanks to God the Highest, dear brother, you did not serve these Moscovites long, while I shall surely be obliged to remain for all these 3 years, unless God's mercy comes. Happy the man who does not serve! More than once have I been convinced of this. Well, what can be done, if such is the will of God that I must serve. Happily one-half of my service has passed; perhaps our Lord God will grant that the other will pass also. This year, if our Lord God keeps me alive, I shall go home on leave, and thus slowly things arrange themselves. . . . . I am glad that you are satisfied with my photograph. The man who is with me in this photograph is my best companion, a Pole from near Warsaw, but he goes to the reserves, i.e., home, in autumn. Send me the soonest possible your photograph and that of Maks. If it is possible, please send me a silver watch and a good razor. But perhaps this will cost much there; if so, don't send. It would be very agreeable to receive such a gift from one's brothers; I should have a remembrance for my whole life. I beg your pardon for daring to write for such things to you. I say only, dear brothers, if it is not expensive and if you think that it is possible, send it. . . . . Brother Wiktor did not write me that he intends to marry in Czyżew, but I know it, for already when I was at home Wiktor drank more than once with her parents and went to them sometimes with his chestnut mare. Indeed it would be a happiness if he could marry there. You can send money [home], for our parents spent their own upon land, and in such a business [as this marriage] money is useful. Write how much you can send him. Did brother Wiktor not write you whether there is anybody to be paid off, and why they need money? . . . .

                                          MICHAŁ MARKIEWICZ

221　　　　　　　　　　　　　　　September 26, 1913

DEAR BROTHERS: . . . . I received the money from you, 10 roubles 1 copeck; just before the maneuvers it was paid to me, and it was very useful during the maneuvers. I thank you heartily, and particularly you, dear brother Stanisław. If it were not for your help I should have suffered much want and misery, while so, thanks to God, the second maneuvers passed neither good nor bad. Thanks to God, there was no rain and no cold. . . . . But, as soldiers say, last year it was terrible; it rained the whole time, and nothing is worse than to be wet during such a wandering. We have wandered like Jews in the desert, all this in memory of the Napoleonic War, and through the same ways as the French in 1812–13. We passed many different villages, and nowhere I have seen any good house or barn, only everything like henhouses. It is easy to notice that these "Kacapy" [nickname for Russians] farm exceedingly badly. What is worse, they have no draw-wells, only the women go for water far away, to some ditch or pit. And they sow whole fields with flax, as in our country with rye, for example.[1] I won't write more about these "Kacapy," I only say that nowhere is it so well as in our country, in the beloved Poland. . . . .

MICHAŁ

As to the watch and razor, you were right in not sending them [probably because of the tax].

222　　　　　　　　　　　　　　　November 22, 1913

DEAR BROTHER: . . . . I received a letter from home, in which they inform me that our father received the money sent by you, precisely that about which you wrote me in your last letter, the 1,000 roubles, and moreover mother received 10 roubles. Father deposited your money in the savings bank of Gombin. Wiktor evidently could not conclude the business in Czyżew, for he wrote that now he is calling upon the Jankowskis in Kielniki, and had even asked already the favor of their daughter. They invited him to call upon her. Very well, but they put off the question of marriage, I don't know why —whether they want to get their sons married first or for some other reason. . . . . They [at home] wrote also that this plague of a Ziółek [second husband of their grandmother] nags our house [family]. For

[1] Cf. Osiński series, No. 131, note.

example, Chojnacki's boy tends his cattle [to graze] and once he pastured them near our windmill. A cow, precisely that of Chojnacki, damaged a wing of the windmill, and brother Ignac beat the boy for it. This "berry" ["peach"] of a Ziółek persuaded Chojnacki to make a complaint against Ignac. The court condemned the latter to 2 weeks of prison, but father appealed, and we don't know what will result. Father in turn lodged a complaint against Chojnacki for damaging the wing. . . . . How do you like our dear grandfather? May—[the devil take] him—! Our brother Wiktor wrote that he slanders and blackens our house before people, and Wiktor intends to reward him for his bad muzzle.

They write to me to come on leave, particularly our dear mother. I have certainly promised to go, but the leave does not depend upon me alone. . . . . I asked the captain here and he promised to let me go, but whether he will or not, I don't know, although I have the full right. . . . . May God grant me to get, for a few days at least, out of this true hell upon earth, this Moscovite's jaw, because I am very worried and longing for my family. And what is worse, they say that the service will be made longer. . . . . People say that in the duma of Petersburg the question is going on. . . . .

Please send to Maks from me my best wishes. May God allow him to attain as soon as possible his noble end [to finish with the college].

MICHAŁ MARKIEWICZ

223 January 11, 1914

DEAR BROTHERS: . . . . I have been on leave. I got home on December 6, and I left on December 30. Our dearest mother was very glad about my coming and greeted me very tenderly. I am sorry that our dear mother was ill twice during these two years since I have been in the army. . . . . Well, thanks to God the Highest, everything passed off and now mother is healthy, although she still suffers constantly from stomach catarrh. Oh, may God grant our dearest mother to recover fully, for our whole happiness, our whole hope and our good rely upon her. As to our father, he complain, now as he always did, but he has not been ill for these two years. When I was at home we received your letter, dear brother Stanisławs in which you abused father for the question of this land from Switkowski. Maks was right in writing to father that he had even less confidence in him than in the worth of a Russian rouble. Father justifies himself, but what he thought was really nothing else than that which mother guesses. Father excuses himself for doing so on the score that it cost less, but in reality I think that it would have been as mother says.[1] As to brother Wiktor, he is neither upon water nor upon ice [insecure]. He calls upon the girl every Sunday, but there is nothing certain. But he excuses himself on the ground that there is nobody to work at home, and that he won't marry until I come back from the army. He is partly right. Well, but nobody knows how God will direct his lot. If he had a good chance he ought not to wait until I come. As to Ignac, Julka and Mania, you would not know them, dear brothers, they have grown so. Ignac is perhaps the biggest among us—a boy like a ladder. May our Lord God give him health! I pity him for falling a victim for the sake of this [Chojnacki] boy's skin. When I came, he had sat in prison, for two weeks. [Farm-work, weather and crops.] Grandmother is also bad, she looks sickly. As to Ziółek, he is healthy like a horse, only he has grown a little older. . . . .

MICHAŁ MARKIEWICZ

224   April 20, 1914

DEAR BROTHER: . . . . You look very nice and young in the photograph. It is somewhat difficult to know you in the photograph, for you have grown so fat; you are not quite like yourself. . . . . W. Borek looks well also. Evidently you are in good companionship with each other, and it is very right and good to have a companion from one's own neighborhood and well known. Do you live together, or do you perhaps work together? . . . . Please write me, and give him my best wishes and greetings. . . . . At home brother Wiktor got married. The wedding took place on February 18, in the church of Radziwie. He married Miss Antonina Oliszewska from Popłacin. I don't know her, but Wiktorek writes that she is a pretty girl, of middle height, 19 years old. She has a sister 17 years, and a brother 10 years old. Both her parents are dead . . . . and left a fortune, 1 włóka [30 morgs] of land and moreover 1,500 roubles cash for the farm-stock, sold after Oliszewskis' death. . . . . This farm lies quite near the Vistula, and a part of the river belongs to this land. . . . .

---

[1] The father probably bought or planned to buy the land in his own name. The "lesser cost" probably refers to notarial expenses.

The place is very good, Wiktorek writes, and he praises the fortune highly enough. I hear that he made indeed a good match, and so unexpectedly. When I was on leave at home, Wiktorek had no girl at all, and then suddenly he writes that he is marrying. May God bless him in his new household. But at home conditions have grown worse, for there is nobody to work. Father wrote me to come "for recovery," at least for half a year. Well, I should be glad to come back once and forever and to get free from this accursed service, but it is not in my power, I guess that things are bad at home without us, but what can I do since I must serve? But you, dear brother Staś, since you have no work now and since there is likely to be war [with Mexico], I would advise you to come home. Please write me, how long do you mean to remain in America? Wiktorek intended before to take [father's] farm himself.[1] . . . .

MICHAŁ MARKIEWICZ

225 July 1, 1914

DEAREST BROTHER: . . . . I received 10 roubles and 1 copeck for which I thank you most heartily. I intended to write home for money, when unexpectedly I received 10 roubles. For me it is a big sum of money. . . . . May God grant me . . . . an occasion to prove to you my gratitude for your well-doing, and your brotherly heart, dear brother Staś. And now, in the last year of service money is very necessary, for we must dress ourselves a little better. For it is impossible to go in the clothes which they give, because people would say that such a man came from some prison or some desert, not from military service. . . . . You ask about the service [how long it will last]. I cannot write anything with certainty. . . . . They kept the recruits of 1910 longer because there was war in the Balkans, the Bulgars with the Turks . . . . and Russia wanted to benefit from this war. . . . . He [the Moscovite] likes to make war against the Turks, for they are not Japanese. . . . . May our Lord God and

---

[1] This last must be understood with reference to the unexpressed question, "Who will take the father's farm, Staś or Michał?" Evidently, Michał would like to have it, for since Wiktor is already married and settled the brother who takes the farm will be favored, particularly so because of the father's attitude. Therefore he tries to learn discreetly whether Staś (who is older) intends to return, and whether he would oppose Michał's taking the farm. There is at the same time a cunning endeavor to learn his brother's intentions, and a mixed feeling, for he evidently loves his brother and would like to have him come.

God's Mother grant me to get free from this Moscovite jaw. . . . .
Believe me, when I went with the recruits, I was not so sad as now,
since I returned from the leave.   I even wept, I was so sorry to return
. . . . among these beasts and wolves the "Kacapy." . . . . From
home they write . . . . that they have a lawsuit about the trees
which grow upon the range between their field and the priest's.   They
won the first time, but they lost the second time, for the court did not
call our witnesses.   The lawyer says that we must win.   It would
be better if they made peace instead of lawsuits, which take money
and time. . . . .

MICHAŁ M.

KOZŁOWSKI SERIES

The Kozłowskis are a poor family in the province of
Łomża. At his death the father left a small farm of two
morgs—possibly inherited from his mother. The widow,
Franciszka, remained on the farm with the youngest
boy, Franek. One daughter (stepdaughter?) of Franciszka
married a shoemaker of the same village. The position of
a village shoemaker is rather bad, and this explains the
apparent cupidity of the daughter. The other children had
gone to America. Meanwhile there had remained undivided
a farm left by Franciszka's late husband's father, and the
trouble begins with the division of this land.   In the division
six morgs of land are added to the small farm of Franciszka.
She has no right to sell these 6 morgs, but at the same time
she wishes to get as much profit from the situation as possible, and, on the other hand, she is really not in a position
to take care of the whole farm until Franek grows up.   The
shoemaker's wife has a right to part of the value of the
whole farm and she claims her share, but Franciszka wants
to pay her only a sum corresponding to her part of the original farm of two morgs, and wishes to drive a sharp bargain
even then. Her first plan is to sell the farm, conceal as
much money as possible for herself, and go to America to be
supported there by her children. But the children are
unwilling to give her power of attorney; they seem rightly
to distrust her.   Then, as the opportunity to marry presents
itself, she changes her plans, sells whatever can be sold
without legal authority, gets money from her children to
join them in America, invents pretexts for not going, gets

married, and tries to keep the whole farm for her youngest son, while getting in addition as much money as possible from the sale of the forest and stock. She succeeds perfectly, and is evidently too clever for her children. They not only get no money from her, but she succeeds in getting some from them. Ultimately she conciliates even her most dangerous antagonists, the shoemaker and his wife.

All this shows no lack of maternal feeling. On the contrary, she shows that feeling on the occasion of her daughter's death. But she has a powerful personality, and she has probably been independent for a long time; she has governed her environment, and she does not wish to fall into the position of an old, helpless, and moneyless mother, supported by her children. And as having some money herself is the only way of keeping her independence, she endeavors by all means to get it. As a woman, she has not the same tradition of familial solidarity as men; she is not the head of the family, the rightful manager of the common property; there are no rights and responsibilities of leadership to set limits to her egotism. The family-group as a distinct whole does not exist for her; she means to deal always only with individuals and opposes to them her own individuality. In so far the case is different from that of the old Wróblewski, who shows a much more far-going moral degeneration, since he is the head of a family and nevertheless breaks off all relations with his sons.

The influence of Franciszka's personality upon her environment is very well shown by the circumstance that everybody who comes into immediate touch with her finally does whatever she wishes. Her youngest son is under her absolute control; her *kuma*, Maryanna Szczepańska, is dominated; her second husband manifests a real devotion to her; even the stepdaughter and the shoemaker are sub-jugated, though not without protest. Her brothers and children in America are, of course, less under her power, but even they cannot quite avoid her influence. The letters give us a good idea of the means by which the social environment may be controlled through merely psychological influences, without any socially acknowledged right to control—one of the practical problems of the peasant woman and solved by many of them in the same way as by Kozłowska.

The fundamental device is, of course, the appeal to sentiment. Kozłowska uses it artistically. In order to appreciate this we must remember the peasants' tendency to schematize people and things. Every person belongs to a certain determined social type and is presumed to have the attitudes of this type; every person has a determined position, and from this position conclusions about his behavior may be drawn. The surest way to provoke a desired sentimental reaction in the environment is therefore to assume and to keep consistently a character corresponding to the sentiment it is desired to provoke. Thus, for example, a noble, a priest, a teacher, an official, a newspaper man, an agitator, wishing to win the attachment of the peasants, must each act in a different way. There are also reactions which only a person in a determined position can arouse. For instance, envy is most easily awakened in peasants by a peasant. A priest or a noble will hardly succeed in provoking pity, etc.

Now, Kozłowska has a determined character and she tries to arouse only such feelings as are habitual with regard to a person of this character. She is a widow and therefore presumed to be helpless. The supposition of helplessness has a stronger basis, because she is old and formally poor, i.e., she has little which is rightfully her own. Further, she is a mother and grandmother, and supposed to have the feelings of love, longing for her absent children, grief for a child's death, anxiety for her grandchildren when they become orphans, etc. The type of favorable reaction which she can easily provoke in her environment is thus predetermined; it is pity for her helplessness and sympathy for her maternal feelings. And, indeed, she plays continually those two chords. And she does it with just the intensity required by the social milieu to which she belongs. In a more cultivated milieu, more accustomed to restrain the feelings, her behavior would appear highly unnatural, distasteful, and hysterical. Perhaps she is in fact a little hysterical, but certainly her behavior is adapted to her social sphere—one accustomed to a display of feelings. She has nothing to lose and much to win by exaggeration; therefore she exaggerates her helplessness as well as her motherly love, her poverty and her (certainly unreal) bad health, her grief and her gratitude.

Of course, her actions are not in accordance with her assumed character; but she knows like a master how to present them in a suitable light. The gradual selling of the forest is given as the result of her poverty and inability to farm. When she wants the farm sold, she appeals to her oldest son as her "guardian" and pretends to acknowledge his authority. When she marries, she pretends that she was forced to it by her helplessness. Her anger against "the shoemaker's wife" is justified by her motherly indignation, because of the invectives and curses which the stepdaughter hurls against her children. And the hardest blow to her is the—just or unjust—allegation of immoral conduct, which tends to wreck completely her assumed character.

But she knows also how to use other weapons. She appeals to religious feelings—by using in a clever way the name of God, by sending religious tokens, by exploiting the magical fear of a mother's curse, by presenting other people's duties toward her in a religious form, etc. Expressions of indignation and pride alternate with appeals to pity and strengthen each other by contrast.

The second typical means of control is the use of the feelings aroused, instead of rational arguments. In asking for anything or in explaining her conduct Kozłowska does not rely upon the strength of her arguments. On the contrary, she seems to avoid intentionally the real issue and instead creates around the problem an atmosphere of sentiment favorable to her. It is hardly a fully conscious, rationally motivated policy, any more than is her ability to provoke the desired feelings; both are certainly naïve. Her use of sentiment instead of argument is also largely due to her insufficient training in argumentation. Most of her arguments, are, in fact, rather weak, and in this respect she is also a type. The essential features of her argumentation are almost universal, not only among women, but also among men of the peasant class, and this is precisely the argumentation which is most efficient with peasants. In order to demonstrate something rationally, we must not only be able to develop a logically perfect chain of reasoning, but must also have an opponent able to follow this reasoning to acknowledge its binding character; and first of all, we must have identical premises. But a peasant opponent is not trained to follow a line of reasoning, is not accustomed to accept a thing as true solely because it has been demonstrated to him. And even if he admits a premise explicitly, he has always some other implicit premises which he keeps intentionally unexpressed and which invalidate in his mind his opponent's conclusion. So it is a difficult task to get the peasant to accept your argument. But if, with regard to a given problem, you succeed in arousing a set of feelings favorable to your view, the work is done, for the peasant will *himself invent* arguments which will persuade him. This is the mechanism used consciously by all those who want to influence the peasant, and they imitate it from the half-conscious procedure of the peasants themselves, of which Kozłowska gives a good example.

The third means which the old woman uses to obtain what she wants is to be as exacting as possible. She not only does not give her children what is due to them, but she continually demands money from them, and not only from them but even from her brothers, who have no obligation whatever toward her. She simply reverses the situation, making demands which the others might naturally make. It can be understood then that under these conditions her son-in-law, instead of claiming his wife's dowry, would be satisfied if she sent him back his own money, or her son would be satisfied if she let him alone. The principle is the same as in bargaining, which is a general characteristic of the peasant as well as of the Jew. In their dealings with the manor-owners the peasants' claims are sometimes impudent. They do not expect those claims to be granted, but they hope to get at least something. In many cases the source of this unlimited exacting is found in a curious psychological identification of wish and right. Thus, the peasants' wish to get the land of the nobility gives rise to a half-determined, sometimes even fully determined and rationally justified, conception that they have the right to this land. In Kozłowska's case certainly there is much of this attitude. We find it also in most family quarrels about property, and in many lawsuits.

Among the other personalities in this series the most interesting is perhaps the *kuma* (Marysia's godmother), Maryanna Szczepańska. She is notable because of the nature of her friendship with Franciszka. This kind of old women's friendship is very frequent. It is based upon a community of interests and attitudes. The women seek in each other a help against their respective families and comfort in domestic troubles, and, being of the same generation and the same social group, they agree perfectly with each other, particularly as there are no practical problems to divide them. The necessity of such a friendship is felt mostly in older age by women who do not know how to adapt themselves to the young generation, and who begin to feel solitary in their own families. Of course if there is a close and harmonious relation between husband and wife such a friendship has less occasion to arise, and indeed we do not find it in most of our series. In their relation the old women manifest much mutual adulation, and this shows that their friendship has still another function; it is their only way of getting social recognition of the kind and degree they desire. It seems to be a tacit pact between them always to praise, never to blame each other. They behave in the same way when speaking about each other, and Maryanna's letters are good examples of this behavior.

Old men, like old bulls, do not care much for society. Their social standing is more assured, their instinct of domination finds place enough in the family, their familial attitude does not allow them to initiate strangers into their home affairs, and they do not need any help against their families. After their retirement the situation changes, and then we find them sometimes associated in friendship with retired neighbors of the same age. The usual consequence of retirement, however, is to strengthen the bonds between husband and wife.

THE FAMILY KOZŁOWSKI

Franciszka Kozłowska, a widow
Antoni (Antoś), her son, living in America
Franek (Franciszek), her son, living with her
Józef Plata, her second husband
Marysia (Mania) Baranowska ⎱
Zosia Bieniewska   ⎰ her daughters, living with their husbands
Julcia Brzostowicz   in America

"The shoemaker's wife," her daughter or stepdaughter
Antoni Hermanowicz, "the shoemaker"

Wincenty ⎫
Antóni ⎭ Franciszka's brothers (or brothers-in-law)

Maryanna Szczepańska, Franciszka's *kuma*

226–45. MAINLY FROM FRANCISZKA KOZŁOWSKA IN POLAND,
TO MEMBERS OF HER FAMILY IN AMERICA. 237–38,
FROM MARYANNA SZCZEPAŃSKA; 230, 239–41, FROM
FRANEK; 242–43, FROM JÓZEF PLATA; 244–45, FROM
ANTONI HERMANOWICZ

226   DANIŁOWO, March 15, 1906

[TO MARYSIA AND JAN BARANOWSKI] In the first words of my
letter I speak to you with these godly words, "Praised be Jesus
Christus,".and I hope that you will answer me "In centuries of
centuries, Amen." . . . .

I inform you, dear children, about my grief. Were it not for
my soul for which I am anxious lest I lose it in eternity, I should
have drowned myself, and you would have nobody to write to any
more. Dear children, I write to you and I don't s   these letters
from crying. I am only glad from your letter that you intend to
take me to America. There perhaps I should still live some years
more. But, dear daughter and son-in-law, make some plan about
all this.

Dear daughter and son-in-law, the worst is the forest, for I could
find some farmer for [renting] the field, but the worst is about the
forest. People would cut it down [steal the wood in my absence].
Dear children, you said in your first letter that you would take me,
so take me indeed, I beg you heartily.

Dear children, I describe to you my grief. On the same day
when I received that letter from you, I received also a notification
from the bailiff that the shoemaker's wife wants it [the farm] sold at
auction, and the auction will be on March 21. Now, dear children,
when we were at the court, I asked them: "How much do you want
to be paid off." She said 60, and he [her husband] said 70. She
said that she wanted not only [the inheritance] after her father, but
also after her grandfather. I offered her 50. But now I will give her
nothing at all. Let her go by [the way of] lawsuits, I will give her

nothing at all.[1] Now, dear children, I inform you that she writes letters to America, and particularly to Antoni. Moreover, through acquaintances she sends messages against me. And now Antoś has not written to me for more than 3 months [as a result of this slandering]. And perhaps, dear daughter and son-in-law, dear children, perhaps they [Antoś and wife] don't know that you wish to take me to America, and they don't know. But, dear daughter and son-in-law, don't be angry with me for the thing which I shall mention. Dear children, I could not get to America for my money. Why, and I should not go without my son who is with me. Dear daughter and son-in-law, perhaps you will send me a ship-ticket. Dear children, sign, all of you, that you want me to come. For perhaps you want me to come, dear daughter and son-in-law, and perhaps those [the son and daughter-in-law] don't want me to come at all.[2] Dear daughter, I ask you whether you received that letter in which were the scapularies and the veil of God's Mother? You say, dear daughter

[1] One of the main sources of the innumerable and interminable lawsuits. Whenever in a dispute one party goes to court, or so much as threatens with a lawsuit, it is enough to harden the other party against all persuasion, even if he knows that he is totally wrong. But at the last moment, before the suit comes to trial a reaction usually comes—reflection and fear of losing—and if there are mediators the matter is frequently settled at this moment. Much depends also upon the judge, whether he is able to give the whole affair an *unofficial* form and to persuade the parties to agree. Therefore the country judges use as little formality as possible, for if once the matter is put upon a formal basis it ceases to be a question of right or wrong and becomes a mere fight. The lawsuits between family members must be considered from this point of view. As long as the matter remains within the family, agreement is always possible upon any basis; the peasant is ready not only to acknowledge any just claim but even to make any sacrifice. But as soon as the question assumes a formal character no considerations of justice, and in general none of the moral norms regulating the family life are applied at all; the law is outside of morals. An attitude which would be judged immoral, unjust, sinful, from the standpoint of familial or communal relations, is *not judged at all,* by any moral standards in legal relations. And this attitude is not always unconscious. A peasant who was in the midst of a lawsuit with his brother, and who was evidently and absolutely in the wrong from the standpoint of justice, replied, when we pointed this out to him: "Why, they did not want it settled *by the way of justice!*" meaning that they went at once to court instead of trying to get his consent in an amiable way.

[2] This request may have two aims. She either wants to be assured that in any case she will be supported in America, or she wants to have a document which, while not equivalent to legal authority, may still enable her to dispose of a part of the property or to persuade the guardians to let her do so.

and son-in-law, that I was angry with you. No, I was not angry at all, I was very much satisfied, only I waited for your answer. Dear children, you are so dear to me, that I kiss these photographs of you upon the wall. . . . .

FRANCISZKA KOZŁOWSKA

227   November 4, 1906

. . . . MY DEAR CHILDREN: . . . . And now I inform you that I am healthy, but scarcely, from all this thinking which I have upon my mind. . . . . I received your letter and 3 photographs; I gave one to Szczepańska and I have two left. I inform you that I am very much satisfied, dear daughter and son-in-law, may our Lord God bless you, and God's Mother. May she help you in your work and in everything. . . . . Now I write, your mother, to all of you, my children, in general. First to you, dear son, and to my daughter-in-law, and to the Bieniewskis and to the Brzostowiczs and to the Baranowskis, and I wish you every good, whatever you want for yourselves, my dear children.

Now I inform you about this land, that to these 2 morgs were added during the new division, 2 morgs of field and 1 morg of forest to each. . . . . So there are now 6 morgs of field and 2 of forest, 8 morgs together. Now I inform you, dear children, on what spots we received this addition. [Describes in detail.] You, Antoś, and you, Marysia, you know where it is and in what position.

Now, my dear children, it would be the best if we sold it, for I have nothing from it except trouble. I don't sow the land, only [strange] people do, for I rented it, for I cannot manage it myself. Even if I wanted to sow myself, you know that there is no barn and there is no place to put the crops. I keep the forest, but again people steal. A man could guard it more easily, while I, a woman, what can I do? I have only trouble. So it would be the best, my dear children, to sell it, for all this is wasted for the land they pay [the rent]; but in the forest whatever anybody snatches is his own, and when I need money, I also sell some tree,[1] and so all this is wasted. If you don't do as I advise you, dear children, after a few years it will be much cheaper [worth less]. Now they would give money, for they

---

[1] She has no right to do this, and she confesses it, for evidently the shoemaker's wife has written more than once to her brother and sisters that the mother is wasting the forest.

want to buy it, as it is in good order, the forest and the field. For the 2 morgs of forest they would give now 400 roubles, and for the 6 morgs of land they would give perhaps 300. And perhaps they would give more.[1]

My dear children, consult one another and write me, how I shall do. But it would be the best, my dear son Antoś, if it were your head, for you are my guardian. Arrange it so that we may sell it and that you may take me and Franek to America, for I don't wish to farm here. I have the land, but I have no barn, nowhere to put [the crops], and you know that there is no place [near the house] to build it. So it would be the best to sell the field, if you don't wish to be upon it [to settle here], and if I must only grieve [have trouble] alone. I can sell it myself, only send me, all you children, an authorization, and let your uncles send me also an authorization, for they belong to the same farm [they have a right to a part of it]. Then I shall sell it and come to you, and we shall live together, and you will get sooner something of it, for now the value is greater as long as the forest is entire and nothing is missing. . . . . I beg you, dear son, if you allow me to sell it, do it at once. . . . . I beg you, dear son, do it for me, and you all, my dear children, and you, my dear brothers, do it for me, for I would see you once more, as long as we are still alive. [Greetings.]

FRANCISZKA KOZŁOWSKA

Dear daughter Marysia and son-in-law: Why are there in the [wedding-] photograph neither the Bieniewskis, nor the Brzostowiczs, nor my brothers, nor my sister-in-law, only strange people? This astonishes me much. What does it mean?

228　　　　　　　　　　　　　　　　　　　　March 4, 1907

. . . . DEAR SON: . . . . You are obstinately bent against me and I am against you. I would not write to you, but I must. I write you only: consult among yourselves [and decide] as you want to. The shoemaker's wife made an inventory [of the farm, for auction]. We stood before the court, and she quarreled with me, tooth against tooth, and moreover she cursed you for neither taking her man to

[1] This phrase is added later, the first statement seeming perhaps too improbable. Even the worst land was worth at this period twice as much, and it would be a very poor forest on which the lumber alone, without the land, would be worth no more than 200 roubles a morg.

America nor paying her off. Our guardians asked her how much she wanted to be paid off. Then this old beggar, this carcass [her husband] wanted 70 roubles, and she asked 60. I will give her 50, and the guardians also tell her to take 50 and no more. But, dear son, I would rather give her nothing. What do you advise? I was everywhere [for advice], and I thought of either renting the field or selling the forest [to pay her]. But, dear son, I wish I had never lived until this new division and addition, since I am a hinderance to all of you and you are angry with me and you don't write me for half a year. Were it not for this affair I would rather have died [zdechła, used here vulgarly like the English "rotted," is properly used only of animals = German krepiren] and would not have written. Now, dear son, come rather to an understanding among yourselves, take it, sell it and make peace with this shoemaker's wife. Let her not call God's vengeance upon you and grieve me. And now after all this she intends to have an auction, for her part of the inheritance from your grandfather and your father. You left me here for sorrow only. Dear children, don't believe anybody, when the shoemaker's wife slanders me to people. Why, you get it [bad words] also from her, dear son, into your eyes, and behind your eyes [proverbial, to your face and behind your back]. And you get still more from her. She says: "Much did he care for his mother! And when he came to Warsaw, he let his nails grow a sążeń long [6 feet] pretending to be a gentleman."

Dear son, I thank you for writing to me so often! But don't think, dear son, that I write it from my whole heart [that I am grieved]. I say it simply because you write once in a year. If I had known that you would guard me so! May our Lord God and your children care for you as much as you do for me! If you had not gone into the world you would have known better what a mother is, while now in return for my education [of you] you are ashamed of me. But Mańka did the same. She accidentally wrote one letter, that we might know only that she got married. Dear son, please say to Mańka about this letter that she rejoiced me awfully, that I don't know what to do in the country, and she gave me precisely such advice as the letters she writes [no letters, no advice]. To the shoemaker's wife she can well send bows and write, but when her godmother sends her a gift—she sent her scapularies and a veil of God's

Mother—she did not even thank her.[1]   Dear son, and all my dear children together, I tell you sincerely I won't write you any more letters since you are so turned to stone against me.   Since you are so little curious to learn what is going on here with us I won't inform you. I bless you all with the holy cross [old habit in bidding farewell].

Dear son, you said to Franek, "If you manage well I will send you some assistance."   And now you don't even send a naked letter [without a stamp].   But if this shoemaker's wife sells our land at auction then our assistance is over.   Dear son, we keep two pigs for ourselves, but there can be no cow from them [probably alluding to some promise to send money for a cow], the less so if the shoemaker's wife drags us about courts, as she is now doing.   Dear son, I ask you, and do you answer me.   Do you agree to pay her 50 roubles, as I wish, or not?   Perhaps you will send us some money for this payment?   For if we sell these pigs, we can have perhaps enough to buy a cow.   I beg you, dear son, for a speedy answer.   I salute you all, yourself and your wife and my grandchildren.

[FRANCISZKA]

229   June 2, 1907

. . . . DEAR CHILDREN: I inform you that I am not very healthy, for even an iron man would have no longer any health.   I thank you heartily for this letter, dear children, which you sent me.[2]   And then, dear children, I received also the letter from Zosia.   Dear children, I beg you all together, answer me, what is this "dirt" which I have on me?[3]   Answer me, who wrote that letter so that this "dirt" may not grieve me longer.   Dear children, I have enough of my own trouble.   Dear children, I can never in the world bear these troubles, for, dear children, in the week when I wrote this letter I went to Czerwin, and I hardly got there, for my feet were covered with blisters.

[1] The members of the family in America are evidently disaffected by reports from the shoemaker's wife and realize that Szczepańska is in the scheme with their mother.

[2] The son has been moved in some way by the preceding letter to write; probably by the mother's words: "May our Lord God and your children care for you as much as you do for me."   This is the kind of mother's curse which never fails to be impressive.

[3] "Dirt" is commonly used in the sense of "immorality."   She has probably been accused of immoral relations with the man who afterward marries her.

And I went in vain, for not all of our guardians were there; 3 were and 3, not.   Now I shall have to go again, and when winter comes and it is necessary to creep upon the snow, surely I shall die.   And since the shoemaker's wife made the inventory, the guardians won't allow me to sell this property, for Franek is a minor.

And now, dear children, could you arrange so: Send me such a decision that I can rent [the farm] for some years.   Now people are afraid to pay money down for some years, lest it be lost.   I should be glad, dear children, to step away from her [the shoemaker's wife's] eyes.   [*Ślepie*, in the original, is properly used only for the eyes of animals.]   Let her not cause me any more grief.   If I went to you perhaps God would guard me for a year or two, while thus, dear children, when these troubles fill my head I have [peace] neither day nor night.   There is no work from me at all, and soon I shall go away from [lose] my reason, and I shall no longer understand any of your writing.   O God my dear, God my dear, why do you keep me in this world?[1]   Dear children, I beg you, take me to you, I want to have one hour of relief at least and not have to listen to this [calling of] vengeance against you, dear son, and against Zosia.   Moreover, she [the daughter] persuades some dogs like herself to write dirt against me.   What dirt do they write against me?   Perhaps she writes against me about this [man]?   I who can hardly walk with my pains, and she writes dirt about me!   For this land I should have more than one purchaser, but when I learned that the guardians won't let it be sold, I have no more strength to bear all this.   Oh, nothing can be done, my dear children, evidently she must kill me with trouble in this country!

Dear brother, you ask me in your letter about money.   I did not see any money and probably I am to see none.   When you sent me some, I saw it, but now when you don't send, I see none.

I greet you also, my dear children.   It is true that I received at last a letter from you, but I will remember it until my death—what [sorrow] you gave me about that dirt.

---

[1] Here the grief, although also affected, seems more real than in the first letter, for besides the quarrel with the "shoemaker's wife" there is another reason, i.e., the matter of the "dirt."   Whether justified or not, such a suspicion is likely to affect a peasant woman more profoundly than anything else.   And the impossibility of selling the land, meaning the failure of her scheme, is a third reason for grief.

I have nothing more to write to you, dear children and brother. Remain with God. May God help you.

[FRANCISZKA]

I salute my sister-in-law and my brother. Sister-in-law, why should we be angry with each other and what for? I have not seen you, sister-in-law, with my very eyes, and I shall die without seeing you. Well, my dear, let us kiss each other, at least by letter, at least through this paper; let us give hands to each other. I thank you so much, sister-in-law, for not forgetting me yet, and that you both remembered me. Dear brother, I thank you for this, for your knowing that I am your sister. Remember, dear, how you cared for me and I cared for you.

[FRANCISZKA]

Dear children, I don't want to make you any trouble about taking me [sending me a ship-ticket]. I should prefer if you sent me a few roubles [in cash], but I should find my way more easily if you take me [if you send me a ticket].

230 [June 2 1907]

DEAR BROTHER AND SISTERS: Have pity and take at least our mother, let her have at least a few easier hours. Dear brother and sisters and brothers-in-law, I beg you, if you want to see your mother before she dies, take her to you. Have pity, for, dear brother and sisters, you have written already 4 letters, thanks to God, and in each of them you say that you will take us to America. So mother waits for this letter like the mercy of God. When the letter comes, mother kisses it from joy and wets it with tears, but when she opens it [she is deceived].

[FRANEK]

231 July 12 [1907]

. . . . DEAR SON ANTONI: Answer me how I shall manage, for my son-in-law Baranowski sent me a letter saying that he is sending me a ship-ticket for myself and for my son, and wishes to take us to America. And you, dear son, come to an understanding yourself with the others, whether all of you know about it or not, for I am not just as I stand, but I have land and forest, and I don't know how to manage. It is true that my son-in-law is good. But you, my son, you are my guardian, and answer me, how I shall have it there [what conditions]. For, my dear son, there is a marriage opportunity for me, with Józef Plata, who is a very good man. So answer me, my son, as soon as possible, whether I may live in our country, for I don't need to wander about the world in my old years, only my [youngest] son wants us to go. Dear son, answer me as soon as possible, for I am awaiting this letter with my journey and with my wedding.[1] . . . . Dear son, reflect all of you only once, but well, for my son-in-law tells me to rent the land and the forest. . . . . I cannot sell it myself, a father can, but not I. I have nothing more to write, only I wish you health, happiness, and good success. . . . . Dear son, when you receive this letter, don't show it to my daughter Mania, and don't tell her anything, for my son-in-law wishes to take me secretly to America [to surprise his wife].

Franciszka Kozłowska

232   September 11 [1907]

. . . . Dear Son: . . . . You advised me to go but now I am not going. I have married that Plata who had Ewa Pieńkos as wife, from the same village I came from. What could I do in this misery ? When I received the ship-tickets I did at once what you ordered me to do. I rented the land for 3 years, I sold the cow which I had and the forest which was left after father's death, while yours [inherited from the grandfather] is still there. I have wasted all the living which I had [store of grain, potatoes, etc.] and I have bought everything for the journey. And now living is expensive, and I spent some money on living, and I had to dress myself and Franek a little before going to you . . . . and I bought 2 shawls for 13 roubles and 15 pounds of feathers for 12 roubles. [Went twice to the doctor, then to Libawa, and was sent back.] This journey cost us much, for everywhere money had to be paid, and I wasted everything. I have not written to you for I fell sick from grief and I waited until our Lord God changed [restored] me. But now I am somewhat better and I describe this to you. Hermanowiczowa [the "shoemaker's wife"] moved to me, to my lodging and I live with Plata. He built a new

---

[1] The letter shows clearly, behind the cautious expressions, a total change of intentions. She no longer wants to go to America, but she does not dare to take a decisive step at once. Probably at the moment of writing this letter the later scheme is not yet ready in her mind.

house, and Franek is with me. How good he [the husband] is to me, thanks to God! May he be always as good! For when I am sick, he at least cares well for me, and it is well now. I had decided to go to America, but when these Baranowskis managed it so badly, I changed my mind, for now I have no land, and therefore I had to marry. Inform the Baranowskis how I did, and let them send their address, then I shall send them the ship-tickets back. Don't be angry with me for having done so, for I have wasted everything through this. And in the office [in Libawa] they said that these are tickets for a working-ship [steerage?]. And you can know what this journey has cost me. From Warsaw to Libawa alone 42 roubles. . . . . [1]

[FRANCISZKA]

[Postscript]

And I inform you that we went [started] to America all three, the shoemaker went with us for money, for he borrowed it. When

---

[1] The story, as related in this and the following letters, is full of contradictions and totally false. In spite of her son's and son-in-law's wish, she decided not to go to America at all, but to marry Plata. She wished evidently to profit from the opportunity, and to get as much money as possible for herself, as a dowry. Thus, according to her son's wish, she rented the land and sold a part of the forest. Evidently, she had to sell also her farm-stock and household effects in order to make it appear that she really intended to go. Then she had to find a pretext for not going, to account for the money, to explain her marriage, and to conciliate her son-in-law, the shoemaker, and his wife—her worst enemies—that they might not betray her but corroborate her story.

She hoped first to be detained on the score of sore eyes (suspicion of trachoma). She went therefore to many oculists, hoping that one of them would tell her that she could not go. It is very probable that she even tried to get her eyelids inflamed, and went to a Jewish barber in Goworowo (the Jewish barbers act secretly as physicians and are ready to do anything—abortion, artificial crippling to exempt young men from military service, etc.), who, as she says in letter No. 233, "almost burned her eyes." She then went to Warsaw hoping to deceive the oculists there. When this plan failed, she invented the story of the tickets, which is wholly false. First, she says that the tickets were for a "working-ship"; now, this term is current only among the peasants to indicate ships which take only steerage passengers, and she could not have heard this term from the steamship agents. Then she says the tickets were not valid at all. But it is evident that the agent in Warsaw would not have sent her to Libawa with such tickets, for he would have been legally responsible. Certainly the tickets were valid, but for steerage; somebody must have told her that steerage traveling was bad, and she profited from this suggestion to stay. Perhaps she would not have gone even to Libawa if she had been alone, we returned he gave this money back at once, for he borrowed it from the priest and wished to go along with us.

I inform you also that when I intended to go to America I went to Goworowo to a doctor. He poured something into my eyes and almost burned my eyes. I went twice to Warsaw, and there the doctor said that I could have been blinded. You say that I did not wish to go. But I went twice to Ostrołęka to the [district-] chief for passports, and I paid once one rouble, then two. So much trouble and cost I had.

. . . . Now I inform you, my dear children, daughter and son-in-law, that I received your letter and we answer you at once and we inform you that we are in good health [wishes]. Now you write to me, son-in-law, and you are angry with me. But nothing can be done. I am not guilty at all in this matter, my dear son-in-law, for I was already on the way, in the last station, in Libawa, and from Libawa we were sent back. Now, my dear children, would I have caused such a cost for you without wishing to go to you? Why, our Lord God would punish me severely for it. And as to this, dear children, that

---

but her son-in-law, the shoemaker, was with her. Then she tries by all means to make it appear that she spent all her money on the journey to Libawa and back. It is easy to calculate how much money she really had with her. The cow, crops, household furniture, must have brought at least 150 to 200 roubles. Rental of 6 morgs for 3 years at least 180 roubles. The son-in-law Baranowski sent 60. The sale of a part of the lumber perhaps 150–200—together about 600. The journey to Libawa and back for 2 persons, 28 roubles. As she writes 42, she must have paid her son-in-law's fare in order to win his discretion. The journeys to Warsaw and back, inspection by the oculists, etc., no more than 20, probably less; buying of the shawls and feathers (which she later kept for herself), 27, passport, 3. If we take into account the living during this time and the son's clothing we have not more than 150 roubles for all the expenses. Thus she had certainly about 450 roubles left. She writes in the letter No. 232 that she was obliged to buy clothing for herself, while later her *kuma* Maryanna Szczepańska says that she was obliged to sell her best petticoat. The *kuma* is evidently "fixed"; the daughter, the "shoemaker's wife," also, for after all the preceding quarrels she comes to live in her mother's house. Thus, the scheme is carried out, and Franciszka must have brought to her husband no less than 400 roubles of dowry. As she was old, the man would never have taken her without money. And all this was so cleverly done that she does not lose her right—a part of the inheritance left by her first husband. Indeed she expects to receive the total income from the land when the period of its rental has expired, for there is mention that her husband must feed her until that time.

I got married, don't persuade [reproach] this to me, for I got married only when I came back from my journey. If the ship-tickets had been good, I should be in America already, with you, for I wanted continuously [sic] to go to you. But since it happened so, nothing can be done, my dear son-in-law. You have made expenses for yourself, and I also, my dear children, have made expenses for myself, and I got totally ruined, for I wanted to go to you within an hour [immediately]. I had a cow; I wasted it. I had some small crops in the field; I wasted them also, for I prepared myself to go, and you don't believe me and are angry with me. As to my getting married, dear children, it was from this misery, when we had been sent back home, for I had wasted everything, so how could I live? And this year all living is expensive here, grain and potatoes are expensive, and so in putting things together it is easier for me to live.

And as to my not having answered you and sent you the tickets back, it was because I had not your address, and I was afraid to send them to these other children, for perhaps they would not have given them back to you. Now as soon as I received your letter, I sent you at once the ship-tickets, and these signs [checks] of these agents from Warsaw, to whom you wrote to care for us, I sent them to you for controlling. Dear children, how much trouble and weeping I had in that Libawa, God forbid! It is impossible to understand these Germans [sic!]. Were it not for an interpreter who explains everything in Polish I should not have got these ship-tickets back, for they threw them away at once and I could not find them. They wanted red ones, and these were black, and therefore they sent us back and we have all so much expense.

And now I inform you, dear children, about these 60 roubles. I have them not, for I have spent them. I inform you that from Warsaw to Libawa the railway cost us 21 roubles and 21 roubles back. Now I bought you, Marysia, 2 shawls, I gave 13 roubles, and 15 pounds of feathers, I gave 12 roubles, and all this is lying here. Now, dear children, I don't know what I shall do with all this myself, for I have my own shawl and I don't want yours. Write me, dear daughter; perhaps I can send you these shawls by somebody. As to the rest, dear children, forgive me. When I have more money, I will send you at least one half. As to my daughter and your wife, don't be angry, my son-in-law, that you did not take any fortune with her.

If you want to come here, sell her part and take it, for it belongs to her. It is as if she had it in her pocket.[1] . . . .

Now I send you a greeting from myself, your mother, and from Franek, and from your father, my husband. Dear children, I did not marry a young man, only a man in the same age as I am, and he is good for me, and he does not hinder you at all, for he won't waste your fortune; he has enough of his own to live. In another letter I will write you still more about my journey, for it is too much writing at once.

Your truly loving mother,

Franciszka Kozłowska

234   December 24, 1908

Dear Son-in-law: I inform you that we received your letter on December 21, for which we thank you heartily. But instead of being comforted, I was grieved, and I should even prefer if you had not answered me so soon, for I should think her still alive. Why did you send me, dear children, such a letter, at once about money and about my dear dead daughter? Probably you intend to push me alive into the tomb through such writing as you write to me! You write, son-in-law, and you trouble me about sending you at least 100 roubles back. But I thank God that I have anything to put into my pot, for I have wasted everything through your fault. I rented the land, and I live now as I can, poor orphan, upon this world of God. And now, dear children, do you think that I grieve only about your money? Oh no, my children, I grieve because my beloved daughter is dead and the orphans are left. How do they live there, my dear little grandchildren? And I grieve, because Franek will have to go to the army, and you all scattered about the world, away from me, poor orphan. And you cause me still more grief by this bit of paper, asking me to give you this money back. I know that you wasted money on me, but I wasted also everything which I owned upon this journey to you. But I don't deny what you sent me. Only, if you want to have this money, come back to our country, as other people do; you have your parts, sell them and you will have your money. But evidently you want to bury me alive into this holy earth, that I

[1]The journey would cost more than this part would be worth. He had evidently complained that he not only got no dowry with his wife, but that he has expenses on account of the mother-in-law.

may not live any more upon this earth with my beloved daughter [*sic!*]. But why should you, dear son-in-law, persuade me that it is time for me to go into this holy earth? When I shall go to my tomb, you won't even know it.[1] So, my dear son-in-law, don't make me grieve any more, for you made me grieve enough in a single letter.

Dear son-in-law B., I beg you, if it is very hard for you to be there with these children, I beg you, if it is possible, send me one child, so I can educate it. I beg you, dear son-in-law, do as you think the best. And I beg you, dear son-in-law Franuś [pet name], if you could send it, write me in a letter whether you will send it or not, my dear son-in-law!

Dear son-in-law [Janek] and daughter, although you are angry with me about this money, I beg you still, care for these orphans, for you see that they have no mother now. And if it is possible, I beg you, dear daughter, send me one child. I would keep it as long as my eyes shine upon this world. I beg you for it, my dear daughter. Reflect how you should act with regard to my words. May God grant us to live until this. Amen.

[FRANCISZKA]

235   April 18, 1909

And now, dear children, we answer you "In centuries of centuries, Amen." And now we inform you that we received your letter on Good Friday, for which we thank you heartily, for not forgetting us. [Health and wishes.] I am healthy, by the grace of God, only this death of Zosia torments me and gives me no peace. How is she buried there, and why was I not there when she was dying? But, dear daughter and son-in-law, try that at least these orphans get on well, that they don't suffer hunger, for you see that they cannot have a mother any more, only you are their guardians. Care for them, and God and Mother Mary will care for you.

And I ask you, my dear children, how do you live without your sister and my dear daughter, for I think continually about her, day and night. I gave money for recording her, and if God helps me I will

---

[1] All this about being buried, etc., is probably nothing but a rhetorical development of her reproach for the grief her son-in-law has caused by his letter, or it may be an indirect allusion to some phrase in his letter. He may have written, for instance, that she was too old to marry.

give also for a holy mass for repose of her soul.[1]   And I pray for her to God and to our Mother Mary, that God may take her to himself. Pray you also to God for her soul, and God will forgive her certainly.

And now, dear daughter, you mention these feathers, asking me to send them to you.   You see, it is so, dear daughter.   These feathers which I had bought began to be eaten by mites, so I sold a part of them, but if somebody happens to go to America, I will buy some and send them to you.[2]   But if nobody goes, then nothing can be done, and don't be angry with me, dear daughter and son-in-law, for I am not guilty at all.   It is true that it costs you a few roubles, but I have also lost everything which I had.   So don't be angry with me, my dear children, for if I cannot reward you, I will pray to God for your health and success, and God will help you in your work. . . . .

[FRANCISZKA]

And I greet you, dear brother Wincenty.   I cannot give you my hand in this [help you], for I have nothing myself, but you, children, do your best and nourish your uncle as you can.   Dear brother, can you not help yourself in any way?   Come to an understanding with our brother and make some plan, so that it may be well.

You see, dear brother, when you were in good condition, you did not want to know anything about your wife and children, and now you remember them!

236   February 9, 1913

. . . . I received your letter, my dear children [Baranowskis], for which I thank you heartily, for I waited for it with longing.   My dear children, you say that I am angry with you.   Oh no, my dear children, I am not angry with you.   You say that I did not answer your letter.   It is true, my dearest children, that I did not answer you, but why?   You see, it is true that you wished to take me to you, and I was glad because of your wish, but I don't know whether that ticket was bad or those guides.   And so you sent me money and I sold everything, or rather wasted everything [sold too cheap] and

---

[1] The priest has a record of those of his parishoners who have died, and between the sermon and the mass prays for their souls, calling their names.   A mass costs from one to three roubles.   A record is cheaper and less efficient than a mass. Franciszka may have had a mass celebrated, but prefers not to acknowledge that she was in a position to spend that amount.

[2] She used the feathers as part of her dowry.

went. And when I was returned, was it my fault? I wasted your money, and very little of mine was left. When I returned home, I found a desert house. What could I begin then, poor orphan? Should I have called to you, my dear children, and related to you my trouble? But my voice could not have reached you, for you are in a far country, and I was left, an orphan, among waste and troubles, and I had slowly to provide myself once more with the outfit which I had wasted. You were angry with me, dear children, as if I did so intentionally in order to take the money without coming to you. Oh my children, our Lord God is above us, He sees and hears everything. Should I lie?[1] Should I have renounced you and not [wanted] to go to you and not [wanted] to see you? Why, you know that I am left now alone, I have none of you, my dearest children, with me, I am left alone, an orphan, and I can see none of you alive, only I look continually upon these dead photographs. But you, dear daughter, surely you forgot me in truth, since you let a year pass without writing to me, and you forgot when I asked you for the photograph of that orphan after [left by] Zosia. You sent one to the shoemaker's wife and you did not even mention me. I asked the shoemaker's wife for this photograph, but she did not wish to give it to me. . . . . Well, and now, dear daughter, you remembered that you have still a mother somewhere in the world, and you write, curious how I live here and how I succeed! . . . .

And now, dear daughter and son-in-law, please don't be angry about that which I shall ask for, and send me a photograph of these orphans; let me see them once more at least.

Now I send an image and a toy for my granddaughter. . . . .

[FRANCISZKA]

237   [November 4, 1906]

I write to you both, my dear goddaughter, I, your godmother Szczep[ańska], and I wish you every good and whatever you want from our Lord God, the best. I thank you for not forgetting about

---

[1] This appeal to God is curious, for a peasant never makes a false oath, unless totally demoralized. But an oath with mental reservation is frequent. In this case the oath does not refer to anything in particular, unless to the following phrase, and as she probably really wanted to see her children, it is in so far true. It may be also that in repeating all her lies she has finally half-forgotten her real intentions, which she had perhaps also never very explicitly stated to herself.

me, so I send you a gift.   These are those scapularies from Częstochowa, and in this one scapulary with the cross there is sewed up a
[part of the] veil of God's Mother of Częstochowa.   This is important.
I send you a blessing for your whole life.   May God bless you, and
God's Mother.   And my daughter Helcia is very glad that you don't
forget her. . . . .
                                                        Szczep[AŃSKA]

238   [December 28, 1908]

   And now I, dear daughter, greet you, I, your godmother, greet
you, Mania!   Dear daughter, I write you about this: Why did you
cause such costs for your mother that she might go to you, to America!
Going to this America, your mother sold the forest and rented the
land, and all the money which she had was wasted in journeying.
She went twice to Ostrołęka; no little money was spent; twice to
Warsaw on account of her eyes.   Then at last they went to Libawa
and there they remained for some time, and the rest of their money
was spent on their living, for the ship-tickets were bad, and they had
to return home.   Your mother had sold everything, she had sold
even her best petticoat for this journey, and when she came back,
if Pl[ata] had not married her, I don't know how she would live, for
she had not a grosz left.   Now, you wrote that Zosia is no longer
alive, and I am also sad, and what do you think about your own
mother?   And you make her grieve still more about this money.
You have no idea what a sad Christmas your mother had this year,
for she is grieved because of the death of her beloved daughter.   And
this field which your mother rented is still sown by strange people,
until the years are ended [the renting-term], and your mother, as
you know, is fed by Pl[ata] until [the end of] this time.   And now,
dear daughter Mania, don't be offended at my writing it to you, but
your mother is almost senseless, and she continually cries and complains, what a bad fortune befell her upon this world.

   I, who love you, my daughter,   Maryanna Szczepańska

   Dear [god]daughter, I have learned to know your mother now.
If she could take her heart out, she would give it to you, but she
cannot take it out and what will she do with her misery?   And now
I bid you all goodbye.   May God grant it.   Amen.[1]

   [1] The letter is evidently written under the influence of Kozłowska, and is
perhaps instigated by her.

239   October 24, 1907

DEAR SISTER AND BROTHER-IN-LAW: I send you holy images.
. . . . Dear sister and brother-in-law, you don't believe us that we
wanted to go to America; but . . . . I, your brother, will draw my
lot [be called to military service] in two years after next spring,
so . . . . I should be glad to see all of you at once. . . . . Dear
brother-in-law, I am very much grieved that you say that you will
tear all the hair from your head [from despair]. Dear brother-in-law,
it is not the fault of my sister. . . . .

FRANEK KOZŁOWSKI

240   [April 18, 1909]

And now I, Franciszek [Franek], thank you, dear brother-in-law
and sister, for at least not forgetting me, for my brother dear [irony]
does not write me a single word. He is angry with me, I don't know
what for. Although we ought to love each other, for we are only two
and I must go to the army instead of him, he does not care for me.
Such a good brother, loving his brother! It is bitter and hard for
me to remember such a brother! What is my fault toward him?
O God, be merciful to us, your sinners![1]

And now, dear brother-in-law and sister, I go to Prussia, so please
write me a letter there. I will send you my address. I was in Częstochowa, but I did not expect that a letter from you, dear sister, would
come, or else I should have brought a greater token. Now I send you
only scapularies of Mary the Virgin, already consecrated, ready to
be put around the neck. . . . .

[FRANEK]

241   June 11, 1911

. . . . DEAR SISTER AND BROTHER-IN-LAW: [Complains about
military service.] May never any good man serve in the army, for
here everybody must be a slave and is not free, as at home. And now
I ask you, my dear sister Mania and brother-in-law, how do you
succeed in that America, whether well or poorly. Write me please,
dear sister, how are these orphans kept after Zosia['s death], ... for

---

[1] A strange phrase for a young boy; a typical phrase for an old woman. The
style of the whole letter is clearly an imitation of the mother's style.

I am very curious [interested].   And answer me, whether our brother-in-law B. married [a second time] or not.   [Describes military life.]

And now, dear Mania and brother-in-law, I beg you write a letter to our sorrowful dear mother, and don't be angry with mother, for she is without guilt toward you, and sinful before God alone.[1]   Dear Mania and brother-in-law, you are probably angry since the time when you wanted to take her to America.   But old mother then wanted to go to you as to God (without comparing it),[2] and she rejoiced that in her old years she was to see her children.   But what could she do when she was unable to go to you?   And now, dear sister Mania and brother-in-law, you are angry with your sorrowful and grieved mother, while perhaps you won't see her any more unless in the next world.   And with this anger you will go into the next world, and so we shall look upon one another—and what will God say to this? How shall we justify ourselves?   Dear sister and brother-in-law, mother writes to me always and says that she has no letter from you, and she always weeps in her letter, so it is not pleasant for me either, for she is my mother and yours. . . . . If you saw our mother, you would never recognize her, how she is now without children, for always something new happens [some new trouble].

Franek Kozłowski

242   [July 12, 1907]

I, Józef Pl[ata], wish to take your dear mother for my wife. Answer as soon as possible whether you will take her or whether you tell her to marry me.   I would give my life for her.   I have nothing more to write, only I send a low bow to you all, to the whole family.[3]

Your well-wishing

Józef Pl[ata]

---

[1] Not to be taken as an admission of any particular sin, but only as the application of the general principle of Christian humility that all men are sinners before God.

[2] The restriction is made because a real comparison would be a sin; the restriction characterizes it as a simple metaphor.

[3] The man simply asks for permission to marry their mother.   This indicates once more the degree to which the family is felt as a reality, and the marriage of any member—father or mother, brother or sister, son or daughter—as affecting immediately this reality, is a familial as well as an individual matter.

243   [April 18, 1909]

And now I, your father, salute you, together with your mother and my son, and we wish you every good, whatever you want for yourself from God. We greet [bless] also those little orphans. May God keep them in His holiest guardianship. And [if] perhaps anything in this letter displeases you, then please forgive, for your mother was terribly grieved. . . . .

[JÓZEF PLATA]

244   March 27, 1912

. . . . DEAR BROTHER-IN-LAW AND DEAR SISTER: It is very painful for me that I cannot see my family, and don't even receive a bit of paper that I might at least by letter speak with you. But God reward you even for this bit of paper which you send to mother, even this rejoices me. I should like to see my family there in America, but as I have no money I can do nothing, and there is nobody to help me. If you put together $10 each you could take me to you. I don't want the wrong of anybody, and would give it back with thanks, if only God grants me health. For when you sent the ship-ticket for mother and for Franek, I told mother as a joke: "Take me with you to America, it will be more pleasant to go together." I had then much running to do and many expenses to bear, for I had to go 3 times to Ostrołęka to take an application for a passport, and twice to Warsaw. At last we three went and I had a ship-ticket, bought from the agent in Warsaw for money, and we went to Libawa. In the office in Libawa they refused to accept these tickets which you sent, and besides my ticket they wanted 21 roubles for a passport. I begged mother to lend me this money since I had had already so many expenses. But she refused to help me; she said, "I cannot." Then I said, "Send Franek instead of me, he will take these tickets with him and will settle the matter by words, and they [in America] won't lose so much." But mother answered, "I am not going and neither of you is going either," and I had to come back. As to this, what mother said, that "The shoemaker drags me about courts," I did not intend lawsuits as other people do, but I had to have a guardianship established, i.e., a family council. For mother received 2 morgs of forest, and wasted it half in vain. What was worth 5 roubles, she sold for 2, while now she must almost buy fuel herself. When I went once to the forest and said, "Why do you waste this timber?" they abused me, she and her son, and denied that there was anything to which I had any right. So I was obliged to have a guardianship established, because Franek was a minor and mother took rather too much liberty. And excuse me, don't be angry with me, dear sister and brother-in-law, for I tell the truth always into one's eyes, not behind one's eyes. For so many years since you have been in America I have never had even a small sheet from you, except now this address, for which may God reward you. I should not go to America, except for my children. My daughter Mania can marry. She is 20 years old. My son Władzio is 16 years old, Zygmunt 6 years, Genia 4 years, and I am very sad that I cannot help them, for in our country there is no work and the expenses are big. What I earn is only enough for living, and when we have to pay the rent we must go hungry. If you could draw me to you I don't know how I could reward you. [I should be so grateful.]

ANTONI HERM[ANOWICZ]

245   May 29, 1912

. . . . DEAR SISTER AND BROTHER-IN-LAW: . . . . As to the ship-ticket which I mentioned, I did not count on you alone, brother-in-law. For there are three of you. I don't count B., for he is like a strange man.[1] I am not acquainted with you, so I did not look [to you alone]. I beg your pardon politely for importuning you. For I believe everything you wrote about Antoni, as if I were there myself. You tell me to borrow 140 roubles, but it is not so easy, for here people lend only to a man who has something to look upon [some property]. Meanwhile, I live only from these five fingers; I have nothing but what I earn. Even so our beloved [="loving," ironical] mother, whenever she sees anything new of clothes upon us, wonders whence we get money for it. Instead of being glad that we manage to dress ourselves as we can, she is angry with us.[2] How can I expect strange people to help us, when our own mother begrudges us a piece of bread? If I had wanted absolutely to be in America, I should have gone about 6 years ago when I went to Libawa with Franek and with

---

[1] The gradual incorporation of the brother-in-law in the family is interrupted by the death of his wife, and he becomes a "stranger."

[2] Probably not envy, but an expression of Kozłowska's general disposition to keep others down.

mother. Then I had all my documents, and I begged mother to help me a little, but she did not want to. I said, "Then send Franek instead of me." But mother said, "I don't go and you shall not go either." And so mothers act toward their own children! Because she ruined herself, she wanted to ruin her children. But she returned to her own house, while I returned like the farmer whose buildings are all burned and who is left without a roof above his head. The few roubles which I had, I lost them for mother's sake, and later I was obliged to earn and economize again. And excuse me for writing this, for I tell the truth. As I believe you, so do you believe me, please. And now mother is angry for your not having sent money for Franek when he was going to the army. . . . . Antoś [her son] sent her 10 roubles, and now Antoni [her brother] sent also 10 roubles, but all this is not enough for them. . . . .

ANTONI HERM—

JACKOWSKI SERIES

These are letters from a plain Galician peasant family. The oldest son, Jan, went, probably very early, to Germany and from there came to America and settled in Chicago. The second son, Stanisław, was with him, and then alone, in Germany, but returned to Austria for his military service. The third son, Franek, is young and stays at home.

The quarrels alluded to in the beginning of the correspondence have their source in economic matters. The conditions must be very bad in Wietrzychowice upon a small piece of land. Jan, who does not seem to be of a generous disposition, is irritated by the demands for money, especially as he suspects that Stanisław has drawn as much money as possible from the parents during his military service, and that he has tried to win the favor of the parents and assure for himself the better share of the inheritance after his return from the army. In addition, Stanisław has evidently been a rather light-headed boy, without much force or practicality, and Jan converts some of his general irritation into personal criticism of his younger brother.

On the other hand, the efforts of Stanisław to introduce harmony into the family are interesting. It frequently happens, as in this case, that when the family begins to dissolve one member holds it together more or less. In the Osiński series the mother does it successfully. In the Terlecki series (below) the mother tries to do it, but without success.

THE FAMILY JACKOWSKI

Jackowski, a farmer
Franciszka, his wife
Jan ⎫
Stanisław ⎬ his sons
Franek ⎭
Marysia, his daughter
Jasiek, a cousin
"The aunt," his mother

Two more aunts and two cousins.

246–67, TO JAN JACKOWSKI, IN AMERICA, FROM FAMILY-MEMBERS, IN POLAND

246   TRAWNIK, August 11, 1909

DEAR BROTHER: A long time has passed since we saw each other and a (relatively) longer time since we wrote. But whose fault is it? Surely not mine. . . . .

On Christmas I came home [from the army] for a ten days' leave, and precisely then we received your letter. Evidently if they had known what was written there, they would certainly not have read that letter. Seeing what was going on, I went into the field, for tears stood in my eyes. Dear brother, what I did, I know it well enough myself, and what you do and will do, you must know it the best yourself, and it concerns nobody else at all. Now, dear brother, you sent a little money home. Don't think that I shall take it. They won't ever give it to me. The second year of my service approaches its end, and during this time they sent me once last year 3 crowns, for which I did not ask. Now, when I went from the Servian frontier, we drank merrily, because we returned in good health from those troubles during the winter in Bosnia. Somebody probably made a mistake and reached in my pocket instead of his own, or I simply lost [my money] somewhere. Then I asked for 4 crowns and they sent me them [from home]. I think it was not much during 2 years.

Now, dear brother, if you have time and wish, please write me a few words and inform me why you don't write home. Perhaps you are angry because I shall return home after my military service [and take over the farm]? Well, don't think it, for I won't be at home, I shall willingly yield to everybody.   The world is wide and high, one can quietly wander through it.   Or perhaps something else happened between you and the home? . . . .

Stanisław J.

247   September 18, 1909

Dear Brother: I received your letter and also a dollar in it, for which I thank you heartily.   Now, dear brother, I asked you why you do not write home, and you answer me that it is not my affair. I confess that it concerns me very little, and I must write also that the other matter was my affair, not yours.   I should not have gone so soon to the army or home, but I had to, for they caught me.   Were it not for this, perhaps we should be now together.   And if you are taken to the army, you cannot hope that you will be set free for a day or half a day.   With me it was the same; they took me and held me until Christmas.   And if my parents came to me at once in the same week, I cannot help it, and it was not my fault.

Now, secondly, when they were with me, I did not boast to them that I had much money and that I knew 4 languages.   They asked me, whether I had money, and I said that I was not without a cent.   It seems to me that it was not a lie.   Later, when they were leaving me, they told me not to do any silly thing, at least in the army [probably meaning that he did silly things before], and to keep well.   I said that nothing bad could happen to me in the army, and I said that I knew German, so it would be always easier for me than for a boy who does not know it and comes immediately from his village.   In these things which I told them there was no lie even for a heller.   But as to what they wrote you, I am not the Holy Spirit that I can know everything, whether they wrote the truth or added something more.   If you wrote in anger, dear brother, that I gave my money to somebody to keep, it was not so much anger as scorn [you said it ironically].

Dear brother, you remind me also of this fault, that though I had not seen my parents for 8 years, I should not have allowed them to come and visit me before I went to them.[1]   But you are mistaken, for if you were in America for 10 years and appointed the day on which you would visit them, and if you came to the frontier and they [the Austrians] caught you, you could offer them thousands, they wouldn't

---

[1] It is not easy to understand the basis of Jan's reproach, but (cf. the following note).

let you go until your time came. Just so it was with me, dear brother.
I was taken not even at the frontier, but in Bremerhafen. From there
they brought me to Eger and thence to Tarnów. What could I do?
I only looked to see that none of my acquaintances saw me, for he
would have thought I had killed or robbed someone.

Now, dear brother, you write me that you have experienced many
lies from me. I am curious how you did it, since we have not written
to each other. You remind me of Plagwitz, where I worked when
14 years old. But now I am a grown-up man and I have different
privileges [*sic?* Probably different character and habits]. What I
said and did at 14, I surely would not do now, at 22.

Dear brother, you write about Jasiek and you say that you cannot
believe that I had no opportunity to write to him. If I had had his
address, surely I would have written. I was at home, and our aunt
asked me to write a letter to Jasiek, but a moment after she went to
Sowa and wrote from there. What can I do if they quarrel between
themselves? Surely it is not my fault.

Dear brother, you write me that in my life you see a whole series
of lies. This only interests me—whence do they come, whether
from me or from somebody else? I did not write to anybody except
3 letters to Jasiek. So you must write me whence these lies come.

Dear brother, you write me that I give you admonitions. These
are not admonitions at all [when I say] that you left nothing [no
money of your own at home?], for I left still less. You could care
only if I took anything from home, but I wrote you clearly that I
take no money from home.[1]

Dear brother, you write me that the world is wider before you. I
believe you, but not strongly. Though I am a slave and servant

---

[1] From the whole letter it is evident that Jan, having an unreasoned grudge
against Stanisław, probably connected with the fact that the latter is nearer home
and more able to control their parents, tries to find some rational cause of his own
feelings, and thus invents various pretexts to explain his animosity. · The case is
perfectly typical for a peasant. The powerful background of traditional attitudes
gives rise to a behavior whose nature and reason are a puzzle to the subject himself.
The latter, when asked for explanation, gives imaginary conscious reasons, more
or less inadequate, depending upon the degree of his intelligence. And a curious
evolution also occurs; the imaginary reason, through the power of expression,
becomes more or less a real reason for the future—a part of the subconscious feeling
flows through this new channel. This factor enters into the evolution of the
peasant's attitude toward the manor-owner, the Jew, the government, and into
many religious and familial attitudes.

of the emperor, yet you are also a slave, a servant of somebody else. Perhaps the same happiness awaits you also—which I don't wish you—that you will be in the same situation as I am, and I in the same as you are. So we cannot speak much about it.

Now, dear brother, I inform you that I am a corporal. I succeed well enough, I can say nothing against it, for in the army it cannot be better. In a few months this slavery will come to an end. Next month I will send you my photograph and I beg you to send me yours, since we have not seen each other for so long a time. Dear brother, let us forget what was before, and perhaps our luck will serve us better in the future. . . . .

STANISŁAW J.

248   October 22, 1909

DEAR BROTHER: I received your photograph, for which I thank you heartily and which rejoiced me very much. Now, dear brother, I ask about your dear health and success. For myself, thanks to our Lord God, I am healthy and my success is good enough; a better one cannot be found in the army. Now, on October 18, I became a *Zugsführer* [sergeant] and I am with the recruits. Dear brother, you have sent me your photograph and probably you await mine, so it will come soon after this letter. You must pardon me, but I don't feel at every moment equally strong in my pocket. . . . . Now, dear brother, here in Bosnia there is no news to write. If I were in our country, I should have more to write you, for there I should sooner meet somebody and talk, while here are only strangers. . . . . Now I ask you, dear brother, what is the news in America, who gets married or will marry.

I greet you kindly and heartily, until I see you again. May God grant it. Amen.

Your loving brother,

STANISŁAW J.

249   December 24, 1909

DEAR BROTHER: In my first words I inform you that I received your letter and a dollar in it, for which I thank you heartily.

Dear brother, you write that they did not inform you by telegram about our father's death. I am quite stupid [I don't understand] myself. When our sister died, I was then in Tarnów, and they wrote

me a card which came on the day of the funeral.   I had then no reason
to go, since the funeral was over.   Now, when our father died I
received a letter from home 4 days after the funeral.   He died on Saturday, and on Thursday I received the news, and I wrote you at once.

Dear brother, I did not write up to the present for I thought . . . .
that I should be transferred to Tarnów and thence I should go on a
leave. . . . . I wrote home asking mother to send a petition to the
regiment that they might transfer me to Tarnów.   But mother went
to ask the post official and teacher for advice, and they told her that
it was impossible, for everybody would like to serve in Tarnów.   She
answered me that it was not worth writing.   Only when I sent her a
second letter, she went and sent the petition, and probably about
January 1, I shall be transferred, and if she had written at once, I
should be at home for Christmas.   Now, dear brother, you write that
it would be good for me to get free for a month from my service, to
sit in warmth behind the stove and to care for my comfort.[1]   Dear
brother, if you think what the service is here in Bosnia!   For two years
to go nowhere, only to sit within the walls of the barracks and to
think about your future lot, this would worry anybody. . . . .

Now, dear brother!   You had feeling and love for our father,
everybody can say it boldly, and I thank you with my heart and
soul [for your expression of it?].   But this is bad, that mother does
not do anything with her own head, but always listens to other people,
and is worse off.

Now, as to the funeral, I don't know myself how it was, but when
I go home, I will describe to you everything. . . . .

STANISŁAW J.

250   February 9, 1910

DEAR BROTHER: [Generalities about health and success; was
not transferred to Tarnów.]   Now, dear brother, I inform you that
my military service is slowly approaching its end.   Now my thoughts
are hesitating what to do after the military service.   I wish to ask to
be accepted as a constable.   What do you say to it?   At home we
have not enough to live without trouble and quietly, and if I wanted
to remain in the country I should have necessarily to get married,
and then to work for the wife and children.   Moreover, if God sends

[1] Probably not irony on the part of Jan, but a momentary softening after
the death of the father.

some illness or some misfortune, it would finally be necessary perhaps to take a bag and a stick and to go begging about villages.[1] Dear brother, I don't know your ideas, for you can remain in America as long as you like it, and when you come back, the military service won't let you escape, but I have served 3 years, and [formerly] I have wandered enough about that Germany, and I have experienced enough of good and evil. But I don't know how it is in America. If I am not accepted as a constable, nothing will be left for me except to go to you. Dear brother, if you receive this letter, please describe to me your condition. What is the news with Jasiek? I sent him a photograph, but I had no answer. . . . .

STANISŁAW J.

[Letter of April 1, 1910, asks for a little money to buy clothes when he leaves the army. States that he has not received more than 10 gulden from home during more than 30 months.]

251　　　　　　　　　　　　　　　　　　　　　　　　　June 9, 1910

DEAR BROTHER: In my first words I thank you heartily for your letter and for $10.00 which I received from you. . . . . My success is good enough, only I am bored; these days go so slowly in the last year. . . . .

Dear brother, I received also letters from home but they don't rejoice me at all, for mother is sick. She wrote me a letter that during the whole month of May she was in bed. Something crept into her arm and she cannot move it. She asked me to write her, when I received your letter, what is going on with you, for she has had no letter from you at all. Dear brother, I don't understand all this. If God allows me to end my service happily and if I go home, I will describe everything in detail. Now I don't even know who is my guardian, although we don't need him now any more. I cannot remain at home after my military service, for what should I have of it? If I wished to remain at home I should have to marry, and it looks silly to keep a wife upon a morg of land and to work like a horse in a threshing-machine. . . . .

STANISŁAW J.

---

[1] A rather unexpected standpoint from a peasant. Cf. the attitude of Aleksander (Osiński series), who dreams of nothing but coming back, settling upon the farm and marrying. Perhaps the reason in the case of Stanisław is to be found in his wandering for eight years in Germany.

252

DEAR BROTHER: . . . . I inform you that my clothes are ready and my shoes also; I wait only for the maneuvers, which will be from August 14 until September 10. We don't know yet when we shall go home. . . . .

As to you, dear brother, mother complains that you wrote her not to write to you any more. Secondly, somebody informed them that you will marry a girl who has [only her] ten fingers, and that everybody laughs at you. As to me, I don't believe it, perhaps somebody said or wrote it in joke, and they believe it.

Now, dear brother, they have very good crops, only they cannot manage alone, and there is lack of people in the village [because of emigration]. When I go there now, I must look well at everything, and go further. Dear brother, in ending these few words I greet you kindly and heartily, and don't be angry with me about what I write, for it does not come from me, but from home. . . . .

STANISŁAW J.

September 1, 1910

DEAR BROTHER: I thank you heartily for your letter and the dollar. . . . . On October 10 I am going home. . . . . The maneuvers were rather short, but helped us enough [tired us]. Now we rest after all this.

I wrote home what they merited. I hope that they won't write such slandering any more [about you]. I don't marvel they did, for you know how people are in the country, particularly in our village. If somebody succeeds well, the others' eyes are aching, and if they cannot annoy him in any other way they talk at least. As to myself, I owe [have wronged] no one either, but their eyes ache because I am a sergeant, so they say in the village that when I came to Tarnów my uniform was full of holes and patches, and that the better guests were ashamed to go with me to the town. But I laugh at them all. Let them talk further. If God grants it, everything will go well. . . . .

STANISŁAW J.

254   WIETRZYCHOWICE, October 21, 1910

DEAR SON AND BROTHER: In my first words: "Praised be Jesus Christus" [etc.].

Dear brother, I inform you that I came home on the 20th in the evening and I am very glad that this military service is ended at last. As to our home, dear brother, I found everything in health and in very good order. Mother is healthy, Franek also, and Marysia keeps well enough.

Dear son and brother, we inform you that up to the present everything is in the same state as it was when our deceased father left it. Here everybody is against us, everybody is envious, one does not yield to another even for a *grajcar* [kreuzer]. Father had been sick for 2 years; an abcess grew on his stomach. He was more than once consulting the doctors, and nobody could help him, only everybody advised him to go to Cracow to a hospital. But father would not agree to it, saying that he preferred to finish his life at home, with his own people, not among strangers and in another city. In the last time he could eat nothing, for it [the illness] did not allow him. At the most he took a glass of wine or of milk every hour, and it threw out of him even this.[1] For some months mother could not leave him for a moment, but sat with him day and night. And when father was giving his spirit to God, he explained to mother all his arrangements, how mother ought to do in order that everything might remain as he left it. Only, dear son, all the relatives and friends forgot about your father, and in the last moment instead of going to the funeral some of them went with oxen to the fair. For example, your aunt from the other house sent Franek [her son] to the fair with a Jew, and when your aunt from Szymonowice mentioned it to her she abused her and said that she [the aunt from S.] had come to the funeral only to eat and to drink. So you can imagine how all this went on. Dear brother, when they related all this to me, tears stood in my eyes. And not only at home, but also in the village I have been told the same.[2]

---

[1] Speaking of sickness as of some impersonal "it" is a vestige of the old magical system in which "it" meant "the evil," the noxious principle.

[2] The greatest disrespect which can be shown a family is lack of eagerness in assisting at the funeral of one of its members. It shows that the social standing of the family must be very low indeed. In this case there were no grown-up sons at home. The son in America sent no money; the one in the army had been away from home a long time and, as a soldier, did not count; the father had been sick for two years. These factors had lowered the standing of the family.

Now, dear brother, I inform you that Nog. from Siedliszowice came here to us and wanted mother to make a marriage-festival, saying that you had married her sister there in America. It is her luck that I was not at home; I would have given her a festival which she would have remembered for a long time. Here in Wietrzychowice they fight among themselves like dogs and cats.

Dear brother, when you receive this letter, please describe everything that is news there with you. Mother is old already. She cannot work as she did before, for she has not strength enough. I think it would be the best for her to sell [or rent ?] the field at auction, and to leave the house and a bit of garden. She could keep a pig and go about the house [keep order], and we could help her a little. When I came home, I pitied her so much that I wept like a child when she told me all this.

Dear brother, I have sent a petition to the constable's department. If I learn that they will accept me, I will remain here, but if not, I will go to you. I will write you later about it.

Now, dear brother, there is work enough. . . . . Times are hard, mother has paid 24 renskis of taxes, and the cattle are sick. Nothing can be sold. Whoever has anything cannot sell it. . . . .

Now, dear brother, finishing these few words, I beg you to write your thoughts, for mother cannot do otherwise. She has worked enough, let her have at least in her old years a few days of rest. I have talked already with mother and she agrees. She wants to keep it for a year still, for she has everything sown. Dear brother, we must try that everything may be well. It won't cost us much, and at least mother will have rest and comfort in her old years. Although we have lost our father, yet our mother lives and we can be proud that she is so good that another could be found with difficulty in the village. She does not ask a cent from anybody and she won't waste her own money on trifles, as others do, for she wants to leave a remembrance [inheritance] to her children after her death.

[STANISŁAW J.]

255 Lwów, March 5, 1911

DEAR BROTHER: [Health and success.] As you know already, I am in Lwów [Lemberg] in a constable school for 5 months, i.e., up to the 1st of August. If I hold out I shall go to a post in August, and if not I must seek for some other bread. . . . . If our Lord God allows, it will go perhaps well, for here discipline is in the first place. As to the school, I don't need to speak. Whether there is holiday or Sunday, you must always look into the books, and even at night.

[Misery at home and in the country; taxes heavy; Franek not diligent or steady.] Now, dear brother, I will mention further the letter which mother wrote to you asking for a few hellers. You got a little angry, but what can be done? When we are in need we look for any means by which we can get something. It was the same here. I did not realize it myself before I left home, but when I came home and mother showed me the accounts, what she spent after father's death, I was astonished; I should never have believed it. But never mind. At last it happened that there was not a heller at home. Only then this letter was written. But since you did not want to send anything, nobody can tear the money away from you. For this money which you sent for *medicine* for father lies in the bank. The last decision of father was, not to touch it. For if they wrote you before to send them some and you did not do it, it was over. It came too late and father thanked for it [refused it]. Now you wrote also that you had worked enough for us, that you must think about yourself. It is all right, but there has not been so very much of it. You earned some money in Prussia, our parents added some of their own and bought a piece of land for it, which you have still. You ought not to make reproaches to mother, for it is not proper. Mother wept more than once and said if you had a little remembrance, at least about our father, you would send at least once in a year [money] for a mass for father. Don't think that I want to teach you. I don't do it ever. But I can write what I hear, for I don't know what is the opinion of anybody [how others look at the question, i.e., I let everyone have his own opinion].

[STANISŁAW]

256   May 5, 1911

DEAR BROTHER: . . . . I am curious why do you not answer me. I wrote first a card, then a letter, and I received no answer; I don't know the cause. Certainly my last letter offended you, for there was nothing else between us. I won't hide [retract] what I wrote you. I wrote what mother told me. If you got angry, it is not my fault. There was surely nothing so disagreeable as to bring anger between us. You are a grown-up man and you can manage according to your own ideas. Up to the present nobody has any right to dispose of others; everybody is his own lord. Now I am a free citizen of the Austrian state; I can do what I like. I can take at any moment what I received after the death of my father, and do with it what pleases me, for in the will it is clearly said that when we become 24 years of age mother has to give each what belongs to him, and each can do according to his will.

I was, it is true, for a few weeks at home and I know very well how everything is going on. Nothing can be said against what is at home. Everything is in the greatest order. But as there is nobody to work at home, I told mother to rent [?] the field, so that only a garden would remain with her; then she would not have to work so hard in her old years. She first asked you for advice, whether you would agree. You answered that you agreed, but as everything was sown she wants to harvest the crops this year and to rent not until the autumn. I don't know yet how she will do. I could take my part now, but what do I care for it? As long as mother lives let it remain with her, let her do with it what pleases her. Meanwhile I can do without it, and later in a year, when I become a real constable and keep [the place], I shall have a nice living. The school is rather hard and there is little time, but nothing can be done, as man can and must get accustomed to everything. And so, dear brother, don't be angry, for we are only three and we don't know what yet awaits us in this life. I say only this, that only concord will bring good results and fruits among us.

[STANISŁAW]

257 June 29, 1911

DEAR BROTHER: I am astonished at your silence. Why have I had no answer from you for so long a time? I cannot imagine it. Four months have passed since I left my home, and as soon as I came to Lwów I wrote you first a card, then a letter, and I received no answer at all. But I hope that this silence between us will not remain. What is my guilt toward you? Have I done you any wrong? Certainly not I. When I wrote you the letter from home, I did not write from myself, but I wrote what mother asked me to. And you know certainly mother as well [as I do], so you should not be angry, but do as you please, for today it is permitted to everybody.

As to myself, I cannot say anything now. On the one hand, when I consider everything, it seems painful and I regret a little having become a constable, but on the other hand, if I reflect, everything ceases and some spark of hope rejoices me. If I remain, I shall have a piece of bread, but earned with difficulty, not on account of heavy labor, but because every inconsiderate step leads the constable to the garrison [military prison], and at last he may be dismissed and go whence he came. In another regard, he is always exposed to danger of life and health. And in the third place, anybody who wants to serve as constable to the end must be deaf, dumb, and blind. Only such a man is a good constable. There are orders enough, and every order must be well executed, and everybody wants to say [to order] something, so nothing remains except to keep your mouth shut and to work. [Describes the school.]

Now, dear brother, if you receive this letter, I beg you be so kind and if you can, send me a few kronen, for after the end of this month I need them very much. I don't know where to turn to get some money, and it is not suitable to go to my post without a kreuzer. I hope, dear brother, that you won't refuse me, and I will also try to requite you later on. You have nothing to fear, for I won't deny any heller which I received from you. . . . .

STANISŁAW J.

258 NADWORNA, October 5 [1911]

DEAR BROTHER: . . . . Why do you not answer me? Don't mind if I wrote to you for money. It was in your hands, you could [have sent it] but you didn't have to. It is your business. I wrote, because I needed it. I did not receive it, so I must get on without it. Don't mind it at all, for if you had sent it I should have paid it back sooner or later. . . . . Don't wonder that I wrote asking for money, for I had just left the school. . . . . So don't be angry, dear brother, only answer me as soon as you receive this letter, and if you have a photograph, send it, for I have left the other at home. Mother asked me to leave it and I could not refuse. . . . .

STANISŁAW J.

259 BEDNARÓW, July 20, 1913

DEAR BROTHER AND SISTER-IN-LAW: I send you hearty thanks for your letter and photograph. . . . . I have had no news from home, although I wrote a letter and a card. Surely they are angry. With them anger is not very difficult. I expect a letter now or later, then I will inform you in another letter what they write about your marriage. As to Stolarz, we don't write, for we are angry with each other ever since my military service. Perhaps he is right and perhaps I am. I won't judge him; let somebody else judge.

You ask in your letter, dear brother, about my position, and in what a condition I am here. [Describes his condition, and politics.]

STANISŁAW J.

260   May 5, of the year of God 1910

First of all we write to you and we speak to you these words: "Praised be Jesus Christus." We hope that you will answer us: "In centuries of centuries. Amen." . . . .

[Health; who was called to the army.] Now, dear son, don't hope for any money from us, for, as you know, your father has been sick for a long time and whatever money there was, it is spent, some on doctors, and then when he died the funeral cost us 50 renskis [100 crowns]. And now, after father's death we made the division [of the inheritance]. We were 5 times in Żabno with the assessors and the guardians, and then we spent also money enough, for we had to give them to eat and to drink. We wrote to Jasiek that he might send us his part [of the expenses], but he answered us so, that it would be easier for him to resign his part of inheritance than to pay his part of the expenses. So I, your poor mother, must pay for everything. I got sick and was sick. And now we do what we can do alone, and we shall learn what we cannot do yet. We expected you to come at least for harvest-time. He [Stanisław] cannot come, for we received a letter from Bosnia that he must serve there up to the end. . . . .

FRANCISZKA J.

261   May 5, 1912

DEAR SON: . . . . [Letter received; health.] There is no news in Wietrzychowice. When there is any, we shall write you. Now a church will be built in W. Now you write us to give the money rather to the poor [beggars] than for a mass. But if you give to the poor [beggar] a few cents or bread, he goes to the Jew and gets so drunk that he lies under a hedge.   So it is better to give for a mass than to the poor. . . . .[1]

Franciszka J.

262   July 4, 1912

Dear Son and Brother: We received your letter and $5.00 for which we thank you. Now, dear brother, you ask about the crops. [Hail ruined the crops.]

Now for these dollars we thank you heartily, for we need them like eyes in the head. Now black pox reigns in our country; it is still worse than cholera. The doctors come and inoculate everybody trying to save them from it. And if anybody dies it is forbidden [to take him] to the church, only directly to the cemetery, and they don't allow him dressed, except in a shroud.

Now, dear son and brother, there is no other news in the village except these two misfortunes. Now there will be calmness for there will be nothing to harvest and nothing to thresh, and at last there will be nothing to eat, except what one buys, if he has money.[2] Now we greet you innumerable times, hoping to see you again. Amen.

[Franciszka J.]

[1] The son in America has evidently developed the idea that giving money for religious purposes is wasting it and that it would be better to honor his father's memory by using the corresponding sum on philanthropy. But the peasant knows no philanthropic ends except helping the beggar. Assistance given to a neighbor or to a family member does not come under the head of philanthropy, but of mutual help. But even the helping of beggars is not a purely philanthropic, but a half-religious act, not only because it is ordered by religion, but because the beggar is bound to say prayers for the giver. In fact, the beggar has somewhat a religious function. (Cf. Wróblewski series, No. 31, note.) If therefore Franciszka explains that it is not well to give money to beggars, the background of her attitude is not merely the feeling that the money is wasted unproductively, but also that the beggars are unworthy of their religious function, and that their prayers, profaned by their going to a Jew, getting drunk, and lying under a hedge, would be less efficient religiously than a mass. For her it is a matter of comparison of homogeneous things, not of heterogeneous, as for her son. This peculiarity of the peasant life—the lack of a purely philanthropic attitude—explains to a great extent the mistrust which the peasant shows toward all philanthropic institutions, organized by the higher classes, unless these are based upon religion. The latter exception shows that the origin of the mistrust does not lie in the general hostility toward the higher classes. Cf. No. 31, note.

[2] The curious feature in this letter is what the Germans call *Galgenhumor*. It is often found in the peasant songs and stories.

263   October 8, 1912

. . . . Dear Son and Brother: [Letter received; health and success.] Now in the village there is no news, for nobody got married. Now we have had rains for 2 months and nothing can be done. Now, dear son, you write about marrying. Well, you can marry, only you must know whom you marry. And now consider that she may be an honest girl, who would respect you and would not throw money away for [just] anything. Now consider that she may have there something [some money], or at least that she may be of an orderly [good] family. Now from Wietrzychowice there is no orderly girl [in America]. Now take care of yourself, for afterward it will be too late. You know that you get married neither for a year nor for two, but for your whole life. Now, when you marry, may our Lord Jesus also bless you for the wedding. And now I, your mother, bless you and wish you good luck in everything. Now there is nothing new or interesting; if there is anything, we will write you. Now we greet you . . . . and we bless you once more in order that you may marry the best possible.

[Franciszka]

264   May 5, 1913

Dear Son and Brother: We received your letter from which we learned about your health and success and marriage. Now we are very much satisfied that you are married. Now, as to the wedding-photograph, my dear son, you ought to send it without asking, for you can know that whoever marries sends a photograph home after his wedding, and a few crowns for his parents in order that they may rejoice [feast] that he got married. So now, dear son and brother, since you ask, we beg you for it, in order that we may see [your wife] at least upon the paper, since we did not see her with our eyes.

Now, dear brother and sister-in-law, I wish you health in your marriage and good success, that you may live the best possible. [Village-news and greetings.]

[Franciszka and Franek]

265   July 19, 1913

Dear Son and Brother: . . . . We received your letter, for which we thank you, and $5.00. Now you write that you sent two photographs, and we received only one, where you are, and Józek, and yours [wife], and the older best-maid, but there is no other. . . . . Now for these dollars, my son, I arranged a marriage-festival. I invited my friends and Marysia's mother and so we amused ourselves. Now, dear son, Koźlok came and said that the guests had a very small feast, and we can even know ourselves, for you sent us a photograph with two pairs, while we have seen weddings where at least 5 or 6 pairs were [photographed]. You have been for 5 years in America and yours [wife] 6, and still you did not make yourselves a decent wedding. Now we learned that you are a Sokół. Well, my son, we would advise you to leave it, for you won't be well off. For nobody has yet been well off for being a Sokół, and you won't either. [Greetings.]

[FRANCISZKA and] F[RANEK] J.

266   September 30, 1913

DEAR SON AND BROTHER: . . . . You ask what was in this [lost] letter. Well, there was this. Don't dare, my son, to sell your field here without my knowing it and don't let yourself be cheated, as Stokłosiak cheated Kazimierz M., who sold him his lot of land half-gratis. So I admonish you, my son, that you may know what to do. If you intend to sell, write home, and I will describe, what and how you should do with all this. [Crops; weather; farm-work.]

Now, dear brother, write us how do you wish and what do you think whether you will return or will stay there. Now as to me, dear brother, I want to go there to you, for here we work but we can produce nothing, for whenever we make a few cents, at once there is an expense, and it looks as if one measured the water, and the water is always there. . . . . So I beg you, describe to me what you think, what you think about yourself and about me. . . . .

[FRANCISZKA and] FRANEK J.

267   June 12, 1914

DEAR SON AND BROTHER: . . . . When you write, describe to us how far from Chicago you will go to this farm. Now describe to us whether this land is fertile, and how many morgs. For we would dissuade you from this intention. In our country there are terrible taxes . . . . and so many different expenses that it is impossible to pay, while the crops are bad, and if rain comes [during the harvest], everything sprouts, so that it is impossible to eat the bread. Now, as you know, two years ago hail beat everything and only the naked soil remained. Last year everything sprouted, and now God alone knows what will be with the crops. So if you have money, it would be perhaps better for you to buy a house in Chicago than a farm. Now don't be angry with me for giving you advice, but I, as your mother, want you to live the best possible. Now, you see, there are many people from our country, but they all settle in Chicago. . . . .

[FRANCISZKA]

KANIKUŁA SERIES

In contrast with the preceding materials—relatively intelligent and showing a great variety of interests—we place here the most stupid series of our whole collection.

The letters—their style, the manner of dating them, etc.—show a very low degree of intellectual development. Two of the letters are dated: "The present day of the present month." On receiving from us a money-order, the son protested, saying that he expected money and received a mere scrap of paper—and this after three years in America. He did not know how to write his own address.

Now this series discloses the meaning of the peasant's stupidity. This does not manifest itself in an inability to manage the normal, habitual business of life. The Kanikułas know well enough how to farm, to make good marriages, to buy land, etc. And the most ignorant peasant may be quite successful within the usual circle of practical problems. Perhaps, indeed, in the peasant tales the success of the youngest, stupid son is precisely the expression of the fact that lack of development of the reflective faculties goes along very well with practical cleverness. (Cf. Introduction: "Theoretic and Aesthetic Interests.") The usually admitted manifestation of stupidity is the inability to adapt one's self to new practical situations. But even this criterion is not exact enough. Indeed, a new situation is seldom immediately imposed by the environment and passively accepted by the individual; usually the latter selects out of a diversity of external circumstances some practical situations among many others equally possible, and tries, consciously or instinctively, to select only such problems as he is more or less able to solve. In this way, for instance,

is to be explained the fact, often noted with astonishment
by the peasants themselves, that the facility of adaptation
of emigrants to their new environment is not proportional to
the degree of their intelligence and culture. It evidently
depends upon the merely negative ability of the man to limit
his sphere of activity.

The only criterion of intelligence is therefore the width of
the sphere of activity within which the man can be successful, the range of problems which he is able to solve.
The mere faculty of adaptation depends only mediately
upon the degree of intelligence. In a completely new
environment an intelligent man will more easily find soluble
problems within his reach than a stupid one. But, on the
other hand, his claims are greater, and thus subjectively
his chances may be equal or less. The stupid Kanikuła
is much happier in America than the intelligent Piotrowski
or Porzycki. (Cf. those series.) And this criterion of
intelligence depends in turn upon a feature with regard to
which the Kanikuła series is particularly instructive—the
range of interest. It could hardly be narrower than it is
here.

To this general point of view we shall return in a later
volume, when we attempt to appreciate the intellectual
evolution of the peasant during the last thirty years under
the influence of the movement of "enlightenment."

The Kanikuła correspondence covers two and a half
years. Four letters, very much like the first, are omitted
—three asking for money and one expressing thanks for
money. The family solidarity seems to be preserved.
The son, indeed, did not send money home at once, but
probably he could not.

268–72, FROM PIOTR KANIKUŁA, IN POLAND, TO HIS SON, IN AMERICA

268　　　　　　　　　Letter written on the present day of the present
month [1912, Spring]

[Usual greetings, wishes; information about weather.] And now, dear son, we inform you about this money that you sent, that we received it and answered you directly. [One page about letter-writing follows.]

[PIOTR KANIKUŁA]

DEAR BROTHER-IN-LAW, I beg you very much, describe to me . . . . how it is there in America, and how is the work now, whether good or bad . . . . because I want to go to you. Dear brother-in-law, I shall ask you to help me in some manner to get to America, because in our country nothing can be done. The wages are now very small. . . . . I have nothing more to write. Goodbye.

[JÓZEF]

269　　　　　　　　　　　Letter written in 1912 [Spring]

[Usual greetings; letter received.] And now, dear son, we beg you very much to send us money. Don't forget about us, because it is more and more difficult for us to work in our old days. Father has sprained his hand and cannot work, and you went away and took with you every penny wherever it was, and you left us without a penny, so if (God forbid!) death comes, we shall have not a penny. . . . . And Józef, your brother-in-law, had no work in the factory during the whole winter, only walked about Huszczka, and now he has gone to Chełm, since Easter. [More asking for money and describing bad conditions.] And now, dear son, I ask you, where did you put the ax? Write, where you put it, so we shall not have to search for it. . . . .

PIOTR KANIKUŁA

270　　　　　　　　　　Letter written on June 8, 1912

. . . . We send you already the third letter and you don't answer. Have you forgotten about us already, or what? And you don't send money, although we need it very much, because Joszt is parceling a field, so we would take some morgs. You don't even send those few roubles back to Hanusia [sister]. Other people have sent some hundred roubles each. Karol Smotryś sent 300 roubles and Piotr Podolak, Paulina's husband, 200, and Piotr, Paweł's son, sent 100, and you don't send anything to us. You know, when you wanted it and you could borrow nowhere a single rouble, we helped you, and you have forgotten about us. When you needed [money] you said you would send it immediately when you got there, and you have been there half a year already and don't send. Other people don't do like you. They have sent already, and you did not. [More complaints and admonitions.]

[PIOTR KANIKUŁA]

271   Letter written on May 20, 1913

. . . . And now we inform you that here Joszt is parceling a field, so if you sent us money, we would take some land, not for anybody else, but for yourself. And Anusia requests you to send her [money] also, because she would also take some land. She needs [money] for everything, because he [her husband] does not serve now. You don't owe her much more, and yet you don't send back those few roubles. Then send money, and we will take some land. [Greetings, wishes; repeated requests for money.]

PIOTR KANIKUŁA

272   Letter written on April 15, 1914

. . . . We are already very bad. Father is ill, our old years are very bad, because we have no health. Now we thank you very much, dear son, for your letter and postcard, we thank you very much for not forgetting that we live in this world. So we wish you blessing from God. Be married, with God, and may God help you to be married happily, and let God bless you first, and then we bless you and wish you every good from God the Merciful. . . . . And don't forget about us as long as we live in the world, and may God allow us to see you, dear children.

You wrote that Smotryś is no longer alive—that his wife poisoned him. It is not true. Who could invent it so and so [in such detail]? How do people make a dead man of a living? What you wrote about Stach—that he married Helena Łoza—it is true. He married her against the will [of her parents], he drove her to Grabowiec and there they got married. Because Łoza did not wish her to marry him, he married her against his will. Now they are sitting in the house of Józwa, but Łoza refuses to give her anything.

[News about weather.] Dear son, don't forget about us. Our dear children, remember about us old people, because you know that we have now to live like small children. As we formerly cared for you, so now it is our turn to be cared for by somebody. I repeat, we are now like small children whom somebody must dress and put their shoes on and feed them. [Greetings, blessings; request for letters.]

[Piotr Kanikuła]

Now the wife of Józef greets very much her husband and the son greets his father.[1] . . . .

---

[1] Kanikuła evidently took his brother-in-law to America.

TOPOLSKI SERIES

The family is now living in a town and working in a factory, but they came from the country. There is therefore some difference between the parents and the children; the latter are already developing to some extent the features of townspeople, while the parents are typical peasants. The relation between parents and children assumes a particular form; the children are totally independent and the parents try to keep up the country-relations, not by authority, but by sentiment.

THE FAMILY TOPOLSKI

Topolski, a factory-worker
His wife
Wacław (Wacek) ⎫
Antek ⎪
Janek ⎬ his sons
Stefek ⎭
Bronka ⎫
Józia ⎬ his daughters
Stasia (Stachna) ⎭
Michałowski, Bronka's husband
G——, an aunt of Stasia
Michał ⎫
Edzio ⎬ cousins

273–80, TO STASIA TOPOLSKA, IN AMERICA, FROM FAMILY-MEMBERS, IN POLAND

273   OSTROWIEC, March 20, 1912

DEAR CHILDREN: . . . . We write this letter on Good Wednesday, for Stefek came for the holidays and he writes it, while Antek does not want to write. He would prefer to be sick for 3 days rather than write one letter. . . . . We gave the process to a lawyer. . . . . Your father aspires and prays to God that he may go to Kujawy [the farm which is the object of the lawsuit], if it were only one hour before dying, and not hear any more this bullying in the factory. . . . .[1] Bronka wrote to us that Michałowski [her husband] teases her in his letters. She complains that she is unhappy. She has always some misunderstandings with him. And you there [Stasia], keep away from Michałowski, lest people ascribe to you some [evil] things, for Malczykowa asked already whether you are not living in the same apartment.[2] Has Michałowski sent some money to his wife? . . . . Write us what work is Wacław doing. . . . . Bronka also wonders that in your letters to her you mention little about Wacław. Janek is such a disorderly boy as he has always been; he does not put any money aside. We had hardly put 40 roubles in the bank for him when he drew it and bought a bicycle.[3] And if he has some trouble in the factory he comes and asks us to gather any money that we have, saying that he will go to America. For the holidays we have 30 pounds of flour, 12 pounds of ham and a leg of veal. Michał brought all this from Iwaniska. . . . .

EVERYBODY FROM HOME

274 December 29, 1912

DEAR STASIA: We received your letter . . . . and we were very much rejoiced, but when we read it we wept. Why did you leave Wacław [brother with whom she went to America] thus? You ought to remain with him and to come back together. God knows what has become of him? Perhaps in such a big city he cannot find you. What did we suffer until we got this letter from you! People said that you were arrested [while crossing the frontier] and put into prison, others said that you were sent back by *etapes* [from prison to prison to the native village]. Jula, from Kielce, said that the ship stopped in the sea and no ship was permitted to go. And now

[1] Longing for land and for independence. The feature is almost universal among peasants who work in factories in Poland, but is weakened or disappears in America.

[2] This suspicion would hardly arise in a village. Bronka is Stasia's sister, and a relation between Stasia and her husband would be felt as almost incestuous.

[3] Were the family living in the country, the father would probably not allow Janek to withdraw the money. For example, the money earned by the children at season-work in Germany, even if not given to the parents for spending, is nevertheless almost always given to them to keep until the son or daughter marries.

the people say that it is bad in America, that this new president is not good, that factories have stopped and only a few of them are active, that he has diminished the pay for work, and that he endeavors not to admit the Poles into America, saying that they spoil the people there.[1] All this is more grief for us, for while you did not lose much, Wacław had money and good work and lost it all. If he does not get work there, it will be bad. Write us about everything. . . . . Did you get acquainted with somebody from Ostrowiec? If not, try to do it.[2] Write us whether you are boarding with somebody else or cooking for yourself, and about Wacek also, whether you both are not homesick. For while you have been away from home for a long time [she was first in Russia], Wacław left the home for the first time so we don't know how he feels. [News about the factory in which the father is working.] Janek [brother] has left that girl in Kunów, for she wanted him to rent an apartment for her in Ostrowiec and to furnish it, while he wanted to go to her [to live in her parents' house] for some time, until they earn and put aside more money. As he had not money enough [for the apartment], they separated.[3] [Politics; calls for military service; condemnations of political offenders.] There is no more news, but you must describe your journey, what they gave you to eat upon the ship, how much money you spent, and everything. . . . . Write us regularly, a letter every two weeks. . . . .

YOUR PARENTS and EVERYBODY FROM HOME

275   February 26, 1913

DEAR CHILDREN: . . . . We are curious how you look now, Stasia. We imagine that you must look very bad, because you grieve [are homesick]. But nothing can be done, it must be so for some time. Antek K. went to America. He did not wish to go to the

---

[1] The childish idea of the president's influence upon social and economic life is evidently the result of two factors—familiarity with the idea of absolutism and the enormous agitation which precedes the presidential election.

[2] Parents are always glad when their children find in America people of their own village or neighborhood. There is thus maintained some semblance of community interest, oversight, and mutual aid.

[3] The reason seems trifling. Among peasants where the question of an independent home is connected with the question of a farm, such an attitude would be justifiable, and even then a girl would hardly object to her husband's living for some time with her parents. Here the evident motive is vanity—a vanity of the type which develops in towns.

army, he preferred America. He took your address. . . . . You cannot imagine how many people go to America. Soon very few will remain in our country. We are curious whether Michałowski sent some money to his wife. Write us exactly about everything, how you like it in America. How does the food taste to you, for we hear that the cooking is different there? Write us whether you did not meet somebody else of your acquaintance. Perhaps you feel better now than in the beginning. Did you dance during the last days of carnival? For Rem. wrote that he danced so much as to lose his heels. My dear Stasia, when you write a letter, write it in the presence of Wacek, that he may dictate a few words in his own name, for it is so painful for us—as if he were not there. We know nothing about him. . . . . And yourself, you write such short letters, there is nothing to read, although you are in such a distant country. . . . . Now we inform you about this lawsuit. The lawyers assure us that we shall win. We have asked two and they both say it. . . . .

YOUR PARENTS and EVERYBODY FROM HOME

276   April 22, 1913

DEAR CHILDREN: . . . . Our lawsuit about Kujawy will be judged on May 5. As soon as it is over we will write you at once· And we beg you, in the case we need money to pay this farmer's part, send us as much as you have. Ask even Michałowski to give you those 100 roubles back. We expect that if we win in Radom he will appeal to Warsaw. Then we should not need the money so soon. But perhaps he won't be able to appeal. . . . . You need not be afraid about your money, for it would not be lost if mortgaged upon the farm. Of the 100 roubles which Wacław left we spent 50 on this lawsuit, but we keep a pig which we bought for $7\frac{1}{2}$ roubles after Christmas. Now we could get more than 30 for it. So if we don't win, we shall sell the pig and put the money in the bank[1] [to Wacław's account]. [News about friends, etc.]

YOUR PARENTS and EVERYBODY FROM HOME

277   DYMINY, August 22, 1913

DEAR STACHNA [STASIA]: I read your letter to Edzio. The content of the letter touched us very much. It is true that you have been courageous in going so far. This only is happy, that you suc-

---

[1] In these money matters the attitude of the parents is typically peasant.

ceeded in persuading Wacław [to go with you]. Probably your time passes more pleasantly together. Are you healthy at least? I really cannot imagine that you are there at the other end of the world; I should not muster courage enough to do it. I admire you. . . . .

God, O my God! What does destiny do with man! He finds himself suddenly there beyond the sea. Man is like a ball. I feel this all, I have experienced it myself to some extent, this working for a piece of bread, ... but I should not have equaled your boldness in leaving your country and your native home.[1] I imagine your fear, your regret, your fears! My dear, God has seen all this. . . . . The Highest Creator will reward you, since he has tried you thus. The confidence in God's mercy never deceives anybody. Perhaps God will grant you some good lot in reward for that trouble and labor which you have borne up to the present.[2] O God! don't fail to come with help to them. From my poor side, I wish you to come back happy and to reach the end for which you left your home, and may the presence of the Highest always be a witness of your lot.

You ask about my children. [Information about children.] Józia [Stasia's sister] was here not long ago and mentioned that you dissuaded her from marrying a widower. But I understand her very well. He is an honest and laborious man, and the children don't play any part. The boy is 5 years old and can even be useful, while both the girls are kept by their grandmother. The girl [Józia] is not in her first youth. Moreover, he liked her [fell in love with her].[3] I advised her to marry him. I told her that if she is good she will be happy [of] herself. Have you no opportunity [to marry] there? I advise you also to marry, not to wait and not to select, for this is the worst. As long as you are in good health all is well. I notice it in myself. Evidently it is easier to hold out someone's else back [to be beaten] than one'-

[1] The difference between the older and younger generations is here clearly expressed. Indeed, the emigration of women (not going to their husbands) is a comparatively recent phenomenon.

[2] The suffering as such is here considered as a sufficient claim on God's reward although no one obliged the girl to go to America.

[3] It is characteristic that the usual term still used in the country for love before marriage (love without either sexual relation or marriage-tie) is "liking," not "loving," while between parents and children or brothers and sisters the term "loving" is current.

own. But I shall wait soon for news about your marriage.[1] It is to be hoped that such a girl as you are should not waste her time there. . . . .

[YOUR AUNT] G.

278   OSTROWIEC, February 9, 1914

DEAR STASIA: We received your letter on Feb. 1, and Wacław came back on Feb. 3. He came in good health, had no accident. The crossing of the frontier cost him 4 roubles. . . . . He says that he is bored here, he regrets that he came back. As to the work, we don't know yet—for he has not yet asked anybody—whether he will get any or not. . . . . Your father keeps well, but he could not be a shooter anymore, for he does not see well. When he comes back from the factory he often falls or jostles people. In Ostrowiec it is as warm as in summer. If we were in Kujawy, we should think about sowing, while as it is probably that farmer will sow for us. We are tired with waiting. It seems to us as if there were 10 years left until the end of this suit. But what can we do? When we were the plaintiffs the suit was soon decided, but now he is the plaintiff, and we can do nothing. . . . . Wacek asks you to thank the agent who said that he would go 6 days [by sea], while he went 10. He regrets now that he came and says that in the spring he will go back. That would be a trouble for us, if he went back, took the money, and we should have nothing to pay for Kujawy. Nobody feels it as much as I do [the mother], for I should like to get there as soon as possible, while it lasts so long. . . . .

YOUR PARENTS

279   May 21 [1914]

DEAR STASIA: You know that you worry me now in writing that we have forgotten about you. Why, we sent two postcards and two letters after Easter. And now I am obliged to send you a letter without a stamp, for evidently you gave a bad address. You may know that there is not an hour during the day without my thinking of

---

[1] The aunt and the parents retain the traditional attitude as to the necessity of marrying, but the aunt cares less than the parents whether the girl makes a good match. Cf. Nos. 279, 280.

you. But since you moved to another lodging evidently the address is bad. And instead of my writing reproaches to her, she writes to us! Instead of describing at length how she succeeds there, she sends a postcard, neither this nor that [without determined news]. Write us about this bachelor, whence is he, what is his name? Is it the same, from the province of Lublin, about whom you wrote, or another? But, my dear, you write that he has neither money nor work. Well, if you get married in America, you should at least make a career [marry well], or else you will both suffer misery. My Stasia, be careful about yourself and don't stain yourself again [?].[1] As long as Wacek was there, I was not so anxious, while now I fear more about you. Write us whether you have seen Michałowski, for his wife was with us when we wrote this letter and said that she knew everything about him from Staszewski, who had lived with him. He sent 100 roubles for her, but has not yet given the debt back to Wacek. . . . .

[YOUR MOTHER and] EVERYBODY FROM HOME

280   July 12 [1914]

DEAR STASIA: We received your letter . . . . with the photograph, but instead of getting comfort, we wept, for probably you won't come back if you marry there. You wrote here once about that bachelor, that he would not come back, so we don't know whether it is the same or another. For your mother and father it is very painful, for they won't remain long upon this world. But what can be done? If you cannot do otherwise, we don't bind you lest you should complain about us later on.[2] You write us nothing about him; we don't know whence he is and what is his name, whether he is some skilled workman, whether he has some money. For when two poor people come together, it is not very good. And he is probably old, for indeed everybody says that he looks [on the photograph] as if he were

[1] In the original it is not clear whether the word *znów* (again) has the meaning, "for the second time," or is used as a particle strengthening the advice.

[2] The parents are evidently opposed to this marriage, but they do not dare to urge their opposition, (1) because a poor marriage is better than none; (2) because they are afraid of a complaint from their daughter (equivalent to a curse) if she should remain an old maid through their interference; and (3) because the girl is already partially independent.

more than forty and as if he had gray hair. He must not have been for a long time in America, for he wears whiskers not in the American fashion, cut and fixed, but hanging down in disorder. But if he is an honest and good man, don't mind anything. For us it matters only that we might see you some day. . . . .

We kiss you a thousand times. We hope that you will send us a letter before your wedding. Don't give him this letter to read, lest he be offended.

YOUR FAMILY

SĘKOWSKI SERIES

Up to the present we have had to do with families of peasant farmers. Here we find a family of manor-employees. Jan Sękowski, the father, is probably a farm-clerk or a land-steward. He has some education. His letters are written in rather good Polish. The other letters of the family are on the average not above the usual level of peasant letters. But a letter which Mania wrote to us in sending the letters shows an astonishing progress made during her four years in America. Perhaps it is due to her husband's influence. She is one of the few of our peasant correspondents showing an interest in our work.

The manor-life develops features which differ to some extent from those of the peasant farmers. The series therefore assumes a particular importance. There are over two million manor-servants (families included) in Poland. The main bulk of them are the so-called *parobeks*, i.e., those who do physical farm-work (plowing, sowing, harvesting, threshing, driving, etc.). Then come the cattle-, pig-, and sheep-herders, forest-guards, watchmen, etc.; then handworkers (black-smiths, carpenters, gardeners, millers), then private servants (butlers, cooks, maids, grooms, laundresses, coachmen), and finally the "officials" (overseers, clerks, stewards, cashiers, managers, distillers, head foresters). A rather small estate has thirty to forty servants, most of them married; a relatively large estate, of some seven or eight thousand acres, has two hundred to three hundred servants; but there are estates which keep many more than this, although the largest ones, from about twenty thousand to three hundred thousand acres (or over) have partly the tenant system. Thus, the manorial organization exerts a powerful influence upon country life, and this extends beyond the sphere of the manor-servants, because there is intermarriage between them and the farmers, and a ruined farmer, or his children, frequently goes into service.

The characteristics which the life of a manor-employee tends to develop are rather negative. The dependence upon the manor-owner is much greater than that of employees upon employer in the city, because the whole life of the manor-employee is spent in the manor, and even his private life is not completely his own. At the same time, we find in addition to the business relation a social hierarchy much more rigid than in the town. A higher employee in a town business may be received in his employer's house, may marry his daughter, may become his equal if he makes money; the manor-official is once and forever outside of the social sphere of his noble employer—unless, of course, he is a ruined noble himself, or his employer's relative. On the other hand, the manor-official tends to keep between himself and the physically working servants the same distance as that which separates him from his employer. In this way the system always keeps alive the idea that social hierarchy is something absolute. In accordance with this idea, humility toward the superior and arrogance toward the inferior appear quite natural; no moral condemnation of any kind is attached to them.

Moreover, while we have distinguished only three degrees in this hierarchy—the employer, the official, the servant— there are in fact many more. On a large estate there is a continuous gradation from the head manager down to the unmarried *posyłka* (servant helping the *parobek*) involving sometimes as many as six or seven degrees of social (not merely business) hierarchy. On the other hand, on a very small estate the distinctions between employees may be rather small, as the highest type of employee may be an overseer or clerk. This is Sękowski's position. It is easy to understand how many insignificant interests, petty vanities, and ridiculous fights result from this system.

Another feature, still more negative, which manorial life tends to develop, is petty dishonesty. The control of the employees in a manor is particularly difficult because of the complexity of the functions, the difficulty of introducing a permanent division of labor, and a corresponding specifica-tion of responsibilities, etc. The temptation to steal is stronger here than anywhere else, because of the old prepos-session that "stealing" means stealing only money, cattle, horses, or manufactured things, while stealing natural products which serve to maintain human or animal life is simply "taking" and hardly reprehensible. It becomes reprehensible when these products are stolen *and sold*, but the difference is easily overlooked.

Egotism is also more easily developed in manorial life than in village life. The idea of *mutual help* and of collabora-tion scarcely exists. The manor-servants look for help to the owner, not to one another; there is no mutuality and no reciprocity, as in help between equals. Instead of this, another solidarity develops—the *complicity* in laziness and stealing. Only during the regenerating movement of the last twenty years has the idea of the *solidarity of general interests* of manor-servants *as workers*—the counter-part of the socialistic idea—succeeded in developing; and it has resulted in many successful strikes, in which, never-theless, only the lower workers, not the manor-officials, took part.

In familial relations the influence of the manorial life is also rather negative as compared with that of the village life. There is indeed no rivalry and no struggle among children for inheritance, but there is also no solidarity resulting from common interests. The father does not look upon his children as upon collaborators and helpers, but as upon a burden of which he tries to get rid as soon as possible (as Sękowski does) by sending them away to work on their own account. When the children have left their parents' home, nothing else keeps them together, and there is no tendency to return. As most of the manor-servants wander from place to place, there are no stable associations with a determined locality. The egotism and hardness of the parents in village life are tempered by the idea that their children will inherit the farm upon which they have worked during their whole life, and will continue their work; the sphere of interest includes the future generations. In manorial life the only interest which makes the parents care for the future of their children is the hope that one of the children will take them when they are unable to work.

THE FAMILY SĘKOWSKI

Jan Sękowski, a manor-employee
His wife
Adam (Adaś) $\Big\}$ his sons
Tadeusz (Tadzio)
Kazia
Mania (Maryanna) $\Big\}$ his daughters
Leosia (Leokadya)
Frania (Franka), Adam's wife
Teodor Kacperski, Kazia's husband
Janek, Mania's husband
Żytniewski and wife, Sękowski's parents-in-law
Mańka, their granddaughter
Staśka, niece of Sękowski's wife
"The aunt," Staśka's mother
Walenty, the aunt's second husband

281–95, LETTERS FROM THE SĘKOWSKI FAMILY, IN POLAND,
TO FAMILY-MEMBERS IN AMERICA

281 ŁAZY, December 5, 1909

DEAR HUSBAND: I inform you that we are in good health, and
we wish to you also the best health and success from our Lord God.
Dear husband, the third star[1] [Christmas] approaches already since
you have been far away from us in that foreign country. Dear
husband, there is no more painful moment for me than when I remember that you are there far away and quite alone. So we send you a
star and at the same time I divide a wafer[2] with you. Dear husband,
as to our coming, you must know first whether we have good eyes.
Dear husband, so we shall go to to Poznań, when we shall know certainly that we are going. Dear husband, I beg you in the name of
everything in the world, don't change your word. For I won't write
you [ask you] any more about it, because you wrote [as if reproaching]
that I wanted absolutely to come to America. Dear husband, it is
true, but don't be afraid [of my coming, for I will be a good wife].
For I know what [a life] I had when you were at home, how you always
made my heart joyful. Dear husband, I did not know at all how to
respect [appreciate] you.[3] But now, dear, and only now, I know

---

[1] The word is used in connection with Christmas ceremonies to indicate (1) the
first star on Christmas eve, with the appearance of which the supper, the most
important ceremony, begins; (2) the Christmas celebration in general; (3) the
Christmas gifts; (4) stars cut out of paper, wafers, etc., hung upon the Christmas
tree or sent in letters as Christmas tokens; (5) a transparent and illuminated star
of paper or glass with which boys walk about the village on Christmas night,
singing, offering wishes, asking for gifts.

[2] The consecrated wafer plays an important, partly magical, rôle. It is consecrated before Christmas and during the eve supper the members of the family
divide a part of it among themselves and, while eating, express wishes, evidently
with a half-conscious idea of a power inherent in the wafer to fulfil wishes, and with
the conscious idea of communion. The rest is kept and used during the year, more
or less with the idea of its healing properties; powders are preferably taken in
connection with it. Preparing and selling wafers is the privilege of organists.

[3] We have seen (Introduction: "Marriage") that "respect" is the fundamental
norm of conjugal relations. The love included within the norm of respect is not
romantic or sensual love. Sensual love as such is clearly outside of the idea of
normal, that is, perfect conjugal relations. And while it exists in young marriages,
it is not to be spoken of; it is considered as being something indecent. There is,
for example, a letter from a peasant in the newspaper *Zaranie* describing how a
priest in his wedding-address condemned sensual abuses, but spoke of them so

how necessary it is to respect the husband, as the conjugal duty orders.

Dear husband, I inform you also about our daughter, how intelligent she is. When I ask her, "What will father buy you?" she says, "Shoes." She says, "Dear papa, Mania will go to papa."

I wish you health and happiness for your name-day, dear Adaś.

Mania [sister] begs you to find a nice boy for her.[1] But she begs you not to write about it, for father reads every letter. When we come to you we shall speak of it. I greet you kindly and heartily, and goodbye.

Your loving wife and daughter,

[FRANIA]

282   February 1 [1910]

DEAR BROTHER: I have a little wish [request] for you. You wrote before that you would send ship-tickets for Frania and for me, and that we should go together to America, and now you sent us such

---

realistically as to make his hearers indignant. This is the reason we so seldom find expressions of love in conjugal letters, particularly if these are dictated. In one letter from America (Struciński series) a husband makes to his wife some sensual allusions but immediately begs her pardon.

The best illustration of the antithesis of conjugal feelings within the norm of respect and outside of this norm is afforded by the practice of *beating*. Beating one's wife is evidently among the worst actions from the standpoint of the norm of respect. But between young people it harmonizes perfectly with *love*. A young woman often likes to be beaten, particularly when the husband beats her because he is jealous, because the wife is not demonstrative enough, or refuses marital relations. Beating is then considered a proof of love; a woman considers herself wronged, not loved, when the husband never beats her. Women speak with pride of being beaten, and are unhappy because of the indifference of husbands who do not beat them. Any interference in these cases ends badly for the interfering person, who may be beaten by man and wife together. Evidently, such an attitude toward beating is to be understood only upon the sexual basis. The attitude is quite the contrary when the pair (or the husband) is old, when the reason of beating has nothing to do with the reciprocal relations of man and wife, as, for example, when the man beats his wife in some quarrel about money or about the children.

[1] There is a general and justified opinion among Polish girls that it is very easy to get married in America and that the Polish-American husbands are better. This explains partly the fact that girls are willing to go to an unknown man who asks them in marriage (cf. the case of Staśka in this series), and in general that they risk going alone to America while they are often afraid to go alone to the nearest town in their own country.

a hopeless letter.   So I beg you, dear brother, if now it is difficult for you, then do it a little later, in the beginning or in the end of May. . . . . Why, I will pay you back as soon as I earn, if I only come happily there.   I have learned sewing and in any case I can do other work also. . . . . I should like to earn a little more, for here I shan't earn anything, even if I go to Prussia.   And in Prussia one must also work, perhaps worse than in America.   Only, dear brother, if I could go together with Frania!   It would be better also for her during the journey, and afterward we could work together. . . . .

Your sister,
MARYANNA [MANIA] SĘKOWSKA

283   February 17, 1910

DEAR SON: I received your last letter.   I am very much pained that you have such bad luck, while others, impotent and lazy fellows, earn nice money.   But nothing can be done.   You ought not to lose hope and courage.   Where fear is the greatest God's help is the nearest.   Who perseveres to the end will be saved, only patience and perseverance are needed.   You know that I also had often hard and painful times, but I suffered and only asked God for any improvement of my lot.   And our Lord God helps willingly, if that improvement is really necessary, for everything is good, whatever God does.   And therefore at the end of such a prayer one must say: "Not mine, but Thy will, O God, be done."

You say that the hernia pains you.   Probably you do not always wear the belt.   I got it also, for during the digging of potatoes I had to put them into the cart . . . . but as soon as I noticed it, I went to Poznań and bought a belt and now I feel very well. . . . . Evidently, if you wish absolutely to come home, I have nothing against it,[1] but is it not a pity to spend more than 100 roubles upon the journey, when you have no money?   And then, what will you do, go to Prussia [for season-work]?[2]   Don't trouble yourself about Franka.   If she is

---

[1] The unwillingness to have his son back and perhaps a burden to himself is in interesting contrast with the attitude of any farmer, who at the worst asks his son to wait until he has earned some money, but always wants him to return ultimately. Cf. Markiewicz series, Osiński series, etc.

[2] The practice of going to Prussia, although very much developed, is not looked upon as desirable in itself, only as a necessity.   It is considered well for a boy or a girl to go for two or three years, get together a dowry, and become a little acquainted with the wide world, but those who make their living in this way are rather despised.

tired with staying in our home she may go to service,[1] and everywhere it will be well.   Thus she ought not to dream about America, but she will go to Prussia.   And then you can write to each other. . . . .

We all greet you most kindly.

Your father,

J. SĘKOWSKI

284   March 18, 1910

DEAR SON: We all at home wept about your misfortune, and we try to find some way to improve your lot, but we are unable to do anything.   God alone is left to you, and He will help you without doubt, only you must pray warmly to Him.   But at the same time don't let your hands fall, try in every way.   Sometimes it is even necessary to humiliate one's self deeply, but one must not mind it. . . . .[2] May God help you.

Your father,

J. SĘKOWSKI

285   March 18, 1910

DEAR HUSBAND: I inform you about our health, that we are in good health, only for me there is no greater pain of the heart than that God has sent you such a sickness in that foreign country.   Dear husband, what may not happen with you there when you are so severely sick!   Who takes care of you in this sickness?   My heart cannot bear any longer this grief about your misfortune!   What conditions do you have there, in that America?   Dear husband, if God grants you to recover, and if you see that the conditions are bad in that America, come home!   I will go again to season-work. Dear husband, I beg you, if God still gives you health, write to me and describe to me everything about your illness.   If this letter [finds] you still alive!   For I think that you are no more alive.   Dear husband!   How I wanted to see you once more before your death! For you know how I have loved you, and I never have lost hope in God, and even now I don't lose it totally.   Perhaps our Lord God

---

[1] A farmer would never allow his daughter-in-law to go into service; he would consider it derogatory to his son and himself.

[2] This is the phrase to which the writer's daughter Kazia Kacperska alludes when she says that "father told Adam to beg."   In fact, this is an advice which a farmer would hardly give his son, while it shows that the writer's attitude in these matters is influenced by his servile position.

will still give you health! Only I am very anxious because of my dreams, for I had them very bad. Dear husband, if you live still, answer me as soon as possible, for my heart will be grieved until I receive news that you live still. Dear husband, I should prefer to die rather than you should die. For what should I do if you were to die?[1] I put all my hope in you! Dear husband, I am even unable to describe this pain which I have upon my heart. But never mind for myself—but the child! If you knew how she rejoiced that she would go to you! These last days she continually pointed at you[r photograph], saying, "This is my papa, and this [the old Sękowski] is papa's papa." And she was so glad that she would go to her papa! And she loved [caressed?] you so, as if someone had ordered her.[2] But we did not tell her at all; she did it of herself. And all this was for this pain and grief! When we tell her that her father is sick and mother will go to Prussia, she says, "Mama won't go Prussia, but will go with Mania to papa." If she sees that I am weeping she begins to cry and does not allow me to weep. Dear husband, I greet you kindly and heartily.

YOUR LOVING WIFE and YOUR DAUGHTER

I commend you to our Lord God and I pray to our Lord God that He may give you health and that we may see one another. And if not upon this world, may we merit to see one another in the other world.

286   December 13, 1910[3]

DEAR SISTER MANIA: . . . . Tadzio is very glad that you will send him money for a new suit. He knows already how to read and to write a little, and now he says that he will learn still better. . . . . We have now two boarders, both from Prussia. One of

---

[1] This letter shows traces of tears and is perhaps the strongest expression of conjugal love in our collection. The traditional form of conjugal relation, as a mere familial relation, here breaks down completely; the married couple becomes a unique, almost isolated, social group. We shall follow later the same process in detail in other series. Here the conjugal relation is more easily liberated from the familial ties because in manorial life those ties themselves are not very strong.

[2] The word "loving" for "caressing" is very often used; the peasants are indeed little inclined to caress, and a caress is always the expression of a strong feeling.

[3] One letter preceding this one is omitted. It contains Jan's enumeration of the expenses of the journey of Mania and Frania to America.

them . . . . speaks Polish, but the other does not. They are the kind of engineers who put water-pipes in the manor. Both are still unmarried. We killed a pig not long ago, and I went to Kazia to take her some [meat]. I was there for a week, and Kazia made a skirt for me and for mother a ———— [illegible word] which I brought home. I had put some money aside for this journey, for I sweep the room of these gentlemen. . . . . Your hen is dead. . . . . Tereska's man has been taken to the army, and her sister has a child [illegal]. Józef went to America, and Zośka will also go before summer, for she was his girl. Kazimierz [Mania's sweetheart] is not taken to the army. . . . . He neither walks nor speaks with any girl, only is always very pensive. . . . . Dear Mania, mother is now so feeble and tired that she cannot work. As long as I am at home I do everything, but father talks already about my going to [season-] work. Could you write that I should not go, for I don't mind anything except mother.[1] Mother longs also for you. . . . .

Your sister,

LEOKADYA SĘKOWSKA

287　　　　　　　　　　　　　　　　　　　　March 20, 1912

DEAR CHILDREN: . . . . Yesterday we had St. Joseph's holiday. In the afternoon we were with Tadeusz in Zagórów, for mother ordered a suit for him there, for 6 roubles. It will be ready for Sunday. We have now such nice and warm days; the pig is well fattened. He will be killed as soon as Kazia comes to help mother work. May God grant, dear children, your wishes to be fulfilled, that you may be able to take us some day to you, for here one cannot count for anything. As long as I can run [work] well they keep me, but when I get older, they will do the same with me as they did with Mr. R.[2]

[1] The situation shows once more the father's egotism and avarice; this attempt to drive the last daughter from the home while the mother needs her help could only exceptionally occur in a farmer's family.

[2] This insecurity of the manor-servant's position justifies to some extent his faults. It had been always the custom to support old manor-servants when they had served long in the same manor, but in later times changing of place has become more and more usual. Ten years ago an association was organized for the pensioning of the old manor-servants. A manor-servant can hardly put aside money enough from his salary to keep him in his old age. The only way to amass some capital is the illicit one, and there are indeed many manor-servants who have bought nice farms and houses in small towns. Sękowski evidently has money, although he does not acknowledge it.

If the Żytniewskis [wife's parents] come we shall be almost obliged to support them. Then I should like your mother and Tadeusz to go to you, and I should still remain for some time with the grandparents, and grandmother would keep my house. . . . . I will tell Tadeusz to write you also something in the evening, for I have nothing more to write. Only he does not want much to write, saying that he has enough of his own writing [for the school].

[J. SĘKOWSKI]

288 [March 20, 1912]

DEAR SISTERS: I received your card, for which I thank you heartily, for remembering me. . . . . And now I beg you, economize as much money as possible, that I may come some day to you with mother and father. And now I inform you also about those ducks of yours. You know, that gray duck, when she sees me far away she quacks and runs toward me.

I remain, your brother,

TADEUSZ SĘKOWSKI

289 April 9, 1912

DEAR FRANIA: I received your letter. . . . . Grandfather and grandmother Żytniewski came to us to stay, and they brought one granddaughter, 10 years old. What can I do? I cannot grudge a little food and a corner. As long as I am in Łazy they can be with me.[1] [News about work, friends, and acquaintances.]

J. SĘKOWSKI

290 January 15, 1913

DEAR DAUGHTER [MANIA]: So at last that time has come to you when the human lot is totally changed. From a maiden you will become a married woman, from a free being a slave of your husband and of fortune, from a merry and lively [girl] you will become sad, for there is no true happiness in this world; it exists only after death, and then only for the chosen ones. In this world there is a valley of tears, nothing but anxiety, suffering, and different troubles which we must bear patiently in order to merit that true happiness. We

---

[1] We see in this example how the supporting of aged parents is felt as an absolute obligation. Even the old miser Sękowski, who drives all his children away to work, cannot begrudge his wife's parents a place with him.

can never avoid misfortunes and we are unable to bear them with patience without the help of God. Therefore, may the Lord God who blessed Abraham, Isaac, and Jacob, this God who blessed our forefathers and who remembered us in His Providence, who will never forget His creatures up to the end of the world—may He bless you until the end of your life as your parents bless you now. In the name of the Father †, the Son †, and the Holy Spirit †, Amen. May God grant it. Amen.[1]

YOUR PARENTS

291   April 8, 1913

DEAR CHILDREN: Yesterday we received your letter and I answer you at once. First I inform you that we, i.e., your father, mother, and grandfather, are in good health and we wish you the same with our whole soul and heart. Grandmother and Mańka went to Kalisz, and Tadeusz is probably in the middle of the sea or already near America, and will be there sooner than this letter. You could have written sooner about feathers [for pillows], then Tadeusz would have taken them. Mańka Kowal won't go now; they have changed their mind, and first Kaziek will go and two daughters of Kamiński the miller.[2] They will surely go to Chicago, because a rich brother of Kamińska lives there, and I believe that the F's borrowed money from him for the exemption of Kazimierz from the army. Moreover mother says that you have enough feathers,[3] while Leosia has nothing, and what will Leosia say to it? Well, perhaps it would not matter much, these few feathers, but there won't be any opportunity [to send them] until I go with your mother. As to the gift from Janek, I did

---

[1] The pompousness of speech and the preaching attitude of this letter, as well as of some other of Sękowski's letters, are explained by the combined influence of religion and manorial life. They imply a relative superiority of the "preacher" over his hearers, and are found most frequently among men who are more or less outside of the proper peasant community and a little above it by their learning— organists, commune secretaries, shop-keepers, manor-employees, etc. As these men having no land property are looked upon by the peasant farmer with a curious mixture of superficial respect and a profound and hidden disdain, the display of their relative learning, particularly in divine and moral matters, is a means of securing and defending their superiority. The peasant is, in fact, much impressed by good speaking.

[2] Kaziek (Kazimierz) was formerly engaged to Sękowski's daughter.

[3] Feathers are the most necessary part of the dowry; the poorest girl must have a good feather-bed. Feathers and pillows are collected beyond the real necessity.

not rejoice [expect] so long as I did not hear anything, but now, since I have been promised, I will wait patiently till it comes. I am very glad that I have a son-in-law who is able to buy a gift for his father, while I must present gifts to Kacperski [other son-in-law]. He does not ask for them, but it would not be suitable otherwise.[1] On Easter they did not come to us, but on Pentecost they will certainly come, and mother always finds something to give them, while I give them 20 marks, as if for their traveling expenses. They don't wish to go to America, and probably they will never go, although a factory-workman like Kacperski would earn more in America than in Prussia. Be energetic with Tadeusz there, and make him learn well; the more and the better he learns the better it will be for him. As to the photograph, it is necessary only to know how to stand and to arrange one's self the best possible. Why does your mother look so well in her photograph ? Because she is taken more from the side. Mother does not look so young today; she did perhaps 20 years ago. If you don't look well in your first photographs, I think that it is not the fault of the photographer, but your own. Still I don't intend to burn these photographs, for in a few years you will look exactly thus, and then they will be good. And now I wish you would have your photo-graph taken once more, but all of you together, and without any strange persons except those who belong now to our family. . . . . Janek's parents asked me to tell them how they could come from their locality to us, for they intend to visit us. But I doubt much whether they will risk it, the more so when I describe [the way] to them, for they are not far away from the railway, while we live about 10 miles [Polish = 50 English] from Kalisz, the nearest station.[2] . . . .

[1] Sękowski gave no dowry to any of his daughters, and even thus he complains of one son-in-law that he must give him presents, whereas he himself accepts presents from the other. Such an attitude would be normal in village life only in an old and helpless widow. A farmer, even a poor one, would accept a present from his son-in-law, but only because he considered that after his death the son-in-law would have the inheritance; and he would never grudge the giving of a present. He would consider Sękowski's attitude humiliating.

[2] The family lives near the German frontier. As the Russian government, for strategical reasons, did not allow the building of railways in this part of the country, while on the German side the railroads were numerous, the life of the frontier-districts is much more closely connected with the life of the Polish provinces in Germany than with that of central Poland. The season-emigration (in the district where the Sękowskis live, 20 per cent of the population goes every year to season-work) develops direct relations with central and western Germany and is a medium of German influence.

My father and mother live in Smulsk still. Some days ago I received a letter from my father in which he asks for a few roubles. I answered him and I promised [to send them] somewhat later, for now I have none, as I spent everything on Tadeusz['s journey]. But my father writes that he is already very feeble, and my mother also. He is 78, and mother 79 years old. If I can, I should be glad to visit them once more. . . . .

Your parents,

[J. SĘKOWSKI]

292   March 4, 1914

DEAR SON: I received all your letters, the maps and the booklet. I looked over all this. At the first sight it seems very good and promising much; even if only one-half were true of what is printed in this booklet it would still be very good. In any case I advise you not to begin anything before you learn the truth. You have time enough, since you have not yet sold your house. So, as I wrote you in my preceding letter, ask your paper for advice. They write there precisely that they don't want to make a fortune from their paper, only to inform the Poles as much as possible. They will neither praise nor blame, but will write you the truth; they will perhaps even print it in the paper. Perhaps in the office of that paper in Chicago they know about these farms, and perhaps not; you could send them one such booklet, if you have any more, for it would be better if they first read the booklet and answered then.[1]

I believe you that factory work can become a bore, and that it will pay less and less, while living will be always more and more expensive, for people continually go to America. Write also to Franek, Leosia's [husband], and send him such a booklet if you can. He has money, and perhaps there, where he works, somebody knows Florida.

About all points it is necessary to ask everybody's advice, but not to listen and not to believe everybody, and above all not to try to catch the pigeon, letting the sparrow go, and then to have nothing.

[1] The old man's conceit is clearly manifested in this giving of advice without knowing the conditions. At the end of this letter he gives the text of the letter which his son ought to write to the paper. Another example is the question of photographs, which recurs in many letters. Evidently the manor-life, developing the tendency to keep as strong as possible small hierarchical distinctions, leads to the custom of asserting one's own superiority in any matters, however trivial.

If it were near you could go there some Sunday and ascertain it personally, but it is very far. I think you would have to travel perhaps 3 days. Perhaps it is not so hot there as it would be if Florida were upon the continent, but it is a peninsula, not very wide, and therefore it may be cooler. At any rate I advise you to think about it day and night and when you have proofs that it is worth doing, then to set to work at once.

Let Tadeusz learn as much as possible, let him be assiduous and obedient, let him never offend Frania, that she may not have to complain about him when we see one another some day. . . . .

[J. SĘKOWSKI]

[Includes the draft of a letter to the Polish paper asking for advice about buying the farm.]

293   June 28, 1914

DEAR MANIA: We received the photograph of this Leonard, and a scrap instead of a letter, upon which you had written about Staśka.[1] . . . . Grandfather is with us, but so weak that it is impossible to use him; so mother went to Kalisz herself and spent a few days. Staśka would like to go, but your aunt is very angry about it. She quarreled at once with your mother, for she exploits Staśka a great deal.[2]

Staśka went to be photographed, but I don't know how she will look, for there was nobody to advise her and she will be photographed in full. Thus the face will be small and indistinct, and if she does not stand sidewise, but straight, the photograph may be quite unlike her. I said at once when your mother came back, "Why did you not advise her how the photograph ought to be and how she ought to stand?" Why is our photograph, i.e., mine and your mother's, so distinct, and why does your mother look in the photograph like a girl, although she is 50 years old? Staśka will send a copy here

[1] Staśka is the writer's wife's niece whom this Leonard, Mania's friend, wants to take to America and to marry without knowing her. For a similar case, cf. Butkowski series.

[2] This kind of parental egotism, where the parents hinder the marriage of their children because they wish to exploit their work, is really rare. The impulse to it is frequent, as we shall see more than once, but is usually counterbalanced by the stronger wish to see the children married. Cf. Introduction: "Marriage."

when it is ready, and I am to send it to you, but if it does not please me I will send it back and let her have another taken.

As to my opinion, I don't like to praise anybody much but I must confess that Staśka is a very good girl, intelligent, working, saving, handsome, only a little too tall and not instructed. But these are secondary faults. At any rate she deserves good luck. Today is precisely the twenty-ninth anniversary of our marriage with your mother. It was also Sunday, and St. Peter's and St. Paul's day on Monday. We have lived together for so many years, struggling with a various fortune [*sc.* rather bad], which is likely to be found in every marriage. Well, good or bad fortune must be accepted alike. . . . .

Our priest is still alive, but very feeble. . . . .

[J. Sękowski]

294   July 5, 1914

Dear Children: . . . . It is perhaps better that you did not succeed in selling your house, for there is no evil which does not turn to good.[1] Perhaps later you will sell it more profitably, and in America when you have money you can buy land at any moment; there is enough of it there. I thank Frania very much for her work upon Tadeusz. It is well that he is now with Leosia. Let everybody have a part of the trouble. And thus a day [will pass] after a day, a year after a year, and you won't even notice how he will reach his 16th year, and then, according to the American laws, he will be able to work himself. [News about acquaintances.]

From Mania I received a very strange letter. She and Leosia like to write much and to add larger and smaller scraps to the letter. And this letter had also such a scrap—and nothing more. . . . . Probably the letter was too thick and somebody hoped that there was money, opened the letter and did not put back the main sheet. . . . . Upon this scrap . . . . Mania writes us to send Józef's [daughter] Staśka to America, saying that she had a boy there who would send Staśka a ship-ticket. Mother was a week ago in Kalisz about this matter.

---

[1] This kind of optimism is nothing but the ultimate expression of the usual peasant resignation to the past and the irreparable which prevents him from being ever discouraged and always enables him to begin again. The emigration to Brazil afforded many such examples. Peasants who were born rich came back completely ruined and began at once as manor-servants to work and to economize with unrelenting energy and vitality.

Staśka would be glad to go but your aunt and her Walenty [her second husband] won't let her go from Kalisz, for Staśka has a good position there, while your aunt and Walenty suffer misery, because they both keep drinking heavily. Your aunt quarreled at once with your mother, so that the latter cried. I don't wonder, for the Żytniewski family [from which the aunt comes] is good only for drinking vodka, quarreling, and discord.[1] Staśka, as it seems, will be something else. As I noticed, she is intelligent, sparing, pretty enough, only somewhat too tall. Grandfather Żytniewski is with us . . . . but quite impotent [feeble *and* useless].

[J. Sękowski]

295 July 19, 1914

Dear Mania: Yesterday we received Staśka's photograph from Kalisz and today we send it to you. I don't know whether all this will succeed and whether Staśka's journey will come about. She wants to go to America; your aunt is not satisfied with it, but she cannot hinder it. Everything will depend upon how they write to each other and how their photographs please them. . . . . If they come to an understanding, I would advise you not to send a ship-ticket, but money . . . . for in the case of some unforeseen hindrance it is easier to get the money back. . . . . But send it to my address, for it is impossible to trust your aunt. They are in a bad situation, and very avaricious. . . . . If you don't receive any answer from Kalisz, don't think that it is Staśka who does not answer, but that perhaps somebody plays bad tricks, i.e., either her employers [she is a housemaid] or your aunt. So write simultaneously here and to Kalisz. Before Staśka leaves, we should like to bring her here and to send her from here upon the journey. . . . .

[J. Sękowski]

296 Bydgoszcz, November 23, 1913

Dear Mania: I received your letter with the photograph and I am very glad that you got such a man. But first of all, let him be good, for money is of no use if your life is not happy. When you

---

[1] This is a hard expression, as his own wife comes from this family and her parents live with him.

wrote that I could also have such luck Teodor [her husband] was terribly angry and is still angry with you. It is true that I could have also such luck. But no, even now I still fear to go to America, and when I was at home I was so timid that I would not have gone to Konin alone. If I had gone when father had ordered me, when Rozyna went from the manor, I should have fallen precisely into that misery. Perhaps I should not even live today, for you know how Adam had it how father told him to beg.[1] And I am so inclined to crying and so timid, I should never have talked to anybody [father or mother] about it. You know how it is with the Bajtlers now, how much Rozyna cost them [how large a dowry they gave] and what a splendid wedding it was. And now what has she?[2] You know that he wanted to shoot her down. Everybody must bear the lot which God designed for him. I have not a gay life either. I did not intend to write of it to you ever, but now over this letter of yours he made me suffer more than ever. You see how it happens. You know him, for he was in our house. Do you remember how good he was—like a child—and now he sins as if he were not the same man. Formerly he mended my stockings and made my bed when I was alone, and now he says that mother and father persuaded him and that we held him in order to make him marry me. And what did he say to me? He said that he would be so good that I should beat him rather than he me, that he would take me even in a single dress if father gave nothing, that he had 1,000 marks and this would be enough for everything. And now he says that it is not true, that he never said so. He reproaches me always that others got so and so much, and what did I get? And he denies that he ever said so [that he would take me without dowry]. May your husband only not be so false! I don't even wish to write home about it, for father would tell it to everybody, and it is a shame for us. Nothing can be done. . . . . I became a guiltless victim, for I thought that he loved me so of himself, while it was mother who persuaded him and gave him more than one glass of liquor. And now he reproaches me with all this. Father also plagued me and I did not have a merry life at home, while he painted everything so sweetly to me—that I should have every-

---

[1] Allusion to No. 284.

[2] Rozyna probably married the man the writer was to marry. Her allusions to dowry mean that a wife with a dowry has an additional right to good treatment.

thing so good.   Do you remember how it was in Ruda at that party, how he danced with all the girls while I stood in the corner and wept? And this was only the first year.   What must it be now, when 5 years have passed?   I cannot write you everything.

I greet you a thousand times and wish you good sleep.   Could you not have sent me at least a dollar, to drink some wine, for I was not at the wedding?

[KAZIA KACPERSKA]

Love each other, that you may have a child, a boy, in a year. Remember me and comfort me.

MAKOWSKI SERIES

We find here again a modification of the fundamental peasant attitudes, due to the fact that the Makowskis are not farmers, but belong to the handworker class in a small town.

The letters of Antoni Makowski give us the expression of a paternal feeling distinct from that which we find in other series; it is a father's love without any assumption of authority or any patronizing. But this simple attitude is less primitive than the complex one of love and authority which we have seen in the earlier series. The lack of paternal authority implies a disintegration of the primitive familial group. This is proved in the present case by the familial quarrels alluded to in Makowski's letters and by the lack of solidarity of which he complains. The causes of this change are: (1) the fact that among the handworkers the old forms of social life, though slower to disappear in provincial towns than in large cities, dissolve more rapidly than in the country; (2) the emigration, both to America and to Prussia, of which the district of Przasnysz is one of the oldest centers. In consequence of this the father, in his relation toward his children, ceases to be the representative of the family-group and becomes a mere individual.

Another interesting point in this series is the attitude toward death. As noted elsewhere, death for the peasant is an important but normal phenomenon—normal not only as to theoretical reflection but also as to the sentimental reaction toward it. In the intelligent classes, on the contrary, the death of a beloved person is always reacted upon as an abnormal fact, in spite of the theoretical reflection. The difference has its source in the social regulation of the attitude toward death which we find among the peasant traditions. Socially, death is a normal fact, and will be such for the individual in the exact measure in which the individual's attitude is socially determined. This view is corroborated by the fact that in any concrete case of death among the peasants today (if we abstract the remnants of the old naturalism and of the magical Christianity) the important part is played by the social-religious system, while the individual mystical attitudes are relatively little developed. Death is viewed by the dying person and by his relatives from the standpoint of the religious community to which the individual and his family belong; the interest in future life, the problem of the relation to God, are less absorbing than the questions of social ceremonies before and after death, and of the attitude of the family and the community toward the dying individual, of the common prayers to be said, masses to be celebrated, etc. This shows the extent to which social regulation of the attitude toward death is dominant.

In the present case, where the familial connection is weakened, one link of this social regulation is lacking. The death of Zygmunt and that of his mother are reacted upon in the socially determined way within the narrow circle of the nearest family on the one hand and within the widest circle of the community on the other, but not by the intermediary circle of the family in the wider sense, as including all relatives. (Cf. the behavior of Walery's father, in the Wróblewski series.) Further, in the case of Zygmunt's death there is a socially abnormal element— the extraordinary nature of his sickness. But otherwise, we find the typical attitudes—the calm, although sorrowful, expectation of death by the dying person and the family; the traditional farewell and blessing given to those who remain; the religious ceremonial before death (with its magical background); the funeral ceremonies, with their social importance, etc.

THE FAMILY MAKOWSKI

Antoni Makowski, a shoemaker
His wife
Stanisław (Staś, Stach) ⎫
Zygmunt ⎪
Wacław (Wacuś, Wacek) ⎬ his sons
Kazio (Kaziek) ⎭
Mania (Marynka), his daughter
W. Makowski, Antoni's brother
Władek (Władysław), a cousin
Grandmother Grudzińska, the mother of Antoni's wife (probably)
Hipek ⎫
Franek ⎬ her sons

297–305, TO STANISŁAW (STAŚ) MAKOWSKI, IN AMERICA, FROM FAMILY-MEMBERS IN POLAND

297 PRZASNYSZ, December 29, 1908

In the first words of our letter "Praised be Jesus Christus."

We received two of your letters, and we are very much satisfied, for in your first letter you wrote that you were sick and we were terribly grieved, but in your second letter you write that you are in good health, and we thank our Lord God, for this [health] is a treasure from God. . . . . We are very much pained that it is already the second Christmas eve that we divide the wafer and you are not here. We said "With whom does our Stach divide the wafer?" and we looked upon your photograph. I shed tears that you are not here, dear Stach, and we cannot divide this dear wafer with you, for we don't know whether we shall live until the next year. May God grant us to see one another as soon as possible! We divided all of us the wafer which you sent among all of us. Kaziek took a bit of it and went to your photograph and pretended to put it into your mouth, saying, "Dear Staś, bite a little of this wafer!" and we wept.[1]

---

[1] Kaziek expressed symbolically the idea of the spiritual participation of the absent brother in the familial festival. We see here how new symbols are created in order to keep up the spirit of the old organization in new conditions.

Dear Staś we received the large photographs, but not the small ones. . . . . Probably they were stolen in the post-office, these photographs and the little crib [a colored paper imitation of a crib, one of the popular Christmas tokens, like stars, angels, Santa Claus, etc.]. We are pained that you have spent money and we have no benefit of it; you must labor for every grosz. It is a pity. . . . . You look very handsome in the photograph. How big you have grown! And this best girl looks rather pretty also. Who is she? Tell us where she comes from.[1]

Dear Staś, why do you reproach us about some gossip? Since you have been [in America], for almost 2 years, you never wrote even two words about people, so what gossip can there be? We are very much astonished and we wonder. Dear Staś, you know the whole Grudziński family. They envy us, they would drown us in a spoon of water if they could—Hipek as well as Franek and the grandmother [so probably they are the source of the gossip].[2] But perhaps our Lord God will grant us to overcome everything with His help. . . . .

Dear Staś, we embrace you innumerable times. May our Lord God help you in everything. We admonish you, save as much money as possible, in order to have a remembrance that you have been in America when you come back to our country. . . . .

A. MAKOWSKI

298   November 8 [1909]

. . . . DEAR STAŚ: Now I shall describe to you Zygmunt's sickness. He was sick with typhoid fever for 17 days. No help could be given. Our doctors could not help. I brought a doctor from Ciechanów, and he could not help either; it only cost much money. But I wanted to save him, for he was the only support of us. Now the three little ones are left with me, and your mother upon the bed.

[1] The photograph was evidently taken at the wedding of some friend where Staś was a best man, and the best men and maids were photographed in pairs. An occasion of this kind is often the beginning of a relation between a best man and a best maid leading to a new marriage. Indeed the pairs are often matched with this in view. Hence the interest of the parents in the girl.

[2] The Grudzińskis are the family of Antoni's wife. We find here a new type of dissolution of familial ties. Up to the present we have seen only individual members losing the attitude of familial solidarity for some particular reasons. Here we find an open fight between two branches of the family, evidently made possible by the growing differentiation of town from country life.

The deceased Zygmunt was a little angry with you for having written him thus, that he behaved badly. Somebody must have informed you falsely, for he was interested in nothing except work and church. He had improved himself for two years and passed the examination in the school. Your father has wept a long time for you, but there remains the hope that at least we receive sometimes a letter from you; this is our whole joy. But from Zygmunt we shall never more receive anything. Before dying, he bade us all farewell, and you also, dear Staś. He asked you not to be angry with him. He had a very nice funeral. There were as many people as on All Saints Day, even many Jews. Four garlands were carried before the coffin, which were made for him in the town, and we received two telegrams, one from Płock, from the priest Królikowski, and one from his companion. I cannot write any more about Zygmunt's funeral, for our heart bursts open with sorrow. . . . .

Dear Staś, you may be exempted [from military service], because Zygmunt is dead, and these others are small. Your father hopes you will come home perhaps. We have nothing more to write. We hope that you will share our sorrow. Now we all greet you. Answer us as soon as possible. As to Władek [cousin], don't answer him at all; why should you have this trouble with him? When Zygmunt was sick he did not even drop in once. . . . .

[Your father]

ANTONI MAKOWSKI

299   November 15, 1909

. . . . DEAR STACH: First I inform you about the sad situation of your parents. Zygmunt is dead, on November 2, after terrible sufferings, for he was terribly ill for 3 weeks and did not speak a word for 2 weeks. I have lived 40 years and I have never seen a man so desperately sick as he was. Your parents did not undress for 17 nights for they both had to sit with him, because he always tried to run away, and beat himself so that his arms and legs were all bruised. And now I write you news which is much sadder still. Your mother fell sick at once after the death of the late Zygmunt and is now severely sick, so that the priest was there with our Lord God [sacrament], and she will soon follow her son. And as to their material situation, they have exhausted whatever they had. Your father walks like a shadow from grief. And you ask why do they not answer you. But perhaps you don't receive our letters; perhaps you are then in the factory and somebody else receives your letters. More-over, somebody has turned your head and you listen to him and write foolish letters to your parents. When they received your last letter they became still more sick. So, dear Staś, forget everything and share the sorrow of your family. Now we, your uncle and aunt, send you sincere greetings. Amen.

W. MAKOWSKI

300 December 8 [1909]

. . . . We received your letter, for which we thank you. Now, when the Christmas holidays are approaching, we send you a wafer and we divide it with you and we wish you merry holidays. We wish you to have merrier holidays than we have here in our country, for we have very sad ones, because we are pained that you are not here and Zygmunt is not here and mother is very sick, so that she cannot rise, and she may not live until the holidays. Now we won't describe any-thing more until the next letter. I, your oldest brother Wacław, and Mania and Kazio, we three little orphans, we divide the wafer with you and wish you a Merry Christmas. And don't for-get us. . . . .

WACŁAW MAKOWSKI

301 January 1, 1910

. . . . DEAR STAŚ: We received your two letters, for which we thank you, for only your letters rejoice us. Your mother was awfully glad to receive this letter; she even kissed it from joy. For your mother is very sick. Dear Staś, don't grieve that you are far away in the world and have nobody except God. Your mother has been sick for more than two years, and has remained in bed for 10 weeks, and thus, dear Staś, I must worry terribly, for I have nobody. I must cook myself, for Marynka is too little yet and needs care herself. And as to the family [relatives], in happiness they are good, but in misfortune they don't even look. I don't know how I shall do now. Your mother won't live long; Mania and Wacek must be sent to school, for they have not yet learned much. But I don't know how I shall manage all this. Our Lord God has put a terrible cross upon me, and I have carried it for 3 months already. I don't work any more at all in my shop. Now I thank you for the money, for it was very useful to me. May God give you health [as reward]. And Kaziek is a pretty boy; you would not recognize him. And he is clever! [Weather.]

Your mother cannot write any more, so she tells me to write you thus: She kisses you with her whole heart and her whole soul, and wishes you every good, whatever you want from God, and success in your intention. "And [she says] I wish you to be my true child, good and religious. And may we see each other in Heaven. And don't forget about your father and these little orphans. And now I bless you in this far world, in the name of the Father and the Son and the Holy Spirit, Amen! And now I bless also my dear brother-in-law. Don't abandon my Stach! And I bless you, my sister, and your children; may God bless you! And also my brother [cousin] G."

Only don't grieve, only don't grieve; perhaps our Lord God will still grant health to your mother. Now we greet you, I your father, wish you a good New Year, and Wacław, and Mania, and Kazio.

ANTONI MAKOWSKI

302   January 14, 1910

DEAR STAŚ: We send you sad news, for we have already buried your mother. A great sorrow reigns over us after the loss of our dearest [wife and] mother and the dear Zygmunt. We have gone through two funerals in so short a time. The funeral was very beautiful, for there were 4 priests. The priests did not cost me very much. And there were many people. Yes, dear Staś, I am totally ruined. Your mother has been sick for more than two years, and the doctors cost, and I could not work, and now I cannot work either, because a terrible sorrow overcomes me for your mother and Zygmunt and you, dear Staś. Now I don't know what to do. If I knew that in America I should be able to educate these three orphans I would go to America. So I beg you, answer me and advise me how to manage all this. Yes, dear Staś, don't grieve, only pray our Lord Jesus for health and don't forget about us and don't be angry with us for writing you so often. Now we greet you, I, your father, kiss you heartily, and Wacław, and Marynka, and Kazio.

ANTONI MAKOWSKI

303   February 15, 1910

DEAR STAŚ: . . . . I thank you heartily for your letter, because only your letter can rejoice us. We cannot cease to long for our beloved Zygmunt and our dear mother who loved us so. And now we must think about ourselves. But nothing can be done. God's will! Your mother was not sick with consumption, but with chronic lung catarrh, so the doctors said. It is only your "dear" grandmother who gossiped that your mother was sick with consumption. She told it everywhere in Przasnysz and even wrote it to America. Such is our dear family!

Now, dear Staś, I shall describe to you our incident—what the Lord God can do! When Zygmunt died, our deceased mother wept terribly, lay down at once and died from this sorrow. On the third day after your mother's funeral Wacuś fell sick with typhoid and had 41° [Centigrade] of fever. What could we do? Marynka and Kazio with tears prayed to God's Mother and devoted him to God's Mother and asked God's Mother for his health, promising that when he recovered, he would go to Częstochowa. The fever disappeared at once. It was at 3 in the afternoon, and at 4 the fever had already yielded. The doctor could not believe that he was better. He was weak after this, but for the last two weeks he has walked and now, thanks to God, he is already going to school and is perfectly healthy.[1]

Dear Staś, I should advise you that it would be better if this Miss Szczepańska went to you. You know her very well, so perhaps she would be good for you. Now she is in Warsaw, and even got a little instructed. As to Miss Drewniacka, I cannot tell you anything, for it could spread about [gossip], only I write you that she wrote a letter to one boy here in the town asking him to come [and marry her].[2]

ANTONI MAKOWSKI

304 April 7, 1910

. . . . I thank you heartily for your letters, for only your letters rejoice me. I should like to have a letter from you every day, but it is impossible. Now, dear Staś, I write you about our holidays. We had very sad holidays, so that I cannot even describe them to you. Nobody from our family calls upon us and nobody helps us. As long

---

[1] Cases like this one are related by the thousands, not only among peasants, but among intelligent classes. The vow of a pilgrimage to Częstochowa is considered particularly effective.

[2] The fact would be considered reprehensible in two respects, (1) as proving that the girl is not really attached to Staś, since not long before becoming engaged to him she wrote to another, and thus she wants to marry just anybody; (2) as proving that she lacks self-appreciation, since she makes advances.

as everything was whole [clothes, etc.] it was only half as bad, but now I don't know what way to turn.   You wrote me to take some woman, but it is not worth while, for I must give her a room and pay her, and the children won't have any benefit.   Probably I shall be obliged to marry.   Up to the present I see nothing convenient.   And the shoemaker's work is bad, there is no earning at all.   I don't know how it will be.   All the men are going to America. . . . .   Now our priest from Przasnysz is going to Częstochowa, and I have devoted Wacek [made a vow in his name that he would go].   But I don't know how to send him alone, and then it will cost about 15 roubles. . . . .

A. Makowski

305   June 21, 1911

. . . . Dear Staś: I won't describe to you my success; you know yourself very well how I succeed.   You write in your letter that when Wacek and Mania grow up it will be very well with me.[1]

And now, dear Staś, I called upon Mrs. Drewniacka on the same day when I received the letter, and Mrs. D., had also received a letter from Mania [her daughter].   So we talked it over and I went to the priest and took both birth-certificates, which I send you.[2]   Why did you not write, when your wedding will be?   I would have gone to your wedding, while now I won't go.   It is very painful to me not to be at the wedding of my first son.   And now describe to me, how the wedding was and who was at it. . . . .   Send me your wedding photograph.   Dear son, I send you my blessing, may Lord God bless you and God's Mother and St. Józef.   I wish you every good [etc.].   In the name of the Father [etc.].   Now I cannot write any more for regret contracted my heart,[3] only I greet you and my dear daughter-in-law.

Your loving father,
Antoni Makowski

[1] Evidently an unfinished reproach.   The father is offered small comfort. The son should have promised to come back, and the following paragraph seems to indicate that he had formerly promised to take his father to America.

[2] The son marries precisely the girl whom the father sought to dissuade him from marrying, and the father complies with the fact without protest.

[3] The letter is one of the best expressions in our collection of paternal resignation and affection in the face of the repudiation by the child of the familial ties. Usually in such cases the father rebukes, threatens, preaches, or curses.

CUGOWSKI SERIES

The author of these letters, Józef Cugowski, is a skilled workman of peasant origin and has evidently some general instruction. His letters are in rather good Polish. He has kept almost all the traditional peasant attitudes, only more individual, conscious, and equilibrated.

After his father's death he assumes immediately, as the oldest brother, the rôle of head of the family, and if he still seems to recognize that his brothers have an equal right of decision and asks for their advice, it is partly a formality, partly a desire to keep harmony, partly, finally, the lack of personal interest in any possible economic arrangement about the fortune left. This lack of personal interest shows that for him the rôle of head of the family is nothing but a social function imposed by circumstances and resulting from the familial unity. But there is one point in which his attitude differs slightly from the average peasant's—he goes further in his patriarchal attitude than is normal in the country by practically excluding from the family-group all the members who do not bear the same name, i.e., married sisters and brothers-in-law. In this respect his (otherwise justified) treatment of Graj, his contemptuous attitude toward Margas, his (probably willing) limitation of the subscription to their parents' monument, are very significant. He goes so far as practically to consider his stepmother and his sisters-in-law more as real members of the family than he does his own sisters. Now, there is of course some superiority of masculine over feminine relationship among the peasants, but not to such an extent; there are localities where no such superiority seems to be acknowledged at all. As to the question of keeping the father's farm—it is evidently Graj who is nearer to the peasant tradition than Cugowski. Since no son can take the whole farm because all the sons have other occupations, according to the peasant's ideas it should be taken by a son-in-law rather than be divided. But Cugowski wants the farm to remain in the hands of some male member of the family, and since this cannot be done he no longer cares for its integrity.

In religious matters Cugowski keeps most of the characteristic features of the actually dominant moral-religious system, particularly the rich formalism and the lack of really mystical or eschatological interests. But religiousness is already much more individualized and internal. Except the mention of the crime in Jasna Góra (Częstochowa), we find nothing in his letters concerning churches, ceremonies, meetings, etc. Thus, we can consider his religion as intermediary between the moral and the mystical system. The same may be said of his attitude toward death; still to some extent socially determined, it leaves much more place for individual sorrow.

One of his features is typically peasant—the pomposity of style so usual in all the peasants who rise intellectually above the average level. In this particular case there is hardly any showing off. We have rather the impression (which all the peasant speeches leave) that the man simply enjoys his own ability of "fine" talking or writing. It must be remembered also that a letter ought to be the best literary work of which the writer is capable.

THE FAMILY CUGOWSKI

Cugowski, a farmer
His second wife
Józef, a skilled workman ⎫
Teoś, a merchant   ⎬ his sons
Staś (Stanisław)   ⎭
Piotr

Wikcia ⎱
Frania ⎰ his daughters
Anusia
Ewcia (Ewa), Józef's second wife
Marya P. (Marynia), Józef's third wife
Romuś ⎱
Micio ⎰ Józef's sons (by his second wife)
Henio
Genia (Geniusia) ⎱
Bogunia
Irenka ⎰ Józef's daughters (by his second wife)
Stasia
Michasia, Teoś' wife
Lucia, Staś's wife
Graj, Wikcia's husband
Ludwik, Frania's husband
Margas, Anusia's husband

306–18, FROM JÓZEF CUGOWSKI, IN POLAND, TO HIS
BROTHER STANISŁAW (STAŚ), IN AMERICA

306 OSTROWIEC, July 25, 1907

"Praised be Jesus Christus!"

DEAR LUCIA AND STAŚ: With a great impatience we awaited the
news from you, whether God had led you happily to the place of your
destination. But glory be to God for having kept you happy and in
health, in spite of great difficulties and dangers. Thanks be to him
for it for eternal times. I received your letter two weeks ago, and I
answer only today because of different circumstances about which I
shall inform you at least partly in this letter.

First, I inform you about a very sad thing concerning our dear
father, that he bade us farewell forever. Tired with his life's work,
the old man moved to a better land, into eternity. [It happened]
soon after your departure, no more than a week, for he died on
May 25. I intended to leave the next day, as we had decided, when
I received suddenly a telegram asking me to come for the funeral. So
we both went and Genia with us. Teoś was also there, but alone.
The funeral was very beautiful. The priest came home for the body
and accompanied it to the cemetery, because Teoś and I attended to
everything ourselves. I don't know how it would have been otherwise, how our good and sentimental [irony] brother-in-law Graj

would have arranged it, for he even refused, or rather did not wish to send a telegram for me and Teoś, but busied himself with everything until the priest and the neighbors forced him. He wished to push his work to the end, but he did not succeed at all. What is worse for him, he has become now in our eyes and conviction our worst enemy forever. When we came everything was ready, i.e., the funeral agreed upon, the coffin bought. But God have pity, what a coffin! First too narrow, but, what is the most important, about 6 inches too short. But it cost only 17 złoty [2 roubles, 55 copecks], so you can imagine what can be had for that money. As soon as I came I ordered at once another made and I took upon myself the decision of everything until Teoś came. Graj was very much dissatisfied and spoke very little with me. But that is not yet the end. After the funeral it was necessary to decide about what was left, of course, with our whole family present, that is, I, Teoś, Graj with Wikcia, Ludwik with Frania, Anusia, mother and Piotr. It was to be divided into equal parts, but as father said while alive that it was to go to one of you two, I don't oppose the will of our father, but respect it and resign my poor part for the benefit of you or Teoś. But as you were not present, I gave it in your name to Teoś. Frania with her husband and Anusia did the same. Only he [Graj] did not want to agree to anything; he wanted to be the farmer after our father's death, to give a few roubles to mother and to drive her out upon the road. But it cannot be and won't be so. I proposed to give him, as remuneration for the pains which he took for our father, one meadow, half of the harvest for this year, one part of the turf and the wood which lies near the house. But he refused to accept it. Then he got a few roubles in cash and such a dismissal that he went home without even bidding us goodbye. After this I called two farmers . . . . and wrote an authorization in favor of our mother, that she was to live in the house until her death, harvest everything, pay the taxes and keep the house in order, with the help and advice of these two farmers. They bound themselves by their own signature that they won't permit anybody to take anything, except Teoś in the future and our mother at present. In case of violence, these two have the right to call on others for help and to prevent positively any abuse.

Now, my Staś, he begins to protest furiously that as the oldest son-in-law he has the right to sell the farm at auction, and he says

that he has your authorization.   But we don't believe that you could
have resigned in his favor, particularly in writing.   I don't expect
it to be possible, knowing his mean intentions with regard to us all.
[Work; condition of the country.]

JÓZEF

307   September 7, 1907

.... DEAR SISTER-IN-LAW AND BROTHER: We received your
letter on Thursday .... for which we thank you very much.   We
waited for some news from you, but alas! such a large space divides
us that no news can come rapidly from the other hemisphere of the
earth.   But glory be to God that you are both in good health, and
that you, my Staś, have some work and can earn for your living and
that of your wife.   I hope that later on you will get better and more
profitable work .... and then you can live better than in our native
country.   You know how it was when you were leaving, and now
things don't seem to get better but rather worse.   The trade and
industry are stopping, particularly now when winter approaches.
Our factory goes on very badly .... and you know, my dear ones,
that there is a numerous family to nourish, so there is enough to
think of when one cannot earn.   And what is the worst, there is no
place to go, for in the whole country it is the same, in some localities
still worse.   Food has become much dearer .... everything costs
about $\frac{1}{3}$ more than before.   It is because in many localities hail has
beaten the crops, in other localities they have rotted, in Russia and
Lithuania there were strikes in many manors, and the crops were
left in the field.   Moreover fires, incendiary and from lightning, have
also destroyed much bread.   In a word, our Lord God took the
bread away and begins to punish these beastlike elements which
now don't acknowledge their Creator as their Lord above them, but
in the most horrible way blaspheme against Him and against everything which is holy, i.e., the faith and His commands.[1]

Dear Staś, you ask me now for the second time to get from
Barański your 40 roubles.   So I shall describe to you now his present
situation.   When he came back he got sick and stayed for some
weeks in bed.   I was just then in their house, but they begged me

---

[1] A good expression of the peasant's hate of revolutionary ideas, not counterbalanced in this case by any reflection on the probable bearing of these ideas upon
the condition of the lower classes or upon the national Polish life.

in the name of everything [and said] that when he was better and began to work somewhere he would try to get money and would give it back. But what happened? A few days later he came to health again, and went in search of work in the direction of the frontier, to Zawiercie. And what did this scoundrel do? A few steps from the railway-station he cut his throat and stabbed himself three times. When people noticed him, he gave few signs of life. They took him . . . . to the hospital . . . . and sent her a telegram asking her to come. I don't know whether he is still alive, and even if he recovers, criminal responsibility awaits him, the scoundrel, for suicide.[1] And thus, my dear ones, your 40 roubles are to be considered lost. In their home is misery, some children, and not a penny put aside. . . . . And you must know, dear Staś, that you are not the only one who is the victim of this cheater. He had borrowed money from many people when coming back from America, and even more than from you. Who is to be made responsible for this money, while this woman and her children ought rather to have some help? You remember probably how I advised you to be careful, for you did not know him, and now my prophecy is almost fulfilled. . . . .

From our mother we have had no news for some weeks. I don't know how Graj treats her there. But it seems to me that he won't get anything by his avarice and wrath. . . . .

Dear brother, I inform you about one thing more. I don't know whether you will both agree. We decided, Teoś and I, to erect a monument to our dear parents. It would cost about 150 roubles, and the local priest would take charge of the matter, for it was he who gave this idea, a very good one. So if you wish to contribute, it would be a monument from the sons, for our sisters refused to take part in it; only the sons with their wives. . . . .

Józef

308   December 29, 1907

Dear Sister-in-law and Brother: [Expression of familial affection; New Year wishes; news about work and factory.] I received a letter from our mother a few days ago. She describes to

---

[1] Technically correct as to the possibility of prosecution, but a more unreserved and self-righteous condemnation of suicide than is usual among peasants. As shown by popular tales and songs the attitude is by no means uniform, but, as in the higher classes, varies with the motive of the suicide, the character of the person, and the social consequences of the act.

me more or less her farming, and writes about Graj, that he took all the clothes of our late father. But no matter; he can take nothing [valuable]. In a few words I shall describe it to you. He wrote a long letter to Teoś, with claims to everything which is left. . . . . He intended to have it sold at auction, and even asked a lawyer's advice. He wished by all means to triumph and to have the upper hand, but he was deceived. Teoś sent me his letter, which he probably did not expect. And of course I gave him a suitable answer, for he slandered me as well as my wife. . . . .

JÓZEF

309 March 25, 1908

Wednesday, Day of the Annunciation of the Holiest Virgin Mary. "Praised be Jesus Christus."

MY DEAR AND BELOVED L[UCIA] AND S[TAŚ] BOTH TOGETHER: [A page about work in America and in Poland.] Dear Staś, I got our last payment from the factory [insurance money, paid out when the workman leaves the factory, becomes unable to work or dies] and I put it into the bank. You will have, as last help, a few hundred roubles secure. And perhaps our Lord God will bless you in your work and your intentions, and you will earn some more money and increase your capital. May God grant it!

Here is misery, as before; nothing has changed. If we work for a week we stop for another or two. And what proscriptions they [the factory-owners] invent! It is awful. But what can we do, since in the whole empire the conditions are the same. And robberies and attacks are the order of the day, although we have a state of war. We don't know when it will be abolished and some rights given to the nation. From our factory many people have been dismissed, the big mill has stood still for some months. . . . .

Now, my Staś, I shall mention something about Graj. He complains awfully to you about me and Ewcia [writer's wife], saying that we have wronged him, that I have abused him in my letter and Ewcia has told him the truth. He says about me that Piotr instigated me, and therefore I acted and decided thus. But I shall tell you only this, that I have acted according to my own reason and conviction; I am not a child that anybody can instigate and persuade to do something which does not agree with the truth and my conscience and my own opinion, for I have my own reason already. If he says that through our fault he got too little, well, I shall try to add some [money] more, that he may have enough and may not complain about me or my wife.   And I will mention, or rather remind him, what he got and what we got.   And I will ask him also who has more rights, whether he, as the oldest son-in-law, or I, as the oldest son.   And if I made such a decision, it was not for my own benefit, but for the benefit of you and Teoś.   This is the first point.   And the second point is that all this [the farm] ought to remain in totality, as the only remembrance of our parents in our native country.   He thought probably that he would inherit all this and would manage it alone, but it cannot be by any means and will not be.   [Easter wishes.]

JÓZEF

310   July 12, 1908

. . . . My dear and beloved L[ucia] and Staś: I received your letter. . . . . Don't be angry with me for not having written to you, but I was sure that you would do as hundreds and thousands of people do who come back in throngs, cold and hungry.   But since your condition is not so bad, and moreover you are both in good health, we are very glad, and thanks be for it to God the Highest.   It would not be a crime if you should come back, but you know how it is now in our country, and so you are right in not moving.   [Describes the economic and political conditions of the country, lack of work, murders.]

Now I inform you, my dear ones, about our success and health at home.   I and my children are now healthy, thanks to God, but with Ewcia things are very bad.   For a long time she had been weak, she walked and did what she could.   But almost since Christmas she has been worse and worse, to such an extent that on Easter there was nobody to make anything [any Easter food].   I don't care for myself, but the children had almost nothing, and I have a heavy sorrow, for she was lying sick during the whole holidays, so weak that she could not come up these few steps.   I asked factory and private doctors, but it did not help at all, for it is a lung disease which requires a special cure.   So a private doctor, after examination, decided that she must go abroad.   So I had to do it, in order to save the health of the mother of the family which God gave us.   Well, without much hesitating I took my wife to Zakopane and placed her in a sanatorium there.   The cost is enormous, for it will cost almost 150 roubles monthly, but nothing can be done, I must comply with it. May God only grant her to recover.[1] I cannot determine today how long she will be there, for it has been only a week and a half. The doctor, after examining her, gave me this comforting hope, that she can recover, but not soon, at least in two months. May God the Omnipotent grant it, for I am unhappy with these small children in such a time as now. Believe me, my dear ones, I cannot keep my ideas together in view of the burden which overwhelms me. I try to get along with these children as well as I can, for it would be impossible to hire anybody. I must hire only for washing, and the rest Genia manages alone, according to my directions. You waited for a letter from me, but I was unable to write even a few words. When I came back from the factory, instead of resting I had to try to give some food to this poor sick woman. But could I do it as it ought to be done? And can one get everything always, even for money?

Yes, dear Lucia and Staś, my destiny strikes me hard, particularly as in the present time, which is so bad, I ought to be thinking about economizing as much as possible, and here, on the contrary, I must take the money which I have put aside in order to save health. But if God gives health, we must live in some way. Meanwhile may Thy will be done, my Lord!

It was at the end of May in Petersburg, I took Romuś [son] to Teoś, that he might learn business and help them. I have received already two letters from them and one from Romuś. He is very much pleased and he understands everything well. Perhaps God will grant him to have a piece of bread in this way in the future. He has not much instruction, but Teoś also has little and he manages

---

[1] From a man in Cugowski's position the sacrifice is great, for it probably means a sacrifice of his whole fortune. A peasant farmer would hardly do this. But it would be a mistake to explain it merely by a stronger affection. Cugowski's affection is probably not much stronger than that of an average peasant, particularly as it is his second wife and as half a year after her death he marries for the third time and seems to be happy again. There is certainly another reason for sacrificing more than a peasant would; he is a hired workman, his whole life is organized upon the basis of salary, and property has for him only the secondary value of a resource in the case of extraordinary expenses; its influence upon his social standing is also very slight. For the peasant, on the contrary, property means a basis, not only of economic life, but of the whole individual and social life. Farm-work is his main interest, land is the essential condition of his social standing in the community. Therefore for a peasant a sacrifice, economically equal to that of Cugowski would be subjectively incomparably greater, almost impossible.

a rather big business. Romuś has finished two classes, and if he is willing he can learn there, for it is easier than in our town. Teoś and his wife don't look well, although they have enough to eat and don't lack money. But they don't lack work and trouble either. They keep ten men, so there is enough to think about. Three good shops and a bakery are upon his head. There is income, but also enormous expenses. I advised them to take a smaller business and to manage it alone, then it would be easier. But they say that everything would be well were it not for those people who don't pay their debts. . . . . I have sent long ago the money for our father's monument, but I have no news yet whether it is ready. . . . . Genia learns very well; she got prizes last year and this year. She passed to the 3d division. . . . .

JÓZEF

311 BOLESŁAWÓW, September 7, 1908

DEAR AND BELOVED LUCIA AND STAŚ: . . . . I am a little comforted in hearing that after so long a time you got some work and you will be able to earn at least for a modest living. . . . . At least you made your wife free from that heavy work. This is your great luck, granted by God, that health favors both of you in these troubles about material existence, for otherwise it would be bad in that distant and foreign country. You write yourself, my Staś, that it is not well to be sick there, because the doctors' treatment is bad. The same usually happens here, with a few exceptions. Whoever has money, has everything, and whoever is poor, the wind always blows into his eyes [Proverb]. And it is no news that the working-class is ill-favored today, not only there but upon the whole earth-sphere.

As I have written you in the last letter, I think, Ewcia is sick. Up to the present she remains in bed, not even at home, but abroad, in Zakopane. . . . . But thanks to God, she feels much better, and perhaps God the Almighty will grant her to recover, although it costs us very much. More than two months have passed since she went there, and I manage to get on alone, as well as I can with my children. . . . . If I could earn more! But work is so bad, that I earn scarcely enough to keep the house, and God sent Ewcia the sickness, for which I spend the rest of the old supplies. I really don't know what will happen when everything is spent, and if health does not come back. I don't know what I shall do alone with these small children. . . . . But Thy will be done, O Lord! [Crops; weather; bad condition of the country.]

Józef

312 January 6, 1909

Day of the Three Kings † G[aspar] † M[elchior] † B[althazar][1]
"Praised be Jesus Christus."

DEAR AND BELOVED LUCIA AND STAŚ: [Two pages about the factory in which he is working and the conditions of the work.] Now I shall describe to you, my dear ones, our present sorrow, which harasses me terribly. Ewcia has been severely sick for the last three weeks, and so feeble that she cannot rise, while there is unhappily nobody to do anything for this poor sick woman and give her even any food. Genia goes to school, and even if she did not, she is still a child and what can be asked from her? I took a maid, but God pity us! She is quite incapable of doing anything. And I go to the factory for the whole day, so you can imagine what care this poor sick woman has. My health is also beginning to be ruined. Four weeks ago I got a spineache which plagued me so much in the beginning that I had to lie down and remained ten days in bed; I was unable to move my hand or foot, and the pain was terrible. Even today I am not quite well, but I cannot remain in bed, I must walk as well as I can, for my duties oblige me to do it. My sickness also has contributed to some extent to make my wife's health worse. And so she is grieved because of my sickness, and I am grieved a hundred fold more by her sickness, for mine can pass with time, while God alone knows how long hers will last. . . . . To complete all this, I received a letter from Teoś before Christmas [informing me] that Michasia [his wife] was dangerously ill with typhoid fever. The letter was full of such a terrible sorrow that we wept over their lot, although ours is not better in this respect. And, so my dear Lucia and Staś, I announce sad news to you. You have wished us a Merry Christmas, but we have spent it almost in tears, particularly I, for there is nobody to do anything. I don't care about myself, but about my children. And so from all sides sorrow and grief harass the man in this poor life, and there is no better hope in any respect. . . . .

Józef and Ewa with Their Family

[1] These three letters are written on January 6, with consecrated chalk, upon the door of every house, and are not to be erased until the following year.

. . . . DEAREST LUCIA AND STAŚ: . . . . I announce to you, my dear ones, a very sad news, a terrible blow that befell me a few weeks ago. Even today I don't know how to describe it to you, because of my heavy sorrow and terrible grief.

As I told you in my last letter, we both were sick, Ewcia and I. Today I am in good health, thanks to God, for my sickness was transitory and through care my pains have disappeared. . . . . But my dear poor Ewcia bade us farewell forever, leaving these little children orphans and me in a heavy sorrow with them. I don't know how to describe to you, my dear ones, what a terrible woe and despair are tossing me. I don't know how to define this terrible blow; I almost lose my senses. After such care on my part, after such enormous expenses, it was impossible to save her by any means from that terrible disease, until it ended with death amid horrible sufferings. She was conscious almost till the last moment, and begged us in the name of everything that is sacred to help her, poor martyr. You can imagine, my dear ones, what was going on within me when my children's mother and my wife implored for help and I could not help her. My heart almost burst open with grief in looking at a dear person whose life was going out forever before my eyes, and who had a right to live, who was very necessary in this world to bring up her children who were so small. You have no idea what a torture it is for the dying person when she is conscious. I cannot describe it and nobody can relate it. But I had no less to suffer in looking at such an agony. For if an old person dies one can more easily comply with it, while my poor Ewcia was still a young woman; she had lived scarcely 36 years, she was in the fulness of life, and she had to die. I was glad when she came back from abroad in September. She looked so well, and she was so full of joy that she had got her health back. But our rejoicing did not last. After a few weeks she began to get worse, and so rapidly that there was no help. Every day she was worse; you could almost see her fade away. I brought doctors again . . . . but it did not help at all. Three weeks before Christmas she lay down and did not rise again. . . . . Sad is my lot, for I am today in such a situation, that I have neither money nor wife, nor, what is the most important, a mother for my children. You must know my dear ones, that the 3 months abroad cost more than 500 roubles and, counting other expenses, I suffered an awful loss. And all this was in vain, for nobody has ever recovered from consumption, and poor Ewcia was sick with this terrible disease. Now, after her death and funeral I had to sell, almost for nothing, her bedding and many other things which she used, and I don't know what to do with the things which are left. It is easy to waste them, while they cost a considerable sum of money. And I have no near friends with me who would give me salutary good advice. Everything has fallen upon my head, troubled with a heavy sorrow. You can agree yourselves, my dear ones, that my present situation is painful above any expression. But Thy will be done, O Lord! I must carry this heavy cross which you have put upon me, O Lord! Give me only strength and patience in order not to fall under its weight!

My dear ones, I should have much to write you still, but excuse me, for even in penning these few words my heart is cut with sorrow, and I write almost without ideas, they have become so entangled. Three weeks have passed today since she left us, i.e., on February 7, at 10 o'clock in the evening, and still I cannot come to myself and I don't know what will be further. I only pray God to give me health in order to earn bread for these poor orphans, and to educate them that they may find their way in life. For myself I don't foresee any happiness upon this miserable world, for I have experienced none up to the present. In less than 17 years I have buried two wives, and in such conditions one may become weary of his life. . . . .

JÓZEF

314 April 2, 1909

. . . . MY BELOVED LUCIA AND STAŚ: . . . . You probably received my letter with the sad news, what a severe blow befell me. The second month since the death of my dear Ewcia will be ended soon, and still I cannot adjust myself to this reality. I feel so lonely. Every object reminds me vividly how great a lack is felt at every step when one has no wife, mother and housekeeper. Still more I feel it now, when the solemn holidays of Easter are approaching. Everybody rejoices, even if he is in misery, on this joyful day, while I, unhappy man, experience for the second time such an awful pain of heart, particularly today, being burdened with so numerous a family and in the critical times which have prevailed in our country during the last few years. But nothing can be done, such is evidently my destiny from God, to bear only heavy crosses and sorrow and toil-some labor.   In a word, it is not granted to me to share bright and pleasant days, but only thick clouds overshadow the horizon of my life and send sometimes strong lightnings which shatter almost totally the remnants of hope of my wretched life in this valley of tears.   And I can say truly "My soul is sorrowful even unto death." But Thy will be done, O Lord!   And although I am so tormented with different kinds of afflictions, still I don't lose hope in the mercy of the Highest, that He will deign to comfort me at least for the short time of my shattered life.   And conscious of the duties which I have, I invigorate myself with this hope and say, after the Lord's Psalmist: "Sursum Corda."

Dear Staś, I inform you moreover that besides the sorrow which I bear one thing still harasses us, i.e., this miserable fortune which was left after the death of our parents.   As you know, my Staś, Graj was the mainspring in trying to manage so that it might not get into your hands or those of Teoś, that it might not be willed to any of you by a notarial act during our father's life.   And thus it happened.   So now Graj gives Teoś no rest, but "dries his head" [annoys him by asking] continually that a division may be made, or that Teoś will give him the power to be a trustee of it.   But I cannot agree to it in any way. He does not write to me, for he is afraid because I have abused him much, once during our dear father's funeral, and then for the second time in my letter.   So he corresponds now only with Teoś and gives him no rest but wants to benefit from it himself and to drive our step-mother away.   But he does not succeed, for I know about everything because Teoś sends me all his letters; he does not suspect it probably. He tries to persuade Anusia's husband also, a man named Margas, to cede him their claims, and proposes to let this Margas live in this house. This Margas wrote already to me and to Teoś that a part is due to him also.   But I don't know him and don't wish to have this pleasure. And so, my Staś, think about it well, how to act.   If you want to keep this farm, I as well as Teoś, will give you a written document that we resign our claims in favor of you, and you may then make some plan with it, that it may remain with you and that in the future our name at least will be there.   To tell the truth, it is not a resting-place for us even in the future, for I suppose that it will end by being equally divided, and then each member of the family will get perhaps 60 roubles or even less, and it will not profit one member to pay all the others off, because there are 8 parts. . . . . You know, my dear ones, that Teoś and I have enough of our own troubles, and I don't want to occupy myself with something which has little material importance for me. And again, to give it to some fool like Graj or to some Margas that he may get the whole benefit is not suitable and I don't think of it. We have resolved that our stepmother shall stay there until her death and shall care for everything, but they don't like it and Graj wants to have the upper hand and to drive her away; but without our permission he can do nothing. . . . . Perhaps our Lord will grant us to meet this year at the consecration of our parent's monument; then we could settle this matter. . . . . I beg you, dear Staś, after receiving this letter write at once to Teoś and me. . . . .

JÓZEF

315   December 12, 1909
"L[audetur] J[esus] Chr[istus]."

DEAR LUCIA AND STAŚ: After so long an interruption I bring it about to write you something about myself, and during so long a time much material of different content has gathered. [Letter and photograph received.]

I inform you first, that I have entered for the third time into the conjugal bond. My wedding was performed on October 31, in the parish Wojciechowice. . . . . My wife's maiden name is Marya P. She is a young person only 26. She is of the size of the deceased, but her character is mild beyond expression, so that in a few days she knew so well how to gain the love of the children, particularly of the little Stasia, that the latter begins to cry aloud at the mention of her leaving. In a word, I thank God and the Holiest Mother for their holy providence. I can say boldly and from my heart that further my life will be lighter and happier, for I have suffered very much in my life, particularly during the last times. I am unable to describe what an enormous burden oppressed my shoulders. But God the Almighty in his Providence deigned to comfort me. It is true that only a few weeks have passed since our wedding, but I am confident that the future will be most certainly light, for such a noble character as that with which my beloved Marynia is endowed can never change. I at least will give not the slightest reason for it but will endeavor by all means to reward her sacrifice, for it is indeed not a small sacrifice, and I shall know how to appreciate it duly after so many troubles and such a heavy sorrow. But I won't describe it in detail; perhaps God will grant us to see one another and then you will get acquainted with my chosen little wife. Meanwhile . . . . we send you our wedding photograph. I dont know whether you will like her in the photograph, although I may say that she is well [pretty] enough.[1] But I inform you at the same time of news sad beyond expression. Genia has been dangerously and severely ill for some weeks, and this grieves us much. May God give her recovery, for it is really a pity. Such a good child. . . . .

MARYA and JÓZEF

316   October 15, 1910

. . . . MY BELOVED LUCIA AND STAŚ: First I inform you, my dear ones, about the very sad accident which happened in that miraculous place, Jasna Gora [Częstochowa], through this scoundrel and murderer, the Paulinist Damazy Macoch, and his mates. They disgraced the miraculous image of the Holiest Mother and robbed it of jewels and costly adornments. Moreover, they have long passed their time in the cloister-cells in revelry, and this year in July they committed a murder in this holy place. It is impossible to describe what a feeling of oppression prevailed in the country. . . . . But thanks to God, the main criminal and his associates have been caught, and justice will measure a merited punishment to them. [News about work, factory, weather.]

Dear Staś, there is the question of this miserable property left by our deceased parents. As you know, it is not willed to anybody, but must be divided into equal parts. Teoś wrote to me asking me to arrange it, but no other arrangement can be made except an equal division. So we came to an understanding with Teoś and it is decided thus, for you must agree yourself that such a situation cannot last long; everything gets wasted, and there is no proprietor to repair. . . . . Write me your opinion. . . . .

MARYA and JÓZEF with THEIR FAMILY

[1] Here the man's conjugal attitude is completely individualized. Although the marriage was probably contracted partly for economic reasons, partly with regard to the children, Cugowski, whose individual feelings are more developed than in the average peasant and less subordinated to the familial attitudes, introduces a sentimental element into his conjugal relations, which is usually lacking even in first marriages of peasants.

317 August 5, 1911

. . . . BELOVED LUCIA AND STAŚ: I beg your pardon for not having given you any news. . . . . It is not a big thing to write a few words and it does not take much time, only the most important part is played here by a thought free [of care], while I have very little of it, for trouble and sorrow have been my continual companions since long ago. Our Lord God does not spare me His crosses in this miserable valley of sorrow. And so, beginning with the sickness and death of my wife Ewcia, a year later [came] the death of my beloved and always regretted daughter Geniusia. She was extinguished like a light while still like a blossoming bud of a pure lily. The sorrow of my heart after the loss of these dear beings is not yet calmed, the wound of the heart is not yet healed, and already a new blow begins to wound my heart, for even if I do not wish it, I must tell you the sad news in order to relieve myself a little at least. Well, it is so, my dear ones. Henio [son] has been sickly for a long time, but now for a few months he has been seriously sick. I don't wish to believe it, but it proves that he has the same symptoms of disease as Ewcia and Geniusia had. Neither medicine nor strengthening food is of any help; he is weaker and weaker, he looks worse and worse, until at last he will end with this sad death.

And so, my beloved Lucia and Staś, this is more or less the first side of the medal of my present life, concerning the feelings of my heart and the moral side. And now as to the material side, I cannot say that it is painted with bright colors. [Work; factory conditions.]

Dear L. and S., inform me what is the news with you. . . . . From Teoś I have had no news lately. They succeed rather well, but health favors neither of them. Romuś and Micio are with them. Romuś has been there for more than three years, and I took Micio last October. Romuś is already a rather good salesman. As to Bogunia, she has finished three divisions [of the village school] and we don't know what to do with her now. Irenka passed into the second division. She does not learn well, but she is healthy and strong. Stasia is also in good health, only my poor dear Henio is very weak and it will clearly be difficult for him to recover. But may God grant it, for I am very sorry for him.

Now I shall mention in short our actual common life. Thanks to God, I cannot complain about my wife. She complies with every-thing as well as she can, not badly. Well, and the fruit of our love came to us, of female kind; she is 6 months old, is healthy and keeps well.

Inform us, my dear ones, what is the news with you, how does your health serve you, how do you succeed, and how about your progeny? Do you think of increasing your family now, or only when you have put some capital aside? . . . .

Marya and Józef with Their Family

318   November 12, 1911

. . . . Beloved Lucia and Staś: . . . We are glad that you are both in good health and success, and the proof of it is that you intend to buy a house. May God help you, my dear ones! Happy the man who does not need to pay this awful tribute of rent, having the opportunity to come to [acquire] his own property.

My dear L. and S., probably you think more than once . . . . why do I write to you so seldom? But you will agree that I have many reasons to be downhearted and sluggish and lazy toward everything, so to speak. I shall explain to you at least some part of these reasons. Well, you know what I passed through after your departure. I lost first my wife, a year later my dear Geniusia. This year a third blow struck me, a not less hard one; my beloved little son Henio bade us farewell forever on September 13. I am unable to describe my woe; you have no idea what sorrow and pain of heart toss me after the loss of these my dearest beings. I should not wish to my worst enemy that which God sends upon me. Among such pains and afflictions one simply does not want to live; the world, even in its most beautiful colors, loses its charm, and one becomes indifferent toward everything. Verily I am that martyr whom God puts to the test and whom destiny strikes heavily. But Thy will be done, O Lord! I say only this: Ill-fated [euphemistically, instead of "accursed"] is this disease against which no remedy has been found up to the present, but whoever is afflicted with it sees an inevitable death before his eyes. And it is the most terrible disease, for it consumes gradually, leaving the mind conscious almost until the moment of agony. And how many victims it swallows at different ages, mostly in youth. I will add only this, that it cannot be described, what a grief tears the heart in looking upon the slow agony of a dear being when you are unable to help, to give some relief or even some hope, while this [being] implores to be saved. My beloved children, how they longed for life! My dear Geniusia mentioned you often, saying that, when you came back she would already be grown up. But when the poor child was sick in bed, she said herself: "I shan't see auntie or uncle any more." And how she wished to see Teoś! In the same way my beloved Henio asked more than once: "Please, father, when will uncle come back from America, for I should like so much to see him." But alas! too large a space divides us, we could not even dream about it. Let us rather leave these sad questions in peace, for tears overflow the eyes and the heart almost bursts open with heavy grief. My dear ones, as to this money of yours, it is sent and probably you will receive it sooner than this letter. I had some trouble with it, for you did not send me any authorization, and I had to show your letter as a proof that you had asked it sent. They did it only for me, out of politeness, because they know me. . . . . This is how your capital stands: I have sent 375 roubles, the sending cost 3 roubles, 94 copecks, 20 roubles are left as your share, which you can receive only after New Year. You have also 20 roubles with me, and as I wrote you, the monument upon the grave of our parents cost 150 roubles, so I, Teoś, and you have contributed 50 roubles each. . . . . I did not use your money on anything else, for it was put in the bank in your name, and I could have put in even the biggest sums, and they would not have given me back even a penny. Such is the law. . . . .

M[ARYA] and Józef with THEIR FAMILY

BARSZCZEWSKI SERIES

The family Barszczewski lives on the limits of ethnographical Poland. The province of Gródno has a mixed Polish, Lithuanian, and White Ruthenian population. As it lies outside of the kingdom of Poland fixed in 1815, the efforts at Russification have always been stronger and more continuous there; thus, there is a certain influence of Russian culture. These two factors explain certain differences in attitudes when compared with the normal psychology of the Polish peasant. The infiltration of eastern influences may perhaps be the reason for the marked dissolution of the family relation which we find here. The father does not live with the mother (No. 322), Stanisław quarrels with Józefa, with Kryszczak, with Aleksander B., and breaks off relations almost completely with his parents—all because of certain economic misunderstandings. Tomasz writes an exceptionally hard letter to his mother when she asks for help (No. 328). Their brother-in-law, Stefan, is accused of indifference by his sister and parents. And it is evident from other facts that this situation is the result of the dissolution of a former state of greater solidarity. Indeed the claims of familial solidarity are the same as in a normal Polish family. For example, everybody asks Stanisław for money on the basis of the familial relations. And those claims are still partly recognized; Tomasz had lent money to Stanisław, Stanisław gives a dowry to his sister. More than this, we find here a typical endeavor to establish a personal connection between two members of the family who do not know each other (No. 328). Thus the fundamental familial organization was evidently the same as everywhere among the Polish peasants. And the disorganization cannot be explained merely by the influence of modern life, since it exists already in the older generation and could hardly develop so rapidly in the young generation if it had not been prepared.

The second feature is the "philosophical" attitude toward social and religious problems which we find in the letters of Tomasz and Aleksander. It is not Polish in its form, but reminds us of the socialistic and mystical reflections, usually clad in poetical expressions, of the Russian home-bred "philosophers of life." The route by which the influence came is easily explained; it can be only the Russian literature. Accordingly, those attitudes are rather superficial, particularly with Tomasz; they do not greatly influence the practical life.

THE FAMILY BARSZCZEWSKI

Jan Barszczewski, a farmer
His wife

Tomasz
Stanisław
Antoni } his sons
Aleksander

Józefa Kryszczak
Wiktora Błaszczuk } his daughters

Antonina, wife of Tomasz
Marya (Wiszniewska), wife of Stanisław
Marya (Górska), wife of Aleksander
Paulina, wife of Antoni
Aleksander Kryszczak, husband of Józefa
Alfons, son of Tomasz
Adela, daughter of Wiktora Błaszczuk
Stefan Górski, brother of Marya, Aleksander's wife
Stefan's father

319-48, TO STANISŁAW BARSZCZEWSKI, IN AMERICA, FROM FAMILY-MEMBERS, IN POLAND

319   GRODNO, November 17, 1906

[To Stanisław Barszczewski. Beginning of the letter missing.] About 70,000 people are tortured in prisons, hundreds have been shot and hanged. The spring . . . . will probably put more innocent victims to the sword than the present winter, for the blood that is shed, the fire of cities and villages, do not subdue the people but rather kindle hatred against their persecutors and oppressors. In our province it is a little quieter but at Indur robbers compelled the post-official to give them all the money from the office. In Sisdra the post-official killed one and wounded another of 12 robbers, and the others fled without money. But it does not matter much as long as there is no army with guns in villages and cities. . . . . Now everything is dear, from salt and matches up to the coat on your shoulders and the wagon of firewood at the market; cheap is only the life of the poor man, because it is taken away without question, without witnesses, without court.

Probably you are longing there, dear brother, and sometimes sorrowful. I anticipate that although such a great distance of land and sea separates you, still in your thought you visit your country, your relatives, and friends; you remember the radiant moments and the painful hours, you imagine the circumstances met long ago; your native country-house with its straw-roof and its dear inhabitants seems lovely to you; perhaps even the curved ridge between the fields or a naked stone upon the stripped soil reminds you sweetly of some mystery of the past. . . . .

TOMASZ BARSZCZEWSKI

320   VILLAGE SYTKI, December 26, 1906

OUR DEAREST SON STANISŁAW: We, your parents, inform you that we are alive and healthy, thanks to our Lord God. We wish to you also good health, and may God's Mother bless you in your health and help you in your plans, and may the Savior of the world not forget you, because you don't forget us. Truly, you are our son, because you remember our family. So we also bless you, at least in a letter, since we cannot speak with you face to face and heart to heart. God alone knows whether we shall yet speak with you, at least once before our death, and embrace you in our parental arms.

[BARSZCZEWSKIS]

[Greetings and wishes from brothers.]

And now I, [your] sister Józefa, I throw myself upon your neck, dear brother, and I kiss innumerable times your brotherly lips, at least by letter. May God keep you, brother, in His care, may God's Mother help you in all your plans, may the Guardian Angel care for you and remember you at every step, as you don't forget about me and help me. You sent me for my dowry such a big sum. I did not hope to receive such a gift, those 100 roubles. Once more I return and kiss your brotherly lips, ten times for every rouble.

Your sister, loving to the grave,

JÓZEFA BARSZCZEWSKA

321 November 10, 1907

Answer: "In centuries of centuries. Amen." In the first words of my letter: "Praised be Jesus Christus."

And then I send you, brother, a low bow, and I wish you from our Lord God every good, first health, then happiness, in a land so far away from your native country. May this God's Mother defend you against every ill. O, Saint Anthony, O Miraculous, hear my prayer! And you, all Saints, help my dear brother in so far a land to pass happily his time of service. And then also I, husband of Józefa from the village Bujak, Aleksander Kryszczak, your future brother-in-law, I send you, dear brother-in-law, my lowest bow and I wish you from our Lord God every good, whatever you ask from God. And then together with my wife, your sister Józefa, we send you the lowest bow and we wish you from our Lord God to live in health and happiness in America.

Now, dear brother, you sent a letter and you speak in it about being angry with me, your sister Józefa, and with brother Aleksander. You have a reason to be angry with our brother, but with me you have no reason to be angry. You write that I took the cow. But I did not take the cow myself, but our parents themselves let me take it. It was a sort of a dowry that I took. I did not demand anything from our parents, and my husband Aleksander did not demand it, because he heard from our parents that you wrote a letter that you would send me money for a cow. And now you write about being angry with me. But I did not take it myself. Our parents said so, "We have, thanks to God, two cows, so take the old one, and the young one will remain with us, and when your brother sends you money, you will buy another, or you will have it for something else."

O, dear brother-in-law, if you knew, what a misfortune I had. A cow, when calving, went away [died], and a young horse, 3 years old, died also. Therefore we beg you, dear brother-in-law, don't be angry with me and with my wife, because we have a farm which, thanks to God, cannot be counted as small—two parts of [my father's] farm (the third is taken away for my uncle), and 10 desiatinas [= 20 morgs = 26 acres] which I bought. . . . . And what you say about taking the cow away, I don't mind it, but your parents said themselves, "For such a large farm it would not be nice of us not to give the cow."[1] And they said, "Take the cow, children, and when Stanisław sends you money, you will buy another, and for us this young one will be enough." I gave them hay and vetch for their cow. So now, my wife and I, we beg you, brother-in-law, to keep your promise. Yes, dear brother, you have no reason to be angry. We beg you, if you cannot give us, then lend us at least, because we need it now very much. Goodbye.

JÓZEFA and ALEKSANDER KRYSZCZAK

322 [Spring, 1908]

[Three-fourths of the letter filled with greetings from all the members of the family.] And I, Aleksander, write further about how all this happened. Brother, you are very angry with me, because it happened so in our life. It is not you and not I who arranged it, but our Lord God himself sent it. In our life we were compelled to bear greater misery than this one, and we bore it; so we must bear this one also. My brother, if we don't forgive each other, our Lord God will not forgive us. You said, brother, to provide for the wedding of Józefa. So I gave such a wedding as was suitable. It cost all together, with the bed-furnishings, about 100 roubles, and the 100 roubles of dowry which you sent and the cow before calving, worth 80 roubles.

I did not write to you, brother, where father lives. Father is in Baciki at home. He does not wish to be with mother.

[ALEKSANDER BARSZCZEWSKI]

[1] The meaning is that Józefa's husband is a rich man, owns a large farm, and it would not be suitable if Józefa had too small a dowry.

323   [July 21, 1908]

DEAR LITTLE BROTHER: It is long that we have had no news from
you, about your health and existence, and we want to know something
about you—how you hammer out your happiness abroad. We know
that in America it is no longer as it used to be, because a multitude of
factories have stopped work. Many of our people have come back
under their native roofs; but you give no news of yourself.

Since spring our parents have been living in Grodno, father with
me, mother with Aleksander. With the present letter I hastily
address myself to you, hoping that I may find in your kindness a gracious help for me in the present moment which is a very difficult one
for me. The question is this: As you know, if you wish to earn a
miserable rouble here, you must bathe it in your sweat before you
receive it. In order to support my small children and my wife and
to assure their existence in the future, I must, according to my obligations, rise when the night with her dark cloak begins to fly before the
light of the coming day. While all people around me calmly sleep
untroubled on their soft couches, I set to work in order to clear the
roads for them, that when the powerful of this world walk in their
leisure they may not hurt their delicate feet against any small lump
of earth, or that the capricious ladies may not soil their many-colored
silk dresses. The whole long day I work like an ant in an ants nest,
until night drives away the last light of the day. And so days, weeks,
months, and years pass, and who knows whether my whole life will
not be like this?[1] Thanks to hard labor I succeeded in putting
aside a small sum out of which I bought a little land and built a small
house, but I cannot finish it because of lack of money; there are

---

[1] On this type of philosophizing, cf. Introduction: "Theoretic and Aesthetic
Interests." The content—the contrast between the rich and powerful, and the
poor workman—shows the influence of city life and of the workman psychology.
We do not find this attitude among the peasant farmers who, even if poor, have in
those matters a psychology of independent proprietors. Socialism finds little
interest among the farmers, not only because of its standpoint in matters of property but also because, since the abolition of serfdom, there has developed a certain self-consciousness and pride in the peasant which render the idea of being a
class oppressed by the capitalist devoid of content and difficult of acceptance.
There is envy, of course, and a sentiment of injustice in the division of property,
but no consciousness of being exploited—except in matters of taxes. Moreover,
the peasant farmer, being the member of a family, does not feel so isolated in his
struggle for life as does the workman. Tomasz is only beginning to develop the
workman psychology.

neither stoves, nor doors, nor windows, nor many other things. I can borrow nowhere, even at 10 per cent, and now the time hurries me to finish it. So I beg you, dear brother, don't refuse my request, send me the soonest possible at least what you owe me, and hereby you will do a great service to myself and to my family. You know, fear comes upon me when I remember that if I don't have my own small home when my strength and my health refuse their service and I shall be compelled to take a stick into my hand as a help to my feet, that I shall then have to spend the rest of my days in some damp and half-dark cellar. I feel ill at this thought. I endeavored to add one penny to another in the measure of my strength and capacity in order to secure myself against any black hour, and to have at any rate a roof of my own.

Besides what you owe, please tell Stefan that we beg him to lend us about 50 roubles, and at the first opportunity we promise to give it back, with our thanks. . . . .

TOMASZ and ANTONINA BARSZCZEWSKI

324   February 4, 1909

. . . . DEAR BROTHER STANISŁAW: . . . . We beg your pardon, don't be angry with us if we offended you about this ship-ticket, because we did not know at whose cost you counted it, and now we thank you for explaining to us how it ought to be. Aleksander says that he will give us 100 roubles [of the debt he owes you] and we thank you for it, for your good will and your good actions. We thank also our brother Aleksander, because he did not disavow that [debt], which he pays us. . . . .

Now it is your parents who write. Dear son, you write to us, your parents, and you ask us about the money which you sent. But you sent us 50 roubles when Aleksander came from the army, which were for his journey, and you sent the rest at our disposition, and now you ask about it. The 150 roubles [additional] which you sent, you wrote and said yourself in your letter that you were providing for the marriage of Józefa, and we did everything, as you wrote, we your father and mother, your parents. And now, Stanisław, you demand 200 roubles from Aleksander. We ask you what [200 roubles]? He is giving 100 roubles to Tomasz, and 100 roubles were spent for our different expenses, for wedding-clothes, marriage-feast, and different things. . . . .

Dear brother, we are not very well satisfied that we have to demand money from Aleksander. It would be much better for us to receive it from those hands into which we gave it [from you directly, since you borrowed it from us].

Dear Brother-in-law Stefan, we, Tomasz and Antonina, send you a low bow, and your not-yet-known brother-in-law Aleksander Barszczewski and your sister Marya send you a low bow also. You ask how is it in Grodno, whether employment can be found. Dear brother-in-law, those employments are very difficult to find. And, dear Stefan, we beg your pardon about this ship-ticket, because you were offended and very angry with us. Now you say, brother and brother-in-law, that we are becoming very full of honor [sensitive]. Oh, no! You have pride and honor, but we don't have honor.[1] . . . .

[TOMASZ, ANTONINA, ALEKSANDER, MARYA]

Dear brother ,Stefan, you ask about father; but why do you not write to father? You have not sent a single letter to father, and father has waited and waits still. Father keeps the farm for you, and you don't think at all about him. Remember about your father. Father remembers about you and takes care of everything. Father ordered the monument, and it is already done, for a deposit has been paid; but it is not yet paid for entirely, because father has now no money, so he is waiting until spring. Perhaps God will give some possibility, or perhaps the son [yourself] will send something. . . . .

[MARYA BARSZCZEWSKA]

325   May 25, 1909

DEAR COMPANION, MR. STANISŁAW: [Usual greetings and wishes.] And now I beg your pardon for not writing for so long a time, but I was on a trip for 3 weeks, and when I came it was just then work, planting season in the garden. You know I have not been at home for two years, so everything was gone to waste. I rested for two days and began to work during the day; and the evenings are short, one must hurry to sleep. . . . . The journey was neither good nor bad, so that, thanks to God, I came through happily, only when I arrived at Grodno, I had a small accident. When I left the car

---

[1] "Honor" means with the peasant personal pride shown in familial and communal relations and mainly in economic matters. It is therefore not always a virtue.

somebody stole my purse with my money. There was not much, five roubles with some copecks, and American, Belgian, Dutch, German, coins. I don't regret the Russian money, but I do those strange coins, because I gathered them for remembrance. And moreover, it was not nice, an American coming home in a cab and asking the landlady to pay the cabman. Everything else I brought arrived safely. . . . . I gave the ear-rings to your sister-in-law, for which she thanks you very much. She is very much pleased. Tomasz bought a lot and built a small house, your second brother bought also and builds, and your parents are in Grodno, your father with Tomasz, mother with the younger son, and so they live. Only they are very angry with Tomasz because you wrote to the younger brother to give Tomasz your money. Tomasz took 100 roubles, and the rest remains with the younger brother, because both of them need it. They both bought [lots] and they are both building.

[Signature missing]

326   September 5, 1910

. . . . We inform you, dear brother, that we received 200 roubles of money, and [we], your brother and sister-in-law, thank you very much for not refusing our request. Now, brother Stanisław, you asked whether our parents are alive, so we answer you and inform you that they left for the country, because mother was very ill and she was afraid of dying in Grodno, so they left for the old place. But, thanks to God, now they are in good health. . . . . Now you ask, brother, about Chodorowski. He is now a great lord, he does not even wish to speak to us, because he has opened a beershop and a store. You say that you sent him 3 letters, and he says that he has received none. . . . .

TOMASZ BARSZCZEWSKI [Probably written by his son.]
Now your [god]son bows to you. He tends the cow.

327   November 7, 1910

DEAR BROTHER: [Generalities about health.] I heard, dear brother, that you wrote that you intended to come in a year. So we beg you, come, and we will live here as best we can. Now I beg you, dear brother, if you can, send me 100 roubles. I don't want them for drinking, but I should like to buy another cow. I have some roubles, but it is not enough. I have a piece of land, but I hate to sell it. If you come you can take it for your house, and if you don't want it I shall then sell it to somebody else and give you the money back. I should like to borrow money here, but nobody will give it to me. Good men have none and bad men are envious. Now I inform you, dear brother, that my house costs me 705 roubles, and the cellar 105 roubles. I beg you, dear brother, together with my wife, don't refuse my request. . . . . Now your [god]son Alfons greets you, wishes you every good and begs you to come.

[Tomasz Barszczewski]

328   [Probably winter, 1910–11]

. . . . I, Aleksander, your brother, and my wife Marya and my children, we Barszczewskis, send you a greeting brother Stanisław and sister-in-law. We don't yet know our sister-in-law, but by letter we kiss you, brother and sister-in-law, and we wish you, in the name of Jesus, health and whatever you want from God. And now I ask you, brother, whether our Lord Jesus loved the world or the man? I say, the man, because for his sake He was hung upon the cross, and He loved the man. When hanging upon the cross, He saw John under the cross, and said to his mother, "There standing near you is your son." And He said to John, "That is your mother." So He called us sons of Mary, and His brothers. Our Lord Jesus says to us, "Brothers, love God, and I will love you." Our Lord Jesus orders men to love one another and to call one another brothers. Why do we, children of the same father and the same mother, not love one another? Why? Because fire is kindled among us, and hell burns, and satans rejoice, that we, brothers, live well and remember one another and love one another in such a way [irony]. Oh, may God and the Holiest Mother grant us, brothers, to love one another; as Mary loved our Lord Jesus, so we ought to love one another and have charity. As Christ our Lord said, "Love one another and have charity, then your Highest will love you."[1] But you, brother, did you remember that you had a father and a mother in your land? You forgot how your mother nursed you, how many nights she did not sleep. You went to make money, and you forgot that you

---

[1] The whole religious introduction may be either an imitation of a sermon or a result of "philosophizing" under Russian influence, as with Tomasz. But from this point to the end the letter is typically Polish and peasant.

left old parents. Do you know, brother, what a sorrow there was when our mother was dying? She called to us, "My sons, why do I not see you? You went far away into the world, and you forgot about us." What a pity it was when our mother was dying that there was nobody to wipe the tears from her eyes. And nevertheless in dying she blessed [her sons], and she blessed you, brother Stanisław. She did not forget you, although you forgot your mother. Before her death she wrote asking for help, then I borrowed some money and sent it to them; but Tomasz wrote such a letter that our father could not listen when they read it to him, so he wrote me. . . . .

ALEKSANDER BARSZCZEWSKI

329   VILLAGE SYTKI, December 29, 1913

MY DEAREST SON STASIO AND MY DAUGHTER-IN-LAW: I, your father, send you my blessing. May God bless you in your intentions and help you; whatever you wish for yourselves, I wish it to you. And now I inform you, dear children, that I am alive, but as to my health, I scarcely live in this world. I cannot nourish myself [take the same food] as before, and to tell the truth, it is very hard for me to live now. And I inform you, dear son, that we buried your mother 3 years ago, but you did not know about mother's death, because you forgot about us. It seems to me that 7 years have passed since we spoke to one another by letters. More than once we wept for you, thinking that you were no longer alive. But at last we received news from you, and I was glad that in my old days I heard at least by letter some words about your life and success. Now I beg you, my son, don't forget about me, your old father, and perhaps God will not forget about you. I wish you, my dear children, every good, and above all health. Your father, old already,

JAN BARSZCZEWSKI

[Follow greetings from brother and an old companion.]

330   May 19, 1914

DEAR BROTHER AND SISTER-IN-LAW: . . . . I, your brother Antoni, address myself to my brother Stanisław with a great request. My dear brother, I, your brother, with great timidity beg you to be so good and to lend me at least 300 roubles. I will give it back, every penny, because, to tell the truth, I have enough to live on from my work, but I want to buy a piece of land. In our village they are making colonies,[1] and it is very difficult to live. I was much better off before, because I had no trouble about pasture, but profited from the common pasture. . . . . But now everybody has his own piece of land in a single lot, and everybody pastures upon his own lot; and as to me, you know that my whole property is a garden, where I must live and plant, and I have no place to pasture. Well, there is in our village a piece of field for sale, I don't know whether you remember or not, left by the old Pietruczak. The youngest son went to another village *w przystępy* [provincialism, meaning probably "joining his wife and her property"], but his own piece of land is a part of his inheritance from his father. But he is too far away to cultivate it, and he wishes to sell it, and he said to me, "Buy this piece of land from me, and you will have a field and a pasture." So, my brother, that is the reason why I beg you and my sister-in-law to help me and to lend me this sum of money. If you are afraid that I will not give it back, I will send you my note, I will certify it with the notary and send it to you beforehand, and then you will send me the money. I beg you, my brother, with my whole heart. I have no money, and what can I do? Among us it is very difficult to borrow. I beg you for a speedy answer, whether you will lend me or not. Answer me with an open heart. . . . .

AN[TONI] [and] PAULINA BARSZCZEWSKI

331   [November 27, 1907]

. . . . DEAR BROTHER STANISŁAW: . . . . We are very unhappy because during this whole year we had not a happy hour, only continuous sorrow. We intended to build a house, but lumber is dear; we must endeavor up to the last [not clear]. Before we began it our mother died; some weeks afterward my husband's brother was called to military service; after some weeks more my husband's father died; some weeks passed after this, and our oldest son died. Such a continuous misery, and tears shed in a stream! Dear brother, I kiss you, at least by letter, and I beg you, don't forget about me, because you know that we come from the same blood. . . . .

Your loving sister,

WIKTORA

---

[1] A "colony," is a new type of peasant farm. Cf. Wróblewski series, No. 53, note.

To my godfather:

DEAR FATHER, I send you my lowest bow, bowing below your knees, and I kiss both your hands. I inform you that I am healthy, thanks to God, and I wish you the same, good health from our Lord God, every virtue and happiness. You ask me whether I learn, so I will tell you that I wish it very much, but now it is cold and snow fell, and I have no shoes, only old slippers. I kiss your hands and I beg you for a pair of shoes, and then I beg your pardon.

The sun is set, the light is out, my pen slipped from my hand, I want to sleep. Goodbye!

Your well-wishing,

ADELA BŁASZCZUK [a very young child]

HALICKI SERIES

In the Barszczewski series we noticed certain effects which Russian influence has upon the peasant on the eastern border of ethnographical Poland. Here we find the German influence manifested in the west. The Halicki's live in a small town in the province of Posen. They are not peasants, but belong to the lower bourgeoisie. The original difference in attitudes between the peasant class and the lower bourgeoisie (handworkers, shopkeepers, etc.) in small towns was, however, rather small. In fact, the Polish bourgeoisie was constituted mainly of two elements—German immigrants of the bourgeois class and Polish peasants settled in towns. In small towns the latter element prevailed. Town life developed, of course, different attitudes in economic, and to some extent in religious, life, but the character of familial life and the relation toward the community remained essentially the same, and even in economic life most of the fundamental features of the peasant are preserved, e.g., quantification of economic values, property as fundamental category. Nevertheless these old attitudes disintegrate more rapidly in towns, and any external influence shows its effects much sooner in a town than in a village.

And this is precisely true in the case of the Halickis. The hard, business-like attitude toward life which characterizes the Prussian organization has been assimilated by the Poles in the province of Posen; this assimilation was necessary in view of the economic and national struggle which they have to carry on. The changed attitudes require a reorganization of the old familial and communal solidarity upon a new basis, and this reorganization is going on. But wherever it is not yet achieved the new attitudes merely dissolve the old social system, and we find such situations as the present one.

One special point is strongly emphasized in this series— the character of a letter as means of literary expression and the feeling of obligation to make the letters as good as possible from the literary point of view.

THE FAMILY HALICKI

R. Halicka, a widow
Polikarp
Kazio (Kazimierz)
Michał ⎱ her sons
Tadek (Tadzio, Tadeusz)
Pela
Jadwiga
Stasia (Stacha, Stanisława) ⎱ her daughters
Mania (Maryśka, Marysia)
Staś (Stanisław) Rakowski, Pela's husband
Krukowski, Jadwiga's betrothed
Grandmother

332–47, TO POLIKARP HALICKI, IN AMERICA, FROM FAMILY-MEMBERS IN POLAND, AND A LETTER (348) FROM HALICKI TO THE AUTHORS.

332 ZALESIE, October 7, 1912

DEAR SON: I thank you for your letter, for which I waited with longing. We knew that one ship sunk with the men. Glory be to God that you are healthy and happy. I beg you, my dear son, write to us as often as you can, you know how glad I am when I can speak with you at least by letters. . . . . My sickness has decreased a little; during the past week I was so sick that I did not recognize my friends. I don't know whence this sickness came . . . . but Stasia knew how to help me, and God is good and let me leave my bed. And you, dear Polikarp, have provided me so well with housegoods that I can have everything, whatever a sick person may need. When I look upon the furniture bought from your economized money I must shed tears. In your room lives your successor, Mr. Frankowski.

. . . . He is quiet and talks little.   He did not wish to take the room without boarding, so he will pay 60 marks.   But I don't know how it will be further, for you know well how our family is.   I told Jadwiga to go away.   Now she weeps and probably she won't go.   Tadzio works in the mill. . . . .

And now I come back to your letter.   How nicely you have described everything as in a book!   May God give you a good place, where you can pay easily the debt for your journey.   You know probably everything, how it is in our country, about the arming. People say that you must also come back.   What a sorrow I feel! Perhaps soon they won't even let your letters come through. . . . .

I finish my plaintive letter, my son.   Praise be to God for your health.   Stasia has written more at length to you;   I don't want us both to bore you with the same things. . . . .

Now, my child, I commend you to God, to His holy care. May everything happen to you, whatever you wish from God. I remain,

Your mother to the grave,

R. HALICKA

Write to Kazio and Michał.   Greetings for everybody.   I am feeble, but I want absolutely to write with my own hand;   it seems to me as if I talked with you.[1]

333   December 5, 1912

[Quotation from a religious song.]

DEAR POLIKARP: Since you left this song always rings in our ears. On Sunday, after you left, it was sung in the choir during the holy mass;   we and mother could not withhold our tears.   Mother in particular is very low in spirits.   She was sick, and I was even afraid that this sickness would take a serious turn.   Now, thanks to God,

---

[1] The mother's familial attitudes remain unchanged, and while Polikarp does not show much solidarity with regard to the other members of the family he keeps the traditional attitude toward his mother.   The particularly near relation between the mother and this son (cf. Nos. 337, 338, 341, 345) is probably due to the fact that he is the oldest and took care of the family after his father's death.   On the side of the son there seems to be a real affection for his mother, but besides this the conscious tendency also to be and to be considered a *model* son.   This feeling of his own righteousness must have been assisted by the attitude of the mother who always gave him as an example to the younger children.

she is somewhat calmer. I would not grieve you with sad news; I think nevertheless that it will be better if I describe to you everything sincerely.

I am very pained that we have spent the last times so sadly. Perhaps you regret it yourself, for if you had known that you would get so far away certainly you would not have acted thus, and you would have spared our mother's tears. And Stasia, and even Jadwiga, is not so bad, although she has a sharp tongue. Particularly, I could not bear it that you hated her so. What should I say? I ought to avenge myself more than you did. Perhaps you won't be pleased with me for mentioning old sins. But I know how much we have all wept when we learned that you were to go away in earnest. It seemed to us so improbable. Jadwiga cried for whole days that she did not bid you goodbye. Everybody said that it would be better if Michał had left, he would have caused less sorrow.

Your place is occupied by a Mr. Frankowski. The boys ought to take him for a model. What a quiet man! For whole evenings he stays at home, reads, plays with the boys at different games. Mother would even prefer sometimes if he went somewhere or shut himself up in his room; she could then do more [housework]. Mania is with me during the day, helps me in everything and waits impatiently for the evening to come—they are so merry and jest so much there at home. But Jadwiga stays with me continually; she helps me in sewing and sleeps here. I have only 3 girls for sewing, and there is very much work. . . . . Don't wonder that we did not answer you sooner. Staś [husband] committed it to me, and I have too much to do. The business goes on very well. . . . . But although we have enough to eat and to drink I am not satisfied with all this. Staś is iniquitous. He never gets drunk but he has such a something in him that more than once the worst ideas come into my mind. I put all the fault upon myself and reproach myself [for having married him], and you would do the same. . . . . You write me that you are pleased there and succeed well. Thanks to God, if it is really so, but it seems to me that you try to stifle yourself [your feelings]. I cannot believe, I know your disposition, I know how much I suffered without showing it, although I was judged very bad. And today, when I reflect, it seems to me that there was nobody worthy of my sufferings. Staś would not be so bad of himself, if he were better educated and did not lack religion. This kills me, that he was able thus to pretend. And today it seems as if he wanted to avenge himself upon my family, as if he hated them. He won't let the children come to our home. Although for the sake of appearances we don't show it to people, yet as we are in business, people notice enough. And for his own family he fights to the last. Surely he would like to have them with him. They moved to Leszno, God knows for how long. If they had known that Staś would come so rapidly to his own business, they would not have done it. What I shall have to struggle with still! And it pains me still more when I see discord at home, lack of attachment of one to another. My heart burst open! I should like to sympathize more with them during my life, but they [the boys] are too hard. Although they have Frankowski's example it is of no use. I don't praise him too much—I know little of his past life—but as far as we know him it is difficult to find such a kind and quiet man. But Michał! If he does not improve he will perish miserably. Nobody praises him.

Perhaps I shall bore you with my scribbling, but I don't know how to compose a letter as well as you do. Moreover I have written it during a whole week, and I have a sore hand. Only I beg you very much, you have already the letter from Krukowski, help them as you can, but keep him in hand. . . . . Don't be obstinately grudging against Jadwiga, for we have enough to suffer from others [outside of the family]. Today I so much want concord among our family. I have always desired it, but today, after a new catastrophe with Staś—perhaps they will write you about it from home. I finish this letter at home, for I cannot do it in my own house from fear of Staś. . . . .

I wish you healthy and merry holidays—health, happiness, and God's blessing in the New Year.

I have still so much to write—but later.

Your loving sister,

PELA

334   December 16, 1912

DEAR POLIKARP: I write to you for the first time. . . . . I wish you a Merry Christmas. . . . . I noticed that you have stopped writing. But you ought to keep in yourself the feeling of a *Poznaniak* [man from Posen] and not to have already that of an American. If

I could find there some suitable position, I should come next spring, for here I am bored to death. . . . .[1]

The [family-] war is a little calmed, but not for long. I hope you don't intend to come back while it lasts. . . . . Mother says that when she receives a letter from you she feels as if she spoke with you. . . . . In the house of Rakowski [brother-in-law, Pela's husband], there was an outbreak lately. R. told mother to get out of his house, without any reason. But don't be anxious about mother; I will avenge her. Pela is much changed, for R. has beaten her severely. A real crazy bandit. If you write to him abuse him soundly. And don't make him a gift of your money [ask him to pay his debt to you], for he has scarcely got feathers, and he wants to fly. [He became arrogant toward his wife's family as soon as his own business developed. Probably he was formerly dependent upon them in financial matters.]

Your brother,

KAZIMIERZ

335   New Year, 1913

DEAR SON: . . . . I was very glad to receive the money, but I felt how parsimoniously you must have lived, dear son, wishing to help me for the holidays. Even if I had not the lord's help [probably a widow's pension], I should not ask anything from you. Try only to put some money aside and to come back as soon as possible to our country, at least for a short time. Naturally only if we have peace, for in the contrary case you must give up coming, for I hope that you won't come here for death. Take care of your health and life. Krukowski and we are waiting for your answer to his letters. It would be better [if it comes] for you would describe everything, but I believe that he won't mind [if it does not come], but will go. He has relatives enough there. Frankowski is no longer here. The reason was that he saw here no future at all. . . . . He noticed it at once and tried secretly to find another place, and he succeeded. . . . . When he bade goodbye to the priest . . . . the latter asked him whether Michał [the writer's son] is able to occupy his [Frankowski's] place.

---

[1] The tendency to get away from home is becoming so general among Polish boys that it may be considered one of the most important causes of emigration. Even in Poland children feel as a burden their dependence on their parents and their obligations to them, and, of course, this feeling can only increase in America.

He said: "He is able, but the lord must control him well." Michał
is preparing my grave. He keeps company with Kostek and does not
care for his own good. Ask Frankowski yourself what will become
of Michał. Tadek will be a man, for he is diligent. . . . . As to
the letter [with gossip] about which you write . . . . don't mind
it at all. We have still much other slandering to bear. We don't
go anywhere, we don't talk with anybody, and people cannot hold
out nevertheless. . . . . Balcer must leave his place, for the lord
noticed that he permitted himself too much with Praska, and both
were dismissed in order not to give scandal to young people. . . . .

YOUR MOTHER

Dear Polikarp, don't wonder if mother does not write herself, but
her eyes are weak and she is continually unwell, and she wishes
nevertheless the letters to be written in her name.

336   February 3, 1913

DEAR POLIKARP: . . . . I shall describe to you shortly the news
from Zalesie. Last month we celebrated the fiftieth anniversary of
the last insurrection. On January 22, there was a divine service,
and the day before, a mass for the dead. Our two veterans [ancient
insurgents who lived in Zalesie] were invited to Posen, but they
remained here. At every meeting of every association they occupy
the first place. . . . .[1]

Yesterday we had a representation, arranged by the united associations, but after this there were no dances, only social plays.
Jadwiga performed her part splendidly. Michał also played in this
theater. . . . . As to the pastoral mass [on Christmas night], I
cannot describe it, for I was not in the church. I know only that they
sang very nicely.

After your departure it was very sad at home, but now it will be
sadder still, for Michał also left us this morning. But we have much
fun with Tadzio. Once during the supper he asked Mr. Frankowski
and Kazimierz, "How much do you pay to your men? For *I* pay

[1] Great respect is shown to the men (of any social class) who took part in the
Polish insurrection of 1863. They are considered in some way as the keepers of
the ideal of Poland's independence and are assumed to have an exceptionally
high moral standard. The interesting point is that in spite of their difficult situation as exiles, almost all of them have grown up to the moral level which the public
respect imposes upon them.

so and so much." .... They have already given him the title "director of the mill." But in the office-work he is very industrious. They are satisfied with him and believe that he will be a good merchant. . . . .

Now sad days will begin here [because of Lent]. We shall spend Sundays only in reading books. . . . .

I finish my short writing. . . . . Correct my faults, for it is my first letter.

I embrace you heartily.

MARYŚKA [MANIA]

337 February 10, 1913

DEAR SON: .... For some days I have had the intention of writing this letter, but I could not gather my thoughts, for my heart was burdened with sorrow, because Michał also was leaving us. I am very anxious that he may get back his good name. You know him very well, so you can guess how he is. He has found a place himself and wanted absolutely to go into the world, but when the moment of separation came, he could not withhold tears. I have at least this one comfort, that he made his peace with God. In the evening he went to town to confession, the next morning he received holy communion, and he left on the third day. . . . . He wrote that he is working with a veteran of the last insurrection. I hope that under the influence of such a man he will be edified.[1] You will receive soon a letter from him. . . . .

Dear son, Stasia and I have had sad dreams. We saw you always gloomy and weeping. But, as I guessed from your letter, you must have borne painful moments when you were leaving the Ganzes.[2] Only take care that these disagreeable things don't happen any more. I beg you for God's sake, don't poison your health with this, that I may see you and embrace you once more, as my most beloved child.

What a joy it was when we received the parcel of tea! It has a very good taste and seems to us more healthful than ours. . . . . I was very glad that you had such an idea. Grandmother even mentioned once that as you remember about your mother, our Lord God won't forget you. . . . .

[1] Cf. No. 336, note.

[2] He was engaged to their daughter and left because of some quarrel. The mother means that the bad dreams are already fulfilled and no further misfortune is to be anticipated.

As to the gossip of Ososka, I have calmed her already. Now they begin to talk about the Ganzes. Ososka said that Mrs. Ganz and her daughter are running after men, and Mr. C. took an aversion to her [the daughter] once and forever.

Dear son, I inform you that Krukowski intends certainly to go to America. Before leaving he will be engaged to Jadwiga, and when he comes happily to America, he will take her at once. Only I am afraid that you won't receive her as a brother [should]. But it is true that her character has changed and she is now very serious. When Krukowski comes show him where he can find the best work. Don't be afraid about money, for he finds his way himself. I think that it would be the best for them if they could settle in Milwaukee, for it is the best to be among one's own people. You know Krukowski, that he is a good man. . . . .

Wherever I go, everybody asks how you succeed. Our priest asks often about you; whether you intend to remain there and how you succeed. I say only that good people get on well everywhere, while bad people are always sour. . . . .

YOUR MOTHER

338   February 19, 1913

DEAR AND BELOVED SON: I received the money for which I send you a hearty "God reward." I rejoice very much, dear child, that being in such a far world, you nevertheless remember about me. I doubt whether any of your brothers will do it. But certainly God will reward you. Dear son, it is not your duty. Why should you ever refuse anything to yourself? And, moreover, you have still the burden of the journey [the debt]. So once more, may God reward you! . . . .

As I have mentioned already, dear son, Krukowski is going on March 8, for he saved so much that now he can boldly go, and if he does not like it he can boldly come back. Before leaving, i.e., next Sunday, he will exchange rings with Jadwiga. So I beg you, consider him a member of our family, i.e., in the beginning, until they marry. Later let them do as they like. Krukowski . . . . confessed to me sincerely that if he had married Jadwiga at once he would be happier today. But it is not his fault. . . . . He told me that he loved you much. And you know how Jadwiga has always intended to go to America. Perhaps fortune will be kind to her. . . . . I shall send you something through Krukowski; I think perhaps cigars and a bottle of cognac. . . . . And I beg you, take care of Krukowski, lest some American girl should seduce him. Well, God's will. . . . .

YOUR MOTHER

339　　　　　　　　　　　　　　　　　　　April 3, 1913

DEAR SCN: . . . . We had here nice [Easter] holidays. Michał was away only 3 days, he couldn't hold out longer. . . . . O my God, how Michał is changed! He sat at home, and when I told him to go and amuse himself he petted me and said, "Eh, mother, I feel the best with you." Imagine this! He, who was so insolent! I won't even describe how they behaved, he and Kazimierz, after your going. And their demands! . . . . Kazimierz is a little angry for the truth which you wrote him. . . . .

Tell me what you want. I will send you everything through Jadwiga. For, as you know, the ship-ticket will come soon. And may God grant it, for I have already spent money enough. And people envy her, marrying Krukowski.

Grandmother is mortally sick. All her children came, and she blessed us all. . . . .

Krukowski wept much in leaving. When Jadwiga receives the ship-ticket, we shall order a mass. The singers here want to sing "Veni Creator" for her.

Your truly loving

MOTHER

340　　　　　　　　　　　　　　　　　　　May 25, 1913

DEAR POLIKARP: I thank you heartily for your letter. You ask me why I have not given any news about myself for so long a time. I think you gave the reason yourself in writing me that I am drinking, loafing about restaurants, etc. . . . . I wonder much that you, being in America, know better what I am doing than myself. Evidently you ought to know that the news of your correspondent (I know even who it is) is not at all in accordance with the truth. [News about his future examination for journeyman-builder; complaints about his master.] Well, but all this will last only for a certain time. I think that this will be the last winter I shall spend at home. I don't know yet where I shall go, but I will *not* remain here.[1] . . . .

KAZIMIERZ

---

[1] Cf. No. 334, note.

341   June 28, 1913

DEAR SON: . . . . I had bad forebodings about Jadwiga's journey, and I was not mistaken, for you probably know already from Krukowski, what a difficult journey she had, and that she is sick. I cannot sleep at night until I receive better news. . . . . It is nobody's fault, she has what she wanted. Well, may God the Highest grant her health! She left with tears and begged my pardon. . . . . You will agree, dear Polikarp, that she has suffered penance enough during this journey. . . . . We received your photographs. They are so natural that Stasia and Mania kissed them. They put them upon a table and adorn you every day with fresh flowers. [Enumerates the gifts which she sent through Jadwiga.] People don't cease to wonder that you remember me so and send money so often.

YOUR MOTHER

342   August 13, 1913

DEAR POLIKARP: . . . . I wonder why you always find in my letter some desire of vengeance, some bitterness, some sharp tone. Even if I had any reason to avenge myself, I am unable to perform any vengeance; I don't know at all to whom my vengeance could be addressed. I am persuaded that only the references of Tadzio about me influence you thus. But I don't wish to write any more upon this subject. Also, I won't inform you about the good and would-be good actions of Tadzio. Be sure that he has remained the same "little angel" [devil] as he was formerly. You write me to accept your model remarks without anger. Was I ever angry about them? From my letters you can conclude that I am angry only with Tadzio's stories about me. Well, I won't exonerate myself before you, for I have no reason. . . . .

Rakowski is now rather calm, but he does not talk with mother. . . . .

KAZIMIERZ

343   August 17, 1913

DEAR BROTHER: You mentioned in your last letters to mother that Marysia and I had forgotten about you. But it is not so bad as you think. I was a little hurt because I was the first who wrote you and I did not receive any answer. . . . . I thought that it was not pleasant for you to receive news written by your sister Stacha. But Tadek came once from the mill asking me whether I knew how to write a letter; if yes, then you ask me to write you a few words, and if not, then he said that he would help me. . . . . So I take the pen, but I have no time to compose a beautiful style, only whatever thoughts come to my head, my hand follows them obediently, in order to describe my life for a rather long time.

I must confess that I have now greater and greater duties, as the oldest in the house. The whole house rests upon me, particularly since we have a strange person at home. Mother is burdened with years, but nevertheless she is always active; she has nobody [else] to help her. Mania is in business (I should like it better if she occupied herself with sewing, for among these people she will get a bad character), and thus she must be rather served at home, ... for even if she wished to help us, she can sometimes scarcely walk, poor girl. And thus we both, mother and I, struggle with the cruel lot. I thought that when Jadwiga left there would be fewer persons at home, but instead of her there is grandmother, who can scarcely breathe. Moreover, I took an apprentice for sewing. You can imagine my yoke. In the morning I comb my ladies [she is a hairdresser], when I come home there is a great hurry about cooking dinner. (I cook myself since we have boarders.) Sometimes I have no time to breakfast. And then cleaning of rooms, the apprentice asks about work—it is maddening! And, as you know, there is no little [farm-] stock. In a word, we have very much to do. But though we work so much, life is calm, for the boys behave well enough. We can thank God that He gives us health. Moreover, you send us from time to time what you can; whatever you do for mother, you do it also for us. Often we have mirth. When your letter comes everybody tries to get it first. For example, when you wrote your last letter to mother you must have been in a splendid humor, and it caused us a great joy. . . . . Now I permit myself also to describe to you how Michał was for two weeks at home. The poor fellow, he has improved very much in his home life; we spent very pleasant hours and days. The poor boy, he looks so bad and does not care for his health. He tried to get a place, but he was dismissed everywhere. You know how mother is. She began to get anxious, he became very irritable lately, and finally he got some place in O., but he will be there only a month. Even if one wanted to put the blame on him, one could not. It is evidently his destiny. I noticed during his stay at home that he never said a prayer, slept over the time of mass. Perhaps he got so Germanized in that last place. I pity him much, but I cannot help him.

Dear Polikarp, in your letters to Michał I read about a secret which you had confided to him. If you will not be angry with me I will tell you. Leave off this intention. The actor's life is miserable and your health is not good enough. If you were in Posen, it would be another question; we should admire you also. It is well that mother does not know about it, for certainly she would have counted it among the worst crimes.[1] This news came to the ears of Pela and Mania; even Kazio and Tadzio know nothing.

Describe to me what coiffure is fashionable in America and what dresses. Jadwiga writes so little that I cannot get an answer to any questions, and Krukowski does not write at all. Soon it will be mother's name-day, and on September 2, that of Frankowski. Don't forget to send him wishes. He got another place. . . . . Everybody invited him, ... but he did not go anywhere, he remained with us. Three days after his departure he came through Zalesie from Posen to his new place, and came to us again. He was angry, for Mrs. Ch. congratulated him on leaving his heart in Zalesie, and in general everybody in Z. says that I go nowhere because I am engaged to him. . . . . I am proud that I became an interesting person in Zalesie. Though never such an idea—to marry Frankowski—came into my head; but people talk. It is true that he got attached to us. He writes often to me, and it is difficult for me to answer him. Often if mother did not oblige me I should not do it. But I doubt whether he will be now equally attached. Probably he will be proud of his luck. . . . . Don't forget about Michał. Give him always good advice. Frankowski himself when he knew him, said that he needed continual advice and remonstrance, for he is very light-headed. . . . . I send you a hearty greeting.

Your sister,

STACHA

[1] The prejudice against the actor's life is not at all based upon any idea of the immoral character of theatrical shows—which does not exist in Poland—but upon the current conception of the actor's private life, as wandering, insecure, immoral in sexual relations, given up to drinking. The conception is drawn from the observation of wandering provincial troops half a century ago. The artistic *Bohême* is precisely the antithesis of the life-ideal of the Poles of Posen. The theater itself in Posen is an exception in public opinion because of its national importance.

344   September 16, 1913

DEAR POLIKARP: I cannot understand how my letter could have angered you so much [the letter referred to is missing], and how the moment after reading that letter could have been the most disagreeable since you have been in America. Don't believe that I, writing that letter with good intentions, wanted to give you any advice or to make any reproaches about your behaving badly. Oh no! I know your character now. I know that you have been not only a good, but a model brother, for I don't know how the others will be but I think that no one of them will behave as you. I have particularly Michał in mind, for although he was able to behave well during the 2 days which he spent at home, in reality he is not like this. Mother grieves now over the lot that awaits him. Now he works in the mill, but I don't know how long it will last. For Tadzio it is disagreeable, for he is more respected than Michał [though he is only a boy], and more than once he complains about him when he comes back home. Michał feels happy with Kostek, with whom he keeps company as if he were dependent upon him. But through this he ruins all his future. Do you know, he has become worse, not better. Even if there are strangers at home he behaves as if he were quite uneducated, and swearing is with him a usual thing. Perhaps he will have more humility when he has not a pfennig in his pockets, as it was in Kamień where he had not even money enough to send a postcard home. Mother did not write you, perhaps, about it, but I am obliged to, for you believe that he has reproaches to hear from us. But you are mistaken, for it is not he, but we who hear reproaches. Mother [does not reproach him, for she] is afraid that he may take his life. I won't write any more, for I don't know what an impression this letter will make upon you, and then it is already 1 o'clock at night and time to sleep. The best time to write is night for me, for nobody hinders me. . . . .

Be healthy, cheerful, keep far from you all troubles and don't get angry.

With kindest greeting and hearty embraces.

Always the same,
MARYŚKA

345   September 29, 1913

DEAR SON: . . . . I received the money for which I thank you heartily. I think, and I explain to your brothers and sisters, how sparing and industrious you must be. The postmen wonder, and some people even envy me. You intended 10 marks for Michał [for his name-day]. You have a truly brotherly heart. But it is sad, for I did not give him this money at once. I could not. He sends almost every day letters with applications [for work] in answer to advertisements, and I must always give him 50 pfennigs or even 1 mark. He has even sent your photograph once, for he had no more of his own. I don't know whether he will give it back to me. If his character does not change he will only spoil your reputation. He could not stay longer in his second place. I asked him to persevere at least for a month, and even this he scarcely did. His clothes were so dirty that I had to wash them like a miller's clothes. . . . . In Posen they know his character already, and then he knows that he cannot get more than 40 or 50 marks there. He won't be able to live upon it poor boy. I spoke about him with the director of the mill. He could be employed there but he made so many mistakes in a week! Tadzio might lose his place through him. The director told me that he preferred Tadzio, and will raise his wages. . . . . Mr. S. told me once upon the street that Michał knows nothing. Now he has work for 2 or 3 weeks in the agricultural shop.

This very day I told all my children that if I turn the money which you send me to the benefit of all of them they all should be grateful to you. Is it not so? . . . .

The girls, i.e., Stasia and Mania, received a letter from you; they refused to show it to me, only they were sad and cried. What did you write them? I don't know up to the present.[1]

God reward you for having remembered your mother's name-day in this far world. Michał asked Tadzio, "Tadzio, when is mother's name-day?" Well, he is intelligent!

[YOUR MOTHER]

I rejoice always in receiving your letter as if I talked with you. You have inherited from your father this faculty of beautifully composing a letter. I notice that none of your brothers have this gift.

[1] Cf. No. 344.

346   February 2, 1914

DEAR BROTHER: Probably you expected to receive my letter sooner, but I could hardly find a quiet moment, for I not only have much work in the shop, it awaits me at home. When a moment comes I profit by it to sew my dresses. And now mother is with Staś and Pela, at a family-festival, for Pela's little son Polikarp is baptized today. Stacha is at a performance at the Sokoły. Everybody is away, and I am glad that I can pen a few words to you.

The winter season [in the shop] was very good, and the proprietor is satisfied. It is perhaps because the expropriation [of Polish land] is postponed and people are less criticized [when they buy in German shops. The girl is in a German shop]. I should never have believed that at such a time people would go to strangers; in our shop . . . . almost two-thirds of the buyers are Poles. Although in Zalesie exceptions are not so much made [Poles who work with Germans are not so despised], nevertheless it is very painful for me that I must be among people who persecute us continually. How glad I should be to stay at home, for there is work enough everywhere. Only mother cannot decide and keep her decision. You don't know what annoyances I must bear sometimes. In one of your letters to mother you wrote that my demands are too great. But you are mistaken. I know that somebody has written false things to you about me. But I will bear patiently everything. For, to tell the truth, I am only a victim, as you mentioned once in a letter, and I must suffer for all the others. Perhaps Jadwiga was also misused in this way and now she must suffer for it, for what nobody was willing [to say] Jadwiga had to say. Therefore it was said that she had a big mouth, and finally she was considered the worst at home.[1] But perhaps the time will come when after getting rid of this scorn she will be considered the best.

It is very difficult for me to talk about Michał, for at this thought my ideas seem to leave my head. I think that you have been also much oppressed by this news. He was always a dreamer, with no seriousness, and he will remain one. After all the letters from mother, after all the begging and imploring he decided, after a long time, to write that he lighted a cigarette with these silly stories [that he does not mind them; he is evidently accused of some dishonesty]. And here the Jew threatens mother again with the court. I don't know

[1] Cf. No. 348.

how this matter will end. Polikarp, make this sacrifice, write him a few words, they will certainly act upon him, I am sure. What a life he must lead now with the Lejowskis, where anger is always boiling. Antek L. and his father pass each other by as if they were not acquainted. How can Michał improve there? So, I beg you, grant my request. [Weather; skating; amusements.] You have forgotten about my name-day; everybody has forgotten except mother. I never remember having such a name-day. . . . .

I finish my splendid writing and kiss you many times.

Always the same,
MARYŚKA

347 February 22, 1914

DEAR POLIKARP: . . . . You ask me whether I am in such a financial position that I could go to the architectural school. Don't you know our condition? Don't you know that the money which I bring home is immediately spent? It is very nice of you that you wanted to deprive yourself and to put aside for me, i.e., to lend me, some money. I am glad that I have at least one such brother. Could not Michał send some money home, for I hear that he gets 140 marks a month? As to me, I shall see later, in May or June. I shall risk writing to Posen [to the school]. . . . . Perhaps Rakowski could also lend me some money, for I have nothing myself. . . . . There was a call to military service yesterday. Everybody was taken except 3 boys. Mother even wept from pity. . . . .

KAZIMIERZ

348 March 4, 1915

DEAR SIR: . . . . The quarrel with my sister Jadwiga arose, in my opinion, from a very trifling cause, although my mother and my sisters ascribed to it more importance.

When we were once together at a party, Jadwiga noticed that my behavior toward one of my friends was too cordial. My brothers and sisters disliked the whole family of this girl for some wrong caused us a few years ago, but I did not care about it. At home they required me to avoid altogether our so-called enemies, but I did not conform to this demand, considering such behavior not suitable in society (in the club). Although I never met this girl intentionally outside of the club meetings, the gossip grew that I was secretly engaged to her. Jadwiga caught this gossip and was the first to inform mother of it. My family would never have consented to such an alliance, and I did not think of it either. In general, there was no love-relation at all with that friend. In view of the gossip, I gave no explanation but demanded that they should not annoy an innocent girl. This only strengthened the suspicions. The whole matter was later cleared up, particularly when, in consequence of this incident, I let myself be persuaded by some persons from America, who were then in Zalesie, and came with them here, leaving a splendid position and my "sweetheart." I succeeded in getting my mother's permission, promising to remember her and to come back after two years. . . . . Jadwiga refused neverthless to bid me goodbye. She is now here in America, and our relations are again harmonious. . . . .

P. HALICKI

RZEPKOWSKI SERIES

The Rzepkowski's are of peasant-noble origin. The father of Emilia and Marya and the grandfather of Zocha were brothers and farmers. The letters show the evolution from peasantry toward the middle class through two generations. The evolution is more rapid in the first branch of the family (Nos. 349, 350) than in the second; Zocha's father is still only a janitor (*stróż*) in Warsaw. Nevertheless there is a curious difference between the two generations (the two aunts on the one hand, the niece on the other) with regard to intellectual and moral refinement and in the attitude toward life-problems. The fundamental attitudes of the old women differ little from those of average peasant women, in spite of their instruction, which is much above the average peasant level. The girl, on the contrary, while preserving still a general peasant background, shows a rare self-consciousness, impressionability, and individualization —manifested, for example, in her attitude toward death. The difference is probably due to the fact that the attitudes of the lower-middle class differed less from the attitudes of the peasants thirty or forty years ago than they do now, and that the old women have lived more in the country and in small towns, while the girl has been reared in Warsaw. Perhaps also the particular sensibility of the girl has its source in her consciousness of approaching death.

THE FAMILY RZEPKOWSKI

August Rzepkowski, an emigrant

Michał
Jakób
Klemens
Staś ⎫ his cousins
Emilia
Marya
Wikcia

Zocha, daughter of another cousin

349–52, TO AUGUST RZEPKOWSKI, IN AMERICA, FROM FAMILY-MEMBERS IN POLAND

349 January 27, 1908

DEAR AUGUST: I lack words to thank you for remembering me. You gave me a great pleasure in sending your photograph and that of your family. When I came to the Radońskis (to Wikcia) and she gave me your photograph saying that it was for me and asking whether I recognized you, I could not recognize you; you have changed very much.[1] And you would not know me either. I am already a gray-haired old woman. My misfortunes, griefs, sorrows about my children ruined my health. It is already 25 years since I married, 7 years since I became a widow. I have five children, three boys and two daughters. The oldest, Kazimierz, is 23 years old. He is in a military school in Czugajewo, government Cherson. When my husband lived he was in the fourth class, and finished it after the death of my husband, but had no great wish to learn and went to the army [as volunteer].[2] But as the number of Poles in the military school is limited, for 3 years he could not pass the examination, only last year he suc-

---

[1] August has renewed relations with his cousins and his brother after more than twenty years of absolute silence. This sudden revival of familial feelings is a frequent case and comes without any apparent reason. Not less frequently it happens that members of a family who have never known one another feel suddenly interested, write and try to meet. This behavior is obviously due to a functioning of infantile memories, and points back to a more communistic familial organization.

[2] It is considered rather bad for a Pole to make a military career in the Russian army. As, moreover, the instruction of the army officers is very insufficient (hardly equal to the gymnasium instruction), this explains why the mother considers her son's choice as a result of his unwillingness to learn.

ceeded after many difficulties. The other son, Bolesław, 22 years, could not learn because of deafness. He finished only two classes in the gymnasium in Kalisz. After his father's death I sent him to the chocolate and candy factory "Cukiernicy Warszawscy," but nobody would accept him because he lacks instruction and is deaf (in one ear). The third, Maryan, 21 years, finished 6 classes in a real gymnasium and is studying in Warsaw, in the school of Wawelberg. He will become a technical engineer, but he is in only the second year, and there are four. The oldest daughter, Janina, is 17 years old; she is in a boarding school in Warsaw in the sixth class. In June she will finish there and will go to the musical conservatory, because she has great ability and talent in music. She has 4 years still to work, and then she must earn her living by lessons. The younger, Wiesława, is 16 years old, she is at the same school in the fifth class. When she finishes I shall try to get a place as teacher for her. After the death of my husband very little [money] remained; were it not for the help of the family I could not educate my children. God took their protector away when he was most necessary for the children. Michał, my youngest brother, is a priest in Dzierżenin. He took me with all my children to himself;[1] and Jakób and Klemens . . . . help with money. Thanks to their good hearts, I can instruct my children. Mother and Karusia had been also with Michał. Four years ago Karusia died. . . . . She was 55 years old. Mother died on November 4, one year ago. One half of her body was paralyzed; she lay months in her bed. Poor thing, she suffered much, but was always calm, submitting to the will of God. Her death was very easy, she slept quietly and left us orphans. God took away from us this beloved bond of the whole family. My husband died also from a heart illness. . . . . He was buried in Warsaw, because there Jakób has his tomb, where his wife is buried. Father, mother, and Karusia

[1] To have a member of the family a priest is considered the greatest luck by the peasants. The fact itself more than anything else raises the social standing of the family; some of the priest's religious character is, in the eyes of the peasant, communicated to his relatives. And in economic matters the priest proves, as we see in the present case, of the greatest help to the family. He has a good income and no personal obligations; he is supposed to preserve the attitude of familial solidarity, and he does preserve it in fact. Therefore every peasant, almost without exception, when giving instruction to his son, dreams that the latter will become a priest. We have here the same attitude which for many centuries the noble families had preserved; one son had to become a priest for the sake of the family, even if it meant a sacrifice of personal aspirations.

are buried in Ciechanów, because Jakób erected a family tomb of the Rzepkowskis there, as uncle Wiktor is a priest there and will be there up to his death. Mother wished father to be buried there and uncle to take care of the chapel and to celebrate the holy mass for the souls of the deceased family as long as he lives.

Lastly I have had trouble because in spite of the deafness of my son Bolesław they insisted on calling him to the army. They kept him in the hospital in the fort of Modlin, and wearied him during 6 weeks. I had much to suffer before I succeeded in getting him free. You have no idea what lawless things are going on here, we are so happy that often the living envy the dead. A small star shone for a moment and again clouds are coming [referring to the promises of autonomy made by Russia in 1906].

Do you correspond with anyone from Lipsk? Do you know that they have been permitted to build a church?[1] I was there a year ago, after 30 years. I had hoped to find a little progress and improvement, but I saw with pain that it is worse than it was when we lived there. The glass [drinking] plays the main part there. The backwardness is enormous. I write this letter in Zaremby, where I have been for a week with [my brother] the priest Klemens. Wikcia came also, and Emilia lives here. We come so very seldom together; we are the only sisters since Karolcia left us [died]. . . . .

Your sister [cousin],

MARYA

350 January 28, 1908

DEAR AUGUST: By a very strange and unexpected accident we got news of where you are living in America; up to the present we did not know where to find you. We take advantage of the address we received and without delay we take the pen in order to inform you what is the news with us. But during such a long past and such a long time of our common silence many changes had to come, very sad changes for our family. Our parents are dead, and sister Karolina, the husband of Auntie Misiewicz, both the Żółkiewskis, the husband of my sister Mania, etc. . . . . Only my husband Paweł is alive . . . . and the young generation, which also is getting old. It is very sad that in Lipsk they devote themselves so much to the glass.

---

[1] The permission to build a (Catholic) church is still difficult to get in Russian Poland, particularly in the east.

If you are curious and if you wish to know about me, I shall try to inform you. I am permanently with my brother, the priest Klemens, who is priest of the parish Zaremby Kościelne, and Paweł, my husband, is with my son in Sosnowiec.[1] They are working at the Nadwiślańska railway station and are getting on very well there. Jadzia, my daughter, has an elementary school in Warsaw and has been doing well, but now she has trouble, because when the government suspended the Polish School Association she had to try to get official permission to have a school, though she has a certificate and has passed the examination. Probably she will receive the permission, but she must wait.

As to myself, for my old years I chose the calm and comfortable retirement with priest Klemens.[2] I am very well situated here. I have comfortable lodging and a quiet life. The church is near, which makes me most joyful and happy for my whole life. What can be more pleasant today, in my old age, than ceaseless prayer on my lips?[3]

[1] A rather exceptional situation, particularly as the letter does not show any hostility between husband and wife. The probable explanation is the following: In peasant marriage the relation often grows rather cool with progressing age, but the tradition of common life is so strong that it is hardly broken, except when the man emigrates to America. But here, in the second, half-educated generation, the sentimental and intellectual ties between man and wife are yet hardly stronger than among peasants, while the tradition has lost its influence. The prestige of her brother, her own prestige as his housekeeper, and economic considerations doubtless play a part. Cf. note 3.

[2] She speaks of her brothers "priest" Klemens and "priest" Michał. In the intelligent class this would be ridiculous. The word "priest" is in Polish an honorific title (in fact, etymologically *ksiądz* priest, is connected with *książe* prince) and is used as equivalent of *Pan* (Mr., Sir). Now, the words "Mr." and "Mrs." are *never* used when speaking about one's own relatives, as they are in English, unless when talking to very inferior persons (master to servants). When a person speaks about his relatives to other relatives, he uses the Christian names; when to strangers, he uses the word which indicates the relation ("my brother," "my wife"). In this case the proper way would be to say simply "Klemens" or "Michał." But the difference is significant. It shows that the writer addresses her own brothers as "priest," when speaking to them. This is a sign of the enormous prestige which a priest has with her. She does not dare to assume any attitude of equality toward her brothers, although she is above the average peasant level. A peasant often does not dare to sit in the presence of her brother-priest if strangers are present.

[3] The position of a priest's housekeeper is envied because of the economic privileges, but particularly because of the nearness of the church, the privileges she enjoys in the church (she has her own bench near the altar), and the respect she receives from the other women in the parish.

The more so as our health is no longer good.   Rheumatism especially
prevails in our whole family.   "Old age is not a joy."   The priest
Michał is the youngest and he was born in 1863; what shall I
say about us older ones?   But I must inform you about my children,
that Janek is still unmarried but already betrothed, and Jadzia,
my daughter, married a student of medicine, so she must work until
he completes his medical studies.   It is only bad that they must live
apart, for he is in Cracow.   If there were a [Polish] university in
Warsaw it would be much easier for them, and much better to be
together.   But probably Mania informed you about our family,
that three brothers are in Warsaw and sister Wiktoria, who is married.
Staś is in Riga in the army, two brothers are priests in their parishes,
and two sisters, myself and Mania, are with them. . . . .

[EMILIA]

351   WARSAW, May 12, 1909

MY DEAR, MY BELOVED UNCLE: I received your letter this week.
It was so sad that it frightened me and therefore I write directly in
order to share my thoughts with you.   I regret that I caused you pain
without even knowing it.   It is true that lately I did not give you any
sign of life but believe me, I was so ill that I could not take a pen in
hand, and [brother] Wacio is as afraid of writing as a Jew is of water,
and moreover nobody can write for me as I write myself.   Therefore
I did not ask either my other brothers or my parents.   I believed that
I should die and then my parents would write to you.   Meanwhile it
has turned out otherwise.   I am still alive, I don't know for how long
a time.   In any case every letter that I write seems to me the last
which I can write.   Therefore you see, dear uncle, in what a position
I am.   Please don't wonder if I am late in writing, although I will
try to avoid it as much as possible.   You don't write whether you are
in good health.   How are auntie and my cousins doing?   I know
only that they are working but that is not enough for me.   With us
there is no news.   My parents and brothers are in good health and in
the best of spirits.   It is always so, only sometimes it changes under
the influence of higher forces, but everything ends happily.

I had lately the honor of getting acquainted with our countryman
from Lipsk, perhaps you remember him—Mr. Adam Chomiczewski.
He deigned to come to us because his cousin Skokowska, who is in
Warsaw for treatment, lives with us.   You have no idea what a man

he is, you cannot remember all the benefits he has done to people, all the wealth and relationships he has! He is a friend of the first persons in Warsaw and in the whole country! He poses egregiously but evidently he does not know that whoever listens to him, says, "Stupid man!" I like people from my country, but this one does not please me. I will write today about no general questions, because to tell the truth I am very sleepy. It is late already, and during the day I have no time to write because I am preparing to go away next week, or some day. Then there is nothing of importance. About personal questions also much cannot be said. I will write to you at length after getting to Wyżarne; I shall have more time there and my thoughts will be freer. I hope to live for those few weeks, and if it happens otherwise, well, then my parents will inform you that your correspondent has removed from here to eternity. But I confess that, if formerly I wished to die, now such an ending is displeasing for I want to live. It seems that I perceived too late that life is beautiful in spite of all. I am curious whether in dying one has all his presence of mind, whether he understands what is going on at that moment with him and around him. If so, I thank very much [wish to be excused]. I don't wish to die in full consciousness. I cannot imagine what occurs in the head, in the thoughts of the dying person, what he feels and thinks. Do you know, I have the intention of dying with a pen in my hand, namely to write what I feel in those last moments. Of course, if it is possible to do it and if regret for the flying life does not oppress me.

I write as if I were already with one foot in the grave, but it is not so, because I don't even lie in bed, but I walk. I even sew sometimes with the sewing-machine; only this "death" persecutes me, and I cannot write more today, because all my faculties are covered with mourning crape. [Greetings and kisses.]

ZOCHA

352 LIPSK, June 20, 1909

MY DEAR UNCLE: Two weeks have passed already since I left Warsaw, and not until today have I found time to write to you, dear uncle. I had to renew my old acquaintances, and had other obligations also, which did not permit me to do until now what I should have begun with. How is your health, dear uncle and auntie? Are my little cousins in good health, do they play or work? I am curious how the weather is, and the temperature in America, because here it is bad, not wet, but very cold. Do you know, not all the potatoes have yet come up? The summer will be very late.

I feel worse than bad in my health. It has come so far that while 5 years ago I weighed 148 pounds, now I weigh scarcely 112; it is perhaps the smallest weight that a grown-up person can have. I have little hope of living for a long time, and still less of having the health and strength, which I need so much for work. That is the reason I cannot follow your advice, dear uncle, about long walks. From Wyżarne to Lipsk is 6 versts; to Prolejki, 4 times as far. It is not for my strength to walk so long a way, since if I walk a little through the forest I feel terribly tired. Corsets and narrow shoes I don't wear even in Warsaw, the less so in the country. I take as much sour and sweet milk as I can and everything made from milk. I also eat all vegetables, but what is the use of all this? In the country, indeed, I get better during the summer, and some pounds are added to my weight, but the winter takes all this away and more still. How long will it last, and what kind of illness is it? No doctor can know it. The home remedies, the so-called old woman's remedies, don't bring the desired results either. I try everything that anybody advises me to do, and in vain. Now somebody got the idea that it is a tapeworm, and they gave me some poison; but I fear to use it lest I may poison myself in reality. Death does not let us wait very long for itself; why should I hasten its visit?

In Lipsk I found everything as it has been from old; no changes reach these retired places. If there were not the frequent, too frequent, emigration to America and back, people here could remain for a long time "as in God's house behind the stove" [Proverb: happy and calm] without knowing that there exists a world besides Suwałki, Grodno, Warsaw, and Częstochowa, and that in this world people are more intelligent, richer and better prepared to live. Here it is that those who have money enough sit every day in the tavern— no, it is not a tavern, these belong to the past—but a "restaurant"! Lipsk has been able to do this much for the comfort of its citizens. And those who have not so much money work the whole week in order that they may at least on Sunday "be equal to men" and sit at the same table—or under the same table. Not everybody is like this, but an enormous majority. The cause of all this is the lack of schools, and therefore people who are a little more intelligent cry "enlightenment," but their voice is a voice calling in the wilderness. The rich and noble are abroad, and only they could do something if they would. And in general people grow indifferent to everything that is Polish and for Poland—not to this brilliant and splendid [Poland] which clinks with its thousands [of roubles], but to this poor, gray, vulgar and stupid [Poland]. What do they care if the children of hired workmen remain poor hired workmen, if for a long time still they will believe that, by charms and curses, illness and different other troubles are chased away? On the contrary, they endeavor to maintain as long as possible this unnatural state, because they know that when there is not a single illiterate, from this moment on the thousands will no more flow so easily as now to their bottomless pockets.

Thence comes this indifference to all exhibitions which have the local industry in view. The rich industrial does not care for such an exhibition, because he will always find a sale for his products, if not here, then elsewhere. And besides, his clients are rich people who imitate what they see abroad. What do they care for local industry? And we poor people, we disregard [this], and do you know why? Because such exhibitions have no practical importance. In America perhaps they are as they ought to be, but with us it is simply a "turning of the head."[1]

Such "turning of the head" is, for instance, our "Association for Knowledge of the Country," to which you wrote once asking what is the object of this Association. If you thought that it is concerned with the question of enriching the country, you erred greatly. They travel through the land, it is true, but for the pleasure of it, not in order to study what is done in this part or the other and what could be done in a given place. They care only for a nice locality, for old ruins of castles, palaces, churches, and nothing more. All this is very nice, but in my opinion it is not the time to do it now; we have so many questions, more important, concerning the present and the future that it is impossible to busy ourselves with the past. So our peasant's reason tells us, which is contrary to the "fine reason of the

---

[1] The reference is to a provincial exhibition in Częstochowa about which the uncle had probably asked, and which was, in fact, very well organized. But the girl's letters betray a general pessimism, probably the result of her personal condition—not only ill-health and fear of death, but also the disharmony between her general culture and her habitual environment.

lords," as the Jews say. In America people are more practical, therefore it is better there than here.

Staying in the country annoys me very much, not because I am without occupation—I have enough for my strength—but much time remains which in Warsaw I spent in reading books, and here I have none. I am robbed of this only pleasure that remained, because I like books better than all amusements and plays or society, all visits, etc. In Warsaw I surrounded myself with books like a true bookworm; here I cannot borrow them anywhere, and I am sad. [Greetings and kisses.]

ZOCHA

KALINOWICZ SERIES

We have here an interesting case of familial solidarity preserved in full strength by the children after the death of their parents, in spite of the usually disintegrating influence of emigration. Affection seems to have grown stronger and has taken the place of the subordination to the head of the family. In this way the moral unity of the group is kept, although there is neither a common economic basis of existence nor any external pressure of the community, and in spite of the fact that the members are separated.

The growth of affection is shown by the exaggerated sentimentality in the letters. The expression of feelings in the peasant is seldom proportionate to their real importance, but, when we find such an exaltation as throughout almost all of the letters of the members of this family, there is certainly a very real intensification of the feelings. There is also a very good opportunity for the familial solidarity to manifest itself in the fact of the marriage of one sister. And, in general, we see this solidarity in its purest form, free from any questions of money, social opinion, etc.

THE FAMILY KALINOWICZ

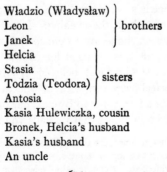

Władzio (Władysław) ⎫
Leon   ⎬ brothers
Janek   ⎭

Helcia   ⎫
Stasia   ⎬
Todzia (Teodora) ⎬ sisters
Antosia   ⎭

Kasia Hulewiczka, cousin
Bronek, Helcia's husband
Kasia's husband
An uncle

675

353–63, TO WŁADZIO (WŁADYSŁAW) KALINOWICZ, IN AMERICA, FROM FAMILY-MEMBERS

353   [December 5, 1913]

DEAR WŁADZIO: We send you a kind and hearty greeting, we embrace you and kiss you innumerable times and we inform you that, thanks to God, we are in good health, and we wish you also with our whole heart the best of health. Dear brother, after a long waiting and a great longing we received your letter which rejoiced us so much that we wept the whole day from joy that you are alive and from sorrow that perhaps you bear there misery, dear Władzio. Today it is December 5, tomorrow we are going home, and I think to myself, O God, even if I had to work as hard until the next December, or even a year more, I would work gladly, if I could help our dear little brother. But nothing can be done.[1] Dear Władzio, when we remember you, we shed bitter tears and we think that there is nothing more left for us upon this world. I would be glad to go to you, dear Władzio. . . . . Now we finish these few words, we greet you once more, kiss you and embrace you. Perhaps God will comfort us and we shall see one another still. When we get home we will write oftener. . . . .

T[EODORA] and J[ANEK] KALINOWICZ

Now we greet dear Hulewiczka [cousin], with her husband and son.

354   [LĄD, end of January, 1914]

MOST BELOVED WŁADZIO: I, Todzia [Teodora] write to you these few words. First, I greet you with my whole heart, I kiss you and embrace you hundreds of times. Now I inform you first, dear Władzio, about Helcia's wedding. The wedding was performed on January 21, at 7 o'clock in the evening. It was very beautiful, all the lights in the church shone, rugs were spread out and singers sang. But, dear Władzio, all this changed for us into a great sorrow and we all wept, because our most beloved Władzio was not there. Dear Władzio, we feel very sad without you and we long for you. Dear Władzio, write a few words to Bronek, our brother-in-law, for he is always very sad; he imagines that perhaps you are angry with him.

---

[1] That is, they must go home, for the Polish season-workers are not permitted to stay in Prussia during two winter months, the Prussians fearing that they will settle in the east provinces and strengthen the Polish element there.

Write to him, dear Władzio, perhaps you will rejoice him.[1] Dear Władzio, we feel very sad without you. We came home not long ago, and we must go soon again. Such is our sad life, for we are scattered about the world. Now I greet you once more, I embrace you and kiss you thousands of times. Later I will write more. . . . . I remain longing.

Your sister,
TEODORA

I will come soon to you.

355   [SIBERIA] January 25, 1914

DEAR BROTHER: Notwithstanding a long time [spent] in longing and awaiting news from you, I am obliged to write a few words coming from the depths of my heart. Dear brother, it will soon be a year since you left the home, and during this whole year I have longed and wished for news from you, but you have forgotten about me totally. And still you know well how sad I feel and how I long for you. Have you no brotherly feeling? Don't you know how I long for you and want to know about you? Nobody knows what is dear to me, but a brotherly heart is dearest of all, and I cannot find it. You know that I have served 2 years and did not ask you for any help, but I want a brotherly heart and a brotherly love. But I know that the time passes rapidly for a man who lives in liberty and can do his will, and if there is bitterness, there is also sweetness. But I have no sweetness at all, I am like a man in a penitentiary. I want brotherly words, I want a brotherly heart and remembrance. If I knew that I had been ever disagreeable to you when we lived together, I would say, "It is my fault." But I loved you more than my life and I love you still. But you, as soon as you got a little liberty, you forgot about everything. So it is now in the world; a brother stabs his brother, a sister drowns her sister for profit's sake. But please forgive me these words, for I write them in longing and sorrow and desire. I don't see anything pleasant, everything which I love is closed and hidden from me. He who has liberty does not know longing or sorrow, but I know them well. For 2 months already I have had no news from home, neither about my sisters nor about my brothers, so my heart is troubled, although my condition is not worse

---

[1] The brother-in-law feels himself more or less an intruder in the family until his marriage has been sanctioned by all the brothers and sisters.

than that of others [my companions].   So I beg you very much, dear
brother, if somebody tells you that you are alone, spit into his eyes,
and remember that you have brothers and sisters who want news
from you.   You wrote in the beginning and you complained about
me, [saying] that it interested you and you wanted to know about my
condition, about my success.   And you think that I am not interested.   But I want very much to know about your health and success,
to know where my dear brothers are.   So I beg you very much, write
me where you are, how do you succeed . . . . for from home they
write me nothing about you;   they say only that you don't succeed
in America.   Such is our lot, that we don't succeed anywhere. . . . .

Your brother,

LEON

356   February 11, 1914

MOST BELOVED BROTHER: . . . . Today I had the happiness to
receive your letter which caused me a great joy. . . . . When I received
it I could not eat my dinner. . . . . You ask me how long I have still
to serve.   I cannot tell you exactly for I don't know it myself.   I was
glad that the last year was coming but now I am very sad . . . . for
people say that there will be a war with Prussia and Austria and
England. . . . . You know what my life is, far away from my dearest
brothers and sisters.   I cannot complain that the conditions are
bad, but what about this slavery?   For what am I a slave in these
Siberian mountains? . . . . I could be something else than I am [not
a simple soldier], but I don't want it, I am weary of life. . . . .

You say that Helcia is getting married.   Yes, she asked me for
advice [permission], and I advised her also to do it, for I pity her very
much, that she remains so alone, while we don't know whether any
one of us will ever come back to our beloved Poland and to our beloved sisters and brothers.   It seems to me as if I never should tear
myself out of this slavery.   Your intentions are very serious [probably
the brother intends to take his family to America], but don't worry
about me as long as I am in service.   When I see that things are bad
I shall address myself to you, but now for a time I will be patient.
The service is easy.   [Expression of brotherly feelings;   news and
request for news about relatives and friends.]

I remain in longing.

Your loving brother,

LEON

357 May 19, 1914

MOST BELOVED BROTHER: . . . . You ask me why I send you letters with stamps, whether I am so rich in money. Well, I don't grudge these 10 copecks. Why, I have 90 roubles—oh, I beg your pardon, 90 copecks—a month. But for this money I can send more letters than my brother-in-law, who has more honor [higher position?] and more money than I.[1] They wrote to me not long ago, complaining that you don't write to him. He says that he is often in despair, because everybody in our family, particularly the brothers, looks at him with an unfavorable eye. Stasia and Todzia complained also that you wrote seldom to them. I told them to write more often, then they will receive more letters. And why does Helcia not write to Hulewiczka? I will learn it and inform you. If it is through him [the brother-in-law], I will thank him when I come back. . . . .[2]

LEON

358 LĄD, March 22, 1914

DEAR WŁADZIO: In our first words to you P[raised] b[e] J[esus] Chr[istus]. We hope that you will answer us: "In centuries of centuries, Amen." [Greetings; health.]

Dear Władzio, we have written 4 letters to you and we don't know what happened, for we received an answer to none. We are very much pained that our most beloved brother forgets about us. Dear Władzio, we love you so much, I pray to our Lord God that I may see you at least in a dream, and you have forgotten about us.

Dear Władzio, don't believe Janka that she is faithful to you. She has already Józef Balczak. She bought a ring for him, and she dares to write to you! Pardon me, dearest Władzio, for writing thus to

[1] The brother-in-law is required to become at once a member of the family in the full sense of this membership.

[2] In spite of the extraordinary efforts to preserve the familial solidarity, the brother-in-law is not assimilated, and the sister is estranged; the family not only does not acquire a new member but is in danger of losing one. The family Kalinowicz is not held together by a community of economic or social interests, but merely by affection, and there seems to be no immediate relation of solidarity between it and the family of the brother-in-law, simply because the family Kalinowicz is no longer a complete and organized family-group, and does not count as such in the eyes of the community. A family must either have a head (or rather, a head-couple) or be composed of married, settled, and socially mature members, in order to have a social standing as a group.

you, but we have a dear brother and we want to have also a dear sister-in-law, and that is the end of it. I write you nothing but the holy truth. I inform you, most beloved Właczio, that we shall go into the world on March 30. We are very sad that we must wander about the world, but nothing can be helped. God's will be done, let it be so for some time. Dear Władzio, don't be angry with Helcia, she grieves very much that you have not written to her for so long a time. Dear Władzio, Helcia longs much for Hulewiczka, sends her a sincere greeting, kisses her and embraces her thousands of times and begs her to write. Dear Władzio, don't be angry with Helcia for having married. She had nothing else to expect but this Prussian grease [figurative for "season-work;" a particular kind of grease is given to the season-workers for cooking], and we don't like this Prussian grease; we are tired of it. Dear Władzio, Janek is a good-for-nothing, he always plays cards, refuses to listen to anybody, is very vulgar, offends everybody; such a rogue as the world has never seen. Write him a few words, dear Władzio, perhaps you will correct him a little in this way.

Dear Władzio, perhaps you are displeased with me for describing everything thus, but what you don't like, forgive me. I write you the sincere truth, because I love you sincerely. . . . .

I remain your truly loving sister,

TEODORA

359   May 8 [1914]

. . . . DEAR WŁADZIO: Don't be angry with us for writing little to you, for it seems to me that we have written more to you than you, dear brother, to us. Believe me, I never felt so sad at home as this winter. You say, dear Władzio, that we have a brother-in-law now and therefore we forget about you. It is not true, we shall never forget you, for you are our most beloved little brother and we long for you as a deer for water, like earth without rain; and we want to see you as soon as possible. Dear Władzio, if you knew how every letter of yours rejoices us you would write more often, our beloved brother. . . . .

I wrote to you after Helcia's wedding, but I don't know whether you received this letter. I pitied [regretted?] Helcia very much, I cried during the whole festival; the festival was not a festival, but a sorrow for me [play of words, *wesele*, marriage-festival, is etymologically identical with *wesele,* joy]. I should have much to describe and to complain about, but I pray to God that He may help me to see you and to relate to you everything by words. Dear Władzio, as to America, I want to go there, for it seems to me that now everything will be different at home. Dear Władzio, I should like to get to you as soon as possible, for I long very much. Or you come to us; then everything will be well, for now we are true orphans. . . . . As soon as you receive this letter, answer us and tell me whether I shall prepare myself for America and when, for I should like to as soon as possible. I should regret very much to leave my sisters and all my beloved ones, but what can be done, since we must go asunder for bread and long for one another as now, when we are scattered, everybody elsewhere. Dear Władzio, Helcia wrote and asked me to greet you as well as her beloved Hulewiczka. . . . . All our girls greet you also [enumerates those who work with her]. . . . . I was very glad that you wrote also something to Janek, for he is very arrogant. Excuse me for having written so much and so badly, but to my dear brother I write boldly, for he will accept everything, even if anything is bad. . . . .

S[TASIA], T[EODORA], and J[ANEK] KALINOWICZ

360 [Summer, 1914]

DEAR BROTHER: [Usual beginning; expression of fraternal feelings.] You ask, dear Władzio, about Antosia. She is with Helcia. Up to the present she has nothing to nurse [as Helcia has no child yet], but we don't know how it will be later on. We intended to take her with us, she had even got the passport, only we pitied her, for she is still too young for such heavy work. [Greetings, love and longing expressions, etc.]

Your loving sisters and brother,

STASIA, T[EODORA], and J[ANEK] KALINOWICZ

361 SIBERIA, June 22, 1914

DEAR BROTHER: . . . . My time passes very slowly, I can compare it to that which we all three spent in Linisberg in Germany. I have had no letter from home since Easter. Since Helcia married she has written to me only twice, and Bolek did not write even once. I don't know what it is, whether they have no time because of work,

or since they lay down for the first time to sleep they have not awakened up to the present. Well, I will arouse them when I go back.
. . . . I received a letter from Mińsk. They wrote me that uncle is getting married and they invite me to come to them after the end of my service. I have had for a long time the idea of visiting them and of getting acquainted with them, for they are very good people.[1] They always ask whether or not I need anything. But they have not sent me anything up to the present, for my character does not permit me to beg. Everybody knows that I am not earning wages, but in slavery [and they ought to send without asking]. . . . .

LEON

362 LĄD, July 13, 1914·

. . . . DEAR WŁADZIO: Your letter found us in good health. [Wishes.] I beg your pardon for not having answered your first letter, but I have no time to write and Helcia does not want to write alone. You were dissatisfied that I did not write. I did not write, it is true, and you were angry with me, it is a fact. But you had no reason. I have more reason [to be angry] but today I beg your pardon for everything. You were dissatisfied with us for not having written to you before our wedding. But you know why we did not write. You did not write to me and therefore I did not write to you.[2] Today I write to you, dear Władzio, and we are very glad that you don't forget about us, and we don't forget about you either. We remember you continually. Now I inform you what is the news here. Wacek is no more with us, because he got totally spoiled. He attempted to violate Mania F. He invited her to his room saying that he would show her the photograph of the young manor-owner; he closed the door with the key and threw her upon the bed. Only she cried very much. With difficulty people forced the door.[3] . . . . There was an

---

[1] The uncle should become the head of the family after the father's death. We see, indeed, that he shows some interest for his nephews. But his long separation from this branch of the family hinders him from assuming any really active rôle.

[2] From the standpoint of the family-relations, Władzio was perfectly right in being angry, for his permission was probably not asked before his sister's marriage, and it was the brother-in-law's duty to write him first after the marriage.

[3] This Wacek is probably an overseer in the manor. The attempt of violation would hardly ever happen in this form in a village, and in general it is one of the rarest crimes. Here it seems to be the result of the influence of season-emigration (about 25 per cent of the population in this locality emigrate for the summer) and the corresponding loosening of morals.

accident: one workman was drowned. He was bathing on Sunday, precisely during the divine service.[1] [Relates who died; weather.]

BRONEK

Dear brother, I greet you also and embrace you and beg your pardon for not having answered you at once. I wanted Bronek to write, but he let one day pass after another. If you knew how much he works you would not wonder at all. . . . . He works in Słupca. He leaves at 4 every morning and comes back at 10. He boarded with Felek, paid him 3 roubles a week, but they gave him very miserable living and he had to stop. [News about friends.] I greet you, dear little brother, I embrace you and kiss you a thousand times, and I beg you very much, write often, for we long much for you. . . . . Antosia greets you. She remembers you often and wishes you to come as soon as possible. . . . .

HELCIA

363   [November] 27, 1914

DEAR BROTHER AND DEAR KASIA: After a painful sighing and a terrible longing [on our part] Todzia [Teodora] sent us two letters which rejoiced us very much. Now we inform you that we, although in great fear and waiting for better times to come, are still alive and healthy, and we wish you the same with our whole heart. Now we inform you that God gave us a son. He is named Stanisław Józef. For the first time he greets his dear uncle and aunt Kasia and the other uncle [Kasia's husband] and his cousin. Dear brother, we pity you very much, we remember you often, saying that perhaps you are hungry sometimes, since your condition is so bad . . . . and you have had no work for 6 months. We are very much pained. And how does my dear Kasia succeed? I long very much for her. Dear brother, we have much news, but all is sad. Now I won't write more, for the day is short, and we spend these long evenings in darkness [no oil because of the war].

[HELCIA]

[Longer or shorter greetings from other members of the family, except those who are in Prussia.]

---

[1] Bathing during the divine service is considered the cause of his drowning—God's punishment.

WICKOWSKI SERIES

The letters depict a typical economic situation, resulting partly from certain traditions, partly from recent legal factors. Traditionally the peasant preferred rather to will his farm to one son than to divide it. But it was not a universal custom. In some cases it was more profitable to divide the farm, particularly if the father died before his children were of age to be settled. The development of emigration during the last twenty years brought a new and important change of conditions. A season-emigrant can live and put money aside upon the smallest bit of land and buy later a larger farm, while if he has no land at all he is hopelessly proletarized. Hence division of land becomes an economic necessity. But it is limited by the Russian law: no new farms below six morgs can be created by division. The law was established during the liberation of the serfs, and its intention was to keep an economically strong peasant class, conservative and true to the Russian government, as against the too patriotic and revolutionary nobility. The result was an enormous and continually growing country proletariat, which partly emigrates to America, and we find more and more frequently situations like the one in the present series, where the heirs live upon an undivided property, ruining the farm or quarreling continually.

In the present case there are four brothers and two sisters. One brother, Józef, is in America. One sister, Mania, is married. The other brothers, Jan, Stanisław, and Antoś, and their sister Helenka, live together and keep the farm. The farm was their mother's, and was a part of the farm of their grandfather; part of it belongs to their uncle. A new survey was made after their mother's death, and now the place upon which their farm buildings stand belongs to their uncle.

The family situation is instructive, particularly if we compare it with that of the family Kalinowicz. Here we find also familial affection as the main bond, unifying the young generation after the parents' death. But this bond proves less effective; the situation requires something more. Indeed, there is a farm left—a common basis of the material existence of the family-group as a whole—and therefore the need of a head of the family is much greater than in the Kalinowicz case; there are not only social, but also economic, functions to perform. In such important social events as the introduction of a new member through marriage, even a headless family can act as a whole, as the Kalinowiczs prove, although a perfect economic co-operation in such conditions is impossible. But in the Wickowski family there is nobody to assume the rôle of the head and manager. The brothers are too old to accept the guardianship of an uncle, while none of them is able to take the responsibility himself. The oldest (probably) is Józef, but he is in America. The second, Jan, in normal conditions would be the head, but he is sick and therefore unfit. Stanisław is not yet serious enough, and Antoś is a child. Thus, in spite of the bond of affection, the family is gradually disaggregated as an economic and social unit, because it is unable to act consistently in economic matters and to behave as a sufficiently harmonious whole with regard to the social environment.

THE FAMILY WICKOWSKI

Józef (Józio)
Jan
Stasiek (Stanisław) } brothers
Antoś

Mania R. } sisters
Helenka

Mania's husband
Władka, his niece
Stanisław Wickowski, **an uncle**
His wife
Wacek his son
Zosia, his daughter
Władysław Wickowski, another **uncle**
Józefa, his wife
Andrzej Wickowski, third uncle
Józef ⎫
Franek ⎬ **his sons**
Wicek ⎭

364–68, TO JÓZEF (JÓZIO) WICKOWSKI, IN AMERICA, FROM
FAMILY-MEMBERS

364   GORZKÓW, March 4, 1914

"Praised be Jesus Christus." . . . .

[DEAR BROTHER JÓZEF]: . . . . You ask whether Antoś is
learning. But we inform you that Antoś is so lazy to learn that there
is nobody in the world like him. Neither beating nor begging can
help. Although he knows how to read a little, it is very little. Moreover, he is a bad boy, disobedient, tearing his clothes, and difficult
to keep at home, for he always loafs about. Uncle's [daughter]
Zosia, although nobody compels her to learn, learns well herself
because she is willing.

We cannot give now anything to our brother-in-law besides this
cow, for we have no money. Perhaps later on. Though we had a
few roubles, they have been spent during the carnival. Stasiek
spent some money on cigarettes and other things, for he is not very
parsimonious. Here he gave a deposit for a suit, there he spent
money during a wedding, for Wicek A. married Wiśniewski's daughter
and went to live with her; she will have 7 morgs of land. And Józef
Lisek bought himself out of the military service [was declared unfit
by bribing the doctor] and is at home, but we don't know how much it
cost him, for he refuses to tell. Perhaps we shall learn some day,
then we will write you. . . . .

[JAN WICKOWSKI]

Now, dear brother, I will write you a few words. Józef A. wants
to rent our land if you take me to America. He says that he will sup-

port Jan [who is sick] and sow the land as we agree.   He is exempted from military service; it costs him about 350 roubles. . . . .

Your loving brother,

STANISŁAW WICKOWSKI

365   April 11 [1914]

. . . . DEAR BROTHER JÓZIO: We inform you about our health. We cannot come to health, and I don't know what will be with us for Antoś is still sick with his leg. . . . . It would be worth while to take him to a doctor, but we always lack money.   And I am tortured by this cough which won't leave off.   It is difficult to get health, and difficult to die.   Miserable is my life, for I see nothing upon this world except misery.

Well, dear Józio, I inform you about our success.   Things go on in a various way, not very well, for young people don't know how to manage as well as old people, for one does not want to listen to the other.   If mother lived it would be different, and the order at home would be better.   Helenka neither sews nor weaves, but wastes her time about cabins [going to neighbors and talking].   And Stasiek does the same.   And they would be glad to dress, but they have not money enough.   But even so they borrow and buy [clothes].   And the buildings are getting ruined.   The roofs are bad.   It would be well worth while to transfer them, for even uncle is not satisfied that we don't take the buildings from their place.   But what?   We cannot do it ourselves, for money is needed for this transferring. [Weather; farm-work.]

You want me to describe all the news.   You ask me why Franciszek, the blacksmith, did not answer you. . . . . He intended to write . . . . but now in the spring he has no time.   He is not angry at all.   Why should he be?

And the Jędrzejskis when they came did not tell anything bad about you.   On the contrary they praised you, saying that you work and are parsimonious and don't loaf after girls, as you loafed here in our country after women and girls.   Only Franek said that you quarreled with Staś so that it came to fighting.   This only I heard from them. . . . .

And now I inform you that Helena S. is marrying immediately after Easter.   The wedding was to be at carnival, but I don't know why they postponed it. But it will certainly be, for they have already bought wedding-dresses now during Lent. [Other news about marriages and deaths.]

Dear brother Józio, our aunt Stanisławowa [Stanisław's wife] asked me to write you, that you might learn about their [son] Wacek. For he wrote them that he suffers a terrible misery in America and begged his parents to send him money for the journey, saying that if they don't send it he would commit suicide, for he had terrible misery. But they did not send him the money, for they had none. The aunt begs you to help him, either to find some work for him, or to lend him money for the journey, then they will pay you back. The aunt begs you very much.

[JAN WICKOWSKI]

366   June 29, 1914

. . . . DEAR BROTHER: . . . . We farm as we can and we eat what we have. We have not much milk, for we milk only one cow. The other is big with a calf, but perhaps she will calve about the end of this month. . . . .

Wacek will come here on July 1, so he wrote. . . . . Our aunt annoys us about taking our buildings away from their place and says that you should send money for transferring them if you intend to remain for some time still in America. And perhaps you have no intention of coming and farming here at all. Then Stasiek would marry and transfer the buildings. Now he does not know what to do, for to remain together thus is bad. The buildings are getting ruined, and lumber is dearer here every year; now a *sqg* of lumber costs 20 roubles. So decide. Either send the money for transferring the buildings, or come yourself and begin to farm. [News about friends.]

JAN WICKOWSKI

367   ORCHOWICE, June 20, 1914

DEAR BROTHER: [Complaints of his not writing news about farm-work, weather, health, etc.] When you receive this letter from us and when you write to us, write us a few words whether you intend to come now, within a short time, or not. For now many people come from America and say that in America things are bad, and we don't know what is your condition. If you come back to

our country now you could marry well enough, if you wished, for my
sister from Plaskowice wishes you to come and to marry Władka.
[Greetings.]

Your well-wishing brother-in-law and sister,

M. R.

368   Borów, March 28, 1914

. . . . [DEAR NEPHEW]: I am very much pained that you have
sent me no letter during 3 years.   Why, I wrote you so many letters
about every stage of your mother's illness and at last about her death,
and you did not even thank me. . . . .

I thank you first for having sent the money to pay me off [his part
of the inheritance which up to then had not been divided among the
writer, his brother and sister, the latter the nephew's deceased
mother].   Now we are at last free of this straitness, everybody has
his own property.   I won't write you who remained in Gorzków, for
you know it yourself.   I have sold my land in Gorzków and Tarnogóra
and bought 15 morgs here, and I made 400 roubles [personal] debt and
pay besides it 36 roubles a year to the bank..   I keep 4 head of cattle
and one horse for which I gave 90 roubles.   Moreover, I had to buy
a plow, a harrow, a cart, and so on.   I had 24 *kop* of wheat
[1 *kopa*=60 sheaves] and now 2½ morgs are sown, and 1½ morgs
prepared for potatoes, and so on.   Now, as you know, I have some
debts, but if our Lord God gives good crops there will be enough to
pay the debt.   So I would ask you, if you have money, send me about
100 roubles, and I will send you a note;   I will write it and sign it and
add interest.   When you come home and when you want it, I will
pay you back.   In the same way Andrzej's [sons] Józef, Franek, and
Wicek sent 300 roubles to their cousin, and they sent him notes.
You ought not to be afraid, for I don't borrow for liquor and cards.
If 100 is too much for you, send at least 50. . . . .

Your uncle and aunt,

WŁADYSŁAW and JÓZEFA

SERCZYŃSKI SERIES

We have here a third type of situation in which the children are left alone after their parents' death. The legal guardians do not seem to perform their duty conscientiously. The two older brothers are in America. Otherwise it would be their normal function to care for the younger children. So there remain the two married sisters, each of whom wants to take care of the three youngest orphans. It is, of course, their familial duty, but the curious struggle which breaks out between the two married couples discloses other motives besides familial solidarity. There is probably some economic background. The Sławińskis as well as the Puchalskis hope that the brothers who are in America will send money for the children, and keeping the latter may thus prove a good business. Perhaps also Puchalski hopes to win in this way the favor of his brothers-in-law and get a ship-ticket from them for himself. But these considerations are evidently too uncertain and would hardly be a sufficient motive to explain the whole situation. The fundamental reason (besides, in the case of the Puchalskis, some real affection and pity) is the consideration of public opinion. The community will certainly praise the couple which shows its feelings of familial solidarity by keeping the children, and it will no less certainly blame the other couple. And we must add that the popular feeling, always appreciative of familial solidarity, is particularly strong where orphans are concerned.

THE FAMILY SERCZYŃSKI

Two brothers Serczyński in America

Tadeusz (Tadzio) }
Maryan } their brothers

Maryanna (Mania) }
Anna (Andzia) } their sisters
Janina }

Franciszek Puchalski, Anna's husband
Sławiński, Maryanna's husband

369-72, TO THE BROTHERS SERCZYŃSKI, IN AMERICA,
FROM FAMILY-MEMBERS IN POLAND.

369   November 6 [1913]

"Praised be Jesus Christus." . . . .

And now I write to you, dear brothers, about our condition, and I beg you to have pity upon us, and I beg you to send me [money] for clothes, because we have nothing to put upon us and nothing to eat. They have sold our beds and we have nothing to sleep upon; we must sleep upon the bed of Andzia. [A part of] our bedding is with Sławińska. I have been there more than once asking her to give me this bedding back. But Mania told me to go to service in Słupca; but I told her, "Have you ever been going around from service to service? I won't go to service." And she said that she won't give me the bedding. So advise me, dear brothers, what shall I do, whether I have to go to service or not. I beg you very much, dear brothers, don't forget about us, the orphans, and send us [money] for clothes because they are worn out. The money which you sent, Sławińska took it and refuses to give it back. She told me that there is no money at all, and moreover she beat me. I cried so much that I could not walk. And that letter which Andzia wrote, that you did not answer at all, she wept very much [*sic*]. And now, dear brothers, I have nothing more to write, but I greet you.

Your sister,

JANINA [about 14 years old]

370   CIĄŻEŃ, February 16, 1914

. . . . DEAREST BROTHERS: . . . . I shall describe to you now the pain of my heart which was caused by you, dear brothers. I see today that I am deserted by you, but I am not astonished, because

I guess that we are slandered by Sławińska, and you believed her false words. But I call God to be my witness that I have been an open-hearted sister to you, and today I remain with the same heart toward the younger children as I have had toward you. When Sławińska said that these small children ought to be given away to service my heart pained me and I took them to me, I feed them and clothe them. You sent some roubles to Sławińska, I don't know even how much. Say, dear brothers, how ungratefully you reward me! I wrote a letter to you, to which I had no answer at all. Do you remember, dear brothers, how I wanted you to be able to get to America; and now I am not worthy to receive a letter from you. I asked you, as my dear brothers, to give us your advice because my husband intends to go to America. I did not ask you to send him a ship-ticket, because he would go on his own money; he wanted only to come to you. But you are so cold that you don't even deign to give us advice. Oh, believe me, dear brothers, my heart pains me heavily, because for my sisterly love you repay me so ungratefully. We inform you, dear brothers, that we are moving to Konin. I want to place these, our little brothers, because if I let them go from under my care a great misery awaits them, since the family is so careless. If I took three children to me, if I feed them and clothe them, ought they not to have beds on which to sleep? But the beds are with Sławińska, and we are crowded. But the family does not care how the children sleep. So I foresee that if I let them go from under my care misery awaits them. So, dear brothers, I would be very satisfied if you could take Tadeusz the soonest possible to you. We planned so, that if you sent a ticket to Tadzio, and if you advise my husband to come, they would journey together. But you, dear brothers, you are so incited by Sławińska and so lied to by her that you don't dare even to send a letter. But I am astonished that you don't deign to investigate it. You could send a letter to some strange person, then you would learn on which side is the truth. Believe me, dear brothers, you will learn yet on which side the false-ness is, because my husband will yet come to America—only not until he places the children well. And when you get acquainted with my husband I hope that you will respect him otherwise than your first brother-in-law, because my husband cares for the children better than their own father did. . . . .

FRANCISZEK [and] ANNA PUCHALSKI

371 April 24 [1914]

DEAR BROTHER: I write you some words on the anniversary of our loving father. Just a year ago I had the great sorrow. Today our loving father came to me in a dream, and I write you these few words, because I intended not to write to you any more, for I am very much grieved by your views. You listen to what that scoundrel Koniński [= from Konin] writes to you, and you don't believe the truth which I write; but if it is true, the thing which people say now, then you will be persuaded. I heard that you had sent a ship-ticket for Tadeusz, and that he [Puchálski, the brother-in-law from Konin] got it and went to America—that lazy fellow. He had intended to go for a long time but he had no money for the journey. Now he has not been at home for 5 days; he is to sit 4 weeks in a prison. The man who smuggled him through the frontier said that some sort of ship-ticket had come from America and that he [the brother-in-law] was going with this ship-ticket. When I heard it, I sent a boy to Słupca for Tadeusz asking him to come. When he came, I told him how it happened and what people were saying. She [the sister Andzia] got the money-order also and wanted this money-order to be signed [probably by the guardians], but they did not sign. I persuaded Tadeusz to go to her and to ask. . . . . But when Tadeusz went to her dear Andzia [ironically] directly influenced him, and my eyes did not see him again. He went with her to the post-office for money. People say that even if there was no money, but only the ship-ticket, she could have cheated Tadeusz. He [her husband] is perhaps concealed abroad, and she can send him this ship-ticket. If it happens so, then it will be your own fault, because it could have been sent for Tadeusz, but to my address. Did you think that I should bite away a piece of the ticket? I am very much astonished that the thief from Konin has more of your confidence than I.

Now I will tell you also about Maryan. I wrote that he was with me, and he was for 4 weeks. Then Staśkiewicz took him and there he went to school up to the holidays. He came to me at the holidays and was here one day. The next day Janina came three times asking him to go to them. He did not want to go, but [the brother-in-law] himself saw him and asked him positively to go to his house. If he were with me he would go to school again. He [the brother-in-law] is showing off with those children.   He thought that you would send him 50 roubles every month [for them].

Your loving sister,
MARYANNA

372   April 26, 1914

DEAREST BROTHERS: In the name of God I speak to you with these godly words, "Praised be Jesus Christus!" . . . .

. . . . I am in good health, thanks to God, only I have hard work, because I am an apprentice with a baker, Smigielski, so I must work hard and without pay.

I am obliged to describe to you our situation.   After the death of our dear father we remained orphans forever, only our brother-in-law Puchalski, and no one else, cared for us.   The guardians rented our land, sold everything in the house, even the furs [sheepskins], after our father's death, and we were left without any support.   So the family wanted to give us into service, but brother-in-law Puchalski prevented it and became our father.   He is certainly as good as a father, because he found this apprenticeship for me;   he clothed me; when winter came, he had his own sheepskin coat made over for me. He feeds and clothes the smaller children, and so we can feel gratitude toward him for being our true guardian and father.   If he is falsely slandered, and you believe it you will find it out later.   Surely we shall see one another in America soon, and you will learn that he is not like Sławiński.

And now, dear brothers, I send you my brotherly thanks for the 15 roubles which you sent us.   Andzia assisted in getting this money from the post.   We bought a suit for me which cost 6 roubles, a dress for Janina which cost 4 roubles, a dress for Maryan, 3 roubles; 2 roubles were left, but we are without shoes, so brother-in-law Puchalski adds from his money and will have shoes made for us all.   They will cost 10 roubles or more, because shoes are very expensive here.   When Janina went to first confession, brother-in-law Puchalski spent more than 12 roubles for her dress. . . . .   Did the family take any interest in buying anything?   You sent one time some roubles to the address of Sławińska, but we have not been clothed from this money.   I am today in an apprenticeship, but they [the appointed guardians] don't think about clothing me, only dear brother-in-law Puchalski comes to see me every week and cares for me.

Now I hear, dear brothers, that I shall receive a ship-ticket from you. Oh, what a happiness for me, that I shall be able to see you! Oh, I see, dear brothers, that your brotherly love is not extinguished, since you intend to send me a ship-ticket. I beg you heartily for it. But it will be difficult for me to go alone. Brother-in-law wrote in his former letter to you that he intends to go to America, but you did not answer anything, dear brothers. How agreeable and pleasant it would be if I could go with brother-in-law. . . . . Surely, dear brothers, if you knew Puchalski . . . . you would try to have him in America; but you believe false letters and you think him to be a beast. Dear brothers, when you answer me, send the letter to Słupca, to the name of Smigielski, because brother-in-law is moving to Konin in order to send the younger children to school. . . . .[1]

TADEUSZ SERCZYŃSKI

[1] The letter is evidently largely inspired or dictated by Puchalski.

TERLECKI SERIES

The familial situation is rather complicated. The father of the family went many years ago to America and took later his son Michał, to whom these letters are written. Then he died. His wife, Apolonia, married Dobrowolski. Her oldest daughter from the first marriage, Zofia, married Michał Skrzypek; they live with the husband's parents. The second daughter, Stasia, married Fijałkowski and went with his parents and her son Antoś to America. The third, Aurelia, stays with her mother. The latter rents a manorial garden on the estate of the Godlewskis. The familial relations of other members (Rózia, Aleksandra, etc.) cannot be exactly determined.

The disintegration of the family is the most complete which we find in the present collection. There is not a single member of the family who does not quarrel with some other member. This disintegration cannot be completely explained by the emigration and subsequent death of the father, head of the family; we have seen other series in which the death of the parents destroys indeed partly the familial unity, but not the reciprocal affection of the members and a certain solidarity among them. The mother's second marriage evidently brought a new factor of disintegration, but again it does not suffice to explain the actual situation. We should have expected indeed the mother's complete isolation as against a relatively stronger solidarity of the children from the first marriage, as in other similar cases; but the ties of affection between the mother and the children are still perhaps the strongest ties remaining. Moreover, a dissolution of the familial life is marked also in collateral branches of the family (Aleksandra; Rózia). We must therefore fall back on a more general factor of dissolution, and this is found in the fact that the whole young generation here is the second generation of peasants established in a town. (The situation is similar in itself to, although different in its origin from, that in the Borkowski series.) The traditional social elements of the familial organization are lost, and in consequence of this the familial connection is reduced to the elementary and universal relations between individuals—maternal feeling, sexual attraction, friendship, economic calculation. Wherever these factors fail, there is no longer any basis of familial unity. The failure of maternal love brings a break of relations between the mother and Zofia Skrzypek; the failure of sexual attraction leads to the behavior of Fijałkowski, Aleksandra, Rózia; the failure of friendship causes the quarrel between Michał T. and Stasia; the failure of economic solidarity between the stepfather, Dobrowolski, and his wife's family causes his attitude in the matter of the inheritance (in which his wife would have no share) after the death of his wife's first husband. The reason for the lack of traditional elements is the relatively rapid dissolution of the old peasant traditions in country people transplanted into a town and having had no time to adapt themselves to a different set of traditions still alive in a provincial town.

THE FAMILY TERLECKI

Apolonia, widow of Terlecki, by second marriage Dobrowolska
Dobrowolski, her second husband
Michał, her son
Zofia (Zosia) Skrzypek ⎫
Stasia (Stanisława) Fijałkowska ⎬ her daughters
Aurelia (Lola) ⎭
Bronisia (Bronisława, Bronia, Bronka), Michał's wife
Michał Skrzypek, Zofia's husband
His parents
Roman, his brother

Fijałkowski, Stasia's husband
His parents
Antoś, son of Stasia and Fijałkowski
Rózia ⎫
Aleksandra ⎪
Maurycy ⎬ relatives
Aleksander ⎭

373

Only don't show it to Roman!

LUBLIN, April 1, 1911

DEAR BRONISIA AND MICHAŁ: We inform you that we are in good health. . . . . We did not write to you for so long a time because . . . . , to tell the truth, we had no time. Because since we bought the linen-press, we have never had time, and when there is no time, there is no head to think about anything else. And now we sold it, because we did not get on well even with it; although we earned a few złoty and sometimes a few roubles, all this means nothing when lodging is expensive . . . . and living is also very expensive here. . . . . And father [Skrzypek] works in a starch-factory. He earns 20 roubles a month, and this can hardly suffice to live, even ·very modestly. . . . . We heard from mother that Roman is getting on very well, that he earns enough, and on the other hand, we heard that he is tempted and intends to leave his employment because he will get another here in the cement-factory. He ought not to be tempted to come back to the old misery when he is getting on better. He should rather take his wife and children there, because in our country life is very hard for poor people—not for those belly-gods whom the devils won't take. If we knew that it would be easier to live there, we should also risk going ourselves. But we are afraid to do as we once did already when we went beyond Warsaw and lost some hundred roubles, and now it is as difficult to live as after a fire; we must earn back [what we lost]. It is easy to lose but too difficult to come back to the lost fortune. Dear Bronisia and Michał, you write to have your mother learn about the inheritance after your father. But it is in vain, because how can mother learn it? She won't learn it here, evidently, but she must go there [to the village from which the father came], and this old man [stepfather] will give her no money, and your mother has no money of her own. If she had she could go against his will. If you saw how your mother now lives I am sure that you would be very much pained. If you saw the lodging where she lives! Only poles with which the ceiling is supported keep it from falling upon their heads; otherwise they would not know where and when to fly. Lola is going to a laundry, but it does not go on very well because her eye hinders her. Stasia's husband intends to go to America, but the whole misfortune is that he has no money for the journey. Whatever he earns he spends on drinking, and if not on drinking, then on girls. Therefore what he earns is not enough for him, and he is dug [sunk] into debts up to his ears. Fijałkowski is such an orderly man that when he leaves the factory after his work at 6 o'clock in the evening he does not even go home to wash himself. She sees him sometimes the next morning at 2 or 3 after midnight, and if not, then at 7 o'clock in the morning when he is going to the factory. His companion went to America last year; now he is writing letters to him asking him to send a ship-ticket. Then he would go.

Sister [probably cousin] Aleksandra, whose husband is in America —her father [or father-in-law?] cannot manage her at all. He beats her as if she were mud, but all this is of no avail. She became acquainted with a married man who had lived already 16 years with his wife. He left his wife, she left her father and those two children whom she had with her husband. She stole 30 roubles from her father and fled with this peasant.

[MICHAŁ and ZOFIA SKRZYPEK]

Dear Bronisia and Michał, now I shall write for myself, that I got married, which you know already. The marriage was celebrated on August 15. Up to the present we are with [my husband's] mother, so it is somewhat easier, but I don't know how long it will be so. Meanwhile I won't write you more because I have nothing particular, only I beg you to answer us soon. Then in another letter I will address myself to you with a request. I don't know whether you will refuse me or not, I am not sure of myself [hardly dare to ask].

[STASIA]

374   [No date]

DEAR BRONISIA AND MICHAŁ: If you believe that it would be easier for us to live there than in our country and we should not be a burden to you, we should be glad to come nearer to you. But we should like to come all of us. Perhaps we could have there some occupation in a factory, myself, father and mother. We kept that linen-press; it was hard for us. Mother then bought 3 pigs which we kept for 6 months. When they grew up, one died, and we have kept the other 2 since October. Up to the present they cost 34 roubles, and they will give me at the fair 40 roubles. [Another page about the pigs, pig-keeping being now a bad business.] Mr. Dobrowolski [the stepfather] said this, that if he wants to, he can spoil everything that is left after your father. He can write that his wife is from Warsaw and born in Warsaw, because you treat him in your letters as if he were some manor-servant and rascal. You don't know who he is. He is not a first best man, because he was born in Warsaw and baptized in the cathedral of Warsaw. If he does not want you to get anything you won't get anything!

The old Fijałkowskis are trying by all means to sell their house and to go to America in the autumn. . . . .

MICHAŁ SKRZYPEK

375   September 16, 1911

DEAR CHILDREN: With your approaching name-day, dear son and daughter-in-law, I send you wishes. . . . . I don't know why you do not write, whether you are offended because I don't inform you about this property. I have been more than once in the lawyer's office, but I did not find him. But evidently the fortune is best which we earn ourselves. And therefore, dear son, pray to God that you may earn a fortune yourself. I pray for you at every mass. And now, dear children, I inform you that Stasia, with the old Fijałkowskis, is coming to you, in spite of my good advice. She won't listen to me, and perhaps she will regret it, as you do. I beg you very much when she comes to you treat her in a brotherly manner. And now with us there is no news. The crops were abundant, but prices are going up. Bread is 1 copeck a pound dearer, meat costs 15 copecks for a pound of beef, and hogs have got much cheaper, so that it is not worth keeping them, because potatoes cost 2 roubles a *korzec* [about 4 bushels] and in autumn they will go up perhaps up to 3 roubles. As to myself, this year my garden failed, and everything gets on badly with me. I don't know what to begin with, because I don't know whether I shall remain long in this garden; we live worse than dogs in a kennel. . . . . And now I have nothing interesting to write you. As to Rózia, she is not worth the pen and ink [to write about her]; you can guess the rest yourself. In the spring I advised her to move nearer, then she could have earned a living, because 5 women are working steadily with me and I pay them 2 złoty each, and in the spring 8 or 10 worked. But she excused herself on account of caring for her children, and not letting them loaf around uncared for, and meanwhile she amuses herself by receiving guests.

And now, dear brother and sister-in-law [I, your sister write]. I send you my wishes; I should like to see you as soon as possible, but circumstances don't permit it. . . . . Perhaps we shall never see one another until the divine judgment. It is difficult to describe openly what I suffer here. And now I have nothing to write you, only I beg you for a speedy answer, at least this letter will comfort me.

Your truly loving mother,

APOLONIA DOBROWOLSKA

I send you flowers. Answer me as soon as possible, I beg you, don't afflict my aching heart.

And your sister,

A[URELIA] TERLECKA

I have no time to write you more, because it is already midnight, and we must go to the cow which is calving.

376   December 10, 1911

DEAR SON: With the approaching holidays I send you my wishes, whatever you wish yourself from God the Highest, and also to my dear grandchildren. In sending this consecrated wafer I want to see you awake, not in my thoughts and dreams, as I see you very often. And now, dear son, I don't know why you do not answer my letter and prayers. Perhaps something displeased you in it, or perhaps somebody told you false tales again. But I beg you once more, whether she [Stasia] is alive or not, inform me and appease my maternal heart. And if she is alive, divide with her this consecrated wafer in my name. The third month has begun already [since her departure], and I don't know what is going on, because you all abandoned me and perhaps you don't even think how your mother lives in ceaseless labor and moreover in torments. You refuse me even this, that I may receive a few words from you. I wait for your letter as for the best thing, because nobody comes to me any more. I dropped totally [relations] with the Skrzypeks [daughter and son-in-law] since Stasia left; probably they won't stand behind my threshold any more. And now, dear children, I have nothing important to write you, except that the winter oppressed us early and the old Godlewski [estate-owner] died on December 2. I cannot give you more information, because I could not tear myself away from home for the funeral, although the funeral was on December 6. . . . .

Your loving mother,

DOBROWOLSKA

377   March 25, 1912

DEAR CHILDREN: I received your letter for which I am grateful to you and I thank you for your memory and wishes; only I don't like you to write me so little, upon postcards, because I don't even know whom I have to thank, because nobody's name was signed. Dear son, I beg you only, in the name of everything, to advise me how to do that it may be well, besides criticizing. You know that everything cannot be perfect at once. In the beginning you yourself did not get on so well as you do now. And moreover nobody knows what will happen in our country, because people murmur secretly, and around Lublin kettles are built [metaphor] and people say that the explosion will happen soon, and perhaps we shall also perish. But you know more than we do. [Allusions to the preparation for an Austro-Russian war and for a Polish insurrection, in 1912.]

Dear Bronia, I address myself as a loving mother to you, and I beg you, if Antoś [Stasia's son] is with you, take care of him. Although Michał says that Antoś was educated in a forest, yet he himself, while born in the same Lublin, had more defects, even in his later years, than Antoś has, but he does not remember them. And now he [Michał] did not know that this criticism would be painful to his [Antoś'] grandmother [to me], because this is my most beloved grandson. Although the others are equally dear to me, yet they did not work with me, as he did during his whole days.

[APOLONIA DOBROWOLSKA]

To my sister it is written upon this side [of the sheet]. Dear Stasia, I beg you very much to write me a few words yourself, because I know nothing about you except through the hands of other people. In spite of your promises that you would write you don't keep your word to anybody, because even Mr. Czepiński came to me in the garden in order to learn the truth, whether you arrived, because different rumors have been spread. Your thick aunt said that you were sent back and that you live in Rury in a farmer's house. Maurycy came to the garden to learn [the truth] because Stepniak said that Aleksander was drowned. Therefore I beg you, write at least to Czepiński and satisfy his curiosity. I don't feel angry and don't claim anything, although you promised me to write, and different other things. I know that probably you long there for us as we long for you. When you gather much money and there is peace in our country, then come back. . . . . [AURELIA TERLECKA]

378 [1912]

DEAR BROTHER AND SISTER-IN-LAW: [Usual beginning, health and wishes.] Dear brother, you write me that you would take me to you, but not so that I should suffer misery. But have I a delightful life in my country? I suffer perhaps a worse misery because I must work heavily and I receive no good word, and I hear reproaches for every bit of bread which I eat. Believe me, dear Michał, I would fly I don't know where. Although this is my native country I have no near persons in this country except mother. And even mother is very often harsh to me, and all this through the instigation of our stepfather, from whom I never have a good word. He pours curses upon me, whatever ones exist in that world of God, so that my tears never wait. Formerly at least Stasia was here; I had somebody to whom I could go, complain, comfort myself, but now I have nobody to go to. I won't go to Zosia, because she said that if I came to her she would drive me away with a broom. And still less will I go to my aunt, since she dared to say to my eyes that mother and I will soon sit before the church [beg]. But perhaps God the Highest won't let this come, and her ugly eyes won't see it.

And now, dear brother, you order me to learn. Learning is good. Above all, not everybody can be alike, because if everybody wanted to work easily who would be left for the heavy work?

Dear brother, pity our poor mother and don't afflict her poor heart, lessen her tears, because poor mother weeps continually and expects every day a letter from you. I beg you once more, answer us as soon as possible. And when you write to me, write upon a separate sheet, that it may not be together. [AURELIA TERLECKA]

379   October 22, 1912

DEAR CHILDREN: I received your letter . . . . which caused me
a great pleasure, but at the same time a great wound in my heart.
Because if you believed such a lie, I will never believe [anything], and
I implore you and adjure you by the ashes of your dead father, don't
believe it. Although it does not matter much to me, yet I want to
know who carried such a false tale to you, because I want to know the
truth. All the children are good [dear] alike to a mother. In the
same way I have wept for many days for you, particularly when I
learned that you wanted to return from the frontier. In the same
way I weep now for her and I shall not be comforted soon. In the
same way as you did not want to listen to me when I advised you not
to leave, so did she also. As always, a good mother would like to
press all the children to her bosom, but not all of them will listen.
Indeed, as you say, in the second and third years I could possibly not
have received all your letters, because my address was not fixed.
From the manor I received some letters opened, so anything could
happen that I did not receive those letters. But it was not as you
write, that Stasia would have taken, torn, and burned those letters,
because they were of no consequence to her. She got what she was
to get, but you would not have got it, because she received [a legacy]
from her godmother. After the death of the latter her godfather
put 100 roubles in the bank. If I had learned that you were in so
critical a position I would have eaten no bread for a month and given
none to the other children, but saved you. But I knew that you went
to your father [in America] and that he would not let you be wronged.
[The father had died in the meantime.] But you are after all a man
and you ought to have more strength and energy, and she is a woman.
I don't require from you, dear son, to spend money on her and to
make expenses for yourself. Only if she needs it, help her with your
advice, as an older brother and a man who has lived there for a longer
time. . . . . As to the Skrzypeks, you are free not to write at all,
because since Stasia left I have dropped all relations with them,
totally, because they stood like a bone in my throat. [Proverb. They
annoyed me too much.] She complained also about you that she
wrote two letters and you didn't answer, that if she sent you 10 or
15 roubles then you would answer. And perhaps you sent to their
address that letter where you complained that you were in such a
difficult position?

And now, dear Bronka, I address myself to you with this request. As a woman, you have more feeling and experience. I don't say that you should do any detriment to yourself for her sake, but in a given case, in a critical situation, please help her to find some employment or simply some service. I did not want to let her go, but she stubbornly resolved to go, saying that if she is to serve here, she prefers to do it there. And now, dear children, answer everything as soon as possible and inform me whether she is alive and healthy and where she is.

Dear son and daughter-in-law, and my dear grandchildren, I send you my heartiest wishes and kisses, and kiss my Antolek in my name when he comes to you. Did he bring an apple for each of you?

We end already our letter. I [your sister] think that it is enough from me, because I want to sleep. The hour is late. I would write something more but I am afraid to sit longer, because the dogs begin to bark and the pigs to squeal, and I fly to sleep.

Your truly loving mother and sister,

APOLONIA [DOBROWOLSKA and] AURELIA TERLECKA

RACZKOWSKI SERIES

These letters show, in a very detailed and varied manner, the influence of emigration upon family life. We see that every individual undergoes a different evolution, but that there are always factors explaining these differences.

In general, emigration, as should be expected, by isolating the individual from the family and from the community, provokes individualization and weakens the control of the primary group; we have found it already in some of the preceding series. But the degrees and varieties of individualization are numerous.

First of all, as we have mentioned in the Introduction, the nature of individualization depends upon the way in which the individual adapts himself to the new conditions. In this respect we find here such instructive differences as those between Adam Raczkowski, Ludwik Wolski, Helena Brylska, and Aleksander Wolski. The first adapted himself rapidly to American life and succeeded without difficulty in attaining a material position, which, when measured by the peasant standard, must have seemed to him almost brilliant. He gradually ceases to consider it his duty to help his family, but he does not break the familial ties, and occasionally—partly from generosity, partly from the desire to manifest his personal importance—responds to the appeals of other members. Ludwik Wolski, who was finally also successful but must have passed through a rather difficult experience before he got his position (the conditions in Russia being unfavorable for the advance of the lower classes), feels the familial ties as a heavy burden and profits from the first opportunity to break them completely. Probably he has not reached the standpoint that familial affection may exist without an obligation of help, and the familial relation still seems to him indissolubly connected with economic solidarity, so he sacrifices the first to get rid of the second. And the sacrifice was not difficult, because of other factors. Helena Brylska was not particularly successful in her adaptation. Apparently she adapted herself rapidly to a certain narrow circle of American life, changed her attitudes just enough to fit this circle, and for the rest, remained stationary. Certainly in important familial problems her attitudes remain traditional, and it seems probable that her estrangement from her children is due, not to an extensive change in her attitudes, but to an element of asperity in her temper and the difficult American conditions which made it impossible for her to prevent her boys from following the natural impulse to vagabondage. (See note to No. 418.) As to Aleksander, except for his rather insignificant economic success he remains completely misadapted, and his familial attitudes do not change at all during the year covered by his letters. They may of course change later.

The facility and range of adaptation depend, not only upon the conditions which the individual finds in his new environment, but also upon the individual himself—upon (1) his practical ability and intelligence and (2) his habits and traditions. We have analyzed the first point in the introduction to the Kanikuła series, and on the second we find data in the present series. Generally speaking, the younger the individual the more rapidly he adapts himself. Children adapt themselves very rapidly, but not always fortunately, as we see in the case of the children of Helena. Franciszek Ołów, who came to America as an elderly man, father of two grown daughters, was unable to adapt himself at all. But in addition to age and its decreasing plasticity the question of the traditions in which the individual grew up—how numerous and powerful they were—is certainly very important. The relatively easy adaptation of Adam Raczkowski and Teofil Wolski is evidently due to the fact that their families had never been very united. Raczkowski's mother was dead, his father did not live with his second wife, his older brother and sister were in America. As to Wolski, his parents were probably dead long ago, his brothers separated. Moreover, both Adam and Teofil had served in the army before coming to America, and thus the influence of all the social traditions was more or less weakened. Meanwhile, Aleksander Wolski had always lived in the same village with his parents, and so all the traditional attitudes were strongly implanted in him.

This series, particularly the case of Adam, illustrates also the effect of economic conditions on the expansion and development of the personality. Economic success is one of the main sources of the feeling of personal importance, and therefore this feeling is found almost universally among American immigrants. It develops also in Poland under the same influence. (In the autobiography which forms the fourth part of this work we see the ups and downs of the feeling of personal importance as a function of the economic condition of the writer at a given moment.) But, generally speaking, the feeling of personal importance can never develop so rapidly and to such a degree under the influence of a merely economic progress in Poland as it does in America; it is hindered by many social traditions. The social standing of the peasant within the community cannot rise very much through his economic progress if his family does not progress economically at the same time. This limitation partly disappears with the dissolution of the old family, but another tradition is incomparably more difficult for an individual to rid himself of—the old hierarchy of classes. This is more and more supplanted by the new social organization on the basis of the middle-class principle, but it still has strength enough to make an individual of the lower class feel at every moment his social inferiority through the infinitely numerous and various details in which the principle of hierarchy has expressed itself during the many centuries of its dominance.

Finally, even within the new social organization mere economic progress is not sufficient to give the individual the full feeling of personal importance, because the new hierarchy is not exclusively based upon economic differences, but, even more, upon differences of intellectual culture.

Now, in America these obstacles do not exist, at least not to such an extent. The individual is isolated almost completely from the family-group. The traditional class-distinctions, even if they exist, are neither old nor important enough to make themselves felt by the lower classes. The new class-organization is based mainly upon economic differences, and thus economic progress seems the only test of individual value. The cultural criteria are developed in particular groups, but do not pervade the society as a whole. Finally, the immigrant has, as a background for his own personality, not only American life, but the life in the old country, and it is the comparison with his own previous condition and the condition of his people at home which makes him feel his personal importance in so strong and exaggerated a way.

Another important problem raised in this series is the relation between parents and children among Polish immigrants in America. The state of things about which Helena so often complains in her letters—the impossibility of controlling the children—is very general, and is probably more serious among the Poles than in any other nationality. While the external factors of emancipation are the same for the children of every race, we must understand exactly the social conditions which make the Poles react differently to these factors. To be sure, the problem is, how far the parents will be able to oppose their authority to the disintegrating influences of the environment, and this depends upon the adaptation of the means of control to the circumstances. In Polish-peasant life this adaptation is sufficient. We have seen in the Introduction that the parental authority finds there its foundation in the whole organization of the family and in the social opinion of the community; the family and the community have a sufficient power of sanction to prevent any revolt of the child and at the same time to hold the parents responsible for any abuse. The parental authority in the eyes of the child seems not only sacred and all-powerful, but also just, and raised above individual caprice.

If we contrast now the conditions at home with those which the emigrants meet in America, we see that a loss of control over the child is inevitable if the parents do not develop new means as substitutes for the old ones. First, there is in America no family in the traditional sense; the married couple and the children are almost completely isolated, and the parental authority has no background. (In a few cases, where many members of the family have settled in the same locality, the control is much stronger.) Again, if there is something equivalent to the community of the old country, i.e., the parish, it is much less closed and concentrated and can hardly have the same influence. Its composition is new, accidental, and changing; moreover, it is composed of various elements, influenced each separately and each somewhat differently by the new environment, and has consequently a rather poor stock of common traditions. Further, the members of the new generation, brought up in this new environment, are more likely to show a solidarity with one another as against the parents than a solidarity with the parents as against the younger members of the family. Finally, economic independence comes much earlier than in the old country and makes a revolt always materially easy. On the other hand, the parents' authority ceases also to be controlled, except by the state in the relatively rare cases of a far-going abuse. The traditional measure of its exertion is lost; the parents have no standard of education, since the old social standard is no longer valid and no new one has been appropriated. The natural result is a free play given to individual caprice, excessive indulgence alternating with unreasonable severity. Thus the moral character of parental authority in the eyes of the children is lost.

The immigrant can therefore control his children only if he is able to substitute individual authority for social authority, to base his influence, not upon his position as representative of the group, but upon his personal superiority. But this, of course, requires a higher degree of individual culture, intellectual and moral, than most of the immigrants can muster. The contrary case is more frequent, where the children assume a real or imagined superiority to the parents on account of their higher instruction, their better acquaintance with American ways, etc.

The same problems confront country people moving to a Polish town; there, however, the break in the social control of family life is neither so rapid nor so complete, the change of the young generation is not so radical, and there are often time and opportunity enough to substitute a sufficient amount of individual authority for the lost part of social authority.

THE FAMILY RACZKOWSKI

Raczkowski, a retired farmer
Wawrzonkowa, his second wife
Franciszek ⎫
Adam   ⎬ his sons
Helena ⎫
Teofila ⎬ his daughters
Franciszek's wife
Her mother
Helcia ⎫
Stanisława |
Władzia |
Mania   ⎬ Franciszek's children
Janek |
Kostusia ⎭
Zofia, Adam's wife
Władek Brylski (deceased), Helena's first husband
Rykaczewski, his cousin
Staś (Stach) ⎫
Józiek (Józef) ⎬ Helena's sons by Brylski
Maniek (Maryan) ⎭
Józef Dąbrowski, Helena's second husband
Their children
Antoni Wolski, Teofila's husband
Olesiek (Aleksander) ⎫
Julek   ⎬ his children
Aniela ⎭
Teofil Wolski ⎫
Ludwik Wolski ⎬ Antoni's brothers
Małgorzata, Ludwik's wife
Bronisława, Antoni's sister
Franciszek Ołów, a cousin of the Raczkowskis

380–445. 380–81, FROM FRANCISZEK RACZKOWSKI, IN
AMERICA, TO HIS BROTHER ADAM, IN POLAND; 382–402,
FROM FRANCISZEK AND ADAM, IN AMERICA, TO THEIR
SISTER TEOFILA WOLSKA, IN POLAND; 403–25, FROM
HELENA BRYLSKA-DĄBROWSKA, IN AMERICA, TO HER
SISTER TEOFILA WOLSKA, IN POLAND; 426–28, FROM
LUDWIK WOLSKI, IN RUSSIA, TO HIS BROTHER ANTONI
AND HIS SISTER-IN-LAW TEOFILA, IN POLAND; 429,
FROM TEOFILA WOLSKA, WIDOW OF ANTONI WOLSKI, TO
LUDWIK WOLSKI; 430–36, FROM ALEKSANDER WOLSKI
(NEPHEW OF HELENA), IN AMERICA, TO HIS MOTHER,
TEOFILA WOLSKA, IN POLAND; 437–45, FROM TEOFIL
WOLSKI, FIRST IN RUSSIA, THEN IN AMERICA, MAINLY
TO HIS BROTHER AND SISTER-IN-LAW, IN POLAND

380 ANSONIA, July 10 [1903]

DEAR BROTHER ADAM: [Usual greeting.] I received [your]
letter which I answer at once. We are in good health, thanks to
our Lord God, and we wish to you the same. Dear brother, you say
that I do not answer your letters; I answer every letter. I received
from you one letter from the army; then I did not answer, because
the address was bad, but I sent money to father and father sent it to
you. If you had written a letter directly when you came to father
I should have sent you money and you would have got it already.
Now it is too late, you would not receive it soon enough. So when
you get to the army, write me a good address, Russian or Polish,
and then, whenever you need [money] I will send it to you. Write
to me in what company and squad and regiment [you serve]. Dear
brother, nothing rejoices me more, neither money nor anything, since
I have neither dear mother nor father in the world, only you, dear
brother.[1] I learned two weeks ago what a death my father died, in

---

[1] He has two sisters, Teofila Wolska and Helena Brylska. He does not mention
the first because of her alleged bad behavior toward their father, but it is difficult
to determine why he excludes Helena, and, contrary to custom, uses her family-
name, Brylska, as if she were a stranger. They had been quarreling, as we learn
from Adam's letters, but are now on relatively good terms, since Franciszek gives
her letters from home, as he says at the close of this letter. Normally when
relatives quarrel they have no communication while the quarrel lasts, and when it
is over they bear no resentment. In the present case the situation is probably
to be explained by the isolation of the two family-members. No gradation of

a pigsty, from hunger. Such food—a pot of gruel—under his bed, which people threw away after his death! A good daughter! When father worked and gave away everything he had then he was good. Without a priest and alone he died in a pigsty! Let her expect the same—to die in a pigsty. And let her children in the house not come to her.[1]

Dear brother, if you have no money for the journey, borrow from anybody, and I will send it back to him with thanks. Write to me from whom you borrowed.

When father wrote to me, as he had nothing to eat, I sent [money] to him. Helena Brylska lives two versts away from me, I give her every letter.

I have nothing more to write, I wish you health and good success.

With respect,

BOTH RACZKOWSKIS [FRANCISZEK and WIFE]

381 February 15 [1904]

. . . . DEAR BROTHER ADAM, AND ALSO DEAR SISTER AND BROTHER-IN-LAW AND YOUR CHILDREN: We are in good health, thanks to our Lord God, and we wish to you the same.

Now, dear brother, I think well [intentions are good] about you. If work were good you would already be in America. I have had no work for four months now, and I wait for better conditions. If the conditions don't improve by Easter, we will go back to our country, and if they improve and I get work, I will immediately send you a ship-ticket, and you will come. There will probably be hard times in America this year because in the autumn they will elect the president. If the same remains who is now, then all will be well, but if they elect a democrat, then there will be hard times in America, and those who have money enough will go back to their

---

intimacy is possible between two individuals so long as they remain integrate members of the same family; the family relationship demands a certain degree of intimacy; it determines the relation. But in isolation their relation becomes merely personal and admits of any gradation possible between individuals.

[1] The father lived with Teofila Wolska. This false report about his death was sent by his second wife, the writer's stepmother, Wawrzonkowa (cf. letters of Helena Brylska), who evidently hates Teofila. Probably the reason of this hate is that the old man left her and went to live with his daughter.

country.[1] You will learn [all] in another letter. Hold out a little, until I bring you to me or until I come myself to you, and then we shall suffer together. Inform me about your health and success, and what kind of winter you have, because we have great cold and snows. I have nothing more to write, I send my good wishes and low bows to brother and to the Wolskis. With respect,

Your brother,

RACZKOWSKI [FRANCISZEK]

Helena Brylska is working and earning well. I beg you, don't refuse me but inform yourself, you Wolskis, or you Adam, what is the news about my wife's mother and how she is, because I don't know what it means. We wrote three letters and we have an answer to none. I request you, let somebody go to mother and tell her that her daughter begged you to get information as to how mother is, and tell me about mother, and what is the news in our country.

382   WILMINGTON, DEL., June 25 [1904]

DEAR SISTER: [Usual greeting to sister and brother-in-law; generalities about health and success.] I am already with my brother, thanks to God and to God's Mother. As to work, I don't hope to work sooner than autumn, because brother also has no work since Christmas and cannot get work, because all factories are stopped and there is no work until they elect the president in autumn. Then perhaps we shall get work. And at present brother has no pleasure in life either, because there are five of them and I make the sixth, and all this means spending money. And you know that when I left you, I had neither clothes nor shirts; so when I came to them, sister-in-law and brother gave me at once clothes of theirs and we all three went to the city and bought clothes, one suit for working days and another for holidays, and everything in the way of clothes. So you can understand that when we bought everything, it cost them about 80 roubles. The watch and the suit for church cost alone 60 roubles.[2] I have nothing more to write, only I bid you goodbye,

---

[1] This connection of hard times with democratic government is a dogma among the Polish immigrants.

[2] Franciszek R. and Helena Brylska have divided between themselves the expense burden of bringing Adam to America. Helena paid for the ship-ticket, Franciszek supports Adam until he gets work. This is still familial solidarity.

dear sister and brother-in-law.   When I get work I won't forget you.
Remain with God.   Both Raczkowskis with their children send also
their bows.   I beg you, answer the soonest possible.

[ADAM RACZKOWSKI]

383   August 15, 1904

DEAR SISTER: . . . . And now I write to you a second letter,
because when I came to America I wrote you a letter but I have
no tidings from you.   I don't know what it means, whether you did
not write or my letter did not reach you; so please, sister, answer
me, and please, sister, tell me what is the news in our country, and
whether they have called me to military service or not.   And please,
sister, tell me what is the news about war in our country.   As to the
work, we are not working yet, because now they are gathering votes
for the new president, so all factories are closed and don't work at
all till the president is elected.   So when I work I will not forget you,
sister dear and brother-in-law.   And as to Władkowa [Helena B.]
she is earning well and the factory where she works is going well.
Władkowa got married [second marriage] on August 17.   She married
a Pole.   And I request you, sister, inform me, how is the weather
in our country, and how are the crops, how are you getting on?
Here, at the end of July and in the beginning of August we had terrible
heat, and rain and thunderstorms.   And I request you, sister, greet
the Kaliszeskis and their daughter from me.   And tell me who reads
your letters to you and answers [them].   And I beg you very politely,
be so kind and go to Imnielski.   Let him give you the address of his
daughter Weronika, who is in Warsaw, and send me this address,
because I want to write her a letter.   And I beg very politely Mr. and
Mrs. Imnielski to give me the address of their daughter Weronika.
I have nothing more to write, only I send lowest bows to you, sister
and brother-in-law, and I salute also Mr. and Mrs. Imnielski and
their daughters.   Remain with God.

Respectfully,

ADAM RACZKOWSKI

384   September 23, 1904

DEAR SISTER: . . . . I received your letter and I thank you
heartily for answering me.   As to what you write, sister, that I may
greet Brylska for you, well, I wrote her three letters and she wrote

me one and sent us her photograph when she got married. As soon as I came to America, I saluted her politely. But brother and sister-in-law related to me how she remembered [forgot] her children and how she began to behave as soon as she came to America. And she complained to us that sister-in-law was not good to her! She behaved so that if it had been I, I should not have kept her [in the house] 24 hours. As it was, they were patient and kept her, and brother tried to find work for her. And about her writing letters to Wawrzonkowa [their stepmother] and sending money to her, well, I shall bow to her [to Brylska] more profoundly [I will despise her for it still more] because if Wawrzonkowa were lying under a hedge and if I were passing by, I would ——— kick her, but would not give my hand to her [assist her].[1] [Usual greetings.]

ADAM RACZKOWSKI

385 February 13 [1905]

DEAR SISTER: . . . . And now I inform you that I have very good work. I have been working for 3 months. I have very good and easy work. I earn $8.00 a week. Brother has work also. And as to Brylska, I don't know how she is getting on, and I don't think about her at all. Inform me what is going on in our country, who has come to America and who got married, and what is the talk in our country about revolution and war, because I have paid for a newspaper for a whole year and the paper comes to me twice a week,[2] so they write that in our country there is misery. They say in Warsaw and Petersburg there is a terrible revolution and many people have perished already. As to the money, I cannot help you now,

---

[1] Adam's behavior toward his sister who had helped him to come to America and had done him no personal wrong seems to be mean ingratitude and would be this if their relation had been merely personal. But Adam evidently occupies not the individual but the familial standpoint. He condemns Brylska impersonally for her alleged lack of familial feelings toward her own children, toward Franciszek and his wife, and from this standpoint the act of solidarity in sending Adam a ship-ticket cannot counterbalance those alleged offenses against the spirit of the family. The familial standpoint becomes still more marked when Adam reproaches Helena for her solidarity with Wawrzonkowa, the stepmother. The latter is for him not only not a member of the family but an element hostile to the family.

[2] This mention, trifling in itself, is a significant expression of the multiplication of contacts which will result in a more and more intense feeling in the man of his own personality, as we shall see in his later letters.

sister.   You will excuse me yourself; I did not work for five months, so I owed for living alone $70.00 and for the ship-ticket $50.00 and for the clothes I borrowed $45.00.   I still have $109 of debt, but I hope in God that by June I shall get rid of my debt.   I request you sister, inform me who married among the young people, which girls got husbands and which boys got wives, and please inform me about Wawrzonkowa.

I have nothing more to write, only I bid farewell to you sister and brother-in-law, and I leave you with respect, and I salute you, Mr. Teacher and Mrs., your wife, and I leave you with respect,

ADAM RACZKOWSKI

386   June 27, 1906

DEAR SISTER: . . . . I received your letter on June 26 and I answered you directly on June 27, and I ask you whether you received the money that I sent you or not, because they sent me a receipt from the post-office that you received the money on March 26, and you did not say in your letter that you received the money.   So I request you to tell me which month you received the money.   And as to the work, I am working in the same factory, and brother also is working in the same factory, where he was working formerly.   And as to our country, brother says he will not return, because there is nothing to return for.   He has no property there, and it is better for him in America, because in our country he could not even earn enough for a loaf of bread.   And I also do not know whether I shall return or not.   If I can return then perhaps I shall return some day or other, and if not I don't mind, because I do ten times better in America than in our country.   I do better today than brother, because I am alone.   As to Borkowianka, I don't know whether she came to America or not, because I sent her neither a ship-ticket nor money.   So I beg you, sister, be so kind and learn from the Borkowskis whether she thinks of coming or not, because if she does not come then I will marry in the autumn or during carnival.[1]   As to what you write to me about the photograph, I will send you my photograph in August, and brother with the whole family [also].

[1] There is no question of love.   There has been mention of Weronika, and probably under the influence of his sister he is thinking of Borkowianka.   He simply wants to marry in general.   Cf. a similar situation in the Butkowski series.

And as to the money I will send it to you together with the photograph. And about Brylska I do not know anything; she wrote to me at Easter, and since then I have no tidings whatever.

And now, sister-in-law and brother are speaking to you: Be so kind and learn where is the mother of sister-in-law and with whom she lives. Answer us, and I will tell you more in another letter. [Usual greetings.]

ADAM RACZKOWSKI

387 August 6, 1906

[Printed greetings.]

And now I inform you, dear brother [cousin-in-law], Teofil, that I intended to send you a ship-ticket, but I wrote to an agent and the agent answered me that now it is too late to send a ship-ticket, because a ship-ticket takes at least 5 weeks or 6 weeks to get to our country and now, from September 15, they intend to admit no more emigrants to America. So if I sent you a ticket perhaps you would not get to the water soon enough. Meanwhile, a letter takes at most 15 days to go to our country, so if you wish to come to America, as soon as your receive this letter, get ready at once, take money and leave, so you will perhaps land before September 15. Within this letter you have an order for all steamship-lines enclosed, you can buy a ticket for any ship you wish, because this order was sent to me by the agent. And don't think, dear brother Teofil, that perhaps I don't wish to send you [a ship-ticket]. I wish you to come to America, dear brother, because up to the present I am doing very well here, and I have no intention of going to our country, because in our country I experienced only misery and poverty, and now I live better than a lord in our country. I work my 9 hours and I have peace; I have enough to drink and to dress well, and I have money. I wish you also to come; and on the way to America explain that you are going to a cousin [exactly: brother, son of an uncle]. If they ask you how long I have been in America, say 10 years and married,[1] and bring so much money that after landing you will have at least $10.00 and during the voyage remember not to spend money. From Castle Garden send me a telegram. Then, if they won't admit you, I will get you out from Castle Garden; even if it should cost me $100

[1] This applies to the older brother.

I would not allow them to send you back.[1]   I have nothing more to write, only I leave you with respect.   May God grant it.   Amen.

ADAM RACZKOWSKI

388   January 28, 1907

DEAR SISTER: . . . . As to work, I work, but very little, because the factory where we worked with brother was burned on Saturday, January 19, at 7 o'clock in the evening, and brother's carpenter's tools were all burned.   He lost $50.00.   And now I inform you about my old Miss Borkowska, whom nobody wants.   I don't care anything about her—such an old maid!   I wrote to her only in jest, because I have in America girls enough and much better than she, and even to them I don't pay compliments.   I care as much for her as for an old torn shoe.   Today I don't need the favor of anybody except God.   May God continue to give me such health as he gives me up to the present day.   I don't want the favors of anybody except God.   As to Teofil, I don't know what he means, and why he will take to himself such a shepherd's bitch.   There is no place in America for her, because in America they don't keep sheep.   Does he want to keep sheep, and to breed rams, and to become a shepherd?   The stupid, where is his reason, since in America there are girls enough.[2]

As to money, I won't send you any now, because we have expenses ourselves, but I will send you for the holidays some more roubles; you may expect it.   You ask, sister, about the children. Will you inform me where is that youngest one, Maryan, and with

[1] Besides a familial feeling and certainly personal attachment, there is much of showing off in Adam's helping Teofil to come, and in this whole letter he is proud of being able to be a benefactor.   This is one of the typical attitudes assumed by the peasant when, under the influence of a growing isolation from the old social groups, the claims of solidarity, put forward by the family or the community, cease to be considered as natural and naturally satisfied.

[2] This abuse is evidently the effect of resentment, particularly as the girl seems to have shown a preference for Teofil. (Borkowska is another name for the Borkowianka whom he has previously mentioned.)   But it shows mainly the degree of self-conceit which the man has already reached.   The feeling of personal importance and exaltation, based on economic success, is here mixed with a feeling of independence, whose source lies probably in the progressive liberation from the bonds of social tradition, including family and traditional attitudes toward marriage, power of the community, and probably also power of the state, which he had experienced during military service.   Cf. 391, note.

whom he is? If you see some misery on him, take him to yourself; I will reward you, and I will send you money for his clothes, and you will have still a profit from him, because I pity him; the child is guilty of nothing. Please, sister, write to me how old he is. If someone is coming to America, then write to me, please. Perhaps he could bring him with him to me. I would send either money or a ship-ticket for him and I would take him to me.[1]

Expect another letter from your brother soon. [Usual ending.]

ADAM RACZKOWSKI

389 [June?] 3, 1907

DEAR SISTER: . . . . I received your letter on May 29. I received it at same time with Teofil, because on the same day I called on Teofil and I read his letter, and when I came home I received also such a "joyous" letter from you. As to the work, brother is working steadily and since the factory was burned I have had work for a month and for another month I have had no work. During the two years I worked steadily in the same factory I had money, and now I earn hardly enough to live. I am working in the same factory as brother. I do carpenter's work and earn $2.00 a day. The work is good and well paid, but only if you work steadily. May God let me work this year during the summer in that factory and earn at least enough to live. Then by winter I shall have steady work.

This letter, which I received from you, grieved me and brother terribly. Dear sister and brother-in-law, you write to us to hold our hands out to you [help you]. It is true that a misfortune befell you, that a misery from God happened to you, and you have not a piece of bread to put in your mouth at times, but with us also it is not easy. Before we earn that cent in the sweat of our brow and get it into our hands, see here, an expense is waiting for it. I don't need to explain everything to you, because you know yourself what expenses are. But in such misfortune we will not refuse you, and not send you any money, but we will not send it now. We will send it to you on June 15, because we cannot do it sooner. I will not write to you how much until a second letter. Expect a second letter soon after you

---

[1] Sincere feeling toward the boy, connected probably with a desire to manifest his own superiority over the boy's mother Helena, and to express his personality and magnificence.

receive this one. I will write also to Teofil in Philadelphia. Inform me whether you have the same horses as when I was there, or other ones; tell me this. And send me the address of sister, because she does not write to me and I have not her address. I have nothing more to write, only I bid you goodbye myself, and brother with his wife and children. And brother's daughter, who came into the world May 21, salutes you. I send low bows to the Imnielskis and to their daughters. Inform me whether Weronika, Imnielski's daughter, got married. Inform me, how are the crops in our country, and what success, and who got married among the young people, and whether my companions came back from the army or not. I leave you with respect and beg for a speedy answer.[1]

ADAM RACZKOWSKI

390   January 24, 1907 [1908]

DEAR SISTER [printed introduction]: We are in good health, thanks to our Lord God, and we wish the same to you—health and good success and everything that you wish for yourself from our Lord God. And now I inform you about work. Work is now very bad. Since Christmas I have worked only three days in the week, and perhaps they will send me away entirely. Brother still works but he expects every day to be sent away. Some works have stopped entirely and some people have nothing more to live on, and the city is feeding some people already. As to sister, I don't know anything, because she doesn't write to me and I don't write to her and we don't know anything about each other, I don't know how she lives and she doesn't know how I live. And as to the cold, we haven't had any cold yet—but it often rains.

And now I beg you, my sister, myself and brother with his wife, to be so gracious and inform us where is the mother of our sister-in-law, whether in Przasnysz or in Bartułty. If you see her ask her, please, whether she received 20 roubles or not. Let her write to us. And inform me who has married among the young people, and whether the daughters of Imnielski have married or not. Dear sister, I will

---

[1] The whole tone of the letter shows a certain lowering of the feeling of personal importance, to be explained probably by (1) worse economic conditions, (2) a certain revival of old memories, which is shown by the interest manifested in the persons and conditions of the "old country," and which brings the man back to his earlier attitude.

tell you about myself, how I am doing in America. I have not yet experienced poverty in America; on the contrary, I am my brother's support. But I am tired of walking about unmarried. Although I could give my wife enough to live, still I fear lest poverty should look me in the eyes. Were it not for the money I have put in my brother's house, which he bought, I could do nothing during a year and live with my wife like a lord. But now I postpone it for a longer time. You write to me that I don't answer you. I answer every letter. I sent you a letter on Christmas, on the same day you sent me one, and I don't know whether you received it or not.

I have nothing more to write, only I send you low bows and I remain respectfully,

ADAM RACZKOWSKI

And I ask you for a speedy answer.

May God allow us to live till Easter, and after Easter I will write to you what girl I shall marry, and I will send you a photograph as soon as I leave the altar. My girl is a cousin of my sister-in-law; her mother and my sister-in-law are born sisters. They are persuading me to marry her, but I still doubt whether it will be so.

ADAM RAKOSKI [sic]

391   March 2, 1908

DEAR SISTER: . . . . As to Teofil I do not know where he is, because he was with me before Christmas and was out of work then, and he intended to go to the mines. So I don't know whether he went or not, because in mines it is this way: One goes there and finds money, another, death. He wanted to go to the mines, so probably he went, because he has not written to me. As to work, I haven't worked for four weeks. There is no work. Brother still works but is not doing well, because almost all factories are closed. Times are so good in America that people are going begging. As to sister, I don't know anything about her, because she does not write to me, and I do not write to her either. In that [former] letter we asked you to inform us where is the mother of our sister-in-law, and whether she received 20 roubles. Let us know, please, where she is, why she does not write to them.

You advise me to marry Księżakówna. Besides Księżakówna I have others [here] even more stately and I do not bestir myself very much about them.[1]   As to Imnielsczanka [daughter of Imnielski], send her to me, and I will marry her and send you the money for the ship-ticket back.[2]   Now is not a very good time to marry, because work is bad and bad times are coming now.

Tell us about your success, how you are getting on.   Have you still a debt, or did you pay it off?   And please write your letters more distinctly, because I cannot read what you write.   All the letters are covered with ink; it is impossible to make out what those letters are.   [Usual ending.]

ADAM RACZKOWSKI

392   March 8 [Probably 1908]

. . . . Dear sister, you write me that for a year you received no letter from me.   But I sent you three (3) letters and I received no answer till I sent you a fourth letter, and only then I received an answer.   And about Teofil I don't know anything.   It is a year since he called on me, and then he intended to go to the mines for work.   I don't know whether he went there or not, because some three months after he had intended to go there those mines fell in completely, and not a single man got out alive.   And moreover there were fire and water which took the rest.   So I cannot tell you whether he worked there or not, because if he worked there under the surface then probably he is also lying there in the ruins.   And as to sister, I don't know how she is doing, because she doesn't write to me and I don't write to her; I don't know where she is.   Sister dear, you write me, "Shall we ever see each other again?"   You know yourself that I will not go to our country because I fear the Russian,[3] and

[1] A curious example of an attitude remaining superficially the same while the social background is completely changed.   As long as the boy is more a member of a family, the familial dignity requires him not to show too much eagerness in his courtship—to hesitate, really or apparently, to make his choice slowly and from among many girls.   When the individual is isolated, we should expect an easier and more rapid decision and more place for personal preferences.   And normally this is so.   But here the feeling of personal importance takes the place of the demands of familial dignity, and the old behavior is kept up while its psychological factors are quite new.

[2] Compare the careless and protective way in which he speaks about the girl here with the humility used three years before in asking the Imnielskis for the address of their daughter (No. 383).

[3] He would be considered a deserter because he did not go when the reserves were called during the Japanese war.

brother also won't go because he has no health, and even if I sent you a ship-ticket that you might come to us it would be difficult for you to come to us, to leave the household and the children, it would be a great ruin for you in the home. But if you wish to come, then come for three months at least. We do not mind the few dollars. The photograph I will send you after Easter certainly—brother with his family and myself. As to marriage, I intend to marry after Easter, but I don't know yet. I cannot find a girl for me. I don't require her to be pretty and rich, but I seek a girl with a good nature. As to fortune, [in my opinion] God has still more than He spent [Proverb].[1]

Inform me how is my mother [stepmother] Wawrzonkowa, and inform me who among the young ones, boys and girls, got married. I have nothing more to write. . . . . ADAM RACZKOWSKI

393 [Probably summer 1908]

DEAR SISTER: . . . . I don't know what it means, whether you are all dead, that I have no letter from you for three months. I sent you a letter before Easter, and I have no word from you. I request you to answer me. In this letter I tell you nothing, because I have no word from you, only I beg you be so good and go to Bogate, to the church, and when the service is over go to the priest and get my birth-certificate and send it to me, because I will need it presently. I have nothing more to write, only I bid you goodbye. In another letter I will tell you everything. ADAM RACZKOWSKI

394 January 30 [Probably 1909]

DEAR SISTER: I received every one of your letters, and the letter which you sent to me, and the receipt I received on January 26. You were not to send me the receipt, and now I send you the receipt back. I was in the post-office and I gave them another address. They are searching for that money and they say that you must receive it there, and if you don't receive it, it will be returned to the same

---

[1] The indifference to dowry which characterizes the immigrant is due mainly to the fact that it is not indispensable here as it was in peasant life—that the man earns more than his old standard of life required. "God has more than He spent," because there are new and unlimited economic possibilities. Evidently also the man in America is not in a position to undertake the routine of selecting and negotiating which is normal at home.

city from which it was sent. It cannot be lost when sent through the post. And if you receive it answer me at once whether you did receive it or not.

As to sister, I don't write to you because I have no word from her at all since the time when you sent me that letter and asked me to send it to sister. Since that time, when I sent that letter, I have had no word from her at all. And as to work, during the whole month of January work is such that we hardly earn enough to live. And as to what you wrote me, that I might send you about 30 roubles for horses, we can speak about that later. I cannot refuse it to you. After Easter I will send you more, but now I cannot, because I intended to marry during the carnival and I spent some money, about $40.00 on account of the wedding, and I gave this up because I did not like the girl. Tell me who has been married among the young people, because one girl wrote two letters to me and I have the wish to bring her to me. She lives near the manor. . . . .

A. R.

395 June 1, 1909

DEAR SISTER: . . . . And now, please, inform me how do you do. As to work, I am working still, but it is hardly enough to live on. All the iron foundries are closed. Poverty in America is getting worse than in our country, living is dear, and generally everything gets dearer. Please, sister, advise me about what I ask, because I had intended to marry in June, but I intend now to go to our country. I think that I shall not be punished severely for going to America. I did not run away from the regiment; they just sent me back to recover. So I went home, but neither father nor mother was alive and I had no property to live on in our country. I had a brother in America, who had been there 10 years. I wrote to him, he sent me a ship-ticket, and I went to America. I think that for anything like this I should not be punished much.

I have nothing more to write, only I bid you goodbye and ask for a speedy answer.

ADAM RACZKOWSKI

396 July 17, 1909

DEAR SISTER: . . . . We received your letter, for which we thank you heartily. And now we inform you about our health and success. Sad is our success dear sister and brother-in-law; we shall not forget this sorrow up to the grave. Our Lord God gave us a daughter, Stanisława, who rejoiced our whole household, and our Lord God took her to Him. We buried her on July 1. Today in our home we have room enough, but without her everywhere it is empty. Whenever we look at her clothes, every dress we wet with tears. She came to us as if on a visit, rejoiced us, and went away. She was two years old. Sister dear, if we should tell you about her, a whole newspaper would not be sufficient—how graceful and clever she was. Sister dear, excuse me for not writing you a letter for so long a time. After her death I wished to write a letter, but I could not from sorrow. [To this point written by Adam, but evidently dictated by the older brother, father of the girl.]

As to work, we both have no work since July 1. As to Ołów, you praised him as a carpenter, and as long as he was with brother he worked, but when they sent him alone into a car to work, he stood as stupid as an ass, and yet he was angry and swore when we taught him how to work. He got $2.50 a day. Then he went away from us and got work on July 15 in an iron-foundry. He carts earth with a wheelbarrow. He gets $1.50 a day and works like an ox in America.[1] I am working in a gabbarnia [?]. I get $10.00 a week and work only $5\frac{1}{2}$ days in a week. As to my marriage, I will marry in August. I have a girl from Płock; she came from our country not long ago. She is a poor girl, because she has still about $50.00 of debt that I must pay back for her. As to what you say about money, I will send you some, but not now, because brother spent all his for this funeral and it cost me also some $10.00 or $20.00. In another letter I will tell you more. . . . .

ADAM RACZKOWSKI

397 December 18, 1909

DEAR SISTER: . . . . I received your letter on December 15, and I answer this letter, thanking you heartily for answering me. As to work, I have had no work for 2 months, since they had a strike. It means that they do not want to work for the same money, but they want more wages. Perhaps I shall begin to work in February. As to the ship-ticket, I would have sent it to her if she had not married,

[1] Ołów is a cousin of Adam, older and married. He was at first docile, owing to his unfamiliarity with America, but later resented the show of superiority on the part of Adam, particularly as married men are accustomed to a certain deference from the unmarried.

but now I don't want to hear anything about it. You ask me, sister, to send you money. I have some dollars with me, but now I have no work, and I am also looking around me [I am careful] because I do not know what will become of me during the carnival. Perhaps I shall marry, and then I shall need money myself. As to those several hundred dollars that I have with brother, on that house which he bought, he will not give them back at once because he has no money now. And as to the money that you gave to Ołów, he did not tell me anything about it. Let me know how much money he got from you, because Tryc wrote to him also about money, asking him to send back what he borrowed from Tryc. You write, sister, that people repay you with wrong for your goodness and that therefore you will be ruined. If you [think that you] got ruined through me, through what I have taken from you, then calculate how much I owe you and for what, and I will send it to you, even if it is two hundred dollars, but don't blame me.[1] As to the photograph, I will send it to you after the New Year. And as to sister, she does not write to me and I do not write to her either; I do not even know where she is. And now you write, sister, that Olesiek [Aleksander] intends to come to America in the spring. Well, you can send him if he is a good carpenter or blacksmith or handworker of any kind. Then he can find work and good money. But if he knows only farm-labor, then let him work on his farm; he will be better off. You have already sent us one and we have too much of this one "well-trained" carpenter. Don't be angry with me, dear sister, for answering you with those words, but people come from our land to America and say that you are not in such misery as you write to me. I don't forget you yet I will send you some dollars some day or other. Answer me, did Weronika Imnielsczanka marry or not? I want to know it. . . . .

ADAM RACZKOWSKI

398   February 25, 1910

. . . . DEAR SISTER: . . . . I received your letter on Christmas, but I did not answer you at once, because I intended to marry, and therefore I waited with the letter, even too long. Excuse me, dear

---

[1] There is a traditional fear of blame, especially from a person wronged, connected on one hand with the dependence of the individual upon social opinion, on the other hand with the idea of a harmful magical influence in words expressing ill-will. At the same time we have here also the feeling of personal importance as background of generosity.

sister and brother-in-law; don't be angry with me. At last I now inform you, that I am married. My wedding was on January 24. I have a wife from the government of Płock, from Sierpc, beyond Mława. And now we send you this letter and the wedding-photograph. I am in this photograph and my wife. After Easter brother will send you also his own with his family. He will send you none now because his wife is not able to go to the photographer. I describe my wedding in another letter. At present I will mention only this, that this wedding cost me $180. The wedding dress alone cost me $30.00, and about the rings and other things I shall not write you. I took her as rich as she walked [having nothing]. I paid $85.00 back for her ship-ticket. In another letter I will tell you everything that is going on in America, and everything in general. I have nothing more to write, only I send you my greetings, I embrace you and kiss you innumerable times, and my wife also salutes sister and brother-in-law, embraces and kisses sister and brother-in-law, and remains with respect, Zofia Raczkowska.

And I ask you for a speedy answer, when you receive the photograph.

ADAM RACZKOWSKI

399 July 25, 1910

DEAR SISTER: .... We received your letter on July 21 for which we thank you heartily. And now I inform you that I send you my photograph with my whole family on July 25. Expect it to arrive, and when you receive it, answer whether you received it or not. And I beg you, be so good and send us your photograph, that I may have you at least on the lifeless paper. I request you to answer me and tell me what that Ołów says when he gets home; because he will boast there; so spit in his eyes as you would to a witch.[1] If he came to America again and begged even on his knees he would not get back the work he was doing. When he had work he ought to have held it with his hands and his feet, and in America he could have carried money in a bag on his back [if he had held the

---

[1] Spitting is primarily an old Slavic counter-charm or spirit-scarer; secondarily, an expression of contempt. The Russians spit after meeting a Russian priest on the street, because meeting a priest, a *pop*, is considered in Russia a bad omen. Since the Russian conquest the Poles have imitated this gesture, but with them it is an expression of contempt, not a counter-charm.

work], but not so in our country. As to the work, I have work, because this factory where I am working will not stop at all during this year, but I will stop work now at least for a month, because I am tired of work. As to brother, in the beginning he did not do very well, but now everything is going very well with him. His wife keeps 8 persons boarding in her home and he earns $2.50 a day. He does piece-work. In the autumn I shall take him with me, and let him learn the same work I am doing, and he will also earn well. As to the weather, up to the present it is very good with us, there are frequent showers and thunderstorms. The heat is not very great.

And now I only name [enumerate] my family: My oldest [daughter] Helcia, Władzia, Mania, Janek, and Kostusia, my youngest. [Usual ending.]

Franciszek Raczkowski

400   May 6, 1912

Dear Sister: . . . . We received your letter, which afflicted us very much. We learned about the misfortune that befell you, and we send you two letters together, one registered and the other an ordinary one. For two years we did not receive any letter from you, and only now we have received one through Helena and we learned about your trouble. We don't know for what reason you did not write to us. It seems to us that we did not do you any wrong. Why did you not write to us for so long a time? Why did you not even inform us when brother-in-law was sick? We spoke every day about you both. Why do you not write to us? We wrote to you more than a dozen letters and did not receive any answer. It was perhaps that humpbacked fellow who slandered us to you. If so, it is not our fault, sister, that you listened to his words and don't write. If we behave so, sister, and if we listen to such scoundrels, death will take us all and we shall not know anything about one another. When I married my wife had a brother, a scoundrel like Ołów. When marrying I paid to that brother $50.00 for her, for her ship-ticket; later on I paid him $30.00 more. I gave him back $80.00 for her ship-ticket, and he claimed $35.00 more, saying that I owed it to him. We had a lawsuit, which God helped me to win, and today he needs my favors, not I his. Now I let wife's mother come from the old country; she is with me, and today her whole family calls on me and

[begs] my favor.[1]   As to health, brother, with his wife and children, is in good health enough and is working, and I, with my wife and child, am in good enough health, and I have good success, but I don't know how God will help me further.   As to our meeting, if you wish, sister, to see us, you can.   Neither myself nor brother will go to our country, but you can come.   And when you answer us then we will tell you more. . . . .[2]

Your brothers, loving you,
ADAM and FRANCISZEK RACZKOWSKI

401   May 6, 1912[3]

In the first words of our letter we speak to you, dear sister . . . . [Usual greetings and wishes.]   We received a letter from you on May 5, because of which we wrung our hands that such a misfortune happened to you.   You write, sister, that we don't write letters to you.   We wrote to you some letters, but to none we received any answer.   When Ołów went home, brother sent you at once his photograph with his whole family, and a letter, and we received from you no answer.   Did you receive the photograph and the letter, or not? Why should we write to you, since you don't answer?

You wrote to us, sister, that Ołów was coming to America to us, that we should meet him as our brother.   We did it at your request; we gave him what a brother could expect from a brother.   And how did he pay us back for our goodness?   I asked him to come to my wedding, he did not come.   Brother invited him to a christening. He did not come then either.[4]   He went away to our country, and he did not even come to bid us farewell.   When he intended to go to our country brother asked him to come and bid us farewell, and said he would give him a gift for our sister; and brother bought a gold

[1] Pride in this situation would be foreign to the peasant in the old country. There the young expect help from the old for a time.   The element of pride here expressed is another factor in the waiving of the dowry in America.

[2] The letter is very cold for a letter of condolence.   The coldness is partly an intentional reaction to the fact that the sister did not write for so long a time and thus almost broke the familial relation.

[3] This is the letter referred to in the last as sent on the same date.

[4] This neglect is in itself a great offense to familial and individual honor, but in addition, the man who assists at a wedding or a christening is traditionally obliged to contribute to the "collection," and not to come is a proof of stinginess or hostility.

ring for you and intended to hand it over to him that he might give it to you when he arrived in our country. But he went away, and we did not even know when; he only said to people that he came to us to get some money that we owed him! Sister, when he tells you about us don't believe him, because he is a first-rate liar—this Prussian gooseman! In our home somebody recognized him as the same man with whom he had driven geese to Prussia. Then he was so angry that he seized a whip, but the other still said that it was true.

Write to us, sister, did you receive the photograph of brother or not, because if you did not receive it we will send you another. And you can write letters to us as often as every week; we will answer every letter. We send you two letters [one] registered, so if you do not receive this letter, you will receive the registered one. And describe to us how long he was sick, and what he died of, and how did he safeguard you with that property, and tell us how old are your oldest and your youngest. Do you intend to farm yourself or to rent? We request you, answer us about everything. Answer us the soonest possible.

[ADAM and FRANCISZEK RACZKOWSKI]

402   November 28 [1912]

. . . . DEAR SISTER: You write to us and ask us to send you a ship-ticket for your boy. We advise you to let him wait until spring, because it is not certain how work will be in the spring for now they have elected a democrat president and when a democrat is president everybody expects misery to come. Let him wait until March, because only from March on this president will begin to govern, and we shall see how work goes when he governs, whether well or ill. Now work is bad. Brother worked for 9 years in the same factory, and this year he has not worked since spring, because work is stopping. We neither advise you nor dissuade. Sister intends to send him a ship-ticket.[1] If he suffers misery he will not complain about us. We also would send him a ship-ticket very gladly but we have also hard times. Brother has work but it is not even sufficient for him to live on, and as to myself, my health is completely broken. During November I am not working at all, because I am sick and sit at home.

---

[1] The personal feelings of women are never so completely subordinated to the forms of social solidarity as are those of the men, and on the disintegration of a family the individual affection of women is less likely to disappear than the group-solidarity of the men.

I do not know what is the matter, whether I am getting consumption, because I look very sick, and I do not know myself what is the matter. And please inform us where is Teofil, because we don't know about him. Send us his address. Dear sister, if we had to describe to you our troubles, we should have to write you five letters at least. . . . .

ADAM and FRANCISZEK RACZKOWSKI

403   UNION CITY, CONN., October 26 [1902]

"Praised be Jesus Christus." . . . .

DEAREST SISTER: I received your letter, for which I thank you kindly and heartily. And now I inform you [generalities about health]. I inform you that I am not with my brother, because I could not get work there, so I left that [city], but I did not go far away; so we can see each other. And now I ask you, my dear [ones], to answer me, because I am very curious to know how that happened, whether a lawyer defended our suit, or whether they judged it themselves, and whether they called me as a witness or not. I beg you, dear sister and brother-in-law, inform me about all this, because I am very curious, and I will reward you soon for everything, so I hope in God.[1] And as to what brother wrote about my intention to marry— I will not marry, I will never marry such a scoundrel, let him—with all his fortune. As to my children, I beg you all, you know yourself what, because I am a mother and my heart pains me. I will pay you back everything, that you spend; may they only not suffer any wrong.[2] And I beg you, inform me whether father received those 30 roubles which I sent him or not, because I have no word at all. Did Bukoski give you back the umbrella that I took from home because I sent it back from the frontier? If you wish, give the fur [sheepskin cloak] back to Helena [illegible name]—just as you will. I have nothing more to write, only I send you my lowest bows.

Your truly loving sister,
HELENA BRYLSKA

May God grant it. Amen.

[1] The lawsuit is about a farm left after the death of Rykaczewski, a relative of Helena's first husband, and her children are entitled to it.

[2] Helena, after the death of her first husband Brylski, went to America, leaving her three boys temporarily with her sister Teofila Wolska.

404   June 7, 1903

Now I, your sister H. Brylska, write to you, dear sister. [Usual greetings and wishes, printed.]

And now, dear sister, I have been informed about the death of our beloved father, that he ended his temporal life, and that he had such nursing, that he even had no place with you d[ear] sister, in your house, but you turned him out into the pigsty, and there our beloved father ended his life without confession and without the Holy Sacraments. So have you paid him [dear] sister, for the bloody sweat that he shed, caring for us that we might not suffer hunger and that vermin might not eat us. And you did not even know, d[ear] sister, when father ended his temporal life. You cursed me, d[ear] sister, because father asked me for a letter, and I did not get any letter [from him]. I wrote 3 letters [to him] and had no answer. So now perhaps I will not return again to our country, because I have nobody to return to. I sent 2 photographs, one for mother and the other— if you will and have the wish, you can take it. And I inform you, d[ear] sister, that I send money for the holy mass to the memory of father and mother and of my husband and the remaining money for my children's dresses.

I have nothing more to write, only I salute you and greet you kindly and heartily. May God grant it. Amen.

Your sincerely well-wishing sister,

H. Brylska

I ask for an answer.[1]

[1] This letter practically breaks off the relation because of Teofila's supposed behavior toward their father. Two points are essential in this respect: Helena's saying that she had no longer anyone to return to in the old country, and the manner in which she puts the question of the photograph. The form of the beginning and ending is in striking contrast with the real content of the letter. The generally moderate style is perhaps partly due to the fact that Helena's children are with her sister and she fears to make her too angry, but at the same time it is traditional. We have not a single really violent letter in our whole collection of family-letters, while among the letters written to the papers, particularly in America, there are many excessively violent ones. And in general, hard swearing and violent expressions are much more seldom found among the peasants than among the lower city classes. This fact seems due to the particularly strong and refined feeling of the value of words which we find among peasants, and which results evidently from the fixed character of expressions in all those social relations which are organized by tradition. Within such a fixed philological system the slightest shading of an expression is immediately felt and reacted upon; there is

405 July 8, 1903

. . . . DEAR SISTER AND BROTHER-IN-LAW: I inform you that I received your letter on July 6, which found me in good health, and for which I thank you very much. Now, dear sister, I am very much astonished at your writing that I do not write letters to you. I do write letters, I have always written to you all, and I also wrote two letters to you, dear sister, and now you tell me that I don't write letters to you. Dear sister, you write to me that you wept over that letter which I wrote to you, but I had to write so, because I wept myself also heartily when I received such a letter [from stepmother], because my heart pained me very much. It is not true that I believe mother in everything; I understand everything myself; you don't need to write me this; I have some sense myself. But why do you [plural] grieve me with such letters? Instead of rejoicing after receiving a letter, one must grieve.

And now, dear sister, I heard from Niedźwiecki of Przasmysz that this land left by Rykaczewski is lying fallow. I beg you, get advice from the lawyer Cybulski what to do with it, whether to rent it, because if it lies so for some time the government will take it for taxes and you will have nothing from it. . . . .

Your well-wishing sister, with respect,

HELENA BRYLSKA

406 July 13, 1903

. . . . And now, dear sister, I beg your pardon, don't be angry with me, for writing you such a letter. It is not my fault, if I received a letter from our country and very bad things were written in it. Then out of impatience and sorrow I wrote to you, dear sister, a letter which was also bad. And about the photograph I wrote because of not sending it to you, but I wrote also that if you wished you could take one. You write, dear sister, that you did not see the

---

no necessity of using strong words. This explains, for example, the apparently trifling causes of many offenses and enmities. The slightest innuendo means very much when the feeling of measure in expression is traditionally developed. We must also take into consideration the general dependence of thought and feeling upon words, which has been mentioned elsewhere. The proportion is lost completely whenever the peasant gets into a new set of interests and attitudes whose expression has not been determined for him traditionally. Cf. Vol. I, Introduction to the Peasant Letter.

way before you out of this sorrow. I believe you, dear sister, because I suffered the same when I received that letter from our country.[1] So I believe you, dear sister, but I can do nothing. I am not guilty. Pardon me all this, I will not write you such letters any more. Forget, dear sister, about all that has happened; let us forget about it and live as we lived.

And I beg you, dear sister, take care of my children and inform me about everything. I will remember you also.[2]

Your sincerely well-wishing sister,

HELENA BRYLSKA

In another letter I will tell you more.

407   March 3 [1904]

[DEAR BROTHER ADAM]: . . . . I received from you the letter in which you wrote about the ship-ticket, so I gave money to brother and asked him to send you [the ticket], because I was ill and I could not. If brother did not send it to you then perhaps sister will give you money for the journey. If she does not then wait a little; perhaps brother will send you the ticket; because I gave him money to send [it] to you. And when you leave go to brother in Ancona, and when you travel say everywhere the same—that you are going to your brother. On the way to Iłłowo wear clothes which you can throw away when they disinfect them, and take good clothes in a valise, because they do not disinfect clean clothes. To live on, take some smoked meat and dry cheese, and try hard to cross the frontier, because if they catch you they will consider you as a deserter and will take you directly to the war; for we have bad tidings, we receive newspapers every day which say there is a great war and many people perish on the water, because ships are wrecked. At the end of April and the beginning of May there will be a great war because Warsaw collected more than a dozen millions for war. And with us it is also bad. We have no work, for there is none anywhere.

And now I write to you, dear sister, that I have sent you 20 roubles. Buy for the children what you think necessary. Are you angry with me, that you don't write? I have written and

[1] She seems to consider her own pain as a kind of a compensation for the pain which she caused, even if the first was not brought upon her by the same person. (See also preceding letter.) This is a very frequent attitude and probably purely naïve, but possibly influenced by the Christian idea of suffering as objectively valuable and propitiating.

[2] "Remember" usually means "send money."

receive no answer. Tell me about this Staś Brylski who married Wiśniewska, whether you were at the wedding and how are they? I send to you and to my sons my kindest salutations. Are my sons in good health?

With respect,

HELENA BRYLSKA

408 April 8 [1904]

. . . . DEAR SISTER: I am working in the same place where I was working, and I live nearer the factory, so my address will be different. I have sent you money, 20 roubles, and I have no word whether you received it or not. I don't know what it means. I have sent a ship-ticket for brother [Adam] and I don't know either what it means that I have no word. Has he left already or not? What does it mean that you don't answer me? Since Christmas I have no word from you. What does it mean? Are you angry with me? I don't know what is going on, whether you got angry, or you don't wish to write to me, or perhaps the address is bad? I beg you, dear sister, inform me about my children, because I think about them very much and I long for them more than in the beginning, because here in America there are rumors that there is war in our country.[1] We know from the papers; papers come every day and we know about everything. Answer me, dear sister and brother-in-law, about your health and success, tell me about everything, whether good or bad, because brother now is far away from me, he went to his wife's family. The ticket in one direction costs $7.00 and the second [brother], if he left for America, I shall not see him either, because he had a ship-ticket bought to them.[2] Perhaps I shall go to them in about half a year. . . . .

HELENA BRYLSKA

[1] The reason of the growing longing is probably not the one given. We see the longing growing continually until the children come, without reference to any question of war or any other cause of anxiety. In the beginning the relative novelty of the practical situation in which she found herself and the necessity of adapting herself to the new conditions left no place for remembrance and sentiment. The more settled the situation becomes, the more normal the life, the greater the margin left for representation of the past and dreams of the future. And we see from many examples that for the fundamentally practical peasant type recollection is essential to the arousing of a pure sentiment, and how much isolation from the disturbances of practical life this recollection requires. Cf. Introduction: "Theoretic and Aesthetic Interests."

[2] The longing is not only for the children, but for the family and the old country in general. She begins to feel lonely.

409   [No date]

. . . . DEAR SISTER: You ask me to send you money. I answer, that now I can send none, because the factories are going bankrupt; it means they are stopping work. So I fear that if I send money home and the factories stop I shall remain without work and without money. I shall see later on; perhaps I shall send you some when work gets better. I work in the same factory. And now I salute you, dear brother, and I request you not to send your photograph. I know you well, and why should you spend money? Buy yourself rather something else. And now you write me that you receive few letters from me; but I write letters to you very often. And now I beg you, dear sister and brother-in-law, send my children to school, and let their eyes be rubbed.[1] . . . .

HELENA BRYLSKA

410   November 5, 1904

DEAR SISTER: . . . . This is the fifth letter that I am writing and I have no word. I don't know what it means, whether you are angry, or what else? For me it is so difficult to write letters, and I have no time, and still I write to you, and you who have more time, do you find it so difficult to write an answer? I beg you very much, answer me, whether good or bad. I beg your pardon, perhaps you will be offended by this that I write, but, dear sister and brother-in-law, don't wonder, because I expect with impatience a letter from you every day.

And please, inform me about my children, how are they? I should like to bring the oldest boy to me, so please, answer me, whether I may bring him to me. I beg you, dear sister and brother-in-law, answer me the soonest possible, in order that I may know what course to take. . . . .

HELENA BRYLSKA

[1] As after sleep, so that they may see clearly. This is a very good expression of the peasant woman's attitude toward learning, when this is appreciative. Instruction is good because it makes brighter in a general way, not because it makes more fit for any practical purpose. It is perhaps the consequence of the fact that the appreciation of women is in general more subjective, bearing on the personality, rather than objective, bearing on work. At the same time the peasant man often shares the same attitude, which was, indeed, our own former attitude toward "academic culture," the "polished man," and the girls' "finishing school."

411 December 20 [1904 ?]

DEAR SISTER: . . . . I received a letter, dear sister, from you,· and a scapulary, a little cross and a [sacred] picture. I thank you very much for these tokens. Now, dear sister, I sent you 20 roubles for my children for clothes. You asked me to send a ship-ticket for them, and said you would bring them. So we send a ship-ticket for the two [older] boys, and you will bring them. Meanwhile, dear sister, I send you this letter [saying] that I sent some money for the children. You will have the ship-ticket soon. Some days after this letter you will receive another letter [saying] for what ship the ship-ticket is sent. Prepare them as best you can and care for them as for your own children. When you write me a letter, I will send more money for them. Add the remainder, what you think necessary, and I will give you back everything, because I did not expect that all this would happen so soon. Please bring me a large shawl. I have nothing more to write. I send low bows. In another letter I will tell you everything, how it ought to be and how you ought to behave on the way, but now I only inform you that the ship-tickets are sent.

Please answer me, how you think [about it].

With respect,

HELENA BRYLSKA

412 December 31 [1904 ?]

DEAR SISTER: . . . . I have already sent ship-tickets for Józio and Staś. Let the person who comes with them buy a ticket for herself on the same ship for which this ticket is sent. She can say that she must take care of the children and go with them on the same ship.

The ship-ticket is paid from Iłłowo up to my house; no need to pay anything anywhere for my children. Dear brother-in-law, when you leave if you have any baggage, I mean any large trunk or large bag, you can give it up, but don't give it into anybody's hands without a receipt. If you have a receipt the baggage will not be lost. Until you take the steamer there will be a receipt for baggage with the ship-ticket or written on the ship-ticket, and when you leave the steamer they will take those receipts and give iron ones. Without an iron receipt don't give up your baggage, because it would be lost, and that would be a pity, as when mine was lost. And give everywhere the same names, that there may not be any trouble about names. Please, if you come, bring me a large shawl, and bring a stone against hernia. Try to buy it somewhere in a pharmacy or to get it from somebody, because here such a stone does not exist at all, and it is almost as necessary as the eye in the head. If the person who brings the children spends some more money on them, let her tell me or write to me on arrival; I will at once give or send everything back, with my thanks. Prepare them as well as you can, as your own, that everything may be well. . . . .

HELENA BRYLSKA

413   January 23, 1905

. . . . DEAR SISTER AND BROTHER-IN-LAW: We received your letter this month and we answer you at once, and we answer your request. You ask for a ship-ticket for brother-in-law Wolski and for the children. But I cannot satisfy all this. I wish with my whole heart and soul I could bring my children to me, but nothing is to be done. I could economize for [the ticket of] the children, but so much I cannot. We wrote to you in our last letter that we sent a ship-ticket for the children, but it was a mistake, because a ship-ticket cannot be sent for children alone; it is necessary to send one for an older person also. And so I cannot. This money which was intended for the ship-ticket was sent in the name of brother-in-law Wolski; there are 78 roubles. This [is to be used] if it is possible to send the children with somebody. And if it is impossible then, perhaps later on, if our Lord God helps us, we will send more, either money or a ship-ticket for brother-in-law, for now we cannot. And further, you ask about brother Adam. I don't know much about him because I did not see him at all with my eyes; he went to our older brother Franciszek and they are there together. And about me, for my goodness [in sending him a ticket] he does not mind much, because when he wrote me a letter, I wept. He thanked me for my goodness by not calling me sister, but madam. And how is he doing, I don't know. [Usual ending, with greetings for all relatives and acquaintances "without exception."]

HELENA and JÓZEF DĄBROWSKI[1]

[1] If there is an earlier mention of Helena's second marriage the letter containing it is missing from our series.

414 April 5 [1905 ?]

. . . . DEAR SISTER AND BROTHER-IN-LAW: We are both in good health, thanks to our Lord God, and we wish you the same. I received the letter, and Adam wrote to me and told me that when he has money he will send it [to you] for now he can scarcely earn for his living. I wrote to him that he might come to me, and he did not come. I also don't send you money, because I was ill. I spent much money and I don't work; I cannot.

As to the children, there is Fadajeski from Dobrzankowo coming with his daughter. They could bring them, because we are living quite near to the Sadłowskis, and they wrote to the Sadłowskis that they will go to them. I know everything, because I am living quite near to the Sadłowskis. Jazoski from Leszno is coming also, so he wrote to Smigłowski and he could also bring them. If not the one then the other, because they are all coming to this city where I am living. I long terribly for the children; almost every day I look out to see if they are not coming. My dear sister and brother-in-law, let either the one or the other bring me my children; I know exactly [that they are coming to America]. Perhaps you will not give them all up. Then send me at least one of them through somebody, because I long for them terribly. I have nothing more to write, only I bow to you, my sister and brother-in-law, and to your children, and I kiss my children and I bow to them and I wish them every happiness. I beg you, dearest, take care of my children as of your own, because I don't know either what is happening to them or what will become of me. I am longing so terribly for them.

Dear sister and brother-in-law, if you cannot send them all, send at least one of them, the older, and if you can, I beg you send me them all. If you wish, you can do it, because many people are coming to America, to this city where I am, and I know they would bring the children to me.

I request you, write to me about the [step]mother, how does she do. Is she alone or with her sons? With respect,

BOTH DĄBROWSKIS

415 June 12 [1905 ?]

. . . . MY DEAR SISTER: I wrote a letter and I have no answer. I don't know what it means, whether you are angry or you don't wish to write letters to me at all? Perhaps you are angry, because I wrote you those rather disagreeable words. But, my sister, you ought to pardon me, because as your soul pains you for your children, so does mine. I want to see them, I don't know [can't express] how much, because my soul aches for them. You probably got angry with me, as I have no letter from you. Well, I can do nothing; when it passes, then answer me, dear sister.

Can they come to me this year or not? Because if they don't come this year, I must buy a whole ship-ticket for Staś, because when he is 11 years old a whole ship-ticket is necessary and he can travel alone.

I haven't written any letter to mother, and mother is angry that I don't send them money and they must keep my children. Whether I send money or not my children must work with uncle. Let them send the children to me; I don't want anything else. With me it is also hard. I am not working myself, and in America it is not as it was. If they believe that they are wronged let them send the children to me and I will take them. And I don't wish to take the children at their expense, but at mine. I will not pay money in addition to the work of my children. I know [everything about them], because many people with whom I am acquainted come here, and just now Kaliszewiak came to America and called on me and told me about everything. I have nothing more to write, only I send you my lowest bows and wishes for every good.

BOTH HELENA and JOSEPH DĄBROWSKI

416　　　　　　　　　　　　　　　　　　October 12, 1906

. . . . DEAR SISTER: . . . . Further, we have heard that brother Teofil wishes to come to America. He wrote about it to Adam and the latter wrote to me. If it is true, then answer, and we will send him a ship-ticket. Let him come and bring my children, because brother Adam wrote that he cannot send a ship-ticket to him because all the money he had he lent to our older brother for his house. He cannot send a ship-ticket and he requested me to take up this question.

So we have nothing more to write, only we beg your pardon. Don't be angry with us. Be good and kind. We send you low bows and good wishes. Your well-wishing sister with husband and little son,

HELENA, JÓZEF, and FRANCISZEK DĄBROWSKI,
With respect forever

417   April 19 [1907 ?]

. . . . You write, dear sister, that Józiek is ill with his eyes. It would be terribly painful for me if you should not send him, dear sister. And [their step]father would be terribly angry and terribly grieved, if they all may not come. He says, "I strive and strive and wish that they may come to us. Although I am not their own father I care for them as for my own [children], and God will not punish me as [he would do] if I did not wish to have anything to do with them." So I beg you very much, sister dear, send him, because I have heard and shall have to hear from my man, "Why should you not have them all with you? Later on any of them could say to himself that through his stepfather he became an orphan and does not see his mother."[1] So send him. If he is so terribly ill they will send him back from Iłłowo, but I do not think that they will send him back. They are on ship-ticket and he goes to his mother, so I do not think that it will be so. Only send him, dear sister, and they will surely let him through. I beg you, Mr. Wiśniewski, very much, don't be anxious and afraid that you will have many difficulties. And at the frontier if you strike a bargain with a smuggler he can get ten persons through the frontier. And I will reward you for this. If he does not come it will be a

---

[1] The stepfather's motive in having the children brought is not affection for the children, whom he does not know, and is something more than attachment to his wife. We have here, in fact, a good insight into the nature of the feeling of moral obligation in the peasant. It is, first, the religious fear of God; second, the fear of a possible blame and reproach of the wronged persons. If there is the usual fear of public opinion, it is not expressed and certainly not very strong, since the man lives almost completely isolated from his community, while in normal peasant life this fear of public opinion is universally connected with the feeling of moral obligation. We have here a good proof that the crisis brought by emigration or any disintegration of communal life does not lead necessarily to a disintegration of morality. The explanation of the various results brought by the dissociation of the community (or family) in this respect, is probably to be found in the fact that social appreciation is not the only sanction for the peasant, but is indissolubly connected, in various proportions, with self-appreciation, and in certain conditions and for certain individuals this element of self-appreciation may develop strongly enough to substitute itself completely for the social appreciation. Thus, as we have seen in Adam Raczkowski, self-appreciation in the form of a feeling of personal importance, by substituting itself for familial solidarity, changes altruism from a duty into an expression of the personality. Here self-appreciation assumes the form of the feeling of righteousness before God and man. The source of the fear of the blame of the person wronged is not the same as that of the fear of social blame; in the first a magical background is still noticeable, while nothing like this can be detected in the second.

terrible sorrow and trial for us, and a large expense, because they will not give us the money for this ship-ticket back; and I shall ever bear a grief in my heart, that I endeavored to have this child and have it not. Remember, dear sister, send him to me, I beg you for the love [of God?]. And now you wrote that you will send me a shawl, but don't make any trouble about it for yourself and for the [man] who comes. May only all my children come; I don't wish anything more. As you grieve about your children, so I grieve about mine. And I beg you once more, send me all the children, because the ship-tickets are sent for all of them in order that they may all come. We salute you all and we wish you every good. Both of us beg for all the children. We will reward you for it. Mr. Wiśniewski, if they ask you during the journey about anything, say only this, that you bring children to their parents. That is all; you don't need any other explanations. And now again, if God leads you happily through the water perhaps they will require somebody, mother or father, to come and meet you in New York; then they will ask, "Is it your father or mother?" Let them [the children] say, "It is our mother or father." And say Mr. Wiśniewski is my brother. Then all will be well, only don't give any other explanation than such as we request you to give. And now, dear sister, you write that perhaps they will send him back from Iłłowo. Well, then nothing can be done. It would be the will of God; he would be an orphan until his death and would never more see his mother. O my God, what a sorrow for me! But perhaps God will grant him to be let through. Prepare them all [for the journey], dear sister, I hope that he will get through.

Your well-wishing and loving,

DĄBROWSKIS

418   June 6 [1908?]

. . . . DEAR SISTER: . . . . I have not written to you for a long time, so that I feel a longing. Is it true, dear sister, that you are angry with me—I don't know for what reason. Dear sister, let us forgive each other, because our Lord God orders us to forgive one another, and we, so far away in the world, should we not forgive? Our Lord God suffered more without guilt and forgave us sinners; should we not forgive each other? Let us forgive each other all griefs, dear sister. Write me a letter about your health and success. It is true that I did not write you any letter for a long time, but you did not write either for a still longer time, so that I could wait no longer for your letter. What is the news with you, my dear [ones], are you in good health? How are you succeeding? I hope that you will answer me in a brief letter after receiving my letter; I will hope this.

Dear sister, I write as to a sister and I complain as to a sister about my children from the old country—those three boys. I did not have them with me, and I grieved continuously about them; and today again, on the other hand, my heart is bleeding. They will not listen to their mother. If they would listen, they would do well with me. But no, they wish only to run everywhere about the world, and I am ashamed before people that they are so bad. They arrived, I sent them to school, because it is obligatory to send them; if you don't do it the teacher comes and takes them by the collar. So they have been going, but the oldest was annoyed with the school: "No, mama, I will go to work." I say, "Go on to school." But "No!" and "No!" Without certificates from the school they won't let them work. I got certificates for the two oldest ones: "Go, if you wish." They worked for some time, but they got tired of work. One went with a Jew to ramble about corners [trading or amusing himself?], and for some days was not to be seen; I had to go and to search for him. The worst one of them is Stach; the two others are a little better. They were good in the beginning but now they know how to speak English, and their goodness is lost. I have no comfort at all. I complain [to you] as to a sister, perhaps you will relieve me at least with a letter, if you write me some words, dear sister.[1]

[1] In this letter we have the whole tragedy of the breakdown of old sentimental habits. There must have been a complex process of weakening relations between mother and children, due to the facts that in the mother there evidently coexist more or less independently the old sentimental habits and some new ones, acquired in America and in her second marriage, while in the children there is a rapid and more or less complete evolution from the old familial life to an individual independence. We shall find elsewhere (letters of Aleksander Wolski) the proof that the children were disappointed in their expectations when they came to their mother; there were in her some new features which made her appear almost a stranger to them. On the other hand, the children lost their primitive attitudes even more rapidly and completely, and after some time the mother, from the standpoint of her old sentimental attitudes, began to see strangers in them. Probably this disintegration of the family was hastened by the lack of a father. At any rate, the result is that the mother feels the old set of her sentimental attitudes to a large extent objectless, and the disappointment with her children makes her cling more eagerly than ever to her sister—the only person of her whole family who

Salutations from us both and from our children to you, sister and brother-in-law, and to your children. We ask for an answer.

We remain, well-wishing,

H. J. DĄBROWSKIS

419 January 10 [1909, 1910, or 1911]

.... DEAR SISTER: .... I received the letter with the wafer and I thank you for thinking of me, dear sister. Now, dear sister and brother-in-law, don't be angry if I don't write to you very often, but I don't know how to write myself and before I ask somebody to write time passes away, but I try to answer you sometimes at least. You ask me how much my boys and my man earn. My man works in an iron-foundry, he earns 9, 10, 12 roubles [dollars] sometimes, and the boys earn 4 or 5 roubles. My dear, in America it is no better than in our country: whoever does well, he does, and whoever does poorly, suffers misery everywhere. I do not suffer misery, thanks to God, but I do not have much pleasure either. Many people in our country think that in America everybody has much pleasure. No, it is just as in our country, and the churches are like ours, and in general everything is alike. I wish to know with which son grandmother is. Write me. And who is farming on that land after Rykaczewski? Perhaps we shall yet meet some day or other, dear sister. I should like to see you, and my native country. I have nothing more to write, I kiss you both and your children. I wish you a happy and merry and good New Year. May this New Year bring you the greatest happiness possible. We wish it to you from our heart. The children kiss auntie and uncle and their cousins.

We remain, well-wishing,

H. J. DĄBROWSKIS

My children, thanks to God, are not the worst now.[1]

---

is still a real link with her old life. This proves at the same time how much stronger the old sentimental habits are as compared with the new ones, and how much more difficult is the adaptation to new conditions for a woman than for a man. Compare her brothers.

[1] The process of readaptation between mother and children begins, but it will never be complete: the mother cannot get rid of her old desire of authority and tendency to a complete unity of familial life, while the children, after their period of wildness, can neither come back to the traditional familial attitudes of the old country nor yet develop a new organization of their familial life in which individualism and solidarity would be harmoniously unified.

If perhaps you have some new [question], write the soonest possible; perhaps something about that property. [Salutations.]

Dear sister, somebody writes your letters very indistinctly. Your boy knows how to write; he can always write your letters.

I would ask you for something which I need very much; please send it to me the soonest possible. It is the birth-certificates of my boys which I need. Get them from the priest for 5 copecks and send them to me, I shall be very grateful to you for it, and later on I will tell you all, why I need them. But I beg you very much, send the soonest possible the birth-certificate of Stach. I wish to know how old he is. Perhaps he will still be a man. I will give him to the school, perhaps he will do better afterward, when he learns to be some kind of craftsman. Later on he can do better. But I want his birth-certificate. Please send me one for 5 copecks.

420 April 5 [1910 or 1911]

.... DEAR SISTER: .... I received your letter from Brodowska. She said: "Mrs. [Wolska], your sister, told me something, but I don't remember what it was she said," and she gave me the letter. I send you hearty thanks for remembering me, for your being so good and gracious and remembering about us and our affairs. May God help you, dear sister, in everything; God will help you for your good and true heart. Now, dear sister, as to that property, we beg you very much, dear sister, go to the notary and ask the notary to explain to you exactly how it is and what consequences can come from it. Try to set aside the decision, and strive, dear sister, that they may do nothing. They took father's [my first husband's] life away from him, let them do penance for it. I have suffered misery enough with my children without a father, let them suffer now with this their property. If they were good they would come to you and say: "Why should we destroy one another endlessly, Madam? Let us reconcile ourselves conscientiously with one another. Write to your sister and we will be reconciled, and then perhaps God will pardon us." They could say, "We will give what we can, be it more or less, but let there be a holy concord." They don't wish to do it. Do your best, dear sister and brother-in-law, let them be able to do nothing, let it be so till the minors come to their majority, let it be for the glory of God, and let them have nothing of it.[1]   Dear sister, if the notary says that you have no right to make a claim because you have no power of attorney, then we will send you a paper which will be valid, if you need it.   Now, dear sister, I wish very much to go to our country, but it is too difficult for me, because the children are little.   Perhaps I shall come some day or other, at least to see you, if God sends us health and long life.   Now, dear sister and brother-in-law, if you manage that they shall not waste it [the property], when our children come of age we can send you a power of attorney and you can get [a part of it] for your trouble and toil. Offer [a part] for the glory of God, and give [the remaining] to them [to my children].   If not yourself, then your children can live long enough and take it, but give nothing to them [the adverse party]. They have much to lose and [still] they do not wish to make peace in a godly manner.   If they wished it they would make peace in a godly manner, but they do not wish it; so don't let them cheat you out of anything on any pretext [technicality].   Tell me everything, how and what the notary speaks.   Even if we should come now to our country it would not pay us to go with small children for this piece of land.   Perhaps we shall come later on, after some years, when the children grow larger and I can take them to our country with me. As to the children, two of them are very good children.   One is working and gives his money [to me], the other is going to school, and learns well, but the third is not at home at all.   Stach has been bad, is bad, and will be bad.   So long as he was smaller, he remained more at home.   I begged him, "Stach, remain at home with your mother." No, he runs away and loafs about.   Well let him run.   I had his eyes wiped [had him instructed] as well as I could; he can read, write, and speak English, quite like a gentleman.   You say, "Beat."   In America you are not allowed to beat; they can put you into a prison. Give them to eat, and don't beat—such is the law in America. Nothing can be done, and you advise to beat!   Nothing can be done; if he is not good of himself, he is lost.

[1] Typical attitude.   The members of Helena's husband's family who sue her have by the fact of this suit taken the standpoint of strangers and enemies, and merit not the slightest regard, while if they had tried to settle the matter in a conciliatory way, they would have put themselves in the same familial group, and thus the family solidarity would have become a principle of the division of the property.   By the lawsuit all ties of group-solidarity are broken, at least for the time.

I have nothing more to write. We wish you a merry holiday of Easter, we wish you every good. The address of our brothers is the same; you can write to them. I also have letters from them seldom. Hearty thanks, sister, for the sacred things, medals and pictures. I regret that I took the children from our country so soon. In our country perhaps they would have had some misery, and in America they have none, and because of this many become dissolute. In America children have a good life; they don't go to any pastures, but to school, and that is their whole work.[1] . . . .

H. J. DĄBROWSKIS

421 August 7, 1911

. . . . DEAR SISTER: . . . . Now, dear sister, I don't know what it means that you did not deign to answer my letter. Perhaps I wrote you something disagreeable. It seems to me that nothing disagreeable was written, but it is long since I have had a letter from you, and you wrote me, dear sister, that you would tell me more in another letter. I am waiting and waiting, and I don't receive any news from you, so I beg you very much for an answer. Perhaps you found something disagreeable in my letter. Then I beg you, excuse me. And perhaps you did not receive, dear sister, that letter at all; but if you have for a long time no letter from me you could write some words just the same. Your children know how to write, so it is not difficult for you. Dear sister, write, how much is this property worth which the children inherit, and how dear are farms at this time; perhaps we shall come some day or other. I beg you, my dear, write me about this property; perhaps there is some news, perhaps they are cheating us there. I will also answer you what I intend to do about all this, whether we shall come or not. And now, dear sister, as to my children, I gave Maniek away to a school for 2 years. If he is good, I will take him [then], if he is not good, he will remain there till his twenty-first year. If he does his best and listens to what they tell him to do they will let him go sooner. If he does not listen,

---

[1] The failure to control children in America, owing to the loss of social authority by the parents and the failure to develop an individual authority, have been discussed page 709. Helena's statement is, however, a good illustration of the changed conditions under which the parental authority is weakened. In Poland the children do light farm-work under the eye of their parents, while the American school is certainly a factor of emancipation.

they will not let him go until his twenty-first year.   I gave him away, dear sister, because he would not go to school and listen.   I have always had trouble with him.   I had to send him there, and perhaps he will become a [good] man.   They teach reading and writing and different kinds of work.   When he is older he will not suffer misery. I call on him frequently.   He feels well.   If he suffered misery there I would not allow this.   The oldest is not with me, the second is not with me, I feared this one would run away from me, and I gave him away.   He will the sooner learn to be reasonable, and he can become a man. . . . .

H. J. Dąbrowskis

422   December 18, 1911

Dear Sister and Brother-in-law: . . . . I received your letter with the Christmas tokens for which I thank you very heartily.   We divide the wafer among ourselves, we wish you a Merry Christmas. May God grant us to live until the next year.   I beg your pardon if my letter arrives too late for Christmas; it was written too late, my dear.   I don't know myself how to write, so I cannot write when I wish, but when that person who writes my letters has time to spare. Now, my dear sister and brother-in-law, you ask my advice about the boy.   It would be very well to give him the school [instruction], because the school is a great fortune, but will it not be too burdensome for you?   Do what you consider right, my dear.   If he learns well and is willing, try to give him the school.   It is not necessary for him to become a priest; he can be something else.   Tne duties of a priest are hard and difficult, and it is better to be a good peasant than a bad priest.[1]   Do what you consider right and what your strength suffices for, my dear.   Now, you will send your oldest son to America. He is a little too young, and in America work is hard and now the times are bad.   In America there are different kinds of work, heavy and light, but a man from our country cannot get the light one, because he does not know the language.   A light-headed person can soon be corrupted in America, especially a young man.   I don't write it about your son, God forbid!   Perhaps your children are not so bad.   Well, my sister and brother-in-law, if you wish, send him to America.   We will try to find work for him, we will care about him, if he listens

---

[1] This reflection shows the influence of American democratism. Perhaps it does not come from Helena herself, but from her husband.

to us. I would care for him as for my own child. If he wishes, let him come. Do what is the best for you. My children are sometimes good and sometimes not good. As to that property about which you write, let it be quiet for some time; I will see later on. Now, my dear, I expect a woman's illness, I don't know how God will deliver me. If I am in good health I will write you something more.

I kiss you, little sister, and your man and children. I wish you good success. Your boy wrote the letter well enough. He can at least write himself. From our brothers I have sometimes a letter.

We remain, well-wishing,

DĄBROWSKIS

I ask for an answer. You weep more than once, dear sister, and I also weep more than once.

423 May 6, 1912

. . . . DEAREST SISTER, WITH CHILDREN: I received from you a letter, but what a letter! With a great regret and sorrow and woe! I shed tears and I could not calm myself from the grief and woe and sorrow which came upon you, dear sister. O my God, my God, what a misfortune has befallen you! At so young an age your husband left you a widow, a lonely orphan, with your children! O my dear, whenever I think of it I shed tears, I grieve, but how can I help you? I cannot help you. I know what a sorrow and misery it is, because I was a widow myself. Oh, that is a burden—an indescribable woe. But, my dear sister, I beg you, don't grieve. There is nothing to do. It is God's will, God governs us, not ourselves. God took from you a husband, a friend, a guide, and the father of your children. Conform yourself to the will of God, adjust yourself the best you can, pray for your father, and you, sister, for your husband, and God will love you and bless you, if you conform yourself to the will of God. So I request you, don't grieve, don't despair, I beg you very much. Could I help and comfort you I would hasten at the same moment to do it, but I cannot. I grieve only about your bad fortune.

You, children, I request you, respect your mother and listen to her, because God left you only a mother as guide and took your father to Him. Listen to your mother, respect her and behave yourselves well. Especially you, oldest son, listen to your mother and respect her. God forbid that you should cause her any sorrow. I, your auntie, beg you, children, very much to do it.[1] I wrote directly a letter to our brothers and I requested them to write a letter to you.

Myself, dear sister, I walk a little already. My health is weak, but I ought to thank God the Merciful for this great grace that I am still alive for the sake of my orphans. But I shall nevermore be so well as before. From Christmas till Easter I did not leave my bed and I could not turn myself in bed. Now I am walking again, but feebly. I ask you for an answer as to how you are getting on after the death of your husband, and whether you received a letter from our brothers. I hasten to comfort you at least with a letter. Remember, don't grieve. I kiss you and your children. Live, you orphans, with God. God bless you.

I remain in sorrow for you, dear sister,

H. J. DĄBROWSKIS

I ask you for an answer.

424   June 12 [1912 ?]

. . . . DEAR SISTER: . . . . You ask me whether I shall come to our country and when. My dear, I will not come to our country, because I have nothing to come for. I wrote you what a misfortune I had with my illness. My illness and the funeral [of the child] cost me much, and in America everything is expensive. Mine [my man] did not work for a long time when I was ill, so I exhausted all my money. My illness and [illegible word], and my children ruined me. They could earn now, but they went away from me. Is it not a sorrow? I brought them here and all this cost me you know how much. Well, I will not tell you much, because it is hard for me. And you wrote me, dear sister, to lend you [money]. But have I money? If I had, certainly I would lend it to you, from my soul, but I cannot. You have property, you can find some way, and myself, what I don't earn here I have not. And you, my dear, you can find

---

[1] From this and the preceding letter it is evident that Helena keeps unchanged the familial attitude, both in matters of solidarity—in deciding to take her nephew, and in the sincere sympathy she expresses with her sister—and in matters of authority, when she demands beforehand that her nephew shall listen to her when he comes, and when she exhorts all the sister's children to listen to their mother after their father's death.

some way; I cannot possibly lend you. Don't be resentful. I will not come to our country. Some day perhaps, but not soon. Do the best you can. I have no health and shall never have; I hardly walk about the house. If I had health I should go and earn, but I cannot. One man works for all our household; you know yourself how it is possible to live [in such conditions], and you ask me to help you. I cannot. I know that you can work and find a good way. You have property, you suffer no misery and cannot suffer it. If only your children are good you can farm. You are doing better than I here in America, because I must live from hand-work.

We greet you, all your household. Be in good health and manage well. Take care of yourself. I kiss you. I pity you, but how can I help? Please answer.

With respect,

H. J. DĄBROWSKIS

425 December 1 [1912]

. . . . Dear Sister, with Children: . . . . I received your letter, my dear, and I will help you in this matter of a ship-ticket for your son.[1] My dear, I wrote directly to our brothers, as you wrote to them, about this ticket and the brothers wrote me, that they answered you also. You know what they wrote you, and to me they answered that they cannot send a ship-ticket. So I answer you at once: If he wishes it and if you wish it, sister, I will send him a ticket [but] only for the water-passage; and through Prussia and from the ship to me, let him pay himself. Give him money, because even if it is paid from place to place they nevertheless demand money. Though everything was paid for my children the man who brought them had to pay nevertheless, and so they exacted some dollars for nothing. Now, dear, you are probably not without a cent. He wants to come. Give him money and let him leave as soon as you receive this letter. It would be the best, because he would come sooner. Now work is good, and later on we don't know. When he comes he can send you the money back in a short time. Then we will provide for him. Let him only be willing to listen and be good. I have not sent the ship-ticket [but wait] until I receive your answer to this letter.

[Helena]

[1] Aleksander Wolski, whose letters are included in this series.

426 [St.] PETERSBURG, October 7, 1905

"Praised be Jesus Christus!" [etc.]

DEAR BROTHER [ANTONI]: [Generalities about health.] I received your letter, but I could not answer, because I had no time. The young lady [daughter of a Russian aristocrat whom he is serving] came and remained for some weeks, and I don't know how to write Polish myself.[1] As to Teofil, I spoke to him when he was with me. I told him something quite different. I advised him to go to Prussia, to earn some money there, and only then to go to America, not so [as he intends]. He has got accustomed to travel in trains and would like to travel more, but on whose money? I had some money, but I went to the country, then to Warsaw. I had to feed him and myself for some time. Whence can I get so much money? My money is exhausted. I have been without money myself, particularly during this year when I have spent some hundred roubles in travel alone. And what about living and clothes? I must buy everything for my own money. My lord and lady are not here. They don't give me money [for living]. In Petersburg money is easily spent; it is not like the country. We have nothing more to write, we send hearty wishes to you, brother, sister-in-law, Teofil, and children.

Your well-wishing brother and sister-in-law,

L. WOLSKIS

You could write a letter to America, to your family, in order that they may send him a ship-ticket. He would be better considered then. There is a man here, with whom I am acquainted, who said that this would do very well—better than money. He would be more respected and would get work more easily.

LUDWIK WOLSKI

Greetings to sister Bronisława. Inform me how she is getting on, because you never write me about her.

427 February 13, 1912

DEAR BROTHER: I received your letter, but I had no time to answer, and the time passes so you don't notice it. I am very much grieved that you feel so sick. You ask me to come, but notwith-

[1] This shows that he either emigrated to Russia as a young boy or, more probably, stayed there after his military service.

standing all my wishes I cannot now, because **I am in service.** If God grants you to live till summer, then perhaps, but even so I cannot say certainly because I don't know what will be. I should like very much to see you, you know it, but nothing can be done; I don't depend upon myself [but on my master]. I am not in very good health either. I live as I lived, nothing new. I had a letter from Teofil; he is in good health, thanks to God, and is doing well; nothing new or particular.

We have had very cold weather during this whole time for three months. I wish you to bear at least your illness easily. It is necessary to agree with the will of God. We shall all be in that other world sooner or later; even the rich cannot buy himself off from sickness and death, and so it is necessary to agree with God's will. Perhaps God will still allow us to see one another, but it would be vain to think of it beforehand, because things never go on as you wish them. I wish you every good; I don't find words to relieve you. We send to everybody greetings and our best wishes. Dear brother, we don't have any anger against you, how can you think it! I kiss and embrace you most heartily, dear brother.

We remain, your loving and well-wishing,

BROTHER LUDWIK and SISTER-IN-LAW MAŁGORZATA WOLSKI

428   April 8, 1912

DEAR BROTHER AND SISTER-IN-LAW: We received your letter and we are very much grieved that you had to spend such sad holidays, but it is necessary to submit to everything. It is the will of God. We shall all die; nothing can be done against it. Notwithstanding all my desires and wishes, I cannot come. If my letter still finds brother alive, please, sister-in-law, explain to him that I cannot leave my place to go. I should not help him in doing it; death will come in any case as it is destined. To us it is very hard and painful and we feel it very much, but we can be of no help. We kiss him and bid him farewell, because probably we shall see him no more. You write and despair, sister-in-law, that you will be left with your children. But the children are big and they can work themselves, and you have a farm. Other widows remain and not a copeck is left after their husbands, and still they find some way; and you have a farm. You need only to work and not to be lazy; there will be enough to live on.

Your son Aleksander writes that he does not know what to do when his father dies, and asks me to advise him. But I do not know what sort of a farm you have, how many cattle and everything. I could give you advice only if I knew how you succeed [in your farming]. And when you write a letter, sister-in-law, request somebody to write it, because it is impossible to understand what is written; it is without sense and one and the same. I wrote in the other letter that I will not come and now you repeat the same things to me. Please tell brother that I and my wife have not any grievance against him; let him rest easy. We send to you all our good wishes on occasion of the past holidays. Submit to the will of God. And I want to know whether you have been away, sister-in-law, because as long as brother was in good health you gave no word of yourself and now, after four years, you have spoken. I received letters from brother and from his children, but you were as if you had never been. It is very disagreeable to me. Probably you acted just so with brother; you could not take care to lengthen his life. As to my coming, I cannot come now. When I am free I will come; only I don't know when, and whether during this year. With us everything is as of old. We are sick a little, but for the time being it is nothing. I remind you once more, request somebody to write your letters, and longer [ones]. It is not necessary to register them, letters arrive so. We wait for your answer and we send greetings to everybody.[1]

We remain, well-wishing,

YOUR BROTHER LUDWIK and YOUR SISTER-IN-LAW WOLSKI

[1] This letter is a plain endeavor to get rid of any familial claims, to isolate himself completely from the familial group. While Ludwik does not dare to break completely the relation with his brother individually, he declines completely any future participation in the life of the brother's wife and children. His sister-in-law and his nephew, according to the tradition, want him to be morally the guardian after Antoni's death. . He declines absolutely to accept this rôle. At the same time, cruelly rebuking the woman, and trying to place the blame on her—pretending that the reason of his coldness is the fact that she had not written to him for four years, while, as we see from other series, it is sufficient for one member of the family to write in order to keep the familial relation between the group and the absent individual. This is, in fact, the only example we have of the complete and conscious severing of familial relations unjustified by any quarrel. The only plausible explanation is the influence of Russian life. We had to make the same supposition in attempting to explain the rapid disintegration of the Barszczewski family. In Ludwik the influence is still more marked because he has probably lived for many years in isolation among the Russians. Besides the lack of familial unity in Russian life, there may be also other factors—the latent or manifest hos-

429   December 20, 1912

"Praised be Jesus Christus!" . . . .

DEAR BROTHER [LUDWIK] AND SISTER-IN-LAW: We inform you
about our success. Our success, you know brother, is very sad.
Dear kindred, you complain about your misery. But nobody writes
to our country such things as you write. Him [my son] strange
people will take, at their expense they take him. He will molest
you no more. He will be there in any case, and you will not see him
again. Because you don't want to see us. May God pay you [with
good] even for this. Farewell, dear brother, for the last time, with
your family. With tears, for the last time.

                                        TEOFILA WOLSKA

I divide with you a wafer through this lifeless paper. Because
surely we shall meet no more. Nor my children either. Remain
with God.[1]

430   [UNION CITY, CONN.] July 14 [1913]

[Usual greetings and wishes.]

Now I inform you, dear mother, that I brought everything with
me, I did not lose even the smallest thing. I got here with $13.00 and
I have bought me a suit and shoes. Of the $44.00 that auntie sent
for the ship-ticket, she intends to make me a present of one half and
I have to work back the other half. I will work hard now in order
that I may be able to send you some 10 or 20 dollars. Now I am
very sorry, because it is harvest time there [with you], and [I don't
know] how you can manage it, mother; and you have no money.[2]

---

tility between Russians and Poles in general, the difference of social conditions,
traditions, etc.—while the greater sociability of the Russians as compared, e.g.,
with that of the Americans and the greater facility which the Pole has in learning
the language makes the assimilation of the immigrant easier, particularly as there
are no large Polish centers in Russia as in America. In this case the particular
egotism of the man and the demoralizing life of a butler may have played a rôle.

[1] Complete breaking of the familial relation, as reaction to Ludwik's hardness.
The contrast between the gentle and sorrowful form and the content is interesting,
particularly as compared with the brutal form of Ludwik's letters.

[2] The boy is evidently young, perhaps eighteen, but he has already the attitude
of the head of a family, mixed with respect for his mother and even some fear of
her. (Cf. No. 436.) There is a seriousness in him hardly ever found in a boy of
the same age whose father is alive. At the same time there is an interesting contrast between his familial attitude and the individualism of his cousins. The

O dear mother, I grieve more than you. Often I weep secretly, and not an hour passes without my thinking about home. Nothing rejoices me in America. May our Lord God give me health that I may get our affairs in order and return to our country the soonest possible. I pay aunt only for board, for nothing more—$3.00 a week, because living is very expensive. Aunt gave $2,700 for this house. She borrowed $700. And those boys whom auntie brought from our country, they did harm. Uncle bought them everything that they wanted, and they did not want to work, although they could already. And then they simply went away.[1] Stasiek went away two years ago, and Józef went away after Stasiek, and since then uncle and auntie have not seen them. I did not see them either, but they are not far away; by street-car from Waterbury it costs only 10 cents. And auntie gave Maniek away to a farm-school; it is so called. It is a sort of a prison where they learn and work. And those who are there are not allowed to speak to one another. He has already been there for 2 years. If aunt wishes he will remain there till his twenty-first year. So I have not seen him either, because [the fare] to him costs half a dollar. I inform you, dear mother, how many hours a day I work and how much a week I earn. I work in an iron-foundry 10 hours a day. Now, in the beginning, I have light work. I choose different irons out [classify], which are good and which not, because now it is terribly hot. Later on I shall try other work. [End missing.]   [ALEKSANDER WOLSKI]

431   July 28 [1913]

[Usual greetings and wishes.]

Now I write to you, mother, about the address of uncle in America; I would have written it from memory, but I do not know the number.

---

difference is probably due to a number of factors: (1) Helena's boys came to America while still children, and thus the familial attitude was not developed and the individualizing influences had a free field; (2) Helena had married for the second time and this hindered the development of any real familial solidarity between her and her children; (3) Aleksander is the heir of his father's farm, and land is the economic nucleus around which the family would remain grouped in this case, at least until the moment of its division.

[1] The boy's view of his cousins' behavior is evidently influenced by his aunt. At the same time he fully shares his aunt's standpoint of appreciation, which is that of familial solidarity. There is no contradiction, as we shall see, between this letter and No. 435, where he takes the side of his cousins.

Now mother, you want me to write letters more often. What shall I write? I will only answer every one of your answers. This costs you enough, and it costs me doubly, when I send [the letter] and when one comes.[1] Dear mother inform me, please, whether the weather during the harvest is good or not, whether all the crops were good, what others came to America after me. Please describe all this to me. And now I inform you that I have a terrible longing and never can I forget our country. What help can you give me? As soon as I recall [our country], tears come to my eyes every time, and also because I have no friend. Aunt also is not very good. When I come from the shop in the evening, if only I do not help her in anything she gets directly angry, and so she scolds and calls God's wrath down on her husband and me for every trifle. I have never heard this at home.[2] In the beginning she said I had to "work back" for half the debt [for the ship-ticket], but now she says for the whole. Four weeks more and I shall work it back. May God only give me health, and I will never forget you and I will further try to behave the best I can. I don't smoke, I don't drink. There are two boarding with aunt. They have been in America ten years, are unmarried and work every day, and they have not a cent in their pocket. I will not do as they do, so that I may earn money and return home.[3] Let Bronisław Tkaczyk come if he wishes; different works are going well everywhere. When the days get cooler I will try harder work; now it is too hot. I will do such work as uncle does. I am nearly as [strong as] uncle.

And you, Julek, write to me, whether they [the boys] beat you there in my absence. When I was there many feared me. For myself, I don't suffer misery here in America, but you do there in our country. I have nothing more to write. I send only, and we all

[1] As in Russia, letters are often lost, the Polish peasants usually send them without stamps, because double postage is then collected from the receiver, and the government safeguards the letter with formalities which are .equivalent to registration. Registration is safer, but in addition to dread of the formality, the peasant does not like to go to *any office*.

[2] Helena's character may have become embittered through her experiences with her children, but probably she has always been more despotic and quarrelsome than her rather meek sister.

[3] His temperance is not the result of moral considerations, but simply that of the seriousness of his attitude toward life and his estimation of the task which he has to accomplish. This is perfectly typical. In spite of the efforts of the clergy there is never any moral reaction toward intemperance as toward something bad in itself, but merely as toward an obstacle in tending to some end.

send, hearty greetings to you and to our acquaintances. May God grant this. Amen.

And that accordeon I brought with me is not spoiled at all. On Sundays I amuse myself, and it plays like a new one.

[ALEKSANDER WOLSKI]

432   September 1 [1913]

. . . . Now, dear mother, I write you once more. Send me, please, the address of my uncle [Teofil] in America. Dear mother, I have already worked back for the ship-ticket, now I will work for you [to send you money], for digging the potatoes in the autumn. We are both working with Ososki from Bartniki; we do the same work one near another. He greets his brother in Leszno. We both long terribly for our country. He left his wife and children on his farm, and we say to each other, "How they are suffering there alone." When he came from our country 2 months ago, he got at first good work in another city, in Naget. From Union City to Naget is one verst. But that factory stopped for a month, so now we are working together. When it starts, if it goes well, we shall both go there to work. We say to each other that when we earn some money we will soon return to our country, because now it is terribly hard in America; everything is dear, and it is difficult to get work. So I work as hard as I can in order to return soon to our country. I long terribly for my country; nothing gives me pleasure in America. We must be very attentive in our work, every hour, because if anything is bad we are without work.[1] We went once with auntie to Waterbury to her boys, to those farms where they are, but we could not see them; on Sunday we walked about for half a day asking for them, but we could not find out where they are. In August terrible rains fell, and the mornings are cold now.

[ALEKSANDER]

---

[1] It is not without significance that he mentions working conditions immediately after speaking of his longing for home. The adjustment to hired factory-work is one of the most difficult which the immigrant has to make. In this case the boy is sustained by the expectation of success and a return home, but in cases where the children of immigrants are compelled to hand to their parents their total earnings (which is the usual practice), they frequently decline to be promoted to work paying more. No factory-work is stimulating, and a new adjustment is felt as an extra burden.

'Now, dear sister, you ask why do I not write to you, you say that I am angry with you. I am not angry. I have nothing to be angry about, and we speak often among ourselves of how much you must suffer alone. You have nobody with you now in our country; you are quite alone, like a single stump in the field. Dear sister, you have a good son in America. I also have begun farming, but in the beginning it is difficult. I lack money for everything.

[HELENA]

433   November 2, 1913

. . . . DEAR MOTHER: Everything rejoices me very much in the letter in which you described everything to me. It was probably Julek who wrote, because I could not read many words; letters were omitted, others were not written distinctly. You wrote that you intended to get lumber. I don't know what for. Or perhaps have someone come to help you? It was not distinctly written. As to what you wrote me to do, I will do everything gladly a little later, because I have not all [the money needed]. Don't be afraid about me, I am trying to have everything come out as well as possible. I cannot cease thinking, not an hour passes without my thinking about home. I have ever in my head this [idea]—how does everything go on there? I don't drink, I don't smoke, I deprive myself of it more easily than in our country. Nor do I go anywhere. I come from work, I wash myself, eat supper and sit down or I help aunt do something, and I go to sleep. In the morning I must rise at half-past five, and get ready for work. During the recent holidays [All-Saints, November 1, and All-Souls days] we worked. Only during English holidays the factory stops and we do not work. Now I would go to uncle, but I cannot, because in other cities work does not go very well; many people are paid off. Therefore one must keep the work he has, because many people are standing near the factories and begging for work, so one must hold on to his work.

I should not be so sad if aunt did not scold and quarrel about every trifle; therefore I am so sad. If it gets worse and worse I will not live there.

And now I request you, Julek, and you, Aniela, listen well to mother, to what she says and what she orders you to do. Learn well, because I am thankful to mother that I know at least how to write and to read a little. May mother's hands become golden in reward for it, for forcing me to learn.[1] It cannot at all be described how well it is in the world when you know how to read and to write yourself and you can write down everything that you think.

Aunt keeps some nice ducks and hens, and she has some pigeons left by her boys. There were 50 ducks. She keeps 7 for breeding, and she has 80 hens. They are doing well, and she has 10 pigeons, but in comparison with ours they are ugly. You, Julek and Aniela, remember well about mine. Close the opening at night so that something may not devour them. You can sell some young ones, Julek, but leave a pair of the young ones, because otherwise they would be played out, if any of the old ones were lost. Write to me whether the old pairs are both doing well, and don't sell the old ones to anybody. And write me, whether Józef Sobiraj finished being sick [got well] or not, and does he work with his mother or is he hired somewhere. If he would come to America in the spring they would get on better. I have nothing more to write. [Usual greetings.]

[ALEKSANDER]

434 December 8, 1913

. . . . Now I inform that I have sent 65 roubles. I would send more, mother, but we have a slack in America; many people are everywhere without work. Our factory has worked 5 weeks for 5 days a week. We don't work on Saturdays, and on some days we don't work during some hours. This Ososki from Bartniki, brother of that one in Leszno, who worked with me, was paid off from one factory and has not worked for a week. He went everywhere, but he could not find work. I am working in the same place where I began. After New Year perhaps it will get better. I shall not see uncle soon, because I must keep terribly close to my work, and it is far; the journey to him and back will cost $5.00 and the city is large and it will be very difficult to find him. That letter rejoiced me

---

[1] "Hands," because she did so by beating him. The attitude of superiority which the boy assumes here toward his younger brother and sister is another sign that he considers himself the head of the family. When he tells them to listen to their mother, his expression is exactly the same as that of a father. We have here one proof more that the old familial solidarity excludes anything like a particular solidarity of the younger generation against the older, but is a kind of hierarchical solidary organization, particularly when there is a material basis of the existence of the group which calls for a manager.

awfully; it is as if I had seen you. And you, Julek [I thank] for writing me about everything. You wrote this letter very distinctly. I am trying to manage so that we may all be together soon. And please, write me about this Zielazczak, whether he helps [you] or not, and whether he does something bad, for there was nothing written about him. Please write me which boys went to the army, which others came to America, whether Józef Sobiraj got rid of his sickness or not, and about those neighbors who live near to us, which of them annoys you. Please, mother, write me, describe to me what is of interest. Here it has rained during the whole autumn. On All Saints Day we had a frost which covered the windows, but now no more frost, only rains are falling. And about aunt I have nothing to write, no news. They have three children [by second husband]. Two are going to the school. I go nowhere myself; we remain together in the evening, we talk and laugh all together. [A man] from uncle's country is also boarding with aunt. He is 30 years old and unmarried. If I want to buy something he leads me everywhere. I have nothing more to write, I send you only hearty salutations and wish you a Merry Christmas. May God grant it. Amen.

[ALEKSANDER]

435   January 11, 1914

. . . . And now I inform you that on Christmas I saw Józef [son of Helena]. He came to us from the farm for the first time. I saw him at home, at dinner. If it had not been at home, I should not have recognized him. He has grown tall, a little taller than I am, and terribly thin and lean. His voice has also changed. He said also he would not have recognized me. We were terribly glad, both of us. He was two days with us, and we both went everywhere. The church is near, so we were both in the church. He related everything to me, and I, everything to him. He left his mother two years ago and had not seen her since. He regretted my father very much. He did not know that he was dead; he will see his uncle [the writer's father] no more.. He told me how his uncle accompanied him to the frontier, and how he himself wanted neither to go away from his uncle nor to remain anywhere else; and tears gushed from his eyes. He was very sorry for you, working there alone and nobody with you at home. He said that he loved his uncle and auntie [the writer's parents] better than his own mother, because when he came to his mother she neither looked at him nor knew him. He wept, and I also shed tears. His mother would have nothing to do with him. He said that if anybody gave him money he would at once go to his auntie, to our country, and help his auntie; if not, he will go with me to our country in the spring after next, and will remain with us until the call for military service; and after the service, if God lets him live, he will take that land back. He says there are few of us in our country, so we will work.[1] When he went away from us and said goodbye to his mother, his mother would not tell him goodbye. So he went away, but nearly fainted from sorrow, and I wept as never [before]. I went with him to the street-car. We went beyond the city, the street-car came, and he bade me farewell. He wept about me and I wept about him, as never yet I wept. Never had I such a sorrow as then. When I returned home I could not walk from sorrow. In our country one does not realize what family is, but in the world, when one sees somebody, it can be neither described nor told. I wept from dinner until evening, and when they asked me at home why I wept, I could not speak from sorrow, till I got a headache. I long terribly, because I have no friend with whom I may rejoice. Bojarski from Gustkowo has been in this city about 20 years, Mańka Leleniewianka from Gustkowo came to him at the end of carnival. It will be two years since she came. Sometimes on Saturdays I go to them. I have nothing more to write, only I send you hearty salutations and ask you for an answer.

[ALEKSANDER]

[1] Józef retains the old attitudes in spite of the evolution he has undergone in America, and though these old attitudes were not exclusive enough to allow him to remain with his mother. It is a case of psychological dissociation or stratification; the new characters are simply superimposed on the old ones without modifying them essentially. The same feature is found in persons of peasant origin who have had American college instruction. The cultural life is here connected with the English language and the American environment, while the Polish language and the Polish environment suggest merely the associations which are inclosed within the sphere of the peasant interests and traditions. These two strata do not interfere with each other and the same person is at one moment a cultivated American, when speaking English, at another moment a Polish peasant, when speaking Polish. Evidently, this situation is possible only because the peasant immigrants were almost completely cut off from the higher culture in Poland. In the present case the dissociation is probably due to the lack of any strong link connecting the previous life with the new one; the only link is the mother. It is very probable that Józef had lived during the past two years without much reflection on the past, absorbed in the actual conditions, and that only the meeting with his cousin and the talk of the latter brought the old attitudes to consciousness again.

436   February 22 [1914]

. . . . DEAR MAMA, I inform you that I am very sad.   She has always cried out on me, but never refused me board, and now she has refused me board and I have gone to board with strange people.   On the same day I found board elsewhere, and I swear by the love of God that I have paid everything as it ought to be.   And aunt came to me for 30 roubles more.   Such a conscience she had!   But I have paid her already 40 roubles more,[1] and I swore by God and beat my breast.[2]   Even strange people wondered that she has such a conscience, that she thinks out untruths and says them to the people. I swear by God that I have paid everything, and moreover she cheated me.   She was that good to me!   I almost burst open with grief.   When auntie writes anything, don't believe a single word.   I write you the whole truth.   Probably she will also levy on my wages, but I don't know.   I shall write to uncle and perhaps go [to him?]. Now I am at work and have 32 dollars.   How it will be further, I don't know.   I had never such a grief as I have now.   I cannot describe all this.   I shall not forget it.   My head is almost bursting from it.[3]   I did not get the letter from you, because I went away and the letter came to them; so they did not give it to me.   From Traczyk also I have no letter.   I have nothing more to write, only I send you hearty salutations.   Another time I will tell you more. She reminded me also about this old man Wiśniewski, who brought her those children, that she buried him at her own expense, and she also made allusions to myself and to you in connection with him.

[ALEKSANDER]

437   NOWY PETERHOF, June 30, 1904

[Greetings and wishes.]

And now I inform you, dear brother and sister-in-law, about my [mis]fortune and the distress that awaits me.   We are now destined to the war.   So now we shall soon go away to the war, only I do not

---

[1] Probably there has been no conscious cheating on either side, but simply some miscalculation, always possible in the complex form which economic relations often assume between peasants when the matter is not mere buying or borrowing.

[2] Beating the breast is a gesture of asseveration.   It is used as a sign of contrition in the church and in confession.

[3] The incoherence of the letter, contrasted with the usually elaborated form of his letters, shows how completely the boy is upset, and the enormous importance of even such a partial breaking of the familial relations.

know on what day and in which month. Dear brother and sister-in-law, I expected a letter from you, because I wrote to you, but I don't know what has become of you. I want at least to receive one letter from you, to speak [communicate] with you before my death, because I don't know the will of God, whether our Lord Jesus will allow me to return or not; I don't know it. And now I beg you, dear brother and sister-in-law, be so gracious and answer me. I don't know whether you are angry with me, because I wrote you a letter and I have no answer. I expect your letter every day and every hour and every minute in vain, and my heart is anxious, because I should be glad to speak with you, at least by letters, before my parting [half a page more about expecting letters and asking for letters]. Dear brother and dear sister-in-law, I beg your pardon, perhaps I did you sometime some wrong, so I ask for your pardon. Forgive me, because I go so far away, as to death. But I do not lose my hope in God, because our Lord Jesus remembers us better than we remember our Lord God, and therefore I pray our Lord God and this God's Mother of Częstochowa. May our Lord Jesus allow me to return, and God's Mother of Częstochowa. I offer myself to [rely on] the will of God and let it be as our Lord Jesus and this God's Mother of Częstochowa will turn me [decide about me]. I am satisfied with everything, because our Lord Jesus sends me such fortune, and nothing can be done against it. And now I bid you farewell, dear brother, I kiss you innumerable times, and I bid you farewell, dear sister-in-law, and I kiss you. Let our Lord Jesus help you for my prayer. And I bid you farewell, little brother Aleksander, and you, Władysław, and you, sister, and the whole household.[1]

I, your truly loving brother,

TEOFIL WOLSKI

[1] The letter has the purely traditional form of a farewell before death; it is a substitute for a spoken farewell. At the same time it shows the particular kind of fatalism of the Polish peasant, which is closely connected with the magical-religious system. Since in magic there is no continuity between cause and effect, the inability to calculate with certainty the effects of a cause and the almost unlimited range of possible events in a given situation open a wide field for fatalism. Man should do what he knows with certainty to be right in this situation, and then commit himself to the will of God but without any certainty of the results, because he never could have done *everything* necessary.

There was no place for fatalism in the old naturalistic religion, and the fatalistic attitude becomes more and more formal when magic loses its influence and the modern practical attitude, based upon the continuity of cause and effect, takes its place. The peasant, when stating a plan, still adds some words about the will

438 November 1 [1904]

In the first words of my letter I say: "Praised be J. C." and I inform you, dear brother and sister-in-law, that I received your letter on November 1, and I was very glad when I learned that you are in good health, thanks to the highest favor of our Lord God. For myself, up to the present I am still alive and in health, thanks to Lord God the highest and to God's Mother. And as to my success and how I am living, I inform you that up to the present, thanks to God, all is well. We have had no hunger yet up to the present and we haven't now, only now it is already a little cold; little morning frosts happen already, but this is no misery yet. May only God and God's Mother grant that it does not become worse.

And as to the war, I should have much to describe, but I cannot write you much about it. I inform you only that we have been in battle for four days, and now we are in camp for some days. What will be further, God alone knows, when and what will be the end of all this. It doesn't seem at all that it will end soon, on the one or on the other side. Our Lord God alone knows what end will result from it. It is God's will. As God Almighty grants, so will it be. Let us only beg our Lord God and the miraculous Mother of God to give us health and to guard us from every misfortune, and commit everything to the will of God.

I inform Brodowski that his son is also alive and healthy, thanks to our Lord God. I will try to inform him as soon as possible and to repeat to him those few words, which you have written to him. I saw them not long ago, Brodowski and also Rykaczewski. They are also in good health, thanks to God the Almighty. [Bows for the whole family and wishes for good health.] TEOFIL WOLSKI

439 January 1, 1905

. . . . And I inform you that now we stand in camp. We digged pits for ourselves, as we do in Poland for potatoes, and we are sitting inside. We have no great fighting now, only skirmishes happen;

---

of God, the weakness of man, etc., but mainly as a manifestation of humility. There seems to be a half-conscious fear that if he does not do it, God may punish him for his presumption, by destroying his plans. But in the matters of death and sickness, which remain the last refuge of magic, and sometimes in matters of marriage, where also magical practices persist even on a higher level of culture, fatalism is still powerful, because precisely in those lines the continuity of cause and effect is the most difficult of prevision.

they are firing one against another every day, but not much. But presently we expect a great fight, and nobody knows what God will send. The air [weather] here up to the present is very good; no snow as yet, but frost began almost two months ago, and we have frost every day, not great, 10° or more [Réaumur], sometimes it reaches 20°. Yes, my dear brother and sister-in-law, up to the present, thanks to our Lord God the Highest and to God's Mother, we have not yet suffered great misery, although you know yourself that it is no pleasure; but in the position in which we find ourselves, up to the present we have but little to complain of. . . . .

Now it is going badly with you also, as you write to me, dear brother, that they are calling the reservists. God forbid them to take you also. I advise you, dear brother, if you feel anything bad, [apprehension], don't tarry long but direct yourself according to your thoughts [fly].

TEOFIL WOLSKI

A SOLDIER ON WAR[1]

After a long and dark night, at last it began to dawn. The day's apparition was so sad that the heart began to weep.

The sun, arising from behind the mountains, threw to us sad rays; and we remained in intrenchments, watching the shadows of the enemy.

We remained there and we turned our eyes to heaven, appealing for help from there, after so many days spent in hunger and so many tedious nights without sleep.

Everybody sends a prayer to God. May He help us to crumble the enemy and to return healthy after so long and heavy sufferings.

Suddenly a crash interrupted the sepulchral silence—the crash of the enemy's shrapnel which burst in our intrenchment, not missing its mark.

I saw before me a column of dark smoke rising up to the clouds. Oh, what a mark it left and what a blow it cast upon us!

I saw before me my companions lying, without hands or feet, and others in the moments preceding their death, gave sad and terrible groans.

There a surgeon binds up the wounds of the injured, others take them to the hospital, and so companions, helping their companion, save at last his life.

---

[1] Poetry, without rhythm but with some rhyme. Doubtful whether written by himself or another soldier.

Suddenly on the right the Japanese attack us. We went joyfully with bayonets; we went to meet them with a cry of joy, to attain sooner our end.

But the will of God was contrary to us, we were obliged to leave the spot in order to hold the honor of the regiment, to save the banner and our life.

Under a hail of enemies' bullets, bombs, grenades, and shrapnel, we withdrew from our positions. Oh, what losses we had!

At every step I took, a dead body lay or a severely wounded groaned. I went along the road with sorrow in my heart, thinking: "Up to the present I am saved."

At last this great tumult ceased, and I went also with slower steps. I looked back at the smoke rising up to the clouds. And I said then with a subdued voice, looking at the blood streaming on the ground: "Deign, O Lord, to give them eternal rest, and let the light of glory shine upon them in [centuries of centuries. Amen]."

[TEOFIL]

[Letter of January 25, 1905, with news of health and safety omitted.]

440 April 20, 1905

. . . . And as to my success, I am alive and in health, thanks to our Lord God the Highest, and that is all my success.

Everything is well, thanks to our Lord God. We are retiring in order toward Harbin. We walk slowly and rest. Only one day, i.e., on March 12, near Mukden, the Japanese gave us such a beating that we fled 77 versts without stopping. And I have nothing more to write you. If God grants me health and allows me to come back safely, I shall have much to relate to you; but what I could write in a letter, you can write me the same. As you write, so it is. We fight well, only it is unfortunate, that we must fly [conscious irony]. [Half a page about letters received and sent.]

And I inform you about Rykaczewski, that he is lost during our retreat without any tidings. And Brodowski is alive and healthy, thanks to our Lord God. . . . . T. W.

441 April 27, 1905

. . . . I am in good health, thanks to our Lord God, and my success is also [good], glory be to God. Now we are quiet, we are in camp. On April 25 a priest visited us and we were at holy confession, all the Catholics.   Up to the present, thanks to our Lord God and to God's Mother, all is well with us.   As to the war, I have nothing to write you, because you know everything there.   What you say, having learned from papers and letters, so it is, and I can write you nothing else.   If God gives me health and allows me happily to return, I shall have much to relate, but it is impossible to write all this.   The fight that lasted for 12 days near Mukden was terrible and obstinate; we fought in it from the beginning to the end.   And the end was that we had to retire, because a little more and we should have nowhere to fly;   the Japanese encircled us so that only a narrow passage remained through which we fled and the Japanese fired upon us with guns. You know, when we fled thus it could not be without losses;   there remained much of everything for the Japanese.   Myself, thanks to our Lord God, I got out safe and healthy, and I·did not throw away my effects, which I need.

You wrote that we cannot dream about attacking, because as soon as we attack we fly still faster.   That we fly is true, but not so fast as you say.   We beat them as we like, but they are stubborn and will not give way;   so when we are bored with beating them, then we fly.   But perhaps we shall fly no more, because we hear that the Japanese have cut us off from Harbin, and we are not so stupid as to fly to Japan.[1]

Now I inform you that I received on April 21 a letter and a package from brother [Ludwik] of Petersburg.   In this packet were shoes, sugar, tobacco, and a shirt.   I have nothing more to write. . . . .

TEOFIL WOLSKI

442   June 28, 1905

. . . . With us now it is calm.   We have been camping for some weeks at the same place and nobody disturbs us;   we walk about all the mountains, wherever we like, and we are occupied with learning. We learn how to attack the Japanese.   We do also some gymnastics in order to make our bones flexible, which are stiffened from sleeping on the naked ground.   We got some fun and training from these occupations, so that now we don't fear much even the Japanese [irony].

[1] An enormous amount of satire developed among the Russian and Polish soldiers during the Japanese war.   With the Russians it was an expression of their habit of satirizing their own nation, particularly in matters connected with the state of government.   With the Poles, as in this case, it was the expression of a latent and open hostility to Russia.

We have no true news at all; what the soldiers say—you hear every moment something new. It is impossible to make anything out of our Manchurian papers which we read every day. From the news of these papers and from the soldiers' tales [one would think that] in one hour the war will end, and then again the fight is beginning and the war going on. So we cannot believe what we hear; we hope in our Lord God that the war will end soon, but up to the present we have no [certain] tidings. What is the news with you about the war? Please inform me, I am very curious. [More about the uncertain news, and about weather.]

As to your hunts, about which you write me, I heard also something, and that the big game is chased and will fall into nets, and with the big game the small will surely have to suffer, because when the hunter is chasing hares and meets partridges, he surely will not let them go.[1] If God grants that the war is over and helps me to get out of this slavery I don't know where to turn myself. My attachment and wishes attract me to my family, but, as it seems, with you it is no worse [no better] than with us. . . . .

TEOFIL WOLSKI

443 PHILADELPHIA, PA., April 8, 1907

. . . . DEAR WALCIA: And now I write you, my dear, an answer to your letter. Some things in this letter are good, and some things of little worth, because of this: If you come to your brother, I will come and get you and we could marry, remain for some years and return with something [some money] to our country, so that later we might not be obliged to earn [as hired laborers]. If I should return in the autumn I should not have much. It was only during the holidays that I sent back the money for the ship-ticket, and by autumn I shall have about 200 roubles. The journey 100, the remainder for the wedding, and what then? Go again to America? That is no business for me, to work and to throw to the winds. Therefore I write to you the exact truth: If you don't come and don't wait for me longer it means that you will not be mine, because I won't return sooner than perhaps on the next holiday of Easter; by no means can I sooner. And you write that you will wait only till autumn, and so the one disagrees with the other. Therefore, I request you, answer me, what will become of us, whether you will come or not,

---

[1] Allusion to the revolution. The hunters are the Russian authorities and the game the revolutionists—or the contrary.

or perhaps you will wait a year still. And now I will write you further that you have done a stupid thing by sending that letter to Kowalski. He is a brute, not a man, he was not even worth receiving that letter, and not worth what I have paid for two letters from him which I received, because he wrote to me now and was quarreling and blustering, as if anybody were afraid of him, and all this because of you. You ought not to wear your cloak on both shoulders [practice duplicity]. I sent [that letter] to you in order that you might know, and you sent it back to him. Now he writes silly things to me. I don't praise this in you. But now no matter; it is done and cannot be undone, so I bid you goodbye. I embrace you and kiss you. Embrace everybody in my name.[1] Now goodbye.

Loving you,

TEOFIL WOLSKI

444   December 12, 1909

MY DEAREST BROTHER AND SISTER-IN-LAW: . . . . I don't know what it means that you forgot so soon about me, orphan [that I am]. How can I call myself, if not an orphan? You know from your own experience that everybody among you is in his own country and on his own piece of land and defends himself against his poverty with God's help. But what do you think about me? What pleasure have I? As soon as God helped me to grow a little they took me in that far world, and what I suffered there I have related to you already [when I saw you], and I will not write about it, because no writer could describe all my ups and downs. Then I came here to this America.

[1] The letter is a very good example of the typical relation between love and economic considerations. We see these factors equilibrated more or less without the subordination of either of them. The love is strong enough to make the man wait indefinitely for the girl and not to consider dowry, but considerations of the future economic situation put a determined limit to the sacrifice which he is ready to make. This equilibration in various proportions is found in most of the marriages in Poland. But in the old country, marriage is conditioned by social factors more than by individual considerations, and the relation between the economic and the sentimental motives is never so plain and isolated as it is here. Teofil is, at the time when this letter is written, almost completely outside of his family and his native, social environment—more so than his cousin Adam Raczkowski, because of his longer military service, his participation in the war, and his solitude in America. Therefore social considerations cease to play any determining part in his attitude toward marriage, and the individual factors—economic welfare and personal preference—remain alone to determine his choice.

Well, here it is all right, although it is also sad, because the land is strange, the language is strange, and it is difficult to converse. And so I live and pass my age, and when I remember my nearest, that is you, my dear little brother, and you, sister-in-law, that you have forgot about me already, my heart bursts open with regret and woe. I do not know what I have done, why God the Highest punishes me so much. And this punishment is precisely your forgetfulness about me, poor pilgrim. But nothing can be done; evidently such is my fortune, coming from God, not from anybody else. But at any rate, please answer at least this letter, and inform me whether you received a letter from me and a photograph which I sent you, I don't know how long ago. Now, with me nothing new has happened. I live simply, according to God's will. And just now I send you this sheet of paper and I send you also my heartiest wishes for this solemn holiday, i.e., Christmas, and I divide with you this great token, i.e., this piece of wafer, and may God bless you.[1] . . . .

TEOFIL WOLSKI

445 March 18 [1914]

MY DEAR BROTHER AND SISTER-IN-LAW: . . . . And now further, my dearest, I do not know how it is, but it is strange that you forgot me so soon and you don't even wish to write a letter to me. I do not merit this. I should willingly do everything for you, but now it is difficult; I cannot help you at all. Therefore I am not even willing to write this letter, because I would indeed help you a little, but there is no possibility. It is now so difficult to earn a little money—God forbid [help us!]. It is already the second year since everyone is trying only to save his own life and there are many people who die from hunger. I feel so ill myself that I don't know what to do. If

---

[1] A purely sentimental manifestation of the familial attitude. Familial affection seems to be here as in other examples (Kalinowicz and Wickowski series) the last substitute for a disappearing familial solidarity. It is either the most persistent element of solidarity, or the new form which familial connection assumes when a process of individualization has destroyed the primitive unity of the group. The second supposition seems more probable if we remember the evolution which familial attitudes undergo when the married couple with children becomes isolated from the rest of the family, and further that there are few signs of affection within the family in the primitive sense, that affection is not necessary to produce the familial unity, as is shown by the rapid assimilation of new members, and that the relation between members of the family is determined by the degree of kinship, not by individual selection.

I had money enough I would return to my country, but for the time being it is difficult to gather so much money, and therefore I must suffer poverty for some time. God only knows how long this will last. We know only that when this man who now, since the 4th of March, is on the throne, became president, we all were glad that there would be work enough. Meanwhile it turns out otherwise, because for poor people the times are getting worse than before. All the prices increase and work is paid less than formerly, and moreover this work cannot be got. And then in our papers it is written that there in our country some mean agents are going around and claiming that in America now work is better than ever before. These agents persuade the people to go and everybody leaves his last possibility of earning his life, sometimes even robs his family and comes here, but why, he does not know himself. Perhaps he seeks his own hunger-death, as many cases happen where in the morning corpses are found lying in the streets and after cutting them open [physicians] come to the conclusion that they died from hunger. So don't listen to these "catch-people." They are sent by the ship-companies, and are well paid to gather passengers who will pay such high rates for the tickets. You must know that a ticket now costs about $60, i.e., 120 roubles. Those agents know that people enough went to America, but they do not know how [otherwise] to take this hard-earned money away from those poor people and therefore they use such means. Let nobody listen to anybody but only to his relatives whom he has here, in this golden America.

Now I request you to inform me what is the news in your country. How is the winter there? With us it is very light. And what about the young men and girls who got married? Who is dead, who lives?

When I receive a letter from you I will send you my photograph. Now we say goodbye to you, dear brother and sister-in-law, and we embrace and kiss millions of times yourselves and your children.

Your brother, loving to the grave,

T. WOLSKI and STEFAN KUCZBORSKI[1]

---

[1] A friend, who signs as a means of "sending his regards."

REMBIEŃSKA SERIES

We have here a case of familial attitudes quite untouched by emigration. The writer seems to represent as perfectly as possible the *ideal* of a peasant girl according to the traditional norms. There is scarcely anything in her behavior that could be blamed from the traditional standpoint, but also hardly any tendency to go beyond this traditional standpoint. Compare her in this respect with the more self-conscious Frania Osińska

THE FAMILY REMBIEŃSKI

Rembieński
His wife
Aleksandra } his daughters
Stasia
Julka, sister of Rembieński's wife
Kubarz, her husband
Olcia, their daughter
Karolska, sister of Rembieński (or of his wife)
Her husband
Mańka, a cousin of Aleksandra

446–48, ALEKSANDRA REMBIEŃSKA, IN AMERICA, TO FAMILY-MEMBERS IN POLAND

446   BROOKLYN, N.Y., October 14 [1911]

MY DEAR FAMILY:[1] In the first words "Praised be Jesus Christus." . . . .

And now, dear parents, I inform you that I am in good health, thanks to God, which I wish you also with my truest heart. And now I am on duty [a maidservant] and I do well, I have fine food, only I must work from 6 o'clock in the morning to 10 o'clock at night and I

---

[1] The use of the word "family" instead of "parents" may be either a provincialism or an individual expression, but certainly it has no particular meaning with regard to the conception of the family.

have $13 a month. And now, dear parents, I implore you don't grieve about me, thinking that I am without money. When I read those letters—because there came four letters in a single week, 2 from Auntie Karolska, 2 from you dear parents, on the same day—so when I read those letters I became very sad, that there in our country is trouble between you, my parents, and the Karolskis. Why do you mind what I say to her? She urged me to send money to her, and not to you and so I sent it to her, but not my last money, only that which I sent. I had still some 10 or 20 roubles, but I wrote intentionally to auntie [that the money I sent was my last]. And you thought, dear parents that I sent my last money away.[1] But you know yourselves that I cannot remain without a cent, because I am in the world [among strangers]. I almost laughed about your sorrow. As it is I have spent more than 50 roubles on myself for the coming winter, and nevertheless I am not so beautifully dressed as all the others. Only I regret to spend money, I prefer to put it away rather than to buy luxurious dresses, like Olcia Kubaczówna who buys herself a new dress every week and doesn't look at money and doesn't think what can happen. She thinks only how to dress and says she does not need to think about anything more. But I am not of the same opinion; I think about my home. I have brothers and sisters and I intend to help them all to come to America.[2] First I will take Stasia, let her hope to come in the early spring, about Easter, and let her be

[1] She had to send the money to her aunt and uncle first because she had borrowed it from them to pay for her journey. The difference in her behavior toward her aunt, whom she tells that she cannot send any more because it is her last money, and toward her parents, whom she asks not to be anxious because she has still a little money left shows very well the different degrees of nearness in the familial relation. We see the eagerness with which the girl desires the good relations between her parents and her aunt and uncle to be re-established, and we find later that her affection toward her aunt is very real. And further, the fact that the parents have quarreled with the aunt because they think that their daughter has wronged herself to fulfil her aunt's desire, is a proof that the familial affection of parents to children is closer than that between brothers and sisters. This is the traditional situation. Only recently we find contrary cases. (Cf., for example, Krupa series.) On the other hand, if the girl had neglected her familial duties toward her aunt, the parents would certainly have sided with the aunt; this is also traditional, and we find also only recently, as a result of another process of evolution, the complete isolation of the marriage-group as against the rest of the family.

[2] An instructive contrast. The cousin Olcia is already partly Americanized. Her parents have lived for a long time in Brooklyn and own a house there

patient and wait. I would take her now, but in winter there is no such work as in spring. And now, dear parents, you may hope that I will send you for Christmas 10 roubles. I would not send them but, thanks to God, I have some, and I have work, so every month money comes to me. I only ask our Lord Jesus for health, and then no bad fortune will overtake me. I go dressed like a lady only I am sad, because I must remain at home and cannot go outside at all. I am not far away from Uncle and Auntie Kubacz, but I cannot see them more than twice a month. Olcia is in service like me and also can see nobody more than twice a month; but she is far away, she must come on the street-car. When we meet together a young man comes directly to us. Now, dear parents, for girls there is work in America, but not for men. Mańka wrote to me a letter also and she wrote to [illegible name] that they had sent him a ship-ticket. But I once heard Mańka say [perhaps jestingly] that Aunt Julka is in the habit of having a good time with other men, and so maybe Mańka is a mischief-maker.[1]

Now, dear parents, I write to you, that you may give nobody my address. When you receive my letter, hide it, in order that nobody may catch the address. And I request you, tell auntie not to give my address to anybody.[2]

Dear parents, I am very sorry; are you indeed angry with Aunt Karolska? What is the trouble? Tell me, do you visit them? Now I beg you, there is no reason for you to be angry; you can call on them, and I will be more than glad to hear that you are not angry.

And now, dear parents, I will write you that I have an opportunity to be married. I have a fine boy, because uncle and auntie have known him for 3 years. He is good, not a drunkard, he does not swear, as others often do. From him I have not yet heard a single bad word or oath; he has not this habit. I don't know whether I shall marry this year or not—just as you advise me, my parents. He wishes that it may be now, and he begs uncle and auntie because he is boarding with them. I don't like in him that he is as small as

---

[1] The passage is not clear. The general meaning is that Mańka is a joker and that she perhaps wrote this also as a joke and the man thinks it is true.

[2] It is not clear why she does not want her address to be known. Perhaps being a maidservant, she does not want anybody to come to her, and perhaps she does not want any "boys" to write to her in view of her probable marriage and the possible jealousy of the man.

Antek Łada. He is pretty, that is true. Wait a little; for Christmas we will send you a photograph; then you will see him. As to what I wrote about your photograph, you need not send it, because it will be very expensive. And now, dear parents, I beg you so very much, let nobody learn that I am going to be married and that I have a young man. Let only my family [yourselves] know everything, no other people, neither brothers nor sisters. I beg you, let nobody know what I wrote in this letter. Say only "She wrote nothing; all's well," and let that be all. Don't say anything about·this matter. And when I send the photograph, hide it also, please, so that nobody may see it.[1]

And now I have nothing more to write, and I bow to you, dear family, and I wish you every good. May God grant that this letter finds you in good health, and I ask you for a quick answer. . . . .

ALEKSANDRA REMBIEŃSKA

And I request you, dear parents, send letters with stamps, because I have great difficulties. A letter with a stamp arrives sooner.

447

O DEAR FAMILY [PARENTS], I write this letter to you on November 20, and I got your letter on November 20, and I begin this letter with the words [usual greeting]. And now, dear family, I inform you that I am in good health, thanks to our Lord God, and I wish to you also happiness, health, and good success. And now, dear family, I let you know that in October I did not work for two weeks because I did not like to work for nothing, and I left this place because

---

[1] Her whole attitude in this matter of marriage shows a slight modification of the tradition, but just to the degree necessitated by the changed conditions of life. She asks for her parents' "advice" as to the time when she should marry, and expresses her readiness to comply with their wish, but she does it with some consciousness of her independence and assumes that the parents will not object to her marrying as soon as she wishes. As to her choice, evidently her parents, not knowing the man, cannot control it personally, and she does not ask them literally for permission to marry this man; but she tries to justify her choice and appeals to the opinion of her uncle and aunt, who under the circumstances are better representatives of the will of the family than the parents. Her wish to keep the engagement secret is justified by the changed conditions of courtship. While in the old country the whole process of courting is necessarily a public affair and leads to a certain degree of social obligation to keep the engagement, here this process is going on almost privately, the engagement may be broken at any moment without important consequences, and therefore the girl does not like to have it known beforehand.

they wouldn't pay me more than $12. And now I am in another place, only far away from uncle, for it is necessary to travel an hour to uncle; but uncle comes to meet me every second Sunday. I am well enough, I receive now $16 for this month. I don't feel lonesome, because there are two of us girls in this household. The master and mistress are Polish. We are near a church and they send us every Sunday at 6 o'clock in the morning to the mass. We have every day 18 rooms to clean, and to cook and to wash linen. It is myself who wash every week about 300 pieces of linen, and iron it. But I have easy washing because I don't wash with my hands; the machine washes alone, I only cover the linen with soap and put 5 pieces into the machine at once. After 15 minutes I take them out and put in new ones, and so by noon I wash all the 300 pieces. I iron 4 days, from 6 [A.M.] to 8 P.M. I do nothing but iron for those 4 days. Dear parents, you admonish me so severely to be on my guard. But I cannot and do not walk about the city. I cannot even go out before the house for a while. I am in America and I do not even know whether it is America, only it seems to me as if there were only a single house in the whole world and nothing more, only walls and very few people. Now you ask about this young man about whom I wrote, whether he is a Catholic. Well, he has been boarding with the Felikses for probably 2 years, and when I was with them I have seen. He says his prayer and wears a cross on his breast. I hope I am not yet so stupid as not to know with whom I have to speak. He is even from a country not far away from ours, government and district of Łomża. And now, dear [sister] Stasia, don't think that I will hurry and have the wedding the soonest possible; perhaps there will be no wedding at all. Don't forget to get ready and come. It will be more lively when we are both together. You ask for my photograph. I have none ready. I will send you one in December. I will go soon to a photographer. And now, dear parents, don't think that I am with nobody to care about me. I have a good uncle and auntie; I did not expect they would be so good. They care about me as about their own child; they will allow nobody to do me any wrong. When I go to them I am as bold and grateful, as in my own parental home, but still more so. If you don't believe me, then, dear family, please ask uncle and auntie. They will tell you that it is true.

And now, dear family, I have nothing more to write, but only I send you low bows and wish you every good.

I have received the photograph, for which I thank you very heartily, and I will send you soon an American one, with this young man. And now I have nothing to write, only I greet you, parents, and brothers and sisters, and I wish you all health and happiness. I greet also Aunt Karolska and ask and beg her pardon. Let her not be angry with me, but I had no time to write another letter particularly to auntie. Be so good, auntie, and accept from my parents this same letter, because I should write to you the same as to my parents. I have nothing more to write, only I ask you, auntie, for a speedy answer, and I beg you once more, auntie, let nobody know from these letters about the young man. I request you, dear parents, give this whole letter to auntie to read.

[ALEKSANDRA REMBIEŃSKA]

448   Year 1912

O DEAR AUNTIE: I received your letter on February 20 and I write you on February 25. Dear auntie, you wrote 3 letters and I know nothing about them; I received only this one. O dear auntie, you write to me that I either don't wish to write or that I have forgotten [you]. O dear auntie, I will not forget until my death. I write letters, one to auntie and the other to my parents. Perhaps somebody has intercepted those letters at the post-office and does not give them to you. Now, dear auntie, I inform you that I am in good health, thanks to our Lord God, which I wish also to you, dear auntie. May God help you the best; may I always hear that you are doing well; I shall be very glad then. And now dear auntie, I inform you that I am in the same place in service with an English[-speaking] master and mistress who don't know a word of Polish, and I don't know English; so we communicate with gestures and I know what to do, that's all. I know the work and therefore I don't mind much about the language. But, dear auntie, I went intentionally into an English household in order that I may learn to speak English, because it is necessary, in America, as the English language reigns. I am in good health, only I am a little ill with my feet, I don't know what it is, whether rheumatism or something else. I walk very much, because from 6 o'clock in the morning till 10 o'clock in the evening I have work and I receive $22 a month, and I have 7 persons, and 16 rooms to clean, and I cook; everything is on my head. And now, dear auntie, you wrote to me about Staś Filinak that he wished to know

my address; you can give it to him.[1] You wrote to me that he said
that our Lord God punished him because he did not take me. It
is not true. He did not do me any wrong. I pity him very much.
You ask me whether my address is the same. It is the same and it
will never change, and secondly, the Kubaczs have lived already 10
years at the same place and the address is the same. And now, dear
auntie, please don't be angry with me for not answering directly, for
I have no time, neither in the day nor the evening. I am always
busy. And now, dear auntie, I thank you very much for the news,
for now I know everything. You ask about that young man, what
happened. Nothing happened, only it is so that I did not wish to
marry him, because I don't wish to marry at all; I will live alone
through this my life to the end. He is a good fellow, nothing can be
said, his name is Tomasz Zylowski. He wants it to be in summer,
after Easter, but I don't think about marrying, I will suffer alone to
the end in this world.[2] O dear auntie, I write you that I have nothing
to write, only I ask you for a quick answer. And now I beg you,
auntie, write me what happened with [two illegible names of boy and
girl]. I wish you a merry holiday of Easter time. O dear God, why
cannot I be with auntie and divide the egg together with parents and
brothers and sisters! When I recall all this, I would not be sorry if
I had to die right now. Dear auntie, Mańka wrote to me a letter;
Jablońska with [illegible masculine name] will come to the Kubaczs.

[ALEKSANDRA REMBIEŃSKA]

[1] Because her relation with the other suitor is interrupted.

[2] A typical momentary reaction to a disappointment. See her allusion to
dying at the end, where this disappointment is combined with the feeling of loneliness.

BUTKOWSKI SERIES

We have here another example of traditional attitudes almost perfectly preserved in emigration—this time in a young man. In this case, as in that of Rembieńska, the familial relations at home were particularly strong, and this is evidently the main reason why the dissolution comes so slowly. (Cf. introduction to the Raczkowski series.) We notice also that the familial feelings seem a little weaker in Antoni than in Konstanty. As we have no further data as to their past we may conjecture that the difference is one of individual character.

449–61, KONSTANTY AND ANTONI BUTKOWSKI, IN
AMERICA, TO THEIR PARENTS, IN POLAND

449   SOUTH CHICAGO, December 6, 1901

DEAR PARENTS: I send you my lowest bow, as to a father and mother, and I greet you and my brothers with these words: "Praised be Jesus Christus," and I hope in God that you will answer me, "For centuries of centuries. Amen."

And now I wish you, dearest parents, and you also, dearest brother, to meet the Christmas eve and merry holidays in good health and happiness. May God help you in your intentions. Be merry, all of you together. [Health and success; letter received.] I could not answer you at once, for you know that when one comes from work he has no wish to occupy himself with writing [particularly] as I work always at night. . . . . I sent you money, 100 roubles, on November 30. I could not send more now, for you know that winter is coming and I must buy clothes. I inform you that Marta has no work yet. She will get work after the holidays, and it may happen that she will marry. . . . . I inform you about Jasiek, my brother, that he wrote me a letter from Prussia asking me to take him to America, but he is still too young. Inform me about Antoni, how his health is, for in the spring I will bring him to me. I will send him a ship-ticket, if God grants me health. [Greetings for family and relatives.]

[KONSTANTY BUTKOWSKI]

450 January 1, 1902

DEAR PARENTS: .... I send you, my dear parents, my photographs, 5 copies. So please, give my aunt Klemensowa that one in which I am with Marta, and leave the other with yourself. From these 3 [where I am alone] give one to the Butkowski's [uncle], the other to whom you wish, and keep the third. For perhaps we shall see one another soon, and perhaps not, so you will have me at least upon this dead paper. But please don't grieve about me; perhaps I have saddened your heart with this letter [the preceding sentence], but, thanks to God we are still alive. I beg you, father and mother, give [money] for a holy mass, for, as you know, in America everything is hypocritical [the priests and their prayers]. As to the apparition, about which you wrote, that in America our Lord Jesus manifested Himself, don't believe in it. Whoever tells you it you may spit into his eyes [as a liar]. It is not true. Those images which are reproduced in your country—don't care for them, for it's not true. So don't believe in it, because it is not valid, it is invented by people. Why, we in America would know it better than they know there in our country. It happened only thus, that in one town, in a church, upon an image above the altar dew appeared. This image was painted red, so people who came to the church early in the morning said that it was blood, while it was not blood, only dew.[1] ....

KONSTANTY BUTKOWSKI

451 February 17, 1902

DEAREST PARENTS: .... I inform you that I have sent a ship-ticket for Antoni. .... Expect to receive it soon. .... And remember, Antoni, don't show your papers to anybody, except in

---

[1] The man is very religious (cf. letter No. 454, where he asks for scapularies, rosaries, etc.) and his unbelief with regard to the alleged miracle is not the result of any critical attitude toward miracles in general, but merely the negation of a particular fact which might have happened elsewhere at some other moment. The background of this negation is clearly the idea that no such miracle can happen in America where "everything is hypocritical." For the same reason he asks for a mass to be said in Poland, not in America. The underlying assumption is that the efficiency of religious values depends upon the moral perfection of the men who manipulate them. This attitude corresponds to the moral-religious system as against the magical one. (Cf. Introduction: "Religious and Magical Attitudes.") It is the attitude which makes possible the whole "Zaranie movement," to be treated in Part II.

places where you must show them. . . . . And if you receive the ticket soon, don't wait, but come at once. And if you receive it a week or so before Easter, then don't leave until after the holidays. But after the holidays don't wait; come at once. . . . . And send me a telegram from the Castle Garden. You won't pay much, and I shall know and will go to the railway-station. Take 15 roubles with you, it will be enough, and change them at once for Prussian money. As to the clothes, take the worst which you have, some three old shirts, that you may have a change on the water. And when you come across the water happily, then throw away all these rags. Bring nothing with you except what you have upon yourself. And don't bring any good shoes either, but everything the worst. As to living, take some dry bread and much sugar, and about half a quart of spirits, and some dry meat. You may take some onions, but don't take any cheese. . . . . And be careful in every place about money. Don't talk to any girls on the water. . . . . Learn in Bzory when Wojtek will come, for he comes to the same place where I am, so you would have a companion. And about Jan Płonka, if he wants to come, he is not to complain about [reproach] me for in America there are neither Sundays nor holidays; he must go and work. I inform [him] that I shall receive him as my brother. If he wishes he may come. . . . .

[KONSTANTY BUTKOWSKI]

452   November 11 [1902]

DEAREST PARENTS: . . . . Now I inform you about Antoni, that he is working in Chicago; it costs 15 cents to go to him. He is boarding, as well as Marta, with acquaintances, with Malewski. He has an easy and clean work, but he earns only enough to live, for he is unable to do heavy work. I see them almost every evening. I go to them. And Marta works in a tailor-shop, but she refuses to listen to me, else she would have been married long ago. So I inform you that I loved her as my own sister, but now I won't talk to her any more, for she refuses to listen. Family remains family only in the first time after coming from home, and later they forget and don't wish any more to acknowledge the familial relations; the American meat inflates them.

I have nothing more to write, except that we are all in good health. Moreover, I declare about your letters, give them to somebody else to write, for neither wise nor fool can read such writing. If such writers are to write you may as well not send letters, for I won't read them, only I will throw them into the fire, for I cannot understand. I beg you, describe to me about our country, how things are going on there. And please don't be angry with me for this which I shall write. I write you that it is hard to live alone, so please find some girl for me, but an orderly [honest] one, for in America there is not even one single orderly girl.[1] . . . .

KONSTANTY BUTKOWSKI

453   December 21 [1902]

I, your son, Konstanty Butkowski, inform you, dear parents, about my health. . . . . I thank you kindly for your letter, for it was happy. As to the girl, although I don't know her, my companion, who knows her, says that she is stately and pretty, I believe him, as well as you, my parents. For although I don't know her, I ask you, my dear parents, and as you will write me so it will be well. Shall I send her a ship-ticket, or how else shall I do? Ask Mr. and Mrs. Sadowski [her parents], what they will say. And I beg you, dear parents, give them my address and let them write a letter to me, then I shall know with certainty. And write me, please, about her

---

[1] Although it is not entirely clear, even to themselves, what immigrants mean when they say that Polish girls "get totally spoiled" in America, that they are not "orderly," etc., the main point is probably the more or less clear consciousness that the girls lose the character which they ought to possess in conformity with the family spirit—that they are too much individualized. This implies more than mere emancipation from the supremacy of man and more than is implied in the explicit reproaches of the men—a tendency to amusement, to infidelity, to finery, etc., though it implies these features also.

At this point—in the allusion to Marta, to illegible letters—and in the earlier allusion to the corruption of religion in America, the writer shows an exasperation not adequately expressed in the translation. It is the result of the awakened consciousness of the disharmony between the man's present individualistic and his former familial environment. The feeling of loneliness must be particularly strong in a man of his psychology when removed from the family-group, and marriage appears here as a substitute for the family in its primitive form and not, as it is in the old country, a widening of the primitive family-group. In Poland the substitution of the marriage-group for the family-group goes on much more slowly, and mainly in city life. The internal evolution—loss of the sentiment of familial solidarity—keeps pace with the slower evolution of the external conditions. But in America the change of external conditions is always in advance of the change of attitudes, and therefore in the present case the substitution of the marriage-group for the family-group is not accompanied by the loss of familial feelings.

age and about everything which concerns her. I don't need to enumerate; you know yourselves, dear parents. For to send a ship-ticket it is not the same as to send a letter which costs a nickel; what is done cannot be undone. So I beg you once more, as my loving parents, go into this matter and do it well, that there may be no cheating. . . . . I shall wait for your letter with great impatience, that I may know what to do. . . . [1]   KONSTANTY BUTKOWSKI

Please inform me, which one is to come, whether the older or the younger one, whether Aleksandra or Stanisława. Inform me exactly.

454   February 14, 1903

DEAREST PARENTS: . . . . As to the Sadowskis, I wrote them a letter, and I inform you that I shall send her a ship-ticket, for they wrote me a letter and all this pleased me very much. So in March I will send her a ship-ticket, but I will wait until you answer this letter, my parents. I will send the ticket to her address. As to the money for the journey, they could give it to her, and if not, I will send it for her, but to your address. As to Jasiek, I inform you, let him not risk coming, for he is still too young. Here in Chicago work is very hard. . . . . Even Antoni scarcely earns for his living, and you write me to take that one. Let him wait at least 2 years, for Antoni has not worked during the whole winter. He would work for 3 days and sit for a month. For you know that here in America one must always work; there is no rest. He has time enough.

And now I inform you that if she comes to me let her bring a belt consecrated to St. Franciscus, one scapulary consecrated to the Immaculate Conception of Mary and two consecrated to God's Mother of Sorrows, and one *koronka* [arrangement of prayers differing from the rosary] consecrated to the Immaculate Conception. And let her bring also one of those booklets with flower-patterns for embroidery. . . . .

                                        KONSTANTY BUTKOWSKI

---

[1] In spite of the fact that the parents are to select the girl, the marriage is here no longer the familial matter it was traditionally. Its aim is here purely individual. The parents are required to select in view of their son's personal happiness, and the girl, who by emigrating will be isolated from her family, is taken into consideration rather as an individual than as a family-member. We find here the intermediary type between familial and properly individual marriage; the form remains familial but the content is already individualistic. In selecting a stress is put upon the family from which the girl comes, not because the alliance with this family is more or less desired, but mainly because the nature of the family forms a basis for conclusions as to the character of the individual.

455   March 28, 1903

DEAR PARENTS: . . . . I sent the ship-ticket on March 26, and I sent to you, father, 20 roubles of money, so you may give her some for the journey. So I commit myself to you, father and mother, for I don't know her. I inform you, dear parents, that not one, but thousands of girls come here to America, get married, live a month or a year or two, and then some scoundrel persuades her and she runs away with him into the world. Thousands of such cases happen. So my dearest parents, I commit myself to you. I embrace you and kiss your hands and I beg your pardon, dear parents, and you, dearest brothers, and my whole family for hazarding myself in such an undertaking. I don't know how God and the Holiest Mother will help me, for it is neither for a year nor for two, but for my whole life. Don't think, father and mother, that when I marry, I shall forget you. Oh no! Whenever I can I will always help you in any case.

As to Sadowska, I have described in my letter to her how she should arrange everything. . . . . And if they ask her to whom she is going, let her answer, to her brother . . . . Konstanty Butkowski. [Similar advice to his brother.]

KONSTANTY BUTKOWSKI

456   June 13 [1902]

DEAREST PARENTS: . . . . Konstanty works in the same factory as before and earns $2 a day. I have yet no work, but don't be anxious about me, dear parents . . . . for I came to a brother and uncle, not to strangers. If our Lord God gives me health, I shall work enough in America. [News about friends and relatives.] Now I inform you, dear parents, about Władysława Butkowska [cousin]. She lives near us, we see each other every day. She is a doctor's servant. And this doctor has left his wife in Chicago and came to South Chicago. She cooks for him, and she is alone in his house, so people talk about her, that she does not behave well. He pays her $5 a week. I don't know whether it is true or not, but people talk thus because he has left his wife. . . . .[1]

[ANTONI BUTKOWSKI]

[1] In Poland the girl would not venture to take or keep such a place in the face of public opinion.

457   Chicago, December 31, 1902

Dear Parents: . . . . If Konstanty wrote you to send him a
girl answer him that he may send a ship-ticket either to the one from
Popów or to the one from Grajewo. Let the one come which is
smarter, for he does not know either of them, so send the one which
pleases you better. For in America it is so: Let her only know how
to prepare for the table, and be beautiful. For in America there is
no need of a girl who knows how to spin and to weave. If she knows
how to sew, it is well. For if he does not marry he will never make a
fortune and will never have anything; he wastes his work and has
nothing. And if he marries he will sooner put something aside. For
he won't come back any more. In America it is so: Whoever does
not intend to return to his country, it is best for him to marry young;
then he will sooner have something, for a bachelor in America will
never have anything, unless he is particularly self-controlled.[1] [Greet-
ings, wishes, etc.]

                                               Antoni Butkowski

458   South Chicago, April 21, 1903

Now I, Antoni, your son, my dearest parents, and my uncle and
the whole family, we inform you that your son Konstanty is no longer
alive. He was killed in the foundry [steel-mills]. Now I inform you,
dear parents, that he was insured in an association for $1,000.[2] His
funeral will cost $300. And the rest which remains, we have the

[1] The emphasis by Antoni of the business side of marriage is probably an
individual feature. Konstanty does not mention the economic side at all.

[2] The immediate passage from the news of death to business seems to show a
particular coldness in the brother. But it is probably rather a lack of tact in letter-
writing, due to his youth. The letter is written on the second day after Konstanty's
death, and this day was probably mainly devoted to business conferences of the
family; so the business problems are put first. At any rate, it is not a proof of
egotism, since Antoni has no personal benefit to expect. Further, we find here in
an exaggerated form a typical peasant attitude. No grief, however great, interferes for a long time with the peasant's practical activity. This is a consequence
of the fact that, as we have noted more than once, the peasant's psychology is
essentially practical; reflection or sentimental brooding always requires a particular
effort and particularly favorable external circumstances, and therefore, in whatever
situation, it is the practical side, the point from which activity can start, which
naturally tends to occupy the first place. Finally, there is for the peasant nothing
mean or low in economic questions in comparison with other and higher interests.
Cf. Osiński series, letters of Baranowski.

right to receive this money. So now I beg you, dear parents, send an authorization and his birth-certificate to my uncle, Piotr Z., for I am still a minor and cannot appear in an American lawsuit. When he joined his association he insured himself for $1,000 . . . . and made a will in your favor, dear parents. But you cannot get it unless you send an authorization to our uncle, for the lawsuit will be here, and it would be difficult for you to get the money [while remaining] in our country, while we shall get it soon and we will send it to you, dear parents. So now, when you receive this letter, send us the papers soon. Only don't listen to stupid people, but ask wise people. . . . .

Now I inform you, dear parents, that strange people will write to you letters. Answer each letter, and answer thus, that you commit everything to Piotr Z. For they will try to deceive you, asking to send the authorization to them. But don't listen to anybody . . . . only listen to me, as your son; then you will receive money paid for your son and my brother. [Repeats the advice; wishes from the whole family.]

Now I beg you, dear parents, don't grieve. For he is no more, and you won't raise him, and I cannot either. For if you had looked at him, I think your heart would have burst open with sorrow [he was so mutilated]. But in this letter I won't describe anything, how it was with him. It killed him on April 20.[1] In the next letter I shall describe to you everything about the funeral. . . . . Well, it is God's will; God has wished thus, and has done it. Only I beg you, dear parents, give for a holy mass, for the sake of his soul. And he will be buried beautifully, on April 22.

[ANTONI BUTKOWSKI]

459 April 26 [1903]

Now I, Antoni Butkowski, speak to you, dearest parents, and to you, my brothers, with these words: "Praised be Jesus Christus."

Now I inform you, dearest parents, and you, my brothers, that Konstanty, your son, dearest parents, and your brother and mine, my brothers, is no more alive. It killed him in the foundry, it tore him in eight parts, it tore his head away and crushed his chest to a mass and broke his arms. But I beg you, dear parents, don't weep and don't grieve. God willed it so and did it so. It killed him on April 20, in the morning and he was buried on April 22. He was

---

[1] For the use of "it" in this connection, cf. Jackowski series, No. 254.

buried beautifully. His funeral cost $225, the casket $60. Now when we win some [money] by law from the company, we will buy a place and transfer him that he may lie quietly, we will surround him with a fence and put a cross, stone, or iron upon his grave. This will cost some $150. For his work, let him at least lie quietly in his own place. It is so, dear parents: Perhaps we shall receive from the [insurance] society $1,000, and from the company we don't know how much, perhaps 2,000, perhaps 3,000, and perhaps 1,000. . . . . Whatever we receive, after paying all the expenses I will send you the rest, dear parents, and I will come myself to my country. . . . . And let Aleksandra not come now, let her send the ship-ticket back and we will send her the money which he promised her. And don't give her these 20 roubles. Once more I tell you, dear parents, don't listen to anybody, to any letters which anybody will write to you, but listen to me, your son. I cannot close the door myself before lawyers. Some advise well, others still better, but I have a wise man. And now I tell you, dear parents, read this note, which is cut out of a paper; you will know who is guilty of his death. But nothing can be done, dear parents. Don't weep, for you won't raise him any more. For if you had looked upon him, I don't know what would have become of you.[1] . . . .

ANTONI BUTKOWSKI

460   May 20 [1903]

DEAREST PARENTS AND BROTHERS: . . . . I received your letter on May 18, for which I thank you kindly and heartily, for I learned at least about your health, that you are all in good health. For when I received that letter by telegram, I grieved much when you wrote that you were losing your reason. But I beg you, dear parents, don't grieve and don't weep, for you won't raise him any more. We regret him and grieve still more, for we have looked at him during 3 days, and now still at whatever we look, that was left after him our heart fills with grief. About his funeral I cannot describe everything, but he was buried beautifully. Now I inform you, dear parents, that Stefan Zal. went back to our country. When he comes there try to meet him, and he will relate to you everything, for Konstanty

---

[1] In this letter the disproportion between the sentimental and the business part is not so great as in the preceding one; the recurring idea is resignation to the fact which cannot be changed and cannot be any basis of practical activity.

had boarded with him for a month. And if God gives me health, perhaps in the autumn I shall come to our country and tell you everything. . . . . As to the company in which Konstanty worked, we don't know how it will be. If they give us $2,000 by good will, we will agree, but if not, we intend a lawsuit But I won't wait for the end of the suit, for in America a suit may last 5 or 7 years. And for a killed man the company cannot be sued for more than $5,000. Then the lawyer will take one half, and will give the other half to us, for such are the laws in America. . . . .

And about Sadowska, let her not come, for when she comes to New York they will send her back. For now it is so, that when anybody comes to New York he must send a telegram to the person to whom he is going. And now, when he is dead, they won't admit her. They know already that he is dead, for we have been in that ship-agent's office, wanting to return the ticket. But it was already delivered. The agent told us that she should not come. If she wants it absolutely, let her ome; but it will be in vain, for she will be sent back. And if she does not come, let her send the ship-ticket back to us. . . . .

ANTONI BUTKOWSKI

461 July 23 [1903]

DEAREST PARENTS AND BROTHERS: . . . . I inform you that we have received already the money from the association on July 22, and on the same day we sent you 800 roubles. As to the rest, we had to give the lawyer $100, and uncle took $300 for the funeral, and the rest remained with me. I inform you, dear parents, that they did not want to pay the money, only we had to take a lawyer. As to the company, we gave the affair up to a lawyer, for we could not come to an understanding. They offered us only $300 by good will, while by law they must pay some thousands. . . . . But I won't wait; I think that on August 25 I shall be at home. . . . .

ANTONI BUTKOWSKI

RADWAŃSKI SERIES

In this series the process of individualization goes on rapidly in Janek Radwański, much more slowly in his brother Antoni, and probably does not touch the third brother, who, contrary to the behavior of so many others (cf., for example, Michał Osiński), returns home after a short time to do his military service. Otherwise he could never return, and the attraction of the old country, family, and community proves stronger than the fear of military service and the hope of a career in America.

462–68, ANTONI RADWAŃSKI, IN AMERICA, TO HIS PARENTS, IN POLAND

462   [Second part of a letter. Date cannot be determined, probably end of 1912.]

And further, dear parents, we answer your parental request, where you ask us to send you money. All right, dear parents, we are glad to fulfil your request at every moment and at every hour, everything that you ask us for, because you have brought us up from childhood, and we have leaned upon your favor. The example you gave us in our younger years we keep in our older years, as God ordered. Dearest parents, to whom shall you appeal for help, if not first to God the Highest and to God's Mother of Częstochowa, Queen of heaven and earth, asking for health for you and your loving children, and then to us for help? We will help you at any time, if only God helps us and the Holy Virgin Mary.[1] So we send you money, 403 roubles, four

[1] The moral character of this familial attitude is already a sign of a beginning disintegration of the familial group. Indeed, there is no question of moral obligation and even little consciousness of the attitude in the really primitive familial solidarity; the relation of the individual to the group is not a moral but a social relation, accepted as a matter of fact. The relation assumes a moral form when it is not the only one psychologically possible, and the number and variety of possible relations grow, together with the progress of individualization. Thus, the moral norm appears as a substitute for the immediate solidarity when the

hundred three roubles. The three roubles give for a holy mass. And further, dear parents, we inform you, buy yourselves a cow as dear as you wish. Of this money Bronek sends 300 roubles, and Janek 100 roubles. Myself, Antosiek, I do not send you now, dear parents, because, first, I have no money on me, but in the bank, and then I will send you for another time. And you, dear sister, we thank you for your good wishes and for your obedience to our parents. Listen well to the parents, then we will send you money for a good dress. [Usual salutations and ending.]

ANTONI RADWAŃSKI

463 BAYONNE, N.J., January 18, 1913

[Usual greetings and wishes]: And now I inform you, dear parents, I, Antosiek, that I send you money, 250 roubles, and I request you, dear parents, very politely, as soon as you receive this money, leave for yourselves as much as you need for your household, and put the rest where you think it the best, either in a bank or somewhere for the case of any misfortune. I inform you, dear parents, I, Antosiek, about my work. I am working near the fire [furnace], as before. I earn $2.50 a day. Ask Grabowski, he will tell you, what sort of work it is. [Salutations for the whole family.]

[ANTONI]

464 April 9, 1913

. . . . If you want money, dear parents, write, and we will send you for your needs. And now we write to you dear parents, that this Stasiek [the son], of our Szymon Krasnosielski, is a clever boy, so if the news in America is better we will send him a ship-ticket, if he wishes to come, because now work is somewhat bad. Tell this to Szymon and his wife, and let them not regret [what happened]. Perhaps he will get them out of this [situation], if he is willing to work.

And now I, Antosiek, write to you, dear parents, how do you advise me, whether to come to our country or not? Because I have

---

traditional unity of the familial group is changed into a personal connection of its members. In the present case the familial disorganization is only beginning; therefore the moral norm is fully and gladly acknowledged for a time, but finally these demands become "too much." In other cases, as we have seen, the duty becomes gradually more painful until it is finally avoided.

now good work and I would like to marry, and now I don't know what to do.[1]

And now, dear parents, Bronek asks what is the date of his call to military service. He is curious and wants to know whether it was in the past autumn or in the next, or after the next. He thinks of going back to our country, only does not yet know when. He and Janek work together in one plant and I work in another. [Usual ending.]

ANTONI RADWAŃSKI

465
June 25, 1913

. . . . And now we inform you that Czesława [Czesia] Jankowska from Karwacz came and related to us about your success and health, and we were very glad that you are all in good health. She gave us the gift that you sent us, 3 cheeses. So we will send you also a gift, but don't know what kind of a gift you wish from us. Now further, dear parents, you asked us for our photographs; so I, Antosiek, send you my photograph, and some other time we will send you perhaps all three, because we could not now. Janek went to another city, and Bronek says you saw him not long ago. Dear parents, could you send me your photograph? I would send you money, as soon as you write. Only, dear parents, Czesia Jankowska told me that you don't allow me to marry but [ask me] to return home. So I intend to return home, but I do not know when, because now I have good work and wages, $75 a month. Therefore I will still work.[2] [Usual salutations and ending.]

[ANTONI]

466
December 2, 1913

[Usual greetings and Christmas wishes; letter from parents received; thanks.] And another letter I received from Brother Bronisław, in which he writes me to come back to our country. But I do not intend to come back to our country at once, but only in the spring, because up to the present my health is favorable so I think

---

[1] Acknowledgment of the parental authority, but this becomes more and more formal, as we see in the following letters.

[2] The will of the parents proves ultimately insufficient to influence him, but there is not yet a conscious attempt to get rid of the control of the parents. Up to the present the whole process of emancipation seems to have gone on unconsciously.

I shall remain longer. And what you write me, dear parents, that if I do not come, the punishment of prison threatens me, I do not mind it and I do not fear it.[1] And now I inform you, dear parents, about sister, and what you wrote about wishing to send her to a dressmaker. You can do it; let her learn. And as to the help, don't be anxious. If only our Lord God gives me health I will help you at every moment. And now I ask about Brother Bronisław. After his arrival in our country we received a letter [from him], and he wrote me that he will be free from military service, so I request you, dearest parents, if you receive this letter, answer me directly, because I am curious about it, and I shall await it with great impatience. And now I inform you, dear parents, about Janek, that we are together, only he asks you for your blessing, because he intends to marry a girl from Przasnysz, daughter of Mr. and Mrs. Leśniewski, who live in Piaski.[2] I pen to you in this letter whatever I can remember. But I have nothing more to write, only I recommend myself to your kind memory and I beg you for a speedy answer. With high respect,

ANTONI RADWAŃSKI

I shake your hands.   Goodbye.[3]

467   [January, 1914]

[Beginning of letter missing.] Now about your request, what you ask. We cannot help you, dear parents, in this, because as to me, dear parents, I am somewhat [illegible word], and about Janek it is not necessary to explain to you because he is now intending to marry. The second banns of his marriage were on January 4, so he needs money. I lent him myself $50 for his wedding, and I do not take money from the bank, because I regret to touch it. Then, dear parents, manage it as you can yourself. I will send you [money] later, if our Lord God gives me health. But, dear parents, I think that you are not wronged by me all the same. I help you in the measure of my ability. Not long ago I sent you 50 roubles for your

---

[1] First conscious, but still only slight, break in obedience.

[2] Janek is the most emancipated of the brothers; he sends the least money home, and decides to marry without consulting his parents.

[3] Shaking hands is a rather disrespectful form of greeting the parents; the normal form is kissing the hands. One of the complaints of old-fashioned parents about the bad influence of emigration is that the children begin to shake hands instead of kissing.

needs, although we were all three in America. So, dearest parents, I
beg very politely your pardon. Don't be angry for what I write you.
I don't remind you of it, because it ought to be so; it is a duty to
respect and help one's parents until the last moment of death
[life], because so says our Lord Jesus and the Holiest Mother Virgin
Mary: "Do not abandon thy parents and remember about them,
and I will not forget about thee." I wear this in my heart and I
remember. Only, dear parents, you demand too much.[1] You
ask for help because you are already in old age and you cannot do
heavy work; sister [asks] also, the brothers also, so my work does
not suffice for all this. I requested Brother Bronisław very kindly:
"Bronuś, little brother, I beg you, remain with us for some time, then
we will go back together." I implored him as a brother, but he did
not listen to my request and did not heed it. Now he longs and
regrets; probably he regrets that for which I begged him so. And he
is longing now himself, and to me he causes pain, because I wept over
that letter when I read it. He caused regrets to himself and to me
also, because after his departure I thought that my heart would
burst open. And I request you, send me his address, where he is in
service. Now, dear parents, I grieved over this letter which you
sent to me recently, that not even money [bribery] can help, but

---

[1] His attitude seems perfectly correct objectively, and still it is quite different
from the traditionally sanctioned one. Here again the moral statement of the
situation is a sign of the dissolution of the old immediacy of social attitudes. In
the old family-group there can be essentially no opposition between the son's and
the parents' economic interests. The property is familial; there is no question
of any justice or injustice, obligation, antagonism, or, in general, of any moral or
immoral relation in economic matters between any two members of the family as
personalities. The parents do not wrong the son in requiring all his earnings to be
given to them; the older brother does not wrong his younger brothers or sisters
in taking the lion's share of the inheritance if it is he who takes the farm; the
children do not wrong the parents when, after retirement of the latter, they refuse
to them the right to own anything personally and acknowledge only their right to
be supported; etc. In all these cases the relation is that between the part and the
whole, not that between independent but connected entities. But, on the other
hand, when an individual, as in the present case, is half emancipated, there is still
no relation between individuals, but between the individual on one side and the
group on the other, and each is right from a different point of view. The parents
are right here in asking continually for money, if we take the standpoint of the
group; the son is right in refusing to send more than he wishes, if we take the
standpoint of the individual. But in the eyes of the individual whose feeling of
familial unity has dissolved, the situation assumes the form of a relation between
individuals, to be regulated by justice.

I must go and serve in the army. Now I cannot assure you when I shall return to our country. If I knew certainly that I should not go to the army I would go back at the same moment; but I am afraid that if I go to serve it would be still more painful for me than here in America. How do you advise me about it?

And now, dear parents, I inform you about myself and Czesia Jankowska. Once I was there with them and she asked my advice. She had an opportunity to marry a boy before the winter; he wanted to marry her. So she asked my advice about the matter. I answered her: "It depends on your wish." And she said to me that if she had an opportunity to marry such a boy as I am, she wouldn't mind anything. Then I said to her laughing: "Well, let us two marry." Then she proposed that we write to our parents whether we two could not marry.[1] Here is the end of my letter. [Usual ending.]

[ANTONI]

468

[Beginning of the letter with date and greetings missing.] I inform you that I received also a letter from Brother Bronisław, from the army, but not a very cheerful one.

Don't be anxious about your old age, that you will have nothing to live on. Only beg God the Highest and the Holiest Mother for health; and I also will help you at every time. Now also I send you some roubles, although not much, only 35, but I cannot send more, because I must support Janek and his wife. He married and has no work, because work is bad. Janek got a good wife, dear parents, she pleased me very much, she has wisdom; but he has been short of reason—is and will be. The wedding was very nice, because I gave him for this wedding $130. If he has a brotherly heart he will give me that back, and if he has a Cainian heart, it will be lost. But nothing can be done. I spent for him $30 when he came from our country, and he did not give them back. And that coat, that shirt, that ribbon and those corals, which Bronisław brought with him, it was I alone who sent them. I bought all that myself.

And now, dear parents, we inform you about our intentions of marriage. With Czesia it would be very well, because we have

[1] His presentation of the matter is as if the plan of marriage arose only incidentally and unintentionally; he wants to diminish his responsibility for the fact, in view of the expressed wish of the parents that he should not marry but return.

talked about it, dear parents, and we have the wish [to marry]. Czesia is a good girl, and wise. She has informed me about everything. If only we could marry, because we know that we are cousins. We are curious what Uncle and Aunt Jankowski say, because they wrote a letter, and I read it, but they wrote us nothing about it. So we beg you very much, speak among yourselves and to uncle and auntie also. We ask for a speedy answer. [End missing.]

[ANTONI]

DOBIECKI SERIES

The relation between an older and a younger member of a family is broken because of the more rapid evolution of the latter. The uncle here assumes with regard to his nephew, who came later to America, the attitude of familial authority usually assumed by the father. The uncle evidently came to this country when already a mature man and has preserved almost wholly the traditional standpoint. His behavior, as related by himself and by his nephew, shows a tendency to despotism. The boy brought also enough of familial spirit as his first letter shows; but his emancipation has been relatively easy. (Cf. the attitude of Aleksander Wolski in an analogous situation.)

469–73, ANTONI (ANTEK) DOBIECKI, IN AMERICA, TO FAMILY-MEMBERS, IN POLAND, AND ONE LETTER (472) FROM THE UNCLE OF ANTONI

469   PHILLIPS, PA., July 16, 1910

[Usual greeting and generalities; letter received]: Now, mother, you write me that you grieve because you cannot pay your debts and you did not pay the money back to brother-in-law. So I send you another 100 roubles. Give back to everybody what you owe, may nobody look angrily at you because of your owing anybody money; get rid of all your debts. Now I inform you that I sent you 100 roubles on July 13. Answer me distinctly with whom you are living. Now I have nothing to write you, only I send you low bows, dear parents. We send also low bows to brother and sister-in-law. I inform you, dear brother, that you manage your household badly if you cannot give our parents enough to live with you, and even two people have no place in your home. It is your wife who walks in the breeches, not you; your wife governs, not you.

Things are bad in a household where the cow shows the way to the ox.[1] [Proverb.]

Now I have nothing more to write you, only I send you low bows, and I send also low bows to sister and brother-in-law, with their children. And I inform you further, dear parents, don't be anxious about the rent. I will send you money and nobody will look angrily at you. . . . .

[ANTONI DOBIECKI]

470   September 26

. . . . And now I inform you that in America things are very bad. Work is bad and living is very dear. We are working 5 days in a week. We earn hardly more than enough to live. You write me to send you a photograph. I will send you a photograph, but only when I have money; then I will send you money and the photograph together, because if I sent you the photograph, and no money, people would laugh at me. [Salutations for the whole family.]

[ANTONI]

471   September 25

. . . . DEAR FATHER AND MOTHER: I pen you some words. First I ask about your health and success. And as to my success, I am in good health, and my success is as ever. I work as before. And now, dear father and mother, why is it that you don't answer? I sent to you 20 roubles and you don't answer whether you received them or not. And now, dear father and mother, I write to you that I am no more with uncle, but with strange people, because he wanted me to get up every day at two or half-past two o'clock after midnight and to go with him to work.[2] I am working hard enough myself, and I want to rest during the night; 11 hours is work enough. I have worked with him many times and enough. Then he said he

---

[1] When the parents of wife or husband live with the young couple it is usually the women who quarrel, and it is the rôle of the men to keep harmony. Note the contrast between this sharp passage and the preceding and following ceremonial ones.

[2] Probably the uncle had a shop of his own and wanted his nephew to help him sometimes.

would credit me with about a dollar on my board, but instead I was obliged to pay all the money that I owed. Afterward he got angry with me because I would not work with him every day, and he told me to go away and to hunt another boarding-house. He thought that I would help him to work, and that he would thus economize and put it in the bank. And now, dear father and mother, I want to ask what about the military service? Write me whether I have to go to our country or how I may do. But now I have no money. Send me the address of the Olszewiakis. I have nothing more of interest to write, only I salute you. [Usual greetings for all the family.] If you don't want me to come back to our country, brother and sister-in-law, then send me your sister Helena.

[ANTONI]

472   October 10, 1911

DEAR SISTER AND BROTHER-IN-LAW: . . . . Now I inform you, dear sister and brother-in-law, when you write letters to Antek again don't address them to my name, but to his own, because you know what his name is. He has no uncle now; he is a greater lord than his uncle. I will tell you, dear sister, why I fell out with him—Antek went once to some house where they gave him beer to drink, and came back drunk and made a fool of himself at home. I said to him: "You did not go to the church, but you got drunk, and now you will play comedies!" And he told me I was not his father and should not order him about. Then I got angry with him and struck him one in the face. When he came from our country he came to me as to a mother or father, and now he tells me that I am not his father, that I did not bring him up and have no rights over him. But when he came from our country he did not wander about without work, but he got work on the second day, and he works above [the earth], drives a pair of horses and hauls coal and firewood. And when another comes and has no friend he has to go to the mine and dig coal under the earth. But he has good work, he is not working hard. And when he came from our country he was as blind as myself, he did not understand what is written, black on white; then my wife did not sleep of nights but taught him where is what number on which house, because he did not know where to take coal, to what number. And now he is a greater lord than myself. And when he came from our country, I cared for him as a father, for his son. I bought him one suit of clothes for my money and gave him another of my own.[1] [End missing.]

[UNCLE OF ANTONI]

473   October 22, 1912

DEAR PARENTS: . . . . What you write me, that I cease to help you, is not true, because I think of you and remember and will not cease to remember you. I would have sent you some roubles long ago, but I had no news about the others, whether you received them or not. Since I have learned that you received them, I send you now 120 roubles, 20 roubles for your expenses, and 100 roubles please lend at interest. And if you have not enough with those 20 roubles, write to me, and I will send you more, but let these 100 roubles remain untouched. [Salutations.]

ANTONI

[1] Probably all the facts related by both of them are true. The uncle has certainly treated his nephew in the traditional way, playing the part of a father making him work, beating him but also helping him and caring for his future.

KONSTANCYA WALERYCH SERIES

Very rapid emancipation of a girl in America is shown in these letters. In less than half a year she is married without asking for her parents' permission. Probably the familial bonds were not particularly strong, and there is an instructive influence of the new environment. The girl comes to her sister's home and finds there the familial attitude very weak, and this example acts more destructively than solitude upon her own familial spirit.

474–76, KONSTANCYA WALERYCH, IN AMERICA, TO HER PARENTS IN POLAND

474   GREENBURG, PA., December 8, 1913

DEAREST PARENTS: To your words, "Praised be Jesus Christus," I answer, "For centuries of centuries. Amen."

Dearest parents, I inform you that I received the letter sent by you from which I got information about your health and success also. As to myself, thanks to God the Highest, I am in good health, which I wish also to you from all my heart. As to my success, it is not very good because I have done housework, and have been paid $10 for this month, but I had too heavy work; I was obliged to work too long. Now, dearest parents, I inform you that I have at present no work and I don't know what will be further.

Dearest parents, you ask to be informed where I have been boarding after coming to America. I was with my sister and now I am with my sister. Dearest parents, don't be angry with me for not sending you anything up to the present, but I inform you that I could not, because when I traveled to America I remained for a week in Antwerp, and when I came to America I had no work for three weeks, and you know well, dearest parents, that I did not come to parents here; in America nothing is to be had without paying.[1]

[1] Allusion to the fact that her sister and brother-in-law take money for board. In the old country they would have given her hospitality at least for some weeks,

Dearest parents, I inform you that I send you meanwhile thirty roubles for Christmas, and by my soul I cannot send you more at present, because I do not work and I need it myself. I have nothing more to write you, only I greet you and send you low salutations, and I wish you a Merry Christmas, and may the Godly Child have you in His care. God grant it. Amen.

Your loving daughter,

KONSTANCYA WALERYCH

Now, dearest parents, I, your daughter, Frankowska, salute you and greet you heartily and I inform you that I was ill and had two boys born, but they were both dead. Now I [son-in-law] greet you and salute you, and all our children bow to you and kiss you.

BRONISŁAW FRANKOWSKI

Dear Zosia [younger sister], I salute you and write to you that you must go to school and learn well, and next year you will come to America, and then you will write letters.

KONSTANCYA WALERYCH

475 January 17, 1914

. . . . DEAR PARENTS: . . . . I inform you that I married a man from Galicia. Our marriage occurred on the 12th of January; my husband is named Jan Czarnecki. Now, dear parents, I beg you heartily, don't be angry with me for marrying so hastily and a man from so far a country and for not even writing to you about it.[1] I inform you, dear parents, that I took a husband from so far a country for this reason, that, as you know, the girls who married with us and took husbands from the same village, were most unhappy afterward.[2]

---

if not months. The American conditions and customs are considered a justification for not fulfilling the duty of hospitality. The main reason of the change is the fact that here food has to be bought instead of being produced, and thus the economic instead of the social point of view is applied to the question of living. Cf. Introduction: "Economic Life."

[1] The only case in our collection where a girl marries without first asking her parents. Of course it is a complete break of tradition (cf. Introduction: "Marriage"), and a conscious one, since she knows and understands the traditional norms.

[2] The justification of the breach of this custom is interesting, because based upon consideration of utility and personal happiness.

And secondly, when I came to America I often wept because I found myself among good people [irony?]. Dearest parents, I inform you that we had a great wedding, only I was so sad that you were not at my wedding and that you did not even know about it, because I did not write to you.

Dearest parents, I, Jan Czarnecki, your son-in-law, bow to you and greet you heartily, and I beg you not to be angry with me for marrying your daughter, because it is God who gives their fortune to men, and to us also He gave such a fortune and we married in conformity with the will of the Highest. Now, dearest parents, we kiss your hands and we bow to your feet and we ask your parental blessing for this our new life. [Usual greetings.]

Your loving children,

Jan and Konstancya Czarnecki

476   March 25, 1914

. . . . Dearest Parents: . . . . We inform you, dearest parents, that we received the letter you sent us, for which we thank you heartily. We thank you for your good hearts, that you sent us your parental blessing. Dearest mother, you think of having sent me to America as if you had sent me to the grave, and you believe that we shall not be able to return to our country; but about this you can be perfectly sure, mother, because if God gives us health and happiness, we can go to our country at any moment.

Now I, your son-in-law, thank you, dear parents, heartily, that you admitted me to the family circle, and at the same time I thank you that you gave your daughter under my care,[1] and I will endeavor that she may ever be satisfied with me. We inform you, dear parents, that we send you 10 roubles and 2 more, one for grandmother, one to sister Zosia; it makes together 12. We inform you that, thanks to God the Highest, we are in good health, which we wish to you also with our whole heart. We are only sad that you grieve too

---

[1] A good expression of the complex meaning which marriage assumes when it is still a familial matter but has become also an individual matter. There is no place for the idea of putting the girl under the man's care in the familial system, because she remains in the care of the group as a whole; there is no place for the idea of being admitted into the family circle in the individualistic marriage-organization, because the marriage-group becomes then an independent entity.

much, but be calm, because our Lord God gives his fortune to every man, and we married in conformity with God's will.

Now I inform you about my parents. Both my parents are still living and they dwell in Galicia, district Ropczyce, village Czarna, post-station Sędziszów. Father's name is Filip, mother's, Dorota. We are nine brothers—four of us are in America, five in our country—and two sisters.

We have nothing more to write. [Usual greetings.]

Your loving children,

JAN and KONSTANCYA CZARNECKI

FELIKS P. SERIES

The letters afford a good example of a conflict between the solidarity of the old familial type (uncle and nephew) and conjugal solidarity. The conflict is both sentimental and economic. We have, unfortunately, only one side of it presented, but it seems that the familial solidarity is here stronger than the conjugal.

477–80, FROM FELIKS P., IN AMERICA, TO A FRIEND
IN POLAND

477 CHICAGO, July 31, 1908

DEAR COMPANION WACŁAW: I have not written to you for so long a time, because I had no reason to boast about my lot. My uncle is very ill, and with his wife, or rather that mad woman. I can do nothing. Work is also difficult to get here. If my uncle were in good health, then at least I could have a job with him, but he must give this business into other hands, because of his illness. I have searched for work 2 days, all in vain. And with my aunt, or mad woman, it is necessary to make order in such a way as if she were not a human being [by beating her]. My uncle had a motorcycle which he bought just before his illness. He lies in the hospital. I called on him for the first time; after some conversation he told me to take the motorcycle and to use it. Do you know what this snake did? She sold it, and she told him that somebody had stolen it. Such [trouble] I have with this woman. Where I live there are no Poles at all; they all live on the other side of the city. I don't know when I shall go to your brother, for my head is totally broken [with trouble]. I can only wait until my uncle recovers; then everything will be in order. If not, I will take the woman by the head, the money in my pocket and run away home. What else can I do here if he dies? . . . . FELIKS P.

478 August 11, 1908

DEAR WACŁAW: . . . . I am without occupation up to the present, but . . . . the brother of my uncle's wife is trying to get me into . . . . the West Pullman shop. . . . . I long much for you, but I hope that we shall yet be here in America together.   Here in Chicago, when I looked about, I was not very much pleased with the nature of the place, but as to distraction and society, the occasions are innumerable.   Naturally I have not been so merry up to the present.   For that it is necessary to shake your pocket out.

FELIKS P.

479   October 10, 1908

DEAR COMPANION: . . . . I have some work, but only a kind from which I can earn a bare living.   All this [lack of work] is through the fault of my uncle, for he lives in a place where there is not a bit of a factory, and he wants me to work near him that I may live in his house and be with him until he recovers.   But I think of making it short and searching for steady and well-paid work, for with him, i.e., with my uncle, one can live as with a man, but when he is ill he cannot govern [his household] as he did before, but his "cholera" [wife] manages everything.   But you understand I treat her shortly [severely].   I intended before this to drive her away to the four winds, but with a woman it is always difficult.   He, i.e., my uncle, is ill of a sickness which needs a long cure, and even then it is not certain whether he will recover.   So this woman thinks so to herself, that if he is cured after a long time all the money will be spent, for it cost them already $560 for 4 months.   And if he dies nevertheless she will have nothing left.   So she wants him to die as soon as possible— such a "cholera."   And he, i.e., my uncle, has here nobody of his own family except me.   So I have cared for him up to the present, but if this lasts longer I must leave them, for I get very nervous through quarreling and this is bad for me. . . . .   FELIKS P.

480   December 16, 1908

DEAR WACŁAW: . . . . I answer you at once, but unhappily the answer is unfavorable, for I have no work.   I worked for 5 weeks only, and I could only buy what I needed for the winter.   It is true that I don't pay board, but then I have been working for only part of the day.   I would not sit here so long, but there is now little hope for my uncle.   At any moment we expect his death, and then, evidently, I have a certain job. . . . . Don't be angry with me.   As soon as I begin to work I must pay you back at once, for I owe nobody else. . . . .

FELIKS P.

WINKOWSKI SERIES

Almost complete disintegration of the whole traditional set of attitudes appears in this series. The cause is certainly the fact that the man finds himself at first almost alone, and then quite alone among Americans, and thus there is lacking the pressure of social opinion, still existing, even if weakened, in American-Polish communities. It cannot, of course, be assumed that there are no egotistic personalities in Poland, but the behavior in this case would be impossible in the native community of the man. However egotistic the individual, the community checks would not permit of this kind and degree of violation of social tradition.

481–88, S. WINKOWSKI, IN AMERICA, TO FAMILY-MEMBERS, IN POLAND

481   July 8, 1907

In the first words of my letter I salute you, dear mother, and you, sister. I inform you that I received your letter, and I inform you that by the favor of God I am well, and I wish you the same. Now I inform you about this, that you write me sad letters. Why do you do it? Write me joyful letters. I do not like it if anybody writes such a sad letter.[1] There is the will of the Highest God, and whatever God grants it is well. You write to me if I will send you the money, but I do not say that I will not send it, but I will tell you that I am in far America. There is a post-office but by this post-office it is impossible to send the money to the old country, but it is necessary to go to the agent. And to go to the city will cost 50 dollars. If you need it immediately then borrow somewhere, and after two months

[1] This is not the first time we meet the request not to write sad letters. (Cf. No. 405.) This shows the impression which the letters make upon the reader and the importance ascribed to the mood expressed in them. At the same time we see a conscious endeavor to escape moral pain.

I will go to the city and then I will send the money, because now I do not have time to go to the city. I am doing carpenter's work, I have 75 dollars a month. There are no Poles here but us two. I have an opportunity to marry, but she is not a Polish girl, and therefore it is likely that I shall not. I intend to go to the old country for a visit, and whoever in the old country wishes me well I will extend my hand to him, and whoever wishes me ill then he will learn who is Stefan [writer's name].[1] I inform you that I have good work. I work only from 8 in the morning to 5 in the evening and afterward we go to learn and to fight and to leap and to weep, as they say in the old country.

I bow to mother and to sister. I ask for a quick reply. Dear mother [find] for me a nice girl in the old country, nice and handsome, whom I greet fondly. I bow to Ososki, to Pawlinow and to all acquaintances. My address . . . .

STEVE [sic] WINKOWSKI

482   IRONWOOD, MICH., September 29, 1908

DEAR MOTHER: I decided to write to you a few words and I greet you with God's words ["Praised be," etc.]. Don't be angry with me for not writing you a letter for such a long time. Because I cannot describe to you my lot where I was. It is likely that if my acquaintances knew it they would never believe it. What a nationality there is in America! If such a man were brought to your village then all the people would run away from fear [alluding to the negroes]. And I am toiling here a second year. I have pretty good work. I work as a butcher.[2] I have a pay day [*peide*] of 75 dollars a month, and I have a further income of 60 dollars, and my brother and Bolesław Kowaleski are working in the iron mine [*mainie*]. I will have a butcher-shop [*bucernie*] of my own.

Now I inform, dear mother, about my great trouble [*trubel*]. I have a great burden upon my heart on account of one girl. I have been acquainted with her for over 10 months. She is very beautiful and [the daughter] of a rich farmer. She is not Polish. When I

---

[1] A self-assertion resulting from his feeling of his own importance, developed by success. This normal attitude here takes a rough form because of the man's low degree of moral culture. Cf. the case of Adam, in the Raczkowski series.

[2] For "butcher" he uses *bucera* and similarly Polonizes a number of words as indicated in brackets. These words will not be understood at home and are a form of showing-off, harmonizing with his lying about his income.

have a butcher-shop [*bucernie*] of my own, then I will get married.
I dressed this girl in silk and gold. We meet once a week. When I
write to you next time then I will send the money, because now I am
in great trouble [*trublu*]. . . . .

STEVE WINKOWSKI

483   December 8, 1909

I inform you, beloved mother, and you, beloved sister Bronisława,
that by the favor of God I am well and the same I wish to you. I
beg mother and you, sister, to bless me and my Miss Bronisława
Dronskowska with whom I shall be married after Christmas
[*Krismusie*]. I ask you to my wedding. She is not Polish. Her
fathers come from under German [rule]. They have lived in America
a long time already. Their grandfather and grand-grandfather [were]
in America. They are Catholics just as we, and she greets you
also.[1] . . . .

STEVE WINKOWSKI

484   January 5, 1910

I inform beloved mother and father, and you, sister, that by the
favor of God I am well and the same I wish to you. I received your
letter. I beg your pardon, don't be angry at me for not writing often
to you. I will always write to you that I am well. Now I write to
you about my success. My success is pretty good. I work always.
I have good work. I have worked in the store [*storze*] long years. I
am very lonesome, I do not hear the Polish language at all.[2] Here
are Poles who have been in America for many years, and therefore
they do not care for the Polish language. This girl whom I am going
to marry, they say she is Polish but I did not hear Polish language
from her.

I greet you fondly and sincerely, mother, father and sister, Aunt
Gricanowska and uncle and your children.

STANLY [*sic*] WINKOWSKY

---

[1] He still asks for a blessing, invites to his wedding, and informs that the girl
is Catholic. In so far the tradition persists, but only its form is left, for he would
not care at all if his mother forbade the marriage.

[2] Some traces of homesickness remain. His special longing for the Polish
language may be connected with the fact that he feels his isolation on account
of his poor English.

485
May 30, 1911

DEAR SISTER AND BROTHER-IN-LAW: I inform you that I am well and the same I wish to you. I greet your children.

Please answer who died and who got married.

Your brother,

S. W.

486
June 19, 1911

DEAR MOTHER, FATHER,[1] AND SISTER: I inform you that by the favor of God I am well and the same I wish to you. My success is very, very good. My address . . . .

S. A. WINKOWSKI

487
Day 10

DEAR MOTHER, SISTER, AND FATHER: I inform you that I received your letter. You write to me that I obtained great wealth after [the death of] my brother, but what is this wealth? I wrote to you that he left 300 dollars, so you may write to Kużeński and even to God himself, then he will tell you that I took 300 dollars. The funeral cost me 200 dollars, the hospital 38 dollars, carriages at the funeral 26, holy mass 16 dollars, the beer for treating 58 dollars, the coffin for him 28, the priest took 35 dollars, the cloth for the deceased 35, lawyer 50 dollars; Kużeński, in whose house he was, took 10 dollars. Now I erected a monument at my expense; it cost me 38 dollars.[2] I sent 75 dollars to the Chieleńskis, because he was her [Mrs. C.'s] real brother. I could not get anything because he was not our brother [only half-brother]. In the court they were saying that if you want to get his wealth then come over here. The journey will not cost you much [irony]. You know how much the trip cost me. Only bring a big bag [to hold the money], because I do not want anybody's money. I have enough of my own. So long as God grants

---

[1] His mother was probably married a second time; hence the addition of "father."

[2] Judging from the general vulgar ostentation and prevarication of the man we cannot accept this as an accurate enumeration of expenses, but the man evidently did conform to the *form* of the old familial attitude by arranging an elaborate funeral for a member of the family. This is a fundamental expression of the solidarity of the family and a sign of its social standing, and Winkowski does it, although his family feelings are almost dead.

me health I make 95 dollars a month. I am a boss [*bosza*] in a big store [*storze*]. You write to me whether I am married. Well, no, America is not the old country where it is necessary to marry for your whole life. Here it is not so.[1]

I beg your pardon dear mother and sister and father. In a short time I will come to you for a visit. I will not stay long with you, and I will go back. I will go to you with the daughter of my landlord. She can speak Polish a little.

I ask for a quick reply.

S. A. WINKOWSKI

488 EVELETH, MINN., March 29, 1912

BELOVED MOTHER, SISTER, AND FATHER: I inform you about my health. By the favor of God I am well, and the same I wish to you, and my success is pretty good. Therefore I inform you that the 10th of May I will be gone to another province, very far away. And what mother wrote me about this money which is for me, the lawyer wants 20 dollars from me for getting this money. I think that there is not any more than that.

I do not have anything to write. I remain, with good health.

S. A. WINKOWSKI

[1] Complete repudiation of the traditional idea of marriage—the more striking if compared with his rather normal attitude less than three years before.

INDIVIDUAL LETTERS AND FRAGMENTS OF LETTERS SHOWING THE DISSOLUTION OF FAMILIAL SOLIDARITY

The dissolution of familial solidarity is not always due exclusively to the member who has emigrated; it may also happen that the group ceases after a time to be interested in its absent member. Or it may happen that the group learns of some real or imaginary break of solidarity on the part of the absent member and repudiates him. In this respect we should remember that sometimes the act of emigration, and always a too prolonged stay abroad, constitute in themselves a break of solidarity. Often the reaction of the group (or of some of its members) is aroused by a false report about the absent member sent by someone from abroad. Gossip, which often forces the individual to remain a solidary member of the group, may become a factor of dissolution when it is false. Finally, it happens also that the emigration of a member of the family-group leads to a breakdown of familial attitudes in another member who stays at home, and whose situation, in consequence of the emigration of the first, becomes abnormal. Thus, for example, a wife left alone by her husband, a child left without the control of the father, become more easily demoralized.

Cases of these various kinds are given in the following.

489–98, ISOLATED LETTERS OR FRAGMENTS OF LETTERS

489

[The group repudiates the member, but the latter has not lost his feeling of solidarity.]

DETROIT, MICH., October 10, 1900

DEAR BROTHER: "Praised be Jesus Christus." . . . .

I inform you, dear brother, that I received your letter for which I thank you from my soul and my heart. May God help you the best possible. And now I inform you that I am in good health, thanks to God, and I wish you the same. And now I admonish you, as my brother, about what you wrote to me—that you will go voluntarily where you may be shot or hung. Remember rather the mercy of Jesus Christ and when this idea [of suicide] visits you, sigh to our Lord God, and it will be better for you.[1] The same ill luck presses heavily upon me also; I suffer poverty and hard words, and I don't know what will become of me, whether I shall ever see you again.

As to the matter which I mentioned to you, about my business, let the clear lightning strike her before she becomes my wife. It would be better for me to break hand and leg than to marry her. I write you so, dear brother, and you can believe me, it will be so. I have other matters in my head than such a crooked stick. And now, dear brother, you write me that paternal and maternal uncles, father and mother, brothers and sisters repudiate me. I don't mind myself; you can repudiate me, because I am an exile and a pilgrim, far away from you, from my father's land and my family, and therefore you repudiate me. Let God repay you all this, good for evil; let it be my wrong and not yours. I beg you, dear brother, salute in my name my parents and thank them that they deigned to repudiate me; but my conscience does not allow me to do it [repudiate them], and God would punish me heavily for it. I beg you for the second time, write a letter to our parents in your own hand in my name, and thank them for everything.[2] I won't forget you, only be patient, I beg you. And now I inform you that I shall send you for Christmas about 20 roubles and to Stasiulek I shall send also for Christmas 10 roubles and that will be all. And now pardon me, dear brother, for writing so poorly, but I have on this account [the bad news] drowned the worm pretty well, for I received your letter precisely on pay day, and I am writing this letter to you at $1\frac{1}{3}$ o'clock in the night.[3] And I bid you

---

[1] The inclination to suicide is very frequently expressed by the peasant in moments of discouragement, and the only reason preventing suicide from being particularly frequent is the religious fear of damnation, since the fear of death itself, as we have seen, is not very strong.

[2] The meekness manifested is not ironical, and is intended to provoke a reaction of compassion and remorse.

[3] The feeling of grief is compared to the gnawing of a worm, and "drowning the worm" is the usual popular expression for drinking in order to forget grief. Socially there is only one form of normal intoxication, that which takes place during ceremonies of any kind, where the purpose of drinking is to maintain a certain intensity of common feelings. But individually drinking has another function,

farewell, dear [brother].   Remain with the Lord God.   And I beg you, write letters to auntie and to our parents from yourself, for I will not write unless I receive an answer, because for 2 months already I have had no letter.   Goodbye.   I remain,

Your loving brother,
A. Rembiński

My address is such, the following one. . . . . Finis.   *Gut naj* [good night].

And I beg you answer the soonest possible and write, my brother, news from [illegible name] and the neighborhood.[1]

A. Remb.

490

[Demoralization of a wife in the absence of her husband.   The latter, in spite of his emigration, shows more familial feeling, even with regard to the children, than the wife.   The letter tends to establish a solidary relation between the husband and the rest of the family as against the wife.]

Letter written the 13th

"Praised be Jesus Christus." . . . .

And now, dear father, what does all this mean that you write me ? Why does my wife not wish to come to America, and writes me such stupid things that I am [illegible word] with her?   I have sent her a ship-ticket for all, and she writes me such silly things and is not ashamed of it.   When I sent the ticket I sent for all, and not for her alone. Could I leave the children ?   My heart does not allow me to leave my own children.   Then, dear father, if she does not wish to listen it will end badly for her.   Dear father, bow to her [ironically] and take the children to yourself, and I will send you directly two hundred roubles for the children, and let her do as she pleases.   And if not, then give

---

it becomes a substitute for action whenever a strong feeling is aroused and for some reason cannot find an immediate expression in activity.   For the eminently practical nature of the peasant a feeling which does not lead to action becomes unbearable, and he is not accustomed to find relief in aesthetic life or in a more or less long process of theoretic reflection which precedes or substitutes itself for action in intellectual people.

[1] The character of his writing shows that he is becoming more and more intoxicated.   He adds some meaningless and corrupted English and German words about "writing letters."

this ship-ticket to [sister] Kostka.   Let Kostka come with this ticket. She has only to give the name and the age of my wife.   Let her come with the children, and when Kostusia [Kostka] comes we will do well together, and my wife, as she was a public woman, so may she remain a public woman.   And if the children fear to go, please, father, take them to your home; I will send you 200 roubles.   Let her not make a fool of me in America, as if I were her servant; this is neither right nor necessary.   When someone read me that letter of hers, finally I did not let him finish, because I was ashamed.

If nobody comes with this ticket, I will get the money back and will send it directly to you, father, for the children.   And if not, let Kostusia come alone if the children don't want to come.

[B. Leszczyc]

491

[Example of the influence of gossip upon the attitude of the family-group toward the absent member.]

Natrona, Pa., December 29

. . . . Dear Parents: You write that I forget about you.   My dearest, my parents, forgive me, but I cannot write myself, and when you ask somebody to write you must go and treat him.   My dear parents, it was very painful for me when I learned—as Frek told me—that I am reveling so in America, that I throw ten roubles away at a baptism.   And I did not spend even ten grosz, because I had nothing to spend.   I had still a debt, and they [my creditors] looked angrily at me; how could I spend anything?   My dearest, my parents, I have had very sad holidays, even in the army I had no such sad holidays, and the first holidays that I had in America were not so sad as now.   I don't know whether something happened in our country, that I have been so sad.   Now I have nothing more to write, only I send you hearty wishes, my dearest, and I kiss the hands and feet of my dearest parents.

[Józek]

And now I, Helena, write to auntie.   Please, auntie, don't believe anybody, who says that Józek is such a reveler.   He did not throw away a single grosz.

Greetings from myself, and also from my man and children.

492

[Fragment of a letter showing the influence of gossip. Author unknown.]

I wrote you 2 letters, and you did not answer me. And now you write me to send you money, so I can send you a few roubles. One woman will go to our country, so you will receive a gift in a month. You ask me whether I will come home. Well, dear wife, we shall meet soon. Put out of your head [the idea] that I have a mistress here; I did not know that you are still so stupid. When I was in America the first time, I was younger, and did not commit this folly; should I commit it now? I should sooner have expected death than to hear this. Inform me who told you about it.

493

[Fragment of a letter showing the influence of gossip and the demoralization of children in the absence of the father.]

June 4, 1914

DEAR WIFE: I inform you that I am in good health, that I left my old place, because there was no work. I came then to Toledo and I have work. I sent you 20 roubles on June 2, because I had no more. You know that in the world it is indispensable to have some money with you. If God helps me, I will send you more. Here in America it begins now to be so that one does not work more than he works. Thousands of people go about without work. And as to our children, I cannot hear any more about it. Give them some of the broomstick and chase them away on the street, because they are so bad. And you I ask, don't write such letters to me any more, because otherwise I will stop writing to you at all.[1] Tell the man who told you all this that I will send him some roubles for beer in reward for it. Let him get drunk [again].

[1] Probably this expression of provocation has some history, and this is not the first complaint of the wife about the children, but we find frequent protests of this kind from peasants, about the communication of disagreeable facts. They say they do not want to be made sad. (Cf. No. 481.) Reflection is painful to the peasant, especially when he has no possibility of action, and by a sort of passive hedonistic selection he demands to be spared disagreeable news. Or he may resort to positive hedonistic selection, e.g., drink. Cf. No. 489, note 3.

494

[Fragment of a letter showing how familial solidarity is stronger than gossip.]

DEAR WIFE: Probably you have received the ship-ticket already; so you can prepare to leave. You know that people have told me bad things about your behavior, but to me it seems otherwise. I will forgive you all your wrongdoing. I only hope our life together may be good in the future. The bed-furnishings, whatever you have, bring with you, because here they are very expensive. And bring also your better dresses with you; the remainder can be left for the present. Put it into a trunk and let it lie there for some time. Conceal also my army-certificate. I will not send you money; manage as you can until you come to me. The agent said you will have no trouble about anything. Take with you a loaf of black bread—it is the best—and also some apples. I wrote you already how you may explain.

495

[Fragment of a letter showing some coldness between husband and wife as the result of emigration.]

June 16

DEAR WIFE: Why do you make such bad allusions to me? Do you know from what family I come? Did you not know whom you took? I have not worked for 7 months, and now times are so bad that in America it gets worse and worse. A lot of people come from our country, and here in America there is no work for them, and thousands walk about without work. But the people in our country imagine that when somebody comes to America he does nothing but make money. But here in America one must work for 3 horses, and yet this work is scarce. With this letter I send you some few złoty [a little money]. I send thirty roubles which you will have for your expenses. About the holiday of God's Mother [patron] of seed-time I will send you perhaps a ship-ticket and then you will come to me. As soon as you receive this letter and the money write me how many geese and young cattle and pigs you have already. Why is it so hard to persuade you to write letters? Is it so hard for you to write?

496   June 7, 1914

[Fragment showing the introduction of an outsider into family quarrels.]

I inform you, Sir, about my health. I am in good health, Mr. M., and I wish you the same. This Smoliniak went away with another man to New Britain, and they wrote about us that we robbed them and their sisters. So if you ever write [to them], as a man knowing our situation, be so kind and abuse them. And please write them the truth, what profit we had of them. When he was ill with his hand, I had his stove heated for 3 weeks, and during the whole time when he did not work he did not pay his [full] board but only $2 for his food. Mańka [his sister], as you know, remained [with him] for days and even weeks, and we asked nothing for it, only what we lent her. As to their education, you know the best about it. The big Sobieski stopped me in the street and asked me whether he was my cousin, and said that probably he was educated among cattle. Please tell him some day or other about it.

497

[The writer of the two following letters is the man referred to in the Raczkowski series, in connection with a quarrel with Adam Raczkowski. He came to America at a mature age and emigration produced hardly any change in his attitudes. The present letters are interesting because of the familial situation. Marriage with a Russian is, of course, forbidden by the community on account of both national and of religious considerations, and the family shares the standpoint of the community. In disowning the daughter, Ołów conforms to the expectation of the community and, as head of the family, orders his wife to do the same. It is true that in writing to his cousins, the Wolskis, he is asking for information, but he wants them, as family-members, to know of the situation, and he expects them to share his position, and invites their intrusion.]

[November, 1909]

MY DEAR WIFE: I received a letter from you which grieved me very much. But I beg you, don't grieve, because this grieving will not help us. If our daughter forsakes you, dear wife, as a good mother, and her father, who wanders about the world for her happiness, and if she despises all this, then nothing can be done. And when she comes from her wedding, from the Russian church, let her immediately go away just as she stands. And you, dear wife, I beg you, live where you are living, because I do not even know where to send my letter. And I inform you, dear wife, that I will soon be in our country. And now I beg you, don't grieve, you, my wife, and you, my daughter Zosia. I don't mention daughter Domicella, because she is not worth it.

I, your loving husband,

FRANCISZEK OŁÓW

I remain in good health, but in sorrow. That is a madness of one's reason! To fall off from God and to take hold of a man!

498   WILMINGTON, DEL., November 3, 1909

To that sad letter I answer: "In centuries of centuries. Amen."

DEAR SISTER [COUSIN]: Forgive me for not having written for so long a time, but you know that I wished to gather some roubles in order to send them back sooner. Now I will send the money very soon. And now, dear sister, I inform you and your husband that I am in good health, and I wish the same to you, dear [sister and] brother-in-law, and to your children. Now I request you, dear sister, and you, dear brother-in-law, inform me what is the news in my home, because I received a letter which grieved me much, that my daughter Domicella will get married, but forsakes her faith; and my wife writes me that she will not be at home, so I don't know, where she is to be. Dear sister and dear brother-in-law, Antoni, I beg you, tell me how this thing is, because I have nobody else to ask except you, dear sister. So I beg you heartily, inform me what has become of my wife and my dear daughter Zosia, because I no longer ask about my daughter Domicella. Since she forsakes God and her parents I cannot even ask about her. I am a wanderer in a strange land for the sake of my children, and hear through a letter that my daughter forsakes her faith and her parents. I wanted to go, but I have money only for my debt, and I must still earn for my journey. If God grants me work and health I will be soon in our country. I have nothing more to write. [Usual ending.]

FRANCISZEK OŁÓW

CORRESPONDENCE BETWEEN HUSBANDS AND WIVES

In this connection we find a great variety of problems, but the common problem in all the series of letters is that of the constitution of what may be termed a "natural" family, i.e., a family based, not upon social traditional attitudes, but only upon the actual relations between its members, and therefore practically limited to a married couple with their children; it is the family as elementary social group of the classical sociological theory. It proves here to be the result of a relatively late social evolution. As the older form of familial unity, in which the family embraced relatives up to the fourth or fifth degree (without very clearly determined limits), decomposes under the influence of new conditions, its parts enter into the composition of different territorial, professional, sometimes national and religious groups, and thus their former connection is loosened. Simultaneously an evolution goes on within each of these parts—each elementary group of married couple+children; the reciprocal relations of its members undergo a change. This may perhaps be best expressed in the following way: As long as the familial group was constituted by all the relatives on the sides of both husband and wife, the fundamental conjugal norm was that of "respect," because the married pair was not an isolated couple related only as individuals, but in them and through them their respective families were united, and the dignity of these families was involved in the conjugal relation. When this large family is dissociated, the fundamental conjugal norm becomes that of love and reciprocal confidence, because the relation is a purely personal one. In the larger family the children were not merely children of the given couple, but in a sense belonged to the family as a whole, and the parents, particularly the father, represented the total group with regard to them, and was to some extent responsible for them before the group. Hence the relation between parents and children was one of authority and obedience, and bore at the same time a certain impersonal character, precisely because it lacked exclusiveness, for the children as members of the larger group had a quality which put them partly outside of the smaller group. The isolation of the latter brought new forms of interior life; the parents' authority and the children's obedience became personal, not social, attitudes, and the individualization called for a new norm— that of reciprocal personal affection.

The Polish peasant is now on the way from the older form of familial life to the new one, and we find in the present volume the two forms mixed in various proportions. But since in the new form individual factors play a much more important part than in the old one, the strength and harmony of familial life begin to depend in a much larger measure upon such factors as character, intellectual development, sentimental refinement, etc. Thus we find examples of a stronger or weaker connection between the members of the new marriage-group, of a more or less perfect harmony in the life of this group, of its more or less solidary behavior with regard to the external world, etc.

In arranging the materials we place first those in which the marriage-group is shown as being merely a part of the family, and later those in which the "natural family" is definitely constituted.

PAWLAK SERIES

The conjugal relation is here very impersonal. There are only a few rather insignificant expressions of affection; business, news about children and relatives constitute the content of the letters. The detailed account which the wife gives of all expenses and other matters of business is significant. In these matters she takes only provisionally the place of her husband as manager of the property which is the basis of the living of the family, and in this respect her position is settled; nothing can be changed. In striking contrast with this behavior stands the fact that she has evidently bought a house, in her own name, with money sent her by the husband. Here a traditional attitude has not yet been sufficiently established with regard to the new property and the money for which it was bought, for the money was earned in a new way—by emigration. Of course the simplest conclusion would be that the rôle of the woman should remain the same, because the new problem is an economic problem like the old ones. But we know that the peasant sees qualitative differences where the economist finds mere quantities, and these qualitative differences in the present case are great enough to lead to a new attitude.

499–505, JÓZEFA PAWLAK, IN POLAND, TO HER HUSBAND, IN AMERICA

499   BUDZIWOJ, August 15, 1912

. . . . DEAR HUSBAND: I received your letter, from which I learned about your dear health and success. We are all in good health. The children long awfully for you. When you went away I could not calm them; they cried so that they almost became sick. Józuś asks always where is father and whether he won't come.

Władzio is already beginning to walk. Anielcia had a good school-certificate and will go to the second class. Franek was at his first confession and communion and will go to the third class. Now you ask how much rye I have harvested. Well, I have harvested 5 kopa [1 kopa = 60 pieces, here sheaves] and 19 sheaves, and of barley 2 kopa and 12 sheaves. I put it into the barn of Ignacy Pasek and I paid him 5 crowns, and the driving cost me 3 gulden, I drove 5 times [carts] of dung. The vegetables cost me 3 renski [gulden]. After the harvest I drove dung again [into the field] 5 times, and it cost 2 renski and 1 szóstka. For the fine I paid 3 renski.[1] The cow gives little milk, because I have no good pasture. I received money from you. Now I inform you that Kustra plagues me much about money [debt]. I should like to buy rye and wheat for sowing. I have spent 15 renski from this money. I have sold that pig. God keep us from such pigs! I took 9 renski for it. You are angry with me for not having answered you. But how could I answer since I received no letter? The money came 3 weeks before the letter, and I was very anxious. Write me whether I should pay for my letters [stamp them] or not . . . . and write me where you are boarding. . . . .

Now I kiss you, most beloved husband.

Your wife,

Józefa Pawlak

500   September 22, 1912

. . . . Now, dear husband, I inform you that I received the money, 102 and 5 crowns. I gave the 5 crowns to mother, as you intended, and the 100, with interest, I paid back to Pieta, for Kustra refused to accept them. She wants all the debt at once. Now, dear husband, you ask me for what fine I paid 3 renski. Well, for what was imposed upon us when the cattle were sick, for you had lost that paper which we received from the *starosta* [chief of district] and I had no proof. I had to pay because they wanted to inscribe [levy on] my cow. Dear husband, I inform you that Magdusia [the husband's sister] intends to go to America. Will you allow me to sell

---

[1] This paragraph shows the extreme complexity of the peasant's counting—the result of a combination of old Polish units with those imposed by the foreign government. In this particular case a new source of complication is the substitution of crowns for gulden, introduced in Austria in the past century. The old units are kept by the peasants.

the cow? For she is so bold that I cannot manage her. She runs away whenever she wants to and goes wherever she will, and does damage to other people, and I must pay. I would sell her and buy some older one; perhaps she would be gentler. Now, I have not yet sown the rye, for it has rained during the whole month and nothing could be done. I have nothing more to write, only I greet you kindly and heartily innumerable times. May I see you soon again! Franuś, Anielcia, Józio, and Władzio kiss the hands of their dear father. . . . .

JÓZEFA PAWLAK

501   January 6 [1913]

. . . . Now, dear husband, I received 250 crowns from you on January 2, for which I thank you heartily. I gave back to the Kustras the sum with interest. They took 12 renski of interest. I have threshed the grain; Wojciech Kret threshed for me. I got 4½ korce [18 bushels] of rye and 4 of barley. The threshing cost me 7 renski and 20 cents [kreuzer]. I have ground in the mill 2 korce of rye and ¾ of barley. For threshed barley I gave mother those 5 crowns which you ordered, and I invited her for Christmas eve, but she did not come; she would have come, but Magdusia did not wish it. . . . . I have bad times now for I have no firewood. I have burned all, and it is far to the forest, difficult to drive, and I have little money left. . . . .

[JÓZEFA]

502   May 18, 1913

. . . . DEAR HUSBAND: I received your letter and 175 renski. I gave mother 5 crowns, and 22½ renski [45 crowns] were left for me. I have spent it all, for I bought dung at 60 cents; I could get it cheaper nowhere. . . . . I had 10 wagons of my own and I bought 10. . . . . Now, dear husband, I wrote you for advice, what to do with this house which is for sale, and you answered me neither so nor otherwise. Now people give [offer] for it 530 renski. It seems to me too expensive, but if you order, dear husband, I shall buy it for this money, because it would be good for us. But if you don't order, I won't buy. But there are people who will buy it, for there are buyers enough. Now, dear husband, upon my land I planted potatoes and I left one bed for cabbage. I gave one bed to mother, and I rented two from Lasota and Pasek. As to the crops, they are very nice; we have also beautiful rye and wheat and barley and clover. Now I inform you that the cow stands in the stable, for they don't let her go upon the manorial pasture and I don't know what will be, how I shall keep her until the harvest, for I have nowhere to pasture her.[1] Moreover I have got a calf, and now it is impossible to get even a handful of grass from the manorial land, for they guard it day and night. . . . .[2]

JÓZEFA PAWLAK

503   November 23, 1913

DEAR HUSBAND: . . . . I have already bought that house. I agreed at 530 and I gave them 400. The contract is settled. I paid 13 renski, and 30 cents for the stamps, and I must still give 130 renski. So send them to me. You ordered me to borrow 200 renski from mother, but she did not give them to me, for she had none. She had lent to Kondratka, for you did not mention anything in your letter to her and she did not know. [Enumerates house expenses.] You ordered me to borrow a machine for straw-chopping, but I did not take it for I have no money. . . . . The pig keeps well enough, but I won't drive it [to the fair] until St. Paul's Day [June 29]. The cow and calf keep well also. Pasek will sell two morgs [of land] quite near this house which we bought. If we could buy at least half a morg, then even if a hen ran about there she would be upon our own land. Pitera is very angry with me for having bought this house and threatens me very much. . . . .[3]

JÓZEFA PAWLAK

[1] The permission to send cattle to the manorial pasture, when not a right of common, is sometimes granted personally by the manor-owner as a reward for some service or as help. Sometimes the arrangement is tacit, but after some time the fact becomes custom and is claimed as a right. A change of manor-owners or officials often leads to serious troubles.

[2] Cutting of manorial grass for the cow, carrying of dry wood from the manorial forests, gathering of mushrooms, berries, nuts, is not considered as in any case reprehensible. But little reprehension is attached to such acts as *cutting* of wood, stealing fruit or vegetables, letting the cattle damage the crops, etc., wherever the damage is done to a manor-owner, not to a neighbor-peasant. Cf. Introduction: "Economic Life."

[3] The peasants in Galicia are more attached to land and more unwilling to move from the country to the towns than in any other part of Poland. Perhaps the slight development of industry is one of the causes. Owing to emigration there is relatively more ready money than purchasable land. So the price of land is enormous, and the rivalry between buyers assumes the extravagant forms exemplified in this letter.

504   March 1, 1914

DEAR HUSBAND: In the first words of my letter I speak to you, dearest husband, with these words: "Praised be Jesus Christus and the Holiest Virgin Mary, glorious through the whole world." May She be with you, dearest husband.

[Generalities about health and success.] I received 320 crowns, from which I gave 20 crowns to mother and 260 crowns I must give to Pasek for this land and house which we bought; 40 crowns will be left for me. I bought 1 korzec of rye for 20 crowns, and I had to give 12 crowns, 20 heller on account of that land which we had bought before from Dala. The notary with whom we made the contract is dead, and they did somewhere some cheating. The successors have now divided the land and for the expense of this division I had to give these 12 crowns. Now you ask in whose name I made this contract about this house. Well, I have written you so many letters asking you whether I should buy it or not, why did you not write me in whose name to do it? [Farming details.] Now, dear husband, you write me to move into this house. But I won't move until you come, for I am afraid lest somebody should do me some harm, for it is near the road. I admitted as lodger Józef Pieskiewicz, the tailor. He will pay me 40 crowns a year. I shall pluck the fruit from the orchard, and he can plant potatoes for himself in the beds which are there. . . . .

JÓZEFA PAWLAK

505   April 17, 1914

DEAR HUSBAND: . . . . You write me that your leg bites [aches] you. Well, I cannot help you, for if you were at home we would find some help for it. Only I advise you that there are doctors, so don't grudge money but go to a doctor; perhaps he will help you. And don't put on leeches lest something bad should happen with your leg. [Farm-work, crops, etc.]

Our children learn well, they don't ever omit the classes. . . . . Józuś will go to church in the summer when it is warm, for if I took him in winter he would catch cold. Władzio cannot yet cross himself, but tries already to do it. [Farm-work; marriages and deaths.]

JÓZEFA PAWLAK

KUKIEŁKA SERIES

The familial character of marriage viewed from the husband's side is depicted in the letters of this series. It is difficult to establish whether in this case the relation is really closer than in that of the Pawlaks. At any rate the letters show much more eagerness to keep the familial solidarity and manifest greater claims on familial affection than those of Pawlak's wife, and it seems that Kukiełka's wife is also less interested in the questions of familial solidarity than her husband. If we compare these facts with the situations found in other series (for example, the Markiewicz series), where the wife evidently does not share her husband's familial attitude, and with other cases where the wife seems rather passive and the husband even writes all the familial letters (Stelmach, Cugowski), a general conclusion seems to present itself: As it is primarily the man, not the woman, who represents and understands the group standpoint, in marriage-groups based upon the familial organization the conjugal affection is maintained much more through the husband than the wife. The attitude of the latter is always personal, and she is never satisfied with being treated by her husband merely as a member of the group with certain functions to perform, and not as an individual. Therefore, after a shorter or longer time, she turns her affection toward her children and becomes often almost indifferent toward her husband, because in the case of the children her individualistic affection finds an easier response. This enables her afterward to assume the rôle of a mediator between her husband and her children when the latter develop an individualistic attitude. (Cf. Osiński series.) Meanwhile the husband shows the same unchanging kind and degree of attachment as prescribed by the organization of the family. Of course the sexual factor must exert a powerful if unconscious influence upon the conjugal relation, but it is not consciously allowed to interfere with the social and moral side of this relation.

The respective rôles of husband and wife change, as we shall see, as soon as marriage becomes an individual matter.

There is no contradiction between the lack of familial solidarity in the married woman and the solidarity which an unmarried girl shows toward her parents, brothers, sisters, and relatives. The unmarried girl has no particular familial function to perform and hence her personal affection to individual members of the family can still easily fit into the familial organization.

506–9, JAN KUKIEŁKA, IN AMERICA, TO HIS WIFE, IN POLAND

506   August 9, 1911

[A page and a half of the usual greetings, wishes, and generalities about health.] Now I inform you, dearest little wife, about what you ask, whether Mańka shall go to Warsaw, although she is the daughter of a farmer. Well, I answer you that she is not to go, because I do not allow this.[1]   Now, as to our son Antoni, with him it's

---

[1] Going to Warsaw means going to serve as a housemaid. The father forbids it as contrary to the peculiar dignity of a farmer as against a landless peasant. We find the same aversion to any hired work for wives. This aversion is weakened, without disappearing, when the child or the wife has to go, not to a Polish estate or city, but abroad—to Germany or to America. Sending children to hired work in the country is not suitable for a farmer who has some 10 morgs of land, while only rich farmers, owning 20 to 30 morgs, consider it below their dignity to send their children to Germany. Evidently the reason of this difference is that the work abroad has some characters of novelty which make the application of traditional inhibitions to it less natural and immediate. Further, the inhibition is not so strong with regard to boys as to girls, not so strong with regard to girls as to wives, and in the process of industrial evolution the first has almost disappeared. But it seems still to be instinctively held with regard to the oldest son or, more exactly, to the son who is to take his father's farm. It is certainly neither by mere sentiment nor by rational calculation that the son who is destined to take the farm is more unwillingly allowed to go to hired work than other sons. The aversion to hired work cer-

going very badly, and in this way, that he does not keep his work, and is without a cent at all, and if anybody says anything to him, he does not listen at all, but is ready to fight. What can be done with such a boy? You can understand, dearest little wife, that it would be quite unsuitable for me to give him money, because you know yourself that I must think of you all, and it would be too much if I had still to have difficulties with him or to be concerned with his difficulties. When I sometimes predicted to him [the bad consequences of his behavior] he took pains not to meet me at all. What more can I do? I inform you however that he is in good health; that is all that I can tell you, dearest little wife.[1] I inform you also, dearest little wife, that I will send you about 100 roubles after some days. So don't answer this letter, because after some days another will come, and then you will answer both. Now I want to say this also, my dear little wife, that I am very much pleased with your doing good farming for me, and keeping the boars, sows, and pigs, and with your having harvested the crops. I am very much pleased with this letter, dearest little wife.[2] Now I inform you about my work. I work in a

---

tainly goes back to the time when the work away from the familial farm was mainly servage work; but this is hardly sufficient by itself to explain the facts. We must take into consideration the distinction, pointed out elsewhere, between farm-income and income from hired labor, the latter being additional and destined primarily to cover such expenses as in the peasant's economy are relatively new, while the farm-income is the essential basis of living of the whole family. All these facts are explained if we remember that economic organization is determined by familial organization. The essentially familial property is the hereditary farm, and against this the money earned outside represents the more individual form of property. Wages, being a relatively recent phenomenon, cannot be as completely subordinated to the familial standpoint as land and land-income, even if their subordination is manifested by the demand that earned money be turned over to the family. Therefore, hired work is felt as particularly unsuitable for those whose connection with the main familial group is particularly close, while a certain relaxation of the inhibition is natural for the members who will sooner or later establish a new branch of the family.

[1] Particularly rapid emancipation of the boy. The father's authority is not sufficient when not supported by the whole family-group and community.

[2] The farm-work done by the wife is presented here as meritorious and as if it were done for the husband and deserved his particular gratitude. This attitude seems contrary to the familial principle, according to which there is no division of property between husband and wife because there is no private property. Kukiełka is also evidently conservative and it is improbable that he would occupy an individualistic standpoint. The explanation is connected with the situation

brick-factory and earn very good money, that is, $2.70 for 13 hours. The work is very heavy, but I don't mind it; let it be heavy, but may it last without interruption. The brick-factories are going all right during the summer but in winter they stop, and I am afraid of it. But let it be as our Lord God sends it. When that day comes, some way will be found. Now I have nothing more to write, only I may add that in America there have been enormous fevers, for some days thousands. . . . [End of the letter missing.]

[Jan Kukiełka]

507   January 6, 1912

[Two pages of greetings, wishes, reproaches, and justifications about writing or not writing letters.] Now, dearest little wife, as to what you write about sending a ship-ticket for [our daughter] Mańka, it is so: As to the ship-ticket, it does not matter much, but I mind most this: If I take Mańka, what will you do there, dearest little wife? You know yourself that she is of great help to you. That is one thing. And secondly I mind that the girl will be very sad and will suffer misery. Here in America it is not the same as in our country. What if she does come to me? She cannot remain with me, but must go into service, and in the service it is necessary to learn the English language, and even to learn washing and cooking. Then there will be misery and weeping, because somebody speaks and you can only look at him. If you want it exceedingly I will send [the ticket], but then don't blame me. Now I inform you also, dearest little wife, that after this letter I will send you some roubles, so wait some days before you answer.

The loving father of our children,[1]

[Jan Kukiełka]

508   December 30, 1913

. . . . And now, dear wife and daughters, write to me, when do you think it best for me to return home? On Easter or at some other time? And now I greet you, dear wife and daughters, and I

---

outlined in the first note on this letter. The husband's emigration and the hired work he is doing, even if necessitated by the situation, are still formally a departure from his familial duty, which would oblige him to remain on the farm. The wife by doing his work performs his duty and is therefore entitled to gratitude. Their arrangement is personal even if its object—farm-work—is familial.

[1] Curious expression of the familial attitude.

greet my dear sisters Katarzyna, Rozalia, Maryanna, with their husbands and children. And now I greet the whole household of father-in-law, father and mother and brothers-in-law. And now, dear wife, I inform you [send you this] through the Mrozys [who are returning], and I send you 4 roubles for your expenses. Buy for yourself, Rózia, a white waist and for Nastusia and Jagusia shawls that you may have them for summer when I come home. And now dear wife, tell my sister Rozalia Figlisz not to allow her daughter Marysia to marry Bzdziuch, because no good will come of it. As the father, so is the son, as the tree, so is the wedge. And then it is a near family, and therefore God will not bless such a marriage, because there are enough people in the world.[1] If she does not believe my words let her be persuaded by the example of those who married their relatives. As a good brother, I admonish Sister Rozalia, let her not do it, what she intends to do. [More greetings for the whole family.]

Your husband,
Jan Kukiełka

Gut bai [goodbye]. It means *do widzenia*. [More wishes of divine blessing for the whole family.] I will ask you only, don't ever quarrel with sister Maryanna, don't abuse her, don't let the children laugh at her, God forbid you this! But on the contrary, as a good mother, you ought more than once to buy either bread or sugar or [illegible word] and to give them to herself and her children, and God will be satisfied with your life and will bless you.[2] [More greetings.]

509 February 15 [1914]

Letter from husband Jan to his wife Rozalia. In the first words of my letter I speak to you, dear wife, with those words that are pleasant to you: "Praised be Jesus Christus" and I hope that you will answer me, "For centuries of centuries. Amen."

And now I inform you, dear wife, that I received your letter on February 13, for which may God reward you, that you wrote me about your dear health and success.[3] And now I inform you, dear

---

[1] God does not need an increase in population badly enough to bless with children a marriage of this kind.

[2] The whole letter is a notable expression of familial solidarity.

[3] The beginning is particularly formal, preparatory to the scolding which is to follow. His masculine vanity is particularly offended by the lack of respect shown in connection with the photograph, especially as the wife of the other man behaved better in this respect.

wife, that that letter did not please me at all, because I asked you to write me when I should come, and you did not answer me, as if you were not my own wife but a cook or some other hired woman   And now I inform you, that you wrote twice for me to send you my photograph, you gave me no peace.   To tell the truth, I did not even wish it, but when you wrote once and then once more, I was obliged to send you the photograph.   But it was expensive for me alone, so I asked my companion, and this cost us cheaper.   My companion sent one at once to our country, and they answered him and thanked him very much, but when I sent it I did not even get an answer.   Such is the gratitude I got.   I had thought that I left a good wife at home, but I was disappointed; the husband is far away.   I wrote letters as to a wife, but I did not receive any good answers for them.   When I was a little boy with my parents I was glad and happy, I had whatever I wished, and now I have a wife who does not even write to me about my daughters.   Such is the reward for one's goodness.

And now, dear wife, you write me that Józef, your brother, writes about those few roubles, asking for them.   So I write you, dear wife, you may write to him that I will send him those few roubles, but only when I am at home.   Now I will not send money home because I need it for my journey, and what is left I will give back.   And now you write, that you have no milk.   Do you think that I have it? You have rye for bread, 10 korcy, and I must buy bread; you have a house, and I must pay rent, 7 roubles a month, and so my work goes on.   And now, dear wife, you write that you have a fat pig [ready] to be killed, so I advise you, if they pay you well, you can sell him, if pigs are dear; but if they are cheap, don't sell.   [End missing.]

[JAN KUKIEŁKA]

JANKOSKI SERIES

A typical conjugal relation upon the familial basis is shown in this series. The wife is a substitute for the husband, performing economic functions; there is a lack of personal interests; the husband's father and wife's sister are in solidary co-operation with the marriage-group.

510–11, FROM SZYMON JANKOSKI, IN AMERICA, TO HIS WIFE, IN POLAND

510   PERTH AMBOY, N.J., August 11, 1913

[Usual greetings and wishes.] And now, dear wife, I inform you about my success, that my success is good enough because I have work and I work every day. Dear wife, if you find an opportunity to buy [a farm] somewhere for about 700 roubles, then buy it, I request you, dear wife and dear father, for the money that is in the bank there, and if some more is needed, write to me. Dear wife and dear father, if you have the opportunity to buy somewhere near a manor, then buy it, either in Chojnowo or in Obrębiec or in Czernice, because it is always better to buy near a manor than somewhere far away, as there is the possibility of earning something. And now, dear wife and dear father, what you write about money, that I might send you, so deprive yourselves of it for some time yet, dear wife and dear father, because now I shall send you none, as it is not worth sending some cents. I have money but I am not willing to send these few cents. I will send you later and more at once, then you will know that you have received [something] and I shall know that I have sent the money. And so I will send you later, but then about 200 roubles. Now, dear wife, I request you to go to Obrębiec, to call on the Adamskis and to ask them the address of their son, and send me this address to America. Now I have nothing more to write but to greet you, dear wife, lovingly and heartily. I greet Stasiek and Antoś, and I greet dear father. [Greetings from some friends.]

[SZYMON JANKOSKI]

Now I request you, dear reader, if you cannot read what I wrote here, do not answer, because I did not learn in a school, but in a barn; so write me, dear reader, did you read it or not.[1]

511   May 13, 1914

. . . . And now I greet you, dear wife, and you, my dear children, I greet you all with those godly words, "Praised be" [etc.]. And now I inform you that I received the letter from you for which I thank you very kindly, dear wife, and you, dear children. And now I inform you, dear wife, that I sent you 20 roubles on the 5th of May. I would have sent you more but my finger was wounded. For three weeks I have not been able to work, and I don't know how it will be further. Now, thanks to God and to God's Mother, this finger does not pain me so much.

And now you ask me, dear wife, how much money Walerka [probably wife's sister] earns, in America. Well, do you know, dear wife, that I spent for her more than $60, and from her wages I have not a cent. She served with a certain master and mistress for a month and they did not give her a cent for all this work of hers, and so $14 was lost. And now, I thank you, dear wife for buying this land, and I request you, dear wife, to describe to me how did you succeed with that business, and what about that annuity? Is it already finished or not? I request you, describe all this. You write, dear wife, about that Stasiek, whether you may take him or not. I leave it to your choice. If you are attached to him take [adopt?] him. And now I inform you, dear wife, that I will send you presently the attorney's power. And now I thank you, dear son, that you don't wish to come to America, because now in America there is terrible poverty. It [work] goes badly. I have nothing more to write, I only wish you all health, happiness and good success; what you wish for yourself from our Lord God and God's Mother, and I ask you for a speedy answer. *Got naj* [good night].

SZYMON JANKOSKI

[1] This is a rhyme in the original, and is proverbial.

ŁAZOWSKA SERIES

The general background of the conjugal relation is here still familial; common interests (children, management of the property) are still the main link between husband and wife, and other members of the family (grandfather, uncle) are still closely connected with the marriage-group. But already some changes can be noticed. The woman's affection for her husband and her grief over her daughter's death seem to be a little stronger than the mere familial connection requires in spite of the fact that she seems to lack the ability of expression. Again, the solidarity of the family is no longer so strong as it should be according to tradition, as is shown by the relative estrangement of the daughter in America.

512–17, FROM MARYANNA ŁAZOWSKA AND CHILDREN, IN POLAND, TO HER HUSBAND AND FAMILY-MEMBERS, IN AMERICA

512   PRZASNYSZ, November 27 [1913]

"Praised be Jesus Christus!" [etc.]

[Health; letter received.] You write me, dear husband, that I forbid you to come to our country. I don't forbid [dissuade] you at all, you may come at any moment, you have your own reason. Don't think that I live here luxuriously with these children. I buy only what they need absolutely. Why, they go to school, the girl goes to sewing [learns sewing]. She has still the same jacket. I only had new overcoats made for the boys. It was absolutely necessary, for now it is very cold. I must buy books and hefts for them. . . . . When one of them had no book the teacher told him not to come to the school. You see yourself how bad it is for you not to be able to write. Why, I don't pay for the school; this means much also. And then the shoes cost me much; we are 6 persons to be shod for winter.

I don't spend a single grosz in vain.   It seems to you that you have sent me much money.   But I have paid so many debts.   I have only trouble with these children, for they don't ask whether I have money or not, but require me to give them.   I know myself that you are working hard, you don't need to admonish [remind?] me, for I did not buy anything for myself.   [Food prices; news about pigs and cow.]   Now, dear husband, I wish you a Merry Christmas.   It would be better if we were together; it would rejoice us more. . . . . In going to bed and in rising remember us always, dear husband.[1]

Your most loving wife,

MARYANNA ŁAZOWSKA

513   January 29, 1914

. . . . DEAR [BROTHER] BOLEK: I inform you about my grief. When you wrote a letter and asked how many there are of our family, she spoke and asked us to write about her also.[2]   She fell sick with measles, then she got inflammation of the lungs.   There were doctors, but they could not save her.   She was awfully clever, it is difficult to relate.[3] . . . . I am terribly pained.   If it were by land, I would go afoot to America. . . . . Grandfather despairs continually after Henka's death and he cannot forget her cleverness.   His health has got very bad; he cannot work and says that he will die soon.

[1] This request tends unconsciously to assimilate the familial and the religious attitudes.   The moments after the end and before the beginning of the daily work are evidently the ones most favorable to an undisturbed and purely sentimental remembrance of home or God in a workman's life.   At the same time the periodical character of this remembrance would tend to make of it both a habit and a duty. We understand better the meaning of this request if we remember that the normal life of the peasant is fully practical and always determined by the actual situation. Reflection and remembrance require in him a particular effort and an almost absolute freedom of mind and body.   Therefore he carefully selects the time and place of reflection or remembrance and makes for these acts a self-conscious, intentional, and sometimes ridiculously ceremonial preparation.   (See Part IV.)   As in letter-writing reflection and remembrance are combined, the same care is shown in the preparation for it.

[2] The meaning is that her anxiety not to be omitted in the enumeration of the members of the family was a foreboding of her death.

[3] Normal idealization after death.   In children it is usually intelligence which is thus idealized, in grown-up persons, character.   Perhaps this idealization in general is an unconscious attempt to justify individual grief when it goes beyond the limit assigned by the social regulation of the attitude toward death.   At any rate it is an attempt to give *objective* reasons for subjective grief.

As to the air [weather], up to the present we had frost, but now it does not freeze any more.

We salute and greet you together with your wife and children. She died on January 19, and was buried on January 20.

MARYANNA ŁAZOWSKA

514   March 20, 1914

. . . . DEAR UNCLE: What does it mean that we have no letter? We have had no letter since December 5. What does it mean? Are they [the father and oldest sister] dead, or what? We wrote 3 letters and we had no answer to any of them. When Henka died we wrote a letter, but there was no answer. So please, uncle, write a letter at our cost—we will pay for it—and describe kindly what is going on, for we don't know, because we have no letter. We beg you for God's sake, tell us how it is. If somebody is sick there, describe everything. What happened with our father, that he does not deign to write a letter? When Genia [the oldest sister] was leaving, mother admonished her not to forget about letters. And she does not even deign to write a letter. We wonder how can a daughter be so mean.[1] So please, uncle, read them this letter. But perhaps they are no more alive. Then, please, describe to us kindly everything. Only we beg you for a speedy answer. We bow to you, uncle and auntie, and to all our acquaintances. We wish you a merry Easter. *Alleluiah!* The end.

[ŁAZOWSKA'S CHILDREN]

515   April 10, 1914

. . . . DEAR HUSBAND AND DAUGHTER: We received your letter, for which we thank you heartily, and the money also. Dear husband, Henka is dead.[2] She fell sick on January 5. . . . . There was one doctor and another and they tried to save her, and she wanted to live. Everything, whatever the doctor prescribed, she took everything. She had 40 cupping-glasses applied. In the last moment, dear daughter, she kissed your photograph, and kissed me on the face,

---

[1] The daughter evidently has not a much-developed familial feeling, or perhaps the fact that she is in America with her father and uncle accounts for her lack of longing for home.

[2] Her first letter with news of the death was evidently not received by the husband, who heard of it through the letter to the brother-in-law.

raised her eyes on high and died. She finished her wandering here and went to eternity, to the Mother and to her Lord. But for me it is a terrible burden, for I loved her and she loved me. When I enter into the house, it is as sad for me as in a den. We grieved because we had no letter, we thought that you were dead. As to the weather in our country, it is so wet that one could drown dogs. In gardens water stands, it is impossible to sow or to plant. Many people died this year. Dear husband and dear daughter, we have sad holidays this year, it is difficult even to describe to you my sad experience of this year. I was in Mława, to buy seeds; I spent 50 roubles. . . . . Grandfather is also impaired in health and cannot work. I thank you heartily for the dollar. Remember, dear husband, not to forget about letters. . . . . Grandmother also grieves that uncle does not write.

[MARYANNA ŁAZOWSKA]

Dear father, what shall mother do with me, for I shall go to the school only till vacation, and mother does not know where to give me [in apprenticeship].

Mother is very angry with you [Genia] for not even sending a bow to the Morawiankis, for when the letter comes they always ask whether you send greetings for them.

[WACEK]

516

April 23, 1914

. . . . DEAR HUSBAND: We are in good health, only grandfather is sick. He made a will, for he is in danger of life. He has willed me everything. This happened on April 22. I am to pay 100 roubles to the B.'s. . . . . So I beg you, dear husband, send me money, for it cost me already some 15 roubles. And I am writing already the sixth letter, and I have an answer to none. You see, dear husband, what difficulties and expenses I have; as soon as one is finished, another comes. So I beg you, send me this debt, for they may make a complaint against me, particularly she. Dear husband, nothing rejoices me [not even this will], for I have not my dear daughter. Wherever I go I am sad. At every moment I think about her and about you.

As to the air, it is warm. There is work to be done, and nobody to work, for grandfather is ill. Fences must be repaired and potatoes planted. The prices are very high in our country . . . . and work is difficult to get; only craftsmen can earn. . . . .

Now, dear daughter, I am writing to you. Why do you not write letters to us? Everybody wonders why do you not write. You know how to write and don't write. This makes me wonder much. I had sad holidays. When you were here it was not so sad, for I had always a companion. Grandfather bids you farewell, for perhaps he won't see you any more. . . . .[1] It is difficult to describe to you my experience which I had this year [the daughter's death].

MARYANNA ŁAZOWSKA

517 June 1, 1914

. . . . DEAR HUSBAND: You write that you earn only for your living. Then come back to our country. Enough of this America. You write that you earn only enough for your own living; but who will earn for us? If you earn only for your own living, I cannot earn for mine. Wacek went to the first confession.

And you, dear daughter, you send only bows. Can you not write with your own hand, that you send only bows, as to strangers? Why, I am not your *kuma;* only a *kuma* sends bows for her *kuma.* When you were not in America I did not wonder that uncle wrote father's letters. But you are now with your father, you ought to write letters. You know how to write, only you don't want to. I was glad that I received a letter but I read it and, see here, from my daughter I have nothing but a bow!

Grandfather has been in bed for six weeks, I don't know whether he will recover. He dried out, he cannot eat any more. And thus I have such experiences and troubles this year. I have sown the garden myself. I have nothing but work and trouble. . . . .

Why, I asked you, dear husband, what to do, and had no answer. Grandfather is sick, money is needed, work must be done, and here there is nobody to work. For here a man is needed. So consider it and come. For it is impossible to live without somebody to work. . . . .

MARYANNA ŁAZOWSKA

Dear father, mother bought me a suit at the fair.

[WACEK]

---

[1] The grandfather's imminent death evidently provokes no grief because of his age. The social normality of death is increased with advancing age, to such an extent that life beyond certain limits becomes an anomaly.

OLSZAK SERIES

The old solidarity of the family-group has not yet been superseded, but there is a marked beginning of the isolation of the marriage-group. Real personal love is expressed in the letters of the wife. The connection between the marriage-group and the rest of the family is relatively loosened, particularly in the case of the wife's family. But here again it is the husband who is more conservative in his familial attitudes. It is he who tries to re-establish a closer connection between his wife and her parents and sisters. Though he may be moved in this case more particularly by the desire to help his wife, this is certainly not his reason for asking his cousin not only to help but also to control her.

518–21, TO PIOTR OLSZAK, IN AMERICA, FROM WIFE
AND FAMILY-MEMBERS, IN POLAND

518   November 12, 1913

. . . . DEAR HUSBAND: [Health and success.] In my field [cousin] Jakób worked $2\frac{1}{2}$ days with a single horse and then one day with two horses. He has not been paid at all and he will wait till you send him something, because I borrowed 25 [gulden] of money and bought a calf. I borrowed this money from Kólupa. And Jakób bought me a pig for 11 gulden. I have dug the potatoes out and have sown 7 measures of wheat and 1 measure of barley and 7 measures of rye. I have dunged and sown the field where the oats were. I borrowed $1\frac{1}{2}$ bushels from Franek Batuch. He wants money [interest] for it, as much as he pays himself for borrowing from Tomasiak.[1] But don't worry, I shall manage everything. Since you went away neither father nor mother has been here yet, only

---

[1] She mentions the fact because it is not according to tradition to take money for lending of grain. Traditionally either nothing or a little grain should be taken as interest.

Maryna; and Rózia also, for a week. I went to them and asked them to give me their daughter [to help]. She was here for a week and cried every evening, and once she went home and did not come any more.[1] The knife which you made has not been found, nor the brush. When I went with you to Sącz, Franek took the brush from the shelf in the lobby, for Maryna and Swidzak saw it. But I don't say anything, because there would be trouble for us. . . . . I dream about you every night. Sometimes I dream that you come back angry and sometimes good, and I long very much. The day passes in working but in the evening I long much and at night I cannot sleep. . . . .

Samek did not thresh . . . . because I wanted him to thresh in the autumn, but he was angry, [saying] that if he did he could not go to Hungary through my fault.[2] In the field nobody does you any damage, nor does anybody damage the hedge. People say about you that you don't need that America, but nobody asked how you would pay the debts of which we have so many. Nobody believed up to the end that you would go. The Gazdas are very curious whether you will write to them. Franek comes here and looks sometimes, and when he has passed by it can always be noticed, for when he sees anything he does not omit the occasion [to take it].

About [your brother] Walek I dream also. He has not written to me; I did not receive any letter from him. . . . . Weddings are numerous in our village, but you will learn about them. Our boys remember you. They ask, "Where is father? Why does he not come?" Now I have nothing more of interest to write, but I greet you a hundred thousand times kindly and heartily, dear husband, and I thank you for that letter for which I have looked for so long a time. Be healthy. Let us see each other. Amen. I greet you [enumeration of all the relatives in America]. And if I don't do anything quite well, don't be angry with me. And it is well that you like it there, because I have grieved enough, thinking that you don't like it there. . . . . And Piotrek went with Samek to Hungary to work. And the Tyrkiels, when they both went to the fair, slipped into a

[1] She speaks here of her own family, not of her husband's. The unwillingness of her sisters to help her and the indifferent attitude of her father (see No. 520) show that a married couple may become isolated, not by their own fault, but by the fault of the family in which the solidarity is weakened.

[2] For season-work. The emigration to Hungary is regarded by the Galician peasants as particularly demoralizing.

tavern, and there a fight began. When Waligóra from Brzegi smashed with a glass upon the table, her [Tyrkiel's wife's] forehead was cut in two spots.[1]

Answer at once.

E. OLSZAK

519   May 23, 1914

. . . . DEAR HUSBAND: . . . . You write that you are worse, but you did not write what befell you, for Wojtek Jakubów wrote that your leg pains you but he did not write what happened to you, and I am so anxious because I don't know. But did you go in search of misfortune there? [To think that you found misfortune there!] I don't know what is going on. Only this I can say, Wojtuś, my dear heart, that when anything bad befalls you, a part of my heart is cut, from longing for you. If you only know that the work won't go or if you cannot work, get a little of that money and come, and if you have none perhaps Jasiek Kuzak will lend it to you. And when you come back, if God the Holiest grants you to come back, we could give back either the field bought from Tyrkiel or the other part. . . . . There is no reason to keep it. Why do you need it, particularly if you have no health? And so it seems to me. Whenever I think about you, my heart is cut. And this buying of land from this Tyrkiel is so useless, because you must work and pay this interest, while they live like lords and you cannot say anything to them.[2] If it were not because of this debt you would not have gone to America and would not suffer misery there. But if you are to suffer there and I here it is better, if you can, to come back. From them [the parents] also [there is no great help, such as was promised]. Sometimes one [sister], sometimes the other comes, but when they are most necessary there is none. When I go anywhere, I take the children, I take them to Popardzina [and] I close the house. I shall have enough grain,

[1] There is a mischievous joy in this description, resulting from the woman's animosity toward the Tyrkiels. The reason of the animosity is stated in the following letter.

[2] The reason of the woman's animosity toward the Tyrkiels is here explained; it is envy, because, by selling their land, that family found itself in a better position than the buyer. There is a peculiar and mixed attitude in these matters. The price of land is out of proportion to any possible income from it, and while the peasant, under the influence of the traditional land-hunger, still buys the land and pays the price, he bears a grudge against the seller who made him pay more than the land is economically worth.

but I have bought one quarter of potatoes more, and I paid 1 gulden because they are that dear. But it does not matter much, for they were as dear in the first year when we were married. [Crops; weather; farm-work.]

E. OLSZAK

520 BRZEŻNA, May 5, 1913

[DEAR BROTHER-IN-LAW]: You write us to help her, but we help her as we can. Father continually abuses mother for going so often to her. When you went away Maryna was with her for four weeks, and we also go to her as often as we can. You know that when you were here you bought [things for her?], but she has no money to buy. Where can she get it? The worst are the children, because when she must go anywhere she takes the children to some house [or other]. If we are there, then it is better. But . . . . we have no hired man and there is never time [to help her in farm-work?], and she is very poor without a servant [passage obscure]. But nevertheless we help her as much as we can. She has no fat [for seasoning food] so we take her some whenever we can, when father does not know about it.[1] Now a pig has been killed, so we are sending her [some fat], because she has no money to buy it. You know, dear brother-in-law, the difference between that which is given and that which is bought [the gift is always of better quality]. [News about relatives and greetings from all the family of the wife.]

I, Rózia, have written this page, but, my dear brother-in-law, I beg you, don't be angry if the writing is bad and ugly. . . . .

ROZALIA [RÓZIA[GANCARCZYK

521

. . . . DEAR FRIEND AND *KUM* . . . . You write me to describe everything, so I will write you the whole truth. . . . . I have sown wheat for her upon the field where potatoes had been, and a measure of barley, and rye upon dung where oats had been, because she took one morg of field from Franek. And now I write you that she dug the potatoes out and has sown. . . . . Now you ask what she says about you. She says that she dreams about you every night. . . . . We have nice and warm weather. Yours [your wife] has called upon

---

[1] Cf. No. 518, p. 843, note 1.

us with your letter, and I did everything in the field for her and I have sown, and Franek keeps it [?] well.   They have not divided it yet. And now I write you that I gave to Tyrkiel those 10 gulden. . . . . You ask whether people from Ciecewina [?] [the wife's family] call upon her.   The girls do come, but nobody else.   And now you ask how yours manages.   So, up to the present she manages well enough, and how it will be further, I don't know. . . . .[1] She bought a calf for 50 crowns and keeps it, and now she intends to buy also a pig, and asks me to lend her money, so I will lend her some.   And now I write you about this field, that I persuaded her to rent it from Franek, because Franek told me that he would let it be rented, and that he had [prospective] tenants, Wojtek Ciula, and Józek Junczak, and Franek Samek.   So it is better if your wife takes it instead of having trouble with them [probably because of a too near neighborship].   So your wife took one morg of this field. . . . .

[JAKÓB]

---

[1] Example of a husband controlling his wife through his friends.   In spite of the conjugal affection the individualization of the marriage-group is still incomplete, since other members of the family or community are not only allowed but asked to interfere.

STARKIEWICZ SERIES

Starkiewicz is not a farmer, but had probably worked in a manor, and when he went to America his wife lived with her relatives. This accounts for the woman's lack of economic interest. In their situation it is really not very important whether they have more or less money, for money assumes a real social importance only when it can be used to buy land or can in any way become a basis of an independent existence. And Starkiewicz can hardly hope to earn enough money to buy a farm.

The marriage-group is more isolated from the rest of the family than in the case of the Olszaks; probably their situation as manor-servants has helped to produce this isolation. Still the familial relations are rather close, since the wife can stay with her relatives. Conjugal affection has evidently considerably transcended the traditional limits.

522–28, FROM ZOFIA STARKIEWICZ, IN POLAND, TO HER
HUSBAND, IN AMERICA

522   Uścimów, April 16, 1914

"Praised be," [etc.].

DEAR HUSBAND: I am very glad that I received your letter, but this kills me, that you don't write me exactly what is going on with you. Here papers write that there is war in New York, that houses are destroyed with bombs, ... that ships are stopped [do not bring emigrants to America] and that they say there: "We won't admit the strangers any more who came to spoil our land of money, they have taken enough of our money from our land." And you don't write me what is going on with you. Please, my dear, what became of Stasiek Olesiuk? Already 15 weeks have passed and he does not write any letter to her. Is he no longer alive, or what else became of him? For she grieves very much. Don't you know anything about him? I beg you, my dear husband, you have enough of this earning; come back to us. It will be sufficient for you. You have more than 300 roubles, and you can earn the rest here. You won't take the money with you when you die, and here you can also earn, if God the Merciful grants you health and allows you to live. Instead of working there and wasting your strength you can have here bread enough. If you don't want to serve [in a manor] go to Lublin, and there you can live. You don't want to have most [money] among other men. If it is difficult to return now, if it is true that there are such troubles, then come about autumn, and if perhaps you have sent me all your money, write me and I will send you for the journey. In our country now it is warm, trees are developing their leaves, people are sowing oats and barley and planting potatoes. . . . .

I inform you, dear husband, that somebody stole 100 roubles from stepmother, father's wife, from her chest. We all went to the priest, father and stepmother and sister Wiśniewska, and Wojciech, and Helena, and I. Stepmother was absolutely determined to have father testify under oath. Then father would say that his children had stolen the money. But the priest forbade him to make the oath.[1] . . . .

[Zofia Starkiewicz]

523 June 2, 1914

Dear Husband: I inform you that I received the money, 101 roubles and 5 copecks, and I thank you heartily, my dear husband, for remembering me. Now I inform you that I will do nothing with this money and I won't lend it to anybody, for I am afraid. I will put it into the bank. Just now your godfather Kunak came to me,

[1] The oath is considered a perfectly sufficient proof even if it is false; the responsibility for its truthfulness falls exclusively upon the person who makes it, and it is a general belief that great calamities and even death are the result of a false oath. (The result is conceived partly as divine punishment, partly as immediate magical consequence of the sacrilege.) In this case the author believes that the stepmother's accusation against her stepchildren is either true or not true. In the first case her satisfaction at the priest's refusal to accept the oath—the only possible proof—shows that she does not consider the robbing of the stepmother a bad act. If she does not believe it is true, then she thinks her father either capable of a false oath or so henpecked that he would believe anything the stepmother says, and in either case absolutely estranged from his own children. In that case we have a situation resembling that in the Wróblewski series.

asking me to lend him 100 roubles, but I am afraid. I said so—that
I won't give them until I write to you and ask you, and he agreed.
. . . . What do you say? Shall I lend it or not? He wants to
borrow it on a note, but I should prefer to put it in the bank. I
am very much satisfied that you intend to come when you have no
work. . . . .

Now I inform you that your niece Kaśka is married already. They
went to be married on Thursday before Pentecost, and the marriage-
festival will be on the Holy Trinity Day. They say that they got
married in Włodawa. The rest I will tell you in my next letter. . . . .

Your wife,

ZOFIA STARKIEWICZ

Read for yourself secretly, that nobody may know. I inform
you about this marriage of Kaśka. They went to the wedding alone,
and they have no sign at all whether they are married or not. When
they came back, only then they went to our priest asking him to
publish the banns. They had to take the certificate to the other
church that their banns had been published, and only then the other
priest was to give them the marriage-certificate. But our priest
refused to accept [money] for the banns. So everybody says as he
pleases—some that they were married, others, that they were not,
for nobody was with them, and he is a true Ruthenian.[1]

524   June 21, 1914

DEAR HUSBAND: . . . . I received your letter. . . . . It made
me very sad that so many people are drowned. I think about your
journey. May God only grant you to come back happily to us, may
God guard you against any accident! . . . . I beg you, my husband,
be so good, listen to me, come back at once. After this letter prepare
yourself directly for the journey. What a life it is that you live!
Your work is heavier than a stone. What of it if you leave your
strength in a foreign country? Shall we take our money with us
after our death? Why should we exert ourselves so? Pray God for

---

[1] The secrecy in which she communicates this news, the nature of the gossip,
and the postscript to No. 528, show clearly the normal attitude of the peasant
toward illegal sexual intercourse. There is no trace of a purely moral or religious
condemnation, but a very strong feeling that such an intercourse, even if finishing
with marriage, is *socially abnormal*. This standpoint will explain many peculiarities
in this connection.

health, then we shall live.   Whether you earn or lose, nobody will add or take away anything from you.   I have a hog.   They offered me 45 roubles; I want 50.   Now I won't sell it until you come.   Then we should have 313 roubles, and if we sold the cow there would be about 400.   We would put it into the bank in Lublin, and we should live much better than now. . . . .

ZOFIA STARKIEWICZ

525   August 9, 1914

In the first words of my letter, dear husband, I inform you about my health and success.   Up to the present we are still in good health, but we don't know how it will be further.   I sent you already one letter in which I bade you farewell, like going to death, but still war is in some way held up for 2 weeks, only throngs of soldiers are passing by us afoot and on horses; we see no end of them.   God forbid, what is going on with everyone of us!   How much crying, how much sorrow!   Everybody is so grieved, if you looked today upon anybody you would not know him.   O my God, what we have lived to see!   May God guard everybody against it!   Now nothing else but everybody prays and prepares himself for death.   The priests listen to confession, and people come during whole days and confess themselves. And nobody knows what will happen, whether we shall be sent away from here or not.   Rich people go to far Russia; there is no war there, while here is the worst fire.   We are all so afraid that we don't know how to live in the world.   The reservists have been sent away. . . . even those are taken who are 48 years old. . . . . And nobody knows what will be.   [The papers] write always that it is a European war, but we don't know. . . . . I beg you, answer this letter as soon as possible.   And perhaps we shall no longer be alive when your letter comes. . . . .[1]

And now I beg you, dear husband, and Józefka, Stasiek's wife, we begged you in some letters to write us about him, but you did not answer this.   We heard from the T.'s that Stasiek has a sweetheart and won't come back any more, for he has a sweetheart and will remain in America.   His mother weeps very much, and his wife also. Answer me, whether it is true, but answer me the truth.   Then we

---

[1] This whole paragraph is a good illustration of the peasant's feeling of incomprehension and impotence with regard to the phenomena of the social world outside of his own community.   Cf. Introduction: "Social Environment."

shall tell it to them. Write us the address of Stasiek. Only tell the truth, what is going on. We believe that it is true, for perhaps he had a very bad life and he attached himself to a sweetheart. . . . .

Your truly loving wife,

ZOFIA STARKIEWICZ

526 November 1, 1914

. . . . DEAR HUSBAND: I inform you that I am in good health and our son is also in good health, and we wish you the same. Dear husband, I have sent you 3 letters, this is the fourth, and I have no answer. Are you no longer alive? I don't know myself what it means. It is not enough that I have grief here; I don't know anything about you. I will write you one letter after another, perhaps one of them will reach you, for I shall not live through this grief, thinking about you. And perhaps you are not there, so whoever opens this letter, please answer me at least a few words, whether he is alive or is no more there. . . . . I give my address. . . . .

ZOFIA STARKIEWICZ

527 November 7, 1914

DEAR HUSBAND: I received your letter. [Health; wishes.] Your son sends you bows and kisses your hands, saying that he is worried without his papa. Yes, dear husband, our son is already big enough and intelligent, he always remembers "Mamma, where is papa? Is it far? When shall we go to him? Perhaps tomorrow? Come, mamma, let us go!" . . . . Józefka thanks you heartily for the address which you sent her, and I thank you also for having written a few words about Stasiek. We are still curious to know what woman sits there with him, what is her name. Write me. What does it matter to you if I know who she is? . . . .

As to the war, there is now no battle near us. The nearest one was about Lublin, 3 versts away. Trawniki is burned, Janów destroyed, of Tomaszów only sky and earth are left. There was such a groan from shots here that the earth trembled. Now the battle is going on beyond the Vistula, toward Częstochowa. Radom is destroyed, but not totally, Puławy destroyed, villages destroyed. There was such a roar at night that it was impossible to sleep. Now no more shots are to be heard, for the German has been driven away. Only there is great misery in our country, everything expensive. . . . . Few people are left, only women, for men have been taken, some to the war, others to digging trenches, others to transports; horses and carts are all taken. . . . .

Your loving wife,
ZOFIA STARKIEWICZ

528   November 26, 1914

. . . . DEAR HUSBAND: . . . . Our son is healthy and rather big; he walks already in trousers. When I ask: "What is father doing in America?" he answers: "He cuts wood." I have a great distraction with him; he always talks to me. Were it not for the child I should perhaps not live through this sorrow. Dear husband, I inform you that I hired myself as a milk-woman, for both brothers-in-law are at the war. I have nowhere to live, and it is difficult to live in the village. And thus they will give me lodging and fuel, 1 cow to keep in the manorial stable, 3 bushels grain every quarter and 100 roods of field [for potatoes]. I take, it is true, a duty upon my head, for I must be there at every call, but at least I shan't have to work during the whole summer [for some neighbor]. For the keeping of one cow and for a few roods of field I had to work during the whole summer, while now I shall have peace with it. Whatever I earn [outside the milking hours] will be mine, and they will give me also 4 roubles a year. Yes, dear husband, it is painful for me, for I did not expect that I should have to serve.

Now I inform you that Józefka, Stasiek's [wife], went as a maid to a *pop* [Russian priest] to Kolechowicze. For the prices of everything are now very high; it is difficult to live in the village, when one cannot earn somewhere. First she had waited for a letter from her husband, but it is a year since she has had no letter from him; what should she expect from him any more? She went away on November 15. When she was leaving she cried very much; she simply could not say a word. She is so grieved, because she has a husband and must serve, while he works for some whore and lives with her. She is very much pained, she can hardly bear it. Yes, my husband, poor is her lot. I wept myself about her lot. . . . .

[Describes who went to war and perished.] Brother-in-law bade us farewell by letter and begged everybody to forgive his sins. . . . .

We simply could not listen to this letter; everybody wept. . . . .
Since then there has been no letter from him, perhaps he is dead.
. . . . Now I inform you that people talked here that all the men have
been driven away from America and that they are going to war. . . . .
I thought that it was true and grieved. . . . .

ZOFIA STARKIEWICZ

Kaśka P. had already a daughter on November 17, while the wedding was in June.

KLUCH SERIES

Partial isolation of the marriage-group, resulting, not from a particularly close relation between husband and wife, but from a disintegration of the family, appears in this series of letters. Already one branch of the family has been spacially isolated from the rest. We find no mention of any other member living in Lublin except the father with his wife and the two daughters with their husbands. And even this small group is dissolved by the father's second marriage. Consequently there remain only three marriage-groups, partly solidary, partly opposed to one another. And again we find the men more conservative, willing to keep at least in a certain measure the old group-connection.

529–32, TO S. KLUCH, IN AMERICA, FROM HIS WIFE AND FAMILY-MEMBERS, IN POLAND; AND ONE LETTER FROM THE SISTER-IN-LAW OF KLUCH TO HER HUSBAND, IN AMERICA

529 [LUBLIN], May 21, 1914

DEAR SON-IN-LAW: You ask me to describe to you the success of your wife, but I can write you no news at all, for I have never any occasion to call upon her, although she is my child. How can I call upon her since she drove me away from her? And secondly, when I go she avoids me as if I had done her some evil. She moved from here to Wesoła Street, there they live near each other, she and Pawłowa [Paweł's wife, the other daughter]. I send you only the news that *kuma* Staśkowa [Stasiek's wife] went to borrow money from her, and she said that she had not a penny; so probably there is misery.

And now, dear son-in-law, I beg you very much, write letters to me oftener, for it is my only comfort, when you send me a letter. For I have no comfort at all from my daughters. I respect you more, both my sons-in-law, than my own children. My older son-in-law wrote to me asking me whether I was not angry. Now probably he is angry with me . . . . because I have no news from him at all and I don't know what has become of him. And now I address myself to you, dear son-in-law Stanisław. You ask me whether I am not afraid that you won't give me the money back. I am not afraid at all, for I understand what work means and what it means to be without work. [Conditions at home are bad.] Write letters to me, oftener, then I will also send you more interesting news, for it is my only diversion when you send me a letter. It is sad and painful to me that my daughters avoid me like some enemy [in return] for my education [of them], for my goodness, for my having fed them for some time when you went away.[1] . . . .

J. Z.

530   March 22, 1914

[Usual greetings; letter and photographs received.] Dear husband, you wrote me to try to get Kocieba's address, so I went to his wife. But she did not want to give it at all. She said: "Perhaps he will go to him." I said: "I don't know." Then she said: "He has had no work himself for two months."[2] And now, dear husband, you wrote me to say to *kum* Paweł that you did not work for 4 months. But *kum* did not believe it at all; he said that it was impossible, that you were not without work for so long a time. Dear husband, people don't believe that there is misery in America; they want to go without reflecting. *Kum* does not earn badly where he is now; he did not tell it, but *kuma* [his wife] told me that he earned up to 20 roubles every two weeks. Perhaps even in America he would not earn more, for people think that in America everybody is filled with cakes [by the employers] while, as we see, even in America it is not so sweet. . . . .

M. KLUCH

---

[1] The strength of the familial attitude is seen in the fact that the old man seeks in his sons-in-law a support when the relation with his daughters is broken off. He needs a sanction for his second marriage and his sons-in-law are a substitute for his daughters.

[2] Not professional jealousy, as this developed only among craftsmen and the persons here are from the peasant class. The unwillingness shown here is therefore the sign of a partial dissolution of the old solidarity and hospitality among peasants. The feeling of obligation cannot be shaken off, but the duty seems burdensome and unpleasant, because no longer adapted to the general conditions of modern life. Cf. No. 474.

531

. . . . And now, dear husband, you ask me how much money I have. I have not so much. In the bank I had only 50 roubles and I had left only a few roubles for myself to live upon, and then you sent 100. So there would have been 150 roubles in the bank, but I did not put them in the bank, for, as you know, nobody accepts money and nobody gives it back [because of war]. Those 100 roubles which I had to pay to my father, I did not pay them either, for my sister had also a few roubles at home which she put in the bank, and now the bank refuses to pay them. She cannot, evidently, die from hunger together with her children [so I lent her money]. The old man, I know, is not without money, and as soon as everything starts again our brother-in-law will send [money to my sister] and I will give [the money] back to the old man. And now, dear husband, perhaps I have spent somewhat too much money, so don't be angry with me, for I was—I don't mean to reproach God with it—in Częstochowa and I bought a few things for myself and for the children, so the money was spent. And now you wrote, why did I not inform you that I was in Częstochowa. How could I have informed you, since you forbade me to write at all, so I waited until all this is changed, and I did not know what was the matter. . . . . But you listened to the absurdities of the old man [my father], and the old one avenges himself on me as much as he can. Surely he is so angry because I don't say "mother" to his linen-press [wife]. But you don't know the old one yet. The old one probably is trying to get us separated. As long as I worked I was good [in his opinion], and although he got married he wanted me to wash, to do everything, while his linen-press would lie and drink milk instead of water.[1] He would like his children to be wasted like salt upon boiling water, as he always said to our brother-in-law, "Well, you will be wasted like salt upon boiling water." . . . . Don't believe the old one, whatever he writes you about me, for he

---

[1] Before his second marriage the father had lived with his daughter and his claims to support and service were considered rightful. (Cf. Jabłkowska series.) But after his second marriage all his rights disappeared. He had not only to pay for his own and his wife's living, but his wife had to share the housework with his daughter. He complains of his daughter's ingratitude, but clearly his appeal is made rather in the name of an abstract morality than of a practically acknowledged social obligation. This is one of the clearest examples of familial dissociation resulting from a second marriage through the difficulty of assimilating the new family-member.

never knows what I do and even where I live. Since he moved away from me he has never yet called upon me. I could die and be buried and he would not know anything. And to you he writes that he knows everything, how I live. Let him rather guard his pile-driver [wife] lest they take it away from him for driving bridge-piles into the river-bed. I return once more, dear husband, to my going to Częstochowa. I went there with this intention, that you might be healthy and succeed well, and that we might see each other once more in our life.[1] And now, dear husband, I inform you about this war, that here nothing terrible has been as yet, but we don't know how it will be further. . . . . Only, wounded men are brought from morning till evening, and even by night, and the villages are burned around us. . . . .

M. KLUCH

532 August 31, 1914

. . . . And now, dear husband, don't grieve and don't be very anxious, but here is a terrible misery in Lublin . . . . terrible trouble. Villages are burning around Lublin, dear husband! And we see so many wounded men when they bring them through the streets that our eyes are aching from looking upon these cripples. . . . . And we are quite stupid, dear husband, we don't know what to do. Some say to fly from the town, others say to sit upon the spot, some say so others so, but nobody knows what will befall us, except perhaps our Lord God alone. . . . . We received now fresh news that the pillows are to be taken for the wounded. From this fright we hid them in cellars, but then we learned that whoever hides the pillows will be beaten by the Cossacks, so we took them from the cellar and buried them in the earth. . . . .[2]

[PAWŁOWA]

[1] This is evidently a pretext. Her excuses show that going to Częstochowa is not a pure religious act—a pilgrimage in the proper sense—but a social and aesthetic enjoyment of the same character as attendance at religious ceremonies and parish festivals. The connection of religious life with aesthetic and hedonistic interests is very close.

[2] The fear of the authorities, as of an incalculable danger, stifles every other feeling; there is no place left for pity toward the wounded. This is probably one of the reasons why the peasant, ready for individual compassion and help, mistrusts absolutely any official charity organization, and is unwilling not only to contribute to it, but even to be helped by it, unless the help takes the form of a gift of money.

STRUCIŃSKI SERIES

The case is interesting on account of the evolution which goes on in the conjugal relation. In the beginning this has evidently a familial character which it gradually drops, leaving only some community of interest, personal affection, and sexual impulse. This change is probably due to the emigration of the man, and not alone to his separation from the family-group, but also to the tendency to economic advance which is expressed in the emigration. We have seen that this tendency always acts more or less destructively upon the familial form of economic life; at the same time it creates a new and exclusive link within the marriage-group, since it affects, of course, this group as a whole. We shall see this very well illustrated in another (Jabłkowska) series. But in the present case the influence of emigration does not express itself in this way. The personal conjugal connection is not strong enough to subsist when its familial basis has been dissolved and without the help of the attachment brought by common life. Gradually, therefore, the relations between husband and wife become cooler and seem to tend to a definite break.

533–46, FROM ADAM STRUCIŃSKI, IN AMERICA, TO HIS WIFE, IN POLAND

533   GLASSPORT, PA., June 9, 1910

In the first words of my letter, "Praised be Jesus Christus."

And now I inform you, beloved wife, that by the favor of God I am well, and the same I wish to you and the whole family. And now I ask whether you received the money, because on April 18 I sent to you 19 roubles and 43 copecks, and I have no information about it for 7 weeks. Now I send 25 roubles again, so when you receive it, then write to me, because I am very much troubled. I do not know what happened. And now I do not have anything more to write, only I would ask you to send to me three little crosses, and one little medallion, because I need only one little cross, but I should like to give it to my colleague, and furthermore I would ask you to put in about 6 hog-bristles, because when sometime my shoe is torn then I do not have any means to mend it, and if I want to buy [bristles] then you cannot find a store that has hog-bristles. Give this letter to my parents, or send it by mail, for maybe you do not go there. And now I kiss you.[1]

ADAM STRUCIŃSKI

534   July 13, 1910

. . . . And now I inform you, beloved wife, about my dear health and success. Thanks to God I am well and the same I wish to you. I received your letter July 4, for which I thank you heartily, and I reply to you at once. July 9 I sent you 50 roubles, so that when you receive it then answer me.

And now, beloved wife, you were writing that you want to come to America, so now I do not advise you to come. It is better if I send you a few roubles for your use and if you stay, for the election of president will be soon and it may even be that I will come back to the old country.[2] And if, after the elections, in America times are good then I can send you a steamship-ticket, and if they are bad, then it may be that next fall I will come back to the old country myself. I pray God to help you just as I pray Him to help me in America. So when I stay in America until next fall and then come back to the old country, we shall have good living just the same. When you reply to me write me whether you received those 19 roubles, 43 copecks. I bow to you, beloved wife, and to the whole family. I wish health, happiness, and good success.

ADAM STRUCIŃSKI

[1] The letter is much more business-like and less personal than the following ones; the request to give it to the parents proves that it is meant to be a purely familial letter.

[2] Probably a pretext for not bringing her to America; possibly he was misinformed about date of elections.

535   November 1, 1910

DEAR WIFE: I greet you at least through this dead paper, and I kiss you, my love, and I inform you that I received a letter from you from which I learned about your dear health and also your success, and therefore I am very glad my beloved Broncia. And I also inform you about my health and success. By the favor of God I am well and the same I wish to you, my love. And my success is pretty good, only this, that I am lonesome without you, for what is the use of this work and money if I do not have and do not see you. So, I ask you, beloved angel, to send me your little face, that is a photograph, just as I send [one] to you. Although we are on the inanimate paper, nevertheless we shall see [each other] and in our souls we shall have our tender kisses, my dear love. Beloved Broncia, I send you my photograph together with that of my cousin whom I want to engage with Wiktorya Dobrzyńska, and I ask you, beloved wife, to take your picture together with Wichta [Wiktorya] and to send it to me, because if you will not take it together with her, then I will be very angry with you, because he [the cousin] sends one of his, for he is very much pleased with my description, and therefore he desires it [the picture],[1] and we will come back together. Now I write to you that with a second letter I will send to you 60 roubles. I do not have anything more to write but to send a bow to your beloved mother, sisters, brothers-in-law, brother, and sister-in-law, in general to the whole family, and I send hearty wishes. Let God grant them everything the best. And I bid you farewell, beloved Broncia, embrace you and kiss you, I, your sincerely loving husband,

ADAM STRUCIŃSKI

You will give one photograph to my parents. There will be 5 altogether, 4 mine and one of my cousin.

I ask you for a quick reply and the photographs. Have photographs taken of both of you at once, and send them to me. I shall wait with impatience.

[1] The whole story of the matchmaking in this and the following letters is perfectly typical. The underlying attitudes are exactly in accordance with the tradition, only the means are new because of the new situation. This type of matchmaking is more conservative than the one which we find in the Butkowski series.

536 December 20, 1910

DEAR BRONCIA: First of all I greet you and I kiss you affably and I inform you that I received the letter and a photograph. This letter and the photograph rejoiced me very much. Those photographs rejoiced me very much more than if I should find a hundred dollars. I am very glad also that you took the picture together with Wichta. And I thank you very heartily for the wafer, and I also mutually divide the wafer with you and the whole family, and I congratulate you on Christmas, and let God grant us to live to see each other next year and to sing together "Glory to God in the highest, and peace to us on earth." That I wish to you, my sweetheart, and to the whole family, and I warmly pray God that he would deign to save us until that time. My dear angel! I inform you about my health as also about my success, that by the favor of God I am well and I wish the same to you, my love. And as to my success, it is just as formerly, only that after New Year the work is to go better. And now you ask, my dear little soul, together with Wichta and her mother, about my colleague—who is he, where does he come from, and what is his occupation, and how long has he been in America: Well, he has been in America as long as I have, and we work together at the same work, only we board separately; and he comes from Obryte in the old country, where he has a farm. He came from the army at once to America. In the army he was a higher hospital attendant, and by his usual trade he is a carpenter. So he can build houses well and do joiner's work, and his farm is not bad, because his father is pretty well off, and he is the only son, and there are two sisters, and the remaining sisters are married. I should not believe that, and would not write it, but I know from those who know him, and they know well what kind of success he has. And I was talking with him and he did not want to praise himself like others, for only those praise themselves who do not have anything. And I wish him for Wichta very much, if she will marry him. Because he is not a drunkard, or a villian either, and, secondly, she and all of you see him on the photograph, and you may judge what kind of man he appears to be. And I was showing him those photographs and he was very much pleased with her, and he says that it would be a pity if she would get into some bloodthirsty hands. And he intends to go to the old country with me after one year, in the fall. And so I ask sister not to let Wichta marry someone else. Also he sends his low bows to Wichta and to her mother and father and to the whole family, and he asks for Wichta's hand. I do not have anything more to describe and I ask you, dearest wife, whether you received those 60 roubles which I sent; so write me about that. And I bid you farewell, beloved Broncia. I send you my heartiest husband's feelings, and sincere wishes and bows. I greet you affectionately and kiss you my little dove. I, your husband, sincerely loving you until the grave-board.

ADAM STRUCIŃSKI

And I send bows and hearty wishes to mother, sister, brother-in-law, Wichta, Stasia, and to the whole home, to brother, sister-in-law, and to the whole home. And I congratulate you for the New Year and new happiness, and God grant my wishes. I, pleasantly recollecting you, and wishing you well.

ADAM STRUCIŃSKI

537 February 12, 1911

.... DEAR WIFE: I inform you that I received your letter, from which I learned about your health as also about success, and that rejoiced me very much. Dear wife, you write to me if [that you wish] this year would pass in one moment, and I also should be glad, only I do not know how it will be further, because I should like to save the most money I can, then it would be better for me than everything, because if I had a great deal of money then I should know how to start farming. So I think of staying some two or three years, because I should like us to have a thousand roubles.[1] Well I do not know how it will be on account of present times, because it is the fifth month since we have worked only half days, and they don't even always allow us to work as much as half a day. Now it is very bad in America. Only in ax-shops the work is going better.

At New Year we did not work for two weeks, and now we receive small working payments. And in regard to winter it is neither winter nor warm, in a word, scabby, with us also. The 9th of January there was a terrible thunder, and hail fell almost like potatoes. I do not have anything more to write, but to send you, beloved wife, bows and my dear greetings, and hearty wishes, and I bid you farewell, beloved

---

[1] The desire to advance is here explicitly limited to the marriage-group, and nothing is left of the familial attitude.

wife. I embrace you and kiss you, I, your husband loving you until the grave-board.

ADAM STRUCIŃSKI

[Greetings for the whole family.] And I ask you kindly to send me your exact name and address, because when I send money, then I will send in brother's hands [name], because it is more convenient for brother than for wife, on this account that there are mistakes. I ask for a quick reply.

538 April 17 [1911]

DEAR WIFE: . . . . You write me to come on your account. So when the work goes worse, then it may be that I will come, but I will work as long as we have not a thousand roubles. I will live in the most economical way, and you also do as you can, because it would not pay me to come [here] for one year. I came in order to earn something. Write to me whether you received 80 roubles that I sent to you. I am very lonesome without you. I kiss you, I, your husband.

ADAM STRUCIŃSKI

539 May 21, 1911

DEAR WIFE: . . . . You write me to come. Well, I would come, but I cannot come because the work is going very weakly, and, secondly, I send you the money, and now it is difficult to earn. I will see later. When I am able to earn at least for a ship-ticket then after All Saints Day I will come back. It is true, my dear wife, that you must worry, but I also worry still more than you, and I have more troubles, because I have to think about myself and about you, but it is difficult if God manages us in this way, that we cannot live in abundance. If it were not for that then we would not separate even for one minute, but for the piece of bread it is necessary to bid farewell to the family. So let God help me to earn and to come back happily to my native country. So, I pray God and do you pray also to this Creator and the holiest Mother, that we may be united together and live together until death. I do not have anything else to write.

ADAM STRUCIŃSKI

540   August 21 [1911]

[Greetings; health; letters.]   You write, "If I would come," and I think myself [it would be best] if I could come the soonest possible to my family, for I did not come to America to drink and lead a merry life, because I have a family in the old country.   When I recall it then the tears run.   But I will work as I am able, and when nothing is left for me [in America], then I will come back.   I inform you that the 15 of August I sent 3 photographs and the 19, 100 roubles. Write whether you received it.   I sent a handkerchief on your name-day, and because I do not know whether it will reach you or not, write to me.   I sent two letters together, one with the handkerchief, and another without a handkerchief.

I do not have anything else to write.

[ADAM STRUCIŃSKI]

541   November 26, 1911

DEAR WIFE: I inform you that I received your two letters, and in both of them I heard nothing else but if I would come back. You see, my dear treasure, although you write to me that I love the money better than you, nevertheless you see that I love you and the money, because if without money then I should not like you either, and when I have a great deal of money then you also will like me still better than without money, because when we have a great deal of money then when we fill ourselves up by eating and drinking, and when we dress up, then it will be pleasant to look at each other; then we will love each other still better and we will put lips on lips, and the heart will beat, and then the love will be better than it was when we were hungry and ragged, because when a man is hungry then he does not like to love.[1]   So you see, I want to work for some time yet because the work is going not the worst, and I may earn as I did not before. So I will stay some couple of weeks, and you, my dear, pray God for health, and this time will fly away for me and for you as one moment. So I send you 25 roubles for the holidays.   Out of this money give 2½ roubles to each mother, and with 20 roubles procure what is necessary for you, and do not walk hungry and cold, because I attempt to provide so that there will not be any hardship.   When

---

[1] This hedonistic attitude, rare among the peasants, shows a relatively far-going individualization.

you receive the money then answer at once.   I congratulate you for the holidays of Christmas.   I do not have anything more to write.

ADAM STRUCIŃSKI

542   1912

. . . . Now I inform you, beloved wife, about your letter, that I received it, from which I learned only that you are well, and about nothing else.   You do not write even whether you received the money and letter.   Whether you are angry, I do not know.   And I ask you whether you wish to come to America to me or not.   So answer me. If you wish, then at once after Whitsuntide I will send you a steamship-ticket, unless you do not want to wait so long.   If so come on yours [at your expense], because I do not have any intention of coming back unless there is great want in America;   then and only then I would come back.   Then answer me about your coming, or perhaps you do not have the desire to come, or perhaps something will hinder you, or perhaps your family does not allow you.   Then answer, and I will know how to arrange.   So if you should not come then I would stay some time, and I would send you [money] for living, just as I used to send to you.

I do not have anything more to write, but to send bows and hearty wishes to the whole family, and especially a bow to you, beloved wife, and also hearty wishes.   I remain sincerely, I, your husband,

ADAM STRUCIŃSKI

543   September 15, 1912

. . . . BELOVED WIFE: . . . . A few days ago I was very ill, and for this reason I did not reply to your letter at once.   And I am very glad of your success, that you behave yourself well and manage well. Because I have also a few pennies, and now I work up to one thousand roubles, and just as soon as I save a thousand roubles, at once, in a short time, I will come back.   And I ask you what kind of crops were this year.   And prepare a lot of potatoes and one barrel of cabbage, and in addition feed up a hog, and when I come then we will kill this hog.   We will boil potatoes and cabbage and we will put the rib pieces into the cabbage; and we will have comfortable shelter for the whole winter.   And see that the feather bed is good, and the bed strong because from [eating] rib pieces, potatoes, and cabbage the man is heavy, and if the bed were weak then it could break down. Only do not take this trick badly [do not be angry at my joke.][1] Now in regard to this man about whom I wrote, I thought that he went to the [old] country, and he is still here, because in the spring, when there was a strike in our factory and he could not get work in the same city he went to another city. And now he wrote a letter to me and he was asking about Wichta, whether she got married. And he sends bows to her, and he wrote that he will soon come to Glassport, and we intend to go together to the old country. So let Wichta write something, and I will send [it] to him. I do not have anything more to write, only I send my bows to brother and sister-in-law, to brothers-in-law, and sisters-in-law; and hearty wishes and a low bow to Wichta's mother and to the whole family, and especially a bow and hearty wishes to you, beloved wife. Remain with God. I, your husband,

ADAM STRUCIŃSKI

I ask for a quick reply. *Gut baj.*

544
October 28, 1912

DEAR WIFE: . . . . I was already starting to go to the old country, but I detained myself in order to earn some 100 roubles more, and because the war is going to be, so that if they should have to take me into the army then it is better to be in America. When there is peace then I will come at once, because I have worked enough. Answer me whether the reservists are taken already, because we read the papers and we know that Russia sent an army of 80,000 to the frontier of Asia. You see, beloved wife, I am afraid of being taken. Now I write you that in two weeks after the letter I will send you the money for "celebration." Beloved Broncia, when there is peace then we shall soon see each other. I do not have anything more to write.

ADAM STRUCIŃSKI

545
February 18, 1913

. . . . DEAR WIFE: I inform you that I received your letter and I am answering you at once and I inform you that we shall not see each other before my brother Andrzej comes to me. I should be

---

[1] Sexual allusions are completely avoided as long as marriage is a familial matter. Here we find only a vestige of the familial attitude in his asking pardon for his joke.

gone already, but I received a letter from my brother to send him a ship-ticket, and he asks about that. He says that he has to work very heavily, and apparently he does not have any possibility of helping our parents. I sent him therefore a ship-ticket and I expect him to come to me in the holidays, and so when he comes then I will be going back to my country at once. Dear wife, you make yourself so mournful that you must suffer. I suffer more, because I must work like a mule, and I do not have any comfort either. So it is not as we want, only it must be as we can. It is true that I promised you too much about my coming, but what could I do if it did not come out as I thought. But I hope that in May I shall be in my home, if not sooner. I beg your pardon, dear Broncia. Do not be angry with me, forgive me, and when I come then we will reconcile. I am ending. I send to you my kiss and embrace. Will it do? Bows to the whole family. I remain sincerely your husband, brother, brother-in-law,

ADAM STRUCIŃSKI

546 [No date]

DEAR WIFE: [Greetings; health and success good.] Don't worry about me, because when I work then I do not want to bring you to America, because here in America it is very difficult for a peasant [man], because as long as he is well then he always works like a mule, and therefore he has something, but if he becomes sick then it is a trouble, because everybody is looking only for money in order to get some of it, and during the sickness the most will be spent, and in old age, when one has not health or money, then there is trouble again. So when I have money today, then if something bad happens, I take a train and go ahead there where I came from, but it is not so with a woman. Now the work will go 2 months at most, because there are elections of the president. As is known, there will be very hard times and want. The fight is seen already among those who run for president of the Republican side. I will not stay and I will run away for the winter to you under the feather bed. I have the money, so that I shall not worry about anything, and as to what you write about what you think, I do not know. So, do not write me that at all unless you think of doing as you did when I was in Prussia. But also about Prussia do not write anything nor about my parents either, for when I received your letter, and I did not have a colleague who would write me a letter, then I answered myself, though with pencil, and you think—God knows what. And if you want money then I will send you a few roubles, because not long ago you were saying that you had [money]. Now you say that you have none. Write me how much money you have. And I did not send to you for such a long time because I wanted to save something. I do not have anything more to write.[1]

[ADAM STRUCIŃSKI]

[1] The last letters are filled with excuses and delays. The man apparently likes to be in America and prefers to be there alone. We are not to assume any definite interest in another woman, but possibly he is sexually demoralized. It is not the character of the peasant to prepare a break with his wife and lead gradually up to it, or to deceive her and at the same time write affectionately. Desertions of wives in Poland by husbands in America are not infrequent. Perhaps usually, as in this case, the desertion (if it comes to that) is not planned, but the moment does not come when the stimulation to go is stronger than the stimulation to stay.

BORKOWSKI SERIES

The Borkowski case is a particularly interesting example of a situation in which the marriage-group has almost ceased to be a part of the family and is no longer kept together by the familial organization, while the personal connection of husband and wife is not yet strong enough to make the group consistent.

The Borkowskis are city people. We do not know when the families of the husband and the wife came to Warsaw—it may have been thirty years ago or three hundred—and their attitudes give us no cue to this problem. The fact is that we find here an almost complete lack of traditional elements, except religion. But this may be the result either of a loss of peasant traditions in the city or of a gradual disintegration of old city traditions under the influence of modern life. At any rate, Borkowski is a factory workman, not a guild member, so he has not even the vestiges of the traditions of the handworker class, which would be slight even if he were a member of a guild, as we see in the case of his friend, Stanisław R.

Although Borkowski and his wife have numerous relatives in the city or in the neighborhood, the members of neither family care much for one another. The lack of solidarity goes so far that Borkowski's brother has not written to him during a period of twenty years; otherwise the letters would have been preserved with the others. Compare this situation with the one which we find in the Markiewicz family. When Teofila, the wife, finds herself in an exceptionally bad situation, no one among her relatives helps her. They avoid even social relations with her, as a boresome, poor, ill-dressed, complaining old woman.

There is also nothing that could take the place of the community which we find in the country or in small towns. To be sure, everyone has a circle of acquaintances within which there is gossip—a poor imitation of social opinion—but there is nothing like the continuous relationship between the inhabitants of a village, and no periodical meetings. Social opinion has therefore little power, consistency, or vitality.

Clearly in these conditions marriage becomes a mere individual matter; its social side is limited to the religious sanction, to the few uncomplicated relations between the marriage-group and the loose social environment, and to an exceptional intervention of this environment and of the state in the rare cases of criminal behavior. Within the large limits marked by these few social forms there is place enough for all the varieties which the relation between two individuals of different sex may assume. The nature of this relation will, of course, depend upon the personalities of the members and the sphere of their common interests. In the actual case, where the personalities of husband and wife are poor in traditions and poor in culture, their connection must be rather weak. When the first sensual attraction has disappeared, habit and the common interests of everyday life are the only links. But the emigration of the husband interrupted both of these, and a gradual dissolution of the conjugal bond became a psychological necessity.

We do not know the evolution through which the husband has passed, but we can easily guess it from the woman's letters. He evidently found a new sphere of interests in America; being a relatively intelligent, although not educated, man, he adapted himself successfully to the new conditions, and his life in Warsaw, where he did the same work but earned less and had less opportunity to express himself, must have appeared to him rather narrow—much more so, indeed, than in the case of a peasant, with the variety of work and the many concrete social interests which village life can give. Further, he seems to have felt rejuvenated in America, away from his wife, who was probably older than he (cf. No. 563). He dresses better, shaves his beard, and, as his wife expresses it, looks ten years younger. Probably, almost certainly, he has here a relation with another woman. Hence after a certain time there is nothing more left of the old affection toward his wife, and though for almost twenty years he writes from time to time and sends some money, he does it partly from pity, partly from a feeling of moral obligation. He does not make any great sacrifice; during the whole time he has sent her less than five hundred dollars, i.e., less than twenty-five dollars a year. But we must remember that he lacks any really strong motive to help her, for the feeling of obligation, not backed by the sanction of social opinion, cannot be strong in a man on this level of culture. And he feels more and more that his wife is a useless burden to him —not only on account of money, but also as the only link with a past life which he evidently wants to forget, and perhaps also as a hindrance to marrying someone else.

As to the influence of social opinion, there is an interesting difference between his behavior and that of a peasant, expressed by the fact that for so long a time he keeps up his relations with old friends of himself and his wife and still does not help her enough to prevent her becoming a pauper. Manifestly he does not care much for the opinion of the people at home, the demands of this opinion on him are neither strong nor consistent (cf. No. 586), and he does not at all identify the social position of his wife with his own. Now, a peasant would either send his wife money enough to satisfy the opinion of the community and to enable her to maintain a social position in accord with his own, or would break off all relations with her, with his friends, and with his family in order to avoid all touch with the opinion and condemnation of his community.

The letters give us a very good insight into the evolution of the woman. Without the backing of a family-group she never feels that she has a right to claim her husband's fidelity, help, and protection. The higher moral view with regard to the conjugal relation is clearly not more strongly developed in her than in her husband and cannot be a substitute for the absent social norms. In the beginning, she assumes implicitly that he will care for her after his emigration, since he cared for her at home. Later, when she realizes that things have changed, she appeals, not to his conjugal duty, but to his promise to help her and to his generosity. Still later, appeals to pity become her only resource, and when even this proves insufficient, she uses additional arguments—promises of God's reward, threats of suicide, etc. Love is at no time appealed to. The nature of her claims changes also. First, she wants and expects her husband to come back rather than to take her to America; later, she would be glad if he let her go to him, under someone's care (her affection is not strong enough to overcome her fear of the journey); still later, she ceases to expect to live with him and hopes only to see him once more; finally, it is enough for her to have from time to time his letters and money.

Another interesting point is her relation to her environment. As she has no social standing as a member of a family-group her social position is based exclusively on her marriage, i.e., upon the position of her husband, upon his attitude toward her, upon their having a home, etc. As soon as her husband leaves, her position is immediately lowered; she has no home and she does not represent much personally. But still he is expected to return or to take her to America, and thus her position is not yet so very low, because provisional. When, however, time passes and she remains alone, her social environment no longer takes her husband's possible return into account, and then her position depends exclusively upon his attitude toward her; every letter, photograph, sum of money, which he sends influences her social standing positively, as proofs that he is still solidary with her, while every proof of his desire to get rid of her pushes her down in social opinion. Naturally, it would be quite different if she were able to fight for a position by herself, without being so exclusively dependent upon him. But, being a city woman, she is afraid of heavy work, not only because of its physical hardship, but also because she believes that it would lower her still more. On the other hand, she is unable to progress by skilled work and, moreover, apparently lacks energy. Being so completely dependent upon her husband, she wants him for herself alone; she seems to feel that every expression of his personality outside is a loss for her, she is hostile to all his friends and relatives.

All these features of the Borkowski marriage-group are typical, because resulting necessarily from the given social situation and the general characteristics of the personalities. Now, if they had children, the whole situation would be different. We shall find, indeed, in the next series analogous characters and an analogous social situation, and we shall see what an enormous importance the children have there— an incomparably greater one than in the traditional familial organization.

547–86,   TO WŁADYSŁAW BORKOWSKI, IN AMERICA, FROM
HIS WIFE, IN POLAND, AND SOME LETTERS (578–86)
FROM ACQUAINTANCES

547

WARSAW, July 21, 1893

DEAR HUSBAND: I received your letter on July 4, which found me in usual health.   Up to the present I live with the Rybickis.   I am not very well satisfied, perhaps because I was accustomed to live for so many years quietly, with you alone.[1]   And today you are at one end of the world and I at the other, so when I look at strange corners [surroundings], I don't know what to do from longing and regret.   I comfort myself only that you won't forget me, that you will remain noble [generous] as you have been.   You wanted me to go to the Borkowskis [his brother].   I was there.   If they had only asked about you themselves!   But nobody said a word, only I related.[2]   Stasiak . . . . asked, but nobody else.   Borkowski's wife said that you took 27 roubles for the wardrobe and 15 roubles for the chest of drawers, and she refused to add anything.   She said to Stanisław that you had taken enough.   The small altar and the clock were taken by Filip from Praga and he gave 20 roubles.   I have nothing more to write, only I beg you, my dear, write to me as often as you can about yourself, whether you are in good health and how you succeed, for this is my only pleasure; I have no other.   I have only the sort of friends who think that I own thousands and from time to time someone comes to me, asking me to lend her a dozen roubles. . . . . And everyone would borrow for eternity; I know them already. . . . .

And now I bid you goodbye and wish you health and every good. Only don't forget me.

Your sincerely well-wishing wife,

[TEOFILA BORKOWSKA]

[1] Isolation has become habitual and desired.   We do not find this in the peasant family.   Of course some privacy is always sought by the marriage-group, but only for matters which, like the sexual relation, are more or less reserved by tradition as beyond the reach of other people's intrusion.   And the amount of privacy claimed by the marriage-group from the family is much smaller than that which it requires from the community.   In short, privacy for the peasant is nothing but a certain socially sanctioned limitation of the social character of individual life.   Here, on the contrary, it becomes a voluntary individual seclusion from the social life in general.

[2] The disintegration of the family is certainly real, even if in the given case the writer puts a particular emphasis upon the indifference of her husband's relatives, in accordance with her tendency to keep him exclusively for herself.

548   April 12, 1894

DEAR HUSBAND: I received your letter on April 2, which found
me in the best of health, and I wish you the same with my whole
heart.   Up to the present I thought and rejoiced that you would still
come back to Warsaw, but since you write that you won't come, I
comply with the will of God and with your will.   I shall now count
the days and weeks [until you take me to America].   May our Lord
God grant it to happen as soon as possible, for I am terribly worried.
Such a sad life!   I go almost to nobody, for as long as you were in
Warsaw everything was different.   Formerly we had friends, and
everybody was glad to see us, while now, if I go to anybody, they are
afraid I need something from them and they show me beforehand an
indifferent face. . . . . They all do it, even those who were so good
formerly.   Now they show themselves, as they are.[1]   You write me
to try to earn something with Władzia.   But I have not earned yet
a grosz from her.   She says that people beg her to give them work for
living alone, while I must pay 2 roubles for lodging, besides board.[2]
So, my dear, I beg you, describe to me everything in detail, what I
can take with me, what clothes, whether it is worth taking the fur,
the [photographs in] frames and other trifles.   I will take the image
and the cross, but I have heard that it was forbidden to take the
chest.   So please describe everything to me exactly.   You write
to the Lukas that I write so seldom, but always when the Lukas
write I ask them to write something from me.   Evidently they
don't do it. . . . .

Your loving wife,

TEOFILA BORKOWSKA

[1] As we have stated in the introduction, Teofila, not being a member of a
family-group, can have no other social recognition than that which results from
her own or her husband's position.   Her husband being away, the recognition
which she had as his wife is reduced to almost nothing as is shown by the behavior
of her environment and of which she complains.   There are still two chances for
her to keep at least some social standing.   One is her husband's fidelity—sending
of money, writing of letters, etc.—in a word, proofs that he remains solidary with
her in spite of the separation and that the separation is only temporary, that he
will either come back or take her to America.   The second chance is to acquire a
personal position by her own work.

[2] Władzia is a cousin who has a millinery or dressmaking shop, in which
Borkowski wants his wife to work as a seamstress.

549 August 8, 1895

DEAR HUSBAND: . . . . You won't believe how much I suffered when you did not write for some months. I thought that I should not live long enough to read your letter, but when I received the letter from you I wept with joy. But after reading it sadness overwhelmed me again. I thought that you had forgotten and would not write your address. But, thanks to God, it seems to me that my heavy sorrow and my terrible want are over. There is no work this year with Dobska at all, so I don't sew there at all. I earn sometimes a few złoty, but what does it mean when I must pay 3 roubles rent a month [in a room with three or four others]. In one place I had no money to pay for the lodging, and they took my bed. Now I sleep upon a borrowed bed. Moreover, they have levied hospital taxes in Warsaw, 1 rouble for a person yearly, so I must pay, for if you do not pay you must pay later 4 roubles of fine.

Before I received your letter, I went to the consul more than once, begging him to find you, what is going on with you. But he did not want to search for you until I paid him 5 roubles. But I did not have them and I had to remain in sadness. My dear, you ask for my photograph, but I can send it only when you send me a few roubles. But I beg you, send me yours as soon as possible. . . . .

[TEOFILA]

550 October 2, 1895

DEAR HUSBAND: To the last letter which you wrote on July 13, I answered at once with great joy, for I thought that after so many months of my sorrow and crying and different other troubles the sun shone for me. But I see that it only joked, that I must suffer so up to my death. Up to the present I have never annoyed you [about money], for I knew that when you could, you would send me a few roubles. So I beg you, if you can, send me a few roubles as soon as possible, for I am in a situation without issue. . . . .

Your loving wife,

TEOFILA BORKOWSKA

551 January 28, 1896

DEAR HUSBAND: . . . . You reproach me for not answering you at once. My dear, I evidently did not do it through negligence, for you won't believe, I have not words enough to tell you, how much good you did me by sending that money, you saved me from some strange despair, because I waited for this money as for the salvation of my soul. Twelve roubles out of this money went for rent alone, for I must pay 3 roubles a month. Now they won't take less for a person, because apartments have gone up. And I have a corner where I must sit upon my bed. And in renting they say at once that I cannot cook, and ask me whether I will sit much at home. I have often such conditions for these 3 roubles that I cannot even boil a little water for my tea, but must remain the whole day living on dry food. The first 11 roubles I received from Berlin, the next time 10 from the consul, both without any letter, so I thought that perhaps it was not from you, this money, and I did not know what to do. You promised me to send your photograph. I hoped always to see you at least upon paper, but I was deceived. I sent you the books; it seems to me that they are good. Now I have nothing more to write you, only I wish you every good and every happiness, whatever you want from our Lord God. For I know this, that if you get on well I shall also get on well; so you said when you were leaving.

Greeting from all acquaintances, the good ones. . . . .

TEOFILA BORKOWSKA

552   May 13 [1896]

DEAR HUSBAND: I received your letter . . . . together with the photographs. You won't believe me what a joy and comfort it was for me when I saw you. It seemed to me in the first moment that I saw you alive. I received the money, i.e., 12 roubles, on April 1. I thank you for it heartily. Dear Władek, you asked me to answer you at once when I received the letter and the money. I wished to answer at once . . . . but I caught such cold that for 3 weeks I did not rise from my bed. Now, thanks to our Lord God, I am better. And so, my dear, from the money which you sent me I intended to pay 4 roubles of rent and to buy shoes for myself, but I had to spend it on medicine and a doctor. So, my dear, I beg you, if you can, send me a little money as soon as you receive this letter, for I need it very much. The Czub. thank you very much for the photograph, Kawecki has probably answered you himself, for he was to write at once. You pleased everybody very much, acquainted as well as unacquainted people, you look so well.

Now, dear Władek, as to my coming to you, if it were possible, I should be very glad, but imagine what a terrible difficulty it would be for me to start quite alone on such a far journey. You know that I am not very bold, nor very talkative either, so it would be very difficult for me to find my way alone.[1] For as to Rafalski, he won't go now; his plans are changed. He is offended with you for having written him about land instead of writing how much you earn and what work is there. He says: "Does he do any favor to me? He will send me a ship-ticket when I send him 20 roubles. But if I wish I can buy a ticket myself." My dear, you ask me why do I not write you about Karol and his wife. I have nothing to write about them, for I know nothing. They don't come to me at all, they are afraid I might want something from them, so I don't go to them either. Since you left they have not invited me to any holidays or little parties which they arrange often. You know, Władek, I pray to God continually that He may inspire you with the wish to come back to Warsaw. After the crowning there will be amnesty, so you can come back, and you would certainly have work, for in the factory they are working on holidays and nights, and everybody says that it will last for some years still. So, my dear, perhaps you will change your mind and long for your native country. I heard that you promised it to Rafalski. I would wait patiently; I have suffered for 3 years, I would bear it for one year more. . . . . I have kept the box, the image of God's Mother, and the photographs as tokens. I did not sell your fur coat either; I keep it, for I think that you will perhaps walk in it about Warsaw. Although I was already in a hard need, I did not sell it. . . . .[2]

My dear, don't forget what I asked you for, because I need it very much and very soon. . . . .

[TEOFILA]

553 July 10, 1896

DEAR WŁADEK: . . . . I don't know what it means that you don't answer the letter in which I thanked you for the photographs and the money which you sent me, 10, 11, and 12 roubles, the last

---

[1] Her helplessness, in contrast with the energy of country girls who undertake the journey to America even to marry unknown men (cf. Butkowski series) is perhaps partly constitutional.

[2] The woman's desire to see her husband back in Warsaw rather than to go to America is probably conditioned by other factors than her fear of traveling alone. She can imagine future happiness only in the same familiar conditions and environment in which she had lived happily before. Perhaps there is also some desire to get restitution for all the humiliations which she has to suffer, to have the same people who now neglect her be the witnesses of her triumph.

before Easter. I sent you a letter on May 13, almost begging for a few roubles, for I spent these on medicines and the doctor, but not only you did not send me anything, you did not even answer, so I don't know what it means, whether you are offended with me for having asked you for these few roubles. But you have written yourself that you will send me [money] every month, and therefore I was more bold in asking you for it.[1] . . . . So please answer me whether you received that letter and the books which I sent you before. The letter was registered, so it must have reached you, and if it did not reach you . . . . write me and I will take a complaint to the post-office. . . . .

Your always loving wife,

TEOFILA BORKOWSKA

554   December 2, 1896

DEAR HUSBAND: I inform you that I have already left the hospital and I am healthy enough, and I wish you the same. I received in the hospital the letter which you wrote on August 31. I rejoiced very much, for every letter from you is a day of joy for me, and I have no other joy now. Only I am very much pained that you reproach me for writing only about myself and nothing about any relatives or acquaintances. But what can I write about them, since they are all *państwo* [originally "lord and lady," then in general, "gentle people" or "rich people"] as compared with me, while I am quite alone, without husband, without home. When I left the hospital I did not know what to do with myself, without money and almost without roof, for I did not know what to do and what to pay for the lodging with. I remained for 2 months in the hospital and had to pay 6 roubles of rent. She remitted one rouble, 5 were left. So I begged her, and promised I would pay her when you send some money. But nobody cares for me, nobody helps me, for they know that I have no chance to pay them back. And you reproach me for not informing you about them. Why, he is your own brother, he could ask sometimes what is going on with you, once at least, send one of the children to me or write to you. And my family is the same; they are afraid I will ask them for something. Czab. came to me once, to the hospital, and I know that they are all in good health.

---

[1] She does not consider it her husband's duty to maintain her, as a peasant woman would do, but appeals merely to his promise.

My Władzio, don't be angry that I send registered letters, but you see you write so seldom I should think that my letter did not reach you and I could not learn, while so I am certain that you received it and I live at least with some hope that you will answer me. And now I am waiting for an answer to that letter which I wrote you when I was in the hospital, and I know that it reached you for it was registered. Evidently, dear Władek, you are so angry with me that you have not written for some months, while I sent you almost not a letter but a petition. So don't be angry with me, my dear husband, for to whom shall I appeal? And you made me bold yourself, for you promised me to send me a little, and I don't ask much, anything [a little] at least. And I beg your pardon once more, Władek, don't be angry with me, but answer me as soon as possible. As to the photograph, perhaps I shall earn a little, but only in the spring; then I would send you one, for now I have no money to go to the photograph[er]. . . . .[1]

[TEOFILA BORKOWSKA]

555   May 19, 1897

DEAR HUSBAND: . . . . I received your letter together with the money, i.e., with 12 roubles . . . . for which I thank you heartily, dear Władek. After receiving those 20 roubles, which you sent me last year, I wrote you 3 letters, two registered, the last with a single stamp, so I beg you much, answer me whether you received them all, particularly that non-registered one, for it seems to me that letters often don't reach you. Now, dear Władek, you write me that you are not sure whether I receive your money, because I don't write myself [with my own hand], only Mrs. Sliwińska [the woman from whom she rents] does. But you can be as sure as if I wrote with my own hand. She gives me every letter as soon as she receives it from the post, whether with money or not, and address them as always, because they are sure people. . . . . I intentionally begged somebody else to write this letter in order that you might believe that I receive your letters and money. I beg you, dear Władek, write to me more often, for now you have not written for so long a time. My dear, write me whether you intend ever to come back to Warsaw? I often hear that some husband comes back to his family, and even whole families return. When I hear it my heart almost bursts open, because

---

[1] The absolute and painful dependence of the wife could hardly be better illustrated than by this letter.

you don't write and won't return to your native country. Why, you are a Pole! . . . . In Warsaw there is an enormous movement, all factories full of work, and for you also work is ready. Only come! . . . .

I thank you once more heartily for the money, and the next time when you send me some money I will go to the photograph[er] and send you [my photograph].

Your loving wife,

TEOFILA BORKOWSKA

556　　　　　　　　　　　　　　　　　　　September 26, 1897

DEAR HUSBAND: For God's sake, what does it mean that you don't answer? Kawecki called on me, for he also wrote to you and you gave him no answer, so he came to ask what you write to me, what is going on with you and how you succeed. He thought that you don't want to write to him because you have got very rich; he was curious, for he did not know how to judge you. Only when I told him that for half a year you have not written to me, he was also pained, fearing that something had happened to you. For I also grieved terribly [thinking] what had happened to you. For I don't think that you could have forgotten me totally, while I write you such supplications every time. So I repeat once more my begging. Answer me as soon as possible and send me anything you can. For if I were not in need I should never annoy you, but our Lord God is the best witness how terribly hard it is for me to live. Those few roubles which you sent me a few times are only enough to pay the rent for some months, because there I must give 3 roubles a month at once. As to board, clothes, and shoes, they are earned with such a difficulty that you have surely no idea. And I must eat every day. There are mostly days in my present situation when I have one small roll and a pot of tea for the whole day, and I must live so. And this has lasted almost 5 years since you left. If I were a plain country woman I would go to wash linen or floors, or in summer to work in a garden, but you know that I am unable to do it and I have no strength, while sewing by hand is terribly hard.[1] So, my dear husband, don't

---

[1] The inability to do hard work is to some extent real, but to some extent only imagined with the women and men who belong to that lower town and city class which is more or less specialized in finer handwork or small trade. There is a peculiar rivalry between this class and the peasants in the country. People of this class feel that only the relatively finer character of their work and dress keeps them in a certain regard above the country peasant, while by hard labor they

be angry with me for writing to you so decidedly, but I have almost nobody except you. Although I have many relatives it is as if I had none, for you remember also what you got from your relatives when you were in need. Although you were only a child. . . . .

And now I bid you goodbye, dear husband. Be healthy, and don't forget me.

Your loving wife,
Teofila Borkowska

557 May 24, 1898

Dear Władek: I received your letter on May 1, i.e., 15 roubles of money. They had searched for me for some weeks and could not find me, because you almost never address to Jan Sliwiński, but to Teofila Borkowska. I should not have received this money . . . . only Sliwińska wondered why you had not written for almost a year. She found the postman and asked him whether he had never had a letter from America to Borkowska, and he said that he had one some weeks ago, but could not find [the person] and gave it back to the post-office. There were two money-orders, one of 15 roubles for Teofila Borkowska, and the other of 25 roubles for Teofila Bartowska [misaddressed]. They refused to give me the second, saying that it was not for me, and kept it at the office. And as you sent no letter, I don't know myself whether these 25 roubles are for me or not. So I beg you, dear Władek, answer me the soonest possible whether you sent me these 25 roubles, and if you did, you must correct the name yourself. . . . . Perhaps I suspect you, dear husband, and grieve that you have forgotten me, while it is perhaps unjust. You have written perhaps, but not to the address of the Sliwińskis, but to mine, and the letter did not reach me. I thank you, dear Władek, for your remembrance and for these 15 roubles with which you have saved me from a great misery. May our Lord God in reward help you in all

---

would fall at once to the lowest degree in the social scale—to that of a *wyrobnik*, having no home and working by the day. Therefore they defend themselves to the last against plain physical work, and often prefer pauperism. The class of city paupers recruits itself mainly, if not exclusively, from these people. The peasant, particularly the farmer, despises heartily this class of people, even if envying sometimes their few external refinements of dress and manners. But this class of people, by real culture hardly superior to the country peasant, forgets every prepossession and works as hard as possible when in America.

your intentions. I pray to Him every day for you. . . . . I greet you heartily.

Your always loving wife,

Teofila Borkowska

Good by [in English; imitated from his letter].

558 September 12, 1898

Dear Husband: First I must thank you heartily for having helped me so much. I did not expect it at all, only I always thought that perhaps you had no money yourself and you could send me none. I only prayed to our Lord God to give you health and to bless you in all your intentions, for I knew that you would not desert me. And so it happened, for which I thank you heartily once more, and may our Lord God help you further in everything.

First I received the 15 roubles about which I wrote you. Then I received 25 roubles, when you corrected the name. And now I received 28 roubles through the Commercial Bank, for which I made some purchases, because for a long time I had bought nothing [no clothes, etc.] for myself. I am very happy through all this, but I should be still more happy if we could see each other some day, and if it were in Warsaw.

You ask me what is the news in Warsaw. You would not recognize Warsaw—such movement and work, hundreds of big new houses. On Marszałkowska Street a score of very splendid houses, and a very beautiful church on Dzielna Street, and in the neighborhood of the Jesus Hospital they begin to build a church, and on Czerniakowska Street a church, and a politechnical school is opened in Warsaw, such as up to the present have been only abroad. Therefore there is movement and in factories everywhere much work. They built a new railway to Wilanów, another is being built to Grójec, many nice small parks are added, before the All-Saints Church and the St. Alexander Church. Where the Ujazdowski place was there is now a very beautiful park. On Krakowskie Przedmieście will stand a monument of Mickiewicz; there will be a consecration on Christmas eve, an enormous meeting; all the windows are already hired. Only you won't be here! And perhaps you will still come back to Warsaw some day? May God grant it.[1] All my brothers came here, some

---

[1] By the description of Warsaw she evidently wishes to attract him home. At the same time we have a manifestation of attachment to the city.

of them to Warsaw, to work at the railway-works, others in Wola, others in Brudno. . . . . The Borkowskis are no longer here. They rented a buffet at a railway-station. [Indifferent news about friends.]

TEOFILA BORKOWSKA

559   May 12, 1899

DEAR HUSBAND: I received your letter . . . . with 20 roubles and three photographs on April 4, for which I send you a hearty "God reward." I bear it always in my heart and thought and I always repeat it to everybody, that you were good and generous and you are so up to the present. I can be proud before everybody that you don't forget me[1] for which once more may our Lord God reward you. I beg only our Lord God that we may yet see each other once more. Write me, dear Władek, can I hope it? When I saw you in a cyclist dress in the photograph, I could hardly recognize you, you have got about 10 years younger, particularly because you had your beard shaved. But did you not regret your beard? Kawecki thanks you much for the photograph and will send you his own soon, together with his wife's. They even wish to give you a surprise and to send you a group of all [the members] of the fraternity [a half-religious fraternity to which he belonged; see Kawecki letters]. And as to me, if God comforts me still on your behalf [if you still send me money], I will send you also my photograph. Don't be angry, dear Władek, for my counting upon you alone. Perhaps now your condition is still difficult, but I beg our Lord God in every prayer that He may help you in all your intentions, and I always feel a comfort and hope, that you are very happy and in a very good condition.[2] . . . . And I think that if our Lord God helps you, for me it will also be better. . . . .

Your loving wife,

TEOFILA BORKOWSKA

[1] We see how her social standing depends exclusively upon her husband's good will toward her. She does not succeed in getting position personally, hardly even tries, but clings desperately to the only thread which keeps her from falling definitely into the class of paupers and outcasts.

[2] We find here a proof that praying to God for the sake of anyone is not a merely formal expression of gratitude, but that the prayer, as well as the blessing, is supposed to be really efficient and a real reward for a benefit received. The existence of beggars is based upon this idea. Cf. Wróblewski series, No. 31, note.

560   June 26, 1901

DEAR WŁADEK: I received the letter with 50 roubles, which you sent on January 25. Later, after many troubles and much walking, at the cost of 10 roubles, I got the pictures, for which I thank you heartily, first for the money, then for the picture. For you not only remember about my needs, but you caused me a great pleasure. But for the picture only I thank you, for Karol [brother] and Lodzia [niece] are not satisfied at all, they would prefer a score or two of roubles.[1] Dear Władek, I have not written for so long a time, for, to tell the truth, I don't dare to importune you so often. But you authorized me yourself, for you wrote me to write you whenever I needed money. So, dear Władek, I write now————.

I don't live any longer with Karol and his wife, for it seemed to them that since I lived with them they ought to have a living out of me. But as I could not give them everything you sent me they began to behave toward me in an awful manner, so that at last they wanted to beat me. So I live now elsewhere. . . . .

O, dear Władek, if it could happen some day, if you could come and take me with you! For myself I would not be able to go alone to you. And perhaps somebody from your side [of your family or friends] will go to America? Then I would willingly go with him to you. . . . .

Your loving wife,
TEOFILA BORKOWSKA

561   July 29, 1902

DEAR HUSBAND: I received your letter . . . . and it grieved me much that you had been so very sick. Well, but thanks to God you are now in good health, and I wish you the same in the future; I pray our Lord God for it every day. [Describes the difficulty she had in getting 60 roubles which he sent her.] Stanisław intends to go to you within a short time. He promised me always that when he went he would take me with him. I rejoiced very much, but they

---

[1] Again she tries, consciously or half-consciously, to weaken still more the connection between her husband and his family, in order to have him exclusively for herself. This method does not seem very wise, if we compare this situation with the peasant series. Since the personal relation between husband and wife is not strong enough, the proper thing would be to strengthen as much as possible all the ties which attach him to his country.

wanted to wheedle me out of the money which you had sent me. And as I could not give it to them they don't speak to me any more. I don't know whether it is possible, but when he goes to America, he wants to marry there his sweetheart with whom he lives and has 5 children. So, dear husband, if it is possible, when he takes her, perhaps I could go with them to you. I desire it very much, even only to see you, my dear! If it is possible, write to him yourself, for he is like a wasp to me now because of my not having given them this money.[1] I thank you once more heartily for the money and I beg you, my dear, although with a great timidity, don't forget about me and send me soon a little at least, for it is already difficult for me to earn anything. They require now machine-sewing. Moreover my eyes ache from crying and from work in these small corners, in the kitchen where I live, because for 3 roubles nobody would receive me into a dwelling-room. And even these 3 roubles I can scarcely pay, and often I suffer hunger, since the rent must be paid. . . . .

Your always loving wife,

TEOFILA BORKOWSKA

562 March 27, 1903

DEAR HUSBAND: Mr. Rupiński called upon me on March 11, and left me 40 roubles, for which may our Lord God reward you. I wanted to answer you at once but I had yet to see Mr. R. before his departure. Meanwhile he probably had some business and could not see me, for during a whole week I went every day to the Karols to see him, for they always told me that he was not yet leaving. . . . . And perhaps they simply deceived me, for they have a pleasure in annoying me in any way. Now, dear Władek, Mr. R. said that you would probably come back to Warsaw. O, dear Władek, a new life entered into me, the whole world appeared to me more gay. Now I shall pray to our Lord God to shorten these months, for you won't believe how happy I am now. I shall live with this idea, that I may see you yet before dying. Now, dear Władek, I will try to find the man who bought the altar, for he said that if we want it he will give it back at any moment. Dear husband, perhaps you will send me an authorization to get back from Stanisław the rest of the money which he owes you. . . . .

TEOFILA BORKOWSKA

[1] Compare this whole story with the letters of Stanisław R.

563   April 23, 1904

DEAR HUSBAND: I received your letter with 60 roubles. . . . . It rejoiced me on the one hand, but on the other hand grieved me very much. Believe me, dear Władek, that I had such a foreboding. When I divided the [Easter] egg with anybody, I wept, for I imagined always that you are so far away, alone, without family, and more than once you must feel very sad, as I do, and perhaps even sick, and there is nobody to care for you of your own people. And so it seemed to me continually, and suddenly Sliwińska brings me a letter. Really, my foreboding proved true. Believe me, dear Władek, that I even was not so glad to receive this money as grieved in learning that you are sick. You are often sick there, probably the climate is bad for you. But I pray and beg our Lord God every day to give you health and to make you still happy in your life. You are still young, and up to the present you have not yet experienced any good in your life. So may our Lord God give you every good, whatever you wish from Him, for your good heart.[1] God reward you for the money which you sent me! Besides you, I had still another sorrow, for my brother Ignacy is dead. . . . . I don't know even whether you remember him. So people of my family begin to die. . . . .

                                                 TEOFILA BORKOWSKA

564   August 8, 1904

DEAR HUSBAND: For God's sake answer, what is going on with you. This is the fourth letter which I send you, begging you for an answer, and you don't answer me even a word. I believe, dear husband, that perhaps you are tired already with writing always and sending money. But perhaps our Lord God will make you free soon. I wish it myself, for I am also tired with worrying myself so in this world and worrying you besides. Although you do not let me feel it, because you are good, yet I feel it myself, and whenever I receive money from you I weep, for I am a burden to you and I can repay you with nothing except by praying God for your health and for happiness in your life. . . . .[2]   Your sincerely loving wife,

Good by.   TEOFILA BORKOWSKA

[1] This is apparently a resignation to the idea of a perpetual separation and perhaps to the possibility of his being happy with another woman.

[2] Her conviction is more outspoken than in the preceding letter. A few words from time to time and a little money to enable her to continue to live is all she can claim.

565   October 16, 1905

DEAR HUSBAND: . . . . I wrote you a letter on August 10, asking you to answer with at least a few words, whether you are in good health and whether you received my letter with thanks for the money. But up to the present I have no answer. It is true, dear Władek, that you have not so much time, but, my dear, write me sometimes a few words; you will cause me a great comfort. For I read your letter like a prayer, because for me, dear Władek, our Lord God is the first and you the second. Don't be angry, if perhaps I bore you with my letters, but it is for me a great comfort to be able to speak with you at least through this paper. Write me, Władek, whether you will come some day to Warsaw. Good by. May our Lord God keep you in His care.

Your loving wife,

TEOFILA BORKOWSKA

566   February 12, 1906

DEAR HUSBAND: . . . . Don't be angry with me for writing to you in such an importunate way and asking always for money, but what can I do, poor woman, when I have no other way except to stretch out my hand on the street and beg. It is quite difficult for me to earn enough for my whole living, because not everybody wants [clothes] sewn by hand but only some poor servant maid, who pays then very little. So, my dear husband, send me what you can, for I have nothing to live on. I even made debts for my rent and a few roubles which I borrowed from Sliwińska on account of the money which you will send me. . . . . I wrote you some letters begging you so much to answer me a few words, whether you are in good health, but you wrote me no letter except that one with money. . . . .

TEOFILA BORKOWSKA

567   November 25, 1906

DEAR HUSBAND: First, may God the Great reward you for your good heart and your care for me, for truly it is nothing else but the Divine Providence which through your person guards me. I had not a whole rouble left, and moreover I got so sick that I was taken unconscious to the hospital; nobody even among my acquaintances knew it. Only when I came back a little to health I asked the nun to telephone to Sliwińska, and the latter when coming to me met the postman who gave her a letter and a money-order for 70 roubles. She brought me at once this comfort to the hospital. Believe me, Władek, when I read your letter, that perhaps I may see you still, it seemed to me that I was healthier. But even so I remained still about a month in the hospital, and when I left it I had money to live and to pay for the lodging, because Sliwińska brought me 75 roubles from the post-office. . . . . So think, dear Władek, is it not a true Providence, Divine and yours, which guards me?

Perhaps you won't come here for ever, dear Władek, but at least perhaps you will visit Warsaw and your friends, and so God will listen to me and I shall see you once more. . . . .[1]

TEOFILA BORKOWSKA

568   March 1, 1907

DEAR HUSBAND: Again some months have passed and I have no news from you. As long as you were in Chicago it seemed as if I felt you nearer, but now [when you are in California] it seems to me that you are so far that even by thought I cannot reach you. O, my dear Władek, you cannot imagine how woeful it is to live so alone, a woman left by everybody in the world. For if a woman is poor she has no friends at all, even her family leaves her. I see nobody but Sliwińska from time to time, and nobody else ever comes to me. So, my dear Władek, although you are so far, don't forget me, for if you forgot me my life would be ended for me. Answer me soon, my only one!

Good by, my dear husband.

Your loving wife,

TEOFILA BORKOWSKA

569   September 2, 1909

DEAR HUSBAND: For God's sake, what has happened? Since you wrote last year and sent money in June . . . . you sent money the second time in December, but no letter. I wrote two letters to you, begging you to write a few words, at least upon a postcard, but you did not write, I don't know why. . . . . You know probably already that [Mr.] Sliwiński is dead, for I wrote you, and even your friend, Mr. Kotowski, told me that he wrote you. I don't see Mr. K. now, for he lives in Praga and I hear intends to go back to America. Mr. K. told me that you would write a letter for me to the address of

---

[1] Complete resignation, placing herself on the same basis as his friends.

his brother on Hoża Street, so I go there very often and ask, but there is never any letter. So, dear Władek, don't be angry for my registering this letter, but from sorrow I don't know what to do. Dear husband, if you send money, send it as before to the address of Mrs. Sliwińska. . . . . And I beg you, dear husband, don't be angry, but I beg you, send as soon as possible, what you can. Dear Władek, I know that you are worth some thousands, for Mr. K. told me so. You could therefore do to yourself and to me and to all your friends this pleasure, and come at least on a visit to Warsaw. Now in Warsaw it is very quiet.

Good by, dear husband, and may God give you everything the best.

Your loving wife,

TEOFILA BORKOWSKA

570   January 20, 1910

DEAR HUSBAND, MY BELOVED WŁADEK: I don't know why you do not want to write to me. Evidently you don't want to, for I have sent you 4 letters and begged and implored you to write at least a few words, but you don't write at all. Never yet, during so many years, has it been so. Now, toward the end of my life, for a year and 8 months you have not written a letter. Why, you could find a little time to write a few words! You sent money a year and two months ago and even then you did not write a word. Evidently you don't wish to care for me any more. And what can I do now, unhappy woman, since I cannot earn enough for my living. Here thousands of young people walk without work, and for me, in my advanced age, it is still more difficult. So I don't know what I shall do with myself, miserable woman, if you cease to care for me and don't send me money any more. Nothing more is left for me except to stretch out my hand and beg on the street, or to take my life away. But I, miserable woman, have not courage enough to do either the one or the other, only I worry and suffer hunger, for I lack a bit of bread. So have pity, dear husband! You have cared for me so many years, don't abandon me in the last years of my life. Send me a little money, and perhaps our Lord God will listen to my prayer—and increase your fortune, your happiness, and your health. . . . .[1]

TEOFILA BORKOWSKA

[1] An unimportant letter follows from which it is evident that he sent her some money before this letter reached him.

571   August 6, 1910

DEAR HUSBAND: I write to you with great timidity, but despair obliges me to write so openly.   I beg you, dear Władek, I beg you for God's sake, have pity and send me a little money, for I can find no way out.   I tried to get from the Philanthropic Association at least a few tickets for a few pounds of bread and a few pints of gruel monthly, but they refused me, for they learned that I have a husband. They say that it is for them all the same whether this husband is in Warsaw or in America, but I have a husband.   So I don't know what to do with myself.   I have no work, for now even a poor servant maid wants [her dresses] to be sewn on a machine with different adornments, for such is the fashion.   And, to tell the truth, I begin to lose my eyes with sewing and crying.   So I only implore first our Lord God, then you for mercy upon me.   Have pity, dear husband, send me [money] as soon as possible, because I owe for rent, I owe to Sliwińska, and I have no possibility of paying them, while every day I must nourish myself, and I have nothing.   Although I economize every grosz from you and nourish myself with anything in order only to live through the day, yet everything is so expensive, particularly rent.   I live in a basement, my bed in a corner, a box and a small table before the bed, and I pay for it 3 roubles and 2 złoty [3 roubles, 30] a month, and they hardly permit me sometimes to cook a little with my own fuel, and so it is everywhere. . . . . .

TEOFILA BORKOWSKA

Dear husband, write me whether you will come some day to Warsaw?   It is true that you have put aside some money, but on the other hand you are far away from your family and from your land.   And after so many years you would have had better conditions even here, and more than one pain would be spared to you. For it seems to me that sometimes it is not very pleasant for you there, and more than once perhaps you long for your people.   Write me, dear Władek; let me at least have some illusion that I shall still see you.

572   October 13, 1910

DEAR HUSBAND: A few weeks ago I sent you a letter, or rather a supplication, asking you to have pity and to send me some money. But you, Władek, did not answer me a word.   I don't know what to think. I think that you are tired perhaps with having cared for me for so long a time. But have pity and send me something and don't forget me. Perhaps soon things will come to an end with me and I shall go aside from your way. Write me, dear Władek, what is the news with you. Perhaps you are sick and therefore don't answer. Answer, my beloved, my dear benefactor, and send me some money. . . . .

TEOFILA BORKOWSKA

573 November 11, 1910

DEAR HUSBAND: You write that I have not answered after receiving your money. But I sent you at once a letter with thanks when I received 75 roubles from the post-office. . . . . You sent this money a year ago, in November, while I received it only in February 1910. . . . . Of the money which you have sent me not a penny was ever lost. If we see each other some day—and I pray always to our Lord God for it, and I hope that it will come—I shall show you all your letters and orders, for I keep them like holy things. . . . . Dear Władek, you make reproaches for my calling on you for money. Look through the letters [you will see] that I beg you and implore you with great timidity, and only because great need forces me. Dear Władek, you won't believe how I beg our Lord God that I may see you still before my death. My dear, write me whether it will ever happen. And write ·me, my dear, whether you know there everything, which happened here upon Jasna Góra [Częstochowa; a monk killed his cousin and robbed the cloister].

TEOFILA BORKOWSKA

574 December 18, 1910

DEAR HUSBAND: I received your letter and 38 roubles. [Details and thanks.]

Dear Władek, are you angry when I write you and ask you to write me a few words, whether you will ever come to Warsaw? For you never answer my begging. Answer at least a few words to my begging, my dear! . . . .

TEOFILA BORKOWSKA

575 April 20, 1911

DEAR HUSBAND: I wrote you four letters and in every one I implored you to write me at least a few words, and I cannot prevail upon you. So, my dear husband, have pity upon me, I implore you, and send me a little money, for strange things come already to my head, and I tell you openly that it is from hunger. For a long time I have not had a penny of my own, only a few roubles of debt which I borrow, a few złoty at once. But as it seems to other people that you won't send me any more, so I don't dare to borrow, and they make excuses and don't want to lend me. So I beg you, send as soon as possible, or else I will probably take my life away. On Easter I should not have had a bit of dry bread if Śliwińska had not given me, and she also has nothing, lives only by the mercy of her children. . . . .[1]

Teofila Borkowska

576   September 8, 1911

Dear Husband: Don't be angry with me, dear Władek, for writing to you too often, but I am always tormented [about you] and I grieve, fearing you may be sick. For the papers write here that in America great heats prevailed and therefore many people are sick; perhaps even therefore I grieve so and have such painful dreams. So, dear Władek, answer me at least a few words, comfort me in my heavy misfortune, for you are my only Providence. . . . . Only you are changed since some time, dear Władek; when you write, your letter is now always angry with me. . . . .

Teofila Borkowska

577   July 12, 1912

Dear Husband: Have pity upon me, for I am already barefooted and naked. They have taken everything for the rent, even the pillow from under my head; only a small pillow is left. Have pity, dear Władek, and send me some money! You won't let me die from hunger, for I know that you have a merciful and noble heart, only perhaps somebody incites you. Why, I have not much longer to live, for with such a hunger as I suffer now I shall not hold out long. So I implore you, dear husband, have pity and listen to my imploring, for you are the second after God, to whom I pray every day.

Good by, dear husband. Be happy.

Your loving wife,
Teofila Borkowska

[1] The next letter, here omitted, shows that he sent her some money.

578

RESPECTED SIR: Your wife is sick, she lies in the St. Roch's Hospital . . . . since August 20. She received the money which you sent, 20 roubles, in August; she was already so sick that she scarcely dragged herself to the post-office. . . . . She is not so dangerously sick, but suffering very much . . . . and in general the whole organism is very weak because of bad nutrition and continuous sorrow. She is so alone and deserted almost by everybody, for the family never comes to see her. Even to the hospital nobody goes except me, who go to her once in a week. Even the Czs. do not, although I informed them. In the hospital she has at least some care, while at home she remained quite alone, for the people with whom she lived left for some weeks. The doctor advised sending her to the hospital that she might have at least a little comfort and care. So please write to her at once. You will thus comfort her a little, for she longs continually for you and your letters. I shall answer you at once, how she is in her health. And please be so good and send her a few roubles when she leaves the hospital, for of those 20 roubles only a few złoty are left, and she must pay the rent for the time during which she remains in the hospital. And please, be so kind, send her [money] regularly every month or every 2 months, for your wife is horribly tormented by this lack of a few złoty and of a letter from you, when you don't write for so long a time. And please, write a little more affectionately. Only do it soon, for it will be the best medicine for your wife, at least for her heart. . . . .

ALEKSANDRA SLIWIŃSKA

579

"Praised be Jesus Christus."

RESPECTED MR. BORKOWSKI: I have received your letter, for which I send you the most hearty "God reward." I was very glad that you deigned to describe the customs of that country and that you are in good health, for which infinite praise be to God who deigns to keep you in His omnipotent guardianship on your long journey. And now, Resp. Sir, in Warsaw there is no news. Food has got cheaper, except sugar and meat. For instance, 2 lbs. of bread cost now 6 copecks, a korzec [250 lbs.] of potatoes 1 rouble, and so on.

As to our singing, all those are there who were there during your presence. We have not learned any new song except this one which we send you. I, my children, and all our brothers and sisters from the choir of the Holy Rosary, are in good health, by the favor of our Lord God, and we wish you the same with our soul and heart. We send up a profound and sincere sigh to the Great Lord of Hosts, that He may bless you in that far and remote country. I send you my photograph and that of the priest S., for remembrance. All your acquaintances greet you, such as [enumeration].

And now, Resp. Mr. Borkowski . . . . nothing remains, except to kiss you, my kindest friend, heartily. I greet you and bid you goodbye in the name of the Holy Trinity, from whose care may you never be removed. And I exhort you to worship this Holy Trinity ceaselessly, and be sure that you won't be deceived. And acting thus, we can secure for ourselves our soul's salvation. I wish it to you, my kindest friend and brother in Christ, and to myself with all my heart.[1]

P. KAWECKI

580   November 24, 1896

RESPECTED MR. WŁADYSŁAW BORKOWSKI: I received your photograph, for which I send you most hearty thanks. I took it to the church and showed it to all your friends, who were very much satisfied, and particularly myself, for it is made very originally. I married Mrs. Józefa P. last year, and now God has given us a third daughter [two from the first marriage]. We are in good health, by the favor of our Lord God, and we wish you the same. Here in Warsaw everything is the same, except [news about priests who died or were transferred]. As to the Rosary-choir, nobody among the priests cares for us, only I teach [the members] to sing, as best I can. From our Rosary-circle died [enumeration]. Your wife longs very much for you, she would like to see you as soon as possible. From this grief

---

[1] The religious fraternities to one of which the writer and Borkowski belonged are very old in Warsaw. They have developed an artificial kind of devotion and a religious jargon of which the first letter of Kawecki is a good example. Outside of the traditional atmosphere of these circles, this way of addressing a friend by a man would be hardly possible in Poland, except perhaps on some very important occasions, in great sorrow, etc. The religiosity is, moreover, hardly connected with a higher morality; Kawecki himself becomes later a habitual drunkard. On the fraternities in general, cf. Osiński series, No. 78, note.

she was very sick, and was obliged to go to the hospital, but now she is already in good health, and implores you for pity's sake to come back to Warsaw ["and implores . . . ." added later]. And now . . . . I commend your person to the Providence of God. May He guard you against any bad accidents and grant you the best health and every good. [Christmas wishes and greetings from friends.]

P. KAWECKI

581　　　November 25, 1894

"Praised be" [etc.].

DEAR FRIEND: [News about the death of the tsar Alexander III, description of the funeral-ceremonies, etc.; news about friends.] In the iron-factories and on the railways there is enormous work. In Sosnowiec lives one of your friends, I forget his name. He says always that you should come, that there is a sure place for you on the railway. So come back to Warsaw now. Because of his ascending the throne the emperor has reduced the punishment of prisoners and offenders, so there will be amnesty for you. And you will revive your wife again from this sorrow, for she torments herself continually. That which you lost you will earn again with the help of our Lord God. And as to the shame, throw it away from you and let it be ended. For people do worse things and they come off easily.[1] So I am persuaded that you will come back soon, and I beg you to answer whether you will come back. And I assure you with all my heart that you won't be deceived at all. . . . .

Your loving and sincere friend,

EMILIAN L.

582　　　October 28, 1900

DEAR WŁADYSŁAW BORKOWSKI: Praised be God. You praise God and I praise him also. But you did not keep the word which you gave me and you did not write me where you are to be found. Only after much begging I received your address [from your wife], and there must be some jealousy, for your wife begged me very much not

---

[1] We do not know his offense. Possibly some small peculation.

to give anybody your address. Only I beg you, don't make any reproaches to your wife in your letters.[1]

Now, dear Władzio, I inform you about my success. I work now in my own shop, and there was a time when 10 journeymen worked with me and I had 1,500 roubles in cash. Counting upon my cash, I took a larger shop, and I lost everything in a year. I have still all my tools, but have that cash no longer, and only 2 journeymen and a boy work with me. So my condition is not very good, and if I knew that there was something good for me in America and if you gave me information in a letter, I would leave Warsaw, for in Warsaw it is more and more difficult to live. Although I became a master and belong to the guild, it is very difficult to get on. I have had losses because of the strike of last year, and the rent is expensive, while I heard from your wife that God has blessed you and you succeed well. May God grant it to you. I wish it, for when you left, it seemed to me as if my brother or father were dead. . . . .

Your true companion,

STANISLAW R.

[1] The situation disclosed in these letters is rather difficult to understand. There is an evident antagonism of interests between Stanisław R. and Teofila B., both of whom rely on Władysław B. in matters of money. Still, for a long time, their relations remain friendly, until apparently they are broken almost entirely. The simplest explanation seems to be the following one. Teofila is jealous of Stanisław, for the social reason stated in the introduction, and for the economic reason, that he wants her husband to lend him money. Yet her hostile feeling is for a long time neutralized by the fact that in Stanisław's home she is relatively well treated and often fed—which in her loneliness and poverty mean much—and that she hopes to go to America under Stanisław's care. This second reason remains even after the breaking of the relation (see her letter No. 561), and therefore the break is not definite. As to Stanisław, it is probable that he may have miscalculated the power of the connection between Teofila and her husband and hoped to influence him through her until he understood that Władysław B. considered his wife rather a burden, and then he lost his interest in her. At any rate, his way of writing about her in the first letters and in the last one seems to express precisely such an evolution. The break, thus prepared, may have been caused really by Teofila's refusal to lend Stanisław money. Nevertheless, it is possible that there was also a feeling of pity, finally tired out by Teofila's continual complaints.

Besides this situation with regard to Teofila, and his own matrimonial relations, the letters of Stanisław are totally insignificant. They show a personality as average and uninteresting as possible, and in this respect precisely typical of his class, which has lost the mediaeval town traditions, has no peasant traditions, remains still untouched by the influence of modern industrialism, and particularly in Warsaw, lacks the ambitious tendencies going along with the constitution of a new social organization.

583   April 6, 1902

DEAR COMPANION: . . . . My work is very bad. You wrote me to come, and then I had still some money, but now I have none. But I would go to you at once if you sent me a ship-ticket. Only I have now a large family, another wife [illegal] who is worthy of respect. So we are two, and 5 children, the oldest 15, the youngest 2 years old. At the same time your wife assures me that if I go she will go with me, but with nobody else. Reflect whether you may help me, for I should risk everything. Warsaw is building up rapidly, but among the middle [really lower] class the misery is awful. If I sell my tools I can get about 400 roubles. Now, dear companion, your wife suffers terribly without money, for she cannot earn much. The money which you sent is spent long ago, and it is very difficult for her to earn. She wrote to you long ago for some help, for she has nothing to live on and to pay the rent. This letter is written in the presence of your wife. [News about friends.] P. Kawecki is in the customs-office, as formerly. He drinks very much. . . . .

Your truly well-wishing,

STANISŁAW R.

584   May 14, 1902

DEAR COMPANION WŁADYSŁAW: . . . . I don't know what is going on with you, why do you not give any news about yourself. This is the 4th letter which I send you and have no answer. . . . . In my last letter I asked you for a ship-ticket for myself and your wife, for your wife has absolutely nothing to live on and to pay for her lodging. Those 50 roubles which you sent so long ago are spent, for more than a year has passed since you sent them. . . . . So I don't know whether you don't receive my letters or don't wish to answer your countryman from Warsaw, a Pole and a companion. Dear Władysław, my companion, perhaps you have read in my letters that I want to go to you at any moment, for in Warsaw, even if I worked my hands away, I could earn only for my living and some clothes, while it does not suffice for the schooling of my children. Many people here in Warsaw walk without work. . . . . As to my character and my disposition, you know well that I have never cheated anybody for a grosz. In the same way I would give you back with thanks the money for the ship-ticket.

Perhaps I have offended you in some way in my letters and therefore you don't answer me.   Pardon me, for I have loved you much because of your devotion. . . . .

Your wife comes every day to me and asks whether you have not given any news about yourself.   She wonders whether perhaps somebody has written some false letters to you [slandering her] and therefore you remember her so little.   For it is difficult for her to live. She says with great crying that now, were it not for the sea, she would go afoot to you.   So she begs you also to send her a ship-ticket. . . . .

STANISŁAW R.

585   May 30, 1902

DEAR COMPANION WŁADYSŁAW: I received your letter on May 29, and I rejoiced much at your good advice.   I am therefore selling my whole business and waiting for your answer and the ship-ticket which you promised me, for I believe that it will be cheaper.   Dear Władzio, could you not send a ticket for me and for my oldest son, 15 years old, for he would perhaps become a loafer during this year of my absence.   And if you think that it is difficult, so I beg you to send a ticket for me alone.   I will take more money with me than 50 roubles [required from every immigrant].   I should like to work together with you as long as I still have some health, by the favor of God. . . . . Your wife received the money, 60 roubles and 1 copeck.   Now I inform you that in Warsaw handworkers are very badly situated. When I see you, I will tell you everything.   So, dear companion, send me a ship-ticket.   I should prefer a more expensive one, for I should not like to go so long through the water.   With your advice and help, God will help me also. . . . .

STANISŁAW R.

586   February 8, 1903

DEAR COMPANION WŁADYSŁAW: . . . . I received your ship-ticket last year . . . . and I am not sure whether it will be valid for this year.   I asked and was informed that it was valid but I don't know whether you did not withdraw it, so I beg you, inform me about it.   This year I am going to see you and to greet you like a brother and companion.   Poland is a country which gets poorer and poorer. Now I inform you why I could not go last year.   I counted that I should finish in time a work for which 275 roubles were due to me, but the bronze-maker did not make the bronzes [for furniture] in time. Moreover, I had an apprentice-boy, for whose learning the parents had paid. So all this hindered my going. Dear companion, answer me what happened with that ship-ticket? I regret having wasted this year in Warsaw. If my ship-ticket is valid this year it would be a great help to me, because I would take my wife and children; I should have money enough. Then we would live merrily, for my wife loves me too much and does not want to let me go alone. Dear Władzio, help me in whatever you think it advisable. Jan K. came here from America and told me that it was the best to go together with one's wife, that there such good housewives are lacking, because the women don't want to work. Now, dear companion, I have very good children, who would love you much. Jan K. said that a woman who wants to work and cooks or bakes well gets on pretty well. And I can boast that I have a wife who is good in this work, and laborious, and affectionate in the case—God forbid!—of a sickness. With my children you would have a distraction, for everybody envies me because of them, they are so pretty and attached.

And now, dear companion, I should like to inform you about your wife, but I don't know what is going on with her, for she does not call upon us any more. Last year she came almost every day. I don't say it as a reproach [boast], but I always asked her to share our dinner and invited her to stay over the supper. I don't know why [she does not come], perhaps because she is angry with me for your having sent me the ship-ticket, for I heard so. I write you the truth. I inform you only that I don't know where she lives now, for Klimek's wife [with whom she lived] told me that nobody wants to lodge her, because she is awfully boresome, and already gray-headed like a mushroom [usual comparison].

STANISŁAW R.

PORZYCKI SERIES

The Porzyckis are another isolated marriage-group whose relation with the family-group of both husband and wife is rather loose, though some assistance is given and received. As in the case of the Borkowskis, there is a notable poverty of traditional materials, but the Porzyckis have preserved somewhat more of the traditional attitudes, because, living in a small town, they are more subject to the pressure of social opinion. The social opinion itself is, however, rather hesitating; even in small towns the traditional standpoint has been abandoned in most of its details. Moreover, it was never very consistent, since the traditions of the city class were always intermingled with those of the peasants. Perhaps the Porzyckis are also of peasant origin; the preceding generation may have moved to the town and there lost all the peasant attitudes which differed from those prevailing in the town without acquiring the traditions of their new environment.

The cultural level is not much higher than in the Borkowski case. Porzycki is a shoemaker, the woman a midwife, and these professions in small towns do not require much instruction. It seems that there is a little more community of interests between the Porzyckis than between the Borkowskis; at least there is a little more real affection. But this would be hardly enough to keep the conjugal connection strong in spite of the separation if there were no other factors.

Finally, the characters are almost alike in both cases. Porzycki, as well as Borkowski, is rather cold; his wife, by her lack of energy and independence, is hardly more able than Borkowska to defend her own cause either in her relation with her husband or with her social environment. And, moreover, she is a neuraesthenic. In short, it seems that the history of this marriage-group should be a repetition of that of the Borkowskis, and of many others from among the lower city class. But it is not so, owing to the children. The children are, first of all, objects of common care, and thus the sphere of interest of husband and wife remains partly the same in spite of their separaton. Further, the common obligation toward the children forces the parents to keep their obligations toward each other. Consequently, the situation of the wife is quite different from that in the Borkowski case. She is not an isolated and passive individual toward whom any attitude is possible from the husband, but an active member of a larger group to which her husband belongs; she performs a function which nobody else could perform, and her husband must be interested in her, if not personally, at least as in a member of the marriage-group. The children themselves grow into active members of the marriage-group and exert a conscious influence on their parents. See particularly the letters of Romek.

With regard to the social environment, the situation of the woman is here also quite different from that in the preceding case. We see that she has sometimes economic difficulties, but there is not a single complaint about any humiliation. The woman is and will always be treated by the environment with some consideration as a member and provisional head of the small group, even if her personality should not command respect. Sympathy with the children, expectation that the children will grow up and possibly become important members of the community, certainty that the husband, even if absent, will never completely break the relation of solidarity, because the ties which unite him with the rest of the marriage-group are too strong— all these considerations, to which may be added the fact that she has a profession, keep the social standing of Porzycka from ever falling even approximately so low as that of Borkowska. Certainly her social standing still depends upon her husband's success and his fidelity to her, but not absolutely, as in the preceding case.

The Porzyckis are thus an example of a relatively solidary family-group of the modern type, in which the solidarity does not result alone from tradition and pressure of social opinion, but from relations between individuals as determined by mere natural bonds. However, the group is neither perfectly solidary nor very harmonious. Common interests have to fight against individual interests, and there are frequent misunderstandings and quarrels. In comparing this case with the peasant families, we see what a powerful factor of harmony is the traditional familial organization.

587–629, TO STANISŁAW PORZYCKI, IN AMERICA, FROM HIS WIFE AND CHILDREN, IN POLAND. THE LAST LETTER IS HIS REPLY TO A REQUEST FOR FURTHER DETAILS ABOUT HIS FAMILY

587   [MŁAWA, autumn, 1910]

DEAR FATHER: I inform you that we are all in good health, thanks to our Lord God. . . . . Don't believe in those dreams, for they only deceive everybody. . . . . Mother must always cry, sometimes even be sick, for when Hela merits a punishment and mother beats her, grandmother at once takes her part, and they both gossip [outside] about mother. This [contemptible] Hela now goes to the teaching in the church,[1] and instead of being better she is still worse. Please, father, advise us, at least in a letter, what to do with this Hela, for mother can no longer hold out with her. . . . .[2]

ROMUALD [ROMEK] P.

[1] Instruction before confession.

[2] It is the familial duty of the son to take the part of the mother against the daughter, but in the whole series the attachment of the son to the mother and of the daughter to the father is so marked as to suggest the Freudian theory. Perhaps the attitude of protector of the family assumed by the boy in the absence of the father is here, as in many of the following letters, merely an objective and conscious form in which the subconscious preference for the mother finds its expression.

588

November 3 [1910]

Dear Husband: In the first words of my letter, "Praised be Jesus Christus. . . . ."[1]

I received the money, 50 roubles, for which I thank you heartily, for I was almost in despair. During the whole of October I earned nothing, and there were always expenses. Were it not for the Rząps, who lent us a few roubles, I don't know how we should have lived. Thanks to God that at least they are our friends, for it would be hard. . . . . These 50 roubles which you sent will be spent at once—15 roubles to Pawłowska, 10 to the Rząps . . . . shoes for us all, a few wagons of turf, potatoes. Believe me, my dear, I should prefer to have you rather than this money, for I had not so much trouble when you were here. Now you write that you won't come back until you pay your debt. But it will soon be a year and there is almost nothing paid of it. . . . . I inform you about Romek, that he is getting awfully spoiled; he does not listen at all, he is worse and worse. Please send him an admonition, but so as if you wrote of yourself, for he does not even want to go to church.[2] Pawłowski writes to his family that he will come back, will sell his property and will take them all to America, for it is so well there. I have nothing more to write, only I wish you, dearest love, good health and success, and may the Lord God help you to pay that debt back.

Your loving wife and children,

Władysława Porzycka

Only, I beg you, write more often.

589

January 7, 1911

And although we cannot be together, yet we can be united in our hearts and thoughts [probably quotation from his letter]. It is true, dear husband, that we are united in our hearts and thoughts, but tell me why does this unity of thoughts not suffice for me? Tell me, why does my heart, although united, long for yours? Oh, it is ter-

[1] The only letter which begins in the typical peasant way, with the greeting, "Praised be," etc. In the following letters the greeting is dropped, probably in imitation of the husband's letters. The omission is itself a sign of the loosening of old traditions.

[2] It is interesting to note that the children rapidly outgrow these childish attitudes, naughtiness, disobedience, etc.; the common difficulties, the common fight with poverty, etc., make of them rather the associates of the mother.

ribly empty here, and I long so much for you, dear husband! The longing and grief devour me slowly. If you knew, dearest, what were our holidays! Perhaps yours were also not merrier, but you are a man and you can bear your lot with more resignation. Can I do it? Oh no, it is difficult to bear this; the wheelbarrow of life is too heavy for my shoulders. So, dear husband, if you wish to lighten our misfortune, take me there, where you are, and perhaps when we are together this weight of life won't seem so heavy to us. For if you don't take us, know it, my dear, that I can still get money for my own journey. I will leave the children and go after you. Otherwise I shall perish, waste away here. Why, Stach dear, you went away with the idea that we should come at once after you, and you don't even mention it but I must be the first [to speak of it]. Klasztor took his wife 9 weeks ago, Mania Pawłowska is going away presently. Only for me there is no place!

Dear Stach, if I found work at least! But I happen to get work as often as a blind hen finds grains [proverb]. And here we lack money, and you say yourself that the children ought not to suffer cold. My dear husband, if I could, if I had [money], surely not only the children but myself would be dressed, for you know that I like it. But when there is no money! Do you know, dear Stach, that since you went away I have not bought anything for myself except shoes, for I cannot walk barefooted. But all this would not be so painful to me if we could be together. So if you love me, arrange for us to be together! Well, dear husband, you won't say now that I write little, will you? Though all these are not merry things, still don't grieve, dearest, for I should not like you to be grieved through me. I should like us to be always merry, always happy, and our letters to be not so sad. But, say, should I lie? You prefer the reality yourself, even if it were the saddest. And then, to whom shall I go, if not to you? To whom shall I complain, if not to you? And when I know that you share my feelings and sympathize with me—oh, then my heart is much lighter. Pardon me, dear Stach, for sending you so much sad news, but all this because I want to be *with you*. What more shall I write you? Only that our children are healthy, thanks to God, and learn well enough. I have nothing more to write. I think it is enough, is it not?

This letter took me very much time, but it is not time that I lack. I received your money for Christmas only after New Year. I send you hearty thanks. We received your letter with the wafer on December 17. . . . .

Your loving, longing, and true-to-death wife, with children,

WŁADYSŁAWA PORZYCKA

590
February 11, 1911

DEAR FATHER: I inform you that I received your letter with wishes and 3 roubles for my name-day on my name-day itself. I thank you very much, father, for the wishes and for these 3 roubles, which came in the worst time, for mother had no money at all, so I took half a rouble for myself and gave 2½ to mother. Mother scarcely saves our life. We paid Pawłowska for the last quarter [rent], and not yet for this quarter. Dear father, take either all of us there or at least me alone. Then we could both earn more than you alone. Dear father, I want to go to school only this year, and then to become a tailor's apprentice, for tailor's work pleases me most, because of the wages and because the work is not hard to learn. I have nothing more to write, only I wish you good health and success.

Your truly loving son,

ROMUALD P.

591
March 15, 1911

DEAR FATHER: I inform you that we are in good health. . . . . Pawłowska rented our lodging, for somebody gave her 70 roubles, and we have not yet rented another. And Rzezuski went to America in the autumn, set up a shoemaker's shop and is getting on pretty well. He has now taken her [his wife] and they left their children with the grandmother. You wrote that Osiecki is to come back. So I would beg you to send me through him a few books, and if you have some old suit send it to me. Mother will have it cut down and I shall have something to walk in. If you went to Pawłowski you would perhaps have better work, for Pawłowski sent 1,000 roubles in all. You wrote us that he perhaps borrowed them, but he answered that he did not borrow a penny. He has paid already 200 roubles to Mr. Tański. Dear father, we still owe Pawłowska for half a year. . . . .[1]

ROMUALD P.

[1] The letter is probably partly dictated by the mother.

592   April 29, 1911

DEAR FATHER: First I inform you that I am in good health, by the grace of Lord God, and I wish you the same with my whole heart. And as to the school, we are going on May 1, and the summer vacation will begin on June 1. And we have no lodging as yet, for all are rented, so we must perhaps take this one after the Kirszenbaums. But it is 80 roubles. Do you allow us to take it or not?

If Mr. Osiecki has not left yet, please father, send me through him an accordeon with bells.

Wishes for name-day: I wish you, father, health, happiness, success, long life, and to see one another soon.

Your truly loving son,
ROMUALD PORZYCKI

DEAR FATHER: If Mr. Osiecki comes back, and if you can, send me through him a ball in a net. [Adds wishes for name-day, copied from a book.]

HELENA P.

593   May 3, 1911

DEAR HUSBAND: First I beg your pardon, Staś dear, that I have so neglected [writing], but, believe me, not from pleasure. It seems to you that I did not write for a long time. Well, but say yourself, what could I write so often? If I had any merry news surely I would hasten with the good tidings, but this monotonous uniformity is always here. Now I have a little more, not merry, but natural news. My dear husband, I received the first 25 roubles in the last week before Easter, and the second 10 roubles only today. . . . . May God reward you. But I must describe to you, what I spent this money on. Well, I bought a suit for Romek, and shoes. This cost me 10 roubles. For Hela I bought a dress, shoes, and a hat, for you know that her nature already claims its own; so I spent for her 11 roubles. I gave 8 roubles to Pawłowska, and what is left? Moreover, I paid some other small debts, so we did not have very merry holidays—sad and modest. If we were together at least, and shared our good or bad fortune, surely it would be merrier. But now, my dear, you are there and I am here, bad fortune separated us. But let us hope in God that we shall once more live together. You ask my advice, dear Stach, what you shall do with your person, come back or not. Oh, if it were in my power, I would add wings that you might return to us. But say, dear, what awaits us here? My dear husband, I don't advise you either so or so, for you know better yourself what to do. You know what we had in our country, and you know what you have there. Do as your reason advises you, and I agree perfectly. As to this debt, it will be as you do it. If you send it partly, I will pay it back; if you put money aside [and send the whole at once], it will be well also. You ask me how much I can spend monthly. I think you know yourself, for we are not more and not less now [than formerly], and we don't spend money for any luxuries. I shall have as much as you send.

So, dear husband, you deceived me, you let me wait 2 months. I waited obediently till at last you wrote me that you could not take me. Thereby I have no lodging now; the lodging we had is rented long ago. I don't know how it will end. . . . . My health is very bad, my strength is leaving me. For a year I have intended to go to a physician, but always something is lacking, either time or money. . . . . And now, dear Staś, I intend to insure myself, for I am afraid for my life, and therefore I intend to insure myself for some hundred roubles. You don't expect to be there long, and cannot, and here we shall not be able to put money aside . . . . and if a black hour comes or if I die, what will be the future of my children? So advise me, dear Staś, what should I do. In my opinion it would be the best if you took us to you. You write that you are anxious about the children, lest they become American [illegible word]. But even in America it cannot be worse than in this accursed Mława. You know yourself that I have nobody here, I am alone, an orphan in the world. I don't go to Piotr [her brother] at all, for you know yourself how good he is. I went once to him, and he was quarreling with her. I could not bear it and said a few words—why does he swear so? When he began to bark against me and you, I thought that I should die from all this. The matter was particularly about you. But don't write him anything.

Dear Staś, believe me that as the fish thirsts for fresh water, so we thirst to be united with you, but not here, only in America. I should prefer to work heavily, and to get away from this hell. . . . . Calculate only what all this costs—living, lodging, fuel, dress. Surely we could live there together. My success is bad, for two more midwives came here, and there is almost nothing to do. So I beg you, dear Staś, consider it in our favor, and take us from here, that I may at least for a moment breathe freely, for I cannot bear all this. . . . .

Your sincerely loving and true wife, with children,

WŁADYSŁAWA P.

Pawłowska agreed with mother for 77 roubles [for the lodging], and she will herself put it into order. But—it would be best, dear father—take us to you.

Your truly loving son,

ROMUALD P.

In Mława it is bad; I should prefer to live in the country.

594   June 27 [1911]

DEAR HUSBAND: I received your letter, which on the one hand rejoiced me, that at last there is a place for me in America, for indeed, dear Staś, in the present state of things my despair goes to my head. If it lasts longer so, I think you will send me to Tworki [insane-hospital], for there is not enough of my head to overcome all this. You have not even an idea how everything has stopped. Whence shall I take [money]? If there were anything to steal, I would steal, but even this is impossible. You always try to comfort me and tell me not to grieve, but all your explanations have had no result yet. You tell me to borrow, but I have already debts enough. Even the Osieckis won't lend me as much as I want, for what are these few roubles when I owe to Pawłowska for a full quarter and she looks sourly at me, and the other quarter is near. Whence shall I take [money]? So I write you the last letter and tell you, let it be once, [for all], either take the children or come yourself and suffer together with us. I write you decidedly, let it be so or so, for here I am neither upon ice nor upon water. I have no lodging. We agreed with Pawłowska about this other lodging, but I did not give her any deposit, for how could I give any? And now she says that she won't give the lodging. So what shall I do with all this? Mad things come to my head with all this. And you tell me to insure myself! Very well, but only where *they will pay me*, for I have nothing to pay with. Osiecki said himself that he would give me money for one ship-ticket, and you could send for the children, but speedily, for the Osieckis intend to leave at the end of July, and I could go with them. But if not, then come yourself, and when you come, it will be more or less better. I don't wish to suffer any more as I do; I have lost my health already. Answer at once, what you intend, for every day is important to me. . . . .

Well-wishing,[1]

WŁADYSŁAWA P.

595 August 17, 1911

DEAR FATHER: I inform you . . . . that the vacation is ending. On September 1 we go to school, and mother does not earn any money now, so when we go to school we need for books and for fees. So I beg you, father, send a few roubles at least for me and for Romuś, so perhaps mother will get somewhere [money for other expenses]. As to these 35 roubles which you sent, mother did not even see them well. Mother owed 12 roubles to Pawłowska from the other quarter and gave her 4 roubles for this quarter and some lesser debts. And mother owes 10 roubles to the Osieckis.[2] Dear father . . . . if you had much money, it would be better to come back to our country, for here it is also well for one who has much money. It is bad only for us, for we have nothing. Write us, is it true that it is so hot in America, for Mania, Mrs. Pawłowska's daughter, writes that it is so hot that people fall down upon the streets. . . . .

Your loving daughter,

HELENA

596 September 23, 1911

DEAR FATHER: I inform you that we received your letters and 20 roubles. You wrote mother to pay my fee from this money . . . . but here is a more necessary debt, that of Pawłowska; she is the first. I shall probably not go to school any more, dear father, for it is too difficult for mother. I must help mother at home. Formerly at least grandmother was in her bed, and it was possible to leave the house, but now [since grandmother is dead] if mother goes somewhere to a sick woman she shuts the house and takes the key with her, and when we come from the school, we must sometimes sit outside till

---

[1] "Well-wishing" (doubly underscored), instead of "Your loving and true wife," as previously. In contrast with the humble and pleading letters of Teofila Borkowska, Porzycka demands to be united with her husband as her *right*, and this right is based on the fact that they have children, and common duties toward them.

[2] Enumeration of expenses probably dictated by the mother.

evening. Romuś passed into the fifth division [grade], but on the condition that he will take private lessons for three months at 3 roubles a month. He is a bad comfort to us, for he is sickly and looks very bad. Mother grieves, for it will probably be consumption. Up to the present he did not cough, but now he coughes terribly. Mother intends to go to the doctor with him. Mother also looks bad; sometimes she groans during the whole night. I alone am in good health, and even I was ill for more than a week. Probably you won't find us all here when you come. But perhaps I write letters too often; if you mind the cost, I won't write letters so often. But these letters don't cost me, for I won the paper at a lottery during the exhibition. I thank you heartily for your wishes, but you were mistaken, for my name-day is on March 2, or on May 22. . . . . But even so it is well.

Your loving daughter,

HELENA

We and uncle sent together a letter to the other uncle in America. Perhaps it did not arrive, so please inform him about grandmother['s death].

597   October 30, 1911

DEAR HUSBAND: First I inform you that we are in good health. . . . . Michalina T. married a Sudzieński, cooper from Mława. . . . . They came to live with us but they won't pay any money; they say that it will be on account of the debt. . . . . Dear Staś, I have earned nothing for 5 weeks already, and here you tell me to drink milk. But a quart costs 12 grosz . . . . and there are so many other expenses. . . . . Helcia, thanks to God, is better, and is going to school, for this is all her dowry, so it is impossible to keep her at home. She learns well, better than Romek. I chose for him such a profession [of barber], I think that it is the best for him, not very hard, and healthy, for he is always in movement. I don't know how you think. He likes it, for it is not heavy and is well paid, and he will be able to do it. Rakoski [the employer] praises him. . . . .

Your sincerely loving wife,

WŁADYSŁAWA P.

DEAR FATHER: . . . . I inform you that after the lessons I go to the barber and learn barber's work. You wrote to send you a photograph, but I have no [Sunday] clothes. So please, father, send me

money for the clothes. . . . . Dear father, I cannot die, for I must
keep you and feed you in your old days, and if I died who would feed
you? . . . . Don't grieve about me, I am healthy, better than before
this illness. . . . .

ROMUALD P.

598   November 3 [1911]

DEAR HUSBAND: First I inform you that I received your letter
on All-Souls Day. I thank you for it heartily. I am very much
pained that you grieve so. We are, thanks to God, in good health,
and Romek looks much better. In the summer he bathed too often
and this must have done him harm. Now I treat him myself with
medical herbs, and he is quite well already, only he requires very good
living, and I have not enough for all this. I don't know myself what
to do; my practice has ceased totally. I accepted these Sudzieńskis
on the condition that I was to receive a few roubles, but the Tańskis
arranged that this money might go on account of the debt. They
agreed upon 30 roubles. O, dear Staś, may God unite us as soon as
possible, for our whole life is only a torture. We are always separated,
the one here, the other there, and always in this longing. You think
about us, and we about you. Dear Staś, you wrote in your last letter
that I ought to pull away from my head this longing and to occupy
myself with my duties and with prayer. O, dear Staś, were it not
for the prayer and the hope in God, I don't know how I should bear
all this. I hope that our Lord God will change it into a better happiness, but meanwhile we must suffer, for such is the will of God.
Dear Staś, I beg you, don't grieve, but have confidence in God, and
God will comfort us in everything. . . . .

Your truly loving wife, with children,

WŁADYSŁAWA P.

599   November 20 [1911]

DEAR HUSBAND: . . . . You write about Romek, that if you
were here everything would be better. That is true, but even 10
fathers cannot take the place of one mother, particularly with our
Romek. He is so delicate and exacting in his constitution that it is
not only necessary but indispensable to have always something good
for him, for he won't take into his mouth anything not perfect. He
cannot eat at all, he is so tired with learning. He must sit till mid-

night and worry himself in learning lessons, and he is weak, so it is indispensable to have for him always something good to eat. If I did not care for him, he would have been in his grave long ago. [Usual ending.]

WŁADYSŁAWA P.

600 January 20, 1912

DEAR HUSBAND: . . . . You have no idea how I am worried. Oh, may God put an end to all this, for I cannot hold out any longer. I have not a happy moment in my life. I have only wasted my young years in longing and grief, alone with these orphans, and I have no hope that it will end soon. Dear Staś, I cannot describe all this to you, for the frame of this letter is too small. If I had wings, like a falcon I would fly to you, even if only for an hour, and tell you everything. Dear Staś, you write me to rent a lodging; I don't think of renting; let it be as it is, for I don't intend to remain here any longer. . . . . The Sudzieńskis don't live with us now. It was too crowded for them. But it is well that they went away, for God forbid living with anybody! . . . . If you send the Tańskis the interest, calculate carefully how much . . . . and as to the whole, they can wait. Better pay Łączyński, for he is at least polite when he comes for money, though he needs it more. . . . .[1] I give you one other advice. Write a letter to Rząp [her cousin] and ask him in my name to help us. He won't refuse us. They are 4 brothers, so even if he has no money he can find a way. Only if you write me anything about Rząp, write upon a separate sheet, for she comes sometimes to me and reads your letter. Let her rather not know, for women are always worse, more avaricious. . . . .[2]

Your sincerely loving wife,

WŁ. PORZYCKA

601 April 4, 1912, Good Thursday

DEAR FATHER: First I inform you that we received today your letter, for which we have waited impatiently, but instead of rejoicing us, it caused us a still greater pain. Mother was already sick and

---

[1] Lending money is still treated as a personal service and paying a debt as a partial reciprocation. Politeness of the creditor heightens the value of the service.

[2] As we have seen more than once, men have a stronger and more persistent feeling of familial solidarity than women. In this case Rząp is the relative of the writer.

got still worse after reading this letter. In a few days the holidays will come, but these holidays, instead of bringing us joy, cause us a still greater pain when we look upon this gay world. Everybody is merry, only we must cry. During the whole of Lent we have fasted truly, and during Easter we shall fast still better, for perhaps we shan't have even a bit of dry bread. You tell us to borrow money from somebody. But why don't you borrow there from somebody? Perhaps somebody there will sooner lend you, for here we are so in debt. We have taken so much on credit in all the shops that nobody wants either to lend us or to give us credit any more, but everybody asks us to pay our debts. You told us not to rent an apartment, and we did not rent any; and now they drive us away from here, for we did not pay the rent for half a year. You travel from town to town and enjoy pleasures, while we die from hunger. It would be better if you sent us the money which you spend on traveling, or if you put it aside. Pawłowski went to Chicago and he stays there and sends her money, though she does not need it as we do, for to whomever she goes among her tenants everybody must give her. Dear father, for the holidays even a beggar clothes his children, while we are like the poorest orphans; we are even ashamed to go out upon the street, for everybody laughs at us. If you could imagine how we look today, as if we had arisen from the tomb, and all this from sorrow. Nothing grieves me so much, even if I were dying from hunger, as the pain and sorrow of my mother, upon which I must look, and already in youth poison my life. As long as I live, I don't remember such a sad time as these holidays which approach for us. I have nothing more to write, only I wish you health and merry holidays.

Your loving son,

Romuald Porzycki

Don't be angry with me for having described so much misery, but you think perhaps that we are well off here.[1]

---

[1] The letter is exceptionally hard. A peasant boy would never dare to write to his father in this way. He would have a certain right of control over his father's behavior, but only in matters which constituted a direct breach of the familial solidarity and to the extent proportionate to their respective importance in the family-group. As the father is the actual, while the son only the prospective, head of the family, this right of control could only find its expression in some humble request addressed by the son to the father. In extraordinary cases the son could appeal to the rest of the family, who would then exert an active control. But here the situation is different. The marriage-group is isolated and the respective positions of its members are no longer determined by social tradition, but by the

Unhappy the hour of my wedding! I pity these orphans, for I am ready to take my life away. I cannot overcome all this any more! Could my tears torment you as much as the pain which you cause me! How have you had the conscience to send such a letter!

Your sorrowful wife

602 April 24, 1912

DEAR HUSBAND: First I inform you that I received the letter with money more than a week ago, I cannot [write further.]

Dear father, I announce to you very sad news: Romuś is severely sick. Three illnesses came upon him at once. His heart is bad, his lungs and stomach have caught cold; we don't know how it will turn out. One doctor said that he must go to Warsaw, and Dr. Korzybski tells us to take him to the country. But first, it is difficult for us, and then he has terrible fever and vomits. Mother has almost lost her senses. She began to write this letter, but she cannot do it from grief. If you could appear today in our home and comfort us! For it is worse here today than in a tomb. We thought that we should soon go to America, and Romuś rejoiced that he would visit such a far world, and then suddenly it happened so. Now he says that even if our Lord God gives him his health back he won't go. Write at least letters more often to us, dear father. Now help is needed, and here we have no money. Please write us, father, whether you had foreboding of our grief. Dear father, Mr. Korzybski said that Romek needed this cure long ago, but as long as he could walk we did not notice it, for he said nothing to mother; only now, when he could walk no more [he spoke]. We should like not to grieve you, father, but we have grieved already for some days. If this letter could come to you the soonest possible! I have nothing more to write, only we wish you health and good success.

Your loving daughter,

HELENA P.

Only don't grieve, father, perhaps our Lord God will grant him to recover. Pray, father, our Lord God for his health.

---

individual characteristics of the members themselves. The father's authority is based upon his physical, moral, and intellectual superiority and upon the fact that he is the support of the family; it decreases as these factors decrease. In the present case it is precisely his moral superiority and his willingness to support the family which are in question. Probably the mother's talk has influenced the boy and undermined the father's authority.

603   May 13, 1912

DEAR HUSBAND: First I inform you that we are in good health, and Romek, thanks to God, walks already, but he is still feeble. He lay more than 2 weeks and was severely ill, he had typhoid and his heart was bad. We doubted whether he would live, but God the Merciful comforted us. I did not know any more what to do with all this; for 2 weeks I neither slept nor ate, for he had great fever and I had always to sit with him, and there was nobody here to take my place in anything. It cost me much, the drugs alone, some roubles. None of the doctors accepted any money from me. Dear Staś, I inform you that I received two letters and 25 roubles, for which I thank you heartily. Don't turn your head about [don't trouble yourself about] taking us to America, and leading yourself into still worse debts. If you have good work, stay there until you pay the debt and come back. . . . .   Your loving wife,

WŁADYSŁAWA P.

604   May 14, 1912

DEAR FATHER: I inform you that I am better already, thanks to our Lord God. I have not yet come to my full strength, but I walk already. . . . . I don't go to the school, for the doctor forbade me to go. Dear father, we inform you that the bishop was here and myself and Hela were at confirmation on May 10. Dear father, don't turn your head about taking us to America, rather pay the debt and then come here. It will be better, for Łączyński doubts whether we shall pay him. . . . . Dear father, I wish to go to school next year, but I have no money. It is not indispensable to pay 100 roubles. Whoever is poorer pays as he can, 50 or 25. Some go without paying. Help me only for the first fee, later I will try to earn for myself with lessons [helping the younger students]. Rząp has come already from America and brought many different things for his wife—a gold watch, a ring, a bracelet, and many other things. I have nothing more to write, only I wish you health, and to see one another soon *in our fatherland*. May God grant it. Amen.   Your truly loving son,

ROMUALD ANTONI PORZYCKI

Dear father, please pay first the debt and then come back to us yourself, for now I will never and for nothing go to a foreign country. Here is my fatherland, here I want to live and to die. I joined a circle of temperance, i.e., of not drinking any alcoholic drinks—brandy, beer, or wine. I hope that I shall hold, for this is an offering for Poland. Dear father, now people begin to think and act better here, even priests inscribe [boys] into secret associations. May God grant a star of a better future to shine for us. . . . . Amen.

> Your son, loving his father and his fatherland
> and ready to give his life for them,[1]
>
> ROMUALD

605   June 7 [1912]

DEAR HUSBAND: . . . . Romek is still feeble and has not the same strength as before, but there is hope in God that he will recover. Only he needs good food now. He would eat even 10 eggs a day, and here eggs cost 5 grosz each. But I don't spare money for him. . . . . Dear Staś, you write us to go to the country, but it is not possible by any means. Our children are rather well developed [intellectually], and what is there? Shall I send them to Prussia [for season-work]? We have no fortune there, nobody has sown grain for us, everything must be bought as here. Hela passed the examination to the fourth division, but Romek must still remain in the fifth. This illness is the cause of all this. He could have got a job, but now nothing can be done. . . . . Dear Staś, what shall I do with this Romek? He aspires to go to the gymnasium, while all this is difficult. . . . .

> Your truly loving wife,
>
> WŁADYSŁAWA P.

Only I beg you, don't grieve, everything will be well, if God grants it.

---

[1] The patriotic spirit of this letter is evidently a result of the influence of the association about which the boy writes. Secret associations in schools have existed in Poland since the loss of her independence; but their character has changed. At first they were mainly devoted to patriotic purposes, but toward the end of the nineteenth century, particularly in Russian Poland, they occupied themselves mainly with self-instruction. They completed the very deficient education of the Russian schools, not only in the subjects of Polish history and literature, but also in other subjects not treated at all, or only poorly treated in the schools—philosophy, biology, sociology, history of western literatures, history of art. The associations were mainly directed by older students. With the introduction of private Polish schools, within the last ten years, the secret associations have turned from self-instruction to self-education upon a patriotic basis. They imitated formally the "scouting" movement in England, but developed their own moral ideal of patriotism, chivalry, purity, and general efficiency. The association, to which Romek, and later Hela, belonged were of this latter type. The vow of temperance is the first degree of initiation.

606 June 24, 1912

DEAR FATHER: I inform you that I am in good health. . . . .
I cannot describe the joy which you caused me by your letter, and
I don't know how to thank you for your goodness and the sacrifice
which you make for my sake. Dear father, I will prepare myself
for the 3d class, but it is not sure whether I shall pass the examination
or not. But I shall surely get into the 2d. When I have any certain
news, I will inform you. . . . . Dear father, only don't deceive me,
for you would then probably cause my early death; I am so given up
with my whole life to this learning. Dear father, do your best, for
the time is short, and the candidates will be examined on August 20.
Dear father, the whole preparation will cost 24 roubles, if I learn
2 hours a day, and 14 roubles if one hour a day. How much the fee
will cost I don't know yet. I will write you in a second letter. Dear
father, we received your letter and 40 roubles, for which we thank you
heartily. . . . .

Your, remaining in uncertainty, truly loving son,

ROMUALD P.

607 [September 16, 1912]

DEAR HUSBAND: I thank you heartily for your kind feelings
toward us. May God grant your intentions to be fulfilled, may
God give us comfort in our children. They both joined a temperance
association. They don't drink even ordinary beer. Romek does
not smoke any cigarettes and does not do any silly things. He is
always occupied with serious things and learning. In that circle
they have their own treasure and library. Romek keeps the library,
so he has enough to read and acquires very much knowledge. Dear
Staś, you would have much to speak with him; probably you would
wonder at his ideas. They have a priest in their association who
leads them. Romek always goes to him and receives different
national books, and the priest has no secrets from him, talks with him
openly about everything [national and moral questions]. And Hela
is in the fourth division. She learns well also. I should be glad if
she finished at least this school; in any case it would be better for
her. Dear Staś, we have begun, but I don't know whether we shall
be able to go on, for all this costs very much. The books alone and
the clothes take much money—the overcoat of Romek alone 18
roubles, and the shoes and summer clothes. Dear Staś, from this

money which you sent 50 roubles must be kept for Romek [for the fee], and the remaining 60 roubles will be spent soon. [Enumerates the expenses.]   Your truly loving wife,

WŁADYSŁAWA PORZYCKA

608   September 16, 1912

DEAR FATHER: . . . . I go to school, I am in the fourth division. . . . . Mother did not want to send me to school this year, but I was stubborn and mother at last agreed. . . . . I thank you a thousand times for remembering me. We don't need anything more, we lack only you, dearest father. I inform you that I joined a circle of temperance. It means not to drink . . . . not to play cards and not to smoke during your whole life. You ask about Romek. He is admitted to the second class of the commercial school and learns well enough. And in the new lodging it is very good for us. Mother has patients. Directly after we moved, the next day, they did not give mother any rest, but she was called to a patient. All would be well, if only our Lord God gave us all health. . . . .   HELENA P.

609   May 22, 1913

DEAR FATHER: I inform you that we received your letter and 50 roubles. . . . . From these 50 roubles we gave to Mr. Tański the interest. Now mother bought for Romek shoes and for herself a dress, and hats for mother and for me. You think perhaps that we spend money here on some unnecessary things, but no, dear father, we spend only on what we need absolutely. Dear father, I am no longer so little, and mother must spend some money on me also, for I cannot walk dressed worse than everybody. . . . . I go to a singing-class, and every Sunday and holiday we sing in the church. . . . . Dear father, Romek teaches four boys and gets from every one of them 1 rouble a month; this money which he earns goes for his school wants. Romek will soon pass an examination, so he must even now worry. Sometimes when he comes from the school he is quite sweating. . . . . Thanks to God, he recovers, he can eat more and has color on his cheeks. He has grown so big that he is already somewhat taller than mother, and I am a little smaller than mother. . . . .

Your sincerely loving daughter,

HELA

610

June 16 [1913]

DEAR AND BELOVED HUSBAND: .... I don't know what it means that you don't receive our letters. .... We wrote you 3 letters and received an answer to none. I had begun to think that you had followed Osiecki in search for pleasures. But excuse me for writing you such silly things. And as to the money, don't worry. If you send it it will come. Only send soon and plenty, for we need it. I paid Łączyński 65 roubles, for he wants money most; Łączyński is sick with consumption. You write that you will take me and Hela to America, and Romek can be left. But where? With him it is still worse than with a small child, for he has no health and has a very delicate nature. He can by no means be left alone. So if we are tó go we will go all together, and if not, then none. .....

Your truly loving wife with children,

W. PORZYCKA

DEAR FATHER: You wrote that mother and Hela might go, and I might remain here. I agree with it, and I can remain in the pension. But for vacation where shall I go? Perhaps to you, for here they all leave for vacation. As to the money, dear father, don't trouble yourself whether we shall get it, whether there is not somebody ill; even if so, for a sick person money is useful.[1] Our lessons end on Saturday, June 21, and on Sunday we shall receive thé certificates with promotion or not. So if I am promoted to the 3d class, I will inform you. ....

ROMUALD

611

June 25, 1913

DEAR FATHER: .... I have been promoted to the 3d class, without a second examination. Dear father, you do ill in postponing the sending of money. You wrote that you would send us 50 roubles monthly, and we believed it. So we gave out most of the money which you had sent before, in paying the debts. The rest was spent

---

[1] There is irony at this point. The father has made some *stupid* excuse for not sending money—that the money might not reach them on account of the probable war, that if the mother was ill there would be no one to go to the post-office for the letter. The remark about vacation above is also ironical. In comparison with No. 601 the moralizing attitude of this and the following letter is more objective and superior. The boy is more under the influence of the patriotic society and of his reading and less under the influence of his mother.

in a short time. Meanwhile a month passes, then another, and you always postpone. Once you are afraid that somebody is ill, then again that somebody is dead, and we are almost dying here of hunger, and we can really fall sick from grief. For you must also know that mother has very little income, while we must eat every day in order not to die. We should have been dead from hunger long ago if nobody had lent us money. But at last people refuse to lend. So, dear father, I beg you very much, send at least a few roubles for living at the appointed time, for, dear father, I can control myself, but mother is despairing and cursing her life and everything, when she does not see any better prospect before her. I beg your pardon, father, for writing this letter with such reproaches, but don't be angry with me, for I must at last write the truth. I send you the medical advice of our school-physician, how I ought to nourish myself. Just think, father, what a day of living would cost if I nourished myself even partly according to this program. . . . .

ROMUALD

612 [June 25, 1913]

DEAR FATHER: . . . . And now I inform you that we received your letter on June 23, for which I thank you. Dear father, misery came to us seriously, for more than once we have gone hungry to bed. Łączyński comes to us now one or two times every week. He is sick with consumption, so when he comes to us the whole lodging is filled with a foul smell. When once he stayed over night here we all got sick, I and Romek even had vomits. May God grant us to settle the matter with him as soon as possible! Mother has given him 65 roubles back already. Mother earns almost nothing, and here everything is so expensive, pork 41 grosz, beef 38 grosz, so we buy only seldom a pound, and of the worst, the cheapest. So please, father, send us at least a few roubles, for we cannot hold out so any longer. . . . .

HELA

613 July 5 [1913]

DEAR HUSBAND: . . . . I received 75 roubles for which I thank you heartily, for we needed it very much. I don't know whether I shall be able to give anything of this money to Łącz., for I have made some debts, and I must pay these first of all. . . . . Dear Staś, don't be angry with us if the children have described to you too much of our misery in that last letter, but I was not at home.   And you know, my dear, that here if one has no money he does not know what to do, for it is even difficult to borrow, because here everybody has scarcely enough to live. . . . .

Dearest Staś, write me how do you live there.   Are you not worried with this solitary life?   For I, when I pass this time in mind, it seems very, very long.   Three years and a half we have led such a martyr life!   For there is nothing worse than longing.   And you are so indifferent, you don't even deign to send us your photograph! Send it, I beg you, at least on a postcard; it will cost cheaper. . . . .

Your truly loving wife,

WŁADYSŁAWA PORZYCKA

My condition is very bad.

614

July 23, 1913

DEAR FATHER: . . . . I inform you that we received 40 roubles, from which we gave 25 to Mr. Łączyński.   [Enumerates all the expenses.]   Dear father, believe now everything that we write you, for we write you the sincere truth.   Even if we wished to add anything, we could not, for you look always at us and see everything, and we can hide nothing at all.   Dear father, we have your picture. Although you did not deign to send us your photograph, we had a larger copy made of an old one.   Dear father, now it is at least a little more gay, we have somebody to speak to.   But what!   We speak, and you don't wish to answer us.[1]   So it would be the best if you earned much money and came to our country, or if we went to you.   And if not, then take me to you.   I could at least cook for you, and you would not have to pay me, and it would be better for us. . . . .

And Romcio always does nothing but go to the forest and read books.   He is already a hundred times fatter than I, and as you know, bigger than mother.

Your truly loving daughter with her mother and

Romciuchno [affectionate diminutive of Romuald]

[1] An example of the primitive attitude toward photographs and pictures. The photograph of the dear person seems for the peasant as well as for the child to mean much more than to a sophisticated man, to convey much more feeling of life and reality.   In *all* the series of peasant letters this is manifested.

615 August 18, 1913

DEAR FATHER: . . . . As to that America, we discussed and decided either to go all together or to remain and not to take upon us the burden of a new debt. This would be still better than to go. Mr. Nowakowski asks you whether work is good and whether it is worth while to go to America. It is also hard for them to live, and the priest [a brother or uncle] cannot suffice for everything.[1] Dear father, when we saw your photograph we were awfully pained that you look so bad, but later we comforted ourselves that the photograph is bad. . . . .

ROMUALD

616 August 18, 1913

DEAR FATHER: . . . . I received one rouble from you, for which I thank you heartily. I am somewhat pained that you always make a difference between us two. We are never equally treated, but he aways gets more than I do, as if I were not your daughter. But nothing can be done. Dear father, if you love Romek more than me, what can I do? Dear father, I lent this rouble to mother, for she had no money, but soon we shall go to school; then mother will give it back. I shall have it for the fee, if you are so gracious as to send me 2 roubles more. For books perhaps mother will give me, if she earns.

HELENA

617 September 10, 1913

DEAR FATHER: . . . . I am in the 3d class and am learning well enough, for I cannot say very well. To Mr. Łączyński we owe still 15 roubles of the sum, and the interest, 28 roubles, together 43. Mr. Ł. is a very good man for he counted the interest only for 3 years, at 8 per cent. Dear father, Mr. Pawłowski came back [from America], but he intends soon to go there again, for he has nothing to do here. He acquired a higher culture [irony]. I send you my photograph and, I beg you, send me yours, but a better one, for I was only grieved in receiving the former one. . . . .

ROMUALD

618 October 20, 1913

DEAR FATHER: . . . . I inform you . . . . that Romek was very ill . . . . and now, although he walks, it is with difficulty. . . . . Dear father, he is a bad comfort for us, for he is always sick, only

[1] For the rôle of a priest in the family cf. Rzepkowski series.

seldom a little better. Mother grieves terribly and weeps continually. Mother weeps from sorrow and sings at the same time. It would be better if you were at home. [Money received; expenses.] Dear father, there would be no misery in our home any more, if only Romcio were in good health. We inform you that Uncle Piotr wrote to Yonkers, to Uncle Jan [both mother's brothers] asking him for a ship-ticket, and he intends to go to America, for his affairs are very bad; he does not keep his shop any more. . . . .

HELENA

619   November 5, 1913

DEAR HUSBAND: . . . . Romek was seriously ill but, thanks to God, it passed, although he is never very well, for his disease remains for his whole life. He suffers with heart-disease, and this cannot be healed. Hard is the life of such a man, for he is unable to work, except with his head . . . . so learning is indispensable to him. Dear Staś, I inform you about my success. My success is so bad that I earn almost nothing. We live only on what you send. Dear Staś, you write that you will come on Christmas. Oh, how glad I should be if this lonely life of ours came to an end! But if you come here and we have not a rouble with us, how shall we live, since this year everything is so dear? Prices were never so high. Do as you think best, my dear, but may you not wish to go for the fifth time [keep going]. Piotr has failed so utterly that he does not even keep his shop. He has many debts, and even 500 roubles mortgage. Janek refused to send him a ship-ticket. He justified himself saying that Piotr won't be admitted, because he lacks fingers on one hand. Now he does not know himself what to begin. And the cause of all this is liquor. . . . .

WŁADYSŁAWA P.

620   January 29, 1914

DEAR FATHER: . . . . We don't know now what to do with this lodging, whether we should remain or not, for it is very small, and if you come, it would be too crowded. So tell us positively whether you will come or not. Then we shall know what to do. Dear father, did you receive our letter for Christmas with a wafer, in which we informed you about the death of F. Łączyński and the illness of Pawłowski? Did Uncle Bogorski from Chicago write to you? He wrote to us and wants us absolutely to come there, for work is very good there. But these are vain dreams. Did you receive a letter from Uncle Piotr [asking for a ship-ticket]? If you received it, please father, don't trouble yourself about him, for he has not deserved it. Mother has wept bitter tears more than once because of him. And he takes now work from Wichrowski. Such is the shop he keeps [i.e. none at all]. Dear father, we overwhelm you with only questions in this letter, but we have nothing to write, so we write at least this. . . . . We are satisfied with your photograph, you look very well . . . . but you look sad and upon your face weariness is marked. [Lessons.] I beg you, father, write more, for when you write this one page we have nothing to read. When Mr. Rzezuski writes a letter, there are at least 5 sheets; she must read it during a whole week. . . . .

HELENA

621   March 20, 1914

DEAR FATHER: . . . . You ask us to reflect about that America. But we can by no means leave Romek here. [Money received; expenses.] Dear father, my studies are going on well enough. I hope that this year I shall finish this school. Now here, in Mława, a new four-class school will be opened. I should be glad if I could finish at least these 4 classes. There it would cost 40 roubles a year in each class. Mother's income is rather bad. You know, sometimes she has so much work that she can find no time, and then for a month there is nothing. . . . .

Your loving daughter Helena . . . . with her mother and Romcio, her dear little brother, who was today at confession. I was last Saturday.[1]

622   March 28, 1914

DEAR HUSBAND: . . . . You write that you are too much disgusted with such a life. Nothing can be done, my dear. For me it is also very painful to worry so alone. Perhaps I must even bear

---

[1] Before going to confession it is the habit to beg the pardon of everybody for any past wrongs, and any evil doing on the day of confession is considered particularly degrading. It is also considered exceptionally mean to wrong anyone who has been recently to confession. Therefore days of confession are days of exceptional harmony in family life. The end of Hela's letter is the expression of this

more pains than you, for I am a woman, and still—and still I accept my lot. Yes, dear, let us sacrifice ourselves for our children, because we live only for them. Were it not for them I should have been with you long ago. Dear Staś, you reflect whether Romek cannot be left alone. This is totally impossible. He needs continuous care, for he has no health. How often it is necessary to rise at night when he has a heart attack, and to help him. He is weak like a small child. He is a good boy and I love him strongly, but unhappily there is no great hope for his future. He learns well. Now we must pay 25 roubles for his second quarter. [Usual ending.]

WŁADYSŁAWA P.

623 April 20, 1914

DEAR FATHER: [Health; money and letter received.] We were very glad when we received your letter on Good Friday, particularly Romek. He ordered us to go at once, before the holidays, saying that he would be alone [for Easter]. Dear father, you write for me and mother to come. Oh, how glad we should be to go at once! But, dear father, it would be difficult for us to part with our sickly fellow Romek. Although he troubles me [teases or beats a little] sometimes, yet I love him and it would be difficult for me to go away from him, and mother also cannot reconcile herself with leaving him alone. . . . .

Your truly loving daughter,

HELENA

624 April 24, 1914

DEAR FATHER: . . . . We received today your letter, in which you write about having sent 53 roubles and in which was a silk handkerchief. I thank you with my whole heart for this handkerchief. I have not even words enough to thank you. Everybody wanted to have this handkerchief, Romek, and even mother. Romek wanted me absolutely to give it to him, but I would not give it even for a thousand roubles, for it is a token from my dear beloved father, and such a token should not be given to anybody, even to the emperor himself. Dear father, you send me always something, and what shall I send to you? Now I cannot yet, but when I grow big, I will try to reward you perhaps, if only with a trifle. . . . .

Just now we received . . . . those 53 roubles. We thank you, father, for this money, which will be very useful to us. Now I shall enumerate what we shall spend it for. First we must pay the rent for a quarter, interest to Tański, mother and Hela [I] have no shoes, Hela has no overcoat. Don't be angry, father, for it is obligatory; I have nothing to wear. Oh! And I have no hat! So calculate please, how much I alone will cost: shoes at least 4 roubles, overcoat some 10 roubles, a hat about 2 roubles, together 16 for me alone. And mother and Romek? Really it is worth crying that you have such spongers who only spend your earnings. And I am the worst. Now they croak against me at home, that they must spend so much for me. But judge yourself, father, can I be the worst [dressed] of all? And now mother is against me for this handkerchief [saying] that you did not send anything to her [favorite] child, but only to your [favorite] child. . . . .

HELENA

625   July 6, 1914

DEAR FATHER: . . . . I have passed to the 4th class with a small second examination in German, but it is no matter, for during the vacation I will learn and later it will be more easy for me with the German. Dear father, aunt [Piotr's wife] died on June 30, and already people are recommending another wife to uncle. Hela has finished her school already, but we don't know what to do with her now, and where to place her. . . . . Dear father, we have not had any letter from you for a long time, so we are grieved, for we don't know whether you are healthy or sick, or perhaps you have no work. We expected a letter from you at least for mother's name-day, but you did not send any even for the name-day, so we make the supposition that something bad happened to you, or perhaps you forgot about us. But this latter supposition is impossible. . . . .

ROMUALD

626   July 29, 1914

DEAR FATHER: First I inform you that we received your letter and 40 roubles in our new apartment. They were just enough for the apartment, for we had to pay 40 roubles for half a year. The apartment is expensive, but what can we do if all the apartments are now expensive. We should perhaps have found a cheaper one, but we learned too late that Rzezuska had rented [our old one].   But, never mind, here we have at least comfort, and even if you came you would have room enough to work, and mother perhaps will have better success than there, in that hole.   Dear father, inform us what is the news in America, for here a terrible war is probable.   They wanted to take Romek to prison, for he went beyond the town with some companions.   The border is now open, and soldiers keep guard in the fields.   Even the farmers who bring their crops in must have papers from the mayor that they have the right to go.   Perhaps we shall be killed here, so please send us, father, some money, 1,000 roubles at least, so we shall be able to fly somewhere before this war, for it is impossible to remain so.   And if with you there is also such misery [as you wrote?] come rather to us; we will put these miseries together.   We live on Niborska Street, facing the hospital; our house is surrounded with a garden.   Romek is so healthy here that we can hardly give him enough to eat, and we eat also rather well; a loaf and a half of bread is used every day, while formerly we took half a loaf for two days. . . . .

HELENA

627   August 10, 1914

DEAR FATHER: . . . . We find ourselves now in a very critical situation, because we are in the midst of the greatest war.   Mława is near the frontier and therefore it is most disturbed.   We received your letter with the handkerchief and 3 roubles on the day before the war, for the next day communication was interrupted and trains no longer come to Mława nor leave it.   The telegraphs [wires] are broken, the post abandoned, the [governmental] bank abandoned, all the officers and all the officials have gone away.   The army has been mobilized, and uncle [Piotr] was also taken, but then set free because of his hand.   The Russian army was in Iłłowo and Działdowo and tried to take Nyborg, but was checked for they had no infantry.   On the very first day the Prussian station in Wólka and the bridges were blown up, and now larger or smaller battles are fought around Mława.   The Russian army is camping now in Mława and in its neighborhood.   German aeroplanes fly every day above our Mława, and just now one of them went away; they are still shooting at it from guns.   This morning, when a German aeroplane flew over Mława and they began to shoot at it from cannons and machine-guns, a score of civilians and children were wounded, we don't know whether from the aeroplane or by the falling bullets. Up to the present we are alive, thanks to God, but we cannot assure you that we shall not perish very soon. The wounded find no longer a place in the hospitals, though there are now two or three of them on every street. Dear father, everything is very dear here now, for no supplies are brought. Many things cannot be bought at all, for they are lacking. Perhaps we shall die not of bullets but of hunger, for this also is quite possible. So we all bid you farewell, for perhaps we shall see one another never more upon this earth. It is a pity that you did not take us to you, perhaps there we should be safer. . . . . Dear father, we have paid all our money to the landlord, as rent for half a year, and now we have nothing to live on. . . . .

Your sincerely loving son,
ROMUALD

628 August 24, 1914

DEAR FATHER: [Repeats in part the news in the letter of August 10.] We stayed at first in Mława, hoping that things would get quiet, and then we had nowhere and no money to fly. Later Mrs. Wasilewska's husband, who is a sergeant and knows about the movements of the army, said that the Russian army would fall back, and told his wife to fly to her family in Kosiny. Mother knows the Wasilewskis well, and Wasilewska wanted to take us with her, so we went also to Kosiny, but after two days we returned on foot to Mława, as it was a little quieter. Meanwhile the Russian army fell back, and Germans, to the number of 20,000, entered Mława and let nobody out. They made trenches around Mława and began to commit different abuses—burned houses and windmills, robbed the farmers, and behaved as if in their own town. In such activities they spent a week in Mława, and on August 20 the Russian cavalry and artillery drove them away from Mława. . . . . Now we need not fear the Germans, but we don't know what will happen next. The Poles are going with the Russians. The Germans threw proclamations from their aeroplanes to the Poles, asking them to help them, and when they win, they will give us Poland back. But they work in vain, for the Russians also wrote a proclamation in which they promise us autonomy and such laws as were during the Polish times, and the Poles believe the Russians rather than the Germans. . . . . Dear

father, you can easily guess that there is now great misery here. . . . .
We live only on what anybody lends or gives us. . . . . So we beg
you, if you can, send us at least a few roubles, or else we shall die from
hunger. We send this letter through Japan, but whether it will reach
you, we don't know. But a drowning man grasps even a razor. . . . .

ROMUALD PORZYCKI

629

January 5, 1915

RESPECTED SIR: . . . . You ask for details concerning my family.
I give them to you. My wife is now 36 years old, my son Romek 17,
my daughter Hela 15. As to my wife, you are not mistaken in saying
that she is very nervous. Any insuccess influences her much, she
gets sick and does not eat for a day or two. As to Romek, he was not
so sick when a child . . . . he had no heart-disease. While I was
still at home, I soothed and softened everything. When I was leaving,
my wife asked me to bring them as soon as possible to America. During the first and second year I could not do it, for I had no steady
work; I could scarcely send them from time to time a few roubles.
I had borrowed money for my journey to America, so there were more
than 200 roubles of debt left. Thus my wife was obliged to pay the
interest and from time to time a few roubles of the sum out of my
small wages. Even today there are more than 100 roubles to pay
back. Thus, during three years I was unable to send a ship-ticket.
After 3 years Romek finished the governmental [town-] school and
wrote me that he wanted more instruction. I permitted him; I
could not refuse to the child the permission to learn. But the expenses
increased, and it was really as bad as they wrote. With my small
earnings I could not send them much. And thus Romek, seeing his
mother always crying from longing and despair, might have got his
heart-illness even through this, for he is very sentimental, like his
mother, while Hela has my iron nature. My wife wished at first to
come to America, because she would have come with them both.
But later Romek did not want for anything in the world to leave off
learning, and his mother did not want to leave him alone with strangers, for, as she mentions to me, he needs care like a small child.
And I agreed and was glad that he did not want to come to America,
only wants to live in his own country, for I don't like the American
education of children. Here the child is not morally educated, it
knows no respect for its elders. It knows only how to throw snow or

stones at the passengers. As to me, I cannot become Americanized, for in the old country I had easier work. There I was a shoemaker, while here I must work in an iron-foundry, and even this goes on feebly. For the last few months I have worked scarcely two or three days in a week. So I sit here as upon sharp nails and wait for the incidents of the war in Poland. I am longing for my family, because I have had no news for more than two months. I don't know whether they are alive or not. Wishing to save my family from hunger, I sent on October 24, 80 roubles, but I have no certitude whether they received them. Probably they did not, for the governmental post-office in Mława is abandoned, and my family may not be there, for Mława, as it seems, has changed her proprietors 4 times already. . . . . As to my verses [a humoristic piece, printed in the Polish paper *Zgoda*], I thank you very much for your praise. . . . . I have never been a man of letters. Perhaps if I had studied in that line I should have some aptitude. This one I composed in free moments and I doubted whether the editors would deign to print it. . . . .

STANISŁAW PORZYCKI

JABŁKOWSKI SERIES

In the present case we have the only example of a perfectly solidary and harmonious "natural family," as the result of an evolution which has substituted individual bonds between the members of a marriage-group for traditional social bonds between the members of the "large family."

We see also an important social consequence of this evolution—the particularly marked isolation of the marriage-group from the rest of the community, even from the relatives who in the old organization would be the most important members of the group, namely, the parents of the man and the woman and the· brothers and sisters. On the one hand, the marriage-group, perfectly solidary within itself, acts in economic and social matters toward the rest of the community as toward strangers, sometimes even with a marked hostility; on the other hand, any action from outside is received as affecting the marriage-group as a whole. In this respect the reactions to external influences tending to disaggregate the group—gossip, efforts to compel the husband or the wife to act in economic matters in a personal way—are significant. These influences themselves, the more or less unfriendly acts of neighbors, acquaintances, relatives, which Jabłkowska attributes to "jealousy," are perhaps better understood if we take into consideration the very natural hostile attitude of the social environment toward so isolated and impenetrable a familial group. The old type of family, at least in Poland, has no place for such an isolation. Under these conditions it is obvious that when for any reason the marriage-group tends to separate itself sharply from the family-group the latter not only shows a sharp resentment, but the smaller group is by the fact of the resentment thrown more and more back upon itself, until its isolation is greater than that of the modern family.

Another interesting point in this connection is the important part played by the woman in the constitution of the new family. This rôle is complicated, as is the situation of the woman itself. In the old group the woman's position in the family was in one respect more secure than in the new one, because she was backed by her group. But, on the other hand, the woman's relation to her husband and children always tended to be as exclusive and personal as possible; she always occupied the standpoint of particular individuals, not that of the group as a whole. And thus the new group appears from this point of view as a realization of a certain tendency of the woman—the tendency to substitute a few subjective personal relations for the many objective social relations. In all the cases in which the new group is or tends to be constituted, the woman seems to be the principal factor of its unity and isolation. But as she has not the help of any social traditions her success depends upon her personality.

The whole evolution in the Jabłkowski case seems relatively recent, for the older generation has preserved much of the traditional peasant attitude. Probably the Jabłkowskis are the children of peasants, who settled in the city.

630–48, TO KONSTANTY JABŁKOWSKI, IN AMERICA, FROM HIS WIFE AND CHILDREN, IN POLAND

630 LUBLIN, December 28, 1913

DEAREST AND MOST BELOVED HUSBAND: I received your letter with Christmas wishes and the postcard with New Year wishes, and I thank you heartily. O dear husband, I thank you once more for your letters, for I was in very great sorrow during the whole holidays, because I had no letters. I wondered much why, and I thought so, that perhaps you were sick from all this sorrow. So when I received the letter, I cried from joy. . . . . You write me not to answer this last letter of yours but I do answer, for some days have passed since I have written you a postcard, and you would have no letter from me for a long time. When I receive another letter from you I shall have also something to write, for now I shall be a little calmer and I will calculate all the money which I spent and what I spent it for. For I tell you, dear husband, I was so grieved after the letter which you wrote me before that I thought I should never calm myself. And after that I had no letter for almost 2 weeks. And moreover I got a letter from Stasiak on December 23, and . . . . I did not send him that letter back, for you told me not to write letters to anybody. Answer me whether you speak [are on speaking terms] with Stasiak, for he wrote me that he is not guilty of the offense against me in Koźlak's letter to his wife. He excused himself that he wrote whatever Koźlak told him to write [dictated], and he said that it was exclusively Koźlak's fault; he [Stasiak] could not go into a cellar and write the letter so that nobody might see it [scil., somebody has read or heard what Koźlak dictated and thus gossip arose]. He wrote many more words, but I don't repeat everything for it would take too much time to write. But he begged my pardon very much and said that he did not [intend to] offend me in that letter in any way. He wrote that he was not a traitor to you and never had been. He is only very pained that Janek [the writer's son] called him in his letter a rascal and a Ham [for having offended Janek's mother], and he wrote a few words to Janek saying that he would remember it. . . . . Finally he wrote thus: "I won't write you any more news; you will learn from your friend [husband?] who is a rascal toward us." And to Janek he wrote: "Don't ever write such letters to anybody, for if I were really such a rascal as you write, this letter would have cost you dear. If you don't believe me, ask your father." And he wished us a Merry Christmas and New Year. So I beg you, dear husband, very much, don't quarrel with these swine. I beg you once more, don't quarrel. Forget your wrong; why should you waste your health in vain? . . . .

MARCYANNA JABŁKOWSKA

631   February 17, 1914

MOST BELOVED FATHER: I thank you very nicely for the scrap upon which you wrote a few words for me. Dear father, you tell me to learn to be an iron-moulder. But I won't learn to be an iron-moulder, for it is a hard speciality. One earns a few roubles more, but he must work like an ox. And here if a moulder is kept anywhere, he is, but if they throw him away he cannot find work, but must work as a simple laborer. Thus it happened with Hojnacki. You write me that any peasant can do the work which I do. But you don't know yet what work it is. Myka wanted to work at the light and said that he had worked at the light in the cement-factory, but they refused to admit him for they were afraid he would spoil something. . . . . I learned for almost half a year in helping an electro-technician, and as he liked me he explained to me everything . . . . so that now if I got a plan, I could instal the light myself, and I can decompose and recompose a dynamo machine. . . . . And if the factory stops I can do locksmith's work. . . . . I earn now almost 25 roubles, and later I shall have almost 35 roubles, or even more. Now, dear father, don't trouble about me. I shall find my way and even help you.[1] Now, dear father, I need a suit for Easter, for this one which I have is quite spoilt . . . . and I need also shoes, for these which I have are torn. . . . . Besides this, dear father, send me some neckties . . . . and if they reach me I shall beg you to send me perhaps 2 stiff shirts, for I have only one such . . . . and it is not enough. I must take it to the laundry too often. . . . .   JAN JABŁKOWSKI

632   February 21, 1914

MOST BELOVED AND DEAREST HUSBAND: I received your letter . . . . written on February 8. . . . . As to lending money, you may be calm, for I am not so silly as to lend money or to warrant for anybody. You know that I am not very eager to do such things. I won't lend to my brother either, for I know how eager he is in paying back. . . . .[2] Now you ask about my overcoat. It is a little worn

---

[1] We have here the new attitude toward work—appreciation of skill and efficiency—as stated in the Introduction: "Economic Attitudes."

[2] A sign of the degree to which the old solidarity is dissolved. In peasant life money should be lent, not only to so near a relative, but to any member of the community, and the question of his paying the debt would hardly be raised as self-evident. So the solidarity between members of the family is here weaker than the traditional solidarity between members of the community.

on the front side, about the pockets and sleeves, but it does not look so bad yet. You write me, dear husband, to buy a fur collar, but now I don't want to buy any, for spring is near. Since I did not buy in the beginning of the winter I won't buy now, for immediately some persons would be found ready to say that I did not buy it for winter, only for summer. . . . . And I shall put this whole 100 roubles into the savings-bank; I won't divide it. As to the debts, I owe 8 roubles to my father, which I lacked to live, for I have not worked for almost a month and Janek's salary does not suffice for our household, because I spend now on everything one rouble a day. Yes, my dear husband. So I took 7 roubles for living and 1 rouble for your mother, together 8 roubles. I have not yet paid these 2 roubles to your mother which I owed her, but I gave her this 1 rouble, for she was at the wedding of your foster-daughter. Tomaszewski came to invite me and mother to that wedding, but what was the need to them of my going there.[1] And now, dear husband, I owe still 10 roubles to Gelblum [Jewish shopkeeper] on the booklet [in which goods taken on credit are inscribed]. So I write you, dear husband, that I shall put these 100 roubles into the bank and I won't pay these debts.[2] Father does not need money much so I will pay him 1 rouble on my pay day and 1 rouble on Janek's pay day and thus I shall pay it back gradually. And from Gelblum I won't take now on the booklet, but as far as possible for cash, until you send me money for the children's clothing; then perhaps a few roubles will remain from the clothing, and these I shall pay to Gelblum. For the children need clothes absolutely. Janek must have another suit for going out, and Oleś has only one which has been repaired already and he has nothing to put on when he goes to church. Now, as to the Jałozos [husband's sister and brother-in-law], I shall write you what a *bryndza* [literally sheep-cheese; slang for "bad condition," "misery" or "disorderly life"] there is now, only in another letter, for now I am not particularly healthy. I have toothache and my arm pains me. . . . . Goodbye, my dear Kostuś, for I long very much without you. I kiss you heartily innumerable times.

Your wife,

MARCYANNA JABŁKOWSKA

Now I kiss you once more strongly. Now, dear husband, Oleś was a little angry, because you did not send kisses for him in your letter.

[1] Another attitude which would be quite incomprehensible in a peasant group.

[2] In order not to destroy the round number. A vestige of the qualitative character of economic quantities. Cf. Introduction: "Economic Attitudes."

633

DEAR AND MOST BELOVED HUSBAND: I beg you, don't forget to write the date of my letter, for I don't know to which of my letters you answer. [Details about health of herself and the boys.] Mania [daughter] is in good health, thanks to God, only her eyes are a little red, as when you were here. If she does not cry they are not red, and as soon as she cries a little they become red again; .... and she is so inclined to cry this daughter of yours. .... She says always that father is not here and there is nobody to dance with her. .... And she is so wrathful that you have no idea. Janek sometimes teases her or tells her something [reprimands her] or gives her a tap—not very much, but he wants her now, when she is bigger, to be more careful and polite, not to play with the first best, not to run about the street, and to learn well. Thus, when he tells her anything and gives her a tap, she flares up and jumps at his eyes and beats him and kicks him with her feet and refuses to yield. I always make remarks to her and tell her not to flare up at Janek, for he is older and big. And she tries to beat Oleś also, and he has to run away from her. Although they strike her sometimes first she pays them twice as much back.[1] If I strike her with a "discipline" [short whip], she begins to cry awfully and runs into the room and calls, "O my God, my God! O father, father!" and she calls as if she were already an orphan. So I cannot beat her often, for I begin immediately to pity her; I prefer rather to beg her. And in the school she is also difficult, for her teacher told me that she is very self-conceited and does not allow anybody to tell her anything; when anybody says a word, she answers him. She wants all other children to respect her, and she is still not wise enough to be proud and not to talk with the first best.[2] So I

[1] In addition to possible constitutional independence, the girl has not been brought up in the custom of obeying her brothers. Cf. the contrary attitude of Stasia in the Krupa series. The custom loses its force in the industrial milieu and in the absence of the large family-group.

[2] Here, as at some other points in this series, we see the principle of social hierarchy applied to children and carried to a ridiculous minuteness. It did not originate in the country, but in towns. It consists, generally speaking, in the selection of playmates for the children by the parents. This selection exists to some extent in the country, but there it is based mainly upon the consideration of a morally good or bad example which the child may have in its playmates, not upon any idea of the latters' social position. Thus, the son or daughter of a noble can play freely with such peasant children as are known to be good and not spoiled (particularly in sexual matters). But the background of this liberty is the unexpressed and sometimes only half-conscious idea that the distance is too great

told her that I would write to you, but she does not know that I write really. So don't write to her all this that I tell you, for she always says that she will improve, and it would be very painful for her. For she is very good and obedient when I send her to do anything, only she is so hasty and wrathful. You may always admonish her in your letter to learn well, to be good, not to fight with boys at home and in the school. [Details about health of the family; page and a half about the clock which is out of order; two pages about floors, windows, and humidity in the apartment.] But perhaps all this will hold until you come back, for I don't want to occupy myself [with repairing]. I have already the whole house upon my head, for although, my dear husband, you keep all our home in your memory, yet it is not as if you

---

for any undesirable familiarity to arise, either between the parents or between the children when they grow up. It is the same principle which allows the country nobleman to be on much more familiar terms with the peasant or the Jew than with anyone of the middle class, and which gives the members of the highest aristocratic families the greatest freedom in selecting friends. But in towns, where social distinctions are very minute and there is a continuous passage from the lowest to the highest class, the task of keeping these distinctions up is a very difficult one, the more so, the lower the given class and the more insignificant the basis of distinction. And as the intimacy of children may lead to an intimacy of parents, and the friendship made in childhood may last in later days, the parents are very careful to select for their children playmates of the same or of a higher social standing and to keep them far from any connection with those of a lower level. A second factor acts here also and compels parents to make the selection. It is the importance of manners. In this respect the country nobility relies upon tradition, heredity, and the general home atmosphere and is not afraid that the children would lose their good manners in playing with peasant children. The same does not hold in towns, particularly in the lower-middle class, where good manners are an artificial and imitated product and can be easily lost. Finally, the moral consideration plays in towns a more important part than in the country, as town-children are generally more spoiled, and it is more difficult to avoid undesirable contact.

The result of all this is, that no child of a "self-respecting" family can select its companions without the control of its parents, not even in school; and particularly no playing upon the street is permitted. And as only those who have little or nothing to lose in social standing let their children play upon the street, the street-children constitute really a dangerous element for the others, from the moral point of view.

Evidently, there is an incalculable but very strong influence of this whole system of control upon the psychology of the young generation. It must be noted, however, that a movement of democratization in the higher classes began some 20 or 30 years ago and is growing. The control of the children in this respect still exists, but is based more and more upon merely moral considerations. But this movement has not yet reached the lower classes, who remain as rigid in their distinctions as formerly.

were at home. . . . . Janek and Oleś exchanged their watches, Oleś himself wanted to change. . . . .

Now, my dear husband, I want to tell you a few words about the Jałozos. Kasia [the wife] does not come to us; Michał came once, but I was not at home. [Your] mother goes sometimes to them. Once, when she came back, she cried so much, saying that they are in such misery. They did not pay the rent and a complaint against them was made. The police wanted to levy on their furniture, but they carried it to another house and have only a bed of boards, while the children sleep upon the floor. And they quarrel among themselves. Michał tells her to go to work, but she says that she had a fortune [dowry] and won't go to work. But he says that he has her fortune in his buttock [despises it]. What [he says] is a fortune worth when she does not know how to manage the household? A woman is worth more who knows how to manage everything, although she is poor.[1] And mother told him to try to get a janitor's job. She [Kasia] has sent a boy twice already asking me to lend them money, but let her wait till I do it. But your mother would carry everything to Kasia. Your mother is just like my father, who would carry everything to———[probably another daughter] and would not say, "You ought not to give." There was a little poppy which they brought from Wola; I don't even know when mother carried it out. But never mind the poppy. She asked me to give her the old shoes of Mania, and I gave them.[2] I shall describe more in another letter. . . . . Goodbye, dear husband, I kiss you heartily.

Your always well-wishing and loving wife,

Marcyanna Jabłkowska

I kiss you once more strongly, dear husband, and goodbye. Work happily with God.

634 March 17, 1914

Most beloved Husband: [Letters received and written; description of her sickness.] Now I tell you, I was so worried when I lay in bed, you have no idea, and it is impossible to describe, because you

---

[1] An appreciation more adapted to the conditions of town-workmen than to those of farmers, for in the first case fortune has merely an additional value as compared with the salary, while in the second it is absolutely fundamental for the whole life-organization.

[2] In this connection the older generation is simply carrying out the ideas of familial solidarity.

were not at home. For it seemed to me that if you said to me even a single word I should be healthier. Moreover, letters are now so late from you; they don't arrive normally. . . . . Now, dear husband, as to the good heart, whether I have a good heart toward you or not, I tell you only this, that as I love God and want my soul's salvation after my death, I always love you and always have a good and constant heart toward you. Yes, my dear husband. And I would never write any testy things in my letters, but yourself, dear husband, you lead [incite] me to do it. And I shall write you, my dear, a few words from a good heart. My dear, when you learn anything about me and it does not please you, you ought to write me at once, "So and so, my dear (or however else, in your manner), and I hear that you have been where I don't wish you to go." For I even acknowledge that you are right when you write that it is not a fit company for me, and I regretted myself that I was there and I said to myself that I will never more go anywhere. And you write me about it after a year, as if you had waited for something more to make a conviction against me. Yes, my dear husband, I shall never be angry with you, even if you write me something like this in every letter and if you make any remarks to me, for you have the right and you ought to make remarks to me without any fear, if you are displeased with anything, and I shall listen to you at any time. Yes, my dearest husband.

[Calculation of income and expenses.] My dear husband, once more I make this remark, for you write precisely that you did not intend to answer my letter. It was very bad of you to think so, and to have written only after listening to the advice of *Kum* Wierzba. My dear husband, I write to you with a good intention, without any wrath, and it seems to me that you will agree with me. Answer me whether I don't write the truth, my dear husband, that you ought to answer without hesitation every letter, good or bad . . . . and that you ought to accept everything from me, whether it is written good or bad [praise or blame], and I must also accept from you good and bad writing. We must listen to each other in order that it may be well, until we are united with each other, for I wish our life to be happy as long as we live upon the world. And don't listen to any Hams whatever they may tell you against me, or to any apes, whatever they may write you in their letters about me. And if anything comes to your ears about me, write me at once and I will listen to you and won't be angry at all if you make any remark to me. For I don't listen to anybody except you. For if we listen to everything that people bark with their tongues, we should be well off! If I wrote to you everything that I hear from women who have their husbands in America! For if their husbands are of a bad conduct, they think and say at once that all are the same. But I don't listen to anybody except you for you have ever written me not to listen. Yes, dear husband. [Usual ending.]   MARCYANNA

MY MOST BELOVED AND DEAREST FATHER: I am healthy and I wish you the same with my whole heart. And now, dear father, you write that you won't come until the next year. But, dear father, don't think this; it won't be so. For mother says that she will not stop working until you come. And do you know, father, that mother is sick, but goes to work nevertheless. And I beg you, father, very much, earn for the journey and come, for I am very much worried. When Sunday comes, mother does not go anywhere, and I have not even 1 companion and must play alone, so I am very much worried. I have nothing more to write, I kiss you innumerable times, your hands and lips. Goodbye.   MARYSIA J.

635   March 22, 1914

DEAREST AND MOST BELOVED HUSBAND: . . . . You ask me why were the children not authorized by me in [writing] their letter. I was working at night when they wrote the letter to you, and when I came back they told me that they wrote to you for money for clothes. I intended myself to write you about it, but they hastened for they were afraid lest the money should be too late and they could not buy before Easter. They told me about it, and I see myself that it is necessary to buy. Janek told me to take money from the bank, but I said that I won't take it. . . . . Seeing that I was not in a hurry to write to you, he wrote. . . . . And Mania did not write to you for anything, for she has with me the 4 roubles which you sent her for her name-day. I took this money for living and now must give it back, for she always asks for it saying that father sent it. . . . . Janek has earned now 11 roubles for he took night-work. . . . . He took 6 roubles of these, for he always takes 1 rouble [for his personal expenses] and bought shoes for 5 roubles, so 5 were left for me. [More about money-matters. Now, dear husband, as to this exchange of watches, Oleś himself wanted to exchange, for his watch is more difficult to wind up, and he was afraid of spoiling it; he changed himself, voluntarily. He has earned already more than a rouble for mending shoes. . . . . You would laugh to see how he mends and quarrels with his grandfather. For now your father is here and always interferes with Oleś, as he likes to interfere with everything, but Oleś does not allow him to tell him anything, saying, "How much do you know about it? I know myself what to do." Now, dear husband, as to the carbolic acid, you can be perfectly sure, for I have poured it out already. I give you my word of honor that I tell the truth; I used it only sometimes for my teeth. [Two pages describing her sickness; concern for her husband's health; hygienic advice.] So please care for yourself that you may come back in good health and looking well. I beg you once more, dear husband, care for your health, for I look bad now also after my sickness, and thus we might both get overworked, my dear husband, and during our work the grave might cover us and we might not rejoice with each other upon this white world. Yes, my dear and beloved husband.

Now as to Rafałowa, about my going there with my children. When I am there nobody else is there except Rafałowa and Mateusz and their children. She buys a small bottle of vodka and a bottle of beer, we put our money together [to buy it]. Oleś plays the accordeon a little; the children dance, we laugh at them, and thus a little time passes. Sometimes they come to me, also alone. But we don't meet so often; during the whole summer I was there 3 times and they were in my house 2 times. They are very polite toward us. This is the only defect, that they are not married and live so. They intend to marry, but they postpone it thus from day to day. . . . .

MARCYANNA JABŁKOWSKA

636   [March 22, 1914]

DEAREST AND MOST BELOVED FATHER: I beg you very much, send me a cream-white ribbon of the same breadth as that one which you sent me for the holidays. Then I shall have a scarf for my dress for the first communion. I beg you very much, be so gracious and buy it and send it to me as soon as possible after you receive this letter. I beg you very much, and I kiss your hands, each finger, and each eye, and each ear, and your nose, and your chin, and your cheeks, and your neck [all the words in diminutive form], everywhere and everywhere, my diamond little father, who loves me. I am in good health, thanks to God, and then goodbye. Written by your loving daughter,

MARYSIA JABŁKOWSKA [10 years old]

Gud baj.

DEAREST AND MOST BELOVED FATHER: I am in good health, thanks to God, and I wish you the same with my whole heart and my whole soul. Now, dear father, I have mended everybody's shoes, and after calculation it amounts to 1 rouble, 50 copecks, and I have calculated everything twice cheaper than a shoemaker would take. So I beg you, dear father, send me either in a letter 2 dollar-notes, then mother would go to the bank and change them, give me 1 rouble 50 copecks and take the rest herself; or when you send money, send also these 1 r. 50 c. for me. . . . . I have nothing more to write only I kiss your dear hands and your dear head and your dear face heartily innumerable times, and once more I kiss you innumerable times. Goodbye, most beloved and dearest father. Written by your son, loving and never forgetting you, and wanting to see you and to kiss you as many times,

ALEKSANDER [OLEŚ] JABŁKOWSKI [12 or 13 years old]

637 April 18, 1914

DEAR HUSBAND: [Long account of renovation of house and furniture.] As to Easter, I was in Rafałowa's home on Good Sunday, for she sent a girl asking us to come. On Monday I stayed at home and slept the whole afternoon, for now there are no holidays for me, nothing rejoices me at all. . . . . On Tuesday the Rafałs called on me, but I was going to night-work and they stayed only one hour and a half. I brought 5 bottles of beer and that was all. . . . . Nobody else comes to us and I go nowhere.[1] [Calculation of income and expenses.] Now again I must buy shoes for your mother, because she has already some patches upon hers and she begins to talk that she won't walk now any more in shoes with patches. I shall describe to you some day what she says, for she does not like to be with us. She wants us to give her the money back and she would rather be free. Yes, my dear husband. [Details about health.] Dear husband, you write me to go sometimes with the children to the high mass. In winter I never went, neither with them nor alone, for it was too cold. Now it is warmer, but I have not much to wear, and Mania has no summer overcoat, and now the weather is cold. . . . . My summer overcoat is quite worn and not nice enough to go to the church. Instead of putting anything whatever on myself, I prefer to stay at home, for

[1] Evidently the husband does not like her to have many social relations. The egotism of the marriage-group asserts itself even in this matter.

at once some people would be found who would say that Jabłkowska walks in such a worn and out-of-fashion overcoat. So I prefer to stay at home, for we are everywhere talked about, that both the Jabłkowskis are clever and laborious people, that you are working in America and sending money which we put into the bank, that I am working, and Janek also, that we dress well and the children are nicely dressed. Thus, they say, clever people do.[1] Now, dear husband, I should like to buy a summer dress and a nice skirt and a nice overcoat, and also an overcoat for Mania. Now I must buy for Mania a white dress and slippers for Pentecost, because she is going to her first confession. My head aches with all this, that always something is needed. So, my dear husband, when you send money some day, if you send me 100 roubles and some more, I will buy something, but if you send only 100, I won't buy anything; I will sit at home and put those 100 roubles into the bank, because I want you to come back as soon as possible, for I worry much without you. Yes, my dear husband. . . . .

Dear husband, I ask you whether it is true that you have killed, in company with Wierzba, a pig, that Wierzba wrote thus. For once Kozak came to me when I was in the factory and asked: "Has *Kum* [your husband] written a letter now?" I say: "Why do you ask? He has." And he laughs: "And what does he write?" I say: "Nothing in particular. He is in good health, thanks to God. And what is the matter?" He says: "Nothing, only mine [my wife] said that Wierzba's wife said that Wierzba wrote that they killed a pig together." So I am curious, whether it is true, for even if you did it it is all right. [Usual ending.]

MARCYANNA JABŁKOWSKA

638 May 8, 1914

DEAR HUSBAND: I received your postcard for which I thank you heartily. . . . . Now, dear husband, to this postcard I answer you by a letter, not by a postcard, because I wrote you a postcard on May 1, and I cannot send you thus one postcard after another, for it ought not to be done so. A postcard ought to be sent after a letter, and not

---

[1] Compare the high social standing of Jabłkowska with the case of Borkowska. The community dislikes and opposes the isolation and egotism of the marriage-group but must respect and acknowledge the superiority which solidarity and efficiency give to this group. The position of the latter is weaker than that of the large family-group, but incomparably stronger than that of an isolated individual.

two postcards one after another. Therefore I write you a letter, dear husband, for I long very much without a letter. I have had no letter from you for 17 days. . . . . I was so anxious and nervous that it was awful, because now there is such trouble in America. I have read in the paper that 30 Americans were shot in Mexico, and many other things . . . . and that a ship was drowned which left America on April 7. . . . . So, my dear husband, I admonish you very much, if you intend to come from America sooner or later inform me exactly when you will leave. And then I shall write you to bring us some token from America. For if only things are bad in America, I beg you, come back. Now, dear husband, I dreamed that you returned home and came to me to the factory and I did not recognize you. It seemed to me that it was you, but I was not certain. And I asked the women, "Look there, this man is like my husband." And you went to the well for water. And Pazuchowa said, "Evidently, it is Konstanty." And you came back, carrying water, and entered into the room and kissed me and began to weep that I did not own you. And I told you nothing, because I was angry with you for not having written to me when you would come back, for I was pained that I had not met you at the railway-station. Then I awoke. So my dream was contrary [bad?], because I dreamed that you kissed me with your tongue.

Miecznik has quarreled with me. They are all mean, for they grudge this heavy work which I have. All this is through envy, for whenever money comes [from you], their eyes sally out of their heads from envy. For we have such luck that people grudge our work. In this quarrel with me he reproached me that I ought not to work, for you send me money from America.[1] He did not say this to my eyes [outright], only he said that I was working for the sake of distraction. We are 4 women who work together, as before. One of them remained at home, and Miecznik went at once to the master asking him to send a woman to us. The master refused, and the 3 of us worked until breakfast. After breakfast he went to the director and said that there were three of us and we could not get along, and the director sent another woman more. He was so mean because he did not want us to earn a złoty more, for he grudges, particularly me. I got very angry at these Hams, for I don't allow anybody to abuse me much

[1] It is traditionally not suitable to a man's dignity to let his wife do hired work and to a woman's dignity to do hired work if she has a husband.

and he cannot offend me in any other way, for I have my honor and I don't care about any conversations. So he was very loud-mouthed and said that I was too great a lady, that such a lady ought not to work in such a black factory room but to sit in her apartments. Yes, my dear husband. And I tell you that I will work only until you come, for it is a pity for [me to lose] my health working with such Hams. [Health details.] Now I write you a few words more about Oleś. He finished the school and we ought to think of his having some occupation. So decide, please, and write me . . . . what to do. He always dreams either about going to a drug-store and learning to be a salesman, or to a press, to be a printer. . . . .

[MARCYANNA]

639   May 26, 1914

DEAR HUSBAND: . . . . I received 100 roubles and put them into the bank, so now there are 700 roubles in the bank. . . . . And for my expenses I took a loan from the bank,[1] but I am not very much satisfied for I have taken the loan and have not bought everything which I needed. . . . . I only got angry in the worst way, nothing more. For if both of us had been here, we should sooner have given good advice to each other, what to do. So I took a loan of 40 roubles. . . . . And there was more trouble than money. It is happy that I know how to write and it makes no difference to me, because I had to sign 6 times. . . . . And those who cannot sign—what a shame it is! The official and the doorkeeper laugh at him. [Enumerates the expenses and describes the clothing bought, upon 4 pages; adds a detailed account.] Now, dear husband, this small bottle of vodka and the *zakąska* [relishes] which you find written upon the scrap, we drank it with Syroka's wife. I shall describe to you in what way. When I had no letter from you for so long a time . . . . I imagined God

---

[1] It would be less troublesome and less expensive to spend a part of these 100 roubles instead of taking a loan, for the interest, taxes, etc., on a loan amount to twice as much as the interest which she can get on her own money. But there is evidently a remainder of the old distinction between property as a fundamental, not purely economic category, and incomes and expenses. The loan is classed with the latter, and not related to the property. It is an exact parallel with the distinction between mortgage and ordinary debt. The latter, in the peasant's eyes, does not harm the property as such, only the income-and-expense system. The other point here is the predilection for a round sum; a hundred is an entity which would be damaged by subtracting anything from it. Cf. note 2, p. 936.

knows what! That you were sick, or that you had got so indifferent. And I went to Syroka and said so: "Tell me my fortune from cards, *kuma*, whether my husband is healthy, for I have had no letter for a long time." And she laid the cards and said: "*Kum* is healthy and works, and during this week you will receive a letter with good news, and a big sum of money is on the way, so don't grieve for on Sunday you will go [to the post-office] for money." And I said: "If your words prove true, *kuma*, I will treat you when the money comes." And thus it happened. I received your letter on Thursday and the post-notification about money on Monday, and I had to treat her. So when I returned from the town with Mania and Oleś, I brought a small bottle of spirits and *zakąska*, and we went to Syroka and drank it. . . . . And please answer me whether you are angry with me or not for having drunk this bottle with Syroka.

Dear husband, I write you a few words about this Wierzba's money. It is so, my dear husband: I don't wish *Kum* Wierzba to send money to my address. First, I don't wish to be at the service of Wierzba. Second, she will bear a savage claim, why Wierzba sends money to my address, not to hers. For even if I talk with her whenever it is necessary, I shall always remember those words which she threw against me unjustly. God is witness whether she was right! And so to speak, I don't wish to cause Wierzba this pain, for you live well with each other and it would not be suitable to offend him, for he is a very fine man. But she is an accomplished swine, although my *kuma*. So when this money comes, I shall draw it from the post-office and immediately there I shall give it to her. And I do it for you, dear husband, and for the *kum*, for he asks me politely. [Church-going; asks for prayer-books.]   [MARCYANNA]

640   March 28, 1914

DEAREST AND MOST BELOVED HUSBAND: [Easter wishes; money received and spent.] Now, dear husband, I write you a few words about Lucek [husband's brother] and his wife, for I was with them just now. Lucek began to abuse us, saying that we lacked confidence in them and were afraid to lend them some money. He was offended with you for not having written the letter to him, but having sent it in my letter, for I gave them this letter without the envelope, because I did not notice the inscription, "To be forwarded to Lucek" and tore the envelope. I did not give them the envelope therefore, but said that the letter was inclosed in mine. And why should we turn our heads [trouble ourselves] about the Luceks? We have enough of our own troubles. We should never come to an end with them. Lucek began at once to worry me, asking me to lend him 100 roubles nevertheless, even without your knowing it. I said that I positively would not lend without your knowing it. Lucek began to laugh at me, saying that I was afraid of you. And I said: "Yes, it is true, I am afraid. My husband wrote me that he confided everything to me but on the condition that I would not lend money to anybody, either of my family or of his own. I write to my husband about every rouble which I spend. I must listen to my husband and nobody else." I had to find an excuse for he worried me about this loan. He said that he will write a letter to you some day, but I don't know what about. He said that we shall still beg his favor some day. Is he our father or what else? Stupid Lucek! . . . .

MARCYANNA JABŁKOWSKA

641   April 7, 1914

BELOVED AND DEAR HUSBAND: . . . . I have already bought suits for the boys. But I feared to do it myself and Janek also. Janek said, "If some man were with us it would be better, for he would see how this suit looks, and whether it fits me well, for you, mother, won't know it as well." We had nobody to ask to go with us except Adam Jabłkowski. So we went to him and I said to him a few words and we went at once to the Jew, and Janek selected a suit which pleased him. . . . . The Jew asked 22 roubles for this suit; Adam offered him 10. The Jew said, "You are joking," and said, "21 roubles." Adam offered 11. The Jew bargained, saying that he could not give it away at such a price and asked 20. Then Adam told him to select another suit for Oleś, then we would come to an agreement on both together. So we selected a suit for Oleś from black cloth. . . . . It pleased Oleś and is nice enough. The Jew asked 20 roubles for both, and Adam offered 18. I did not bargain, for I did not feel quite well, only Adam. They agreed upon 20 roubles and I paid 20 roubles, 14 for Janek's and 6 for Oleś' suit. I did not expect that we should buy at such a price, for the stuff is better than in the old ones, although they cost more. [Enumerates other expenses.] Now, dear husband, when we bought the suit, Janek said, "Now, mother, let us take a drink on this occasion." Though I could not have acted otherwise myself, for it would not be nice of me, because Adam got muddy enough in walking with us, for it rained—God forbid! And we felt cold all of us. So we went to Adam's house and I bought a pint of vodka and a pound and a half of a good *zakąska* [probably ham and sausage] and 5 bottles of beer and rolls for 10 copecks, and I gave to the children 10 copecks each, and Mania asked me to buy oranges . . . . and all this cost me 2 roubles 15 copecks. [Enumerates on 3 pages various expenses and makes a general calculation.] So you can calculate, dear husband, whether I have calculated well. Perhaps I have made some mistakes, then write me; I won't be angry at all, for we ought precisely to control each other's expenses, for this is good order. . . . . I shall describe to you many other things, but in another letter. . . . . Answer me whether you are quite healthy for I dream often about you, and I shall describe to you how I dream about you. But you are always bad toward me in my dreams and I always cry awfully. . . . .

Marcyanna Jabłkowska

642   June 3, 1914

Dearest Father: [Thanks for gifts; describes how he earned more money by working nights.] I put 10 roubles from this money aside and intended to add 10 roubles later on and to buy myself a black suit. But it happened otherwise. On Pentecost morning, coming from the post-office, I met Adam Jabłkowski and he asked me absolutely to come to him with mother in the afternoon. I did not want to go, but he began to talk, that we despise his house. So we went. We went, and he had said nothing, and we found a christening [of his child]. Adam's brother was to be his *kum*, but he did not come, and Adam asked me absolutely to be his child's godfather. I was not prepared and refused, but he begged me and mother, and I had to hold the child at the baptism, together with Majewska, whose husband had a cab. . . . . And on Monday we had a *poprawiny* [supper in celebration], and I spent 6 roubles of my money on the christening-festival and *poprawiny*. And to the 4 roubles which were left I added 2 roubles more and bought shoes. . . . . Now I will begin to work at night again and will buy a black suit. . . . . Then I will get 6 photographs in my summer suit and 6 in my black suit and I will send you one of each; you will see what suits I have and how I look now. . . . .

Jan Jabłkowski

643   June 7, 1914

DEAREST AND MOST BELOVED HUSBAND: [Letters delayed.] I
write you a few words precisely about this christening in Adam's
house.   I am not satisfied with it at all, for I grudge these 6 roubles
which we have spent, for each rouble is awfully necessary to me.   But
it was impossible to act otherwise for there would be more talking
than all this is worth.   For if he had said to Janek that it was a
christening we should not have gone at all.   But I cannot say that
they have treated us badly—God forbid!   They behaved very
politely, for the christening was on Sunday, and on Monday *poprawiny*
and we returned rather late on both evenings, about midnight, and
he brought us home in a cab both times.   I was there and Janek and
Mania, while Oleś . . . . was in the country with his companion.
[Describes with whom and how long he stayed; why she permitted
him to go, etc.]   And these Majewskis [Adam's friends] admired
[wondered] that I am still so young and have such big and handsome
and good children.   And they wondered that Janek was going out
with me; they said that another boy would not be willing.   [Money-
matters; choice of career for Oleś.]

Now, dear husband, I write you a few words, that Golasıowa has
asked my pardon, for she was in Częstochowa [on a pilgrimage], and
after this she came to me and began to cry and to beg my pardon,
and she wanted to kiss my hand, but I did not allow her, and we
kissed each other in the face.   And she asked me to beg your pardon,
that you might not be angry with her.   Now I inform you, dear
husband, what a misfortune befell Brzozowski. . . . .   He went also
to America and his wife died here . . . . and 4 small children
remained.   People wrote for him to come.   Only don't be impressed
with it, my dear husband, for we are in good health, thanks to God.
If I am a little unwell, never mind, for I am not very sick either; I
walk, I work, perhaps gradually this sickness will pass.   I write you
on a separate scrap what is the matter with me.   [The scrap was
probably destroyed by the sender of the letters.]   And if I write you
that she is dead, why, you don't need to grieve about anybody else
except yourself and your family.   So don't mind it much.   I write
you this news that you may know, for I am also curious when you
write me anything like this.   Now, dear husband, I write you about
this sickness of mine, since what time I have not felt well.   My dear
husband [it has been] since you wrote me disagreeable letters about

this whole trouble. When Wierzba's wife told us nothing, and you were in such a wrath against me unjustly. Only don't be angry with me again for mentioning this, for I don't remember it any more [I have forgiven]. But when you ask me since what time I have been unwell, I write you the positive truth. If you had not asked me I would not have written at all. So it was, my dear husband, that I cried very much and could not eat and could not sleep, only grieved that you had so little confidence in me and listened to gossip. And I worked more than ever. [Describes her work; writes what the factory-doctor prescribed.] And the doctor told me that if I don't feel better, I must go to a specialist for women's diseases, and I should go and should not grudge the money, but, to tell the truth, dear husband, I am ashamed. . . . .

[MARCYANNA]

644 June 17, 1914

DEAREST AND MOST BELOVED HUSBAND: [Two pages describing receipt of a letter in a torn envelope and asking him not to send such thick letters because the post-officials think they contain money. Three pages itemizing expenditures, etc.] I write you a few words about Mania. Write a sheet to her and admonish her to be more polite and not to fight with Janek, for when he makes any remark to her and pushes her a little, she begins at once to cry awfully and jumps at him. Once he told her not to eat in the courtyard, for I worked at night, and she went into the courtyard with a pot [of food]. She did not listen, and he struck her a little on the face. She came immediately to me to the factory, weeping, and said that Janek had beaten her on the face. I got angry, went home and asked who was guilty. They told me so and so. Thus she had merited to be struck a little. I got angry and said that by the love of God I would write to you. And I must write because I have said so. Now write her not to cry thus about any trifle, for I tell you, dear husband, that she is such a weeper that it is awful. She cries about anything. When I have worked over night, I am unwilling to go anywhere, I lay down and tell her, "Mania, don't go anywhere into the field alone." Then she begins to weep at once saying that she is worried, and sometimes she listens, sometimes not, and does not tell me where she is going. And I am afraid, for now different accidents happen; I read in the paper what is going on in the world. Therefore I don't allow her to

go alone into the field. But she says: "When the boys go out you
are not angry." And I say: "It is permitted to the boys, for they
are boys, and you are a girl, you ought not to walk alone." So, my
dear husband, admonish her always, perhaps then she will sooner
listen, for this crying of hers angers me awfully. More than once I
got so angry that I had to strike her, but I should prefer to have her
listen to me when I tell her anything, rather than to beat her, for it is
not a pleasure to beat a child. . . . .

Now, dear husband, I write you about Oleś, that he finished his
school and received a very good certificate . . . . nothing but fives
and two fours [5 is the highest mark]. He received a book as reward
for having learned well. This book costs perhaps 2 roubles, but
unhappily it is Russian. When he was leaving the teacher kissed him
on the head and said that he would try perhaps to get a job for him.
And Oleś came home and said: "Well, mother, give me a few copecks
for having passed the examination." And he was so glad that he had
passed it! I kissed him and gave him only 15 copecks, for I had little
money, but he was glad even thus, went at once and hired a bicycle
and took a ride. And you, dear husband, when you send money, set
aside a rouble or a half for him, for his having passed the examination;
then he will be glad. . . . . He wants to go to the country for a week.
I permit him; let him rest a little. [Relates how she tried to get a
job for him at once.] Now, dear husband, I write you a few words
about *Kum* Wierzba and this pig. You ought to have known yourself that you are not in your own home but with strangers, and that
this does not pay; for you write that it did not pay. Nowadays
nobody is ever to be believed. When I hear [read] what you write I
say [to myself] that I did not expect anything like this from Wierzba—
that you would not come to an understanding. But such are the
times today. Describe to me everything you had between yourselves
[the whole quarrel]. But I would beg you, dear husband, not to
quarrel. Let him manage his own pocket and not profit from you.
And don't ever hasten to such common undertakings. Yes, my dear
husband. But it is always more pleasant to have somebody to talk
with. Manage things as your reason advises you, that it may be
well. Don't have any common undertakings and don't quarrel with
each other. . . . . Now, dear husband, as to Syroka, don't fear that
I tell anything there. I only listen to what she tells me and I laugh,
for she says that those two [women] are very angry because you send
100 roubles every two months, and they write to their husbands, and

these are angry that you send so much, for their wives write them that you send money and they do not. Petruniowa has only 100 roubles. Syroka said it herself, for I don't ask. . . . .

MARCYANNA JABŁKOWSKA

645 June 28, 1914

DEAREST AND MOST BELOVED HUSBAND: . . . . Your last letter was also half-opened and then sealed by the post. . . . . I inform you what a question I had with the factory-porter about that letter which, as I wrote you, was opened; I write it upon a scrap and when you read this scrap, burn it. Now I write you, dear husband, a few words about Oleś. . . . . He began to work in the same factory as Janek; instead of loafing about, let him rather work, then he will even eat better. For when he did nothing he ate little, for he had no time because of loafing. He has no hard work . . . . and earns 50 copecks. . . . . Mania passed the examination to the second division, but her certificate is not very good; she is so unwilling to learn that it is awful. [Six pages of money-accounts; 2 pages of health; usual ending.]

MARCYANNA JABŁKOWSKA

Now, dear husband, I write you a few words about this porter. He has read my letter. I made him awfully ashamed and talked much [abused him] and said that he ought not to be curious to read my letters for I receive letters from my husband, and my husband writes his letters home and they are not interesting to him. This is fortunate, that he did not tell anything more to this——[illegible word, probably a contemptful term for a woman about whose husband Jabłkowski wrote something bad] except that——[her husband?] suffers such misery. He [the porter] told her that I had read this aloud in the factory. And I, far from reading your letters to anybody, don't even tell what you wrote. I guessed at once that he had read my letter and said to him: "How did you dare to read my letter and moreover to spread gossip among the women?" . . . . He excused himself and said that he will not do it any more. So I beg you, if you write anything bad about anybody, send this letter registered. . . . .

646 July 5, 1914

DEAREST AND MOST BELOVED HUSBAND: . . . . I received from you money, 110 roubles . . . . only I am very anxious why I have got no letter. . . . . The porter went to the country for a few days, and the doorkeeper who took his place may have opened and read it from curiosity. . . . . For some people lie in wait for these letters like dogs, because they can learn nothing from me. Other men who are in America don't send so much money, so they are curious why you send so often. Parzuch has sent only 200 roubles, a watch and a pin during a year. . . . . Now, dear husband, I inform you what I did with this money for I have no letter and I don't know your decision. . . . . I asked you for 120, but evidently you could not; nothing can be done. . . . . I put 100 roubles into the bank, and we have there already 800. . . . .

Oleś is still working in the factory. . . . . I shall write you when he gets some other job. Only I beg you, dear husband, write Oleś a few words and tell him to listen to me, for when he goes to the town and I tell him to be back at such a time for dinner, he does not listen; twice already he has not been in time for dinner. And he smokes cigarettes secretly. He kept company with Lutek. I abused him, and he got a little away from Lutek, but now again he walks [associates] with Stadolak. I am not satisfied with it, for the boy is not orderly; I don't need to explain much, but [the fact is that] he is not orderly and everything pleases him. Therefore I don't want Oleś to walk with him. [Oleś] had a good companion, but he is now with his father in the country. [News about poultry; 2 pages about her health.] So I must go to a specialist for women's diseases, but for me it is a great shame, for, as you know, up to the present I have never known such a doctor, and it makes a terrible impression upon me. Stanisławowa was sick and went to such a doctor, and she told me that there is a sofa and he orders to lie down and puts his hand inside, for he must inspect. . . . . But you know me [and you understand] that it is for me fearful and disgusting. . . . .[1]

MARCYANNA JABŁKOWSKA

647

July 22, 1914

DEAREST AND MOST BELOVED HUSBAND: [Letter received; thanks for a prayer-book; health.] As to my not going to work, don't write me anything about it and don't stir up Janek still more, for even now I must dispute with him. He does not want me to work,

---

[1] The attitude of the peasant woman on this point is even more extreme. Not only is the idea of medical inspection revolting, but she would not venture to write of it to her husband.

he says that he is ashamed that I am working. He has talked so for a year. And more than once he gets angry, particularly if I am sick. Now also he has talked much when he read this letter saying that you don't allow me to go to work. I did not want him to read this letter and I hid it in a drawer, but he found it. And they all began to clamor: "Mother won't work any more, father writes well; enough of this work." And Janek said: "Father writes you not to work, and you don't listen." And he talked much, and said that if I work he won't give me all his money, only 4 roubles [on each pay day]. But he has said so more than once, and still I work and he gives me his money. So I write you thus, dear husband. I should like myself not to work any more, for you know that people often abuse those women who work in the factory. Even now more than one tell [bad things] about Parzuchowa and Piotrowska, because they are so hot tempered. And people say: "Jabłkowska alone is an orderly [good] woman, and it is a pity for her to work here with them." But I should like to help you still to put these 1,000 roubles aside, as you desire yourself. So if I work for some time still it is some help for you, because I have fuel and a few roubles for living, and the expense is big, for everybody wants to dress and to eat well, and here everything is expensive. Yes, my dear husband. You see, we still lack 200 roubles. So I will work for some time still, we shall put it aside sooner. And I should like you to come back at last, for I am tired already with all this. I don't promise you to work for a long time, only till you come back. Yes, my dear husband. Now you write me not to go to work and not to do anything [at home], for there are people to do the work for me. Well, bad is my "ladyship" now. When you come, then I shall be a lady [do no housework]. But now grandmothers want to be ladies. Well, my mother may be excused sometimes, for she is right when she complains that [your mother] does not want to help her to do anything in the kitchen.[1] When we drink tea in the evening your mother takes her own pot and washes it, but leaves the glasses from which I and the children drank. And it is always so. I don't say anything until you come back; let all this go on, for it is nearer than farther [nearer to the end than to the beginning]. And she always holds up her nose saying that she gave her money here, that she is not here from pity. If there is sometimes

---

[1] Both the grandmothers are kept in the home, the wife's in return for doing the housework, and the husband's in return for money lent. The latter, therefore, does not feel obliged to help with the work.

something worse at dinner, they all know how to be squeamish—the children, particularly Janek and Oleś, and your mother also lets her nose fall. I don't wonder at the children . . . . but your mother wants to be a lady. Now she does not know herself how to walk [she is so proud]. If you were at home you would laugh. And she always reproaches us about this money, saying that we have risen to our feet for her money. And she says that she ought to have interest on these 300 roubles. And she does not like to be with us; she wants only to have those 300 roubles back, and she does not know herself how to tear this money away. For once she said that Tomaszewski wanted her to lend him 300 roubles and promised her to take her to his home. Then again she said that Antek wants to borrow this money and will give a big interest. But I say so: I won't lend until you come back, and then it will be as you do. And she is tired of staying with us, she wants to go to Józef. She was always calling on Kasia, until once they almost fought about this money. For she [your mother] said that she had lost her money. And she [Kasia] said: "Where do you have your money? Why have you given me nothing." And so always. Once she began to reproach me about this money, and I told her to be silent, when you come, you will give her these 300 roubles back and let her go wherever she will be better off. And she said: "What does it matter if I have 300 roubles? And where is my interest?" And she said that you went to America on her money, and that money makes money.[1] And thus, dear husband. But she has got calmer since I told her that you will pay her back and now she says nothing, only that if she doesn't stay with us she will go to Józef. Only I beg you very much, don't be angry, for I write to you as to my husband, for I have nobody to talk to. [Four pages about Oleś' apprenticeship in a jeweler's shop.]

MARCYANNA JABŁKOWSKA

648   August 28, 1914

DEAREST AND MOST BELOVED HUSBAND: . . . . I thank you once more [for the letters] for I don't know what will be our further destiny. Perhaps because of this trouble [war] it will be difficult to

---

[1] She gets her living instead of interest and this is three or four times as much as the money would bring in cash. But the mother retains the attitude of the peasant, with whom the lending of money is not considered as a purely economic investment but as a personal help to be subjectively appreciated.

get even a letter.   But nothing can be done, we must comply with God's will, we must bear steadfastly everything.   Pray to God that He may keep us all in good health, and you, my dear husband, remember about your health and be steadfast, don't grieve about us. Why, we are not alone, whatever happens to everybody else here will happen also to us.   And I write you once more and beg you, dear husband, don't grieve, that you may not fall sick, for you know very well that I want to see you, and the children want it also.   Yes, my dear husband, pray only to the Holiest Mother to care for us and to defend us, and don't grieve so, dear husband.   For when I received the postcard with your last farewell, I fell upon my knees before the image of God's Mother and, crying, I prayed to God and to God's Mother to guard you from any misfortune, as well as our children and our parents.   And you see that up to the present God keeps us in His care and in health, so He won't leave us further on.   Dear husband, be steadfast and work happily with God, and care for yourself and don't forget us. . . . . And I beg you, dear husband, don't send any money at all . . . . although I wrote you in my preceding letter for money. . . . . Now I receive a few roubles from the bank every week. . . . . I have taken already 40 roubles.   Yes, dear husband, there is no work, and living must be bought. . . . . If we had no money in the bank, we should perhaps die from hunger, for it would be impossible even to borrow. . . . . Our bad enemies rejoiced [thinking] that when there is no work and I take the money from the bank they would come surely and rob me of the money. But I went to the cashier and asked him what to do, whether I should take money from the bank.   But he reprimanded me and said, God forbid me to take money, for some misfortune might befall me.   He said that the money in the bank will never be lost. . . . . So I write you, dear husband, don't grieve about our money, for not we alone have those few hundred roubles.   People from the high sphere have thousands and they don't get it all, only a few roubles at once. . . . . So don't send me any money, put it into the bank, don't keep it with you, so that somebody may not take it.   And keep the bank book carefully.   Care for your labor's fruit, dear husband, for you work hard. . . . . Don't be angry with me, dear husband, for not sending you any money-accounts, but I have not a calm head. . . . . And if sometimes letters don't reach you and you have no news from us, I beg you for God's sake, don't grieve, only pray to God for patience

and health, and I must be patient here also with our children. . . . .
Goodbye, my dear and beloved husband.   Be calm about us, I beg
you very much, dear husband.   Don't lose your courage, comply
with God's will, and I and our children we must also comply with
God's will, since we have lived to see such things.[1]   I kiss you and I
press you in my embrace, and I kiss your face, the dearest one for
me.   And once more I kiss you heartily, my dear husband.

Your wife, always well-wishing and loving you,

MARCYANNA JABŁKOWSKA

[1] Compare the fortitude of this letter with that in Starkiewicz series, No. 525,
Kluch series, No. 532, and Porzycki series, No. 627.

PERSONAL RELATIONS OUTSIDE OF MARRIAGE AND THE FAMILY

We have seen that the familial and communal system of life does not leave much place for relations of individual friendship and love. The closeness of friendship is determined by the strength of social, objective bonds which exist between the individuals, and not by their personal affinity. Friends are, first of all, members of the family, then any inhabitants of the village, parish, community. Of course there is some liberty of individual selection, but only in so far as it does not interfere with the recognized objective bonds. The subject can be in a closer friendship with one inhabitant of his village than with another, or with one cousin than with another, but he has no right to prefer a cousin to a brother, an unrelated inhabitant of his village to a cousin, a member of another community to a member of his own community, a foreigner to a Pole. Since, evidently, such norms seldom completely determined the real conduct, we find the interesting fact that in all cases where individual preference is not based upon the objective bonds certain other social bonds are substituted to justify it, and assume thus a social importance which they would hardly attain otherwise. Here belongs, first of all, the god-relation. A *kum* is equivalent to a relative, under the pretext that it is spiritual relationship. Therefore, a man who has a close friend sanctions this friendship by asking him to be his *kum* or by holding his child at baptism. He then has the right to prefer him to his real relatives. Another objective bond used to justify friendship is that between a *swat* (matchmaker) and the bride, the groom, or their parents. If neither of these social bonds is available, there remains the weakest and least recognized one, companionship in some social activity—school, military service, work. Perhaps the frequent endeavor to have a friend marry one's relative is in a large measure due to the desire to sanction the friendship by a familial relation.

Naturally, when the family dissolves, personal friendship assumes a greater independence. But again, as we have seen, the constitution of a strong marriage-group puts new hindrances in its way. (Cf. Jabłkowski series.) Thus it seems that free friendship is limited socially to the intermediary period between the dissolution of the old family and the constitution of the independent marriage-group. Individually the only favorable time for it is the time before marriage, and sometimes there are friendships in old age, after retiring from the active family life.

As to love, we know that it is always, in the traditional organization, related to the question of marriage, and since marriage is a familial matter, love remains subordinated to familial considerations and to the control of the community. Here again a partial dissolution of the family and, moreover, a disintegration of the forms of social control are necessary in order to make place for a free individual relation which may last for a certain time before culminating in marriage. And, of course, a certain degree of individual culture is also indispensable to make this relation interesting in itself.

The following series do not lend themselves to a systematic arrangement, but we place first the cases in which the personal relations are still somewhat under the influence of the traditional attitudes.

HEJMEJ SERIES

It will be noted that each letter is from a different person and shows a different kind of relation. They are from (1) cousin and friend, (2) sister, (3) mayor of the commune, (4) a Jew, (5) father. All these relations are here still typical for the primitive social organization of peasant life; no evolution toward the modern individualistic form is manifested.

649-53, TO WOJCIECH HEJMEJ, IN AMERICA, FROM FAMILY-MEMBERS AND FRIENDS, IN POLAND

649 MOKRAWIEŚ, 1913

DEAR WOJCIECH: [Usual beginning; health and success.] You ask how I am getting on with my work. You can know yourself, that formerly there were two of us and now I am alone, so more than once I have to do without breakfast or even dispense with dinner, because there is no time to eat. You ask about your wife, but I don't know anything. I have been there often, every second or third day, but I don't see anything [wrong]; I see only that she bought one calf and put another to suckle, and is managing [the farm-work] well. If she buys sometimes a pound or two of flour, don't be angry, because now everybody buys; you know well how the grain is now, that it is impossible to bake any bread without buying flour [and mixing it with the homemade flour]. It is not well to believe everything that people say, for you would never come to the truth by this way. At present there are people who write even if they did not see [anything bad], while they ought to think well before they begin to write without knowing the thing with certainty. And then you are tormented without need, because you cannot learn [the truth] exactly at once, for it is far away. You ask what people say about you. Nobody says anything, and your parents-in-law don't say anything bad either. And as to myself, since I undertook this work, I must do it, although it is very hard . . . . you are to understand, that I do it only for your sake. [Weather.]

I don't have anything more to write you, dear Wojtuś, because I don't want to write you lies and don't want to invent, and I don't know anything bad. When I don't know anything with certainty, I don't believe anybody; but here I did not even hear anything from anybody. . . . .[1]

FRANCISZEK WITKOWSKI

650

December 28, 1913

"Praised be Jesus Christus!" . . . .

Now, dear brother, I thank you for the letter and for these 100 crowns which you sent us We were very glad because they will be very useful to us now. This year was very wet and all the grain got rotten in the field . . . . and there is a great misery among us. And now we inform you, dear brother, that on Christmas we had a nice young man from America! He came with our father when he was returning from Nowy Sącz, and he said that he married Kaśka in New York, that she came with him and is now in Stary Sącz, and brings a big trunk which they cannot lift, and there are 60 crowns to be paid for it, and she has no change, only a whole 3,000, and nobody in the town can change it. But our father did not want to give him [money] nor to believe him, but said: "Come here both of you. Then we will go for this trunk and pay for it." Then he went, saying that he would bring Kaśka. But he did not go to Sącz, only to the house of Paszon in Osowo, and there told him the same—that he married Paszon's daughter Halka in Cleveland in America, that he is his son-in-law. Paszon drew the money out and gave it him. He took it and went. Paszon waited one day, two days, three days—

[1] The friendship between Hejmej and Witkowski is certainly based upon some kind of relationship, probably cousinship; the allusions to common work prove that there was also some business-partnership, perhaps renting of land. The relation is close enough to involve some sacrifice and interference with the marriage-group. The control which Hejmej exerts upon his wife through his relatives and friends is not an isolated case; we have seen other instances of it. It does not mean that the relation between the husband and the controlling friend is closer than that between the husband and the wife, but merely that since marriage is a familial and social matter, the conjugal relation can be controlled by any member of the family or community, even spontaneously, the more so when in the name of the husband. The friend acts as substitute of the husband and representative of the group. And accordingly the husband never asks that the side of his wife's life be controlled which is reserved for conjugal privacy and has not a social character, i.e., sexual fidelity. There is gossip, of course, when a break of fidelity is suspected, but only because such a break brings the sexual problem out of the sphere of conjugal privacy.

neither son-in-law nor daughter! It was some thief. Only he must have learned somewhere what he knew—that our Kaśka is in New York and Paszon's Halka in Cleveland. Paszon did not even have the money but borrowed it and gave it to such a thief. . . . .[1]

And now the price of vodka has gone up here to 1 crown 20 hellers for a liter, and formerly, as you know, it was 40 cents [80 hellers]. And there are much fewer taverns than formerly, and now it is no longer called a tavern, but a *consens*, as formerly *propinacya*. And therefore they have imposed higher taxes, and whoever makes anything, either tailor or shoemaker or blacksmith or potter, when he wants to work must have a trade-permission which costs up to 30 gulden or 60 crowns. And whoever does not pay, all his tools are taken away from him, and a constable with a mayor goes to him and he can make nothing until he has paid the tax. Such a misery is now here, in this poor Galicia. . . . .

Your sister,

ROZALIA HEJMEJ

651   January 22, 1914

RESPECTED WOJCIECH: We speak to you these words: "Praised be Jesus Christus, born of the Holiest Virgin Mary" [rhymed].

Dear Wojciech, we write to you this letter and we ask you about your dear health and success. As to us all in the commune, we are in good health, except Michał Bodziony who is ill, and our success is as usual in Mokrawieś.

Now we inform you that we received your letter for which we are very glad in the whole community, and we thank you for writing to us. Dear Wojciech, we inform you that winter is severe in our country, severe cold and enough of snow-hills, for we cannot go through by any way. Now we inform you that we divided the birchwood near

---

[1] The credulity of the old man, so contrary to the usual suspiciousness of the peasant, is due to the revolution which American emigration has brought into the peasant life. While in normal condition a marriage of the daughter without the parents' knowledge and with a man absolutely unknown would be impossible, everything seems possible in America. As we have said elsewhere, the peasant's ideas and prepossessions are so completely adapted to his normal conditions of life, that once outside of these conditions he loses all feeling of proportion, all appreciation of probability and improbability. Extremely difficult to cheat within the sphere of his habitual acts and conceptions, he becomes the prey of any stupid combination when he can no longer apply his usual criteria.

Wrzary, but not the pinewood, because winter interrupted us. As to Franek, up to the present, he manages well enough, and we don't know how it will be further. Now we inform you that Józek Hejmejak is getting married in Gostwina, in the house of Plata, and Wojtek Stawczak married Kubalanka, that one in the house of Jasiek Bodziony.

Dear Wojciech, we are glad that you intend to stay only long enough to pay back your worst debts. We all wish you it with our whole heart, may God the Holiest help you and grant you happiness, health and good success, that you may return sound to your native village, because although it seems that there is misery in the village, at least it is gay.

We end our words and we all, farmers and friends, greet you, together with our wives, most heartily innumerable times, and we wish you for this New Year happiness, health, fortune and after leaving this world a Heavenly crown [rhymed].

Now I greet you, Wojciech, I, son of Maciuś from Rogi, i.e., the Mayor, and I greet you also heartily, I, the Mayor's wife, i.e., Zwolińska. Now I greet you, Wojtuś, I, Jan Hejmej, very heartily. Be healthy, dear Wojciech, until we see you again. May God grant it.[1]

Yours forever well-wishing,

JAN ZWOLIŃSKI, Mayor

I signed,

J[AN] H[EJMEJ]

Our [J. H.'s ?] grandmother greets you.

[Communal seal.]

652　　　　　　　　　　　　　WOJAKOWA, July 15, 1914

DEAR WOJCIECH: First I thank you for your letter which I received on July 2, and I thank you for remembering us. As to our health, about which you ask, it is as usual, and our success, as in Galicia; it cannot be praised, because in Galicia there has been always misery and there will be further misery. Money is always lacking.

---

[1] The letter is written in the name of the whole commune. In Galicia, where the commune is autonomous, it plays a much greater rôle than in Russian Poland, where it is controlled by the Russian government. We have no other example of such a letter, and probably in this case the fact that it was written is due to the familial relation between the secretary of the commune and Wojciech Hejmej. It is a very good manifestation of the attitude of the social community toward its individual member.

There is nothing new. As to weddings .... we covered [with a veil=married] today the daughter of Kacola from Mośkówka. We have a new priest. And there is nothing more of interest to write. We have very nice crops, and harvest is beginning. And I inform you that I received 120 crowns by money-order from you on July 15, for which I thank you heartily. And there is great heat in our country. And you ask why I did not want to accept 20 gulden from your wife. You ought to know yourself that she did not offer me any. If she had offered me, I would surely have accepted, even a single gulden, for who is the Jew who does not want money? And you write me not to give anything on credit [to your wife]. I don't want to give on credit much, and your wife owes me already for a shawl and for different smaller things. And if you send any money for me, send it to my address, it will be the best.[1] .... My wife greets you and thanks you for the letter that you wrote to us, and we beg you to write us more, whether your condition is getting better. And when you have money, send it to us, because we need it much and we have waited a long time. And when God grants you to come back to our country, then I will relate to you everything. And I write you that you have a nice daughter, because when there was a May-festival, she came to us for candies.

I finish this letter. Be healthy and please answer to your Jew who is very well-wishing for you.

KALMAN METZENDORF

Git baj [goodbye].

653 September 1, 1914

.... DEAR SON: .... Don't be angry with us for not having answered you at once, but we had no time at all. We managed as we could, because now it has been very narrow [much work] during the harvest and up to the present, because men have been taken to the army. And now we inform you that we gave Kaśka away [lost] for eternal times. But don't grieve, because she had suffered enough, poor girl. She was sick for more than a year, and so she knew so much [suffering] that she was weary of living upon the world. We

---

[1] This second expression of a lack of confidence does not necessarily mean more than that the woman does not usually occupy so consistently the familial point of view as the man and is more likely to yield to individual interests or to the temptation of the moment.

inform you that she died on August 23, but don't grieve, dear son, for all this comes from God. When somebody said that your arm was torn away this poor girl wept so much because of you that we could not appease her in any way. When she was dying she asked about you, where you were, because she had already forgotten herself [her mind wandered]. So she asked where you were, and when we told her that you were in America, she said: "Then we shall not see each other any more." She kept her reason up to her death. But don't grieve, dear son, because she is happy already, since she died, for she won't have any more terror, while we don't know of what a death we shall perish [because of the war]. I don't write you any more about it, for you know better than we do, only I inform you that there is no man among us except the old ones; all the others went to the army. . . . . Now we beg you, answer us at once when you receive this letter, because we are curious where you find yourself. If you are getting on well, thank God, if badly, then it is the same as here.

We greet you, all of us, dear brother. Answer us at once in order that we may still read a letter from you. Don't be angry, dear brother, with me for having not written nicely, but all this is from grief. Amen.

[Your father,

HEJMEJ][1]

[1] Dictated by the father to the daughter.

PEDEWSKI SERIES

A typical situation, showing the persistence of the old attitudes in courtship. The girls in question evidently do not lack suitors, as they have two proposals within a short time from America. This, upon the ground of the familial psychology, explains the lack of encouragement of which Pedewski complains in his letters. At the same time Pedewski's own attitude is also characteristic. He wants to marry into the family, and it is for him a secondary matter which one of the sisters accepts him, though he shows a marked preference for one of them. His rival, although he asks explicitly for the favor of one of the sisters, puts the matter upon a familial basis.

654–56, FROM STANISŁAW PEDEWSKI AND BRONISŁAW KOWALSKI, IN AMERICA, TO THE FAMILY JAZOSKI AND TO OTHERS, IN POLAND

654 TITUSVILLE, PA., April 27, 1913

In the first words of my letter I speak to you, Julcia and Kostusia, with those godly words: "Praised be Jesus Christus."

Now I inform you about my success. Thanks to God, I am doing very well because there is sufficient work, and it will continue so in America, and bosses will go out to Castle Garden seeking workmen. Now I beg you to write me what is to be heard in the old country. And now I ask you what I am [what you take me for] and what is this you are speaking against me. I do not think that I have merited so badly. I never did you any harm. When I was at home, I would have given everything to you, even if you had asked for my blood. And now, when I wrote you a letter, you go about the village and you tell everybody that if it were not for your dislike of making something of nothing you would send it back to America. Was there something disagreeable in that letter? I do not know. See here, you know that I am such a man that if somebody turns me in any way, I go

967

there.   You asked me to write.   I wrote.   But if you ladies are not
quite satisfied with it, then I can do nothing more.   I shall still find
a girl for me.   The reason of my writing is only the fact that I called
so often upon you, Kostusia, that I considered your parents like my
own.   I always said that I must be a son-in-law of the Jazoskis.
Although Julcia did not care for me, I said that if not her, I should
marry Kostusia.   But clearly you despise me, because Julcia turned
up her nose at me too, when I was in the old country.   [Unintelligible
sentence.]   But I do not care what people are saying and I do what
I wish.   And now, dear Julcia and Kostusia, don't mind about what
I wrote; you answered me and so I write this letter.   But as to the
Michalskis [the girls who did the gossiping], I wish that as they have
already become old they may further become public women, as a
reward for this barking of theirs, for it is the Michalskis who barked
all this.   When Siembozak left they told him that you spoke badly
about me, and Siembozak, when he came here, repeated it to me.
And now, if you have the wish to come to me, write, but not directly,
only after I send you a second letter, because I am going to another
city and your letter will possibly not find me.   I have nothing more
to write, only I salute you and your parents.   I hope to see you soon
and happy in America.

STANISŁAW PE[DEWSKI]

[An unintelligible sentence follows.]

655   September 2, 1913

[Usual greetings to his friends Franciszek and Juliusz.]   I got
your letter for which I thank you heartily.   And now, dear companion, you ask me about my success in America.   Well, let God help
you in our country, that you may do as well; then you would not
lack anything.   I do very well.   In the beginning I was a little
homesick, but now I have already forgotten about it.   I have very
good and easy work; I can say that I don't work at all, I only stand
in an iron-foundry.   I am working in a bolersap [boiler-shop].   I
have 26 roubles wages weekly, counting in our country's money.
Time goes on very quickly in America, you don't notice when the
week is passed, and of money we have our pockets full.   Three of us
are here from one village, Siembozak, and Wojteczek Zegleniak.
We have music every day.   Wojteczek organized a quartet, taking
besides himself a clarinet, an accordeon and a trumpet, and they play

in saloons. If they played in our country the whole village would listen. Dear companion, now that I am acquainted with America, for no money would I return to our country, because there on Sunday it is not so joyful as here every day. You ask me to inform you about your sister. What information can I give you? When your sister came, I saw her, but now we don't see each other. They are far from us. When I was there she said all was well, but now I don't know. And now, dear companion, you ask me to send you some gift, but I can send you nothing by letter. When somebody goes home, then I shall know what to send you, but now I don't know, because by letter nothing will arrive. And what you write about the Jazoskis, why should I write to them in vain? If I write they do as if they would not know me at all. Were it not for [a word erased] even now there would be nothing. Old [Jazoski] and Kostusia seem not to be acquainted with me. Well, I didn't expect it. I don't mind it very much, only it is painful. And now, my companion, I beg you to inform me what is the news with you and at the Jazoskis, and inform me what do they say about me, and how everything goes on in the country. Please write me everything that is to be heard and who are your companions, because you two will not remain companions for a long time. And say, what do the Jazoskis say about me, good or ill? I have nothing more to write, only I greet you and *gud baj* [goodbye].

STANISŁAW PEDEWSKI

And now I write to Franek Jazoski [brother of the girls]. I write to you, my companion, about my success. My success is pretty good, only it is terribly sad, there is not a single girl; boys alone. And so perhaps we shall soon see ourselves as brothers-in-law. Don't be in a hurry in coming to America before I come back.

My Julcia, I don't know if you will become my sister.

My dearest sister Kostusia, do you remember how we loved each other one Sunday? Why do you not answer me? Oh, how I like you, my Kostusia!

STANISŁAW PEDEWSKI

656 BAYONNA, June, 1913

In the first words of my letter I speak some words to Mr. and Mrs. Jazoski, and before all these godly words: "Praised be Jesus Christus," and I hope that you will answer me "For centuries of centuries. Amen."

And now I speak to your daughters and sons and in general [*sic*] to Miss Konstancya. Very politely I beg you to excuse me for not writing for so long a time, but it was because I have the intention of returning to our country and then we shall speak together by words. And now I announce to Miss Konstancya and to Mr. and Mrs. Jazoski that I should be glad to live in the family Jazoski, but I do not know sufficiently if I can beg very politely Miss Konstancya to give me a good word, and also Mr. and Mrs. Jazoski, because I think now of returning soon to my country. That is the end of my letter. What more I have to write I shall do it in another letter, only I request you to answer me quickly. And now I have nothing more to write. [Usual greetings.]

BRONISŁAW KOWALSKI

KAZIMIERZ F. SERIES

This is the only case we have in which a girl plans to bring her betrothed to America, and we have never heard of a similar case. At any rate, a manor-servant like Kazimierz F., lacking strong familial consciousness and having the habit of dependence, would lend himself more readily to a situation of this kind than the farming peasant, with his characteristic pride in money matters. The girl who sent us the letters evidently felt some shame in doing so, as she had attempted to erase the phrases relating to the marriage question, as well as everything indicating a familiar relation. But the erasures are not complete and not systematic. A remnant of this feeling is left in the man also, but rather in the form of yielding to social opinion. (Cf. Nos. 659, 660.)

The girl married another man two years later, and Kazimierz came to America helped by his relatives. The girl's husband has read the letters, as it was he who sent them in her name. Clearly there is no retrospective jealousy, since he allowed her to keep them after the marriage.

657–60, FROM KAZIMIERZ F., IN POLAND, TO HIS
BETROTHED, IN AMERICA

657   ŁAZY, October 10, 1910

DEAR MANIECZKA: I received the postcards from you on the way and also one from America. Pardon me, dear Manieczka for not having answered you at once, but I expected soon to have a letter [from you], but I have none and I am obliged to write. Dear Manieczka, don't believe that I forgot about you, or anything like this. No, I don't expect ever to forget you. If you knew how I am longing without you! Not a single hour passes without my thinking of you, not an evening passes without my remembering those moments which we spent in the garden every evening ["which . . . . evening" erased by the owner of the letters]. Don't forget about me, don't allow anybody to turn your head. Be true to me in America as [you were] in our country ["as . . . . country" erased]. You are for me ["You . . . . me" erased] the only one, and I ["and I" erased] ought to be also [the only one] for you. Dear Manieczka, such is my love for you ["such . . . . you" erased], that wherever I am, whether at some entertainment or in some conversation, I am always thinking ["always thinking" erased] about you. Yes, dear Manieczka, nothing interests me now any more. I think only of you, my thoughts fled with you. Dear Manieczka, on the following Sunday, October 23, I shall go to Turek [military call]. What will be the result for me, I don't know yet. As soon as I learn I will write you at once. I beg you for an answer. Write me how do you like America. Are you merry, have you already any job and how much do you earn ["job . . . . earn" erased]? Please write me . . . . about your journey, how long did you both go? Send me your photograph, only the soonest possible. I have now nothing more to write, only I send you salutations from [your?] parents. I send also salutations for your brother and sister-in-law, and for you, Manieczka, hearty greeting, a low bow, a kiss ["low . . . . kiss" erased] and a hearty hand shake. . . . . I wish you good success and [I add] the old Polish "God make you happy."

With respect,

I, your ["I, your" erased]

KAZIMIERZ

658   November 20, 1910

DEAR MERKA: [erased; probably because pet name for "Marya," "Manieczka."] I received your letter . . . . and I answer you at once. First I must write you about my military service, how I succeeded. I can now be happy. I don't know whether our Lord God guarded me or what else, but I was exempted. . . . . Don't be angry, dear Merka [erased], for my not having written to you anything from Turek, but I was not sure of your first address . . . . only now I can write to you more often ["I can . . . . often" erased]. I am very glad that you arrived so happily . . . . and that you got work at once. Dear Manieczka, I was about a month in Turek, but

I did not amuse myself at all. First, my head was turned with the military service, secondly, my thoughts fled after you, and nothing interests me, except the wish to come to you the soonest possible. . . . . You ask me for my photograph. Well, I will send you one, but . . . . later on, not now, for I look very bad; you know how I looked last year, and this year I am still worse ["you . . . . worse" erased]. As soon as I recover a little, I will think about it. . . . .

KAZIMIERZ

659   January 27, 1911

DEAR MANIECZKA: . . . . Your letter rejoiced me much, but not completely. For I expected that you would say something about the ship-ticket or that you would send me money for the journey, while you write me in a totally different way. You write me, dear Manieczka, that for America a man must be healthy and strong in order to earn. But how many people go to America, and everybody works and comes back healthy, and brings nice money with him besides. Why should it be the worst with me? Don't think, dear Manieczka, that I am so weak or sickly. Don't fear. It is not so bad. I was sick only before the [call to] military service, but now my illness is over, it is not so bad.[1] And it seems that in America I should not have more work than I must often work here in vain. You write me, dear Manieczka, that it is not worth while to come, for in 2 years the president will be elected. But do you think, dear Manieczka, that I would go there for some ten years? I should like to go for just two years, in order to earn a few roubles. Moreover, I should like to see something of the world, for today people say: "Don't try to be educated behind the stove." Moreover, I should like, dear Manieczka, to have a few roubles when we marry. If you have money, I must have some also, for it is not nice at all if the boy marries and has no money for what he needs to get married [wedding-expenses].

You see, dear Manieczka, such are my intentions, and it seems to me that you will agree with me. Dear Manieczka, I hope that you will certainly find some way, that I may be with you in America. I beg you for it very much, and I believe that you cannot refuse. . . . . Don't be anxious about my finding work. I shall find my way, and

---

[1] The illness was evidently caused intentionally, in order to avoid the military service.

it will be good for us both some day.   You know well my thoughts, my dear Mania, I don't need to write you much, for I think always one and the same.   I would write you more, but I leave it for another time. . . . .

KAZIMIERZ

660

March 1, 1911

DEAR MANIECZKA: I received both your letters. . . . . After receiving the first I was somewhat grieved, but when I got the second I was relieved and very glad.   Evidently you wanted only to frighten me with that first letter.   But I did not lose hope even so, because I knew that you only feigned, that you wanted to convince yourself what thoughts I have.   Dear Manieczka, don't think that I am also feigning like some clown.   No, it is not so bad!   I remember up to the present what we so often spoke about, and up to the present I keep the same line of conduct.   Dear Manieczka, you write me that you intend to send me $50.   I thank you very much.   My father here will give me the rest. $50 would not be enough but I will try to get the remainder ["to send . . . . remainder" erased], so that I may have money enough for the journey and something left in America.   Dear Manieczka, I beg you also, as soon as you get this letter, write me at once, that I may be sure how to manage.   As to sending money [home], why are you so much disturbed, while I don't hear your father murmuring at all.   If you are afraid people will talk too much about us in Łazy, I advise you to send the money to Lotka's address.   She will go to Słupca to the post-office, will get it and nobody will know.   I beg you, dear Manieczka, don't disappoint me, for I confide in you totally and I think that I can do so, that I don't err in this. . . . .   Dear Manieczka, I won't write you any love-words about this.   We will talk when we see each other in America.   What is the use of scribbling this upon the paper?   Nothing can result from it.   But I give you my word of honor that all will be well.   I beg you, dear Manieczka, for a speedy and good answer, that we may see each other the soonest possible. . . . .

KAZIMIERZ

ARCISZEWSKI SERIES

These letters, written by and addressed to various persons, have one common feature. They show a very general type of friendly relation among young boys of the present generation who have already dropped most of the traditional attitudes and feel rather free from familial rigorism, who are in a period of life when practical interests do not yet constitute the main aim of life, and who have neither tendencies to self-development nor social ideals. In these conditions, their main interest is amusement—dancing, flirting, merry conversations, etc. And this is also the basis of their friendship. An interesting point is that all three, at the period when these letters were written, have confronted for the first time different serious problems of life—Stefan, the problem of adaptation to American conditions; J. Wiater, that of military service; Borowski, the problems which the revolution of 1905 put before the Polish youth. And, as should be expected, all three of them react negatively. Wiater's reaction is rather normal, but Stefan shows a more than normal inaptitude for sentimental adaptation, while Borowski remains almost completely passive in the midst of powerful national and social movements.

The love-relation, which constituted so important a part of the content of the letters, has also the character of play. It is no longer a mere preparation for marriage, and not yet a serious matter in itself.

661-65, FROM STEFAN ARCISZEWSKI, IN AMERICA, TO FRIENDS, IN POLAND, AND TWO LETTERS (664, 665) REPRESENTING THE SAME TYPE OF ATTITUDES IN OTHER BOYS

661   BREMEN, November 28 [1913]

[Greetings and wishes.]

DEAR COMPANION: I inform you about my health and success. I am in good health, which I wish to you also with all my heart. Now, dear companion, Czesio, I am now near the sea, in Bremen; the city is so called. I got over the frontier all right, and from Iłłowo also I got on well enough, and I don't know how it will be from now on. Dear companion Czesio, please write me the news about yourself. As to me, I am very sad here. And I request you, dear companion, learn how my betrothed, Miss Helena is behaving, whether she is pining or not. I beg you, my companion, write me about her, because I am very sad without her. You know well that I love her. But no matter, the dog may have her. [I don't care.] When you write to me, get her address, and I request you, dear companion, send me the address of Miss Zaleska. I beg you once more, dear companion, let me know how Helena is behaving. I request you, Czesio, write to me whether she wept or not after my departure. I have nothing more to write, but only I send you, dear companion, and to all my acquaintances, the lowest bow.

I, truly well-wishing,

STEFAN ARCISZEWSKI

662   AMSTERDAM, N.Y., March 2, 1914

RESPECTED COMPANION: Since the moment we parted, I have received one letter and have no tidings since. I came to this massive, golden whore [America], but I feel terribly sad, because here if you have no money, "Don't put your nose" [anywhere]. I am sitting without work and I don't know what will happen, whether things will get better or not. A terribly great number of people walk about without work. Now, before *Zapusty* [last six days before Lent] they go and break railway-cars, because they have nothing to eat. Michał works a little, but I cannot get work. What is the news in our country? Is there any probability of war? For here it is heard that in our country there will be war. If only there were a change in our country! I wish I could return home at once, because here I have nothing to do. Now, dear companion Czesio, please tell me what is the good news about yourself. Rumors have reached me that Helena got married, but I don't know with whom, whether with Kozak or with somebody else. Please write me whether there will be a call now, in March, to military service, or not, and whether any girls got married or not. With us now, on the 14th and 15th of February, terrible snows fell, so that it was impossible to crawl out from home.

I sent a letter to Miss Klimaszewska on February 24, but she has not yet answered me. I don't know what it means. It seems as if she did not know me, and as if she was afraid on that account. And perhaps Serafin saw her and did not allow her to send her address. In April, I think of going nearer to New York; perhaps there I shall learn something more.

Now I am complimenting [flirting] with Miss Szewczak. She lives not far from me, in Philadelphia. We write each other terrible [declarations of] love. She believes that I write all this in earnest. I request you, Czesio, send me the address of Julka Zaleska. I beg you, write to me what you hear about town, how the boys amuse themselves there. Because when I recall those plays, how often we amused ourselves together, tears stand in my eyes. Please tell me what is to be heard with us at home [what is the news]. Once more I ask you, what about Helena, how does she do, whether her success [with boys] is good or bad, and how many amusements [dances] there were. Here I was at two dances and was lucky enough at them. End.

My lowest bow to all our acquaintants, to Miss Piotrowska and Miss Bojarska.

I remain, truly well-wishing, yours. I kiss you.

STEFAN

663 [1914]

RESPECTED COMPANION: . . . . Now dear companion, I am writing you a second letter and I have no answer to my first, so I don't know how it is with you and in our country. Here with us it is very sad. I am without work and Michał also works irregularly, because factories are closed. I have received a letter from Kostek and Paweł. They have no work. Kostek has not worked for 6 weeks and Paweł for 12. And so it is very bad with us, I don't know what will happen; bad times are coming. Now, dear Czesio, I beg you, describe what is the news about yourself, because I am curious. If I had not listened to my mother I should have earned more. Mother wanted me to go to America, and I didn't want to go. If I had not come, I should have done better. I didn't intend to come to America before spring and now here it is very bad. Factories are stopped, there is no work. Now, dear companion Czesio, write to me about the girls, whether they long for me or not, because I am very curious. Tell me about them, and particularly about Miss Sobierajska. Is she longing for me or not? I beg you with all my heart. My best companion, I beg you now once more, Czesio, what success does my old girl have now in the carnival? If there are to be weddings, please inform me who has got married either near the barracks or in the town, or in the village among our acquaintances. Here I have no acquaintance, and therefore I am very sad and I long terribly for my native country.

Now, dear companion Czesio, I beg you, send me, if you can, some nice Polish recitals [poems for recital] and some new waltzes.

Lowest bow to you, Czesio. Lowest bow from Michał.

I, truly well-wishing,

STEFAN

Now, dear companion Czesio, please salute from me Miss Bronisława Piotroska, and all the girls with whom we are acquainted. Now, dear companion Czesio, you have no idea what a longing got me. I don't regret anything else, but only the carnival. Now in our country they will amuse and rejoice themselves, and myself, I am sitting here, as in a prison. If I had known it, I would never in the world have sacrificed myself and come to America.

Now, dear companion Czesio, lowest bow to yourself and to your sister and parents, and to Władysław and Franuś, and to all our acquaintances.

I, truly well-wishing, and loving you,

STEV ARTER

664   ZAMOSTEK, October 27, 1913

DEAREST COMPANION: First I thank you for your memory. . . . . I got your address from your brother Stanisław and I answer you. . . . . I have been at home for 6 weeks after coming from America.

As to the lots, I drew No. 51 and I am received into the army. . . . .
Know it, dear companion, that if I had not to go to the army I should
not hold out at home; there are no companions, nowhere to go. Our
Gorzków has quite declined.[1] But what a girl I have found now!
I will write you in another letter, for I don't know yet whether she
will wait for me [until my return from the army].

[Enumerates those taken into the army and those exempted.]
We shall have still 9 days for revelry at home, and then to Chełm.
[Enumerates the marriages and betrothals.] People marry, dog's
blood! [*Psiakrew*, popular oath.] And I shall also have a wedding
in Chelm, but with the accursed *Kacap* [nickname for "Russian"].
Send me to the army 10 gallons of whiskey. I will feed these Moscovites so that cholera will take them! Pardon me, dear companion,
for writing you in such an ugly way, but the devils almost take me
[I am furious]. Why should I serve these whores' sons? Dam
it.[2] . . . .

I wish you every good with my whole heart.

Yours,

Jan Wiater

665 Przasnysz, October 12, 1906

Dear Staś: I begin this letter with the words, "Praised be
Jesus Christus," and surely, were it not for the far space which does
not let me hear your answer, I should hear, "In centuries of centuries.
Amen." . . . .

I have been working for two months in a notary's office. I
have had not much work up to the present, but although I have a
little free time I cannot enjoy evening walks as during your presence
here, for there is a state of war and it is forbidden to walk without a
lantern and a passport. There are patrols upon the street who arrest
those who walk without lanterns. . . . . I do it and I succeed.
Terrible things are going on in our country, beyond description. In
Warsaw nothing but bombs and brownings. . . . . Constables are

[1] It is an evident sign of the decline of the old territorial group when young
people need the attraction of companionship and amusements in order to stay at
home. This decline is one of the factors making emigration so easy and is itself
hastened by emigration.

[2] The hate of the Russians is particularly strong among the peasants of this
province, which suffered a very violent religious persecution during the second half
of the nineteenth century. It was mainly inhabited by Uniates.

killed, as well as the bigger fishes. . . . . Not long ago our military governor was killed. In Łódź there is a general strike and court-martial. Every day a few men are hung or shot. The prisons are overfilled. . . . . In our town a school-association has been organized, but the Sokols have been dissolved by the government. . . . .

The girls look very well, particularly Walercia. Boleś K. preaches morals to her in a way which seems very pleasant for her. . . . . Polcia looks as you have never seen her—a dress two yards and a half, a hat three yards in circumference, and herself grown up, a yard and a half tall, and she dreams already about everything that is suitable. In general the girls are nice, but they will probably be obliged to hire us for talking, for they are eager to talk, and the boys won't. . . . . Walercia feels a terrible sympathy for you. And how is the matter with you? Inform me, for if you feel anything toward her I will try, for my friend's sake, to send Boleś away in some way; why should he spoil the matter? It seems to me that the thing ought to be taken up at once, for he tramples much around her. May he not succeed at last. . . . .

Your truly loving companion,

BOROWSKI

KOWALSKI SERIES

This series is interesting in two respects: (1) The familial relation has degenerated to a mere business relation, so that the two letters from brother and sister-in-law can be used as typical examples of business letters. (2) Personal friendship has assumed the function traditionally performed by the familial relation; there is much more community of interests between Antoni Kowalski and Stanisław than between Antoni and his brother, and much more real affection. Stanisław is, indeed, a cousin of Antoni Kowalski, but by its personal character their connection is qualitatively different from traditional cousinship.

The evolution is probably due to the influence of the middle-class environment in Posen. The family is beginning to get into this class.

666–71, TO ANTONI KOWALSKI, IN AMERICA, FROM FAMILY-MEMBERS AND A FRIEND, IN POLAND

666   MIŁOSŁAW, June 15, 1913

DEAR BROTHER [-IN-LAW]: We received your letter . . . . but you wrote us so little. We don't know whether they inspected your things [baggage] or not, and how it was on the ship. Kazimierz [husband of the writer] is still working in Nerengow, but he will have only four weeks more to work and he is afraid that after this he will have no work. . . . . Nothing worth writing has happened during this time. . . . . I thought that Kazimierz would think more about everything and would exert himself more [with regard to their common property] when you, Antoni, were not here. But now, just as before, he does not think anything beforehand and he has not done anything yet, because when he comes late, he says that he won't. It was I who painted the door, and everything that was left [I did]. Nobody has bought the table yet . . . . and the wheel [?]. Now times are hard and everybody does without. And Kazimierz goes nowhere and speaks with nobody, so nobody knows; but perhaps somebody will yet happen [to buy them]. When anything new happens I will write. I urged Kazimierz to write, but the lazy fellow did not wish to do it; he preferred to read papers and told me to write. . . . .[1]

KAZIMIERZ and WŁADYSŁAWA [KOWALSKI]

667 March 15, 1914

DEAR BROTHER: . . . . Before all I must answer about this contract. You say that it is our own fault, for renting it. It is true. But if Kazimierz had looked into it himself and had relied upon nobody else, it would not be so bad. But he relied upon our uncle; he took uncle with him and was sure that everything was all right. But it is not as when you were here, Antoni, because you did [for us] as for yourself, and our uncle cannot know how it will fall out for us, whether good or bad. And then, all this was done without any reflection, because it was so: One afternoon Nowicki came with the Neumanns and asked whether we would not rent [the property], but [said] that they wanted absolutely to live in it themselves. But as the Maślińskis intended to move away we said to each other that it would be very well, since it happened that one person wanted to take it all [the whole place] and at least there would be no trouble with the lodgers. We were to reflect how to do, and they went away. In the evening they came back and said that it would be well to make the contract at once. . . . . Kazimierz went directly to our uncle in order to ask his advice, and took uncle with him and relied upon him entirely, thinking that when he looked into it everything would be all right. But with uncle it is not as with you; uncle does not mind much what is better and what worse for us. He knows only how to say [after the thing is done] what somebody did bad and what good. . . . . If Kazimierz had more thought about everything himself instead of looking to and relying upon other people, everything would have turned out differently, because nobody can advise him [properly] in everything; he alone can know everything himself, since he knows all his own conditions the best. . . . . He complains that you told him always to ask uncle's advice, and that uncle did not

---

[1] The complaint in this and the following letter of the negligent behavior of the husband is to be qualified by the fact that she addresses herself to the husband's brother and not to an outsider. Even so, it is not in accordance with the tradition.

advise him. . . . . We had no time to ask your advice, and we did not think that the contract was already valid; we thought that it must still be approved by the court, and that up to that time it was possible to draw back. . . . . Since you went away we have been in a worse situation than in the year when we got married, because we had to pay all the expenses alone, and Kazimierz did not work in the winter and worked badly in the summer, ... and there is no other income. If I only could earn something! But in Miłosław there is nothing to be done; I will not go and steal from the forest. . . . .

Zosia Kupś got married in the winter. . . . . And Marynia is getting ready to go to the convent. She sends greetings to you and said that you caused her much grief . . . . but she is no longer angry. Perhaps you want to see the last of her; I have her photograph, taken not long ago . . . . so I send it to you . . . . but please send it back, because if I don't have it she can be angry with me for having sent it so far away. In a year she will certainly [she says], go to the convent, but I don't know whether it is not feigned. A man courted her lately, but she refused him. . . . . If you wish, write some words to Marynia; she will be glad, I think.[1]

KAZIMIERZ and WŁADYSŁAWA

668 PALCZYN, January 5, 1913

DEAR ANTONI: . . . . I ask you now whether you spent the holidays happily and gaily, and what served for amusement, cards or dances. But that is perhaps not fashionable in America. We played cards during both holidays, for what could we do? It rained and snowed—impossible to go anywhere. On the first day we could hardly get to Mr. Przybysz's to amuse ourselves a little there. It is a pity, dear Antoni, that you are not here. But nothing can be done. Perhaps we shall yet live together and amuse ourselves, as we did formerly. Lucyan came also for the holidays, but for 3 days only. We have amused ourselves for the last time in the house of the Przybyszs, because I must also inform you that poor Mr. Przybysz is very unfortunate. He has convulsions, and therefore he ceased to

---

[1] The romantic attachment here is completely different from what we find normally among peasants. No peasant girl would be heartbroken through the failure of the man for whom she cared to marry her, because no strong love can grow out of mere acquaintance on the basis of the traditional peasant attitude, unless it has terminated in sexual relations, and we have no ground to assume that this is the case here.

perform his [government?] service and must move away from here. So after the holidays I went with him to the house of Drzewiecki. He lives now quietly there.   He is not so bad, but after these attacks he speaks wanderingly.   It is a pity, because he was a good man; he wished nobody any wrong.   Miss Bronia was also with the Przybyszs until Christmas, so I went there often and we amused ourselves nicely.   But now all this has come to an end; Mr. Przybysz is in Miłosław, Bronia in Jaworów.   It is a pity, for all is over.

Yesterday I was also with Kazimierz and his wife, and I saw at last that they had decided to answer your four letters—so they said. Isn't that a villany!   When they want something they know how to write but when they have got what they want it is difficult for them to send you their note [promise to pay].   As if you did not figure in it at all!   I told them it was not nice of them.   Władzia answered that it was the affair of Kazimierz.   But I said that they both deserved a good beating, because Kazimierz is an exceedingly negligent fellow, and she is such a bad "muzzle."   But you know yourself, my dear, how it was; it is the same now.   She read me your letter, and they said that you want a note from them but according to their calculation you still owe them 300 marks.   But what is the need of those other expenses besides the new building?   A nice administration is it not? Do as you will, but I tell you that you will never come to an understanding with them.   When you were here you had trouble and grief more than once, and now they do as they please.   If I were you, after receiving that note I would send them nothing, but I would demand the interest, and then we should see how it would go with them.   As long as you associate with them you will never have money; you will work for the benefit of others.   Evidently, it is not my affair, but as I promised you, I inform you.   But please don't betray me, because Janczak lives in good friendship with them. . . . .

Your true and well-wishing friend,

Stanisław R.

669   October 10, 1913

[Greetings; generalities about health; letters written and received; harvest was good.]   Now I write you about Kazimierz and his wife. As you know already, they rented that farm.   For 10 years he [the tenant] will pay 700 marks yearly.   My father assisted, so I inform you more exactly about it, because from what you wrote to them and to Janczak I see that you did not understand it well and that you are very angry. It is true it is too cheap, but they have it as they wished it. They thought only about America, and they did not think about reserving a lodging for themselves. Afterward they asked for the lodging upstairs, and the tenant allowed them to live there, but I think that it will not go well. My father advised them to ask 850 marks rent, but Kazimierz would have been glad to have even 600, and my father could not say anything against it, since he is neither a child nor a woman. But Kazimierz and his wife are not fit to manage this property. It would be the best to let them be simply lodgers, and to give them no right to dispose of it, because they don't do as they promised. He works, it is true, but his work amounts to nothing. [Detailed conditions of the rent-contract.]

Now I write you about our neighbors. Marynia Przybysz got married. The wedding was August 19. We were at the marriage-feast and had a pretty good time. There is nothing else new. Please write me how it is in America, whether you really do not like it, and whether you wish me to come and to earn well. But write me from your true heart. . . : .

STANISŁAW R.

670   November 19, 1913

DEAR FRIEND: With us everything is as from old. I would gladly go to you, but my father is opposed to it. He says that although I could get out, the Germans would afterward take my part [confiscate my fortune]. Even if I refused to be a German citizen it would not help. But no matter, let it be so till spring, and then I shall know how it will be with my military service. Lucyan says that it is not so bad in that nice army, but he says that he regrets those two years. He is getting on well; every four weeks he is at home. Last week we were in Cieśle at a wedding. Lucyanek was also there; he had a leave of 8 days. He butchered for the feast, and soon after he butchered also for another neighbor. He earned some money and amused himself. He would have been at the second wedding, but he had no leave for so long a time. The wedding was very nice, we amused ourselves "up to the ears." It lasted two days—time enough to dance. It was not as in Skotniki or with the Przybyszs, because while it was nice with the latter it was short; we could not amuse ourselves so well. . . . . It is sad among us; the dances are ended.

. . . . I live like Adam driven away from Paradise. I have few friends, so I don't know where to go. Sometimes I go to Janczak and we play the violin a little. As to those tenants, they are getting on badly. It seems to me that they will not remain for a long time. He paid little to Kazimierz, because his situation is bad. . . . . Now I ask you, dear Antoni, whether that gun has been of any use to you . . . . and whether that suit is fashionable now in America. . . . . Here it rains continually . . . . mud up to the knees. Frost and snow would be preferable; one could kill some game more easily. But the hares have all been shot, and there are very few deer. My shooting is bad this year. I have a bad gun. I miss yours. . . . .

Stanisław R.

671 April 6, 1914

Dear Friend: First of all I wish you, dear friend, healthy and merry holidays. Perhaps you will spend better holidays than I here, and particularly Kazimierz, for an accident happened to him, because he is too good, and moreover a fool. On the first of the month he needed money. He went to his tenant, who owed him 350 marks of rent for half a year. But Neumann was not at home. He went on the 2d. Neumann was eating dinner and said that he must finish it. All this because he had no money. On the third day at 7 o'clock P.M. [Neumann] sent his servant-girl asking Kazimierz to come for the money. Kazimierz, as you know, is good natured. Though it was the duty of Neumann to bring him money, because the law is so, Kazimierz went for the money. Neumann put the money on the table and told him to take it. Kazimierz said: "I must first count it, whether there is enough." . . . . And K. counted the money. Suddenly N. seized him and pushed him away from the table. They began to push each other and suddenly N. seized a stick and wounded K. on the head badly enough. K. went bleeding to the doctor, and the next day also he wanted the doctor to come. So Władzia came here and related all this to my father. And father said: "You see, that is what you get for your kindness. Why did not Kazimierz take a chair and split his head? Moreover, what do you want? You wished to go to America, and now you complain [you were in a hurry to rent the house and to leave]." Then Władzia said: "You were present when we made the contract. Why did you not say anything?" Father got so angry that he cursed her and swore at her, for you know how he can do it. Władzia fled. . . . . The next day K. went to a lawyer and told the whole matter. Neumann had already entered a suit on the ground of the invasion of his home. I don't know how it will end. I will write you more later. Neumann is a strong antagonist and it is a pity that you are not here; you would perhaps defeat him. . . . .[1] I called yesterday on Kazimierz, but I did not find him or his wife at home, but my aunt [mother of Antoni and Kazimierz] told me the whole affair and asked me to inform you. She said that she herself took the money for the holy mass [to the priest]. She said that with you she had it much better and that she does not like very much [to live with Kazimierz].

STANISŁAW R.

[1] This whole quarrel has probably also a racial background. Neumann is a German or of German extraction.

FRYZOWICZ SERIES

Type of sentimental friendship, rare among country people but found sometimes among town people of the hand-worker class. This form of sentimentality is probably due to the influence of religious life in towns—bigotry, ceremoniousness, fraternities with their superficial humanitarianism, complicated devotion, and lack of practical interests. At the same time the sedentary occupation favors reflective attitudes. Consequently among this class of people sentiment as such assumes a value which it never has among peasants, where it is immediately converted into a motive of action. The same can be said about intellectual life. An impersonal interest in the same phenomena is sufficient to create a communion between individuals, while among peasants there must be always a certain solidarity of personal interests to give rise to a friendship.

In the present case the type is not perfectly pure. Fryzowicz is indeed a small handworker and a typical town inhabitant, but his correspondent, Wojciech, besides his handwork has a farm, as frequently happens in small towns. These townsmen-farmers are the natural intermediary class between the peasants and the lower bourgeoisie, although they are not numerous enough to play an important part in social organization.

672-75, JAKÓB FRYZOWICZ, IN POLAND, TO A FRIEND, IN
AMERICA.   THE FRIEND IS ADDRESSED AS "BROTHER":
HE IS POSSIBLY A COUSIN

672   GOSTWICA, February 23, 1914

"Praised be Jesus Christus." . . . .

MY HEARTILY BELOVED BROTHER: [Greetings; wishes; letter
received.]   I love you also very much, because you are always well-
wishing toward me.   I remember the day of September 23, it was
very sad for me, because on that day you left for America, and moreover you did not come to us to bid us goodbye.   I had prepared something for you, in order to thank you for having always made things
for me, without accepting any payment.   I expected you to come on
that day and I waited for you from morning till noon, and you did
not come.   I said: "Ah, perhaps he did not go today," and our host
said: "He went probably, because I saw somebody going in a wagon,
and two men following the wagon."   I was afraid and ran to your
house.   I entered and asked your wife what was the news, and she
said: "Well, there is the news that he went."   And she said to me:
"It is well that you came, because you will take your watch; he told
me to take it directly to you."   And so on the one hand, I was glad
that I had the watch repaired, and on the other hand, I was very
grieved that you did not come to us at least for half an hour to bid us
farewell, because perhaps we shall see one another, and perhaps not.
I thank you very nicely for this letter because I have expected it
the whole time with great longing, and when I read it it seemed to me
as if my health had increased.   Because now, since Christmas, I have
been seriously ill.   I thought that I must die; my legs were so swollen
that I could not move. . . . .   Now I can walk with a stick . . . .
and, thanks to our Lord God, I can sew already, a little sitting and a
little standing.   And now I thank you very much for wanting to give
me that diamond for cutting glass, but it is no longer there, because
somebody has stolen it from you.   Our Jasiek went with your letter
to your wife that she might believe that you want to give me this
diamond indeed.   She searched for it but she did not find it.   Surely
somebody has stolen it.   This was a man without conscience.   I
thank you also very nicely for this panorama.   I wished to give it
back to your wife, but she said: "If he gave it to you, keep it."   So

may our Lord God give you health for a hundred years, since you treat me so nicely. . . . .[1]

Now I inform you . . . . that the winter here is very good . . . . nice weather during the whole carnival; so beautiful that it is a joy to live in the world!

And then I inform you who got married. [Enumerates 10 weddings.] And Józek Hejmejak [son of Hejmej] was to marry in Gostwica, in the house of [the daughter of] the former mayor Plata; the wedding was to be on Wednesday before the end of the carnival. But it got spoiled because they could not come to an understanding, for Hejmej refused to will [to his son] the whole *półrolek* [ancient division of land; literally "half a field"; now it means a farm of a certain size].

And then I inform you who died. [Enumerates seven persons. Greetings and wishes.]

JAKÓB FRYZOWICZ

673   April 19, 1913

. . . . Go, little letter, on the journey, because I cannot go myself. Fly, little letter, across mountains and valleys to the distant country, fly across waters and rivers as far as America. When you find the house of my brother, stand at the threshold and praise our Lord God. When you are near, bow low to my brother, and when you are nearer, bow still lower, and stand in a corner and say in a low voice into my brother's ear that you come from Little Kubina [contemptful form of Kuba, itself diminutive form of Jakób] from Łyskownice, from the one who sews *górnice* [kind of clothes] and beg him, little letter, to accept you, beg my brother to take you in his hands, and tell him that Kuba wrote below whatever [news] he heard.[2]

First of all, my heartily beloved brother I greet you. . . . . My legs are not yet quite well, but perhaps I shall recover slowly. May God reward you a hundred fold for your advice, what to do in order to recover sooner. And [I wish] heartily that God may reward you for your letter. . . . . And I thank you very nicely for the snuff-tobacco

---

[1] Accepting the gifts in this case puts the man in a certain situation of inferiority. He is a *komornik*, without land, while his friend is a farmer. The gifts belong to the class of property, not of income, and the reason for giving them is not social solidarity, but personal friendship.

[2] The whole of the preceding introduction is in verse.

which you sent me in the letter. I laughed that you are such a frolic-some fellow and knew how to rejoice me. And I thank you for answering me at once.

And now I must speak with you and have an explanation. Why are you not satisfied when I speak or write to you *wy* and not *ty* ["you" and not "thou"]. I think it [W.] is a very nice letter. Why do you not like it? You cannot do without it at any rate, because how can anybody omit it in speaking to you, either "Wojciech" [more reverential, full form of the name] or "Wojtek" [more familiar form]. But I cannot agree with you [about speaking "thou" instead of "you"], unless—if our Lord God gives health to us both and we live long enough—when you return from America we shall both tend hornless animals [pigs]. Then I shall have more boldness and I will say "thou" to you.[1] So now I love you with my heart and I respect you with my love, and I wish you every good. [More wishes.] Now I inform you that in Kalwarya † Priest Podworski is dead, the same who sent us images . . . . and in Lwów † is dead Priest Adam Weszolicki, editor of *Gazeta Niedzielna*. [Four more priests who died.] And now in Podegrodzie we have another priest-vicar. . . . . And in Nowy Sącz a student tried to drown himself on a fair-day. . . . . And in Stary Sącz a thief stole 400 crowns from a shoemaker. . . . . And the weather is very beautiful. . . . . And the watches which you repaired keep going. . . . . And the highway is made now near Józek Duda['s farm]. [Wishes and greetings.]

KUBA FRYZOWICZ

674 June 12, 1914

[General introduction in very bad verse; greetings; health; etc.]. I love you heartily, so I ought to write more often to you, but I am so hindered, because I must sew the whole day, and when Sunday comes I have also occupation; some come to speak about work, others to take the clothes. So I write you down whatever I heard from other people. In Podegrodzie there will be a cloister [a church] founded, on the spot where Mrs. Stroska has a small shop. . . . . They will pay her as much as she asks, but she must move away from that place and field, because at that place was born Jan Papczyński,

---

[1] "Did he tend pigs with you?" is a proverbial saying, used when an inferior assumes undue familiarity with his superior. The whole paragraph is, of course, a manifestation of the writer's humility.

and he is a saint.   He was born 213 years ago, he founded a cloister of Marians under the Muscovite, and now two are left from this congregation.   The Muscovite drove them away from his land, and they came to Cracow and they are in Cracow, and on St. Jakób's Day they will come to Podegrodzie, and one of them will preach, and they will settle in Podegrodzie forever. . . . .   And this I inform you, that our priest went with pilgrims from Cracow to Jerusalem, to Bethlehem, to Nazareth, to the mountain of St. John.   The land Palestina is in Turkey. . . . .   And further I inform you that in Podegrodzie there is an orchestra of twenty musicians. . . . .   And further I inform you that 7 men have been called to the army from Gostwica. . . . .   And our Jasiek lost his watch; they went for birch-wood . . . . and he lost it in the bushes.   He went twice to search for it, but he did not find it, and he promised the people who gather wood money for finding it . . . . and he went to a fortune-teller in Sącz that she might foretell whether he would find it or not, and she told him that he would find it, and indeed 3 weeks later . . . . a man found it and Józef gave him 2 *szóstki* and got the watch. . . . .   And Błasiak Michał . . . . sits in prison. . . . .   He is to sit 4 months for having wounded the hands of Plata with a knife, and he is also to pay him 150 gulden for cutting his hands.   [Describes in two pages how the man was arrested.]

Jakób Fryzowicz

675   August 2, 1914

My dearly beloved Brother: . . . . I was very glad when I received your letter and I read it with joy, but when I came to the passage about your accident, your misfortune, that your leg has been so injured, then I wept.   But nobody saw it except our Lord God alone, because nobody was looking when I read the letter; nobody knows and nobody will know what you wrote to me, because not every-body ought to know what your condition is.[1]   I love you heartily and I pity you because your strength is so weakened for how can you walk and work when your legs are aching.   But nothing can be done.

---

[1] We find here the implicit admission that sickness, and misfortune in general, are things to be ashamed of and not to be spoken of before strangers.   This attitude may be perhaps explained by individual psychology, but it is possible that it points back to the more primitive social identification of physical and moral evil in a unique magical evil principle.

We must agree with the will of God, because whom God loves upon him He sends crosses. My leg pained me also very much, but our Lord God granted me to recover passably. [Crops and weather.]

And further I inform you that the parish-festival on St. Jakób's Day had three meanings. The first meaning, as usually, every year. The second meaning, that on this day 900 years had passed since the first church was established in Podegrodzie. The great portal was adorned with flowers and pine trees, and of them the figures 1014–1914 were made. The third meaning is the reception of these Marians about whom I wrote in the last letter that they would come on St. Jakób's Day. Two of them came, one had a sermon about this St. Jan Papczyński and St. Kunegunda. [Details of the ceremony.] They brought from Cracow many books, biographies of St. Jan Papczyński, and whoever gave 2 crowns for the cloister-fund received this book, and our priest had pictures of St. Jan P. printed. People took so many of these books and pictures that a big fund was gathered, and I don't know who gave money for a big picture of St. Jan P. in a gilded frame. [Description of the service.]

And now, when I write this letter, I inform you what is going on in our country. Well, a terrible war has begun with Servia, and on August 2, when I write this, all the recruits and reservists belonging to the army have gone to Bosnia to the war. . . . . What a crying and lamenting there is in our country! It cannot be described. From Stodoły a ferryman was taken with his boat somewhere to the Vistula; he will there carry the army across the river. Chmura has been taken, the same who came from America. He had sold his farm and intended to go back to America; meanwhile he was seized and taken to the war. Now they are to take from the farmers, horses for transports and cattle for meat. . . . . In Wieliczka and Bochnia the salt [mines] will be closed and people will eat gruel, cabbage, etc., without salt. If only the Muscovite goes to help Servia, there will be a terrible war. And I inform you that our host has been called to the army and designated to be a constable. It is somewhat better because he won't go under fire, only he will go where he is ordered. And now I inform you who died. [List of dead; repetition of the same news about the war, and particularly about the taking of horses and cattle from the peasants.] On August 1, telegrams came for all those who belong to the army to go at once . . . . and so some of them threw away scythes, others sickles, others rakes, and went to the church, to confession, and on Sunday to the army and to the war!

And so, dear brother, it looks in our country. What will follow, God only knows—how it will end. The priests and the papers say that people ought not to care about it, because such is the will of God, and everybody must agree with the will of God.

And now . . . . you write me not to pay for my letters. But I should be ashamed to do it; even if the postage cost a crown, what does it mean in comparison with brotherly love. You pay also when you write to me, and surely you don't regret it, because it is done willingly and freely, without any compulsion. . . . .

JAKÓB FRYZOWICZ

OSINIAK SERIES

The letters of Osiniak, with the introductory letter of his friend, Leon Mazanek, present in an isolated and magnified form two attitudes which, while seldom quite conscious, play an important part in the life of the Polish country-people, particularly when it comes to an adjustment to modern conditions. Those attitudes are love of nature and love of personal independence.

The aesthetic love of nature arises when for some reason the utilitarian and the mythical attitudes disappear. One example of this evolution is shown in the peasant literary production. Here the imitation of existing literary models develops an aesthetic attitude, and immediately we find a very intense productivity in the line of descriptions of nature. Another example is the life of which Osiniak's letters give us a description—the life of poachers, foresters, bee-keepers, etc., whose utilitarian attitude toward nature finds a much narrower field than that of a farmer, and in whom some instruction has destroyed the mythical beliefs without destroying the feelings which accompanied them. In the case of Osiniak and his friend the aesthetic attitude could develop particularly easily because they are sons of town inhabitants and had not the traditional utilitarianism of the farmer to overcome.

As to the love of personal independence, it is perfectly natural among handworkers of a small town, who have for many generations worked at their own risk and profit in their own small shops. It would seem, on the contrary, that this feature could hardly have developed among peasants under conditions of serfdom. But this is not the case, and for the following reasons: (1) Serfdom had innumerable degrees, from the absolute subordination, amounting to slavery, of the landless personal servant of the lord, up to the almost complete liberty of the crown and church peasants. (2) In the normal type of serfdom the peasant-farmer had only to give a part of his time to the lord, while he disposed freely of the rest, and this continual contrast between compulsory work and free work must have helped to originate and to keep alive a conscious appreciation of independence. (3) The interference of the lord or the government with the peasant's personal life was limited to important and rare occasions, while in his everyday life the peasant was bound only by the social opinion of his equals. This explains the fact that the peasant appreciates much more this liberty of the everyday life than more important social and political liberties, and at the same time the seeming paradox that he hates the detailed organization and limitation of individual life in modern industrial cities, while he complies with it almost without opposition. He hates it because he sees no equivalent in free citizenship for the lost independence of everyday life, and he complies with it because he is accustomed to comply with any authority, for during centuries the authority had exerted itself only on important occasions and inspired a hereditary awe.

So in this respect, as well as in the attitude toward nature, Osiniak and Mazanek, although of the handworker class, are good representatives also of the peasants. The usually less marked misadaptation of Polish country-people to city life is, however, magnified in their case almost to a tragical degree. Osiniak never became adapted at all, while Mazanek, through his marriage, seems forced to bear it. And certainly, in many of the non-specified complaints which we find in letters from America, as well as in the longing of Polish city-workers for country and land, the two elements analyzed above—love of nature and love of independence—play an important rôle.

The nature of the friendship which united the men is of interest. While the actual homosexual relation seems to be almost never found among the Polish peasants, there is evidently in the present case a distinct feeling of the homosexual kind. In Osiniak it expresses itself in the lack of any heterosexual relation (stated in a letter of his friend to the authors) and in the distinct jealousy with which he dissuades his friend from marrying. In Mazanek we find a romantic idealization of his friend, of the classical type. This idealization, as contrasted with the prosaic attitude toward his own married life, is evidently assisted by the poetical remembrance of the surroundings in which they had spent their youth, as well as by the subsequent death of his friend. Nevertheless it is an interesting manifestation, in relatively primitive conditions of life, of the "Greek love."

As to poaching, described in detail in some of these letters, there is of course little prejudice against it, since game is not considered the property of anyone. The spirit of adventure was not developed among the peasants until some thirty or forty years ago, and poaching was quite sufficient to satisfy it.

676–82, FROM WŁADEK OSINIAK, IN GALICIA, TO LEON MAZANEK, IN AMERICA, WITH A LETTER (676) FROM THE LATTER TO THE AUTHORS

676 CHICAGO, ILL., November, 1914

DEAR SIR: Having read the advertisement in *Dziennik Związkowy* I send you six (6) letters which I received from the friend of my first youth, who has not been alive for some years. If you can profit from them, please notice that in the first letter, of May 26, 1903, some phrases are written in numbers, which can be read by putting numbers to correspond with the letters, i.e., 1–a, 2–b, 3–c, etc. The author of these letters, Władysław Osiniak, as well as myself, signed below, was born in Głogów, Galicia, 1½ [Polish] miles from Rzeszów. Głogów is a small town inhabited by poor but independent handworkers, who have not even an idea of the slavery of an American factory workman. The town is situated in a very beautiful country, groves and pine forests surround it with a green and black ring, ponds overflowing with fish glisten in some places. Streams and rivulets flow from the forests into the ponds and out of them, gathering themselves into a river, Szlachcianka. (This river is called "Szlachcianka" [noble girl] because the daughter of a nobleman, proprietor of a manor, was drowned in it—so says the legend.)

Władek (so I briefly called my friend) was the son of a shoemaker, I was the son of a tailor. We lived in the same street, our houses faced each other. Our parents lived in great friendship. My father and Władek's father were seated every summer evening in the garden under an old widespreading lime tree (near every house in the town there is a smaller or larger orchard, even the public roads are planted with fruit trees) smoking their pipes. My father took part in the last Polish revolution [1863] and he related his adventures during this revolution and his 12 years of service in the Austrian army. Władek, a great dreamer, as a boy 14–15 years old roamed with me around the neighboring forests. Often we slept in the forest. In the morning, about sunrise, we arose, awakened by the morning cold, we admired the sunrise, sitting upon big oak trunks on the highest hillock, situated above a pond. In the east cultivated fields are seen and a rising sun which is reflected in the pond; in a half-circle a glade planted with young pines, about 6 years old, and farther another half-circle, all this inclosed by a great mixed forest of oaks, pines, firs, alders, full of big game. In the brushwood are hidden hundreds of hares, foxes, martens. Oh, what a delightful impression one felt in walking during the night, by the light of the moon, along the hills, with a true friend at one's side who adored nature—playing flute and ocarina! The moon reflected itself in the pond; the echo of the flute flowed far away up the dew. Sometimes we could hear the barking of foxes, or the bleating of roes who called one another, or the hooting of an owl. We dreamed about far countries, about travels among American prairies, African deserts, and the jungles of India. These dreams drew me here, where bad fortune torments me, penury annoys me, 3 children cry for bread, a wife complains, and I myself have lost all shame to such a degree that for the vain profit of a few cents I send those letters from my best and only friend, which I have kept in a good hiding-place for many years and read hundreds of times. But I hope that I shall receive them back. . . . .

LEON M.

677 GŁOGÓW, May 26, 1903

DEAR FRIEND: You ask what is the news in Głogów. Everything is as it has been from old; one can say, "Old misery." [Letters written and received; general news about acquaintances.] As I see, you want to fill your pocket at once with dollars, for when you had easy work you kept it for a short time, and now you remain longer in the factories, which, I believe, must be like hell. Perhaps you have now more money; it ought to be so. But perhaps not? It is also true that writing is tiresome enough, particularly for the eyes. I don't even want to read books any more, and I marvel how you could read so much when you were writing [as a clerk] in Głogów. When I arise from this paper I go home in the evening like a blind hen. Oh, there is no better, more joyous moment than to go with a stick [a gun; poachers' jargon] to the forest. But they guard it well! I shall write you below about different adventures, because now I should like to find something to say about Głogów, but I can find nothing; without joking, I cannot. [Some news about people who intend to go to America.] In your home all are in good health. This winter we celebrated in Głogów the 40th anniversary of the insurrection of 1863. In the town there is no news at all. If you write soon, use numbers in some words. And now I will tell you something about shooting [the word ciphered]. First I tell you the fate of Fr. Morarski, like that which happened to us. Somebody from Głogów, probably W. M., killed a deer [cipher] in January and the gamekeeper [cipher] drove him away, so that he had to throw the gun away, or he hid it after shooting, and the keeper saw this and found it later. It was a double-barreled gun. He imagined that it was Fr. Mor. And moreover, the deer disappeared, because another companion of the man fled and carried it away while the keeper was pursuing the first one. . . . . The keeper took the gun to the chief forester and drew up a complaint against Morarski, who proved that he was in Rzeszów at the time, and the keeper will probably sit [in prison for false complaint]. Then he drew up a complaint against Bartuzel, but this also resulted in nothing. Then against the man who was there really. But who can prove it? The only result is that they now guard the forest of Głogów better. The second thing will be interesting enough. Listen. St. Zaj. and Wl. Zaj. killed a roe . . . . about 5 o'clock in the evening and, as they like to do, wanted to take it home right then. They came to the meadow near the spring. . . . . Suddenly about 20 paces back of them somebody called: "Hello, thieves!" and so on. What could they do? It was not very dark, so they could only leave [the roe] and fly, before he recognized them. And so they did. He [the keeper] could indeed have tried the plan: "Stop, or I will shoot," but he did not think of it. Only later we learned that it was [not the keeper but] Józef Jaroński and Jan Domański who were setting traps for martens. They took the roe and ate it, but at least everything was quiet. Now another [story] still. On Sunday evening after 10 o'clock we went to the forest on the other side of the fields, by the light of the moon. We were 4: two had to drive [the game], two to stand [and shoot]. When we came to the fields there was fog. You could not see another man at 5 paces. So we walked close to one another in order not to get lost. . . . . We came to the forest, but in the fog we did not see much; it was cold—snow up to the knees. If I had not remembered to take the compass we should not have found the way to the forest. After $1\frac{1}{2}$ hours of driving, those who stood were frozen and moved, intending to go home, and only then we came, having driven nothing. We hastened then to our house as to a friend. As to the gamekeeper, with whom we are acquainted, probably you don't know him. He often comes to Mr. R's . . . . with a cart; he is keeper in his forest. He was a good fellow more than once with us. I shot only once at the deer, and it was so: I walked a long time about the forest, I went beyond the last hill . . . . ; they were there. I moved toward them for half an hour perhaps, and it was difficult, because there were 5 of them, 2 lying down and the others loafing around. It was necessary to conceal myself carefully and to advance cautiously, lest they notice me. I came to 45 paces, I leaned against a tree and shot. I missed, as it proved afterward—about 10 inches too high, for the bullet was in the tree under which the deer lay. But nothing could be done, I had to be reconciled to my fate. At other times it was different. Once we ran through the whole forest of Głogów following the traces of a bleeding deer which did not fall. Then it stopped bleeding, and that was the end of our chase. Even worse things happened. Not long ago, on March 8, "it" [a deer] got a good one. "It" could not jump a moat and fell into the water and was no more to be seen. . . . . And another time things did not go better. St. Zaj. and Wl. Zaj., on Good Friday afternoon, went to the forest in search of "this." They came across a "big one." The first time the gun did not go off, only the second time, but he missed, being in a hurry, and this saved him. He hid the gun and marked [the place] by breaking a branch. They went a few steps and suddenly the gamekeeper appeared from behind a thicket. They could not run, because he was near. He approached and whistled. The son of the chief forester appeared with a gun and threatened to shoot at them. But as they found nothing, they only quarrelled and wanted to take [the poachers] with them, but they did not go, and so the question was left. But they [the keepers] went to search for the gun, and because there was a branch broken, they found it, as they are practiced in the matter. There was a lawsuit, but nothing can be proved against them. If they had looked into their pockets and found the peas and sand [buck-shot and powder], it would have been worse. . . . .

Your friend,
Wł. Osiniak

678   Przemyśl, March 29, 1905

DEAR FRIEND: Well, so you are still alive. . . . . I could not believe I saw your handwriting. Perhaps you reminded yourself about our young years? Alas, they won't return again! But nevertheless you could have written at least once in half a year. I think that you don't regret a few cents, and if indeed you have little time there, you can still make an hour's sacrifice for your old friend. You don't need to make efforts to write poetically or in some new style, but quite simply. I cannot explain to myself what was the reason of your long silence—whether you cannot get accustomed to the American ink or pen, or perhaps you belong to some sect which abhors writing, because in the New World even this is possible. . . . . What do you expect to do about the military service? Write me what you think about it. I am now in Przemyśl, in the post-office. It is not so bad, only there are no holidays, only half a day every Sunday. They pay for it, it is true, but it would be better to get a few gulden less and to be freer. It is so difficult to get a leave that I could not even be at home for Christmas, although it is only 12 [Polish] miles from home.   I am in a storehouse, delivering parcels, because I read well; so sitting in the lawyer's office has proved of some use.   Besides, I have learned to read Ruthenian.   I do nothing but deliver parcels, sometimes 1,000,000 crowns worth.   After New Year I hope to deliver letters in Przemyśl.   Evidently I have no time now to amuse myself like a nobleman [to poach].   On the day before going to Przemyśl we got horns [killed a hart].   It was on Easter, in the thicket where hazel-shrubs grow, with St. Zając.   Since then nothing more; he is in the army in Rzeszów, and I am here. . . . . You see that I know how it tastes to be alone in a strange town; how much worse it must be in a foreign country!   But I hope that you are getting on better now, because you can speak more easily.   Describe what vicissitudes of fortune you have passed through during this time. Are you not married perhaps, like Józef Podo and Dragulski?   I should not wish it so soon to you, as to a friend.   But don't conclude that I experienced it upon my own skin; I am still free as a bird in the sky.   I don't know what to write further, nor what you want to know. . . . . I wait for a big letter. . . . .

WŁADYSŁAW

679   June 9, 1906

DEAR FRIEND: . . . . Don't despise writing; force yourself to do it.   To me you can write with a pencil upon any bit of paper. . . . . I won't be angry, and it will cost you much less trouble.   It happens sometimes that you sit somewhere in a garden, you are bored, you have nothing to do and nobody to speak with; there is a pencil and paper—because you don't wear ink with you.   You compose a letter, you come home and either copy it with ink or put the same writing into a cover, address it with ink and on the first occasion put it into a mail box.   I perform this duty in this way even in writing to my people in Głogów.   I don't lose my free moments on your letter, I write it during the time I am on duty in the post-office.   Even now a salesman is interrupting me.   The devil brought him to annoy me, but I must be patient.

You are right in not thinking of returning home for military service and wasting the precious time in putting your mouth under the fist of Mr. Sergeant.   Something can still happen during your pursuit of happiness [e.g., you might become crippled], and then they must free you from this honor of serving the "fatherland"; and if not, you will still have time to receive such dainties. Even the dog does not put his back under the stick; how much less the man who is not menaced by the honorable authorities [who is out of reach]. Think of it as if a trap had been set here, and be careful not to step into it, at least not at once. I don't find anything interesting around me, as in service one always tries to rise above the others. I have been beaten enough in my youth [disciplined by the rough life of a poacher] so that I don't need to take much pains in competition with an old gendarme or an ex-corporal. . . . . You ask what I am doing now. Well, it is enough to say, as in any post-office. I don't know what I shall do in the future, I live without any aim and I don't try to find any—if only for that reason that I missed once. You can't imagine perhaps how hard it is to resign a thing about which one has thought for a long time. I kill my free time going on a bicycle around the neighboring villages and towns. Up to the present I could not believe that Lajos Dragulski is bound [married] already, but I must believe your words. Perhaps he will regret it some day—or perhaps not; it cannot be foreseen. My sister Bronka got married also . . . . and I could not even be at the wedding because it was difficult to get leave. . . . . I can go home very seldom, though it is only 12 miles and the fare is 5 crowns there and back. I am quite bound—free time only on Sunday afternoon—and every day I must rise at 5 in the morning; two hours for dinner; till 6 in the evening. It is perhaps better than to do handwork, but one is not free. I am paid 1 gulden 15 kreuzer a day and the uniform; on the side I get only a few crowns a month [tips]. But here everything is so expensive that almost nothing is left, and when holidays come, Christ our Lord! one becomes almost enraged. Other people amuse themselves, and the post-officials labor in the sweat of their brow, so that one does not want to eat when he comes home for half an hour at noon. I think that you don't work there much more heavily in your factory. Well, in a mine evidently one must labor hard. . . . .

W. Osiniak

680 September 21, 1906

Dear Friend: I received your letter for which I thank you most heartily. I am glad that you did not begrudge the time or paper, as before, to your old friend. But perhaps we shall yet see one another once more. What do you think? It seems improbable indeed, but nothing in the world is impossible; so perhaps even here the government will change some day, and then perhaps it won't be so difficult to live as it is now. Well, and perhaps the Polish girl [you are to marry] in America won't be able finally to bear the wandering in a strange land. Take this also into account, because you would be badly off if she sweetened your free moments with dreams about returning home. And I should not advise you either to marry one who is born there, because it would be like fastening one's self with a nail to that world there. Again as to character and birth there are great difficulties; the man ought to know the woman well before marrying her. Well, I think that you won't bind yourself so soon, because it was only a hasty thought, a consequence of your longing for your country. But you must persevere. And perhaps you want to deceive me? For a year or three, since people say that it is possible there [to marry for so short a time] I should like to try such delights, in spite of the Christian principles. I ought not to be afraid, because in your preceding letters you wrote that at least you don't think of doing this foolish thing just now. It is also not right [to object], because the world could not exist if all those [who marry] were fools. But one ought to look soberly at such questions.

In Głogów there is not much news. Dragula, Bałaban, Grodecki . . . . and other men of my age have already come back from the army, having served three years each. . . . . Władek Grodecki plans only now to marry Kościuszkówna; he ought to know her well enough, even from under. This year big rains have fallen, the pond in Stykow overflowed its banks, so that water ran through the road. The beech tree upon which you cut your name for the last time stands safe, the spring is in the same place, only we are farther away from it than before. I have not forgotten the last day either. Don't drop the thought of returning just because you don't know any trade. You can set up a shop or a tavern if you have a few ten-gulden pieces, and you can live freely, as, for example, Sokołowski, Żywiec, Pado, and many others in Głogów. It is easier than handwork and does not need protection. Only look into this American citizenship, so that it may not be anything like a mousetrap [whether American citizenship frees from the duties of an Austrian subject]. So you could come back, and I say it is worth while, though I don't try to persuade you to do it. [You say] "Learn! learn!" We cannot take all the fault upon us [for not having learned], although we are also guilty a little. Only think, what did my father or your father earn! Could we have learned, even in a *bursa* [where poor boys are boarded and schooled]. I could have realized my dreams even without learning, I could have been happy in simplicity, but bad fortune persecutes me even here, so that I look unwillingly and almost with anger upon this world, as you noticed in that last letter. I would undertake mad things which would guarantee a rapid end. And you, fall mortally in love if you will, but after some weeks of love, don't marry, but when the first love passes, then reflect, look well at this creature before and behind, and then act according to your will.

I forgot to write you that I have seen living Indians here in Przemyśl. There was an American circus named Buffalo Bill. [Describes the performance; admires particularly the good shooting.] What is the news in America? In Russia there is revolution. Nobody in Warsaw is sure of the next day, and the government does not want to give the constitution and we cannot foresee what will come of it. Every day some policemen and their superiors perish. But the "heroism" of the Russian soldiers shows itself upon the innocent population; those who make the attempts are usually safe, and the innocent people are arrested. You can guess how the Russian officials treat them there [in prison]; it needs not to be explained to a man who reads the papers. They are braver now than against the Japanese! . . . .

WŁADEK OSINIAK

681 December 17, 1906

DEAR FRIEND: I received your letter. Oh, what a wedge you drove into my head [distressed me]! But don't let us lose our balance, but discuss things in their order. First, I rejoice that your health is good. As to weariness or despair, don't think that I am free of them. If I am not at least three times more weary than you I ought to thank God. Perhaps you no longer believe in such a being from beyond the world, but you mentioned something about the devil in your letter, and since you believe in the latter, you ought the more in the former. I am almost alone here, like a finger, because my associates look crossly at me, and if I had not been beaten [and hardened as a poacher], more than once I should be ready to weep. It is also difficult to find such a friend as I want. Here I think frequently about myself, whether I am so fit for nothing, or why I have such a bad opinion of this world, and I can find no other reason except that I have a feeling of beauty and a love of beautiful views of nature too strongly implanted in my soul. We spent too much time in the forest, dear friend, when we were young, and it is difficult to tear these memories out. I see here well-instructed men who have not one hundreth part of such aspirations [love of nature], and how much more difficult is it to find a desirable friend among the "paupers" [intellectually poor] or how else do you call them? And I don't expect to find any, except . . . . I meet somebody, for example, and say, "Let us go outside of the town." "Why," he answers "isn't it all right here?" "Well," I answer, "if you are suited, then goodbye." And the devils take him! Let thunder strike such a life, since you wish it also! I no longer expect to find happiness, it is not suitable to dream about it. To see the world? At present it is an unrealizable wish for me, so I did not even mention it to you. There is only one reason why I hope that it won't be too late, that is if only I don't marry, I shall have free will, and then we shall see. I don't want to work up to my death either, I don't even think of it. Some years ago I should have clung to such words without reflection [probably to the invitation to come], but just then there was no money. Now money is more easy to get, but the conditions are such that I must consider everything well. It is true that I did not bind myself, but what of that? We are matched, it is true; we suffer through it; this is also true. And what will happen later on—I am stupid and I don't know, as I don't know what I shall be in the other world, a horse or a dog. You speak about getting sickly [in order to become free from military service]. It seems to me also that I got too sickly, I am not quite well now with my breast, perhaps it will pass away; I don't know. This call to military service made me suffer much. I did not spare my health, I thought: "Either [I will be free]—or [I will risk my life?]." I walked during severe cold at night, my toes froze, and who knows whether I had not inflammation of the lungs, but did not lie in bed. The military examination passed happily, but I can no longer believe in my health. Well, but I don't mind it much, perhaps in this way I shall reach the end, because why should I live? If it were only for this reason, I cannot say "Yes" or "No" [to your proposal to come to America]. Don't be angry or

discouraged from living because of this, and at least don't stop
writing, because I should like to have at least your address from time
to time, because nobody can guess the future. So I don't need to
write you more clearly. At present I cannot answer or undertake
anything positive. You ought to forgive me and to understand why
I am a little too lazy. I hope that it will pass. Finally, I wish you
happiness and good luck in 1907.

Your true friend,
WŁADEK

682 February 2, 1907

DEAR FRIEND: I received such a letter as I did not even expect,
and I am very grateful to you for it. I am doubly sad that I disappointed your expectation, but in spite of my best wish I cannot
fulfil our old promises at the present time. Perhaps God will grant
that it will be possible later on. Don't imagine that I have changed
completely. I have only passed, or rather experienced, some dis-
appointments, and therefore it is possible that I am somewhat more
peevish than during my youth, but I hope that you will forgive me
such a sin. I wrote that I don't think of marrying, and you need not
suspect me of falling in love with an inhabitant of Przemyśl, although
it is not a crime and I would confess it to you, my most tender friend,
at the first occasion. As to carrying letters [becoming postman] it
is also very doubtful. I don't see anything ahead. I stand as before
a cross-way. I believe it will be necessary to do any silly thing in
order to end this uncertainty. . . . . And don't forget me entirely
even in California. I thank you for the photograph. I will perhaps
put it into a frame and will wear it hanging with my watch; it is
suitable for that. You have changed hardly at all in these 2 or 3
years, but as you say yourself, it was made 2 years ago. I expected
rather to see big whiskers, and I see a young American. Well, may
fortune favor you. I can inform you also . . . . that our Milka
[probably younger sister] has also got married. Here in Galicia there
is nothing new, only at the university [of Lemberg] Ruthenian students, *hajdamaki* [=robbers; old nickname of Ruthenian insurgents]
beat the professors, broke and tore valuable pictures, and now sit
[in prison]. There is even the son of an usher from Przemyśl, a
Ruthenian, who sits on account of the Polish university in Lemberg.
His father does not mind it very much, but he will probably be driven

away from Lemberg.   Well, in the devil's name, this won't cost me anything.

I am tired of such a life under an ax [like a slave].   Neither holiday nor freedom.   Let the clear lightning strike it!   When holidays come, other people breathe [rest], even a horse, even a Jewish one, has holidays sometimes, and here in this post-office one goes almost mad.   For example, I have not been in a church at mass for almost a year.   Well, I shall get to heaven!   I have nothing more to write, especially since I have written six letters this evening—home sending wishes for the wedding at which I was not present, to Jasło, etc.   I greet you most heartily.

Your friend,
WŁADEK

KRUPA SERIES

We place this series at this point as illustrating the friendship arising between members of the same family, in addition to the familial relation, upon the basis of a community of cultural life.

The situation in the Krupa family is that of a growing separation between the old and the young generations and a new kind of solidarity (although only a partial one) between the young people. We find this dissociation of interests between parents and children in some other series (Markiewicz), but there its basis is the struggle of different social and economic forms of life (familial organization and individualism, old and new class-divisions, property and salary as foundations of economic life), while here the dissociation has its source in new moral ideals which the young generation develops, and other differences are only secondary.

The essential ideals of the young generation are those of individual intellectual development and of active service to the national idea—both rather strange to the parents. We have translated three letters of the latter in order to show how completely their circle of interests is limited to the traditional conditions of peasant life. The only reason compelling the parents to give their children instruction is the economic one; they have too many children to keep at home and they hope that through education the children will be able to attain a better position in life. But even this consideration is not always sufficient to move them to spend money on instruction. Thus, only through the promise of Józia's help are the old Krupas moved to send their third daughter, Basia, to a school, and over Stasia's going to Kruszynek there has been a long struggle, while the parents of Karolcia S. [a cousin] refuse to send her at all. As to the national idea, in the old Krupas there is a passive clinging to the Polish nationality, but not a trace of any thought of contributing actively to Poland's progress or to Poland's liberty.

On the contrary, the young people show a real enthusiasm for both ideals. In Józia this enthusiasm is already equili-brated and self-conscious; she is the oldest and best in-structed. The advice and the occasional scolding which she gives to her brother show her eagerness to see him become an educated man and an active patriot. In Stanisława (Stasia) the enthusiasm is still naïve. Her admiration of the country between Cracow and Warsaw (aesthetically the ugliest part of Poland), the pride with which she enumerates the sub-jects she is beginning to study (whose names she cannot even record without error), her plans as quickly formed as dropped, show that the desire to attain some superior ends is formed before the ends themselves are clearly conceived. Finally, in the brother there is evidently a great vitality and enthusiasm, but connected with an adventurous spirit and an insufficient determination of his own attitudes with regard to various possible ends.

These three individuals are typical, each in his own way, for the development of this kind of idealistic attitudes, both in the lower classes under the influence of the higher classes and in young people of any class under the influence of their elders. The simplest case is that in which the individual by his previous life has been prepared to accept consciously a determined end—intellectual or moral self-development, realization of certain social and political desiderata—and gradually subordinates to it his lower egotistic tendencies and his traditional attitudes. This case seems to be realized exactly in Józia, whose moral and social ideals are such that they could be fully adopted by any individual of the peasant class as soon as he understood the necessity of substituting conscious efforts toward individual and social development for passivity and tradition. Her intellectual and patriotic ideals are limited and determined by a strong religiosity (of a more profound and personal character than the usual peasant religiosity). The qualities which she wants to see her brother develop are those most useful in a peasant community—laboriousness, parsimony, sobriety, practical energy, and wisdom. Aesthetically she enjoys most, in full consciousness, those phenomena which appeal the most to the half-conscious aesthetic sense of the peasant —nature and religious ceremonies.

The second typical way in which idealistic attitudes are developed (most frequent in women) is represented by Stanisława. The individual becomes conscious of the existence of a certain sphere of interests and aspirations higher than his own. He understands at first only its superiority, without really understanding its content, without discriminating between various ideals. A desire to rise to this higher sphere develops, and with it the consciousness (often exaggerated) of his own imperfection in comparison with the superior men who are at home in this higher sphere. Then come strenuous efforts toward self-development, always accompanied by the feeling of humility. The nature of the ideals which the individual will make his own depends in this case, not upon the individual's past, but almost exclusively upon the content of the set of ideal interests and tendencies which he has first begun to understand, i.e., ultimately upon the group of intellectual, aesthetic, moral, or religious workers which he happened to encounter and which first introduced him into this new world. Of course it may happen later that the individual meets a different set of men and ideals which seem to him again superior, and then the same process is repeated, but it is the first awakening of ideal interests as we find it here which is particularly important for further development.

The third type (more frequent among men) is given in the brother to whom the letters are written. Here the attitudes are determined, not with regard to the higher sphere of idealistic interests, but with regard to the lower sphere above which the individual rises. Any new and higher idealistic attitude acquired appears as the ground of an attitude of superiority assumed toward the materialistic tendencies, the apparent meanness of everyday life, the traditional customs and beliefs, etc., and toward the men who are their representatives. Sometimes a mere theoretical or verbal acknowledgment of a higher end, without any effort toward its practical realization, satisfies the individual and suffices in his own eyes to justify his superiority. There is in the beginning hardly any selection of the idealistic attitudes; any attitude may be accepted which fulfils the condition of being a basis of superiority in any regard, and frequent and apparently illogical changes may occur, determined often by the fact that the influence of a given attitude has been exhausted, that it has ceased to provoke admiration or to make the individual feel his superiority—as every emotional reaction is weakened by habit. If the individual finally selects a definite end, it is, consciously or not, the end which seems best to justify the permanent attitude of a superior man, a reformer, a prophet, etc. Evidently, there may be more or less sincerity mixed with vanity, and frequently an evolution toward a greater sincerity is noticeable as the individual progresses in age.

The solidarity among the young people upon the basis of their new ideals as against the old generation is well expressed in its evolution. Józia is first alone. Then she sees with particular joy that her brother has developed a sphere of interest more or less common with hers, and she tries to make this community as close as possible. She, and in a measure her brother, are glad to see that Stasia will soon become one of them, and Stasia understands it and feels proud and humble at the same time, until, in her last letter, she begins to show a greater independence and self-consciousness. Finally, Józia helps to attract Basia into their circle. This solidarity is not limited to their immediate family. Franciszek, the instructed peasant, sends at his own expense his betrothed, Karolcia, to the school when her parents refuse to do so.

Nevertheless, the solidarity is not perfect. The brother in America not only shows tendencies to develop certain attitudes in disaccord with those of young people in his own country, but does not seem to acknowledge fully Stasia's rights to independence of views and of life. Perhaps it is his situation as presumptive heir of the farm which leaves, in spite of all his "progressiveness," a certain background of the plain peasant materialism in economic and familial matters.

These attitudes, here only incidentally mentioned, will be illustrated in another collection of materials (Part II), treating the actual evolution of the peasant and the movement of social idealism.

683–94, TO WOJTUŚ KRUPA, IN AMERICA, FROM FAMILY-MEMBERS IN POLAND

683   KROŚNICA, November 30, 1912

DEAR LITTLE BROTHER: I intended to write you long ago, but I was always hindered by the lack of your exact address. I have received it from home only now. So I hasten to talk with you by letter, since it is impossible to do it by speech. And I want so much to have this talk with you, but a sincere, hearty talk, a truly brotherly one. I should like to tell you what lies upon my heart, and to receive your confession in turn.   I hope that you won't refuse my request and that this letter will be the beginning of our understanding.   Do you agree?

Time has flown already since we saw each other.   When you were going to America we could not even bid goodbye to each other. When I learned from our parents that you had gone away I was very much grieved, for knowing your hot nature I was afraid some misfortune might befall you, which is not difficult in a strange country for a young and inexperienced man.   But, thanks to God, I hear that everything is going on well with you, and I pray always the Holiest Mother to keep you under her protection.   Meanwhile, thanks to the help of God, I passed my examination happily and am working now for the second year as a teacher.   I teach in the district of Nowy Targ; so it is among mountaineers.   I am alone in a small mountain village.   The work is rather difficult and tedious, but the people and the children are very well-disposed toward me.   And so we are both working independently for our piece of bread, we are thinking of our future.   We are both far away from the native home but I am at least among my own people while you are far away beyond the ocean, surrounded by people who speak to you a strange language, and often pray to a different God.   So don't wonder, brother, if I feel often anxious lest you forget that you are a Pole and a Catholic.   But this will never happen.   You will always remember our native village and the small church, our old house and our parents.   Stasia wrote to me just now that you have joined the Polish "sokols."   This is precisely a proof that you remember that you are a Pole.   I hear also that you learn English.   Evidently this will make your stay in America easier, but don't forget to read Polish books also.   Dear Wojtuś, I hope that you will answer me at once.   I shall wait impatiently for your letter.   Write me at length, how and where you work, and how you are succeeding.   Are you in good health?   What do you do on Sundays?   Whom do you visit there?   And in general everything about yourself.   In our country there is trouble now; everybody speaks of war which may come.   The Christmas holidays, so dear to us, are approaching.   I wish you to spend them in the merriest possible manner, and remember how they are spent in our country.   I wish you so, as if I broke the wafer with you at Christmas eve dinner. . . . . I embrace you and greet you heartily.

Your loving sister,

Józefa

684

DEAR LITTLE BROTHER: . . . . I inform you that your letter rejoiced me very much, for I see from your words that although in a foreign country and among so many dangers, you have still remained true to all that you took with you from your native home. I am glad that you always feel a Pole and a Catholic, that you work and economize in the thought of your fatherland and family, that you avoid bad society and try to instruct yourself and to develop intellectually. We need precisely such men today, who are not only able to work hard, but also to economize and to use their money properly. And this will come as soon as our people get at least enlightenment enough to understand that a man ought not to work simply in order to drink and to waste his money later. Unhappily today it is usually so, both here in our country and there in foreign countries. So nothing more is left for me than to encourage you to go farther on the way which you have chosen. Read and learn as much as you can, particularly in your native language, though the English may be useful to you there. And then, put aside as much money as you can, of course not being too parsimonious about your food or any honest amusement. And God preserve you from the idea that you might remain in America forever! How many of the strongest and healthiest men our fatherland loses every year! Oh, may nobody make this already large number still larger, but after earning some money and getting more experience may everyone return speedily to his native threshold and use them here in an intelligent work for the good of his fatherland!

Probably they have written you from home that Stasia went to an agricultural school in the Kingdom [Russian Poland]. It is of course very happy news to us, for our Stasia will be able to learn farming and housekeeping. And today everybody is proclaiming that an agricultural school is indispensable for country girls. But I was quite astonished that our parents, particularly father, agreed to it. At any rate it leads to expenses, and we both know that when money is mentioned in our home the question goes as upon clods. [Proverbial.] Well, thanks to God, that it ended so. May she only happily finish this school, then the three of us could talk among ourselves about everything and understand one another. . . . . Aunt Grabowska will perhaps come to me in the spring, for now I am very lonely among the mountaineers. I live alone in the school, but I am not bored, for there is always work. I have 80 children, so my head scarcely holds out. We have now severe winter; sledging is very good. If you knew how pleasant it is to go thus with sledges on Sunday to church in the midst of these white fields of ours, and then to kneel down before our Lord Jesus and to sing with one's full voice, *Gorzkie żale!* ["Bitter Regrets," a religious hymn for Lent]. Do you, Wojtuś, ever hear there our beautiful *Gorzkie żale?* Probably not, for where should you? [Rumors about Balkan war.]

JÓZEFA

685   May 19, 1913

MY DEAR LITTLE BROTHER: . . . . Accept for your letter a hearty "God reward." Every one of your letters causes me an enormous joy, and makes me still nearer to you, if it is possible. I am still more thankful to you because, though not having much time, you nevertheless write me such long letters and confide to me everything so willingly. I wait impatiently for each letter, and when I receive it, I read it more than once. I am very glad that your health serves you well. Still I would advise you to change your occupation and, if possible, to work somewhere in the fresh air, the more so as, according to your own words, you intend to visit America a little; so perhaps you will find somewhere such an occupation, even if for smaller wages. For, you see, nothing spoils health so much as staying in a sultry place. . . . . And remember that you are still a young boy and that our fatherland needs healthy and strong sons. I not only do not blame your [intention of] visiting America and becoming better acquainted with it, that is with the United States, but on the contrary, I encourage you. Trips and changes of this sort are very instructive. So if there is no difficulty about it, do it. Probably you will regret leaving your *drużyny sokole* [friendly sokol associations],[1] but it seems to me likely that there are also branches of the sokols in other localities. As to the English language, certainly, since you are there and have the opportunity to learn, it is worth while to profit by it, for everything you learn may be useful at an opportune moment. How glad I am that my brother is a *druh sokół*, for our whole hope today is in these "friendly associations." I would beg you also very earnestly to send me your photograph in a sokol's uniform—for probably you are having yourselves photographed. Or if you have

---

[1] The word *sokół* means "falcon," and under the name are organized societies, mainly of young men, for athletic and patriotic purposes. *Druh* is an old Polish word meaning "friend"; *drużyna*, "associations of friends."

none of that kind, then send me any. You sent some home, but I did not see them. . . . . What did they write you from home? To me nothing, and I don't wonder, for father is busy from dawn till dark with work in the field and has no time to take up a pen. How do they manage there, poor people? Here it is now very nice, for this is the month of May, the most beautiful in the year, consecrated to the Holiest Virgin, the Polish queen.[1] Therefore children adorn her statues and pictures, and everywhere songs in her honor resound. . . . . It is splendid everywhere, the larks sing, the cuckoo calls, the frogs croak, and a single great choir resounds. In our Krośnica it is so beautiful, so green, that I want always to run about the fields and mountains. Alas! I must sit in the cabin, for *primo* [I must] teach the children, *secundo* prepare myself for the examination which I have to pass in the autumn. But though I sit at home, I see through the windows splendid mountains around me. I hear the murmur of the stream and the singing of the birds. I tell you beforehand that as soon as you come back you must at once come to me, and then we shall enjoy different mountain-trips. Staśka intends now to come to Zakopane and visit the Tatras, of course with a tourist party. Only she is anxious, poor girl, whether she will have the time.

For the news about Władek W., I thank you heartily. I was very pained when I read it. For I believe (and it seems to me that I make no mistake) that Władek is lost to us. For, as a married man, he surely will not wish to go to the army, and this awaits him certainly if he comes back. And if he does not serve his time he will never be able to come back. And what a grief it is for his parents, who had quite different hopes about him. I won't tell it to anybody, for only gossip would result. It is a sad fact, for in this way hundreds of Polish men and women are lost to their fatherland, settling forever in America, or—what is worse—getting morally lost there. And meanwhile in our fatherland there are simply not hands enough to work. In recent times emigration has even increased because of these different troubles. Here in our country [Galicia] as in the whole empire, the disorder is terrible—the struggle of parties, our local parliament dissolved, new elections, a new governor. May God only grant that the Poles get no harm from all this. May the Polish Catholics win, and not the Jews and Socialists. . . . . Did you

---

[1] Allusion to the symbolic crowning of the Virgin as Polish queen by King John Casimir in the seventeenth century.

celebrate there the anniversary of the constitution of May 3 ?[1] Here it was everywhere solemnly celebrated. . . . .

JÓZEFA

686   August 1, 1913

DEAR LITTLE BROTHER: . . . . I received your letter and photograph. . . . . Judging by the photograph you are a nice boy, but very childish. I thought that you were already more serious. And see here, such a child wants to consider himself already as a citizen of the United States, and dreams I don't know what projects. You will think probably, what do I want from you? Nothing more, dear brother, than that you may not forget there, in this exile, about our holy faith and our mother-country, that you may be always a true Catholic and Pole. For, O my dear, whoever is not a good Catholic will not be a good Pole. Without God there is no fatherland, and even if we bring I don't know what offerings to this fatherland, we shall not get our liberty back without God's blessing. Dear Wojtuś, I was very much pained to learn that you do not fulfil there in the foreign country our religious practices and duties, which every Christian Catholic ought to fulfil. But it is really impossible! I cannot believe that my brother has forgotten his prayers, which his mother taught him. It is true that you are young and inexperienced and bad society can do much evil, but I don't believe that you went so far as to lose your faith. Oh, this would be worse than anything! And another question, no less disagreeable. I learn that you intend to become an American subject [sic], and then again to join the American army. It would mean the same as to renounce your fatherland. My dear, in America only the men can settle who have here nothing to lose, but you have, I think, your whole future here. There is work enough and honest earning in our country, only people don't know how to take care of their money. And if you want to serve in the army, here you won't escape that pleasure either. I think so: earn as much as you can, learn as much as possible; in a word, profit well from your stay there, and then back to us, and don't

[1] The constitution of May 3, 1791, was an endeavor to reorganize Poland upon a new basis. It failed because of the subsequent division of Poland. The anniversary is always celebrated in Poland as a claim that (after a century of decay) the nation gave proof of its capacity for self-government (by the provision of a more democratic and centralized organization) and that the partition was contrived by hostile states precisely because Poland had demonstrated that capacity.

look again at America. For it is not worth regretting. And I think it is more gay here, in spite of our misery, than there, with their riches. You guess probably that I got the news about you from Kasia W., whom I met in Podgórze. Well, she is quite fit for America! I beg you very much, Wojtuś, don't give her my letters to read and don't tell her what I write you, particularly about her, for there would be only useless anger. It is true that they are our family, but they belong to those who don't care about their native country and see their happiness only in America. We cannot improve them, so let us rather be silent and do what is our duty without listening to their principles, often erroneous. And I should prefer if you kept far from them, though politely. Were it not true, what I heard about you! I shall wait impatiently for your answer to this letter. And I beg you very much, as your loving sister, write me the sincere truth, confide in me everything, as a good brother to his sister, for I am very much grieved. . . . .

Józefa

687 Gołotczyzna, March 2 [1913]

Dear little Brother: How happy I am that I can at last write to you. You don't know how I was pained that in such an important change of my life I could neither talk with you nor even write to you. . . . . I took your address from home . . . . but unhappily I lost it . . . . and only now that Józia sends it to me I hasten to write and to describe to you everything, and also to learn how you get on, how you succeed. . . . . Dear brother, how do you like my going to this school? Are you perhaps very dissatisfied? For on the one hand the fee in this school costs somewhat too much, and a year of time will be wasted. But I think that I shan't regret it. For now learning gives the means to live and is everywhere the best foundation, particularly when this enlightenment is lacking among our women in the country. Now, when people begin to think about learning, it begins to get better and better in this world. But unhappily there is still very little of this learning. And then, I did not decide alone about myself. I wanted very much to go and I begged [my parents] for a long time to be permitted. And they did not wish to give their consent, but only when Karolka's betrothed began to persuade them. Perhaps you remember him, Franciszek, who was farm-manager in Czasław. He had been himself in such a school, and he held out very much for Karolka and me to go to the school, and he made different efforts to this effect. And our uncle and aunt from Kamienice praised [the plan] much and advised us to go. And when Józia wrote a letter, that if I went her [greatest] wish would be accomplished, and that she would help me all in her power [they agreed]. But we were to go and then again not, from fear of the war which might break out from moment to moment. As things became quieter, we went, but what of it, since that war was not settled finally, but it can still break out, and will almost certainly do so in March. Oh, it is horrible. In Galicia they begin to take [to the army] boys from 18 years up. May God the Good keep this war far from us, for it never brings happiness, even if it is the best. Were it at least a war for our country, for our Poland! But for the sake of some ports, etc., it is not very pleasant to go to war. But you are probably more curious about other things, so I will describe my journey, the surroundings here, and whatever I can.

Perhaps you received my letter in which I wrote you that I go to an agricultural school in the Kingdom. I wrote you that we were going to Kruszynek, but in Kruszynek there was no more room, so we came to Gołotczyzna. We left on January 15, amid leave-taking and crying, so losing our heads that we did not know which way to take, whether to go or not. Some people began to dissuade, others frightened us with war, others still that it is hard to cross the frontier. Well, but we went, and upon the frontier there was no big terror at all, we were treated politely. We went through Częstochowa and Warsaw, for Gołotczyzna is in the province of Płock, and the province of Płock is still far enough beyond Warsaw. If you knew, dear brother, what a beautiful country it is, such plains that you cannot see the end, big villages, a multitude of brick houses, one village far enough from another, and exceedingly many of the most various mills, windmills, factories. The farmers are richer than in Galicia. In some houses the order is quite exemplary. In a word, we were well pleased here. We saw the cloister of Częstochowa, and we were in Warsaw for some hours, and saw many things. It is a very beautiful city, this Warsaw, situated in a splendid lowland and the Vistula flows near it as a wonderful wide girdle. Dear brother! How happy I should be if you could come to me, visit this country. But alas! these are dreams which will turn into nothing. Józia wrote me that she wished greatly to come to the Kingdom, but that she cannot, for you know what she is occupied with, and in vacation she must pass her examination, and surely nobody will come here to me. Well, nothing can be done, the journey to me is too far. If God grants me to pass this year happily I shall see everybody again, and perhaps you will come then— so you also. But now I must think about study and work, for here we have study and work above the ears, so that we have not even time to worry. For the first month we worried [were homesick] a little, but now already less for, as I wrote, we have plenty of work and many companions. I have a few such good and hearty companions that if we had to leave one another now we should surely cry. Now, as to the studies, we are studying many things. Besides the usual farm-studies, we have lectures about agriculture and we learn all the natural sciences, i.e., geology, chemistry, physics, astrology [sic], and so on; also writing, arithmetic, geography, sewing, cutting, and different small handicrafts, so that the whole day is filled, and there is not even time to write letters. But this does not matter, for on Sundays we have a little time, and then we write letters. On ordinary days we rise at 6, on Sundays at 7. We go to sleep at 10. We go every Sunday to the church; we have a church near. Besides this, the Sundays are spent merrily; we make trips to different places, we arrange different theatrical plays. [Greetings, request for letters, etc.]

STANISŁAWA

688 April 10, 1913

DEAR LITTLE BROTHER: . . . . I was very glad on receiving your letter and the news that you are in good health and not displeased with all this. . . . . Your letter, though short, is so kind, good, and sincere that it was a pleasure for me to read it. So once more I thank you a hundred fold for your letter, for your recognition of me, your advice, and the proofs of your brotherly love and good will. You even guess [more than I expressed], dear little brother. Up to the present, indeed, I did not need money very much, so I did not beg for it expressly; and then, I was afraid that my letter would not reach you. . . . . But you must know that whatever you send . . . . you must send it to the address of the school-superior. [Exact address and details.] Perhaps it will seem ridiculous that I give you only addresses [without asking what I want]. But it did not suit me to write [more clearly]. Well, though I did not ask you formerly, now I beg you very much indeed. It is true that our parents send money to pay the school, but this year there is to be a general excursion of the students to Galicia, and this will cost about 20 crowns. So I am afraid to ask our parents, for indeed there might be too much of all this for them. If you are so kind, dear brother, as to fulfil my request, I shall be very, very grateful to you. For I want very much to be on that trip, and I reflected to whom I might address my humble request, and I mentioned it in my first letter to you. When you expressed the readiness to do it I rejoiced very much that I can beg you and not be disappointed.

Dear brother, how is your life going on, whether sad or gay, or simply monotonous and indifferent? Have you got accustomed to your life? For up to the present I had no idea of any other life than that which I led at home. Well, and now I have got a little acquainted with a different life. For some people it may be splendid, for others merry, for others indifferent, for still others sad. My life here is various; sometimes merry in a group of companions, satisfied while I am studying, and at other moments if not sad, then indifferent. And the days pass with a mad rapidity; I don't know whether yours also? I have not any pains here; we live in rather good concord. I have only some contrarieties about religion, for here some subversive spirit prevails. I shall describe it more exactly another time. As to my study about God [of theology], it goes on well enough. I have nothing more of interest to write you, only I embrace you heartily. . . . .

[STANISŁAWA]

689 June 3, 1913

DEAR LITTLE BROTHER: Hiding myself in the garden (for if I did not I should have to work in the garden and there would be no time to write), holding the letter upon my knee, I begin to write. Pardon me, if it is so scribbled. . . . . I am very glad that you are healthy and that you succeed well, for, as I see from your letter, God the Merciful does not desert you, and though you must work heavily the fruits of your labor are to be seen. And the work did not make you a light-headed man nor a spendthrift, for when one has to work hard for his money he learns better how to manage it. It seems to me that you don't look upon this question in a different way, for it manifests itself in many things. You don't act as other emigrants, our acquaintances, do, but on the contrary, you remember your fatherland, for you joined the sokols. I like it very, very much, and surely it won't have bad results for you, for it makes your life more various, gives you various knowledge and develops your spirit and your courage. Moreover you remember to learn, and in these times it is perhaps still more important than the preceding thing, for now the struggle by means of knowledge is easier than with the fists. At any rate, knowledge is indispensable. And then, dear brother, you remember about your parents and send them money, for perhaps now they need it, and when you return they will give it back with interest. I heard something like this, that you intend to remain in America, but I don't believe it, for what would then be the use of sending money home? And moreover should you not long for your country, would it not be hard to work during your whole life and never to breathe any more the free air of your fatherland? No, dear brother, it cannot and ought not to be so. I think that you work there heavily only in order to enrich your country, your family and yourself, but not to leave this money in the foreign land. Well, I will give you here a plan. Perhaps it will seem ridiculous to you, but I consider it very suitable. Save, dear brother, as soon and as much money as you can; then come back and we will go to Lithuania and buy land there, for there is land enough and cheap—no more than 150 gulden a morg. I have here a few companions from Lithuania. They are very rich and honest girls. They tell me everything and persuade me to go with them to Lithuania. I should like to persuade our parents also to do it, but it would be difficult, for they are no more in the strength of their age and cannot so easily leave their country. And it seems to me that for us it would be very well, for there in Galicia, particularly in our district, the land is expensive and there is very little of it, so that farming is not splendid there at all; one must continually add one penny to another in order to defend one's self against misery. It is difficult even to think about enlarging one's farm. For me therefore nothing is left except to choose some career, to study a little more after leaving the school and to work in my chosen career, for there is not much at home to return for, while thus, by putting our strength and our fortunes together, we could buy something. But more about it later; we have time enough. Meanwhile I would learn whether it is true that Władek W. got married? They have written it to me from home. We will not go on a trip to Galicia, but we will travel about the Kingdom, but this is good, that we shall learn to know the Kingdom well.

I have here such religious contrarieties, because there is too great a subversion. Some of my companions, though not all of them, believe that man is created from the ape. Besides this, they consider different prayers useless, etc. And it troubles me much, for it is not so. But now things are greatly changed, and when they learn better then such absurdities will evaporate from their heads. I did not write anything home about it. I wrote only to Józia, and don't you write either. You wonder perhaps why I don't mention anything about money up to the end of my letter, but I knew nothing yet up to the last moment, till the post came and brought the money, for which I thank you most heartily, my golden little brother.

Your loving sister,

S[TANISŁAWA]

690
July 14, 1913

DEAR LITTLE BROTHER: . . . . What lies upon our heart, we write it first. So you did, and I will do the same. As you, dear brother, cared most about cleaning yourself from the reproaches which people made to you, even so I must present to you more clearly the conclusion which you drew from my own letter.

My dear brother, don't think at all that the thought of leaving my native roof, my native home, the parents, etc., is so pleasant to me. If you knew how hard a struggle I must fight [with myself when I think] that this will happen really some day and that I must go away— if you knew all this, surely you would not think that I don't want to return home.

But I don't wonder at all at your thinking that my head is turned and therefore I don't wish to come back home, for from my letter this was clearly to be seen, and you don't know the conditions well enough on the basis of which I came to this school, so I will explain them a little better.

As you know, our parents don't get on easily [alone] and surely they would prefer if I remained at home, but the economic conditions don't permit it. Our parents have reflected enough about it even before my departure to the school, and they were convinced beforehand that it won't be worth while for me to come back home after finishing this school. Mother advised me to choose some career, and our parents almost agreed that I shall not return home, except for a short time. Then I wished more to be somewhere in the world, but now, on the contrary, I have a hot wish to return home. And perhaps I shall return, for it is not yet at all decided that I am not to return. It will depend upon our parents, and upon this—where I shall be able to use better the learning which I shall acquire here, whether at home in farming or in some other occupation.

Dear brother, pardon me for writing all this, but please don't think that you have such an unreasonable sister in whose head sits only worldly emptiness. Forget, little brother, everything that I wrote in that letter, for it was written perhaps too unreasonably and mechanically, so it is useless to attach a great importance to it. And don't take, God forbid, that which I wrote formerly and what I write now in bad part, for I write you all this heartily and truly, as to a brother. Don't think that I am perhaps offended for these few words. As many admonitions as you may give me, I will be only grateful to you. I should like to explain all this to you the best possible, only it is too difficult in a letter.

But probably you are weary of reading these excuses, which are much like reproaches, so let us pass to another subject. Dear brother, how is your work? It seems to me that it goes on pretty well, since you earn nice money. They wrote me from home that you sent money and how much you sent. Józia is very much satisfied with you. She wrote me that she noticed from your letters that you did not get spoiled at all in the world, but, on the contrary, you are an orderly [good] boy. And Aunt Grabowska is proud that you are among the sokols. Basia wrote that you intend to send them your photograph in a sokol uniform. I would beg you very much to send me also such a photograph if you can; I should be very glad. I wanted to take your photograph from home, but they did not permit me. Karolka here adds her request to mine, for she also wants you to send a photograph. . . . .

I have nothing more of interest to write, for different trifles about the school probably don't interest you, such as, for example, that we arrange organization-meetings and we want to organize a scouting association. I don't know whether you have heard anything about such associations. Their end is also a better lot for Poland. Then, we publish a paper in common called *Dźwignia* ["The Lever"].

Your loving sister,

S[TANISŁAWA]

691

DEAR WOJTUŚ: . . . . Why don't you write? Have you really forgotten us? Perhaps you are angry with us. But I consider it impossible. What should you be angry for? Such trifles as, for example, that we don't answer your letter soon? Perhaps I have expressed myself a little inconsiderately, for such things may be very unpleasant, even painful. But even to strangers such things can be forgiven to some extent, and it is so unjustified to be angry with one's parents or sisters for such things that I cannot believe that you would do it.

But I suppose another cause of anger, which I don't know even, only guess. It may be possibly our home conditions, magnified by human talking and presented to you in a colored light. I don't write it clearly, do I? But it is only because, first, it is simply difficult to explain it clearly in a letter. Secondly, I don't know whether this letter will fall at once into proper hands (i.e., yours). So you must remember and guess many things, and ask for others in a letter, and then I will explain them better. . . . .

I came from the school in January and will return to the Kingdom in August. This time I shall go to Warsaw, to the Teachers' Seminary. If I finish this course, which lasts 3 years, I shall receive a place in the Kingdom as a teacher. All this business will cost me about 500 gulden. It is a big sum indeed, but what can I do? I shall have at least a secure existence and shall be able to help our parents at some moments. . . . .

You have heard perhaps that Karolka Stoyka is getting married in two weeks. . . . . She marries Franciszek, the man whom you knew, I think, and who sent her to that school.

STANISŁAWA

692

January 1, 1912

. . . . DEAR SON: [Letters received and written.] Józia is already a teacher; she is in the mountains, 3 miles beyond Nowy Targ and 12 miles from us. She did not come for the holidays to us, but to your aunt in Podgórze [either because it was nearer, or because of disharmony between her and her parents]. We heard that she has 30 reński of salary [a month], but she did not write how she succeeds there, she wrote only a small card, "Merry holidays," and nothing more. . . . . Now your·uncle from Bieżanow is selling that cabin with that piece of land and we are buying it. So if you can earn some money, dear son, send it to us, then I would buy it at once in your name.   Even if you don't send, we shall buy it, but it would be better if you sent us something, for your uncle wants 225 [gulden] for it and we have only a little more than a hundred, and we must borrow the rest.   I don't write anything more of interest.   Thanks to God, nobody among your relatives and acquaintances died.   At home we are in good health, thanks to God, only Józiek was a little sick.   He caught cold when he went to church on Sunday. . . . . Now I ask you still about one thing.   When you write to us, tell us whether you have seen anywhere Władek Wolski, or heard about him, where he is, for your aunt Wolska begs you very much.   He has not written to them since last spring, and people send various news about him that he is getting on [or: behaving ?] very badly there.   They had informed us in the same way about you when you did not write to us for so long a time, having lost your work.   They said that Jędrek, your uncle's [son] pushed you down from a tramway, that you lay sick in a hospital.   Was it true?   We are very curious.   I asked you about the same in the preceding letter, but you write that you have not received any letter. . . . . I wonder very much who devours or holds up all those letters. . . . .

Jakób and Franciszka Krupa

693   October 20 [1912]

. . . . Dear Son: [Letters sent and received; farm-work; weather.] Now, dear son, I beg you, if you can put aside some money, send it to me.   I would buy a colt, for now we have gathered hay and clover enough at the second harvest, only I lack money, for we have spent on that piece of land which we bought from your uncle, and we spent those 100 reński which you sent also on this.   We had borrowed about that much money, and we paid the debt as soon as you sent it.   And if you send some money now, even if not for the horse, we may put it into the bank, for your uncle wanted us absolutely to put those 200 crowns of yours [100 reński] also into the bank, and if our Lord God grants it, we shall put them yet.   For when you went away people said that it was a pity that we had sent you, that you won't pay us back even the journey.   So now, when you send money, everybody wonders.   And we need much for our farming, as it usually happens.   Moreover, this year the crops are bad.   The grain is not very bad, but we did not dig more than 20 korcy of potatoes.   As to Józia, she does not need any more money.   She sent a nice gift on mother's name-day and asked us now to give Basia to the school, promising to help her. So we gave her, and this will also cost. And now I also [Stanisława] prepare to go to an agricultural school. We both, I and Karolka Stoyka, will go to Kruszynek. . . . . If we can and if my parents allow me, we shall go perhaps on New Year. It will cost us 150 crowns each. Karolka's father won't allow her to go and won't give her any money, but her sister-in-law's brother, who is a post-official in Biała, advises her to go and will send her money. And I have hope in you. [Family news; marriages.] Dear brother, mother is glad that you are learning, and does not blame you at all for having inscribed yourself [in a school?], only she is still curious whether you read any Polish books and go sometimes to the church and hear sermons. Our parents request you to go to the church as much as possible, for without God all your efforts will be of no avail. . . . .

[PARENTS]

694   May 11 [1913]

DEAR SON: We received your letter . . . . and the money, 410 [written: 400 10] crowns for which we thank you. . . . . Now, dear son, we think about it, how to use this money, whether to put it into the savings bank or to pay our useless debt back. For if I put this money into the bank, I should have only 20 crowns of interest in a year, while I must pay 26 crowns on 400 crowns, so in this way 6 crowns a year would be saved. For you I can put money into the bank in partial payments, or to buy a piece of land if there is some opportunity, for this is most secure. Last year, when we bought this half a morg from your uncle it cost 250 reński and, thanks to God, we have paid it already and now we have a wider lot in a single piece. But there is now no opportunity to buy a small piece of land, and for a large one we have no money. Antek and Józiek thank you for that money which you sent [for them]. We bought clothes and shoes for them. Zośka and Stefka thank you also and rejoice that mother will buy for them some nice stuff for dresses. [Weather; farm-work.] We greet you heartily, we your parents and all your sisters and brothers, and the grandmother from near the forest and the [paternal] uncle from near the forest and the [paternal] uncle and aunt from the field and the [maternal] uncle and aunt from the big house, and all your relatives and acquaintances. . . . .

JAKÓB and FRANCISZKA KRUPA

PIOTROWSKI SERIES

The man Walenty Piotrowski, to whom these letters are written, is a type whose characteristic features are present to some degree everywhere at a certain stage in the process of rising from a lower class to a higher level. Two varieties of this type have found their expression in the French terms *rastaquouère* (or *rasta*) and *cabotin*. The *rastaquouère* imitates the refined attitudes of the aristocratic class while lacking the innate refinement of character which would make these attitudes natural; the *cabotin* assumes the intense and refined feelings, the high ideals, and heroic efforts of a superior man, while he is, in fact, essentially commonplace. As the aristocratic refinement finds its expression in social forms, the *rastaquouère* begins by imitating these forms; as the type of a superior man is most explicitly and accessibly expressed in literature and art, the *cabotin* begins by using these expressions. The *rasta* and the *cabotin* have to be distinguished from the snob and the hypocrite. The snob seeks mainly to get recognition or toleration from a group to which he does not hope fully to belong (the dog is the pre-eminent snob); the hypocrite uses the socially sanctioned attitudes of his own class. Neither of them tries really to assimilate any superior attitudes and to get thus into a higher class. Both lack one interesting feature of the *rasta* and *cabotin*, who play the comedy of higher attitudes not only before others but before themselves.

There is a great field for cabotinism among the lower classes of Polish society, because the higher classes have developed, in addition to their refinement of manners, many attitudes which in the lower classes are almost lacking, or were lacking until half a century ago. These are, particularly, intellectual and artistic interest (to a certain extent present among the peasants, but without the tendency to develop along these lines); social idealism (nationalistic and also recently socialistic ideals); romantic love; and, finally, the general attitude of superiority toward the lower classes, based upon the preceding attitudes. Now, whenever an individual of a lower class tries to get into a higher class he has not only to rise economically and intellectually and to imitate the external forms of the life of the higher class, but he must also assimilate the attitudes of this class. And this always gives rise to a certain amount of cabotinism. Sometimes the attitudes are assimilated really and easily (Zygmunt and Hanka in this series) because of a natural or social preadaptation in the individual, or the assimilation of some attitudes may be real and sincere, while in others the individual becomes a *cabotin*.

But Walenty P., as he appears in this correspondence, is a perfect *cabotin* along all lines. First, he imitates the intellectual interest; he writes about general problems; he probably reads a little. But in comparison with Zygmunt it is evident that this interest exerts no real influence upon his life. In spite of Zygmunt's advice and the example of his enthusiasm for knowledge and intellectual self-development, it does not seem that Walenty tries seriously to develop himself. His work, amusements, and excessive letter-writing leave him hardly any time for this. His own letters show a much lower degree of culture than those of Zygmunt, who is younger. His display of interest in this line is evidently artificial. Nor is there more of sincerity and depth in his aesthetic interests. He takes part in amateur plays, but without real interest, as Zygmunt points out. He shows off in the literary line and sends poetical letters to everybody. But we have a good proof of the lack of originality of his literary composition, for we find among his papers a rough draft of a letter in verse which he sent, or planned to send, to his parents, and it is nothing but a copy of one of the schematic poetic addresses to parents printed upon the sheets of letter-paper sold in America. Walenty, instead of sending a letter with such a printed introduction, evidently copied the latter in order to pass it off as his own composition.

Again, in the line of social idealism, he pretends to be interested in the socialistic idea. But he does nothing for this; he does not even belong to a party, for this requires some sacrifice. He is satisfied with occupying in form the attitude of an enlightened and self-conscious workman, and he does not even try to rise higher in the workman class, nor to exert any positive influence upon others.

The attitude of romantic love, sincere with Hanka, half-sincere with Stasia (who seems to be much of a female *cabotin*), is clearly imitated and insincere with Walenty, who is continually playing before the girls, his friends, and himself the fine rôle of lover. Flirting with both girls at the same time, he affects heartbreak, first, after the marriage of Stasia, and then after the death of Hanka.

We have no data as to his imitation of the refined manners of the higher classes. But there are many hints about the attitude of superiority which he occupies toward his fellow-workmen in America and of the isolation in which he pretends to find himself because of the low cultural level of his environment.

Finally, there is one general feature of the *cabotin* which Walenty has to the highest degree. It is the interest—the only sincere one—which the *cabotin* naïvely takes in himself and in his various attitudes. It is the necessary accompaniment of the whole process of conscious imitation of a higher type of life.

The situation found in the letters of Stasia and Hanka is peculiar. Each of the girls knows of Walenty's flirtation with the other; both are in love with him, Stasia more superficially, Hanka more profoundly. There is jealousy between them, but neither dares to claim the man exclusively for herself; each accepts his indecision as a matter of fact. And the man hesitates to the end. He does not seem to be very much in love with either of the girls, and still he is serious with both. His relation with Hanka is closer and more friendly; his attitude toward Stasia more romantic. And while he makes declarations of love to both, he proposes to neither.

This situation can be fully understood only if we consider the social background upon which it developed. The persons involved are of the working class, passing into the lower middle class. Now the traditional set of attitudes in the working class is drawn from two sources—the peasant life and the life of the crafts-corporations. Into this mixture is here infused the ideology of the upper classes, partly through books, partly through the medium of the lower middle class. And it is this mixture of heterogeneous elements which explains the present situation.

As we know from the peasant letters, love, as idealization and individualization of sexual attraction, does not exist in peasant life in the form of a socially acknowledged and sanctioned attitude—though this does not mean that it does not exist as individual fact. The fundamentally sanctioned attitude before marriage is "liking" (friendship); after marriage "respect." The sexual life before marriage is socially condemned, after marriage ignored. (Incidentally, this may also explain to a certain extent why the loss of virginity is not so definite an obstacle to marriage as in social groups where sexual life itself is socially acknowledged as a basis of marriage.)

But the relation of "liking" demands no exclusiveness. The claim for exclusiveness appears only as a result of a contractual relation—marriage or official betrothal—or of a concrete sexual relation (if the latter has results), because through the child the sexual relation becomes mediately a social fact. Thus a man may court many girls and a girl may have many suitors—not only *may* but *ought to* do so— each knowing about the others, and the indecision has to be accepted as a matter of fact. No claim to exclusiveness is put forward and no feeling of personal dignity can object to hesitation in the other party.

But if the peasant tradition acted alone in the present case, it would not be sufficient to explain the situation. Indeed, the peasant courtship requires much finer distinctions, much more weighing of words, etc., than we find in these letters. Expressions as far-going as are used here would certainly be equivalent to betrothal if used among peasants. They are in fact imitated from the higher classes and mainly derived from books. But in a higher class also they would be equivalent to a proposal, and at this point we must take into account the other body of tradition—that of the old lower bourgeoisie, i.e., the craftsmen and hand-workers.

In certain respects there is incomparably more freedom in sexual matters within this class than within the peasant class, though this freedom is, of course, only before marriage, as in the corresponding German (lower middle) class. Perhaps also there has been an influence of the German mores, as a part of this class is of German extraction and the town-organization was imitated from Germany. But certainly the wandering life of the journeyman and the small trader must have contributed to the development of the freedom of sexual relations by lessening the responsibility of the man and by allowing him to break off any engagement.

Marriage itself is here more an individual than a familial matter—at least more so than in peasant life. The economic basis of marriage is also different; work and craftsmanship count more in comparison with property than in peasant life, and in general the personal life has much more importance. These, and perhaps other factors, have contributed to the result that in the lower bourgeoisie sexual relations with girls are much more frequent than among peasants, and engagement and betrothal have a much less definite character. Nevertheless, while the relation—courtship, betrothal, sexual intercourse—lasts it is exclusive; it may be broken off, but not shared with another. Thus the situation which we find in the present case would be scarcely possible if the traditions of the lower bourgeoisie were acting alone, not in combination with the peasant traditions.

Finally, we have a third element—the expression of romantic love, imitated from the upper classes. And it is curious how insufficiently assimilated this form is. There is a peculiar lack of harmony and of adequate expression in every letter, and judging from certain statements the same feature must have characterized the letters of the man. A perfectly cold and formal letter may be followed by another in which love is expressly declared. Or in a single letter a quite ceremonious form of address may be followed by declarations which would require the dropping of all formalities (particularly in Stasia's letters). Or, again, phrases of love may alternate with others which seem to exclude any love-relation. Phrases which express confidence in the man's reciprocity are found along with others in which the contrary opinion is stated, and without any adequate transition. Or the most burning expressions of gratitude and devotion are wasted upon such trifles as receiving cards, photographs, or a ribbon, while constraint and coldness characterize many phrases which should be written in a totally different way. In short, the real situation would require letters intermediary between more or less ceremonious friendship- and acquaintance-letters and open love-letters—a type which in the upper classes would characterize the beginning of a love-relation. But here no intermediary form is found. Instead, there is a most unharmonious mixture of isolated expressions, each of which would be adequate only in either a love-letter or a ceremonious letter. It seems as if there were in the girls and in the man a strange alternation of contrary attitudes following one another immediately and without transition, while in reality we see here only the result of the inadequacy of the form, imitated from the upper classes, to the content, originating in the attitudes of the lower classes.

Curiously enough, both girls attain finally a more or less adequate expression and in quite contrary ways. Stasia finds it by eliminating the element of love and by dropping into an attitude of cold acquaintance. Hanka, on the contrary, finds it by rising above all the traditional attitudes of her class and by developing really and unreservedly the attitude of romantic love characteristic of the higher classes. Her evolution is due to two factors—book-culture and an isolation from her usual milieu, which in the beginning may have been affected but finally becomes real. Perhaps her sickness has contributed also, for we notice more than once a higher refinement developing in sick girls, precisely because they are more isolated and live a more intense sentimental and intellectual life.

The main interest of the letters of Zygmunt lies, (1) in the kind of relation which unites the two men; (2) in the type of Zygmunt as a "climber" in the better sense of the word.

1. The relation is one of close friendship, with a background of homosexual affection on the part of the older

Walenty which Zygmunt evidently does not share. As far as he is conscious of the other man's tendencies he tries to check them at once and to give to their relation a character of normal friendship. The relation as we find it here is typical. (Compare the Osiniak series.) Perhaps, indeed, there is a little of homosexual affection in every close friendship which is not based essentially upon a community of interests. A mediate proof of it seems to be that marriage usually either interrupts friendship or changes its character, makes it more like a business friendship. On the other hand, a proof that the homosexual tendency almost never passes into act is that the closest friendship does not interfere with normal relations with girls. The existence of this homosexual element is more easily detected in Poland than elsewhere because, particularly in the lower classes, there is no inhibition imposed upon the expression of a man's feelings in general. In this respect it is interesting to compare Zygmunt and Walenty. The first begins to develop such inhibitions owing to the influence of a higher intellectual milieu, of his social ideals, and mainly of his aspirations to self-development, and he tries to impart the same inhibitions to his friend—not very successfully, as it seems. Walenty appears here, as well as in his correspondence with the girls, as an effeminate, vain, impressionable person, devoid of self-control, and living for show.

2. Zygmunt is not a peasant, but a workman. It is therefore not strange if very few of the typical peasant attitudes are found in him. But it seems strange that not even the workman psychology can characterize him. He has indeed workman ideas, explicitly socialistic, and a few attitudes which could hardly be found in another class, but his stock of traditional characters is very limited. This is the fundamental difference between him and such men as Maks or Wacław Markiewicz, who in order to climb the

social ladder must get rid of a great deal of the traditional elements. This (in addition to the irreducible individual difference of character) explains the fact that the "climbing" in Zygmunt assumes the particular form in which the tendency to rise socially, to get instruction in order to pass into a higher class and get a higher position, is closely allied with, and partly subordinated to, a general disinterested tendency to self-development, while both these tendencies were dissociated in Maks and Wacław M., each of whom developed only one of them. There is more plasticity in Zygmunt, and the intellectual and moral influence to which he is subjected can act more freely upon him. For example, the economic problem, which determines to such an extent the life of peasant climbers, plays a very small part with him. He has neither to develop nor to overcome the traditional yearning for property. Again, he does not need to spend his energy on the religious problem, as the religious life never determined his personality to such an extent as it does with the peasant. But he remains in a general way religious, and his socialism does not interfere with his religious tendency, such as it is.

Henryk is a more ordinary fellow than Zygmunt, but has come under the same general influences. His life-plans are much more determined by his actual situation and by the problem of *work* than by his aspiration to a higher culture. In love matters his attitude is typically that of a workman. His behavior in matters of gossip is that of a man whose sphere of interest is inclosed by the limits of his community, although it is not so fixed a community as that of the peasant.

The girl A. P. is Walenty's cousin. She is also much more of a peasant than Walenty himself, or the two girls Hanka and Stasia. The introduction in verse to the first letter, the religious attitude, the attitude toward priests, the manner in which she speaks of her wedding, the importance given to letter-writing and to the photographs—all this is purely peasant. Even the closeness of the familial relation is so.

Jula's letters are the only example we have of a mere friendly correspondence between girl and boy. In all other cases there is either family-relation or flirtation, or at least a relation preliminary to an eventual engagement. None of all these relations exists here. Such a correspondence as we find here would be hardly possible in a pure peasant milieu.

695–747, TO WALENTY PIOTROWSKI, IN AMERICA, FROM VARIOUS PERSONS IN POLAND. 695–705, FROM STASIA G.; 706–17, FROM HANKA; 718–36, FROM ZYGMUNT; 737–40, FROM HENRYK; 741–42, FROM A. P.; 743–45, FROM JULA; 746–47, FROM THE PARENTS OF WALENTY

695 ZAGŁOBA, June 9, 1912

RESPECTED SIR: I thank you very, very much for the card. For indeed I don't know how I merited your remembrance. There is no news with me, except that I long for Rytwiany, and still more for your society, in which my time was spent so pleasantly and agreeably as it never can be spent in Zagłoba.

Andzia [Hanka] intends to go to Rytwiany for a church festival. I should be glad to go, but alas! my duties don't allow me to take this pleasure.

I should like to write more, but I must be satisfied with this until we get better acquainted, or rather until you know me better, for I know already very well your upright character from the representation of Andzia, and also a little personally. *Then* I shall write you very much, though I don't know whether it will give you any pleasure. . . . .

STASIA G.

696 August 2, 1912

RESPECTED SIR: In the introduction to my letter I beg your pardon very much for daring to delay my answer for so long a time.

But please forgive me this fault, for I could not answer because of lack of time.

Respected sir! I send you my hearty thanks for your letter, so dear to my heart. Sir! You wrote so wonderfully and charmingly about love that your letter may be read with a true satisfaction. I tell you that more than one renowned poet could envy you this faculty. For who, who would represent to himself love so attractively? (Perhaps only the man who has already once loved.) But as to myself, I do not believe much in it, for love is often deceitful and without reciprocity, though it happens that it is also holy and innocent; yet in these times that is very seldom. Respected sir! You write me precisely that you feel unhappy to the highest degree because of not possessing the reciprocity of Miss ——. Sir! You ought not to lose hope, you ought not to give yourself up to despair. Only you ought to try with all your power that everything might be again as it was before. And because you are a man, all this will come easily. Respected sir! The greatest burden fell from my heart at the moment when I learned from your letter that you have not yet a betrothed. In that case I won't be afraid lest——

Respected sir! I never thought that your heart and your reciprocal love must be conquered with such difficulty as you write. If so, it seems to me that nobody will conquer your heart, for a woman has not strength enough for such a heroic effort, while a man—— Please tell me with what weapons can your heart be conquered? Whether with humility, or with jealousy, or with flattery, or with kindness, etc.? Or with the most dangerous arms of a woman—tears? Please write me, with what? Perhaps I will adapt myself. Respected, sir! You ask whether "I have at least a spark of love?" Sir! If I knew how to give love such a charming shape, how to make it so beautiful, it is possible that you would—— Alas! The gracious Heaven did not grant me any poetical faculty. So I can tell you only one word— that I . . . . ["love you" omitted, but marked by as many points as there are letters in the respective Polish words] more than my life. But these words are not cold although breathing simplicity. Although they are short, yet for a lov[er] they contain very, very much. Respected sir, I beg you very much, answer me kindly by a letter soon. For I shall wait for it with an enormous impatience and lon[ging]. Your letter is the only medicine against my lon[ging]. Oh, blessed be the hour in which I knew you. I owe this happiness to Andzia and I am infinitely grateful to her for having made me acquainted with you. I commend myself to your kind memory.

Respectfully yours,

STASIA G.

More news about you, respected sir, A[ndzia] will furnish me, for I don't yet know anything certain. I will write her a letter on Sunday.

And perhaps there is no woman who is worthy of possessing your heart? In such a case—— I beg your pardon. [Irony.]

697   September 9, 1912

RESPECTED SIR: I received your letter and your cards, for which I thank you much. I beg your pardon for having let you wait so long for my letters. But I hope that you won't take it in bad part, for it was difficult for me to answer, having such a terrible sorrow, about which you heard probably from Miss Anna [Hanka].

Respected sir! Your letter before the last one grieved me much, for you wrote it with a terrible irony; every word in this letter wounds my heart profoundly. But what can I do? I tried to be sincere and open-hearted, and you took all this for false money. But now I will calculate my words, in order surely not to offend you for the second time.

Again, with your last letter you comforted me much. Respected sir! You write me not to mind that you did not inform me about your leaving Wil——. I did not mind it at all, for I understand and know the proverb, "The heart is not a servant" . . . . But at any rate it would be more agreeable for me if I had received the news also. And so I learned only by accident, from Andzia, that you had left.

It is painful to me that you have so bad an opinion of me, that you believe me deceitful. Oh, no! I am completely constant, inconstancy is unknown to me. In order to make you sure of it I should like to give you a proof, but unhappily I don't know in what way to do it, and for that very reason you can be sure. For if I knew it would be a sign that I have spoken already with somebody about things like this.

How do you spend your time? I think very pleasantly, because in the presence of your beloved. With my whole heart I wish you amusement and a pleasant passage of your time. I have no further news at all. Only I beg you for a kind answer, for which I shall be very grateful to you.

With respect,
STASIA G.

698 November 18, 1912

RESPECTED SIR: I inform you that I had the happiness to receive the letter which you sent me from America. For this letter and for your remembering me I express to you my hearty thanks.

Respected sir! What good did you gain by leaving your country? You were getting on here pretty well; why do you search for happiness among foreign gods? It seems to me that here in Poland it can also be found. But this depends upon the form in which one finds it. Some people consider happiness in the form of money, others in the form of something else. You belong surely to the former, since everybody goes to America only for money. But money does not always give happiness. With my whole heart I wish you may put aside much, much money and come back to our country as soon as possible. How long do you intend to stay in America? Have you any friend there, or do you spend your time lonely? You are very impolite, for you did not write any letter for so long a time, and this one which you sent could therefore have been written somewhat more at length. And in general you used to write your letters in a some-what different way. Evidently America is beginning to change you. But alas! not for the better. In your letter you mentioned something about a photograph. So, if you are so gracious, I would ask for it very urgently and the soonest possible. I am curious whether America has changed you. It could not have changed you for the better, for in your person culminate all the good qualities, and in general you can be counted among the best, etc. You will think probably that this is an empty compliment, but I speak the sincere truth. And I am not the only one who has this opinion about your person, but another very near to your heart, Miss A[ndzia], also praises you to the skies. There is no news with me, everything is as it was. I am not marrying yet, for nobody wants me.

Up to the time I received your letter I was very longing and sad. But your letter rejoiced me completely. And if I receive your photograph also I shall feel completely happy.

If you spend as few hours on your work as you write, then I beg you to write me many letters, at least twice a month; it would not be so very much. Is it true? I don't send you Christmas wishes yet, for surely you will write again before the holidays.

I have nothing more of interest to communicate. I wish you success and merry distraction with my whole heart. I beg you for a kind answer as soon as possible. I shall wait with long[ing] both for your letter and for your photograph. I send you a hearty handshake.

I remain always one and the same,

STASIA G.

699   December 4, 1912

INFLUENTIAL [WIELMOŻNY] SIR: I inform you that I had the honor of receiving from you a few days ago a new letter from America. [Letters sent; asks for answer.] Please describe to me everything. How do you succeed in America? Do you amuse yourself merrily? And then, when do you intend to come back to our country? And perhaps you think of remaining there forever? It would be a pity if you settled there. Rather come back to our country.

Please be so kind and send me your photograph. You asked whether I correspond with Miss Anna [Hanka]. Well, I must tell you that since you left Rytwiany, I sent her no less and no more, but eight letters. But she did not even begin to answer any of them. Then I ceased writing to her. And now I don't know at all what is going on with her. With me there is no news either. Mortal tediousness. Your letters are the only distraction for me. So I beg you very much, be so kind and write to me as soon as possible. With great longing I shall wait for your letter. And I beg you, don't refuse me this grace. Probably you will receive this letter before Christmas. So I send you my best wishes for the approaching holidays. I have nothing more to write, only I commend myself to your kind memory.

I remain always the same,

STASIA G.

P.S. I remind you about the photograph.

700   January 9, 1913

RESPECTED SIR: I inform you that I received your letter, for which I give you hearty thanks. Sir! I am very grateful to you for this letter. But while on the one hand you gave me much pleasure with it, on the other hand it was very painful to me. For how could you have suspected me of anything like this, that I am so indelicate as not to answer your letters. You offended me much, for I did not even think about anything like this, much less realize it. I inform you that I send answers at once after receiving every one of your letters. Why you did not receive the former remains a puzzle to me. To your letter before the last I sent answers twice, but having no news from you I did not write any more. I thought that you were occupied with somebody and I did not want to interrupt a pleasant idyl with my tedious letters. In a word, I did not wish you to suspect me of importunity. This was the reason why I did not dare to send you wishes for New Year. Now please accept my late wishes. And I wish you to get as soon as possible renown and millions in America and to come as soon as possible back to our country.

I was pained when for so many months I had no letter from you. I thought that you had already forgotten. You ask me whether I wish to stop my correspondence with you. Sir! If it were possible, I would correspond with you steadily. But this evidently depends only upon you. I count my correspondence with you among the greatest pleasures. So I hope that you won't refuse me this pleasure, but that you will reciprocate by correspondence.

With me there is no news. I have not married yet, unfortunately, and it is not likely to happen soon, for it is now more and more difficult to find a husband.

What is the news with you? Do you remain a bachelor up to the present? I beg you once more, send me your photograph. In the name of my parents I thank you for the greetings which you sent. They reciprocate in the same way. . . . .

I commend myself to your kind memory.

With respect,
STASIA G.

P.S. I wish you to amuse yourself merrily during the whole carnival.

701   January 29, 1913

SIR: A month has passed and I have no news from you. Don't forget that a month has many, many more days when they are counted with impatience and anxiety. So I will still wait and deceive myself that perhaps I don't wait in vain.

STASIA G.

702   March 14, 1913

RESPECTED SIR: [Letters received.] I beg your pardon for not having answered your letters for so long a time. But please forgive me this momentary inconsistency. I could not answer sooner because I was very sick for almost a month, and in spite of my wish I was unable to answer sooner. But now, when I am in health, my first act is to take a pen in order to excuse myself to you. . . . . How do you spend your time? Certainly more merrily than I do, for in a city one can amuse himself better than in the country. With me everything is as formerly. I am bored, nothing more. And the time passes so monotonously. I have nothing more to write. . . . . I take the liberty of bidding you goodbye. . . . . I send you a hearty handshake.

With respect,

STASIA G.

703   May 14, 1913

RESPECTED SIR: I inform you that I received your letter, your cards, a photograph, and ribbons. . . . . Answer me please, how did I merit to be remembered by you so particularly? For besides the letters and the photograph, these ribbons have confused me, for I don't know, in fact, under what pretext I may accept them. They will be for me a very dear remembrance. I don't think that you will be angry.[1] As to the photograph, I thank you very much. It was a very pleasant surprise for me. I have asked for it so often, and nevertheless I did not receive it, and I thought already that I should not have the honor of owning your photograph; meanwhile, I received it on my name-day. I must confess that you look very well upon it. . . . . With me there is no news at all; always the old story. . . . .

I thank you once more for your kind remembrance . . . . and for all these objects, which caused me an incomparable pleasure.

With respect,

STACHA G.

704   [Without date]

RESPECTED SIR: I have the honor to inform you that I received your postcard a few days ago and your letter, for which I send you hearty thanks.

---

[1] She will treat them as a gift too precious to be used. Cf. the behavior of Hanka under similar circumstances (No. 716).

You ask me why I have not written to you for so long a time. Well, I must inform you that in this case I am not led by anything particular, only one day passes after another and then weeks pass. I am now somewhat occupied with work, for a few months ago I accepted the place of salesgirl in the local shop, so my duties are much greater. And so on working days I have no time, and Sunday passes so rapidly in amusing myself in a very agreeable society that I have absolutely never the time to think about correspondence. You write something about anger. I don't even think of being angry. God forbid! For in general I don't like to be angry with anybody. I prefer to live in harmony with everybody. As far as it seems to me you have no reason either to be offended with me. For if I don't write letters often it is not a cause to be angry. What is the news with you? How do you amuse yourself? As to me, you can envy me, for I spend the time very merrily. I have a small group, but well adapted to one another, and perfectly satisfying my demands.[1] I am just now writing to Andzia one letter after another, asking her to come also. But it seems to me that she will not come. In case she does not come, I intend to go to her when there is a parish-festival in Rytwiany. Perhaps then you will be present also? I have nothing more to write, I mention only that if you wish me to send you my photograph—for I have just been photographed—then please send me yours first. . . . . I beg you for a word of news.

With respect,

STASIA G.

P.S. I am charmed with these cards which you send me. If you are so kind, please send me more. Anything of the same kind. . . . .

---

[1] This letter is clearly intended to break off the relation. Particularly the phrases concerning her amusements and the "pleasant society" aim at this. And if we compare this letter with Hanka's letters in which she protests against suppositions that she is going into society, or excuses herself for having amused herself, we see the real meaning of social life and entertainment in this class—the same as in the peasant class, although still more evident in the latter. A social entertainment in which both sexes take part is seldom disinterested, as far as young people are concerned, i.e., the mere pleasure of society is never the real end. All parties are either traditional ceremonial meetings with a religious background (wedding, christening, funeral, holiday, festival) or they develop out of the reception of the eventual bridegroom or matchmaker in the eventual bride's house, and retain always the character of virtual or actual matching. This is the meaning of all

                                               [July or August 1913]

RESPECTED SIR: . . . . You ask me what is the news with me. Well, first I must inform you that I am getting married. This information will not be news to you, for from your letter I learned that you are very well informed about it. I wonder who was so serviceable and saved me the trouble of informing you about this fact. Excuse me for not informing you about it sooner, but I did not believe myself that it would happen. My banns have only just been published, and the wedding will be on August 10. You wonder that I am getting married so young. But I believe, on the contrary, that it is time for me to get married. I have begun my eighteenth year already, twenty is not so far, and I am very much afraid of remaining an old maid. Moreover, I don't marry because forced to, only from love. I get an ideal husband, who satisfies all my demands —modest enough, evidently. You are interested to know whence my future husband comes? He was born in the province of Radom, and educated in Warsaw. We have known each other more than a year and a half, for he now works in Zagłoba. He is a railway engineer and locksmith. We will not remain here long. I think that we shall go to Warsaw. I regret very much that you are not in our country. I hope that you would not have refused me the pleasure and would have been at my wedding. While now, unhappily, too wide a space divides us.

I intended to go to Rytwiany, but now I will not go, for Andzia will come.

I have nothing more to write you. I want only to beg your pardon if I ever caused you any pain, and to ask your forgiveness. Write me that you are not angry with me. But I believe that I have not merited your anger.

Perhaps this is the last letter which I shall write you. For now of what use would my letters be to you? Surely they would give you no pleasure, for as long as I was a girl it was different, but now my

---

the receptions in private houses (outside of ceremonial festivals), of all dances, walks, etc. Therefore a girl or a boy "amusing" himself is always understood to be in search of a match, and therefore a girl or a boy engaged or half-engaged ought never to "go into society" or to seek "amusement" when the other is absent. Stacha's explicit acknowledgment that she amuses herself means therefore that she no longer expects a proposal from Walenty, but is in search of another match or even already engaged.

rôle is completely changed. So I must be satisfied with one thing. I have no more news. I bid you farewell, respected sir.

With respect,

STASIA G.

I beg you, do not refuse me this grace, and destroy all my letters.

706 RYTWIANY, November 8, 1912

RESPECTED SIR: Oh, how happy I feel after receiving your letter, for which I waited with much longing, but with uncertainty. I imagined that when you went to America, I should have to bid you farewell forever, so this day of separation was for me as [illegible; terrible?] a day as if I bade farewell to everything that was dear to me upon the earth, as if I were at the funeral of my happiness and nothing were left for me except to put on mourning and to wear it the rest of my life upon the earth.

Dear sir, I have no words to describe and I cannot even express all that I feel, so terrible is your departure for me. So whenever I met your brother, I always asked him to give me your address if you wrote first to your parents. I intended to write the first, but since I received a letter myself, I have your address. Dear *kum*,[1] you wrote me about those strikes, and while nobody knew yet that you wrote to me, on the same day I learned that you wrote to your parents also, and that your parents grieve very much about your being in such misery. It would be the best if you could refrain from writing to your parents [such things], for when you write you cause only grief, weeping, and nothing more. This is perfectly useless and your parents grieve enormously about you. But as to me, you can be sure that nobody will learn [that you have written] anything bad; if I tell anybody that you wrote I will always say that it is all right. For not even my parents know what you write to me. As to the money, you may not trouble yourself, for we don't need it. You will give it back when you can. You may keep it with you, for in the case of some accident it may always be useful. Don't send it back until you think that you are in such a good condition as no longer to be afraid of misery. [Send it] only then, or else I would be ready to send it back. Dear friend, you ask about Miss Stanisława

---

[1] Probably the god-relation exists, if at all, only between the parents of the boy and girl, and she transfers it half jokingly to their relation.

[Stasia]. I don't know anything, for since she wrote me that letter which you saw, she afterward wrote only one postcard. After your departure I wrote her a letter, registered, and she did not answer. Then I wrote 2 cards, and she did not answer either. Sister-in-law has written me two letters already, and she [Stasia] did not. So I don't write to her any more and don't intend to unless she writes to me. Then I will inform you about anything. If you want me to be the intermediary [between you] further I will sacrifice myself [half ironical?] with pleasure. Dear sir, please excuse me for not having answered at once, but you understand that I desire so much to answer you immediately, on the same day on which I receive your letter. But everything was so unfavorable that I could not answer at once, and now I have answered you, but not to everything. My mother has been sick with inflammation of the kidneys for 5 weeks, and I am so occupied with the household and with sewing that really it is difficult for me to afford writing a letter. You must comply with it, and you will kindly forgive me. In the next [letter] I will write more and I will try [to write] a little better, for I wrote this one so badly that I am ashamed to send it. Really I don't know what is the fault, whether the pen is bad, or the ink, or the one who wrote. Probably it is my fault, that I don't know how to write [nicely], but I will try some day. We thank you heartily for having sent the photograph, for from sister we had a letter in which they wrote that they received your photograph and letter, and asked me to come.

Greetings from my parents, and from me hearty embraces. [The Polish word for "shake" (hands) and "embrace" is the same—from *ściskać*, "to press." Here it means formally "handshake," really "embrace."] I beg you for a kind answer.

[Your] l . . . . . [oving],

ANNA [HANKA]

707   January 30, 1913

DEAR SIR: I inform you that I received on January 16 the letter for which I had waited with great impatience and uncertainty. I send you a hearty "God reward" for it, and for the good wishes. Dear sir, that letter comforted me very much, so I thank you very much for the reciprocal feelings expressed in it, and about which I doubted much, for you did not give any sign for so long a time. Dear sir, I am really very pained and I regret very much that I sent you a letter which made upon you a sad impression and took away from you a merry moment in which you could have felt yourself happy. Though you may be confident that the feelings which I share with you are sincere. I live alone also. I keep company with absolutely nobody, I go nowhere, to no parties, and nobody comes to me, so I have got accustomed to being interested in no society. I take no walks either. If I have a moment free, I spend it in reading books. If you do not believe me I can confidently appeal to your brother. He can inform you. Dear sir! perhaps you will not believe what I write, but I feel such a lack of you that I can never forget for a moment what you did in going to America. When you were in Rytwiany I walked every evening, I wanted always to see you, to exchange a few words, and so I spent my time pleasantly. But now it is a veritable grave in Rytwiany for me. But nothing can be done, I must accept my fate and be patient, and perhaps our Lord God will grant moments like those to return again. What do you think? I should have much to write, but I am afraid, for you begin immediately to think too much, and something still worse may result from it. If I thought about you and about a stranger [the writer] at the same time it would be too much for you. Why, you find yourself in a rather disagreeable situation, for if you are not working, you have enough to think about.

Dear sir, I want to justify myself, so that you will forgive me for having postponed my answer somewhat long. My sir, on the evening when I received your letter my mother was very sick. She almost struggled with death; so I was very much impressed with it. Moreover, during the whole night I ran like mad, now to the surgeon-assistant, now again to the factory, to my father, and so on. I had to go wherever it was necessary. I did not cover myself as I ought to in winter, only as if it were spring, and I caught a rather serious cold, so that I was afraid I should go to the cemetery. But I was well cared for at once, and in some way it passed off, so that I am in good health now. Mother cannot yet rise from her bed, for she is very weak. I won't bore you longer with this story, I only wanted to explain to you why I did not answer at once. It was only because I was sick, and my mother was even very sick; so I could not write, for I had no time.

And now I inform you what you asked me about. Stacha writes to me very seldom, for when she does I have never any time to answer her. But now I have written to her and I asked whether she had

written to you. I don't know yet what she will answer. As to
Miss N., we are not angry with each other, but we don't keep company since I came from Zagłoba. Only when we meet, we have to
talk with each other. Since you left I have spoken only 3 times with
her. She is [pretends to be] a lady, and I cannot bear such people.
[Information about acquaintances.]

Your lov[ing],

ANNA

708   February 18, 1913

WORTHY FRIEND: I inform you that I received 2 letters and a
card. [One page about writing letters and answering.] Your
brother is very anxious lest you marry some pretty American girl, and
I think also much about it, that perhaps you will fall in love and get
into a marriage bond there in America. [News about marriages and
acquaintances]. T. Sz. wrote that she does not wish to her worst
enemy to make the journey to America. She was very seasick upon
the ship, and in America she is immeasurably homesick. My brother
wrote now that if I wanted to see America he would take me in the
spring. But I would decide to go solely in order to see more often
my beloved, i.e., my *kum*, but my parents don't allow me to dream
about America, and mother faints at the mention of it. So it seems
that I shan't see America. As long as my parents are alive I must
remain nearer to them. [Repeats the news about Miss N. playing a
lady; news about other friends.]

[HANKA]

709   March 2, 1913

DEAR SIR: I inform you that I answered your letters very long
ago, and I am sure that you must have received them. And you
don't deign to answer me.

Dear! In spite of not receiving any answer, I cannot wait longer,
for my heart which is wounded since the moment of your departure
shows me itself the way to pen a few words far away beyond the sea,
where the man is who could heal it. [Evidently imitated.] But
when, when? Alas!

Now I sit musing alone and I think how often I had the pleasure
of spending such evenings as this one in talking with you. Oh, how
pleasant it was to live then! Today the tediousness is beyond

description. I am tortured. Wherever I look—emptiness every-where. Always I feel the lack of someone. Nothing can make me cheerful. Nothing except this one thought, when I remember that perhaps sometime we shall see each other. But this will not come soon probably, will it? And I do not know how I shall be able to live thus any longer. I imagine it will not be very cheerful. But nothing can be done. I must accept my fate.

Then I want to know of your health. I am in good health, thanks to our Lord God, and I wish you the same, with a true heart. I beg you, deign to inform me how you are succeeding, how you spend your moments, whether merrily, surrounded by pretty foreigners or acquaintances. I am curious what influence [impression] the American girls have made upon you? I think not a bad one, for there all the women are elegant, though I should not envy them, for perhaps I could also be in their company. My sister in America and her husband wrote me. I received their letter this week. They ask me to come without fail. They almost implore me. Moreover, my sir, they wrote me that they had there for me a boy who knew me from my photograph, and is so rich, for he has $2,000, and when I came, he would marry me at once. But I answered them that if he had so many thousands let him search for a wife more worthy of him, for I will not marry for the sake of thousands, but of love. I always repeat it to myself, that happiness is only in love, not in any amount of money, for money is a thing which may be acquired, while nothing will change me. I asked them where he got his assurance that I would marry him at once, since he let them write so? It is not enough that I pleased him, for I don't know him, and I don't know whether he would please me. Well, I don't know what they will answer to this. In this way, dear sir, I could have seen America. But I don't know whether this nice gentleman who is so sure of himself will still want me after what I answered them, and so I have a fresh grief. [Irony.]

With the approaching Easter holidays I wish you the fulfilment of your dearest wishes and merry amusement in the most numerous society possible.[1] But please do not forget your truly l[oving]

HANKA

[1] This paragraph shows clearly the modesty of Hanka's claims. A girl claiming exclusive rights to the man would never wish him "merry amusement in a numerous society," because of the meaning of social entertainments, explained above.

710   [Probably end of March or beginning of April 1913]

DEAR *Kum:* You write that I have forgotten you already, for I don't write to you. Oh, it never was so and I am sure that it never can happen, for it is not permitted to forget about such a true friend as you are to me. You suspect me of getting married perhaps, and that therefore I don't write. It is awful to tease in so terrible a way one who can love nobody besides you and who certainly would never decide to marry some man whom she could never love! And even if I married, I could not always feign that I love him, while thinking about someone else. This would not be right. It is much better to suffer now instead of suffering later, making somebody else suffer besides, and betraying him—which would be more probable than the contrary. Therefore I promised myself to marry no sooner than you come from America, and perhaps not at all. Since you went to this unhappy America, I prepare myself seriously for the life of an old maid, and as far as it seems, I shan't be deceived. . . . .

Please don't forget me and write as soon as possible. Your letters are my only comfort and distraction. . . . . And don't write me any more that you bore me with your letters, for it offends me much. I wait for your letters as for salvation, and you write such taunts. . . . .

Your loving,

HANKA

711   [April] 30, 1913

DEAR SIR: I have the honor to inform you that before the holidays, on Good Thursday, I received your letter with the wishes, and 3 cards. Today I received another letter and I am very much pleased. After reading these letters I feel very happy. Because your letters, dear *kum*, make upon me a very kind impression. I read them with great pleasure every evening, for they alone can calm my heart. For these letters, so dear to me, and for your reciprocal feelings expressed in them, I have the honor to thank you heartily, dear *kum*. For the cards I give you also a hearty "God reward." I should be glad to thank you in a more hearty manner, but really I don't know how to express how grateful I feel to you, dear *kum*, for these cards, for they have a great value for me and I will keep them in remembrance. I am very much pained that I cannot reciprocate in the same way, but it seems to me that our Kingdom has no cards like these.

Then I inform you, dear *kum*, about my dear health and success. Well, thanks to God the Highest, I am in good health, and I wish you the same with my whole heart and soul. As to my success, it is not the worst, but I cannot say that it is good. We live so as to push misery before us and to go along in some way or other, though it is useless for me to describe it. You know how it has always been in Rytwiany, and so it is now. I work faithfully, but I have little profit from my work. Therefore I am so discouraged that I don't even want to work, although, to tell the truth, I did not get discouraged [merely] because I profit little from my work. You are probably curious why. Well, if I may tell you, or rather confess truly, I have been in so strange a disposition for some time that wherever I go, wherever I look, I see nothing which amuses or distracts me. I remember only the moments long ago which we often spent so pleasantly together. Everything makes upon me such a painful impression that really life itself has no attraction for me. I am so lonely that I would go to the end of the world to find the person who is so dear to me and to confess this terrible torture and suffering which my heart suffers after the loss of the person who made a glimmering small spark in my heart glow into a burning fire of love. [Evidently from a romance.] And your absence has made it [the love] so strong that nobody will be able to separate [me from you].

Dear Mr. Walenty! How did you spend your holidays, merrily or not? For I, though I was in my *kum's* [Walenty's parents] and our neighbors' houses and they were in our house, yet I only pretended to be merry, and in reality I was as sad as I seemed merry. Nothing amused me. I did it only in order not to make any enemies, else I would have gone nowhere. On the third day of Easter your mother, my *kum*, was with us. The time passed pleasantly enough. Your brother was to come; I looked for him during the whole holidays, but he did not come. Whenever I meet him I ask him to come, but he always promises me and never comes. I have already abused him a little, but he does not seem to be very much afraid of me. Your mother, Mr. Walenty, is in despair about your going so far away, and because she cannot see her dear son. Dear *kum*, really I envy you that your mother loves you so much, even more than my own mother loves me. That a man should have such luck with certain persons, is really to be envied. I told your mother not to grieve, that our Lord God will help her to live until you come with some pretty rich

American, i.e., daughter-in-law, and she will feel happy by the side of your wife. I see that your mother has nothing against it; on the contrary, she says that she would like to see you happy, and to have a daughter-in-law. Dear Mr. Walenty, I thank you much for the money which you sent back, but I am much astonished that you were so anxious about these few roubles and sent them so hurriedly. You hurried quite uselessly. It would be better if you had kept them until I go to America; then you could send them for my journey.

Dear Mr. Walenty, I won't write any more today, but in the next letter. I have been sitting too long already. It is night, one o'clock, and if my mother awakes she will scold me for not sleeping. My parents send you greetings and salutations, and I a hot kiss.

Thy truly loving,

HANKA

712   May 20, 1913

RESPECTED SIR: I have the honor to inform you that I received your letter and your photograph, for which I give you a hearty "God reward."

Dear Mr. Walenty! How glad I am that at every moment I can look at least upon a picture of a person so dear to my heart. Dear Walek! I lack the words to express how happy I felt after receiving those photographs and also after reading your letter, for this letter, written by you,[1] my Walek, is my only comfort. Perhaps you are offended with me for having postponed the answer, but if you knew, my Walek, how sad it is to live without you, you would not wait for an answer, but would come yourself. Then I am sure that I could send a letter to you to Rytwiany every day, while now, when I sit down to write a letter to you, my dear, I first read all your letters, and before I think what to write a late hour approaches and so a day passes after another. Today I at last decided to pen a few words which might assure you that I love you more than life. But what of it, since God the Merciless separated us and condemned to long sufferings? Though this which happened, my Walek, is your fault only, for I did whatever I could; it was not suitable for me to do more. But you did not mind anything. You believed that if you went to America you would forget there your country and your friends and

---

[1] At this point Hanka uses the form "thee" (used also at the end of the preceding letter), and continues to use "thee" and "thou" to the end.

would be happy then. Though perhaps it is so, I think that still if you come back and the persons whom you know stand before your eyes, then you will be obliged to live as we do now, my Walek. Dear Walek, you ask me what is the use of my longing for you. I see that you don't like it much, since you advise me to gather society [about me]. Well, I will try to do it as I can, for up to the present I have still none. And to you, my Walek, I won't describe any more my feelings, even if I am mad with despair. Now I will only describe what is the news in Rytwiany, and in general about acquaintances. Do you agree to it? I must still mention about that unknown American. As to this, you can be calm, my Walek, that you won't have any rival. The matter is not about some marvel of beauty that there might be rivalry. The one from America does not write since I answered them, and here in Rytwiany and the neighborhood nobody gives any attention to me. . . . .

Your truly loving,

HANKA

713   June 4 [1913]

DEAR WALEK: . . . . I see from your letters and you also write me on these postcards some reproaches about something. I see that for some time you are very nervous. I don't understand why. You write to me with so great "respect" that really it causes me great pain. If you think, my Walek, that it is not suitable for us to write "thou" to one another, say so, for it was I who began it, and I can change it. I will write you in the same way as you write on the cards. Listen, my Walek! You are offended because I did not write you what you asked—what people say about you. Well, my dear, I tried to do it. I saw Mr. M. and Mr. Dz. and in general the others, and I began to speak with them about different subjects, and I did not notice anything. Everybody expressed himself so well about you that there is no suspicion whatever [of their thinking anything bad]. So I noticed, at least. As to Mr. M. who lives near the main road, I have spoken with him more than once, and I hear also from Hela P., who always tells me what she knows about you from M. As far as I know, M. always expresses himself in a very flattering manner; he does not find words enough to praise you and he speaks always of you as of a progressive man. And what other people say, never mind. Let them talk. You cannot be an exception, my Walek. They have something to say about everybody, so what does it matter if they talk a little about you also? And you, my Walek, be a little less sensitive about these things. It will be better for you. Don't be impressed with such things, for it is not worth while.[1] You ask me, my Walek, whether I will go to Zagłoba. Well, be calm, for if it matters anything to you, perhaps I won't go, for I am not very anxious to go there and my parents don't allow me either, only Stacha always asks me to come, and my sister-in-law wants me also to come and to see her new son, who will be only 3 months old on June 8. I did not want to go as a *kuma* [of the sister = godmother of the baby], so they want me to come now to them, and only then they will come to Rytwiany with all their children, and Stasia also intends to come. But probably I won't go. Dear Walek! I am curious why you do not want me to go to Zagłoba. Surely you have nothing to fear, for I am not a man and I won't fall in love with Stasia, and if I read the letters which you wrote to her it would be nothing, for I know even now what you write to her and still I don't mind it. On the contrary, I am pleased that you correspond with each other. So be calm about this, for nothing bad will result from it. Don't be angry, my dear, for I feel that there is something the matter with you, but really I don't know what. I should be very grateful to you for kindly informing me. Dear Walek! You write me something about burning of photographs, so I beg you very much, don't write such things any more, for they cause me great pain unless you want to tease me, then do. . . . . So, my dear Walek, if you burn my photograph, I will do then as you advise me to do. Then you ask me whether I have well-suited company. Up to the present I have none and I don't know what will be further on. What does it mean, this well-suited company? For, so to speak, I am too stupid, I cannot understand what it means. And I am also at a guess to know why you asked me to answer you during this season. I don't know what is the matter at this point, for I have written more than once during this summer and before the season ends you will receive more than one letter from me, and you will even not want to answer me any more, for you will certainly be bored if I begin to write too much. There is no news at all, everything is the same. Only this is new, that Miss Nowak is married.

---

[1] The fellow is exceptionally vain, but his interest in public opinion is perfectly normal and typical for his class. Its origin lies in peasant life, not in town life. The attitude of the girl is above the normal, in this respect as in others, and even she is later most profoundly affected by the gossip about herself.

I envy her, for they love each other much. And Stefcia feels as happy as if she were in the seventh heaven. I was at her wedding, but I did not amuse myself very merrily. I did not want to go at all, ... but it was impossible, for she was dressed in my home and she refused to go without me. I wanted to go as a guest, but they refused also, and at last I had to agree to be a best maid. I had a groom [best man] for whom I did not care at all. It was a certain Mr. S. Well, never mind how it was, but he asked for my hand even there, without waiting, but I asked him how old he was, and I told him that he was too young for such things, let him still grow to be a comfort to his mamma. . . . .[1] I envy you very much, my dear, your spending your time there so merrily. Who knows whether I won't go to you some day. . . . .

I send you a few kisses.

Your loving,

HANKA

714 June 30, 1913

RESPECTED SIR: I inform you that I am now in Zagłoba. Before leaving Rytwiany I received your letter with wishes, and at the same time a ribbon, for which I thank you heartily. From Rytwiany I sent you a letter. When you receive it, please answer me. I wait for your answer in Rytwiany. What is the news with you? With me nothing. I am healthy, and merry enough in Zagłoba.[2]

With respect,

HANKA

715 July 20, 1913

MY DEAR WALEK: . . . . Forgive my postponing my answer, but I am in so strange a mood that even today I don't know how to arrange the letter, what to begin with and what to end with in the writing of this letter. First I must begin with the beginning. Well,

---

[1] The wedding-festival, like all ceremonies with a religious source, has primitively not the same meaning as non-ceremonial social entertainments; it does not involve matchmaking. To be at a wedding-festival is not a matter of choice, but to some extent a matter of obligation. The only and important exception concerns the best men and best maids, who are usually paired with regard to a possible marriage. This explains why Hanka, in her desire to be absolutely faithful to Walek, tries to avoid being a best maid, while she cannot refuse to be at the festival.

[2] Postcard; ceremonial form.

my Walek, I won't describe it to you so exactly, for I should have to write for a whole week and there is not time enough. And I am sure that you know already everything, for probably somebody has written to you. First I inform you that I was in Cracow. I should never have gone, the idea would not even have come to my head to go to Cracow, were it not for this, that Mrs. Rog. went to bring her daughter Stasia and they persuaded me and I went with her. I wished to see whether it is possible to live in the farther world, not in Rytwiany only. Well, and it seems to me that it is better to live anywhere than in Rytwiany. On this occasion I called on a doctor in Cracow, for I caught cold in the winter, and I did not care for being cured; I did not believe in it. Then I went to the wedding of Staśka N. and I fixed myself better still [I got worse] through dancing, for I had to dance more than the other girls. I did not mind it either until my side began to ache severely. Only then a doctor was called. He frightened me by saying there would be inflammation of the lungs, and talked a great deal, but gave me no medicine at all, only some powders and cupping-glasses. But this helped little. So the doctor in Cracow, after examining me, told me that it was a very [illegible word] cold and gave me medicines, and now I am getting much better. But since I came back whoever meets me asks why I was in Cracow. When I tell them that I called on a doctor, they say everywhere that I am sick with consumption. And I don't say anything, for what shall I say to stupid people who think that since I went to Cracow there can be nothing else but consumption? I only laugh at it and say, let them blame me, so that no boy will want to marry me.[1] I should be very glad, for I don't want anybody to call on me or to court me. And Stasia Rog. is sick with a nervous disease, so everybody says already that she has gone mad. But she does not even dream of going mad, for this needs some time, while she is already so bad that for three days she has been in convulsions. The doctors say that if she lives until the ninth day, this can pass, but if not, she will die on one of these days. I sit with her continually, for she does not allow anybody to be with her except me and Kazia, and she does not want to take any medicine from anybody except me. I tell you, Walek, people say that nobody has yet seen such a disease. When she sleeps she

---

[1] The attitude toward sickness seems to be exactly the same as toward some moral fault or sin (cf. Fryzowicz series). This evidently goes back to the peasant life, and still further back to the identification of sickness with possession by the evil principle, of which we find numerous traces in the peasant language and magic.

is quiet, but she sleeps only if they make her sleep with powders. But when she has slept for these hours, she awakes and has convulsions so constantly that three persons have to hold her in bed. She asks herself to be held for she would kill herself if she hit her head. She is quite conscious and knows everything. She knows that her nerves and heart torment her so, and when anyone comes she asks him to pray that she may die and suffer no longer. Yesterday, when she could still speak, she called me and told me everything, how she wanted to be dressed for death and how I was to sew her dress. She wants me to do everything. Do you know, Walek, that I am already so afraid of her that instead of going to Zagłoba later I shall go perhaps this week. I am so tired with her that I am even afraid of her, for she calls me continually, and therefore perhaps later she will come to me.[1] Then I inform you, my Walek, that Stasia writes me one letter after another, asking me to come to her wedding. The banns have been proclaimed already, and the marriage-ceremony will be on August 10. My brother and his wife write also, asking me to come and stay for a longer time, and have some vacation. I intend to go this week and will remain there about a month. You wrote, my Walek, making a supposition about falling in love. Well, you can be perfectly calm, for I love only you and I am not going there to hunt for a husband, but only to get some rest, and to give Stasia the pleasure of being at her wedding. I will not dance much, for mother wrote already to my brother to take care of me and not let me amuse myself too wildly and catch cold again. So even if I wished it they won't allow me. I foresee that you will be offended, dear W., with my going to this wedding, but you see that I cannot excuse myself. If I had not my brother's home there I would not go, but since they write also, why should I not, if they give me to eat?

I am sure, my Walek, that you won't be satisfied with this letter, for I only worry you. But I must describe to you what pains me the most. It is this, dear Walek, that you could believe some finished [absolute] fool about my having walked with Kawal. and Kacz.! I don't say that I am above them, but I tell you, my Walek, that no friendship unites me with these boys. I have never in my life spoken with Kawal. and I am not acquainted with him at all. As to Kacz.,

[1] After her death, as a ghost, because in her last moments she has been particularly attached to Hanka, and because this attachment itself in a person sick with such a strange disease must have had some abnormal, "uncanny" character.

once he was in our house in the winter with your brother, and they accompanied the girls who sew with me. Since then I have not spoken with him at all. I only want to know who wrote you this tale. I would not treat him very politely, for it disparages me greatly when it is said that a band of boys is walking after me and moreover throwing dirty words. Really, Walek, I cannot live through it. I am in such a mood that sometimes I rage with anger, sometimes again cry. How can people speak badly about me when nobody ever sees me? . . . . If I am so lightly treated in Rytwiany, I ought not to live at all, for why should I? If a poor girl loses her opinion [good name] it is almost as much as if she killed herself.[1] . . . .

I kiss you.

Hanka

I have not seen your mother, but my parents and yours were together at a fair and treated themselves so well that my father got quite drunk.

716   September 10 [1913]

My dear Walek: I will mention first your preceding letter in which you sent me a ribbon. I thank you for it heartily, my Walek.

[1] It is an interesting problem whether the origin of the enormous importance which any bad gossip assumes in the eyes of the person gossiped about does not lie in the primitive magical belief in the real influence of words. We have an analogy in the importance ascribed to the curse. The expression of any bad wish provokes the utmost wrath, and bad gossip seems to be (in addition to its ordinary social meaning) a weaker and less explicit form of the curse. This supposition seems to be corroborated by two facts. First, there is always an apparent disproportion between the content of the gossip and the reaction which it provokes in the wronged person. Even if we take into account the fear of ridicule which makes the sting of trifling gossip particularly sharp, there remains the fact that the reaction is always too strong if judged from the objective standpoint. The most vainglorious man of the intelligent class will hardly react to a bit of gossip which would exasperate a not at all conceited peasant. Again, some old proverbs and customary sayings, show a tendency to neutralize the magical influence of bad words by denying them any meaning, by treating them as mere noise, likening them to the blowing of the wind, by assimilating them to the voices of animals of good omen (the dog, the magpie), and by denying that they can reach heaven or God—just as a curse is neutralized. Evidently this neutralization is quite different from a negation of the fact itself stated in the gossip.

All this does not mean that the reaction toward gossip is not now mainly determined by the purely social attitude, only that this social attitude may have been preceded by a more primitive magical one and that the traces of this magical attitude linger still unconsciously behind the explicit desire for social appreciation.

Really I have not words enough to thank, for it is very nice. I wished to take it for my hat, but mother did not allow me; she told me to keep it as a token, and so I did. My Walek, really I don't know any other way to thank you, but when you come, you can ask for something [kisses]. Is it all right?

Then, you write, dear Walek, about some boys of Zagłoba, who are absolutely indifferent to me. First, G. married during the carnival. He got a woman like a *cacko* [originally child's toy; now any small elegant article], so evidently I could not flirt with him for his wife would have seen it at once. It was at his wedding that Stacha got acquainted with her husband, or rather she did not get acquainted, for they have known each other since last year, but fell in love with him. I don't know how true it is, but she told me that they loved each other very much. He is 30 years old. Believe me, Walek, that notwithstanding everything about him, notwithstanding he is quite well to do and rather fine looking, yet his character and his whole behavior don't please me at all. It must be a courageous woman to risk marrying him. Well, but they have like characters and she is also energetic and will not let herself be too much subjected. Well, it will be as it will be. Now they love each other and before the wedding they loved each other also. When Stacha related it to me, I only listened and learned from her. I wondered whence such an innocent being got so much boldness and experience. Well, and soon. The festival was very large, all the workmen and employees were there, and at the marriage-ceremony also, and they amused themselves during the whole night. Some of them were with their wives, and the bachelors flirted on a very large scale with whomever they could. When I dressed Stacha in her wedding-dress, she was so wonderfully beautiful, that I had to say, "If Mr. Walenty saw you now, I don't know what would happen." I teased her as much as I could, for why did she write to you since she had a betrothed? I minded it very much. Moreover she received from you a card with [wedding] wishes which I stole from her. I have it now. Perhaps some day I will adapt a similar one [to the occasion] and send it to you.

Walek, my dear! You write me so much about this Zagłoba. It is true that I wrote you that I felt very gay. Tell me, if I had written as soon as I got there that I was sad you would have said, "If she was going to be worried, she would not have gone." Is it not true? So at first, in the circle of my family who love me so much, I felt gay, but my thoughts are always directed to the place where you are, my W. But what could I write upon a card? Moreover, my sister-in-law could not live without my giving her to read what I write to anybody. Therefore I did not write a letter to you, for as soon as I began to write she read it. Well, what could I do? I did not want to offend her, but I don't want them to know either what I write to anybody, for then she would laugh at me and remind me always of what I wrote.

As to nice boys whom you mentioned, they were numberless! *Nice* boys flirted with *nice* girls, while I behaved as usual. I must boast that if you come you won't know me, I have grown so very serious. I was left behind all the others. I even avoided the honor of being the older [first] "best girl," but was the younger [second] one. I did not want to have a "best man" [accompanying me], but to be only a guest. Well, I succeeded in the house, but not in the church, for one of these "nice" boys came to me and said that the whole wedding group would not allow me, dressed in wedding-clothes, not to belong to them. So I had him as a "best man." This man is the second engineer, a friend of Stacha's husband. But I did not amuse myself much, although it only depended upon myself. Whenever I could I ran home for awhile, and on the second night I slept, while everybody danced till 7 o'clock in the morning. It was no novelty for me; have I been at few weddings? So it was enough for me to have been there [for a relatively short time], because now no parties amuse me any more, they only annoy me.

I will tell you about your photographs also. I asked Stacha to give them to me, but she said that she wouldn't give them up at all, and she did not. She keeps them hidden. And I will write you this also, that Stacha's husband, ten days after the wedding, went to [military] drill for 6 weeks [as a reservist], and she went to him once, for it was not far away, in Pulawy. She stayed there for 3 days in a hotel. She did not want to go, but the old people [parents] drove her out.[1]

I remain, your truly loving,

HANKA

---

[1] Hanka has apparently throughout no reservations and no subtlety of calculation. Otherwise she would have recognized that this information would turn Walek's head again toward Stasia.

717   October 8, 1913

DEAR WALEK: I inform you that I received your card for which—
for which I thank you heartily, and . . . . and [kiss you].   My dear
Walek! I should really prefer if you came.   Then I could explain
[express] myself once, and I think that you would believe in my
feelings, while as it is, notwithstanding my effusions, you always
imagine something, that I betray you, and you always suspect me.
The same about that card I sent you from Zagłoba.   I could not have
written otherwise, for Stacha was there, and I would not let her know
what relations our correspondence includes, for I told her always
that nothing but friendship unites us, and therefore I did not wish to
betray myself.   And even if I had confessed, what could I boast of,
unless something of which I am not sure?   Even if I had told her that
I "love" you, she would surely have asked me, "And does he reciprocate?"   What could I have answered her, since I don't know myself?

For in truth, my Walek, you must agree with me that—I don't say
now, but formerly—when you were still in Rytwiany, certainly not
the smallest spark of love for me glowed in your heart.   I say it from
my own conviction.   When I could suffer no more, I resolved to
confess to you what had tormented me for so long a time.   Well, and
probably from pity, you have tried to reciprocate.   I love you madly
for it, for not having trampled my feelings, for having a little pity on
me.   And I will write you something more; I hope that you will not
be offended with me, as once with Stacha, do you remember?   Well,
long ago I wanted to ask you, my Walek, but I had no courage to do it
sooner.   When do you think of coming back to our country?

You want me, dear Walek, to tell you something about Zagłoba.
[News without importance.]   I don't know what more to write.   If
you come some day, I will perhaps tell you something fresh, for now in
Rytwiany I don't see anything worth communicating.   The eyes
ache to look at this stupidity, therefore I don't go for any walks, but
I sit of evenings and read.   Even so I hear enough of this gaiety
through the window.   I wait for an answer.

Your loving,

HANKA

718   April 22 [1915]

INFLUENTIAL [WIELMOŻNY] SIR: Wishing to satisfy your desire, I
hasten to express my feelings. . . . .

Miss Anna [Hanka] was an ideal girl. She loved me madly, but she was not left without reciprocity on my part. I loved her with my whole heart. She was for me a balm, healing the wounds of my heart. In a word, she was everything to me.

Miss Anna had an unbowed character. She surmounted everything, she knew how to provide against everything, and therefore I loved her. She was given up to me with her whole heart and soul, but during all this time I never provoked a blush upon her pretty face, I never tried to do it.

As to proposing, you know that it is a big question! Without having a position suitable to give one's wife a more or less good support it would be useless to propose. And in spite of all, I have parents far advanced in years, and I must endeavor to help them in their old age and to assure existence for myself. I am not so many years old, and she was also young, so we could come to an understanding, for she felt instinctively that I loved her, that I would not leave her, and everything would come in right time!

And now I must mention that I have a companion with whom I lived in one and the same idea and one aspiration. He had also Miss Anna in his eye, but as he came from a richer family and had a higher instruction than I, she had in mind that it would not be an equal love, and she kept far from him. Her maxim was to have a husband of her own social position. . . . . And I . . . . have temperance and limited myself always to words, personally or in correspondence, for I knew and I know that whatever was for me was not for anybody else. I was always sure of myself.

But, alas! The beginning is gay, but the end is sad. For on February 13, 1914, my dearest being bade farewell to this world and evidently to me also. The news about the death of Miss Anna made upon me the impression of a thunderstroke. I lost everything, nothing is left for me. I am now *alone*.

You can see also from these letters which I send you now how my companions write to me, how they express themselves about Miss Anna and how they regret her, how they persuade me not to grieve. But all this is because of that "tomorrow" [probable meaning: "because I left the country under the influence of social ideals"]. I felt particularly bound by the lack of [liberty of] "word," I aspired for a "free" word, and therefore I left my native country. But I felt deeply this American loneliness.

As to Miss Stanisława, I did not know her until she came on vacation to Miss Anna. She was then 15 years old, she had a higher instruction, was of well-to-do parents, so I did not court her much, for I feared I might be mistaken. When after going back to her parents she wrote a letter to me first, I reciprocated, and later I came to the conclusion that Miss Stanisława was in love with me. Then I doubled my affection toward her [probably: "the expressions of my affection"], but she was so naïve in matters of love that she simply obtruded her person upon me; she wanted me absolutely to marry her. And as I had a companion whom I also loved, knowing well that he had a feeling for Miss Anna, I was ready to yield to him and to give my heart to Miss Stanisława. Once I received from her a letter with the question whether I lived still in "celibacy" and what I was thinking, for she feared to remain an old maid. To this question I remained deaf and cold-blooded.

Then, I had her picture and she had not mine, so for some time she urged me to send her my photograph. As I could not dissuade her, I satisfied her wish a few days before her marriage (without knowing it). And when Miss Anna went to Miss Stanisława's wedding and wanted to take my photograph, Miss St. answered her that nothing was yet lost, "for he can still become mine." . . . . Thus our correspondence finished. Now she lives with her husband well enough, but she has me still in her heart, for I received a post-card from her and I know that she has something in her mind. But I remain deaf to it. Certainly you will agree that she was too naïve. She sacrificed more time to reflecting about love than to widening the experience of her life!

You want to know, respected sir, my opinion, how America influences the Polish girls. You may be sure, not positively, but a hundred times negatively. I have observed it and I observe it still enough to get acquainted with the life of the Polish girls in America, but I have not yet had the luck to meet in America a girl who would be even an imitation of those girls whom I knew in the old country, because few intelligent girls come from Europe, and even if they happen to come they find at once companions who impart to them information which will have a very bad influence on their future, and they soon become tools of demoralization, and so on. And I assure you that I won't marry any girl in America, for it is difficult, very difficult, to find an ideal girl. Every girl upon whom I look has an idiotic, not at all a logical, attitude [sic]! I have not met in America a single girl to be compared with those in the old country. I feel [the lack of] the pleasant life in the old country as compared with America, but I hope that this pleasant life will come back. Perhaps I shall merit that friends will surround me, as formerly. I hope that in the old country I shall still find a companion by the side of whom I shall lead a more pleasant life than now. I have been already long enough in America, but I cannot find, even for a few minutes, the pleasure of social conversation or flirtation. I don't know how it is in Chicago, Detroit, or other cities, but I think that there is no difference, for I can conclude from papers and understand. Here I finish, although I could write much, very much, more, but I fear importuning you too much. If you wish something more, all right. I won't remain deaf or lazy. I would ask you to correspond with me from time to time, for it would be a great pleasure for me, if it is not too difficult for you and if it does not occupy too much of your time. I receive correspondence from the old country, written on various subjects. I will be able therefore to inform you, as far as you wish.

I had some other letters, very important ones, kept hidden, but one of the boarders stole them. Why? What for? I don't understand what they mattered for him. I have still over 100 letters, but they have very little content which could interest you, so I do not send them. I have a girl in the old country with whom I only began to correspond, but now the post functions so lazily that I don't even wish to write! . . . .

WALENTY PIOTROWSKI

719   SICHOW, December 22, 1912

DEAR WALENTY: . . . . I received your letter, but it is rather late, so that . . . . you won't receive my answer until after the holidays. But since I write it before the holidays, I wish you first a Merry Christmas, a gay and pleasant amusement in an agreeable company, then health and every good, light work, big pay, and at last a big capital and a pretty American girl. You asked me to write you how I succeed. Well, I succeed pretty well. I was already a few times in Warsaw [as chauffeur-assistant]. Only, you know, one becomes so muddy and sometimes so cold. When we come to Warsaw, particularly if there is rain and mud, people look at us as at fools, for we are hardly to be seen from behind the mud, our automobile is so spattered.   During the holidays I shall be at home, and afterward I shall go to Warsaw and stay there during the winter in an automobile garage, and sometime in the spring I hope to get a place somewhere and to drive alone [probably as a cab-driver].   If you write [advise] me so, as soon as I come to Warsaw I will try to take lessons somewhere in German, or I will learn alone. . . . . You ask what is the news in Rytwiany.   Well, nothing except that many people have left for America since you went. . . . . The turbine upon the dam is already working.   In the place of that machine at which you were there is an electric motor, and in general motors are put in instead of all the machines. . . . . But how silly, I am!   Why do I talk about the turbine?   What do you care there about any turbine? Well, but listen.   Going once by this electric machine I forgot entirely that I should not meet you there, and only when I saw Nowak and some other boy there with him, I remembered. . . . . I ask you also whether you receive any correspondence from Rytwiany?   Ah, yes, from Miss G. [Hanka], don't you? . . . .

Well, what more?   I have nothing to write you at this moment, only I send you greetings from my parents, my sister, and my brother-in-law.

Your loving and sincerely well-wishing friend,

ZYGMUNT

720   February 10, 1913

DEAR WALENTY: Having now nothing to do because of bad roads, I sit at home.   I am in good health and I wish to you the same. Everything is all right with me, only I am a little offended with your reproaches.   If I felt guilty I would admit it, but since I don't feel guilty of anything like this it is very painful to me.   I received 3 letters and 3 cards from you, and I sent you also 3 letters and one card, and in none I made any such reproaches as you did.   Is it my fault that you must write first a letter to me, and a few days later, writing another letter, you make reproaches already for my not writing to you, while your first letter to me was still on the way?   Only when, after more than 20 days, I received your first letter, i.e., the one which you wrote on November 25, I sent you an answer which you received in the beginning of January.   So during this time you wrote [as you say] these 6 letters and 7 cards, each full of reproaches about my not writing, as if I got these letters in a week's time.   And now in this fourth letter you write that you have sent already 6 letters. I received only 4 and 3 cards, and I have sent you also 4 letters and 1 card, but whether these letters follow one another every week or not, I don't count. I know only that I answer every one of your letters. So why do you fly out, why are you angry and suspect me about things of which I don't feel guilty? . . . .

Your companion,

ZYGMUNT

721   January 22, 1913

DEAR COMPANION: [Letters received and written.] I am in good health and I wish you the same with my whole heart. Now, having no other occupation, we drive beets from Łubnice to Rytwiany with that big automobile . . . . day and night. In our factory there was a wedding and in Rytwiany also; people amuse themselves, profiting from the short carnival.

I want to answer more or less your letter. Well, being working people, oppressed with exploitation in their fatherland, harassed in their native village by the uncertainty of tomorrow, and hearing about this gold-flowing America of their dreams, sure of an improvement of their existence, they go there. But what befalls them? The same, even a still harder labor, sometimes complete lack of work, and then again appears this specter of uncertainty of tomorrow, harassing the man. And such people, being in such a condition, commit often unheard-of things; some of them poison and kill themselves in different ways, others attack and rob merchants and other rich people, and most often they commit robbery and murder upon their own working companions. Such people have still an ineffaceable animality in themselves. But we young men, we ought not to look with cold blood upon the wasting of our bloody labor by these exploiters. Don't think that we alone, the Poles, work hard and are exploited. How many working people are there of English, or German, or of other nationalities! They all have their capitalists, their squanderers, and all this working people constitutes a single invincible power. Only now this working people begins to know this power which it possesses, and by the means of trade-unions it provides itself with capital, in order to be able to begin a struggle with the exploitation. . . . .

Your, always the same, loving companion,

Z.

722   RYTWIANY, January 28, 1913

DEAR WALENTY: Having learned about your present situation, I am very pained . . . . and still more because knowing it I cannot help my dear companion, for I have yet no steady work. I think that besides myself nobody yet knows about your situation, although people know here that you have no work.

So, dear companion, for you, who think more broadly and who are in insecurity about tomorrow, may this present situation be for you an experience for the future. May it be a lesson for you that our mortal enemy is capitalism. May it be at the same time the end of such a life, full of misfortune, wandering, and misery. Yes, dear companion, such is the life of us workers. But our duty is not to let our hands drop impotently, but to make the strongest resistance. So, dear companion, accept these few words of sympathy, as from your true companion. . . . .

ZYGMUNT

723   WARSAW, March 15, 1913

DEAR COMPANION: Let it be so, for I am sure that if I had with anybody else such relations as with you he certainly would not let me call him "companion."[1] And now, dear companion, I want to answer more or less the series of your letters, containing mostly one subject, to which I have never yet answered you according to each letter in particular. So, dear companion, don't be angry with the truest of your friends and don't give too much importance to what I will write you here. You will be convinced that I am sincere. First, dear companion, you do harm to yourself by this your—how shall I call it —this absent-minded behavior. For in writing a letter you are made nervous and distracted by my half-sympathetic, half-cold letters. You think probably: "I love you, I long for you and write it to you so often, while you put me off in any way with evasive letters. It is true that I have your word, which I drew from you once near the machine during pleasant talks, but a long bit of time has flown since then and I want to know with certainty, I want you to love me surely." Don't you think so? Well, and I, when I received your first letter—I confess that it was sincerely awaited—after reading it I felt such a sympathy that if I could I would have flown to you with an aeroplane.

[1] This refers probably to the fact that Walenty is older and was his superior in work.

But alas! I am a poor man who knows nothing, so I hastened at least to comfort you by written words. Meanwhile a second letter comes, then a card, then a third letter, then two more cards, and all these on one subject: "You don't write, and I love you." I give you my word that at last I was even angry, for when I sent you the answer after receiving your first letter, before this first letter reached you I had already 3 letters and some cards, all of them full of reproaches about my not writing. Who will not agree with me that even enchanted lovers would be angry? So you see what results from too frequent writing. And now let us come back to this loving. I tell you sincerely, when I read that letter in which you wrote that you would put all the crowns of the world at my feet, I threw the letter away and did not read further. I thought: "How is it possible to write anything like this?" But after reading all that letter and reflecting, I forgive you, for I let myself often be transported also by feeling, but mostly I prevail over such feelings. So you see, dear companion, after this sharp letter, and you understand it very well; you know even already my idea, for I want you to know it; by the power of my will I want you to understand my idea.[1] And precisely by it you see that I am various [in variable moods?] and why I am various I will describe to you in another letter which I will send you within a short time after this one. So, dear companion, let it be the first letter of our real, progressive correspondence, for this past correspondence was some strain which must have broken in a short time. I finish this letter, for I have no place to write more, but even so you will have much to think over, although it is so short.

Your (*variously*)[2] loving and true companion and friend,

ZYGMUNT

[1] The sense is clear. Zygmunt understands the background of the other's "love-letters" and wants him to understand that those feelings should be suppressed. He confesses having had them himself in a slight degree. All this, nevertheless, should not be taken too radically; most certainly there has never been an actual homosexual relation, and Zygmunt does not allude to the possibility of such a relation, but merely to the *type of feelings* of the other man. Probably the reason of his condemning and controlling those feelings is much more their effeminating influence and the weakening of the power of will which they cause and denote than any moral judgment of the homosexual relation to which they may lead and which is probably not even explicitly thought of.

[2] "Variously" here, as well as above, may mean either that his feelings are not yet quite determined, that sometimes he yields to the sentimental friendship, sometimes again feels more manly and intellectual; or that he is ready to be Walenty's friend only in so far as the sentimental affection is excluded. As he never wrote the promised explanatory letter, we do not know which interpretation is the true one.

724 March 17, 1913

DEAR COMPANION: I ask you whether you received my letter of March 15. This letter is very important, although not finished yet, so if you receive it inform me at once, and I will send you the continuation of this letter, and if you don't receive it try to get it, for it won't be withheld at the post, as it is well addressed and has a stamp. You won't receive any news from me until you inform me that you received the letter of March 15. They wrote me from home that you have sent me a view of a drowning ship [evidently symbolic], but they did not send it to me, they sent me only 2 of your letters and a card. Remember about this letter, for it is very important. I compose already the continuation. ZYGMUNT

725 RYTWIANY, April 21, 1913

DEAR COMPANION: . . . . I will write you about one question which is worth being considered by you. Don't hinder your brother from going to America, for in this way you will be the cause of his bad future. You have no idea how many people went to America and are going still. If you don't take him, he will remain almost alone in Rytwiany, for all his companions will leave soon. You ought to take him, if it were only for this reason, that so many people go to America this spring and everybody gets work, even not bad work, so he would not perish either. I don't know whether it is true, whether you know really all the cities and even all the localities of North America or you only write so. Please don't be angry, but it is only my conclusion from the letters which you write me, criticizing America in every regard.[1] You ask me whether Stach [a common friend who is in America] is working or not. My word! I am really ashamed of you both; being so near to one another, in comparison with the distance which separates me from you, you want me to inform you about each other! Really, something extraordinary must have happened between you, since you are so angry that you do not even write to each other.[2] . . . . And now I inform you that Miss G. [Hanka], according to your wish, saw me, but I don't understand what for. . . . .[3] I resent your

[1] Another example of the difference between the impressionable, sentimental, and unreflective character of Walenty and the more intellectual and equilibrated nature of Zygmunt.

[2] Probably some petty quarrel, easily leading to the breaking of relations with natures such as Walenty's.

[3] Apparently connected with Hanka's conscientious effort to report to Walenty the opinions current about him.

absence in different respects, particularly now in one, i.e., that I am loafing awfully after girls. If you were here you would certainly dissuade me from it.[1] You ask me to send you my photograph. What can I do, if I have no money to have myself photographed? This is one [reason], and the second is that I have more important things to buy [books?] than to spend money on photographs. Excuse me for expressing myself in so hard a way, but man is often obliged to accept even the most painful things.[2] Your brother told me that you intended to send him photographs. Be so kind and put in one for me. And he told me that you have sent already $50, i.e., 100 roubles. This made me reflect, and I was pained, for you write such monotonous letters and never even mention what you do, what work you have, how much you earn. You omit the things which are the most important at the present time.

> Always the same, your loving companion,
>
> ZYGMUNT

But there are moments when he is different.

726   May 14, 1913

DEAR COMPANION: Since Easter I have had no news from you.[3] I waited for a long time for an answer to my last letter from Warsaw, written rather at length. Evidently it did not reach you. For two weeks already I have waited for your wishes [for my name-day]. But you could not guess what news I will give you. Well, you see, I intend to go to America, evidently not immediately, but after some time, when I get more exact information with regard to this. During this time could you try to get for me, if possible, work in some automobile factory?

> ZYGMUNT

727   Warsaw, May 29, 1913

DEAR COMPANION: I beg your pardon very much for not having informed you about anything. It was because of different reasons

---

[1] The homosexual background of the friendship is evidently strong in Walenty, but this passage probably means no more than that the sentimental friendship of the two men would exclude other sentimental relations.

[2] Knowing the importance of the photograph in the psychology of the peasant and the working man, this is an indication of the degree to which Zygmunt is emancipated from the traditions of his class.

[3] The effect of letter 723, which evidently offended Walenty.

which happened during my stay in Rytwiany. So you see, dear companion, what this feverish correspondence can lead to. You always suspect me of such stupid things, about which you ought not even to write me, and you always write one and the same, as if it were my duty to listen to it and to answer you correspondingly. If you feel the need of unbosoming your ailments before someone first reflect whether it is possible [suitable] to unbosom them before anybody. But I see that you don't reflect at all about anything, but if something does not please you, then in your opinion it is bad, but only in your opinion, you may be sure. But in answer to these complaints I advise you to get acquainted as well as you can with the actual problems and institutions, and in general to read scientific works. Advice like this has been given to me, and I give it to you.

Now I am in Warsaw and I work in a garage. I earn 50 copecks a day, and the Prince gives me lodging. . . . . And if you analyze the whole thing you won't wonder if I tell you that in the beginning of my work I had an impression under the influence of which I did not want to live upon the world. But it was only the first moment, and after considering the matter everything got changed and everything goes on well enough, only I have a very long distance to go to the work. . . . . I don't know whether you received the postcard in which I asked you to try to get some work for me in America. But I beg your pardon now, for I must still remain for some time in Warsaw. Write me whether you will take your brother to America or not. You have sent your photographs home and to Miss G. [Hanka], while I asked you and you don't send any.

Your loving [companion],

ZYGMUNT

728   June 1, 1913

DEAR COMPANION: I received a letter from you sent to Rytwiany, so I answer you at least on a simple postcard, for not long ago I sent you a letter. As to this that you write, that American life is not agreeable to you, it is to be seen even on your photograph that you lie, for you look even better than you did in our country. Finally, why should we complain to one another about our troubles? We are young, so we ought to try to get on the best possible, for what will be later, when we grow older if we complain now when we are young? You write me that I may know how you are living. But if I write you how I am living you will surely say that you are better off in America than I am in Warsaw. Certainly, I earn enough to live [to board], I have a place to lodge. Well, but I need clothes, and I won't give myself totally up to this work alone; I want to study, and nobody will give me books gratis. I won't sit [at home?] like a man who knows neither how to write nor how to read. Well, and then I must change my heart into a stone and write: "Dear parents, send me money," while I know that it is my duty and it is time for me to help my parents, instead. . . . . So don't be angry, dear companion, if I teased you sometimes, for you know what it means to be forced against one's [will]. Let us then stop mutual complaints, for it does not suit us. Instead of writing bad things only, rather let us inform one another about good ones. Describe to me this theater in which you played a part. . . . .

ZYGMUNT

729   August 8, 1913

DEAR COMPANION: I beg your pardon very much for having offended you during these last times in writing you nothing, but excuse me, for I don't depend yet upon myself, but I must still be subject to these stupid laws and absurd institutions for some time, because I am in training. I should wish nobody to be in training in such conditions as I find myself at present. It would need much writing if I wished to describe all this, while I, my dear Walek, have as little time as you can ever imagine. Some day when we meet we shall relate to each other the impressions and troubles experienced during this time. And now we ought not to let our hands fall impotently, commending ourselves to destiny, we ought not to lose hope, and we ought to keep a strong will, for if we lose all this and doubt everything, then it will be still worse. We must think that we are not alone in bad conditions. How many people suffer a hundred times worse than we do, and nevertheless there are many among them who defend themselves with energy against this bad lot. Should we, young men, ever doubt about carrying out our plans? No, we have never doubted and won't doubt that youth is strength, the more so if it is organized and unified; then it is a power which yields before nothing.

And now, dear companion, I shall at last describe to you my conditions, how I spend my time and what company I have. As you know already, when we were still in Rytwiany we all three wrote, I, Stach, and Henryk, to Uncle Wincenty. You know him probably from our talk—the same who learned in Belgium and who is forbidden to come back to Russia. So we wrote to him asking him to help us, by correspondence, in self-education. He had a job and probably no time, but he sent us the address of a lady, his good friend and companion from old times, who is now a private teacher. The lady showed a great readiness to give us advice and information; she even sent us to Rytwiany a few very good books. But although I knew her by letters for more than half a year, I never had any occasion to see her; when I was in Warsaw, she was abroad. Now she is also abroad occupying the place of a teacher. Not long ago she made me acquainted by letter with one of her friends here in Warsaw. It is a young man of 20, son of an official; his father is no longer alive, only the mother is left and receives the pension. This young man has two younger brothers, they are all studying, and he, although so young, has finished 8 classes already [a gymnasium]. But I got acquainted with him before he went away for the summer to the country, and now we only correspond with each other. After so short an acquaintance we are already "companions." And if you are curious in what way we became companions, write to Stach and let him send you a letter—the first which I got from this companion—in which he expresses himself for the first time as my companion, and at the same time informs me about different questions.[1] I had no time to describe to Stasiek my acquaintance with this companion and sent him that letter, but I don't know whether he received it or not, for I send him letters without stamps, in the same way as to you. So, as you see, I have relations with good men. For think of it, how should such a highly educated man enter into relations with such a dirty and moreover ignorant boy as I am? And nevertheless he, being such a man and coming from a higher family, was not ashamed, but came to the shop and in getting acquainted with me shook my dirty hand. So it is possible to conclude that there are still good men in the world, since such a man became more generous through his studies. For usually men now get instruction for business, in order to exploit the ignorant ones, which is ignoble. . . . .

[1] The importance attached to these apparently trifling facts—the use of the term "companion," and the condescension of the student in shaking hands—by a young man of Zygmunt's solid character shows how profound is the difference between even the middle class and the workman class.

You ask me how I spend my moments. If I only had as much of these moments as I need! You can guess that if I had more of them I would write to you more often. . . . . And now excuse me for making a small remonstrance. But don't be angry. You write me that you belong to an amateur theater, but that you don't find in it good company [amusement?] because of some feeling. This reminds me of romantic novels from old times, when men did not know yet how to govern their feelings; but men who are in such conditions as ours ought to govern any feeling, particularly for such a good thing as an amateur theater. All associations, amateur theaters as well, are useful for our end; it is our duty to give them as much good will and energy as we can. You see I receive advice like this from my new companion who does not spare it to me. . . . .

I remain your loving companion,

ZYGMUNT

How about your romance with Miss Stasia or Miss Hanka?

730   August 15, 1913

DEAR WALEK: I cannot take part in the solemnity of our parish-festival. I wish at least to write a few words home on this day of August 15. How painful it is to spend the time far away from our native country, and still more painful on a day which is solemnly celebrated in our native country.[1]

And precisely while writing these few words to my parents I received your card, in which you inform me about the wedding of Miss Stasia. But probably the wedding is already over, for it was to be on August 10. You guess probably that this news made upon me not a small impression. But precisely on that account write me what she could have written you. I am very curious.

You ask me to write you something about Warsaw. I can write you only this, that Warsaw is full of various kinds of revelry and drinking. If a woman's body can be bought, well, then you can get everything for roubles. But besides all this Warsaw has also good men and good things, as, for example, this companion . . . . about whom I wrote you already. . . . .

Your loving companion,

Zygmunt

[1] This paragraph discloses Zygmunt's attitude toward religion, as stated in the introduction. A socialist like S. Jasiński (cf. that series) would certainly profit from the occasion of this parish-festival to write a declamatory invective against the stupidity of the people—the priests keeping them in "darkness" etc.

September 18, 1913

DEAR COMPANION WALEK: I beg your pardon, but I will make a reproach. Why have you written nothing for so long a time? Are you embittered against me, or do you want to vex me in this way, or perhaps to gratify me? Oh, don't ever think that you will gratify me in such a way; be sure that slowly we should get accustomed to it and at last we should forget each other. So, dear Walek, I beg your pardon, for I am conscious that sometimes I forget you, but I forget you only to remember you again, to remember those times of our acquaintance and of our friendship then so strongly linked. But these times passed, opening before us the road of our life, wide but full of thorns. But are we to let our hands drop impotently and commit ourselves to the will of fortune? No! We are young, we have great strength and energy, therefore we ought to go forward boldly and perseveringly, pulling the thorns aside from our road. Yes, dear companion, a hard fate threw us away from our native country, so far, leaving us a remembrance pleasant and dear to our heart. But if we want to understand all this and to give ourselves an account of it, we need learning.

My training goes on well enough. If I can only hold out for some time everything will be well. Now I have inscribed myself for the evening courses of a technical school.

Stach wrote to me that everything is not well with him, and nevertheless he does not lose his hope, but looks always confidently at the intended aim. Oh, how unjust fortune is for having thrown us about the world so far from one another! Nevertheless, we shall be able to bear everything.

So, dear companion, let us renounce all these suspicions, all these [complaints about] pains caused by one to another. Have we not pains enough in our struggle about tomorrow? We have even too much of these different contrarieties and misunderstandings, and it would be bad of us if we continued to act so. What wonder if in the present conditions one does not write to another for some time? Instead of it, one writes, after a longer interruption, really sincerely, truly, with effusion, rapidly and longingly.

So—I beg your pardon once more—be cheerful, don't ever lose hope and strong will. You know, I am very curious and I should be glad if you described to me your whole romance with Miss S. [Stacha] G., and how it ended. Or perhaps it is not ended yet. . . . . .

I send greetings for all our acquaintances from Rytwiany, our native nest, but still dark enough. The function of spreading our enlightenment in our native nest belongs to us, as to its sons, who look upon the wider world. . . . . I send you a hearty handshake.

Your loving companion,

ZYGMUNT

732   October 27, 1913

DEAR COMPANION: I received your letter in which you express [relate] to me your secret. I was very grieved, dear companion, and I sympathize with you. Forgive me, please, if I recall something from the past. Do you remember at one of our meetings upon the dam I said to you something in this sense about your romance, which had only begun then, while you assured me that nothing like this would happen—that I should not even think of it? And still my guesses were just, though I never guessed that anything might happen like this which has happened now. I did not guess it, for I counted more upon her. Who could indeed have suspected anything like this from such a serious young person? But, dear companion, I confess that I don't wonder. Knowing already life more or less and human relations, it does not seem to me strange at all. But in any case notice how weak in spirit are these women. Only consider it well and you will see that any of them is as weak as any other. Oh, excuse me, dear companion, but I express myself like some conservative critic of *love*, of these youthful impulses, of this beauty of youth. But, on the contrary, I am a partisan of it. How beautiful, how simple it is! Should I be a persecutor of love? Oh, no, I am not this! And do you know, dear companion, that when I received that letter from you I had such a wish to write her a letter that would give her back the past assurance which now has fled away, a letter which would render her more firm, more strong in love, a letter which would incite her to confront the greatest impediments and dangers in order to reach the point where the heart beats warmer.[1] But after considering it reasonably I could not do it. And you consider it also reasonably and act as you think the best.

---

[1] The whole paragraph refers to the marriage of Stasia. We may be sure that Walenty in appealing to Zygmunt for sympathy did not represent the incident frankly. To him, indeed, any preference of another man would seem in Stasia infamous.

As to myself, besides the usual work, all the evenings of the week are occupied with study, so I have often not even time enough to satisfy the indispensable needs. Forgive me, therefore, if I don't answer your letters at once. Do you know, dear companion, how attractive science is, how great, how much it forces us to think about ourselves? Great things, simply miracles, can be seen in science, things which in the future will be of ordinary use to men. But evidently it must be first more or less known.

As to my environment and society, I have a good, intelligent, and instructed society, which I imitate and benefit much from, for I receive from those generous men scientific help. But bad environment is not lacking either; I find myself in it during whole days. . . . .

[Your] l[oving] c[ompanion],

ZYGMUNT

733   December 7, 1913

DEAR COMPANION: [Excuses himself for not writing.] You will wonder probably why I complain so continually about lack of time. I must inform you at least partly about all this. You know already that we have a [maternal] uncle who finished the university while he was a simple locksmith. He read many books, knew intelligent men, he benefited much, understood the necessity of learning, and decided to go on in this direction. Really he undertook great labors, but with the help of very generous and instructed men he attained his aim. And now, as a licensed engineer, he advises me and wishes me, since I want to learn, not to wear myself out working for my bread and at the same time learning of evenings, as I do now. He was able to finish the university although he began to learn when he was already about 30 years old, and only with the help of strangers who lent him money for living and instruction and to whom he now pays back, in parts, the debt contracted. And I am still so young, and I don't need the help of strangers, since I have so rich a [paternal] uncle. So why should I weary myself so, while I could go to some technical school and after finishing it be an instructed and intelligent proletarian? I should really not even be a proletarian any longer, but being from proletarian extraction, I would not be ashamed even then of proletarians. But you see, my uncle refused me this. I am even ashamed to confess that I have such an uncle. Although we know how much he has he was able to say that he had only enough to give instruction to his son and to live in his old days.   And I did not want any gift from him; I wanted only as much as I need for studying and for living during my studies.   After finishing the studies I would have paid back the debt either to himself or to his son.   And would it not have been very profitable for me and a noble act of citizenship from him?   I am very pained, not so much because he does not want to help me as because he does not understand it; he is still so dark and backward.   Therefore I must weary on now in this way.   The studies take my time until 12 or 1 o'clock in the night and in the morning I must rise at 6:30, for although my work begins at 8, I have so far to go that I must rise sooner.

Well, enough of these complaints and these contrarieties of which our life is composed. . . . . The Christmas holidays are not far away, holidays which awaken in all of us children, far away from their families, dear remembrances of the past years, of the moments spent in the family circle.   But things are now taking such a turn in the world that not all children can spend the holidays in their native homes.   I am very pained to think that you and Stach belong to these. And so on the approach of the holidays I wish you to spend them merrily, and also I wish you that thought which comforts you when you remember that you are so far away from your home.   Excuse me for expressing my wishes upon ordinary paper, but be sure that they are warmer and more sincere than others, written upon showy material. . . . .

Your loving companion,

ZYGMUNT

734   March 5, 1914

DEAR COMPANION: . . . . I am now in Warsaw, I am working as before, only in another shop.   The conditions are somewhat better and the work much nearer. . . . .

I think you know already that Miss G. [Hanka] is dead.   I was leaving for Warsaw on the very day of her funeral.   It was very painful for me not to be at the funeral, but nothing can be done; duties and conditions oblige a man to act. . . . .   I regret Miss Anna very, very much, for she was one of the good, model girls.   Well, but nothing can be done, we must persuade ourselves of it in some way. And now I will mention to you something about Kalina.   As I wrote you, we met once accidentally at Rytwiany.   We walked for a long time about the factory, talking a little about old times. When I asked him whether he was corresponding with you, he answered that he had not corresponded for a long time. I did not ask him why. . . . . He then told me only that Miss G. had been very sick, but was already better. But I learned afterward that he called on Miss G. during the whole time of her sickness, and before her death, i.e., a few days after our meeting, was there very often. I have been told that she, feeling very feeble, asked him to go away. Then he began to cry, so that later they both cried about themselves [or "about each other?"]. Really a very painful rôle was played if he was really in love with her.

Well, but enough of these sad things. Now I will write you something about myself. First, I go to courses in the school, and for 3 subjects to my acquaintances who are absolutely good to me. I have one course in the school about machinery, another under the title "How to Keep Health during Work," i.e., in general a course in hygiene. It is very curious and interesting. Besides this I receive from my acquaintances very scientific books and papers containing many things of which I knew nothing. Only now I begin to take a wider look about the world. If we met somewhere I should have much to tell you. It is difficult to write all this. So I only advise you with my whole heart, don't waste your time, but try to read social things, for in reading about any science you will be able to explain to yourself many, many contradictions of life. . . . .[1]

                                                    ZYGMUNT

735   April 7, 1914

DEAR COMPANION: After so long a silence at last I bring it about to write a letter. . . . . It could seem as if the subject of our

[1] This and the following letters, except for the reference to Hanka, do not contribute any new incidents but show the progressive development of Zygmunt's self-consciousness and social idealism, and thus help to understand the type of man. This type is and was very frequent in Poland in association with the development of national and socialistic ideas. Up to the last quarter of the nineteenth century it was limited almost exclusively to the intelligent classes, and the social idealism assumed mainly the form of nationalism. Since 1870–80 the type has become frequent among workmen, in connection with socialism. Since about 1890 it has become more and more frequent among peasants and assumes the forms found in the newspapers *Gazeta Swiateczna* and *Zaranie* (cf. Part II). But, as our collection shows, it is both less frequent and less thoroughly developed among peasants, probably because of the stronger economic and traditional determinism. This type and the corresponding type among women will be more systematically treated in Part II.

correspondence were exhausted, as if our correspondence were declining. It happens thus with most friends who after separating for some time, get accustomed to it and finally forget about each other, about the friendship which united them formerly. But this happens only between friends who are not conscious of themselves, who gave themselves too much up to fate and fate precisely tears the bonds of their friendship. But you, dear companion, don't suppose that this should ever happen between us. You see, I was silent because just now is the time of my great effort to understand, i.e., I am reflecting about all the phenomena which are found in the course of the day and which interest me very much. Up to the present I am able to explain many things to myself, to judge many things and to appreciate those which are good.

I am only pained that whenever I receive a letter from you it is always full of some sadness, always full of a great longing. It is therefore not strange if every such letter influences me painfully. So it is my duty to provide against it, realizing that I am your friend but one whom fortune set upon a different way.

Well, dear Walek, give an account to yourself, of what circumstances obliged you to emigrate. Did you go of your own wish or were you really forced to it? Then reflect well what was the difference between your home and your new system of life, and if you suffered because of it was it not possible to remedy it, and in what way. You see, you can draw a lesson from your own life. Meanwhile you grieve and complain so endlessly that even a man burdened with a wife and children would complain less. I know, my dear, that you are pained by the actual relations between men and by all this arrangement. But you can persuade yourself that it is a powerful strain due to the development of everything, and without this development nothing could be done. Capitalism develops, immorality and degeneration develop also, but at the same time science develops on a great scale, a great self-consciousness develops among workmen, and in general everything develops. Should we stand with broken hands and grieve? It would be absolutely unsuitable. It is time to shake off these old prejudices. Why, you are young, and true youth is not subject to these prepossessions. . . . . If you can, read some day Mickiewicz's "Ode to Youth" and reflect well about it, for it serves as a watchword for the young people of lower and higher schools in Warsaw. . . . .

ZYGMUNT

736   May 4, 1914

DEAR COMPANION: I inform you that I received two of your letters which I answer only now, for they were at a short interval. . . . . In the first you write me about your trouble, your loneliness, and every letter is full of some sorrow, some doubt in your force and your intentions. Is it not time to leave this sorrow? It is of no benefit to us at all, but on the contrary, we lose much through it. I repeat, dear companion, we lose much through it, for even if our tendency were realizable it would never come to an effect through our doubts of its realization. In the same way, you remember perhaps, when Moses led the Israelites and, wanting to do a miracle before the Israelites, struck three times a rock from which water gushed out. Why did he need to strike three times, since the water could have gushed out the first time? If you have learned it you remember probably that Moses doubted the first and the second time that the water could gush on his order. This comparison will appear strange to you, for Moses was an envoy of God to liberate the people from slavery (I suppose you will think so). I don't deny it, but does slavery not exist now? Still worse, for there exists a spiritual slavery of whole masses of people, and thus a man conscious of this slavery has to wait for this mission. The main cause of our sorrow is that we always think and complain about our own distress. But if we saw not only our distress but also that of other people and if we tried to help them, we should forget absolutely our own. In that case we should say that we think socially. O dear companion, it is very beautiful and lofty to think socially. The people who think socially and give themselves up to social problems, forgetting about their own, reach great things. I should like very much, dear companion, to make you understand as well as possible, so that you might think differently and not grieve, but one is not always able to express what he wishes. . . . .

ZYGMUNT

737   RYTWIANY, February 14, 1913

DEAR WALEK: . . . . I thank you for not forgetting me. . . . . I beg you, dear W., be so kind and write me a letter and describe the news there in America . . . . and whether it seems to you better than in Rytwiany, for I am tired of staying in Rytwiany. . . . . I work in the same shop, but it is very boresome, for you know that old beggar [his superior], how he is; so there is not a single quiet day. I must bear all this for some time still, and next month . . . . I will ask for an advance. I don't know how I shall succeed, but it seems to me that they will give whatever I ask, for in winter good work opens up, and they have no men. And now you know perhaps that Władek M. got married. . . . . The wedding was first rate, people of higher class alone, few friends, for that Hela of his wanted it so. . . . . The music was the kind we had a better variety of sometimes years ago. Three musicians played, two violins and a drum. I don't write you any more about it, for I don't know; they got married, they embrace, and it goes on well up to the present; what the future will be we don't know. I don't know whether you received the cards which I sent you, two of them. In one I wrote you that I intended to marry during carnival, but it was only because I had nothing to write upon such a small card where there is not even space, and I wrote you this in order that you might have something to laugh at, for I know how you talked to me about my intentions. But up to the present I still remain the same. If I go away I don't know what will happen with us both, for up to the present we love each other madly and when we meet we give a kiss. But now we don't meet often, and I don't go to her home; we meet only upon the street, or when she goes to the church. And all this because many misunderstandings happened with her mother, and my sister does not go there and she says that she probably won't ever go again. . . . .

Now I inform you about the illness of Rog. She was very sick because she wanted to poison in herself a small engineer who is to come into the world. The younger of those two who were in Rytwiany in your times made it. He promised to marry her and did whatever he wished with her. At last, when he could not get rid of her after this, he had to go to Warsaw and calmed himself ["gave no news" or "died"?] and so she was left a widow.

And now I inform you that we both, I and Zygmunt, will receive books from my brother, who was in a school in Belgium. These books are to be instructive in our specialities. So now I think more about studying a little, and later perhaps I will go to him, or if not, then to you to America. We haven't the books yet, but we expect them from day to day, and if I receive them I will begin again to love books and will think about them more than about my girl. But I won't leave her as long as I am in Rytwiany. . . . .

HENRYK

738

DEAR COMPANION WALEK: I beg your pardon for not having answered. . . . . There is no news in Rytwiany . . . . only I inform you, though probably you know it already, that Miss G. [Hanka] is dead. I was at the funeral. . . . . I saw Kalina, for he was also there. We talked a little about you, among others. He asked how you are succeeding there in America, for he said he had had no letter from you since you left. . . . . As to Stach [the writer's cousin], he certainly has forgotten about me already, for I don't know what he is doing there and why it is so difficult for him to write. But I am not eager either to write him the first, and positively it won't happen, for I know that now one can sooner profit from a stranger than from one's brother. But I don't care for it at all; let him do what he wants, I won't go to him for anything. [News about work and factory.]

And now, as to the girls, they all sit like hens upon eggs and wait to see how soon the happy moment will appear for them. But it is not so easy. They will sit for some time still. I am still with my Halka as before—sometimes bad, sometimes good, moments, but still nothing is certain in our affair, for we have many impediments. So I behave as I can and as is suitable for me, although, as you know, I am very much in love with her and I should like the things not to pass away so lightly, for now she begins already to confess a little her reciprocation. But her mother does not please me, for she has a mouth rather too big, and therefore she likes sometimes to cause a misunderstanding. If anything results from it you will learn it, for I shall write you everything, but only about May or June. Up to the present I don't know anything, only I guess, but nobody can know somebody else's thoughts. Well, but probably it will end about those months, one way or the other. . . . . And now I inform you also about her sister, that in May will be her wedding with Mr. C. There is yet no certainty, for the divorce-suit is to be ended this month, but he is sure to win, and we shall dance in May.

I have nothing more to write, for you will be even weary with reading this; you will say that these are only trifles, nothing serious. Well, don't believe that I think it; I described all this precisely because I know that you like to read and to know everything.

Your loving c[ompanion],

HENRYK

739   [April, 1913]

DEAR WALEK: . . . . I received your card and letter. . . . .
I inform you now about my success. I work as before. I received
an advance on April 1; . . . . I have now 20 roubles instead of 16.
. . . . I asked for 25, but they gave me only 20 for the present. . . . .
I must still push my misery before me for some time in Rytwiany.

As to you, dear Walek, you tell me that you have already heard
there that people here speak badly about you. I am astonished, how
you know immediately in America what is going on in our country.
I won't write you much, for you would think that I laugh at you, but
it is true that I myself heard people saying that you are nowhere
satisfied, when you were in Rytwiany you only looked for easy bread,
and just so they think that if you are in bad conditions there it is
because you don't wish to work. They say that you do nothing
there, that you loaf about and think that it will drop from heaven.
But excuse me if I dare to write so about you. I won't say any more,
for you would be very angry. But don't mind at all what they say
about you, for now you can whistle at them and they can do nothing
against you there.

As to me . . . . I was a little angry with my betrothed, as you
call her. For a month we did not speak, but during the holidays we
made apologies and now everything goes on well, as before. But we
see each other very seldom, only on holidays, for, as you know already,
. . . . Zygmunt brought books from Warsaw, and now I don't loaf
about any more of evenings, but read. I don't go to her house, but
when we meet on the street we talk a little, and nothing more. Her
older sister is marrying . . . . that German engineer who was here
when you were still at home, ... and if I don't leave Rytwiany
my wedding will be next spring, and only then I shall live with a wife.
But if I leave, then everything will be lost, like a stone in water, for
I hope to go to my brother abroad. . . . .

Your loving,

HENRYK

740   April 16, 1914

DEAR COMPANION WALEK: . . . . You say that it is painful for
you that I don't write, but I wrote 2 letters, ... so certainly letters
don't reach you. In my first letter there was much news, among
other things that Miss G. was dead, and in the second various local

news. . . . . I don't forget either what we talked before separating. Don't think that I am forgetting you. I considered you my first companion when you were in Rytwiany, for as to these companions whom I have now, I don't care much for them, except Miciek. I keep very little company with them. I stay mostly at home, and if not in my own home, then with my girl. But things go on very badly with us; every short time some anger comes. Just tonight, when I am writing this letter to you, there is again some misunderstanding with her. But I don't know how it will be further. Sometimes, when it is all right with us she arouses in me so much love that I should be glad to give my life for her. I don't understand whether she only excites me thus or it is a fact [that she loves me]. But, as it seems to me, she has fallen very much in love with me, for if I go anywhere or talk with any other girl, I don't know what becomes of her and then she gets angry. I won't write any more about her, for I don't know how it will turn out. [Indifferent news.]

And now I beg you, tell me about America in general, everything. How do the workmen stand there, how do our Poles behave in America, what girls are there, whether they are worth something or nothing. . . . . I have heard here that you have there very good [pleasant] society. . . . . And inform me whether it is calm there or they are thinking about some trouble, for there is always something new. . . . .

HENRYK

741 October 26 [1913]

I begin my letter with these godly words "P[raised] b[e] J. Ch."
I sit to the table,
I unfold the paper,
And I write a letter.
I don't write it with pen and ink alone,
But with a sweet heart, a dear diamond.
My pen wrote
My heart wept
For it has not seen you since long ago.
[Generalities about health and success.] We wish you also health and good success from God's Mother of Sulislawice, whom you did not see—how she was crowned. May this God's Mother help you in that America. We received your letter on October 24, for which we thank you heartily. . . . . When I read this letter I wept so that I hardly

could read it, and father and mother also, for [we were touched that] you don't forget us. [News about family and friends.]

I describe to you what a church festival we saw, such as perhaps nobody will live to see any more. Our Lord God allowed you to live at this time, but nothing can be done, since you did not see it. But I was there and I will describe everything to you, as to my dear brother. There were 250 priests, two bishops, and so many people that it was impossible to see over them. They conducted the Holiest Mother, and four orchestras played behind the procession when they brought her to a pavilion beyond Sulislawice. And the pavilion was so beautifully adorned that the heart burst open with regret [emotion]. The priests sang alone and the bishop crowned God's Mother, and the whole people lay crosswise [arms extended] upon the earth. Priests carried this image, and lords and peasants, everybody a little. I am unable to describe to you, dear brother, this miraculous festival.[1] Our vicar was with the company [of pilgrims from the village]. We lead him, in a crown. We have now such a nice [handsome] vicar. Priest Kow. went away. He said a mass for the whole parish and asked us to greet all you who are in America. He wept during the mass, and the people in the church wept so and were so crowded around him that he could hardly leave us.[2]

Remember, dear brother, don't marry in America, for I should like to be at your wedding, for I rejoice about you as about my own brother, and still more. I should be glad if you were at my wedding, but I don't know, for mine will be probably during the carnival. And to your brother girls come themselves—such luck he has among girls. We were at his name-day in his house, but we said to ourselves: "It is not the same as with Waluś." There were guests enough, but he is not the same as you are. . . . .

[A. P.]

[1] This part of the letter is one of the best expressions of religious feelings which we have. Particularly the influence of the ceremonial and that of the crowd, leading almost to ecstasis, is most naïvely manifested. It shows the extent to which the influence of religion in peasant life depends upon aesthetic and social factors.

[2] The personality of the priest plays an important rôle in religious life. We have seen in other series the influence of the personal factor upon the attitude of the peasant toward church and religion; this influence is still more manifest in the letters to the newspapers, for it grows with the modern religious evolution.

742   January 3, 1914

DEAR BROTHER [COUSIN]: [Usual greeting, wishes; letter and photograph received.] I am very glad that you look so beautiful upon the photograph. Everybody wonders much. Please inform me whether you look really so as upon the photograph, or not, for my father takes it always and looks [wondering] that you don't seem like yourself. Only, dearest brother, you look very sad and I was grieved that you were sick. I beg you, dear brother, when do you intend to come to our country? For I should like you to be at my wedding, and if not, then perhaps at my funeral, for this is more probable than the wedding. But I beg you, write me. I long for you, dear brother, for we have not seen one another for very long and I should like to see you alive. Although I see you upon the paper, you don't speak to me. [Weather; holidays; news about friends.] Come, dear brother, to our country, for it is our beloved country, and perhaps you are homesick there and sad, and here you will have whatever you need for eternity. Our priest said that there is not long to wait until the end of the world. You have a father who is old; it would be sad if you were not at his funeral, for your brother is not like you; everybody regrets you, while many complain about him. [Greetings.]

                                                        A. P.

743   May 26, 1913

DEAR *Swat:*[1] I speak to you with these words: "P[raised] b[e] J. Ch. and Mary, the Holiest Mother, queen of the Polish crown." [Health, wishes; letter received.] And now I inform you that there is no news with us, everything is as it was, only Rytwiany seems empty and sad. But on the other hand in this beloved month of May we borrow mirth and a soft comfort at the feet of God's Mother of Incessant Help and we live with hope from day to day. Dear *swat*, you did not write whether the May service[2] is performed there, at least on Sundays. And then, you look very sad on the photographs. [News about family.] I have nothing more of interest to write, dear *swat*, for there is nothing; sad and tedious, as usually in Rytwiany.

[1] Literally "matchmaker," "bridesman," *swat* is used here to indicate an indefinite near relation.

[2] A religious service performed in the evening during the whole month of May, in honor of Mary.

[I have] no beauty, no money, it is difficult to get married, but may thy will, O Lord, be done. . . . .

Describe to us everything in detail after receiving this letter, what is the news, did you marry, and who got married there. [Greetings and wishes.]

JULA

744　　　　　　　　　　　　　　　　　　　July 12, 1913

DEAR WALENTY: [Beginning as in the preceding letter; health, wishes.] Praise be to God for your good success. As to the longing [homesickness] about which you complain, this longing will leave you soon, for people say that wherever is bread and well-being there the man has delight. [Weather; crops.] I am always equally bored in this Rytwiany. I should like also to go to America, but they [the parents] won't permit me. . . . . You promised us to describe exactly the conditions in America, but you don't seem to be in a hurry. You did not deign to write us either in what sort of factory you work and what your work is at present. Excuse me, dear *swat*, for requiring too much, but all this is because if one is not somewhere one would like to do everything. I am very curious why Marylka does not write to me, for I have had no letter from her since long ago. Surely she has a big society. You must also have a large society, and it is very praiseworthy. . . . .

[Greetings from the whole family.] Greet Marylka also from us all, embrace her and kiss her in my name as many times as she will let you. . . . .

JULA

745　　　　　　　　　　　　　　　　　September 12, 1913

DEAR FRIEND: [Beginning as before.] We inform you, dear friend, that there is a papal jubilee appointed for a whole month, from August 15 till September 15, and in the diocese of Sandomierz full absolution is granted for being 6 times in a church and confessing. And then, on the solemn day of birth of God's Mother [September 8] a crowning of the image of God's Mother in Sulislawice has been performed. The weather was splendid, and the meeting numerous. There were 3 bishops, 150 priests who took part in the crowning, and 180 companies [of pilgrims] came from all the sides of the world. The crowning of the image was performed in the field, a pavilion was built $1\frac{1}{2}$ versts from the cloister. The image was taken away from the altar, and with great solemnity and ceremony they proceeded to the pavilion—the whole train of clergy, princes, nobility, and all. The bishop of Sandomierz celebrated the full service and delivered the sermon in that pavilion, and after the ceremony of crowning the image was taken back to the cloister. We send you a small image [photograph] in the new crown; you will learn better details about this crowning from the papers. And then, dear Walenty, our friend, we inform you that Rytwiany will be scattered, for they are making "colonies" already and they are very much against us, the *komorniks;* they want absolutely to drive us away from these sands and from Rytwiany in general, so we don't know what will happen with us. You say that I have a boy and don't write you anything about it. Well, I know nothing, and I am very curious whence you got the news. As to Marylka, I answer every letter, but she is now occupied with her boy and does not deign to write me. Please congratulate her privately from me about her [future] marriage. . . . .

JULA

746   June 18, 1913

. . . . "Praised be" [etc., usual beginning; health; wishes.]

DEAR SON: We inform you that we received 2 letters, ... for which we thank you heartily, for we learned many curious things from these letters. Dear son, you write us that you have no money. How could you have money, since on the letters alone which you write about the world you spend perhaps 3 or 4 dollars a week. Write to us as often as possible, but don't send letters everywhere about the world. Only think how much money has gone already on these letters. Dear son, you grieved us in writing that you had no money. It is bad, dear son. As it seems, therefore, you won't send your debt back in time, for the end of the year [since you borrowed it] is not far, and you write that you have no money. We are glad that you are in good health and that you earn more now, but this grieves us, that you have no money. For if you put a few dollars aside and instead of keeping them, send them here, you would have more. Having $50, if you send them here, you would have 100 [roubles]. Dear son, you write that your boss likes you. Surely you must treat him with drink very much, and therefore he likes you. Whatever you earn, you pour out [liquor] for this money into him, and therefore he likes you, and therefore you have no money. You tell me not to send you either a pillow or tea. I should have a great pleasure in sending them to you, I should like to gratify you, but what can I do when there is nobody through whom [I can send]. Mańka and Stefan S. intend to go, but they prepare themselves for the journey like Jews for a war [proverb: slowly and unwillingly]. And even if I sent it through her she would do the same as Szym. did, for she is a terrible idiot, totally stupid.

Dear brother, you write me to leave my work here. But if I leave this work who will work? Father is old, and he works hard. Everybody tells him: "You ought not to work so hard, you have two sons, one here, the other in America. You ought to sit at home.". . . .

Dear son, don't be openhearted [generous], for openhearted people have empty pockets. You write us, dear son, about your dream, but I don't know what I dream and I don't describe it to you, for it is not to be described. Once already I opened the door [in a dream], for you called through the window, but you did not want to come in. Then I cried till the morning. . . . .

[Your mother],
W. P.

747   November 9, 1913

DEAR SON: . . . . You write that the food does not taste good to you. But from this consumption may seize you in a short time, so put some money aside and come back to our country. . . . . You write us that you are in good conditions. What is the goodness if you cannot eat? We inform you, dear son, that from America there came back [enumeration], and that on November 3 at noon 2 houses were burned, Chmiel's and Jastrząb's. On Monday they were burned down, and on Tuesday Chmiel got his son married. . . . . They baked cakes and smoked sausage during the whole night, and probably from this the fire arose.

But if you knew, dear brother, how much groaning and weeping there was! You have no idea. The hair stood upon one's head. The people of whole Piaski knelt and begged for a change, that our Lord God might stop the calamity. But nothing helped, what was to burn was burned, and we saved the other houses, for I am now in the fire-guard. . . . . Three days later a man died who had been frightened by the cries of the wailing people.

Wojtuś wrote that $30 has been stolen from him in America, so be on your guard lest somebody circumvent you. If you have money, hide it; let nobody know about it, not even your companion. . . . .

W. P.

LIPNIACKI SERIES

Letters from a manor-owner, G. T., to his former employee, Lipniacki, probably a farm-clerk, who must have played some part in the revolution of 1905–6 obliging him to go to America.

This kind of relation between a manor-owner and his servant can arise only if the manor-owner is unmarried. The woman introduces at once the question of class-distinction, which makes such an intimacy impossible and removes the main factor of familiarity—the solitude of country life. In this particular case the intimacy is favored by the fact that the manor-owner is old and sick, does not leave his house, and receives few guests. Perhaps the revolution, in which both are interested—the servant openly, the master secretly —creates a new tie between them.

748–56, FROM A MANOR-OWNER IN POLAND, TO HIS FORMER
SERVANT, IN AMERICA, AND TWO LETTERS FROM
A FARM-MANAGER TO THE LATTER

748   Rysiów, July 3, 1908

Mr. Jan: I received your last letter from Swansborough, ... and then for some months there has been no news at all, so that we made different suppositions . . . . —that you went to Australia, were sick or even dead. In the winter the blacksmith M. started the rumor that he had met you one evening in the forest. We thought that you had returned secretly and didn't show yourself, wishing to learn first what is the news. Your father came to us, thinking that perhaps you were hidden here. Only at the end of March or in April, Stanisław [the farm-manager] received the works of Sienkiewicz and we guessed that they were from you, for there was not a word, and the wrapping was so torn that only the address, written by a strange hand, remained intact. No wonder, for they tore it first at the frontier, then in the censure through which all the books must pass. We could not find even the stamp.   Only a few weeks ago we received 7 cards from you from Baltimore. . . . .

You write that in October you will go to school.   All right, learn, for learning is always useful.   But your project to join the army does not seem good to me.   First, the time spent in the army is lost. Then, in the United States military service does not pay, they consider the army to be a throng of sluggards and spongers.   Finally, in a few years a war between the United States and Japan will surely break out, as a result of commercial rivalry, so you may lay down your head [perish] for a foreign business.   [Death of the writer's friend and neighbor.]

In our neighborhood things are more quiet, although in the Kingdom and in Warsaw attacks still happen.   Every town is full of constables.   In Michów there are 12, in Kamionka 12, in Firlej 8. The suit about Kaluzyński is not yet settled.   I hear that [the accused] excuse themselves by saying that it was you who made most of the trouble in Firlej.[1]   You are searched for by [advertisements in] papers.   Near Lublin there are still attacks of bandits.   A week ago, during a fair, a dozen farmers were robbed and one killed.

Stanisław has sold a part of your clothes for about 40 roubles, and lent the money at interest.   He still has the rest.   People say that he asks too much, and don't buy.   In your home everything is well. [Describes his sickness.]   Now, after 4 months, it is better, but I cannot stand; two men raise me and seat upon a rolling-chair. . . . . My fingers are quite cramped . . . . but I can still hold a pen or a spoon. . . . . But probably all this will end soon. . . . .

G. T.

749   August 13, 1908

MR. JAN: I received your letter yesterday and I answer you at once. . . . . As to "Kazio," I would not advise you to write about him for two reasons.   First, I have no possibility of ascertaining whether it was he or somebody else among this company who talked about you, and what was said about you in general.   What I heard comes from different persons who may for some reasons tell untruth, but there is a great probability that [the prisoners], wishing to defend themselves and counting upon it that the government can do nothing against you and that you won't come back to this country, put their

---

[1] It was usual in political trials to put the blame on any one of the number who succeeded in escaping the authorities.

own guilt upon you. . . . . And then, it seems to me that ["Kazio"] in particular has some favors from the authorities, for his affair stuck in some strange way and nothing is to be heard about it, and there are also other things which show that he belongs to the s[pies]. People say so; perhaps it is not true.

In the beginning of July there appeared in Firlej 5 young men two of whom killed a police officer and a constable, ... the third killed the lawyer M., and the last two fired at other constables in the town, but without result. . . . . Some dozens of men have been arrested in Michów and the neighborhood, and all of them have been taken to Warsaw in irons. Probably they won't return any more, at least not soon.

If people say here different absurd things about you it can be explained by two causes. First, your going to America makes them think that you ran away from some punishment, and again, you have quarrelled with many people, so they speak absurdities from anger. There is one man, and of the intelligent class, who says that all these who have served with me [on my estate] became bandits.[1] Whence such an opinion? He has been no more than a year in this country.

In your home there is no news. Your father was here and asked about you. I told him you had written that everything was well with you. Your friend, the locksmith Zdunek, is dead of consumption. You ought also to be careful, for remember that in your family two persons died of consumption. . . . .

I greet you heartily,
G. T.

750   October 17, 1908

MR. JAN: . . . . I have sent you 60 roubles. There was not so much money got for your clothes, but I sent more, supposing that slowly more will be gathered. . . . . After this card which you wrote about the slaughter in Firlej a new police officer came to us and asked Stanisław who wrote it. Stanisław answered that he did not get any such letter and did not know who wrote it. But the policeman said that they knew that you had written it. What wrong had these men who were killed done to you? Why did you rejoice in their death? So be more careful in the future. You wrote it without thinking, and

---

[1] During and after the revolution of 1905–6 many plain robbers assumed the rôle of revolutionists and many revolutionists (especially after the execution of their leaders) dropped into banditism. This situation will be treated in **Part II.**

here they annoy the persons to whom you wrote. The information of the papers about the murderers in Firlej was false. In two houses near Lublin some bandits were killed, some arrested, and among the latter, two confessed that they had killed the constables in Firlej; the revolver of a dead constable was found with them. . . . . Lately there was an attack upon the manor in Krasinin. They stole some money and jewelry and wounded the proprietor with his own gun. The attacks upon governmental liquor-shops and upon inhabitants in their houses, and highway-robberies do not cease. . . . .

Why do you spend money in subscribing to a paper for Stanisław? Probably you have not much money to spend yourself, and Stanisław cannot demand such gifts from you. [Weather; crops and harvest; cholera in Russia; farming news.]

Jaś Górnik [a manor-servant] became stubborn and went away for the second time. Later on he wanted to come back, but I thanked him [refused]. Now he is marrying a widow of 36 and will have at once a boy 6 years old (there were more, but they are dead). But the widow has 600 roubles, people say. Well, may he only not be deceived, and get the money of which he is so greedy. The woman, I hear, is a loafer and in spite of her 36 years runs to musics [dancing parties] and after boys. But he seems not to mind it if only she has money.[1] May he not be deceived like Kozik, who was to get 500 roubles with his wife, got nothing, and now beats his wife for it. [Enumerates his house-servants; news about neighbors.]

The new priest in Rudno, Tel., is very kind, and people like him. They decided to give money for repairing the two houses and building a new one for him. . . . .

I greet you,

G. T.

751

January 11, 1909

Mr. Jan: Being in bed for three months, I have had no possibility of answering you. Now, sitting again in the rolling-chair, I take my pen to thank you for your last long letter in which you describe the farming in America. Well, the customs change from land to land, but evidently the people work better than in our country. [Describes new murders and robberies.]

---

[1] As a farm-servant, particularly a teamster like this one, has little chance to put enough money aside to buy land, and as land-hunger is a prevalent feature of the true peasant, such a marriage does not prove that the man is avaricious, for the idea of land-property is not a purely economic factor.

Górnik has married the widow, almost twice older than himself . . . . and now he loafs about and weeps for marrying her.

The priest Tel. left Rudno and moved to Opole, to a better parish. He began to repair the houses but did not finish it. Another priest came, an old man with a numerous family—with the organist and beadle 18 persons. He does not enjoy a good opinion. The parishioners did not want him and say that they won't give any money for repairing.[1] And one of the houses is almost ruined. The other is without doors, windows, floors, stoves, or ceilings. I don't know how it will end. . . . .

G. T.

752 February 24, 1909

Mr. Jan: I received your letter. . . . . In the post-office there is a parcel for Stanisław and they make trouble about delivering it. Perhaps it is books from you. But why do you spend money in sending gifts? . . . .

The affair of "Kazio" & Co. was judged a month ago by the court-martial in Warsaw. They were all declared not guilty in this affair, but have been sent to Russia for belonging to the socialistic party, except "Kazio," who did not belong to any party. [New robberies; some bandits caught.] It is only strange that all these bandits are caught by the detachment of police sent from Lublin, while the local police . . . . has never yet discovered any of them [because bribed]. . . . .

Stanisław has sold of your clothes to the amount of 54 roubles 68 copecks; there are still left 25 collars, 5 pairs of cuffs, 1 bedsheet, 5 pillowcases, a yellow waistcoat, a summer overcoat, green trousers and vest, 4 neckties, almost all the shirt-buttons, a pair of scissors, a comb, envelopes, photographs of girls [probably actresses], a hat, a box, a valise, a pillow, a lamp, the books, *Secretary* [models of letters], *Sexual Life, Atlas of Russia, The Honeymoon,* and 5 small booklets.[2] . . . .

I greet you,

G. T.

---

[1] This paragraph, connected with the corresponding one in No. 750, shows to what an extent the attitude of the peasants toward the priest depends upon the personality of the latter.

[2] The enumeration shows clearly that the man was a coxcomb in his social sphere. This is typical for a farm-clerk, who is generally an unmarried man (when

753   May 2, 1909

MR. JAN: . . . . Stanisław will buy the books for which you asked when he goes to Lublin. But why do you need the book *Bezwyznaniowość* ["Freethinking"; literally, "being without a confession"]. Whoever does not believe does not need the book, and I think it is not you, for since you ask the priest in Firlej for a mass, you must belong to the believers. . . . .

For a month there has been a new judge in Michów, sent by the government, a Russian, Mr. Trabuchow, elder of the Don-Cossacks. He walks dressed like a Cossack, with a sword at his side. He punishes severely. He fined Okoń [a peasant] 20 roubles for having taken a piece of wood from the governmental forest in Lubartów, besides the value of the wood. A peasant said, "Thief" to another. He got a month of prison, etc. But as it is a Russian judge, and moreover a soldier, the peasants sit quiet and say nothing. He called on me and said that he would keep the court in order. He forbids the assistants to go to beerhouses with the parties, he dismisses constables when they don't keep order. In short, he is full of energy. . . . . The peasants now regret the deceased Mr. Zaleski. As long as he lived they did with him whatever they wanted. . . . . Only now they understand what they have lost.

Katarzyna, our cook, whom you certainly remember, was often sick and wished to leave. Stanisław searched for another in her place. When Mr. K. called once upon me Stanisław asked him about Marcela, whether she was in Jawidz. He answered that she had found a boy and must leave, because she expected an addition [child]. I tried to learn what became of her, according to your wish. I heard that she went to Kock, where she is now, and whether there was or will be something [immoral], people don't know. At any rate, whatever has been, such things are usual. . . . .

                   I greet you,

                       G. T.

———

he marries, he tries to get an advance and to become a farm-manager) and being in a superior position and better dressed and educated than the simple teamster, has a good chance with the farm-girls. He wears clothes and ties of the most extraordinary colors, uses very strong perfumes, has always a stiff collar, which the peasant wears only on Sundays, uses pomade on his hair and beard, copies pretentious love-letters from special handbooks, etc., and by these means exerts a great influence upon girls.

[The following, No. 754, is composed of passages selected from letters of various dates.]

754 October 18, 1909

MR. JAN: . . . . I have been in bed again until yesterday, and therefore I did not write to you. . . . . What was the reason of the bluff about your coming back? If you wished to make a joke with other people, never mind; but why did you lead me into error? I was troubled, thinking that after your return you might be arrested. I don't say that you are guilty.[1] But you emigrated to America, and people immediately concluded that you must have taken part in something. And as you did not lack various enemies, who pretended to be your friends as long as you were here but attacked you as soon as you left, you might have been arrested and kept in prison for a few or for many months, until the matter was cleared, for although the state of war is abolished, there is still a state of "strengthened protection," which is almost the same. . . . .

[June 25, 1910]

Although you are already a grown-up man and you have your own reason, don't be angry if I warn you about your matrimonial intentions. Remember that you may easily wander alone, in case of necessity, from place to place, but with a wife and children it is difficult, often quite impossible. And then one does not know what to do with this pawn. It is easy to get married, but it is very difficult, if not impossible, to get unmarried again. . . . .

[February 8, 1911]

Your preceding cards informed us laconically that you traveled, but you did not write what for. It is very agreeable to travel for the pleasure of it, but I know from my own experience that it costs very much. Did your financial position allow you to do it? We are not curious to investigate your mysteries, but if it is not a secret we should be glad to learn where you have been and why. . . . .

Different people ask here sometimes for your address. We answer that we don't know. Shall we give it or not? . . . .

Among the people who are serving with us probably you don't know many now. . . . . Perhaps you remember that small boy Konrad who came to Marysia from Łukowiec. Now he is 18 and is

[1] He evidently was so in political matters, but the writer pretends to be ignorant or writes in this way fearing the letter will be opened by the police.

my waiter, together with another man. He is a good and clever boy. Wójtowiczówna married Kozioł from Baran [pun: the man's name means "buck," the village's, "ram"] and they get on miserably, for they are both poor. Andzia launches herself powerfully [is dissolute]. Her younger sister Felka is serving here since New Year, but surely she will go home, for she is in a very romantic mood and I am afraid it will happen as with Kukrzycka, who left on January 1, thick [pregnant]. . . . .[1]

G. T.

755

June 5, 1909

RESPECTED SIR: . . . . There is nothing new and nothing good with us. The judge [the manor-owner] is very bad; he coughs worse and worse, he complains about pain in the lungs, and in general he is downhearted and dissatisfied. For, indeed, everything is going on so badly. The spring is awful. Nobody remembers such an other. The flowers and tomatoes froze on May 24, there was such a frost. . . . . My bees are almost wasted through this accursed cold. . . . . Now it is a little warmer, but what of it since there is no rain and the wind blows and dries everything, ... and it is to be expected that the whole summer will be awful. But what can we do against it? We are not strong enough, and we must wait for God's mercy. . . . .

Your father is in good health. I hear that he is plowing the new land. . . . . I see him seldom. Sometimes he comes to learn whether you wrote to me. He asked for your address, but I could not give it to him for I did not know myself, and I think that even now I won't tell him, for perhaps you don't wish it. . . . .

Mr. Zaborski lived in the winter in Oziora's house. He complains much, the poor man, about his wife; he says that he is the most unhappy man in the world. Well, he chose her himself and had known her perfectly, and he was caught in this way. . . . . He has bought a place in Sobolew . . . . built a rather nice house, fenced the garden, moved the beehives. Sobolew looks now very nice from far away, for seen from near, there is enormous misery, stupidity, and ignorance. It does not go forward, but backward, to the oldest savage customs. . . . .

STANISŁAW L.

[1] Dissolute sexual life in manors is much greater than in villages, partly because the opinion of the community is not so strong, since the community is unstable, partly because the girls are more independent of their families, and, in general, because the opportunity is greater and the control looser.

756   January 24, 1913

RESPECTED SIR: I will give you a little information, whatever I can. [News about acquaintances, such as] Madejska got a boy; the child is dead, and she married some man from Kock. Stefan G. went to the army and did not come back; people say that he married a Russian. Julka B. married Majcher and lives on poorly in the colony. Her brother Stefan is finishing the eighth class [gymnasium]. He is very clever, and will probably go to the university. . . . .

I send you inclosed a letter from your father. I did not give him your address. He comes often, asks about you and complains that you never write to him. You could do him this pleasure. Why, it is always a father's heart [in spite of his faults].

Two months ago the priest of Firlej died suddenly. His parishioners have stolen everything. A woman took even his trousers, and when they were taken away from her she said that she took them as a remembrance of the priest. Such is the culture in our country. . . . .

STANISŁAW L.

JASIŃSKI SERIES

The particular interest of these letters is connected with the fact that their author is a peasant who through his instruction and his social and political ideals has gotten completely outside of the peasant class and has degenerated, physically and morally, the double strain of intellectual life and of a complete change of social and moral attitudes having proved too much for him. The question whether a peasant will be able to keep his equilibrium upon a new basis of life depends, of course, upon the rapidity and the character of the change. A peasant like Wacław Markiewicz has indeed an entirely new sphere of intellectual interests and convictions, but through his occupation and his family-relations he retains enough connection with the peasant life to preserve his balance. A man like Maks Markiewicz, or any peasant who by his culture and occupation passes into a higher class, even if he loses his connection with the peasant life, gets into an environment which has a moral and social organization different from that of the peasant class but still strong enough to keep the new member from degenerating. (See Markiewicz series.) Zygmunt, the friend of Walenty Piotrowski, was already prepared to accept to some extent many of the new ideals which were given to him, and continued to adapt himself gradually. (See Piotrowski series.) And again in other cases there are elements in the new environment which were already latent in the old. Thus, for example, peasants and workmen do not lose their moral self-control when belonging to revolutionary parties with a patriotic character, because patriotism is always latent in the lower classes. But in the case of Jasiński none of the factors which are able to preserve equilibrium in a new sphere of intellectual and moral life was present. Unlike Wacław, he has no connection with the peasant life; unlike most of the climbers, he did not get into a class with a strong traditional organization to which he could adapt himself, but into a circle of socialist-revolutionaries whose norms of conduct are still somewhat fluid and whose set of ideas is not elaborated thoroughly enough to organize intellectual life as completely as it is organized by religion among the peasants. Jasiński was a country teacher, and as the schools provide no preparation for change he was probably introduced into a new sphere of life without the proper preadaptation. In this respect he differs from Zygmunt, who introduced himself into a new sphere informally, and through the selection of his personal relations. Finally, the system of Polish national ideals does not seem to influence Jasiński strongly. Note his relation to the Russian socialists.

The matter is quite different with a man of a higher social class who becomes a socialist. He is accustomed to a greater individual autonomy in intellectual and moral problems and is therefore much more able to keep his equilibrium upon the slippery ground of revolutionism. But the peasant's intellectual and moral life has always been so absolutely controlled by public opinion that individual autonomy cannot take the place of social control if the latter is lacking. And Jasiński in this respect is in a worse position than most of the socialists, for he is for long periods isolated from his companions.

It is interesting to observe how the peasant, in a kind of half-conscious moral self-defense, endeavors in every new environment to find some substitute, however imperfect, for the lost system of social traditions; how he tries to have some kind of social opinion upon which he can lean. In the present case Jasiński is in his socialistic ideas a perfect echo of his party. His very words are typical formulae, repeated identically innumerable times by socialists from the lower classes, particularly by women, who share with the peasants this imitative tendency. Not a single personal note rings in them. It seems as if the peasant wished to extract and to assimilate from socialism everything that is fixed, determined, commonplace, traditional—as if he sought in this fluid milieu the greatest possible stability. And at the same time he adapts himself rapidly to a new socialistic group (to the Russian socialists during his exile), which shows precisely that the choice of his ideas is not determined by rational consideration, but merely by his environment.

757–64, FROM S. JASIŃSKI, IN POLAND AND RUSSIA, TO WACŁAW MARKIEWICZ, IN AMERICA. NO. 764 IS A LETTER TO MARKIEWICZ FROM ANOTHER SOURCE, COMPLETING THE CHARACTERIZATION OF JASIŃSKI

757   ZDWÓRZ, May 17, 1906

DEAR MR. WACŁAW: I don't know what it means. Have you forgotten about me or what? Neither letter nor even greeting. One sees at once that you are changed into an American, occupied only with calculations about your business. . . . . But never mind, I like it. We all ought to break the stupid and simply idiotic European ice and [stop] lying, because no honest understanding can be reached by formalities, only empty lying to one another, and imbecility.[1]

And now I describe to you my lot.

I left the prison of Mokotów after 3 months, on April 20. I have suffered since then real torments. First, I was obliged, against my convictions, to send a petition that my place might be restored to me, for people gave me no job.[2] It is true that they had none. Then

---

[1] This ideal of absolute sincerity and abandonment of formalities was developed among Polish socialists under the influence of Russian socialism, which was rather strong during the revolution of 1905–6. American life is here viewed through the prism of this ideal.

[2] The sending of the petition was "against his conviction" as a socialist, for the position depended either upon the government, or, more probably, upon the National Democratic and Conservative parties, for it seems that the school was supported by the Polish School Association, which was controlled by these parties.

in Z. I had trouble with the old mean and abject beast—old Palimoda, who uses different arms against me. As he could do nothing else against me, he slandered me to the mayor, whose boots he licks [in original an indecent expression], because he wants to borrow money from the communal bank. Then he contrived with the manorial spies and wrote a complaint against me to the National Democratic party. In short, it would take whole quires of paper to describe the meanness of such a man-beast. And why? I feel no guilt in myself, unless it is that I wanted the good of the community.[1] In a word, a general reaction had set in; the National Democratic party was victorious at the elections in Poland, in Russia the Constitutional Democrats. But the end is not yet. The devil knows what will follow.

I always want to go to America. I thought I should go surely now, but since I got the place again, I am waiting from moment to moment. But the wish remains to go, to go the soonest possible. If some misfortune befalls me—for different things can happen—I shall go at once. When I come I will send a telegram to you asking you kindly to meet me. Meanwhile please answer me whether it is easy to find a job, what are the conditions—lodging, boarding, work, pay, journey. Could I hold out [at the work] or would it be difficult? Please tell me this, for in our shriveled and impotent Europe a somewhat more energetic man has nothing to do. In order to live, one must have the mind of a goose, the patience of a stone, and be an ox—devout, obedient, polite, etc. . . . .   ST. JASIŃSKI

758   KADNIKOW, PROVINCE OF VOLOGDA [RUSSIA]
                                        February 1, 1907

DEAR COMPANION WACŁAW: Only yesterday I received your letter written in June last year. . . . . As you probably know, after 33 days of liberty—if this can be called liberty—I was arrested once more, and this time condemned to be exiled to the government of Vologda, [the exact place] at the decision of the governor. I passed during this time through different prisons, *étapes*, and adventures, starting from Gostynin, via Kutno, Warsaw, Praga, Minsk, Smolensk, to Moscow, where I remained for a month, lying sick in the central prison Butyrki. There I had the time to get acquainted with many

---

[1] The story concerns probably some local struggle between socialists and National Democrats and is exaggerated by the writer who seems to be somewhat hysterical and to have a slight mania of persecution.

Russian revolutionists and parties.   On June 30, I was transported to Vologda.   Here I was at first designated to live in Solwyczegradsk [far to the north], but I made a petition and the governor sent me instead to Kadnikow, 47 versts from Vologda.   Here I have lived for 8 months, without any occupation, like all the political exiles. There are 170 of us here and 70 more escaped.   I should have done it long ago if I had money.   In the beginning we got from the police 2 roubles 70 copecks monthly for living, but after a demonstration from all the colonies of the province of Vologda they began to give us 8 roubles, then 7 roubles 70 copecks, and today only 7 roubles 40 copecks.   Live, as you can, upon this. . . . .

It is difficult to describe what I passed through during this time. I mention that I was near to sending a bullet through my head to end this once for all and to get peace. . . . . But slowly all this cleared up a little, and now I live, giving myself quite up to the study of social and political sciences and of Esperanto.   I already read novels and newspapers in this language.   I sit the whole day in the cabin, for the cold here, falling to 40° R. below the freezing-point, no longer permits even walking, for the feet and ears freeze.   I expect to remain here not longer than 2 months.   We shall see what the new duma does, and then I shall give myself amnesty.   Even if we get it I could by no means live in our country, for I cannot even earn enough for black bread.   I have Paranà still in view, but to go there one must have at least 300 roubles, while I haven't even a single spare rouble. . . . .

Your condition there is now probably good enough, for the strikes have passed and the factories are going full speed.   Moreover you are better acquainted with the conditions and you belong to the socialist club. . . . . Could you not do as the Russian proverb says: "Take a thread from everybody in the community, and the naked man has a shirt," and send me a ship-ticket to my old address?

You will say that it is not noble of me to fly from the battlefield. But I answer that the field for activity is as wide there as here, and I can do much more there than here, being half-legal or illegal [under suspicion].   Think and answer me the soonest possible. . . . .

ST. J.

P.S.   You complain of capitalistic oppression and religious and national separatism.   It is true.   And therefore the Russian revolution won't limit itself to taking only the liberty of which you know the consequences, but will have the people take all the land, the factories, the capital, and will introduce, first in the east, holy socialism. After it the other nations will follow. A near future will show it to us, and we, the proletarians, shall yet admire and live in a socialist society, which for tens and hundreds of years has been screened from us by all the religions with their gods, and the states with their laws and armies.[1] I am very much astonished that the people there [in America] are still so religious and on the side of the *pops*,[2] at the mention of whom I think of the middle ages and the holy inquisition. Is it so difficult to overcome this with the liberty you have? I don't think so. It is true that English people are very religious, but today this ardor, I believe, is subdued even among them. I should like to write you very much here, but unhappily the lack of space does not permit me, so I limit myself to what I can put here. Do you correspond with anybody? Do you learn? Did anybody write you about me as about a heretic, a godless man, a socialist-revolutionist or even anarchist, whom in the name of God the base old Paliwoda and Bala delivered into the hands of justice?[3] So it goes on in the world, my dear. Not long ago we were almost all together, and today Mil. is in W[arsaw], Zal. and Zold. in Argentine, you in the United States, I in Vologda, etc. What a fate! Does there not stick one general cause of all behind this—liberty and bread!

Yours,

St. J.

759 March 16, 1907

DEAR WACŁAW: I received your letter just now. . . . . I thank you heartily for having . . . . offered me your help in such a difficult moment of my life. I did not write to you sooner, ... first because I did not know your address . . . . and then I believed that upon American soil you had become an idealist of the dollar, as most of the Americans . . . . and I thought that it was not worth while writing. I was very much mistaken; I got a lesson, never to judge anybody beforehand. . . . . It would be better to send money instead of a ticket, for if I should not go I could easily later send the

[1] Socialism became in Poland (still more in Russia) a new and perfectly typical religion. Here this is quite naïvely expressed.

[2] *Pop* is the Russian popular name for an orthodox priest. In Poland it is now an extremely contemptuous word for priests in general.

[3] Here, as in the quarrel in the last letter, we have a trace of the mania of persecution.

money back to your parents, and if I should go, I could choose the ship I wanted. . . . . Then write whether I could get some job there, manual or intellectual, be for example, a teacher, a clerk, or perhaps an agitator, a reporter. . . . . If not, I shall direct my eyes toward Paranà, New Zealand, or Australia. . . . . I should advise you to get acquainted with some Russian colony in America and to study the last works of Tolstoi, and many other things. . . . . About any amnesty and in general any peaceful negotiations with the government there is no question at all. . . . . Soon the judgment of the people on the bureaucratic and bourgeois order of things will begin. . . . . Now a moment, a great moment is coming for Russia. . . . .

STANISŁAW JAS[IŃSKI]

760 PETERSBURG, July 21, 1907

DEAR COMPANION: I write this letter to you, but you don't know what is going on at this moment with me. You see, I am in Petersburg. I came here hoping to go abroad, but as far as matters have cleared up during my journey, I cannot go further. I see it myself. I have entirely given up the plan of going to America, for I see myself that there is no place for me either there or in South America. I am totally "out of tune" nervously, my memory does not act at all, I cannot work, I am quite unfit for the struggle for life.[1]

As you know, I was accustomed to live in a different manner, and today I am obliged to adapt myself bitterly. It is painful indeed, but never mind, I count this as life's experience. I am looking for an occupation. It is a question whether I shall find it, and even if I find it there is the other question of the passport.[2] I am lying, but I don't know how long I shall succeed. I have still 10 days' time, and I have some hope, though very small, that I shall get something by lying. If I don't succeed, I shall be obliged to return and to sit quietly [in exile].

Almost one-half of the money which you sent me will be spent. What shall I do if I don't find a place? Will you abuse me very much if I cannot give it back? Say, I don't want to wrong you, but what can I do? I am convinced that if I dare to go to you there will

[1] The breakdown is rather sudden, and the explanation seems to be that however miserable the conditions of life in exile, he did not in fact have to struggle for life, but when suddenly faced by the problem of work he collapses.

[2] A political exile has a passport which permits him to live only in a designated place, and he must report to the police on appointed days.

be nothing of me. I shall be totally unable to work, and why should I be a burden or a trouble to you?[1] I fear it, and I prefer to die here, for things are bad with me. I live meanwhile, waiting for something, with a companion-runaway who has something like a job, but the gods pity him! What is his life worth? He is a clerk in a bourgeois lawyer's office for 20 roubles a month, and for this he must be everything also in the line of politeness, for [the employer] asks him to reach him cigarettes, etc. It is sad, but true. To be a servant, a

[1] The relation of the two men, the "intellectualist" and the workman, is here perfectly typical for certain kinds of characters and conditions. The high appreciation which the half-educated or uneducated Polish peasant or workman shows of any intellectual superiority (particularly when the latter is not allied with a too marked class-distinction, which makes it then appear too *natural*) and in general the importance which instruction receives in Polish society, makes this kind of relation rather frequent when an instructed man, even if poor, weak, or immoral, comes into a near relation with rich peasants or with workmen. The result is parasitism in various degrees. The case has been witnessed hundreds of times among socialists. The workmen supported their leaders and speakers quite disinterestedly and individually (not from the party-funds). On emigration to the United States, to Brazil, to Western Europe, almost every colony of workmen or farmers has such temporary or permanent parasites—half-instructed "intellectuals" who scorn or are unfit for any physical labor and live at the expense of the laboring people. The case is particularly frequent on emigration, because in that case a man can hardly earn anything by intellectual work, and because the intelligent Poles who emigrate are recruited, with a few exceptions, from the least valuable elements. The attitude of the peasant or workman toward such an intelligent parasite is very curious. It is a mixture of real generosity, compassion, admiration, contempt, calculation, and vanity, in the most various proportions, depending upon the character of the parasite, his conditions, the degree of appreciation which the uninstructed man shows for instruction, etc. In general the uninstructed man (besides purely disinterested motives, which are never lacking) is at the same time glad to show off before his companions his intimate relation with a superior man, and in his relation with the latter is glad to show his own superiority in economic matters while acknowledging the intellectual superiority of the other. Sometimes there are also services which the intelligent man is expected to give in exchange—letter-writing, some teaching, entertainment. But mainly the benefit which the peasant or workman expects to draw from him is the enlightening influence of his company. Unfortunately the same attitude is often assumed toward really useful and intellectual men who come into contact with the peasant and workman—teachers, agricultural instructors, journalists, etc., with the exception of the priests. This is manifested most typically in Brazil, where every man who goes with ideal purposes is treated by the colonists, more or less benevolently, as a parasite, and thus loses the opportunity of exerting a serious influence. In Poland itself this attitude is found wherever the consciousness of the value of instruction is only half-developed.

slave for a few poor grosz—it does not conform with my character. And whose servant? Some exploiter's.[1]

I will see what can be done, but please don't consider it a crime in me if it happens that I cannot give you [the money] back. I did not wish to cheat you, I intended to do without begging anybody, but unhappily I cannot get on any further. You know me, that I never wished and don't wish any wrong to anybody. Write me, please, how you are succeeding. I am pained. I have paid back the whole amount of money borrowed from the priest. Perhaps I shall pay back yours also. . . . .

St. J.

761   August 3, 1907

DEAR FRIEND AND COMPANION: Two weeks ago I sent you a letter with news of the breaking up of my plans. Now I have received your letter. . . . . My health does not improve, I live in a "black melancholy" or neurasthenia, which expresses itself in a physical weakness of the organism. I am terribly nervous, I get easily tired and every trifle annoys me. When I am in such a state nothing interests me; I can do nothing. Even writing a letter is difficult. . . . . I consulted a physician, he advised me to nourish myself well, but alas! He said that it came from abnormal conditions. I expected to change my conditions by leaving Kadnikow, but it proved that I cannot go further than Petersburg. I have been here for 2 weeks waiting for my passport. I got it by lying, but what is the benefit if I have no job and cannot get any. There are hopes for some 15 to 20 roubles [a month], but imagine whether it is possible to exist upon it, when lodging alone, a corner [in a room with others] costs 5 roubles. I was at the teachers' association. They told me it was possible to get a place as teacher, but near the [North] sea-shore, in the province

---

[1] It is a peculiar feature of many men with high social ideals in Poland—and not alone in Poland—that while talking and even acting most sincerely in the interest of a high social end, and while making sacrifices for it, they neglect simple duties of honesty in everyday life. They seem to feel exempted from the common morality by the fact of their superior morality. In Russia the same feature can be observed in an exaggerated degree. The source of this discrepancy seems to lie in the loss of moral equilibrium which new ideals, particularly revolutionary ideals, brings to an unprepared and insufficiently preadapted consciousness. The radical and drastic expression of the loss of this equilibrium is found in the conversion of revolutionism into banditism—a situation treated in Part II.

of Archangel . . . . among Samoyeds, or in the province of Vologda, among Zyrans, for 12 roubles a month. And what a place! I did not even thank them for such a proposal. I will still appeal for protection to one place which is not very promising. If I don't succeed I think of going back to Kadnikow, adding something to the governmental expenses and living there for some time. In the Kingdom [of Poland] it is very difficult to earn one's living, and I don't think at all of going back. As to Galicia, it is a good place to learn, but only for those who have money. . . . . And so, dear Wacław . . . . here it is bad, there it is not good. . . . . Were it not for your money, I would have taken to stealing long ago. I cannot "expropriate" [rob], for I don't know how to shoot. It is bad to be a man good for nothing. As to Petersburg, it is a colossus glittering with gold, but on the other hand terrifying with its misery and drunkenness. There are good things, schools, libraries, but [the influence of] all this is not to be noticed among the public. Everything governmental smells of militarism, everything private of exploitation, cynicism, and frantic enjoyment of life. I don't wish to insult the Russian civilization and culture, but except the samovar and the *rysak* [Russian breed of trotting-horses] nothing else pleased me. These two things merit attention. Well, yes, and the singing. . . . . The song about Stenka Razin . . . . lives up to the present among the people, ... as well as about Pugaczow.[1] The revolution of today waits for precisely a hero like these two. We hope that moment will soon come, for time feeds the masses with hate which grows at every moment and which must express itself at last in terror and destruction. And then, although many will fall, a new world will blossom, and there will be bread enough for everybody, no more misery upon the streets, fewer weak and sick people. I believe in it; this is my religion. I believe in science, the leader of mankind. I believe in the brotherhood of peoples. Let us work as long as we can.

Yours,

St. J.

Don't be angry and don't abuse me if I spent one-half the money without your permission. If I live, I will give it back, and if not, then, although you won't speak well of me, don't speak badly. I kiss you and embrace you.

[1] Leaders of popular Russian revolutions in the seventeenth and eighteenth centuries.

762   KADNIKOW, March 10, 1908

DEAR FRIEND AND COMPANION: I received your letter . . . .
which was for me a true surprise, for I thought that you were angry
with me for life and death.   All this [friendship] is very well, but up
to some time [to a certain point] particularly when the question is a
material one.   Then friends become enemies, and states make wars.
I thought it likely that you occupied the same standpoint with regard
to me, for I got no answer to two of my letters from Petersburg,
except this letter, in which you don't mention whether you received
those letters or not.   You must know that this question is not yet
settled, and even today I am delaying about sending this money back,
for in the spring I think of going away from here. . . . . My health
is much improved, and one of these days I will go to Vologda and
ask the physician . . . . whether I shall be able to go to Brazil, to
Paranà.   In that case I will go in the beginning of May or at the end
of April. . . . . You sit there, silly people in North America, groaning.
Go to South America.   You will be better off immediately.   The
Brazilian government . . . . is beginning to colonize, the Poles are
very much wanted.   A special office is even organized in Warsaw to
this end, and our press speaks much about it and even advises [going],
although the gentlemen of the National Democratic party shed
crocodile tears that our fatherland will remain without working hands.
Vive Brazil!   You have only to go with a woman and you will get
a ready farm with a house and farm-buildings. . . . . The *Macierz*
[Polish school-association] has been closed; you know it certainly.
As to myself, even if I returned to our country I could get no place,
for I remain here under the "special care" of the police. . . . .

                                                                  ST. J.

763   WOLA SEROCKA, July 29, 1913

DEAR MR. WACŁAW, COMPANION AND FRIEND: A few days ago
I received your letter from which I understand that it is bad with you.
I guess you must be seriously wounded, since you lost the ability to
work and you lie in the hospital for some months, without knowing
whether you will ever recover. . . . . Something like this has been
going on with me for 4 years already.   At the end of my exile and on
the way back I caught cold, I began to cough, but I did not heed it.
They called me to the army, I served for 5 months, but I came back
so ill that I did not expect to recover.   It was in 1910.   But during

the summer, doing nothing, only walking through fields and forests, I grew somewhat stronger, and in the winter I began to give private lessons. Evidently, being already experienced, I was so economical that I put aside 50 roubles in 6 months. I resigned about this time the hope of going to America, for with such health it was impossible to go. But the opportunity of a great future presented itself to popular teachers in acting as emigrant guides—a second-class passage to Brazil, with the return passage paid if you do not like Brazil. I wrote a letter to the Emigration Society in Cracow which arranged the trip for me, but third class and without the provision for return. I went therefore to Brazil in July, 1911 and I settled in Paranà. Certainly my hopes and rosy expectations were broken and pulverized. Why? The main cause was my bad health, so that after 10 months I resolved to come back to Europe—after having spent 2 months in the hospital of Curityba. My material situation was such that I received help for the journey back from voluntary contributions of companion-workmen. In short, I returned home to die. . . . . After my return [June, 1912] I lay down and I am lying the whole time. . . . . I rise sometimes now, in the summer, in order to warm myself in the sun. I feel better, but I cannot walk, for my lungs—oh, these lungs!—are very small today and I am afraid of the winter—whether I shall hold out. Such is the state of my health. My material state is no better, for besides my debt, about 300 roubles in all, I have 4 roubles in cash, which I would send you at once if you were here in our country. I have no moral right to the inheritance [from my father], and even if I have a legal right it gives me only the possibility of living and boarding with my brother. If I wanted to tear these 150 roubles away from him, I should then be obliged to go and beg my living. So imagine my situation. And my brother himself has not much more besides debts; the misery is the same as in your home. . . . . Write me, what do you want me to do? I know that you have earned this money in bloody sweat, but . . . . I wanted to pay first my debt to those who did not earn it so hard and lent it to me,[1] but, alas, I can do no more. I don't know what you will think of me.

Yours sincerely,

ST. JASIŃSKI

[1] It is a matter of "pride" among socialists not to remain under an obligation to a member of a class sharing other convictions, and in this respect his attitude is normal. At the same time his "pride" did not prevent his accepting obligations from this class.

764   March 8, 1907

DEAR MR. WACŁAW: . . . . I am in Ojców. I don't know what will be further. Jasiński writes to me sometimes, but whether he is crazy or something else, I don't understand. Once he wrote me a letter advising me to get from Moscow or Petersburg Russian papers and books—as he says, very good ones. What do I want with them? I am not even yet perfectly well acquainted with the Polish literature. . . . . I try to avoid any mention of politics in my letters to him, for I know that if anybody does not agree with him he is furious at once. Not long ago I got a postcard from him, full of dirty calumnies. In this postcard he calls me a denouncer.

I don't know why. He says that I, together with some society whose activity he conjectures, betrayed him. It fell upon me like thunder from a clear sky. I, who correspond with him and send him a few roubles from time to time, I—to denounce him? And to denounce—what? A few days afterward he writes another postcard in which he does not mention that affair at all. . . . .

W. GOSZEWSKI

INDEX TO LETTER SERIES